Student Quick Tips

Use this Student Quick Tips guide for a quick and easy start with McGraw-Hill Connect. You'll get valuable tips on registering, doing assignments, and accessing resources, as well as information about the support center hours.

Getting Started

TIP: To get started in Connect, you will need the following:

- Your instructor's Connect Web Address

   Sample of Connect Web Address:

   http://www.mcgrawhillconnect.com/class/instructorname_section_name

- Connect Access Code

TIP: If you do not have an access code or have not yet secured your tuition funds, you can click "Free Trial" during registration. This trial will provide temporary Connect access (typically three weeks) and will remind you to purchase online access before the end of your trial.

Registration and Sign In

1. Go to the Connect Web Address provided by your instructor
2. Click on **Register Now**
3. Enter your email address

TIP: If you already have a McGraw-Hill account, you will be asked for your password and will not be required to create a new account.

4. Enter a registration code or choose **Buy Online** to purchase access online

(Continued: **Registration and Sign In**)

5. Follow the on-screen directions

TIP: Please choose your Security Question and Answer carefully. We will ask you for this information if you forget your password.

6. When registration is complete, click on **Go to Connect Now**

7. You are now ready to use **Connect**

Trouble Logging In?

- Ensure you are using the same email address you used during registration

- If you have forgotten your password, click on the "Forgot Password?" link at your Instructor's Connect Course Web Address

- When logged into Connect, you can update your account information (e.g. email address, password, and security question/answer) by clicking on the "My Account" link located at the top-right corner

Home (Assignments)

TIP: If you are unable to begin an assignment, verify the following:

- The assignment is available (start and due dates)

- That you have not exceeded the maximum number of attempts

- That you have not achieved a score of 100%

- If your assignment contains questions that require manual grading, you will not be able to begin your next attempt until your instructor has graded those questions

(Continued: **Home Assignments**)

> **TIP:** Based on the assignment policy settings established by your Instructor, you may encounter the following limitations when working on your assignment(s):

- Ability to Print Assignment

- Timed assignments – once you begin a "*timed assignment*," the timer will not stop by design

> **TIP:** "*Save & Exit*" vs. "*Submit*" button

- If you are unable to complete your assignment in one sitting, utilize the "*Save & Exit*" button to save your work and complete it at a later time

- Once you have completed your assignment, utilize the "*Submit*" button in order for your assignment to be graded

Library

> **TIP:** The *Library* section of your Connect account provides shortcuts to various resources.

- If you purchased ConnectPlus, you will see an *eBook* link, which can also be accessed from the section information widget of the *Home* tab

- *Recorded Lectures* can be accessed if your instructor is using *Tegrity Campus* to capture lectures. You may also access recorded lectures when taking an assignment by clicking on the projector icon in the navigation bar

- Many McGraw-Hill textbooks offer additional resources such as narrated slides and additional problems, which are accessible through the *Student Resources* link

Reports

TIP: Once you submit your assignment, you can view your available results in the *Reports* tab.

- If you see a dash (-) as your score, your instructor has either delayed or restricted your ability to see the assignment feedback

- Your instructor has the ability to limit the amount of information (e.g. questions, answers, scores) you can view for each submitted assignment

Need More Help?

CONTACT US ONLINE

Visit us at:

www.mcgrawhillconnect.com/support

Browse our support materials including tutorial videos and our searchable Connect knowledge base. If you cannot find an answer to your question, click on "Contact Us" button to send us an email.

GIVE US A CALL

Call us at:

1-800-331-5094

Our live support is available:

Mon-Thurs: 8 am – 11 pm CT
Friday: 8 am – 6 pm CT
Sunday: 6 pm – 11 pm CT

Brooker | Widmaier | Graham | Stiling

BIOLOGY

THIRD EDITION

Robert J. Brooker
University of Minnesota - Twin Cities

Eric P. Widmaier
Boston University

Linda E. Graham
University of Wisconsin - Madison

Peter D. Stiling
University of South Florida

BIO 120

Brigham Young University - Provo

Mc
Graw
Hill
Education

2 3 4 5 6 7 8 9 0 DCM DCM 16 15 14

ISBN-13: 978-0-07-352108-4
ISBN-10: 0-07-352108-6

Learning Solutions Consultant: Darlene Bahr
Project Manager: Jennifer Bartell
Cover Photo Credits:
135165667.tif–Clint Spencer
86805319.tif–Comstock Images
87483499.tif–Hemera Technologies
160106131.tif–Dragana Jokmanovic
86810367.tif–Polka Dot Images
87755539.tif–Jupiterimages
87690711.tif–Hemera Technologies

Brief Contents

About the Authors

Robert J. Brooker

Rob Brooker (Ph.D., Yale University) received his B.A. in biology at Wittenberg University, Springfield, Ohio, in 1978. At Harvard, he studied lactose permease, the product of the *lacY* gene of the *lac* operon. He continues working on transporters at the University of Minnesota, where he is a Professor in the Department of Genetics, Cell Biology, and Development and has an active research laboratory. At the University of Minnesota, Dr. Brooker teaches undergraduate courses in biology, genetics, and cell biology. In addition to many other publications, he has written two undergraduate genetics texts published by McGraw-Hill: *Genetics: Analysis & Principles*, 4th edition, copyright 2012, and *Concepts of Genetics*, copyright 2012.

Eric P. Widmaier

Eric Widmaier received his Ph.D. in 1984 in endocrinology from the University of California at San Francisco. His research focuses on the control of body mass and metabolism in mammals, the hormonal correlates of obesity, and the effects of high-fat diets on intestinal cell function. Dr. Widmaier is currently Professor of Biology at Boston University, where he teaches undergraduate human physiology and recently received the university's highest honor for excellence in teaching. Among other publications, he is a coauthor of *Vander's Human Physiology: The Mechanisms of Body Function*, 13th edition, published by McGraw-Hill, copyright 2014.

Linda E. Graham

Linda Graham received her Ph.D. in botany from the University of Michigan, Ann Arbor. Her research explores the evolutionary origin of land-adapted plants, focusing on their cell and molecular biology as well as ecological interactions. Dr. Graham is now Professor of Botany at the University of Wisconsin-Madison. She teaches undergraduate courses in biology and plant biology. She is the coauthor of, among other publications, *Algae*, 2nd edition, copyright 2008, a major's textbook on algal biology, and *Plant Biology*, 2nd edition, copyright 2006, both published by Prentice Hall/Pearson.

Left to right: Eric Widmaier, Linda Graham, Peter Stiling, and Rob Brooker

Peter D. Stiling

Peter Stiling obtained his Ph.D. from University College, Cardiff, Wales, in 1979. Subsequently, he became a postdoctoral fellow at Florida State University and later spent two years as a lecturer at the University of the West Indies, Trinidad. During this time, he began photographing and writing about butterflies and other insects, which led to publication of several books on local insects. Dr. Stiling is currently a Professor of Biology at the University of South Florida at Tampa. His research interests include plant-insect relationships, parasite-host relationships, biological control, restoration ecology, and the effects of elevated carbon dioxide levels on plant herbivore interactions. He teaches graduate and undergraduate courses in ecology and environmental science as well as introductory biology. He has published many scientific papers and is the author of *Ecology: Global Insights and Investigations*, published by McGraw-Hill, copyright 2012.

The authors are grateful for the help, support, and patience of their families, friends, and students, Deb, Dan, Nate, and Sarah Brooker, Maria, Rick, and Carrie Widmaier, Jim, Michael, and Melissa Graham, and Jacqui, Zoe, Leah, and Jenna Stiling.

The Learning Continues in the Digital Environment

The digital offerings for the study of biology have become a key component of both instructional and learning environments. In response to this, the author team welcomes Dr. Ian Quitadamo as Lead Digital Author for *Biology*, 3rd edition. As Lead Digital Author, Ian oversaw the development of digital assessment tools in Connect®. Ian's background makes him a uniquely valuable addition to the third edition of *Biology*.

Ian Quitadamo

Ian Quitadamo is an Associate Professor with a dual appointment in Biological Sciences and Science Education at Central Washington University in Ellensburg, Washington. He teaches introductory and majors biology courses and cell biology, genetics, and biotechnology, as well as science teaching methods courses for future science teachers and interdisciplinary content courses in alternative energy and sustainability. Dr. Quitadamo was educated at Washington State University and holds a BA in biology, Masters degree in genetics and cell biology, and an interdisciplinary Ph.D. in science, education, and technology. Previously a researcher of tumor angiogenesis, he now investigates critical thinking and has published numerous studies of factors that affect student critical thinking performance. He has received the Crystal Apple award for teaching excellence, led various initiatives in critical thinking and assessment, and is active in training future and currently practicing science teachers. He served as a coauthor on *Biology*, 11th edition, by Mader and Windelspecht, copyright 2013 and is the lead digital author for *Biology*, 10th edition by Raven, copyright 2014, both published by McGraw-Hill.

Improving Biology Education: We Listened to You

A New Vision for Learning

A New Vision for Learning describes what we set out to accomplish with this third edition of our textbook. As authors and educators, we know your goal is to ensure your students are prepared for the future—their future course work, lab experiences, and careers in the sciences. Building a strong foundation in biology for your students required a new vision for how they learn.

Through our classroom experiences and research work, we became inspired by the prospect that the first and second editions of *Biology* could move biology education forward. We are confident that this new edition of *Biology* is another step in the right direction because we listened to you. Based on our own experience and our discussions with educators and students, we continue to concentrate our efforts on these crucial areas:

- Experimentation and the process of science
- Modern content
- Evolutionary perspective
- Emphasis on visuals
- Accuracy and consistency
- Critical thinking
- Media—Active teaching and learning with technology

The figures are of excellent quality and one of the reasons we switched to Brooker.

Michael Cullen, *University of Evansville*

The visuals are definitely a strength for this chapter. They are easy to interpret and illustrate the basic themes in genetic engineering in a way that students can comprehend.

Kim Risley, *University of Mount Union*

Continued feedback from instructors using this textbook and other educators in the field of biology has been extremely valuable in refining the presentation of the material. Likewise, we have used the textbook in our own classrooms. This hands-on experience has provided much insight for areas for improvement. Our textbook continues to be comprehensive and cutting-edge, featuring an evolutionary focus and an emphasis on scientific inquiry.

The first edition of *Biology* was truly innovative in its visual program, and the third edition continues to emphasize this highly instructional visual program. In watching students study as well as in extensive interviews, it is clear that students rely heavily on the artwork as their primary study tool. As you will see when you scan through our book, the illustrations have been crafted with the student's perspective in mind. They are very easy to follow, particularly those that have multiple steps, and have very complete explanations of key concepts. We have taken the approach that students should be able to look at the figures and understand the key concepts, without having to glance back and forth between the text and art. Many figures contain text boxes that explain what the illustration is showing. In those figures with multiple steps, the boxes are numbered and thereby guide the students through biological processes.

A New Vision Serving Teachers and Learners

To accurately and thoroughly cover a course as wide-ranging as biology, we felt it was essential that our team reflect the diversity of the field. We saw an opportunity to reach students at an early stage in their education and provide their biology training with a solid and up-to-date foundation. We have worked to balance coverage of classic research with recent discoveries that extend biological concepts in surprising new directions or that forge new concepts. Some new discoveries were selected because they highlight scientific controversies, showing students that we don't have all the answers yet. There is still a lot of work for new generations of biologists. With this in mind, we've also spotlighted discoveries made by diverse people doing research in different countries to illustrate the global nature of modern biological science.

This is an excellent textbook for biology majors, and the students should keep the book as a future reference. The thoughts flow very well from one topic to the next.

Gary Walker, Youngstown State University

As active teachers and writers, one of the great joys of this process for us is that we have been able to meet many more educators and students during the creation of this textbook. It is humbling to see the level of dedication our peers bring to their teaching. Likewise, it is encouraging to see the energy and enthusiasm so many students bring to their studies. We hope this book and its media package will serve to aid both faculty and students in meeting the challenges of this dynamic and exciting course. For us, this remains a work in progress, and we encourage you to let us know what you think of our efforts and what we can do to serve you better.

Rob Brooker, Eric Widmaier, Linda Graham, Peter Stiling

CHANGES TO THIS EDITION

The author team is dedicated to producing the most engaging and current text that is available for undergraduate students who are majoring in biology. We have listened to educators and reviewed documents, such as *Vision and Change, A Call to Action*, which includes a summary of recommendations made at a national conference organized by the American Association for the Advancement of Science (see www.visionandchange.org). We want our textbook to reflect core competencies and provide a more learner-centered approach. To achieve these goals, we have made the following innovations to *Biology*, third edition.

- **Principles of Biology:** Based on educational literature and feedback from biology educators, we have listed 12 Principles of Biology in Chapter 1. These 12 principles align with the overarching core concepts described in *Vision and Change*, with 1 to 3 principles included per core concept.
- The Principles of Biology are threaded throughout the entire textbook. This is achieved in two ways. First, the principles are explicitly stated in selected figure legends in every chapter. Such legends are given a Principle of Biology icon. In addition, a question at the end of each chapter is directly aimed at a particular principle.
- **Unit openers:** We have added Unit openers to the third edition. These openers serve two purposes. They allow the student to see the "big picture" of the unit. In addition, the unit openers draw attention to the principles of biology that will be emphasized in that unit.
- **BioConnections:** We have also added a new feature called BioConnections, which are found in selected figure legends in each chapter. The BioConnections inform students of how a topic in one chapter is connected to a topic in another.
- **Learning Outcomes:** As advocated in *Vision and Change*, educational materials should have well-defined learning goals. In this third edition of *Biology*, we begin each section of every chapter with a set of Learning Outcomes. These outcomes inform students of the skills they will acquire when mastering the material and provide a tangible understanding of how such skills may be assessed. The assessment in Connect was developed using these Learning Outcomes as a guide in formulating online questions, thereby linking the learning goals of the text with the assessment in Connect.

With regard to the scientific content in the textbook, the author team has worked with hundreds of faculty reviewers to refine this new edition and to update the content so that our students are exposed to the most current material. Some of the key changes that have occurred are summarized below.

- **Chapter 1. An Introduction to Biology:** As mentioned earlier, we have explicitly stated 12 Principles of Biology in Figure 1.4 and described them on pages 2 through 5.

Chemistry Unit

- **Chapter 2. The Chemical Basis of Life I: Atoms, Molecules, and Water:** Figure 2.1 (diagram of simple atoms) is now introduced before the Rutherford experiment, so that students are exposed immediately to the basic nature of atoms. In addition, Figure 2.16 has been revised (spatially) to better represent partial charges on water molecules to make it clear how attractive forces occur between water molecules.
- **Chapter 3. The Chemical Basis of Life II: Organic Molecules:** We expanded the discussion of protein domains in the context of evolution and adjusted Figure 3.21 to more accurately reflect domains of STAT, including the addition of the Linker Domain. We also improved color coding of pentoses and hexoses as well as amino acid side chains, and other chemical groups, throughout the chapter to maintain consistency.

Cell Unit

- **Chapter 4. General Features of Cells:** A new figure has been added that illustrates the relationship between cell size and the surface area/volume ratio (see Figure 4.8). Several BioConnections are made between figures in this chapter and topics in other units, thereby bridging the gap between cell biology and life at the organismal level.

- **Chapter 5. Membrane Structure, Synthesis, and Transport:** The section on Membrane Structure is now divided into two sections: one that emphasizes structure and another that emphasizes fluidity. Similarly, the section on Membrane Transport is now divided into two sections: an overview of membrane transport and then a section that describes how transport proteins function.
- **Chapter 6. An Introduction to Energy, Enzymes, and Metabolism:** The added learning outcomes to this chapter inform the student of the key concepts and how they relate to the laws of chemistry and physics. The discussion of reversible and irreversible inhibitors of enzymes has been expanded.
- **Chapter 7. Cellular Respiration and Fermentation:** The discussion of cellular respiration from the previous edition is now separated into six sections that begin with an overview and then emphasize different processes of cell respiration, such as glycolysis, citric acid cycle, and oxidative phosphorylation. A greater emphasis is placed on how these processes are regulated. Also, a new figure has been added that describes the mechanism of ATP synthesis via ATP synthase (see Figure 7.12).
- **Chapter 8. Photosynthesis:** BioConnections in this chapter connect photosynthesis at the cellular level to topics described in the Plant Biology unit.
- **Chapter 9. Cell Communication:** The initial discussion of cellular receptors and their activation has been subdivided into two topics: how signaling molecules bind to receptors and how receptors undergo conformational changes. A brief description of the intrinsic pathway of apoptosis has also been added.
- **Chapter 10. Multicellularity:** BioConnections in figure legends have been added to connect this cell biology chapter to topics in the Animal and Plant Biology units. Biology Principle legends remind students that "Structure determines function" and that "New properties emerge from complex interactions."

Genetics Unit

- **Chapter 11. Nucleic Acid Structure, DNA Replication, and Chromosome Structure:** A new illustration has been added that shows how two replication forks emanate from an origin of replication (see Figure 11.19b).
- **Chapter 12. Gene Expression at the Molecular Level:** Several illustrations have been revised for student clarity. BioConnections in figure legends relate gene transcription to other topics such as DNA replication.
- **Chapter 13. Gene Regulation:** The section on eukaryotic gene regulation has been divided into two sections: one section emphasizes regulatory transcription factors and the other emphasizes changes in chromatin structure. Three new figures have been added to this chapter that pertain to chromatin remodeling (see Figure 13.17), nucleosome arrangements in the vicinity of a structural gene (see Figure 13.19), and the most current model for how eukaryotic genes are activated (see Figure 13.20).
- **Chapter 14. Mutation, DNA Repair, and Cancer:** Several illustrations have been revised to match presentation styles in other chapters. BioConnections relate information in this genetics chapter to topics in previous cell biology chapters.
- **Chapter 15. The Eukaryotic Cell Cycle, Mitosis, and Meiosis:** At the request of reviewers, a new illustration has been added that shows how nondisjunction can occur during meiosis (see Figure 15.18).
- **Chapter 16. Simple Patterns of Inheritance:** The section on Variations in Inheritance Patterns and Their Molecular Basis has been streamlined to have fewer types of inheritance patterns.
- **Chapter 17. Complex Patterns of Inheritance:** The topic of maternal effect has been moved to Chapter 19, where it is discussed at the molecular level. The last section of this chapter focuses on epigenetics.
- **Chapter 18. Genetics of Viruses and Bacteria:** BioConnections relate the genetics of viruses and bacteria to the structure and function of cells.
- **Chapter 19. Developmental Genetics:** New insets describing the radial pattern of plant growth have been added to Figures 19.2 and 19.22. Biology principle legends remind students that developmental biology is an experimental science that uses model organisms, and that new properties of life arise by complex interactions.
- **Chapter 20. Genetic Technology:** The technique of DNA sequencing now emphasizes the more modern approach of using fluorescently labeled nucleotides (see Figure 20.9). BioConnections relate the techniques described in this chapter to topics found in other chapters, such as DNA replication.
- **Chapter 21. Genomes, Proteomes, and Bioinformatics:** Biology principle legends help students understand how bioinformatics techniques illuminate principles of evolution.

Evolution Unit

- **Chapter 22. The Origin and History of Life:** New information regarding the experiments of Urey and Miller has been added. Figure 22.12 has been revised to reflect the importance of endocytosis for the emergence of the first eukaryotic cells.
- **Chapter 23. An Introduction to Evolution:** The historical development of Darwin's theory of evolution has been set off in its own subsection. BioConnections relate the study of evolution to bioinformatics techniques.
- **Chapter 24. Population Genetics:** The introductory material on natural selection has been revised to better emphasize that natural selection is typically related to two aspects of reproductive success: traits that are directly associated with reproduction, such as gamete viability, and the ability to survive to reproductive age.
- **Chapter 25. Origin of Species and Macroevolution:** The topic of species concepts has been highlighted in its own separate subsection. Biology principle legends remind students that populations of organisms evolve from one generation to the next.
- **Chapter 26. Taxonomy and Systematics:** Phylogenetic trees have been revised to include more plant examples and to include changes in the environment (see Figures 26.3 and 26.7). The use of DNA sequence changes in primates to hypothesize a phylogenetic tree has been moved to the molecular clock section of the this chapter, which reflects how the data relate to neutral changes in DNA sequences (see Figure 26.13).

Diversity Unit

- **Chapter 27. Bacteria and Archaea:** A new Feature Investigation has been added that highlights the recent discovery that soil bacteria from diverse habitats are able to break down and consume a wide variety of commonly used antibiotics and in the process become resistant to them. This new feature reinforces the general concept that heterotrophic organisms require an organic carbon food source and reiterates the roles of natural selection and horizontal gene transfer in the evolution and spread of traits such as antibiotic resistance. A new illustration has been added that compares and contrasts the structure of bacterial and archaeal membranes, thereby building student knowledge about cell membrane structure and function.

- **Chapter 28. Protists:** This chapter includes an updated concept of protist diversification based on recent research findings. New information about malarial disease development reinforces earlier chapter content on the process and significance of phagocytosis, important both in the lives of protists and immune function in humans.
- **Chapter 29. Plants and the Conquest of Land:** Art specially produced for this edition illustrates a new concept of vegetation spacing in landscapes of the Carboniferous (coal age), a time period when plants dramatically changed Earth's atmospheric chemistry and climate, thereby setting the stage for modern ecosystems. The new illustration helps to emphasize human need to understand past interactions of biology and physical environment as one way to predict future change. A new Genomes and Proteomes feature focuses on the evolutionary and potential pharmaceutical value of comparative genomic analyses leveraged by the availability of increasing numbers of plant genomes. This new material reinforces the concept that plants produce many types of secondary chemical compounds that influence humans and other organisms.
- **Chapter 30. The Evolution and Diversity of Modern Gymnosperms and Angiosperms:** The discussion has been expanded to emphasize the roles of whole-genome duplication and polyploidy in the diversification of the flowering plants on which humans depend.
- **Chapter 31. Fungi:** This chapter includes updated concepts of fungal diversification based on recent research, accompanied by new illustrations of cryptomycota and microsporidia and descriptions of their evolutionary and ecological significance.
- **Chapter 32. An Introduction to Animal Diversity:** The chapter now presents a single unified animal phylogeny rather than two alternate versions based on body plans or molecular data. In addition, the section on animal characteristics has been rewritten, as has the section on specific features of embryonic development. New conceptual questions were added.
- **Chapter 33. The Invertebrates:** The section on Lophotrochozoa has been reorganized, and new photographs have been added. The section on annelids has been completely modernized and rewritten.
- **Chapter 34. The Vertebrates:** The treatment of early vertebrates, the hagfish and lamprey has undergone a major revision, and new phylogenies have been constructed and used throughout. Mammal phylogeny has been rewritten to include information from new molecular studies, and a new figure has been added (Figure 34.26). Bird taxonomy has also been updated in the text and tables. New conceptual questions have been added.

Plant Unit

- **Chapter 36. Flowering Plants: Behavior:** The chapter features new material on the function of circadian rhythms, displayed not only in plants, but also in animals and microorganisms.

- **Chapter 38. Flowering Plants: Transport:** The Feature Investigation on xylem transport has been updated to reflect recent research results.
- **Chapter 39. Flowering Plants: Reproduction:** A new Feature Investigation has been added that focuses on how physics and mathematical modeling can be used to explain how flowers bloom. This new material is a response to recent pedagogical motivation to more effectively integrate physics and mathematics into biology training at an early stage.

Animal Unit

Key changes to the Animal Unit include updating statistics on human disease to reflect current numbers. Cross references have been modified to give specific figure and table numbers rather than simply "see Chapter XX." In many chapters, the end-of-chapter Conceptual Questions were altered to make them more challenging and thought-provoking.

- **Chapter 40. Animal Bodies and Homeostasis:** The discussion of *Hox* genes and their role in organ development was simplified. The chapter-opening introduction was revised to more closely relate to the opening photo and to better tie in with a main theme of the chapter (Homeostasis).
- **Chapter 41. Neuroscience I: Cells of the Nervous System:** The chapter was reorganized to cover resting potentials, action potentials, and synapses in separate sections. The description of microelectrodes and membrane potential recording in squid giant axons was revised to improve understanding. In Figure 41.5 a preimpaled tracing of membrane potential was added to emphasize the negative resting potential in this experiment, and the experimental tracing was adjusted to better reflect what is actually seen in such an experiment. The five keyed steps associated with Figure 41.10 now have headers to help emphasize what is happening at each of those steps. Figures 41.11 and 41.12, showing movement of positive charges along an axon in action potential propagation, were improved. In Figure 41.14, voltage-gated calcium channels were added to the active zone of the axon terminal to reflect recent advances in our understanding of their location on presynaptic cells. In Figure 41.17 trimeric G protein was added to its metabotropic receptor to emphasize its mechanism of action. Table 41.3 was altered such that drugs are organized into subcategories according to therapeutic value, or as illicit or recreational drugs.
- **Chapter 42. Neuroscience II: Evolution and Function of the Brain and Nervous System:** Many of the figures were improved. Figure 42.5 now shows a side-by-side comparison of human and frog nervous systems, emphasizing their similarities. In Figure 42.7, meninges layers were enhanced for visual clarity. Figure 42.9 was redrawn and relabeled to more clearly identify the parts of the human brain. Figure 42.12, showing the lobes of the cortex, is a new figure (formerly part of another figure) and now includes the major functions of each lobe. Figure 42.14a includes an improved photo of *Aplysia*. In Figure 42.15, the presynaptic cell changes that occur with learning are now identified using color and line coding. In Figure 42.18, a new line art illustration of plaques and tangles in the brain of a person with Alzheimer's disease now accompanies the light-micrograph.

- **Chapter 43. Neuroscience III: Sensory Systems:** The Genomes and Proteomes Connection was expanded to describe the evolution of color vision (including the genetics of color blindness). The descriptions of the evolution of eyes and vision was expanded. In Figure 43.5 and elsewhere, the middle ear bones are now color-coded to help distinguish them. Improved color matching in small and large (blow-ups) images of fly ommatidium has been incorporated into Figure 43.14. In Figure 43.15, the macula is now labeled on the illustration of the eye/retina. Figures 43.21, 43.25 and 43.27 were improved with better sizing, labeling, color, and detail for realism.

- **Chapter 44. The Muscular-Skeletal System and Locomotion:** In Figure 44.5, an SEM of a sarcomere (relaxed vs. contracted) was added to the line art to provide a real-life image of sliding filaments. The labeling of Figure 44.6 was improved to help clarify this complex figure. Figure 44.8 was improved for clarity and accuracy of cross-bridge cycling. In Figure 44.10, the sarcoplasmic reticulum and T-tubules of muscle were redrawn to include lateral sacs, and to improve clarity, accuracy, and detail. In Figure 44.15b, better comparison photos were provided to illustrate the differences between normal and osteoporotic bone. The Genomes and Proteomes Connection was updated with more recent data.

- **Chapter 45. Nutrition and Animal Digestive Systems:** The chapter has been reorganized so that it begins with a new section that provides an overview of nutrition and ingestion. The layout for Figure 45.3 was revised for easier flow and clarity. Figure 45.4b now includes a very clear and dramatic new photo of leech mouthparts. Figure 45.8, the digestive system of a ruminant, was simplified for clarity. In Figures 45.9, 45.10, 45.11, and 45.15, the labeling was improved for greater detail.

- **Chapter 46. Control of Energy Balance, Metabolic Rate, and Body Temperature:** Figure 46.16 is a new CDC-derived figure showing rates of obesity in U.S. counties across the country. The discussion of brown adipose tissue has been simplified.

- **Chapter 47. Circulatory Systems:** Several figures were enlarged and simplified to improve clarity. In many cases, additional labels and leader lines have been added or modified to improve accuracy and clarity. The distinguishing anatomic and physiologic features of cardiac muscle are now reviewed early in the chapter (with reference back to Chapter 44). The Genomes and Proteomes Connection was changed from the genetics of hemophilia (some of this information was retained in the main text) to a new feature: A Four-Chambered Heart Evolved from Simple Contractile Tubes. This new Genomes and Proteomes Connection also includes a new Figure 47.4).

- **Chapter 48. Respiratory Systems:** The chapter was reorganized so that the Mechanisms of Oxygen Transport section precedes the section on Control of Ventilation. This is consistent now with other chapters in this unit in which mechanisms are described before control. A new SEM photomicrograph was added to Figure 48.7, showing a spiracle on the body surface of an insect.

- **Chapter 49. Excretory Systems and Salt and Water Balance:** In Figure 49.14, tight junctions were added to cells in the epithelia. Figure 49.9 was improved by making the Malpighian tubules more visible. Figure 49.10c was improved by more accurate and visible labeling, by extending the collecting duct, and by removing the background coloring so that this complex image is much more easily viewed. Figures 49.11 and 49.12 were improved with better labels and leaders. New Figure 49.15 was added, showing the mechanism of action of antidiuretic hormone on medullary collecting duct cells, including aquaporin migration.

- **Chapter 50. Endocrine Systems:** Figure 50.5b (thyroid hormone synthesis) was simplified to improve clarity. A new photo of a flounder was added to Figure 50.14b, to show thyroid-induced effects on eye development. The Genomes and Proteomes Connection was moved to later in the chapter after a discussion of steroid hormones.

- **Chapter 51. Animal Reproduction:** Several discussions were clarified and enhanced with more specific detail, including various morphologic and functional aspects of ovarian cycle, follicular development, and parturition. Figure 51.7 (flow chart of endocrine control of male reproduction) was improved by a new drawing and now includes the hormone inhibin.

- **Chapter 53. Immune Systems:** A new section and Feature Investigation on Toll-Like Receptors and pathogen-associated molecular patterns (PAMPs) were added. Figure 53.2 was enhanced with additional detail to include the presence of nitric oxide and macrophages. Figure 53.7, the structure of immunoglobulin, was simplified for clarity. In Figure 53.8, the number of "variable" segments of an immunoglobulin was changed to reflect more recent understanding of structure. Former Figure 53.9 was split into two figures (Figures 53.10 and 53.11) to help walk the reader through this complex material. A new figure was added to the Public Health section, showing the number of people living with HIV infection over the past 20 years.

Ecology Unit

- **Chapter 54. An Introduction to Ecology and Biomes:** A new section on Continental Drift and Biogeography was added, which addresses the importance of evolution and dispersal on the distribution of life on Earth.

- **Chapter 55. Behavioral Ecology:** The discussion on mating systems has been reorganized and a new figure added to better explain the concepts. The Genomes and Proteomes Connection was updated. Two new conceptual questions have been included.

- **Chapter 56. Population Ecology:** Section 56.3, How Populations Grow, has been expanded slightly. In addition, the data on human population growth has been updated. Two new conceptual questions have been included.

- **Chapter 57. Species Interactions:** The information on enslaver parasites and the section on Parasitism have been expanded to include more detail. The Genomes and Proteomes Connection was updated. Two new conceptual questions have been included.

- **Chapter 58. Community Ecology:** The Genomes and Proteomes Connection was updated. Two new conceptual questions have been included.

- **Chapter 59. Ecosystem Ecology:** The section on biogeochemical cycles was reorganized, and some figures have been updated. The Genomes and Proteomes Connection was replaced with a newer, relevant topic.

- **Chapter 60. Biodiversity and Conservation Biology:** The chapter opens with new introductory material and the section "Why Conserve Biodiversity?" has been updated. New information on conservation strategies has been added.

A NEW VISION FOR LEARNING: PREPARING STUDENTS FOR THE FUTURE

MAKING CONNECTIONS

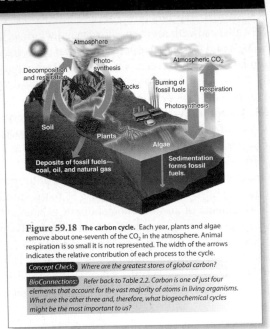

Figure 59.18 The carbon cycle. Each year, plants and algae remove about one-seventh of the CO_2 in the atmosphere. Animal respiration is so small it is not represented. The width of the arrows indicates the relative contribution of each process to the cycle.

Concept Check: Where are the greatest stores of global carbon?

BioConnections: Refer back to Table 2.2. Carbon is one of just four elements that account for the vast majority of atoms in living organisms. What are the other three and, therefore, what biogeochemical cycles might be the most important to us?

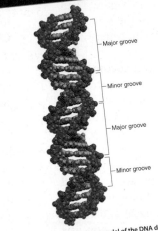

Figure 11.11 A space-filling model of the DNA double helix. In the sugar-phosphate backbone, sugar molecules are shown in blue, and phosphate groups are yellow. The backbone is on the outermost surface of the double helix. The atoms of the bases, shown in green, are more internally located within the double-stranded structure. Notice the major and minor grooves that are formed by this arrangement.

BIOLOGY PRINCIPLE Structure determines function. The major groove provides a binding site for proteins that control the expression of genes.

Principles of Biology are introduced in Chapter 1 and are then threaded throughout the entire textbook. This is achieved in two ways. First, the principles are explicitly stated in selected figure legends for figures in which the specific principle is illustrated. The legends that relate to a Principle of Biology are highlighted with an icon.

In addition, a Conceptual Question at the end of each chapter is directly aimed at exploring a particular principle related to the content of the chapter.

BioConnections New in the third edition, BioConnections are questions found in selected figure legends in each chapter that help students make connections between biological concepts. BioConnections help students understand that their study of biology involves linking concepts together and building on previously learned information. Answers to the BioConnections are found in Appendix B.

Conceptual Questions

1. What are the four key characteristics of the genetic material? What was Frederick Griffith's contribution to the study of DNA, and why was it so important?

2. The Hershey and Chase experiment used radioactive isotopes to track the DNA and protein of phages as they infected bacterial cells. Explain how this procedure allowed them to determine that DNA is the genetic material of this particular virus.

3. A principle of biology is that *structure determines function.* Discuss how the structure of DNA underlies different aspects of its function.

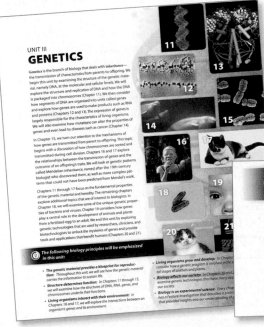

UNIT III
GENETICS

Genetics is the branch of biology that deals with inheritance—the transmission of characteristics from parents to offspring. We begin this unit by examining the structure of the genetic material, namely DNA, at the molecular and cellular levels. We will explore the structure and replication of DNA and how the DNA is packaged into chromosomes (Chapter 11). We then consider how segments of DNA are organized into units called genes and explore how genes are used to make products such as RNA and proteins (Chapters 12 and 13). The expression of genes is largely responsible for the characteristics of living organisms. We will also examine how mutations can alter the properties of genes and even lead to diseases such as cancer (Chapter 14).

In Chapter 15, we turn our attention to the mechanisms of how genes are transmitted from parents to offspring. This topic begins with a discussion of how chromosomes are sorted and transmitted during cell division. Chapters 16 and 17 explore the relationships between the transmission of genes and the outcome of an offspring's traits. We will look at genetic patterns called Mendelian inheritance, named after the 19th-century biologist who discovered them, as well as more complex patterns that could not have been predicted from Mendel's work.

Chapters 11 through 17 focus on the fundamental properties of the genetic material and heredity. The remaining chapters explore additional topics that are of interest to biologists. In Chapter 18, we will examine some of the unique genetic properties of bacteria and viruses. Chapter 19 considers how genes play a central role in the development of animals and plants from a fertilized egg to an adult. We end this unit by exploring genetic technologies that are used by researchers, clinicians, and biotechnologists to unlock the mysteries of genes and provide tools and applications that benefit humans (Chapters 20 and 21).

The following biology principles will be emphasized in this unit:

- **The genetic material provides a blueprint for reproduction:** Throughout this unit, we will see how the genetic material carries the information to sustain life.
- **Structure determines function:** In Chapters 11 through 15, we will examine how the structures of DNA, RNA, genes, and chromosomes underlie their function.
- **Living organisms interact with their environment:** In Chapters 16 and 17, we will explore the interactions between an organism's genes and its environment.

Unit openers have been added in the third edition and serve two purposes. They allow the student to see the "big picture" of the unit. In addition, the unit openers draw attention to the principles of biology that will be emphasized in that unit.

The following biology principles will be emphasized in this unit:

- **The genetic material provides a blueprint for reproduction:** Throughout this unit, we will see how the genetic material carries the information to sustain life.
- **Structure determines function:** In Chapters 11 through 15, we will examine how the structures of DNA, RNA, genes, and chromosomes underlie their functions.
- **Living organisms interact with their environment:** In Chapters 16 and 17, we will explore the interactions between an organism's genes and its environment.
- **Living organisms grow and develop:** In Chapter 19, we will consider how a genetic program is involved in the developmental stages of animals and plants.
- **Biology affects our society:** In Chapters 20 and 21, we will examine genetic technologies that have many applications in our society.
- **Biology is an experimental science:** Every chapter in this unit has a Feature Investigation that describes a pivotal experiment that provided insights into our understanding of genetics.

A GUIDED LEARNING SYSTEM AND CRITICAL THINKING

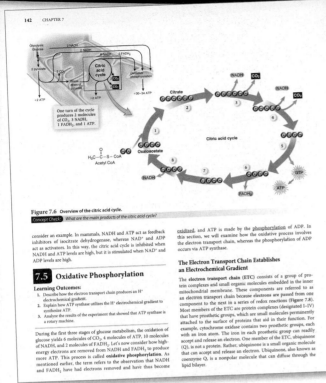

Figure 7.6 Overview of the citric acid cycle.

Concept Check: *What are the main products of the citric acid cycle?*

consider an example. In mammals, NADH and ATP act as feedback inhibitors of isocitrate dehydrogenase, whereas NAD⁺ and ADP act as activators. In this way, the citric acid cycle is inhibited when NADH and ATP levels are high, but it is stimulated when NAD⁺ and ADP levels are high.

7.5 Oxidative Phosphorylation

Learning Outcomes:
1. Describe how the electron transport chain produces an H⁺ electrochemical gradient.
2. Explain how ATP synthase utilizes the H⁺ electrochemical gradient to synthesize ATP.
3. Analyze the results of the experiment that showed that ATP synthase is a rotary machine.

During the first three stages of glucose metabolism, the oxidation of glucose yields 6 molecules of CO₂, 4 molecules of ATP, 10 molecules of NADH, and 2 molecules of FADH₂. Let's now consider how high-energy electrons are removed from NADH and FADH₂ to produce more ATP. This process is called **oxidative phosphorylation**. As mentioned earlier, the term refers to the observation that NADH and FADH₂ have had electrons removed and have thus become

oxidized, and ATP is made by the phosphorylation of ADP. In this section, we will examine how the oxidative process involves the electron transport chain, whereas the phosphorylation of ADP occurs via ATP synthase.

The Electron Transport Chain Establishes an Electrochemical Gradient

The **electron transport chain** (ETC) consists of a group of protein complexes and small organic molecules embedded in the inner mitochondrial membrane. These components are referred to as an electron transport chain because electrons are passed from one component to the next in a series of redox reactions (**Figure 7.8**). Most members of the ETC are protein complexes (designated I–IV) that have prosthetic groups, which are small molecules permanently attached to the surface of proteins that aid in their function. For example, cytochrome oxidase contains two prosthetic groups, each with an iron atom. The iron in each prosthetic group can readily accept and release an electron. One member of the ETC, ubiquinone (Q), is not a protein. Rather, ubiquinone is a small organic molecule that can accept and release an electron. Ubiquinone, also known as coenzyme Q, is a nonpolar molecule that can diffuse through the lipid bilayer.

At the beginning of each section, **Learning Outcomes** have been added in the third edition that inform students of the skills they will acquire when mastering the material and provide a specific understanding of how such skills may be assessed. The assessments in Connect use these Learning Outcomes as a guide to developing online questions.

Critical Thinking—in the text . . .

- **ConceptChecks** are questions that go beyond simple recall of information and ask students to apply or interpret information presented in the illustrations.

- Questions with the **Feature Investigations** continually ask the student to check their understanding and push a bit further.

. . . continued online

- *NEW! Quantitative Question Bank in Connect*® Developing quantitative reasoning skills is important to the success of today's students. In addition to the Question Bank and Test Bank in Connect® a separate bank of quantitative questions is readily available for seamless use in homework/practice assignments, quizzes, and exams. These algorithmic-style questions provide an opportunity for students to more deeply explore quantitative concepts and to experience repeated practice that enables quantitative skill building over time.

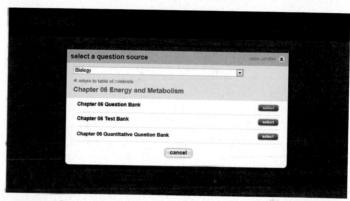

EXPERIMENTAL APPROACH

Feature Investigations provide a complete description of experiments, including data analysis, so students can understand how experimentation leads to an understanding of biological concepts. There are two types of *Feature Investigations*. Most describe experiments according to the scientific method. They begin with observations and then progress through the hypothesis, experiment, data, and the interpretation of the data (conclusion). Some *Feature Investigations* involve discovery-based science, which does not rely on a preconceived hypothesis. The illustrations of the Feature Investigations are particularly innovative by having parallel drawings at the experimental and conceptual levels. By comparing the two levels, students will be able to understand how the researchers were able to interpret the data and arrive at their conclusions.

> *I really like the Feature Investigation so students can begin to grasp how scientists come to the conclusions that are simply presented as facts in these introductory texts.*
>
> Richard Murray, Hendrix College

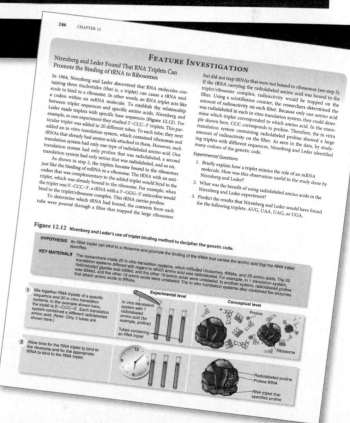

EVOLUTIONARY PERSPECTIVE

Modern techniques have enabled researchers to study many genes simultaneously, allowing them to explore genomes (all the genes an organism has) and proteomes (all the proteins encoded by those genes). This allows us to understand biology in a broader way. Beginning in Chapter 3, each chapter contains a topic called the *Genomes & Proteomes Connection* that provides an understanding of how genomes and proteomes underlie the inner workings of cells and explains how evolution works at the molecular level. The topics that are covered in the *Genomes & Proteomes Connection* are very useful in preparing students for future careers in biology. The study of genomes and proteomes has revolutionized many careers in biology, including those in medicine, research, biotechnology, to name a few.

This is one of the best features of these chapters. It is absolutely important to emphasize evolution themes at the molecular level in undergraduate biology courses.

Jorge Busciglio, University of California—Irvine

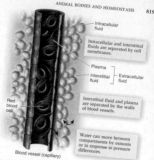

GENOMES & PROTEOMES CONNECTION

Organ Development and Function Are Controlled by *Hox* Genes

Body Fluids Are Distributed into Compartments

A VISUAL OUTLINE

Because students rely on the art as a primary study tool, the authors worked with a team of editors, scientific illustrators, educators, and students to create an accurate, up-to-date, realistic, and visually appealing illustration program that is also easy to follow and instructive. The artwork and photos serve as a visual outline and guide students through complex processes.

The illustrations were very effective in detailing the processes. The drawings were more detailed than our current book, which allowed for a better idea of what the proteins (or whatever the object) structure was.

Amy Weber, student, Ohio University

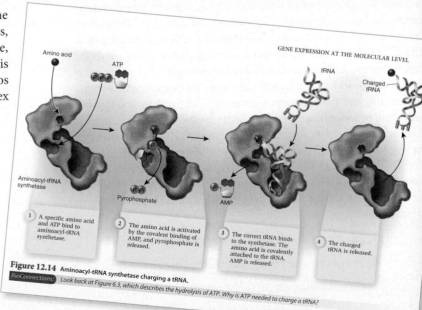

Figure 12.14 Aminoacyl-tRNA synthetase charging a tRNA.

BioConnections: Look back at Figure 6.3, which describes the hydrolysis of ATP. Why is ATP needed to charge a tRNA?

THE DIGITAL STORY...

Digital assessment is a major focus in higher education. Online tools promise anywhere, anytime access combined with the possibility of learning tailored to individual student needs. Digital assessments should span the spectrum of Bloom's taxonomy within the context of best-practice pedagogy. The increased challenge at higher Bloom's levels will help students grow intellectually and be better prepared to contribute to society.

Significant faculty demand for content at higher Bloom's levels led us to examine assessment quality and consistency of our Connect® content and to develop a scientific approach to systematically increase Bloom's levels and develop internally consistent and balanced digital assessments that promote student learning.

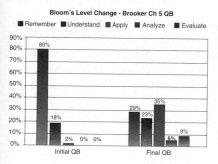

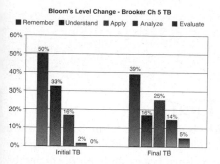

Our goal was to increase assessment quality of our Connect content to meet faculty and student needs. Our objective was to have 30% of all digital assessment questions in Connect at the Apply, Analyze, or Evaluate levels of Bloom's taxonomy. With thousands of existing questions, that is no small task. Consistent with best-practices research on how students learn, we took a comprehensive look at our existing digital assessments to determine Bloom's levels across our assignable content. Because this project was too extensive for a single person to accomplish, we assembled a team of faculty from research, comprehensive, liberal arts universities, and community colleges. Digital team members were selected based on commitment to student learning, biology content expertise, openness to a new vision for digital assessment and professional development, and question-writing skills.

Under the direction of lead digital author, Ian Quitadamo, team members were calibrated to a common perception of Bloom's taxonomy. The team then evaluated our existing Question Bank, Test Bank, Animation Quizzes, and Video Quizzes for appropriate level of Bloom's and compiled the results into a comprehensive database that was statistically analyzed. Results showed adequate coverage at the lower level of Bloom's taxonomy but less so at the higher levels of Bloom's. Knowing that assessment drives learning

quality, we focused our efforts on "Blooming up" existing content and developing new assessments that examine students' problem-solving skills. The end result of our team's scientific approach to developing digital content is a collection of engaging, diagnostic assessments that strengthen student ability to think critically, build connections across biology concepts, and develop quantitative reasoning skills that ultimately underlie student academic success and ability to contribute to society.

We would like to acknowledge our digital team and thank them for their tireless efforts:

Kerry Bohl, *University of South Florida*
David Bos, *Purdue University*
Scott Bowling, *Auburn University*
Scott Cooper, *University of Wisconsin, La Crosse*
Cynthia Dadmun, *Freelance content expert*
Jenny Dechaine, *Central Washington University*
Elizabeth Drumm, *Oakland Community College-Orchard Ridge Campus*
Susan Edwards, *Appalachian State University*
Julie Emerson, *Amherst College*
Brent Ewers, *University of Wyoming*
Chris Himes, *Massachusetts College of Liberal Arts*
Cintia Hongay, *Clarkson University*
Heather Jezorek, *University of South Florida*
Kristy Kappenman, *Central Washington University*
Jamie Kneitel, *California State University, Sacramento*
Marcy Lowenstein, *Florida International University*
Carolyn Martineau, *DePaul University*
Christin Munkittrick, *Freelance content expert*
Chris Osovitz, *University of South Florida*
Anneke Padolina, *Virginia Commonwealth University*
Marius Pfeiffer, *Tarrant County College*
Marceau Ratard, *Delgado Community College*
Nicolle Romero, *Freelance content expert*
Amanda Rosenzweig, *Delgado Community College*
Kathryn Spilios, *Boston University*
Jen Stanford, *Drexel University*
Martin St. Maurice, *Marquette University*
Salvatore Tavormina, *Austin Community College*
Sharon Thoma, *University of Wisconsin, Madison*
Gloriana Trujillo, *University of New Mexico*
Jennifer Wiatrowski, *Pasco-Hernando Community College*

Quantitative question bank

David Bos, *Purdue University*
Chris Osovitz, *University of South Florida*
Martin St. Maurice, *Marquette University*

A NEW VISION IN PREPARING YOUR COURSE

MCGRAW-HILL HIGHER EDUCATION AND BLACKBOARD HAVE TEAMED UP

Blackboard®, the Web-based course management system, has partnered with McGraw-Hill to better allow students and faculty to use online materials and activities to complement face-to-face teaching. Blackboard features exciting social learning and teaching tools that foster more logical, visually impactful, and active learning opportunities for students. You'll transform your closed-door classrooms into communities where students remain connected to their educational experience 24 hours a day.

Do More

This partnership allows you and your students access to McGraw-Hill's Connect® and McGraw-Hill Create™ right from within your Blackboard course—all with one single sign-on. Not only do you get single sign-on with Connect and Create, you also get deep integration of McGraw-Hill content and content engines right in Blackboard. Whether you're choosing a book for your course or building Connect assignments, all the tools you need are right where you want them—inside of Blackboard.

Gradebooks are now seamless. When a student completes an integrated Connect assignment, the grade for that assignment automatically (and instantly) feeds your Blackboard grade center.

McGraw-Hill and Blackboard can now offer you easy access to industry leading technology and content, whether your campus hosts it or we do. Be sure to ask your local McGraw-Hill representative for details.

MCGRAW-HILL CONNECT® BIOLOGY

McGraw-Hill Connect® Biology provides online presentation, assignment, and assessment solutions. It connects your students with the tools and resources they'll need to achieve success. With Connect Biology you can deliver assignments, quizzes, and tests online. A robust set of questions and activities are presented and aligned with the textbook's learning outcomes. As an instructor, you can edit existing questions and author entirely new problems. Track individual student performance—by question, assignment, or in relation to the class overall—with detailed grade reports. Integrate grade reports easily with Learning Management Systems (LMS), such as WebCT and Blackboard—and much more. ConnectPlus Biology provides students with all the advantages of Connect Biology plus 24/7 online access to an eBook. This media-rich version of the book is available through the McGraw-Hill Connect platform and allows seamless integration of text, media, and assessments.

To learn more, visit www.mcgrawhillconnect.com

MY LECTURES—TEGRITY®

McGraw-Hill Tegrity® records and distributes your class lecture with just a click of a button. Students can view them anytime/anywhere via computer, iPod, or mobile device. It indexes as it records your PowerPoint® presentations and anything shown on your computer so students can use keywords to find exactly what they want to study. Tegrity is available as an integrated feature of McGraw-Hill Connect Biology and as a standalone.

PERSONALIZED AND ADAPTIVE LEARNING

McGraw-Hill LearnSmart™ is available as an integrated feature of McGraw-Hill Connect® Biology. It is an adaptive learning system designed to help students learn faster, study more efficiently, and retain more knowledge for greater success. LearnSmart assesses a student's knowledge of course content through a series of adaptive questions. It pinpoints concepts the student does not understand and maps out a personalized study plan for success. This innovative study tool also has features that allow instructors to see exactly what students have accomplished and a built-in assessment tool for grading assignments. Visit the following site for a demonstration. www.mhlearnsmart.com

LabSmart™

Based on the same world-class super-adaptive technology as LearnSmart, McGraw-Hill LabSmart is a must-see, outcomes-based lab simulation. It assesses a student's knowledge and adaptively corrects deficiencies, allowing the student to learn faster and retain more knowledge with greater success.

First, a student's knowledge is adaptively leveled on core learning outcomes: Questioning reveals knowledge deficiencies that are corrected by the delivery of content that is conditional on a student's response. Then, a simulated lab experience requires the student to think and act like a scientist: Recording, interpreting, and analyzing data using simulated equipment found in labs and clinics. The student is allowed to make mistakes—a powerful part of the learning experience! A virtual coach provides subtle hints when needed; asks questions about the student's choices; and allows the student to reflect on and correct those mistakes. Whether your need is to overcome the logistical challenges of a traditional lab, provide better lab prep, improve student performance, or make your online experience one that rivals the real world, LabSmart accomplishes it all.

Learn more at www.mhlabsmart.com

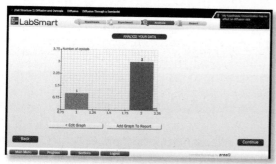

An initial diagnostic establishes a student's baseline comprehension and knowledge; then the program generates a learning plan tailored to the student's academic needs and schedule. As the student works through the learning plan, the program tracks the student's progress, delivering appropriate assessment and learning resources (e.g., tutorials, figures, animations, etc.) as needed. If students incorrectly answer questions around a particular learning objective, they are asked to review learning resources around that objective before re-assessing their mastery of the objective.

Using this program, students can identify the content they don't understand, focus their time on content they need to know but don't, and therefore improve their chances of success in the Majors Biology course.

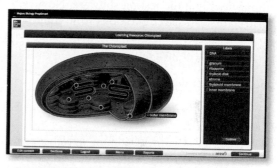

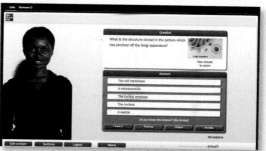

POWERFUL PRESENTATION TOOLS IN CONNECT BIOLOGY

Everything you need for outstanding presentation in one place!

- FlexArt Image PowerPoints—including every piece of art that has been sized and cropped specifically for superior presentations as well as labels that you can edit, flexible art that can be picked up and moved, tables, and photographs.

- Animation PowerPoints—Numerous full-color animations illustrating important processes. Harness the visual impact of concepts in motion by importing these slides into classroom presentations or online course materials.

- Lecture PowerPoints with animations fully embedded.

- Labeled and unlabeled JPEG images—Full-color digital files of all illustrations that can be readily incorporated into presentations, exams, or custom-made classroom materials.

Preparing for Majors Biology

Do your Majors Biology students struggle the first few weeks of class, trying to get up to speed? McGraw-Hill can help.

McGraw-Hill has developed an adaptive learning tool designed to increase student success and aid retention through the first few weeks of class. Using this digital tool Majors Biology students can master some of the most fundamental and challenging principles of biology before they might begin to struggle in the first few weeks of class.

FULLY DEVELOPED TEST BANK

The Digital Team revised the Test Bank to fully align with the learning outcomes and complement questions written for the Question Bank intended for homework assignments. A thorough review process has been implemented to ensure accuracy. Provided within a computerized test bank powered by McGraw-Hill's flexible electronic testing program EZ Test Online, instructors can create paper and online tests or quizzes in this easy-to-use program! A new tagging scheme allows you to sort questions by Learning Outcome, Bloom's level, topic, and section. Imagine being able to create and access your test or quiz anywhere, at any time, without installing the testing software. Now, with EZ Test Online, instructors can select questions from multiple McGraw-Hill test banks or create their own, and then either print the test for paper distribution or give it online.

Contributors for other digital assets:

FlexArt Image PowerPoints—Sharon Thoma, *University of Wisconsin, Madison*

Lecture PowerPoints—Cynthia Dadmun, *freelance content expert*

eBook Quizzes—Nancy Boury, *Iowa State University* and Lisa Bonneau, *Mount Marty College*

Website—Kathleen Broomall, *University of Cincinnati, Clermont College* and Carla Reinstadtler, *freelance content expert*

LearnSmart™—Lead: Laurie Russell, *St. Louis University*, Authors and reviewers: Isaac Barjis, *New York City College of Technology*; Tonya Bates, *University of North Carolina, Charlotte*; Kerry Bohl, *University of South Florida*; Johnny El-Rady, *University of South Florida*; Elizabeth Harris, *Appalachian State University*; Shelley Jansky, *University of Wisconsin, Madison*; Teresa McElhinny, *Michigan State University*; Murad Odeh, *South Texas College*; Nilo Marin, *Broward College*

Flexible Delivery Options

Brooker et al. *Biology* is available in many formats in addition to the traditional textbook to give instructors and students more choices when deciding on the format of their biology text.

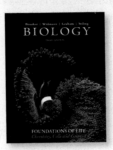

Foundations of Life—Chemistry, Cells, and Genetics

ISBN: 007777583X

Units 1, 2, and 3

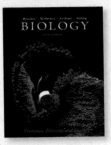

Evolution, Diversity, and Ecology

ISBN: 0077775848

Units 4, 5, and 8

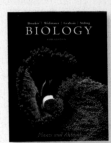

Plants and Animals

ISBN: 0077775856

Units 6 and 7

Also available, customized versions for all of your course needs. You're in charge of your course, so why not be in control of the content of your textbook? At McGraw-Hill Custom Publishing, we can help you create the ideal text—the one you've always imagined. Quickly. Easily. With more than 20 years of experience in custom publishing, we're experts. But at McGraw-Hill we're also innovators, leading the way with new methods and means for creating simplified value-added custom textbooks.

The options are never-ending when you work with McGraw-Hill. You already know what will work best for you and your students. And here, you can choose it.

MCGRAW-HILL CREATE™

With *McGraw-Hill Create*™, you can easily rearrange chapters, combine material from other content sources, and quickly upload content you have written, like your course syllabus or teaching notes. Find the content you need in Create by searching through thousands of leading McGraw-Hill textbooks. Arrange your book to fit your teaching style. Create even allows you to personalize your book's appearance by selecting the cover and adding your name, school, and course information. Order a Create book and you'll receive a complimentary print review copy in 3–5 business days or a complimentary electronic review copy (eComp) via e-mail in minutes. Go to www.mcgrawhillcreate.com today and register to experience how McGraw-Hill Create empowers you to teach *your* students *your* way. **www.mcgrawhillcreate.com**

LABORATORY MANUALS

Biology Laboratory Manual, Tenth Edition
Vodopich/Moore
ISBN: 0-07-353225-8

This laboratory manual is designed for an introductory majors-level biology course with a broad survey of basic laboratory techniques. The experiments and procedures are simple, safe, easy to perform, and especially appropriate for large classes. Few experiments require a second class meeting to complete the procedure. Each exercise includes many photographs, traditional topics, and experiments that help students learn about life. Procedures within each exercise are numerous and discrete so that an exercise can be tailored to the needs of the students, the style of the instructor, and the facilities available.

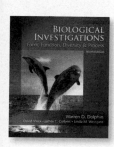

Biological Investigations Lab Manual,
Ninth Edition
Dolphin
ISBN: 0-07-338305-8

This independent lab manual can be used for a one- or two-semester majors-level general biology lab and can be used with any majors-level general biology textbook. The labs are investigative and ask students to use more critical thinking and hands-on learning. The author emphasizes investigative, quantitative, and comparative approaches to studying the life sciences.

McGraw-Hill LabSmart

Based on the same world-class super-adaptive technology as LearnSmart, McGraw-Hill LabSmart is a must-see, outcomes-based lab simulation. It assesses a student's knowledge and adaptively corrects deficiencies, allowing the student to learn faster and retain more knowledge with greater success. Whether your need is to overcome the logistical challenges of a traditional lab, provide better lab prep, improve student performance, or create an online experience that rivals the real world, LabSmart accomplishes it all.

A STEP AHEAD IN QUALITY

360° DEVELOPMENT PROCESS

McGraw-Hill's 360° Development Process is an ongoing, never-ending, education-oriented approach to building accurate and innovative print and digital products. It is dedicated to continual large-scale and incremental improvement, driven by multiple user feedback loops and checkpoints. This is initiated during the early planning stages of our new products, and intensifies during the development and production stages, then begins again upon publication in anticipation of the next edition.

This process is designed to provide a broad, comprehensive spectrum of feedback for refinement and innovation of our learning tools, for both student and instructor. The 360° Development Process includes market research, content reviews, course- and product-specific symposia, accuracy checks, and art reviews. We appreciate the expertise of the many individuals involved in this process.

General Biology Symposia

Every year McGraw-Hill conducts several General Biology Symposia, which are attended by instructors from across the country. These events are an opportunity for editors from McGraw-Hill to gather information about the needs and challenges of instructors teaching the major's biology course. It also offers a forum for the attendees to exchange ideas and experiences with colleagues they might not have otherwise met. The feedback we have received has been invaluable, and has contributed to the development of Biology and its supplements. A special thank you to recent attendees:

Thomas Abbott, *University of Connecticut*
Sylvester Allred, *Northern Arizona University*
Julie Anderson, *University of Wisconsin–Eau Claire*
Kim Baker, *University of Wisconsin–Green Bay*
Michael Bell, *Richland College*
Brian Berthelsen, *Iowa Western Community College*
Joe Beuchel, *Triton College*
Arlene Billock, *University of Louisiana–Lafayette*
Stephane Boissinot, *Queens College, the City University of New York*
David Bos, *Purdue University*
Scott Bowling, *Auburn University*
Jacqueline Bowman, *Arkansas Technical University*
Randy Brooks, *Florida Atlantic University*
Arthur Buikema, *Virginia Polytechnic Institute*
Anne Bullerjahn, *Owens Community College*
Helaine Burstein, *Ohio University*
Raymond Burton, *Germanna Community College*
Peter Busher, *Boston University*
Ruth Buskirk, *University of Texas–Austin*
Richard Cardullo, *University of California–Riverside*
Frank Cantelmo, *St. Johns University*
Jennifer Ciaccio, *Dixie State College*
Anne Barrett Clark, *Binghamton University*
Allison Cleveland, *University of South Florida–Tampa*
Clark Coffman, *Iowa State University*
Jennifer Coleman, *University of Massachusetts–Amherst*
Sehoya Cotner, *University of Minnesota*
Mitch Cruzan, *Portland State University*
Karen A. Curto, *University of Pittsburgh*

Rona Delay, *University of Vermont*
Mary Dettman, *Seminole State College of Florida*
Laura DiCaprio, *Ohio University*
Kathryn Dickson, *California State College–Fullerton*
Cathy Donald-Whitney, *Collin County Community College*
Moon Draper, *University of Texas–Austin*
Tod Duncan, *University of Colorado–Denver*
Brent Ewers, *University of Wyoming*
Stanley Faeth, *Arizona State University*
Michael Ferrari, *University of Missouri–Kansas City*
David Fitch, *New York University*
Donald French, *Oklahoma State University*
Douglas Gaffin, *University of Oklahoma*
John Geiser, *Western Michigan University*
Karen Gerhart, *University of California–Davis*
Julie Gibbs, *College of DuPage*
Cynthia Giffen, *University of Wisconsin–Madison*
Sharon Gill, *Western Michigan University*
William Glider, *University of Nebraska–Lincoln*
Steven Gorsich, *Central Michigan University*
Christopher Gregg, *Louisiana State University*
Stan Guffey, *The University of Tennessee*
Sally Harmych, *University of Toledo*
Bernard Hauser, *University of Florida–Gainesville*
Jean Heitz, *University of Wisconsin–Madison*
Mark Hens, *University of North Carolina–Greensboro*
Albert Herrera, *University of Southern California*
Ralph James Hickey, *Miami University of Ohio–Oxford*
Jodi Huggenvik, *Southern Illinois University–Carbondale*
Brad Hyman, *University of California–Riverside*
Rick Jellen, *Brigham Young University*
Michael Kempf, *University of Tennessee–Martin*
Kyoungtae Kim, *Missouri State University*
Sherry Krayesky, *University of Louisiana–Lafayette*
Jerry Kudenov, *University of Alaska–Anchorage*
Josephine Kurdziel, *University of Michigan*
Ellen Lamb, *University of North Carolina–Greensboro*
Brenda Leady, *University of Toledo*
Graeme Lindbeck, *Valencia Community College*
David Longstreth, *Louisiana State University*
Lucile McCook, *University of Mississippi*
Susan Meiers, *Western Illinois University*
Michael Meighan, *University of California–Berkeley*
John Merrill, *Michigan State University*

John Mersfelder, *Sinclair Community College*
Melissa Michael, *University of Illinois–Urbana-Champaign*
Michelle Mynlieff, *Marquette University*
Leonore Neary, *Joliet Junior College*
Shawn Nordell, *Saint Louis University*
John Osterman, *University of Nebraska–Lincoln*
Stephanie Pandolfi, *Michigan State University*
Anneke Padolina, *Virginia Commonwealth University*
C.O. Patterson, *Texas A&M University*
Nancy Pencoe, *University of West Georgia*
Roger Persell, *Hunter College*
Marius Pfeiffer, *Tarrant County College NE*
Steve Phelps, *University of Florida*
Debra Pires, *University of California–Los Angeles*
Thomas Pitzer, *Florida International University*
Steven Pomarico, *Louisiana State University*
Jo Anne Powell-Coffman, *Iowa State University*
Lynn Preston, *Tarrant County College*
Ian Quitadamo, *Central Washington University*
Rajinder Ranu, *Colorado State University*
Marceau Ratard, *Delgado Community College–City Park*
Melanie Rathburn, *Boston University*
Robin Richardson, *Winona State University*
Mike Robinson, *University of Miami*
Amanda Rosenzweig, *Delgado Community College–City Park*
Connie Russell, *Angelo State University*
Laurie Russell, *St. Louis University*
David Scicchitano, *New York University*
Timothy Shannon, *Francis Marion University*
Brian Shmaefsky, *Lone Star College–Kingwood*
Richard Showman, *University of South Carolina*
Allison Silveus, *Tarrant County College–Trinity River Campus*
Robert Simons, *University of California–Los Angeles*
Steve Skarda, *Linn Benton Community College*
Steven D. Skopik, *University of Delaware*
Phillip Sokolove, *University of Maryland–Baltimore County*
Martin St. Maurice, *Marquette University*
Brad Swanson, *Cental Michigan University*
David Thompson, *Northern Kentucky University*
Maureen Tubbiola, *St. Cloud State University*
Ashok Upadhyaya, *University of South Florida–Tampa*
Anthony Uzwiak, *Rutgers University*

Rani Vajravelu, *University of Central Florida*
Gary Walker, *Appalachian State University*
Pat Walsh, *University of Delaware*
Elizabeth Weiss-Kuziel, *University of Texas–Austin*
Clay White, *Lone Star College–CyFair*
Leslie Whiteman, *Virginia State University*
Jennifer Wiatrowski, *Pasco-Hernando Community College*
David Williams, *Valencia Community College, East Campus*
Holly Williams, *Seminole Community College*
Michael Windelspecht, *Appalachian State University*
Robert Winning, *Eastern Michigan University*
Mary Wisgirda, *San Jacinto College, South Campus*
Michelle Withers, *West Virginia University*
Kevin Wolbach, *University of the Sciences in Philadelphia*
Jay Zimmerman, *St. John's University*

Third Edition Reviewers

John Alcock, *Arizona State University*
Brian Ashburner, *University of Toledo*
Elizabeth A. Bailey, *Alamance Community College*
Arlene Billock, *University of Louisiana–Lafayette*
Bronwyn Bleakley, *Stonehill College*
Randy Brewton, *University of Tennessee–Knoxville*
Becky Brown, *College of Marin*
Carolyn J. W. Bunde, *Idaho State University*
Joseph Bundy, *University of North Carolina–Greensboro*
Romi Burks, *Southwestern University*
Genevieve Chung, *Broward College*
Joe Coelho, *Quincy University*
Michael Cullen, *University of Evansville*
Cynthia Doffitt, *Mississippi State University*
David W. Eldridge, *Baylor University*
Teresa Fischer, *Indian River State College*
Greg Fox, *College of the Canyons*
Arundhati Ghosh, *University of Pittsburgh*
Leonard Ginsberg, *Western Michigan University*
Elizabeth Godrick, *Boston University*
Robert Greene, *Niagara University*
Timothy Grogan, *Valencia Community College*
Theresa Grove, *Valdosta State University*
Jane Henry, *Baton Rouge Community College*
Margaret Horton, *The University of North Carolina–Greensboro*
Jerry Kaster, *University of Wisconsin–Milwaukee*
Bryan Krall, *Parkland College*
Craig Longtine, *North Hennepin Community College*
Kathryn Nette, *Cuyamaca College*
Deb Pires, *University of California–Los Angeles*
Nicola Plowes, *Arizona State University*
Kim Risley, *University of Mount Union*
Laurel Roberts, *University of Pittsburgh*
Rebecca Sheller, *Southwestern University*
Mark A. Shoop, *Tennessee Wesleyan College*
Om Singh, *University of Pittsburgh–Bradford*
Keith Snyder, *Southern Adventist University*
Hattie Spencer, *Mississippi Valley State University*
Ken Spitze, *University of West Georgia*
Joyce Stamm, *University of Evansville*
Ivan Still, *Arkansas Tech University*
Mark Sturtevant, *Oakland University*
Scott Tiegs, *Oakland University*
D. Alexander Wait, *Missouri State University*
Delon Washo-Krupps, *Arizona State University*
Chad Wayne, *University of Houston*

Mollie Wegner, *University of California–Davis*
Emily Williamson, *Mississippi State University*
Erica B. Young, *University of Wisconsin–Milwaukee*

First and Second Edition Reviewers and Contributors

Eyualem Abebe, *Elizabeth City State University*
James K. Adams, *Dalton State College*
Nihal Ahmad, *University of Wisconsin–Madison*
John Alcock, *Arizona State University*
Myriam Alhadefl-Feldman, *Lake Washington Technical College*
Sylvester Allred, *Northern Arizona University*
Jonathan W. Armbruster, *Auburn University*
Joseph E. Armstrong, *Illinois State University*
Dennis Arvidson, *Michigan State University*
David K. Asch, *Youngstown State University*
Tami Asplin, *North Dakota State University*
Amir Assadi-Rad, *Delta College*
Karl Aufderheide, *Texas A&M University*
Idelisa Ayala, *Broward Community College*
Lisa M. Baird, *University of San Diego*
Adebiyi Banjoko, *Chandler-Gilbert Community College*
Gerry Barclay, *Highline Community College*
Susan Barrett, *Massasoit Community College*
Diane Bassham, *Iowa State University*
Donald Reon Baud, *University of Memphis*
Vernon Bauer, *Francis Marion University*
Chris Bazinet, *St. John's University*
Ruth E. Beattie, *University of Kentucky*
Michael C. Bell, *Richland College*
Steve Berg, *Winona State University*
Giacomo Bernardi, *University of California–Santa Cruz*
Deborah Bielser, *University of Illinois–Urbana–Champaign*
Arlene G. Billock, *University of Louisiana–Lafayette*
Eric Blackwell, *Delta State University*
Andrew R. Blaustein, *Oregon State University*
Kristopher A. Blee, *California State University–Chico*
Steve Blumenshine, *California State University–Fresno*
Jason Bond, *East Carolina University*
Heidi B. Borgeas, *University of Tampa*
Russell Borski, *North Carolina State University*
James Bottesch, *Brevard Community College/Cocoa Campus*
Scott Bowling, *Auburn University*
Robert S. Boyd, *Auburn University*
Eldon J. Braun, *University of Arizona*
Michael Breed, *University of Colorado–Boulder*
Robert Brewer, *Cleveland State Community College*
Randy Brewton, *University of Tennessee*
Peggy Brickman, *University of Georgia*
Cheryl Briggs, *University of California–Berkeley*
George Briggs, *State University College–Geneseo*
Mirjana M. Brockett, *Georgia Institute of Technology*
W. Randy Brooks, *Florida Atlantic University*
Jack Brown, *Paris Junior College*
Peter S. Brown, *Mesa Community College*
Mark Browning, *Purdue University*
Cedric O. Buckley, *Jackson State University*
Don Buckley, *Quinnipiac University*
Arthur L. Buikema, Jr., *Virginia Tech University*
Rodolfo Buiser, *University of Wisconsin–Eau Claire*
Anne Bullerjahn, *Owens Community College*
Carolyn J.W. Bunde, *Idaho State University*
Ray D. Burkett, *Southeast Tennessee Community College*

Scott Burt, *Truman State University*
Stephen R. Burton, *Grand Valley State University*
Jorge Busciglio, *University of California*
Stephen P. Bush, *Coastal Carolina University*
Thomas Bushart, *University of Texas–Austin*
Peter E. Busher, *Boston University*
Malcolm Butler, *North Dakota State University*
David Byres, *Florida Community College South Campus*
Jennifer Campbell, *North Carolina State University*
Jeff Carmichael, *University of North Dakota*
Clint E. Carter, *Vanderbilt University*
Patrick A. Carter, *Washington State University*
Timothy H. Carter, *St. John's University*
Merri Lynn Casem, *California State University–Fullerton*
Domenic Castignetti, *Loyola University of Chicago*
Deborah A. Cato, *Wheaton College*
Maria V. Cattell, *University of Colorado*
David T. Champlin, *University of Southern Maine*
Tien-Hsien Chang, *Ohio State University*
Estella Chen, *Kennesaw State University*
Sixue Chen, *University of Florida*
Brenda Chinnery-Allgeier, *University of Texas–Austin*
Young Cho, *Eastern New Mexico University*
Jung H. Choi, *Georgia Institute of Technology*
Genevieve Chung, *Broward Community College–Central*
Philip Clampitt, *Oakland University*
Curtis Clark, *Cal Poly–Pomona*
T. Denise Clark, *Mesa Community College*
Allison Cleveland Roberts, *University of South Florida–Tampa*
Janice J. Clymer, *San Diego Mesa College*
Randy W. Cohen, *California State University–Northridge*
Patricia Colberg, *University of Wyoming*
Craig Coleman, *Brigham Young University–Provo*
Linda T. Collins, *University of Tennessee–Chattanooga*
William Collins, *Stony Brook University*
Jay L. Comeaux, *Louisiana State University*
Bob Connor II, *Owens Community College*
Joanne Conover, *University of Connecticut*
John Cooley, *Yale University*
Ronald H. Cooper, *University of California–Los Angeles*
Vicki Corbin, *University of Kansas–Lawrence*
Anthony Cornett, *Valencia Community College*
Daniel Costa, *University of California–Santa Cruz*
Sehoya Cotner, *University of Minnesota*
Will Crampton, *University of Central Florida*
Mack E. Crayton III, *Xavier University of Louisiana*
Louis Crescitelli, *Bergen Community College*
Charles Creutz, *University of Toledo*
Karen Curto, *University of Pittsburgh*
Kenneth A. Cutler, *North Carolina Central University*
Anita Davelos Baines, *University of Texas–Pan American*
Cara Davies, *Ohio Northern University*
Mark A. Davis, *Macalester College*
Donald H. Dean, *The Ohio State University*
James Dearworth, *Lafayette College*
Mark D. Decker, *University of Minnesota*
Jeffery P. Demuth, *Indiana University*
Phil Denette, *Delgado Community College*
John Dennehy, *Queens College*
William Dentler, *University of Kansas*
Smruti A. Desai, *Lonestar College–Cy Fair*
Donald Deters, *Bowling Green State University*

Hudson R. DeYoe, *University of Texas–Pan American*
Laura DiCaprio, *Ohio University*
Randy DiDomenico, *University of Colorado–Boulder*
Robert S. Dill, *Bergen Community College*
Kevin Dixon, *University of Illinois–Urbana–Champaign*
John S. Doctor, *Duquesne University*
Warren D. Dolphin, *Iowa State University*
David S. Domozych, *Skidmore College*
Robert P. Donaldson, *George Washington University*
Cathy A. Donald-Whitney, *Collin County Community College*
Kristiann M. Dougherty, *Valencia Community College*
Kari M.H. Doyle, *San Jacinto College*
Marjorie Doyle, *University of Wisconsin–Madison*
John Drummond, *Lafayette College*
Ernest Dubrul, *University of Toledo*
Jeffry L. Dudycha, *William Patterson University of New Jersey*
Charles Duggins, Jr., *University of South Carolina*
Richard Duhrkopf, *Baylor University*
James N. Dumond, *Texas Southern University*
Tod Duncan, *University of Colorado–Denver*
Susan Dunford, *University of Cincinnati*
Roland Dute, *Auburn University*
Ralph P. Eckerlin, *Northern Virginia Community College*
Jose L. Egremy, *Northwest Vista College*
William D. Eldred, *Boston University*
David W. Eldridge, *Baylor University*
Inge Eley, *Hudson Valley Community College*
Lisa K. Elfring, *University of Arizona*
Kurt J. Elliot, *Northwest Vista College*
Johnny El-Rady, *University of South Florida*
Seema Endley, *Blinn College*
Bill Ensign, *Kennesaw State University*
David S. Epstein, *J. Sergeant Reynolds Community College*
Shannon Erickson Lee, *California State University–Northridge*
Gary N. Ervin, *Mississippi State University*
Frederick Essig, *University of Southern Florida*
Sharon Eversman, *Montana State University*
Brent E. Ewers, *University of Wyoming*
Stan Faeth, *Arizona State University*
Susan Fahrbach, *Wake Forest University*
Peter Fajer, *Florida State University*
Paul Farnsworth, *University of Texas–San Antonio*
Zen Faulkes, *University of Texas–Pan American*
Paul D. Ferguson, *University of Illinois–Urbana–Champaign*
Fleur Ferro, *Community College of Denver*
Miriam Ferzli, *North Carolina State University*
Margaret F. Field, *Saint Mary's College of California*
Jose Fierro, *Florida State College–Jacksonville*
Melanie Fierro, *Florida State College–Jacksonville*
Teresa G. Fischer, *Indian River College*
David Fitch, *New York University*
Jorge A. Flores, *West Virginia University*
Irwin Forseth, *University of Maryland*
David Foster, *North Idaho College*
Paul Fox, *Danville Community College*
Sandra Fraley, *Dutchess Community College*
Pete Franco, *University of Minnesota*
Steven N. Francoeur, *Eastern Michigan University*
Wayne D. Frasch, *Arizona State University*
Barbara Frase, *Bradley University*
Robert Friedman, *University of South Carolina*
Adam J. Fry, *University of Connecticut*

Bernard L. Frye, *University of Texas–Arlington*
Caitlin Gabor, *Texas State University–San Marcos*
Anne M. Galbraith, *University of Wisconsin–La Crosse*
Mike Ganger, *Gannon University*
Deborah Garrity, *Colorado State University*
John R. Geiser, *Western Michigan University*
Nicholas R. Geist, *Sonoma State University*
Patricia A. Geppert, *University of Texas–San Antonio*
Shannon Gerry, *Wellesley College*
Cindee Giffen, *University of Wisconsin–Madison*
Frank S. Gilliam, *Marshall University*
Chris Gissendanner, *University of Louisiana at Monroe*
Jon Glase, *Cornell University*
Florence K. Gleason, *University of Minnesota*
Elmer Godeny, *Baton Rouge Community College*
Elizabeth Godrick, *Boston University*
Robert Gorham, *Northern Virginia Community College*
James M. Grady, *University of New Orleans*
Brian Grafton, *Kent State University*
John Graham, *Bowling Green State University*
Barbara E. Graham-Evans, *Jackson State University*
Christine E. Gray, *Blinn College*
Christopher Gregg, *Louisiana State University*
John Griffis, *Joliet Junior College*
LeeAnn Griggs, *Massasoit Community College*
Tim Grogan, *Valencia Community College–Osceola*
Richard S. Groover, *J. Sergeant Reynolds Community College*
Gretel Guest, *Durham Technical Community College*
Stan Guffey, *University of Tennessee*
Cameron Gundersen, *University of California*
Rodney D. Hagley, *University of North Carolina–Wilmington*
George Hale, *University of West Georgia*
Patricia Halpin, *University of California–Los Angeles*
William Hanna, *Massasoit Community College*
Gary L. Hannan, *Eastern Michigan University*
David T. Hanson, *University of New Mexico*
Christopher J. Harendza, *Montgomery County Community College*
Kyle E. Harms, *Louisiana State University*
Sally E. Harmych, *University of Toledo*
Betsy Harris, *Appalachian State University*
M.C. Hart, *Minnesota State University–Mankato*
Barbara Harvey, *Kirkwood Community College*
Carla Ann Hass, *The Pennsylvania State University*
Mary Beth Hawkins, *North Carolina State University*
Brian T. Hazlett, *Briar Cliff University*
Harold Heatwole, *North Carolina State University*
Cheryl Heinz, *Benedictine University*
Jutta B. Heller, *Loyola University–Chicago*
Susan Hengeveld, *Indiana University–Bloomington*
Mark Hens, *University of North Carolina–Greensboro*
Steven K. Herbert, *University of Wyoming–Laramie*
Edgar Javier Hernandez, *University of Missouri–St. Louis*
Albert A. Herrera, *University of Southern California*
David L. Herrin, *University of Texas–Austin*
Helen Hess, *College of the Atlantic*
David S. Hibbert, *Clark University*
R. James Hickey, *Miami University of Ohio–Oxford*
Tracey E. Hickox, *University of Illinois–Urbana–Champaign*
Terri Hildebrand, *Southern Utah University*
Juliana Hinton, *McNeese State University*
Anne Hitt, *Oakland University*
Mark A. Holbrook, *University of Iowa*

Robert D. Hollister, *Grand Valley State University*
Richard G. Holloway, *Northern Arizona University*
Harriette Howard-Lee Block, *Prairie View A&M University*
Dianella Howarth, *St. John's University*
Kelly Howe, *University of New Mexico*
Carrie Hughes, *San Jacinto College*
Barbara Hunnicutt, *Seminole Community College*
Bradley Hyman, *University of California–Riverside*
Ella Ingram, *Rose-Hulman Institute of Technology*
Vicki J. Isola, *Hope College*
Jeffrey Jack, *University of Louisville*
Desirée Jackson, *Texas Southern University*
Joseph J. Jacquot, *Grand Valley State University*
John Jaenike, *University of Rochester*
Ashok Jain, *Albany State University*
Eric Jellen, *Brigham Young University*
Judy Jernstedt, *University of California–Davis*
Lee Johnson, *Ohio State University*
Elizabeth A. Jordan, *Moorpark College*
Robyn Jordan, *University of Louisiana at Monroe*
Susan Jorstad, *University of Arizona*
Walter S. Judd, *University of Florida*
David Julian, *University of Florida*
Nick Kaplinsky, *Swarthmore College*
Vesna Karaman, *University of Texas at El Paso*
Istvan Karsai, *East Tennessee State University*
Nancy Kaufmann, *University of Pittsburgh*
Stephen R. Kelso, *University of Illinois–Chicago*
Heather R. Ketchum, *Blinn College*
Eunsoo Kim, *University of Wisconsin–Madison*
Denice D. King, *Cleveland State Community College*
Stephen J. King, *University of Missouri–Kansas City*
Bridgette Kirkpatrick, *Collin County Community College*
John Z. Kiss, *Miami University*
Ted Klenk, *Valencia Community College–West*
David M. Kohl, *University of California–Santa Barbara*
Anna Koshy, *Houston Community College–NW*
David Krauss, *Borough of Manhattan Community College*
Sherry Krayesky, *University of Louisiana–Lafayette*
John Krenetsky, *Metropolitan State College–Denver*
Karin E. Krieger, *University of Wisconsin–Green Bay*
William Kroll, *Loyola University–Chicago*
Paul Kugrens, *Colorado State University*
Pramod Kumar, *University of Texas–San Antonio*
Josephine Kurdziel, *University of Michigan*
David T. Kurjiaka, *Ohio University*
Allen Kurta, *Eastern Michigan University*
Paul K. Lago, *University of Mississippi*
William Lamberts, *College of St. Benedict/Saint John's University*
David Lampe, *Duquesne University*
Pamela Lanford, *University of Maryland*
Marianne M. Laporte, *Eastern Michigan University*
Arlen T. Larson, *University of Colorado–Denver*
John Latto, *University of California–Berkeley*
John C. Law, *Community College of Allegheny County*
Jonathan N. Lawson, *Collin County Community College*
Brenda Leady, *University of Toledo*
Tali D. Lee, *University of Wisconsin–Eau Claire*
Hugh Lefcort, *Gonzaga University*
Michael Lentz, *University of North Florida*
John Lepri, *University of North Carolina–Greensboro*
Army Lester, *Kennesaw State University*
Jennifer J. Lewis, *San Juan College*

Q Quinn Li, *Miami University, Ohio*
Nardos Lijam, *Columbus State Community College*
Yusheng Liu, *East Tennessee State University*
Pauline A. Lizotte, *Valencia Community College*
Jason L. Locklin, *Temple College*
Robert Locy, *Auburn University*
Albert R. Loeblich III, *University of Houston*
Thomas A. Lonergan, *University of New Orleans*
James A. Long, *Boise State University*
Craig Longtine, *North Hennepin Community College*
David Lonzarich, *University of Wisconsin–Eau Claire*
Donald Lovett, *The College of New Jersey*
James B. Ludden, *College of DuPage*
Albert MacKrell, *Bradley University*
Paul T. Magee, *University of Minnesota–Minneapolis*
Jay Mager, *Ohio Northern University*
Christi Magrath, *Troy University*
Richard Malkin, *University of California–Berkeley*
Charles H. Mallery, *University of Miami*
Nilo Marin, *Broward College*
Kathleen A. Marrs, *IUPUI–Indianapolis*
Diane L. Marshall, *University of New Mexico*
Peter J. Martinat, *Xavier University of Louisiana*
Cindy Martinez Wedig, *University of Texas–Pan American*
Joel Maruniak, *University of Missouri*
Joe Matanoski, *Stevenson University*
Patricia Matthews, *Grand Valley State University*
Barbara May, *College of St. Benedict/St. John's University*
Kamau Mbuthia, *Bowling Green State University*
Norah McCabe, *Washington State University*
Chuck McClaugherty, *Mount Union College*
Regina S. McClinton, *Grand Valley State University*
Greg McCormac, *American River College*
Andrew McCubbin, *Washington State University*
David L. McCulloch, *Collin County Community College*
Mark A. McGinley, *Texas Tech University*
Kerry McKenna, *Lord Fairfax College*
Tanya K. McKinney, *Xavier University of Louisiana*
Carrie McMahon Hughes, *San Jacinto College–Central Campus*
Joseph McPhee, *LaGuardia Community College*
Judith Megaw, *Indian River Community College*
Mona C. Mehdy, *University of Texas–Austin*
Brad Mehrtens, *University of Illinois–Urbana–Champaign*
Susan Meiers, *Western Illinois University*
Michael Meighan, *University of California–Berkeley*
Douglas Meikle, *Miami University*
Allen F. Mensinger, *University of Minnesota–Duluth*
Catherine Merovich, *West Virginia University*
John Merrill, *Michigan State University*
Richard Merritt, *Houston Community College*
Jennifer Metzler, *Ball State University*
Melissa Michael, *University of Illinois–Urbana–Champaign*
James Mickle, *North Carolina State University*
Brian T. Miller, *Middle Tennessee State University*
Hugh A. Miller III, *East Tennessee State University*
Thomas E. Miller, *Florida State University*
Sarah L. Milton, *Florida Atlantic University*
Dennis J. Minchella, *Purdue University*
Subhash C. Minocha, *University of New Hampshire*
Manuel Miranda-Arango, *University of Texas at El Paso*
Patricia Mire, *University of Louisiana–Lafayette*
Michael Misamore, *Texas Christian University*

Jasleen Mishra, *Houston Community College–Southwest*
Alan Molumby, *University of Illinois, Chicago*
Daniela S. Monk, *Washington State University*
W. Linn Montgomery, *Northern Arizona University*
Daniel Moon, *University of North Florida*
Jennifer Moon, *University of Texas–Austin*
Janice Moore, *Colorado State University*
Richard C. Moore, *Miami University*
Mathew D. Moran, *Hendrix College*
Jorge A. Moreno, *University of Colorado–Boulder*
David Morgan, *University of West Georgia*
Roderick M. Morgan, *Grand Valley State University*
James V. Moroney, *Louisiana State University*
Ann C. Morris, *Florida State University*
Molly R. Morris, *Ohio University*
Christa P.H. Mulder, *University of Alaska–Fairbanks*
Mike Muller, *University of Illinois–Chicago*
Darrel C. Murray, *University of Illinois–Chicago*
Richard J. Murray, *Hendrix College*
Melissa Murray Reedy, *University of Illinois–Urbana–Champaign*
Michelle Mynlieff, *Marquette University*
Jennifer Nauen, *University of Delaware*
Allan D. Nelson, *Tarleton State University*
Raymond Neubauer, *University of Texas–Austin*
Jacalyn Newman, *University of Pittsburgh*
Robert Newman, *University of North Dakota*
Laila Nimri, *Seminole Community College*
Colleen J. Nolan, *St. Mary's University*
Shawn E. Nordell, *St. Louis University*
Margaret Nsofor, *Southern Illinois University–Carbondale*
Dennis W. Nyberg, *University of Illinois–Chicago*
Nicole S. Obert, *University of Illinois–Urbana–Champaign*
Olumide Ogunmosin, *Texas Southern University*
Wan Ooi, *Houston Community College–Central*
David G. Oppenheimer, *University of Florida*
John C. Osterman, *University of Nebraska–Lincoln*
Brian Palestis, *Wagner College*
Ravishankar Palanivelu, *University of Arizona*
Julie M. Palmer, *University of Texas–Austin*
Peter Pappas, *Community College of Morris*
Lisa Parks, *North Carolina State University*
C. O. Patterson, *Texas A&M University*
Ronald J. Patterson, *Michigan State University*
Linda M. Peck, *University of Findlay*
David Pennock, *Miami University*
Shelley W. Penrod, *North Harris College*
Beverly Perry, *Houston Community College*
John S. Peters, *College of Charleston*
Chris Petersen, *College of the Atlantic*
David K. Peyton, *Morehead State University*
Marius Pfeiffer, *Tarrant County College NE*
Jay Phelan, *University of California–Los Angeles*
Jerry Phillips, *University of Colorado–Colorado Springs*
Susan Phillips, *Brevard Community College*
Randall Phillis, *University of Massachusetts–Amherst*
Eric R. Pianka, *The University of Texas–Austin*
Paul Pilliterri, *Southern Utah University*
Debra B. Pires, *University of California–Los Angeles*
Thomas Pitzer, *Florida International University*
Terry Platt, *University of Rochester*
Peggy E. Pollak, *Northern Arizona University*
Uwe Pott, *University of Wisconsin–Green Bay*
Linda F. Potts, *University of North Carolina–Wilmington*

Jessica Poulin, *University at Buffalo, SUNY*
Kumkum Prabhakar, *Nassau Community College*
Joelle Presson, *University of Maryland*
Mitch Price, *Pennsylvania State University*
Richard B. Primack, *Boston University*
Gregory Pryor, *Francis Marion University*
Penny L. Ragland, *Auburn University*
Lynda Randa, *College of Dupage*
Rajinder S. Ranu, *Colorado State University*
Marceau Ratard, *Delgado Community College*
Melanie K. Rathburn, *Boston University*
Robert S. Rawding, *Gannon University*
Flona Redway, *Barry University*
Jennifer Regan, *University of Southern Mississippi*
Stuart Reichler, *University of Texas–Austin*
Jill D. Reid, *Virginia Commonwealth University*
Anne E. Reilly, *Florida Atlantic University*
Linda R. Richardson, *Blinn College*
Kim Risley, *Mount Union College*
Elisa Rivera-Boyles, *Valencia Community College*
Laurel B. Roberts, *University of Pittsburgh*
James V. Robinson, *University of Texas–Arlington*
Kenneth R. Robinson, *Purdue University*
Luis A. Rodriguez, *San Antonio College*
Chris Romero, *Front Range Community College–Larimer Campus*
Chris Ross, *Kansas State University*
Anthony M. Rossi, *University of North Florida*
Doug Rouse, *University of Wisconsin–Madison*
Kenneth H. Roux, *Florida State University*
Ann E. Rushing, *Baylor University*
Laurie K. Russell, *St. Louis University*
Scott Russell, *University of Oklahoma*
Christina T. Russin, *Northwestern University*
Charles L. Rutherford, *Virginia Tech University*
Margaret Saha, *College of William and Mary*
Sheridan Samano, *Community College of Aurora*
Hildegarde Sanders, *Stevenson University*
Kanagasabapathi Sathasivan, *University of Texas–Austin*
David K. Saunders, *Augusta State University*
Stephen G. Saupe, *College of St. Benedict*
Jon B. Scales, *Midwestern State University*
Daniel C. Scheirer, *Northeastern University*
H. Jochen Schenk, *California State University–Fullerton*
John Schiefelbein, *University of Michigan*
Deemah Schirf, *University of Texas–San Antonio*
Mark Schlueter, *College of Saint Mary*
Chris Schneider, *Boston University*
Susan Schreier, *Towson University*
Scott Schuette, *Southern Illinois University–Carbondale*
David Schwartz, *Houston Community College–Southwest*
Dean D. Schwartz, *Auburn University*
David A. Scicchitano, *New York University*
Erik Scully, *Towson University*
Robin Searles-Adenegan, *University of Maryland*
Pat Selelyo, *College of Southern Idaho*
Pramila Sen, *Houston Community College–Central*
Tim Shannon, *Francis Marion University*
Jonathan Shaver, *North Hennepin Community College*
Brandon Sheafor, *Mount Union College*
Ellen Shepherd Lamb, *University of North Carolina–Greensboro*
Mark Sheridan, *North Dakota State University*
Dennis Shevlin, *The College of New Jersey*
Patty Shields, *University of Maryland*

Cara Shillington, *Eastern Michigan University*
Richard M. Showman, *University of South Carolina*
Michele Shuster, *New Mexico State University*
Scott Siechen, *University of Illinois–Urbana-Champaign*
Martin Silberberg, *McGraw-Hill chemistry author*
Anne Simon, *University of Maryland*
Sue Simon Westendorf, *Ohio University–Athens*
Robert Simons, *University of California–Los Angeles*
John B. Skillman, *California State University–San Bernadino*
J. Henry Slone, *Francis Marion University*
Lee Smee, *Texas A&M University*
Phillip Snider, Jr., *Gadsden State Community College*
Dianne Snyder, *Augusta State University*
Nancy Solomon, *Miami University*
Sally Sommers Smith, *Boston University*
Punnee Soonthornpoct, *Blinn College*
Vladimir Spiegelman, *University of Wisconsin–Madison*
Bryan Spohn, *Florida State College at Jacksonville*
Lekha Sreedhar, *University of Missouri–Kansas City*
Bruce Stallsmith, *University of Alabama–Huntsville*
Richard Stalter, *St. John's University*
Susan J. Stamler, *College of Dupage*
Mark P. Staves, *Grand Valley State University*
William Stein, *Binghamton University*
Mark E. Stephansky, *Massasoit Community College*
Philip J. Stephens, *Villanova University*
Dean Stetler, *University of Kansas–Lawrence*
Brian Stout, *Northwest Vista College*
Kevin Strang, *University of Wisconsin–Madison*
Antony Stretton, *University of Wisconsin–Madison*
Gregory W. Stunz, *Texas A&M University–Corpus Christi*
Mark Sturtevant, *Oakland University*
C.B. Subrahmanyam, *Florida A&M University*
Julie Sutherland, *College of Dupage*
Mark Sutherland, *Hendrix College*
Brook Swanson, *Gonzaga University*
Debbie Swarthout, *Hope College*
David Tam, *University of North Texas*
Roy A. Tassava, *Ohio State University*
Judy Taylor, *Motlow State Community College*
Randall G. Terry, *Lamar University*
Sharon Thoma, *University of Wisconsin*
Shawn A. Thomas, *College of St. Benedict/St. John's University*
Carol Thornber, *University of Rhode Island*
Patrick A. Thorpe, *Grand Valley State University*
Scott Tiegs, *Oakland University*
Kristina Timmerman, *St. John's University*
Daniel B. Tinker, *University of Wyoming*
Marty Tracey, *Florida International University*
Paul Trombley, *Florida State University*

John R. True, *Stony Brook University*
Encarni Trueba, *Community College of Baltimore County Essex*
Cathy Tugmon, *Augusta State University*
J. M. Turbeville, *Virginia Commonwealth University*
Marshall Turell, *Houston Community College*
Ashok Upadhyaya, *University of South Florida–Tampa*
Anthony J. Uzwiak, *Rutgers University*
Rani Vajravelu, *University of Central Florida*
William Velhagen, *New York University*
Wendy Vermillion, *Columbus State Community College*
Sara Via, *University of Maryland*
Neal J. Voelz, *St. Cloud State University*
Thomas V. Vogel, *Western Illinois University*
Samuel E. Wages, *South Plains College*
Jyoti R. Wagle, *Houston Community College System–Central*
R. Steven Wagner, *Central Washington University–Ellensburg*
Charles Walcott, *Cornell University*
John Waldman, *Queens College–CUNY*
Randall Walikonis, *University of Connecticut*
Gary R. Walker, *Youngstown State University*
Jeffrey A. Walker, *University of Southern Maine*
Sean E. Walker, *California State University–Fullerton*
Delon E. Washo-Krupps, *Arizona State University*
Fred Wasserman, *Boston University*
Steven A. Wasserman, *University of California–San Diego*
R. Douglas Watson, *University of Alabama–Birmingham*
Arthur E. Weis, *University of California–Irvine*
Doug Wendell, *Oakland University*
Howard Whiteman, *Murray State University*
Susan Whittemore, *Keene State College*
Jennifer Wiatrowski, *Pasco-Hernando Community College*
Sheila Wicks, *Malcolm X College*
Donna Wiersema, *Houston Community College*
Regina Wiggins-Speights, *Houston Community College–Northeast*
David H. Williams, *Valencia Community College*
Lawrence R. Williams, *University of Houston*
Ned Williams, *Minnesota State University–Mankato*
E. Gay Williamson, *Mississippi State University*
David L. Wilson, *University of Miami*
Mark S. Wilson, *Humboldt State University*
Bob Winning, *Eastern Michigan University*
Jane E. Wissinger, *University of Minnesota*
Michelle D. Withers, *Louisiana State University*
Clarence C. Wolfe, *Northern Virginia Community College*
Gene K. Wong, *Quinnipiac University*
David Wood, *California State University–Chico*

Bruce Wunder, *Colorado State University*
Richard P. Wunderlin, *University of South Florida*
Mark Wygoda, *McNeese State University*
Joanna Wysocka-Diller, *Auburn University*
H. Randall Yoder, *Lamar University*
Marilyn Yoder, *University of Missouri–Kansas City*
Marlena Yost, *Mississippi State University*
Robert Yost, *Indiana University–Purdue*
Kelly Young, *California State University–Long Beach*
Linda Young, *Ohio Northern University*
Ted Zerucha, *Appalachian State University*
Scott D. Zimmerman, *Southwest Missouri State University*

International Reviewers

Dr. Alyaa Ragaei, *Future University, Cairo*
Heather Addy, *University of Calgary*
Mari L. Acevedo, *University of Puerto Rico at Arecibo*
Heather E. Allison, *University of Liverpool, UK*
David Backhouse, *University of New England*
Andrew Bendall, *University of Guelph*
Marinda Bloom, *Stellenbosch University, South Africa*
Tony Bradshaw, *Oxford-Brookes University, UK*
Alison Campbell, *University of Waikato*
Bruce Campbell, *Okanagan College*
Clara E. Carrasco, Ph.D., *University of Puerto Rico–Ponce Campus*
Keith Charnley, *University of Bath, UK*
Ian Cock, *Griffith University*
Margaret Cooley, *University of NSW*
R. S. Currah, *University of Alberta*
Logan Donaldson, *York University*
Theo Elzenga, *Rijks Universiteit Groningen, Netherlands*
Neil C. Haave, *University of Alberta*
Tom Haffie, *University of Western Ontario*
Louise M. Hafner, *Queensland University of Technology*
Annika F. M. Haywood, *Memorial University of Newfoundland*
William Huddleston, *University of Calgary*
Shin-Sung Kang, *KyungBuk University*
Wendy J. Keenleyside, *University of Guelph*
Christopher J. Kennedy, *Simon Fraser University*
Bob Lauder, *Lancaster University*
Richard C. Leegood, *Sheffield University, UK*
Thomas H. MacRae, *Dalhousie University*
R. Ian Menz, *Flinders University*
Kirsten Poling, *University of Windsor*
Jim Provan, *Queens University, Belfast, UK*
Richard Roy, *McGill University*
Han A.B. Wösten, *Utrecht University, Netherlands*

A NOTE FROM THE AUTHORS

The lives of most science-textbook authors do not revolve around an analysis of writing techniques. Instead, we are people who understand science and are inspired by it, and we want to communicate that information to our students. Simply put, we need a lot of help to get it right.

Editors are a key component that help the authors modify the content of their book so it is logical, easy to read, and inspiring. The editorial team for this *Biology* textbook has been a catalyst that kept this project rolling. The members played various roles in the editorial process. Rebecca Olsen, Sponsoring Editor (Major Biology) did an outstanding job of overseeing the third edition. Her insights with regard to pedagogy, content, and organization have been invaluable. Elizabeth Sievers, Director of Development-Biology, has been the master organizer. Liz's success at keeping us on schedule is greatly appreciated.

Our Freelance Developmental Editor, Joni Frasier, worked directly with the authors to greatly improve the presentation of the textbook's content. She did a great job of editing chapters and advising the authors on improvements for the third edition. We would also like to acknowledge our copy editor, Linda Davoli, for keeping our grammar on track.

Another important aspect of the editorial process is the actual design, presentation, and layout of materials. It's confusing if the text and art aren't on the same page, or if a figure is too large or too small. We are indebted to the tireless efforts of Sandy Wille, Content Project Manager; and David Hash, Senior Designer at McGraw-Hill. Likewise, our production company, Lachina Publishing Services, did an excellent job with the paging, revision of existing art, and the creation of new art for the third edition. Their artistic talents, ability to size and arrange figures, and attention to the consistency of the figures have been remarkable.

We would like to acknowledge the ongoing efforts of the superb marketing staff at McGraw-Hill. Special thanks to Patrick Reidy, Executive Marketing Manager-Life Sciences, for his ideas and enthusiasm for this book.

Finally, other staff members at McGraw-Hill Higher Education have ensured that the authors and editors were provided with adequate resources to achieve the goal of producing a superior textbook. These include Kurt Strand, Senior Vice President, Products & Markets, and Marty Lange, Vice President, General Manager, Products & Markets, and Michael Hackett, Director for Life Sciences.

Contents

UNIT I   Chemistry

UNIT II   Cell

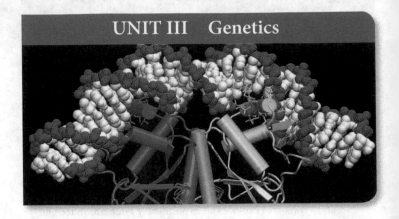

UNIT III   Genetics

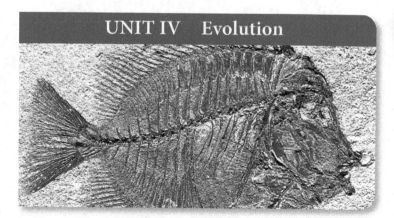

UNIT IV Evolution

An Introduction to Biology

1

B **iology** is the study of life. The diverse forms of life found on
Earth provide biologists with an amazing array of organisms
to study. In many cases, the investigation of living things leads to discoveries that no one would have imagined. For example, researchers determined that the venom from certain poisonous snakes contains a chemical
that lowers blood pressure in humans. By analyzing that chemical, scientists developed drugs to treat high blood pressure (**Figure 1.1**).

Certain ancient civilizations, such as the Greeks, Romans, and Egyptians, discovered that the bark of the white willow tree can be used
to fight fever. Modern chemists determined that willow bark contains
a substance called salicylic acid, which led to the development of the
related compound acetylsalicylic acid, more commonly known as aspirin
(**Figure 1.2**).

In the 20th century, biologists studied soil bacteria that naturally produce "chemical weapons" to kill competing bacteria in their native environment. These chemicals have been characterized and used to develop
antibiotics such as streptomycin to treat bacterial infections (**Figure 1.3**).

Clownfish and anemones. The habits of clownfish and anemones
present biologists with interesting mysteries to solve. Why doesn't
the anemone sting the clownfish? How does a male clownfish
transform its body into a female clownfish?

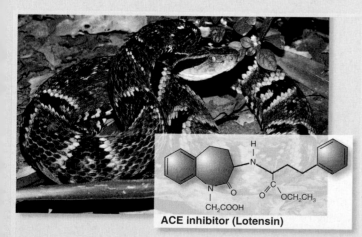

ACE inhibitor (Lotensin)

Figure 1.1 **The Brazilian arrowhead viper and inhibitors of high
blood pressure.** Derivatives of a chemical, called an angiotensin-converting enzyme (ACE) inhibitor, are found in the venom of the
Brazilian arrowhead viper and are commonly used to treat high blood
pressure.

Aspirin

Figure 1.2 **The white willow and aspirin.** Modern aspirin,
acetylsalicylic acid, was developed after analyzing a chemical found in
the bark of the white willow tree.

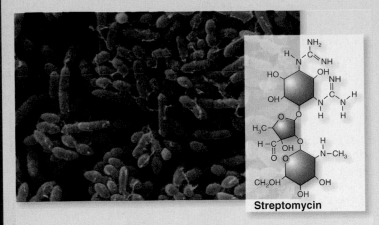

Figure 1.3 The soil bacterium *Streptomyces griseus*, which naturally produces the antibiotic streptomycin, kills competing bacteria in the soil. Doctors administer streptomycin to treat bacterial infections.

These are but a few of the many discoveries that make biology an intriguing discipline. The study of life not only reveals the fascinating characteristics of living species but also leads to the development of medicines and research tools that benefit the lives of people.

To make new discoveries, biologists view life from many different perspectives. What is the composition of living things? How is life organized? How do organisms reproduce? Sometimes the questions posed by biologists are fundamental and even philosophical in nature. How did living organisms originate? Can we live forever? What is the physical basis for memory? Can we save endangered species? Can we understand intriguing aspects of body form and function, such as the ability of clownfish to change from a male to a female?

Future biologists will continue to make important advances. Biologists are scientific explorers looking for answers to some of life's most enduring mysteries. Unraveling these mysteries presents an exciting challenge to the best and brightest minds. The rewards of a career in biology include the excitement of forging into uncharted territory, the thrill of making discoveries that can improve the health and lives of people, and the impact of trying to preserve the environment and protect endangered species. For these and many other compelling reasons, students seeking challenging and rewarding careers may wish to choose biology as a lifelong pursuit.

In this chapter, we will begin our survey of biology by examining the basic principles that underlie the characteristics of all living organisms and the fields of biology. We will then take a deeper look at the process of evolution and how it has led to the development of genomes—the entire genetic compositions of living organisms—which explains the unity and diversity that we observe among living species. Finally, we will explore the general approaches that scientists follow when making new discoveries.

1.1 Principles of Biology and the Levels of Biological Organization

Learning Outcomes:

1. Describe the principles of biology.
2. Explain how life can be viewed at different levels of biological complexity.

Since biology is the study of life, a good way to begin a biology textbook is to distinguish living organisms from nonliving objects. At first, the distinction might seem obvious. A person is alive, but a rock is not. However, the distinction between living and nonliving may seem less obvious when we consider microscopic entities. Is a bacterium alive? What about a virus or a chromosome? In this section, we will examine the principles that underlie the characteristics of all forms of life and explore other broad principles in biology. We will then consider the levels of organization that biologists study, ranging from atoms and small molecules to very large geographical areas.

The Study of Life Has Revealed a Set of Unifying Principles

Biologists have studied many different species and learned that a set of principles applies to all fields of biology. Twelve broad principles are described in **Figure 1.4**. The first eight principles are often used as criteria to define the basic features of life. You will see these principles at many points as you progress through this textbook and they are indicated with

the ⊙ icon. In particular, we will draw your attention to them at the beginning of each unit, and we will refer to them within particular figures in Chapters 3 through 60. It should be noted that the principles of biology are also governed by the laws of chemistry and physics, which are discussed in Chapters 2, 3, and 6.

Principle 1: Cells are the simplest units of life. The term **organism** can be applied to all living things. Organisms maintain an internal order that is separated from the environment (Figure 1.4a). The simplest unit of such organization is the **cell**, which we will examine in Unit II. One of the foundations of biology is the **cell theory**, which states that (1) all organisms are composed of cells, (2) cells are the smallest units of life, and (3) new cells come from pre-existing cells via cell division. Unicellular organisms are composed of one cell, whereas multicellular organisms such as plants and animals contain many cells. In plants and animals, each cell has an internal order, and the cells within the body have specific arrangements and functions.

Principle 2: Living organisms use energy. The maintenance of organization requires energy. Therefore, all living organisms acquire energy from the environment and use that energy to maintain their internal order. Cells carry out a variety of chemical reactions that are responsible for the breakdown of nutrients. Such reactions often release energy in a process called **respiration**. The energy may be used to synthesize the components that make up individual cells and living organisms. Chemical reactions involved with the breakdown and synthesis of cellular molecules are collectively known as **metabolism**. Plants, algae, and certain bacteria can directly harness light energy to produce their own nutrients in the process of **photosynthesis**

(a) Cells are the simplest unit of life:
Organisms maintain an internal order. The simplest unit of organization is the cell. Yeast cells are shown here.

13.7 μm

(b) Living organisms use energy:
Organisms need energy to maintain internal order. These algae harness light energy via photosynthesis. Energy is used in chemical reactions collectively known as metabolism.

(c) Living organisms interact with their environment:
Organisms respond to environmental changes. These plants are growing toward the light.

(d) Living organisms maintain homeostasis:
Organisms regulate their cells and bodies, maintaining relatively stable internal conditions, a process called homeostasis.

(e) Living organisms grow and develop:
Growth produces more or larger cells, whereas development produces organisms with a defined set of characteristics.

(f) The genetic material provides a blueprint for reproduction:
To sustain life over many generations, organisms must reproduce. Due to the transmission of genetic material, offspring tend to have traits like their parents.

(g) Populations of organisms evolve from one generation to the next:
Populations of organisms change over the course of many generations. Evolution results in traits that promote survival and reproductive success.

(h) All species (past and present) are related by an evolutionary history:
The three mammal species shown here share a common ancestor, which was also a mammal.

(i) Structure determines function:
In the example seen here, webbed feet (on ducks) function as paddles for swimming. Nonwebbed feet (on chickens) function better for walking on the ground.

(j) New properties of life emerge from complex interactions:
Our ability to see is an emergent property due to interactions among many types of cells in the eye and neurons that send signals to the brain.

(k) Biology is an experimental science:
The discoveries of biology are made via experimentation, which leads to theories and biological principles.

(l) Biology affects our society:
Many discoveries in biology have had major effects on our society. For example, biologists developed Bt-corn, which is resistant to insect pests and widely planted by farmers.

Figure 1.4 **Twelve principles of biology.** The first eight principles are often used as criteria for defining the basic features of life. Note: The principles described here are considered very broad. Biologists have determined many others that have a more defined focus.

BioConnections: *Look ahead to Figure 52.11. Which of these principles is this figure emphasizing?*

(Figure 1.4b). They are the primary producers of food on Earth. In contrast, some organisms, such as animals and fungi, are consumers—they must use other organisms as food to obtain energy.

Principle 3: Living organisms interact with their environment. To survive, living organisms must be able to interact with their environment, which includes other organisms they may encounter. All organisms must respond to environmental changes. For example, bacterial cells have mechanisms to detect that certain nutrients in the environment are in short supply, whereas others are readily available. In the winter, many species of mammals develop a thicker coat of fur that protects them from the cold temperatures. Plants respond to changes in the angle of the sun. If you place a plant in a window, it will grow toward the light (Figure 1.4c).

Principle 4: Living organisms maintain homeostasis.
As we have just seen, one way that organisms respond to environmental variation is to change their characteristics. Although life is a dynamic process, living cells and organisms regulate their cells and bodies to maintain relatively stable internal conditions, a process called **homeostasis** (from the Greek, meaning to stay the same). The degree to which homeostasis is achieved varies among different organisms. For example, most mammals and birds maintain a relatively stable body temperature in spite of changing environmental temperatures (Figure 1.4d), whereas reptiles and amphibians tolerate a wider fluctuation in body temperature. By comparison, all organisms continually regulate their cellular metabolism so nutrient molecules are used at an appropriate rate and new cellular components are synthesized when they are needed.

Principle 5: Living organisms grow and develop.
All living organisms have an ability to grow and develop. **Growth** produces more or larger cells. In plants and animals, a fertilized egg undergoes multiple cell divisions to develop into a mature organism with many cells. Among unicellular organisms such as bacteria, new cells are relatively small, and they increase in volume by the synthesis of additional cellular components. **Development** is a series of changes in the state of a cell, tissue, organ, or organism, eventually resulting in organisms with a defined set of characteristics (Figure 1.4e).

Principle 6: The genetic material provides a blueprint for reproduction.
All living organisms have a finite life span. To sustain life, organisms must **reproduce**, or generate offspring (Figure 1.4f). A key feature of reproduction is that offspring tend to have characteristics that greatly resemble those of their parent(s). How is this possible? All living organisms contain genetic material composed of **DNA (deoxyribonucleic acid)**, which provides a blueprint for the organization, development, and function of living things. During reproduction, a copy of this blueprint is transmitted from parent to offspring. DNA is **heritable**, which means that offspring inherit DNA from their parents.

As discussed in Unit III, **genes**, which are segments of DNA, govern the characteristics, or traits, of organisms. Most genes are transcribed into a type of **RNA (ribonucleic acid)** molecule called messenger RNA (mRNA) that is then translated into a **polypeptide** with a specific amino acid sequence. A **protein** is composed of one or more polypeptides. The structures and functions of proteins are largely responsible for the traits of living organisms.

Principle 7: Populations of organisms evolve from one generation to the next.
The first six characteristics of life, which we have just considered, apply to individual organisms over the short run. Over the long run, another universal characteristic of life is **biological evolution**, or simply **evolution**, which refers to a heritable change in a population of organisms from generation to generation. As a result of evolution, populations become better adapted to the environment in which they live. For example, the long snout of an anteater is an adaptation that enhances its ability to obtain food, namely ants, from hard-to-reach places (Figure 1.4g). Over the course of many generations, the fossil record suggests that the long snout occurred via biological evolution in which modern anteaters evolved from populations of organisms with shorter snouts.

Principle 8: All species (past and present) are related by an evolutionary history.
Principle 7 considers evolution as an ongoing process that happens from one generation to the next. Evidence from a variety of sources, including the fossil record and DNA sequences, also indicates that all organisms on Earth share a common ancestry. For example, the three species of mammals shown in Figure 1.4h shared a common ancestor in the past, which was also a mammal. We will discuss evolutionary relationships later in Section 1.2 and more thoroughly in Chapter 26.

As described later in this chapter, biologists often view evolution within the context of genomes and proteomes. The term **genome** refers to the complete genetic composition of an organism or species. Because most genes encode proteins, these genetic changes are often associated with changes in the **proteome**, which is the complete protein composition of a cell or organism. By studying how evolution affects genomes and proteomes, biologists can better understand how the changes that occur during evolution affect the characteristics of species. Because evolution is a core unifying principle in biology, we will draw your attention to it in Chapters 4 through 60 by having a brief topic that we call *Genomes and Proteomes Connection*. This topic connects the principle of evolution to the subject matter in that chapter.

Principle 9: Structure determines function.
In addition to the preceding eight characteristics of life, biologists have identified other principles that are important in all fields of biology. The principle "structure determines function" pertains to very tiny biological molecules and to very large biological structures. For example, at the microscopic level, a cellular protein called actin naturally assembles into structures that are long filaments. The function of these filaments is to provide support and shape to cells. At the macroscopic level, let's consider the feet of different birds (Figure 1.4i). Aquatic birds have webbed feet that function as paddles for swimming. By comparison, the feet of nonaquatic birds are not webbed and are better adapted for grasping food, perching on branches, and running along the ground. In this case, the structure of a bird's feet, webbed versus nonwebbed, is a critical feature that affects their function.

Principle 10: New properties of life emerge from complex interactions.
In biology, when individual components in an organism interact with each other or with the external environment to create novel structures and functions, the resulting characteristics are called **emergent properties**. For example, the human eye is composed of many different types of cells that are organized to sense incoming light and transmit signals to the brain (Figure 1.4j). Our ability to see is an emergent property of this complex arrangement of different cell types. As discussed later in this chapter, biologists use the term **systems biology** to describe the study of how new properties of life arise by complex interactions of its components.

Principle 11: Biology is as an experimental science.
Biology is an inquiry process. Biologists are curious about the characteristics of living organisms and ask questions about those characteristics. For example, a cell biologist may wonder why a cell produces a specific protein when it is confronted with high temperature. An ecologist may ask herself why a particular bird eats insects in the summer

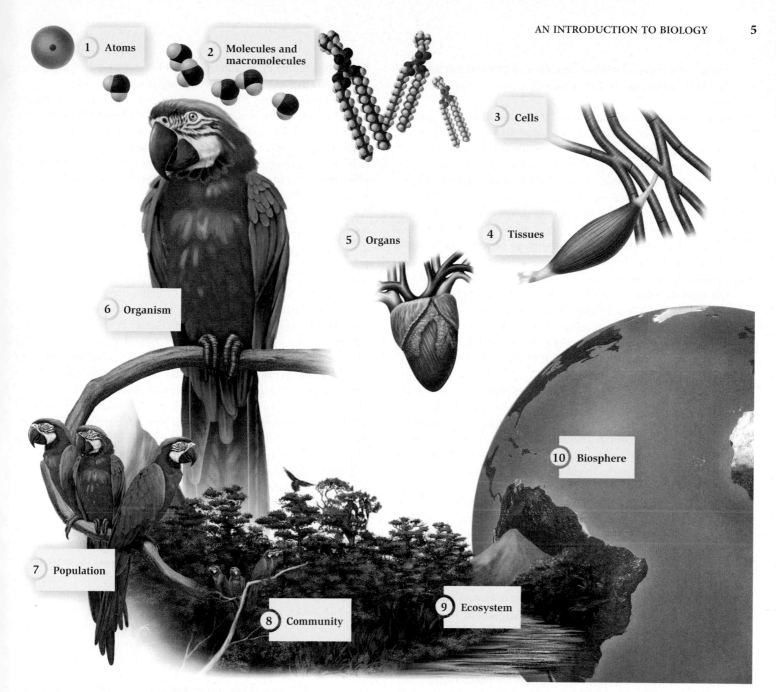

Figure 1.5 The levels of biological organization.

Concept Check: *At which level of biological organization would you place a herd of buffalo?*

and seeds in the winter. To answer such questions, biologists typically gather additional information and ultimately form a hypothesis, which is a proposed explanation for a natural phenomenon. The next stage is to design one or more experiments to test the validity of a hypothesis (Figure 1.4k).

Like evolution, experimentation is such a key aspect of biology that the authors of this textbook have emphasized it in every chapter. As discussed later, a consistent element in Chapters 2 through 60 is a "Feature Investigation"—an actual study by current or past researchers that showcases the experimental approach.

Principle 12: Biology affects our society.   The influence of biology is not confined to textbooks and classrooms. The work of biologists has far-reaching effects in our society. For example, biologists have

discovered drugs that are used to treat many different human diseases. Likewise, biologists have created technologies that have many uses. Examples include the use of microorganisms to make medical products, such as human insulin, and the genetic engineering of crops to make them resistant to particular types of insect pests (Figure 1.4l).

Living Organisms Can Be Studied at Different Levels of Organization

The organization of living organisms can be analyzed at different levels of biological complexity, starting with the smallest level of organization and progressing to levels that are physically much larger and more complex. **Figure 1.5** depicts a scientist's view of the levels of biological organization.

1. **Atoms:** An **atom** is the smallest unit of an element that has the chemical properties of the element. All matter is composed of atoms.

2. **Molecules and macromolecules:** As discussed in Unit I, atoms bond with each other to form **molecules**. Many molecules bonded together to form a polymer such as a polypeptide is called a **macromolecule**. Carbohydrates, proteins, and nucleic acids (for example, DNA and RNA) are important macromolecules found in living organisms.

3. **Cells:** Molecules and macromolecules associate with each other to form larger structures such as membranes. A **cell** is surrounded by a membrane and contains a variety of molecules and macromolecules. A cell is the simplest unit of life.

4. **Tissues:** In the case of multicellular organisms such as plants and animals, many cells of the same type associate with each other to form **tissues**. An example is muscle tissue.

5. **Organs:** In complex multicellular organisms, an **organ** is composed of two or more types of tissue. For example, the heart is composed of several types of tissues, including muscle, nervous, and connective tissue.

6. **Organism:** All living things can be called **organisms**. Biologists classify organisms as belonging to a particular **species**, which is a related group of organisms that share a distinctive form and set of attributes in nature. The members of the same species are closely related genetically. In Units VI and VII, we will examine plants and animals at the level of cells, tissues, organs, and complete organisms.

7. **Population:** A group of organisms of the same species that occupy the same environment is called a **population**.

8. **Community:** A biological **community** is an assemblage of populations of different species. The types of species found in a community are determined by the environment and by the interactions of species with each other.

9. **Ecosystem:** Researchers may extend their work beyond living organisms and also study the physical environment. Ecologists analyze **ecosystems**, which are formed by interactions of a community of organisms with their physical environment. Unit VIII considers biology from populations to ecosystems.

10. **Biosphere:** The **biosphere** includes all of the places on the Earth where living organisms exist. Life is found in the air, in bodies of water, on the land, and in the soil.

1.2 Unity and Diversity of Life

Learning Outcomes:

1. Explain the two basic mechanisms by which evolutionary change occurs: vertical descent with mutation and horizontal gene transfer.
2. Outline how organisms are classified (taxonomy).
3. Describe how changes in genomes and proteomes underlie evolutionary changes.

Unity and diversity are two words that often are used to describe the living world. As we have seen, all modern forms of life display a common set of characteristics that distinguish them from nonliving objects. In this section, we will explore how this unity of common traits is rooted in the phenomenon of biological evolution. Life on

Earth is united by an evolutionary past in which modern organisms have evolved from populations of pre-existing organisms.

Evolutionary unity does not mean that organisms are exactly alike. The Earth has many different types of environments, ranging from tropical rain forests to salty oceans, hot and dry deserts, and cold mountaintops. Diverse forms of life have evolved in ways that help them prosper in the different environments the Earth has to offer. In this section, we will begin to examine the unity and diversity that exists within the biological world.

Modern Forms of Life Are Connected by an Evolutionary History

Life began on Earth as primitive cells about 3.5–4 billion years ago (bya). Since that time, populations of living organisms underwent evolutionary changes that ultimately gave rise to the species we see today. Understanding the evolutionary history of species can provide key insights into the structure and function of an organism's body, because evolutionary change frequently involves modifications of characteristics in pre-existing populations. Over long periods of time, populations may change so that structures with a particular function become modified to serve a new function. For example, the wing of a bat is used for flying, and the flipper of a dolphin is used for swimming. Evidence from the fossil record indicates that both structures were modified from a limb that was used for walking in a pre-existing ancestor (**Figure 1.6**).

Evolutionary change occurs by two mechanisms: vertical descent with mutation and horizontal gene transfer. Let's take a brief look at each of these mechanisms.

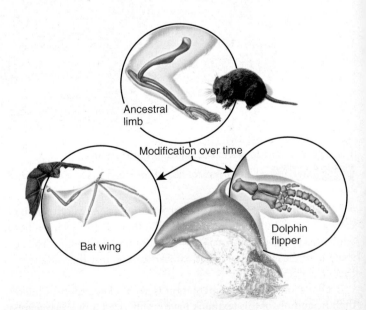

Figure 1.6 An example showing a modification that has occurred as a result of biological evolution. The wing of a bat and the flipper of a dolphin are modifications of a limb that was used for walking in a pre-existing ancestor.

Concept Check: *Among mammals, give two examples of how the tail has been modified and has different purposes.*

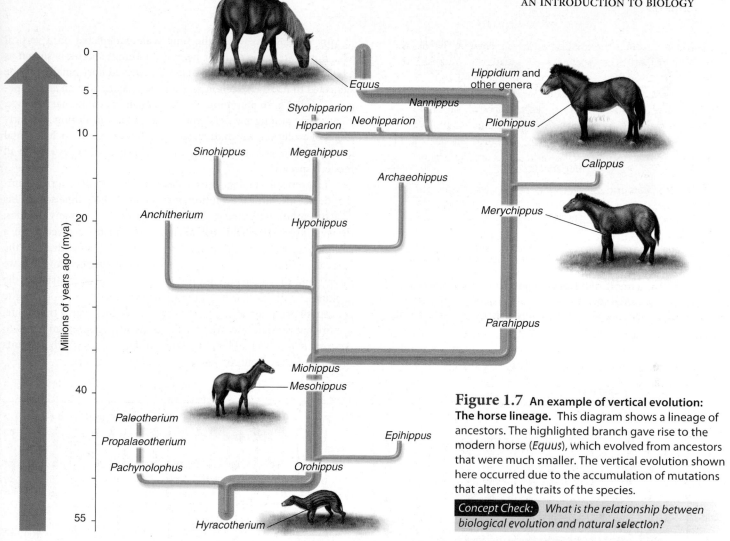

Figure 1.7 **An example of vertical evolution: The horse lineage.** This diagram shows a lineage of ancestors. The highlighted branch gave rise to the modern horse (*Equus*), which evolved from ancestors that were much smaller. The vertical evolution shown here occurred due to the accumulation of mutations that altered the traits of the species.

Concept Check: *What is the relationship between biological evolution and natural selection?*

Vertical Descent with Mutation   The traditional way to study evolution is to examine a progression of changes in a series of ancestors. Such a series is called a **lineage**. **Figure 1.7** shows a portion of the lineage that gave rise to modern horses. This type of evolution is called **vertical evolution** because it occurs in a lineage. Biologists have traditionally depicted such evolutionary change in a diagram like the one shown in Figure 1.7. In this mechanism of evolution, new species evolve from pre-existing ones by the accumulation of **mutations**, which are random changes in the genetic material of organisms. But why would some mutations accumulate in a population and eventually change the characteristics of an entire species? One reason is that a mutation may alter the traits of organisms in a way that increases their chances of survival and reproduction. When a mutation causes such a beneficial change, the frequency of the mutation may increase in a population from one generation to the next, a process called **natural selection**. This topic is discussed in Units IV and V. Evolution also involves the accumulation of neutral changes that do not benefit or harm a species, and evolution sometimes involves rare changes that may be harmful.

With regard to the horses shown in Figure 1.7, the fossil record has revealed adaptive changes in various traits such as size and tooth morphology. The first horses were the size of dogs, whereas modern horses typically weigh more than a half ton. The teeth of *Hyracotherium* were relatively small compared with those of modern horses. Over the course of millions of years, horse teeth have increased in size, and a complex pattern of ridges has developed on the molars. How do evolutionary biologists explain these changes in horse characteristics? They can be attributed to natural selection producing adaptations to changing global climates. Over North America, where much of horse evolution occurred, large areas changed from dense forests to grasslands. The horses' increase in size allowed them to escape predators and travel greater distances in search of food. The changes seen in horses' teeth are consistent with a dietary shift from eating tender leaves to eating grasses and other vegetation that are more abrasive and require more chewing.

Horizontal Gene Transfer   The most common way for genes to be transferred is in a vertical manner. This can involve the transfer of genetic material from a mother cell to daughter cells, or it can occur via gametes—sperm and egg—that unite to form a new organism. However, as discussed in later chapters, genes are sometimes transferred between organisms by other mechanisms. These other mechanisms are collectively known as **horizontal gene transfer**. In some cases, horizontal gene transfer can occur between members of different species. For example, you may have heard in the news media that resistance to antibiotics among bacteria is a growing medical problem. As discussed in Chapter 18, genes that confer antibiotic resistance are sometimes transferred between different bacterial species (**Figure 1.8**).

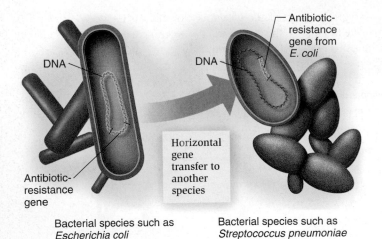

Bacterial species such as
Escherichia coli

Bacterial species such as
Streptococcus pneumoniae

Figure 1.8 An example of horizontal gene transfer: Antibiotic resistance. One bacterial species may transfer a gene to a different bacterial species, such as a gene that confers resistance to an antibiotic.

In a lineage in which the time scale is depicted on a vertical axis, horizontal gene transfer between different species is shown as a horizontal line (**Figure 1.9**). Genes transferred horizontally may be subjected to natural selection and promote changes in an entire species. This has been an important mechanism of evolutionary change, particularly among bacterial species. In addition, during the early stages of evolution, which occurred a few billion years ago, horizontal gene transfer was an important part of the process that gave rise to all modern species.

Traditionally, biologists have described evolution using diagrams that depict the vertical evolution of species on a long time scale. This type of evolutionary tree is shown in Figure 1.7. For many decades, the simplistic view held that all living organisms evolved from a common ancestor, resulting in a "tree of life" that could describe the vertical evolution that gave rise to all modern species. Now that we understand the great importance of horizontal gene transfer in the evolution of life on Earth, biologists have needed to re-evaluate the concept of evolution as it occurs over time. Rather than a tree of life, a more appropriate way to view the unity of living organisms is to describe it as a "web of life," as shown in Figure 1.9, which accounts for both vertical evolution and horizontal gene transfer.

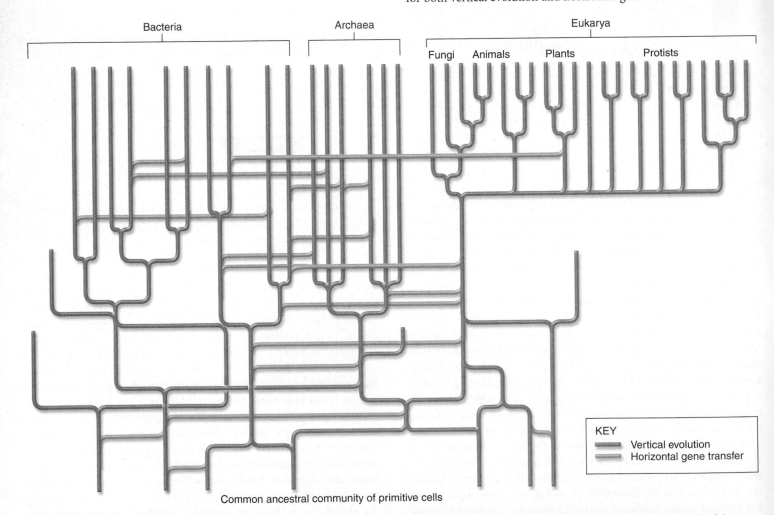

Figure 1.9 The web of life, showing both vertical evolution and horizontal gene transfer. This diagram of evolution includes both of these important mechanisms in the evolution of life on Earth. Note: Archaea are unicellular species that are similar in cell structure to bacteria.

Concept Check: *How does the concept of a tree of life differ from that of a web of life?*

The Classification of Living Organisms Allows Biologists to Appreciate the Unity and Diversity of Life

As biologists discover new species, they try to place them in groups based on their evolutionary history. This is a difficult task because researchers estimate that the Earth has between 10 and 100 million different species! The rationale for categorization is based on vertical descent. Species with a recent common ancestor are grouped together, whereas species whose common ancestor was in the very distant past are placed into different groups. The grouping of species is termed **taxonomy**.

Let's first consider taxonomy on a broad scale. You may have noticed that Figure 1.9 showed three main groups of organisms. From an evolutionary perspective, all forms of life can be placed into those three large categories, or domains, called **Bacteria**, **Archaea**, and **Eukarya** (**Figure 1.10**). Bacteria and archaea are microorganisms that are also termed **prokaryotic** because their cell structure is relatively simple. At the molecular level, bacterial and archaeal cells show significant differences in their compositions. By comparison, organisms in domain Eukarya are **eukaryotic** and have larger cells with internal compartments that serve various functions. A defining distinction between prokaryotic and eukaryotic cells is that eukaryotic cells have a **cell nucleus** in which the genetic material is surrounded by a membrane. The organisms in domain Eukarya were once subdivided into four major categories, or kingdoms, called Protista (protists), Plantae (plants), Fungi, and Animalia (animals). However, as discussed in Chapter 26 and Unit V, this traditional view became invalid as biologists gathered new information regarding the evolutionary relationships of these organisms. We now know the protists do not form a single kingdom but instead are divided into several broad categories called supergroups.

Taxonomy involves multiple levels in which particular species are placed into progressively smaller and smaller groups of organisms that are more closely related to each other evolutionarily. Such an approach emphasizes the unity and diversity of different species. As an example, let's consider the clownfish, which is shown on the textbook cover and examined in **Figure 1.11**. Several species of clownfish have been identified. One species of clownfish, which is orange with white stripes, has several common names, including Ocellaris clownfish. The broadest grouping for this clownfish is the domain, namely, Eukarya, followed by progressively smaller divisions, from kingdom (Animalia) to species. In the animal kingdom, clownfish are part of a phylum, Chordata, the chordates, which is subdivided into classes. Clownfish are in a class called Actinopterygii, which includes all ray-finned fishes. The common ancestor that gave rise to ray-finned fishes arose about 420 million years ago (mya). Actinopterygii is subdivided into several smaller orders. The clownfish are in the order Perciformes (bony fish). The order is, in turn, divided into families; the clownfish belong to the family of marine fish called Pomacentridae, which are often brightly colored. Families are divided into genera (singular, genus). The genus *Amphiprion* is composed of 28 different species; these are various types of clownfish. Therefore, the genus contains species that are very similar to each other in form and have evolved from a common (extinct) ancestor that lived relatively recently on an evolutionary time scale.

Biologists use a two-part description, called **binomial nomenclature**, to provide each species with a unique scientific name. The scientific name of the Ocellaris clownfish is *Amphiprion ocellaris*. The first part is the genus, and the second part is the specific epithet, or species descriptor. By convention, the genus name is capitalized, whereas the specific epithet is not. Both names are italicized. Scientific names are usually Latinized, which means they are made similar in appearance to Latin words. The origins of scientific names are typically Latin or Greek, but they can come from a variety of sources, including a person's name.

GENOMES & PROTEOMES CONNECTION

The Study of Genomes and Proteomes Provides an Evolutionary Foundation for Our Understanding of Biology

The unifying concept in biology is evolution. We can understand the unity of modern organisms by realizing that all living species evolved from an interrelated group of ancestors. However, from an experimental perspective, this realization presents a dilemma—we cannot take a time machine back over the course of 4 billion years to carefully study the characteristics of extinct organisms and fully appreciate the series of changes that have led to modern species. Fortunately, though, evolution has given biologists some wonderful puzzles to study, including the fossil record and the genomes of modern species. As mentioned, the term genome refers to the complete genetic composition of an organism or species (**Figure 1.12a**). The genomes of bacteria and archaea usually contain a few thousand genes, whereas those of eukaryotes may contain tens of thousands. The genome is critical to life because it performs these functions:

- *Stores information in a stable form:* The genome of every organism stores information that provides a blueprint for producing its characteristics.

- *Provides continuity from generation to generation:* The genome is copied and transmitted from generation to generation.

- *Acts as an instrument of evolutionary change:* Every now and then, the genome undergoes a mutation that may alter the characteristics of an organism. In addition, a genome may acquire new genes by horizontal gene transfer. The accumulation of such changes from generation to generation produces the evolutionary changes that alter species and produce new species.

An exciting advance in biology over the past couple of decades has been the ability to analyze the DNA sequence of genomes, a technology called **genomics**. For instance, we can compare the genomes of a frog, a giraffe, and a petunia and discover intriguing similarities and differences. These comparisons help us to understand how new traits evolved. For example, all three types of organisms have the same kinds of genes needed for the breakdown of nutrients such as sugars. In contrast, only the petunia has genes that allow it to carry out photosynthesis.

An extension of genome analysis is the study of **proteomes**, which refers to all of the proteins that a cell or organism makes. The function of most genes is to encode polypeptides that become units in proteins. As shown in **Figure 1.12b**, these include proteins that form

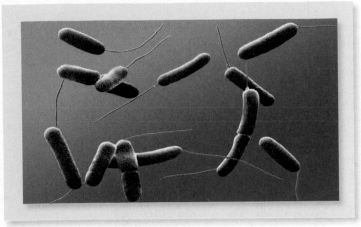

(a) Domain Bacteria: Mostly unicellular prokaryotes that inhabit many diverse environments on Earth.

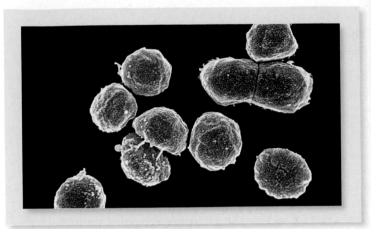

(b) Domain Archaea: Unicellular prokaryotes that often live in extreme environments, such as hot springs.

Protists: Unicellular and small multicellular organisms that are now subdivided into seven broad groups based on their evolutionary relationships.

Plants: Multicellular organisms that can carry out photosynthesis.

Fungi: Unicellular and multicellular organisms that have a cell wall but cannot carry out photosynthesis. Fungi usually survive on decaying organic material.

Animals: Multicellular organisms that usually have a nervous system and are capable of locomotion. They must eat other organisms or the products of other organisms to live.

(c) Domain Eukarya: Unicellular and multicellular organisms having cells with internal compartments that serve various functions.

Figure 1.10 The three domains of life. Two of these domains, **(a)** Bacteria and **(b)** Archaea, are prokaryotic cells. The third domain, **(c)** Eukarya, comprises species that are eukaryotes.

BioConnections: *Look ahead to Figure 26.1. Are fungi more closely related to plants or animals?*

Taxonomic group	Clown anemonefish is found in	Approximate time when the common ancestor for this group arose	Approximate number of modern species in this group	Examples
Domain	Eukarya	2,000 mya	> 5,000,000	
Kingdom	Animalia	600 mya	> 1,000,000	
Phylum	Chordata	525 mya	50,000	
Class	Actinopterygii	420 mya	30,000	
Order	Perciformes	80 mya	7,000	
Family	Pomacentridae	~ 40 mya	360	
Genus	*Amphiprion*	~ 9 mya	28	
Species	*ocellaris*	< 3 mya	1	

Figure 1.11 **Taxonomic classification of the clownfish.** This simplified classification does not include a taxonomic group, called a supergroup, which is described in Chapter 26.

Concept Check: *Why is it useful to place organisms into taxonomic groupings?*

a cytoskeleton and proteins that function in cell organization and as enzymes, transport proteins, cell-signaling proteins, and extracellular proteins. The genome of each species carries the information to make its proteome—the hundreds or thousands of proteins that each cell of that species makes. Proteins are largely responsible for the structures and functions of cells and organisms. The technical approach called **proteomics** involves the analysis of the proteome of a single species and the comparison of the proteomes of different species. Proteomics helps us understand how the various levels of biology are related to one another, from the molecular level—at the level of protein molecules—to the higher levels, such as how the functioning of proteins produces the characteristics of cells and organisms and affects the ability of populations of organisms to survive in their natural environments.

In the chapters that follow, we use a recurring theme in a brief topic called "Genomes & Proteomes Connection" as a concrete way of understanding the unifying concept of evolution in biology. These brief topics will allow you to appreciate how evolution produced the characteristics of modern species. These topics explore how the genomes of different species are similar to each other and how they are different. You will learn how genome changes affect the proteome and thereby control the traits of modern species. Ultimately, these concepts provide you with a way to relate information at the molecular level to the traits of organisms and their survival within ecosystems.

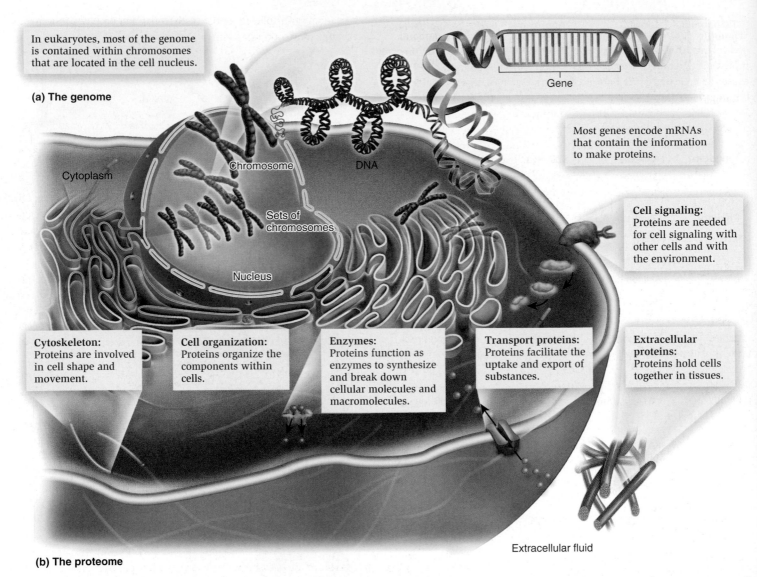

(a) The genome

In eukaryotes, most of the genome is contained within chromosomes that are located in the cell nucleus.

Cytoplasm

Chromosome   DNA

Sets of chromosomes

Nucleus

Gene

Most genes encode mRNAs that contain the information to make proteins.

Cell signaling: Proteins are needed for cell signaling with other cells and with the environment.

Cytoskeleton: Proteins are involved in cell shape and movement.

Cell organization: Proteins organize the components within cells.

Enzymes: Proteins function as enzymes to synthesize and break down cellular molecules and macromolecules.

Transport proteins: Proteins facilitate the uptake and export of substances.

Extracellular proteins: Proteins hold cells together in tissues.

Extracellular fluid

(b) The proteome

Figure 1.12 Genomes and proteomes. (a) The genome, which is composed of DNA, is the entire genetic composition of an organism. Most of the genetic material in eukaryotic cells is found in the cell nucleus. The primary function of the genome is to encode the proteome **(b)**, which is the entire protein complement of a cell or organism. Six general categories of proteins are illustrated. Proteins are largely responsible for the structure and function of cells and complete organisms.

Concept Check: *Biologists sometimes say the genome is a storage unit of life, whereas the proteome is largely the functional unit of life. Explain this statement.*

Genomes and Proteomes Are Fundamental to an Organism's Characteristics

Clownfish (*Amphiprion ocellaris*), which we considered earlier in Figure 1.11, are coral reef fish that live among anemones on the ocean floor (see textbook cover). Normally, the nematocysts (stinging cells) of an anemone's tentacles discharge when fish brush against the tentacles, paralyzing the fish. However, clownfish are not routinely stung by the anemone's tentacles. The mechanism that makes this possible is not clearly established, but one widely held view is that the biochemical makeup of the clownfishes' mucus layer provides protection from the stinging cells. The relationship between the clownfish and anemone is symbiotic—it is an advantage to both species. Anemones provide clownfish with a safe refuge. The clownfish drive away but-

terfly fish that eat anemones, and they also may clean away debris and parasites from the anemone.

One anemone is typically surrounded by a harem of clownfish consisting of a large female, a smaller reproductive male, and even smaller nonreproductive juveniles. Clownfish are protandrous hermaphrodites—that is, they can switch from male to female! When the female of a harem dies, the reproductive male changes sex to become a female and the largest of the juveniles matures into a reproductive male. How does this occur? Unlike male and female humans that differ in their sex chromosomes (XY males and XX females), the genomes of male and female clownfish don't contain different sex chromosomes. In contrast to humans, the opposite sexes of clownfish are not determined by genome differences. Instead, sex differences in clownfish arise solely as a result of proteome differences (**Figure 1.13**).

A juvenile clownfish has both male and female immature sex organs. Hormone levels, particularly those of testosterone and 17-estradiol, control particular genes in the genome. High levels of testosterone promote the expression of genes in the genome that encode proteins that cause the male organs to mature. Alternatively, if the 17-estradiol level becomes high and testosterone is decreased, gene expression is altered in a way that leads to the synthesis of some new types of proteins and prevents the synthesis of others. In other words, changes in hormones alter the composition of the proteome. When this occurs, the female organs grow, and the male reproductive system degenerates; the male fish becomes female. These sex changes, which are irreversible, are due to sequential changes in the proteomes of clownfish.

What factor determines the hormone levels in clownfish? Females seem to control the other clownfish in the harem through aggressive behavior, thereby preventing the formation of other females. This aggressive behavior suppresses an area of the brain in the other clownfish that is responsible for the production of certain hormones that are needed to promote female development. If a clownfish is left by itself in an aquarium, it will automatically develop into a female because this suppression does not occur.

Is there a survival or reproductive advantage of protandrous hermaphroditism? Though various hypotheses have been proposed, the answer is not well understood. Perhaps someone reading this textbook will one day conduct research that will answer this question. When this question is answered, biologists may understand how

natural selection played a role in the phenomenon of protandrous hermaphroditism observed in clownfish.

1.3   Biology as a Scientific Discipline

Learning Outcomes:

1. Explain how researchers study biology at different levels, ranging from molecules to ecosystems.
2. Distinguish between discovery-based science and hypothesis testing, and describe the steps of the scientific method.

What is science? Surprisingly, the definition of science is not easy to state. Most people have an idea of what science is, but actually articulating that idea proves difficult. In biology, we can define **science** as the observation, identification, experimental investigation, and theoretical explanation of natural phenomena.

Science is conducted in different ways and at different levels. Some biologists study the molecules that compose life, and others try to understand how organisms survive in their natural environments. Experimentally, researchers often focus their efforts on **model organisms**—organisms studied by many different researchers so they can compare their results and determine scientific principles that apply more broadly to other species. Examples include *Escherichia coli* (a bacterium), *Saccharomyces cerevisiae* (a yeast), *Drosophila melanogaster* (fruit fly), *Caenorhabditis elegans* (a nematode worm), *Mus musculus* (mouse), and *Arabidopsis thaliana* (a flowering plant). Model organisms offer experimental advantages over other species. For example, *E. coli* is a very simple organism that can be easily grown in the laboratory. By limiting their work to a few such model organisms, researchers can gain a deeper understanding of these species. Importantly, the discoveries made using model organisms help us to understand how biological processes work in other species, including humans.

In this section, we will examine how biologists follow a standard approach, called the **scientific method**, to test their ideas. We will explore how scientific knowledge makes predictions that can be experimentally tested. Even so, not all discoveries are the result of researchers following the scientific method. Some discoveries are simply made by gathering new information. For example, as described earlier in Figures 1.1 to 1.3, the characterization of many plants and animals has led to the development of important medicines. In this section, we will also consider how researchers often set out on "fact-finding missions" aimed at uncovering new information that may eventually lead to modern discoveries in biology.

A harem of clownfish contains a single large female. The large female prevents other members of the harem from developing into females through aggressive dominance, which affects their hormone levels.

The other members of the harem are sexually immature juveniles.

The second largest fish is a mature male. When the female dies, this male will develop into a female.

Figure 1.13 How an understanding of genomes and proteomes provides us with a foundation to understand the characteristics of living organisms.

Concept Check: *What determines the morphological differences between male and female clownfish? Is it a difference between their genomes, their proteomes, or both?*

Biologists Investigate Life at Different Levels of Organization

In Figure 1.5, we examined the various levels of biological organization. The study of these different levels depends not only on the scientific interests of biologists but also on the tools available to them. The study of organisms in their natural environments is a branch of biology called **ecology**, which considers populations, communities, and ecosystems (**Figure 1.14a**). In addition, researchers examine the structures and functions of plants and animals, which are disciplines called **anatomy** and **physiology** (**Figure 1.14b**). With the advent of microscopy, **cell biology**, which is the study of cells, became an important branch of biology in the early 1900s and remains so today (**Figure 1.14c**). In the 1970s, genetic tools became available for studying single genes and the proteins they encode. This genetic technology enabled researchers to study individual molecules, such as proteins, in living cells and thereby spawned the field of **molecular biology**. Together with chemists and biochemists, molecular biologists focus their efforts on the structure and function of the molecules of life (**Figure 1.14d**). Such researchers want to understand how biology works at the molecular and even atomic levels. Overall, the 20th century saw a progressive increase in the number of biologists who used an approach to understanding biology called **reductionism**—reducing complex systems to simpler components as a way to understand how the system works. In biology, reductionists study the parts of a cell or organism as individual units.

In the 1980s, the pendulum began to swing in the other direction. Scientists have invented new tools that allow them to study groups of genes (genomic techniques) and groups of proteins (proteomic techniques). As mentioned earlier, biologists now use the term **systems biology** to describe research aimed at understanding how emergent properties arise. This term is often applied to the study of cells. In this context, systems biology may involve the investigation of groups of genes that encode proteins with a common purpose (**Figure 1.14e**). For example, a systems biologist may conduct experiments that try to characterize an entire cellular process, which is driven by dozens of different proteins. However, systems biology is not new. Animal and plant physiologists have been studying the functions of complex organ systems for centuries. Likewise, ecologists have been characterizing ecosystems for a very long time. The novelty and excitement of systems biology in recent years have been the result of new experimental tools that allow us to study complex interactions at the molecular level. As described throughout this textbook, the investigation of genomes and proteomes has provided important insights into many interesting topics in systems biology.

A Hypothesis Is a Proposed Idea, Whereas a Theory Is a Broad Explanation Backed by Extensive Evidence

Let's now consider the process of science. In biology, a **hypothesis** is a proposed explanation for a natural phenomenon. It is a proposition based on previous observations or experimental studies. For example, with knowledge of seasonal changes, you might hypothesize that maple trees drop their leaves in the autumn because of the shortened amount of daylight. An alternative hypothesis might be that the trees drop their leaves because of colder temperatures. In biology, a hypothesis requires more work by researchers to evaluate its validity.

Ecologists study species in their native environments.

(a) Ecology—population/ community/ecosystem levels

Anatomists and physiologists study how the structures of organisms are related to their functions.

(b) Anatomy and physiology— tissue/organ/organism levels

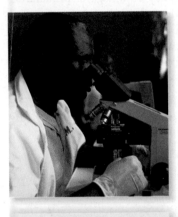

Cell biologists often use microscopes to learn how cells function.

(c) Cell biology—cellular levels

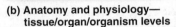

Molecular biologists and biochemists study the molecules and macromolecules that make up cells.

(d) Molecular biology— atomic/molecular levels

Systems biologists may study groups of molecules. The microarray shown in the inset determines the expression of many genes simultaneously.

(e) Systems biology—all levels, shown here at the molecular level

Figure 1.14 Biological investigation at different levels.

A useful hypothesis must make **predictions**—expected outcomes that can be shown to be correct or incorrect. In other words, a useful hypothesis is testable. If a hypothesis is incorrect, it should be **falsifiable**, which means that it can be shown to be incorrect by additional observations or experimentation. Alternatively, a hypothesis may be correct, so further work will not disprove it. In such cases, we would say that the researcher(s) has failed to reject the hypothesis. Even so, in science, a hypothesis is never really proven but rather always remains provisional. Researchers accept the possibility that perhaps they have not yet conceived of the correct hypothesis. After many experiments, biologists may conclude their hypothesis is consistent with known data, but they should never say the hypothesis is proven.

By comparison, the term **theory**, as it is used in biology, is a broad explanation of some aspect of the natural world that is substantiated by a large body of evidence. Biological theories incorporate observations, hypothesis testing, and the laws of other disciplines such as chemistry and physics. Theories are powerful because they allow us to make many predictions about the properties of living organisms. As an example, let's consider the theory that DNA is the genetic material and that it is organized into units called genes. An overwhelming body of evidence has substantiated this theory. Thousands of living species have been analyzed at the molecular level. All of them have been found to use DNA as their genetic material and to express genes that produce the proteins that lead to their characteristics. This theory makes many valid predictions. For example, certain types of mutations in genes are expected to affect the traits of organisms. This prediction has been confirmed experimentally. Similarly, this theory predicts that genetic material is copied and transmitted from parents to offspring. By comparing the DNA of parents and offspring, this prediction has also been confirmed. Furthermore, the theory explains the observation that offspring resemble their parents. Overall, two key attributes of a scientific theory are (1) consistency with a vast amount of known data and (2) the ability to make many correct predictions. Two other important biological theories we touched on in this chapter are the cell theory and the theory of evolution by natural selection.

The meaning of the term "theory" is sometimes muddled because it is used in different situations. In everyday language, a theory is often viewed as little more than a guess. For example, a person might say, "My theory is that Professor Simpson did not come to class today because he went to the beach." However, in biology, a theory is much more than a guess. A theory is an established set of ideas that explains a vast amount of data and offers valid predictions that can be tested. Like a hypothesis, a theory can never be proven to be true. Scientists acknowledge that they do not know everything. Even so, biologists would say that theories are extremely likely to be true, based on all known information. In this regard, theories are viewed as **knowledge**, which is the awareness and understanding of information.

Discovery-Based Science and Hypothesis Testing Are Scientific Approaches That Help Us Understand Biology

The path that leads to an important discovery is rarely a straight line. Rather, scientists ask questions, make observations, ask modified questions, and may eventually conduct experiments to test their hypotheses. The first attempts at experimentation may fail, and new experimental approaches may be needed. To suggest that scientists follow a rigid scientific method is an oversimplification of the process of science. Scientific advances often occur as scientists dig deeper and deeper into a topic that interests them. Curiosity is the key phenomenon that sparks scientific inquiry. How is biology actually conducted? As discussed next, researchers typically follow two general types of approaches: discovery-based science and hypothesis testing.

Discovery-Based Science   The collection and analysis of data without the need for a preconceived hypothesis is called **discovery-based science**, or simply **discovery science**. Why is discovery-based science carried out? The information gained from discovery-based science may lead to the formation of new hypotheses and, in the long run, may have practical applications that benefit people. Researchers, for example, have identified and begun to investigate newly discovered genes within the human genome without already knowing the function of the gene they are studying. The goal is to gather additional clues that may eventually allow them to propose a hypothesis that explains the gene's function. Discovery-based science often leads to hypothesis testing.

Hypothesis Testing   In biological science, the scientific method, also known as **hypothesis testing**, is usually followed to formulate and test the validity of a hypothesis. This strategy may be described as a five-step method:

1. Observations are made regarding natural phenomena.
2. These observations lead to a hypothesis that tries to explain the phenomena. A useful hypothesis is one that is testable because it makes specific predictions.
3. Experimentation is conducted to determine if the predictions are correct.
4. The data from the experiment are analyzed.
5. The hypothesis is considered to be consistent with the data, or it is rejected.

The scientific method is intended to be an objective way to gather knowledge. As an example, let's return to our scenario of maple trees dropping their leaves in autumn. By observing the length of daylight throughout the year and comparing that data with the time of the year when leaves fall, one hypothesis might be that leaves fall in response to a shorter amount of daylight (**Figure 1.15**). This hypothesis makes a prediction—exposure of maple trees to shorter daylight will cause their leaves to fall. To test this prediction, researchers would design and conduct an experiment.

How is hypothesis testing conducted? Although hypothesis testing may follow many paths, certain experimental features are common to this approach. First, data are often collected in two parallel manners. One set of experiments is done on the **control group**, while another set is conducted on the **experimental group**. In an ideal experiment, the control and experimental groups differ by only one factor. For example, an experiment could be conducted in which two groups of trees are observed, and the only difference between their environments is the length of light each day. To conduct such an experiment, researchers would grow small trees in a greenhouse where they could keep other factors such as temperature, water, and nutrients the same between the control and experimental groups, while providing them with different amounts of daylight. In the control group, the number

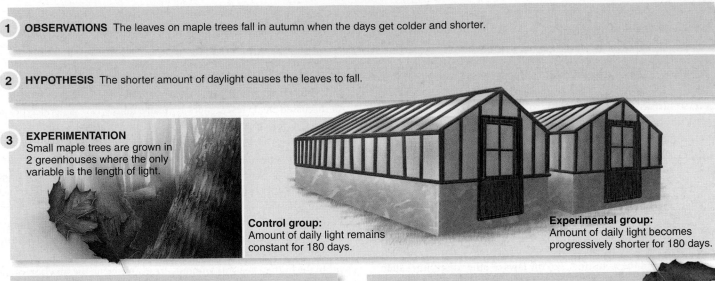

1 OBSERVATIONS The leaves on maple trees fall in autumn when the days get colder and shorter.

2 HYPOTHESIS The shorter amount of daylight causes the leaves to fall.

3 EXPERIMENTATION
Small maple trees are grown in 2 greenhouses where the only variable is the length of light.

Control group:
Amount of daily light remains constant for 180 days.

Experimental group:
Amount of daily light becomes progressively shorter for 180 days.

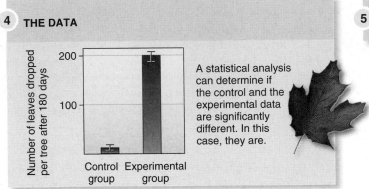

4 THE DATA

A statistical analysis can determine if the control and the experimental data are significantly different. In this case, they are.

5 CONCLUSION The hypothesis cannot be rejected.

Figure 1.15 **The steps of the scientific method, also known as hypothesis testing.** In this example, the goal is to test the hypothesis that maple trees drop their leaves in the autumn due to shortening length of daylight.

Concept Check: *What is the purpose of a control group in hypothesis testing?*

of hours of light provided by lightbulbs is kept constant each day, whereas in the experimental group, the amount of light each day becomes progressively shorter to mimic seasonal light changes. The researchers would then record the number of leaves dropped by the two groups of trees over a certain period of time.

Another key feature of hypothesis testing is data analysis. The result of experimentation is a set of data from which a biologist tries to draw conclusions. Biology is a quantitative science. When experimentation involves control and experimental groups, a common form of analysis is to determine if the data collected from the two groups are truly different from each other. Biologists apply statistical analyses to their data to determine if the control and experimental groups are likely to be different from each other because of the single variable that is different between the two groups. When they are statistically significant, the differences between the control and experimental data are not likely to have occurred as a matter of random chance.

In our tree example shown in Figure 1.15, the trees in the control group dropped far fewer leaves than did those in the experimental group. A statistical analysis could determine if the data collected from the two greenhouses are significantly different from each other. If the two sets of data are found not to be significantly different, the hypothesis would be rejected. Alternatively, if the differences between the two sets of data are significant, as shown in Figure 1.15, biologists would conclude that the hypothesis is consistent with the data, though it is not proven. A hallmark of science is that valid experiments are **repeatable**, which means that similar results are obtained when the experiment is conducted on multiple occasions. For our

example in Figure 1.15, the data would be valid only if the experiment was repeatable.

As described next, discovery-based science and hypothesis testing are often used together to learn more about a particular scientific topic. As an example, let's look at how both approaches have led to successes in the study of the disease called cystic fibrosis.

The Study of Cystic Fibrosis Provides Examples of Discovery-Based Science and Hypothesis Testing

Let's consider how biologists made discoveries related to the disease cystic fibrosis (CF), which affects about 1 in every 3,500 Americans. Persons with CF produce abnormally thick and sticky mucus that obstructs the lungs and leads to life-threatening lung infections. The thick mucus also blocks ducts in the pancreas, which prevents the digestive enzymes this organ produces from reaching the intestine. Without these enzymes, the intestine cannot fully absorb proteins and fats, which can cause malnutrition. Persons with this disease may also experience liver damage because the thick mucus can obstruct the liver. On average, people with CF in the United States currently live into their late 30s. Fortunately, as more advances have been made in treatment, this number has steadily increased.

Because of its medical significance, many scientists are interested in CF and are conducting studies aimed at gaining greater information regarding its underlying cause. The hope is that knowing more about the disease may lead to improved treatment options, and perhaps even a cure. As described next, discovery-based science and hypothesis testing have been critical to gaining a better understanding of this disease.

The CFTR Gene and Discovery-Based Science

In 1935, Dorothy Andersen determined that cystic fibrosis is a genetic disorder. Persons with CF have inherited two faulty *CFTR* genes, one from each parent. (We now know this gene encodes a protein named the cystic fibrosis transmembrane regulator, abbreviated CFTR.) In the 1980s, researchers used discovery-based science to identify this gene. Their search for the *CFTR* gene did not require any preconceived hypothesis regarding the function of the gene. Rather, they used genetic strategies similar to those described in Chapter 20. Research groups headed by Lap-Chee Tsui, Francis Collins, and John Riordan identified the *CFTR* gene in 1989.

The discovery of the gene made it possible to devise diagnostic testing methods to determine if a person carries a faulty *CFTR* gene. In addition, the characterization of the *CFTR* gene provided important clues about its function. Researchers observed striking similarities between the *CFTR* gene and other genes that were already known to encode proteins that function in the transport of substances across membranes. Based on this observation, as well as other kinds of data, the scientists hypothesized that the function of the normal *CFTR* gene is to encode a transport protein. In this way, the identification of the *CFTR* gene led them to conduct experiments aimed at testing a hypothesis of its function.

The CFTR Gene and Hypothesis Testing

Researchers considered the characterization of the *CFTR* gene along with other studies showing that patients with the disorder have an abnormal regulation of salt balance across their plasma membranes. They hypothesized that the normal *CFTR* gene encodes a protein that functions in the transport of chloride ions (Cl⁻) across the membranes of cells (**Figure 1.16**). This hypothesis led to experimentation in which they tested normal cells and cells from CF patients for their ability to transport Cl⁻. The CF cells were found to be defective in chloride transport. In 1990,

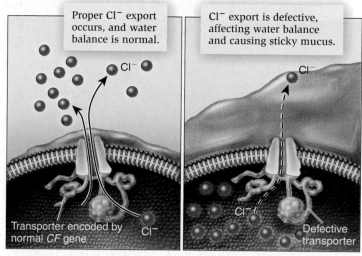

Proper Cl⁻ export occurs, and water balance is normal.	**Cl⁻ export is defective, affecting water balance and causing sticky mucus.**

Transporter encoded by normal *CF* gene

Defective transporter

Lung cell with normal *CF* gene   Lung cell with faulty *CF* gene

Figure 1.16 **A hypothesis suggesting an explanation for the function of a gene defective in patients with cystic fibrosis.** The normal *CFTR* gene, which does not carry a mutation, encodes a protein that transports chloride ions (Cl⁻) across the plasma membrane to the outside of the cell. In persons with CF, this protein is defective due to a mutation in the *CFTR* gene.

Concept Check: *Explain how discovery-based science helped researchers to hypothesize that the CFTR gene encodes a transport protein.*

scientists successfully transferred the normal *CFTR* gene into CF cells in the laboratory. The introduction of the normal gene corrected the cells' defect in chloride transport. Overall, the results showed that the *CFTR* gene encodes a protein that transports Cl⁻ across the plasma membrane. A mutation in this gene causes it to encode a defective protein, leading to a salt imbalance that affects water levels outside the cell, which explains the thick and sticky mucus in CF patients. In this example, hypothesis testing has provided a way to evaluate a hypothesis about how a disease is caused by a genetic change.

FEATURE INVESTIGATION

Observation and Experimentation Form the Core of Biology

Biology is largely about the process of discovery. Therefore, a recurring theme of this textbook is how scientists design experiments, analyze data, and draw conclusions. Although each chapter contains many examples of data collection and experiments, a consistent element is a "Feature Investigation"—an actual study by current or past researchers. Some of these involve discovery-based science, in which biologists collect and interpret data in an attempt to make discoveries that are not hypothesis driven. Most Feature Investigations, however, involve hypothesis testing in which a hypothesis is stated and the experiment and resulting data are presented. Figure 1.15 shows the general form of Feature Investigations.

The Feature Investigations allow you to appreciate the connection between science and scientific theories. As you read a Fea-

ture Investigation, you may find yourself thinking about different approaches and alternative hypotheses. Different people can view the same data and arrive at very different conclusions. As you progress through the experiments in this textbook, we hope you will try to develop your own skills at formulating hypotheses, designing experiments, and interpreting data.

Experimental Questions

1. Discuss the difference between discovery-based science and hypothesis testing.

2. What are the steps in the scientific method, also called hypothesis testing?

3. When conducting an experiment, explain how a control group and an experimental group differ from each other.

Figure 1.17 **The social aspects of science.** At scientific meetings, researchers gather together to discuss new data and discoveries. Research that is conducted by professors, students, lab technicians, and industrial participants is sometimes hotly debated.

Science as a Social Discipline

Finally, it is worthwhile to point out that biology is a social as well as a scientific discipline. Different laboratories often collaborate on scientific projects. After performing observations and experiments, biologists communicate their results in different ways. Most importantly, papers are submitted to scientific journals. Following submission, papers usually undergo a **peer-review process** in which other scientists, who are experts in the area, evaluate the paper and make suggestions regarding its quality. As a result of peer review, a paper is either accepted for publication, rejected, or the authors of the paper may be given suggestions for how to revise the work or conduct additional experiments before it is acceptable for publication.

Another social aspect of research is that biologists often attend meetings where they report their most recent work to the scientific community (**Figure 1.17**). They comment on each other's ideas and work, eventually shaping together the information that builds into scientific theories over many years. As you develop your skills at scrutinizing experiments, it is helpful to discuss your ideas with other people, including fellow students and faculty members. Importantly, you do not need to "know all the answers" before you enter into a scientific discussion. Instead, a more realistic way to view science is as an ongoing and never-ending series of questions.

 Summary of Key Concepts

Biology is the study of life. Discoveries in biology help us understand how life exists, and they also have many practical applications, such as the development of drugs to treat human diseases. (Figures 1.1, 1.2, 1.3)

1.1 Principles of Biology and the Levels of Biological Organization

- Eight principles underlie the characteristics that are common to all forms of life. All living things (1) are composed of cells as their simplest unit; (2) use energy; (3) interact with their environment; (4) maintain homeostasis; (5) grow and develop; and (6) have genetic material for reproduction. Also, (7) populations of organisms evolve from one generation to the next, and (8) are connected by an evolutionary history (Figure 1.4).

- Additional principles include (9) structure determines function; (10) new properties of life emerge from complex interactions; (11) biology is an experimental science; and (12) biology influences our society.

- Living organisms can be viewed at different levels of biological organization: atoms, molecules and macromolecules, cells, tissues, organs, organisms, populations, communities, ecosystems, and the biosphere (Figure 1.5).

1.2 Unity and Diversity of Life

- Changes in species often occur as a result of modification of pre-existing structures (Figure 1.6).

- During vertical evolution, mutations in a lineage alter the characteristics of species from one generation to the next. Individuals with greater reproductive success are more likely to contribute to future generations, a process known as natural selection. Over the long run, this process alters species and may produce new species (Figure 1.7).

- Horizontal gene transfer may involve the transfer of genes between different species. Along with vertical evolution, it is an important process in biological evolution, producing a web of life (Figures 1.8, 1.9).

- Taxonomy is the grouping of species according to their evolutionary relatedness to other species. Going from broad to narrow groups, each species is placed into a domain, kingdom, phylum, class, order, family, and genus (Figures 1.10, 1.11).

- The genome is the genetic composition of a species. It provides a blueprint for the traits of an organism, is transmitted from parents to offspring, and acts as an instrument for evolutionary change. The proteome is the collection of proteins that a cell or organism makes (Figure 1.12).

- An analysis of genomes and proteomes helps us to understand how information at the molecular level relates to the characteristics of individuals and how they survive in their native environments (Figure 1.13).

1.3 Biology as a Scientific Discipline

- Biological science is the observation, identification, experimental investigation, and theoretical explanation of natural phenomena.

- Biologists study life at different levels, ranging from ecosystems to the molecular components in cells (Figure 1.14).

- A hypothesis is a proposal to explain a natural phenomenon. A useful hypothesis makes a testable prediction. A biological theory is a broad explanation that is substantiated by a large body of evidence.

- Discovery-based science is an approach in which researchers conduct experiments and analyze data without a preconceived hypothesis.

- The scientific method, also called hypothesis testing, is a series of steps to formulate and test the validity of a hypothesis. The experimentation often involves a comparison between control and experimental groups (Figure 1.15).

- The study of cystic fibrosis provides an example in which both discovery-based science and hypothesis testing led to key insights regarding the nature of the disease (Figure 1.16).

- Each chapter in this textbook has a "Feature Investigation," an actual study by current or past researchers that highlights the experimental approach and helps you appreciate how science has led to key discoveries in biology.
- Biology is a social discipline in which scientists often work in teams. To be published, a scientific paper is usually subjected to a peer-review process in which other scientists evaluate the paper and make suggestions regarding its quality. Advances in science often occur when scientists gather and discuss their data (Figure 1.17).

Assess and Discuss

Test Yourself

1. The process in which living organisms maintain a relatively stable internal condition is
   a. adaptation.
   b. evolution.
   c. metabolism.
   d. homeostasis.
   e. development.

2. Populations of organisms change over the course of many generations. Many of these changes result in increased survival and reproduction. This phenomenon is
   a. evolution.
   b. homeostasis.
   c. development.
   d. genetics.
   e. metabolism.

3. All of the places on Earth where living organisms are found is termed
   a. the ecosystem.
   b. a community.
   c. the biosphere.
   d. a viable land mass.
   e. a population.

4. Which of the following is an example of horizontal gene transfer?
   a. the transmission of an eye color gene from father to daughter
   b. the transmission of a mutant gene causing cystic fibrosis from father to daughter
   c. the transmission of a gene conferring pathogenicity (the ability to cause disease) from one bacterial species to another
   d. the transmission of a gene conferring antibiotic resistance from a mother cell to its two daughter cells
   e. all of the above

5. The scientific name for humans is *Homo sapiens*. The name *Homo* is the _____ to which humans are classified.
   a. kingdom
   b. phylum
   c. order
   d. genus
   e. species

6. The complete genetic makeup of an organism is called
   a. the genus.
   b. the genome.
   c. the proteome.
   d. the genotype.
   e. the phenotype.

7. A proposed explanation for a natural phenomenon is
   a. a theory.
   b. a law.
   c. a prediction.
   d. a hypothesis.
   e. an assay.

8. In science, a theory should
   a. be equated with knowledge.
   b. be supported by a substantial body of evidence.
   c. provide the ability to make many correct predictions.
   d. do all of the above.
   e. b and c only

9. Conducting research without a preconceived hypothesis is called
   a. discovery-based science.
   b. the scientific method.
   c. hypothesis testing.
   d. a control experiment.
   e. none of the above.

10. What is the purpose of using a control group in scientific experiments?
    a. A control group allows the researcher to practice the experiment first before actually conducting it.
    b. A researcher can compare the results in the experimental group and control group to determine if a single variable is causing a particular outcome in the experimental group.
    c. A control group provides the framework for the entire experiment so the researcher can recall the procedures that should be conducted.
    d. A control group allows the researcher to conduct other experimental changes without disturbing the original experiment.
    e. All of the above are correct.

Conceptual Questions

1. Of the first eight principles of biology described in Figure 1.4, which apply to individuals and which apply to populations?

2. Explain how it is possible for evolution to result in unity among different species yet also produce amazing diversity.

3. In your own words, describe the twelve principles of biology that are detailed at the beginning of this chapter.

Collaborative Questions

1. Discuss whether or not you think that theories in biology are true. Outside of biology, how do you decide if something is true?

2. In certain animals, such as alligators, sex is determined by temperature. When alligator eggs are exposed to low temperatures, most alligator embryos develop into females. Discuss how this phenomenon is related to genomes and proteomes.

Online Resource

www.brookerbiology.com

Stay a step ahead in your studies with animations that bring concepts to life and practice tests to assess your understanding. Your instructor may also recommend the interactive eBook, individualized learning tools, and more.

UNIT I
CHEMISTRY

Living organisms can be thought of as collections of discrete packages—one or more cells—within which occur a wide array of chemical reactions. These reactions occur between atoms and molecules and may require, or in some cases release, energy. Chemical reactions and interactions between molecules play a role in virtually all aspects of a cell's activities. In order to understand how living organisms function, grow, develop, behave, and interact with their environments, therefore, we first need to understand some basic principles of atomic and molecular structure and the forces that allow them to interact with each other. We begin this unit with an overview of **inorganic chemistry**—that is, the nature of atoms and molecules, with the exception of those that contain rings or chains of carbon. Such carbon-containing molecules form the basis of **organic chemistry** and are covered in Chapter 3.

💡 *The following biology principles will be emphasized in this unit:*

- **Living organisms use energy:** *We will see how the chemical energy stored in certain of the bonds of molecules such as sugars and fats can be released and used by living organisms to perform numerous functions that support life, including growth, digestion, and locomotion, among many others.*

- **Structure determines function:** *As described in Chapter 3, the three-dimensional structure of molecules is critical in enabling them to specifically interact with each other.*

- **The genetic material provides a blueprint for reproduction, and all species (past and present) are related by an evolutionary history:** *Nucleic acids, the basis of inherited genetic material, are first introduced in Chapter 3.*

- **New properties emerge from complex interactions:** *You will learn in this unit how various types of forces create complex molecules from simple atoms and impart precise shapes on these molecules. The newly created molecule has properties that are different from those of its component atoms.*

- **Biology affects our society:** *In Chapter 2, we will see how an understanding of chemistry has transformed the ability of physicians to diagnose disease in humans. One example of an application of chemistry to medicine discussed in Chapter 2 is the PET scan.*

The Chemical Basis of Life I:
Atoms, Molecules, and Water

2

Biology—the study of life—is founded on the principles of chemistry and physics. All living organisms are a collection of atoms and molecules bound together and interacting with each other through the forces of nature. Throughout this textbook, we will see how chemistry can be applied to living organisms as we discuss the components of cells, the functions of proteins, the flow of nutrients in plants and animals, and the evolution of new genes. This chapter lays the groundwork for understanding these and other concepts. We begin with an overview of the nature of atoms and molecules, focusing on the structure of the atom and how it was discovered. We next explore the various ways that atoms combine with other atoms to create molecules, looking at the different types of chemical bonds between atoms, how these bonds form, and how they determine the structures of molecules. We end with an examination of the water molecule and the properties that make it a crucial component of living organisms and their environment.

Crystals of sodium chloride (NaCl), a molecule composed of two elements.

2.1 Atoms

Learning Outcomes:

1. Describe the general structure of atoms and their constituent particles.
2. Discuss the way electrons orbit the nucleus of an atom within discrete energy levels.
3. Relate atomic structure to the periodic table of the elements.
4. Quantify atomic mass using units such as daltons and moles.
5. Explain how a single element may exist in more than one form, called isotopes, and how certain isotopes have importance in human medicine.
6. List the elements that make up most of the mass of all living organisms.

All life-forms are composed of **matter**, which is defined as anything that contains mass and occupies space. In living organisms, matter may exist in any of three states: solid, liquid, or gas. All matter is composed of **atoms**, which are the smallest functional units of matter that form all chemical substances and ultimately all organisms; they cannot be further broken down into other substances by ordinary chemical or physical means. Atoms, in turn, are composed of smaller, subatomic components, collectively referred to as particles. Chemists study the properties of atoms and **molecules**, which are two or more atoms bonded together. A major interest of the physicist, by contrast, is to uncover the properties of subatomic particles. Chemistry and physics merge when one attempts to understand the mechanisms by which atoms and molecules interact. When atoms and molecules are studied in the context of a living organism, the science of biochemistry emerges. In this section, we explore the physical properties of atoms so we can understand how atoms combine to form molecules of biological importance.

Atoms Are Composed of Subatomic Particles

There are many types of atoms in living organisms. The simplest atom, hydrogen, is approximately 0.1 nanometers (nm, 1×10^{-10} meters) in diameter, roughly one-millionth the diameter of a human hair. Each specific type of atom—nitrogen, hydrogen, oxygen, and so on—is called an **element** (or chemical element), which is defined as a pure substance of only one kind of atom.

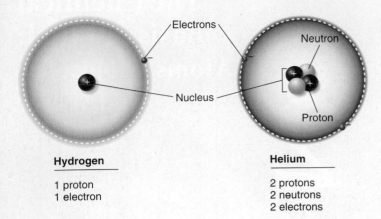

Hydrogen

1 proton
1 electron

Helium

2 protons
2 neutrons
2 electrons

Figure 2.1 **Diagrams of two simple atoms.** This is a model of the two simplest atoms, hydrogen and helium. The nucleus consists of protons and neutrons, and electrons are found outside the nucleus. Note: In all figures of atoms, the sizes and distances are not to scale.

Three subatomic particles—**protons** (p^+), **neutrons** (n^0), and **electrons** (e^-)—are found within atoms (**Figure 2.1**). The protons and neutrons are confined to a very small volume at the center of an atom, the **atomic nucleus**, whereas the electrons are found in regions at various distances from the nucleus. With the exception of ions—atoms that have gained or lost one or more electrons (described later in this chapter)—the numbers of protons and electrons in a given type of atom are identical, but the number of neutrons may vary. Each of the subatomic particles has a different electric charge. Protons have one unit of positive charge, electrons have one unit of negative charge, and neutrons are electrically neutral. Like charges always repel each other, and opposite charges always attract each other. It is the opposite charges of the protons and electrons that create an atom—the positive charges in the nucleus attract the negatively charged electrons.

Because the protons are located in the atomic nucleus, the nucleus has a net positive charge equal to the number of protons it contains. The entire atom has no net electric charge, however, because the number of negatively charged electrons around the nucleus is equal to the number of positively charged protons in the nucleus.

This basic concept of the structure of the atom was not established until a landmark experiment conducted by Ernest Rutherford during the years 1909–1911, as described next.

FEATURE INVESTIGATION

Rutherford Determined the Modern Model of the Atom

Nobel laureate Ernest Rutherford was born in 1871 in New Zealand, but he did his greatest work at McGill University in Montreal, Canada, and later at the University of Manchester in England. At that time, scientists knew that atoms contained charged particles but had no idea how those particles were distributed. Neutrons had not yet been discovered, and many scientists, including Rutherford, hypothesized that the positive charge and the mass of an atom were evenly dispersed throughout the atom.

In a now-classic experiment, Rutherford aimed a fine beam of positively charged α (alpha) particles at an extremely thin sheet of gold foil only 400 atoms thick (**Figure 2.2**). Alpha particles are the two protons and two neutrons that comprise the nuclei of helium atoms; you can think of them as helium atoms without their electrons (see Figure 2.1). Surrounding the gold foil were zinc sulfide screens that registered any α particles passing through or bouncing off the foil, much like film in a camera detects light. Rutherford hypothesized that if the positive charges of the gold atoms were uniformly distributed, many of the positively charged α particles would be slightly deflected, because one of the most important features of electric charge is that like charges repel each other. Due to their much smaller mass, he did not expect electrons in the gold atoms to have any effect on the ability of an α particle to move through the metal foil.

Surprisingly, Rutherford discovered that more than 98% of the α particles passed right through as if the foil was not there and only

Figure 2.2 Rutherford's gold foil experiment, demonstrating that most of the volume of an atom is empty space.

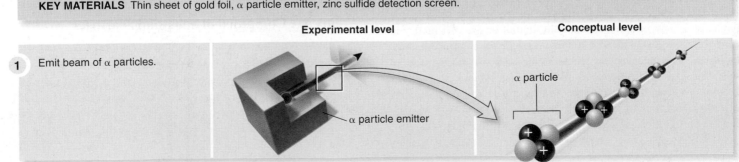

HYPOTHESIS Atoms in gold foil are composed of diffuse, evenly distributed positive charges that should usually cause α particles to be slightly deflected as they pass through.

KEY MATERIALS Thin sheet of gold foil, α particle emitter, zinc sulfide detection screen.

Experimental level   **Conceptual level**

1   Emit beam of α particles.

α particle emitter

α particle

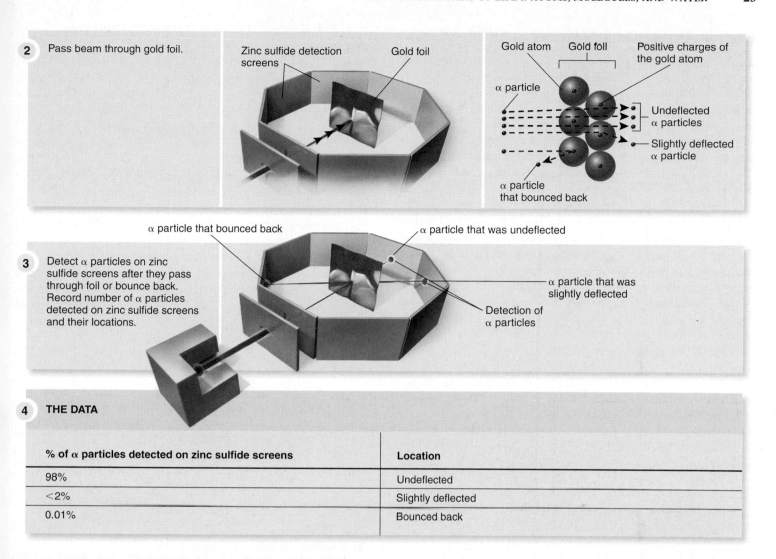

2 Pass beam through gold foil.

Zinc sulfide detection screens

Gold foil

Gold atom   Gold foil   Positive charges of the gold atom

α particle

Undeflected α particles

Slightly deflected α particle

α particle that bounced back

3 Detect α particles on zinc sulfide screens after they pass through foil or bounce back. Record number of α particles detected on zinc sulfide screens and their locations.

α particle that bounced back

α particle that was undeflected

α particle that was slightly deflected

Detection of α particles

4   THE DATA

% of α particles detected on zinc sulfide screens	Location
98%	Undeflected
<2%	Slightly deflected
0.01%	Bounced back

5   CONCLUSION Most of the volume of an atom is empty space, with the positive charges concentrated in a small volume.

6   SOURCE Rutherford, E. 1911. The scattering of α and β particles by matter and the structure of the atom. *Philosophical Magazine* 21:669–688.

a small percentage was slightly deflected; a few even bounced back at a sharp angle! To explain the 98% that passed right through, Rutherford concluded that most of the volume of an atom is empty space. To explain the few α particles that bounced back at a sharp angle, he postulated that most of the atom's positive charge was localized in a highly compact area at the center of the atom. The existence of this small, dense region of highly concentrated positive charge—which today we call the atomic nucleus—explains how some α particles could be so strongly deflected by the gold foil. The α particles would bounce back on the rare occasion when they directly collided with an atomic nucleus. Therefore, based on these results, Rutherford rejected his original hypothesis that atoms are composed of diffuse, evenly distributed positive charges.

From this experiment, without being able to actually visualize an atom, Rutherford proposed a transitional model of an atom, with its small, positively charged nucleus surrounded at relatively great distances by negatively charged electrons. Today we know that more than 99.99% of an atom's volume is outside the nucleus. Indeed, the nucleus accounts for only about 1/10,000 of an atom's diameter—most of an atom is empty space!

Experimental Questions

1. Before the experiment conducted by Ernest Rutherford, how did many scientists envision the structure of an atom?

2. What was the hypothesis tested by Rutherford?

3. What were the results of the experiment? How did Rutherford interpret the results?

Electrons Occupy Orbitals Around an Atom's Nucleus

At one time, scientists visualized an atom as a mini–solar system, with the nucleus being the Sun and the electrons traveling in clearly defined orbits around it. A diagram of the two simplest atoms—hydrogen and helium—which have the smallest numbers of protons, was shown in Figure 2.1. This model of the atom is now known to be an oversimplification, because as described shortly, electrons do not actually orbit the nucleus in a defined path like planets around the Sun. However, this depiction of an atom remains a convenient way to diagram atoms in two dimensions.

Electrons move at terrific speeds. Some estimates suggest that the electron in a typical hydrogen atom could circle the Earth in less than 20 seconds! Partly for this reason, it is difficult to precisely predict the exact location of a given electron. In fact, we can only describe the region of space surrounding the nucleus in which there is a high probability of finding that electron. These regions are called **orbitals**. A better model of an atom, therefore, is a central nucleus surrounded by cloudlike orbitals. The cloud represents the region in which a given electron is most likely to be found. Some orbitals are spherical, called *s* orbitals, whereas others assume a shape that is often described as similar to a propeller or dumbbell and are called *p* orbitals (**Figure 2.3**). An orbital can contain a maximum of two electrons. Consequently, any atom with more than two electrons must contain additional orbitals.

Orbitals occupy so-called **electron shells**, or energy levels. **Energy** can be defined as the capacity to do work or effect a change. In biology, we often refer to various types of energy, such as light energy, mechanical energy, and chemical energy. Electrons orbiting a nucleus have kinetic energy, that is, the energy of moving matter. Atoms with progressively more electrons have orbitals within electron shells that are at greater and greater distances from the nucleus. These shells are numbered, with shell number 1 being closest to the nucleus. Different electron shells may contain one or more orbitals, each orbital with up to two electrons. The innermost electron shell of all atoms has room for only two electrons, which spin in opposite directions within a spherical *s* orbital (1*s*). The second electron shell is composed of one spherical *s* orbital (2*s*) and three dumbbell-shaped *p* orbitals (2*p*). Therefore, the second shell can hold up to four pairs of electrons, or eight electrons altogether (see Figure 2.3).

Electrons vary in the amount of energy they have. The shell closest to the nucleus fills up with the lowest energy electrons first, and then each subsequent shell fills with higher and higher energy electrons, one shell at a time. Within a given shell, the energy of electrons can also vary among different orbitals. In the second shell, for example, the *s* orbital has lower energy, whereas the three *p* orbitals have slightly higher and roughly equal energies. In that case, two electrons fill the *s* orbital first. Any additional electrons fill the *p* orbitals one electron at a time.

Although electrons are actually found in orbitals of varying shapes, as shown in Figure 2.3, scientists often use more simplified diagrams when depicting the electron shells of atoms. **Figure 2.4a** illustrates an

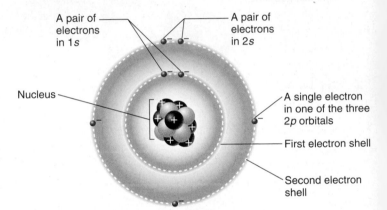

(a) Simplified depiction of a nitrogen atom (7 electrons; 2 electrons in first electron shell, 5 in second electron shell)

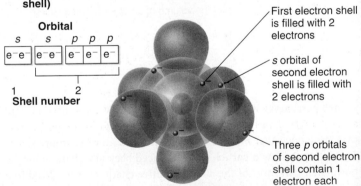

(b) Nitrogen atom showing electrons in orbitals

Figure 2.4 Diagrams showing the multiple electron shells and orbitals of a nitrogen atom. The nitrogen atom is shown **(a)** simplified and **(b)** with all of its orbitals and shells. An atom's shells fill up one by one. In shells containing more than one orbital, the orbital with lowest energy fills first. Subsequent orbitals gain one electron at a time, shown schematically in boxes, where *e*⁻ represents an electron. Heavier elements contain additional shells and orbitals.

Concept Check: *Explain the difference between an electron shell and an orbital.*

Orbital name	1*s*	2*s*	2*p*
	Nucleus		
Number of electrons per electron shell	2	2 per orbital; 8 total	
Orbital shape	Spherical	First orbital: spherical	Second to fourth orbital: dumbbell-shaped

Figure 2.3 Diagrams of individual electron orbitals. Electrons are found outside the nucleus in orbitals that may resemble spherical or dumbbell-shaped clouds. The orbital cloud represents a region in which the probability is high of locating a particular electron. For this illustration, only two shells are shown; the heaviest elements contain a total of seven shells.

example involving the element nitrogen. An atom of this element has seven protons and seven electrons. Two electrons fill the first shell, and five electrons are found in the outer shell. Two of these fill the 2s orbital and are shown as a pair of electrons in the second shell. The other three electrons in the second shell are found singly in each of the three p orbitals. The diagram in Figure 2.4a makes it easy to see whether electrons are paired within the same orbital and whether the outer shell is full. Figure 2.4b shows a more scientifically accurate depiction of a nitrogen atom, showing how the electrons occupy orbitals with different shapes.

Most atoms have outer shells that are not completely filled with electrons. Nitrogen, as we just saw, has a first shell filled with two electrons and a second shell with five electrons (see Figure 2.4a). Because the second shell can actually hold eight electrons, the outer shell of a nitrogen atom is not full. As discussed later in this chapter, atoms that have unfilled electron shells tend to share, release, or obtain electrons to fill their outer shell. Those electrons in the outermost shell are called the **valence electrons**. As you will learn shortly, in certain cases such electrons allow atoms to form chemical bonds with each other, in which two or more atoms become joined together to create a new substance.

Each Element Has a Unique Number of Protons

Each chemical element has a specific and unique number of protons in its nucleus that distinguishes it from another element. The number of protons in an atom is its **atomic number**. For example, hydrogen, the simplest atom, has an atomic number of 1, corresponding to its single proton. Magnesium has an atomic number of 12, corresponding to its 12 protons. Recall that with the exception of ions, the number of protons and electrons in a given atom are identical. Therefore, the atomic number is also equal to the number of electrons in the atom, resulting in a net electric charge of zero.

Figure 2.5 shows the first three rows of the periodic table of the elements, which arranges the known elements according to their atomic number and electron shells (see Appendix A for the complete periodic table). A one- or two-letter symbol is used as an abbreviation for each element. The rows (known as "periods") indicate the number of electron shells. For example, hydrogen (H) has one shell, lithium (Li) has two shells, and sodium (Na) has three shells. The columns (called "groups"), from left to right, indicate the numbers of electrons in the outer shell. The outer shell of lithium (Li) has one electron, beryllium (Be) has two, boron (B) has three, and so forth. This

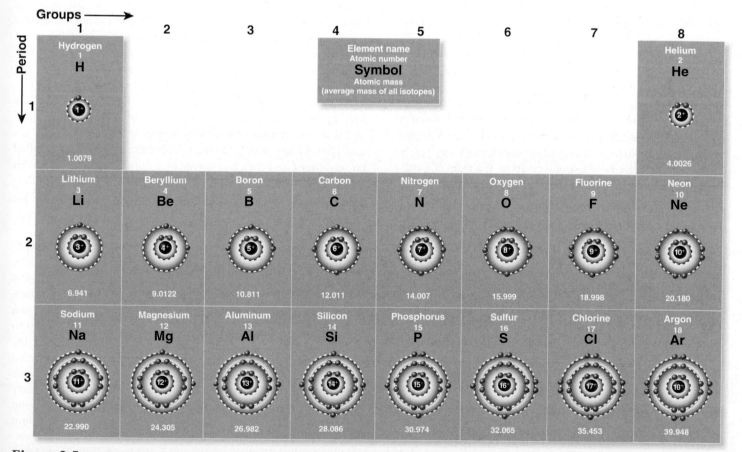

Figure 2.5 The first three rows of the periodic table of the elements. The elements are shown in models that depict the electron shells in different colors and the total number of electrons in each shell. The occupancy of orbitals is that of the elements in their pure state. The red sphere represents the nucleus of the atom, and the numerical value with the + designation represents the number of protons and, therefore, the positive charge of the nucleus. Elements are arranged in groups (columns) and periods (rows). For the complete periodic table, see Appendix A.

organization of the periodic table tends to arrange elements based on similar chemical properties. The similarities of elements within a group occur because they have the same number of valence electrons, and therefore, they have similar chemical bonding properties.

Atoms Have a Small but Measurable Mass

Atoms are extremely small and thus have very little mass. A single hydrogen atom, for example, has a mass of about 1.67×10^{-24} g (grams). Protons and neutrons are nearly equal in mass, and each are more than 1,800 times the mass of an electron (**Table 2.1**). Because of their tiny size relative to protons and neutrons, the mass of the electrons in an atom is ignored in calculations of atomic mass.

The **atomic mass** scale indicates an atom's mass relative to the mass of other atoms. By convention, the most common type of carbon atom, which has six protons and six neutrons, is assigned an atomic mass of exactly 12. On this scale, a hydrogen atom has an atomic mass of 1, indicating that it has 1/12 the mass of a carbon atom. A magnesium atom, with an atomic mass of 24, has twice the mass of a carbon atom.

The term mass is sometimes confused with weight, but these two terms refer to different features of matter. Weight is derived from the gravitational pull on a given mass. For example, a man who weighs 154 pounds on Earth would weigh only 25 pounds if he were standing on the Moon, and he would weigh 21 trillion pounds if he could stand on a neutron star. However, his mass is the same in all locations because he has the same amount of matter. Because we are discussing mass on Earth, we can assume that the gravitational tug on all matter is roughly equivalent, and thus the terms become essentially interchangeable for our purpose.

Atomic mass is measured in units called daltons, after the English chemist John Dalton, who, in postulating that matter is composed of tiny indivisible units he called atoms, laid the groundwork for atomic theory. One **dalton (Da)**, also known as an atomic mass unit (amu), equals 1/12 the mass of a carbon atom, or about the mass of a proton or a hydrogen atom. Therefore, the most common type of carbon atom has an atomic mass of 12 Da.

Because atoms such as hydrogen have a small mass, but atoms such as carbon have a larger mass, 1 g of hydrogen contains more atoms than 1 g of carbon. A mole (mol) of any substance contains the same number of particles as there are atoms in exactly 12 g of carbon. Twelve grams of carbon equals 1 mol of carbon, and 1 g of hydrogen equals 1 mol of hydrogen. As first described by Italian physicist Amedeo Avogadro, 1 mol of any element contains the same number of atoms—6.022×10^{23}. For example, 12 g of carbon contain 6.022×10^{23} atoms, and 1 g of hydrogen, whose atoms have 1/12 the mass of a carbon atom, also contains 6.022×10^{23} atoms. This number, which is known today as Avogadro's number, is large enough to be somewhat mind-boggling, and thus gives us an idea of just how small atoms really are. To visualize the enormity of this number, imagine that people could move through a turnstile at a rate of 1 million people per second. Even at that incredible rate, it would require almost 20 billion years for 6.022×10^{23} people to move through that turnstile!

Isotopes Vary in Their Number of Neutrons

Although the number of neutrons in most biologically relevant atoms is often equal to the number of protons, many elements can exist in multiple forms, called **isotopes**, that differ in the number of neutrons they contain. For example, the most abundant form of the carbon atom, ^{12}C, contains six protons and six neutrons, and thus has an atomic number of 6 and an atomic mass of 12 Da, as described earlier. The superscript placed to the left of ^{12}C is the sum of the protons and neutrons. The rare carbon isotope ^{14}C, however, contains six protons and eight neutrons. Although ^{14}C has an atomic number of 6, it has an atomic mass of 14 Da. Nearly 99% of the carbon in living organisms is ^{12}C. Consequently, the *average* atomic mass of carbon is very close to, but actually slightly greater than, 12 Da because of the existence of a small amount of heavier isotopes. This explains why the atomic masses given in the periodic table do not add up exactly to the predicted masses based on the atomic number and the number of neutrons of a given atom (for example, see carbon in Figure 2.5).

Isotopes of an atom often have similar chemical properties but may have very different physical properties. For example, many isotopes found in nature are inherently unstable; the length of time they persist is measured in half-lives—the time it takes for 50% of the isotope to decay. Some persist for very long times; for example, ^{14}C has a half-life of more than 5,000 years. Such unstable isotopes are called **radioisotopes**, and they lose energy by emitting subatomic particles and/or radiation. At the very low amounts found in nature, radioisotopes usually pose no serious threat to life, but exposure of living organisms to high amounts of radioactivity can result in the disruption of cellular function, cancer, and even death.

Modern medical treatment and diagnosis make use of the special properties of radioactive compounds in many ways. For example, beams of high-energy radiation can be directed onto cancerous parts of the body to kill cancer cells. In another example, one or more atoms in a metabolically important molecule, such as the sugar glucose, can be chemically replaced with a radioactive isotope of fluorine (^{18}F) to create a molecule called fluorodeoxyglucose (FDG). ^{18}F has a half-life of about 110 minutes. When a solution containing such a modified radioactive glucose is injected into a person's bloodstream, the organs of the body take it up from the blood just as they would ordinary glucose. Special imaging techniques, such as the positron-emission tomography (PET) scan shown in **Figure 2.6**, can detect the amount of the radioactive FDG in the body's organs. In this way, it is possible to visualize whether organs such as the heart or brain are functioning normally, or at an increased or decreased rate. A PET scan of the heart that showed reduced uptake of glucose from the blood might indicate the blood vessels of the heart were damaged and are

Table 2.1		Characteristics of Major Subatomic Particles		
Particle		Location	Charge	Mass relative to electron
Proton	+	Nucleus	+1	1,836
Neutron		Nucleus	0	1,839
Electron	−	Around the nucleus	−1	1

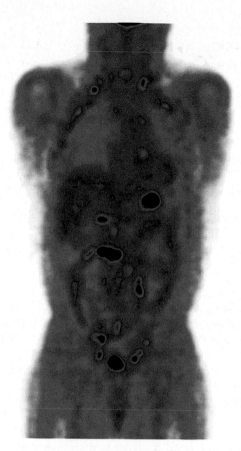

Figure 2.6 **Diagnostic image of the human body using radioisotopes.** A procedure called positron-emission tomography (PET) scanning highlights regions of the body that are actively using glucose, the body's major energy source. Radioactivity in this image shows up as a color. The dark patches are regions of extremely intense activity, which were later determined to be cancer in this patient.

BIOLOGY PRINCIPLE **Biology affects our society.** Applying an understanding of chemistry to biology has transformed the ability of physicians to diagnose disease in humans. In the United States alone, between 1 and 2 million PET scans such as this one are performed each year, helping to localize the sites and extent of diseased structures, greatly facilitating subsequent drug or surgical treatments.

Table 2.2	Chemical Elements Essential for Life in Many Organisms*		
Element	**Symbol**	**% Human body mass**	**% All atoms in human body**
Most abundant in living organisms (approximately 95% of total mass)			
Oxygen	O	65	25.5
Carbon	C	18	9.5
Hydrogen	H	9	63.0
Nitrogen	N	3	1.4
Mineral elements (less than 1% of total mass)			
Calcium	Ca		
Chlorine	Cl		
Magnesium	Mg		
Phosphorus	P		
Potassium	K		
Sodium	Na		
Sulfur	S		
Trace elements (less than 0.01% of total mass)			
Boron	B		
Chromium	Ch		
Cobalt	Co		
Copper	Cu		
Fluorine	F		
Iodine	I		
Iron	Fe		
Manganese	Mn		
Molybdenum	Mo		
Selenium	Se		
Silicon	Si		
Tin	Sn		
Vanadium	V		
Zinc	Zn		

*Although these are the most common elements in living organisms, many other trace and mineral elements have reported functions. For example, aluminum is believed to be a cofactor for certain chemical reactions in animals, but it is generally toxic to plants.

therefore depriving the heart of nutrients. PET scans can also reveal the presence of cancer—a disease characterized by uncontrolled cell growth. The scan of the individual shown in Figure 2.6, for example, identified numerous regions of high activity, suggestive of cancer.

The Mass of All Living Organisms Is Largely Composed of Four Elements

Just four elements—oxygen, carbon, hydrogen, and nitrogen—account for the vast majority of atoms in living organisms (**Table 2.2**). These elements typically make up about 95% of the mass of living organisms. Much of the oxygen and hydrogen occur in the form of water, which accounts for approximately 60% of the mass of most animals and up to 95% or more in some plants. Carbon is a major building block of all living matter, and nitrogen is a vital element in all proteins. Note in Table 2.2 that although hydrogen accounts for about 63% of all the atoms in the body, it makes up only a small percentage of the mass of the human body. That is because the atomic mass of hydrogen is so much smaller than that of heavier elements such as oxygen.

Other important elements in living organisms include the mineral elements. Calcium and phosphorus, for example, are important constituents of the skeletons and shells of animals. Minerals such as potassium and sodium are key regulators of water movement and electric currents that occur across the surfaces of many cells.

In addition, all living organisms require **trace elements**. These elements are present in extremely small quantities but still are essential for normal growth and function. For example, iron plays an important role in how vertebrates transport oxygen in their blood, and copper serves a similar role in some invertebrates.

2.2 Chemical Bonds and Molecules

Learning Outcomes:

1. Compare and contrast the types of atomic interactions that lead to the formation of molecules.
2. Explain the concept of electronegativity and how it contributes to the formation of polar and nonpolar covalent bonds.
3. Describe how a molecule's shape is important for its ability to interact with other molecules.
4. Relate the concepts of a chemical reaction and chemical equilibrium.

The linkage of atoms with other atoms serves as the basis for life and also gives life its great diversity. Two or more atoms bonded together make up a molecule. Atoms can combine with each other in several ways. For example, two oxygen atoms can combine to form one oxygen molecule, represented as O_2. This representation is called a **molecular formula**. It consists of the chemical symbols for all of the atoms that are present (here, O for oxygen) and a subscript that tells you how many of those atoms are present in the molecule (in this case, two). The term **compound** refers to a molecule composed of two or more different elements. Examples include water (H_2O), with two hydrogen atoms and one oxygen atom, and the sugar glucose ($C_6H_{12}O_6$), which has 6 carbon atoms, 12 hydrogen atoms, and 6 oxygen atoms.

One of the most important features of compounds is their emergent physical properties. This means that the properties of a compound differ greatly from those of its elements. Let's consider sodium as an example. Pure sodium (Na) is a soft, silvery white metal that can be cut with a knife. When sodium forms a compound with chlorine (Cl), table salt (NaCl) results. NaCl is a white, relatively hard crystal (as seen in the chapter opening photo) that dissolves in water. Thus, the properties of sodium in a compound can be dramatically different from its properties as a pure element.

The atoms in molecules are held together by chemical bonds. In this section, we will examine the different types of chemical bonds, how these bonds form, and how they determine the structures of molecules.

Covalent Bonds Join Atoms Through the Sharing of Electrons

Covalent bonds, in which atoms share a pair of electrons, can occur between atoms whose outer shells are not full. A fundamental principle of chemistry is that *atoms tend to be most stable when their outer shells are filled with electrons.* **Figure 2.7** shows this principle as it applies to the formation of hydrogen fluoride (HF), a molecule with many important industrial and medical applications such as petroleum refining, fluorocarbon formation, and pharmaceutical production. The outer shell of a hydrogen atom is full when it contains two electrons, though a hydrogen atom has only one electron. The outer shell of a fluorine atom is full when it contains eight electrons, though a fluorine atom has only seven electrons in its outer shell. When HF is made, the two atoms share a pair of electrons, which spend time orbiting both nuclei. This allows both of the outer shells of those atoms to be full. Covalent bonds are strong chemical bonds, because the shared electrons behave as if they belong to each atom.

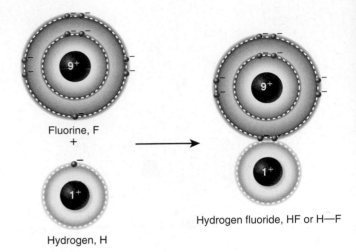

Fluorine, F
+

Hydrogen, H

Hydrogen fluoride, HF or H—F

Figure 2.7 The formation of covalent bonds. In covalent bonds, electrons from the outer shell of two atoms are shared with each other in order to complete the outer shells of both atoms. This simplified illustration shows hydrogen forming a covalent bond with fluorine.

When the structure of a molecule is diagrammed, each covalent bond is represented by a line indicating a pair of shared electrons. For example, HF is diagrammed as

H—F

A molecule of water (H_2O) can be diagrammed as

H—O—H

The structural formula of water indicates that the oxygen atom is covalently bound to two hydrogen atoms.

Each atom forms a characteristic number of covalent bonds, which depends on the number of electrons required to fill the outer shell. The atoms of some elements important for life, notably carbon, form more than one covalent bond and become linked simultaneously to two or more other atoms. **Figure 2.8** shows the number of covalent bonds formed by several atoms commonly found in the molecules of living cells—hydrogen, oxygen, nitrogen, and carbon.

For many types of atoms, their outermost shell is full when they contain eight electrons, an octet. The **octet rule** states that many atoms are most stable when they have eight electrons in their outermost electron shell. This rule applies to most atoms found in living organisms, including oxygen, nitrogen, carbon, phosphorus, and sulfur. These atoms form a characteristic number of covalent bonds to make an octet in their outermost shell (see Figure 2.8). However, the octet rule does not always apply. For example, hydrogen has an outermost shell that can contain only two electrons, not eight.

In some molecules, a **double bond** occurs when atoms share two pairs of electrons (four electrons) rather than one pair. As shown in **Figure 2.9**, this is the case for an oxygen molecule (O_2), which can be diagrammed as

O=O

Another common example occurs when two carbon atoms form bonds in compounds. They may share one pair of electrons (single bond) or two pairs (double bond), depending on how many other covalent bonds each carbon forms with other atoms. In rare cases,

Atom name	Hydrogen	Oxygen	Nitrogen	Carbon
	Nucleus Electron 1^+	8^+	7^+	6^+
Electron number needed to complete outer shell (typical number of covalent bonds)	1	2	3	4

Figure 2.8 **The number of covalent bonds formed by common essential elements found in living organisms.** These elements form different numbers of covalent bonds due to the electron configurations in their outer shells.

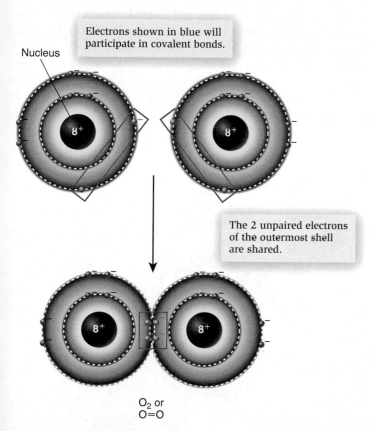

Nucleus

Electrons shown in blue will participate in covalent bonds.

The 2 unpaired electrons of the outermost shell are shared.

O_2 or
$O=O$

Figure 2.9 **A double bond between two oxygen atoms.**

Concept Check: *Explain how an oxygen molecule obeys the octet rule.*

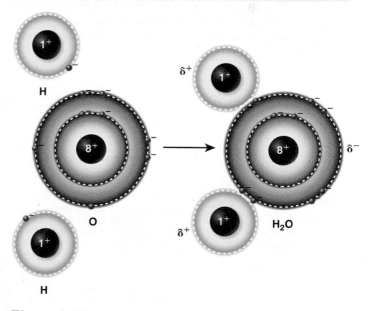

In water, the shared electrons spend more time near the oxygen atom. This gives oxygen a partial negative charge (δ^-) and each hydrogen a partial positive charge (δ^+).

H

δ^+

δ^-

δ^+

O

H

H_2O

Figure 2.10 **Polar covalent bonds in water molecules.** In a water molecule, two hydrogen atoms share electrons with an oxygen atom. Because oxygen has a higher electronegativity, the shared electrons spend more time closer to oxygen. This gives oxygen a partial negative charge, designated δ^-, and each hydrogen a partial positive charge, designated δ^+.

carbon can even form triple bonds, in which three pairs of electrons are shared between two atoms.

Some atoms attract shared electrons more readily than do other atoms. The **electronegativity** of an atom is a measure of its ability to attract electrons in a bond with another atom. When two atoms with different electronegativities form a covalent bond, the shared electrons are more likely to be closer to the nucleus of the atom of higher electronegativity than to the atom of lower electronegativity. Such bonds are called **polar covalent bonds**, because the distribution of electrons around the nuclei creates a polarity, or difference in electric

charge, across the molecule. Water is a classic example of a molecule containing polar covalent bonds. Since oxygen is much more electronegative than hydrogen, the shared electrons tend to be pulled closer to the oxygen nucleus than to either of the hydrogens. This unequal sharing of electrons gives the molecule a region of partial negative charge (indicated by the Greek letter δ and a minus sign, δ^-) and two regions of partial positive charge (δ^+) (**Figure 2.10**).

Atoms with high electronegativity, such as oxygen and nitrogen, have a relatively strong attraction for electrons. These atoms form polar covalent bonds with hydrogen atoms, which have low electronegativity. Examples of polar covalent bonds include O—H and N—H. In contrast, bonds between atoms with similar electronegativities, for example between two carbon atoms (C—C) or between carbon and hydrogen atoms (C—H), are called **nonpolar covalent bonds**. Molecules containing significant numbers of polar bonds are known as **polar molecules**, whereas molecules composed predominantly of nonpolar bonds are called **nonpolar molecules**. A single molecule may have different regions with nonpolar bonds and polar bonds. As we will explore later, the physical characteristics of polar and nonpolar molecules, especially their solubility in water, are quite different.

Hydrogen Bonds Allow Interactions Between and Within Molecules

An important result of certain polar covalent bonds is the ability of one molecule to loosely associate with another molecule through a weak interaction called a **hydrogen bond**. A hydrogen bond forms when a hydrogen atom from one polar molecule becomes electrically attracted to an electronegative atom, such as an oxygen or nitrogen atom, in another polar molecule. Hydrogen bonds, like those between water molecules, are represented in diagrams by dashed or dotted lines to distinguish them from covalent bonds (**Figure 2.11a**). A single hydrogen bond is very weak. The strength of a hydrogen bond is only a small percentage of the strength of the polar covalent bonds linking the hydrogen and oxygen within a water molecule.

Hydrogen bonds can also occur within a single large molecule. Many large molecules may have dozens, hundreds, or more hydrogen bonds within their structure. Collectively, many hydrogen bonds add up to a strong force that helps maintain the three-dimensional structure of a molecule. This is particularly true in deoxyribonucleic acid (DNA)—the molecule that makes up the genetic material of living organisms. DNA exists as two long, twisting strands of many millions of atoms. The two strands are held together along their length by hydrogen bonds between different portions of the molecule (Figure 2.11b). Due to the large number of hydrogen bonds, it takes considerable energy to separate the strands of DNA.

In contrast to the cumulative strength of many hydrogen bonds, the weakness of individual bonds is also important. When an interaction between two molecules involves relatively few hydrogen bonds, such interactions tend to be weak and readily broken. The reversible nature of hydrogen bonds allows molecules to interact and then to become separated again. For example, small molecules may bind to proteins called enzymes via hydrogen bonds. **Enzymes** are molecules found in all cells that facilitate or catalyze many biologically important chemical reactions. The small molecules are later released after the enzymes have changed their structure.

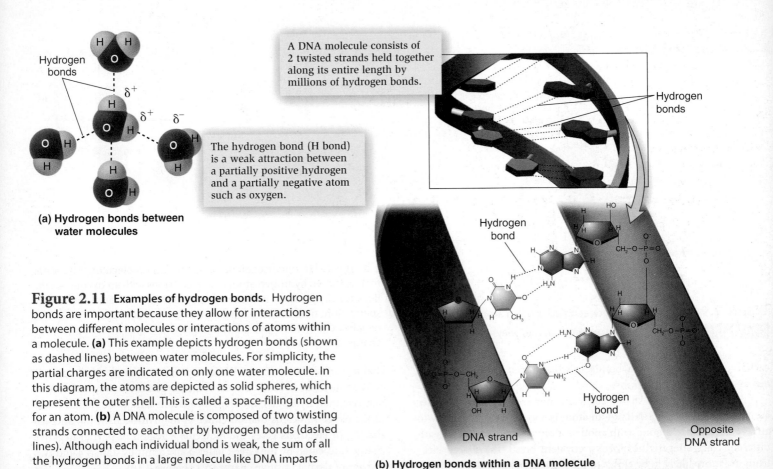

Figure 2.11 Examples of hydrogen bonds. Hydrogen bonds are important because they allow for interactions between different molecules or interactions of atoms within a molecule. **(a)** This example depicts hydrogen bonds (shown as dashed lines) between water molecules. For simplicity, the partial charges are indicated on only one water molecule. In this diagram, the atoms are depicted as solid spheres, which represent the outer shell. This is called a space-filling model for an atom. **(b)** A DNA molecule is composed of two twisting strands connected to each other by hydrogen bonds (dashed lines). Although each individual bond is weak, the sum of all the hydrogen bonds in a large molecule like DNA imparts considerable stability to the molecule.

(a) Hydrogen bonds between water molecules

(b) Hydrogen bonds within a DNA molecule

Concept Check: In Chapter 11, you will learn that the two DNA strands must first separate into two single strands for DNA to be replicated. Do you think the process of strand separation requires energy, or do you think the strands can separate spontaneously?

Hydrogen bonds are similar to a special class of bonds that are collectively known as **van der Waals forces**. In some cases, temporary attractive forces that are even weaker than hydrogen bonds form between molecules. These van der Waals forces arise because electrons orbit atomic nuclei in a random, probabilistic way, as described previously. At any moment, the electrons in the outer shells of the atoms in a nonpolar molecule may be evenly distributed or unevenly distributed. In the latter case, a fleeting electrical attraction may arise with other nearby molecules. Like hydrogen bonds, the collective strength of these temporary attractive forces between molecules can be quite strong.

Ionic Bonds Involve an Attraction Between Positive and Negative Ions

Atoms are electrically neutral because they contain equal numbers of negative electrons and positive protons. If an atom or molecule gains or loses one or more electrons, it acquires a net electric charge and becomes an **ion** (**Figure 2.12a**). For example, when a sodium atom (Na), which has 11 electrons, loses one electron, it becomes a sodium ion (Na^+) with a net positive charge. Ions that have a net positive charge are called **cations**. A sodium ion still has 11 protons, but only 10 electrons. Ions such as Na^+ are depicted with a superscript that indicates the net charge of the ion. A chlorine atom (Cl), which has 17 electrons, can gain an electron and become a chloride ion (Cl^-) with a net negative charge—it still has 17 protons but now has 18 electrons. Ions with a net negative charge are called **anions**.

Table 2.3 lists the ionic forms of several elements. Hydrogen atoms and most mineral and trace elements readily form ions. The ions listed in this table are relatively stable because the outer electron shells of the ions are full. For example, a sodium atom has one

Table 2.3		Ionic Forms of Some Common Elements in Living Organisms		
Atom	Chemical symbol	Ion	Ion symbol	Electrons gained or lost
Calcium	Ca	Calcium ion	Ca^{2+}	2 lost
Chlorine	Cl	Chloride ion	Cl^-	1 gained
Hydrogen	H	Hydrogen ion	H^+	1 lost
Magnesium	Mg	Magnesium ion	Mg^{2+}	2 lost
Potassium	K	Potassium ion	K^+	1 lost
Sodium	Na	Sodium ion	Na^+	1 lost

electron in its third (outermost) shell. If it loses this electron to become Na^+, it no longer has a third shell, and the second shell, which is full, becomes its outermost shell (see Figure 2.12).

Alternatively, a Cl atom has seven electrons in its outermost shell. If it gains an electron to become a chloride ion (Cl^-), its outer shell becomes full with eight electrons. Some atoms can gain or lose more than one electron. For instance, a calcium atom, which has 20 electrons, loses 2 electrons to become a calcium ion, depicted as Ca^{2+}.

An **ionic bond** occurs when a cation binds to an anion. Figure 2.12a shows an ionic bond between Na^+ and Cl^- to form NaCl. Salt is the general name given to compounds formed from an attraction between a positively charged ion (a cation) and negatively charged ion (an anion). Examples of salts include NaCl, KCl, and $CaCl_2$. Salts may form crystals in which the cations and anions form a regular array. Figure 2.12b shows a NaCl crystal, in which the sodium and chloride ions are held together by ionic bonds. Ionic bonds are easily broken in water—the environment of the cell—releasing the individual ions.

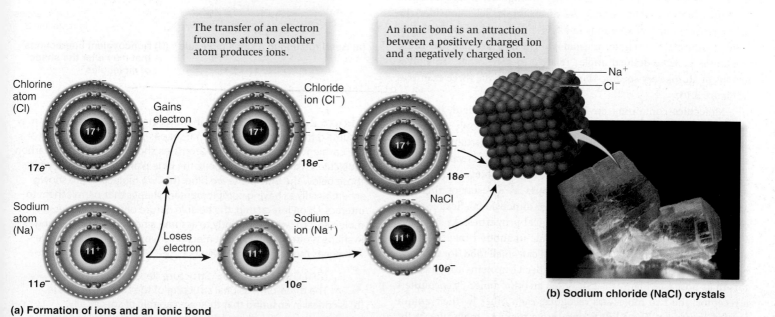

The transfer of an electron from one atom to another atom produces ions.

An ionic bond is an attraction between a positively charged ion and a negatively charged ion.

Chlorine atom (Cl)   17e⁻

Gains electron

Chloride ion (Cl⁻)   18e⁻

Sodium atom (Na)   11e⁻

Loses electron

Sodium ion (Na⁺)   10e⁻

NaCl

Na⁺
Cl⁻

(b) Sodium chloride (NaCl) crystals

(a) Formation of ions and an ionic bond

Figure 2.12 Ionic bonding in table salt (NaCl). (a) When an electron is transferred from a sodium atom to a chlorine atom, the resulting ions are attracted to each other via an ionic bond. **(b)** In a salt crystal, a lattice is formed in which the positively charged sodium ions (Na^+) are attracted to negatively charged chloride ions (Cl^-).

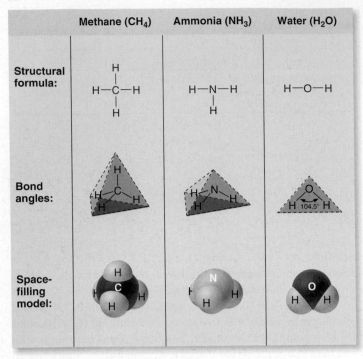

Figure 2.13 Shapes of molecules. Molecules may assume different shapes, depending on the types of bonds between their atoms. The angles between groups of atoms are well defined. For example, in liquid water at room temperature, the angle formed by the covalent bonds between the two hydrogen atoms and the oxygen atom is approximately 104.5°. This bond angle can vary slightly, depending on the temperature and degree of hydrogen bonding between adjacent water molecules.

Molecules May Change Their Shapes

When atoms combine, they can form molecules with various three-dimensional shapes, depending on the arrangements and numbers of bonds between their atoms. As an example, let's consider the arrangements of covalent bonds in a few simple molecules, including water (**Figure 2.13**). These molecules form new orbitals that cause the atoms to have defined angles relative to each other. This gives groups of atoms very specific shapes, as shown in the three examples of Figure 2.13.

Molecules containing covalent bonds are not rigid, inflexible structures. Think of a single covalent bond, for example, as an axle around which the joined atoms can rotate. Within certain limits, the shape of a molecule can change without breaking its covalent bonds. As illustrated in **Figure 2.14a**, a molecule of six carbon atoms bonded together can assume a number of shapes as a result of rotations around various covalent bonds. The three-dimensional, flexible shape of molecules contributes to their biological properties. As shown in Figure 2.14b, the binding of one molecule to another may affect the shape of one of the molecules. An animal can smell food, for instance, because odor molecules interact with special proteins called receptors in its nose (see Figure 43.25). When an odor molecule encounters a receptor, the two molecules recognize each other by their unique shapes, somewhat like a key fitting into a lock. As molecules in the food interact with the receptor, the shape of the receptor changes. When we look at how an animal's brain receives information from

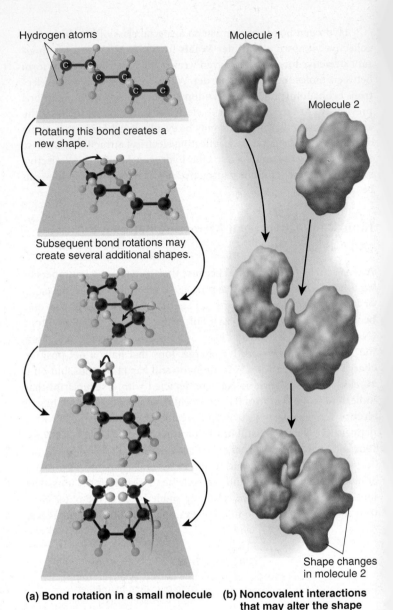

(a) Bond rotation in a small molecule

(b) Noncovalent interactions that may alter the shape of molecules

Figure 2.14 Shape changes in molecules. A single molecule may assume different three-dimensional shapes without breaking any of the covalent bonds between its atoms, as shown in **(a)** for a six-carbon molecule. Hydrogen atoms above the blue plane are shown in white; those below the blue plane are blue. **(b)** Two molecules are shown schematically as having complementary shapes that permit them to interact. Upon interacting, the flexible nature of the molecules causes molecule 2 to twist sufficiently to assume a new shape. This change in shape is often an important mechanism by which one molecule influences the activity of another.

BIOLOGY PRINCIPLE Structure determines function.
The three-dimensional structure of the two molecules in (b) is critical in ensuring that they are capable of specifically interacting with each other and not with other molecules. Thus, the function of the molecules is defined by their abilities to bind to each other, which in turn depends on their unique structures.

other parts of the body, we will see that the altered shape of the receptor initiates a signal that communicates information about the smell of the food to the animal's brain (look ahead to Chapter 43).

Free Radicals Are a Special Class of Highly Reactive Molecules

Recall that an atom or an ion is most stable when each of its orbitals is occupied by its full complement of electrons. A molecule containing an atom with a single, unpaired electron in its outer shell is known as a **free radical**. Free radicals can react with other molecules to "steal" an electron from one of their atoms, thereby filling the orbital in the free radical. In the process, this may create a new free radical in the donor molecule, setting off a chain reaction.

Free radicals can be formed in several ways, including exposure of cells to radiation and toxins. Free radicals can do considerable harm to living cells—for example, by causing a cell to rupture or by damaging the genetic material. Surprisingly, the lethal effect of free radicals is sometimes put to good use. Some cells in animals' bodies create free radicals and use them to kill invading cells such as bacteria. Likewise, for many years people have used weak solutions of hydrogen peroxide to kill bacteria, as in a dirty skin wound. When applied to the wound, hydrogen peroxide can break down to create free radicals, which can then attack bacteria (this practice is no longer recommended because of the possibility of damage to skin cells).

Despite the exceptional case of fighting off bacteria, though, most free radicals that arise in an organism need to be inactivated so they do not kill healthy cells. Protection from free radicals is afforded by molecules that can donate electrons to the free radicals without becoming highly reactive themselves. Examples of such protective compounds are certain vitamins known as antioxidants (for example, vitamins C and E), which are found in fruits and vegetables, and the numerous plant compounds known as flavonoids. This is one reason why a diet rich in fruits and vegetables is beneficial to our health.

Free radicals are diagrammed with a dot next to the atomic symbol. Examples of biologically important free radicals are superoxide anion, $O_2^{\cdot-}$; hydroxyl radical, $\cdot OH$; and nitric oxide, $NO\cdot$. Note that free radicals can be either charged or neutral.

Chemical Reactions Change Elements or Compounds into Different Compounds

A **chemical reaction** occurs when one or more substances are changed into other substances by the making or breaking of chemical bonds. This can happen when two or more elements or compounds combine to form a new compound, when one compound breaks down into two or more molecules, or when electrons are added to or removed from an atom.

Chemical reactions share many similar properties. First, they all require a source of energy for molecules to encounter each other. The energy required for atoms and molecules to interact is provided partly by heat, or thermal, energy. In the complete absence of any heat (a temperature called absolute zero), atoms and molecules would be totally stationary and unable to interact. Heat energy causes atoms and molecules to vibrate and move, a phenomenon known as

Brownian motion. Second, chemical reactions that occur in living organisms often require more than just Brownian motion to proceed at a reasonable rate. Such reactions need to be catalyzed. As discussed in Chapter 6, a **catalyst** is a substance that speeds up the rate of a chemical reaction. Enzymes are proteins found in all cells that catalyze important chemical reactions. Third, chemical reactions tend to proceed in a particular direction but eventually reach a state of equilibrium.

To understand what we mean by "direction" and "equilibrium" in this context, let's consider a chemical reaction between methane (a component of natural gas) and oxygen. When a single molecule of methane reacts with two molecules of oxygen, one molecule of carbon dioxide and two molecules of water are produced:

$$\underset{\text{(methane)}}{CH_4} + \underset{\text{(oxygen)}}{2\,O_2} \;\rightleftharpoons\; \underset{\text{(carbon dioxide)}}{CO_2} + \underset{\text{(water)}}{2\,H_2O}$$

As it is written here, methane and oxygen are the starting materials, or **reactants**, and carbon dioxide and water are the **products**. The bidirectional arrows indicate that this reaction can proceed in both directions. Whether a chemical reaction is likely to proceed in a forward ("left to right") or reverse ("right to left") direction depends on changes in free energy, which you will learn about in Chapter 6. If we began with only methane and oxygen, the forward reaction would be very favorable. The reaction would produce a large amount of carbon dioxide and water, as well as heat. This is why natural gas is used as a fuel to heat homes. However, all chemical reactions eventually reach **chemical equilibrium**, in which the rate of the formation of products equals the rate of the formation of reactants; in other words, there is no longer a change in the concentrations of products and reactants. In the case of the reaction involving methane and oxygen, this equilibrium occurs when nearly all of the reactants have been converted to products. In biological systems, however, many reactions do not have a chance to reach chemical equilibrium. For example, the products of a reaction may immediately be converted within a cell to a different product through a second reaction, or used by a cell to carry out some function. When a product is removed from a reaction as fast as it is formed, the reactants continue to form new product until all the reactants are used up.

A final feature common to chemical reactions in living organisms is that many reactions occur in watery environments. Such chemical reactions involve reactants and products that are dissolved in water. Next, we will examine the properties of this amazing liquid and its importance to biology.

2.3 Properties of Water

Learning Outcomes:

1. Describe how hydrogen bonding determines many properties of water.
2. List the properties of water that make it a valuable solvent, and distinguish between hydrophilic and hydrophobic substances.
3. Explain how the molarity of a solution—the number of moles of a solute per liter of solution—is used to measure the concentration of solutes in solution.
4. Discuss the properties of water that are critical for the survival of living organisms.

5. Explain how water has the ability to ionize into hydroxide ions (OH^-) and into hydrogen ions (H^+), and how the H^+ concentration is expressed as a solution's pH.
6. Give examples of how buffers maintain a stable environment in an animal's body fluids.

It would be difficult to imagine life without water. People can survive for a month or more without food but usually die in less than a week without water. The bodies of all organisms are composed largely of water; most of the cells in an organism's body are filled with water and surrounded by it. Up to 95% of the weight of certain plants comes from water. In humans, typically 60–70% of body weight is from water. The brain is roughly 70% water, blood is about 80% water, and the lungs are nearly 90% water. Even our bones are about 20% water! In addition, water is an important liquid in the surrounding environments of living organisms. For example, vast numbers of species are aquatic organisms that live in watery environments.

Thus far in this chapter, we have considered the features of atoms and molecules and the nature of bonds and chemical reactions between atoms and molecules. In this section, we will turn our attention to issues related to the liquid properties of living organisms and the environment in which they live. Most of the chemical reactions that occur in nature involve molecules that are dissolved in water, including those reactions that happen inside the cells of living organisms and in the spaces that surround them (**Figure 2.15**).

However, not all molecules dissolve in water. In this section, we will examine the properties of chemicals that influence whether they dissolve in water, and we consider how biologists measure the amounts of dissolved substances. In addition, we will examine some of the other special properties of water that make it a vital component of living organisms and their environments.

Ions and Polar Molecules Readily Dissolve in Water

Substances dissolved in a liquid are known as **solutes**, and the liquid in which they are dissolved is the **solvent**. In all living organisms, the solvent for chemical reactions is water, which is the most abundant solvent in nature. Solutes dissolve in a solvent to form a **solution**.

Solutions made with water are called **aqueous solutions**. To understand why a substance dissolves in water, we need to consider the chemical bonds in the solute molecule and those in water. As discussed earlier, the covalent bonds linking the two hydrogen atoms to the oxygen atom in a water molecule are polar. Therefore, the oxygen in water has a slight negative charge, and each hydrogen has a slight positive charge. To dissolve in water, a substance must be electrically attracted to water molecules. For example, table salt (NaCl) is a solid crystalline substance because of the strong ionic bonds between positive sodium ions (Na^+) and negative chloride ions (Cl^-). When a crystal of sodium chloride is placed in water, the partially negatively charged oxygens of water molecules are attracted to the Na^+, and the partially positively charged hydrogens are attracted to the Cl^- (**Figure 2.16**). Clusters of water molecules surround the ions, allowing the Na^+ and Cl^- to separate from each other and enter the water—that is, to dissolve.

Generally, molecules that contain ionic and/or polar covalent bonds dissolve in water. Such molecules are said to be **hydrophilic**, which literally means "water-loving." In contrast, molecules composed predominantly of carbon and hydrogen are relatively insoluble in water, because carbon-carbon and carbon-hydrogen bonds are nonpolar. These molecules do not have partial positive and negative charges and, therefore, are not attracted to water molecules. Such molecules are **hydrophobic**, or "water-fearing." Oils are a familiar example of hydrophobic molecules. Try mixing vegetable oil with water and observe the result. The two liquids separate into an oil layer and water layer, with very little oil dissolving in the water.

Although hydrophobic molecules dissolve poorly in water, they normally dissolve readily in nonpolar solvents. For example, cholesterol is a compound found in the blood and cells of animals. It is a hydrophobic molecule that is barely soluble in water but easily dissolves in nonpolar solvents used in chemical and biological

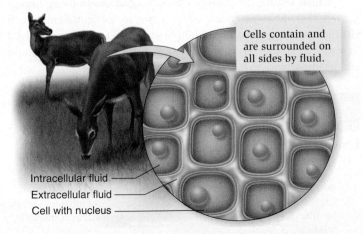

Figure 2.15 **Fluids inside and outside of cells.** Aqueous solutions exist in the intracellular fluid and in the extracellular fluid. Chemical reactions are always ongoing in both fluids.

Figure 2.16 **Table salt (NaCl crystals) dissolving in water.** The ability of water to dissolve sodium chloride crystals depends on the electrical attraction between the polar water molecules and the charged sodium (Na^+) and chloride ions (Cl^-). Water molecules surround each ion as it becomes dissolved. For simplicity, the partial charges are indicated for only two water molecules.

laboratories, such as acetone or chloroform. Biological membranes like those that encase cells are made up in large part of nonpolar compounds. Because of this, cholesterol also inserts itself into biological membranes, where it helps to maintain the membrane structure.

Molecules that have both polar or ionized regions at one or more sites and nonpolar regions at other sites are called **amphipathic** (or amphiphilic, from the Greek for "both loves"). When mixed with water, long amphipathic molecules may aggregate into spheres called **micelles**, with their polar (hydrophilic) regions at the surface of the micelle, where they are attracted to the surrounding water molecules. The nonpolar (hydrophobic) ends are oriented toward the interior of the micelle (**Figure 2.17**). Such an arrangement minimizes the interaction between water molecules and the nonpolar ends of the amphipathic molecules, which face inward. Nonpolar molecules can dissolve in the central nonpolar regions of these clusters and thus exist in an aqueous environment in far higher amounts than would otherwise be possible based on their low solubility in water. Familiar examples of amphipathic molecules are those in detergents, which can form micelles that help to dissolve oils and nonpolar molecules found in dirt. The detergent molecules found in soap have polar and nonpolar ends. Oils on your skin dissolve in the nonpolar regions of the detergent, and the polar ends help the detergent rinse off in water, taking the oil with it.

In addition to micelles, amphipathic molecules may form structures consisting of double layers of molecules called bilayers. Such bilayers have two hydrophilic surfaces facing outside, in contact with water, and a hydrophobic interior facing away from water. As you will learn in Chapter 5, bilayers play a key role in cellular membrane structure (look ahead to Figure 5.1).

The Amount of a Dissolved Solute per Unit Volume of Liquid Is Its Concentration

Solute **concentration** is defined as the amount of a solute dissolved in a unit volume of solution. For example, if 1 gram (g) of NaCl were dissolved in enough water to make 1 liter (L) of solution, we would say that its solute concentration is 1 g/L.

A comparison of the concentrations of two different substances on the basis of the number of grams per liter of solution does not directly indicate how many molecules of each substance are present. For example, let's compare 10 g each of glucose ($C_6H_{12}O_6$) and sodium chloride (NaCl). Because the individual molecules of glucose have more mass than those of NaCl, 10 g of glucose contains fewer molecules than 10 g of NaCl. Therefore, another way to describe solute concentration is according to the moles of dissolved solute per volume of solution. To make this calculation, we must know three things: the amount of dissolved solute, the molecular mass of the dissolved solute, and the volume of the solution.

The **molecular mass** of a molecule is equal to the sum of the atomic masses of all the atoms in the molecule. For example, glucose ($C_6H_{12}O_6$) has a molecular mass of 180 ([6×12] + [12×1] + [6×16] = 180).

As mentioned earlier, 1 mole (abbreviated mol) of a substance is the amount of the substance in grams equal to its atomic or molecular mass. The **molarity** of a solution is defined as the number of moles of a solute dissolved in 1 L of solution. A solution containing 180 g of

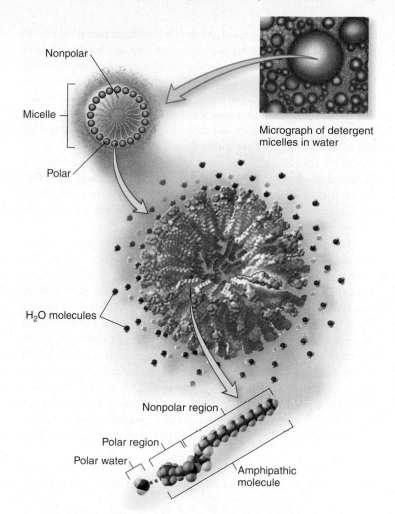

Figure 2.17 **The formation of micelles by amphipathic molecules.** In water, amphipathic molecules tend to arrange themselves so their nonpolar regions are directed away from water molecules and the polar regions are directed toward the water and can form hydrogen bonds with it.

Concept Check: *When oil dissolves in soap, where is the oil found?*

glucose (1 mol) dissolved in enough water to make 1 L is a 1 **molar** solution of glucose (1 mol/L). By convention, a 1 mol/L solution is usually written as 1 M, where the capital M stands for molar and is defined as mol/L. If 90 g of glucose (half its molecular mass) were dissolved in enough water to make 1 L, the solution would have a solute concentration of 0.5 mol/L, or 0.5 M.

The concentrations of solutes dissolved in the fluids of living organisms are usually much less than 1 M. Many have concentrations in the range of millimoles per liter (1 mM = 0.001 M = 10^{-3} M), and others are present in even smaller concentrations—micromoles per liter (1 μM = 0.000001 M = 10^{-6} M) or nanomoles per liter (1 nM = 0.000000001 M = 10^{-9} M), or even less.

Water Exists in Three States

Let's now consider some general features of water and how dissolved solutes affect its properties. Water is an abundant compound on Earth that exists in all three states of matter—solid (ice), liquid

Labels on figure: Nonpolar; Micelle; Polar; Micrograph of detergent micelles in water; H₂O molecules; Nonpolar region; Polar region; Polar water; Amphipathic molecule

(water), and gas (water vapor). At the temperatures found over most regions of the planet, water is found primarily as a liquid in which the weak hydrogen bonds between molecules are continuously being formed, broken, and formed again. If the temperature rises, the rate at which hydrogen bonds break increases, and molecules of water escape into the gaseous state, becoming water vapor. If the temperature falls, hydrogen bonds are broken less frequently, so larger and larger clusters of water molecules are formed, until at 0°C water freezes into a crystalline matrix—ice. The water molecules in ice tend to lie in a more orderly and "open" arrangement, that is, with greater intermolecular distances, which makes ice less dense than water. This is why ice floats on water (**Figure 2.18**). Compared with water, ice is also less likely to participate in most types of chemical reactions.

Changes in state, such as changes between the solid, liquid, and gaseous states of water, involve an input or a release of energy. For example, when energy is supplied to make water boil, it changes from the liquid to the gaseous state—a process called vaporization. The heat required to vaporize 1 mole of any substance at its boiling point is called the substance's **heat of vaporization**. For water, this value is very high, because of the high number of hydrogen bonds between the molecules. It takes more than five times as much heat to vaporize water than it does to raise the temperature of water from 0°C to 100°C. In contrast, energy is released when water freezes to form ice. A substance's **heat of fusion** is the amount of heat energy that must be withdrawn or released from a substance to cause it to change from the liquid to the solid state. For water, this value is also high.

Another important feature for living organisms is that water has a very high **specific heat**, defined as the amount of heat energy required to raise the temperature of 1 gram of a substance by 1°C (or conversely, the amount of heat energy that must be lost to lower the temperature by 1°C). A high specific heat means that it takes considerable heat to raise the temperature of water. A related concept is heat capacity, which refers to the amount of heat energy required to raise the temperature of an entire object or substance. A lake has a greater heat capacity than does a bathtub filled with water, but both have the same specific heat because both are the same substance (ignoring for the moment that neither are pure H_2O). These properties of water contribute to the relatively stable temperatures of large bodies of water compared with inland temperatures. Large bodies of water tend to have a moderating effect on the temperature of nearby land masses. These three features, the high heats of vaporization and fusion, and the high specific heat of water, mean that water is extremely stable as a liquid. Not surprisingly, therefore, living organisms have evolved to function best within a range of temperatures consistent with the liquid phase of water.

The temperature at which a solution freezes or vaporizes is influenced by the amounts of dissolved solutes. These are examples of a solution's **colligative properties**, defined as those properties that depend strictly on the total number of dissolved solutes, not on the specific type of solute. Pure water freezes at 0°C and vaporizes at 100°C. Addition of solutes to water lowers its freezing point below 0°C and raises its boiling point to above 100°C. Adding a small amount of the compound ethylene glycol—antifreeze—to the water in a car's radiator, for instance, lowers the freezing point of the water and consequently prevents it from freezing in cold weather. Similarly, the presence of large amounts of solutes partly explains why the oceans do not freeze when the temperature falls below 0°C.

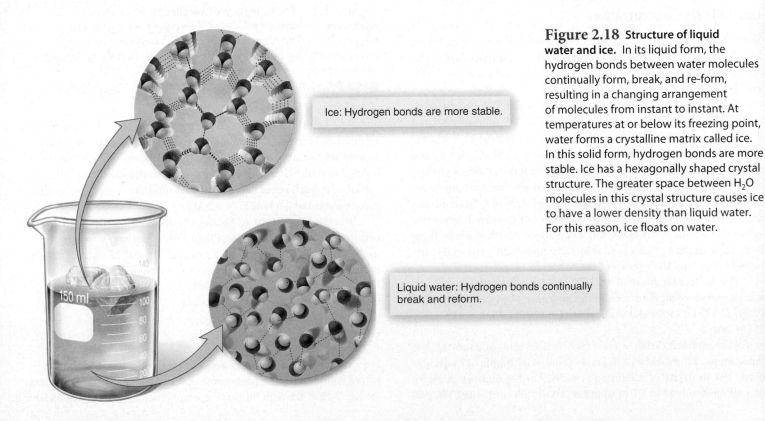

Ice: Hydrogen bonds are more stable.

Liquid water: Hydrogen bonds continually break and reform.

Figure 2.18 **Structure of liquid water and ice.** In its liquid form, the hydrogen bonds between water molecules continually form, break, and re-form, resulting in a changing arrangement of molecules from instant to instant. At temperatures at or below its freezing point, water forms a crystalline matrix called ice. In this solid form, hydrogen bonds are more stable. Ice has a hexagonally shaped crystal structure. The greater space between H_2O molecules in this crystal structure causes ice to have a lower density than liquid water. For this reason, ice floats on water.

Water Performs Many Important Tasks in Living Organisms

As discussed previously, water is the primary solvent in the fluids of all living organisms, from unicellular bacteria to the largest sequoia tree. Water permits atoms and molecules to interact in ways that would be impossible in their nondissolved states. In Unit II, we will consider many ions and molecules that are solutes in living cells.

Even so, it is important to recognize that in addition to acting as a solvent, water serves many other remarkable functions that are critical for the survival of living organisms. For example, water molecules participate in many chemical reactions of this general type:

$$R_1—R_2 + H—O—H \rightarrow R_1—OH + H—R_2$$

R is a general symbol used in this case to represent a group of atoms. In this equation, R_1 and R_2 are distinct groups of atoms. On the left side, $R_1—R_2$ is a compound in which the groups of atoms are connected by a covalent bond. To be converted to products, a covalent bond is broken in each reactant, $R_1—R_2$ and H—O—H, and OH and H (from water) form covalent bonds with R_1 and R_2, respectively. Reactions of this type are known as **hydrolysis reactions** (from the Greek *hydro*, meaning water, and *lysis*, meaning to break apart), because water is used to break apart another molecule (**Figure 2.19a**). As discussed in Chapter 3 and later chapters, many large molecules are broken down into smaller, biologically important units by hydrolysis reactions.

Alternatively, other chemical reactions in living organisms involve the removal of a water molecule so that a covalent bond can be formed between two separate molecules. For example, let's consider a chemical reaction that is the reverse of our previous hydrolysis reaction:

$$R_1—OH + H—R_2 \rightarrow R_1—R_2 + H—O—H$$

Such a reaction involves the formation of a covalent bond between two molecules. Two or more molecules combining to form one larger molecule with the loss of a small molecule is called a **condensation reaction**. In the example shown here, a molecule of water is lost during the reaction; this is a specific type of condensation reaction called a **dehydration reaction**. As discussed in later chapters, this is a common reaction used to build larger molecules in living organisms.

Another feature of water is that it is incompressible—its volume does not significantly decrease when subjected to high pressure. This has biological importance for many organisms that use water to provide force or support. For example, water supports the bodies of worms and some other invertebrates, in a structure called a hydrostatic skeleton, and it provides turgidity (stiffness) and support for plants (Figure 2.19b).

Water is also the means by which unneeded and potentially toxic waste compounds are eliminated from an animal's body (Figure 2.19c). In mammals, for example, the kidneys filter out soluble waste products derived from the breakdown of proteins and other compounds. The filtered products remain in solution in a watery fluid, which eventually becomes urine and is excreted.

Recall from our discussion of water's properties that it takes considerable energy in the form of heat to convert water from a liquid to a gas. This feature has great biological significance. Although everyone

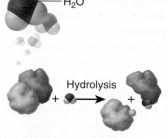

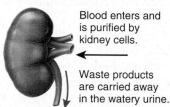

(a) Water participates in chemical reactions.

Blood enters and is purified by kidney cells.

Waste products are carried away in the watery urine.

(c) Water is used to eliminate soluble wastes.

(b) Water provides support. The plant on the right is wilting due to lack of water.

(d) Evaporation helps some animals dissipate body heat.

(e) The cohesive force of water molecules aids in the movement of fluid through vessels in plants.

(g) The surface tension of water explains why this water strider doesn't sink.

(f) Water in saliva serves as a lubricant during—or as shown here, in anticipation of—feeding.

Figure 2.19 Some of the amazing functions of water in biology. In addition to acting as a solvent, water serves many crucial functions in nature.

BIOLOGY PRINCIPLE Living organisms maintain homeostasis. Healthy organisms have a normal supply of water that maintains such homeostatic functions as body temperature, salt balance, and waste levels.

is familiar with the fact that boiling water is converted to water vapor, water can vaporize into the gaseous state even at ordinary temperatures. This process is known as **evaporation**. The simplest way to understand this is to imagine that in any volume of water at any temperature, some vibrating water molecules have higher energy than others. Those with the highest energy break their hydrogen bonds and escape into the gaseous state. The important point, however, is that even at ordinary temperatures, it still requires the same energy to change water from liquid to gas. Therefore, the evaporation of sweat from an animal's skin requires considerable energy in the form of body heat, which is then lost to the environment. Evaporation is an important mechanism by which many animals cool themselves on hot days (Figure 2.19d).

The hydrogen-bonding properties of water affect its ability to form droplets and to adhere to surfaces. The phenomenon of water molecules attracting each other is called **cohesion**. Water exhibits strong cohesion due to hydrogen bonding. Cohesion aids in the movement of water through the vessels of plants (Figure 2.19e). A property similar to cohesion is **adhesion**, which refers to the ability of water to be attracted to, and thus adhere to, a surface that is not electrically neutral. Water tends to cling to surfaces to which it can hydrogen bond, such as a paper towel. In organisms, the adhesive properties of water allow it, for example, to coat the surfaces of the digestive tract of animals and act as a lubricant for the passage of food (Figure 2.19f).

Surface tension is a measure of the attraction between molecules at the surface of a liquid. In the case of water, the attractive force between hydrogen-bonded water molecules at the interface between water and air is what causes water to form droplets. The surface water molecules attract each other into a configuration (roughly that of a sphere) that reduces the number of water molecules in contact with air. You can see this by slightly overfilling a glass with water; the water forms an oval shape above the rim. Likewise, surface tension allows certain insects, such as water striders, to walk on the surface of a pond without sinking (Figure 2.19g).

Hydrogen Ion Concentrations Are Changed by Acids and Bases

Pure water has the ability to ionize to a very small extent into **hydroxide ions (OH^-)** and into hydrogen ions that exist as single protons (H^+). (In nature or in laboratory conditions, hydrogen atoms may exist as any of several rare types of positively or negatively charged ions; in this text, we will use the term hydrogen ion to refer to the common H^+ form.) In pure water, the concentrations of H^+ and OH^- are both 10^{-7} mol/L, or 10^{-7} M. An inherent property of water is that the product of the concentrations of H^+ and OH^- is always 10^{-14} M at 25°C. Therefore, in pure water, $[H^+][OH^-] = [10^{-7}$ M$][10^{-7}$ M$] = 10^{-14}$ M. (The brackets around the symbols for the hydrogen and hydroxide ions indicate concentration.)

When certain substances are dissolved in water, they may release or absorb H^+ or OH^-, thereby altering the relative concentrations of these ions. Substances that release hydrogen ions in solution are called **acids**. Two examples are hydrochloric acid and carbonic acid:

$$HCl \rightarrow H^+ + Cl^-$$
(hydrochloric acid)   (chloride ion)

$$H_2CO_3 \rightleftharpoons H^+ + HCO_3^-$$
(carbonic acid)   (bicarbonate ion)

Hydrochloric acid is called a **strong acid** because it almost completely dissociates into H^+ and Cl^- when added to water (which is why the arrow is not bidirectional in this reaction). By comparison, carbonic acid is a **weak acid** because some of it remains in the H_2CO_3 state when dissolved in water (note the bidirectional arrows $\rightleftharpoons$).

Compared with an acid, a **base** has the opposite effect when dissolved in water—it absorbs hydrogen ions in solution. This can occur in different ways. Some bases, such as sodium hydroxide (NaOH), release OH^- when dissolved in water:

$$NaOH \rightarrow Na^+ + OH^-$$
(sodium hydroxide)   (sodium ion)

Recall that the product of $[H^+]$ and $[OH^-]$ is always 10^{-14} M. When a base such as NaOH raises the OH^- concentration, some of the hydrogen ions bind to these hydroxide ions to form water. Therefore, increasing the OH^- concentration lowers the H^+ concentration. In another example, ammonia reacts with water to produce ammonium ion:

$$NH_3 + H_2O \rightleftharpoons NH_4^+ + OH^-$$
(ammonia)   (ammonium ion)

Both NaOH and ammonia have the same effect—they lower the concentration of H^+. NaOH achieves this by directly increasing the OH^- concentration, whereas NH_3 reacts with water to produce OH^-.

The H^+ Concentration of a Solution Determines the Solution's pH

The addition of acids and bases to water can greatly change the H^+ and OH^- concentrations over a very broad range. Therefore, scientists use a log scale to describe the concentrations of these ions. The H^+ concentration is expressed as the solution's **pH**, which is defined as the negative logarithm to the base 10 of the H^+ concentration (a logarithmic scale is used because the concentrations of hydrogen ions can vary over a very wide range).

$$pH = -\log_{10}[H^+]$$

To understand what this equation means, let's consider a few examples. A solution with a H^+ concentration of 10^{-7} M has a pH of 7. A concentration of 10^{-7} M is the same as 0.1 μM. A solution in which $[H^+] = 10^{-6}$ M has a pH of 6. 10^{-6} M is the same as 1.0 μM. A solution at pH 6 is said to be **acidic**, because it contains more H^+ ions than OH^- ions. Note that as the acidity increases, the pH decreases. A solution in which the pH is 7 is said to be neutral because $[H^+]$ and $[OH^-]$ are equal. A solution with a pH above 7 is considered to be **alkaline**. **Figure 2.20** considers the pH values of some familiar fluids. Keep in mind that each change of one pH unit represents a 10-fold difference in H^+ concentration.

Why is pH of importance to biologists? The answer lies in the observation that H^+ and OH^- can readily bind to many kinds of ions and molecules. For this reason, the pH of a solution can affect:

- the shapes and functions of molecules
- the rates of many chemical reactions
- the ability of two molecules to bind to each other
- the ability of ions or molecules to dissolve in water

Due to the various effects of pH, many biological processes function best within very narrow ranges of pH, and even small shifts can have a negative effect. In living cells, the pH ranges from about 6.5 to 7.8 and is carefully regulated to avoid major shifts in pH. The blood of the human body has a normal range of about pH 7.35 to 7.45 and is therefore slightly alkaline. Certain diseases, such as kidney disease, can decrease or increase blood pH by a few tenths of a unit. When this happens, the enzymes in the body that are required for normal metabolism can no longer function optimally, leading to additional illness. As described next, living organisms have molecules called buffers to help prevent such changes in pH.

Buffers Minimize Fluctuations in the pH of Fluids

What factors might alter the pH of an organism's fluids? In plants, external factors such as acid rain and other forms of pollution can reduce the pH of water entering the roots. In animals, exercise generates lactic acid, and certain disease states can raise or lower the pH of blood.

Organisms have several ways to cope with changes in pH. In vertebrate animals such as mammals, for example, structures like the kidney secrete acidic or alkaline compounds into the bloodstream when the blood pH becomes imbalanced. Similarly, the kidneys can transfer hydrogen ions from the fluids of the body into the urine and adjust the pH of the body's fluids in that way. Another mechanism by which pH balance is regulated in diverse organisms involves the actions of acid-base buffers. A **buffer** is a compound that minimizes pH fluctuations in the fluids of living organisms. A buffer solution is composed of a weak acid and its related base. One such buffer solution contains carbonic acid (H_2CO_3) and bicarbonate ions (HCO_3^-), called the bicarbonate pathway, which functions to keep the pH of an animal's body fluids within a narrow range:

$$CO_2 + H_2O \rightleftharpoons H_2CO_3 \rightleftharpoons H^+ + HCO_3^-$$

$$\text{(carbonic acid)} \qquad \text{(bicarbonate)}$$

This buffer system can work in both directions. For example, if the pH of an animal's body fluids were to increase (that is, the H^+ concentration decreased), the bicarbonate pathway would proceed from left to right. Carbon dioxide would combine with water to make carbonic acid, and then the carbonic acid would dissociate into H^+ and HCO_3^-. This would increase the H^+ concentration and thereby decrease the pH. Alternatively, when the pH of an animal's blood decreases (that is, the H^+ concentration increases), this pathway runs in reverse. Bicarbonate combines with H^+ to make H_2CO_3, which then dissociates to CO_2 and H_2O. This process removes H^+ from the blood, restoring it to its normal pH, and the CO_2 is exhaled from the lungs. Many buffers exist in nature. Buffers found in living organisms function most efficiently at the normal range of pH values found in that organism.

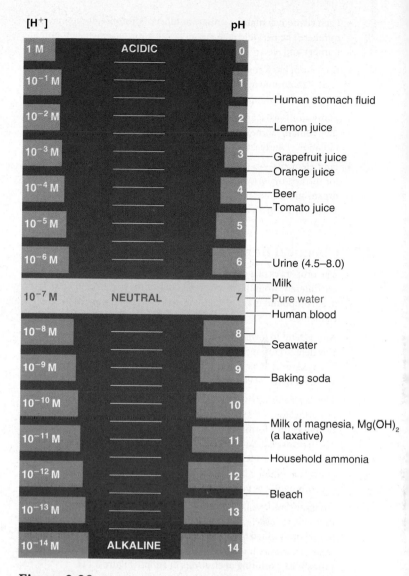

Figure 2.20 The pH scale and the relative acidities of common substances.

Concept Check: What is the OH^- concentration at pH 8?

BioConnections: Look ahead to Figure 54.16. The plant life shown growing in part (b) of that figure has been exposed to rain that was acidified due to contaminants arising from the burning of fossil fuels. If the pH of the soil were 5.0, what would the H^+ concentration be?

Summary of Key Concepts

2.1 Atoms

- Atoms are the smallest functional units of matter that form all chemical elements and cannot be further broken down into other substances by ordinary chemical or physical means. Atoms are composed of protons (p^+, positive charge), electrons (e^-, negative charge), and (except for hydrogen) neutrons (n^0, electrically neutral). Electrons are found in orbitals around the nucleus (Table 2.1, Figures 2.1, 2.2, 2.3, 2.4).

- Each element contains a unique number of protons—its atomic number. The periodic table organizes all known elements by atomic number and electron shells (Figure 2.5).

- Each atom has a small but measurable mass, measured in daltons (Da). The atomic mass scale indicates an atom's mass relative to the mass of other atoms.

- Many atoms exist as isotopes, which differ in the number of neutrons they contain. Some isotopes are unstable radioisotopes and emit radiation (Figure 2.6).

- Four elements—oxygen, carbon, hydrogen, and nitrogen—account for the vast majority of atoms in living organisms. In addition, living organisms require mineral and trace elements that are essential for growth and function (Table 2.2).

2.2 Chemical Bonds and Molecules

- The properties of a molecule—two or more atoms bonded together—are different from the properties of the atoms that combined to form it. A compound is a molecule composed of two or more different elements.

- Atoms tend to form bonds that fill their outer shell with electrons. Covalent bonds, in which atoms share electrons, are strong chemical bonds. Atoms form two covalent bonds—a double bond—when they share two pairs of electrons (Figures 2.7, 2.8, 2.9).

- The electronegativity of an atom is a measure of its ability to attract bonded electrons. When two atoms with different electronegativities combine, they form a polar covalent bond because the distribution of electrons around the atoms creates a difference in electric charge across the molecule. Polar molecules, such as water, are largely composed of polar bonds, and nonpolar molecules are composed predominantly of nonpolar bonds (Figure 2.10).

- An important result of polar covalent bonds is the ability of one molecule to loosely associate with another molecule through weak interactions called hydrogen bonds. The van der Waals forces are weak electrical attractions that arise between molecules due to the probabilistic orbiting of electrons in atoms (Figure 2.11).

- If an atom or molecule gains or loses one or more electrons, it acquires a net electric charge and becomes an ion. The strong attraction between two oppositely charged ions forms an ionic bond (Table 2.3, Figure 2.12).

- The three-dimensional, flexible shape of molecules allows them to interact and contributes to their biological properties (Figures 2.13, 2.14).

- A free radical is an unstable molecule that interacts with other molecules by taking away electrons from their atoms.

- A chemical reaction occurs when one or more substances are changed into different substances. All chemical reactions eventually reach an equilibrium, unless the products of the reaction are continually removed.

2.3 Properties of Water

- Water is the solvent for most chemical reactions in all living organisms, both inside and outside of cells. Atoms and molecules dissolved in water interact in ways that would be impossible in their nondissolved states (Figure 2.15).

- Solutes dissolve in a solvent to form a solution. Solute concentration refers to the amount of a solute dissolved in a unit volume of solution. The molarity of a solution is defined as the number of moles of a solute dissolved in 1 L of solution (Figure 2.16).

- Molecules with ionic and polar covalent bonds generally are hydrophilic, whereas nonpolar molecules, composed predominantly of carbon and hydrogen, are hydrophobic. Amphipathic molecules, such as detergents, have polar and nonpolar regions (Figure 2.17).

- H_2O exists as ice, liquid water, and water vapor (gas) (Figure 2.18).

- The colligative properties of water depend on the number of dissolved solutes and allow it to function as an antifreeze in certain organisms.

- Water's high heat of vaporization and high heat of fusion make it very stable in liquid form.

- Water molecules participate in many chemical reactions in living organisms. Hydrolysis breaks down large molecules into smaller units, and dehydration reactions combine two smaller molecules into one larger one. In living organisms, water provides support, is used to eliminate wastes, dissipates body heat, aids in the movement of liquid through vessels, serves as a lubricant, and its surface tension allows certain insects to walk on water (Figure 2.19).

- The pH of a solution refers to its hydrogen ion concentration. The pH of pure water is 7 (a neutral solution). Alkaline solutions have a pH higher than 7, and acidic solutions have a pH lower than 7 (Figure 2.20).

- Buffers are compounds that minimize pH fluctuations in the fluids of living organisms. Buffer systems in animals can raise or lower pH to keep the pH of body fluids within a narrow range.

Assess and Discuss

Test Yourself

1. _____ make(s) up the nucleus of an atom.
   a. Protons and electrons
   b. Protons and neutrons
   c. DNA and RNA
   d. Neutrons and electrons
   e. DNA only

2. Living organisms are composed mainly of which atoms?
   a. calcium, hydrogen, nitrogen, and oxygen
   b. carbon, hydrogen, nitrogen, and oxygen
   c. hydrogen, nitrogen, oxygen, and helium
   d. carbon, helium, nitrogen, and oxygen
   e. carbon, calcium, hydrogen, and oxygen

3. The ability of an atom to attract electrons in a bond with another atom is termed its
   a. hydrophobicity.
   b. electronegativity.
   c. solubility.
   d. valence.
   e. both a and b.

4. Hydrogen bonds differ from covalent bonds in that
   a. covalent bonds can form between any type of atom, and hydrogen bonds form only between H and O.
   b. covalent bonds involve sharing of electrons, and hydrogen bonds involve the complete transfer of electrons.
   c. covalent bonds result from equal sharing of electrons, but hydrogen bonds involve unequal sharing of electrons.
   d. covalent bonds involve sharing of electrons between atoms, but hydrogen bonds are the result of weak attractions between a hydrogen atom of a polar molecule and an electronegative atom of another polar molecule.
   e. covalent bonds are weak bonds that break easily, but hydrogen bonds are strong links between atoms that are not easily broken.

5. A free radical
   a. is a positively charged ion.
   b. is an atom with one unpaired electron in its outer shell.
   c. is a stable atom that is not bonded to another atom.
   d. can cause considerable cellular damage.
   e. both b and d.

6. Chemical reactions in living organisms
   a. require energy to begin.
   b. usually require a catalyst to speed up the process.
   c. are usually reversible.
   d. occur in liquid environments, such as water.
   e. all of the above.

7. Solutes that easily dissolve in water are said to be
   a. hydrophobic.
   b. hydrophilic.
   c. polar molecules.
   d. all of the above.
   e. b and c only.

8. The sum of the atomic masses of all the atoms of a molecule is its
   a. atomic weight.
   b. molarity.
   c. molecular mass.
   d. concentration.
   e. polarity.

9. Reactions that involve water in the breaking apart of other molecules are known as _____ reactions.
   a. hydrophilic
   b. hydrophobic
   c. dehydration
   d. anabolic
   e. hydrolytic

10. A difference between a strong acid and a weak acid is
    a. strong acids have a higher molecular mass than weak acids.
    b. strong acids completely (or almost completely) ionize in solution, but weak acids do not completely ionize in solution.
    c. strong acids give off two hydrogen ions per molecule, but weak acids give off only one hydrogen ion per molecule.
    d. strong acids are water-soluble, but weak acids are not.
    e. strong acids give off hydrogen ions, and weak acids give off hydroxyl groups.

Conceptual Questions

1. Distinguish between the types of bonds commonly found in biological molecules.

2. What is the significance of molecular shape, and what may change the shape of molecules?

3. A principle of biology is that *new properties emerge from complex interactions*. How is this principle evident even at the molecular level? What examples of emergent properties of molecules can you find in this chapter, in which atoms with one type of property combine to form molecules with completely different properties?

Collaborative Questions

1. Discuss the properties of the three subatomic particles of atoms.

2. Discuss several properties of water that make it possible for life to exist.

Online Resource

www.brookerbiology.com

Stay a step ahead in your studies with animations that bring concepts to life and practice tests to assess your understanding. Your instructor may also recommend the interactive eBook, individualized learning tools, and more.

The Chemical Basis of Life II: Organic Molecules

3

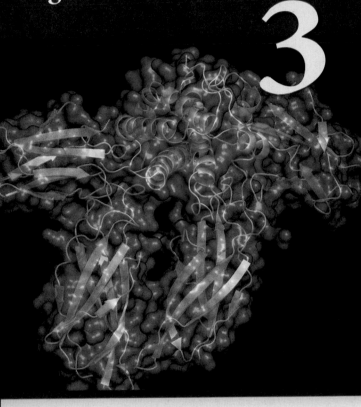

A model showing the structure of a protein—a type of organic macromolecule.

In Chapter 2, we learned that all life is composed of subatomic particles that form atoms, which, in turn, combine to form molecules. Molecules may be simple in atomic composition, as in water (H_2O) or hydrogen gas (H_2), or may bind with other molecules to form larger ones. Of the countless possible molecules that can be produced from the known elements in nature, certain types contain carbon and are found in all forms of life. These carbon-containing molecules are collectively referred to as **organic molecules**, so named because they were first discovered in living organisms. Among these are lipids and large, complex compounds called **macromolecules**, which include carbohydrates, proteins, and nucleic acids. In this chapter, we will survey the structures of these molecules and examine their chief functions. We begin with the element whose chemical properties are fundamental to the formation of biologically important molecules: carbon. This element provides the atomic scaffold on which life is built.

3.1 | The Carbon Atom and the Study of Organic Molecules

Learning Outcomes:

1. Explain the properties of carbon that make it the chemical basis of all life.
2. Describe the variety and chemical characteristics of common functional groups of organic compounds.
3. Compare and contrast the different types of isomeric compounds.

The science of carbon-containing molecules is known as **organic chemistry**. In this section, we will examine the bonding properties of carbon that create molecules with distinct functions and shapes.

Interestingly, the study of organic molecules was long considered a fruitless endeavor because of a concept called vitalism, which persisted into the 19th century. Vitalism held that organic molecules were created by, and therefore imparted with, a vital life force that was contained within a plant or an animal's body. Supporters of vitalism argued there was no point in trying to synthesize an organic compound, because such molecules could arise only through the intervention of mysterious qualities associated with life. As described next, this would all change due to the pioneering experiments of Friedrich Wöhler in 1828.

Wöhler's Synthesis of an Organic Compound Transformed Misconceptions About the Molecules of Life

Friedrich Wöhler was a German physician and chemist interested in the properties of inorganic and organic compounds. He spent some time studying urea ($(NH_2)_2CO$), a natural organic product formed from the breakdown of proteins in an animal's body. In mammals, urea accumulates in the urine formed by the kidneys, and then is excreted from the body. During the course of his studies, Wöhler purified urea from the urine of mammals. He noted the color, size, shape, and other characteristics of the crystals that formed when urea was isolated. This experience would serve him well in later years when he quite accidentally helped to put the concept of vitalism to rest.

Figure 3.1 Crystals of urea as viewed with a polarizing microscope (approximately 80× magnification).

Concept Check: *How did prior knowledge of urea allow Wöhler to realize he had synthesized urea from ammonia and cyanic acid?*

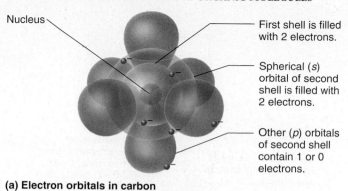

(a) Electron orbitals in carbon

Nucleus

First shell is filled with 2 electrons.

Spherical (*s*) orbital of second shell is filled with 2 electrons.

Other (*p*) orbitals of second shell contain 1 or 0 electrons.

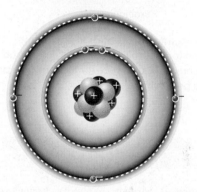

(b) Simplified depiction of carbon's electron shells

Figure 3.2 Models for the electron orbitals and shells of carbon. Carbon atoms have only four electrons in their outer (second) electron shell, which allows carbon to form four covalent bonds. When carbon forms four covalent bonds, the result is four hybrid orbitals of equal energy.

In 1828, while exploring the reactive properties of ammonia and cyanic acid, Wöhler attempted to synthesize an inorganic molecule, ammonium cyanate (NH_4OCN), which is not found in living organisms. Instead, to his surprise, Wöhler discovered that ammonia and cyanic acid reacted to produce a third compound, which, when heated, formed familiar-looking crystals (**Figure 3.1**). After careful analysis, he concluded that these crystals were in fact urea. In short, no mysterious life force was required to create this organic molecule. Other scientists, such as Hermann Kolbe, would soon demonstrate that organic compounds such as acetic acid (CH_3COOH) could be synthesized directly from simpler molecules. These studies were a major breakthrough in the way in which scientists viewed life, and so began the field of science now called organic chemistry. Since that time, the fields of chemistry and biology have been understood to be intricately related.

Central to Wöhler's and Kolbe's reactions is the carbon atom. Urea and acetic acid, like all organic compounds, contain carbon atoms bound to other atoms. Let's now consider the chemical features of carbon that make it such an important element in living organisms.

Carbon Forms Four Covalent Bonds with Other Atoms

One of the properties of the carbon atom that makes life possible is its ability to form four covalent bonds with other atoms, including other carbon atoms. This occurs because carbon has four electrons in its outer (second) shell, and it requires eight electrons, or four additional electrons, to fill its second shell (**Figure 3.2**). In living organisms, carbon atoms most commonly form covalent bonds with other carbon atoms and with hydrogen, oxygen, nitrogen, and sulfur atoms. Bonds between two carbon atoms, between carbon and oxygen, or between carbon and nitrogen can be single or double, or in the case of certain C≡C and C≡N bonds, triple. The variation in bonding of carbon with other carbon atoms and with different elements allows a vast number of organic compounds to be formed from only a few chemical elements. This is made all the more impressive because carbon bonds may occur in configurations that are linear, ringlike, or highly branched. Such molecular shapes can produce molecules with a variety of functions.

Carbon and hydrogen have similar electronegativities (see Chapter 2); therefore, carbon-carbon and carbon-hydrogen bonds are nonpolar. As a consequence, molecules with predominantly or entirely hydrogen-carbon bonds, called **hydrocarbons**, are hydrophobic and poorly soluble in water. In contrast, when carbon forms polar covalent bonds with more electronegative atoms, such as oxygen or nitrogen, the molecule is much more soluble in water due to the electrical attraction of polar water molecules. The ability of carbon to form

both polar and nonpolar bonds (**Figure 3.3**) contributes to its ability to serve as the backbone for an astonishing variety of biologically important molecules.

One last feature of carbon that is important to biology is that carbon bonds are stable within the large range of temperatures associated with life. This property arises in part because the carbon atom is very small relative to most other atoms; therefore, the distance between carbon atoms forming a carbon-carbon bond is quite short. Shorter bonds tend to be stronger and more stable than longer bonds between two large atoms. Thus, carbon bonds are compatible with what we observe about life-forms today; namely, living organisms can inhabit environments with a range of temperatures, from the Earth's frigid icy poles to the superheated water of deep-sea vents.

Carbon Atoms Can Bond to Several Biologically Important Functional Groups

Aside from the simplest hydrocarbons, most organic molecules and macromolecules contain **functional groups**—groups of atoms with characteristic chemical features and properties. Each type of functional group exhibits similar chemical properties in all molecules in which it occurs. For example, the amino group (NH_2) acts like a base. At the pH found in living organisms, amino groups readily bind H^+ to become NH_3^+, thereby removing H^+ from an aqueous solution and raising the pH. As discussed later in this chapter, amino groups are widely found in proteins and also in other types of organic molecules.

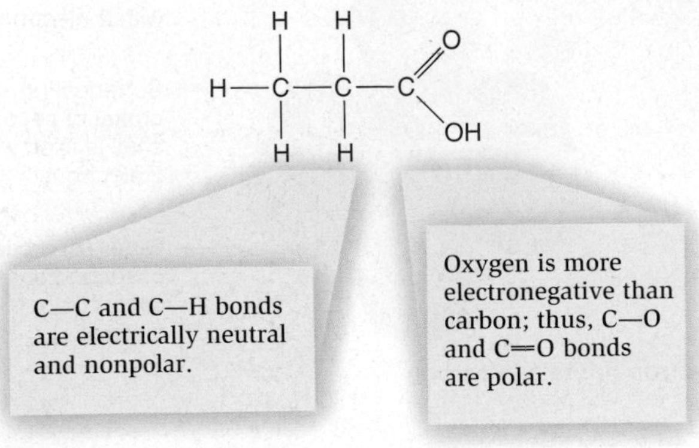

H H O
| | ‖
H—C—C—C
| | \
H H OH

C—C and C—H bonds are electrically neutral and nonpolar.

Oxygen is more electronegative than carbon; thus, C—O and C=O bonds are polar.

Propionic acid

Figure 3.3 Nonpolar and polar bonds in an organic molecule. Carbon can form both nonpolar and polar bonds, and both single and double bonds, as shown here for the molecule propionic acid, a common food preservative.

Table 3.1 describes examples of functional groups found in many different types of organic molecules. We will discuss each of these groups at numerous points throughout this textbook.

Carbon-Containing Molecules May Exist in Multiple Forms Called Isomers

When Wöhler did his now-famous experiment, he was surprised to discover that urea, $((NH_2)_2CO)$, and ammonium cyanate, (NH_4OCN), apparently contained the exact same ratio of carbon, nitrogen, hydrogen, and oxygen atoms, yet they were different molecules with distinct chemical and biological properties. Two molecules with an identical chemical formula but different structures and characteristics are called **isomers**.

Figure 3.4 depicts three ways in which isomers may occur. **Structural isomers** contain the same atoms but in different bonding relationships. Urea and ammonium cyanate fall into this category; a simpler example of structural isomers (isopropyl alcohol and propyl alcohol) is illustrated in Figure 3.4a.

Table 3.1	Some Biologically Important Functional Groups That Bond to Carbon		
Functional group* (with shorthand notation)	**Formula**	**Examples of where they are found**	**Properties**
Amino –NH_2	R—N with two H	Amino acids (proteins)	Weakly basic (can accept H$^+$); polar; forms part of peptide bonds
†Carbonyl (–CO) Ketone	O ‖ R—C—R'	Steroids, waxes, and proteins	Polar; highly chemically reactive; forms hydrogen bonds
Aldehyde	O ‖ R—C—H	Linear forms of sugars and some odor molecules	Polar; highly chemically reactive, forms hydrogen bonds
Carboxyl (–COOH)	O ‖ R—C—OH	Amino acids, fatty acids	Acidic (gives up H$^+$ in water); forms part of peptide bonds
Hydroxyl (–OH)	R—OH	Steroids, alcohol, carbohydrates, some amino acids	Polar; forms hydrogen bonds with water
Methyl (–CH_3)	H | R—C—H | H	May be attached to DNA, proteins, and carbohydrates	Nonpolar
Phosphate (–PO_4^{2-})	O ‖ R—O—P—O$^-$ | O$^-$	Nucleic acids, ATP, phospholipids	Polar; weakly acidic and thus negatively charged at typical pH of living organisms
Sulfate (–SO_4^-)	O ‖ R—O—S—O$^-$ ‖ O	May be attached to carbohydrates, proteins, and lipids	Polar; negatively charged at typical pH
Sulfhydryl (–SH)	R—SH	Proteins that contain the amino acid cysteine	Polar; forms disulfide bridges in many proteins

†A carbonyl group is C=O. In a ketone, the carbon forms covalent bonds with two other carbon atoms. In an aldehyde, the carbon is linked to a hydrogen atom.
*This list contains many of the functional groups that are important in biology. However, many more functional groups have been identified by biochemists. R and R' represent the remainder of the molecule.

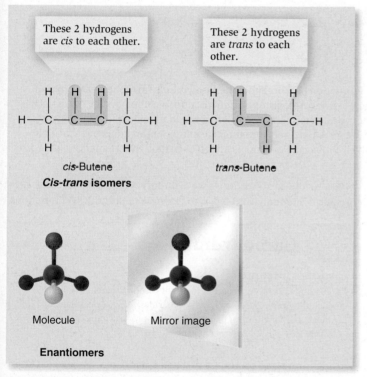

Because this –OH group is attached to a different carbon, these 2 molecules are structural isomers.

Isopropyl alcohol

Propyl alcohol

(a) Structural isomers

These 2 hydrogens are *cis* to each other.

These 2 hydrogens are *trans* to each other.

cis-Butene

trans-Butene

***Cis-trans* isomers**

Molecule

Mirror image

Enantiomers

(b) Two types of stereoisomers

Figure 3.4 Types of isomers. Isomers are molecules with the same chemical formula but different structures. The differences in structure, though small, are sufficient to result in very different biological properties. Isomers can be grouped into **(a)** structural isomers and **(b)** stereoisomers.

Stereoisomers have identical bonding relationships, but the spatial positioning of their atoms differs. Two types of stereoisomers are *cis-trans* isomers and enantiomers. In ***cis-trans* isomers**, like those shown in Figure 3.4b, the two hydrogen atoms linked to the two carbons of a C=C double bond may be on the same side of the carbons, in which case the C=C bond is called a *cis* double bond. If the hydrogens are on opposite sides, it is a *trans* double bond. *Cis-trans* isomers may have very different chemical properties from each other, most notably their stability and sensitivity to heat and light. For instance, the light-sensitive region of your eye contains a molecule called

retinal, which may exist in either a *cis* or *trans* form because of a pair of double-bonded carbons in its string of carbon atoms. In darkness, the *cis*-retinal form predominates. The energy of sunlight, however, causes retinal to isomerize to the *trans* form. The *trans*-retinal activates the light-capturing cells in the eye.

A second type of stereoisomer, called an **enantiomer**, exists as a pair of molecules that are mirror images. Four different atoms can bind to a single carbon atom in two possible ways, designated a left-handed and a right-handed structure. The resulting structures are not identical, but instead are mirror images of each other (Figure 3.4b). A convenient way to visualize the mirror-image properties of enantiomers is to look at a pair of gloves. No matter which way you turn or hold a left-hand glove, for example, it cannot fit properly on your right hand. Any given pair of enantiomers shares identical chemical properties, such as solubility and melting point. However, due to the different orientation of atoms in space, their ability to noncovalently bind to other molecules can be strikingly different. For example, as you learned in Chapter 2, **enzymes** are molecules that catalyze (speed up) the rates of many biologically important chemical reactions. Typically, a given enzyme is very specific in its action, and an enzyme that recognizes one enantiomer of a pair often does not recognize the other. That is because the actions of enzymes depend on the spatial arrangements of the particular atoms in a molecule.

3.2 Formation of Organic Molecules and Macromolecules

Learning Outcomes:
1. Diagram how small molecules may be assembled into larger ones by dehydration reactions and how hydrolysis reactions can reverse this process.
2. List the four major classes of organic molecules and macromolecules found in living organisms.

As we have seen, organic molecules have various shapes due to the bonding properties of carbon. During the past two centuries, biochemists have studied many organic molecules found in living organisms and determined their structures at the molecular level. Many of these compounds are relatively small molecules, containing a few or a few dozen atoms. However, some organic molecules are extremely large macromolecules composed of thousands or even millions of atoms. Such large molecules are formed by linking together many smaller molecules called **monomers** (meaning one part) and are thus also known as **polymers** (meaning many parts). The structure of macromolecules depends on the structure of their monomers, the number of monomers linked together, and the three-dimensional way in which the monomers are linked.

As introduced in Chapter 2, the process by which two or more molecules combine into a larger one, with the loss of a small molecule, is called a **condensation reaction**. When an organic macromolecule is formed, two smaller molecules combine by condensation, producing a larger molecule along with a molecule of water. This specific type of condensation reaction is called a **dehydration reaction**, because a molecule of water is removed when the monomers combine.

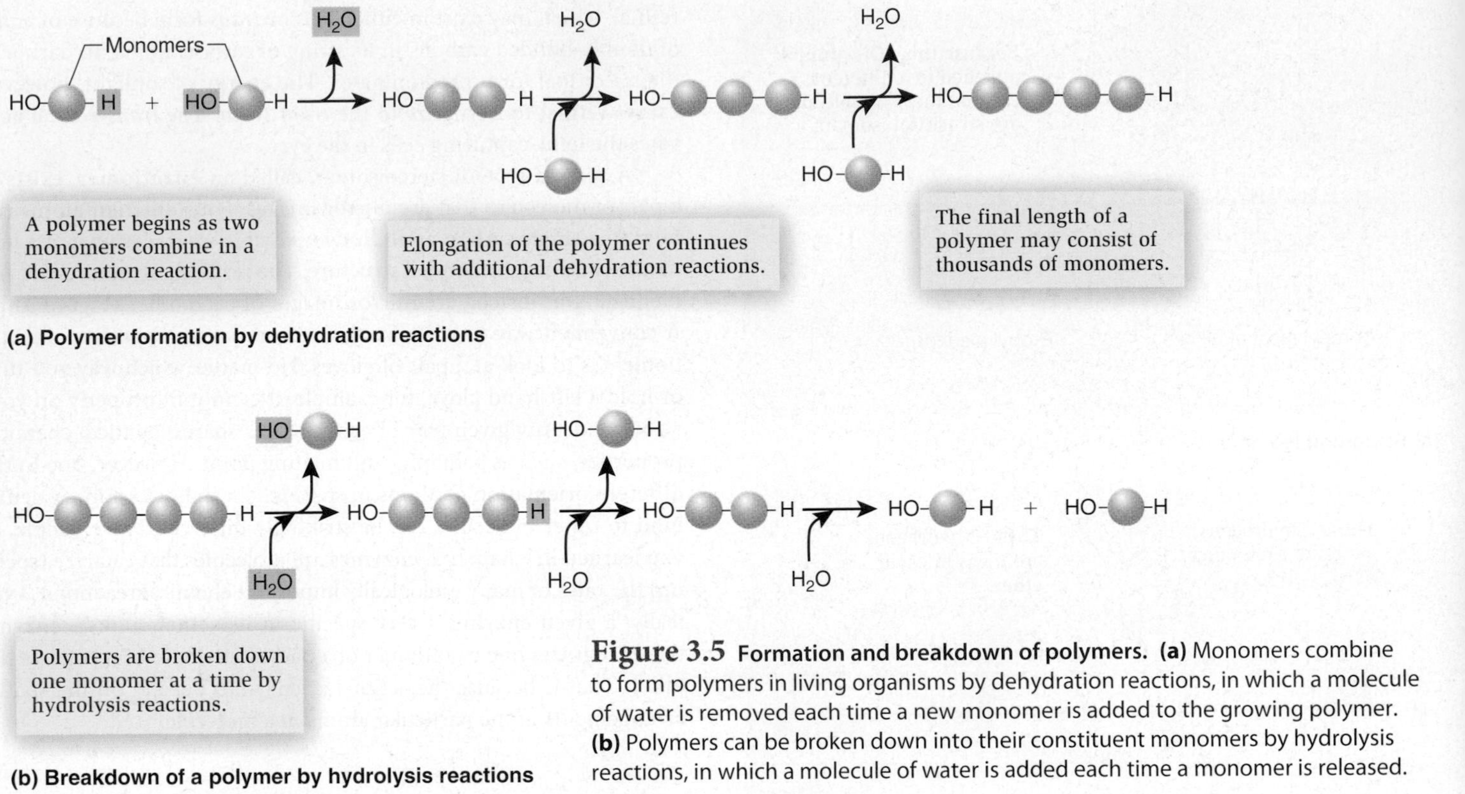

A polymer begins as two monomers combine in a dehydration reaction.

Elongation of the polymer continues with additional dehydration reactions.

The final length of a polymer may consist of thousands of monomers.

(a) Polymer formation by dehydration reactions

Polymers are broken down one monomer at a time by hydrolysis reactions.

(b) Breakdown of a polymer by hydrolysis reactions

Figure 3.5 **Formation and breakdown of polymers. (a)** Monomers combine to form polymers in living organisms by dehydration reactions, in which a molecule of water is removed each time a new monomer is added to the growing polymer. **(b)** Polymers can be broken down into their constituent monomers by hydrolysis reactions, in which a molecule of water is added each time a monomer is released.

An idealized dehydration reaction is illustrated in **Figure 3.5a**. Notice that the length of a polymer may be extended again and again with additional dehydration reactions. Some polymers can reach great lengths by this mechanism. For example, as you will learn in Chapter 46, nutrients in an animal's food are transported out of the digestive tract into the body fluids as monomers. If more energy-yielding nutrients are consumed than are required for the animal's activities, the excess nutrients may be processed by certain organs into extremely long polymers consisting of tens of thousands of monomers. The polymers are then stored in this convenient form to provide a source of energy when food is not available, such as during sleep, when the animal is not eating but nevertheless still requires energy to carry out all the various activities required to maintain cellular function.

Polymers, however, are not recognized by the cellular machinery that functions to release the chemical energy stored in the bonds of molecules. Consequently, polymers must first be broken down into their constituent monomers, which then, under the right conditions, can release some of the energy stored in their bonds. As you learned in Chapter 2, the process by which a polymer is broken down into monomers is called a **hydrolysis reaction**, because a molecule of water is added back each time a monomer is released (Figure 3.5b). Therefore, the formation of polymers in organisms is generally reversible; once formed, a polymer can later be broken down. These processes may repeat themselves over and over again as dictated by changes in the various cellular activities of an organism. Dehydration and hydrolysis reactions are both catalyzed by enzymes.

By analyzing the cells of many different species, researchers have determined that all forms of life have organic molecules and macromolecules that fall into four broad categories, based on their chemical and biological properties: carbohydrates, lipids, proteins, and nucleic acids. In the next sections, we will survey the structures of these organic compounds and begin to examine their biological functions.

3.3 Carbohydrates

Learning Outcomes:
1. Distinguish among different forms of carbohydrate molecules, including monosaccharides, disaccharides, and polysaccharides.
2. Relate the functions of plant and animal polysaccharides to their structure.

Carbohydrates are composed of carbon, hydrogen, and oxygen atoms in or close to the proportions represented by the general formula $C_n(H_2O)_n$, where n is a whole number. This formula gives carbohydrates their name—carbon-containing compounds that are hydrated, that is, contain water. Most of the carbon atoms in a carbohydrate are linked to a hydrogen atom and a hydroxyl functional group. However, other functional groups, such as amino and carboxyl groups, are also found in certain carbohydrates. As discussed next, sugars are relatively small carbohydrates, whereas polysaccharides are large macromolecules.

Sugars Are Small Carbohydrates That May Taste Sweet

Sugars are small carbohydrates that in many, but not all, cases taste sweet. The simplest sugars are the monomers known as **monosaccharides** (from the Greek, meaning single sugars). The most common types are molecules with five carbons, called pentoses, and those with six carbons, called hexoses. Important pentoses are ribose ($C_5H_{10}O_5$) and the closely related deoxyribose ($C_5H_{10}O_4$), which are part of RNA and DNA molecules, respectively, and are described later in this chapter. The most common hexose is glucose ($C_6H_{12}O_6$). Like other monosaccharides, glucose is very water-soluble and thus circulates in the blood or fluids of animals, where it can be transported across cell membranes. Once inside a cell, enzymes can break down glucose into smaller molecules, releasing energy that was stored in the chemical bonds of glucose. This energy is then stored in the bonds of another molecule, called adenosine triphosphate, or ATP (see Chapter 7), which, in turn, powers a variety of cellular processes. In this way, sugar is often used as a source of energy by living organisms.

Figure 3.6a depicts the bonds between atoms in a monosaccharide in both linear and ring forms. The ring structure is a better approximation of the true shape of the molecule as it mostly exists in solution, with the carbon atoms numbered by convention, as shown. The ring is made from the linear structure by an oxygen atom, which forms a bond that bridges two carbons in which carbon 1 binds to the oxygen of carbon 5. The hydrogen atoms and the hydroxyl groups may lie above or below the plane of the ring structure.

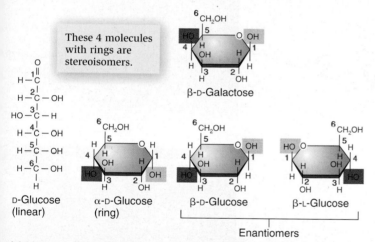

(a) Linear and ring structures of D-glucose

(b) Isomers of glucose

Figure 3.6 Monosaccharide structure. (a) A comparison of the linear and ring structures of glucose. In solution, such as the fluids of organisms, nearly all glucose is in the ring form. (b) Isomers of glucose. The locations of the C-1 and C-4 hydroxyl groups are emphasized with green and orange boxes, respectively. Glucose exists as stereoisomers designated α- and β-glucose, which differ in the position of the —OH group attached to carbon atom number 1. Glucose and galactose differ in the position of the —OH group attached to carbon atom number 4. Enantiomers of glucose, called D-glucose and L-glucose, are mirror images of each other. D-Glucose is the form used by living cells.

BIOLOGY PRINCIPLE Living organisms use energy. The chemical energy stored in certain of the bonds of glucose molecules can be harnessed by living organisms. This energy can be used to perform numerous functions that support life, including the synthesis of new molecules, growth, digestion, locomotion, and many others.

Concept Check: With regard to their binding to enzymes, why do enantiomers such as D- and L-glucose have different biological properties?

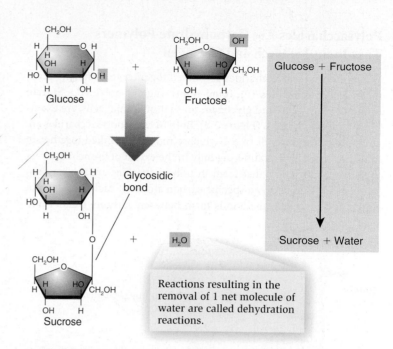

Figure 3.7 Formation of a disaccharide. Two monosaccharides can bond to each other to form a disaccharide, such as sucrose, maltose, or lactose, by a dehydration reaction.

Concept Check: What type of reaction is the reverse of the one shown here, in which a disaccharide is broken down into two monosaccharides?

Figure 3.6b compares different types of isomers of glucose. Glucose can exist as D- and L-glucose, which are mirror images of each other, or enantiomers. Other types of isomers are formed by changing the relative positions of the hydrogens and hydroxyl groups along the sugar ring. For example, glucose exists in two interconvertible forms, with the hydroxyl group attached to the number 1 carbon atom lying either above (the β form of glucose, Figure 3.6b) or below (the α form, Figure 3.6a) the plane of the ring. As discussed later, the isomers of glucose have different biological properties. In another example, if the hydroxyl group on carbon atom number 4 of glucose is above the plane of the ring, the sugar called galactose is created (Figure 3.6b).

Monosaccharides can join together by dehydration to form larger carbohydrates. **Disaccharides** (meaning two sugars) are carbohydrates composed of two monosaccharides. A familiar disaccharide is sucrose, or table sugar, which is composed of the monomers glucose and fructose (**Figure 3.7**). Sucrose is the major transport form of sugar in plants. The linking together of most monosaccharides involves the removal of a hydroxyl group from one monosaccharide and a hydrogen atom from the other, giving rise to a molecule of water and covalently bonding the two sugars together through an oxygen atom. The bond formed between two sugar molecules by such a dehydration reaction is called a **glycosidic bond**. Conversely, hydrolysis of a glycosidic bond in a disaccharide breaks the bond by adding back the water, thereby uncoupling the two monosaccharides. Other disaccharides frequently found in nature are maltose, formed in animals during the digestion of large carbohydrates in the intestinal tract, and lactose, present in the milk of mammals. Maltose is α-D-glucose linked to α-D-glucose, and lactose is β-D-galactose linked to β-D-glucose.

Polysaccharides Are Carbohydrate Polymers That Include Starch and Glycogen

When many monosaccharides are linked together to form long polymers, **polysaccharides** (meaning many sugars) are made. **Starch**, found in plant cells, and **glycogen**, present in animal cells, are examples of polysaccharides (**Figure 3.8**). Both of these polysaccharides are composed of thousands of α-D-glucose molecules linked together in long, branched chains, differing only in the extent of branching along the chain. The bonds that form in polysaccharides are not random but instead form between specific carbon atoms of each molecule. In starch and glycogen, the bonds form between carbons 1 and 4 and

between carbons 1 and 6. The high degree of branching in glycogen contributes to its solubility in animal tissues, such as muscle tissue. This is because the extensive branching creates a more open structure, in which many hydrophilic hydroxyl (—OH) side groups have access to water and can hydrogen-bond with it. Starch, because it is less branched, is less soluble, which contributes to the properties of plant structures (think of a potato or a kernel of corn).

Some polysaccharides, such as starch and glycogen, are used to store energy in cells. Like disaccharides, polysaccharides can be hydrolyzed in the presence of water to yield monosaccharides, which are broken down to provide the energy that can be stored in ATP. Starch and glycogen, the polymers of α-glucose, provide an efficient

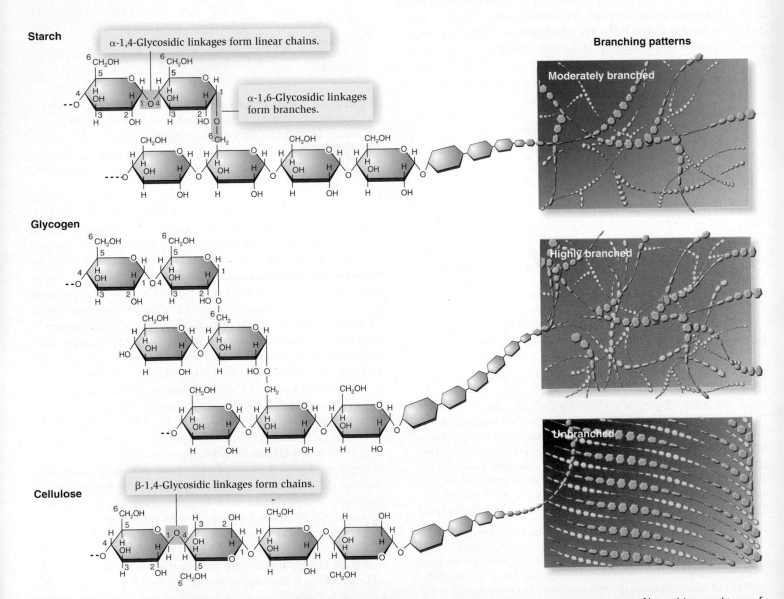

Figure 3.8 Polysaccharides that are polymers of glucose. These polysaccharides differ in their arrangement, extent of branching, and type of glucose isomer. Note: In cellulose, the bonding arrangements cause every other glucose to be upside down with respect to its neighbors.

BioConnections: *Look ahead to Figures 10.5 and 10.6 for its role in plant structure and to Figures 35.10 and 35.11 for the role of cellulose in plant growth. Considering the amount of plant life on Earth, what might you conclude about the abundance of cellulose on the planet?*

means of storing energy for those times when a plant or animal cannot obtain sufficient energy from its environment or diet for its metabolic requirements.

Other polysaccharides provide a structural role, rather than storing energy. The plant polysaccharide **cellulose** is a polymer of β-D-glucose, with a linear arrangement of carbon-carbon bonds and no branching (see Figure 3.8). Each glucose monomer in cellulose is in an opposite orientation from its adjacent monomers ("flipped over"), forming long chains of several thousand glucose monomers. The bond orientations in β-D-glucose prevent cellulose from being hydrolyzed for ATP production in most types of organisms. As noted earlier, this is because many enzymes are highly specific for one type of molecule. The enzymes that break the bonds between monomers of α-D-glucose in starch do not recognize the shape of the polymer made by the bonds between β-D-glucose monomers in cellulose. Therefore, plant cells can break down starch without breaking down cellulose. In this way, cellulose can be used for other functions, notably in the formation of the rigid cell-wall structure characteristic of plants. The linear arrangement of bonds in cellulose provides opportunities for vast numbers of hydrogen bonds between cellulose molecules, which stack together in sheets and provide great strength to structures like plant cell walls. The hydrogen bonds form between hydroxyl groups on carbons 3 and 6.

Unlike most animals and plants, some organisms do have an enzyme capable of breaking down cellulose. For example, certain bacteria present in the gastrointestinal tracts of grass and wood eaters, such as cows and termites, respectively, can digest cellulose into usable monosaccharides because they contain an enzyme that can hydrolyze the bonds between β-D-glucose monomers. Humans lack this enzyme; therefore, we eliminate in the feces most of the cellulose ingested in our diet. Undigestible plant matter we consume is commonly referred to as fiber.

Other polysaccharides also play structural roles. **Chitin**, a tough, structural polysaccharide, forms the external skeleton of insects and crustaceans (shrimp and lobsters) as well as the cell walls of fungi. The sugar monomers within chitin have nitrogen-containing groups attached to them. **Glycosaminoglycans** are large polysaccharides that play a structural role in animals. For example, they are abundantly found in cartilage, the tough, fibrous material found in bone and certain other animal structures. Glycosaminoglycans are also abundant in the extracellular matrix that provides a structural framework surrounding many of the cells in an animal's body (see Figure 10.4).

3.4 Lipids

Learning Outcomes:
1. List the several different classes of lipid molecules important in living organisms.
2. Diagram the structure of a triglyceride and explain how it is affected by the presence of saturated and unsaturated fatty acids.
3. Explain why some fats are solid at room temperature, and others are liquid.
4. Discuss how fats function as energy-storage molecules.
5. Apply knowledge of the structure of phospholipids to the formation of cellular membranes.
6. Describe the chemical nature of steroids and give an example of their biological importance.

Lipids are hydrophobic molecules composed mainly of hydrogen and carbon atoms, and some oxygen. The defining feature of lipids is that they are nonpolar and therefore insoluble in water. Lipids account for about 40% of the organic matter in the average human body and include fats, phospholipids, steroids, and waxes.

Triglycerides Are Made from Glycerol and Fatty Acids

Triglycerides or triacylglycerols (often simply called "fats"), are formed by bonding glycerol to three fatty acids (**Figure 3.9**). Glycerol is a three-carbon molecule with one hydroxyl group (—OH) bonded to each carbon. A fatty acid is a chain of carbon and hydrogen atoms with a carboxyl group (—COOH) at one end. Each of the hydroxyl groups in glycerol is linked to the carboxyl group of a fatty acid by the removal of a molecule of water by a dehydration reaction. The resulting bond is an example of a type of chemical bond called an ester bond.

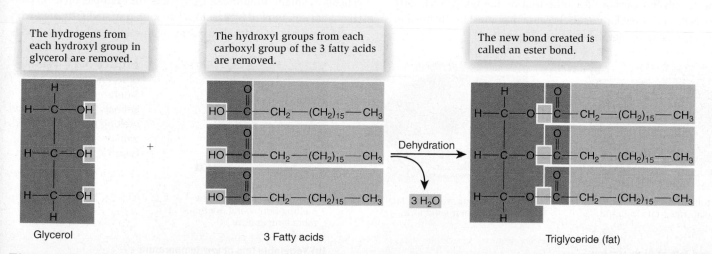

Figure 3.9 The formation of a triglyceride. The formation of a triglyceride requires three dehydration reactions in which fatty acids are bonded to glycerol. Note in this figure and in Figure 3.10, a common shorthand notation is used for depicting fatty acid chains, in which a portion of the CH_2 groups are illustrated as $(CH_2)_n$, where n may be 2 or greater.

Carboxyl group

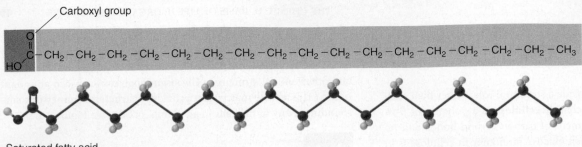

Saturated fatty acid
(Stearic acid)

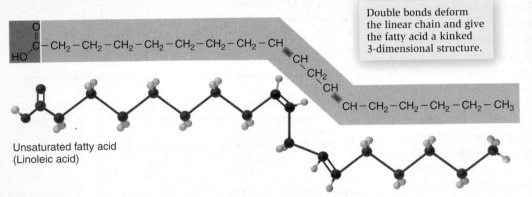

Double bonds deform
the linear chain and give
the fatty acid a kinked
3-dimensional structure.

Unsaturated fatty acid
(Linoleic acid)

Figure 3.10 Examples of fatty acids. Fatty acids are hydrocarbon chains with a carboxyl functional group at one end and either no double-bonded carbons (saturated) or one or more double bonds (unsaturated). Stearic acid, for example, is an abundant saturated fatty acid in animals, whereas linoleic acid is an unsaturated fatty acid found in plants. Note that the presence of two C=C double bonds introduces two kinks into the shape of linoleic acid. As a consequence, unsaturated fatty acids are not able to pack together as tightly as saturated fatty acids.

The fatty acids found in fats and other lipids may differ with regard to their lengths and the presence of double bonds (**Figure 3.10**). Most fatty acids in nature have an even number of carbon atoms, with 16- and 18-carbon fatty acids being the most common in the cells of plants and animals. Fatty acids also differ with regard to the presence of double bonds. When all the carbons in a fatty acid are linked by single covalent bonds, the fatty acid is said to be a **saturated fatty acid**, because all the carbons are saturated with covalently bound hydrogen. Alternatively, some fatty acids contain one or more C=C double bonds and consequently fewer C—H bonds; these fatty acids are known as **unsaturated fatty acids**. The C=C double bond introduces a kink into the linear shape of a fatty acid. A fatty acid with one C=C bond is a monounsaturated fatty acid, whereas a fatty acid with two or more C=C bonds constitutes a polyunsaturated fatty acid. In organisms such as mammals, certain fatty acids are necessary for good health but cannot be synthesized by the body. Such fatty acids are called essential fatty acids, because they must be obtained in the diet; one example is linoleic acid (see Figure 3.10).

Fats (triglycerides) that contain high amounts of saturated fatty acids can pack together tightly, resulting in numerous intermolecular interactions that stabilize the fat. Saturated fats have a high melting point and tend to be solid at room temperature. Animal fats generally contain a high proportion of saturated fatty acids. For example, beef fat contains high amounts of stearic acid, a saturated fatty acid with a melting point of 70°C (see Figure 3.10). When you heat a hamburger on the stove, the stearic acid and other saturated animal fats melt, and liquid grease appears in the frying pan (**Figure 3.11**). When allowed to cool to room temperature, however, the liquid grease in the pan returns to its solid form.

Because of kinks in their chains, unsaturated fatty acids cannot stack together as tightly as saturated fatty acids. Fats high in unsaturated fatty acids usually have low melting points and are liquids at room temperature. Such fats are called oils. Fats derived from plants generally contain unsaturated fatty acids. For example, olive oil contains high amounts of oleic acid, a monounsaturated fatty acid with a melting point of 16°C. Fatty acids with additional double bonds

Figure 3.11 Fats at different temperatures. Saturated fats found in animals tend to have high melting points compared with unsaturated fats found in plants.

High temperature converts solid, saturated fats to liquid.

After cooling, saturated fats return to their solid form.

(a) Animal fats at high and low temperatures

Unsaturated fats have low melting points and are liquid at room temperature.

(b) Vegetable fats at low temperature

Concept Check: Certain types of fats used in baking are called shortenings. Shortenings are often made from vegetable oils by a process called hydrogenation, in which hydrogen causes double bonds to become single bonds. What do you think happens to such oils when they are hydrogenated?

have even lower melting points; linoleic acid (see Figure 3.10) has two double bonds and melts at –5°C. Safflower and sunflower oils contain high amounts of linoleic acid.

Most unsaturated fatty acids, including linoleic acid, exist in nature in the *cis* form (see Figure 3.4). Of particular importance to human health, however, are *trans* fatty acids, which are formed by an artificial process in which the natural *cis* form is altered to a *trans* configuration. This gives the fats that contain such fatty acids a more compact, linear structure and, therefore, a higher melting point. Although this process has been used for many years to produce fats with a longer shelf-life and with better characteristics for baking, it is now understood that *trans* fats are linked with human disease. Notable among these is coronary artery disease, caused by a narrowing of the blood vessels that supply the heart with blood.

Like starch and glycogen, fats are important for storing energy. The hydrolysis of triglycerides releases the fatty acids from glycerol, and these products can then be metabolized to provide energy to make ATP. Certain organisms, most notably mammals, have the ability to store large amounts of energy by accumulating fats. The number of C—H bonds in a molecule of fat or carbohydrate determines in part how much energy the molecule can yield. Fats are primarily long

chains of C—H bonds, whereas glucose and other carbohydrates have numerous C—OH bonds. Consequently, 1 gram of fat stores more energy than does 1 gram of starch or glycogen. Fat is therefore an efficient means of energy storage for mobile organisms in which excess body mass may be a disadvantage. In animals, fats can also play a structural role by forming cushions that support organs. In addition, fats provide insulation under the skin that helps protect many terrestrial animals during cold weather and marine mammals in cold water.

Phospholipids Are Amphipathic Lipids

Phospholipids, another class of lipids, are similar in structure to triglycerides but with one important difference. The third hydroxyl group of glycerol is linked to a phosphate group instead of a fatty acid. In most phospholipids, a small polar or charged nitrogen-containing molecule is attached to this phosphate (**Figure 3.12a**). The glycerol backbone, phosphate group, and charged molecule constitute a polar hydrophilic region at one end of the phospholipid, whereas the fatty acid chains provide a nonpolar hydrophobic region at the opposite end. Recall from Chapter 2 that molecules with polar and nonpolar regions are called amphipathic molecules.

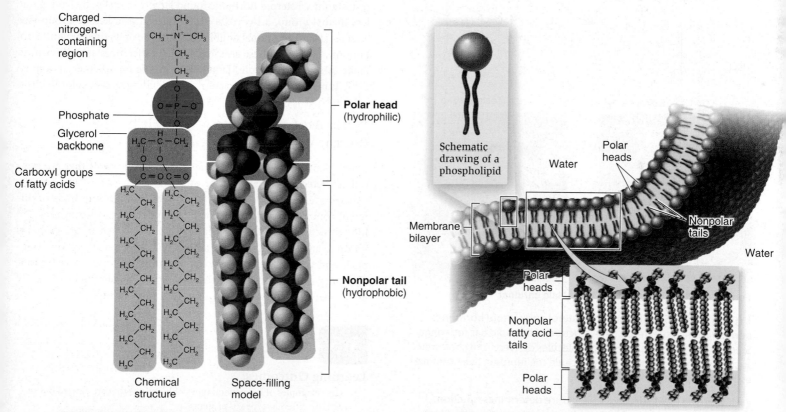

(a) Structure and model of a phospholipid

(b) Arrangement of phospholipids in a bilayer

Figure 3.12 Structure of phospholipids. (a) Chemical structure and space-filling model of phosphatidylcholine, a common phospholipid found in living organisms. Phospholipids contain both polar and nonpolar regions, making them amphipathic. The fatty-acid tails are the nonpolar region. The rest of the molecule is polar. **(b)** Arrangement of phospholipids in a biological membrane, such as the plasma membrane that encloses cells. The hydrophilic regions of the phospholipid face the watery environments on either side of the membrane, whereas the hydrophobic regions associate with each other in the interior of the membrane, forming a bilayer.

Concept Check: *When water and oil are added to a test tube, the two liquids form two separate layers (think of oil and vinegar in a bottle of salad dressing). If a solution of phospholipids was added to a mixture of water and oil, where would the phospholipids dissolve?*

BioConnections: *For a more detailed view of the components of cellular membranes, including the phospholipid bilayer, look ahead to Figure 5.1.*

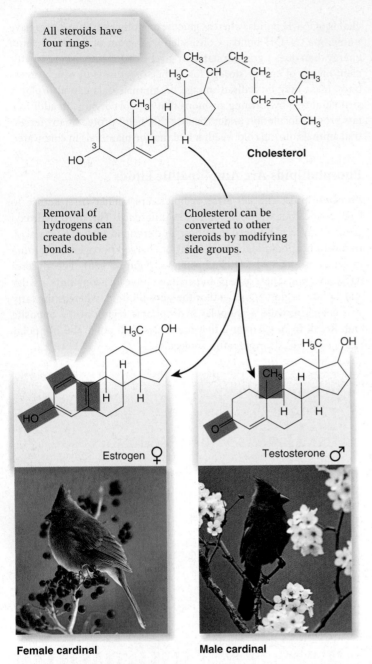

All steroids have four rings.

Cholesterol

Removal of hydrogens can create double bonds.

Cholesterol can be converted to other steroids by modifying side groups.

Estrogen ♀

Testosterone ♂

Female cardinal

Male cardinal

Figure 3.13 **Structure of cholesterol and steroid hormones derived from cholesterol.** The structure of a steroid has four rings. Steroids include cholesterol and molecules derived from cholesterol, such as steroid hormones. These include the reproductive hormones estrogen and testosterone.

BIOLOGY PRINCIPLE Structure determines function. The few seemingly minor chemical (structural) differences between estrogen and testosterone are sufficient to completely alter their biological functions. The striking differences in appearance of these two cardinals are just one example of sex-dependent differences in form and function in the animal world that are due to these two molecules.

In water, phospholipids become organized into bilayers, with their hydrophilic polar ends interacting with the water molecules and their hydrophobic nonpolar ends facing the interior, where they

are shielded from water. As you will learn in detail in Chapter 5, this bilayer arrangement of phospholipids is critical for determining the structure of cellular membranes, as shown in Figure 3.12b.

Steroids Contain Ring Structures

Steroids have a distinctly different chemical structure from that of the other types of lipid molecules discussed thus far. Four fused rings of carbon atoms form the skeleton of all steroids. One or more polar hydroxyl groups are attached to this ring structure, but they are not numerous enough to make a steroid highly water-soluble. For example, steroids with a hydroxyl group are known as sterols—one of the most well known being cholesterol (**Figure 3.13**, top). Cholesterol is found in the blood and cellular membranes of animals. Due to its low solubility in water, at high concentrations cholesterol can contribute to the formation of blockages in major blood vessels.

In steroids, tiny differences in chemical structure can lead to profoundly different biological properties. For example, all steroid hormones are derived from cholesterol and share similarities in structure, but with some important differences. Estrogen is a steroid hormone found in high amounts in female vertebrates. Estrogen differs from testosterone, a steroid hormone found largely in males, by having one less methyl group, a hydroxyl group instead of a ketone group (see Table 3.1), and additional double bonds in one of its rings (Figure 3.13, bottom). However, these seemingly small differences are sufficient to make these two molecules largely responsible for whether an animal exhibits male or female characteristics, including feather color in birds.

Waxes Are Complex Lipids That Help Prevent Water Loss from Organisms

Many plants and animals produce lipids called waxes that are typically secreted onto their surface, such as the leaves of plants and the cuticles of insects. Although any wax may contain hundreds of different compounds, all waxes contain one or more hydrocarbons and long structures that resemble a fatty acid attached by its carboxyl group to another long hydrocarbon chain. Most waxes are very nonpolar and therefore exclude water, providing a barrier to water loss. They may also be used as structural elements in colonies like those of bees, where beeswax forms the honeycomb of the hive.

3.5 Proteins

Learning Outcomes:
1. Give examples of the general types of functions that are carried out in cells by different types of proteins.
2. Explain how amino acids are joined to form a polypeptide, and distinguish between a polypeptide and protein.
3. Describe the levels of protein structure and the factors that determine them.
4. Outline the bonding forces important in determining protein shape and function.
5. Explain what domains are and their importance in proteins.

Proteins are polymers found in all cells and play critical roles in nearly all life processes (**Table 3.2**). The word protein comes from the

Table 3.2   Major Categories and Functions of Proteins

Category	Functions	Examples
Proteins involved in gene expression and regulation	Make mRNA from a DNA template; synthesize polypeptides from mRNA; regulate genes	RNA polymerase assists in synthesizing RNA from DNA.
Motor proteins	Initiate movement	Myosin provides the contractile force of muscles.
Defense proteins	Protect organisms against disease	Antibodies help destroy bacteria or viruses.
Metabolic enzymes	Increase rates of chemical reactions	Hexokinase is an enzyme involved in sugar metabolism.
Cell signaling proteins	Enable cells to communicate with each other and with the environment	Taste receptors in the tongue allow animals to taste molecules in food.
Structural proteins	Support and strengthen structures	Actin provides shape to the cytoplasm of plant and animal cells. Collagen gives strength to tendons.
Transporters	Promote movement of solutes across plasma membranes	Glucose transporters move glucose from outside cells to inside cells, where it can be used for energy.

Greek *proteios* (meaning of the first rank), which aptly describes their importance. Proteins account for about 50% of the organic material in a typical animal's body.

Proteins Are Made Up of Amino Acid Monomers

Proteins are composed of carbon, hydrogen, oxygen, nitrogen, and small amounts of other elements, notably sulfur. The building blocks of proteins are **amino acids**, compounds with a structure in which a carbon atom, called the α-carbon, is linked to an amino group (NH_2) and a carboxyl group (COOH). The α-carbon also is linked to a hydrogen atom and a side chain, which is given a general designation R. Proteins are polymers of amino acids.

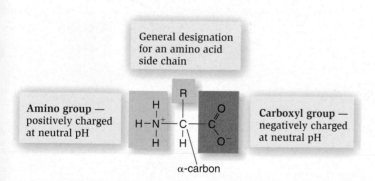

General designation for an amino acid side chain

Amino group — positively charged at neutral pH

Carboxyl group — negatively charged at neutral pH

α-carbon

When an amino acid is dissolved in water at neutral pH, the amino group accepts a hydrogen ion and is positively charged, whereas the carboxyl group loses a hydrogen ion and is negatively charged. The term amino acid is the name given to such molecules because they have an amino group and also a carboxyl group that acts as an acid.

All amino acids except glycine may exist in more than one isomeric form, called the D and L forms, which are enantiomers. Note that glycine cannot exist in D and L forms because there are two hydrogens bound to its α-carbon, making it symmetric. Only L-amino acids and glycine are found in proteins. D-isomers are found in the cell walls of certain bacteria, where they may play a protective role against molecules secreted by the host organism in which the bacteria live.

The 20 amino acids found in proteins are distinguished by their side chains (**Figure 3.14**). The amino acids are categorized by the properties of their side chains, whether nonpolar, polar and uncharged, or polar and charged. The varying structures of the side chains are critical features of protein structure and function. The arrangement and chemical features of the side chains cause proteins to fold and adopt their three-dimensional shapes. In addition, certain amino acids may be critical in protein function. For example, amino acid side chains found within the active sites of enzymes are important in catalyzing chemical reactions.

Amino acids are joined together by a dehydration reaction that links the carboxyl group of one amino acid to the amino group of another (**Figure 3.15a**). The covalent bond formed between a carboxyl and amino group is called a **peptide bond**. When multiple amino acids are joined by peptide bonds, the resulting molecule is called a **polypeptide** (Figure 3.15b). The backbone of the polypeptide in Figure 3.15 is highlighted in yellow. The amino acid side chains project from the backbone. When two or more amino acids are linked together, one end of the resulting molecule has a free amino group. This is the amino end, or **N-terminus**. The other end of the polypeptide, called the carboxyl end, or **C-terminus**, has a free carboxyl group. As shown in Figure 3.15c, amino acids within a polypeptide are numbered from the N-terminus to the C-terminus.

The term polypeptide refers to a structural unit composed of a linear sequence of amino acids and does not imply anything about functionality. In other words, an artificial molecule with a random sequence of amino acids could be synthesized experimentally in the laboratory; this molecule would be a polypeptide but would have no function. In contrast, a **protein** is a molecule composed of one or more polypeptides that have been folded and twisted into a precise three-dimensional shape that carries out a particular function or functions. Many proteins also have carbohydrates (glycoproteins) or lipids (lipoproteins) attached at various points along their amino acid chain; these modifications impart unique functions to such proteins.

Proteins Have a Hierarchy of Structure

Scientists view protein structure at four progressive levels: primary, secondary, tertiary, and quaternary, shown schematically in **Figure 3.16**. Each higher level of structure depends on the preceding levels. For example, changing the primary structure may affect the secondary, tertiary, and quaternary structures. Let's now consider each level separately.

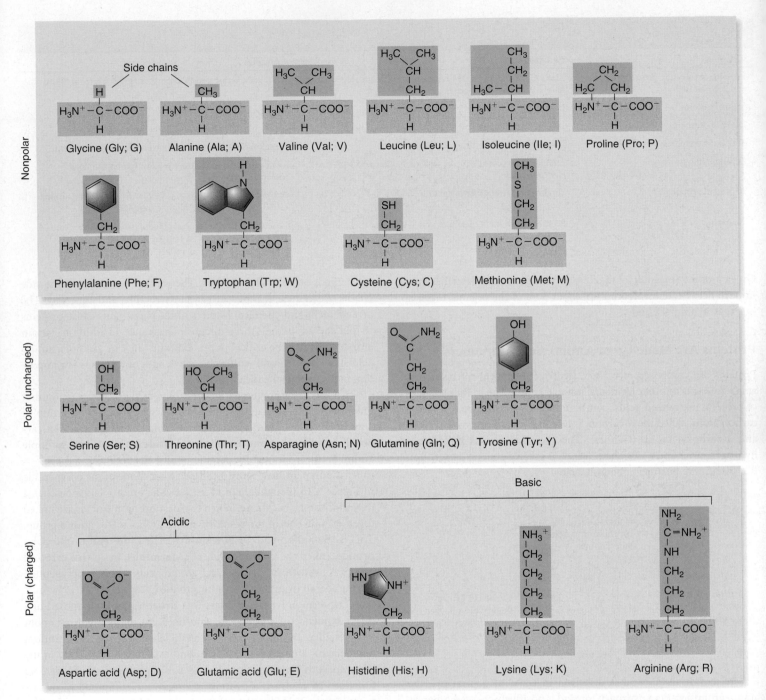

Figure 3.14 The 20 amino acids found in living organisms. The various amino acids have different chemical properties (for example, nonpolar versus polar) due to the nature of their different side chains. These properties contribute to the differences in the three-dimensional shapes and chemical properties of proteins, which, in turn, influence their biological functions. Tyrosine has both polar and nonpolar characteristics and is listed in just one category for simplicity. The common three-letter and one-letter abbreviations for each amino acid are shown in parentheses.

Primary Structure The **primary structure** (see Figure 3.16) of a protein is its amino acid sequence, from beginning to end. The primary structures of proteins are determined by genes. As we will explore in Chapter 12, genes carry the information for the production of polypeptides with specific amino acid sequences.

Figure 3.17 shows the primary structure of ribonuclease, which functions as an enzyme to degrade ribonucleic acid (RNA) molecules after they are no longer required by a cell. As described later

and in Unit III of this textbook, RNA is a key part of the mechanism of protein synthesis. Ribonuclease is composed of a relatively short polypeptide consisting of 124 amino acids. An average polypeptide is about 300 to 500 amino acids in length, but some polypeptides form proteins that are a few thousand amino acids long.

Secondary Structure The amino acid sequence of a polypeptide, together with the fundamental constraints of chemistry and physics,

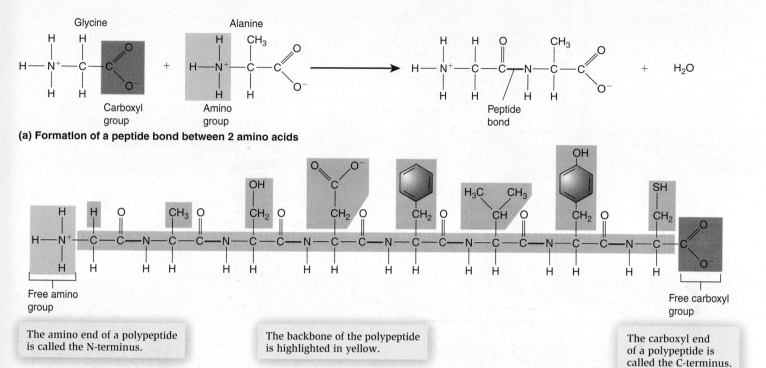

(a) Formation of a peptide bond between 2 amino acids

(b) Polypeptide—a linear chain of amino acids

The amino end of a polypeptide is called the N-terminus.

The backbone of the polypeptide is highlighted in yellow.

The carboxyl end of a polypeptide is called the C-terminus.

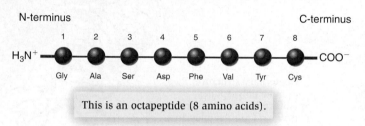

This is an octapeptide (8 amino acids).

(c) Numbering system of amino acids in a polypeptide

Figure 3.15 **The chemistry of polypeptide formation.** Polypeptides are polymers of amino acids. They are formed by linking amino acids via dehydration reactions to make peptide bonds. Every polypeptide has an amino end, or N-terminus, and a carboxyl end, or C-terminus.

Concept Check: *How many water molecules would be produced in making a polypeptide that is 72 amino acids long by dehydration reactions?*

cause a protein to fold into a more compact structure. Amino acids can rotate around bonds within a polypeptide. Consequently, proteins are flexible and can fold into a number of shapes, just as a string of beads can be twisted into many configurations. Folding can be irregular, or certain regions can have a repeating folding pattern. Such repeating patterns are called **secondary structure**. The two basic types of a protein's secondary structure are the α helix and the β pleated sheet.

In an α helix, the polypeptide backbone forms a repeating helical structure that is stabilized by hydrogen bonds along the length of the backbone. As shown in Figure 3.16, the hydrogen linked to a nitrogen atom forms a hydrogen bond with an oxygen atom that is double-bonded to a carbon atom. These hydrogen bonds occur at regular intervals within the polypeptide backbone and cause the backbone to twist into a helix.

In a β pleated sheet, regions of the polypeptide backbone come to lie parallel to each other. Hydrogen bonds between a hydrogen linked to a nitrogen atom and a double-bonded oxygen form between these adjacent, parallel regions. When this occurs, the polypeptide backbone adopts a repeating zigzag, or pleated, shape.

The α helices and β pleated sheets are key determinants of a protein's characteristics. For example, α helices in certain proteins are

composed primarily of nonpolar amino acids. Proteins containing many such regions with an α helix structure tend to anchor themselves into a lipid-rich environment, such as a cell's plasma membrane. In this way, a protein whose function is required in a specific location such as a plasma membrane can be retained there. Secondary structure also contributes to the great strength of certain proteins, including the keratins found in hair and hooves; the proteins that make up the silk webs of spiders; and collagen, the chief component of cartilage in vertebrate animals.

Some regions along a polypeptide chain do not assume an α helix or β pleated sheet conformation and consequently do not have a secondary structure. These regions are sometimes called random coiled regions. However, this term is somewhat misleading because the shapes of random coiled regions are usually very specific and important for the protein's function.

Tertiary Structure   As the secondary structure of a polypeptide becomes established due to the particular primary structure, side chains of amino acids interact with each other. The polypeptide folds and refolds upon itself to assume a complex three-dimensional shape—its **tertiary structure** (see Figure 3.16). The tertiary structure is the three-dimensional shape of a single polypeptide. Tertiary

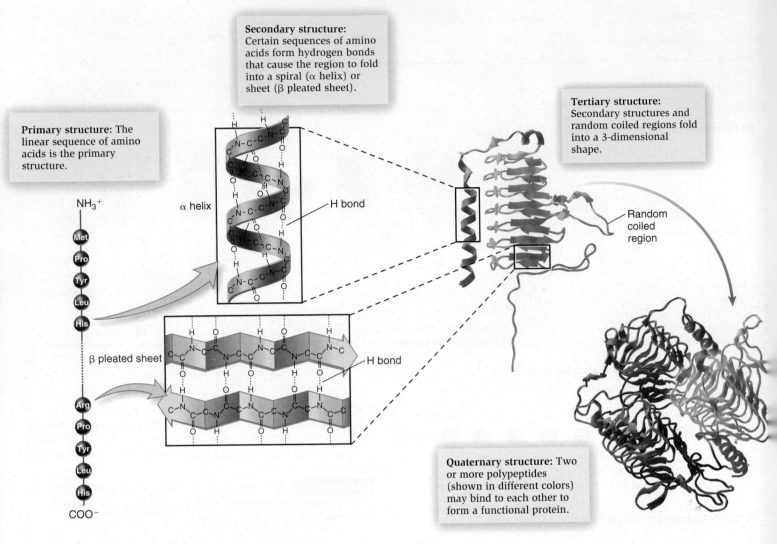

Figure 3.16 **The hierarchy of protein structure.** The R groups are omitted for simplicity.

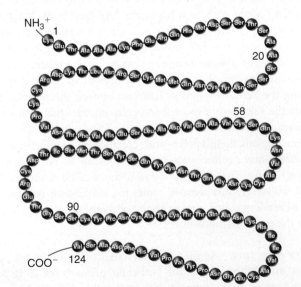

Figure 3.17 **The primary structure of ribonuclease.** The example shown here is ribonuclease from cows, which contains 124 amino acids.

structure includes all secondary structures plus any interactions involving amino acid side chains. For some proteins, such as ribonuclease, the tertiary structure is the final structure of a functional protein. However, as described next, other proteins are composed of two or more polypeptides and adopt a quaternary structure.

Quaternary Structure Many functional proteins are composed of two or more polypeptide chains that each adopt a tertiary structure and then assemble with each other (see Figure 3.16). The individual polypeptide chains are called **protein subunits**. Subunits may be identical polypeptides or they may be different. When proteins consist of more than one polypeptide chain, they are said to have **quaternary structure** and are also known as **multimeric proteins** (meaning multiple parts). Multimeric proteins are widespread in organisms. A common example is the oxygen-binding protein called hemoglobin, found in the red blood cells of vertebrate animals. Four protein subunits combine to form one hemoglobin protein. Each subunit can bind a single molecule of oxygen; therefore, each hemoglobin protein can carry four molecules of oxygen in the blood.

Protein Structure Is Influenced by Several Factors

The amino acid sequences of polypeptides are the features that distinguish the structure of one protein from another. As polypeptides are synthesized in a cell, they fold into secondary and tertiary structures, which assemble into quaternary structures for many proteins. Several factors determine the way proteins adopt their secondary, tertiary, and quaternary structures. As mentioned, the laws of chemistry and physics, together with the amino acid sequence, govern this process. As shown in **Figure 3.18**, five factors are critical for protein folding and stability:

1. *Hydrogen bonds*—The large number of weak hydrogen bonds within a polypeptide and between polypeptide chains adds up to a collectively strong force that promotes protein folding and stability. As we already learned, hydrogen bonding is a critical determinant of protein secondary structure and also is important in tertiary and quaternary structure.

2. *Ionic bonds and other polar interactions*—Some amino acid side chains are positively or negatively charged. Positively charged side chains may bind to negatively charged side chains via ionic bonds. Similarly, uncharged polar side chains in a protein may bind to ionic amino acids. Ionic bonds and polar interactions are particularly important in tertiary and quaternary structure.

3. *Hydrophobic effect*—Some amino acid side chains are nonpolar. These amino acids tend to exclude water. As a protein folds, the hydrophobic amino acids are likely to be found in the center of the protein, minimizing contact with water. As mentioned, some proteins have stretches of nonpolar amino acids that anchor them in the hydrophobic portion of membranes. The hydrophobic effect plays a major role in tertiary and quaternary structures.

4. *van der Waals forces*—Atoms within molecules have temporary weak attractions for each other if they are an optimal distance apart. This weak attraction is termed the van der Waals force (see Chapter 2). If two atoms are very close together, their electron clouds will repel each other. If they are far apart, the van der Waals force will diminish. The van der Waals forces are particularly important in determining tertiary structures.

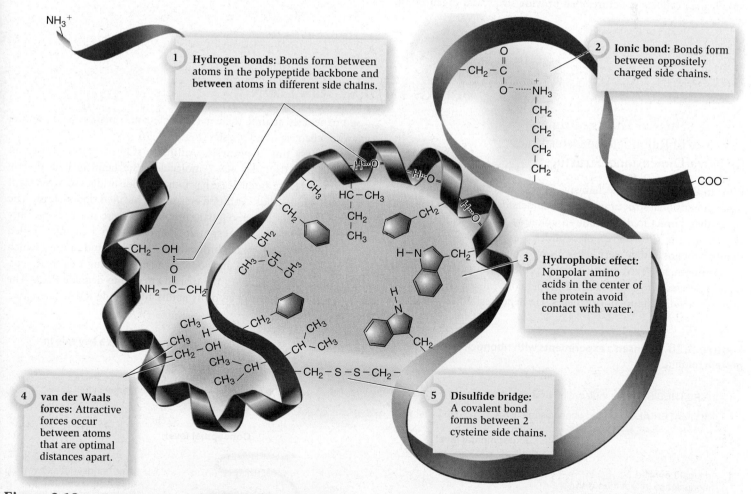

Figure 3.18 Factors that influence protein folding and stability.

BIOLOGY PRINCIPLE New properties emerge from complex interactions. This key principle of biology is apparent even at the molecular level. Note in this figure how several distinct types of chemical interactions can produce a protein with a complex shape. Compare this with the chapter-opening photo of a real protein, and the several intermediate levels of protein structure shown in Figure 3.16. It is the three-dimensional shape of different proteins that determines their ability to interact with other molecules, including other proteins.

5. *Disulfide bridges*—The side chain of the amino acid cysteine contains a sulfhydryl group (—SH), which can react with a sulfhydryl group in another cysteine side chain (see Figure 3.14). The result is a **disulfide bridge** or disulfide bond, which links the two amino acid side chains together (—S—S—). Disulfide bridges are covalent bonds that can occur within a polypeptide or between different polypeptides. Though other forces are usually more important in protein folding, the covalent nature of disulfide bridges can help to stabilize the tertiary structure of a protein.

The first four factors just described are also important in the ability of different proteins to interact with each other. As discussed throughout Unit II and other parts of this textbook, many cellular processes involve steps in which two or more different proteins interact with each other. For this to occur, one protein must recognize and bind to the surface of the other. Such binding is usually very specific. The surface of one protein precisely fits into the surface of another (**Figure 3.19**). Such **protein-protein interactions** are critically important so that cellular processes can occur in a series of defined steps. In addition, protein-protein interactions are important in building complicated cellular structures that provide shape and organization to cells.

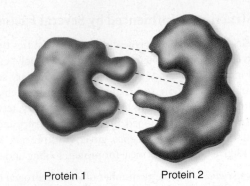

Protein 1   Protein 2

Figure 3.19 Protein-protein interaction. Two different proteins may interact with each other due to hydrogen bonding, ionic bonding, the hydrophobic effect, and van der Waals forces.

Concept Check: *If the primary structure of protein 1 in this figure were experimentally altered by the substitution of several incorrect amino acids for the correct ones, would protein 1 still be able to interact with protein 2?*

FEATURE INVESTIGATION

Anfinsen Showed That the Primary Structure of Ribonuclease Determines Its Three-Dimensional Structure

Prior to the 1960s, the mechanisms by which proteins assume their three-dimensional structures were not understood. Scientists believed either that correct folding required unknown cellular factors or that ribosomes, the site where polypeptides are synthesized, somehow shaped proteins as they were being made. American researcher Christian Anfinsen, however, postulated that proteins contain all the information necessary to fold into their proper conformation without the need for cellular factors or organelles. He hypothesized that proteins

spontaneously assume their most stable conformation based on the laws of chemistry and physics (**Figure 3.20**).

To test this hypothesis, Anfinsen studied ribonuclease, an enzyme that degrades RNA molecules. Biochemists had already determined that ribonuclease has four disulfide bridges between eight cysteine amino acids. Anfinsen began with purified ribonuclease. The key point is that other cellular components were not present, only the purified protein. He exposed ribonuclease to a chemical called β-mercaptoethanol, which broke the S—S bonds, and to urea, which disrupted the hydrogen and ionic bonds. Following this treatment, he measured the ability of the treated enzyme to degrade RNA. The enzyme had lost nearly all of its ability to degrade RNA. Therefore,

Figure 3.20 Anfinsen's experiments with ribonuclease, demonstrating that the primary structure of a polypeptide plays a key role in protein folding.

HYPOTHESIS Within their amino acid sequence, proteins contain all the information needed to fold into their correct, three-dimensional shapes.

KEY MATERIALS Purified ribonuclease, RNA, denaturing chemicals, size-exclusion columns.

Experimental level	Conceptual level

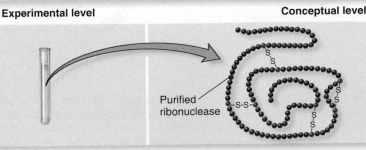

1   Incubate purified ribonuclease in test tube with RNA, and measure its ability to degrade RNA.

Purified ribonuclease

Numerous H bonds and ionic bonds (not shown) and 4 S—S bonds. Protein is properly folded.

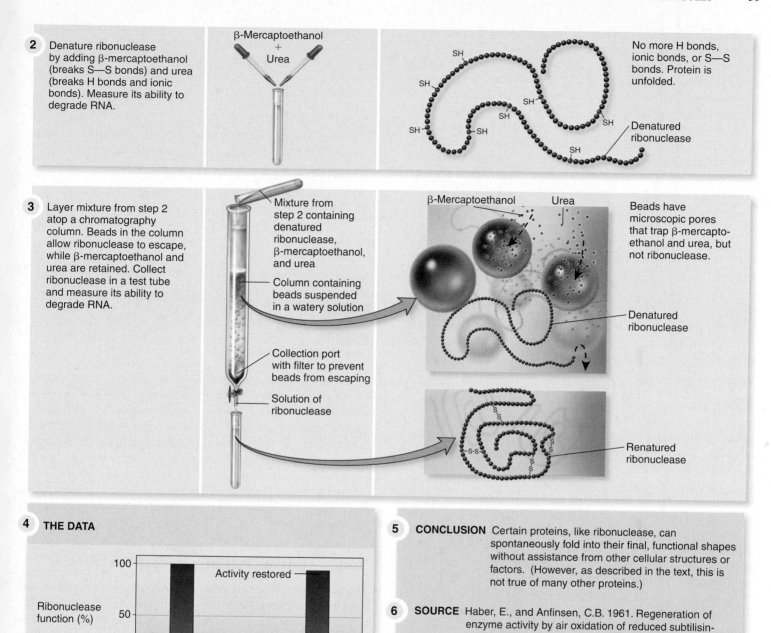

2 Denature ribonuclease by adding β-mercaptoethanol (breaks S—S bonds) and urea (breaks H bonds and ionic bonds). Measure its ability to degrade RNA.

β-Mercaptoethanol + Urea

No more H bonds, ionic bonds, or S—S bonds. Protein is unfolded.

SH ... Denatured ribonuclease

3 Layer mixture from step 2 atop a chromatography column. Beads in the column allow ribonuclease to escape, while β-mercaptoethanol and urea are retained. Collect ribonuclease in a test tube and measure its ability to degrade RNA.

Mixture from step 2 containing denatured ribonuclease, β-mercaptoethanol, and urea

Column containing beads suspended in a watery solution

Collection port with filter to prevent beads from escaping

Solution of ribonuclease

β-Mercaptoethanol   Urea

Beads have microscopic pores that trap β-mercaptoethanol and urea, but not ribonuclease.

Denatured ribonuclease

Renatured ribonuclease

4 THE DATA

Ribonuclease function (%)

100

Activity restored

50

0

Purified ribonuclease (step 1)

Denatured ribonuclease (step 2)

Ribonuclease after column chromatography (step 3)

5 CONCLUSION Certain proteins, like ribonuclease, can spontaneously fold into their final, functional shapes without assistance from other cellular structures or factors. (However, as described in the text, this is not true of many other proteins.)

6 SOURCE Haber, E., and Anfinsen, C.B. 1961. Regeneration of enzyme activity by air oxidation of reduced subtilisin-modified ribonuclease. *Journal of Biological Chemistry* 236:422–424.

Anfinsen concluded that when ribonuclease was unfolded or denatured, it was no longer functional.

The key step in this experiment came when Anfinsen removed the urea and β-mercaptoethanol from the solution. Because these molecules are much smaller than ribonuclease, removing them from the solution was accomplished with a technique called size-exclusion chromatography. In size-exclusion chromatography, solutions are layered atop a glass column of beadlike particles and allowed to filter down through the column to an open collection port at the bottom. The particles in the column have microscopic pores that trap small molecules like urea and mercaptoethanol but that permit large molecules such as ribonuclease to pass down the length of the column and out the collection port.

Using size-exclusion chromatography, Anfinsen was able to purify the ribonuclease out of the original solution. He then allowed the purified enzyme to sit in water for up to 20 hours, after which he retested the ribonuclease for its ability to degrade RNA. The result revolutionized our understanding of proteins. The activity of the ribonuclease was almost completely restored! This meant that even in the complete absence of any cellular factors or organelles, an unfolded protein can refold into its correct, functional structure. This was later confirmed by chemical analyses that demonstrated the disulfide bridges had re-formed at the proper locations.

Since Anfinsen's time, we have learned that ribonuclease's ability to refold into its functional structure is not seen in all proteins. Some proteins do require enzymes and other proteins to assist in their proper folding. Nonetheless, Anfinsen's experiments provided compelling evidence that the primary structure of a polypeptide is the key determinant of a protein's tertiary structure, an observation that earned him the Nobel Prize in Chemistry for 1972.

As investigations into the properties of proteins have continued since Anfinsen's classic experiments, it has become clear that most proteins contain within their structure one or more substructures, or domains, each of which is folded into a characteristic shape that imparts special functions to that region of the protein. This knowledge has greatly changed scientists' understanding of the ways in which proteins function and interact, as described next.

Experimental Questions

1. Before the experiments conducted by Anfinsen, what were the common beliefs among scientists about protein folding?

2. Explain the hypothesis tested by Anfinsen.

3. Why did Anfinsen use urea and β-mercaptoethanol in his experiments? Explain the result that was crucial to the discovery that the tertiary structure of ribonuclease may depend entirely on the primary structure.

GENOMES & PROTEOMES CONNECTION

Proteins Contain Functional Domains Within Their Structures

Modern research into the functions of proteins has revealed that many proteins have a modular design. This means that portions within proteins, called **domains**, modules, or motifs, have distinct structures and functions. These units of amino acid sequences have been duplicated during evolution so that the same kind of domain may be found in several different proteins. When the same domain is found in different proteins, the domain has the same three-dimensional tertiary structure and performs a function that is characteristic of that domain.

As an example, **Figure 3.21** shows a member of a family of related proteins that are known to play critical roles in regulating how certain genes are turned on and off in living cells. This protein is called a signal transducer and activator of transcription (STAT) protein.

Each domain of this protein is involved in a distinct biological function, a common occurrence in proteins with multiple domains. For example, one of the domains is labeled the SH2 domain (see Figure 3.21). Many different proteins contain this domain. It allows such proteins to recognize other proteins in a very specific way. The function of SH2 domains is to bind to tyrosine amino acids to which phosphate groups have been added by cellular enzymes. When an amino acid receives a phosphate group in this way, it is said to be phosphorylated. As might be predicted, proteins that contain SH2 domains all bind to phosphorylated tyrosines in the proteins they recognize. As a second example, a STAT protein has another domain called a DNA-binding domain. This portion of the protein has a structure that specifically binds to DNA.

Overall, the domain structure of proteins enables them to have multiple, discrete regions, each with its own structure and purpose in the functioning of the protein. Individual domain sequences and structures are often highly conserved across all life and can be thought of as evolutionary modules; they may have originated as discrete proteins of their own that were later combined and rearranged in multiple, different ways to produce new proteins.

3.6 Nucleic Acids

Learning Outcomes:

1. Describe the three components of nucleotides.
2. Distinguish between the structures of DNA and RNA.
3. Describe how certain bases pair with others in DNA and RNA.

Nucleic acids account for only about 2% of the weight of animals like humans, yet these molecules are extremely important because they are responsible for the storage, expression, and transmission of genetic information. The expression of genetic information in the form of specific proteins determines whether an organism is a human, a frog, an onion, or a bacterium. Likewise, genetic information determines whether a cell is part of a muscle or a bone, a leaf or a root.

Nucleic Acids Are Polymers Made of Nucleotides

The two classes of nucleic acids are **deoxyribonucleic acid (DNA)** and **ribonucleic acid (RNA)**. DNA molecules store genetic information coded in the sequence of their monomer building blocks. RNA molecules are involved in decoding this information into instructions for linking a specific sequence of amino acids to form a polypeptide chain. The monomers in DNA must be arranged in a precise way so that the correct code can be read. As an analogy, think of the difference in the meanings of the words "marital" and "martial," in which the sequence of two letters is altered.

Like other macromolecules, both types of nucleic acids are polymers consisting of linear sequences of repeating monomers. Each monomer, known as a **nucleotide**, has three components: (1) a phosphate group, (2) a pentose (five-carbon) sugar (either ribose or deoxyribose), and (3) a single or a double ring of carbon and nitrogen atoms known as a base (Figure 3.22). A nucleotide of DNA is called a deoxyribonucleotide; that of RNA is a ribonucleotide. The phosphates and sugar molecules form the backbone of a DNA or RNA strand, with the bases projecting from the backbone. The carbon atoms of the sugar are numbered 1'–5' (**Figure 3.23**). The phosphate groups link the 3' carbon of one nucleotide to the 5' carbon of the next (see Figure 3.23).

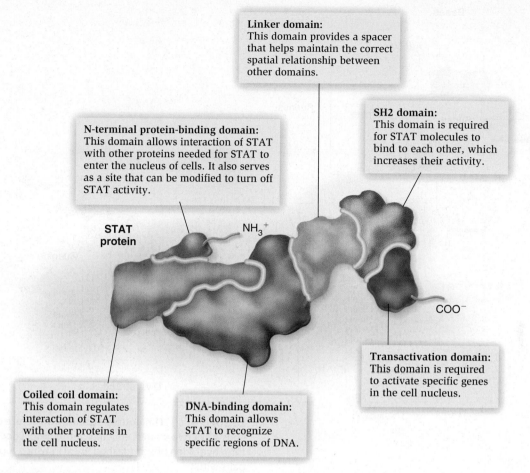

Linker domain:
This domain provides a spacer that helps maintain the correct spatial relationship between other domains.

N-terminal protein-binding domain:
This domain allows interaction of STAT with other proteins needed for STAT to enter the nucleus of cells. It also serves as a site that can be modified to turn off STAT activity.

SH2 domain:
This domain is required for STAT molecules to bind to each other, which increases their activity.

STAT protein

NH₃⁺

COO⁻

Transactivation domain:
This domain is required to activate specific genes in the cell nucleus.

Coiled coil domain:
This domain regulates interaction of STAT with other proteins in the cell nucleus.

DNA-binding domain:
This domain allows STAT to recognize specific regions of DNA.

Figure 3.21 The domain structure of a signal transducer and activator of transcription (STAT) protein.

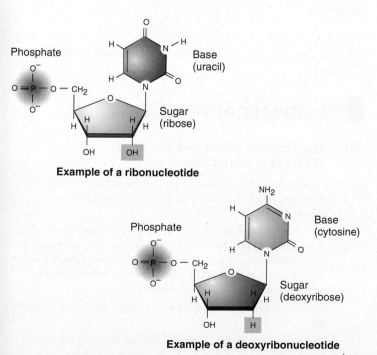

Phosphate

Base (uracil)

Sugar (ribose)

Example of a ribonucleotide

Phosphate

Base (cytosine)

Sugar (deoxyribose)

Example of a deoxyribonucleotide

Figure 3.22 **Examples of two nucleotides.** A nucleotide has a phosphate group, a five-carbon sugar, and a nitrogenous base.

DNA Is Composed of Purines and Pyrimidines

The nucleotides in DNA contain the five-carbon sugar **deoxyribose**. Four different nucleotides are present in DNA, corresponding to the four different bases that can be linked to deoxyribose. The **purine** bases, **adenine (A)** and **guanine (G)**, have fused double rings of carbon and nitrogen atoms, and the **pyrimidine** bases, **cytosine (C)** and **thymine (T)**, have a single-ring structure (see Figure 3.23).

A DNA molecule consists of two strands of nucleotides coiled around each other to form a double helix (Figure 3.24). Purines and pyrimidines occur in both strands. The two strands are held together by hydrogen bonds between a purine base in one strand and a pyrimidine base in the opposite strand. The ring structure of each base lies in a flat plane perpendicular to the sugar-phosphate backbone, somewhat like steps on a spiral staircase.

As we will see in Chapter 11, only certain bases can pair with others, due to the location of the hydrogen-bonding groups in the four bases (see Figure 3.24). Two hydrogen bonds can be formed between adenine and thymine (A-T pairing), but three hydrogen bonds are formed between guanine and cytosine (G-C pairing). In a DNA molecule, A on one strand is always paired with T on another strand, and G with C. This base pairing maintains a constant distance between the sugar-phosphate backbones of the two strands as they coil around each other. If we know the amount of one type of base

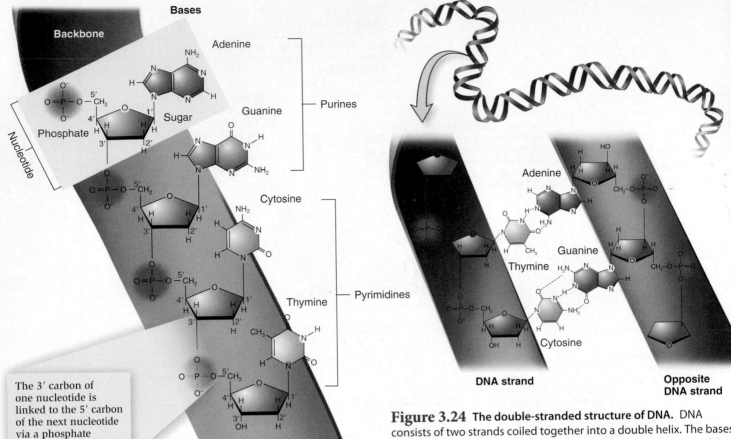

Figure 3.23 **Structure of a DNA strand.** Nucleotides are linked to each other to form a strand of DNA. The four bases found in DNA are shown. A strand of RNA is similar except the sugar is ribose, and uracil is substituted for thymine.

The 3′ carbon of one nucleotide is linked to the 5′ carbon of the next nucleotide via a phosphate group.

Figure 3.24 **The double-stranded structure of DNA.** DNA consists of two strands coiled together into a double helix. The bases form hydrogen bonds (dashed lines) in which A pairs with T, and G pairs with C.

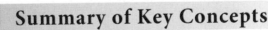 *If the sequence of bases in one strand of a DNA double helix is known, can the base sequence of the opposite strand be predicted?*

in a DNA molecule, we can predict the relative amounts of each of the other three bases. For example, if a DNA molecule were composed of 20% A bases, then there must also be 20% T bases. That leaves 60% of the bases that must be G and C combined. Because the amounts of G and C must be equal, this particular DNA molecule must be composed of 30% each of G and C. This specificity provides the mechanism for duplicating and transferring genetic information (see Chapter 11).

RNA Is Usually Single Stranded and Comes in Several Forms

RNA molecules differ in only a few respects from DNA. Except in some viruses, RNA consists of a single rather than double strand of nucleotides. In RNA, the sugar in each nucleotide is **ribose** rather than deoxyribose. Also, the pyrimidine base thymine in DNA is replaced in RNA with the pyrimidine base **uracil (U)** (see Figure 3.22). The other three bases—adenine, guanine, and cytosine—are found in both DNA and RNA. Certain forms of RNA called messenger RNA (mRNA), ribosomal RNA (rRNA), and transfer RNA (tRNA) are responsible for converting the information contained in DNA into

the formation of a new polypeptide. This topic will be discussed in Chapter 12.

Summary of Key Concepts

3.1 The Carbon Atom and the Study of Organic Molecules

- Organic chemistry is the science of studying carbon-containing molecules, which are compounds found in living organisms (Figure 3.1).

- One property of the carbon atom that makes life possible is its ability to form four covalent bonds (polar or nonpolar) with other atoms. The combination of different elements and different types of bonds allows a vast number of organic compounds to be formed from a relatively few chemical elements (Figures 3.2, 3.3).

- Carbon bonds are stable at the different temperatures associated with life.

- Organic compounds may contain functional groups (Table 3.1).

- Carbon-containing molecules can exist as isomers, which have identical molecular composition but different structures and characteristics. Structural isomers contain the same atoms but in different bonding relationships. Stereoisomers have identical bonding relationships but different spatial positioning of their atoms. Two types of stereoisomers are *cis-trans* isomers and enantiomers (Figure 3.4).

3.2   Formation of Organic Molecules and Macromolecules

- The four major classes of organic molecules are carbohydrates, lipids, proteins, and nucleic acids. Organic molecules exist as monomers or polymers. Polymers are large macromolecules built up by a type of condensation reaction called a dehydration reaction, in which individual monomers combine with each other. Polymers are broken down into monomers by hydrolysis reactions (Figure 3.5).

3.3   Carbohydrates

- Carbohydrates are composed of carbon, hydrogen, and oxygen atoms. Cells can break down glucose, an important carbohydrate, releasing energy which is then stored in the bonds of ATP.

- Carbohydrates include monosaccharides (the simplest sugars), disaccharides, and polysaccharides. The polysaccharides starch (in plant cells) and glycogen (in animal cells) store energy in cells. Some polysaccharides, notably cellulose, serve a support or structural function (Figures 3.6, 3.7, 3.8).

3.4   Lipids

- Lipids, composed predominantly of hydrogen and carbon atoms, are nonpolar and very insoluble in water. Major classes of lipids include fats, phospholipids, steroids, and waxes.

- Fats, also called triglycerides, are formed by bonding glycerol with three fatty acids. In a saturated fatty acid, all the carbons are linked by single covalent bonds. Unsaturated fatty acids contain one or more C=C double bonds. Animal fats generally contain a high proportion of saturated fatty acids, and vegetable fats contain more unsaturated fatty acids (Figures 3.9, 3.10, 3.11).

- Phospholipids are similar in structure to triglycerides, except that one glycerol is linked to a phosphate group instead of a fatty acid. They contain both polar and nonpolar regions, making them amphipathic (Figure 3.12).

- Steroids are constructed of four fused rings of carbon atoms. Small differences in steroid structure can lead to profoundly different biological properties, such as the differences between estrogen and testosterone (Figure 3.13).

- Waxes, another class of lipids, are nonpolar and repel water, and are often found as protective coatings on the leaves of plants and the outer surfaces of animals' bodies.

3.5   Proteins

- Proteins are composed of carbon, hydrogen, oxygen, nitrogen, and small amounts of other elements such as sulfur. Proteins are macromolecules that play critical roles in almost all life processes. The proteins of all living organisms are composed of the same set of 20 amino acids, corresponding to 20 different side chains (Figure 3.14, Table 3.2).

- Amino acids are joined by linking the carboxyl group of one amino acid to the amino group of another, forming a peptide bond. A polypeptide is a structural unit composed of amino acids. A protein is a functional unit composed of one or more polypeptides that have been folded and twisted into precise three-dimensional shapes (Figure 3.15).

- The four levels of protein structure are primary (its amino acid sequence), secondary (α helices or β pleated sheets), tertiary (folding to assume a three-dimensional shape), and quaternary (multimeric proteins that consist of more than one polypeptide chain). The three-dimensional structure of a protein determines its function—for example, by creating binding sites for other molecules (Figures 3.16, 3.17, 3.18, 3.19, 3.20, 3.21).

3.6   Nucleic Acids

- Nucleic acids are responsible for the storage, expression, and transmission of genetic information. The two types of nucleic acids are deoxyribonucleic acid (DNA) and ribonucleic acid (RNA). Both are molecules consisting of repeating monomers known as nucleotides. Each nucleotide is composed of a phosphate group, a five-carbon sugar (either ribose or deoxyribose), and a single or double ring of carbon and nitrogen atoms called a base (Figures 3.22, 3.23).

- A DNA molecule consists of two strands of nucleotides coiled around each other to form a double helix, held together by hydrogen bonds between a purine base (adenine or guanine) on one strand and a pyrimidine base (cytosine or thymine) on the opposite strand. DNA molecules store genetic information coded in the sequence of their monomers (Figure 3.24).

- RNA consists of a single strand of nucleotides. The sugar in each nucleotide is ribose rather than deoxyribose, and the base uracil replaces thymine. RNA molecules are involved in decoding this information into instructions for linking amino acids in a specific sequence to form a polypeptide chain.

Assess and Discuss

Test Yourself

1. Molecules that contain the element _____ are considered organic molecules.
   a. hydrogen
   b. carbon
   c. oxygen
   d. nitrogen
   e. calcium

2. _____ was the first scientist to synthesize an organic molecule. The organic molecule synthesized was _____.
   a. Kolbe, urea
   b. Wöhler, urea
   c. Wöhler, acetic acid
   d. Kolbe, acetic acid
   e. Wöhler, glucose

3. The versatility of carbon to serve as the backbone for a variety of different molecules is due to
   a. the ability of carbon atoms to form four covalent bonds.
   b. the fact that carbon usually forms ionic bonds with many different atoms.
   c. the abundance of carbon in the environment.
   d. the ability of carbon to form covalent bonds with many different types of atoms.
   e. both a and d.

4. _____ are molecules that have the same molecular composition but differ in structure and/or bonding association.
   a. Isotopes
   b. Isomers
   c. Free radicals
   d. Analogues
   e. Ions

5. _____ is a storage polysaccharide commonly found in the cells of animals.
   a. Glucose
   b. Sucrose
   c. Glycogen
   d. Starch
   e. Cellulose

6. In contrast to other fatty acids, essential fatty acids
   a. are always saturated fats.
   b. cannot be synthesized by the organism and are necessary for survival.
   c. can act as building blocks for large, more complex macromolecules.
   d. are the simplest form of lipids found in plant cells.
   e. are structural components of plasma membranes.

7. Phospholipids are amphipathic, which means they
   a. are partially hydrolyzed during cellular metabolism.
   b. are composed of a hydrophilic portion and a hydrophobic portion.
   c. may be poisonous to organisms if in combination with certain other molecules.
   d. are molecules composed of lipids and proteins.
   e. are all of the above.

8. The monomers of proteins are _____, and these are linked by polar covalent bonds commonly referred to as _____ bonds.
   a. nucleotides, peptide
   b. amino acids, ester
   c. hydroxyl groups, ester
   d. amino acids, peptide
   e. monosaccharides, glycosidic

9. A _____ is a portion of protein with a particular structure and function.
   a. peptide bond
   b. domain
   c. phospholipids
   d. wax
   e. monosaccharide

10. The _____ of a nucleotide determines whether it is a component of DNA or a component of RNA.
    a. phosphate group
    b. five-carbon sugar
    c. side chain
    d. fatty acid
    e. Both b and d are correct.

Conceptual Questions

1. Distinguish between different types of isomers.

2. Explain the difference between saturated and unsaturated fatty acids, and how the structural differences between them contribute to differences in their properties.

3. A principle of biology is that *structure determines function*. What does this mean for organic molecules such as carbohydrates, lipids, and proteins?

Collaborative Questions

1. Discuss the differences between different types of carbohydrates.

2. Discuss some of the roles that proteins play in organisms.

Online Resource

www.brookerbiology.com

Stay a step ahead in your studies with animations that bring concepts to life and practice tests to assess your understanding. Your instructor may also recommend the interactive eBook, individualized learning tools, and more.

UNIT II
CELL

Cell biology is the study of life at the cellular level. Although cells are the simplest units of life, biologists have come to realize that they are wonderfully complex and interesting, providing information about all living things. In this unit, Chapter 4 begins with an overview of cell structure and function and explores the technique of microscopy. In Chapter 5, we will examine the structure and synthesis of cell membranes and the transport of substances in and out of the cell. Chapters 6, 7, and 8 are largely devoted to metabolism, the sum of the chemical reactions in a cell or organism. Chapter 6 explores the topic of energy and considers how enzymes facilitate chemical reactions in a cell. Chapter 7 examines the pathways for carbohydrate breakdown and how those pathways are used to make an energy intermediate called ATP. In Chapter 8, we will explore the process of photosynthesis in which the energy of sunlight drives the synthesis of carbohydrates. Finally, Chapters 9 and 10 consider the ways that cells interact with their environment and with each other. In Chapter 9, we will examine how cells respond to signals, either those that come directly from their environment or those that are made by other cells. In Chapter 10, we will explore how cells interact with each other to produce a multicellular organism.

The following biology principles will be emphasized in this unit:

- **Cells are the simplest units of life:** *Throughout this unit, we will examine how life exists at the cellular level.*

- **Living organisms use energy:** *Chapters 6, 7, and 8 examine how cells utilize and store energy contained within organic molecules such as glucose.*

- **Living organisms interact with their environment:** *Chapters 5 and 9 largely focus on the plasma membrane of the cell and how it provides an interface between the cell and its environment.*

- **Structure determines function:** *Throughout this unit, we will see many examples in which the structure of proteins determines their cellular functions.*

- **Biology is an experimental science:** *Every chapter has a Feature Investigation that describes a pivotal experiment that provided insights into the workings of cells.*

General Features of Cells

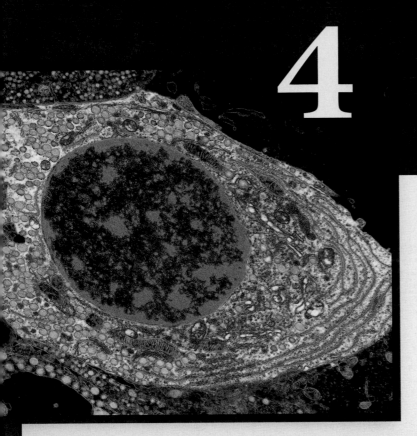

4

A cell from the pituitary gland. The cell in this micrograph was viewed by a technique called transmission electron microscopy, which is described in this chapter. The micrograph was artificially colored using a computer to enhance the visualization of certain cell structures.

Emily had a persistent cough ever since she started smoking cigarettes in college. However, at age 35, it seemed to be getting worse, and she was alarmed by the occasional pain in her chest. When she began to lose weight and noticed that she became easily fatigued, Emily decided to see a doctor. The diagnosis was lung cancer. Despite aggressive treatment of the disease with chemotherapy and radiation therapy, she succumbed to lung cancer 14 months after the initial diagnosis. Emily was 36.

Topics such as cancer are within the field of **cell biology**—the study of individual cells and their interactions with each other. Researchers in this field want to understand the basic features of cells and apply their knowledge in the treatment of diseases such as cystic fibrosis, sickle-cell disease, and lung cancer.

The idea that organisms are composed of cells originated in the mid-1800s. German botanist Matthias Schleiden studied plant material under the microscope and was struck by the presence of many similar-looking

compartments, each of which contained a dark area. Today we call those compartments cells and the dark area the nucleus. In 1838, Schleiden speculated that cells are living entities and that plants are aggregates of cells arranged according to definite laws.

Schleiden was a good friend of the German physiologist Theodor Schwann. Over dinner one evening, their conversation turned to the nuclei of plant cells, and Schwann remembered having seen similar structures in animal tissue. Schwann conducted additional studies that showed large numbers of nuclei in animal tissue at regular intervals and also located in cell-like compartments. In 1839, Schwann extended Schleiden's hypothesis to animals. About two decades later, German biologist Rudolf Virchow proposed that *omnis cellula e cellula*, or "every cell originates from another cell." This idea arose from his research, which showed that diseased cells divide to produce more diseased cells.

The **cell theory**, which is credited to both Schleiden and Schwann with contributions from Virchow, has three parts.

1. All living organisms are composed of one or more cells.
2. Cells are the smallest units of life.
3. New cells come only from pre-existing cells by cell division.

Most cells are so small they cannot be seen with the unaided eye. However, as cell biologists have begun to unravel cell structure and function at the molecular level, the cell has emerged as a unit of incredible complexity and adaptability. In this chapter, we will begin our examination of cells with an overview of their structures and functions. Later chapters in this unit will explore certain aspects of cell biology in greater detail. But first, let's look at the tools and techniques that allow us to observe cells.

4.1   Microscopy

Learning Outcomes:
1. Explain the three important parameters in microscopy: resolution, contrast, and magnification.
2. Compare and contrast the different types of light and electron microscopes and their uses.

The **microscope** is a magnification tool that enables researchers to study the structure and function of cells. A **micrograph** is an image taken with the aid of a microscope. The first compound microscope—a

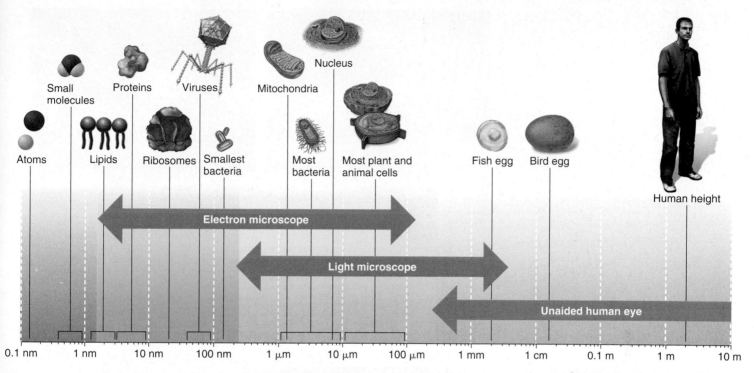

Figure 4.1 A comparison of the sizes of various chemical and biological structures, and the resolving power of the unaided eye, light microscope, and electron microscope. The scale at the bottom is logarithmic to accommodate the wide range of sizes in this drawing.

Concept Check: *Which type of microscopy would you use to observe a virus?*

microscope with more than one lens—was invented in 1595 by Zacharias Jansen of Holland. In 1665, an English biologist, Robert Hooke, studied cork under a primitive compound microscope he had made. He actually observed cell walls because cork cells are dead and have lost their internal components. Hooke coined the word *cell*, derived from the Latin word *cellula*, meaning small compartment, to describe the structures he observed. Ten years later, the Dutch merchant Anton van Leeuwenhoek refined techniques of making lenses and was able to observe single-celled microorganisms such as bacteria.

Three important parameters in microscopy are resolution, contrast, and magnification. **Resolution**, a measure of the clarity of an image, is the ability to observe two adjacent objects as distinct from one another. For example, a microscope with good resolution enables a researcher to distinguish two adjacent chromosomes as separate objects, which would appear as a single object under a microscope with poor resolution. The second important parameter in microscopy is **contrast**. The ability to visualize a particular cell structure may depend on how different it looks from an adjacent structure. Staining the cellular structure of interest with a dye can make viewing much easier. The application of stains, which selectively label individual components of the cell, greatly improves contrast. As described later, fluorescent molecules are often used to selectively stain cellular components. However, staining should not be confused with colorization. Many of the micrographs shown in this textbook are colorized, or artificially colored, to emphasize certain cellular structures, such as different parts of a cell (see the chapter opener, for example). In colorization, particular colors are added to micrographs with the aid of a computer. Finally, **magnification** is the ratio between the size of an image produced by a microscope and its actual size. For example, if

the image size is 100 times larger than its actual size, the magnification is designated 100×. Depending on the quality of the lens and illumination source, every microscope has an optimal range of magnification before objects appear too blurry to be readily observed.

Microscopes are categorized into two groups based on the source of illumination. A **light microscope** utilizes light for illumination, whereas an **electron microscope** uses a beam of electrons for illumination. Very good light microscopes resolve structures that are as close as 0.2 μm (micron, or micrometer) from each other. The resolving power of a microscope depends on several factors, including the wavelength of the source of illumination. Resolution is improved when the illumination source has a shorter wavelength. A major advance in microscopy occurred in 1931 when Max Knoll and Ernst Ruska invented the first electron microscope. Because the wavelength of an electron beam is much shorter than visible light, the resolution of the electron microscope is far better than any light microscope. For biological samples, the resolution limit is typically around 2 nm (nanometers), which is about 100 times better than the light microscope. **Figure 4.1** shows the range of resolving powers of the electron microscope, light microscope, and unaided eye and compares them with various cells and cell structures.

Over the past several decades, enormous technological advances have made light microscopy a powerful research tool. Improvements in lens technology, microscope organization, sample preparation, sample illumination, and computerized image processing have enabled researchers to invent different types of light microscopes, each with its own advantages and disadvantages (**Figure 4.2**).

Similarly, improvements in electron microscopy occurred during the 1930s and 1940s, and by the 1950s, the electron microscope

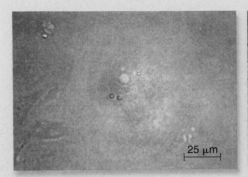
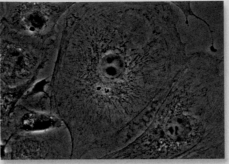

Standard light microscopy (bright field, unstained sample).
Light is passed directly through a sample, and the light is focused using glass lenses. Simple, inexpensive, and easy to use but offers little contrast with unstained samples.

Phase contrast microscopy.
As an alternative to staining, this microscope controls the path of light and amplifies differences in the phase of light transmitted or reflected by a sample. The dense structures appear darker than the background, thereby improving the contrast in different parts of the specimen. Can be used to view living, unstained cells.

Differential interference contrast (Nomarski) microscopy.
Similar to a phase contrast microscope in that it uses optical modifications to improve contrast in unstained specimens. Can be used to visualize the internal structures of cells and is commonly used to view whole cells or large cell structures such as nuclei.

(a) Light microscopy on unstained samples

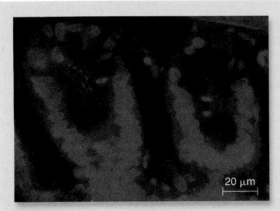
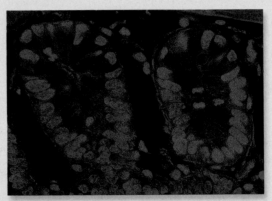

Standard (wide-field) fluorescence microscopy.
Fluorescent molecules specifically label a particular type of cellular protein or organelle. A fluorescent molecule absorbs light at a particular wavelength and emits light at a longer wavelength. This microscope has filters that illuminate the sample with the wavelength of light that a fluorescent molecule absorbs, and then only the light that is emitted by the fluorescent molecules is allowed to reach the observer. To detect their cellular location, researchers often label specific cellular proteins using fluorescent antibodies that bind specifically to a particular protein.

Confocal fluorescence microscopy.
Uses lasers that illuminate various points in the sample. These points are processed by a computer to give a very sharp focal plane. In this example, this microscope technique is used in conjunction with fluorescence microscopy to view fluorescent molecules within a cell.

(b) Fluorescence microscopy

Figure 4.2 Examples of light microscopy. (a) These micrographs compare three microscopic techniques on the same unstained sample of cells. These are endothelial cells that line the interior surface of arteries in the lungs. **(b)** These two micrographs compare standard (wide-field) fluorescence microscopy with confocal fluorescence microscopy. The sample is a section through a mouse intestine, showing two villi, projections from the small intestine that are described in Chapter 45. In this sample, the nuclei are stained green, and the actin filaments (discussed later in this chapter) are stained red.

was playing a major role in advancing our understanding of cell structure. Two general types of electron microscopy have been developed: transmission electron microscopy and scanning electron microscopy. In **transmission electron microscopy (TEM)**, a beam of electrons is transmitted through a biological sample. To provide contrast, the sample is stained with a heavy metal, which binds to certain cellular structures such as membranes. The sample is then adhered to a copper grid and placed in a transmission electron microscope. When the beam of electrons strikes the sample, some of them hit the heavy metal and are scattered, while those that pass through without being

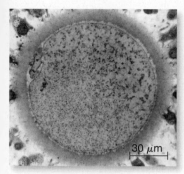

(a) Transmission electron micrograph (TEM)

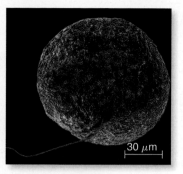

(b) Scanning electron micrograph (SEM)

Figure 4.3 **A comparison of transmission and scanning electron microscopy.** **(a)** Section through a developing human egg cell, observed by TEM, shortly before it was released from an ovary. **(b)** An egg cell, with an attached sperm, was coated with heavy metal and observed via SEM. This SEM is colorized.

Concept Check: *What is the primary advantage of SEM?*

scattered are focused to form an image on a photographic plate or screen (**Figure 4.3a**). The metal-stained regions of the sample that scatter electrons appear as darker areas, due to reduced electron penetration. TEM provides a cross-sectional view of a cell and its organelles and gives the best resolution compared with other forms of microscopy. However, such microscopes are expensive and cannot be used to view living cells.

Scanning electron microscopy (SEM) is used to view the surface of a sample. A biological sample is coated with a thin layer of heavy metal, such as gold or palladium, and then is exposed to an electron beam that scans its surface. Secondary electrons are emitted from the sample, which are detected and create an image of the three-dimensional surface of the sample (**Figure 4.3b**).

4.2 Overview of Cell Structure

Learning Outcomes:
1. Compare and contrast the general structural features of prokaryotic and eukaryotic cells.
2. Explain how the proteome underlies the structure and function of cells.
3. Analyze how cell size and shape affect the surface area/volume ratio.

Cell structure is primarily determined by four factors: (1) matter, (2) energy, (3) organization, and (4) information. In Chapters 2 and 3, we considered the first factor. The matter found in living organisms is composed of atoms, molecules, and macromolecules. Each type of cell synthesizes a unique set of molecules and macromolecules that contribute to cell structure. We will discuss the second factor, energy, throughout this unit, particularly in Chapters 6 through 8. Energy is needed to produce molecules and macromolecules and to carry out many cellular functions.

The third phenomenon that underlies cell structure is organization. A cell is not a haphazard bag of components. The molecules and macromolecules that constitute cells are found at specific sites. For instance, if we compare the structure of a muscle cell in two different humans, or two muscle cells within the same individual, we would

see striking similarities in their overall structures. All living cells have the ability to build and maintain their internal organization. Proteins often bind to each other in much the same way that building blocks snap together. These types of **protein-protein interactions** create intricate cell structures and also facilitate processes in which proteins interact in a consistent series of steps.

The fourth critical factor of cell structure is information. Cell structure requires instructions. These instructions are found in the blueprint of life, namely, the genetic material, which is discussed in Unit III. Every species has a distinctive **genome**, the entire complement of its genetic material. Likewise, each living cell has a copy of the genome. The **genes** within each species' genome contain the information to produce cells with particular structures and functions. This information is passed from cell to cell and from parent to offspring to yield new generations of cells and new generations of offspring. In this section, we will explore the general structure of cells and examine how the genome contributes to cell structure and function.

Prokaryotic Cells Have a Simple Structure

Based on cell structure, all forms of life can be placed into two categories called prokaryotes and eukaryotes. We will first consider **prokaryotic cells**, which have a relatively simple structure. The term comes from the Greek *pro* and *karyon*, which means before a kernel—a reference to the kernel-like appearance of what would later be named the cell nucleus. Prokaryotic cells lack a membrane-enclosed nucleus.

From an evolutionary perspective, the two categories of organisms that have prokaryotic cells are **bacteria** and **archaea**. Both types are microorganisms that are relatively small with cell sizes that usually range between 1 micrometer (μm) and 10 μm in diameter. Bacteria are abundant throughout the world, being found in soil, water, and even our digestive tracts. Most bacterial species are not harmful to humans, and they play vital roles in ecology. However, some species are pathogenic—they cause disease. Examples of pathogenic bacteria include *Vibrio cholerae*, the source of cholera, and *Bacillus anthracis*, which causes anthrax. Archaea are also widely found throughout the world, though they are less common than bacteria and often occupy extreme environments such as hot springs and deep-sea vents.

Figure 4.4 shows a typical bacterial cell. The **plasma membrane**, which is a double layer of phospholipids and embedded proteins, forms an important barrier between the cell and its external environment. The **cytoplasm** is the region of the cell contained within the plasma membrane. Certain structures in the bacterial cytoplasm are visible via microscopy. These include the **nucleoid region**, where the genetic material (DNA) is located, and **ribosomes**, which are involved in polypeptide synthesis.

Some bacterial structures are located outside the plasma membrane. Nearly all species of bacteria and archaea have a relatively rigid **cell wall** that supports and protects the plasma membrane and cytoplasm. The cell-wall composition varies widely among prokaryotic cells but commonly contains peptides and carbohydrates. The cell wall, which is relatively porous, allows most nutrients in the environment to reach the plasma membrane. Many bacteria also secrete a **glycocalyx**, an outer viscous covering surrounding the bacterium. The glycocalyx traps water and helps protect bacteria from drying out. Certain strains of bacteria that invade animals' bodies produce a very thick, gelatinous glycocalyx called a **capsule** that may help them

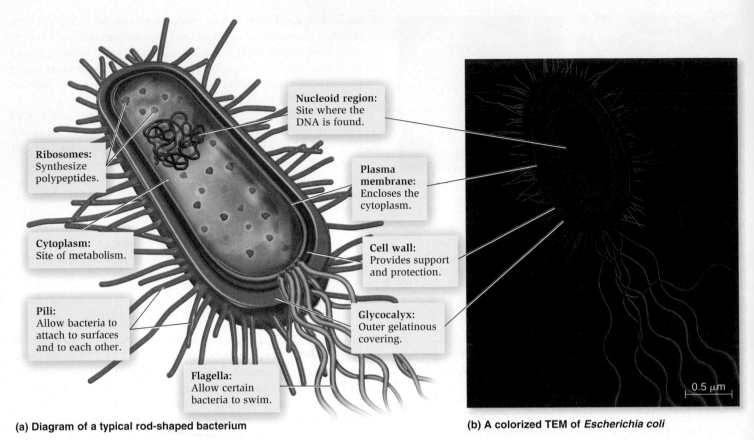

Nucleoid region: Site where the DNA is found.

Ribosomes: Synthesize polypeptides.

Plasma membrane: Encloses the cytoplasm.

Cytoplasm: Site of metabolism.

Cell wall: Provides support and protection.

Pili: Allow bacteria to attach to surfaces and to each other.

Glycocalyx: Outer gelatinous covering.

Flagella: Allow certain bacteria to swim.

0.5 μm

(a) Diagram of a typical rod-shaped bacterium

(b) A colorized TEM of *Escherichia coli*

Figure 4.4 Structure of a typical bacterial cell. Prokaryotic cells, which include bacteria and archaea, lack internal compartmentalization.

avoid being destroyed by the animal's immune (defense) system or may aid in the attachment to cell surfaces. Finally, many prokaryotic cells have appendages such as pili and flagella. **Pili** allow cells to attach to surfaces and to each other. **Flagella** provide prokaryotic cells with a way to move, also called motility.

Eukaryotic Cells Are Compartmentalized by Internal Membranes to Create Organelles

Aside from bacteria and archaea, all other species are **eukaryotes** (from the Greek, meaning true nucleus), which include protists, fungi, plants, and animals. Paramecia and algae are types of protists; yeasts and molds are types of fungi. **Figure 4.5** illustrates the morphology of a typical animal cell. Eukaryotic cells possess a true nucleus, where most of the DNA is housed. A nucleus is a type of **organelle**—a membrane-bound compartment with its own unique structure and function. Like prokaryotic cells, all eukaryotic cells have a plasma membrane. In contrast to prokaryotic cells, eukaryotic cells exhibit extensive **compartmentalization**, which means they have many membrane-bound organelles that separate the cell into different regions. Cellular compartmentalization allows a cell to carry out specialized chemical reactions in different places.

Some general features of cell organization, such as a nucleus, are found in nearly all eukaryotic cells. Even so, the shape, size, and organization of cells vary considerably among different species and even among different cell types of the same species. For example, micrographs of a human skin cell and a human neuron show that, although these cells contain the same types of organelles, their overall morphologies are quite different (**Figure 4.6**).

Plant cells possess a collection of organelles similar to animal cells (**Figure 4.7**). Additional structures found in plant cells but not animal cells include chloroplasts, a central vacuole, and a cell wall.

GENOMES & PROTEOMES CONNECTION

The Proteome Largely Determines the Characteristics of a Cell

Many organisms, such as animals and plants, are multicellular, meaning that a single organism is composed of many cells. However, the cells of most multicellular organisms are not all identical. For example, your body contains skin cells, neurons, muscle cells, and many other types. An intriguing question, therefore, is how does a single organism produce different types of cells?

To answer this question, we need to consider the distinction between an individual's genome and proteome. Recall that the genome constitutes all types of genetic material, namely DNA, that an organism has. Most genes encode the production of polypeptides, which assemble into functional proteins. The **proteome** is defined as the complete protein composition of a cell or organism. A recurring biological principle is *structure determines function*. As discussed in this unit, the structures and functions of proteins are primarily responsible for the structures and functions of cells.

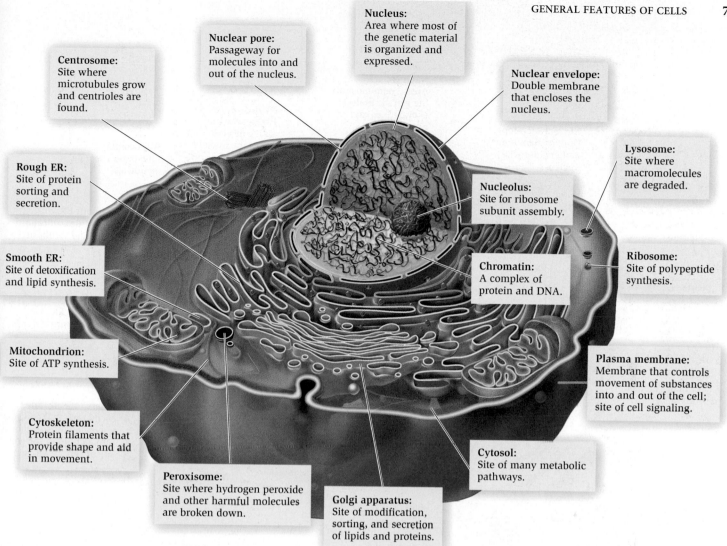

Centrosome:
Site where microtubules grow and centrioles are found.

Nuclear pore:
Passageway for molecules into and out of the nucleus.

Nucleus:
Area where most of the genetic material is organized and expressed.

Nuclear envelope:
Double membrane that encloses the nucleus.

Rough ER:
Site of protein sorting and secretion.

Lysosome:
Site where macromolecules are degraded.

Nucleolus:
Site for ribosome subunit assembly.

Smooth ER:
Site of detoxification and lipid synthesis.

Ribosome:
Site of polypeptide synthesis.

Chromatin:
A complex of protein and DNA.

Mitochondrion:
Site of ATP synthesis.

Plasma membrane:
Membrane that controls movement of substances into and out of the cell; site of cell signaling.

Cytoskeleton:
Protein filaments that provide shape and aid in movement.

Peroxisome:
Site where hydrogen peroxide and other harmful molecules are broken down.

Golgi apparatus:
Site of modification, sorting, and secretion of lipids and proteins.

Cytosol:
Site of many metabolic pathways.

Figure 4.5 General structure of an animal cell.

 BIOLOGY PRINCIPLE Cells are the simplest units of life. A cell, such as the animal cell illustrated here, is the smallest unit that satisfies all of the characteristics of living organisms. These characteristics are discussed in Chapter 1 (see Figure 1.4).

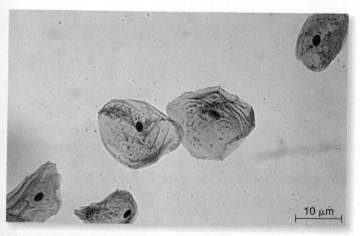

(a) Human skin cell

10 μm

(b) Human nerve cell

46 μm

Figure 4.6 **Variation in morphology of eukaryotic cells.** Light micrographs of **(a)** a human skin cell and **(b)** a human neuron (a cell of the nervous system). Although these cells have the same genome and same types of organelles, their general morphologies are quite different.

BioConnections: *Look ahead to Figure 13.21. How does alternative splicing affect protein structure and function?*

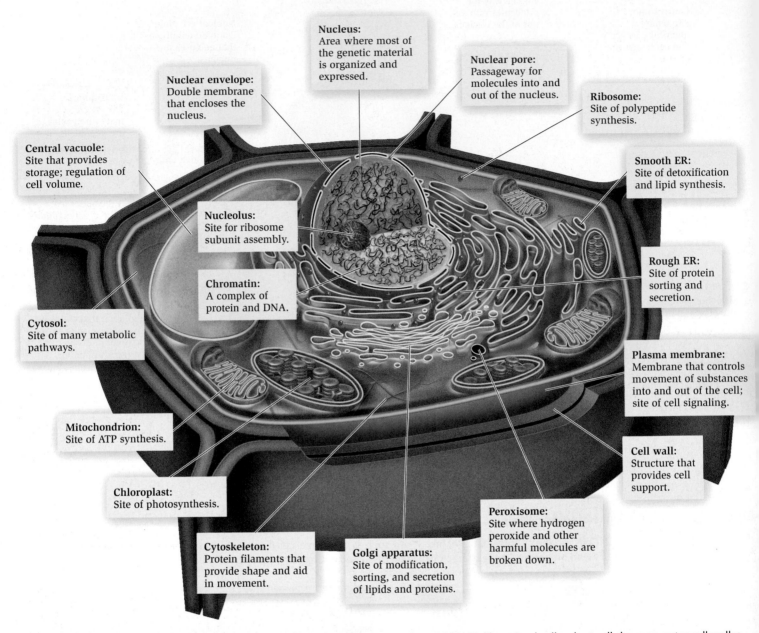

Nucleus: Area where most of the genetic material is organized and expressed.

Nuclear pore: Passageway for molecules into and out of the nucleus.

Ribosome: Site of polypeptide synthesis.

Nuclear envelope: Double membrane that encloses the nucleus.

Smooth ER: Site of detoxification and lipid synthesis.

Central vacuole: Site that provides storage; regulation of cell volume.

Nucleolus: Site for ribosome subunit assembly.

Rough ER: Site of protein sorting and secretion.

Cytosol: Site of many metabolic pathways.

Chromatin: A complex of protein and DNA.

Plasma membrane: Membrane that controls movement of substances into and out of the cell; site of cell signaling.

Mitochondrion: Site of ATP synthesis.

Cell wall: Structure that provides cell support.

Chloroplast: Site of photosynthesis.

Peroxisome: Site where hydrogen peroxide and other harmful molecules are broken down.

Cytoskeleton: Protein filaments that provide shape and aid in movement.

Golgi apparatus: Site of modification, sorting, and secretion of lipids and proteins.

Figure 4.7 General structure of a plant cell. Plant cells lack lysosomes and centrioles. Unlike animal cells, plant cells have an outer cell wall; a large central vacuole that functions in storage and the regulation of cell volume; and chloroplasts, which carry out photosynthesis.

Concept Check: What are the functions of the cell structures and organelles that are (1) found in animal cells but not plant cells and (2) found in plant cells but not animal cells?

As an example, let's consider skin cells and neurons—two cell types that have dramatically different organization and structure (see Figure 4.6). In any particular individual, the genes in a human skin cell are identical to those in a human neuron. However, their proteomes are different. The proteome of a cell largely determines its structure and function. Several phenomena underlie the differences observed in the proteomes of different cell types.

1. *Certain proteins found in one cell type may not be produced in another cell type.* This phenomenon is due to differential gene regulation, discussed in Chapter 13.

2. *Two cell types may produce the same protein but in different amounts.* This is also due to gene regulation and to the rates at which a protein is synthesized and degraded.

3. *The amino acid sequences of particular proteins can vary in different cell types.* As discussed in Chapter 13, the mRNA from a single gene can produce two or more polypeptides with different amino acid sequences via a process called alternative splicing.

4. *Two cell types may alter their proteins in different ways.* After a protein is made, its structure may be changed in a variety of ways. These include the covalent attachment of molecules, such as

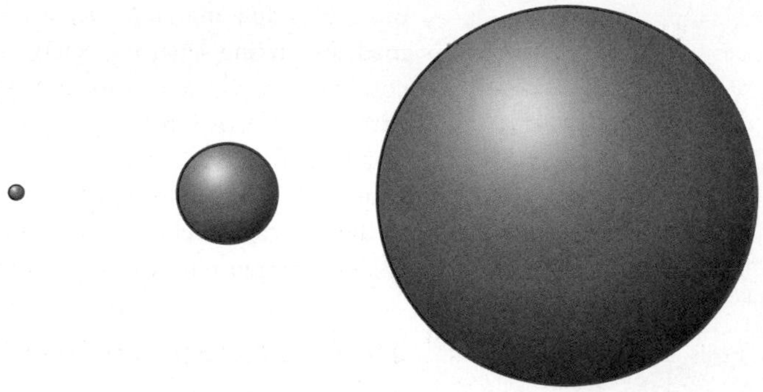

Figure 4.8 Relationship between cell size and the surface area/volume ratio. As cells get larger, the surface area/volume ratio gets smaller. Note: The three spheres shown here are not drawn precisely to scale.

Radius (μm):	1	10	100
Surface area (μm²) ($A = 4\pi r^2$):	12.6	~ 1260	~ 124,600
Volume (μm³) ($V = \frac{4}{3}\pi r^3$)	4.2	~ 4200	~ 4,200,000
Surface area/volume ratio:	3.0 : 1	0.3 : 1	0.03 : 1

BioConnections: Look ahead to Figure 40.9. How does the surface area/volume ratio affect the shapes of structures involved with gas exchange?

phosphate and carbohydrates, and the cleavage of a protein to a smaller size, which are discussed in Chapter 21.

These four phenomena enable skin cells and neurons to produce different proteomes and therefore different structures with different functions. Likewise, the proteomes of skin cells and neurons differ from those of other cell types such as muscle and liver cells. Ultimately, the proteomes of cells are largely responsible for producing the traits of organisms, such as the color of a person's eyes.

During the last few decades, researchers have also discovered an association between proteome changes and disease. For example, the proteomes of healthy lung cells are different from the proteomes of lung cancer cells. Furthermore, the proteomes of cancer cells change as the disease progresses. A key challenge for biologists is to understand the synthesis and function of proteomes in different cell types and how proteome changes may lead to disease conditions such as cancer.

Surface Area and Volume Are Critical Parameters That Affect Cell Sizes and Shapes

As we have seen, a common feature of most cells is their small size. For example, most bacterial cells are about 1–10 μm in diameter, and a typical eukaryotic cell is 10–100 μm in diameter (see Figure 4.1). Though some exceptions are known, such as an ostrich egg, small size is a nearly universal characteristic of cells. In general, large organisms attain their large sizes by having more cells, not by having larger cells. For example, the various types of cells found in an elephant and a mouse are roughly the same sizes. However, an elephant has many more cells than a mouse.

Why are cells usually small? One key factor is the interface between a cell and its extracellular environment, which is the plasma membrane. For cells to survive, they must import substances across their plasma membranes and export waste products. If the internal volume of a cell is large, it will require a greater amount of nutrient uptake and waste export. The rate of transport of substances across

the plasma membrane, however, is limited by its surface area. Therefore, a critical issue for sustaining a cell is the surface area/volume ratio. This concept is illustrated in **Figure 4.8**, which considers a simplified case in which cells are spherical. As cells get larger, the surface area of their plasma membrane increases with the square of the radius ($A = 4\pi r^2$), whereas the volume increases with the cube of the radius ($V = 4/3\pi r^3$). Therefore, as the radius of the cell gets larger, the surface area-to-volume ratio gets smaller. Biologists hypothesize that most cells are small because a high surface area/volume ratio is needed for cells to sustain an adequate level of nutrient uptake and waste export.

One way for cells to partially overcome the dilemma posed by the surface area-to-volume ratio is to have elongated and irregularly shaped surfaces. For example, look back at Figure 4.6. The skin cell is roughly spherical, whereas the neuron is very elongated and has an irregularly shaped surface. If a skin cell and a neuron cell had the same internal volume, the neuron would have a much higher surface area/volume ratio.

4.3 The Cytosol

Learning Outcomes:

1. Identify the location of the cytosol in a eukaryotic cell and list its general functions.
2. Describe the three types of protein filaments that make up the cytoskeleton.
3. Explain how motor proteins interact with microtubules or actin filaments to promote cellular movement.

Thus far, we have focused on the general features of prokaryotic and eukaryotic cells. In the rest of this chapter, we will survey the various compartments of eukaryotic cells with a greater emphasis on structure and function. **Figure 4.9** highlights an animal and plant cell according to four different regions. We will start with the **cytosol** (shown in yellow), the region of a eukaryotic cell that is outside the membrane-bound organelles but inside the plasma membrane. The other regions of the cell, which we will examine later in this chapter, include the

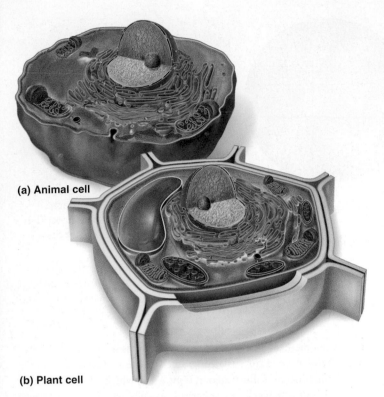

(a) Animal cell

(b) Plant cell

Figure 4.9 **Compartments within (a) animal and (b) plant cells.** The cytosol, which is outside the organelles but inside the plasma membrane, is shown in yellow. The membranes of the endomembrane system are shown in purple, and the fluid-filled interiors are pink. The peroxisome is dark purple. The interior of the nucleus is blue. Semiautonomous organelles are shown in orange (mitochondria) and green (chloroplasts).

interior of the nucleus (blue), the endomembrane system (purple and pink), and the semiautonomous organelles (orange and green). As in prokaryotic cells, the term cytoplasm refers to the region enclosed by the plasma membrane. This includes the cytosol and the organelles.

Synthesis and Breakdown of Molecules Occur in the Cytosol

Metabolism is defined as the sum of the chemical reactions by which cells produce the materials and utilize the energy necessary to sustain life. Although specific steps of metabolism also occur in cell organelles, the cytosol is a central coordinating region for many metabolic activities of eukaryotic cells. Metabolism often involves a series of steps called a metabolic pathway. Each step in a metabolic pathway is catalyzed by a specific **enzyme**—a protein that accelerates the rate of a chemical reaction. In Chapters 6 and 7, we will examine the functional properties of enzymes and consider a few metabolic pathways that occur in the cytosol and cell organelles.

Some pathways involve the breakdown of a molecule into smaller components, a process termed **catabolism**. Such pathways are needed by the cell to utilize energy and also to generate molecules that provide the building blocks to construct macromolecules. Conversely, other pathways are involved in **anabolism**, the synthesis of

molecules and macromolecules. For example, polysaccharides are made by linking sugar molecules. To make proteins, amino acids are covalently connected to form a polypeptide, using the information within an mRNA (see Chapter 12). Translation occurs on ribosomes, which are found in various locations in the cell. Some ribosomes may float freely in the cytosol, others are attached to the outer membrane of the nuclear envelope and endoplasmic reticulum membrane, and still others are found within the mitochondria or chloroplasts.

The Cytoskeleton Provides Cell Shape, Organization, and Movement

The **cytoskeleton** is a network of three different types of protein filaments: **microtubules**, **intermediate filaments**, and **actin filaments** (**Table 4.1**). Each type is constructed from many protein monomers. The cytoskeleton is a striking example of protein-protein interactions. The cytoskeleton is found primarily in the cytosol and also in the nucleus along the inner nuclear membrane. Let's first consider the structure of cytoskeletal filaments and their roles in the construction and organization of cells. Later, we will examine how they are involved in cell movement.

Microtubules Microtubules are long, hollow, cylindrical structures about 25 nm in diameter composed of protein subunits called α and β tubulin. The assembly of tubulin to form a microtubule results in a polar structure with a plus end and a minus end (see Table 4.1). Microtubules grow only at the plus end, but can shorten at either the plus or minus end. A single microtubule can oscillate between growing and shortening phases, a phenomenon termed **dynamic instability**. Dynamic instability is important in many cellular activities, including the sorting of chromosomes during cell division.

The sites where microtubules form within a cell vary among different types of organisms. Nondividing animal cells contain a single structure near their nucleus called the **centrosome**, also called the microtubule-organizing center (see Table 4.1). Within the centrosome are the **centrioles**, a conspicuous pair of structures arranged perpendicular to each other. In animal cells, microtubule growth typically starts at the centrosome in such a way that the minus end is anchored there. In contrast, most plant cells and many protists lack centrosomes and centrioles. Microtubules are created at many sites that are scattered throughout a plant cell. In plants, the nuclear membrane appears to function as a microtubule-organizing center.

Microtubules are important for cell shape and organization. Organelles such as the Golgi apparatus are attached to microtubules. In addition, microtubules are involved in the organization and movement of chromosomes during mitosis and in the orientation of cells during cell division, events we will examine in Chapter 15.

Intermediate Filaments Intermediate filaments are another class of cytoskeletal filament found in the cells of many but not all animal species. Their name is derived from the observation that they are intermediate in diameter between actin filaments and microtubules. Intermediate filament proteins bind to each other in a staggered array to form a twisted, ropelike structure with a diameter of approximately 10 nm (see Table 4.1). They function as tension-bearing fibers that help maintain cell shape and rigidity. Intermediate filaments tend to

Table 4.1	Types of Cytoskeletal Filaments Found in Eukaryotic Cells		
Characteristic	**Microtubules**	**Intermediate filaments**	**Actin filaments**
Diameter	25 nm	10 nm	7 nm
Structure	Hollow tubule	Twisted filament	Spiral filament

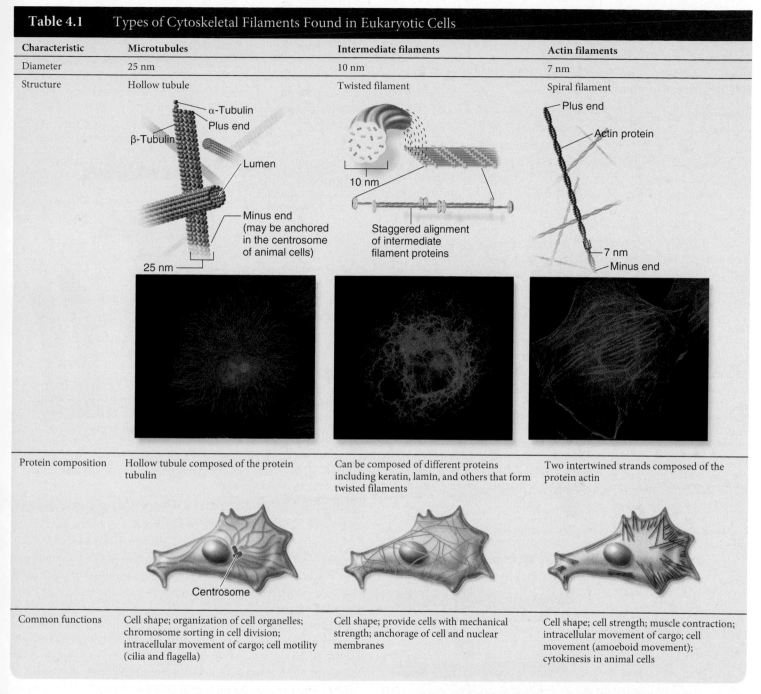

Protein composition	Hollow tubule composed of the protein tubulin	Can be composed of different proteins including keratin, lamin, and others that form twisted filaments	Two intertwined strands composed of the protein actin
Common functions	Cell shape; organization of cell organelles; chromosome sorting in cell division; intracellular movement of cargo; cell motility (cilia and flagella)	Cell shape; provide cells with mechanical strength; anchorage of cell and nuclear membranes	Cell shape; cell strength; muscle contraction; intracellular movement of cargo; cell movement (amoeboid movement); cytokinesis in animal cells

be relatively permanent. By comparison, microtubules and actin filaments readily lengthen and shorten in cells.

Several types of proteins assemble into intermediate filaments. Keratins form intermediate filaments in skin, intestinal, and kidney cells, where they are important for cell shape and mechanical strength. They are also a major constituent of hair and nails. In addition, intermediate filaments are found inside the cell nucleus. As discussed later in this chapter, nuclear lamins form a network of intermediate filaments that line the inner nuclear membrane and provide anchorage points for the nuclear pores.

Actin Filaments Actin filaments are also known as **microfilaments**, because they are the thinnest cytoskeletal filaments. They are

long, thin fibers approximately 7 nm in diameter (see Table 4.1). Like microtubules, actin filaments have plus and minus ends, and they are very dynamic structures in which each strand grows at the plus end by the addition of actin monomers. This assembly process produces a fiber composed of two strands of actin monomers that spiral around each other.

Despite their thinness, actin filaments play a key role in cell shape and strength. Although actin filaments are dispersed throughout the cytosol, they tend to be highly concentrated near the plasma membrane. In many types of cells, actin filaments support the plasma membrane and provide shape and strength to the cell. The sides of actin filaments are often anchored to other proteins near the plasma membrane, which explains why actin filaments are typically found there. The plus ends grow toward the plasma membrane and play a key role in cell shape and movement.

Motor Proteins Interact with Cytoskeletal Filaments to Promote Movements

Motor proteins are a category of proteins that use ATP as a source of energy to promote various types of movements. As shown in **Figure 4.10a**, a motor protein consists of three domains: the head, hinge, and tail. The head is the site where ATP binds and is hydrolyzed to adenosine diphosphate (ADP) and inorganic phosphate (P_i). ATP binding and hydrolysis cause a bend in the hinge, which results in movement. The tail region is attached to other proteins or to other kinds of cellular molecules.

To promote movement, the head region of a motor protein interacts with a cytoskeletal filament, such as an actin filament (**Figure 4.10b**). When ATP binds and is hydrolyzed, the motor protein attempts to "walk" along the filament. The head of the motor protein is initially attached to a filament. To move forward, the head detaches from the filament, cocks forward, binds to the filament, and cocks backward. To picture how this works, consider the act of walking and imagine that the ground is a cytoskeletal filament, your leg is the head of the motor protein, and your hip is the hinge. To walk, you

Tail — binds to other components

Hinge — region that bends

Head — binds to cytoskeletal filament; site of ATP binding and hydrolysis

(a) Three-domain structure of myosin, a motor protein

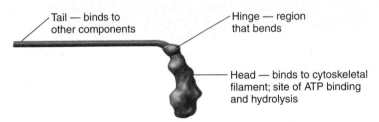

Actin filament

Minus end

1 Head is released from cytoskeletal filament.

2 Head cocks forward and binds to filament.

3 Head cocks backward (this moves the tail from left to right).

(b) Movement of a motor protein along a cytoskeletal filament

Figure 4.10 Motor proteins and their interactions with cytoskeletal filaments. The example illustrated here is the motor protein myosin (discussed in Chapter 44), which interacts with actin filaments. **(a)** Three-domain structure of myosin. **(b)** Conformational changes in a motor protein that allow it to "walk" along a cytoskeletal filament.

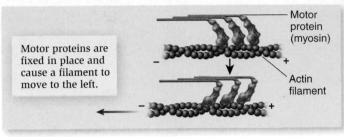

Motor proteins "walk" along a microtubule from the minus end to the plus end carrying a cargo.

Cargo

Motor protein (kinesin)

Microtubule

(a) Motor protein moves

Motor proteins are fixed in place and cause a filament to move to the left.

Motor protein (myosin)

Actin filament

(b) Filament moves

Both the motor proteins and filaments are fixed in place so the actions of the motor proteins cause the microtubules to bend.

Motor protein (dynein)

Linking protein

(c) Filaments bend

Figure 4.11 Three ways that motor proteins and cytoskeletal filaments cause movement.

BioConnections: Look ahead to Figure 44.6. Which of these three types of movements occurs during muscle contraction?

lift your leg up, you move it forward, you place it on the ground, and then you cock it backward (which propels you forward). This series of events is analogous to how a motor protein moves along a cytoskeletal filament.

Interestingly, cells have utilized the actions of motor proteins to promote three different kinds of movements: movement of cargo via the motor protein, movement of the filament, or bending of the filament. In the example shown in **Figure 4.11a**, the tail region of a motor protein called kinesin is attached to a cargo, so the motor protein moves the cargo from one location to another. Alternatively, a motor protein called myosin can remain in place and cause the filament to move (**Figure 4.11b**). This occurs during muscle contraction, which is described in Chapter 44.

A third possibility is that both the motor protein and filament are restricted in their movement due to the presence of linking proteins. In this case, when motor proteins called dynein attempt to walk toward the minus end, they exert a force that causes the microtubules to bend (**Figure 4.11c**). In certain kinds of cells, microtubules and motor proteins facilitate movement involving cell appendages called **flagella** and **cilia** (singular, flagellum and cilium). The difference between the two is that flagella are usually longer than cilia and are typically found singly or in pairs. Both flagella and cilia cause movement by a bending motion. In flagella, movement occurs by a

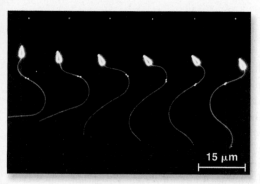

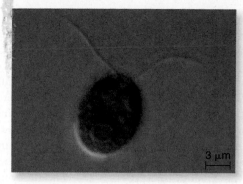

15 µm

3 µm

70 µm

(a) Time-lapse photography of a human sperm moving its flagellum

(b) *Chlamydomonas* with 2 flagella

(c) *Paramecium* with many cilia

Figure 4.12 **Cellular movements due to the actions of flagella and cilia.** **(a)** Sperm swim by means of a single, long flagellum that moves in a whiplike motion, as shown by this human sperm. **(b)** The swimming of *Chlamydomonas reinhardtii*, a unicellular green algae, also involves a whiplike motion at the base, but the motion is precisely coordinated between two flagella. This results in swimming behavior that resembles a breaststroke. **(c)** Ciliated protozoa such as this *Paramecium* swim via many shorter cilia.

Concept Check: *During the movement of a cilium or flagellum, describe the type of movements that occur between the motor proteins and microtubules.*

whiplike motion that is due to the propagation of a bend from the base to the tip. A single flagellum may propel a cell such as a sperm cell with a whiplike motion (**Figure 4.12a**). Alternatively, a pair of flagella may move in a synchronized manner to pull a microorganism through the water (think of a human swimmer doing the breaststroke). Certain unicellular algae swim in this manner (**Figure 4.12b**).

By comparison, cilia are often shorter than flagella and tend to cover all or part of the surface of a cell. Protists such as paramecia may have hundreds of adjacent cilia that beat in a coordinated fashion to propel the organism through the water (**Figure 4.12c**).

Despite their differences in length, flagella and cilia share the same internal structure called the **axoneme**. The axoneme contains microtubules, the motor protein dynein, and linking proteins (**Figure 4.13**). In the cilia and flagella of most eukaryotic organisms, the microtubules form an arrangement called a 9 + 2 array. The outer nine are doublet microtubules, which are composed of a partial

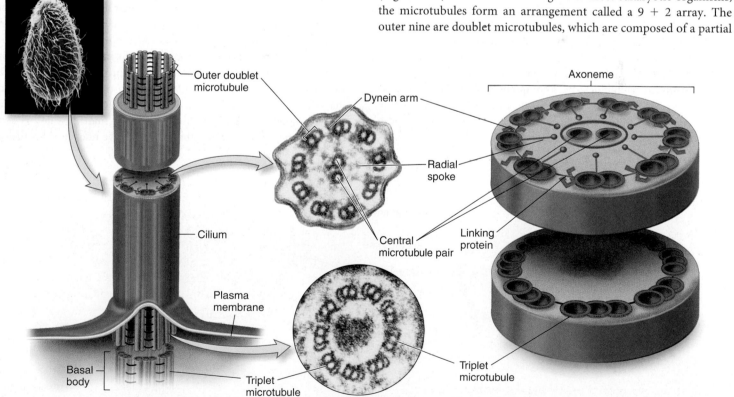

Outer doublet microtubule

Dynein arm

Axoneme

Cilium

Radial spoke

Central microtubule pair

Linking protein

Plasma membrane

Basal body

Triplet microtubule

Triplet microtubule

Figure 4.13 **Structure of a eukaryotic cilium or flagellum.** The structure of a cilium of a protist, *Tetrahymena thermophila* (see inset), consists of a 9 + 2 arrangement of nine outer doublet microtubules and two central microtubules. This structure is anchored to the basal body, which has nine triplet microtubules, in which three microtubules are fused together. Note: The structure of the basal body is very similar to centrioles in animal cells.

BioConnections: *Look ahead to Figures 28.4, 28.7, and 28.8. What are some different uses of cilia and flagella among protists?*

microtubule attached to a complete microtubule. Each of the two central microtubules consists of a single microtubule. Radial spokes project from the outer doublet microtubules toward the central pair. The microtubules in flagella and cilia emanate from **basal bodies**, which are anchored to the cytoplasmic side of the plasma membrane. At the basal body, the microtubules form a triplet structure. Much like the centrosome of animal cells, the basal bodies provide a site for microtubules to grow.

The movement of both flagella and cilia involves the propagation of a bend, which begins at the base of the structure and proceeds toward the tip (see Figure 4.12a). The bending occurs because dynein is activated to walk toward the minus end of the microtubules. ATP hydrolysis is required for this process. However, the microtubules and dynein are not free to move relative to each other because of linking proteins. Therefore, instead of dyneins freely walking along the microtubules, they exert a force that bends the microtubules (see Figure 4.11c). The dyneins at the base of the flagellum or cilium are activated first, followed by dyneins that are progressively closer to the tip, and the resulting movement propels the organism.

4.4 The Nucleus and Endomembrane System

Learning Outcomes:

1. Describe the structure and organization of the cell nucleus.
2. Outline the structures and general functions of the components of the endomembrane system.
3. Distinguish between the rough endoplasmic reticulum and the smooth endoplasmic reticulum.
4. Identify three important functions of the plasma membrane.

In Chapter 2, we learned that the nucleus of an atom contains protons and neutrons. In cell biology, the term **nucleus** has a different meaning. It is an organelle found in eukaryotic cells that contains most of the cell's genetic material. A small amount of genetic material is also found outside the nucleus, in mitochondria and chloroplasts.

The membranes that enclose the nucleus are part of a larger network of membranes called the **endomembrane system**. This system includes not only the nuclear envelope, which encloses the nucleus, but also the endoplasmic reticulum, Golgi apparatus, lysosomes, vacuoles, and peroxisomes. The prefix *endo* (from the Greek, meaning inside) originally referred only to these organelles and internal membranes. However, we now know that the plasma membrane is also part of this integrated membrane system (**Figure 4.14**). Some of these membranes, such as the outer membrane of the nuclear envelope and the membrane of the endoplasmic reticulum, have direct connections to one another. Other organelles of the endomembrane system pass materials to each other via **vesicles**—small membrane-enclosed spheres. In this section, we will examine the nucleus and survey the structures and functions of the organelles and membranes of the endomembrane system.

The Eukaryotic Nucleus Contains Chromosomes

The nucleus is the internal compartment that is enclosed by a double-membrane structure termed the **nuclear envelope** (**Figure 4.15**). In most cells, the nucleus is a relatively large organelle that typically occupies 10–20% of the total cell volume. **Nuclear pores** are formed where the inner and outer nuclear membranes make contact with each other. The pores provide a passageway for the movement of molecules and macromolecules into and out of the nucleus. Although cell biologists view the nuclear envelope as part of the endomembrane system, the materials within the nucleus are not (see Figure 4.15).

Inside the nucleus are the chromosomes and a filamentous network of proteins called the nuclear matrix. Each **chromosome** is composed of genetic material, namely DNA, and many types of proteins that help to compact the chromosome to fit inside the nucleus. The complex formed between DNA and such proteins is termed **chromatin**. The **nuclear matrix** consists of two parts: the nuclear lamina, which is composed of intermediate filaments that line the inner nuclear membrane, and an internal nuclear matrix, which is connected to the lamina and fills the interior of the nucleus. The nuclear

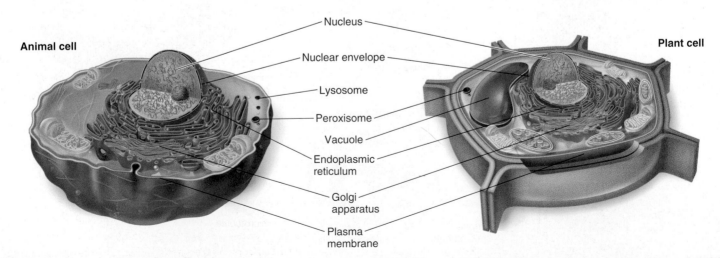

Figure 4.14 The nucleus and endomembrane system. This figure highlights the internal compartment of the nucleus (blue), the membranes of the endomembrane system (purple), and the fluid-filled interiors of the endomembrane system (pink). The nuclear envelope is part of the endomembrane system, but the interior of the nucleus is not.

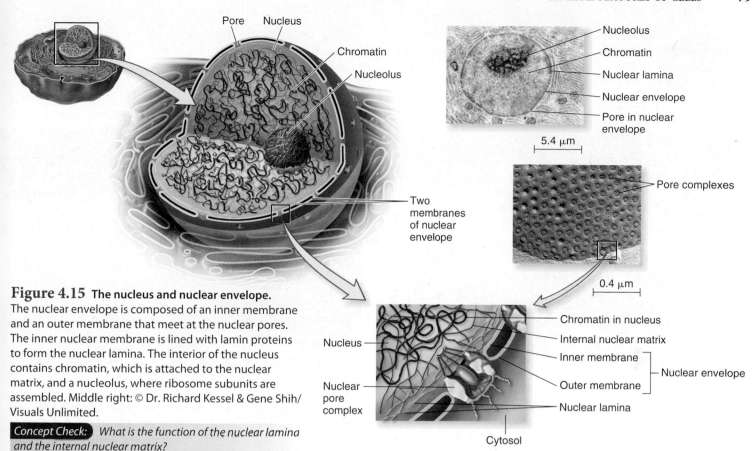

Figure 4.15 The nucleus and nuclear envelope.
The nuclear envelope is composed of an inner membrane and an outer membrane that meet at the nuclear pores. The inner nuclear membrane is lined with lamin proteins to form the nuclear lamina. The interior of the nucleus contains chromatin, which is attached to the nuclear matrix, and a nucleolus, where ribosome subunits are assembled. Middle right: © Dr. Richard Kessel & Gene Shih/Visuals Unlimited.

Concept Check: *What is the function of the nuclear lamina and the internal nuclear matrix?*

Figure 4.16 Chromosome territories in the cell nucleus.
Chromosomes from a chicken were labeled with chromosome-specific probes. Seven types of chicken chromosomes are stained with a different dye. Each chromosome occupies its own distinct, nonoverlapping territory within the cell nucleus. Reprinted by permission from Macmillan Publishers Ltd. Cremer, T., and Cremer, C. Chromosome territories, nuclear architecture and gene regulation in mammalian cells. *Nature Reviews/Genetics*, Vol. 2(4), Figure 2, 292–301, 2001.

BioConnections: *Look ahead to Figure 15.8. What happens to chromosome territories during cell division?*

matrix serves to organize the chromosomes within the nucleus. Each chromosome is located in a distinct, nonoverlapping **chromosome territory**, which is visible when cells are exposed to dyes that label specific types of chromosomes (**Figure 4.16**).

The primary function of the nucleus is the protection, organization, replication, and expression of the genetic material. These topics are discussed in Unit III. Another important function is the assembly of ribosome subunits—cellular structures involved in producing polypeptides during the process of translation. The assembly of ribosome subunits occurs in the **nucleolus** (plural, nucleoli), a prominent region in the nucleus of nondividing cells. A ribosome is composed of two subunits: one small and one large (see Chapter 12, Table 12.3). Each subunit contains one or more RNA molecules and several types of proteins. Most of the RNA molecules that are components of ribosomes are made in the vicinity of the nucleolus. By comparison, the ribosomal proteins are produced in the cytosol and then imported into the nucleus through the nuclear pores. The ribosomal proteins and RNA molecules then assemble in the nucleolus to form the ribosomal subunits. Finally, the subunits exit through the nuclear pores into the cytosol, where they are needed for protein synthesis.

The Endoplasmic Reticulum Initiates Protein Sorting and Carries Out Metabolic Functions

The **endoplasmic reticulum (ER)** is a network of membranes that form flattened, fluid-filled tubules, or **cisternae** (**Figure 4.17**). The terms endoplasmic (Greek, for in the cytoplasm) and reticulum (Latin, for little net) refer to the location and shape of this organelle when viewed under a microscope. The term **lumen** describes the internal space of an organelle. The ER membrane encloses a single compartment called the **ER lumen**. There are two distinct, but continuous types of ER: rough ER and smooth ER.

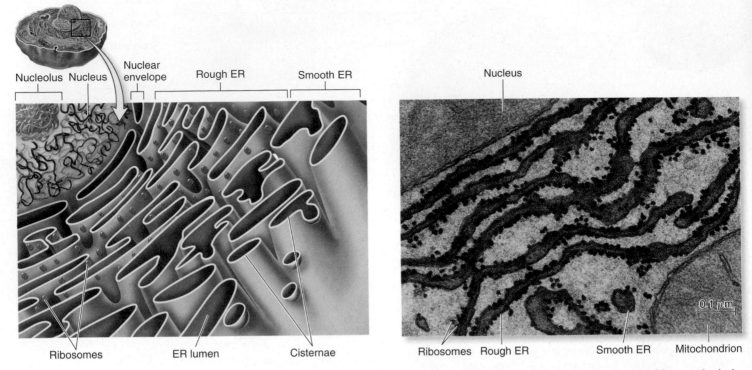

Figure 4.17 Structure of the endoplasmic reticulum. (Left side) The endoplasmic reticulum (ER) is composed of a network of flattened tubules called cisternae that enclose a continuous ER lumen. The rough ER is studded with ribosomes, whereas the smooth ER lacks ribosomes. The rough ER is continuous with the outer nuclear membrane. (Right side) A colorized TEM of the ER. The lumen of the ER is colored yellow and the ribosomes are red.

Rough ER   The outer surface of the **rough endoplasmic reticulum (rough ER)** is studded with ribosomes, giving it a bumpy appearance. Rough ER plays a key role in the sorting of proteins that are destined for the ER, Golgi apparatus, lysosomes, vacuoles, plasma membrane, or outside of the cell. This topic is described later in Section 4.6. In conjunction with protein sorting, a second function of the rough ER is the insertion of certain newly made proteins into the ER membrane. A third important function of the rough ER is the attachment of carbohydrates to proteins and lipids. This process is called **glycosylation**. The topics of membrane protein insertion and protein glycosylation will be discussed in Chapter 5, because they are important features of cell membranes.

Smooth ER   The **smooth endoplasmic reticulum (smooth ER)**, which lacks ribosomes, functions in diverse metabolic processes. The extensive network of smooth ER membranes provides an increased surface area for key enzymes that play important metabolic roles. In liver cells, enzymes in the smooth ER detoxify many potentially harmful organic molecules, including barbiturate drugs and ethanol. These enzymes convert hydrophobic toxic molecules into more hydrophilic molecules, which are easily excreted from the body. Chronic alcohol consumption, as in alcoholics, leads to a greater amount of smooth ER in liver cells, which increases the rate of alcohol breakdown. This explains why people who consume alcohol regularly must ingest more alcohol to experience its effects. It also explains why alcoholics often have enlarged livers.

The smooth ER of liver cells also plays a role in carbohydrate metabolism. The liver cells of animals store energy in the form of glycogen, which is a polymer of glucose. Glycogen granules, which

are in the cytosol, sit very close to the smooth ER membrane. When chemical energy is needed, enzymes are activated that break down the glycogen to glucose-6-phosphate. Then, an enzyme in the smooth ER called glucose-6-phosphatase removes the phosphate group, and glucose is released into the bloodstream.

Another important function of the smooth ER in all eukaryotes is the accumulation of calcium ions (Ca^{2+}). The smooth ER contains calcium pumps that transport Ca^{2+} into the ER lumen. The regulated release of Ca^{2+} into the cytosol is involved in many vital cellular processes, including muscle contraction in animals.

Finally, enzymes in the smooth ER are critical in the synthesis and modification of lipids. For example, the smooth ER is the primary site for the synthesis of phospholipids, which are the main lipid component of eukaryotic cell membranes. This topic is described in Chapter 5. In addition, enzymes in the smooth ER are necessary for certain modifications of the lipid cholesterol that are needed to produce steroid hormones such as estrogen and testosterone.

The Golgi Apparatus Directs the Processing, Sorting, and Secretion of Cellular Molecules

The **Golgi apparatus** (also called the Golgi body, Golgi complex, or simply Golgi) was discovered by the Italian microscopist Camillo Golgi in 1898. It consists of a stack of flattened membranes, with each flattened membrane enclosing a single compartment. The Golgi stacks are named according to their orientation in the cell. The *cis* Golgi is near the ER membrane, the *trans* Golgi is closest to the plasma membrane, and the medial Golgi is found in the middle. Materials are transported between the Golgi stacks via membrane vesicles that bud

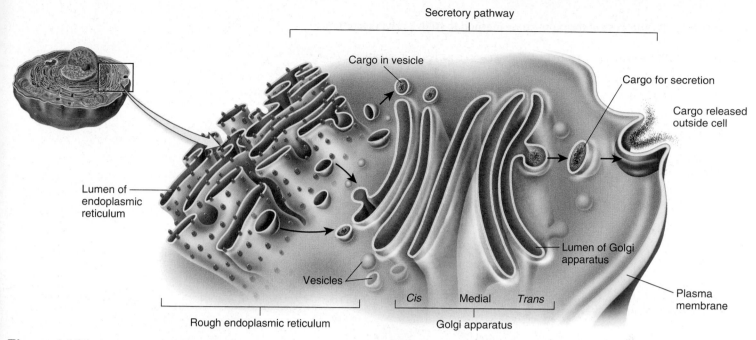

Figure 4.18 **The Golgi apparatus and secretory pathway.** The Golgi is composed of stacks of membranes that enclose separate compartments. Transport to and from the Golgi compartments occurs via membrane vesicles. Vesicles bud from the ER and go to the Golgi, and vesicles from the Golgi fuse with the plasma membrane to release cargo to the outside. The pathway from the ER to the Golgi to the plasma membrane is termed the secretory pathway.

Concept Check: *If we consider the Golgi apparatus as three compartments (cis, medial, and trans), describe the compartments that a protein travels through to be secreted.*

from one compartment in the Golgi (for example, the *cis* Golgi) and fuse with another compartment (for example, the medial Golgi).

The Golgi apparatus performs three overlapping functions: (1) processing, (2) protein sorting, and (3) secretion. We will discuss protein sorting in Section 4.6. Enzymes in the Golgi apparatus process, or modify, certain proteins and lipids. As mentioned earlier, carbohydrates can be attached to proteins and lipids in the endoplasmic reticulum. Glycosylation continues in the Golgi. For this to occur, a protein or lipid is transported via vesicles from the ER to the *cis* Golgi. Most of the glycosylation occurs in the medial Golgi.

A second type of processing event is **proteolysis**, whereby enzymes called **proteases** make cuts in polypeptides. For example, the hormone insulin is first made as a large precursor termed proinsulin.

In the Golgi apparatus, proinsulin is packaged with proteases into vesicles. The proteases cut out a portion of the proinsulin to create a smaller insulin polypeptide that is a functional hormone. This happens just prior to secretion, which is described next.

The Golgi apparatus packages different types of materials (cargo) into **secretory vesicles** that fuse with the plasma membrane, thereby releasing their contents outside the cell. Proteins destined for secretion are synthesized into the ER, travel to the Golgi, and then are transported by vesicles to the plasma membrane. The vesicles then fuse with the plasma membrane, and the proteins are secreted to the outside of the cell. The entire route is called the **secretory pathway** (**Figure 4.18**). In addition to secretory vesicles, the Golgi also produces vesicles that travel to other parts of the cell, such as the lysosomes.

FEATURE INVESTIGATION

Palade Demonstrated That Secreted Proteins Move Sequentially Through Organelles of the Endomembrane System

As we have seen, one of the key functions of the endomembrane system is protein secretion. The identification of the secretory pathway came from studies of George Palade and his colleagues in the 1960s. He hypothesized that proteins follow a particular intracellular pathway to be secreted. Palade's team conducted pulse-chase experiments, in which the researchers administered a pulse of radioactive amino acids to cells so they made radioactive proteins. A few minutes later, the cells were given a large amount of nonradioactive amino acids. This is

called a "chase" because it chases away the ability of the cells to make any more radioactive proteins. In this way, radioactive proteins were produced only briefly. Because they were labeled with radioactivity, the fate of these proteins could be monitored over time. The goal of a pulse-chase experiment is to determine where the radioactive proteins are produced and the pathway they take as they travel through a cell.

Palade chose to study the cells of the pancreas. This organ secretes enzymes and protein hormones that play a role in digestion and metabolism. Therefore, these cells were chosen because their primary activity is protein secretion. To study the pathway for protein secretion, Palade and colleagues injected a radioactive version of the amino acid leucine into the bloodstream of male guinea pigs.

Figure 4.19 Palade's use of the pulse-chase method to study protein secretion.

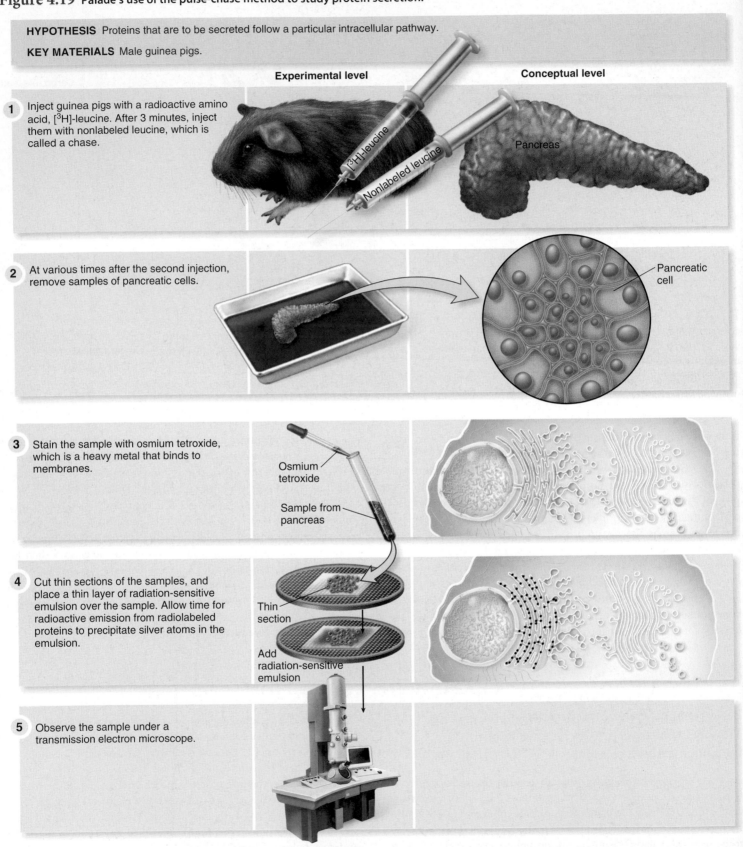

HYPOTHESIS Proteins that are to be secreted follow a particular intracellular pathway.

KEY MATERIALS Male guinea pigs.

Experimental level   Conceptual level

1 Inject guinea pigs with a radioactive amino acid, [³H]-leucine. After 3 minutes, inject them with nonlabeled leucine, which is called a chase.

[³H]-leucine

Nonlabeled leucine

Pancreas

2 At various times after the second injection, remove samples of pancreatic cells.

Pancreatic cell

3 Stain the sample with osmium tetroxide, which is a heavy metal that binds to membranes.

Osmium tetroxide

Sample from pancreas

4 Cut thin sections of the samples, and place a thin layer of radiation-sensitive emulsion over the sample. Allow time for radioactive emission from radiolabeled proteins to precipitate silver atoms in the emulsion.

Thin section

Add radiation-sensitive emulsion

5 Observe the sample under a transmission electron microscope.

6 THE DATA

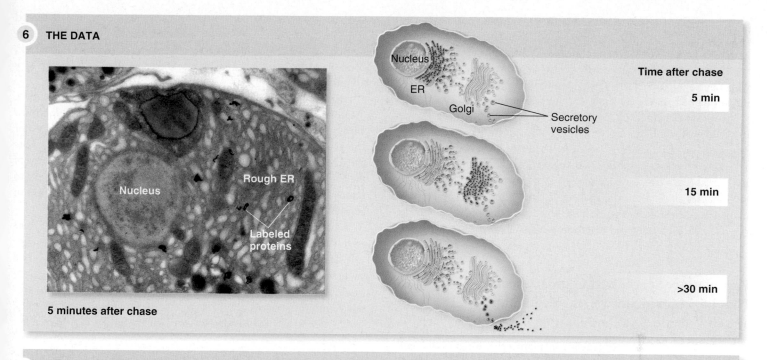

Nucleus

ER

Golgi

Secretory vesicles

Time after chase

5 min

15 min

>30 min

Nucleus

Rough ER

Labeled proteins

5 minutes after chase

7 CONCLUSION To be secreted, proteins move from the ER to the Golgi to secretory vesicles and then to the plasma membrane, where they are released to the outside of the cell.

8 SOURCE Caro, L.G., and Palade, G.E. 1964. Protein synthesis, storage, and discharge in the pancreatic exocrine cell. An autoradiographic study. *Journal of Cell Biology* 20:473–495.

The radiolabeled leucine traveled in the bloodstream and was quickly taken up by cells of the body, including those in the pancreas. Three minutes later, they injected nonradioactive leucine (**Figure 4.19**). At various times after the second injection, samples of pancreatic cells were removed from the animals. The cells were then prepared for transmission electron microscopy (TEM). The sample was stained with osmium tetroxide, a heavy metal that became bound to membranes and showed the locations of the cell organelles. In addition, the sample was coated with a radiation-sensitive emulsion containing silver. When radiation was emitted from radioactive proteins, it interacted with the emulsion in a way that caused the precipitation of silver, which became tightly bound to the sample. In this way, the precipitated silver marked the location of the radiolabeled proteins. Unprecipitated silver in the emulsion was later washed away. Because silver atoms are electron dense, they produce dark spots in a TEM. Therefore, dark spots revealed the locations of radioactive proteins.

The micrograph in the data of Figure 4.19 illustrates the results that were observed 5 minutes after the completion of the pulse-chase injections. Very dark objects, namely radioactive proteins, were observed in the rough ER. As shown schematically to the right of the actual data, later time points indicated that the radioactive proteins moved from the ER to the Golgi, and then to secretory vesicles near the plasma membrane. In this way, Palade followed the intracellular pathway of protein movement. His experiments provided the first evidence that secreted proteins are synthesized into the rough ER and move through a series of cellular compartments before they are secreted. These findings also caused researchers to wonder how proteins are targeted to particular organelles and how they move from one compartment to another, topics that are described in Section 4.6.

Experimental Questions

1. Explain the procedure of a pulse-chase experiment. What is the pulse, and what is the chase? What was the purpose of the approach?

2. Why were pancreatic cells used for this investigation?

3. What were the key results of the experiment of Figure 4.19? What did the researchers conclude?

Lysosomes Are Involved in the Intracellular Digestion of Macromolecules

We now turn to another organelle of the endomembrane system, **lysosomes**, which are small organelles found in animal cells that break down macromolecules. Lysosomes contain many **acid hydrolases**, which are hydrolytic enzymes that use a molecule of water to break a covalent bond. This type of chemical reaction is called hydrolysis:

$$R_1 - R_2 + H_2O \xrightarrow{\text{Acid hydrolase}} R_1 - OH + R_2 - H$$

The acid hydrolases found in a lysosome function optimally at an acidic pH. The fluid-filled interior of a lysosome has a pH of approximately 4.8. If a lysosomal membrane breaks, releasing acid hydrolases into the cytosol, the enzymes are not very active because the cytosolic pH is neutral (approximately pH 7.2) and buffered. This prevents significant damage to the cell from accidental leakage.

Lysosomes contain many different types of acid hydrolases that break down carbohydrates, proteins, lipids, and nucleic acids. This enzymatic function enables lysosomes to break down complex materials. One function of lysosomes involves the digestion of substances that are taken up from outside the cell via a process called endocytosis (see Chapter 5). In addition, lysosomes help to break down intracellular molecules and macromolecules to recycle their building blocks to make new molecules and macromolecules in a process called autophagy (see Chapter 6).

Vacuoles Are Specialized Compartments That Function in Storage, the Regulation of Cell Volume, and Degradation

Vacuoles are prominent organelles in plant cells, fungal cells, and certain protists. In animal cells, vacuoles tend to be smaller and are more commonly used to temporarily store materials or transport substances. In animals, such vacuoles are sometimes called storage vesicles. The term vacuole (Latin, for empty space) came from early microscopic observations of these compartments. We now know that vacuoles are not empty but instead contain fluid and sometimes even solid substances. Most vacuoles are made from the fusion of many smaller membrane vesicles.

The functions of vacuoles are extremely varied, and they differ among cell types and even environmental conditions. The best way to appreciate vacuole function is to consider a few examples. Mature plant cells often have a large **central vacuole** that occupies 80% or more of the cell volume (**Figure 4.20a**). The central vacuole serves two important purposes. First, it stores a large amount of water, enzymes, and inorganic ions such as calcium. It also stores other materials including proteins and pigments. Second, it performs a space-filling function. The large size of the vacuole exerts a pressure on the cell wall, called turgor pressure. If a plant becomes dehydrated and this pressure is lost, a plant will wilt. Turgor pressure is important in maintaining the structure of plant cells and the plant itself, and it helps to drive the expansion of the cell wall, which is necessary for growth.

Certain species of protists use vacuoles to maintain cell volume. Freshwater organisms such as the alga *Chlamydomonas reinhardtii* have small, water-filled **contractile vacuoles** that expand as water enters the cell (**Figure 4.20b**). Once they reach a certain size, the vacuoles suddenly contract, expelling their contents to the exterior of the cell (look ahead to Figure 5.16). This mechanism is necessary to remove the excess water that continually enters the cell by diffusion across the plasma membrane.

Another function of vacuoles is degradation. Some protists engulf their food into large food vacuoles in the process of phagocytosis (**Figure 4.20c**). As in the lysosomes of animal cells, food vacuoles contain hydrolytic enzymes that break down the macromolecules within the food. Macrophages, a type of cell found in animals' immune systems, engulf bacterial cells into phagocytic vacuoles, which then fuse with lysosomes, where the bacteria are destroyed.

Peroxisomes Catalyze Detoxifying Reactions

Peroxisomes, discovered by Christian de Duve in 1965, are relatively small organelles found in all eukaryotic cells. Peroxisomes consist of a single membrane that encloses a fluid-filled lumen. A typical eukaryotic cell contains several hundred of them.

Peroxisomes catalyze a variety of chemical reactions, including some reactions that break down organic molecules and others that are biosynthetic. In mammals, for example, large numbers of peroxisomes are found in liver cells, where toxic molecules accumulate and are broken down. A common by-product of the breakdown of toxins is hydrogen peroxide, H_2O_2:

$$\underset{\text{(toxin)}}{RH_2} + O_2 \longrightarrow R + H_2O_2$$

Hydrogen peroxide has the potential to damage cellular components. In the presence of metals such as iron (Fe^{2+}), which are found

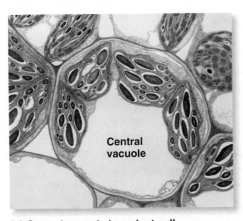

(a) Central vacuole in a plant cell

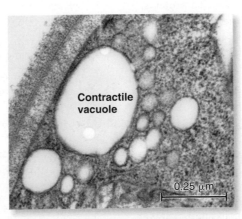

0.25 μm

(b) Contractile vacuoles in an algal cell

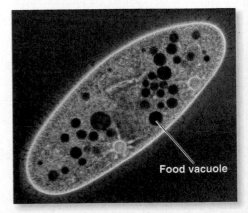

(c) Food vacuoles in a paramecium

Figure 4.20 **Examples of vacuoles.** These are TEMs. Part (c) is colorized.

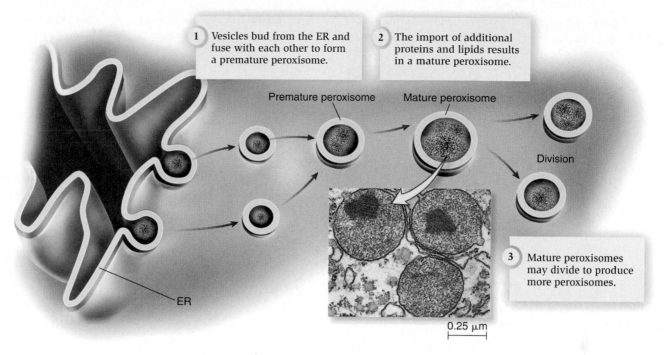

Figure 4.21 **Formation of peroxisomes.** The inset is a TEM of mature peroxisomes.

naturally in living cells, H_2O_2 is broken down to form a hydroxide ion ($OH-$) and a molecule called a hydroxide free-radical ($\cdot OH$):

$$Fe^{2+} + H_2O_2 \rightarrow Fe^{3+} + OH^- + \cdot OH \text{ (hydroxide free-radical)}$$

The $\cdot OH$ is highly reactive and can damage proteins, lipids, and DNA. Therefore, it is beneficial for cells to break down H_2O_2 in an alternative manner that does not form a $\cdot OH$. Peroxisomes contain an enzyme called **catalase** that breaks down H_2O_2 to make water and oxygen gas (hence the name peroxisome):

$$2\,H_2O_2 \xrightarrow{\text{Catalase}} 2\,H_2O + O_2$$

Aside from detoxification, peroxisomes usually contain enzymes involved in the metabolism of fats and amino acids. For example, plant seeds contain specialized organelles called **glyoxysomes**, which are similar to peroxisomes. Seeds often store fats instead of carbohydrates. Because fats have higher energy per unit mass, a plant can make seeds that are smaller and less heavy. Glyoxysomes contain enzymes that are needed to convert fats to sugars. These enzymes become active when a seed germinates and the seedling begins to grow.

Peroxisomes were once viewed as semiautonomous organelles like mitochondria and chloroplasts, because they appeared to be self-replicating, that is, produced by the division of pre-existing peroxisomes. However, recent research indicates that peroxisomes are derived from the endomembrane system. A general model for peroxisome formation is shown in **Figure 4.21**, though the details may differ among animal, plant, and fungal cells. To initiate peroxisome formation, vesicles bud from the ER membrane and form a premature peroxisome. Following the import of additional proteins, the premature peroxisome becomes a mature peroxisome. Once the mature peroxisome has formed, it may then divide to further increase the number of peroxisomes in the cell.

The Plasma Membrane Is the Interface Between a Cell and Its Environment

The cytoplasm of eukaryotic cells is surrounded by a plasma membrane, which is part of the endomembrane system and provides a boundary between a cell and the extracellular environment. Proteins in the plasma membrane perform many important functions that affect the activities inside the cell (**Figure 4.22**). First, many plasma membrane proteins are involved in **membrane transport**. Some of these proteins function to transport essential nutrients or ions into the cell, and others are involved in the export of substances. Due to the functioning of these protein transporters, the plasma membrane is selectively permeable; it allows only certain substances in and out. We will examine the structure and function of the plasma membrane, as well as a variety of transporters, in Chapter 5.

A second vital function of the plasma membrane is **cell signaling**. To survive and adapt to changing conditions, cells must be able to sense changes in their environment. In addition, the cells of a multicellular organism need to communicate with each other to coordinate their activities. The plasma membrane of all cells contains receptors that recognize signals—either environmental agents or molecules secreted by other cells. When a signaling molecule binds to a receptor, it activates a signal transduction pathway—a series of steps that cause the cell to respond to the signal. For example, when you eat a meal, the hormone insulin is secreted into your bloodstream. This hormone binds to receptors in the plasma membrane of your cells, which results in a cellular response that allows your cells to increase their uptake of certain molecules found in food, such as glucose. We will explore the details of cell signaling in Chapter 9.

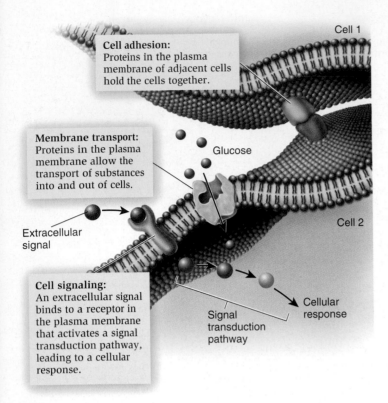

Figure 4.22 Major functions of the plasma membrane. Three important roles are membrane transport, cell signaling, and cell adhesion.

Concept Check: *Which of these three functions do you think is the most important for cell metabolism?*

A third important role of the plasma membrane in animal cells is **cell adhesion**. Protein-protein interactions among proteins in the plasma membranes of adjacent cells promote cell-to-cell adhesion. This phenomenon is critical for animal cells to properly interact to form a multicellular organism and allows cells to recognize each other. The structures and functions of proteins involved in cell adhesion will be examined in Chapter 10.

4.5   Semiautonomous Organelles

Learning Outcomes:

1. Outline the structures and general functions of mitochondria and chloroplasts.
2. Discuss the evidence for the endosymbiosis theory.

We now turn to those organelles in eukaryotic cells that are considered semiautonomous: mitochondria and chloroplasts. These organelles grow and divide, but they are not completely autonomous because they depend on other parts of the cell for their internal components (**Figure 4.23**). For example, most of the proteins found in mitochondria are imported from the cytosol. In this section, we will survey the structures and functions of the semiautonomous organelles in eukaryotic cells and consider their evolutionary origins. In Chapters 7 and 8, we will explore the functions of mitochondria and chloroplasts in greater depth.

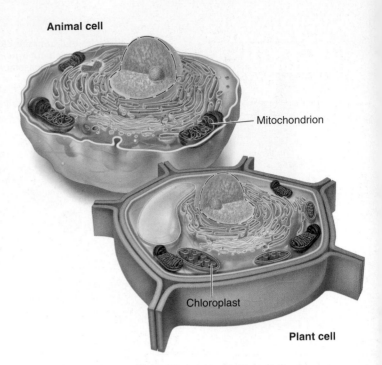

Figure 4.23 Semiautonomous organelles. These are the mitochondria and chloroplasts.

BIOLOGY PRINCIPLE Living organisms use energy. Chloroplasts capture light energy and synthesize organic molecules. Mitochondria break down organic molecules and make ATP that is used as an energy source to drive many different cellular processes.

Mitochondria Supply Cells with Most of Their ATP

Mitochondrion (plural, mitochondria) literally means thread granule, which is what mitochondria look like under a light microscope—either threadlike or granular-shaped. They are similar in size to bacteria. A typical cell may contain a few hundred to a few thousand mitochondria. Cells with particularly heavy energy demands, such as muscle cells, have more mitochondria than other cells. Research has shown that regular exercise increases the number and size of mitochondria in human muscle cells to meet the expanded demand for energy.

A mitochondrion has an outer membrane and an inner membrane separated by a region called the intermembrane space (**Figure 4.24**). The inner membrane is highly invaginated (folded) to form projections called **cristae**. The cristae greatly increase the surface area of the inner membrane, which is the site where ATP is made. The compartment enclosed by the inner membrane is the **mitochondrial matrix**.

The primary role of mitochondria is to make ATP. Even though mitochondria produce most of a cell's ATP, mitochondria do not create energy. Rather, their primary function is to convert chemical energy that is stored within the covalent bonds of organic molecules into a form that can be readily used by cells. Covalent bonds in sugars, fats, and amino acids store a large amount of energy. The breakdown of these molecules into simpler molecules releases energy that is used to make ATP. Many proteins in living cells utilize ATP to carry out

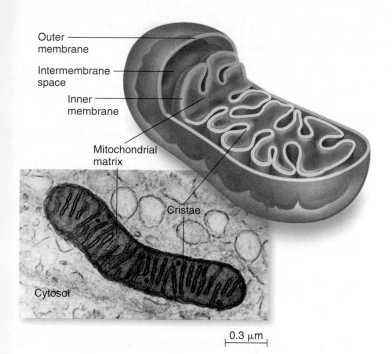

Figure 4.24 **Structure of a mitochondrion.** This figure emphasizes the membrane organization of a mitochondrion, which has an outer and inner membrane. The invaginations of the inner membrane are called cristae. The mitochondrial matrix lies inside the inner membrane. The micrograph is a colorized TEM.

Concept Check: *What is the advantage of having a highly invaginated inner membrane?*

their functions, such as muscle contraction, uptake of nutrients, cell division, and many other cellular processes.

Mitochondria perform other functions as well. They are involved in the synthesis, modification, and breakdown of several types of cellular molecules. For example, the synthesis of certain hormones requires enzymes that are found in mitochondria. Another interesting role of mitochondria is to generate heat in specialized fat cells known as brown fat cells. Groups of brown fat cells serve as "heating pads" that help to revive hibernating animals and protect sensitive areas of young animals from the cold.

Chloroplasts Carry Out Photosynthesis

Chloroplasts are organelles that capture light energy and use some of that energy to synthesize organic molecules such as glucose. This process, called **photosynthesis**, is described in Chapter 8. Chloroplasts are found in nearly all species of plants and algae. **Figure 4.25** shows the structure of a typical chloroplast. Like the mitochondrion, a chloroplast contains an outer and inner membrane. An intermembrane space lies between these two membranes. A third system of membranes, the **thylakoid membrane**, forms many flattened, fluid-filled tubules that enclose a single, convoluted compartment called the thylakoid lumen. These tubules tend to stack on top of each other to form a structure called a **granum** (plural, grana). The **stroma** is the compartment of the chloroplast that is enclosed by the inner membrane but outside the thylakoid membrane.

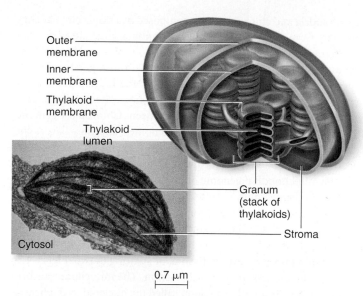

Figure 4.25 **Structure of a chloroplast.** Like a mitochondrion, a chloroplast is enclosed in a double membrane. In addition, it has an internal thylakoid membrane system that forms flattened compartments. These compartments stack on each other to form grana. The stroma is located inside the inner membrane but outside the thylakoid membrane. This micrograph is a colorized TEM.

Chloroplasts are a specialized version of plant organelles that are more generally known as **plastids**. All plastids are derived from unspecialized **proplastids**. The various types of plastids are distinguished by their synthetic abilities and the types of pigments they contain. Chloroplasts, which carry out photosynthesis, contain the green pigment chlorophyll. The abundant number of chloroplasts in the leaves of plants gives them their green color. Chromoplasts, a second type of plastid, function in synthesizing and storing the yellow, orange, and red pigments known as carotenoids. Chromoplasts give many fruits and flowers their colors. In autumn, the chromoplasts also give many leaves their yellow, orange, and red colors. A third type of plastid, leucoplasts, typically lacks pigment molecules. An amyloplast is a leucoplast that synthesizes and stores starch. Amyloplasts are common in underground structures such as roots and tubers.

Mitochondria and Chloroplasts Contain Their Own Genetic Material and Divide by Binary Fission

To fully appreciate the structure and organization of mitochondria and chloroplasts, we also need to briefly examine their genetic properties. In 1951, Yasutane Chiba exposed plant cells to Feulgen, a DNA-specific dye, and discovered that the chloroplasts became stained. Based on this observation, he was the first to suggest that chloroplasts contain their own DNA. Researchers in the 1970s and 1980s isolated DNA from both chloroplasts and mitochondria. These studies revealed that the DNA of these organelles resembled smaller versions of bacterial chromosomes.

The chromosomes found in mitochondria and chloroplasts are referred to as the **mitochondrial genome** and **chloroplast genome**, respectively, and the chromosomes found in the nucleus of the cell constitute the **nuclear genome**. Like bacteria, the genomes of most mitochondria and chloroplasts are composed of a single circular chromosome. Compared with the nuclear genome, they are very small. For example, the amount of DNA in the human nuclear genome (about 3 billion base pairs) is about 200,000 times greater than the mitochondrial genome. In terms of genes, the human genome has approximately 20,000–25,000 different genes, whereas the human mitochondrial genome has only a few dozen. Chloroplast genomes tend to be larger than mitochondrial genomes, and they have a correspondingly greater number of genes. Depending on the particular species of plant or algae, a chloroplast genome is about 10 times larger than the mitochondrial genome of human cells.

Just as the genomes of mitochondria and chloroplasts resemble bacterial genomes, the production of new mitochondria and chloroplasts bears a striking resemblance to the division of bacterial cells. Like their bacterial counterparts, mitochondria and chloroplasts increase in number via **binary fission**, or splitting in two. **Figure 4.26** illustrates the process for a mitochondrion. The mitochondrial chromosome, which is found in a region called the nucleoid, is duplicated, and the organelle divides into two separate organelles. Mitochondrial and chloroplast division are needed to maintain a full complement of these organelles when cell growth occurs following cell division. In addition, environmental conditions may influence the sizes and numbers of these organelles. For example, when plants are exposed to more sunlight, the number of chloroplasts in leaf cells increases.

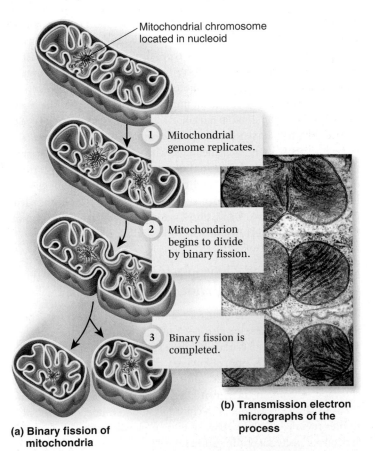

Mitochondrial chromosome located in nucleoid

1 Mitochondrial genome replicates.

2 Mitochondrion begins to divide by binary fission.

3 Binary fission is completed.

(b) Transmission electron micrographs of the process

(a) Binary fission of mitochondria

Figure 4.26 Division of mitochondria by binary fission.

BioConnections: *Look ahead to Figure 18.14. How is this process similar to bacterial cell division, and how is it different?*

Mitochondria and Chloroplasts Are Derived from Ancient Symbiotic Relationships

The observation that mitochondria and chloroplasts contain their own genetic material may seem puzzling. Perhaps you might think that it would be simpler for a eukaryotic cell to have all of its genetic material in one place—the nucleus. The distinct genomes of mitochondria and chloroplasts can be traced to their evolutionary origin, which involved an ancient symbiotic association.

A symbiotic relationship occurs when two different species live in direct contact with each other. **Endosymbiosis** describes a symbiotic relationship in which the smaller species—the symbiont—actually lives inside the larger species. In 1883, Andreas Schimper proposed that chloroplasts were descended from an endosymbiotic relationship between cyanobacteria (a bacterium capable of photosynthesis) and eukaryotic cells. In 1922, Ivan Wallin also hypothesized an endosymbiotic origin for mitochondria.

In spite of these interesting ideas, the question of endosymbiosis was largely ignored until the discovery that mitochondria and chloroplasts contain their own genetic material. In 1970, the issue of endosymbiosis as the origin of mitochondria and chloroplasts was revived by Lynn Margulis in her book *Origin of Eukaryotic Cells*. During the 1970s and 1980s, the advent of molecular genetic techniques allowed researchers to analyze genes from mitochondria, chloroplasts, bacteria, and eukaryotic nuclear genomes. Researchers discovered that genes in mitochondria and chloroplasts are very similar to bacterial genes. Likewise, mitochondria and chloroplasts are strikingly similar in size and shape to certain bacterial species. These observations provided strong support for the **endosymbiosis theory**, which proposes that mitochondria and chloroplasts originated from bacteria that took up residence within a primordial eukaryotic cell (**Figure 4.27**). Over the next 2 billion years, the characteristics of these intracellular bacterial cells gradually changed to those of a mitochondrion or chloroplast. The origin of eukaryotic cells is discussed in more detail in Chapter 22.

Symbiosis occurs because the relationship is beneficial to one or both species. According to the endosymbiosis theory, this relationship provided eukaryotic cells with useful cellular characteristics. Chloroplasts, which were derived from cyanobacteria, have the ability to carry out photosynthesis. This benefits plant cells by giving them the ability to use the energy from sunlight. By comparison, mitochondria are thought to have been derived from a different type of bacteria known as purple bacteria or α-proteobacteria. In this case, the endosymbiotic relationship enabled eukaryotic cells to synthesize greater amounts of ATP. How the relationship would have been beneficial to a cyanobacterium or purple bacterium is less clear, though the cytosol of a eukaryotic cell may have provided a stable environment with an adequate supply of nutrients.

During the evolution of eukaryotic species, many genes that were originally found in the genome of the primordial purple bacteria and cyanobacteria have been transferred from the organelles to the nucleus. This has occurred many times throughout evolution, so modern mitochondria and chloroplasts have lost most of the genes that still exist in present-day purple bacteria and cyanobacteria. Some researchers speculate that the movement of genes into the nucleus makes it easier for the cell to control the structure, function, and

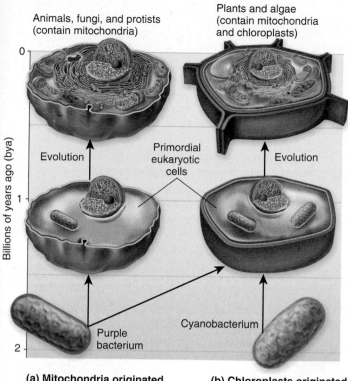

Figure 4.27 A simplified view of the endosymbiosis theory. (a) According to this concept, modern mitochondria were derived from purple bacteria, also called α-proteobacteria. Over the course of evolution, their characteristics changed into those found in mitochondria today. **(b)** A similar phenomenon occurred for chloroplasts, which were derived from cyanobacteria (blue-green bacteria), a bacterium that is capable of photosynthesis.

Concept Check: *Discuss the similarities and differences between modern bacteria and mitochondria.*

division of mitochondria and chloroplasts. In modern cells, hundreds of different proteins that make up these organelles are encoded by genes that have been transferred to the nucleus. These proteins are made in the cytosol and then taken up into mitochondria or chloroplasts. We will discuss this topic next.

4.6 Protein Sorting to Organelles

Learning Outcomes:

1. List which categories of proteins are sorted cotranslationally and which are sorted post-translationally.
2. Describe the steps that occur during the cotranslational sorting of proteins to the endoplasmic reticulum.
3. Explain how proteins are moved via vesicles through the endomembrane system.
4. Outline the steps of post-translational sorting of proteins to mitochondria.

As we have seen, eukaryotic cells contain a variety of membrane-bound organelles. Each protein that a cell makes usually functions within one cellular compartment or is secreted from the cell. How does each protein reach its appropriate destination? For example,

how does a mitochondrial protein get sent to the mitochondrion rather than to a different organelle such as a lysosome? In eukaryotes, most proteins contain short stretches of amino acid sequences that direct them to their correct cellular location. These sequences are called **sorting signals**, or **traffic signals**. Each sorting signal is recognized by specific cellular components that facilitate the proper routing of that protein to its correct location.

Most eukaryotic proteins begin their synthesis on ribosomes in the cytosol, using messenger RNA (mRNA) that contains the information for polypeptide synthesis (**Figure 4.28**). The cytosol provides amino acids, which are used as building blocks to make these proteins during translation. Cytosolic proteins lack any sorting signal, so they remain there. By comparison, the synthesis of proteins destined for the ER, Golgi, lysosomes, vacuoles, or secretory vesicles begins in the cytosol and then halts temporarily until the ribosome has become bound to the ER membrane. After this occurs, translation resumes and the polypeptide is synthesized into the ER. Proteins that are destined for the ER, Golgi, lysosome, vacuole, plasma membrane, or secretion are first directed to the ER. This is called **cotranslational sorting** because the first step in the sorting process begins while translation is occurring. Finally, the uptake of most proteins into the nucleus, mitochondria, chloroplasts, and peroxisomes occurs after the protein is completely made (that is, completely translated) in the cytosol. This is called **post-translational sorting** because sorting does not happen until translation is finished. In this section, we will consider how cells carry out cotranslational and post-translational sorting.

The Cotranslational Sorting of Some Proteins Occurs at the Endoplasmic Reticulum Membrane

The concept of sorting signals in proteins was first proposed by Günter Blobel in the 1970s. Blobel and colleagues discovered a sorting signal in proteins that sends them to the ER membrane, which is the first step in cotranslational sorting (**Figure 4.29**). To be directed to the rough ER membrane, a polypeptide must contain a sorting signal called an **ER signal sequence**, which is a sequence of about 6–12 amino acids that are predominantly hydrophobic and usually located near the N-terminus. As the ribosome is making the polypeptide in the cytosol, the ER signal sequence emerges from the ribosome and is recognized by a protein-RNA complex called **signal recognition particle (SRP)**. SRP has two functions. First, it recognizes the ER signal sequence and pauses translation. Second, SRP binds to an SRP receptor in the ER membrane, which docks the ribosome over a channel. At this stage, SRP is released and translation resumes. The growing polypeptide is threaded through the channel to cross the ER membrane. If the protein is not a membrane protein, it will be released into the lumen of the ER. In most cases, the ER signal sequence is removed by an enzyme, signal peptidase. In 1999, Blobel won the Nobel Prize for Physiology or Medicine for his discovery of sorting signals in proteins. The process shown in Figure 4.29 illustrates another important role of protein-protein interactions—a series of interactions causes the steps of a process to occur in a specific order.

Some proteins are meant to function in the ER. Such proteins contain ER retention signals in addition to the ER signal sequence.

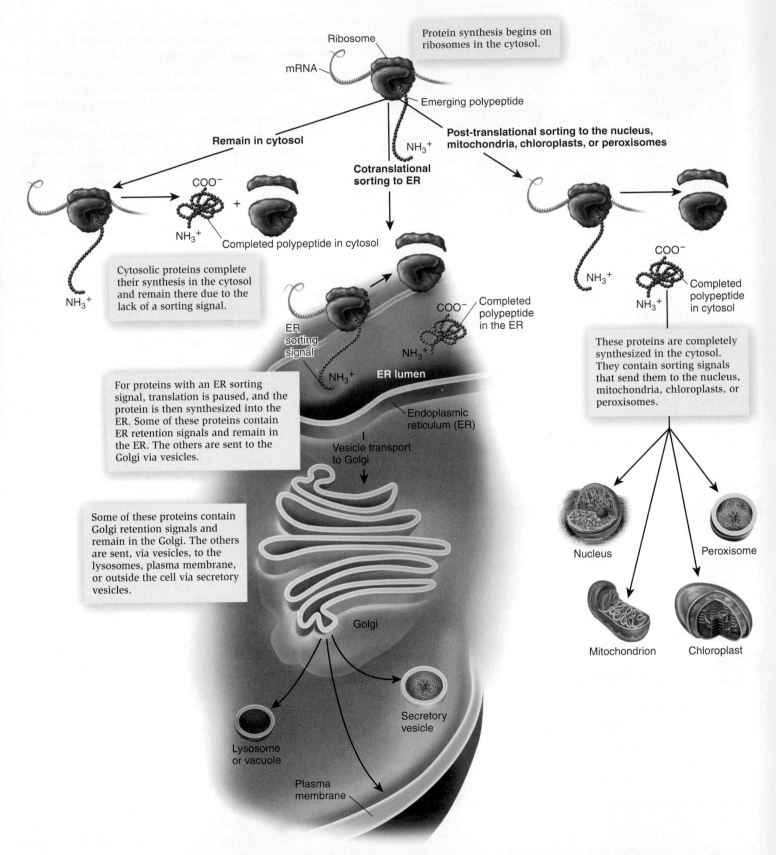

Ribosome

mRNA

Protein synthesis begins on ribosomes in the cytosol.

Emerging polypeptide

Remain in cytosol

NH_3^+

Post-translational sorting to the nucleus, mitochondria, chloroplasts, or peroxisomes

Cotranslational sorting to ER

COO^-

NH_3^+

+

Completed polypeptide in cytosol

NH_3^+

Completed polypeptide in the ER

COO^-

NH_3^+

NH_3^+

COO^-

Completed polypeptide in cytosol

Cytosolic proteins complete their synthesis in the cytosol and remain there due to the lack of a sorting signal.

ER sorting signal

NH_3^+

ER lumen

These proteins are completely synthesized in the cytosol. They contain sorting signals that send them to the nucleus, mitochondria, chloroplasts, or peroxisomes.

For proteins with an ER sorting signal, translation is paused, and the protein is then synthesized into the ER. Some of these proteins contain ER retention signals and remain in the ER. The others are sent to the Golgi via vesicles.

Endoplasmic reticulum (ER)

Vesicle transport to Golgi

Some of these proteins contain Golgi retention signals and remain in the Golgi. The others are sent, via vesicles, to the lysosomes, plasma membrane, or outside the cell via secretory vesicles.

Nucleus

Peroxisome

Mitochondrion

Chloroplast

Golgi

Secretory vesicle

Lysosome or vacuole

Plasma membrane

Figure 4.28 Three pathways for protein sorting in a eukaryotic cell. Proteins either remain in the cytosol, or they are sorted to the ER (cotranslational sorting), or sorted after the protein is completely made (post-translational sorting).

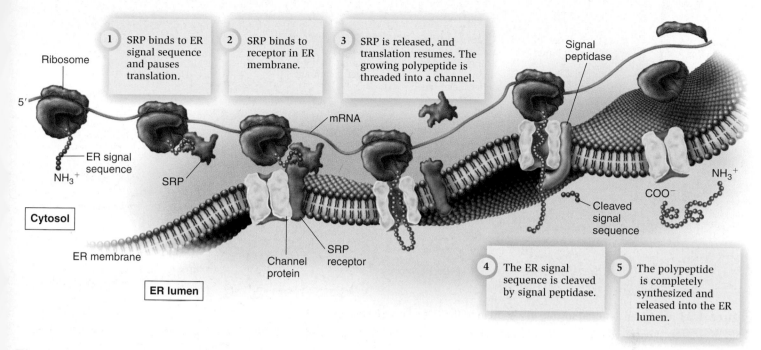

Figure 4.29 First step in cotranslational sorting: sending proteins to the ER.

Concept Check: *What prevents an ER protein from being completely synthesized in the cytosol?*

Alternatively, other proteins that are destined for the Golgi, lysosomes, vacuoles, plasma membrane, or secretion leave the ER and are transported to their correct location (see Figure 4.28). This transport process occurs via vesicles that are formed from one compartment and then move through the cytosol and fuse with another compartment. Vesicles from the ER may go to the Golgi, and then vesicles from the Golgi may go to the lysosomes, vacuoles, or plasma membrane. Sorting signals within proteins' amino acid sequences are responsible for directing them to the correct location.

Figure 4.30 describes the second step in cotranslational sorting, vesicle transport from the ER to the Golgi. A cargo, such as protein molecules, is loaded into a developing vesicle by binding to cargo receptors in the ER membrane. Vesicle formation is facilitated by the binding of coat proteins, which, by shaping the surrounding membrane into a sphere, helps a vesicle to bud from a given membrane. As a vesicle forms, other proteins called V-snares are incorporated into the vesicle membrane (hence the name V-snare). Many types of V-snares are known to exist. The particular V-snare that is found in

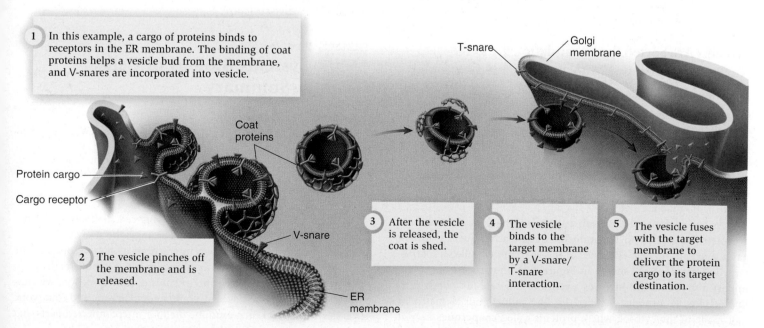

Figure 4.30 Second step in cotranslational sorting: vesicle transport from the ER to the Golgi.

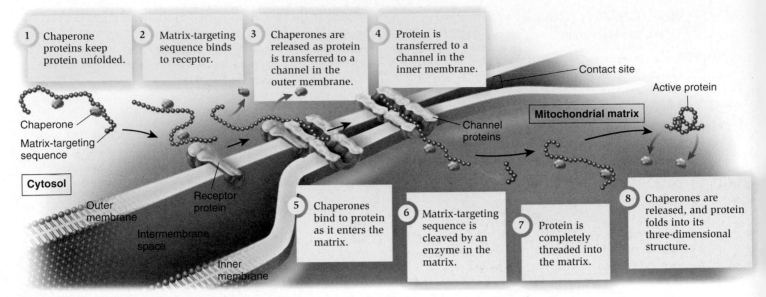

Figure 4.31 Post-translational sorting of a protein to the mitochondrial matrix.

Concept Check: What do you think would happen if chaperone proteins did not bind to a mitochondrial matrix protein before it was imported into the mitochondrion?

a vesicle membrane depends on the type of cargo it carries. After a vesicle is released from one compartment, such as the ER, the coat is shed. The vesicle then travels through the cytosol. But how does the vesicle know where to go? The answer is that the V-snares in the vesicle membrane are recognized by T-snares in a target membrane. After V-snares recognize T-snares, the vesicle fuses with the membrane containing the T-snares. The recognition between V-snares and T-snares ensures that a vesicle carrying a specific cargo moves to the correct target membrane in the cell. Like the sorting of proteins to the ER membrane, the formation and sorting of vesicles also involves a series of protein-protein interactions that cause the steps to occur in a defined manner.

Proteins Are Sorted Post-Translationally to the Nucleus, Peroxisomes, Mitochondria, and Chloroplasts

The organization and function of the nucleus, peroxisomes, mitochondria, and chloroplasts depend on the uptake of proteins from the cytosol. Most of their proteins are synthesized in the cytosol and then taken up into their respective organelles. For example, most proteins involved in ATP synthesis are made in the cytosol and taken up into mitochondria after they have been completely synthesized. For this to occur, a protein must have the appropriate sorting signal as part of its amino acid sequence.

As one example of post-translational sorting, let's consider how a protein is directed to the mitochondrial matrix. Such a protein has a short amino acid sequence at the N-terminus called a matrix-targeting sequence. As shown in **Figure 4.31**, the process of protein import into the matrix involves a series of intricate protein-protein interactions. A protein destined for the mitochondrial matrix is first made in the cytosol, where proteins called **chaperones** keep it in an unfolded state. A receptor protein in the outer mitochondrial

membrane recognizes the matrix-targeting sequence. The protein is released from the chaperone as it is transferred to a channel in the outer mitochondrial membrane. Because it is in an unfolded state, the mitochondrial protein can be threaded through this channel, and then through another channel in the inner mitochondrial membrane. These channels lie close to each other at contact sites between the outer and inner membranes. As the protein emerges in the matrix, other chaperone proteins already in the matrix continue to keep it unfolded. Eventually, the matrix-targeting sequence is cleaved, and the entire protein is threaded into the matrix. At this stage, the chaperone proteins are released, and the protein can fold into its three-dimensional active structure.

4.7 Systems Biology of Cells: A Summary

Learning Outcomes:

1. Outline the differences in complexity among bacteria, animal, and plant cells.
2. Describe how a eukaryotic cell can be viewed as four interacting systems: the nucleus, cytosol, endomembrane system, and semiautonomous organelles.

We will conclude this chapter by reviewing cell structure and function from a perspective called **systems biology**, the study of how new properties of life arise by complex interactions of its components. The "system" being studied can be anything from a metabolic pathway to a cell, an organ, or even an entire organism. In this section, we view the cell as a system. First, we will compare prokaryotic and eukaryotic cells as systems, and then examine the four interconnected parts that make up the system that is the eukaryotic cell.

Bacterial Cells Are Relatively Simple Systems Compared to Eukaryotic Cells

Bacterial cells are relatively small and lack the extensive internal compartmentalization characteristic of eukaryotic cells (**Table 4.2**). On the outside, bacterial cells are surrounded by a cell wall, and many species have flagella. Animal cells lack a cell wall, and only certain cell types have flagella or cilia. Like bacteria, plant cells also have cell walls but their chemical composition is different from that of bacterial cells. Plant cells rarely have flagella.

As mentioned earlier in this chapter, the cytoplasm is the region of the cell enclosed by the plasma membrane. Ribosomes are found in the cytoplasm of all cell types. In bacteria, the cytoplasm is a single compartment. The bacterial genetic material, usually a single chromosome, is found in the nucleoid region, which is not surrounded by a membrane. By comparison, the cytoplasm of eukaryotic cells is highly compartmentalized. The cytosol is the area that surrounds many different types of membrane-bound organelles. For example, eukaryotic chromosomes are found in the nucleus that is surrounded by a double membrane. In addition, all eukaryotic cells have an endomembrane system and mitochondria, and plant cells also have chloroplasts.

A Eukaryotic Cell Is a System with Four Interacting Parts

We can view a eukaryotic cell as a system with four interacting parts: the interior of the nucleus, the cytosol, the endomembrane system, and the semiautonomous organelles (**Figure 4.32**). These four regions have their own structure and organization, while also playing a role in the structure and organization of the entire cell.

Nucleus   The nucleus houses the genome. Earlier in this chapter, we learned how the genome plays a key role in producing the proteome through the process of gene expression. The collection of proteins that a cell makes is primarily responsible for the structure and function of the entire cell. Gene regulation, which occurs in the cell nucleus, is very important in producing specific cell types and enabling cells to respond to environmental changes. The collection of filamentous proteins called the nuclear matrix serves to organize and protect the chromosomes within the nucleus.

Cytosol   The cytosol is the region that is enclosed by the plasma membrane but outside the organelles. It is an important coordination center for cell function and organization. Along with the plasma membrane, the cytosol coordinates responses to the environment. Factors in the environment may stimulate signaling pathways in the cytosol that affect the functions of cellular proteins and the regulation of genes in the cell nucleus.

The cytosol also has a large influence on cell structure because it is the compartment where many small molecules are metabolized in the cell. This region receives molecules that are taken up from the environment. In addition, many metabolic pathways for the synthesis and breakdown of cellular molecules are found in the cytosol, and pathways in organelles are often regulated by events there. Most of the proteins that constitute the proteome are made in the cytosol.

A particularly important component of the eukaryotic cell is the cytoskeleton, which provides organization to the cell and facilitates cellular movements. The formation and function of the cytoskeleton is caused by an amazing series of protein-protein interactions. In most cells, the cytoskeleton is a dynamic structure, enabling its composition to respond to environmental and developmental changes.

Endomembrane System   The endomembrane system can be viewed as a smaller system within the confines of the eukaryotic cell. The endomembrane system includes the nuclear envelope, endoplasmic reticulum (ER), Golgi apparatus, lysosomes, vacuoles, peroxisomes,

Table 4.2	A Comparison of Cell Complexity Among Bacterial, Animal, and Plant Cells		
Structures	**Bacteria**	**Animal cells**	**Plant cells**
Extracellular structures			
Cell wall*	Present	Absent	Present
Flagella/cilia	Flagella sometimes present	Cilia or flagella present on certain cell types	Rarely present†
Plasma membrane	Present	Present	Present
Interior structures			
Cytoplasm	Usually a single compartment inside the plasma membrane	Composed of membrane-bound organelles that are surrounded by the cytosol	Composed of membrane-bound organelles that are surrounded by the cytosol
Ribosomes	Present	Present	Present
Chromosomes and their location	Typically one circular chromosome per nucleoid region; a nucleoid region is not a separate compartment.	Multiple linear chromosomes in the nucleus; nucleus is surrounded by a double membrane. Mitochondria also have chromosomes.	Multiple linear chromosomes in the nucleus; nucleus is surrounded by a double membrane. Mitochondria and chloroplasts also have chromosomes.
Endomembrane system	Absent	Present	Present
Mitochondria	Absent	Present	Present
Chloroplasts	Absent	Absent	Present

* Note that the biochemical composition of bacterial cell walls is very different from plant cell walls.
†Some plant species produce sperm cells with flagella, but flowering plants produce sperm within pollen grains that lack flagella.

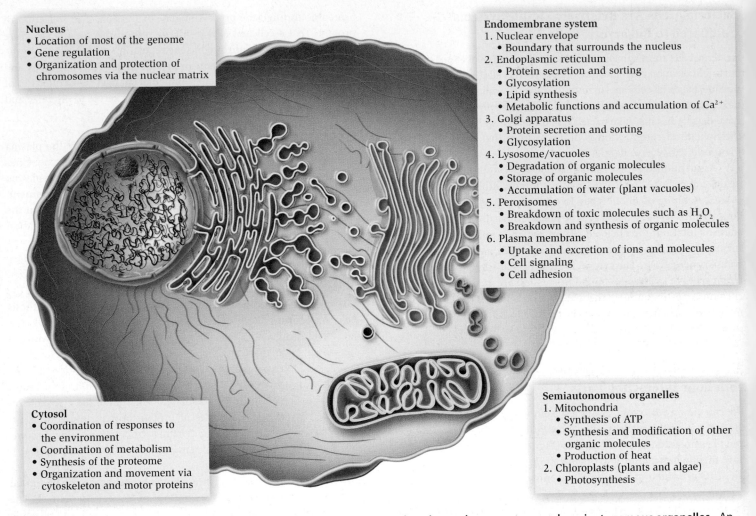

Nucleus
- Location of most of the genome
- Gene regulation
- Organization and protection of chromosomes via the nuclear matrix

Endomembrane system
1. Nuclear envelope
   - Boundary that surrounds the nucleus
2. Endoplasmic reticulum
   - Protein secretion and sorting
   - Glycosylation
   - Lipid synthesis
   - Metabolic functions and accumulation of Ca^{2+}
3. Golgi apparatus
   - Protein secretion and sorting
   - Glycosylation
4. Lysosome/vacuoles
   - Degradation of organic molecules
   - Storage of organic molecules
   - Accumulation of water (plant vacuoles)
5. Peroxisomes
   - Breakdown of toxic molecules such as H_2O_2
   - Breakdown and synthesis of organic molecules
6. Plasma membrane
   - Uptake and excretion of ions and molecules
   - Cell signaling
   - Cell adhesion

Cytosol
- Coordination of responses to the environment
- Coordination of metabolism
- Synthesis of the proteome
- Organization and movement via cytoskeleton and motor proteins

Semiautonomous organelles
1. Mitochondria
   - Synthesis of ATP
   - Synthesis and modification of other organic molecules
   - Production of heat
2. Chloroplasts (plants and algae)
   - Photosynthesis

Figure 4.32 The four interacting parts of eukaryotic cells: nucleus, cytosol, endomembrane system, and semiautonomous organelles. An animal cell is illustrated here.

and plasma membrane. This system forms a secretory pathway that is crucial in the movement of larger substances, such as carbohydrates and proteins, out of the cell. The export of carbohydrates and proteins plays a key role in the organization of materials that surround cells.

The endomembrane system also contributes to the overall structure and organization of eukaryotic cells in other ways. The ER and Golgi are involved in protein sorting and in the attachment of carbohydrates to lipids and proteins. In addition, most of a cell's lipids are made in the smooth ER membrane and distributed to other parts of the cell. The smooth ER also plays a role in certain metabolic functions, such as the elimination of alcohol, and is important in the accumulation of Ca^{2+}.

Another important function of the endomembrane system that serves the needs of the entire cell is the breakdown and storage of organic molecules. Lysosomes in animal cells and vacuoles in the cells of other organisms assist in breaking down various types of macromolecules. The building blocks are then recycled back to the cytosol and used to construct new macromolecules. Vacuoles often play a role in the storage of organic molecules such as carbohydrates, proteins, and fats. In plants, vacuoles may store large amounts of water. Peroxisomes are involved in the breakdown and synthesis of organic molecules and degrade toxic molecules such as hydrogen peroxide.

The plasma membrane is also considered a part of the endomembrane system. It plays an important role as a selective barrier that allows the uptake of nutrients and the excretion of waste products. Proteins in the plasma membrane facilitate the transport of substances into and out of cells. The plasma membrane contains different types of receptors that provide a way for a cell to sense changes in its environment and communicate with other cells. Finally, in animals, proteins in the plasma membrane promote the adhesion of adjacent cells.

Semiautonomous Organelles   The semiautonomous organelles include the mitochondria and chloroplasts. Regarding organization, these organelles tend to be rather independent. They exist in the cytosol much like a bacterium would grow in a laboratory medium. Whereas a bacterium takes up essential nutrients from the growth medium, the semiautonomous organelles take up molecules from the cytosol. The organelles use these molecules to carry out their functions and maintain their organization. Like bacteria, the semiautonomous organelles divide by binary fission to produce more of themselves.

Although the semiautonomous organelles rely on the rest of the cell for many of their key components, they also give back to the cell in ways that are vital to maintaining cell organization. Mitochondria take up organic molecules from the cytosol and give back ATP, which is used throughout the cell to drive processes that are energetically unfavorable. This energy is vital for cell structure and function. Mitochondria also modify certain organic molecules and may produce heat. By comparison, the chloroplasts capture light energy and synthesize organic molecules. These organic molecules store energy and are broken down when energy is needed. In addition, organic molecules, such as sugars and amino acids, are used as building blocks to synthesize many different types of cellular molecules, such as carbohydrate polymers and proteins.

Summary of Key Concepts

4.1 Microscopy

- Three important parameters in microscopy are magnification, resolution, and contrast. A light microscope utilizes light for illumination, whereas an electron microscope uses an electron beam. Transmission electron microscopy (TEM) provides the best resolution of any form of microscopy, and scanning electron microscopy (SEM) produces an image of a three-dimensional surface (Figures 4.1, 4.2, 4.3).

4.2 Overview of Cell Structure

- Cell structure is determined by four factors: matter, energy, organization, and information. Every living organism has a genome. The genes within the genome contain the information to produce cells with particular structures and functions.
- We can classify all forms of life into two categories based on cell structure: prokaryotic and eukaryotic cells.
- Bacteria and archaea have prokaryotic cells with a relatively simple structure that lacks a membrane-enclosed nucleus. Structures in prokaryotic cells include the plasma membrane, cytoplasm, nucleoid region, and ribosomes. Prokaryotic cells also have a cell wall and many have a glycocalyx (Figure 4.4).
- Eukaryotic cells are compartmentalized into organelles and contain a nucleus that houses most of the DNA. The surface area/volume ratio is thought to limit cell size (Figures 4.5, 4.6, 4.7, 4.8).
- The proteome of a cell determines its structure and function.

4.3 The Cytosol

- The cytosol is a central coordinating region for many metabolic activities of eukaryotic cells, including polypeptide synthesis (Figure 4.9).
- The cytoskeleton is a network of three different types of protein filaments: microtubules, intermediate filaments, and actin filaments. Microtubules are important for cell shape, organization, and movement. Intermediate filaments help maintain cell shape, rigidity, and strength. Actin filaments support the plasma membrane and play a key role in cell strength, shape, and movement (Table 4.1, Figures 4.10, 4.11, 4.12, 4.13).

4.4 The Nucleus and Endomembrane System

- The primary function of the nucleus is the organization and expression of the genetic material. A second important function is the assembly of ribosomes in the nucleolus (Figures 4.14, 4.15, 4.16).

- The endomembrane system includes the nuclear envelope, endoplasmic reticulum (ER), Golgi apparatus, lysosomes, vacuoles, peroxisomes, and plasma membrane. The rough endoplasmic reticulum (rough ER) plays a key role in the initial sorting of proteins. The smooth endoplasmic reticulum (smooth ER) functions in metabolic processes such as detoxification, carbohydrate metabolism, accumulation of calcium ions, and synthesis and modification of lipids. The Golgi apparatus performs three overlapping functions: processing, protein sorting, and secretion. Lysosomes degrade macromolecules and help digest substances taken up from outside the cell (endocytosis) and inside the cell (autophagy) (Figures 4.17, 4.18).
- Palade's pulse-chase experiments demonstrated that secreted proteins move sequentially through the ER and Golgi apparatus (Figure 4.19).
- Types and functions of vacuoles include central vacuoles; contractile vacuoles; and phagocytic, or food, vacuoles (Figure 4.20).
- Peroxisomes catalyze a variety of chemical reactions, including those involved with the breakdown of toxic molecules such as hydrogen peroxide, and also typically contain enzymes involved in the metabolism of fats and amino acids. Peroxisomes are made via budding from the ER, followed by maturation and division (Figure 4.21).
- Proteins in the plasma membrane perform many important roles that affect activities inside the cell, including membrane transport, cell signaling, and cell adhesion (Figure 4.22).

4.5 Semiautonomous Organelles

- Mitochondria and chloroplasts are considered semiautonomous because they grow and divide, but they still depend on other parts of the cell for their internal components (Figure 4.23).
- Mitochondria produce most of a cell's ATP, which is utilized by many proteins to carry out their functions. Other mitochondrial functions include the synthesis, modification, and breakdown of cellular molecules and the generation of heat in specialized fat cells (Figure 4.24).
- Chloroplasts, which are found in nearly all species of plants and algae, carry out photosynthesis (Figure 4.25).
- Mitochondria and chloroplasts contain their own genetic material and divide by binary fission (Figure 4.26).
- According to the endosymbiosis theory, mitochondria and chloroplasts originated from bacteria that took up residence in early eukaryotic cells (Figure 4.27).

4.6 Protein Sorting to Organelles

- Eukaryotic proteins are sorted to their correct cellular destination (Figure 4.28).
- The cotranslational sorting of ER, Golgi, lysosomal, vacuolar, plasma membrane, and secreted proteins begins in the cytosol, while translation is occurring, and involves sorting signals and vesicle transport (Figures 4.29, 4.30).
- Most proteins of the nucleus, mitochondria, chloroplasts, and peroxisomes are synthesized in the cytosol and taken up after the protein is completely made; this is called post-translational sorting (Figure 4.31).

4.7 Systems Biology of Cells: A Summary

- Systems biology is the study of how new properties of life arise by complex interactions of its components. In systems biology, the cell is viewed in terms of its structural and functional connections, rather than its individual molecular components.

- Prokaryotic and eukaryotic cells differ in their levels of organization. In eukaryotic cells, four regions—the nucleus, cytosol, endomembrane system, and semiautonomous organelles—work together to produce dynamic organization (Table 4.2, Figure 4.32).

Assess & Discuss

Test Yourself

1. The cell doctrine states that
   a. all living things are composed of cells.
   b. cells are the smallest units of living organisms.
   c. new cells come from pre-existing cells by cell division.
   d. all of the above.
   e. a and b only.

2. When using microscopes, the resolution refers to
   a. the ratio between the size of the image produced by the microscope and the actual size of the object.
   b. the degree to which a particular structure looks different from other structures around it.
   c. how well a structure takes up certain dyes.
   d. the ability to observe two adjacent objects as being distinct from each other.
   e. the degree to which the image is magnified.

3. If a motor protein was held in place and a cytoskeletal filament was free to move, what type of motion would occur when the motor protein was active?
   a. The motor protein would "walk" along the filament.
   b. The filament would move.
   c. The filament would bend.
   d. All of the above would happen.
   e. Only b and c would happen.

4. The process of polypeptide synthesis is called
   a. metabolism.   d. hydrolysis.
   b. transcription.   e. both c and d.
   c. translation.

5. Each of the following is part of the endomembrane system except
   a. the nuclear envelope.
   b. the endoplasmic reticulum.
   c. the Golgi apparatus.
   d. lysosomes.
   e. mitochondria.

6. Vesicle transport occurs between the ER and the Golgi in both directions. Let's suppose a researcher added a drug to cells that inhibited vesicle transport from the Golgi to the ER but did not affect vesicle transport from the ER to the Golgi. If you observed cells microscopically after the drug was added, what would you expect to see happen over the course of 1 hour?
   a. The ER would get smaller, and the Golgi would get larger.
   b. The ER would get larger, and the Golgi would get smaller.
   c. The ER and Golgi would stay the same size.
   d. Both the ER and Golgi would get larger.
   e. Both the ER and Golgi would get smaller.

7. Functions of the smooth endoplasmic reticulum include
   a. detoxification of harmful organic molecules.
   b. metabolism of carbohydrates.
   c. protein sorting.
   d. all of the above.
   e. a and b only.

8. The central vacuole in many plant cells is important for
   a. storage.   d. all of the above.
   b. photosynthesis.   e. a and c only.
   c. structural support.

9. Let's suppose an abnormal protein contains three targeting sequences: an ER signal sequence, an ER retention sequence, and a mitochondrial matrix-targeting sequence. The ER retention sequence is supposed to keep proteins within the ER. Where would you expect this abnormal protein to go? Note: Think carefully about the timing of events in protein sorting and which events occur cotranslationally and which occur post-translationally.
   a. It would go to the ER.
   b. It would go the mitochondria.
   c. It would go to both the ER and mitochondria equally.
   d. It would remain in the cytosol.
   e. It would be secreted.

10. Which of the following observations would not be considered evidence for the endosymbiosis theory?
    a. Mitochondria and chloroplasts have genomes that resemble smaller versions of bacterial genomes.
    b. Mitochondria, chloroplasts, and bacteria all divide by binary fission.
    c. Mitochondria, chloroplasts, and bacteria all have ribosomes.
    d. Mitochondria, chloroplasts, and bacteria all have similar sizes and shapes.
    e. all of the above

Conceptual Questions

1. Describe two specific ways that protein-protein interactions are involved with cell structure or cell function.

2. Explain how motor proteins and cytoskeletal filaments interact to promote three different types of movements: movement of a cargo, movement of a filament, and bending of a filament.

3. A principle of biology is that *structure determines function.* Explain how the invaginations of the inner mitochondrial membrane are related to mitochondrial function.

Collaborative Questions

1. Discuss the roles of the genome and proteome in determining cell structure and function.

2. Discuss and draw the structural relationship between the nucleus, the rough endoplasmic reticulum, and the Golgi apparatus.

Online Resource

www.brookerbiology.com

Stay a step ahead in your studies with animations that bring concepts to life and practice tests to assess your understanding. Your instructor may also recommend the interactive eBook, individualized learning tools, and more.

Membrane Structure, Synthesis, and Transport

5

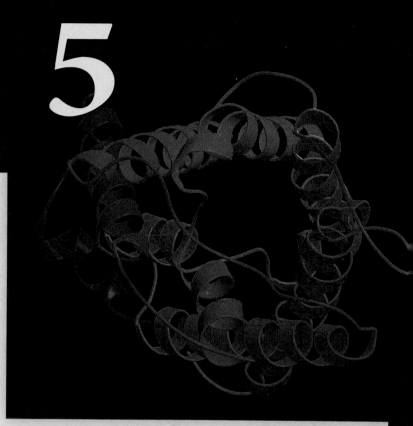

When he was 28, Andrew began to develop a combination of symptoms that included fatigue, joint pain, abdominal pain, and a loss of sex drive. His doctor conducted some tests and discovered that Andrew had abnormally high levels of iron in his body. Iron is a mineral found in many foods. Andrew was diagnosed with a genetic disease called hemochromatosis, which caused him to absorb more iron than he needed. This was due to an overactive protein involved in the transport of iron through the membranes of intestinal cells and into the body. Unfortunately, when the human body takes up too much iron, it is stored in body tissues, especially the liver, heart, pancreas, and joints. The extra iron can damage a person's organs. In Andrew's case, the disease was caught relatively early, and treatment—which includes a modification in diet along with medication that inhibits the absorption of iron—prevented more severe symptoms. Without treatment, however, hemochromatosis can cause organ failure. Later signs and symptoms include skin discoloration, arthritis, liver disease, diabetes mellitus, and heart failure.

The disease hemochromatosis illustrates the importance of membranes in regulating the traffic of ions and molecules into and out of cells. Cellular membranes, also known as biological membranes, are an essential characteristic of all living cells. The **plasma membrane** separates the internal contents of a cell from its external environment. With such a role, you might imagine that the plasma membrane would be thick and rigid. Remarkably, the opposite is true. All cellular membranes, including the plasma membrane, are thin (typically 5–10 nm) and somewhat fluid. It would take 5,000–10,000 membranes stacked on top of each other to equal the thickness of the page you are reading! Despite their thinness, membranes are impressively dynamic structures that effectively maintain the separation between a cell and its surroundings. Membranes provide an interface to carry out many vital cellular activities (**Table 5.1**).

In this chapter, we will begin by considering the components that provide the structure and fluid properties of membranes and then explore how they are synthesized. Finally, we will examine one of a membrane's primary functions—membrane transport. Biological membranes

A model for the structure of aquaporin. This protein, found in the plasma membrane of many cell types, such as red blood cells and plant cells, allows the rapid movement of water molecules across the membrane.

regulate the traffic of substances into and out of the cell and its organelles. As you will learn, this occurs via transport proteins and via exocytosis and endocytosis.

Table 5.1	Important Functions of Cellular Membranes
Function	
Selective uptake and export of ions and molecules	
Cell compartmentalization	
Protein sorting	
Anchoring of the cytoskeleton	
Production of energy intermediates such as ATP and NADPH	
Cell signaling	
Cell and nuclear division	
Adhesion of cells to each other and to the extracellular matrix	

5.1   Membrane Structure

Learning Outcomes:

1. Describe the fluid-mosaic model of membrane structure.
2. Identify the three different types of membrane proteins.
3. Explain the technique of freeze-fracture electron microscopy.

An important biological principle is that *structure determines function*. Throughout this chapter, we will see how the structure of cellular membranes enables them to compartmentalize the cell while selectively importing and exporting vital substances. The two primary components of membranes are phospholipids, which form the basic matrix of a membrane, and proteins, which are embedded in the membrane or loosely attached to its surface. A third component is carbohydrate, which may be attached to membrane lipids and proteins. In this section, we will be mainly concerned with the organization of these components to form a biological membrane and how they are important in the overall function of membranes.

Biological Membranes Are a Mosaic of Lipids, Proteins, and Carbohydrates

Figure 5.1 shows the biochemical organization of a membrane, which is similar in composition among all living organisms. The framework of the membrane is the **phospholipid bilayer**, which consists of two layers of phospholipids. Recall from Chapter 3 that phospholipids are **amphipathic** molecules. They have a hydrophobic (water-fearing) or nonpolar region, and also a hydrophilic (water-loving) or polar region. The hydrophobic tails of the lipids, referred to as fatty acyl tails, are found in the interior of the membrane, and the hydrophilic

heads are on the surface. Biological membranes also contain proteins, and most membranes have carbohydrates attached to lipids and proteins. Overall, the membrane is considered a mosaic of lipid, protein, and carbohydrate molecules. The membrane structure illustrated in Figure 5.1 is referred to as the **fluid-mosaic model**, originally proposed by S. Jonathan Singer and Garth Nicolson in 1972. As discussed later, the membrane exhibits properties that resemble a fluid because lipids and proteins can move relative to each other within the membrane. **Table 5.2** summarizes some of the historical experiments that led to the formulation of the fluid-mosaic model.

Half of a phospholipid bilayer is termed a **leaflet**. Each leaflet faces a different region. For example, the plasma membrane contains a cytosolic leaflet and an extracellular leaflet (see Figure 5.1). With regard to lipid composition, the two leaflets of cellular membranes are highly asymmetrical. Certain types of lipids may be more abundant in one leaflet compared to the other. A striking asymmetry occurs with glycolipids—lipids with carbohydrate attached. These are found primarily in the extracellular leaflet. The carbohydrate portion of a glycolipid protrudes into the extracellular medium.

Proteins Associate with Membranes in Three Different Ways

Although the phospholipid bilayer forms the basic foundation of cellular membranes, the protein component carries out many key functions. Some of these functions were considered in Chapter 4. For example, we saw how membrane proteins in the smooth ER membrane function as enzymes that break down glycogen. Later in this chapter, we will explore how membrane proteins are involved in transporting ions and molecules across membranes. In later chapters, we will examine how membrane proteins are responsible for other functions,

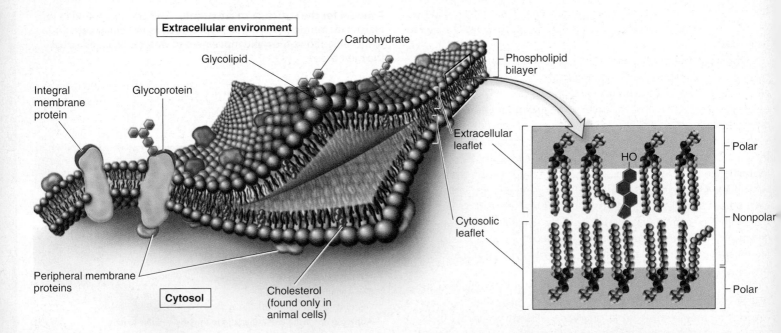

Figure 5.1   Fluid-mosaic model of membrane structure. The basic framework of a plasma membrane is a phospholipid bilayer. Proteins may span the membrane and may be bound on the surface to other proteins or to lipids. Proteins and lipids, which have covalently bound carbohydrates, are called glycoproteins and glycolipids, respectively. The inset shows nine phospholipids and one cholesterol molecule in a bilayer, and it emphasizes the two leaflets and the polar and nonpolar regions of the bilayer.

Table 5.2	Historical Developments That Led to the Formulation of the Fluid-Mosaic Model
Date	**Description**
1917	Irving Langmuir made artificial membranes experimentally by creating a monolayer of lipids on the surface of water. The polar heads interacted with water, and nonpolar tails projected into the air.
1925	Evert Gorter and F. Grendel proposed that lipids form bilayers around cells. This was based on measurements of lipid content enclosing red blood cells that showed there was just enough lipid to surround the cell with two layers.
1950s	Electron microscopy studies carried out by J.D. Robertson and others revealed that membranes look like a train track—two dark lines separated by a light space (look ahead to Figure 5.3a). Researchers determined that the dark lines in these experiments are the phospholipid heads, which were heavily stained, whereas the light region between them is their phospholipid tails.
1966	Using freeze fracture electron microscopy (look ahead to Figure 5.3b), Daniel Branton concluded that membranes are bilayers, because the freeze fracture procedure splits membranes in half, thus revealing proteins in the two membrane leaflets.
1972	S. Jonathan Singer and Garth Nicolson proposed the fluid-mosaic model described in Figure 5.1. Their model was consistent with the observation that membrane proteins are globular, and some are known to span the phospholipid bilayer and project from both sides.

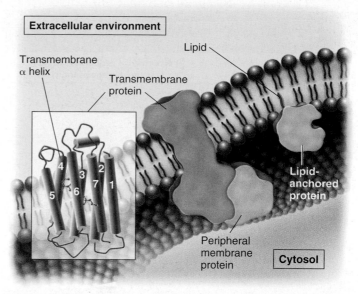

Figure 5.2 Types of membrane proteins. Integral membrane proteins are of two types: transmembrane proteins and lipid-anchored proteins. Peripheral membrane proteins are noncovalently bound to the hydrophilic regions of integral membrane proteins or to the polar head groups of lipids. Inset: The protein bacteriorhodopsin contains seven transmembrane segments, depicted as cylinders, in an α helix structure. Bacteriorhodopsin is found in halophilic (salt-loving) archaea.

including ATP synthesis (Chapter 7), photosynthesis (Chapter 8), cell signaling (Chapter 9), and cell-to-cell adhesion (Chapter 10).

Membrane proteins have three different ways of associating with a membrane (**Figure 5.2**). An **integral membrane protein** cannot be released from the membrane unless the membrane is dissolved with an organic solvent or detergent—in other words, you have to disrupt the integrity of the membrane to remove it. An integral membrane protein can associate with a membrane in two ways. **Transmembrane proteins**, the most common type, have one or more regions that are physically inserted into the hydrophobic interior of the phospholipid bilayer. These regions, the transmembrane segments, are stretches of nonpolar amino acids that span or traverse the membrane from one leaflet to the other. In most transmembrane proteins, each transmembrane segment is folded into an α helix structure. Such a segment is stable in a membrane because the nonpolar amino acids interact favorably with the hydrophobic fatty acyl tails of the lipid molecules.

A second type of integral membrane protein is a **lipid-anchored protein**. This type of protein associates with a membrane because it has a lipid molecule that is covalently attached to an amino acid side chain within the protein. The fatty acyl tails are inserted into the hydrophobic portion of the membrane and thereby keep the protein firmly attached to the membrane.

Peripheral membrane proteins, also called extrinsic proteins, represent a third way that proteins can associate with membranes. They do not interact with the hydrophobic interior of the phospholipid bilayer. Instead, they are noncovalently bound to regions of integral membrane proteins that project out from the membrane (see Figure 5.2), or they are bound to the polar head groups of phospholipids. Peripheral membrane proteins are typically bound to the membrane by hydrogen and/or ionic bonds.

GENOMES & PROTEOMES CONNECTION

Approximately 25% of All Genes Encode Transmembrane Proteins

Membrane proteins participate in some of the most important cellular processes, including transport, energy transduction, cell signaling, secretion, cell recognition, metabolism, and cell-to-cell contact. Research studies have revealed that cells devote a sizeable fraction of their energy and metabolic machinery to the synthesis of membrane proteins. These proteins are particularly important in human medicine—approximately 70% of all medications exert their effects by binding to membrane proteins. Examples include the drugs aspirin, ibuprofen, and acetaminophen, which are widely used to relieve pain and inflammatory conditions such as arthritis. These drugs bind to cyclooxygenase, a protein in the ER membrane that is necessary for the synthesis of chemicals that play a role in pain sensation and inflammation.

Because membrane proteins are so important biologically and medically, researchers have analyzed the genomes of many species and asked the question, "What percentage of genes encodes transmembrane proteins?" To answer this question, they have developed tools to predict the likelihood that a gene encodes a transmembrane protein. For example, the occurrence of transmembrane α helices can be predicted from the amino acid sequence of a protein. All 20 amino acids can be ranked according to their tendency to enter a hydrophobic or hydrophilic environment. With these values, the amino acid sequence of a protein can be analyzed using computer software to determine the average hydrophobicity of short amino acid sequences within the protein. A stretch of 18 to 20 amino acids in an α helix is long enough to span the membrane. If such a stretch contains a high percentage of hydrophobic amino acids, it is predicted to be a

Table 5.3	Estimated Percentage of Genes That Encode Transmembrane Proteins*
Organism	**Percentage of genes that encode transmembrane proteins**
Archaea	
Archaeoglobus fulgidus	24.2
Methanococcus jannaschii	20.4
Pyrococcus horikoshii	29.9
Bacteria	
Escherichia coli	29.9
Bacillus subtilis	29.2
Haemophilus influenzae	25.3
Eukaryotes	
Homo sapiens	29.7
Drosophila melanogaster	24.9
Arabidopsis thaliana	30.5
Saccharomyces cerevisiae	28.2

* Data from Stevens and Arkin (2000) Do more complex organisms have a greater proportion of membrane proteins in their genomes? *Proteins* 39: 417–420. Although the numbers may vary due to different computer programs and estimation techniques, the same general trends have been observed in other similar studies.

transmembrane α helix. However, such computer predictions must eventually be verified by experimentation.

Using a computer approach, many research groups have attempted to calculate the percentage of genes that encode transmembrane proteins in various species. **Table 5.3** shows the results of one such study. The estimated percentage of transmembrane proteins is substantial: 20–30% of all genes may encode transmembrane proteins. This trend is found throughout all domains of life, including archaea, bacteria, and eukaryotes. For example, about 30% of human genes encode transmembrane proteins. With a genome size of 20,000 to 25,000 different genes, the total number of genes that encode different transmembrane proteins is estimated to be 6,000 to 7,500. The functions of many of them have yet to be determined. Identifying their functions will help researchers gain a better understanding of human biology. Likewise, medical researchers and pharmaceutical companies are interested in the identification of new transmembrane proteins that could be targets for effective new medications.

Membrane Structure Can Be Viewed with an Electron Microscope

Electron microscopy, discussed in Chapter 4, is a valuable tool to probe membrane structure and function. In transmission electron microscopy (TEM), a biological sample is thin sectioned and stained with heavy-metal dyes such as osmium tetroxide. This compound binds tightly to the polar head groups of phospholipids, but it does not bind well to the fatty acyl tails. As shown in **Figure 5.3a**, membranes stained with osmium tetroxide resemble a railroad track. Two thin dark lines, which are the stained polar head groups, are separated by a

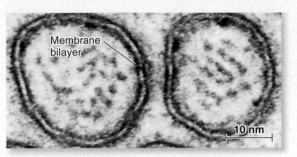

(a) Transmission electron microscopy (TEM)

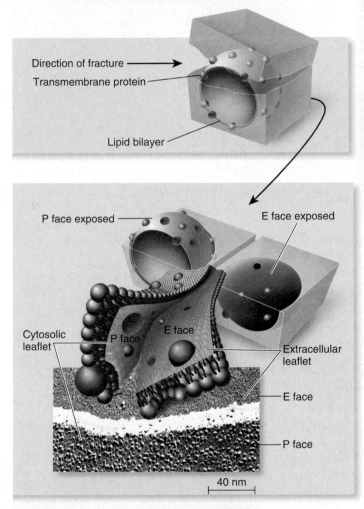

(b) Freeze fracture electron microscopy (FFEM)

Figure 5.3 Electron micrographs of a biological membrane. **(a)** In the standard form of TEM, a membrane appears as two dark parallel lines. These lines are the lipid head groups, which stain darkly with osmium tetroxide. The fatty acyl tails do not stain well and appear as a light region sandwiched between the dark lines. **(b)** In the technique of freeze fracture electron microscopy (FFEM), a sample is frozen in liquid nitrogen and fractured. The sample is then coated with metal and viewed under the electron microscope.

Concept Check: *If a heavy metal labeled the hydrophobic tails rather than the polar head groups (as osmium tetroxide does), do you think you would see a bilayer (that is, a railroad track) under TEM?*

uniform light space about 2 nm thick. This railroad track morphology is seen when cell membranes are subjected to electron microscopy.

A specialized form of TEM, freeze fracture electron microscopy (FFEM), is used to analyze the interiors of phospholipid bilayers. Russell Steere invented this method in 1957. In FFEM, a sample is frozen in liquid nitrogen and split with a knife (**Figure 5.3b**). The knife does not actually cut through the bilayer, but it fractures the frozen sample. Due to the weakness of the central membrane region, the leaflets separate into a P face (the protoplasmic face that was next to the cytosol) and the E face (the extracellular face). Most transmembrane proteins do not break in half. They remain embedded within one of the leaflets, usually in the P face. The samples, which are under a vacuum, are then sprayed with a heavy metal such as platinum, which coats the sample and reveals architectural features within each leaflet. When viewed with an electron microscope, membrane proteins are visible as bumps that provide significant three-dimensional detail about their form and shape.

5.2   Fluidity of Membranes

Learning Outcomes:

1. Describe the fluidity of membranes.
2. Analyze how membrane fluidity is affected by lipid composition.

Let's now turn our attention to the dynamic properties of membranes. Although a membrane provides a critical interface between a cell and its environment, it is not a solid, rigid structure. Rather, biological membranes exhibit properties of **fluidity**, which means that individual molecules remain in close association yet have the ability to readily move within the membrane. In this section, we will examine the fluid properties of biological membranes.

Membranes Are Semifluid

Though membranes are often described as fluid, it is more appropriate to say they are **semifluid**. In a fluid substance, molecules can move in three dimensions. By comparison, most phospholipids can rotate freely around their long axes and move laterally within the membrane leaflet (**Figure 5.4a**). This type of motion is considered two-dimensional, which means it occurs within the plane of the membrane. Because rotational and lateral movements keep the fatty acyl tails within the hydrophobic interior, such movements are energetically favorable. At 37°C, a typical lipid molecule exchanges places with its neighbors about 10^7 times per second, and it can move several micrometers per second. At this rate, a lipid can traverse the length of a bacterial cell (approximately 1 μm) in only 1 second and the length of a typical animal cell in 10 to 20 seconds.

In contrast to rotational and lateral movements, the "flip-flop" of lipids from one leaflet to the opposite leaflet does not occur spontaneously. Flip-flop is energetically unfavorable because the hydrophilic polar head of a phospholipid would have to travel through the hydrophobic interior of the membrane. How are lipids moved from one leaflet to the other? The transport of lipids between leaflets requires the action of the enzyme flippase, which requires energy input in the form of ATP (**Figure 5.4b**).

Although most lipids diffuse rotationally and laterally within the plane of the lipid bilayer, researchers have discovered that certain types of lipids in animal cells tend to strongly associate with each other to form structures called lipid rafts. As the term raft suggests, a **lipid raft** is a group of lipids that float together as a unit within a larger sea of lipids. Lipid rafts have a lipid composition that differs from the surrounding membrane. For example, they usually have a high amount of cholesterol. In addition, lipid rafts may contain unique sets of lipid-anchored proteins and transmembrane proteins.

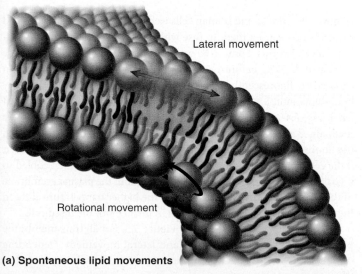

(a) Spontaneous lipid movements

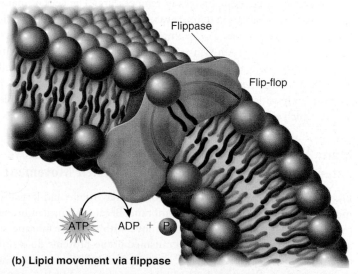

(b) Lipid movement via flippase

Figure 5.4   Semifluidity of the lipid bilayer.   (a) Spontaneous movements in the bilayer. Lipids can rotate (that is, move 360°) and move laterally (for example, from left to right in the plane of the bilayer). **(b)** Flip-flop does not happen spontaneously, because the polar head group would have to pass through the hydrophobic region of the bilayer. Instead, the enzyme flippase uses ATP to flip phospholipids from one leaflet to the other.

Concept Check: *In an animal cell, how can changes in lipid composition affect membrane fluidity?*

The functional importance of lipid rafts is the subject of a large amount of current research. Lipid rafts may play an important role in endocytosis (discussed later in this chapter) and cell signaling.

Lipid Composition Affects Membrane Fluidity

The biochemical properties of phospholipids affect the fluidity of the phospholipid bilayer. One key factor is the length of fatty acyl tails, which range from 14 to 24 carbon atoms, with 18 to 20 carbons being the most common. Shorter acyl tails are less likely to interact with each other, which makes the membrane more fluid.

A second important factor is the presence of double bonds in the acyl tails. When a double bond is present, the lipid is said to be **unsaturated** with respect to the number of hydrogens that are bound to the carbon atoms (refer back to Figure 3.10). A double bond creates a kink in the fatty acyl tail (see inset to Figure 5.1), making it more difficult for neighboring tails to interact and making the bilayer more fluid. As described in Chapter 3, unsaturated lipids tend to be more liquid than saturated lipids, which often form solids at room temperature (refer back to Figure 3.11).

A third factor affecting fluidity is the presence of cholesterol, a short and rigid molecule produced by animal cells (see inset to Figure 5.1). Plant cell membranes contain phytosterols that resemble cholesterol in their chemical structure. Cholesterol tends to stabilize membranes; its effects depend on temperature. At higher temperatures, such as those observed in mammals that maintain a constant body temperature, cholesterol makes the membrane less fluid. At lower temperatures, such as icy water, cholesterol has the opposite effect. It makes the membrane more fluid and prevents it from freezing.

An optimal level of bilayer fluidity is essential for normal cell function, growth, and division. If a membrane is too fluid, which may occur at higher temperatures, it can become leaky. However, if a membrane becomes too solid, which may occur at lower temperatures, the functioning of membrane proteins will be inhibited. How can organisms cope with changes in temperature? The cells of many species adapt to changes in temperature by altering the lipid composition of their membranes. For example, when the water temperature drops, the cells of certain fish will incorporate more cholesterol in their membranes, making the membrane more fluid. If a plant cell is exposed to high temperatures for many hours or days, it will alter its lipid composition to have longer fatty acyl tails and fewer double bonds, which will make the membrane less fluid.

Many Transmembrane Proteins Can Rotate and Move Laterally, But Some Are Restricted in Their Movement

Like lipids, many transmembrane proteins may rotate and laterally move throughout the plane of a membrane. Because transmembrane proteins are larger than lipids, they move within the membrane at a much slower rate. Flip-flop of transmembrane proteins does not occur, because the proteins also contain hydrophilic regions that project out from the phospholipid bilayer, and it would be energetically unfavorable for the hydrophilic regions of membrane proteins to pass through the hydrophobic portion of the phospholipid bilayer.

In 1970, Larry Frye and Michael Edidin conducted an experiment that verified the lateral movement of transmembrane proteins

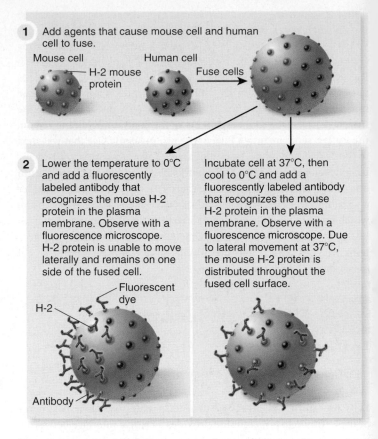

1 Add agents that cause mouse cell and human cell to fuse.

Mouse cell   Human cell

H-2 mouse protein   Fuse cells

2 Lower the temperature to 0°C and add a fluorescently labeled antibody that recognizes the mouse H-2 protein in the plasma membrane. Observe with a fluorescence microscope. H-2 protein is unable to move laterally and remains on one side of the fused cell.

Incubate cell at 37°C, then cool to 0°C and add a fluorescently labeled antibody that recognizes the mouse H-2 protein in the plasma membrane. Observe with a fluorescence microscope. Due to lateral movement at 37°C, the mouse H-2 protein is distributed throughout the fused cell surface.

Fluorescent dye

H-2

Antibody

Figure 5.5 **A method to measure the lateral movement of membrane proteins.**

BIOLOGY PRINCIPLE Biology is an experimental science. This experiment verified that membrane proteins can diffuse laterally within the plane of the lipid bilayer.

Concept Check: *Explain why the H-2 proteins are found on only one side of the cell when the cells were incubated at 0°C.*

(**Figure 5.5**). Mouse and human cells were mixed together and exposed to agents that caused them to fuse with each other to produce mouse-human cell hybrids. Some cells were cooled to 0°C, while others were incubated at 37°C before being cooled. Both sets of cells were then exposed to fluorescently labeled antibodies that became specifically bound to a mouse transmembrane protein called H-2. The fluorescent label was observed with a fluorescence microscope. If the cells were maintained at 0°C, a temperature that greatly inhibits lateral movement, the fluorescence was seen on only one side of the fused cell. However, if the cells were incubated for several hours at 37°C and then cooled to 0°C, the fluorescence was distributed throughout the plasma membrane of the fused cell. This occurred because the higher temperature allowed the lateral movement of the H-2 protein throughout the fused cell.

Unlike the example shown in Figure 5.5, not all transmembrane proteins are capable of rotational and lateral movement. Depending on the cell type, 10–70% of membrane proteins may be restricted in their movement. Transmembrane proteins may be bound to components of the cytoskeleton, which restricts the proteins from moving (**Figure 5.6**), or may be attached to molecules that are outside the cell, such as the interconnected network of proteins that forms the extracellular matrix of animal cells (see Chapter 10).

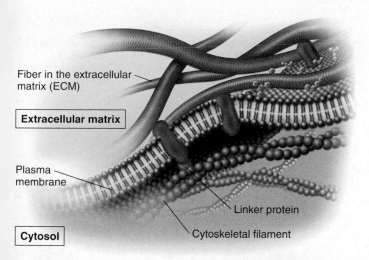

Fiber in the extracellular matrix (ECM)

Extracellular matrix

Plasma membrane

Linker protein

Cytoskeletal filament

Cytosol

Figure 5.6 Attachment of transmembrane proteins to the cytoskeleton and extracellular matrix of an animal cell. Some transmembrane proteins have regions that extend into the cytosol and are anchored to large cytoskeletal filaments via linker proteins. Being bound to these large filaments restricts the movement of these proteins. Similarly, some transmembrane proteins are bound to large, immobile fibers in the extracellular matrix, which restricts their movements.

BioConnections: *Look ahead to Figure 10.8. Discuss how transmembrane proteins are important in the binding of cells to each other and the binding of cells to the extracellular matrix.*

5.3 Synthesis of Membrane Components in Eukaryotic Cells

Learning Outcomes:
1. Outline the synthesis of lipids at the ER membrane.
2. Explain how transmembrane proteins are inserted into the ER membrane.
3. Describe the process of glycosylation and its functional consequences.

As we have seen, cellular membranes are composed of lipids, proteins, and carbohydrates. Most of the membrane components of eukaryotic cells are made at the endoplasmic reticulum (ER). In this section, we will begin by considering how phospholipids are synthesized at the ER membrane. We will then examine the process by which transmembrane proteins are inserted into the ER membrane and explore how some proteins are glycosylated.

Lipid Synthesis Occurs at the ER Membrane

In eukaryotic cells, the cytosol and endomembrane system work together to synthesize most lipids. This process occurs at the cytosolic leaflet of the smooth ER membrane. **Figure 5.7** shows a simplified pathway for the synthesis of phospholipids. The building blocks for a phospholipid are two fatty acids, each with an acyl tail, one glycerol molecule, one phosphate, and a polar head group. These building blocks are made via enzymes in the cytosol, or they are taken into cells from food. To begin the process of phospholipid synthesis, the fatty acids are activated by attachment to an organic molecule called

coenzyme A (CoA). This activation promotes the bonding of the two fatty acids to a glycerol-phosphate molecule, and the resulting molecule is inserted into the cytosolic leaflet of the ER membrane. The phosphate is removed from glycerol, and then a polar molecule already linked to phosphate is attached to glycerol. In the example shown in Figure 5.7, the polar head group contains choline, but many other types are possible. Phospholipids are initially inserted into the cytosolic leaflet. Flippases in the ER membrane transfer some of the newly made lipids to the other leaflet so similar amounts of lipids are found in both leaflets.

The lipids made in the ER membrane are transferred to other membranes in the cell by a variety of mechanisms. Phospholipids in the ER can diffuse laterally to the nuclear envelope. In addition, lipids are transported via vesicles to the Golgi, lysosomes, vacuoles, or plasma membrane. A third mode of lipid transfer involves **lipid exchange proteins**, which extract a lipid from one membrane, diffuse through the cell, and insert the lipid into another membrane. Such transfer can occur between any two membranes, even between the endomembrane system and semiautonomous organelles. For example, lipid exchange proteins transfer lipids between the ER and mitochondria. In addition, chloroplasts and mitochondria synthesize certain types of lipids that are transferred from these organelles to other cellular membranes via lipid exchange proteins.

Most Transmembrane Proteins Are First Inserted into the ER Membrane

In Chapter 4, we learned that eukaryotic proteins contain sorting signals that direct them to their proper destination (see Figure 4.28). With the exception of proteins destined for semiautonomous organelles, most transmembrane proteins contain an ER signal sequence that directs them to the ER membrane. If a polypeptide also contains a stretch of 20 amino acids that are mostly hydrophobic and form an α helix, this region will become a transmembrane segment. In the example shown in **Figure 5.8**, the polypeptide contains one such sequence. After the ER signal sequence is removed by signal peptidase (refer back to Figure 4.29), a membrane protein with a single transmembrane segment is the result. Other polypeptides may contain more than one transmembrane segment. Each time a polypeptide sequence contains a stretch of 20 hydrophobic amino acids that forms an α helix, an additional transmembrane segment is synthesized into the membrane. From the ER, membrane proteins can be transferred via vesicles to other regions of the cell, such as the Golgi, lysosomes, vacuoles, or plasma membrane.

Glycosylation of Proteins Occurs in the ER and Golgi Apparatus

Glycosylation refers to the process of covalently attaching a carbohydrate to a lipid or protein. When a carbohydrate is attached to a lipid, a **glycolipid** is created, whereas attachment of a carbohydrate to a protein produces a **glycoprotein**.

What is the function of glycosylation? Though the roles of carbohydrate in cell structure and function are not entirely understood, some functional consequences of glycosylation have emerged. Glycolipids and glycoproteins often play a role in cell surface recognition.

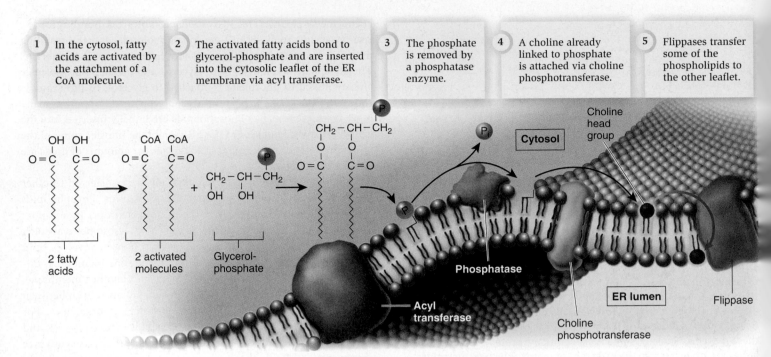

1 In the cytosol, fatty acids are activated by the attachment of a CoA molecule.

2 The activated fatty acids bond to glycerol-phosphate and are inserted into the cytosolic leaflet of the ER membrane via acyl transferase.

3 The phosphate is removed by a phosphatase enzyme.

4 A choline already linked to phosphate is attached via choline phosphotransferase.

5 Flippases transfer some of the phospholipids to the other leaflet.

Figure 5.7 **A simplified pathway for the synthesis of membrane phospholipids at the ER membrane.** Note: Phosphate is abbreviated P when it is attached to an organic molecule and P_i when it is unattached. The subscript i refers to the inorganic form of phosphate.

Concept Check: *How are phospholipids transferred to the leaflet of the ER membrane that faces the ER lumen?*

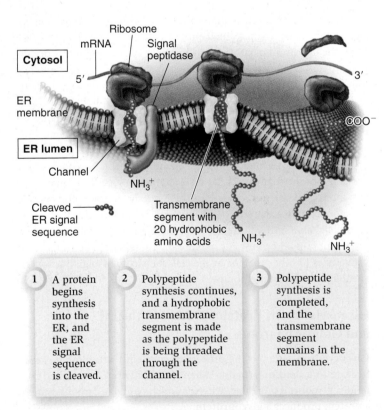

1 A protein begins synthesis into the ER, and the ER signal sequence is cleaved.

2 Polypeptide synthesis continues, and a hydrophobic transmembrane segment is made as the polypeptide is being threaded through the channel.

3 Polypeptide synthesis is completed, and the transmembrane segment remains in the membrane.

Figure 5.8 **Insertion of membrane proteins into the ER membrane.**

Concept Check: *What structural feature of a protein causes a region to form a transmembrane segment?*

When glycolipids and glycoproteins are found in the plasma membrane, the carbohydrate portion is located in the extracellular region. During embryonic development in animals, significant cell movement occurs. Layers of cells slide over each other to create body structures such as the spinal cord and internal organs. The proper migration of individual cells and cell layers relies on the recognition of cell types via the carbohydrates on their cell surfaces.

Carbohydrates often have a protective effect. The carbohydrate-rich zone on the surface of certain animal cells shields the cell from mechanical and physical damage. Similarly, the carbohydrate portion of glycosylated proteins protects them from the harsh conditions of the extracellular environment and degradation by extracellular proteases, which are enzymes that digest proteins.

Two forms of protein glycosylation occur in eukaryotes: N-linked and O-linked. N-linked glycosylation, which also occurs in archaea, involves the attachment of a carbohydrate to the amino acid asparagine in a polypeptide chain. It is called N-linked because the carbohydrate attaches to a nitrogen atom of the asparagine side chain. For this to occur, a group of 14 sugar molecules are built onto a lipid called dolichol, which is found in the ER membrane. This carbohydrate tree is then transferred to an asparagine as a polypeptide is synthesized into the ER lumen through a channel protein (**Figure 5.9**). It attaches only to asparagines occurring in the sequence asparagine–X–threonine or asparagine–X–serine, where X can be any amino acid except proline. An enzyme in the ER, oligosaccharide transferase, recognizes this sequence and transfers the carbohydrate tree from dolichol to the asparagine. Following this initial glycosylation step, the carbohydrate tree is further modified as other enzymes in the ER attach additional sugars or remove sugars. After a glycosylated protein is transferred to the Golgi by vesicle transport, enzymes in the

Golgi usually modify the carbohydrate tree as well. N-linked glycosylation commonly occurs on membrane proteins that are transported to the cell surface.

The second form of glycosylation, O-linked glycosylation, occurs only in the Golgi apparatus. This form involves the addition of a string of sugars to the oxygen atom of serine or threonine side chains in polypeptides. In animals, O-linked glycosylation is important for the production of proteoglycans, which are highly glycosylated proteins that are secreted from cells and help to organize the extracellular

matrix that surrounds cells. Proteoglycans are also a component of mucus, a slimy material that coats many cell surfaces and is secreted into fluids such as saliva. High concentrations of carbohydrates give mucus its slimy texture.

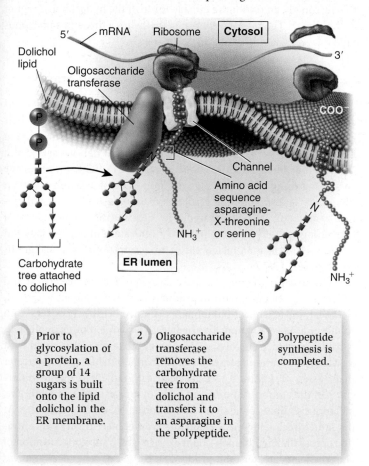

Dolichol lipid · mRNA · Ribosome · Cytosol · Oligosaccharide transferase · COO · Channel · Amino acid sequence asparagine-X-threonine or serine · NH3+ · ER lumen · Carbohydrate tree attached to dolichol · NH3+

1. Prior to glycosylation of a protein, a group of 14 sugars is built onto the lipid dolichol in the ER membrane.

2. Oligosaccharide transferase removes the carbohydrate tree from dolichol and transfers it to an asparagine in the polypeptide.

3. Polypeptide synthesis is completed.

Figure 5.9 N-linked glycosylation in the endoplasmic reticulum.

5.4 Overview of Membrane Transport

Learning Outcomes:
1. Compare and contrast diffusion, facilitated diffusion, passive transport, and active transport.
2. Explain the process of osmosis and how it affects cell structure.

We now turn to one of the key functions of membranes, **membrane transport**—the movement of ions and molecules across biological membranes. All cells contain a plasma membrane that exhibits **selective permeability**, allowing the passage of some ions and molecules but not others. As a protective envelope, its structure ensures that essential molecules such as glucose and amino acids enter the cell, metabolic intermediates remain in the cell, and waste products exit. The selective permeability of the plasma membrane allows the cell to maintain a favorable internal environment.

Substances can move directly across a membrane in three general ways (Figure 5.10). **Diffusion** occurs when a substance moves from a region of high concentration to a region of lower concentration. Some substances can move directly through a biological membrane via diffusion. In **facilitated diffusion**, a transport protein provides a passageway for a substance to diffuse across a membrane. Diffusion and facilitated diffusion are examples of **passive transport**—the transport of a substance across a membrane that does not require an input of energy. In contrast, a third mode of transport, called **active transport**, moves a substance from an area of low concentration to one of high concentration with the aid of a transport protein. Active transport requires an input of energy from a source such as ATP.

In this section, we will begin with a discussion of how the phospholipid bilayer presents a barrier to the movement of ions and molecules across membranes. We will then consider the concept of gradients across membranes and how such gradients affect the movement of water.

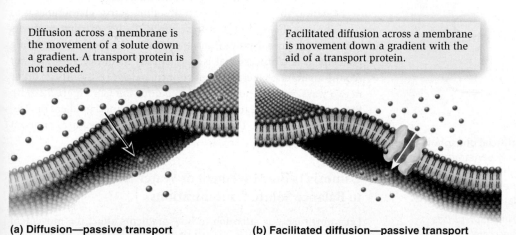
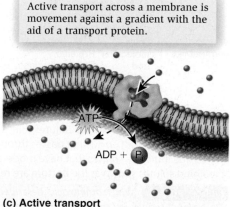

(a) Diffusion across a membrane is the movement of a solute down a gradient. A transport protein is not needed.

(b) Facilitated diffusion across a membrane is movement down a gradient with the aid of a transport protein.

(c) Active transport across a membrane is movement against a gradient with the aid of a transport protein.

ATP · ADP + P

(a) Diffusion—passive transport   (b) Facilitated diffusion—passive transport   (c) Active transport

Figure 5.10 Three general types of membrane transport.

The Phospholipid Bilayer Is a Barrier to the Diffusion of Hydrophilic Solutes

Because of their hydrophobic interiors, phospholipid bilayers are a barrier to the movement of ions and hydrophilic molecules. Such ions and molecules are called **solutes**; they are dissolved in water, which is a solvent. The rate of diffusion across a phospholipid bilayer depends on the chemistry of the solute and its concentration. **Figure 5.11** compares the relative permeabilities of various solutes through an artificial phospholipid bilayer that does not contain any proteins or carbohydrates. Gases and a few small, uncharged molecules can readily diffuse across the bilayer. However, the permeability of ions and larger polar molecules, such as sugars, is relatively low, and the permeability of macromolecules, such as proteins and polysaccharides, is even lower.

When we consider the steps of diffusion among different solutes, the greatest variation occurs in the ability of solutes to enter the hydrophobic interior of the bilayer. As an example, let's compare urea and diethylurea. Diethylurea is much more hydrophobic because it contains two nonpolar ethyl groups ($-CH_2CH_3$) (**Figure 5.12**). For

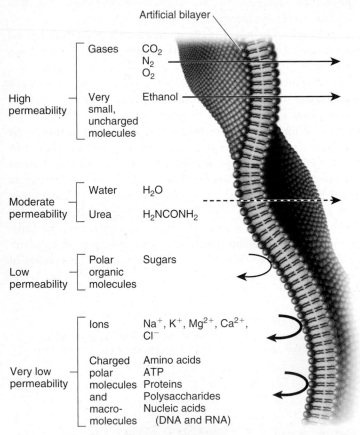

Figure 5.11 **Relative permeability of an artificial phospholipid bilayer to a variety of solutes.** Solutes that easily penetrate are shown with a straight arrow that passes through the bilayer. The dotted line indicates solutes that have moderate permeability. The remaining solutes shown at the bottom are relatively impermeable.

BioConnections: *Which amino acid, described in Chapter 3 (see Figure 3.14), would you expect to cross an artificial membrane more quickly, leucine or lysine?*

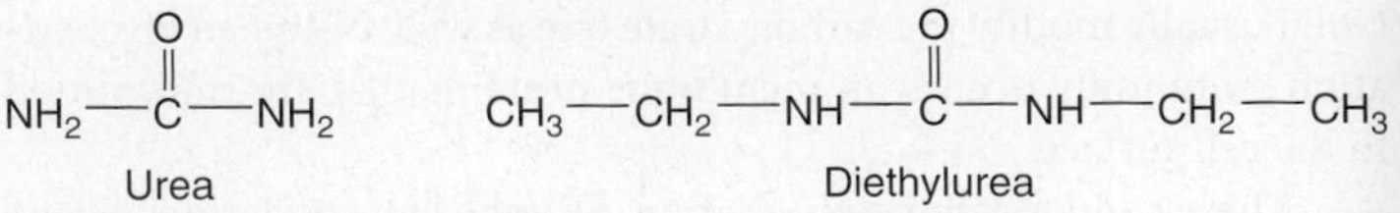

Figure 5.12 **Structures of urea and diethylurea.**

Concept Check: *Which molecule would you expect to pass through a phospholipid bilayer more quickly, methanol (CH_3OH) or methane (CH_4)?*

this reason, it can pass more quickly through the hydrophobic region of the bilayer. The rate of diffusion of diethylurea through a phospholipid bilayer is about 50 times faster than urea.

Cells Maintain Gradients Across Their Membranes

A hallmark of living cells is their ability to maintain a relatively constant internal environment that is distinctively different from their external environment. Solute gradients are formed across the plasma membrane and across organellar membranes. When we speak of a **transmembrane gradient** or **concentration gradient**, we mean the concentration of a solute is higher on one side of a membrane than the other. Transmembrane gradients of solutes are a universal feature of all living cells. For example, immediately after you eat a meal containing carbohydrates, a higher concentration of glucose is found outside your cells than inside; this is an example of a chemical gradient (**Figure 5.13a**).

Gradients involving ions have two components—electrical and chemical. An **electrochemical gradient** is a dual gradient with both electrical and chemical components (**Figure 5.13b**). It occurs with solutes that have a net positive or negative charge. For example, let's consider a gradient involving Na^+. An electrical gradient could exist in which the amount of net positive charge outside a cell is greater than inside. In Figure 5.13b, an electrical gradient is due to differences in the amounts of different types of ions across the membrane, including sodium, potassium, and chlorine (Na^+, K^+, and Cl^-). At the same time, a chemical gradient—a difference in Na^+ concentration across the membrane—could exist in which the concentration of Na^+ outside is greater than inside. The Na^+ electrochemical gradient is composed of both an electrical gradient due to charge differences across the membrane along with a chemical gradient for Na^+.

One way to view the transport of solutes across membranes is to consider how the transport process affects the pre-existing gradients across membranes. Passive transport tends to dissipate a pre-existing gradient. It is a process that is energetically favorable and does not require an input of energy. As mentioned, passive transport can occur in two ways, via diffusion or facilitated diffusion (see Figure 5.10a,b). By comparison, active transport produces a chemical gradient or electrochemical gradient. The formation of a gradient requires an input of energy.

Osmosis Is the Movement of Water Across Membranes to Balance Solute Concentrations

Let's now turn our attention to how gradients affect the movement of water across membranes. When the concentrations of dissolved particles (solutes) on both sides of the plasma membrane are equal,

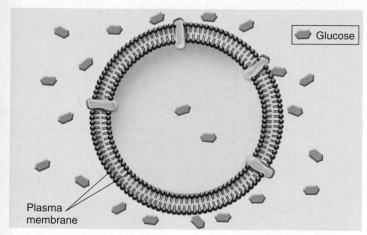

(a) **Chemical gradient for glucose—a higher glucose concentration outside the cell**

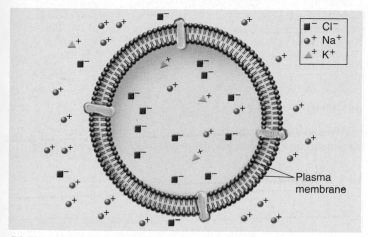

(b) **Electrochemical gradient for Na⁺—more positive charges outside the cell and a higher Na⁺ concentration outside the cell**

Figure 5.13 Gradients across cell membranes.

BioConnections: *Look ahead to Figure 41.10. What types of ion gradients are important for the conduction of an action potential across the plasma membrane of a neuron?*

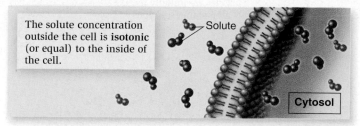

(a) **Outside isotonic**

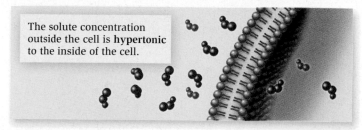

(b) **Outside hypertonic**

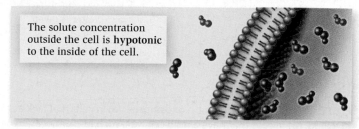

(c) **Outside hypotonic**

Figure 5.14 Relative solute concentrations outside and inside cells.

the two solutions are said to be **isotonic** (**Figure 5.14a**). However, we have also seen that transmembrane gradients commonly exist across membranes. When the concentration of solutes outside the cell is higher, it is said to be **hypertonic** relative to the inside of the cell (**Figure 5.14b**). Alternatively, the outside of the cell could be **hypotonic**—have a lower concentration of solutes relative to the inside (**Figure 5.14c**).

If solutes cannot readily move across the membrane, water will move and tend to balance the solute concentrations. In this process, called **osmosis**, water diffuses across a membrane from the hypotonic compartment (a lower concentration) into the hypertonic compartment (a higher concentration). Animal cells, which are not surrounded by a rigid cell wall, must maintain a balance between the extracellular and intracellular solute concentrations; they are isotonic. Animal cells contain a variety of transport proteins that sense changes in cell volume and allow the necessary movements of solutes across

the membrane to prevent osmotic changes and maintain normal cell shape. However, if animal cells are placed in a hypotonic medium, water will diffuse into them to equalize solute concentrations on both sides of the membrane. In extreme cases, a cell may take up so much water that it ruptures, a phenomenon called osmotic lysis (**Figure 5.15a**). Alternatively, if animal cells are placed in a hypertonic medium, water will exit the cells via osmosis and equalize solute concentrations on both sides of the membrane, causing them to shrink in a process called crenation.

How does osmosis affect cells with a rigid cell wall, such as bacteria, fungi, algae, and plant cells? If the extracellular fluid is hypotonic, a plant cell will take up a small amount of water, but the cell wall prevents osmotic lysis from occurring (**Figure 5.15b**). Alternatively, if the extracellular fluid surrounding a plant cell is hypertonic, water will exit the cell and the plasma membrane will pull away from the cell wall, a process called **plasmolysis**.

Some freshwater microorganisms, such as amoebae and paramecia, are found in extremely hypotonic environments where the external solute concentration is always much lower than the concentration of solutes in their cytosol. Because of the great tendency for water to move into the cell by osmosis, such organisms contain one or more contractile vacuoles to prevent osmotic lysis. A contractile vacuole takes up water from the cytosol and periodically discharges it by fusing the vacuole with the plasma membrane (**Figure 5.16**).

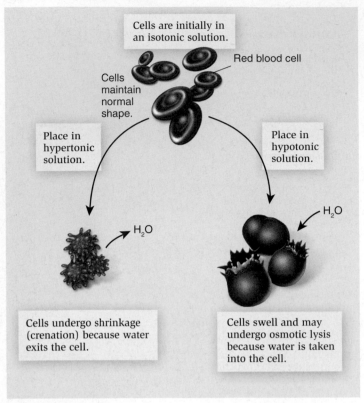

Cells are initially in an isotonic solution.

Red blood cell

Cells maintain normal shape.

Place in hypertonic solution.

Place in hypotonic solution.

H_2O

H_2O

Cells undergo shrinkage (crenation) because water exits the cell.

Cells swell and may undergo osmotic lysis because water is taken into the cell.

(a) Osmosis in animal cells

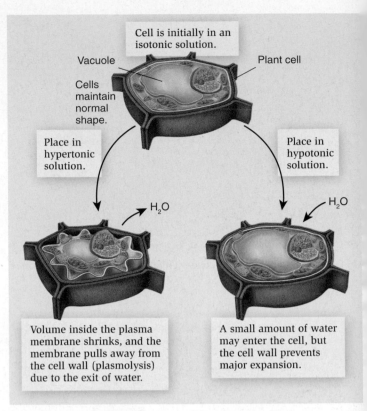

Cell is initially in an isotonic solution.

Vacuole

Plant cell

Cells maintain normal shape.

Place in hypertonic solution.

Place in hypotonic solution.

H_2O

H_2O

Volume inside the plasma membrane shrinks, and the membrane pulls away from the cell wall (plasmolysis) due to the exit of water.

A small amount of water may enter the cell, but the cell wall prevents major expansion.

(b) Osmosis in plant cells

Figure 5.15 The phenomenon of osmosis. **(a)** In cells that lack a cell wall, such as animal cells, osmosis may promote cell shrinkage (crenation) or swelling. **(b)** In cells that have a rigid cell wall, such as plant cells, hypertonic medium causes the plasma membrane to pull away from the cell wall, whereas a hypotonic medium causes only a minor amount of expansion.

Concept Check: *Let's suppose the inside of a cell has a solute concentration of 0.3 M, and the outside is 0.2 M. If the membrane is impermeable to solutes, which direction will water move?*

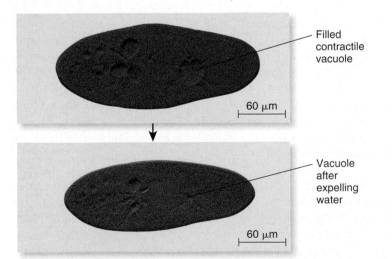

Filled contractile vacuole

60 μm

Vacuole after expelling water

60 μm

Figure 5.16 The contractile vacuole in *Paramecium caudatum*. In the upper photo, a contractile vacuole is filled with water from radiating canals that collect fluid from the cytosol. The lower photo shows the cell after the contractile vacuole has fused with the plasma membrane (which would be above the plane of this page) and released the water from the cell.

BIOLOGY PRINCIPLE Living organisms maintain homeostasis. In this example, the paramecium maintains a relatively constant internal volume by using contractile vacuoles to remove excess water.

5.5 Transport Proteins

Learning Outcomes:
1. Outline the functional differences between channels and transporters.
2. Compare and contrast uniporters, symporters, and antiporters.
3. Explain the difference between primary active transport and secondary active transport.
4. Describe the structure and function of pumps.

Because the phospholipid bilayer is a physical barrier to the diffusion of most hydrophilic molecules and ions, cells can separate their internal contents from the external environment. However, this barrier also poses a potential problem because cells must take up nutrients from the environment and export waste products. How do cells overcome this dilemma? Over the course of millions of years, species have evolved a multitude of **transport proteins**—transmembrane proteins that provide a passageway for the movement of ions and hydrophilic molecules across the phospholipid bilayer. Transport proteins play a central role in the selective permeability of biological membranes. In this section, we will examine the two categories of transport proteins—channels and transporters—based on the manner in which they move solutes across the membrane.

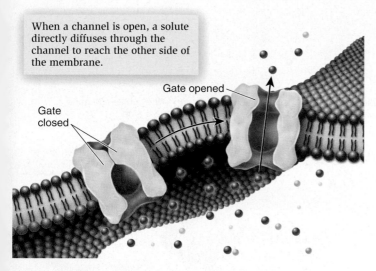

When a channel is open, a solute directly diffuses through the channel to reach the other side of the membrane.

Gate opened

Gate closed

Figure 5.17 Mechanism of transport by a channel protein.

Concept Check: *What is the purpose of gating?*

Channels Provide an Open Passageway for Solute Movement

A **channel** is a transmembrane protein that forms an open passageway for the facilitated diffusion of ions or molecules across the membrane (**Figure 5.17**). Solutes move directly through a channel to get to the other side. When a channel is open, the transmembrane movement of solutes can be extremely rapid, up to 100 million ions or molecules per second!

Most channels are **gated**, which means they open to allow the diffusion of solutes and close to prohibit diffusion. The phenomenon of gating allows cells to regulate the movement of solutes. For example, gating may involve the direct binding of a molecule to the channel protein itself. These gated channels are controlled by the noncovalent binding of small molecules—called ligands—such as hormones or neurotransmitters. The ligands are often important in the transmission of signals between neurons and muscle cells or between two neurons.

FEATURE INVESTIGATION

Agre Discovered That Osmosis Occurs More Quickly in Cells with a Channel That Allows the Facilitated Diffusion of Water

As discussed earlier in this chapter, osmosis is the flow of water to balance solute concentrations. Water can slowly cross biological membranes by diffusion through the phospholipid bilayer. However, in the 1980s, researchers discovered that certain cell types allow water to move across the plasma membrane at a much faster rate than would be predicted by diffusion. For example, water moves very quickly across the membrane of red blood cells, which causes them to shrink and swell in response to changes in extracellular solute concentrations. Likewise, bladder and kidney cells, which play a key role in regulating water balance in the bodies of vertebrates, allow the rapid movement of water across their membranes. Based on these observations, researchers speculated that certain cell types might have channel proteins in their plasma membranes that enable the rapid movement of water.

One approach to characterizing a new protein is to first identify a protein based on its relative abundance in a particular cell type and then attempt to determine the protein's function. This rationale was applied to the discovery of proteins that allow the rapid movement of water across membranes. Peter Agre and his colleagues first identified a protein that was abundant in red blood cells and kidney cells but not found in high amounts in many other cell types. Though they initially did not know the function of the protein, its physical structure was similar to other proteins that were already known to function as channels. They named this protein CHIP28, which stands for channel-forming integral membrane protein with a molecular mass of 28,000 daltons (Da). During the course of their studies, they also identified and isolated the gene that encodes CHIP28.

In 1992, Agre and his colleagues conducted experiments to determine if CHIP28 functions in the transport of water across membranes (**Figure 5.18**). Because they already had isolated the gene that encodes CHIP28, they could make many copies of this gene in a test tube (in vitro) using gene cloning techniques (see Chapter 20). Starting with many copies of the gene in vitro, they added an enzyme to transcribe the gene into mRNA that encodes the CHIP28 protein. This mRNA was then injected into frog oocytes, chosen because frog oocytes are large, easy to inject, and lack pre-existing proteins in their plasma membranes that allow the rapid movement of water. Following injection, the mRNA was translated into CHIP28 proteins that were inserted into the plasma membrane of the oocytes. After allowing sufficient time for this to occur, the oocytes were placed in a hypotonic medium. As a control, oocytes that had not been injected with CHIP28 mRNA were also exposed to a hypotonic medium.

As you can see in the data, a striking difference was observed between oocytes that expressed CHIP28 versus the control. Within minutes, oocytes that contained the CHIP28 protein were seen to swell due to the rapid uptake of water. Three to five minutes after being placed in a hypotonic medium, they actually lysed! By comparison, the control oocytes did not swell as rapidly, and they did not rupture even after 1 hour. Taken together, these results are consistent with the hypothesis that CHIP28 functions as a channel that allows the facilitated diffusion of water across the membrane. Many subsequent studies confirmed this observation. Later, CHIP28 was renamed **aquaporin** to indicate its newly identified function of allowing water to diffuse through a channel in the membrane. More recently, the three-dimensional structure of aquaporin was determined (see chapter opening figure). In 2003, Agre was awarded the Nobel Prize in Chemistry for this work.

Experimental Questions

1. What observations about particular cell types in the human body led to the experimental strategy of Figure 5.18?

2. What were the characteristics of CHIP28 that made Agre and associates speculate that it may transport water? In your own words, briefly explain how they tested the hypothesis that CHIP28 has this function.

3. Explain how the results of the experiment of Figure 5.18 support the proposed hypothesis.

Figure 5.18 The discovery of water channels (aquaporins) by Agre.

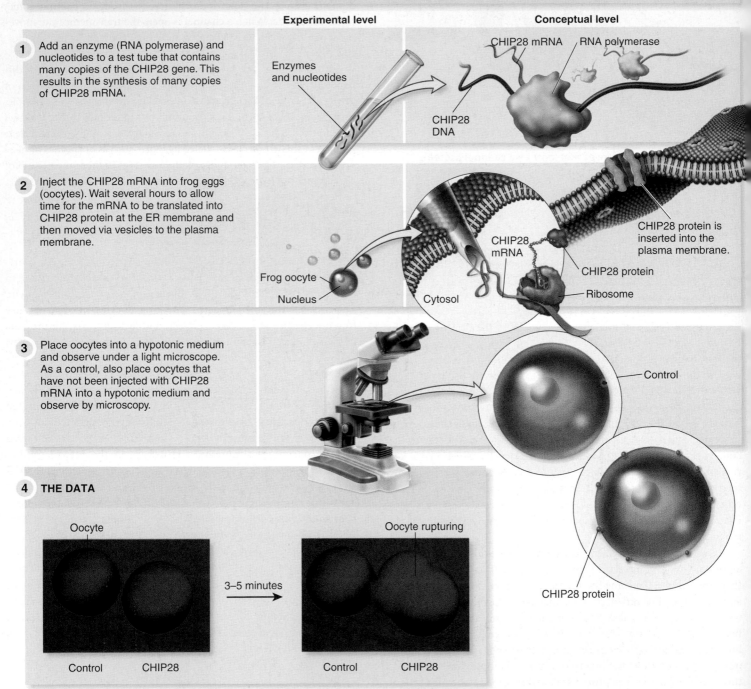

HYPOTHESIS CHIP28 may function as a water channel.

KEY MATERIALS Prior to this work, a protein called CHIP28 was identified that is abundant in red blood cells and kidney cells. The gene that encodes this protein was cloned, which means that many copies of the gene were made in a test tube.

Experimental level   Conceptual level

1 Add an enzyme (RNA polymerase) and nucleotides to a test tube that contains many copies of the CHIP28 gene. This results in the synthesis of many copies of CHIP28 mRNA.

Enzymes and nucleotides

CHIP28 DNA

CHIP28 mRNA   RNA polymerase

2 Inject the CHIP28 mRNA into frog eggs (oocytes). Wait several hours to allow time for the mRNA to be translated into CHIP28 protein at the ER membrane and then moved via vesicles to the plasma membrane.

Frog oocyte

Nucleus

Cytosol

CHIP28 mRNA

CHIP28 protein is inserted into the plasma membrane.

CHIP28 protein

Ribosome

3 Place oocytes into a hypotonic medium and observe under a light microscope. As a control, also place oocytes that have not been injected with CHIP28 mRNA into a hypotonic medium and observe by microscopy.

Control

CHIP28 protein

4 **THE DATA**

Oocyte

3–5 minutes

Oocyte rupturing

Control   CHIP28

Control   CHIP28

5 **CONCLUSION** The CHIP28 protein, now called aquaporin, allows the rapid movement of water across the membrane.

6 **SOURCE** Preston, G.M., Carroll, T.P., Guggino, W.B., and Agre, P. 1992. Appearance of water channels in *Xenopus* oocytes expressing red cell CHIP28 protein. *Science* 256:385–387.

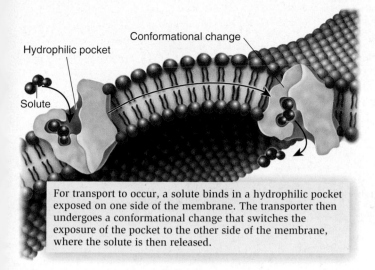

For transport to occur, a solute binds in a hydrophilic pocket exposed on one side of the membrane. The transporter then undergoes a conformational change that switches the exposure of the pocket to the other side of the membrane, where the solute is then released.

Figure 5.19 Mechanism of transport by a transporter, also called a carrier.

BIOLOGY PRINCIPLE Structure determines function. Two structural features—a hydrophilic pocket and the ability to wobble back and forth between two conformations—allow transporters to move ions and molecules across the membrane.

Transporters Bind Their Solutes and Undergo Conformational Changes

Let's now turn our attention to a second category of transport proteins known as **transporters.*** These transmembrane proteins bind their solutes in a hydrophilic pocket and undergo a conformational change that switches the exposure of the pocket from one side of the membrane to the other side (**Figure 5.19**). For example, in 1995, American biologist Robert Brooker and colleagues proposed that a transporter called lactose permease, which is found in the bacterium *E. coli*, has a hydrophilic pocket that binds lactose. They further proposed that the two halves of the transporter protein come together at an interface that moves in such a way that the lactose-binding site alternates between an outwardly accessible pocket and an inwardly accessible pocket, as shown in Figure 5.19. This idea was later confirmed by studies that determined the structure of the lactose permease and related transporters.

Transporters provide the principal pathway for the uptake of organic molecules, such as sugars, amino acids, and nucleotides. In animals, they also allow cells to take up certain hormones and neurotransmitters. In addition, many transporters play a key role in export. Waste products of cellular metabolism must be released from cells before they reach toxic levels. For example, a transporter removes lactic acid, a by-product of muscle cells during exercise. Other transporters, which are involved with ion transport, play an important role in regulating internal pH and controlling cell volume. Transporters tend to be much slower than channels. Their rate of transport is typically 100 to 1,000 ions or molecules per second.

Transporters are named according to the number of solutes they bind and the direction in which they transport those solutes (**Figure 5.20**). **Uniporters** bind a single ion or molecule and transport

* Transporters are also called carriers. However, this term is misleading because transporters do not physically carry their solutes across the membrane.

A single solute moves in one direction.

(a) Uniporter

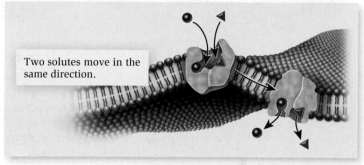

Two solutes move in the same direction.

(b) Symporter

Two solutes move in opposite directions.

(c) Antiporter

Figure 5.20 Types of transporters based on the direction of transport.

it across the membrane. **Symporters** bind two or more ions or molecules and transport them in the same direction. **Antiporters** bind two or more ions or molecules and transport them in opposite directions.

Active Transport Is the Movement of Solutes Against a Gradient

As mentioned, active transport is the movement of a solute across a membrane against its concentration gradient—that is, from a region of low concentration to higher concentration. Active transport is energetically unfavorable and requires an input of energy. **Primary active transport** involves the functioning of a **pump**—a type of transporter that directly uses energy to transport a solute against a concentration gradient. **Figure 5.21a** shows a pump that uses ATP to transport H^+ against a gradient. Such a pump can establish an H^+ electrochemical gradient across a membrane.

Secondary active transport involves the use of a pre-existing gradient to drive the active transport of another solute. For example, an H^+/sucrose symporter uses an H^+ electrochemical gradient,

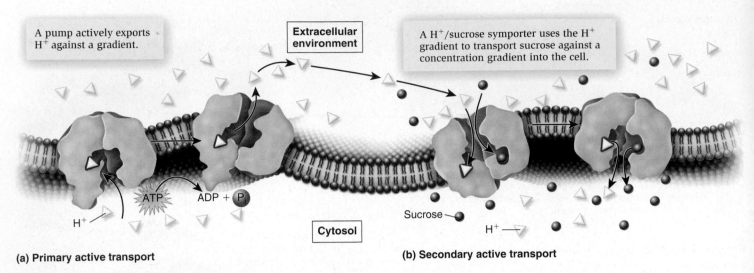

A pump actively exports H$^+$ against a gradient.

Extracellular environment

A H$^+$/sucrose symporter uses the H$^+$ gradient to transport sucrose against a concentration gradient into the cell.

ATP

ADP + P$_i$

H$^+$

Cytosol

Sucrose

H$^+$

(a) Primary active transport

(b) Secondary active transport

Figure 5.21 Types of active transport. (a) During primary active transport, a pump directly uses energy, in this case from ATP, to transport a solute against a concentration gradient. The pump shown here uses ATP to establish an H$^+$ electrochemical gradient. **(b)** Secondary active transport via symport involves the use of this gradient to drive the active transport of a solute, such as sucrose.

established by a pump, to move sucrose against its concentration gradient (**Figure 5.21b**). In this regard, only sucrose is actively transported. Hydrogen ions move down their electrochemical gradient. H$^+$/solute symporters are more common in bacteria, fungi, algae, and plant cells, because H$^+$ pumps are found in their plasma membranes. In animal cells, a pump that exports Na$^+$ maintains a Na$^+$ gradient across the plasma membrane. Na$^+$/solute symporters are prevalent in animal cells.

Symporters enable cells to actively import nutrients against a gradient. These proteins use the energy stored in the electrochemical gradient of H$^+$ or Na$^+$ to power the uphill movement of organic solutes such as sugars, amino acids, and other needed molecules. Therefore, with symporters in their plasma membrane, cells can scavenge nutrients from the extracellular environment and accumulate them to high levels within the cytoplasm.

ATP-Driven Ion Pumps Generate Ion Electrochemical Gradients

The phenomenon of active transport was discovered in the 1940s based on the study of the transport of sodium ions (Na$^+$) and potassium ions (K$^+$). In animal cells, the concentration of Na$^+$ is lower inside the cell than outside, whereas the concentration of K$^+$ is higher inside the cell than outside. After analyzing the movement of these ions across the plasma membrane of muscle cells, neurons, and red blood cells, researchers determined that the export of Na$^+$ is coupled to the import of K$^+$. In the late 1950s, Danish biochemist Jens Skou proposed that a single transporter is responsible for this phenomenon. He was the first to describe an ATP-driven ion pump, which was later named the Na$^+$/K$^+$-ATPase. This pump actively transports Na$^+$ and K$^+$ against their gradients by using the energy from ATP hydrolysis. The plasma membrane of a typical animal cell contains thousands of Na$^+$/K$^+$-ATPase pumps that maintain large concentration gradients in which the concentration of Na$^+$ is

higher outside the cell and the concentration of K$^+$ is higher inside the cell.

Let's take a closer look at the Na$^+$/K$^+$-ATPase that Skou discovered. Every time one ATP is hydrolyzed, the Na$^+$/K$^+$-ATPase functions as an antiporter that pumps three Na$^+$ into the extracellular environment and two K$^+$ into the cytosol (**Figure 5.22a**). Because one cycle of pumping results in the net export of one positive charge, the Na$^+$/K$^+$-ATPase also produces an electrical gradient across the membrane. For this reason, it is called an **electrogenic pump**, because it generates an electrical gradient.

By studying the interactions of Na$^+$, K$^+$, and ATP with the Na$^+$/K$^+$-ATPase, researchers have pieced together a molecular road map of the steps that direct the pumping of ions across the membrane (**Figure 5.22b**). The Na$^+$/K$^+$-ATPase alternates between two conformations, designated E1 and E2. In E1, the ion-binding sites are accessible from the cytosol—Na$^+$ binds tightly to this conformation, whereas K$^+$ has a low affinity. In E2, the ion-binding sites are accessible from the extracellular environment—Na$^+$ has a low affinity, and K$^+$ binds tightly.

To examine the pumping mechanism of the Na$^+$/K$^+$-ATPase, let's begin with the E1 conformation. Three Na$^+$ bind to the Na$^+$/K$^+$-ATPase from the cytosol (Figure 5.22b). When this occurs, ATP is hydrolyzed to ADP and phosphate. Temporarily, the phosphate is covalently bound to the pump, an event called phosphorylation. The pump then switches to the E2 conformation. The three Na$^+$ are released into the extracellular environment, because they have a lower affinity for the E2 conformation. In this conformation, two K$^+$ bind from the outside. The binding of two K$^+$ causes the release of phosphate, which, in turn, causes a switch to E1. Because the E1 conformation has a low affinity for K$^+$ the two K$^+$ are released into the cytosol. The Na$^+$/K$^+$-ATPase is now ready for another round of pumping.

The Na$^+$/K$^+$-ATPase is a critical ion pump in animal cells because it maintains Na$^+$ and K$^+$ gradients across the plasma

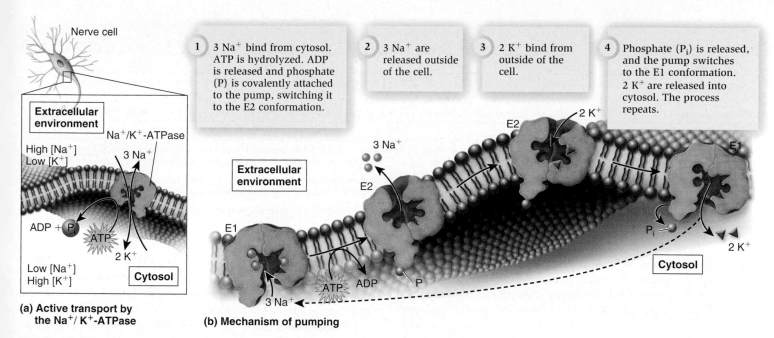

1 3 Na$^+$ bind from cytosol. ATP is hydrolyzed. ADP is released and phosphate (P) is covalently attached to the pump, switching it to the E2 conformation.

2 3 Na$^+$ are released outside of the cell.

3 2 K$^+$ bind from outside of the cell.

4 Phosphate (P$_i$) is released, and the pump switches to the E1 conformation. 2 K$^+$ are released into cytosol. The process repeats.

(a) Active transport by the Na$^+$/K$^+$-ATPase

(b) Mechanism of pumping

Figure 5.22 Structure and function of the Na$^+$/K$^+$-ATPase. **(a)** Active transport by the Na$^+$/K$^+$-ATPase. Each time this protein hydrolyzes one ATP molecule, it pumps out three Na$^+$ and pumps in two K$^+$. **(b)** Pumping mechanism. This figure illustrates the protein conformational changes between E1 and E2. As this occurs, ATP is hydrolyzed to ADP and phosphate. During the process, phosphate is covalently attached to the protein but is released after two K$^+$ bind.

Concept Check: *If a cell contained ATP and Na$^+$, but K$^+$ were missing from the extracellular medium, how far through these steps could the Na$^+$/K$^+$-ATPase proceed?*

membrane. Many other types of ion pumps are also found in the plasma membrane and in organellar membranes. Ion pumps play the primary role in the formation and maintenance of ion gradients that drive many important cellular processes (**Table 5.4**). ATP is commonly the source of energy to drive ion pumps, and cells typically use a substantial portion of their ATP to keep them working. For example, neurons use up to 70% of their ATP just to operate ion pumps!

Table 5.4	Important Functions of Ion Electrochemical Gradients
Function	**Description**
Transport of ions and molecules	Symporters and antiporters use H$^+$ and Na$^+$ gradients to take up nutrients and export waste products (see Figure 5.21).
Production of energy intermediates	In the mitochondrion and chloroplast, H$^+$ gradients are used to synthesize ATP.
Osmotic regulation	Animal cells control their internal volume by regulating ion gradients between the cytosol and extracellular fluid.
Neuronal signaling	Na$^+$ and K$^+$ gradients are involved in conducting action potentials, the signals transmitted by neurons.
Muscle contraction	Ca^{2+} gradients regulate the ability of muscle fibers to contract.
Bacterial swimming	H$^+$ gradients drive the rotation of bacterial flagella.

5.6 Exocytosis and Endocytosis

Learning Outcome:

1. Describe the steps in exocytosis and endocytosis.

We have seen that most small substances are transported via membrane proteins such as channels and transporters, which provide a passageway for the movement of ions and molecules directly across the membrane. Eukaryotic cells have two other mechanisms, exocytosis and endocytosis, to transport larger molecules such as proteins and polysaccharides, and even very large particles. Both mechanisms involve the packaging of the transported substance, sometimes called the cargo, into a membrane vesicle or vacuole. **Table 5.5** describes some examples.

Exocytosis   During **exocytosis**, material inside the cell is packaged into vesicles and then excreted into the extracellular environment (**Figure 5.23**). These vesicles are usually derived from the Golgi apparatus. As the vesicles form, a specific cargo is loaded into their interior. The budding process involves the formation of a protein coat around the emerging vesicle. The assembly of coat proteins on the surface of the Golgi membrane causes the bud to form. Eventually, the bud separates from the membrane to form a vesicle. After the vesicle is released, the coat is shed. Finally, the vesicle fuses with the plasma membrane and releases the cargo into the extracellular environment.

Endocytosis   During **endocytosis**, the plasma membrane invaginates, or folds inward, to form a vesicle that brings substances into

Table 5.5   Examples of Exocytosis and Endocytosis

Exocytosis	Description
Hormones	Certain hormones, such as insulin, are composed of polypeptides. To exert its effect, insulin is secreted via exocytosis into the bloodstream from beta cells of the pancreas.
Digestive enzymes	Digestive enzymes that function in the lumen of the small intestine are secreted via exocytosis from exocrine cells of the pancreas.

Endocytosis	Description
Uptake of vital nutrients	Many important nutrients are very insoluble in the bloodstream. Therefore, they are bound to proteins in the blood and then taken into cells via endocytosis. Examples include the uptake of lipids (bound to low-density lipoprotein) and iron (bound to transferrin protein).
Root nodules	Nitrogen-fixing root nodules found in certain species of plants, such as legumes, are formed by the endocytosis of bacteria. After endocytosis, the bacterial cells are contained within a membrane-enclosed compartment in the nitrogen-fixing tissue of root nodules.
Immune system	Cells of the immune system, known as macrophages, engulf and destroy bacteria via phagocytosis.

the cell. Three types of endocytosis are receptor-mediated endocytosis, pinocytosis, and phagocytosis. In **receptor-mediated endocytosis**, a receptor in the plasma membrane is specific for a given cargo (**Figure 5.24**). Cargo molecules binding to their specific receptors stimulate many receptors to aggregate, and then coat proteins bind to the membrane. The protein coat causes the membrane to invaginate and form a vesicle. Once it is released into the cell, the vesicle sheds its coat. In most cases, the vesicle fuses with an internal membrane organelle, such as a lysosome, and the receptor releases its cargo. Depending on the cargo, the lysosome may release it directly into the cytosol or digest it into simpler building blocks before releasing it.

Other specialized forms of endocytosis occur in certain types of cells. **Pinocytosis** (from the Greek, meaning cell-drinking) involves the formation of membrane vesicles from the plasma membrane as a way for cells to internalize the extracellular fluid. This allows cells to sample the extracellular solutes. Pinocytosis is particularly important in cells that are actively involved in nutrient absorption, such as cells that line the intestine in animals.

Phagocytosis (from the Greek, meaning cell-eating) involves the formation of an enormous membrane vesicle called a phagosome, or phagocytic vacuole, which engulfs a large particle such as a bacterium. Only certain kinds of cells can carry out phagocytosis. For example, macrophages, which are cells of the immune system in mammals, kill bacteria via phagocytosis. Macrophages engulf bacterial cells into phagosomes. Once inside the cell, the phagosome fuses with a lysosome, and the digestive enzymes within the lysosome destroy the bacterium.

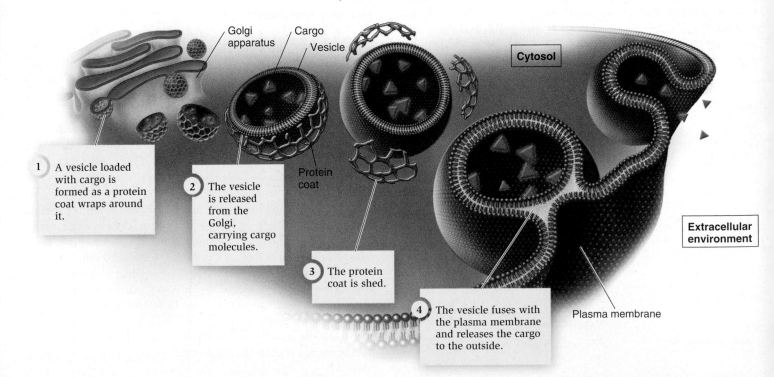

Golgi apparatus   Cargo   Vesicle   **Cytosol**   Protein coat   **Extracellular environment**   Plasma membrane

1 A vesicle loaded with cargo is formed as a protein coat wraps around it.

2 The vesicle is released from the Golgi, carrying cargo molecules.

3 The protein coat is shed.

4 The vesicle fuses with the plasma membrane and releases the cargo to the outside.

Figure 5.23 Exocytosis.

Concept Check: *What is the function of the protein coat?*

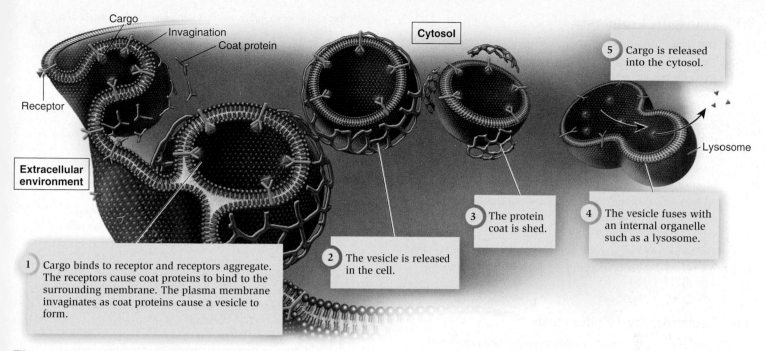

Cargo

Invagination

Coat protein

Cytosol

Receptor

5 Cargo is released into the cytosol.

Extracellular environment

Lysosome

3 The protein coat is shed.

4 The vesicle fuses with an internal organelle such as a lysosome.

1 Cargo binds to receptor and receptors aggregate. The receptors cause coat proteins to bind to the surrounding membrane. The plasma membrane invaginates as coat proteins cause a vesicle to form.

2 The vesicle is released in the cell.

Figure 5.24 Receptor-mediated endocytosis.

Summary of Key Concepts

5.1 Membrane Structure

- A plasma membrane separates a cell from its surroundings. The plasma membrane and organellar membranes provide interfaces for carrying out vital cellular activities (Table 5.1).

- The accepted model of membranes is the fluid-mosaic model, and its basic framework is the phospholipid bilayer. Cellular membranes also contain proteins, and most membranes have attached carbohydrates (Figure 5.1, Table 5.2).

- The three main types of membrane proteins are transmembrane proteins, lipid-anchored proteins, and peripheral membrane proteins. Transmembrane proteins and lipid-anchored proteins are classified as integral membrane proteins. Researchers are working to identify new membrane proteins and their functions because these proteins are important biologically and medically (Figure 5.2, Table 5.3).

- Electron microscopy is a valuable tool for studying membrane structure and function. Freeze fracture electron microscopy (FFEM) is used to analyze the interiors of phospholipid bilayers (Figure 5.3).

5.2 Fluidity of Membranes

- Bilayer semifluidity is essential for normal cell function, growth, and division. Lipids and many proteins can move rotationally and laterally, but the flip-flop of lipids from one leaflet to the opposite does not occur spontaneously. Some membrane proteins are restricted in their movements (Figures 5.4, 5.5, 5.6).

- The chemical properties of phospholipids—such as tail length and the presence of double bonds—and the amount of cholesterol affect the fluidity of membranes.

5.3 Synthesis of Membrane Components in Eukaryotic Cells

- In eukaryotic cells, most membrane phospholipids are synthesized at the cytosolic leaflet of the smooth ER membrane. Flippases move some phospholipids to the other leaflet (Figure 5.7).

- Most transmembrane proteins are first inserted into the ER membrane (Figure 5.8).

- Glycosylation of proteins occurs in the ER and Golgi apparatus (Figure 5.9).

5.4 Overview of Membrane Transport

- Biological membranes exhibit selective permeability. Diffusion occurs when a solute moves from a region of high concentration to a region of lower concentration. Passive transport of a solute across a membrane can occur via diffusion or facilitated diffusion. Active transport is the movement of a substance against a gradient (Figure 5.10).

- The phospholipid bilayer is relatively impermeable to many substances (Figures 5.11, 5.12).

- Living cells maintain an internal environment that is separated from their external environment. Transmembrane gradients are established across the plasma membrane and across organellar membranes (Figure 5.13, Table 5.4).

- In the process of osmosis, water diffuses through a membrane from a solution that is hypotonic (lower concentration of dissolved particles) into a solution that is hypertonic (higher concentration of dissolved particles). Solutions with identical concentrations are isotonic. Some cells have contractile vacuoles to eliminate excess water (Figures 5.14, 5.15, 5.16).

5.5   Transport Proteins

- Two classes of transport proteins are channels and transporters.
- Channels form an open passageway for the direct diffusion of solutes across the membrane. One example is aquaporin, which allows the movement of water. Most channels are gated, which allows cells to regulate the movement of solutes (Figures 5.17, 5.18).
- Transporters, which tend to be slower than channels, bind their solutes in a hydrophilic pocket and undergo a conformational change that switches the exposure of the pocket to the other side of the membrane. They can be uniporters, symporters, or antiporters (Figures 5.19, 5.20).
- Primary active transport involves pumps that directly use energy to generate a solute gradient. Secondary active transport uses a pre-existing gradient (Figure 5.21).
- The Na^+/K^+-ATPase is an electrogenic pump that uses energy in the form of ATP to transport ions across the membrane (Figure 5.22, Table 5.4).

5.6   Exocytosis and Endocytosis

- In eukaryotes, exocytosis and endocytosis are used to transport large molecules and particles. Exocytosis is a process in which material inside the cell is packaged into vesicles and excreted into the extracellular environment. During endocytosis, the plasma membrane folds inward to form a vesicle that brings substances into the cell. Receptor-mediated endocytosis, pinocytosis, and phagocytosis are forms of endocytosis (Figures 5.23, 5.24, Table 5.5).

Assess and Discuss

Test Yourself

1. Which of the following statements best describes the chemical composition of biological membranes?
   a. Biological membranes are bilayers of proteins with associated lipids and carbohydrates.
   b. Biological membranes are composed of two layers—one layer of phospholipids and one layer of proteins.
   c. Biological membranes are bilayers of phospholipids with associated proteins and carbohydrates.
   d. Biological membranes are composed of equal numbers of phospholipids, proteins, and carbohydrates.
   e. Biological membranes are composed of lipids with proteins attached to the outer surface.

2. Which of the following events in a biological membrane would not be energetically favorable and therefore not occur spontaneously?
   a. the rotation of phospholipids
   b. the lateral movement of phospholipids
   c. the flip-flop of phospholipids to the opposite leaflet
   d. the rotation of membrane proteins
   e. the lateral movement of membrane proteins

3. Let's suppose an insect, which doesn't maintain a constant body temperature, was exposed to a shift in temperature from 60°F to 80°F. Which of the following types of membrane changes would be the most beneficial to help this animal cope with the temperature shift?
   a. increase the number of double bonds in the fatty acyl tails of phospholipids
   b. increase the length of the fatty acyl tails of phospholipids
   c. decrease the amount of cholesterol in the membrane
   d. decrease the amount of carbohydrate attached to membrane proteins
   e. decrease the amount of carbohydrate attached to phospholipids

4. Carbohydrates of the plasma membrane
   a. are bonded to a protein or lipid.
   b. are located on the outer surface of the plasma membrane.
   c. can function as cell markers for recognition by other cells.
   d. all of the above
   e. a and c only

5. A transmembrane protein in the plasma membrane is glycosylated at two sites in the polypeptide sequence. One site is Asn—Val—Ser and the other site is Asn—Gly—Thr. Where in this protein would you expect these two sites to be found?
   a. in transmembrane segments
   b. in hydrophilic regions that project into the extracellular environment
   c. in hydrophilic regions that project into the cytosol
   d. could be anywhere
   e. b and c only

6. The tendency for Na^+ to move into the cell could be due to
   a. the higher numbers of Na^+ outside the cell, resulting in a chemical concentration gradient.
   b. the net negative charge inside the cell attracting the positively charged Na^+.
   c. the attractive force of K^+ inside the cell pulling Na^+ into the cell.
   d. all of the above.
   e. a and b only.

7. Let's suppose the solute concentration inside the cells of a plant is 0.3 M and outside is 0.2 M. If we assume that the solutes do not readily cross the membrane, which of the following statements best describes what will happen?
   a. The plant cells will lose water, and the plant will wilt.
   b. The plant cells will lose water, which will result in a higher turgor pressure.
   c. The plant cells will take up a lot of water and undergo osmotic lysis.
   d. The plant cells will take up a little water and have a higher turgor pressure.
   e. Both a and b are correct.

8. What features of a membrane are major contributors to its selective permeability?
   a. phospholipid bilayer
   b. transport proteins
   c. glycolipids on the outer surface of the membrane
   d. peripheral membrane proteins
   e. both a and b

9. What is the name given to the process in which solutes are moved across a membrane against their concentration gradient?
   a. diffusion
   b. facilitated diffusion
   c. osmosis
   d. passive diffusion
   e. active transport

10. Large particles or large volumes of fluid can be brought into the cell by
    a. facilitated diffusion.
    b. active transport.
    c. endocytosis.
    d. exocytosis.
    e. all of the above.

Conceptual Questions

1. With your textbook closed, draw and describe the fluid-mosaic model of membrane structure.

2. Describe two different ways that integral membrane proteins associate with a membrane. How do peripheral membrane proteins associate with a membrane?

3. A principle of biology is that *living organisms interact with their environment*. Discuss how lipid bilayers, channels, and transporters influence the ability of cells to interact with their environment.

Collaborative Questions

1. Proteins in the plasma membrane are often the target of medicines. Discuss why you think this is the case. How would you determine experimentally that a specific membrane protein was the target of a drug?

2. With regard to bringing solutes into the cell across the plasma membrane, discuss the advantages and disadvantages of diffusion, facilitated diffusion, active transport, and endocytosis.

Online Resource

www.brookerbiology.com

Stay a step ahead in your studies with animations that bring concepts to life and practice tests to assess your understanding. Your instructor may also recommend the interactive eBook, individualized learning tools, and more.

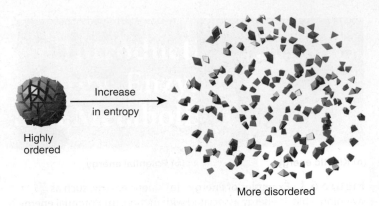

Figure 6.2 **Entropy, a measure of the disorder of a system.** An increase in entropy means an increase in disorder.

Concept Check: *Which do you think has more entropy, a NaCl crystal at the bottom of a beaker of water or the same beaker of water after the Na⁺ and Cl⁻ in the crystal have dissolved in the water?*

promote change or do work (usable energy) and the energy that cannot (unusable energy).

$$\text{Total energy} = \text{Usable energy} + \text{Unusable energy}$$

Why is some energy unusable? The main culprit is entropy. As stated by the second law of thermodynamics, energy transfers or transformations involve an increase in entropy, a degree of disorder that cannot be harnessed in a useful way. The total energy is termed **enthalpy** (**H**), and the usable energy—the amount of available energy that can be used to promote change or do work—is called the **free energy (G)**. The letter *G* is in recognition of the American physicist J. Willard Gibbs, who proposed the concept of free energy in 1878. The unusable energy is the system's entropy (*S*). Gibbs proposed that these three factors are related to each other in the following way:

$$H = G + TS$$

where *T* is the absolute temperature in kelvins (K). Because our focus is on free energy, we can rearrange this equation as

$$G = H - TS$$

A critical issue in biology is whether a process does or does not occur spontaneously. For example, will glucose be broken down into carbon dioxide and water? Another way of framing this question is to ask: "Is the breakdown of glucose a spontaneous reaction?" A spontaneous reaction or process is one that occurs without being driven by an input of energy. However, a spontaneous reaction does not necessarily proceed quickly. In some cases, the rate of a spontaneous reaction can be quite slow. For example, the breakdown of sugar is a spontaneous reaction, but the rate at which sugar in a sugar bowl breaks down into CO_2 and H_2O is very slow.

The key way to evaluate if a chemical reaction is spontaneous is to determine the free-energy change that occurs as a result of the reaction:

$$\Delta G = \Delta H - T\Delta S$$

where the Δ sign (the Greek letter delta) indicates a change, such as before and after a chemical reaction. If a chemical reaction has a

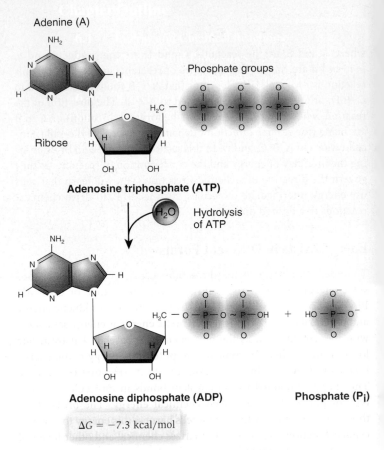

$$\Delta G = -7.3 \text{ kcal/mol}$$

Figure 6.3 **The hydrolysis of ATP to ADP and P$_i$.** As shown in this figure, ATP has a net charge of −4, while ADP and P$_i$ are shown with net charges of −2 each. When these compounds are shown in chemical reactions with other molecules, the net charges are also indicated. Otherwise, these compounds are simply designated ATP, ADP, and P$_i$. At neutral pH, ADP²⁻dissociates to ADP³⁻ and H⁺.

BIOLOGY PRINCIPLE **Living organisms use energy.** The hydrolysis of ATP is an exergonic reaction that is used to drive many cellular reactions.

negative free-energy change ($\Delta G < 0$), the products have less free energy than the reactants, and, therefore, free energy is released during product formation. Such a reaction is said to be **exergonic**. Exergonic reactions are spontaneous. Alternatively, if a reaction has a positive free-energy change ($\Delta G > 0$), requiring the addition of free energy from the environment, it is termed **endergonic**. An endergonic reaction is not a spontaneous reaction.

If ΔG for a chemical reaction is negative, the reaction favors the conversion of reactants to products, whereas a reaction with a positive ΔG favors the formation of reactants. Chemists have determined free-energy changes for a variety of chemical reactions, which allows them to predict their direction. As an example, let's consider **adenosine triphosphate (ATP)**, which is a molecule that is a common energy source for all cells. ATP is broken down to adenosine diphosphate (ADP) and inorganic phosphate (HPO_4^{2-}, abbreviated to P$_i$). Because water is used to remove a phosphate group, chemists refer to this as the hydrolysis of ATP (**Figure 6.3**). In the reaction of converting 1 mole of ATP to 1 mole of ADP and P$_i$, ΔG equals −7.3 kcal/mol. Because this is a negative value, the reaction strongly favors the formation of products. As discussed later, the energy liberated by the hydrolysis of ATP is used to drive a variety of cellular processes.

Chemical Reactions Eventually Reach a State of Equilibrium

Even when a chemical reaction is associated with a negative free-energy change, not all of the reactants are converted to products. The reaction reaches a state of **chemical equilibrium** in which the rate of formation of products equals the rate of formation of reactants. Let's consider the generalized reaction

$$aA + bB \rightleftharpoons cC + dD$$

where again A and B are the reactants, C and D are the products, and a, b, c, and d are the number of moles of reactants and products. An equilibrium occurs, such that

$$K_{eq} = \frac{[C]^c[D]^d}{[A]^a[B]^b}$$

where K_{eq} is the equilibrium constant. Each type of chemical reaction has a specific value for K_{eq}.

Biologists make two simplifying assumptions when determining values for equilibrium constants. First, the concentration of water does not change during the reaction, and the pH remains constant at pH 7. The equilibrium constant under these conditions is designated with a prime symbol, K_{eq}'. If water is one of the reactants, as in a hydrolysis reaction, it is not included in the chemical equilibrium equation. As an example, let's consider the chemical equilibrium for the hydrolysis of ATP.

$$ATP^{4-} + H_2O \rightleftharpoons ADP^{2-} + P_i^{2-}$$

$$K_{eq}' = \frac{[ADP][P_i]}{[ATP]}$$

Experimentally, the value for K_{eq}' for this reaction has been determined to be approximately 1,650,000 M. Such a large value indicates that the equilibrium greatly favors the formation of products—ADP and P_i.

Cells Use ATP to Drive Endergonic Reactions

In living organisms, many vital processes require the addition of free energy; that is, they are endergonic and do not occur spontaneously. Fortunately, organisms have a way to overcome this problem. Cells often couple exergonic reactions with endergonic reactions. If an exergonic reaction is coupled with an endergonic reaction, the endergonic reaction will proceed spontaneously if the net free-energy change for both processes combined is negative. For example, consider the following reactions:

$$Glucose + Phosphate^{2-} \rightarrow Glucose\text{-}6\text{-}phosphate^{2-} + H_2O$$
$$\Delta G = +3.3 \text{ kcal/mol}$$

$$ATP^{4-} + H_2O \rightarrow ADP^{2-} + P_i^{2-} \qquad \Delta G = -7.3 \text{ kcal/mol}$$

Coupled reaction:

$$Glucose + ATP^{4-} \rightarrow Glucose\text{-}6\text{-}phosphate^{2-} + ADP^{2-}$$
$$\Delta G = -4.0 \text{ kcal/mol}$$

The first reaction, in which phosphate is covalently attached to glucose, is endergonic, and by itself is not spontaneous. The second, the hydrolysis of ATP, is exergonic. If the two reactions are coupled, however, the net free-energy change for both reactions combined is exergonic ($\Delta G = -4.0$ kcal/mol). In the coupled reaction, a phosphate is directly transferred from ATP to glucose, in a process called **phosphorylation**. This coupled reaction proceeds spontaneously because the net free-energy change is negative. Exergonic reactions, such as the breakdown of ATP, are commonly coupled to chemical reactions and other cellular processes that would otherwise be endergonic.

GENOMES & PROTEOMES CONNECTION

Many Proteins Bind ATP and Use That ATP as a Source of Energy

Over the past several decades, researchers have studied the functions of many types of proteins and discovered numerous examples in which a protein uses the hydrolysis of ATP to drive a chemical reaction or cellular process (**Table 6.2**). In humans, a typical cell uses millions of ATP molecules per second. At the same time, the breakdown of food molecules to form smaller molecules (an exergonic reaction) releases energy that allows cells to make more ATP from the phosphorylation of ADP (an endergonic reaction). The recycling of ATP occurs at a remarkable pace. An average person hydrolyzes about 100 pounds of ATP per day, yet at any given time we do not have 100 pounds of ATP in our bodies. For this to happen, each molecule of

Table 6.2	Examples of Proteins That Use ATP for Energy
Type	**Description**
Metabolic enzymes	Many enzymes use ATP to catalyze endergonic reactions. For example, hexokinase uses ATP to attach phosphate to glucose, producing glucose-6-phosphate.
Transporters	Ion pumps, such as the Na^+/K^+-ATPase, use ATP to pump ions against a gradient (see Chapter 5).
Motor proteins	Motor proteins such as myosin use ATP to facilitate cellular movement, as in muscle contraction (see Chapter 44).
Chaperones	Chaperones are proteins that use ATP to aid in the folding and unfolding of cellular proteins (see Chapter 4).
DNA-modifying enzymes	Many proteins such as helicases and topoisomerases use ATP to modify the conformation of DNA (see Chapter 11).
Aminoacyl-tRNA synthetases	These enzymes use ATP to attach amino acids to tRNAs (see Chapter 12).
Protein kinases	Protein kinases are regulatory proteins that use ATP to attach a phosphate to proteins, thereby phosphorylating the protein and affecting its function (see Chapter 9).

ATP, adenosine triphosphate; tRNA, transfer RNA.

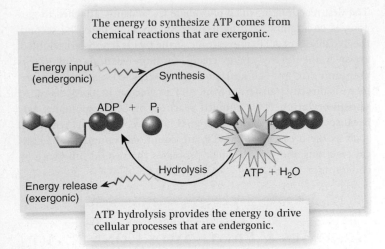

Figure 6.4   The ATP cycle. Living cells continuously recycle ATP. The energy released from the breakdown of food molecules into smaller molecules is used to synthesize ATP from ADP and P_i. The hydrolysis of ATP to ADP and P_i is used to drive many different endergonic reactions and processes that occur in cells.

Concept Check: *If a large amount of ADP was broken down in the cell, how would this affect the ATP cycle?*

ATP undergoes about 10,000 cycles of hydrolysis and regeneration during an ordinary day (**Figure 6.4**).

By studying the structures of many proteins that use ATP, biochemists have discovered that particular amino acid sequences within proteins function as ATP-binding sites. This information has allowed researchers to predict whether a newly discovered protein uses ATP or not. When an entire genome sequence of a species has been determined, the genes that encode proteins can be analyzed to find out if the encoded proteins have ATP-binding sites in their amino acid sequences. Using this approach, researchers have been able to analyze **proteomes**—all of the proteins that a given cell makes—and estimate the percentage of proteins that are able to bind ATP. This approach has been applied to the proteomes of bacteria, archaea, and eukaryotes.

Researchers have discovered that, on average, over 20% of all proteins bind ATP. However, this number is likely to underestimate the total percentage of ATP-utilizing proteins because we may not have identified all of the types of ATP-binding sites in proteins. In humans, who have an estimated genome size of 20,000 to 25,000 different genes, a minimum of 4,000 to 5,000 of those genes encode proteins that use ATP. From these numbers, we can see the enormous importance of ATP as a source of energy for living cells.

6.2   Enzymes and Ribozymes

Learning Outcomes:

1. Explain how enzymes increase the rates of chemical reactions by lowering the activation energy.
2. Describe how enzymes bind their substrates with high specificity and undergo induced fit.

3. Analyze the velocity of chemical reactions and evaluate the effects of competitive and noncompetitive inhibitors.
4. Explain how additional factors, such as nonprotein molecules or ions, temperature, and pH, influence enzyme activity.
5. Identify the unique feature of ribozymes.

For most chemical reactions in cells to proceed at a rapid pace, such as the breakdown of glucose, a catalyst is needed. A **catalyst** is an agent that speeds up the rate of a chemical reaction without being permanently changed or consumed by it. In living cells, the most common catalysts are **enzymes**, which are proteins. The term was coined in 1876 by a German physiologist, Wilhelm Kühne, who discovered trypsin, an enzyme in pancreatic juice that is needed for the digestion of food proteins. In this section, we will explore how enzymes increase the rates of chemical reactions. Interestingly, some biological catalysts are RNA molecules called ribozymes. We will examine a few examples in which RNA molecules carry out catalytic functions.

Enzymes Increase the Rates of Chemical Reactions

Thus far, we have examined aspects of energy and considered how the laws of thermodynamics are related to the direction of chemical reactions. If a chemical reaction has a negative free-energy change, the reaction will be spontaneous; it will tend to proceed in the direction of reactants to products. Although thermodynamics governs the direction of an energy transformation, it does not control the rate of a chemical reaction. For example, the breakdown of the molecules in gasoline to smaller molecules is an exergonic reaction. Even so, we could place gasoline and oxygen in a container and nothing much would happen (provided it wasn't near a flame). If we came back several days later, we would expect to see the gasoline still sitting there. Perhaps if we came back in a few million years, the gasoline would have been broken down. On a timescale of months or a few years, however, the chemical reaction would proceed very slowly.

In living cells, the rates of enzyme-catalyzed reactions typically occur millions of times faster than the corresponding uncatalyzed reactions. An extreme example is the enzyme catalase, which is found in peroxisomes, organelles responsible for the breakdown of toxic molecules such as hydrogen peroxide (see Chapter 4). This enzyme catalyzes the breakdown of hydrogen peroxide (H_2O_2) into water and oxygen. Catalase speeds up this reaction 10^{15}-fold faster than the uncatalyzed reaction!

Why are catalysts necessary to speed up a chemical reaction? Chemical reactions between molecules involve bond breaking and bond forming. When a covalent bond is broken or formed, this process initially involves the straining or stretching of one or more bonds in the starting molecule(s), and/or it may involve the positioning of two molecules so they interact with each other properly. Let's consider the reaction in which ATP is used to phosphorylate glucose:

$$\text{Glucose} + \text{ATP}^{4-} \rightarrow \text{Glucose-6-phosphate}^{2-} + \text{ADP}^{2-}$$

For a reaction to occur between glucose and ATP, the molecules must collide in the correct orientation and possess enough energy so the chemical bonds can be changed. As glucose and ATP approach each other, their electron clouds cause repulsion. To overcome this repulsion, an initial input of energy, called the **activation energy**, is

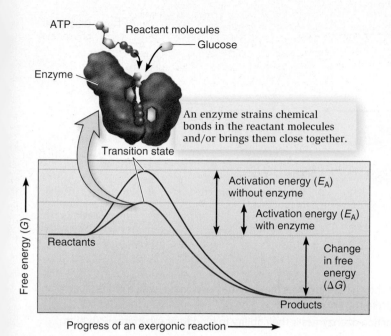

Figure 6.5   Activation energy of a chemical reaction. This figure depicts an exergonic reaction. The activation energy (E_A) is needed for molecules to achieve a transition state. One way that enzymes lower the activation energy is by straining chemical bonds in the reactants so less energy is required to attain the transition state. A second way is by binding two reactants so they are close to each other and in a favorable orientation.

Concept Check: *How does lowering the activation energy affect the rate of a chemical reaction? How does it affect the direction?*

required (**Figure 6.5**). Activation energy (E_A) allows the molecules to get close enough to cause a rearrangement of bonds. With the input of activation energy, glucose and ATP can achieve a **transition state** in which the original bonds have stretched to their limit. Once the reactants have reached the transition state, the chemical reaction can readily proceed to the formation of products, which in this case is glucose-6-phosphate and ADP.

The activation energy required to achieve the transition state is a barrier to the formation of products. This barrier is the reason why the rate of many chemical reactions is very slow. Two common mechanisms can overcome this barrier and thereby accelerate a chemical reaction. First, the reactants could be exposed to a large amount of heat. For example, as we noted previously, if gasoline is sitting at room temperature, nothing much happens. However, if the gasoline is exposed to a flame or spark, it breaks down rapidly, perhaps at an explosive rate! Alternatively, a second strategy is to lower the activation energy barrier. Enzymes lower the activation energy to a point where a small amount of available heat can push the reactants to a transition state.

How do enzymes lower the activation energy barrier of chemical reactions? Enzymes are generally large proteins that bind relatively small reactants. When bound to an enzyme, the bonds in the reactants can be strained, thereby making it easier for them to achieve the transition state (see Figure 6.5). This is one way that enzymes lower

the activation energy. In addition, when a chemical reaction involves two or more reactants, the enzyme provides a site in which the reactants are positioned very close to each other in an orientation that facilitates the formation of new covalent bonds. This also lowers the necessary activation energy for a chemical reaction.

Straining the reactants and bringing them close together are two common ways that enzymes lower the activation energy barrier. In addition, enzymes may facilitate a chemical reaction by changing the local environment of the reactants. For example, amino acids in an enzyme may have charges that affect the chemistry of the reactants. In some cases, enzymes lower the activation energy by directly participating in the chemical reaction. For example, certain enzymes that hydrolyze ATP form a covalent bond between phosphate and an amino acid in the enzyme. However, this is a temporary condition. The covalent bond between phosphate and the amino acid is quickly broken, releasing the phosphate and returning the amino acid back to its original condition. An example of such an enzyme is Na^+/K^+-ATPase, described in Chapter 5.

Enzymes Recognize Their Substrates with High Specificity and Undergo Conformational Changes

Thus far, we have considered how enzymes lower the activation energy of a chemical reaction, and thereby increase its rate. Let's consider some other features of enzymes that enable them to serve as effective catalysts in chemical reactions. The **active site** is the location in an enzyme where the chemical reaction takes place. The **substrates** for an enzyme are the reactant molecules that bind to an enzyme at the active site and participate in the chemical reaction. For example, hexokinase is an enzyme whose substrates are glucose and ATP (**Figure 6.6**). The binding between an enzyme and substrate produces an **enzyme-substrate complex**.

A key feature of nearly all enzymes is their ability to bind their substrates with a high degree of specificity. For example, hexokinase recognizes glucose but does not recognize other similar sugars, such as fructose and galactose, very well. In 1894, the German chemist Emil Fischer proposed that the recognition of a substrate by an enzyme resembles the interaction between a lock and key: only the right-sized key (the substrate) will fit into the keyhole (active site) of the lock (the enzyme). Further research revealed that the interaction between an enzyme and its substrates also involves movements or conformational changes in the enzyme itself. As shown in Figure 6.6 step 2, these conformational changes cause the substrates to bind more tightly to the enzyme, a phenomenon called **induced fit**, which was proposed by American biochemist Daniel Koshland in 1958. Only after this induced fit takes place does the enzyme catalyze the conversion of reactants to products. Induced fit is a key phenomenon that lowers the activation energy.

Enzyme Function Is Influenced by the Substrate Concentration and by Inhibitors

The degree of attraction between an enzyme and its substrate(s) is called the **affinity** of the enzyme for its substrate(s). Some enzymes recognize their substrates with very high affinity, which means they have a strong attraction for their substrates. Such enzymes bind their

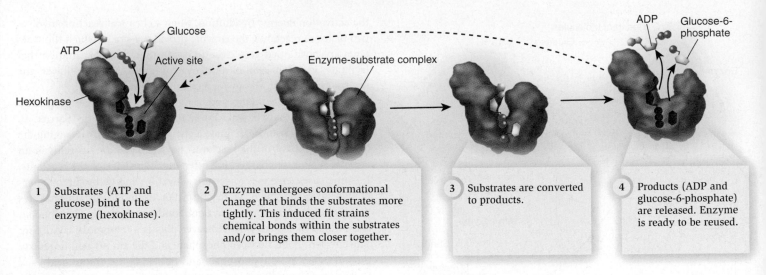

1. Substrates (ATP and glucose) bind to the enzyme (hexokinase).

2. Enzyme undergoes conformational change that binds the substrates more tightly. This induced fit strains chemical bonds within the substrates and/or brings them closer together.

3. Substrates are converted to products.

4. Products (ADP and glucose-6-phosphate) are released. Enzyme is ready to be reused.

Figure 6.6 **The steps of an enzyme-catalyzed reaction.** The example shown here involves the enzyme hexokinase, which binds glucose and ATP. The products are glucose-6-phosphate and ADP, which are released from the enzyme.

BIOLOGY PRINCIPLE **Structure determines function.** A key function of enzymes is their ability to bind their substrates with high specificity. This is due to the structure of the enzyme's active site.

Concept Check: *During which step is the activation energy lowered?*

substrates even when the substrate concentration is relatively low. Other enzymes recognize their substrates with lower affinity; the enzyme-substrate complex is likely to form when the substrate concentration is higher.

Let's consider how biologists analyze the relationship between substrate concentration and enzyme function. In the experiment of **Figure 6.7a**, tubes labeled A, B, C, and D each contained 1 µg of enzyme but they varied in the amount of substrate that was added. This enzyme recognizes a single type of substrate and converts it to a product. The samples were incubated for 60 seconds, and then the amount of product in each tube was measured. In this example, the velocity or rate of the chemical reaction is expressed as the amount of product produced per second. As we see in Figure 6.7a, the velocity increases as the substrate concentration increases, but eventually reaches a plateau. Why does the plateau occur? At high substrate concentrations, nearly all of the active sites of the enzyme are occupied with substrate, so increasing the substrate concentration further has a negligible effect. At this point, the enzyme is saturated with substrate, and the velocity of the chemical reaction is near its maximal rate, called its V_{max}.

Figure 6.7a also helps us understand the relationship between substrate concentration and velocity. The K_M is the substrate concentration at which the velocity is half its maximal value. The K_M is also called the Michaelis constant in honor of the German biochemist Leonor Michaelis, who carried out pioneering work with the Canadian biochemist Maud Menten on the study of enzymes. The K_M is a measure of the substrate concentration required for a chemical reaction to occur. An enzyme with a high K_M requires a higher substrate concentration to achieve a particular reaction velocity compared to an enzyme with a lower K_M.

For an enzyme-catalyzed reaction, we can view the formation of product as occurring in two steps: (1) binding or release of substrate and (2) formation of product:

$$E + S \rightleftharpoons ES \rightarrow E + P$$

where E is the enzyme, S is the substrate, ES is the enzyme-substrate complex, and P is the product.

If the second step—the rate of product formation—is much slower than the rate of substrate release, the K_M is inversely related to the affinity between the enzyme and substrate. For example, let's consider an enzyme that breaks down ATP into ADP and P_i. If the rate of formation of ADP and P_i is much slower than the rate of ATP release, the K_M and affinity show an inverse relationship. Enzymes with a high K_M have a low affinity for their substrates—they bind them more weakly. By comparison, enzymes with a low K_M have a high affinity for their substrates—they bind them more strongly.

Now that we understand the relationship between substrate concentration and the velocity of an enzyme-catalyzed reaction, we can explore how inhibitors may affect enzyme function. These can be categorized as reversible inhibitors that bind noncovalently to an enzyme or irreversible inhibitors that usually bind covalently to an enzyme and permanently inactivate its function.

Reversible Inhibitors Cells often use reversible inhibitors to modulate enzyme function. We will consider examples in Chapter 7 in our discussion of glucose metabolism. **Competitive inhibitors** are molecules that bind noncovalently to the active site of an enzyme and inhibit the ability of the substrate to bind. Such inhibitors compete with the substrate for the ability to bind to the enzyme. Competitive inhibitors usually have a structure or a portion of their structure that mimics the structure of the enzyme's substrate. As seen in

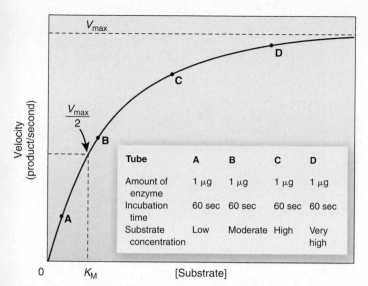

(a) Reaction velocity in the absence of inhibitors

Tube	A	B	C	D
Amount of enzyme	1 µg	1 µg	1 µg	1 µg
Incubation time	60 sec	60 sec	60 sec	60 sec
Substrate concentration	Low	Moderate	High	Very high

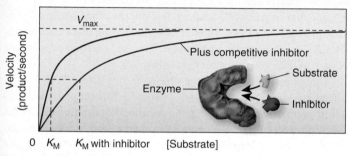

(b) Competitive inhibition

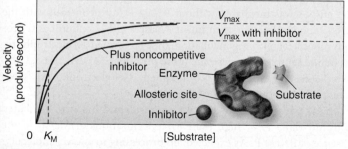

(c) Noncompetitive inhibition

Figure 6.7 **The relationship between velocity and substrate concentration in an enzyme-catalyzed reaction, and the effects of inhibitors.** **(a)** In the absence of an inhibitor, the maximal velocity (V_{max}) is achieved when the substrate concentration is high enough to be saturating. The K_M value is the substrate concentration at which the velocity is half the maximal velocity. **(b)** A competitive inhibitor binds to the active site of an enzyme and raises the K_M for the substrate. **(c)** A noncompetitive inhibitor binds to an allosteric site outside the active site and lowers the V_{max} for the reaction.

Concept Check: Enzyme A has a K_M of 0.1 mM, whereas enzyme B has a K_M of 1.0 mM. They both have the same V_{max}. If the substrate concentration was 0.5 mM, which reaction—the one catalyzed by enzyme A or B—would have the higher velocity?

Figure 6.7b, when competitive inhibitors are present, the apparent K_M for the substrate increases—a higher concentration of substrate is needed to achieve the same rate of the chemical reaction. In this case, the effects of the competitive inhibitor can be overcome by increasing the concentration of the substrate.

By comparison, **Figure 6.7c** illustrates the effects of a **noncompetitive inhibitor.** As seen here, this type of inhibitor lowers the V_{max} for the reaction without affecting the K_M. A noncompetitive inhibitor binds noncovalently to an enzyme at a location outside the active site, called an **allosteric site**, and inhibits the enzyme's function.

Irreversible Inhibitors Irreversible inhibitors usually bind covalently to an enzyme to inhibit its function. For example, some irreversible inhibitors bind covalently to an amino acid at the active site of an enzyme, thereby preventing it from catalyzing a chemical reaction. An example of an irreversible inhibitor is diisopropyl phosphorofluoridate (DIFP). DIFP is a type of nerve gas that was developed as a chemical weapon. This molecule covalently reacts with the enzyme, acetylcholinesterase, which is important for the proper functioning of neurons.

Irreversible inhibition is not a common way for cells to control enzyme function. Why do cells usually control enzymes via reversible inhibitors? The answer is that a reversible inhibitor allows an enzyme to be used again, when the inhibitor concentration becomes lowered. Being able to reuse an enzyme is energy-efficient. In contrast, irreversible inhibitors permanently inactivate an enzyme, thereby preventing its further use.

Additional Factors Influence Enzyme Function

Enzymes, which are proteins, sometimes require nonprotein molecules or ions to carry out their functions. **Prosthetic groups** are small molecules that are permanently attached to the surface of an enzyme and aid in enzyme function. **Cofactors** are usually inorganic ions, such as Fe^{3+} or Zn^{2+}, that temporarily bind to the surface of an enzyme and promote a chemical reaction. Finally, some enzymes use **coenzymes**, organic molecules that temporarily bind to an enzyme and participate in the chemical reaction but are left unchanged after the reaction is completed. Some of these coenzymes are synthesized by cells, but many of them are taken in as dietary vitamins by animal cells.

The ability of enzymes to increase the rate of a chemical reaction is also affected by the surrounding environment. In particular, the temperature, pH, and ionic conditions play an important role in the proper functioning of enzymes. Most enzymes function maximally in a narrow range of temperature and pH. For example, many human enzymes work best at 37°C (98.6°F), which is the normal body temperature. If the temperature is several degrees above or below an enzyme's optimum temperature due to infection or environmental causes, the function of many enzymes is greatly inhibited (**Figure 6.8**). Very high temperatures may denature a protein, causing it to unfold and lose its three-dimensional shape, thereby inhibiting its function.

Enzyme function is also sensitive to pH. Certain enzymes in the stomach function best at the acidic pH found in this organ. For example, pepsin is a protease—an enzyme that digests proteins into peptides—that is released into the stomach. The optimal pH for pepsin function is around pH 2.0, which is extremely acidic. By comparison, many cytosolic enzymes function optimally at a more neutral pH, such as pH 7.2, which is the pH normally found in the cytosol of human cells. If the pH was significantly above or below this value, enzyme function would be decreased for cytosolic enzymes.

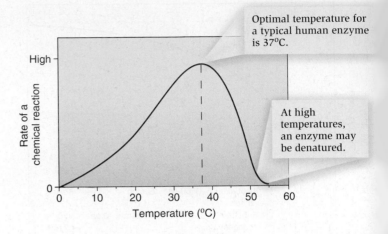

Figure 6.8 **Effects of temperature on a typical human enzyme.** Most enzymes function optimally within a narrow range of temperature. Many human enzymes function best at 37°C, which is body temperature.

FEATURE INVESTIGATION

The Discovery of Ribozymes by Sidney Altman Revealed That RNA Molecules May Also Function as Catalysts

Until the 1980s, scientists thought that all biological catalysts are proteins. One avenue of study that dramatically changed this view came from the analysis of ribonuclease P (RNase P), a catalyst initially found in the bacterium *Escherichia coli* and later identified in all species examined. RNase P is involved in the processing of tRNA molecules—a type of molecule required for protein synthesis. Such tRNA molecules are synthesized as longer precursor molecules called ptRNAs, which have 5′ and 3′ ends. (The 5′ and 3′ directionality of RNA molecules is described in Chapter 11.) RNase P breaks a covalent bond at a specific site in precursor tRNAs, which releases a fragment at the 5′ end and makes them shorter (**Figure 6.9**).

Sidney Altman and his colleagues became interested in the processing of tRNA molecules and turned their attention to RNase P in

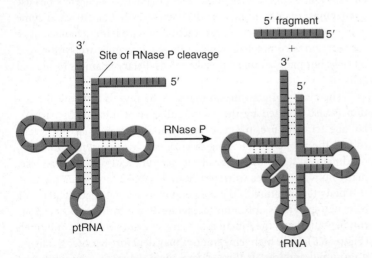

Figure 6.9 **The function of RNase P.** A specific bond in a precursor tRNA (ptRNA) is cleaved by RNase P, which releases a small fragment at the 5′ end. This results in the formation of a mature tRNA.

BioConnections: *Look ahead to Figure 12.19. How do you imagine translation would be affected if RNase P did not work properly?*

E. coli. During the course of their studies, they purified this enzyme and, to their surprise, discovered it has two subunits—one is an RNA molecule that contains 377 nucleotides, and the other is a small protein with a mass of 14 kDa. In the 1980s, the finding that a catalyst has an RNA subunit was very unexpected. Even so, a second property of RNase P would prove even more exciting.

Altman and colleagues were able to purify RNase P and study its properties in vitro. As mentioned earlier in this chapter, the functioning of enzymes is affected by the surrounding conditions. Cecilia Guerrier-Takada in Altman's laboratory determined that magnesium ion (Mg^{2+}) had a stimulatory effect on RNase P function. In the experiment described in **Figure 6.10**, the effects of Mg^{2+} were studied in greater detail. The researchers analyzed the effects of low (10 mM $MgCl_2$) and high (100 mM $MgCl_2$) magnesium concentrations on the processing of a ptRNA. At low or high magnesium concentrations, the ptRNA was incubated without RNase P (as a control); with the RNA subunit alone; or with intact RNase P (RNA subunit and protein subunit). Following incubation, they performed gel electrophoresis on the samples to determine if the ptRNAs had been cleaved into two pieces—the tRNA and a 5′ fragment. Gel electrophoresis separates molecules on the basis of their masses.

Let's now look at the data. As a control, ptRNAs were incubated with low (lane 1) or high (lane 4) concentrations of $MgCl_2$ in the absence of RNase P. As expected, no processing to a lower molecular mass tRNA was observed. When the RNA subunit alone was incubated with ptRNA molecules in the presence of low $MgCl_2$ (lane 2), no processing occurred, but it did occur if the protein subunit was also included (lane 3).

The surprising result is shown in lane 5, in which the ptRNA was incubated with the RNA subunit alone in the presence of a high concentration of $MgCl_2$. The RNA subunit by itself was sufficient to cleave the ptRNA to a smaller tRNA and a 5′ fragment! Presumably, the high $MgCl_2$ concentration helps to keep the RNA subunit in a conformation that is catalytically active. Alternatively, the protein subunit plays a similar role in a living cell.

Subsequent work confirmed these observations and showed that the RNA subunit of RNase P is a true catalyst—it accelerates the rate of a chemical reaction and is not permanently altered by it. Around

Figure 6.10 The discovery that the RNA subunit of RNase P is a catalyst.

HYPOTHESIS The catalytic function of RNase P could be carried out by its RNA subunit or by its protein subunit.

KEY MATERIALS Purified precursor tRNA (ptRNA) and purified RNA and protein subunits of RNase P from *E. coli*.

		Experimental level	Conceptual level

1 Into each of five tubes, add ptRNA.

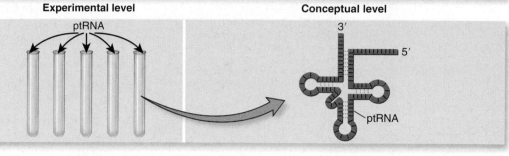

2 In tubes 1–3, add a low concentration of MgCl$_2$; in tubes 4 and 5, add a high MgCl$_2$ concentration.

Low MgCl$_2$ (10 mM)   High MgCl$_2$ (100 mM)

3 Into tubes 2 and 5, add the RNA subunit of RNase P alone; into tube 3, add both the RNA subunit and the protein subunit of RNase P. Incubate to allow digestion to occur. Note: Tubes 1 and 4 are controls that have no added subunits of RNase P.

RNA subunit alone   RNA subunit plus protein subunit

RNA subunit alone cuts here

5' fragment

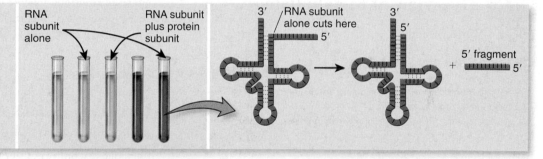

4 Carry out gel electrophoresis on each sample. In this technique, samples are loaded into a well on a gel and exposed to an electric field as described in Chapter 20. The molecules move toward the bottom of the gel and are separated according to their masses: Molecules with higher masses are closer to the top of the gel. The gel is exposed to ethidium bromide, which stains RNA.

Higher mass

Lower mass

ptRNA

tRNA

5' fragment

Catalytic function will result in the digestion of ptRNA into tRNA and a smaller 5' fragment.

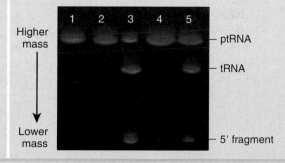

5 **THE DATA**

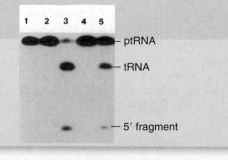

ptRNA

tRNA

5' fragment

6 **CONCLUSION** The RNA subunit alone can catalyze the breakage of a covalent bond in ptRNA at high Mg concentrations. It is a ribozyme.

7 **SOURCE** Altman, S. 1990. Enzymatic cleavage of RNA by RNA. *Bioscience Reports* 10:317–337.

Table 6.3	Types of Ribozymes
General function	**Biological examples**
Processing of RNA molecules	1. RNase P: As described in this chapter, RNase P cleaves precursor tRNA molecules (ptRNAs) to a mature tRNAs.
	2. Spliceosomal RNA: As described in Chapter 12, eukaryotic pre-mRNAs often have regions called introns that are later removed. These introns are removed by a spliceosome that is composed of RNA and protein subunits. The RNA within the spliceosome is believed to function as a ribozyme that removes the introns from pre-mRNA.
	3. Certain introns found in mitochondrial, chloroplast, and bacterial RNAs are removed by a self-splicing mechanism.
Synthesis of polypeptides	The ribosome has an RNA component that catalyzes the formation of covalent bonds between adjacent amino acids during polypeptide synthesis.

the same time, Thomas Cech and colleagues determined that a different RNA molecule found in the protist *Tetrahymena thermophila* also has catalytic activity. The term **ribozyme** is now used to describe an RNA molecule that catalyzes a chemical reaction. In 1989, Altman

and Cech received the Nobel Prize in Chemistry for their discovery of ribozymes.

Since the pioneering work of Altman and Cech, researchers have discovered that ribozymes play key catalytic roles in cells (**Table 6.3**). They are primarily involved in the processing of RNA molecules from precursor to mature forms. In addition, a ribozyme in the ribosome catalyzes the formation of covalent bonds between adjacent amino acids during polypeptide synthesis.

Experimental Questions

1. Briefly explain why it was necessary to purify the individual subunits of RNase P to show that it is a ribozyme.

2. In the Altman experiment involving RNase P, explain how the researchers experimentally determined if RNase P or subunits of RNase P were catalytically active or not. Explain why the researchers conducted experiments in which they measured the formation of mature tRNA without adding the protein subunit or without adding the RNA subunit.

3. Describe the critical results that showed RNase P is a ribozyme. How does the concentration of Mg^{2+} affect the function of the RNA in RNase P?

6.3 Overview of Metabolism

Learning Outcomes:

1. Describe the concept of a metabolic pathway and distinguish between catabolic and anabolic reactions.
2. Explain how catabolic reactions are used to generate building blocks to make larger molecules and to produce energy intermediates.
3. Define redox reaction.
4. Compare and contrast the three ways that metabolic pathways are regulated.

In the previous sections, we examined the underlying factors that govern individual chemical reactions and explored the properties of enzymes and ribozymes. In living cells, chemical reactions are often coordinated with each other and occur in sequences called **metabolic pathways**, each step of which is catalyzed by a specific enzyme (**Figure 6.11**). These pathways are categorized according to whether the reactions lead to the breakdown or synthesis of substances. **Catabolic reactions** result in the breakdown of larger molecules into

smaller ones. Such reactions are often exergonic. By comparison, **anabolic reactions** involve the synthesis of larger molecules from smaller precursor molecules. This process usually is endergonic and, in living cells, must be coupled to an exergonic reaction. In this section, we will survey the general features of catabolic and anabolic reactions and explore the ways in which metabolic pathways are controlled.

Catabolic Reactions Recycle Organic Building Blocks and Produce Energy Intermediates Such as ATP

Catabolic reactions result in the breakdown of larger molecules into smaller ones. One reason for the breakdown of macromolecules is to recycle their organic molecules, which are used as building blocks to construct new molecules and macromolecules. For example, polypeptides, which make up proteins, are composed of a linear sequence of amino acids. When a protein is improperly folded or is no longer needed by a cell, the peptide bonds between the amino acids in the protein are broken by enzymes called proteases. This generates amino acids that can be used in the construction of new proteins.

$$\text{Protein} \xrightarrow{\text{Proteases}} \rightarrow \rightarrow \rightarrow \rightarrow \rightarrow \rightarrow \rightarrow \rightarrow \text{Many individual amino acids}$$

We will consider the mechanisms of recycling later in Section 6.4.

A second reason for the breakdown of macromolecules and smaller organic molecules is to obtain energy that is used to drive endergonic processes in the cell. Covalent bonds store a large amount of energy. However, when cells break covalent bonds in organic molecules such as glucose, they do not directly use the energy released in this process. Instead, the released energy is stored in **energy intermediates**, molecules such as ATP, which are directly used to drive endergonic reactions in cells.

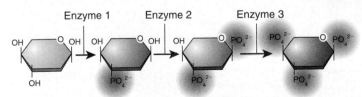

Figure 6.11 A metabolic pathway. In this metabolic pathway, a series of different enzymes catalyze the attachment of phosphate groups to various sugars, beginning with a starting substrate and ending with a final product.

As an example, let's consider the breakdown of glucose into two molecules of pyruvate. As discussed in Chapter 7, the breakdown of glucose to pyruvate involves a catabolic pathway called glycolysis. Some of the energy released during the breakage of covalent bonds in glucose is harnessed to synthesize ATP. However, this does not occur in a single step. Rather, glycolysis involves a series of steps in which covalent bonds are broken and rearranged. This process produces molecules that can readily donate a phosphate group to ADP, thereby producing ATP. For example, phosphoenolpyruvate has a phosphate group attached to pyruvate. Due to the arrangement of bonds in phosphoenolpyruvate, this phosphate bond is unstable and easily broken. Therefore, the phosphate can be readily transferred from phosphoenolpyruvate to ADP:

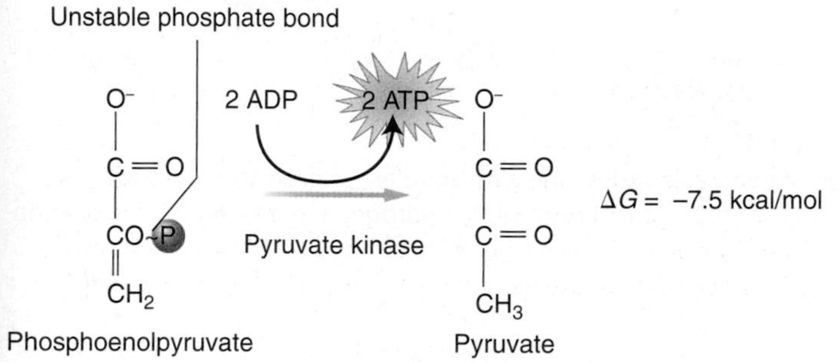

This is an exergonic reaction and therefore favors the formation of products. In this step of glycolysis, the breakdown of an organic molecule, namely phosphoenolpyruvate, results in the formation of pyruvate and the synthesis of an energy intermediate molecule, ATP, which can then be used by a cell to drive endergonic reactions. This way of synthesizing ATP, termed **substrate-level phosphorylation**, occurs when an enzyme directly transfers a phosphate from an organic molecule to ADP, thereby making ATP. In this case, the enzyme pyruvate kinase transfers a phosphate from phosphoenolpyruvate to ADP. Another way to make ATP is via **chemiosmosis**. In this process, energy stored in an ion electrochemical gradient is used to make ATP from ADP and P_i. We will consider this other mechanism in Chapter 7.

Redox Reactions Are Important in the Metabolism of Small Organic Molecules

During the breakdown of small organic molecules, **oxidation**—the removal of one or more electrons from an atom or molecule—may occur. This process is called oxidation because oxygen is frequently involved in chemical reactions that remove electrons from other molecules. By comparison, **reduction** is the addition of electrons to an atom or molecule. Reduction is so named because the addition of a negatively charged electron reduces the net charge of a molecule.

Electrons do not exist freely in solution. When an atom or molecule is oxidized, the electron that is removed must be transferred to another atom or molecule, which becomes reduced. This type of reaction is termed a **redox reaction**, which is short for a reduction-oxidation reaction. As a generalized equation, an electron may be transferred from molecule A to molecule B as follows:

$$Ae^- \quad + \quad B \quad \rightarrow \quad A \quad + \quad Be^-$$
$$\text{(oxidized)} \quad \text{(reduced)}$$

As shown in the right side of this reaction, A has been oxidized (that is, had an electron removed), and B has been reduced (that is, had an electron added). In general, a substance that has been oxidized has less energy, whereas a substance that has been reduced has more energy.

During the oxidation of organic molecules such as glucose, the electrons are used to produce energy intermediates such as NADH (**Figure 6.12**). In this process, an organic molecule has been oxidized, and **NAD$^+$ (nicotinamide adenine dinucleotide)** has been reduced to NADH. Cells use NADH in two common ways. First, as we will see in Chapter 7, the oxidation of NADH is a highly exergonic reaction that can be used to make ATP. Second, NADH can donate electrons to other organic molecules and thereby energize them. Such energized molecules can more readily form covalent bonds. Therefore, as described next, NADH is often needed in reactions that involve the synthesis of larger molecules through the formation of covalent bonds between smaller molecules.

Anabolic Reactions Require an Input of Energy to Make Larger Molecules

Anabolic reactions are also called **biosynthetic reactions**, because they are necessary to make larger molecules and macromolecules. We will examine the synthesis of macromolecules in several chapters of this textbook. For example, RNA and protein biosynthesis are described in Chapter 12. Cells also need to synthesize small organic molecules, such as amino acids and fats, if they are not readily available from food sources. Such molecules are made by the formation of covalent linkages between precursor molecules. For example, glutamate (an amino acid) is made by the covalent linkage between α-ketoglutarate (a product of sugar metabolism) and ammonium (NH_4^+).

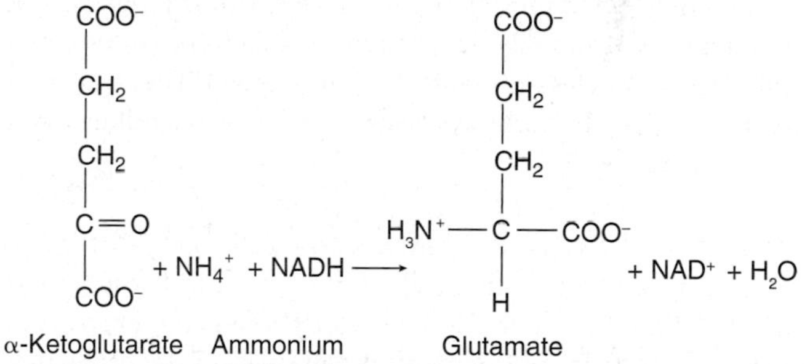

Subsequently, another amino acid, glutamine, is made from glutamate and ammonium.

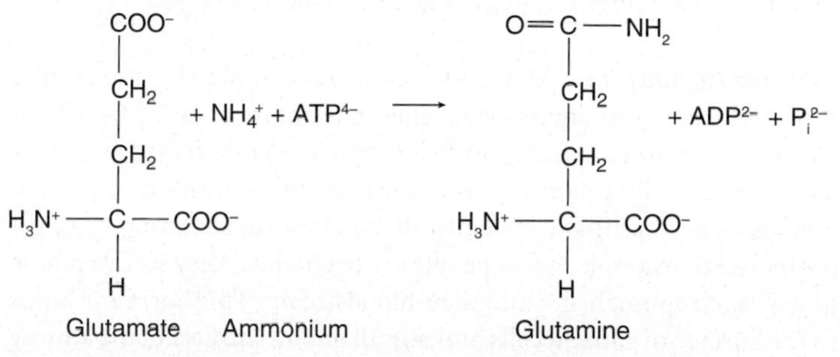

In both reactions, an energy intermediate molecule such as NADH or ATP is needed to drive the reaction forward.

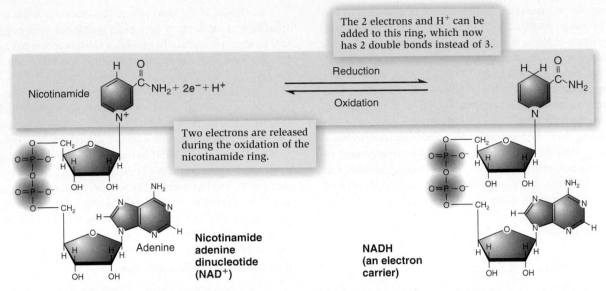

Figure 6.12 **The reduction of NAD⁺ to produce NADH.** NAD⁺ is composed of two nucleotides, one with an adenine base and one with a nicotinamide base. The oxidation of organic molecules releases electrons that bind to NAD⁺ (and along with a hydrogen ion) result in the formation of NADH. The two electrons and H⁺ are incorporated into the nicotinamide ring. Note: The actual net charges of NAD⁺ and NADH are minus one and minus two, respectively. They are designated NAD⁺ and NADH to emphasize the net charge of the nicotinamide ring, which is involved in oxidation-reduction reactions.

Concept Check: *Which is the oxidized form, NAD⁺ or NADH?*

Metabolic Pathways Are Regulated in Three General Ways

The regulation of metabolic pathways is important for a variety of reasons. Catabolic pathways are regulated so organic molecules are broken down only when they are no longer needed or when the cell requires energy. During anabolic reactions, regulation ensures that a cell synthesizes molecules only when they are needed. The regulation of catabolic and anabolic pathways occurs at the genetic, cellular, and biochemical levels.

Gene Regulation Because enzymes in every metabolic pathway are encoded by genes, one way that cells control chemical reactions is via gene regulation. For example, if a bacterial cell is not exposed to a particular sugar in its environment, it will turn off the genes that encode the enzymes that are needed to break down that sugar. Alternatively, if the sugar becomes available, the genes are switched on. Chapter 13 examines the steps of gene regulation in detail.

Cellular Regulation Metabolism is also coordinated at the cellular level. Cells integrate signals from their environment and adjust their chemical reactions to adapt to those signals. As discussed in Chapter 9, cell-signaling pathways often lead to the activation of protein kinases—enzymes that covalently attach a phosphate group to target proteins. For example, when people are frightened, they secrete a hormone called epinephrine into their bloodstream. This hormone binds to the surface of muscle cells and stimulates an intracellular pathway that leads to the phosphorylation of several intracellular proteins, including enzymes involved in carbohydrate metabolism. These activated enzymes promote the breakdown of carbohydrates, an event

that supplies the frightened individual with more energy. Epinephrine is sometimes called the "fight-or-flight" hormone because the added energy prepares an individual to either stay and fight or run away quickly. After a person is no longer frightened, hormone levels drop, and other enzymes called phosphatases remove the phosphate groups from enzymes, thereby restoring the original level of carbohydrate metabolism.

Another way that cells control metabolic pathways is via compartmentalization. The membrane-bound organelles of eukaryotic cells, such as the endoplasmic reticulum and mitochondria, serve to compartmentalize the cell. As discussed in Chapter 7, this allows specific metabolic pathways to occur in one compartment in the cell but not in others.

Biochemical Regulation A third and very prominent way that metabolic pathways are controlled is at the biochemical level. In this case, the noncovalent binding of a molecule to an enzyme directly regulates its function. As discussed earlier, one form of biochemical regulation involves the binding of molecules such as competitive or noncompetitive inhibitors (see Figure 6.7). An example of noncompetitive inhibition is a type of regulation called **feedback inhibition**, in which the product of a metabolic pathway inhibits an enzyme that acts early in the pathway, thus preventing the overaccumulation of the product (**Figure 6.13**).

Many metabolic pathways use feedback inhibition as a form of biochemical regulation. In such cases, the inhibited enzyme has two binding sites. One site is the active site, where the reactants are converted to products. In addition, enzymes controlled by feedback inhibition also have an allosteric site, where a molecule can bind noncovalently and affect the function of the active site. The binding of a

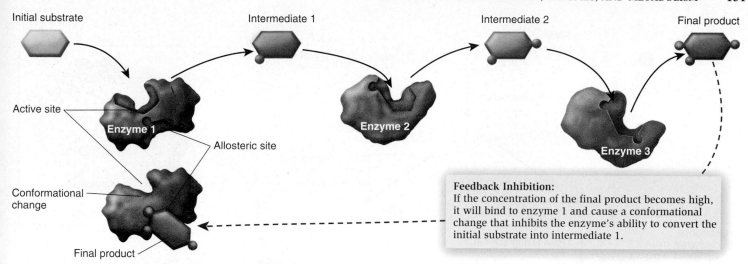

Feedback Inhibition:
If the concentration of the final product becomes high, it will bind to enzyme 1 and cause a conformational change that inhibits the enzyme's ability to convert the initial substrate into intermediate 1.

Figure 6.13 **Feedback inhibition.** In this process, the final product of a metabolic pathway inhibits an enzyme that functions in the pathway, thereby preventing the overaccumulation of the product.

 BIOLOGY PRINCIPLE **Living organisms maintain homeostasis.** In this example, feedback inhibition prevents the formation of too much product of a metabolic pathway.

BioConnections: *Look ahead to Figure 7.3, which describes a metabolic pathway called glycolysis. Feedback inhibition occurs such that high levels of ATP inhibit phosphofructokinase, an enzyme that catalyzes the conversion of fructose-6-phosphate and ATP to fructose 1,6-bisphosphate and ADP. How is this beneficial to the cell?*

molecule to an allosteric site causes a conformational change in the enzyme that inhibits its catalytic function. Allosteric sites are often found in the enzymes that catalyze the early steps in a metabolic pathway. Such allosteric sites typically bind molecules that are the products of the metabolic pathway. When the products bind to these sites, they inhibit the function of these enzymes, thereby preventing the formation of too much product.

Cellular and biochemical regulation are important and rapid ways to control chemical reactions in a cell. For a metabolic pathway composed of several enzymes, which enzyme in a pathway should be controlled? In many cases, a metabolic pathway has a **rate-limiting step**, which is the slowest step in a pathway. If the rate-limiting step is inhibited or enhanced, such changes will have the greatest influence on the formation of the product of the metabolic pathway. Rather than affecting all of the enzymes in a metabolic pathway, cellular and biochemical regulation are often directed at the enzyme that catalyzes the rate-limiting step. This is an efficient and rapid way to control the amount of product of a pathway.

6.4 Recycling of Organic Molecules

Learning Outcomes:

1. Evaluate the relationship between the recycling of organic molecules and cellular efficiency.
2. Outline how the building blocks of mRNAs and proteins are recycled.
3. Describe how the components of cellular organelles are recycled via autophagy.

As mentioned earlier in this chapter, another important feature of metabolism is the recycling of organic molecules, such as nucleotides and amino acids, which are the building blocks of larger molecules.

Except for DNA, which is stably maintained and inherited from cell to cell, other large molecules such as RNA, proteins, lipids, and polysaccharides typically exist for a relatively short period of time. Biologists often speak of the **half-life** of molecules, which is the time it takes for 50% of the molecules to be broken down and recycled. For example, a population of messenger RNA molecules in bacteria has an average half-life of about 5 minutes, whereas mRNAs in eukaryotes tend to exist for longer periods of time, on the order of 30 minutes to 24 hours or even several days.

Why is recycling important? To compete effectively in their native environments, all living organisms must efficiently use and recycle the organic molecules that are needed as building blocks to construct larger molecules and macromolecules. Otherwise, they would waste a great deal of energy making such building blocks. For example, organisms conserve an enormous amount of energy by reusing the amino acids that are needed to construct proteins. In this section, we will explore how nucleotides and amino acids are recycled and consider a mechanism for the recycling of materials found in an entire organelle.

The Nucleotides Within Messenger RNA Molecules in Eukaryotes Are Recycled by Two Mechanisms

The genome of every cell contains many genes that are transcribed into RNA. Most of these RNA molecules, called messenger RNA, or mRNA, encode proteins that ultimately determine the structure and function of cells. As described in Chapter 12, eukaryotic mRNAs contain a cap at their 5′ end. A tail is found at their 3′ end consisting of many adenine bases (look ahead to Figure 12.9). In most cases, degradation of mRNA begins with the removal of nucleotides in the poly A tail at the 3′ end (**Figure 6.14**). After the tail gets shorter, two mechanisms of degradation may occur.

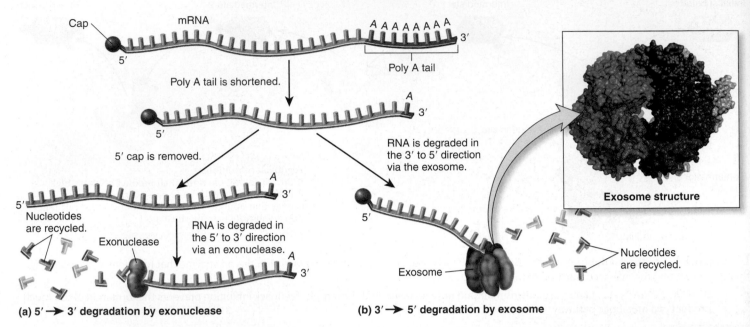

Figure 6.14 Two pathways for mRNA degradation in eukaryotic cells. Degradation usually begins with a shortening of the poly A tail. After tail shortening, either **(a)** the 5′ cap is removed and the RNA is degraded in a 5′ to 3′ direction by an exonuclease, or **(b)** the mRNA is degraded in the 3′ to 5′ direction via an exosome. The reason why cells have two different mechanisms for RNA degradation is not well understood.

In one mechanism, the 5′ cap is removed, and the mRNA is degraded by an **exonuclease**—an enzyme that cleaves off nucleotides, one at a time. In this case, the exonuclease removes nucleotides starting at the 5′ end and moving toward the 3′. The nucleotides can then be reused to make new RNA molecules.

The other mechanism involves mRNA being degraded by an **exosome**, a multiprotein complex discovered in 1997. Exosomes are found in eukaryotic cells and some archaeal cells, whereas in bacterial cells a simpler complex called the degradosome carries out a similar function. The core of the exosome is a six-membered protein ring to which other proteins are attached (see inset to Figure 6.14). Certain proteins within the exosome are exonucleases that degrade the mRNA starting at the 3′ end and moving toward the 5′ end, thereby releasing nucleotides that can be recycled.

Proteins in Eukaryotes and Archaea Are Broken Down in the Proteasome

Cells continually degrade proteins that are faulty or no longer needed. To be degraded, proteins are recognized by **proteases**—enzymes that cleave the bonds between adjacent amino acids. The primary pathway for protein degradation in archaea and eukaryotic cells is via a protein complex called a **proteasome**. Similar to the exosome, which has a central cavity surrounded by a ring of proteins, the core of the proteasome consists of four stacked rings, each composed of seven protein subunits (**Figure 6.15a**). The proteasomes of eukaryotic cells also contain caps at each end that control the entry of proteins into the proteasome.

Figure 6.15b describes the steps of protein degradation via eukaryotic proteasomes. A string of proteins called **ubiquitin** is covalently attached to the target protein. This event directs the target protein to a proteasome cap, which has binding sites for ubiquitin. The cap also has enzymes that unfold the protein and inject it into the internal cavity of the proteasome core. The ubiquitin proteins are removed during entry and released to the cytosol for reuse. Inside the proteasome, proteases degrade the protein into small peptides and amino acids. The process is completed when the peptides and amino acids are recycled back into the cytosol. The amino acids can be reused to make new proteins.

Ubiquitin targeting has two functions. First, the enzymes that attach ubiquitin to its target recognize improperly folded proteins, allowing cells to identify and degrade nonfunctional proteins. Second, changes in cellular conditions may warrant the rapid breakdown of particular proteins. For example, cell division requires a series of stages called the cell cycle, which depends on the degradation of specific proteins. After these proteins perform their functions in the cycle, ubiquitin targeting directs them to the proteasome for degradation.

Autophagy Recycles the Contents of Entire Organelles

As described in Chapter 4, lysosomes contain many different types of acid hydrolases that break down proteins, carbohydrates, nucleic acids, and lipids. This enzymatic function enables lysosomes to break down complex materials. One function of lysosomes involves the digestion of substances that are taken up from outside the cell. This process, called endocytosis, is described in Chapter 5. In addition, lysosomes help digest intracellular materials. In a process known as **autophagy** (from the Greek, meaning eating one's self), cellular material, such as a worn-out organelle, becomes enclosed in a double

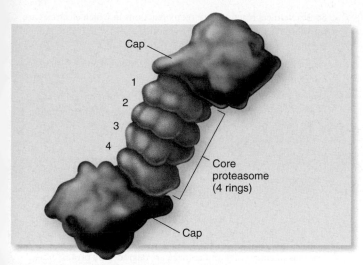

(a) Structure of the eukaryotic proteasome

Figure 6.15 Protein degradation via the proteasome.

Concept Check: What are advantages of protein degradation?

membrane (**Figure 6.16**). This double membrane is formed from a tubule that elongates and eventually wraps around the organelle to form an **autophagosome**. The autophagosome then fuses with a lysosome, and the material inside the autophagosome is digested. The small molecules released from this digestion are recycled back into the cytosol.

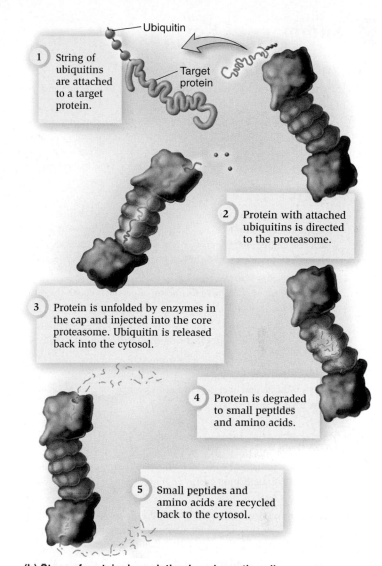

1 String of ubiquitins are attached to a target protein.

2 Protein with attached ubiquitins is directed to the proteasome.

3 Protein is unfolded by enzymes in the cap and injected into the core proteasome. Ubiquitin is released back into the cytosol.

4 Protein is degraded to small peptides and amino acids.

5 Small peptides and amino acids are recycled back to the cytosol.

(b) Steps of protein degradation in eukaryotic cells

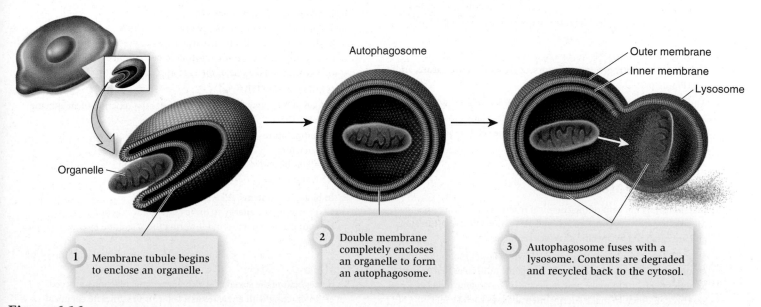

1 Membrane tubule begins to enclose an organelle.

2 Double membrane completely encloses an organelle to form an autophagosome.

3 Autophagosome fuses with a lysosome. Contents are degraded and recycled back to the cytosol.

Figure 6.16 Autophagy.

Summary of Key Concepts

6.1 Energy and Chemical Reactions

- The fate of a chemical reaction is determined by its direction and rate.

- Energy, the ability to promote change or do work, exists in many forms. According to the first law of thermodynamics, energy cannot be created or destroyed, but it can be converted from one form to another. The second law of thermodynamics states that energy interconversions involve an increase in entropy (Figures 6.1, 6.2, Table 6.1).

- Free energy is the amount of available energy that can be used to promote change or do work. Spontaneous or exergonic reactions, which release free energy, have a negative free-energy change, whereas endergonic reactions have a positive change (Figure 6.3).

- Chemical reactions proceed until they reach a state of chemical equilibrium, where the rate of formation of products equals the rate of formation of reactants.

- Exergonic reactions, such as the hydrolysis of ATP, are commonly coupled to cellular processes that would otherwise be endergonic.

- Cells continuously synthesize ATP from ADP and P_i and then hydrolyze it to drive endergonic reactions. Estimates from genome analysis indicate that over 20% of a cell's proteins use ATP (Table 6.2, Figure 6.4).

6.2 Enzymes and Ribozymes

- Enzymes are proteins that speed up the rate of a chemical reaction by lowering the activation energy (E_A) needed to achieve a transition state (Figure 6.5).

- Enzymes recognize reactant molecules, also called substrates, with a high specificity. Conformational changes cause substrates to bind more tightly to enzymes, called induced fit (Figure 6.6).

- Each enzyme-catalyzed reaction exhibits a maximal velocity (V_{max}). The K_M is the substrate concentration at which the velocity of the chemical reaction is half of the V_{max} value. Competitive inhibitors raise the apparent K_M for the substrate, whereas noncompetitive inhibitors lower the V_{max} (Figure 6.7).

- Enzyme function may be affected by a variety of other factors, including prosthetic groups, cofactors, coenzymes, temperature, and pH (Figure 6.8).

- Altman and colleagues discovered that the RNA subunit within RNase P is a ribozyme, an RNA molecule that catalyzes a chemical reaction. Other ribozymes play key roles in the cell (Figures 6.9, 6.10, Table 6.3).

6.3 Overview of Metabolism

- Metabolism is the sum of the chemical reactions in a living organism. Metabolic pathways consist of chemical reactions that occur in steps and are catalyzed by specific enzymes (Figure 6.11).

- Catabolic reactions involve the breakdown of larger molecules into smaller ones. These reactions recycle organic molecules that are used as building blocks to make new molecules. The organic molecules are also broken down to make energy intermediates such as ATP.

- Some chemical reactions are redox reactions in which electrons are transferred from one molecule to another. These can be used to make energy intermediates such as NADH (Figure 6.12).

- Anabolic reactions require an input of energy to synthesize larger molecules and macromolecules.

- Metabolic pathways are controlled by gene regulation, cellular regulation, and biochemical regulation. An example of biochemical regulation is feedback inhibition (Figure 6.13).

6.4 Recycling of Organic Molecules

- Recycling of organic molecules saves a great deal of energy for living organisms.

- Messenger RNAs in eukaryotes are degraded by 5′ to 3′ exonucleases or by exosomes (Figure 6.14).

- Proteins in eukaryotes and archaea are degraded by proteasomes (Figure 6.15).

- Lysosomes digest intracellular material through the process of autophagy (Figure 6.16).

Assess and Discuss

Test Yourself

1. According to the second law of thermodynamics,
   a. energy cannot be created or destroyed.
   b. each energy transfer decreases the disorder of a system.
   c. energy is constant in the universe.
   d. each energy transfer increases the disorder of a system.
   e. chemical energy is a form of potential energy.

2. Reactions that release free energy are
   a. exergonic.
   b. spontaneous.
   c. endergonic.
   d. endothermic.
   e. both a and b.

3. Enzymes speed up reactions by
   a. providing chemical energy to fuel a reaction.
   b. lowering the activation energy necessary to initiate the reaction.
   c. causing an endergonic reaction to become an exergonic reaction.
   d. substituting for one of the reactants necessary for the reaction.
   e. none of the above.

4. Which of the following factors may alter the function of an enzyme?
   a. pH
   b. temperature
   c. cofactors
   d. all of the above
   e. b and c only

5. In biological systems, ATP functions by
   a. providing the energy to drive endergonic reactions.
   b. acting as an enzyme and lowering the activation energy of certain reactions.
   c. adjusting the pH of solutions to maintain optimal conditions for enzyme activity.
   d. regulating the speed at which endergonic reactions proceed.
   e. interacting with enzymes as a cofactor to stimulate chemical reactions.

6. In a chemical reaction, NADH is converted to $NAD^+ + H^+$. We would say that NADH has been
   a. reduced.
   b. phosphorylated.
   c. oxidized.
   d. decarboxylated.
   e. methylated.

7. Currently, scientists are identifying proteins that use ATP as an energy source by
   a. determining whether those proteins function in anabolic or catabolic reactions.
   b. determining if the protein has a known ATP-binding site.
   c. predicting the free energy necessary for the protein to function.
   d. determining if the protein has an ATP synthase subunit.
   e. all of the above.

8. With regard to its effects on an enzyme-catalyzed reaction, a competitive inhibitor
   a. lowers the K_M only.
   b. lowers the K_M and lowers the V_{max}.
   c. raises the K_M only.
   d. raises the K_M and lowers the V_{max}.
   e. raises the K_M and raises the V_{max}.

9. In eukaryotes, mRNAs may be degraded by
   a. a 5′ to 3′ exonuclease.
   b. the exosome.
   c. the proteasome.
   d. all of the above.
   e. a and b only.

10. Autophagy provides a way for cells to
   a. degrade entire organelles and recycle their components.
   b. control the level of ATP.
   c. engulf bacterial cells.
   d. export unwanted organelles out of the cell.
   e. inhibit the first enzyme in a metabolic pathway.

Conceptual Questions

1. With regard to rate and direction, discuss the differences between endergonic and exergonic reactions.

2. Describe the mechanism and purpose of feedback inhibition in a metabolic pathway.

3. A principle of biology is that *living organisms use energy*. Discuss how the recycling of amino acids and nucleotides is energy efficient.

Collaborative Questions

1. Living cells are highly ordered units, yet the universe is heading toward higher entropy. Discuss how life can maintain its order in spite of the second law of thermodynamics. Are we defying this law?

2. What is the advantage of using ATP as a common energy source? Another way of asking this question is, "Why does ATP provide an advantage over using a bunch of different food molecules?" For example, instead of just having a Na^+/K^+-ATPase in a cell, why not have many different ion pumps, each driven by a different food molecule, like a Na^+/K^+-glucosase (a pump that uses glucose), a Na^+/K^+-sucrase (a pump that uses sucrose), a Na^+/K^+-fatty acidase (a pump that uses fatty acids), and so on?

Online Resource

www.brookerbiology.com

Stay a step ahead in your studies with animations that bring concepts to life and practice tests to assess your understanding. Your instructor may also recommend the interactive eBook, individualized learning tools, and more.

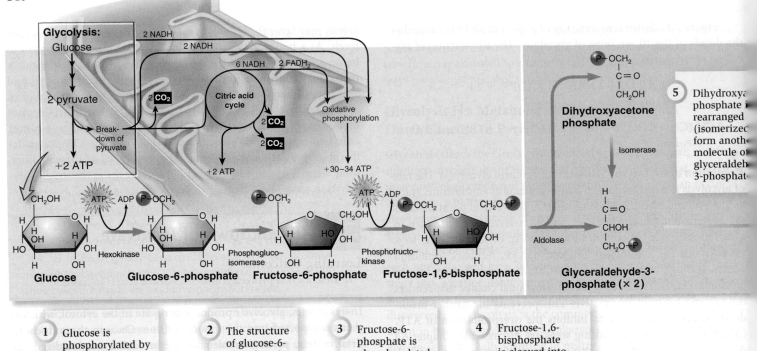

① Glucose is phosphorylated by ATP. Glucose-6-phosphate is more easily trapped in the cell than glucose.

② The structure of glucose-6-phosphate is rearranged to fructose-6-phosphate.

③ Fructose-6-phosphate is phosphorylated to make fructose-1,6-bisphosphate.

④ Fructose-1,6-bisphosphate is cleaved into dihydroxyacetone phosphate and glyceraldehyde-3-phosphate.

Figure 7.3 **A detailed look at the steps of glycolysis.** The pathway begins with a 6-carbon molecule (glucose) that is eventually broken down into 2 molecules that contain 3 carbons each. The notation **x 2** in the figure indicates that 2 of these 3-carbon molecules are produced from each glucose molecule.

BIOLOGY PRINCIPLE **Living organisms maintain homeostasis.** To maintain a relatively constant level of ATP in the cytosol, the activity of phosphofructokinase is controlled by feedback inhibition. A high level of ATP inhibits its function.

Concept Check: *Which of these organic molecules donate a phosphate group to ADP during substrate-level phosphorylation?*

an enzyme complex called pyruvate dehydrogenase (**Figure 7.5**). A molecule of CO_2 is removed from each pyruvate, and the remaining acetyl group is attached to an organic molecule called coenzyme A (CoA) to produce acetyl CoA. (In chemical equations, CoA is depicted as CoA—SH to emphasize how the SH group participates in the chemical reaction.) During this process, two high-energy electrons are removed from pyruvate and transferred to NAD^+ and together with H^+ produce a molecule of NADH. For each pyruvate, the net reaction is as follows:

$$^-O-\overset{O}{\overset{\|}{C}}-\overset{O}{\overset{\|}{C}}-CH_3 + CoA-SH + NAD^+ \rightarrow$$

Pyruvate   CoA

$$CoA-S-\overset{O}{\overset{\|}{C}}-CH_3 + CO_2 + NADH$$

Acetyl CoA

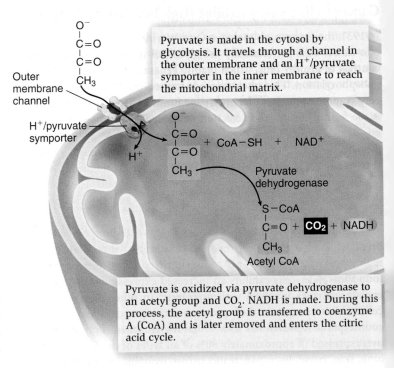

Pyruvate is made in the cytosol by glycolysis. It travels through a channel in the outer membrane and an H^+/pyruvate symporter in the inner membrane to reach the mitochondrial matrix.

Pyruvate is oxidized via pyruvate dehydrogenase to an acetyl group and CO_2. NADH is made. During this process, the acetyl group is transferred to coenzyme A (CoA) and is later removed and enters the citric acid cycle.

Figure 7.5 **Breakdown of pyruvate and the attachment of an acetyl group to CoA.**

The acetyl group is attached to CoA via a covalent bond to a sulfur atom. The hydrolysis of this bond releases a large amount of free energy, making it possible for the acetyl group to be transferred to other organic molecules. As described next, the acetyl group is removed from CoA and enters the citric acid cycle.

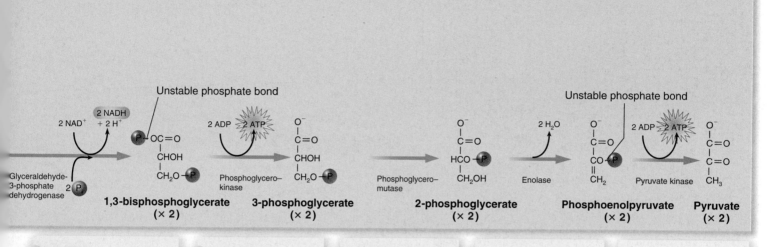

6 Glyceraldehyde-3-phosphate is oxidized to 1,3-bisphosphoglycerate. NADH is produced. In 1,3-bisphosphoglycerate, the phosphate group in the upper left is destabilized, meaning that the bond will break in a highly exergonic reaction.	**7** A phosphate is removed from 1,3-bisphosphoglycerate to form 3-phosphoglycerate. The removed phosphate is transferred to ADP to make ATP via substrate-level phosphorylation.	**8** The phosphate group in 3-phosphoglycerate is moved to a new location, creating 2-phosphoglycerate.	**9** A water molecule is removed from 2-phosphoglycerate to form phosphoenol-pyruvate. In phosphoenol-pyruvate, the phosphate group is destabilized, meaning that the bond will break in a highly exergonic reaction.	**10** A phosphate is removed from phosphoenolpyruvate to form pyruvate. The removed phosphate is transferred to ADP to make ATP via substrate-level phosphorylation.

7.4 Citric Acid Cycle

Learning Outcomes:

1. Discuss the concept of a metabolic cycle.
2. Describe how an acetyl group enters the citric acid cycle and identify the net products of the cycle.

The third stage of glucose metabolism introduces a new concept, that of a **metabolic cycle**. During a metabolic cycle, particular molecules enter the cycle while others leave. The process is cyclical because it involves a series of organic molecules that are regenerated with each turn of the cycle. The idea of a metabolic cycle was first proposed in the early 1930s by the German biochemist Hans Krebs. While studying carbohydrate metabolism in England, he analyzed cell extracts from pigeon muscle and determined that citric acid and other organic molecules participated in a cycle that resulted in the breakdown of carbohydrates to carbon dioxide. This cycle is called the **citric acid cycle**, or the Krebs cycle, in honor of Krebs, who was awarded the Nobel Prize in Physiology or Medicine in 1953.

An overview of the citric acid cycle is shown in **Figure 7.6**. In the first step of the cycle, the acetyl group (with two carbons) is removed from acetyl CoA and attached to oxaloacetate (with four carbons) to form citrate (with six carbons), also called citric acid. Then in a series of several steps, two CO_2 molecules are released. As this occurs, a total of three molecules of NADH, one molecule of $FADH_2$, and one molecule of guanine triphosphate (GTP) are made. The GTP, which is made via substrate-level phosphorylation, is used to make ATP. After a total of eight steps, oxaloacetate is regenerated so the cycle can begin again, provided acetyl CoA is available. **Figure 7.7** shows a more detailed view of the citric acid cycle. For each acetyl group attached to CoA, the net reaction of the citric acid cycle is as follows:

$$\text{Acetyl-CoA} + 2\,H_2O + 3\,NAD^+ + FAD + GDP^{2-} + P_i^{2-} \rightarrow$$

$$\text{CoA—SH} + 2\,CO_2 + 3\,NADH + FADH_2 + GTP^{4-} + 3\,H^+$$

Regulation of the Citric Acid Cycle How is the citric acid cycle controlled? The rate of the cycle is largely regulated by the availability of substrates, such as acetyl-CoA and NAD^+, and by feedback inhibition. The three steps in the cycle that are highly exergonic are those catalyzed by citrate synthase, isocitrate dehydrogenase, and α-ketoglutarate dehydrogenase (see Figure 7.7). Each of these steps can become rate-limiting under certain circumstances, and the way that each enzyme is regulated varies among different species. Let's

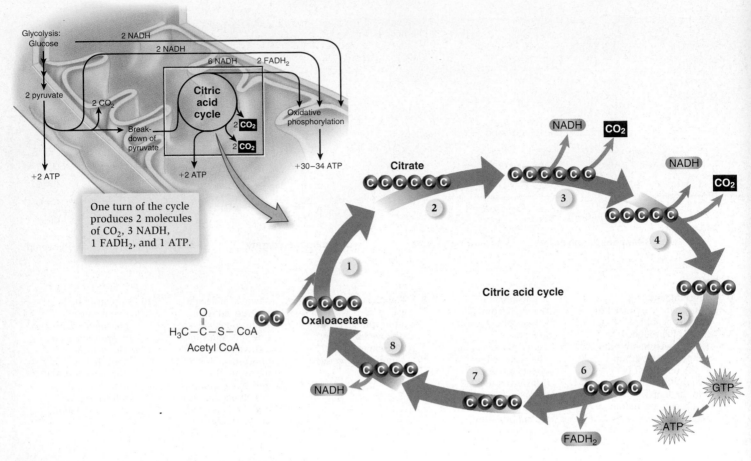

Figure 7.6 Overview of the citric acid cycle.

Concept Check: What are the main products of the citric acid cycle?

consider an example. In mammals, NADH and ATP act as feedback inhibitors of isocitrate dehydrogenase, whereas NAD⁺ and ADP act as activators. In this way, the citric acid cycle is inhibited when NADH and ATP levels are high, but it is stimulated when NAD⁺ and ADP levels are high.

7.5 Oxidative Phosphorylation

Learning Outcomes:

1. Describe how the electron transport chain produces an H⁺ electrochemical gradient.
2. Explain how ATP synthase utilizes the H⁺ electrochemical gradient to synthesize ATP.
3. Analyze the results of the experiment that showed that ATP synthase is a rotary machine.

During the first three stages of glucose metabolism, the oxidation of glucose yields 6 molecules of CO_2, 4 molecules of ATP, 10 molecules of NADH, and 2 molecules of $FADH_2$. Let's now consider how high-energy electrons are removed from NADH and $FADH_2$ to produce more ATP. This process is called **oxidative phosphorylation**. As mentioned earlier, the term refers to the observation that NADH and $FADH_2$ have had electrons removed and have thus become

oxidized, and ATP is made by the phosphorylation of ADP. In this section, we will examine how the oxidative process involves the electron transport chain, whereas the phosphorylation of ADP occurs via ATP synthase.

The Electron Transport Chain Establishes an Electrochemical Gradient

The **electron transport chain (ETC)** consists of a group of protein complexes and small organic molecules embedded in the inner mitochondrial membrane. These components are referred to as an electron transport chain because electrons are passed from one component to the next in a series of redox reactions (**Figure 7.8**). Most members of the ETC are protein complexes (designated I–IV) that have prosthetic groups, which are small molecules permanently attached to the surface of proteins that aid in their function. For example, cytochrome oxidase contains two prosthetic groups, each with an iron atom. The iron in each prosthetic group can readily accept and release an electron. One member of the ETC, ubiquinone (Q), is not a protein. Rather, ubiquinone is a small organic molecule that can accept and release an electron. Ubiquinone, also known as coenzyme Q, is a nonpolar molecule that can diffuse through the lipid bilayer.

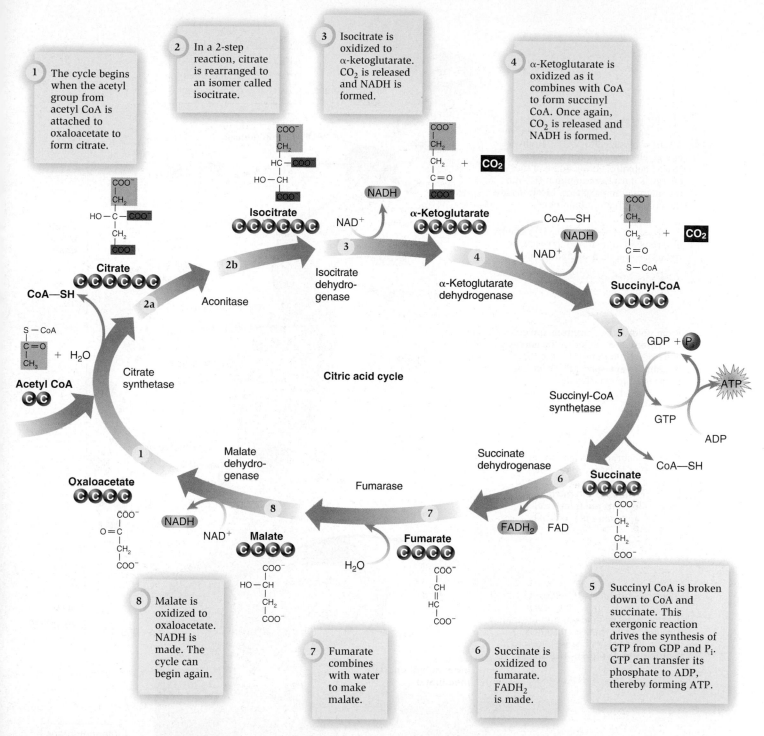

Figure 7.7 **A detailed look at the steps of the citric acid cycle.** The blue boxes indicate the location of the acetyl group, which is oxidized at step 6. (It is oxidized again in step 8.) The green boxes indicate the locations where CO_2 molecules are removed.

The red line in Figure 7.8 shows the path of electron flow. The electrons, which are originally located on NADH or $FADH_2$, are transferred to components of the ETC. The electron path is a series of redox reactions in which electrons are transferred to components with increasingly higher electronegativity. As discussed in Chapter 2, electronegativity is a measure of an atom's ability to attract electrons. At the end of the chain is oxygen, which is the most electronegative

and the final electron acceptor. The ETC is also called the **respiratory chain** because the oxygen we breathe is used in this process.

NADH and $FADH_2$ donate their electrons at different points in the ETC. Two high-energy electrons from NADH are first transferred one at a time to NADH dehydrogenase (complex I). They are then transferred to ubiquinone (Q), cytochrome b-c_1 (complex III), cytochrome c, and cytochrome oxidase (complex IV). The final electron

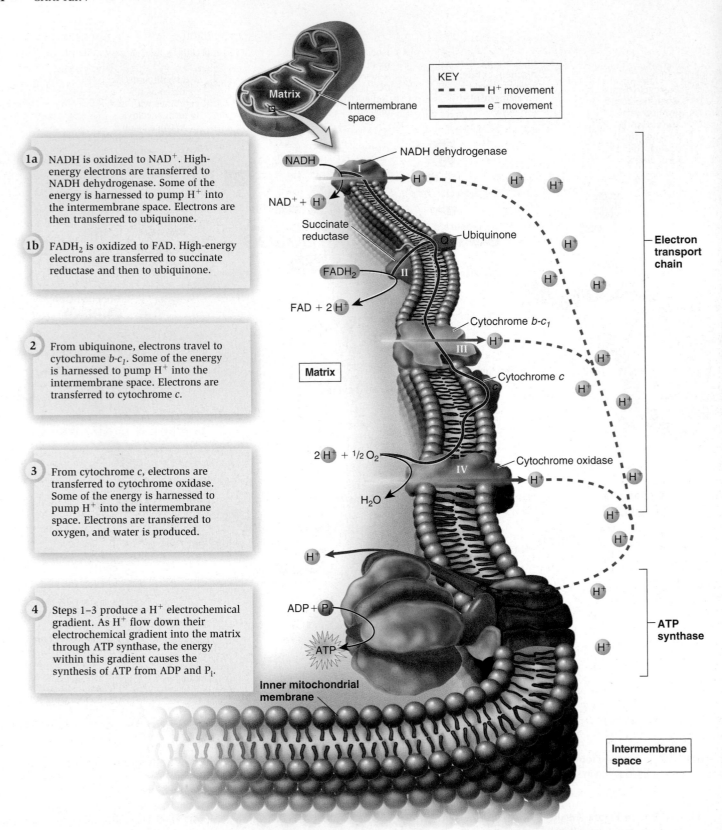

1a NADH is oxidized to NAD$^+$. High-energy electrons are transferred to NADH dehydrogenase. Some of the energy is harnessed to pump H$^+$ into the intermembrane space. Electrons are then transferred to ubiquinone.

1b FADH$_2$ is oxidized to FAD. High-energy electrons are transferred to succinate reductase and then to ubiquinone.

2 From ubiquinone, electrons travel to cytochrome b-c_1. Some of the energy is harnessed to pump H$^+$ into the intermembrane space. Electrons are transferred to cytochrome c.

3 From cytochrome c, electrons are transferred to cytochrome oxidase. Some of the energy is harnessed to pump H$^+$ into the intermembrane space. Electrons are transferred to oxygen, and water is produced.

4 Steps 1–3 produce a H$^+$ electrochemical gradient. As H$^+$ flow down their electrochemical gradient into the matrix through ATP synthase, the energy within this gradient causes the synthesis of ATP from ADP and P$_i$.

KEY
- - - - H$^+$ movement
——— e$^-$ movement

Matrix

Intermembrane space

NADH

NADH dehydrogenase

NAD$^+$ + H$^+$

Succinate reductase

FADH$_2$

FAD + 2 H$^+$

Q Ubiquinone

Cytochrome b-c_1

Matrix

Cytochrome c

2 H$^+$ + ½ O$_2$

Cytochrome oxidase

H$_2$O

ADP + P$_i$

ATP

Inner mitochondrial membrane

Intermembrane space

Electron transport chain

ATP synthase

Figure 7.8 Oxidative phosphorylation. This process consists of two distinct events: the electron transport chain (ETC) and ATP synthesis. The ETC oxidizes, or removes electrons from, NADH or FADH$_2$ and pumps H$^+$ across the inner mitochondrial membrane. In chemiosmosis, ATP synthase uses the energy in this H$^+$ electrochemical gradient to phosphorylate ADP, thereby synthesizing ATP. In this figure, an O$_2$ atom is represented as ½ O$_2$ to emphasize that the ETC reduces oxygen when it is in its molecular (O$_2$) form.

Concept Check: *Can you explain the name of cytochrome oxidase? Can you think of another appropriate name?*

acceptor is O_2. By comparison, $FADH_2$ transfers electrons to succinate reductase (complex II), then to ubiquinone, and the rest of the chain.

As shown in Figure 7.8, some of the energy that is released during the movement of electrons is used to pump H^+ across the inner mitochondrial membrane, from the matrix and into the intermembrane space. This active transport establishes a large **H^+ electrochemical gradient**, in which the concentration of H^+ is higher outside of the matrix than inside and an excess of positive charge exists outside the matrix. Because hydrogen ions consist of protons, the H^+ electrochemical gradient is also called the **proton-motive force**. NADH dehydrogenase, cytochrome b-c_1, and cytochrome oxidase are H^+ pumps. While traveling along the electron transport chain, electrons release free energy, and some of this energy is captured by these proteins to actively transport H^+ out of the matrix into the intermembrane space against the H^+ electrochemical gradient. Because the electrons from $FADH_2$ enter the chain at an intermediate step, they release less energy and so result in fewer hydrogen ions being pumped out of the matrix than do electrons from NADH.

Why do electrons travel from NADH or $FADH_2$ to the ETC and then to O_2? As you might expect, the answer lies in free-energy changes. The electrons found on the energy intermediates have a high amount of energy. As they travel along the ETC, free energy is released (**Figure 7.9**). The movement of one electron from NADH to O_2 results in a very negative free-energy change of approximately –25 kcal/mol. That is why the process is spontaneous and proceeds in the forward direction. Because it is a highly exergonic reaction, some of the free energy can be harnessed to do cellular work. In this case, some energy is used to pump H^+ across the inner mitochondrial membrane and establish an H^+ electrochemical gradient that is then used to power ATP synthesis.

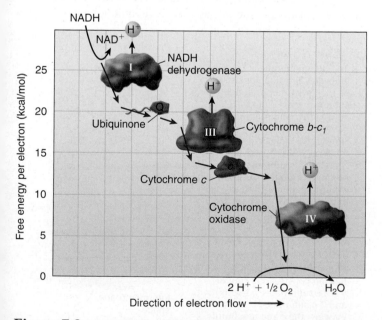

Figure 7.9 **The relationship between free energy and electron movement along the electron transport chain.** As electrons hop from one site to another along the electron transport chain, they release energy. Some of this energy is harnessed to pump H^+ across the inner mitochondrial membrane. The total energy released by a single electron is approximately –25 kcal/mol.

Chemicals that inhibit the flow of electrons along the ETC can have lethal effects. For example, one component of the ETC, cytochrome oxidase (complex IV), is inhibited by cyanide. The deadly effects of cyanide ingestion occur because the ETC is shut down, preventing cells from making enough ATP for survival.

ATP Synthase Makes ATP via Chemiosmosis

The second event of oxidative phosphorylation is the synthesis of ATP by an enzyme called **ATP synthase**. The H^+ electrochemical gradient across the inner mitochondrial membrane is a source of potential energy. How is this energy used? The passive flow of H^+ back into the matrix is an exergonic process. The lipid bilayer is relatively impermeable to H^+. However, H^+ can pass through the membrane-embedded portion of ATP synthase. This enzyme harnesses some of the free energy that is released as the ions flow through its membrane-embedded region to synthesize ATP from ADP and P_i (see bottom of Figure 7.8). This is an example of an energy conversion: Energy in the form of an H^+ gradient is converted to chemical bond energy in ATP. The synthesis of ATP that occurs as a result of pushing H^+ across a membrane is called chemiosmosis (from the Greek *osmos*, meaning to push). The theory behind it was proposed by Peter Mitchell, a British biochemist who was awarded the Nobel Prize in Chemistry in 1978.

Regulation of Oxidative Phosphorylation How is oxidative phosphorylation controlled? This process is regulated by a variety of factors, including the availability of ETC substrates, such as NADH and O_2, and by the ATP/ADP ratio. When ATP levels are high, ATP binds to a subunit of cytochrome oxidase (complex IV), thereby inhibiting the ETC and oxidative phosphorylation. By comparison, when ADP levels are high, oxidative phosphorylation is stimulated for two reasons: (1) ADP stimulates cytochrome oxidase, and (2) ADP is a substrate that is used (with P_i) to make ATP.

NADH Oxidation Makes a Large Proportion of a Cell's ATP

For each molecule of NADH that is oxidized and each molecule of ATP that is made, the two chemical reactions of oxidative phosphorylation can be represented as follows:

$$NADH + H^+ + \tfrac{1}{2}O_2 \rightarrow NAD^+ + H_2O$$

$$ADP^{2-} + P_i^{2-} \rightarrow ATP^{4-} + H_2O$$

The oxidation of NADH to NAD^+ results in an H^+ electrochemical gradient in which more hydrogen ions are in the intermembrane space than are in the matrix. The synthesis of one ATP molecule is thought to require the movement of three to four ions down their H^+ electrochemical gradient into the matrix.

When we add up the maximal amount of ATP that can be made by oxidative phosphorylation, most researchers agree it is in the range of 30 to 34 ATP molecules for each glucose molecule that is broken down to CO_2 and H_2O. However, the maximum amount of ATP is rarely achieved, for two reasons. First, although 10 NADH and 2 $FADH_2$ are available to make the H^+ electrochemical gradient across the inner mitochondrial membrane, a cell uses some of these molecules for anabolic pathways. For example, NADH is used in the synthesis of organic molecules such as glycerol (a component of phospholipids). It is also used to make lactic acid, which is secreted from muscle cells during strenuous exercise (described later in Figure 7.16a). Second, the mitochondrion may use some of the H^+ electrochemical gradient for other purposes. For example, the gradient is used for the uptake of pyruvate into the matrix via an H^+/pyruvate symporter (see Figure 7.5). Therefore, the actual amount of ATP synthesis is usually a little less than the maximum number of 30 to 34. Even so, when we compare the amount of ATP that is made by glycolysis (2), the citric acid cycle (2), and oxidative phosphorylation (30–34), we see that oxidative phosphorylation provides a cell with a much greater capacity to make ATP.

Experiments with Purified Proteins in Membrane Vesicles Verified Chemiosmosis

To show experimentally that ATP synthase directly uses an H^+ electrochemical gradient to make ATP, researchers needed to purify the enzyme and study its function in vitro. In 1974, Efraim Racker and

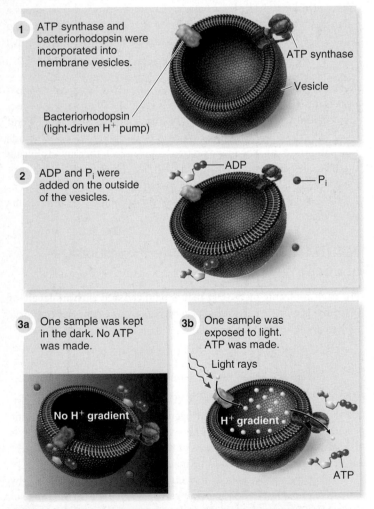

1 ATP synthase and bacteriorhodopsin were incorporated into membrane vesicles.

ATP synthase

Vesicle

Bacteriorhodopsin (light-driven H^+ pump)

2 ADP and P_i were added on the outside of the vesicles.

ADP

P_i

3a One sample was kept in the dark. No ATP was made.

No H^+ gradient

3b One sample was exposed to light. ATP was made.

Light rays

H^+ gradient

ATP

Figure 7.10 The Racker and Stoeckenius experiment. In this experiment, bacteriorhodopsin pumped H^+ into vesicles, and the resulting H^+ electrochemical gradient was sufficient to drive ATP synthesis via ATP synthase.

Concept Check: Is the functioning of the electron transport chain always needed to make ATP via ATP synthase?

Walther Stoeckenius purified ATP synthase and another protein called bacteriorhodopsin, which is found in certain species of archaea. Previous research had shown that bacteriorhodopsin is a light-driven H^+ pump. Racker and Stoeckenius took both purified proteins and inserted them into membrane vesicles (**Figure 7.10**). ATP synthase was oriented so its ATP-synthesizing region was on the outside of the vesicles. Bacteriorhodopsin was oriented so it would pump H^+ into the vesicles. They added ADP and P_i on the outside of the vesicles. In the dark, no ATP was made. However, when they shone light on the vesicles, a substantial amount of ATP was synthesized. Because bacteriorhodopsin was already known to be a light-driven H^+ pump, these results convinced researchers that ATP synthase uses an H^+ electrochemical gradient as an energy source to make ATP.

ATP Synthase Is a Rotary Machine That Makes ATP as It Spins

The structure and function of ATP synthase are particularly intriguing and have received much attention over the past few decades. ATP synthase is a rotary machine (**Figure 7.11**). The region embedded in the membrane is composed of three types of subunits called *a*, *b*, and *c*. Approximately 10 to 14 *c* subunits form a ring in the membrane. One *a* subunit is bound to this ring, and two *b* subunits are attached to the *a* subunit and protrude from the membrane. The nonmembrane-embedded subunits are designated with Greek letters. One ε and one γ subunit bind to the ring of *c* subunits. The γ subunit forms a long stalk that pokes into the center of another ring of three α and three β subunits. Each β subunit contains a catalytic site where ATP is made. Finally, the δ subunit forms a connection between the ring of α and β subunits and the two *b* subunits.

When hydrogen ions pass through a narrow channel at the contact site between a *c* subunit and the *a* subunit, a conformational

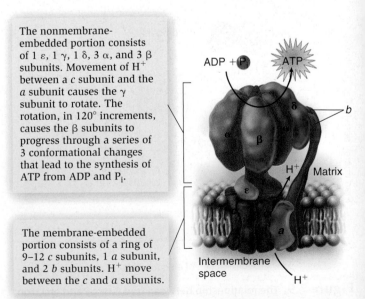

The nonmembrane-embedded portion consists of 1 ε, 1 γ, 1 δ, 3 α, and 3 β subunits. Movement of H^+ between a *c* subunit and the *a* subunit causes the γ subunit to rotate. The rotation, in 120° increments, causes the β subunits to progress through a series of 3 conformational changes that lead to the synthesis of ATP from ADP and P_i.

The membrane-embedded portion consists of a ring of 9–12 *c* subunits, 1 *a* subunit, and 2 *b* subunits. H^+ move between the *c* and *a* subunits.

ADP + P_i

ATP

δ

b

α

β

H^+ Matrix

ε

a

Intermembrane space

H^+

Figure 7.11 The subunit structure and function of ATP synthase.

Concept Check: If the β subunit in the front center of this figure is in conformation 2, what are the conformations of the β subunit on the left and the β subunit on the back right?

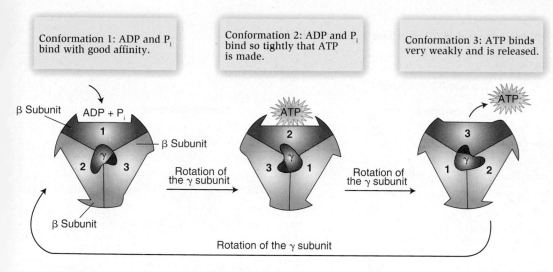

Conformation 1: ADP and P_i bind with good affinity.

Conformation 2: ADP and P_i bind so tightly that ATP is made.

Conformation 3: ATP binds very weakly and is released.

Figure 7.12 **Conformational changes that result in ATP synthesis.** For simplicity, the α subunits are not shown. This drawing emphasizes the conformational changes in the β subunit shown at the top. The other two β subunits also make ATP. All three β subunits alternate between three conformational states due to their interactions with the γ subunit.

change causes the γ subunit to turn clockwise (when viewed from the intermembrane space). Each time the γ subunit turns 120°, it changes its contacts with the three β subunits, which, in turn, causes the β subunits to change their conformations. How do these conformational changes promote ATP synthesis? The answer is that the conformational changes occur in a way that favors ATP synthesis and release. As shown in **Figure 7.12**, the conformational changes in the β subunits happen in the following order:

- Conformation 1: ADP and P_i bind with good affinity.
- Conformation 2: ADP and P_i bind so tightly that ATP is made.
- Conformation 3: ATP (and ADP and P_i) bind very weakly, and ATP is released.

Each time the γ subunit turns 120°, it causes a β subunit to change to the next conformation. After conformation 3, a 120° turn by the γ subunit returns a β subunit back to conformation 1, and the cycle of

ATP synthesis can begin again. Because ATP synthase has three β subunits, each subunit is in a different conformation at any given time.

American biochemist Paul Boyer proposed the concept of a rotary machine in the late 1970s. In his model, the three β subunits alternate between three conformations, as described previously. Boyer's original idea was met with great skepticism, because the concept that part of an enzyme could spin was very novel, to say the least. In 1994, British biochemist John Walker and his colleagues determined the three-dimensional structure of the nonmembrane-embedded portion of the ATP synthase. The structure revealed that each of the three β subunits had a different conformation—one with ADP bound, one with ATP bound, and one without any nucleotide bound. This result supported Boyer's model. In 1997, Boyer and Walker shared the Nobel Prize in Chemistry for their work on ATP synthase. As described next in the Feature Investigation, other researchers subsequently visualized the rotation of the γ subunit.

FEATURE INVESTIGATION

Yoshida and Kinosita Demonstrated That the γ Subunit of ATP Synthase Spins

In 1997, Japanese biochemist Masasuke Yoshida, physicist Kazuhiko Kinosita, and colleagues set out to experimentally visualize the rotary nature of ATP synthase (**Figure 7.13**). The membrane-embedded region of ATP synthase can be separated from the rest of the protein by treatment of mitochondrial membranes with a high concentration of salt, releasing the portion of the protein containing one γ, three α, and three β subunits. The researchers adhered the $\gamma\alpha_3\beta_3$ complex to a glass slide so the γ subunit was protruding upward. Because the γ subunit is too small to be seen with a light microscope, the rotation of the γ subunit cannot be visualized directly. To circumvent this problem, the researchers attached a large, fluorescently labeled actin filament to the γ subunit via linker proteins. The fluorescently labeled actin filament is very long compared with the γ subunit and can be readily seen with a fluorescence microscope.

Because the membrane-embedded portion of the protein is missing, you may be wondering how the researchers could get the γ subunit to rotate. The answer is they added ATP. Although the normal function

of the ATP synthase is to make ATP, it can also hydrolyze ATP. In other words, ATP synthase can run backwards. As shown in the data for Figure 7.13, when the researchers added ATP, they observed that the fluorescently labeled actin filament rotated in a counterclockwise direction, which is opposite to the direction that the γ subunit rotates when ATP is synthesized. Actin filaments were observed to rotate for more than 100 revolutions in the presence of ATP. These results convinced the scientific community that ATP synthase is a rotary machine.

Experimental Questions

1. The components of ATP synthase are too small to be visualized by light microscopy. For the experiment of Figure 7.13, how did the researchers observe the movement of ATP synthase?

2. In the experiment of Figure 7.13, what observation did the researchers make that indicated ATP synthase is a rotary machine? What was the control of this experiment? What did it indicate?

3. Were the rotations seen by the researchers in the data of Figure 7.13 in the same direction as expected in the mitochondria during ATP synthesis? Why or why not?

Figure 7.13 Yoshida and Kinosita provide evidence that ATP synthase is a rotary machine.

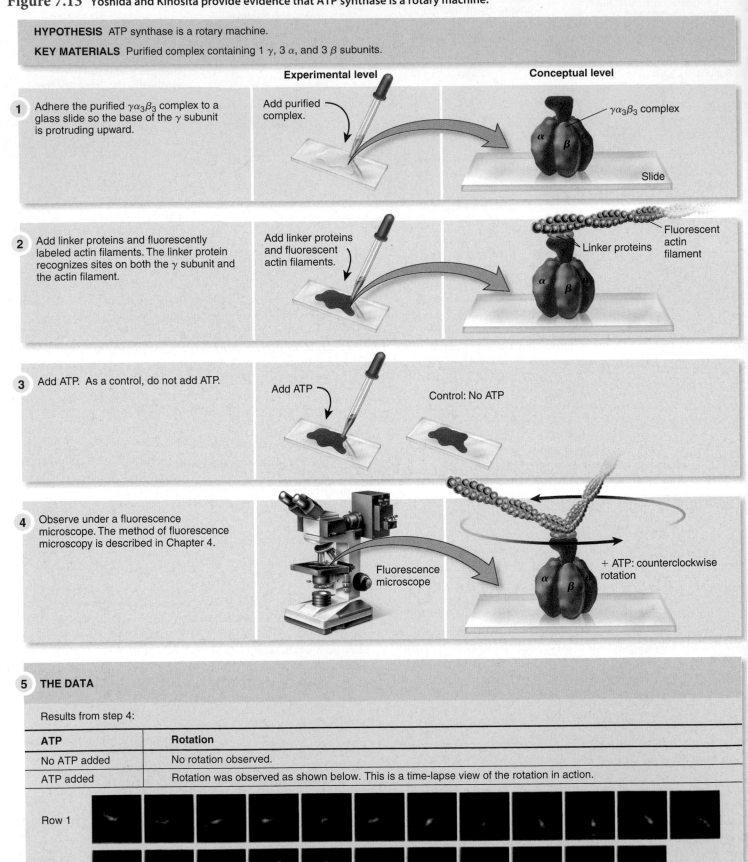

HYPOTHESIS ATP synthase is a rotary machine.

KEY MATERIALS Purified complex containing 1 γ, 3 α, and 3 β subunits.

Experimental level — Conceptual level

1 Adhere the purified $\gamma\alpha_3\beta_3$ complex to a glass slide so the base of the γ subunit is protruding upward.

Add purified complex.

$\gamma\alpha_3\beta_3$ complex

Slide

2 Add linker proteins and fluorescently labeled actin filaments. The linker protein recognizes sites on both the γ subunit and the actin filament.

Add linker proteins and fluorescent actin filaments.

Fluorescent actin filament

Linker proteins

3 Add ATP. As a control, do not add ATP.

Add ATP

Control: No ATP

4 Observe under a fluorescence microscope. The method of fluorescence microscopy is described in Chapter 4.

Fluorescence microscope

+ ATP: counterclockwise rotation

5 **THE DATA**

Results from step 4:

ATP	Rotation
No ATP added	No rotation observed.
ATP added	Rotation was observed as shown below. This is a time-lapse view of the rotation in action.

Row 1

Row 2

6 **CONCLUSION** The γ subunit rotates counterclockwise when ATP is hydrolyzed. It would be expected to rotate clockwise when ATP is synthesized.

7 **SOURCE** Reprinted by permission from Macmillan Publishers Ltd. Noji, H., Yasuda, R.,Yoshida, M., and Kinosita, K. 1997. Direct observation of the rotation of F$_1$-ATPase. *Nature* 386:299–303.

7.6 Connections Among Carbohydrate, Protein, and Fat Metabolism

Learning Outcome:

1. Explain how carbohydrate, protein, and fat metabolism are interconnected.

When you eat a meal, it usually contains not only carbohydrates (including glucose) but also proteins and fats. These molecules are broken down by some of the same enzymes involved with glucose metabolism.

As shown in **Figure 7.14**, proteins and fats can enter into glycolysis or the citric acid cycle at different points. Proteins are first acted on by enzymes, either in digestive juices or within cells, that cleave the bonds connecting individual amino acids. Because the 20 amino acids differ in their side chains, amino acids and their breakdown products can enter at different points in the pathway. Breakdown products of some amino acids can enter at later steps of glycolysis, or an acetyl group can be removed from certain amino acids and become attached to CoA and then enter the citric acid cycle (see Figure 7.14). Other amino acids are modified and enter the citric acid cycle.

Fats are typically broken down to glycerol and fatty acids. Glycerol can be modified to glyceraldehyde-3-phosphate and enter glycolysis. Fatty acyl tails can have two carbon acetyl units removed, which bind to CoA and enter the citric acid cycle. By using the same pathways for the breakdown of sugars, amino acids, and fats, cellular metabolism is more efficient because the same enzymes are used for the breakdown of different starting molecules.

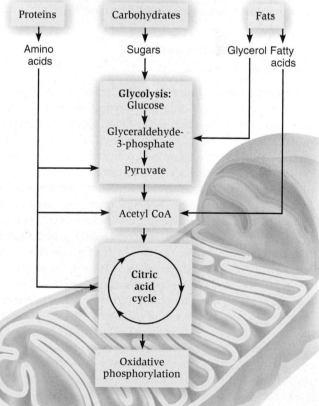

Figure 7.14 **Integration of carbohydrate, protein, and fat metabolism.** Breakdown products of proteins and fats are used as fuel for cellular respiration, entering the same pathway used to break down carbohydrates.

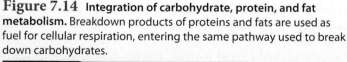

Concept Check: *What is a cellular advantage of integrating protein, carbohydrate, and fat metabolism?*

7.7 Anaerobic Respiration and Fermentation

Learning Outcomes:

1. Describe how certain microorganisms make ATP using a final electron acceptor of their electron transport chain that is not oxygen.
2. Explain how muscle and yeast cells use fermentation to synthesize ATP under anaerobic conditions.

Thus far, we have surveyed catabolic pathways that result in the complete breakdown of glucose in the presence of oxygen. Cells also commonly metabolize organic molecules in the absence of oxygen. The term **anaerobic** is used to describe an environment that lacks oxygen. Many bacteria and archaea and some fungi exist in anaerobic environments but still have to oxidize organic molecules to obtain sufficient amounts of energy. Examples include microbes living in your intestinal tract and those living deep in the soil. Similarly, when a person exercises strenuously, the rate of oxygen consumption by muscle cells may greatly exceed the rate of oxygen delivery—particularly at the start of strenuous exercise. Under these conditions, muscle cells become anaerobic and must obtain sufficient energy in the absence of oxygen to maintain their level of activity.

Organisms have evolved two different strategies to metabolize organic molecules in the absence of oxygen. One mechanism is to use a substance other than O_2 as the final electron acceptor of an electron transport chain, a process called **anaerobic respiration**. A second approach is to produce ATP only via substrate-level phosphorylation without any net oxidation of organic molecules, a process called fermentation. In this section, we will consider examples of both strategies.

Some Microorganisms Carry Out Anaerobic Respiration

At the end of the ETC discussed earlier in Figure 7.8, cytochrome oxidase recognizes O_2 and catalyzes its reduction to H_2O. The final electron acceptor of the chain is O_2. Many species of bacteria that live under anaerobic conditions have evolved enzymes that function similarly to cytochrome oxidase but recognize molecules other than O_2 and use them as the final electron acceptor.

For example, under anaerobic conditions *Escherichia coli*, a bacterial species found in your intestinal tract, produces an enzyme called nitrate reductase. This enzyme uses nitrate (NO_3^-) as the final electron acceptor of an electron transport chain. **Figure 7.15** shows a simplified ETC in *E. coli* in which nitrate is the final electron acceptor. In *E. coli* and other bacterial species, the ETC is in the plasma membrane that surrounds the cytoplasm. Electrons travel from NADH to NADH dehydrogenase to ubiquinone (Q) to cytochrome *b* and then to nitrate reductase. At the end of the chain, NO_3^- is converted to nitrite (NO_2^-). This process generates an H^+ electrochemical gradient in three ways. First, NADH dehydrogenase pumps H^+ out of the cytoplasm. Second, ubiquinone picks up H^+ in the cytoplasm and carries it to the other side of the membrane. Third, the reduction of nitrate to nitrite consumes H^+ in the cytoplasm. The generation of an H^+ gradient via these three processes allows *E. coli* cells to make ATP via chemiosmosis under anaerobic conditions.

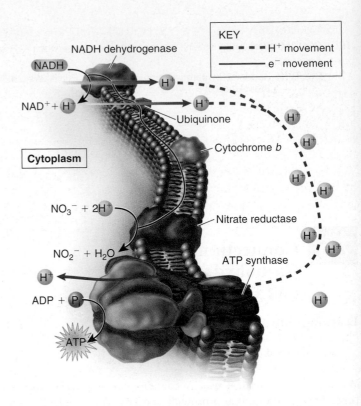

Figure 7.15 **An example of anaerobic respiration in *E. coli*.** When oxygen is absent, *E. coli* can use nitrate instead of oxygen as the final electron acceptor in an electron transport chain. This generates an H^+ electrochemical gradient that is used to make ATP via chemiosmosis. Note: As shown in this figure, ubiquinone (Q) picks up H^+ on one side of the membrane and deposits it on the other side. A similar event happens during aerobic respiration in mitochondria (see Figure 7.8), except that ubiquinone transfers H^+ to cytochrome *b*-c_1, which pumps it into the intermembrane space.

Fermentation Is the Breakdown of Organic Molecules Without Net Oxidation

Many organisms, including animals and yeast, use only O_2 as the final electron acceptor of their ETCs. When confronted with anaerobic conditions, these organisms must have a different way of producing sufficient ATP. One strategy is to make ATP via glycolysis, which can occur under both anaerobic or aerobic conditions. Under anaerobic conditions, cells do not use the citric acid cycle or the ETC, but make ATP only via glycolysis.

A key issue is that glycolysis requires NAD^+ and generates NADH. Under aerobic conditions, oxygen acts as a final electron acceptor, and the high-energy electrons from NADH can be used to make more ATP. To make ATP, NADH is oxidized to NAD^+. However, this cannot occur under anaerobic conditions in yeast and animals, and, as a result, NADH builds up and NAD^+ decreases. This is a potential problem for two reasons. First, at high concentrations, NADH haphazardly donates its electrons to other molecules and promotes the formation of free radicals, highly reactive chemicals that damage DNA and cellular proteins. For this reason, yeast and animal cells exposed to anaerobic conditions must have a way to remove the excess NADH generated from the breakdown of glucose. The second problem is the decrease in NAD^+. Cells need to regenerate NAD^+ to keep glycolysis running and make ATP via substrate-level phosphorylation.

How do muscle cells cope with the buildup of NADH and decrease in NAD^+? When a muscle is working strenuously and becomes anaerobic, as in high-intensity exercise, the pyruvate from glycolysis is reduced to make lactate. (The uncharged, or protonated, form is called lactic acid.) The electrons to reduce pyruvate are derived from NADH, which is oxidized to NAD^+ (**Figure 7.16a**). Therefore, this process decreases NADH and reduces its potentially harmful effects. It also increases the level of NAD^+, thereby allowing glycolysis to continue. The lactate is secreted from muscle cells. Once sufficient oxygen is restored, the lactate produced during strenuous exercise can be taken up by cells, converted back to pyruvate, and used for energy, or it may be used to make glucose by the liver and other tissues.

Yeast cells cope with anaerobic conditions differently. During wine making, a yeast cell metabolizes sugar under anaerobic conditions. The pyruvate is broken down to CO_2 and a two-carbon molecule called acetaldehyde. The acetaldehyde is then reduced by NADH

to make ethanol, while NADH is oxidized to NAD^+ (**Figure 7.16b**). Similar to lactate production in muscle cells, this decreases NADH and increases NAD^+, thereby preventing the harmful effects of NADH and allowing glycolysis to continue.

The term **fermentation** is used to describe the breakdown of organic molecules to harness energy without any net oxidation (that is, without any removal of electrons). The pathways of breaking down glucose to lactate or ethanol are examples of fermentation. Although electrons are removed from an organic molecule such as glucose to make pyruvate and NADH, the electrons are donated back to an organic molecule in the production of lactate or ethanol. Therefore, there is no net removal of electrons from an organic molecule. Compared with oxidative phosphorylation, fermentation produces far less ATP, for two reasons. First, glucose is not oxidized completely to CO_2 and H_2O. Second, the NADH made during glycolysis cannot be used to make more ATP. Overall, the complete breakdown of glucose in the presence of oxygen yields 34 to 38 ATP molecules. By comparison, the anaerobic breakdown of glucose to lactate or ethanol yields only 2 ATP molecules.

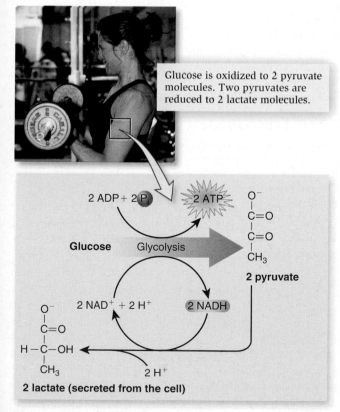

Glucose is oxidized to 2 pyruvate molecules. Two pyruvates are reduced to 2 lactate molecules.

Glucose is oxidized to 2 pyruvate molecules. Two acetaldehyde molecules are reduced to 2 ethanol molecules.

(a) Production of lactic acid

(b) Production of ethanol

Figure 7.16 Examples of fermentation. In these examples, NADH is produced by the oxidation of an organic molecule, and then the NADH is converted back to NAD^+ by donating electrons to a different organic molecule such as pyruvate **(a)** or acetaldehyde **(b)**.

 BIOLOGY PRINCIPLE Biology affects our society. Fermentation by microorganisms is used in wine making, beer brewing, and bread making.

Summary of Key Concepts

7.1   Overview of Cellular Respiration

- Cells obtain energy via cellular respiration, which involves the breakdown of organic molecules and the export of waste products.

- The breakdown of glucose occurs in four stages: glycolysis, pyruvate breakdown, citric acid cycle, and oxidative phosphorylation (Figure 7.1).

7.2   Glycolysis

- During glycolysis, which occurs in the cytosol, glucose is split into two molecules of pyruvate, with a net yield of 2 molecules of ATP and 2 of NADH. ATP is made by substrate-level phosphorylation (Figures 7.2, 7.3).

- Cancer cells preferentially carry out glycolysis, which enables the detection of tumors via a procedure called positron-emission tomography (PET) (Figure 7.4).

7.3   Breakdown of Pyruvate

- Pyruvate is broken down to CO_2 and an acetyl group that becomes attached to CoA. NADH is made during this process (Figure 7.5).

7.4   Citric Acid Cycle

- During the citric acid cycle, an acetyl group is removed from acetyl CoA and attached to oxaloacetate to make citrate. In a series of steps, 2 CO_2 molecules, 3 NADH, 1 $FADH_2$, and 1 ATP are made, after which the cycle begins again (Figures 7.6, 7.7).

7.5   Oxidative Phosphorylation

- Oxidative phosphorylation involves two events: (1) The electron transport chain (ETC) oxidizes NADH or $FADH_2$ and generates an H^+ electrochemical gradient, and (2) this gradient is used by ATP synthase to make ATP via chemiosmosis (Figures 7.8, 7.9).

- Racker and Stoeckenius showed that ATP synthase uses an H^+ gradient by reconstituting ATP synthase with a light-driven H^+ pump (Figure 7.10).

- ATP synthase is a rotary machine. The rotation is triggered by the passage of H^+ through a channel between a c subunit and the a subunit that causes the γ subunit to spin, resulting in three conformational changes in the β subunits that promote ATP synthesis (Figures 7.11, 7.12).

- Yoshida and Kinosita demonstrated rotation of the γ subunit by attaching a fluorescently labeled actin filament and observing its movement during the hydrolysis of ATP (Figure 7.13).

7.6   Connections Among Carbohydrate, Protein, and Fat Metabolism

- Proteins and fats can enter into glycolysis or the citric acid cycle at different points (Figure 7.14).

7.7   Anaerobic Respiration and Fermentation

- Anaerobic respiration occurs in the absence of oxygen. Certain microorganisms carry out anaerobic respiration in which the final electron acceptor of the ETC is a substance other than oxygen, such as nitrate (Figure 7.15).

- During fermentation, organic molecules are broken down without any net oxidation (that is, without any net removal of electrons). Examples include lactic acid production in muscle cells and ethanol production in yeast cells (Figure 7.16).

Assess and Discuss

Test Yourself

1. Which of the following pathways occurs in the cytosol?
   a. glycolysis
   b. breakdown of pyruvate to an acetyl group
   c. citric acid cycle
   d. oxidative phosphorylation
   e. all of the above

2. To break down glucose to CO_2 and H_2O, which of the following metabolic pathways is *not* involved?
   a. glycolysis
   b. breakdown of pyruvate to an acetyl group
   c. citric acid cycle
   d. photosynthesis
   e. c and d only

3. The net products of glycolysis are
   a. 6 CO_2, 4 ATP, and 2 NADH.
   b. 2 pyruvate, 2 ATP, and 2 NADH.
   c. 2 pyruvate, 4 ATP, and 2 NADH.
   d. 2 pyruvate, 2 GTP, and 2 CO_2.
   e. 2 CO_2, 2 ATP, and glucose.

4. During glycolysis, ATP is produced by
   a. oxidative phosphorylation.
   b. substrate-level phosphorylation.
   c. redox reactions.
   d. all of the above.
   e. both a and b.

5. The ability to diagnose tumors using [^{18}F]-fluorodeoxyglucose (FDG) is based on the phenomenon that most types of cancer cells exhibit higher levels of
   a. glycolysis.
   b. pyruvate breakdown.
   c. citric acid metabolism.
   d. oxidative phosphorylation.
   e. all of the above.

6. ATP is made via chemiosmosis during
   a. glycolysis.
   b. the breakdown of pyruvate.
   c. the citric acid cycle.
   d. oxidative phosphorylation.
   e. all of the above.

7. Certain drugs act as ionophores that cause the mitochondrial membrane to be highly permeable to H⁺. How would such drugs affect oxidative phosphorylation?
   a. Movement of electrons down the ETC would be inhibited.
   b. ATP synthesis would be inhibited.
   c. ATP synthesis would be unaffected.
   d. ATP synthesis would be stimulated.
   e. Both a and b are correct.

8. The source of energy that *directly* drives the synthesis of ATP during oxidative phosphorylation is
   a. the oxidation of NADH.
   b. the oxidation of glucose.
   c. the oxidation of pyruvate.
   d. the H⁺ gradient.
   e. the reduction of O_2.

9. Compared with oxidative phosphorylation in mitochondria, a key difference of anaerobic respiration in bacteria is that
   a. more ATP is made.
   b. ATP is made only via substrate-level phosphorylation.
   c. O_2 is converted to H_2O_2 rather than H_2O.
   d. something other than O_2 acts as a final electron acceptor of the ETC.
   e. b and d.

10. When a muscle becomes anaerobic during strenuous exercise, why is it necessary to convert pyruvate to lactate?
    a. to decrease NAD⁺ and increase NADH
    b. to decrease NADH and increase NAD⁺
    c. to increase NADH and increase NAD⁺
    d. to decrease NADH and decrease NAD⁺
    e. to keep oxidative phosphorylation running

Conceptual Questions

1. The electron transport chain is so named because electrons are transported from one component to another. Describe the purpose of the ETC.

2. What causes the rotation of the γ subunit of the ATP synthase? How does this rotation promote ATP synthesis?

3. A principle of biology is that *living organisms maintain homeostasis*. How is glucose breakdown regulated to maintain homeostasis? What would be some potentially harmful consequences if glucose metabolism was not regulated properly?

Collaborative Questions

1. Discuss the advantages and disadvantages of aerobic respiration, anaerobic respiration, and fermentation.

2. Read more about PET scans from other sources. Which types of cancers are most easily detected by this procedure and which types are not? Is the ability to detect cancer via a PET scan related to the state of hypoxia?

Online Resource

www.brookerbiology.com

Stay a step ahead in your studies with animations that bring concepts to life and practice tests to assess your understanding. Your instructor may also recommend the interactive eBook, individualized learning tools, and more.

Photosynthesis

8

A tropical rain forest in the Amazon. Plant life in tropical rain forests carries out a large amount of the world's photosynthesis and supplies the atmosphere with a sizeable fraction of its oxygen.

Take a deep breath. Nearly all of the oxygen in every breath you take is made by the abundant plant life, algae, and cyanobacteria on Earth. More than 20% of the world's oxygen is produced in the Amazon rain forest in South America alone (see chapter opening photo). Biologists are alarmed about the rate at which such forests are being destroyed by human activities such as logging, mining, and oil extraction. Rain forests once covered 14% of the Earth's land surface, but they now occupy less than 6%. At their current rate of destruction, rain forests may be nearly eliminated in less than 40 years. Such an event may lower the level of oxygen in the atmosphere and thereby have a harmful effect on living organisms on a global scale.

In rain forests and across all of the Earth, the most visible color on land is green. The green color of plants is due to a pigment called chlorophyll. This pigment provides the starting point for the process of **photosynthesis**, in which the energy from light is captured and used to synthesize glucose and other organic molecules. Nearly all living organisms ultimately rely on photosynthesis for their nourishment, either directly or indirectly.

Photosynthesis is also responsible for producing the oxygen that makes up a large portion of the Earth's atmosphere. Therefore, all aerobic organisms rely on photosynthesis for cellular respiration.

We begin this chapter with an overview of photosynthesis as it occurs in green plants and algae. We will then explore the two stages of photosynthesis in more detail. In the first stage, called the **light reactions**, light energy is absorbed by chlorophyll and converted to chemical energy in the form of two energy intermediates: ATP and NADPH. During the second stage, known as the **Calvin cycle**, ATP and NADPH are used to drive the synthesis of carbohydrates. We conclude with a consideration of the variations in photosynthesis that occur in plants existing in hot and dry conditions.

8.1 Overview of Photosynthesis

Learning Outcomes:

1. Write the general equations that represent the process of photosynthesis.
2. Explain how photosynthesis powers the biosphere.
3. Describe the general structure of chloroplasts.
4. Compare and contrast the two phases of photosynthesis: the light reactions and carbon fixation.

In the mid-1600s, a Flemish physician, Jan Baptista Van Helmont, conducted an experiment in which he transplanted the shoot of a young willow tree into a bucket of soil and allowed it to grow for 5 years. After this time, the willow tree had added 164 pounds to its original weight, but the soil had lost only 2 ounces. Van Helmont correctly concluded that the willow tree did not get most of its nutrients from the soil. He also hypothesized that the mass of the tree came from the water he had added over the 5 years. This hypothesis was partially correct, but we now know that CO_2 from the air is also a major contributor to the growth and mass of plants.

In the 1770s, Jan Ingenhousz, a Dutch physician, immersed green plants under water and discovered they released bubbles of oxygen. Ingenhousz determined that sunlight was necessary for oxygen production. During this same period, Jean Senebier, a Swiss botanist, found that CO_2 is required for plant growth. With this accumulating information, Julius von Mayer, a German physicist, proposed in 1845 that plants convert light energy from the Sun into chemical energy.

For the next several decades, plant biologists studied photosynthesis in plants, algae, and bacteria. Researchers discovered that some photosynthetic bacteria use hydrogen sulfide (H_2S) instead of water (H_2O) for photosynthesis, and these organisms release sulfur instead of oxygen. In the 1930s, based on this information, Dutch-American microbiologist Cornelis van Niel proposed a general equation for photosynthesis that applies to plants, algae, and photosynthetic bacteria alike.

$$CO_2 + 2\,H_2A + \text{Light energy} \rightarrow CH_2O + A_2 + H_2O$$

where A is oxygen (O) or sulfur (S) and CH_2O is the general formula for a carbohydrate. This is a redox reaction in which CO_2 is reduced and H_2A is oxidized.

In green plants, A is oxygen and 2 A is a molecule of oxygen that is designated O_2. Therefore, this equation becomes

$$CO_2 + 2\,H_2O + \text{Light energy} \rightarrow CH_2O + O_2 + H_2O$$

When the carbohydrate produced is glucose ($C_6H_{12}O_6$), we multiply each side of the equation by 6 to obtain:

$$6\,CO_2 + 12\,H_2O + \text{Light energy} \rightarrow C_6H_{12}O_6 + 6\,O_2 + 6\,H_2O$$

$$\Delta G = +685 \text{ kcal/mol}$$

In this redox reaction, CO_2 is reduced during the formation of glucose, and H_2O is oxidized during the formation of O_2. Notice that the free-energy change required for the production of 1 mole of glucose from carbon dioxide and water is a whopping +685 kcal/mol! As we learned in Chapter 6, endergonic reactions are driven forward by coupling the reaction with an exergonic process that releases free energy. In this case, the energy from sunlight ultimately drives the synthesis of glucose.

In this section, we will survey the general features of photosynthesis as it occurs in green plants and algae. Later sections will examine the various steps in this process.

Photosynthesis Powers the Biosphere

The term **biosphere** describes the regions on the surface of the Earth and in the atmosphere where living organisms exist. Organisms can be categorized as heterotrophs and autotrophs. **Heterotrophs** must consume food—organic molecules from their environment—to sustain life. Most species of bacteria and protists, as well as all species of fungi and animals, are heterotrophs. By comparison, **autotrophs** sustain themselves by producing organic molecules from inorganic sources such as CO_2 and H_2O. **Photoautotrophs** are autotrophs that use light as a source of energy to make organic molecules. These include green plants, algae, and some bacterial species such as cyanobacteria.

Life in the biosphere is largely driven by the photosynthetic power of green plants and algae. The existence of most species relies on a key energy cycle that involves the interplay between organic molecules (such as glucose) and inorganic molecules, namely, O_2, CO_2, and H_2O (**Figure 8.1**). Photoautotrophs make a large proportion of the Earth's organic molecules via photosynthesis, using light energy, CO_2, and H_2O. During this process, they also produce O_2. To supply their energy needs, both photoautotrophs and heterotrophs metabolize organic molecules via cellular respiration. As described in

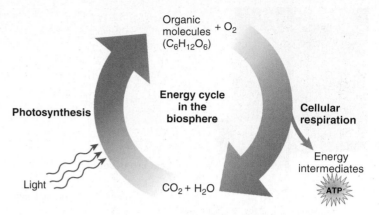

Figure 8.1 **An important energy cycle between photosynthesis and cellular respiration.** Photosynthesis uses light, CO_2 and H_2O to produce O_2 and organic molecules. The organic molecules can be broken down to CO_2 and H_2O via cellular respiration to supply energy in the form of ATP; O_2 is reduced to H_2O.

BIOLOGY PRINCIPLE Living organisms use energy. Photosynthetic species capture light energy and store it in organic molecules, which are used by photosynthetic and nonphotosynthetic species as sources of energy.

Concept Check: *Which types of organisms carry out cellular respiration? Is it heterotrophs, autotrophs, or both?*

Chapter 7, cellular respiration generates CO_2 and H_2O and is used to make ATP. The CO_2 is released into the atmosphere and can be reused by photoautotrophs to make more organic molecules such as glucose. In this way, an energy cycle between photosynthesis and cellular respiration sustains life on our planet.

In Plants and Algae, Photosynthesis Occurs in the Chloroplast

Chloroplasts are organelles found in plant and algal cells that carry out photosynthesis. These organelles contain large quantities of **chlorophyll**, which is a pigment that gives plants their green color. All green parts of a plant contain chloroplasts and can perform photosynthesis, although the majority of photosynthesis occurs in the leaves (**Figure 8.2**). The tissue in the internal part of the leaf, called the **mesophyll**, contains cells with chloroplasts. For photosynthesis to occur, the mesophyll cells must obtain water and carbon dioxide. The water is taken up by the roots of the plant and is transported to the leaves by small veins. Carbon dioxide gas enters the leaf, and oxygen exits via pores called stomata (singular, stoma or stomate; from the Greek, meaning mouth).

Like the mitochondrion, a chloroplast contains an outer and inner membrane, with an intermembrane space lying between the two. A third membrane, called the **thylakoid membrane**, contains pigment molecules, including chlorophyll. The thylakoid membrane forms many flattened, fluid-filled tubules called **thylakoids**, which enclose a single, convoluted compartment known as the **thylakoid lumen**. Thylakoids stack on top of each other to form a structure called a **granum** (plural, grana). The **stroma** is the fluid-filled region of the chloroplast between the thylakoid membrane and the inner membrane (see Figure 8.2).

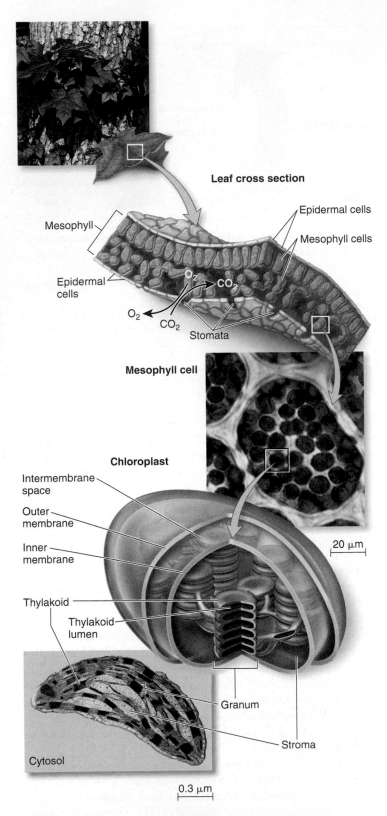

Leaf cross section

Epidermal cells

Mesophyll

Mesophyll cells

Epidermal cells

O_2 CO_2

O_2

CO_2

Stomata

Mesophyll cell

Chloroplast

Intermembrane space

Outer membrane

Inner membrane

Thylakoid

Thylakoid lumen

20 μm

Cytosol

Granum

Stroma

0.3 μm

Figure 8.2 Leaf organization. Leaves are composed of layers of cells. The epidermal cells are on the outer surface, both top and bottom, with mesophyll cells sandwiched in the middle. The mesophyll cells contain chloroplasts and are the primary sites of photosynthesis in most plants.

BioConnections: *Look ahead to Figure 38.17. How many guard cells make up a stoma (plural, stomata)?*

Photosynthesis Occurs in Two Stages: Light Reactions and the Calvin Cycle

How does photosynthesis take place? As mentioned, the process of photosynthesis occurs in two stages called the light reactions and the Calvin cycle. The term photosynthesis is derived from the association between these two stages: The prefix <u>photo</u> refers to the light reactions that capture the energy from sunlight needed for the <u>synthesis</u> of carbohydrates that occurs in the Calvin cycle. The light reactions take place at the thylakoid membrane, and the Calvin cycle occurs in the stroma (**Figure 8.3**).

The light reactions involve an amazing series of energy conversions, starting with light energy and ending with chemical energy that is stored in the form of covalent bonds. The light reactions produce three chemical products: ATP, NADPH, and O_2. ATP and NADPH are energy intermediates that provide the needed energy and electrons to drive the Calvin cycle. Like NADH, **NADPH (nicotinamide adenine dinucleotide phosphate)** is an electron carrier that can accept two electrons. Its structure differs from NADH by the presence of an additional phosphate group. The structure of NADH is described in Chapter 6 (see Figure 6.12).

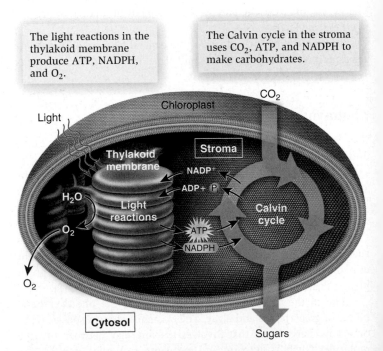

The light reactions in the thylakoid membrane produce ATP, NADPH, and O_2.

The Calvin cycle in the stroma uses CO_2, ATP, and NADPH to make carbohydrates.

CO_2

Chloroplast

Light

Thylakoid membrane

Stroma

$NADP^+$

$ADP + P$

H_2O

Light reactions

O_2

Calvin cycle

ATP

NADPH

Cytosol

O_2

Sugars

Figure 8.3 An overview of the two stages of photosynthesis: light reactions and the Calvin cycle. The light reactions, through which ATP, NADPH, and O_2 are made, occur at the thylakoid membrane. The Calvin cycle, in which enzymes use ATP and NADPH to incorporate CO_2 into carbohydrate, occurs in the stroma.

Concept Check: *Can the Calvin cycle occur in the dark?*

8.2 Reactions That Harness Light Energy

Learning Outcomes:

1. Define the general properties of light.
2. Describe how pigments absorb light energy and the types of pigments found in plants and green algae.
3. Outline the steps in which photosystem II and I capture light energy and produce O_2, ATP, and NADPH.
4. Explain the process of cyclic photophosphorylation in which only ATP is made.

According to the first law of thermodynamics discussed in Chapter 6, energy cannot be created or destroyed, but it can be transferred from one place to another and transformed from one form to another. During photosynthesis, energy in the form of light is transferred from the Sun, some 92 million miles away, to a pigment molecule in a photosynthetic organism such as a plant. What follows is an interesting series of energy transformations in which light energy is transformed into electrochemical energy and then into energy stored within chemical bonds.

In this section, we will explore this series of transformations, collectively called the light reactions of photosynthesis. We begin by examining the properties of light and then consider the features of chloroplasts that allow them to capture light energy. The remainder of this section focuses on how the light reactions of photosynthesis generate three important products: ATP, NADPH, and O_2.

Light Energy Is a Form of Electromagnetic Radiation

Light is essential to support life on Earth. Light is a type of electromagnetic radiation, so named because it consists of energy in the form of electric and magnetic fields. Electromagnetic radiation travels as waves caused by the oscillation of the electric and magnetic fields. The **wavelength** is the distance between the peaks in a wave pattern. The **electromagnetic spectrum** encompasses all possible wavelengths of electromagnetic radiation, from relatively short wavelengths (gamma rays) to much longer wavelengths (radio waves) (**Figure 8.4**). Visible light is the range of wavelengths detected by the human eye, commonly between 380–740 nm. As discussed later, visible light provides the energy to drive photosynthesis.

Physicists have also discovered that light has properties that are characteristic of particles. Albert Einstein formulated the photon theory of light in which he proposed that light is composed of discrete particles called **photons**—massless particles traveling in a wavelike pattern and moving at the speed of light (about 300 million m/sec). Each photon contains a specific amount of energy. An important difference between the various types of electromagnetic radiation, shown in Figure 8.4, is the amount of energy found in the photons. Shorter wavelength radiation carries more energy per unit of time than longer wavelength radiation. For example, the photons of gamma rays carry more energy than those of radio waves.

The Sun radiates the entire spectrum of electromagnetic radiation, but the atmosphere prevents much of this radiation from reaching the Earth's surface. For example, the ozone layer forms a thin shield in the upper atmosphere, protecting life on Earth from much

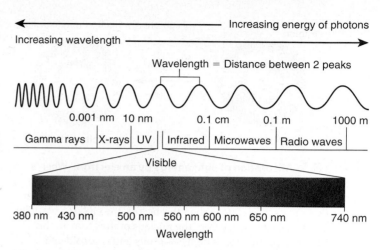

Figure 8.4 The electromagnetic spectrum. The bottom portion of this figure emphasizes visible light—the wavelengths of electromagnetic radiation visible to the human eye. Light in the visible portion of the electromagnetic spectrum drives photosynthesis.

Concept Check: *Which has higher energy, gamma rays or radio waves?*

of the Sun's ultraviolet (UV) rays. Even so, a substantial amount of electromagnetic radiation does reach the Earth's surface. The effect of light on living organisms is critically dependent on the energy of the photons that reach them. The photons found in gamma rays, X-rays, and UV rays have very high energy. When molecules in cells absorb such energy, the effects can be devastating. Such radiation can cause mutations in DNA and even lead to cancer. By comparison, the energy of photons found in visible light is much milder. Molecules can absorb this energy in a way that does not cause damage. Next, we will consider how molecules in living cells absorb the energy within visible light.

Pigments Absorb Light Energy

When light strikes an object, one of three things happens. First, light may simply pass through the object. Second, the object may change the path of light toward a different direction. A third possibility is that the object may absorb the light. The term **pigment** is used to describe a molecule that can absorb light energy. When light strikes a pigment, some of the wavelengths of light energy are absorbed, while others are reflected. For example, leaves look green to us because they reflect radiant energy of the green wavelength. Various pigments in the leaves absorb the energy of other wavelengths. At the extremes of color reflection are white and black. A white object reflects nearly all of the visible light energy falling on it, whereas a black object absorbs nearly all of the light energy. This is why it is coolest to wear white clothes on a sunny, hot day.

What do we mean when we say that light energy is absorbed? In the visible spectrum, light energy may be absorbed by boosting electrons to higher energy levels (**Figure 8.5**). Recall from Chapter 2 that electrons are located around the nucleus of an atom (refer back to Figure 2.4). The location in which an electron is likely to be found is called its orbital. Electrons in different orbitals possess different amounts of energy. For an electron to absorb light energy and be boosted to an orbital with a higher energy, it must overcome

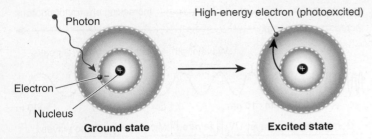

Figure 8.5 **Absorption of light energy by an electron.** When a photon of light of the correct amount of energy strikes an electron, the electron is boosted from the ground (unexcited) state to a higher energy level (an excited state). When this occurs, the electron occupies an orbital that is farther away from the nucleus of the atom. At this farther distance, the electron is held less firmly and is considered unstable.

Concept Check: *Describe the three things that could happen to enable a photoexcited electron to become more stable.*

the difference in energy between the orbital it is in and the orbital to which it is going. For this to happen, an electron must absorb a photon that contains precisely that amount of energy. Different pigment molecules contain a variety of electrons that can be shifted to different energy levels. Therefore, the wavelength of light that a pigment absorbs depends on the amount of energy needed to boost an electron to a higher orbital.

After an electron absorbs energy, it is said to be in an excited state. Usually, this is an unstable condition. The electron may release the energy in different ways. First, when an excited electron drops back down to a lower energy level, it may release heat. For example, on a sunny day, the sidewalk heats up because it absorbs light energy that is released as heat. A second way that an electron can release energy is in the form of light. Certain organisms, such as jellyfish, possess molecules that make them glow. This glow is due to the release of light when electrons drop down to lower energy levels, a phenomenon called fluorescence.

In the case of photosynthetic pigments, however, a different event happens that is critical for the process of photosynthesis. Rather than releasing energy, an excited electron in a photosynthetic pigment is removed from that molecule and transferred to another molecule where the electron is more stable. When this occurs, the energy in the electron is said to be "captured," because the electron does not readily drop down to a lower energy level and release heat or light.

Plants Contain Different Types of Photosynthetic Pigments

In plants, different pigment molecules absorb the light energy used to drive photosynthesis. Two types of chlorophyll pigments, termed **chlorophyll *a*** and **chlorophyll *b***, are found in green plants and green algae. Their structure was determined in the 1930s by German chemist Hans Fischer (**Figure 8.6a**). In the chloroplast, both chlorophylls *a* and *b* are bound to integral membrane proteins in the thylakoid membrane.

The chlorophylls contain a porphyrin ring and a phytol tail. A magnesium ion (Mg^{2+}) is bound to the porphyrin ring. An electron in

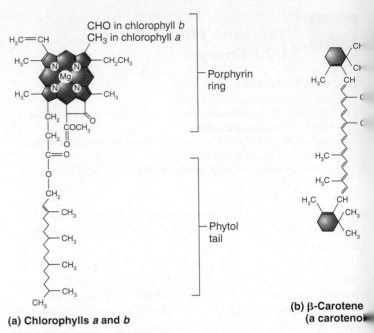

(a) Chlorophylls *a* and *b*

(b) β-Carotene (a carotenoid)

Figure 8.6 **Structures of pigment molecules.** **(a)** The structure of chlorophylls *a* and *b*. As indicated, chlorophylls *a* and *b* differ only at a single site, at which chlorophyll *a* has a —CH_3 group and chlorophyll *b* has a —CHO group. **(b)** The structure of β-carotene, an example of a carotenoid. The dark green and light green areas in parts (a) and (b) are the regions where a delocalized electron can hop from one atom to another.

the porphyrin ring follows a path in which it spends some of its time around several different atoms. Because this electron isn't restricted to a single atom, it is called a delocalized electron. The delocalized electron can absorb light energy. The phytol tail in chlorophyll is a long hydrocarbon structure that is hydrophobic. Its function is to anchor the pigment to the surface of hydrophobic proteins within the thylakoid membrane of chloroplasts.

Carotenoids are another type of pigment found in chloroplasts (**Figure 8.6b**). These pigments impart a color that ranges from yellow to orange to red. Carotenoids are often the major pigments in flowers and fruits. In leaves, the more abundant chlorophylls usually mask the colors of carotenoids. In temperate climates where the leaves change colors, the quantity of chlorophyll in the leaf declines during autumn. The carotenoids become readily visible and produce the yellows and oranges of autumn foliage.

An **absorption** spectrum is a graph that plots a pigment's light absorption as a function of wavelength. Each of the photosynthetic pigments shown in **Figure 8.7a** absorbs light in different regions of the visible spectrum. The absorption spectra of chlorophylls *a* and *b* are slightly different, though both chlorophylls absorb light most strongly in the red and violet parts of the visible spectrum and absorb green light poorly. Green light is reflected, which is why leaves appear green during the growing season. Carotenoids absorb light in the blue and blue-green regions of the visible spectrum, reflecting yellow and red.

Why do plants have different pigments? Having different pigments allows plants to absorb light at many different wavelengths. In this way, plants are more efficient at capturing the energy in sunlight.

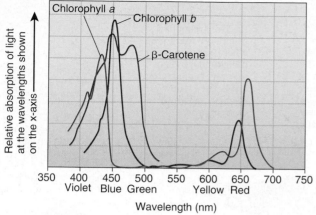

(a) Absorption spectra

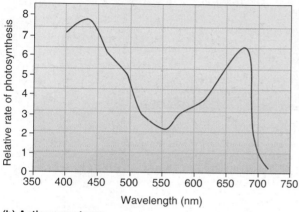

(b) Action spectrum

Figure 8.7 Properties of pigment function: absorption and action spectra. **(a)** These absorption spectra show the absorption of light by chlorophyll *a*, chlorophyll *b*, and β-carotene. **(b)** An action spectrum of photosynthesis depicting the relative rate of photosynthesis in green plants at different wavelengths of light.

Concept Check: *What is the advantage of having different pigment molecules?*

This phenomenon is highlighted in an **action spectrum**, which plots the rate of photosynthesis as a function of wavelength (**Figure 8.7b**). The highest rates of photosynthesis in green plants correlate with the wavelengths that are strongly absorbed by the chlorophylls and carotenoids. Photosynthesis is poor in the green region of the spectrum, because these pigments do not readily absorb this wavelength of light.

Photosystems II and I Work Together to Produce ATP and NADPH

As noted previously, photosynthetic organisms have the unique ability not only to absorb light energy but also to capture that energy in a stable way. Many organic molecules can absorb light energy. For example, on a sunny day, molecules in your skin absorb light energy and release the energy as heat. The heat that is released, however, cannot be harnessed to do useful work. A key feature of photosynthesis is the ability of pigments to capture light energy and transfer it to

other molecules that can hold on to the energy in a stable fashion and ultimately produce energy-intermediate molecules that can do cellular work.

Let's now consider how chloroplasts capture light energy. The thylakoid membranes of the chloroplast contain two distinct complexes of proteins and pigment molecules called **photosystem I (PSI)** and **photosystem II (PSII)** (**Figure 8.8**). Photosystem I was discovered before photosystem II, but photosystem II is the initial step in photosynthesis. We will consider the structure and function of PSII in greater detail later in this chapter.

As described in steps 1 and 2 of Figure 8.8, light excites electrons in pigment molecules, such as chlorophylls, which are located in regions of PSII and PSI called light-harvesting complexes. Rather than releasing their energy in the form of heat, the excited electrons follow a path shown by the red arrow. The combined action of photosystem II and photosystem I is termed **noncyclic electron flow** because the electrons move linearly from PSII to PSI and ultimately reduce $NADP^+$ to NADPH.

Initially, the excited electrons move from a pigment molecule called P680 in PSII to other electron carriers called pheophytin (Pp), Q_A, and Q_B. The excited electrons are moved out of PSII by Q_B. PSII also oxidizes water, which generates O_2 and adds H^+ into the thylakoid lumen. The electrons released from the oxidized water molecules are used to replenish the electrons that leave PSII via Q_B.

After a pair of electrons reaches Q_B, each one enters an electron transport chain (ETC)—a series of electron carriers—located in the thylakoid membrane. The ETC functions similarly to the one found in mitochondria. From Q_B, an electron goes to a cytochrome complex; then to plastocyanin (Pc), a small protein; and then to photosystem I. Along its journey from photosystem II to photosystem I, the electron releases some of its energy at particular steps and is transferred to the next component that has a higher electronegativity. The energy released is harnessed to pump H^+ into the thylakoid lumen.

A key role of photosystem I is to make NADPH (see Figure 8.8, step 3). When light strikes the light-harvesting complex of photosystem I, this energy is also transferred to a reaction center, where a high-energy electron is removed from a pigment molecule, designated P700, and transferred to a primary electron acceptor. A protein called ferredoxin (Fd) can accept two high-energy electrons, one at a time, from the primary electron acceptor. Fd then transfers the two electrons to the enzyme $NADP^+$ reductase. This enzyme transfers the two electrons to $NADP^+$ and together with an H^+ produces NADPH. The formation of NADPH results in fewer H^+ in the stroma.

The synthesis of ATP in chloroplasts is achieved by a chemiosmotic mechanism called **photophosphorylation**, which is similar to that used to make ATP in mitochondria. In chloroplasts, ATP synthesis is driven by the flow of H^+ from the thylakoid lumen into the stroma via ATP synthase (Figure 8.8, step 4). An H^+ electrochemical gradient is generated in three ways: (1) the splitting of water, which places H^+ in the thylakoid lumen; (2) the movement of high-energy electrons from photosystem II to photosystem I, which pumps H^+ into the thylakoid lumen; and (3) the formation of NADPH, which consumes H^+ in the stroma.

A key difference between photosystem II and photosystem I is how the pigment molecules receive electrons. As discussed in more detail later, $P680^+$ receives an electron from water. By comparison,

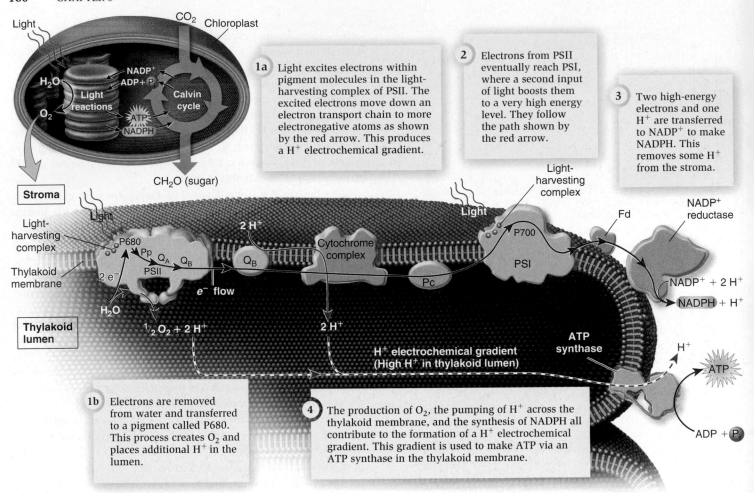

Figure 8.8 **The synthesis of ATP, NADPH, and O₂ by the concerted actions of photosystems II and I.** The linear process of electron movement from photosystem II to photosystem I to NADPH is called noncyclic electron flow.

Concept Check: *Are ATP, NADPH, and O₂ produced in the stroma or in the thylakoid lumen?*

P700⁺—the oxidized form of P700—receives an electron from Pc. Therefore, photosystem I does not need to split water to reduce P700⁺ and does not generate oxygen.

In summary, the steps of the light reactions of photosynthesis produce three chemical products: O₂, NADPH, and ATP:

1. O₂ is produced in the thylakoid lumen by the oxidation of water by photosystem II. Two electrons are removed from water, which produces 2 H⁺ and ¹/₂ O₂. The two electrons are transferred to P680⁺ molecules.
2. NADPH is produced in the stroma from high-energy electrons that start in photosystem II and are boosted a second time in photosystem I. Two high-energy electrons and one H⁺ are transferred to NADP⁺ to produce NADPH.
3. ATP is produced in the stroma via ATP synthase that uses an H⁺ electrochemical gradient.

Cyclic Electron Flow Produces Only ATP

As mentioned, the mechanism of harvesting light energy described in Figure 8.8 is called noncyclic electron flow because it is a linear process. This electron flow produces ATP and NADPH in roughly equal amounts. However, as we will see later, the Calvin cycle uses

more ATP than NADPH. How can plant cells avoid making too much NADPH and not enough ATP? In 1959, Daniel Arnon discovered a pattern of electron flow that is cyclic and generates only ATP (**Figure 8.9**). Arnon termed the process **cyclic photophosphorylation** because (1) the path of electrons is cyclic, (2) light energizes the electrons, and (3) ATP is made via the phosphorylation of ADP. Due to the path of electrons, the mechanism is also called **cyclic electron flow**.

When light strikes photosystem I, high-energy electrons are sent to the primary electron acceptor and then to ferredoxin (Fd). The key difference in cyclic photophosphorylation is that the high-energy electrons are transferred from Fd to Q_B. From Q_B, the electrons then go to the cytochrome complex, then to plastocyanin (Pc), and back to photosystem I. As the electrons travel along this cyclic route, they release energy, and some of this energy is used to transport H⁺ into the thylakoid lumen. The resulting H⁺ gradient drives the synthesis of ATP via ATP synthase.

Cyclic electron flow is favored when the level of NADP⁺ is low and NADPH is high. Under these conditions, there is sufficient NADPH to run the Calvin cycle, which is described later. Alternatively, when NADP⁺ is high and NADPH is low, noncyclic electron flow is favored, so more NADPH can be made. Cyclic electron flow is also favored when ATP levels are low.

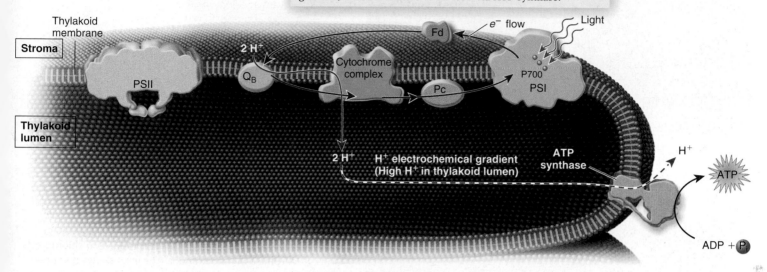

When light strikes photosystem I, electrons are excited and sent to ferredoxin (Fd). From Fd, the electrons are then transferred to Q_B, to the cytochrome complex, to plastocyanin (Pc), and back to photosystem I. This produces a H^+ electrochemical gradient, which is used to make ATP via ATP synthase.

Figure 8.9 Cyclic photophosphorylation. In this process, an electron follows a cyclic path that is powered by photosystem I (PSI). This contributes to the formation of an H^+ electrochemical gradient, which is then used to make ATP by ATP synthase.

Concept Check: *Why is having cyclic photophosphorylation an advantage to a plant over having only noncyclic electron flow?*

GENOMES & PROTEOMES CONNECTION

The Cytochrome Complexes of Mitochondria and Chloroplasts Contain Evolutionarily Related Proteins

A recurring theme in cell biology is that evolution has resulted in groups of genes that encode proteins that play similar but specialized roles in cells—an example of descent with modification. When two or more genes are similar because they are derived from the same ancestral gene, they are called **homologous genes**. As discussed in Chapter 23, homologous genes encode proteins that have similar amino acid sequences and often perform similar functions.

A comparison of the electron transport chains of mitochondria and chloroplasts reveals homologous genes. In particular, let's consider the cytochrome complex found in the thylakoid membrane of plants and algae, called cytochrome b_6-f (**Figure 8.10a**) and cytochrome b-c_1, which is found in the ETC of mitochondria (**Figure 8.10b**; also refer back to Figure 7.9). Both cytochromes b_6-f and b-c_1 are composed of several protein subunits. One of those proteins is called cytochrome b_6 in cytochrome b_6-f and cytochrome b in cytochrome b-c_1.

By analyzing the sequences of the genes that encode these proteins, researchers discovered that cytochrome b_6 and cytochrome b are homologous proteins. These proteins carry out similar functions: Both of them accept electrons from a quinone (Q_B or ubiquinone) and both donate an electron to another protein within their respective complexes (cytochrome f or cytochrome c_1). Likewise, both proteins function as H^+ pumps that capture some of the energy that is released from electrons to transport H^+ across the membrane. In this way, evolution has produced a family of cytochrome b-type proteins that play similar but specialized roles.

8.3 Molecular Features of Photosystems

Learning Outcomes:

1. Describe how the light-harvesting complex absorbs light energy and how it is transferred via resonance energy transfer.
2. Diagram the path of electron flow through photosystem II.
3. Explain how O_2 is produced by photosystem II.

The previous section provided an overview of how chloroplasts absorb light energy and produce ATP, NADPH, and O_2. As you have learned, two photosystems—PSI and PSII—play critical roles in two aspects of photosynthesis. First, both PSI and PSII absorb light energy and capture that energy in the form of excited electrons. Second, PSII oxidizes water, thereby producing O_2. In this section, we will take a closer look at how these events occur at the molecular level.

Photosystem II Captures Light Energy and Produces O_2

PSI and PSII have two main components: a light-harvesting complex and a reaction center. **Figure 8.11** shows how these components function in PSII. In 1932, American biologist Robert Emerson and an undergraduate student, William Arnold, originally discovered the **light-harvesting complex** in the thylakoid membrane. It is composed of several dozen pigment molecules that are anchored to transmembrane proteins. The role of the complex is to directly absorb photons of light. When a pigment molecule absorbs a photon, an electron is boosted to a higher energy level. As shown in Figure 8.11, the energy (not the electron itself) is transferred to adjacent pigment molecules by a process called **resonance energy transfer**. The energy may be

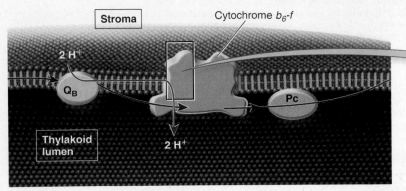

(a) Cytochrome b_6-f in the chloroplast

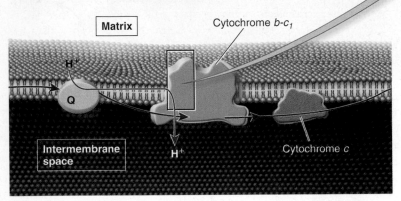

(b) Cytochrome b-c_1 in the mitochondrion

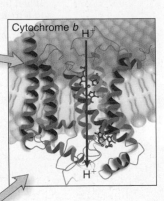

Figure 8.10 **Homologous proteins in the electron transport chains of chloroplasts and mitochondria. (a)** Cytochrome b_6-f is a complex involved in electron and H^+ transport in chloroplasts, and **(b)** cytochrome b-c_1 is a complex involved in electron and H^+ transport in mitochondria. These complexes contain homologous proteins designated cytochrome b_6 in chloroplasts and cytochrome b in mitochondria. The inset shows the three-dimensional structure of cytochrome b, which was determined by X-ray crystallography. It is an integral membrane protein with several transmembrane helices and two heme groups, which are prosthetic groups involved in electron transfer. The structure of cytochrome b_6 has also been determined and found to be very similar.

BIOLOGY PRINCIPLE **Populations of organisms evolve from one generation to the next.** Evolution has resulted in proteins with similar but specialized functions to perform cellular work. As discussed earlier, the work it performs is to synthesize the energy intermediates ATP and NADPH.

Concept Check: *Explain why the three-dimensional structures of cytochrome b and cytochrome b_6 are very similar.*

transferred among multiple pigment molecules until it is eventually transferred to a special pigment molecule designated P680, which is located within the reaction center of PSII. The P680 pigment is so named because it can directly absorb light at a wavelength of 680 nm. However, P680 is more commonly excited by resonance energy transfer from another chlorophyll pigment. In either case, when an electron in P680 is excited, it is designated P680*. The light-harvesting complex is also called the antenna complex because it acts like an antenna that absorbs energy from light and funnels that energy to P680 in the reaction center.

A high-energy (photoexcited) electron in a pigment molecule is relatively unstable. It may abruptly release its energy by giving off heat or light. Unlike the pigments in the light-harvesting complex that undergo resonance energy transfer, P680* can actually release its high-energy electron and become P680+.

$$P680^* \rightarrow P680^+ + e^-$$

The role of the reaction center is to quickly remove the high-energy electron from P680* and transfer it to another molecule, where the electron is more stable. This molecule is called the **primary electron acceptor** (see Figure 8.11). The transfer of the electron from P680* to the primary electron acceptor is remarkably fast. It occurs in less than a few picoseconds! (One picosecond equals one-trillionth of a second, also noted as 10^{-12} sec.) Because this occurs so quickly, the excited electron does not have much time to release its energy in the form of heat or light.

After the primary electron acceptor has received this high-energy electron, the light energy has been captured and can be used

Let's now consider what happens to P680+, which has given up its high-energy electron. After P680+ is formed, it is necessary to replace the electron so that P680 can function again. Therefore, another role of the reaction center is to replace the electron that is removed when P680* becomes P680+. This missing electron of P680+ is replaced with a low-energy electron from water (see Figure 8.11).

$$H_2O \rightarrow 2\,H^+ + {}^1/_2\,O_2 + 2\,e^-$$

$$2\,P680^+ + 2\,e^- \rightarrow 2\,P680$$
$$\text{(from water)}$$

The oxidation of water results in the formation of oxygen gas (O_2), which is used by many organisms for cellular respiration. Photosystem II is the only known protein complex that can oxidize water, resulting in the release of O_2 into the atmosphere.

Photosystem II Is an Amazing Redox Machine

All cells rely on redox reactions to store and utilize energy and to form covalent bonds in organic molecules. Photosystem II is a particularly remarkable example of a redox machine. As we have learned, this complex of proteins removes high-energy electrons from a pigment

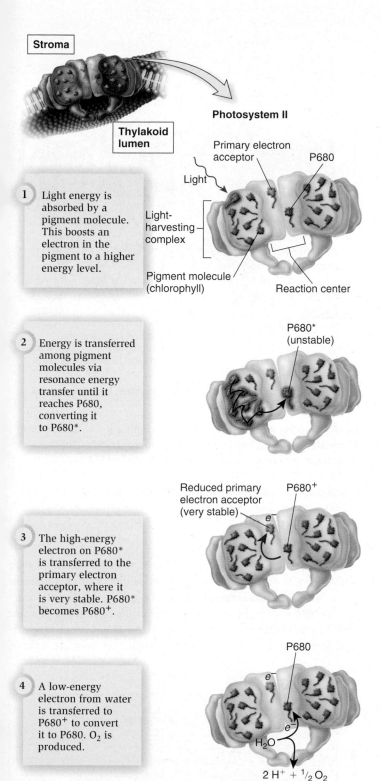

Photosystem II

Primary electron acceptor

P680

Light

Light-harvesting complex

Pigment molecule (chlorophyll)

Reaction center

1. Light energy is absorbed by a pigment molecule. This boosts an electron in the pigment to a higher energy level.

P680* (unstable)

2. Energy is transferred among pigment molecules via resonance energy transfer until it reaches P680, converting it to P680*.

Reduced primary electron acceptor (very stable)

$P680^+$

e^-

3. The high-energy electron on P680* is transferred to the primary electron acceptor, where it is very stable. P680* becomes $P680^+$.

P680

e^-

4. A low-energy electron from water is transferred to $P680^+$ to convert it to P680. O_2 is produced.

H_2O

e^-

$2 H^+ + \frac{1}{2} O_2$

Figure 8.11 **A closer look at how photosystem II harvests light energy and oxidizes water.** Note: Two electrons are released during the oxidation of water, but they are transferred one at a time to $P680^+$.

molecule and transfers them to a primary electron acceptor. Perhaps even more remarkable is that photosystem II can remove low-energy electrons from water—a very stable molecule that holds onto its electrons tightly. The removal of electrons from water results in the formation of oxygen (O_2).

Many approaches have been used to study how photosystem II works. In recent years, much effort has been aimed at determining the biochemical composition of the protein complex and the roles of its individual components. The number of protein subunits varies somewhat from species to species and may vary due to environmental changes. Typically, photosystem II is composed of approximately 19 different protein subunits. Two subunits, designated D1 and D2, contain the reaction center, which carries out the redox reactions (**Figure 8.12a**). Two other subunits, called CP43 and CP47, bind the pigment molecules that form the light-harvesting complex. Many additional subunits regulate the function of photosystem II and provide structural support.

Figure 8.12a illustrates the pathway of electron movement through photosystem II. The red arrows indicate the movement of a high-energy electron, and the black arrows show the path of a low-energy electron. Let's begin with a high-energy electron. When the electron on P680 becomes boosted to a higher energy level, usually by resonance energy transfer, this high-energy electron then moves to the primary electron acceptor, which is a chlorophyll molecule lacking Mg^{2+}, called pheophytin (Pp). Pheophytin is permanently bound to photosystem II and transfers the electron to a plastoquinone molecule, designated Q_A, which is also permanently bound to photosystem II. Next, the electron is transferred to another plastoquinone molecule designated Q_B, which can accept two high-energy electrons and bind two H^+. As shown earlier in Figure 8.8, Q_B can diffuse away from the reaction center.

Let's now consider the path of a low-energy electron. The oxidation of water occurs in a region called the **manganese cluster**. This site is located on the side of D1 that faces the thylakoid lumen. The manganese cluster has four Mn^{2+}, one Ca^{2+}, and one Cl^-. Two water molecules bind to this site. D1 catalyzes the removal of four low-energy electrons from the two H_2O molecules to produce O_2 and four H^+. Each low-energy electron is transferred, one at a time, to an amino acid in D1 (a tyrosine, Tyr) and then to $P680^+$ to produce P680.

In 2004, So Iwata, James Barber, and colleagues determined the three-dimensional structure of photosystem II using a technique called **X-ray crystallography**. In this method, researchers must purify a protein or protein complex and expose it to conditions that cause the proteins to associate with each other in an ordered array. In other words, the proteins form a crystal. When a crystal is exposed to X-rays, the resulting pattern can be analyzed mathematically to determine the three-dimensional structure of the crystal's components. Major advances in this technique over the last couple of decades have enabled researchers to determine the structures of relatively large macromolecular complexes such as photosystem II (**Figure 8.12b**). The structure shown there is a dimer: it has two PSII complexes, each with 19 protein subunits. As seen in Figure 8.12b, the intricacy of the structure of photosystem II rivals the complexity of its function.

The Use of Light Flashes of Specific Wavelengths Provided Experimental Evidence for the Existence of PSII and PSI

An experimental technique that uses light flashes at particular wavelengths has been important in helping researchers to understand the function of photosystems. In this method, pioneered by Robert Emerson,

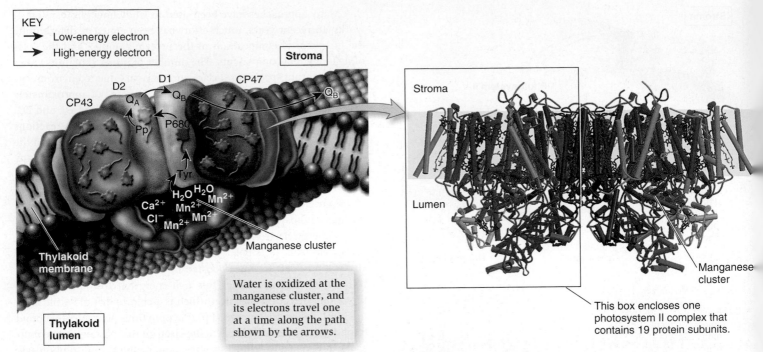

KEY
→ Low-energy electron
→ High-energy electron

Stroma

CP43   D2   D1   CP47

Q_A Q_B Q_B

Pp   P680

Tyr

H_2O H_2O Mn^{2+}
Ca^{2+} Mn^{2+}
Cl^- Mn^{2+} Mn^{2+}

Manganese cluster

Thylakoid
membrane

**Thylakoid
lumen**

Water is oxidized at the
manganese cluster, and
its electrons travel one
at a time along the path
shown by the arrows.

(a) The path of electron flow through photosystem II

Stroma

Lumen

Manganese
cluster

This box encloses one
photosystem II complex that
contains 19 protein subunits.

**(b) Three-dimensional structure of photosystem II as determined
by X-ray crystallography**

Figure 8.12 **The molecular structure of photosystem II. (a)** Schematic drawing showing the path of electron flow from water to Q_B. The CP43 and CP47 protein subunits wrap around D1 and D2. Pigments in CP43 and CP47 transfer energy to P680 by resonance energy transfer. **(b)** The three-dimensional structure of photosystem II as determined by X-ray crystallography. In the crystal structure, the colors are CP43 (green), D2 (orange), D1 (yellow), and CP47 (red).

 BIOLOGY PRINCIPLE Structure determines function. The structural arrangement of the manganese cluster, P680, pheophytin, Q_A, and Q_B provides a pathway of electron movement from photosystem II to the electron transport chain.

a photosynthetic organism is exposed to a particular wavelength of light, after which the rate of photosynthesis is measured by the amount of CO_2 consumed or the amount of O_2 produced. In the 1950s, Emerson performed a particularly intriguing experiment that greatly stimulated photosynthesis research (**Figure 8.13**). He subjected algae to light flashes of different wavelengths and obtained a mysterious result. When he exposed algae to a wavelength of 680 nm, he observed a low rate of photosynthesis. A similarly low rate of photosynthesis occurred when he exposed algae to a wavelength of 700 nm. However, when he exposed the algae to both wavelengths

of light simultaneously, the rate of photosynthesis was more than double the rate observed at only one wavelength. This phenomenon was termed the **enhancement effect**. We know now that it occurs because light of 680-nm wavelength can readily activate the pigment (P680) in the reaction center in photosystem II but is not very efficient at activating pigments in photosystem I. In contrast, light of

Figure 8.13 **The enhancement effect observed by Emerson.** When photosynthetic organisms such as green plants and algae are exposed to 680-nm and 700-nm light simultaneously, the resulting rate of photosynthesis is much more than double the rate produced by each wavelength individually.

 BIOLOGY PRINCIPLE Biology is as an experimental science. This experiment provided key evidence for the existence of two photosystems.

Concept Check: *Would the enhancement effect be observed if two consecutive flashes of light occurred at 680 nm?*

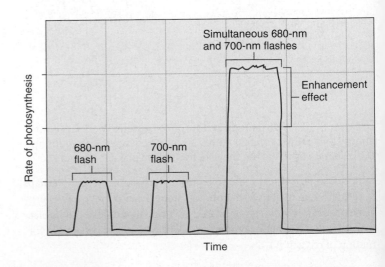

Simultaneous 680-nm
and 700-nm flashes

Enhancement
effect

Rate of photosynthesis

680-nm
flash

700-nm
flash

Time

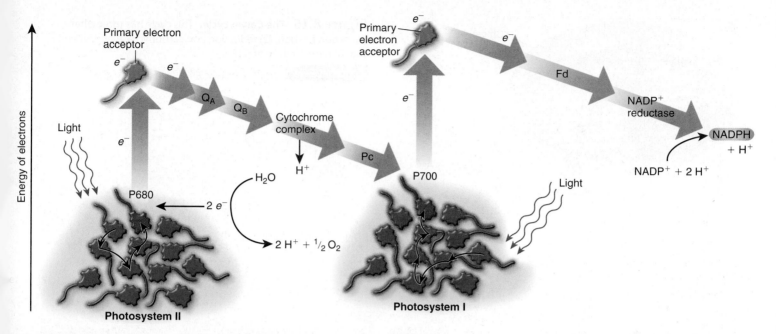

Figure 8.14 **The Z scheme, showing the energy of an electron moving from photosystem II to NADP⁺.** The oxidation of water releases two electrons that travel one at a time from photosystem II to NADP⁺. As seen here, the input of light boosts the energy of the electron twice. At the end of the pathway, two electrons are used to make NADPH.

Concept Check: *During its journey from photosystem II to NADP⁺, at what point does an electron have the highest amount of energy?*

700-nm wavelength is optimal at activating the pigments in photosystem I but not those in photosystem II. When algae are exposed to both wavelengths, however, the pigments in both photosystems are maximally activated.

When researchers began to understand that photosynthesis results in the production of both ATP and NADPH, Robin Hill and Fay Bendall also proposed that photosynthesis involves two photoactivation events. According to their model, known as the **Z scheme**, an electron proceeds through a series of energy changes during photosynthesis (**Figure 8.14**). The Z refers to the zigzag shape of this energy curve. Based on our modern understanding of photosynthesis, we now know these events involve increases and decreases in the energy of an electron as it moves from photosystem II through photosystem I to NADP⁺ during noncyclic electron flow. An electron on a non-excited pigment molecule in photosystem II has the lowest energy. In photosystem II, light boosts an electron to a much higher energy level. As the electron travels from photosystem II to photosystem I, some of the energy is released. The input of light in photosystem I boosts the electron to an even higher energy than it attained in photosystem II. The electron releases a little energy before it is eventually transferred to NADP⁺.

8.4 Synthesizing Carbohydrates via the Calvin Cycle

Learning Outcomes:

1. Outline the three phases of the Calvin cycle.
2. Explain how Calvin and Benson identified the components of the Calvin cycle.

In the previous sections, we learned how the light reactions of photosynthesis produce ATP, NADPH, and O_2. We will now turn our attention to the second phase of photosynthesis, the Calvin cycle, in which ATP and NADPH are used to make carbohydrates. The Calvin cycle consists of a series of steps that occur in a metabolic cycle. In plants and algae, it occurs in the stroma of chloroplasts. In cyanobacteria, the Calvin cycle occurs in the cytoplasm of the bacterial cells.

The Calvin cycle takes CO_2 from the atmosphere and incorporates the carbon into organic molecules, namely, carbohydrates. As mentioned earlier, carbohydrates are critical for two reasons. First, they provide the precursors to make the organic molecules and macromolecules of nearly all living cells. The second key reason is the storage of energy. The Calvin cycle produces carbohydrates, which store energy. These carbohydrates are accumulated inside plant cells. When a plant is in the dark and not carrying out photosynthesis, the stored carbohydrates are used as a source of energy. Similarly, when an animal consumes a plant, it uses the carbohydrates as an energy source.

In this section, we will examine the three phases of the Calvin cycle. We will also explore the experimental approach of Melvin Calvin and his colleagues that enabled them to elucidate the steps of this cycle.

The Calvin Cycle Incorporates CO_2 into Carbohydrate

The Calvin cycle, also called the Calvin-Benson cycle, was determined by chemists Melvin Calvin and Andrew Adam Benson and their colleagues in the 1940s and 1950s. This cycle requires a massive input of energy. For every 6 carbon dioxide molecules that are incorporated into a carbohydrate such as glucose ($C_6H_{12}O_6$), 18 ATP molecules are hydrolyzed and 12 NADPH molecules are oxidized:

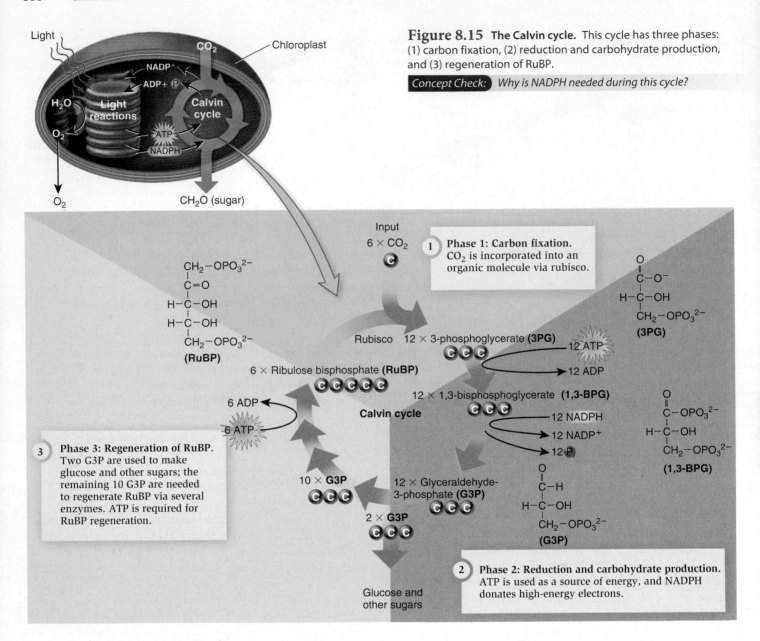

Figure 8.15 The Calvin cycle. This cycle has three phases: (1) carbon fixation, (2) reduction and carbohydrate production, and (3) regeneration of RuBP.

Concept Check: Why is NADPH needed during this cycle?

① Phase 1: Carbon fixation. CO_2 is incorporated into an organic molecule via rubisco.

③ Phase 3: Regeneration of RuBP. Two G3P are used to make glucose and other sugars; the remaining 10 G3P are needed to regenerate RuBP via several enzymes. ATP is required for RuBP regeneration.

② Phase 2: Reduction and carbohydrate production. ATP is used as a source of energy, and NADPH donates high-energy electrons.

$$6\ CO_2 + 12\ H_2O \rightarrow C_6H_{12}O_6 + 6\ O_2 + 6\ H_2O\ .$$

$$18\ ATP + 18\ H_2O \rightarrow 18\ ADP + 18\ P_i$$

$$12\ NADPH \rightarrow 12\ NADP^+ + 12\ H^+ + 24\ e^-$$

Although biologists commonly describe glucose as a product of photosynthesis, glucose is not directly made by the Calvin cycle. Instead, molecules of glyceraldehyde-3-phosphate, which are products of the Calvin cycle, are used as starting materials for the synthesis of glucose and other molecules, including sucrose. After glucose molecules are made, they may be linked together to form a polymer of glucose called starch, which is stored in the chloroplast for later use. Alternatively, the disaccharide sucrose may be made and transported out of the leaf to other parts of the plant.

The Calvin cycle can be divided into three phases. These phases are carbon fixation, reduction and carbohydrate production, and regeneration of ribulose bisphosphate (RuBP) (**Figure 8.15**).

Carbon Fixation (Phase 1) During **carbon fixation**, CO_2 is incorporated into RuBP, a five-carbon sugar. The term *fixation* means that the carbon has been removed from the atmosphere and fixed into an organic molecule that is not a gas. More specifically, the product of the reaction is a six-carbon intermediate that immediately splits in half to form two molecules of 3-phosphoglycerate (3PG). The enzyme that catalyzes this step is named RuBP carboxylase/oxygenase, or **rubisco**. It is the most abundant protein in chloroplasts and perhaps the most abundant protein on Earth! This observation underscores the massive amount of carbon fixation that happens in the biosphere.

Reduction and Carbohydrate Production (Phase 2) In the second phase, ATP is used to convert 3PG to 1,3-bisphosphoglycerate (1,3-BPG). Next, electrons from NADPH reduce 1,3-BPG to glyceraldehyde-3-phosphate (G3P). G3P is a carbohydrate with three carbon atoms. The key difference between 3PG and G3P is that 3PG has a C—O bond, whereas the analogous carbon in G3P is a C—H bond (see Figure 8.15). The C—H bond occurs because the G3P molecule has been reduced by the addition of two electrons from NADPH. Compared with 3PG, the bonds in G3P store more energy and enable G3P to readily form larger organic molecules such as glucose.

As shown in Figure 8.15, only some of the G3P molecules are used to make glucose or other carbohydrates. Phase 1 begins with 6 RuBP molecules and 6 CO_2 molecules. Twelve G3P molecules are made at the end of phase 2, and only two of these G3P molecules are used in carbohydrate production. As described next, the other 10 G3P molecules are needed to keep the Calvin cycle turning by regenerating RuBP.

Regeneration of RuBP (Phase 3)

In the last phase of the Calvin cycle, a series of enzymatic steps converts the 10 G3P molecules into 6 RuBP molecules, using 6 molecules of ATP. After the RuBP molecules are regenerated, they serve as acceptors for CO_2, thereby allowing the cycle to continue.

As we have just seen, the Calvin cycle begins by using carbon from an inorganic source, that is, CO_2, and ends with organic molecules that will be used by the plant to make other molecules. You may be wondering why CO_2 molecules cannot be directly linked to form these larger molecules. The answer lies in the number of electrons that orbit carbon atoms. In CO_2, the carbon atom is considered electron poor. Oxygen is a very electronegative atom that monopolizes the electrons it shares with other atoms. In a covalent bond between carbon and oxygen, the shared electrons are closer to the oxygen atom.

By comparison, in an organic molecule, the carbon atom is electron rich. During the Calvin cycle, ATP provides energy and NADPH donates high-energy electrons, so the carbon originally in CO_2 has been reduced. The Calvin cycle combines less electronegative atoms with carbon atoms so that C—H and C—C bonds are formed. This allows the eventual synthesis of larger organic molecules, including glucose, amino acids, and so on. In addition, the covalent bonds within these molecules are capable of storing large amounts of energy.

FEATURE INVESTIGATION

The Calvin Cycle Was Determined by Isotope-Labeling Methods

The steps in the Calvin cycle involve the conversion of one type of molecule to another, eventually regenerating the starting material, RuBP. In the 1940s and 1950s, Calvin and his colleagues used ^{14}C, a radioisotope of carbon, to label and trace molecules produced during the cycle (**Figure 8.16**). They injected ^{14}C-labeled CO_2 into cultures of the green algae *Chlorella pyrenoidosa* grown in an apparatus called a "lollipop" (because of its shape). The *Chlorella* cells were given different lengths of time to incorporate the ^{14}C-labeled carbon, ranging from fractions of a second to many minutes. After this incubation period, the cells were abruptly placed into a solution of alcohol to inhibit enzymatic reactions and thereby stop the cycle.

The researchers separated the newly made radiolabeled molecules by a variety of methods. The most commonly used method was two-dimensional paper chromatography. In this approach, a sample containing radiolabeled molecules was spotted onto a corner of the paper at a location called the origin. The edge of the paper was placed in a solvent, such as phenol-water. As the solvent rose through the paper, so did the radiolabeled molecules. The rate at which they rose depended on their structures, which determined how strongly they interacted with the paper. This step separated the mixture of molecules spotted onto the paper at the origin.

The paper was then dried, turned 90°, and then the edge was placed in a different solvent, such as butanol-propionic acid-water. Again, the solvent rose through the paper (in a second dimension), thereby separating molecules that may not have been adequately separated during the first separation step. After this second separation step, the paper was dried and exposed to X-ray film, a procedure called autoradiography. Radioactive emission from the ^{14}C-labeled molecules caused dark spots to appear on the film.

The pattern of spots changed depending on the length of time the cells were incubated with ^{14}C-labeled CO_2. When the incubation period was short, only molecules that were made in the first steps of the Calvin cycle were seen—3-phosphoglycerate (3PG) and 1,3-bisphosphoglycerate (1,3-BPG). Longer incubations revealed molecules synthesized in later steps—glyceraldehyde-3-phosphate (G3P) and ribulose bisphosphate (RuBP).

A challenge for Calvin and his colleagues was to identify the chemical nature of each spot. They achieved this by a variety of chemical methods. For example, a spot could be cut out of the paper, the molecule within the paper could be washed out or eluted, and then the eluted molecule could be subjected to the same procedure that included a radiolabeled molecule whose structure was already known. If the unknown molecule and known molecule migrated to the same spot in the paper, this indicated they were likely to be the same molecule. During the late 1940s and 1950s, Calvin and his coworkers identified all of the ^{14}C-labeled spots and the order in which they appeared. In this way, they determined the series of reactions of what we now know as the Calvin cycle. For this work, Calvin was awarded the Nobel Prize in Chemistry in 1961.

Experimental Questions

1. What was the purpose of the study conducted by Calvin and his colleagues?

2. In Calvin's experiments shown in Figure 8.15, why did the researchers use ^{14}C? Why did they examine samples at several different time periods? How were the different molecules in the samples identified?

3. What were the results of Calvin's study?

Figure 8.16 The determination of the Calvin cycle using ^{14}C-labeled CO_2 and paper chromatography.

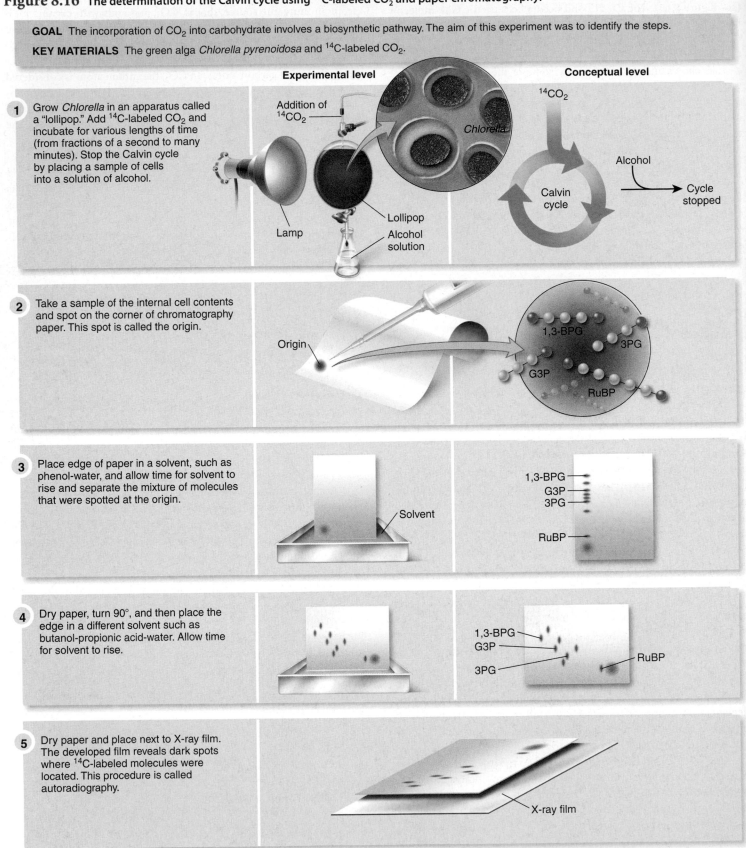

GOAL The incorporation of CO_2 into carbohydrate involves a biosynthetic pathway. The aim of this experiment was to identify the steps.

KEY MATERIALS The green alga *Chlorella pyrenoidosa* and ^{14}C-labeled CO_2.

Experimental level

Conceptual level

1   Grow *Chlorella* in an apparatus called a "lollipop." Add ^{14}C-labeled CO_2 and incubate for various lengths of time (from fractions of a second to many minutes). Stop the Calvin cycle by placing a sample of cells into a solution of alcohol.

Addition of $^{14}CO_2$

Chlorella

Lamp

Lollipop

Alcohol solution

$^{14}CO_2$

Alcohol

Calvin cycle

Cycle stopped

2   Take a sample of the internal cell contents and spot on the corner of chromatography paper. This spot is called the origin.

Origin

1,3-BPG

3PG

G3P

RuBP

3   Place edge of paper in a solvent, such as phenol-water, and allow time for solvent to rise and separate the mixture of molecules that were spotted at the origin.

Solvent

1,3-BPG
G3P
3PG

RuBP

4   Dry paper, turn 90°, and then place the edge in a different solvent such as butanol-propionic acid-water. Allow time for solvent to rise.

1,3-BPG
G3P

3PG

RuBP

5   Dry paper and place next to X-ray film. The developed film reveals dark spots where ^{14}C-labeled molecules were located. This procedure is called autoradiography.

X-ray film

6 THE DATA*

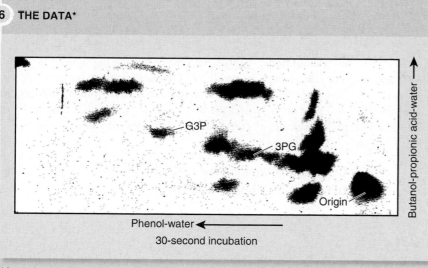

Butanol-propionic acid-water →

G3P

3PG

Origin

Phenol-water ←

30-second incubation

7 CONCLUSION The identification of the molecules in each spot elucidated the steps of the Calvin cycle.

8 SOURCE Calvin, M. December 11, 1961. The path of carbon in photosynthesis. Nobel Lecture.

*An autoradiograph from one of Calvin's experiments.

8.5   Variations in Photosynthesis

Learning Outcomes:

1. Explain the concept of photorespiration.
2. Compare and contrast how C_4 and CAM plants avoid photorespiration and conserve water.

Thus far, we have considered photosynthesis as a two-stage process in which the light reactions produce ATP, NADPH, and O_2, and the Calvin cycle uses the ATP and NADPH in the synthesis of carbohydrates. This two-stage process is a universal feature of photosynthesis in all green plants, algae, and cyanobacteria. However, certain environmental conditions such as temperature, water availability, and light intensity alter the way in which the Calvin cycle operates. In this section, we begin by examining how hot and dry conditions may reduce the output of photosynthesis. We then explore two adaptations that certain plant species have evolved that conserve water and help to maximize photosynthetic efficiency in such environments.

Photorespiration Decreases the Efficiency of Photosynthesis

In the previous section, we learned that rubisco adds a CO_2 molecule to an organic molecule, RuBP, to produce two molecules of 3-phosphoglycerate (3PG):

$$RuBP + CO_2 \rightarrow 2\ 3PG$$

For most species of plants, the incorporation of CO_2 into RuBP is the only way for carbon fixation to occur. Because 3PG is a three-carbon molecule, these plants are called **C_3 plants**. Examples of C_3 plants include wheat and oak trees (**Figure 8.17**). About 90% of the plant species on Earth are C_3 plants.

(a) Wheat plants

(b) Oak leaves

Figure 8.17 Examples of C_3 plants. The structures of **(a)** wheat and **(b)** white oak leaves are similar to that shown in Figure 8.2.

Researchers have discovered that the active site of rubisco can also add O_2 to RuBP, although its affinity for CO_2 is over 10-fold better than that for O_2. Even so, when CO_2 levels are low and O_2 levels are high, rubisco adds an O_2 molecule to RuBP. This produces only one molecule of 3PG and a two-carbon molecule called phosphoglycolate. The phosphoglycolate is then dephosphorylated to glycolate, which is released from the chloroplast. In a series of several steps, the two-carbon glycolate is eventually oxidized in peroxisomes and mitochondria to produce an organic molecule plus a molecule of CO_2:

$$RuBP + O_2 \rightarrow 3PG + Phosphoglycolate$$

$$Phosphoglycolate \rightarrow Glycolate \rightarrow \rightarrow Organic\ molecule + CO_2$$

This process, called **photorespiration**, uses O_2 and liberates CO_2. Photorespiration is considered wasteful because it releases CO_2, thereby limiting plant growth.

Photorespiration is more likely to occur when plants are exposed to a hot and dry environment. To conserve water, the stomata of the leaves close, inhibiting the uptake of CO_2 from the air and trapping the O_2 that is produced by photosynthesis. When the level of CO_2 is low and O_2 is high, photorespiration is favored. If C_3 plants are subjected to hot and dry environmental conditions, as much as 25–50% of their photosynthetic work is reversed by the process of photorespiration.

Why do plants carry out photorespiration? The answer is not entirely clear. One common view is that photorespiration is an evolutionary relic. When rubisco first evolved some 3 billion years ago,

the atmospheric oxygen level was low, so photorespiration would not have been a problem. Another view is that photorespiration may have a protective advantage. On hot and dry days when the stomata are closed, CO_2 levels within the leaves fall, and O_2 levels rise. Under these conditions, highly toxic oxygen-containing molecules such as free radicals may be produced that could damage the plant. Therefore, plant biologists have hypothesized that the role of photorespiration may be to protect the plant against the harmful effects of such toxic molecules by consuming O_2 and releasing CO_2.

C_4 Plants Have Evolved a Mechanism to Minimize Photorespiration

Certain species of plants have developed a way to minimize photorespiration. In the early 1960s, Hugo Kortschak discovered that the first product of carbon fixation in sugarcane is not 3GP but instead is a molecule with four carbon atoms. Species such as sugarcane are called **C_4 plants** because of this four-carbon molecule. Later, Marshall Hatch and Roger Slack confirmed this result and identified the molecule as oxaloacetate. For this reason, the pathway is sometimes called the Hatch-Slack pathway.

Some C_4 plants have a unique leaf anatomy that allows them to avoid photorespiration (**Figure 8.18**). An interior layer in the leaves of many C_4 plants has a two-cell organization composed of mesophyll cells and bundle-sheath cells. CO_2 from the atmosphere enters the mesophyll cells via stomata. Once inside, the enzyme PEP carboxylase adds CO_2 to phosphoenolpyruvate (PEP), a three-carbon molecule,

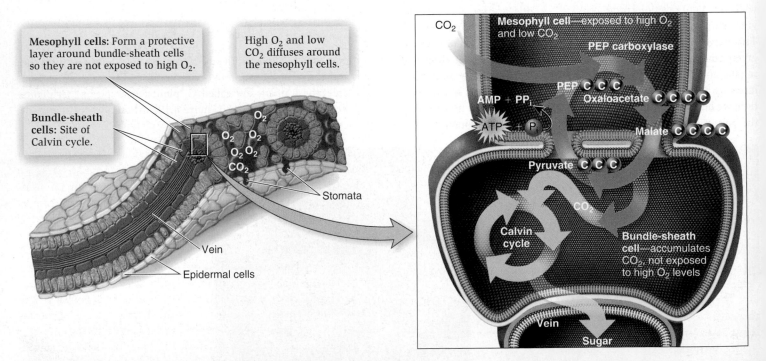

Figure 8.18 **Leaf structure and its relationship to the C_4 cycle.** C_4 plants have mesophyll cells, which initially take up CO_2, and bundle-sheath cells, where much of the carbohydrate synthesis occurs. Compare this leaf structure with the structure of C_3 leaves shown in Figure 8.2.

Concept Check: How does this cellular arrangement minimize photorespiration?

BioConnections: Look ahead to Figure 38.9. How do plants get water needed for photosynthesis into their leaves?

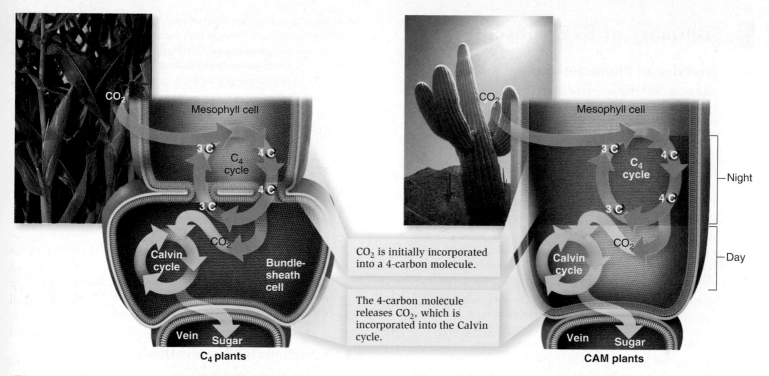

Figure 8.19 **A comparison of C₄ and CAM plants.** The name C₄ plant describes those plants in which the first organic product of carbon fixation is a four-carbon molecule. Using this definition, CAM plants are a type of C₄ plant. CAM plants, however, do not separate the functions of making a four-carbon molecule and the Calvin cycle into different types of cells. Instead, they make a four-carbon molecule at night and break down that molecule during the day so the CO₂ can be incorporated into the Calvin cycle.

Concept Check: *What are the advantages and disadvantages among C₃, C₄, and CAM plants?*

to produce oxaloacetate, a four-carbon molecule. PEP carboxylase does not recognize O₂. Therefore, unlike rubisco, PEP carboxylase does not promote photorespiration when CO₂ is low and O₂ is high. Instead, PEP carboxylase continues to fix CO₂.

As shown in Figure 8.18, oxaloacetate is converted to the four-carbon molecule malate, which is transported into the bundle-sheath cell. Malate is then broken down into pyruvate and CO₂. The pyruvate returns to the mesophyll cell, where it is converted to PEP via ATP, and the cycle in the mesophyll cell can begin again. The CO₂ enters the Calvin cycle in the chloroplasts of the bundle-sheath cells. Because the mesophyll cell supplies the bundle-sheath cell with a steady supply of CO₂, the concentration of CO₂ remains high in the bundle-sheath cell. Also, the mesophyll cells shield the bundle-sheath cells from high levels of O₂. This strategy minimizes photorespiration, which requires low CO₂ and high O₂ levels to proceed.

Which is better—being a C₃ or a C₄ plant? The answer is that it depends on the environment. In warm and dry climates, C₄ plants have an advantage. During the day, they can keep their stomata partially closed to conserve water. Furthermore, they minimize photorespiration. Examples of C₄ plants are sugarcane, crabgrass, and corn. In cooler climates, C₃ plants have the edge because they use less energy to fix CO₂. The process of carbon fixation that occurs in C₄ plants uses ATP to regenerate PEP from pyruvate (see Figure 8.18), which C₃ plants do not have to expend.

CAM Plants Are C₄ Plants That Take Up CO₂ at Night

We have just learned that certain C₄ plants prevent photorespiration by providing CO₂ to the bundle-sheath cells, where the Calvin cycle occurs. This mechanism spatially separates the processes of carbon fixation and the Calvin cycle. Another strategy followed by other C₄ plants, called **CAM plants**, separates these processes in time. CAM stands for <u>c</u>rassulacean <u>a</u>cid <u>m</u>etabolism, because the process was first studied in members of the plant family Crassulaceae. CAM plants are water-storing succulents such as cacti, bromeliads (including pineapple), and sedums. To avoid water loss, CAM plants keep their stomata closed during the day and open them at night, when it is cooler and the relative humidity is higher.

How, then, do CAM plants carry out photosynthesis? **Figure 8.19** compares CAM plants with the other type of C₄ plants we considered in Figure 8.18. Photosynthesis in CAM plants occur entirely within mesophyll cells, but the synthesis of a C₄ molecule and the Calvin cycle occur at different times. During the night, the stomata of CAM plants open, thereby allowing the entry of CO₂ into mesophyll cells. CO₂ is joined with PEP to form the four-carbon molecule oxaloacetate. This is then converted to malate, which accumulates during the night in the central vacuoles of the cells. In the morning, the stomata close to conserve moisture. The accumulated malate in the mesophyll cells leaves the vacuole and is broken down to release CO₂, which then drives the Calvin cycle during the daytime.

Summary of Key Concepts

8.1   Overview of Photosynthesis

- Photosynthesis is the process by which plants, algae, and cyanobacteria capture light energy that is used to synthesize carbohydrates.

- During photosynthesis, carbon dioxide, water, and energy are used to make carbohydrates and oxygen.

- Heterotrophs must obtain organic molecules in their food, whereas autotrophs make organic molecules from inorganic sources. Photoautotrophs use the energy from light to make organic molecules.

- An energy cycle occurs in the biosphere in which photosynthesis uses light, CO_2, and H_2O to make organic molecules, and the organic molecules are broken back down to CO_2 and H_2O via cellular respiration to supply energy in the form of ATP (Figure 8.1).

- In plants and algae, photosynthesis occurs within chloroplasts, organelles with an outer membrane, inner membrane, and thylakoid membrane. The stroma is the fluid-filled region between the thylakoid membrane and inner membrane. In plants, the leaves are the major site of photosynthesis (Figure 8.2).

- The light reactions of photosynthesis capture light energy to make ATP, NADPH, and O_2. These reactions occur at the thylakoid membrane. Carbohydrate synthesis via the Calvin cycle uses ATP and NADPH from the light reactions and happens in the stroma (Figure 8.3).

8.2   Reactions That Harness Light Energy

- Light is a form of electromagnetic radiation that travels in waves and is composed of photons with discrete amounts of energy (Figure 8.4).

- Electrons can absorb light energy and be boosted to a higher energy level—an excited state (Figure 8.5).

- Photosynthetic pigments include chlorophylls *a* and *b* and carotenoids. These pigments absorb light energy in the visible spectrum to drive photosynthesis (Figures 8.6, 8.7).

- During noncyclic electron flow, electrons from photosystem II follow a pathway along an electron transport chain (ETC) in the thylakoid membrane. This pathway generates an H^+ gradient that is used to make ATP. In addition, light energy striking photosystem I (PSI) boosts electrons to a very high energy level that allows the synthesis of NADPH (Figure 8.8).

- During cyclic photophosphorylation, electrons are activated in PSI and flow through the ETC back to PSI. This cyclic electron route produces an H^+ gradient that is used to make ATP (Figure 8.9).

- Cytochrome b_6 in chloroplasts and cytochrome *b* in mitochondria are homologous proteins involved in electron transport and H^+ pumping (Figure 8.10).

8.3   Molecular Features of Photosystems

- In the light-harvesting complex of photosystem II (PSII), pigment molecules absorb light energy that is transferred to the reaction center via resonance energy transfer. A high-energy electron from P680* is transferred to a primary electron acceptor. An electron from water is then used to replenish the electron lost from P680* (Figures 8.11, 8.12).

- Emerson showed that compared with single light flashes at 680 nm and 700 nm, light flashes at both wavelengths more than doubled the amount of photosynthesis, a result called the enhancement effect. This occurred because these wavelengths activate pigments in PSII and PSI, respectively (Figure 8.13).

- The Z scheme proposes that an electron absorbs light energy twice, at both PSII and PSI, losing some of that energy as it flows along the ETC in the thylakoid membrane (Figure 8.14).

8.4   Synthesizing Carbohydrates via the Calvin Cycle

- The Calvin cycle is composed of three phases: carbon fixation, reduction and carbohydrate production, and regeneration of ribulose bisphosphate (RuBP). In the cycle, ATP is used as a source of energy, and NADPH is used as a source of high-energy electrons to incorporate CO_2 into carbohydrate (Figure 8.15).

- Calvin and Benson determined the steps in the Calvin cycle by isotope-labeling methods in which the products of the Calvin cycle were separated by chromatography (Figure 8.16).

8.5   Variations in Photosynthesis

- C_3 plants incorporate CO_2 only into RuBP to make 3PG, a three-carbon molecule (Figure 8.17).

- Photorespiration occurs when the level of O_2 is high and CO_2 is low, which happens under hot and dry conditions. During this process, some O_2 is used and CO_2 is liberated. Photorespiration is inefficient because it reverses the incorporation of CO_2 into an organic molecule.

- Some C_4 plants avoid photorespiration because the CO_2 is first incorporated, via PEP carboxylase, into a four-carbon molecule, which is pumped from mesophyll cells into bundle-sheath cells. This maintains a high concentration of CO_2 in the bundle-sheath cells, where the Calvin cycle occurs. The high CO_2 concentration minimizes photorespiration (Figure 8.18).

- CAM plants, a type of C_4 plant, prevent photorespiration by fixing CO_2 into a four-carbon molecule at night and then running the Calvin cycle during the day with their stomata closed to reduce water loss (Figure 8.19).

Assess and Discuss

Test Yourself

1. The water necessary for photosynthesis
   a. is split into H_2 and O_2.
   b. is directly involved in the synthesis of carbohydrate.
   c. provides the electrons to replace lost electrons in photosystem II.
   d. provides H^+ needed to synthesize G3P.
   e. does none of the above.

2. The reaction center pigment differs from the other pigment molecules of the light-harvesting complex in that
   a. the reaction center pigment is a carotenoid.
   b. the reaction center pigment absorbs light energy and transfers that energy to other molecules without the transfer of electrons.
   c. the reaction center pigment transfers excited electrons to the primary electron acceptor.

d. the reaction center pigment does not transfer excited electrons to the primary electron acceptor.

e. the reaction center acts as an ATP synthase to produce ATP.

3. The cyclic electron flow that occurs via photosystem I produces
   a. NADPH.
   b. oxygen.
   c. ATP.
   d. all of the above.
   e. a and c only.

4. During noncyclic electron flow, the high-energy electron from P680*
   a. eventually moves to NADP⁺.
   b. becomes incorporated in water molecules.
   c. is pumped into the thylakoid space to drive ATP production.
   d. provides the energy necessary to split water molecules.
   e. falls back to the low-energy state in photosystem II.

5. During the first phase of the Calvin cycle, carbon dioxide is incorporated into ribulose bisphosphate (RuBP) by
   a. oxaloacetate.
   b. rubisco.
   c. RuBP.
   d. quinone.
   e. G3P.

6. The NADPH produced during the light reactions is necessary for
   a. the carbon fixation phase, which incorporates carbon dioxide into an organic molecule of the Calvin cycle.
   b. the reduction phase, which produces carbohydrates in the Calvin cycle.
   c. the regeneration of RuBP of the Calvin cycle.
   d. all of the above.
   e. a and b only.

7. The majority of the G3P produced during the reduction and carbohydrate production phase is used to produce
   a. glucose.
   b. ATP.
   c. RuBP to continue the cycle.
   d. rubisco.
   e. all of the above.

8. Photorespiration
   a. is the process where plants use sunlight to make ATP.
   b. is an inefficient way plants can produce organic molecules and in the process use O_2 and release CO_2.
   c. is a process that plants use to convert light energy to NADPH.
   d. occurs in the thylakoid lumen.
   e. is the normal process of carbohydrate production in cool, moist environments.

9. Photorespiration is avoided in C_4 plants because
   a. these plants separate the formation of a four-carbon molecule from the rest of the Calvin cycle in different cells.
   b. these plants carry out only anaerobic respiration.
   c. the enzyme PEP functions to maintain high CO_2 concentrations in the bundle-sheath cells.
   d. all of the above.
   e. a and c only.

10. Plants commonly found in hot and dry environments that carry out carbon fixation at night are
    a. oak trees.
    b. C_3 plants.
    c. CAM plants.
    d. all of the above.
    e. a and b only.

Conceptual Questions

1. What are the two stages of photosynthesis? What are the key products of each stage?

2. What is the function of NADPH in the Calvin cycle?

3. A principle of biology is that *living organisms use energy*. At the level of the biosphere, what is the role of photosynthesis in the utilization of energy by living organisms?

Collaborative Questions

1. Discuss the advantages and disadvantages of being a heterotroph or a photoautotroph.

2. Biotechnologists are trying to genetically modify C_3 plants to convert them to C_4 or CAM plants. Why would this be useful? What genes might you introduce into C_3 plants to convert them to C_4 or CAM plants?

Online Resource

www.brookerbiology.com

Stay a step ahead in your studies with animations that bring concepts to life and practice tests to assess your understanding. Your instructor may also recommend the interactive eBook, individualized learning tools, and more.

UNIT III
GENETICS

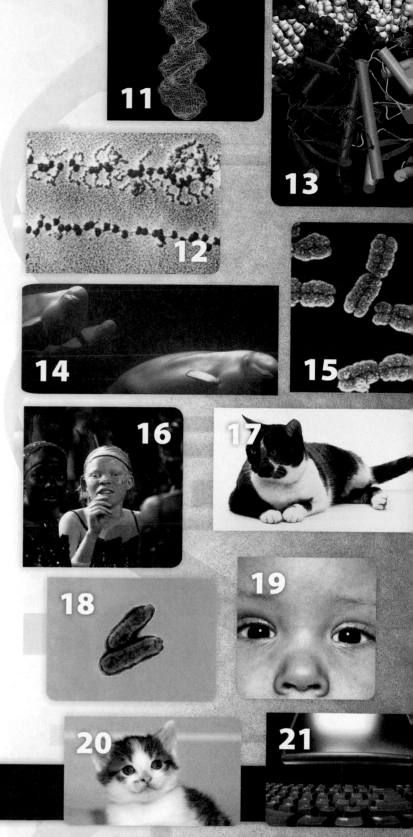

Genetics is the branch of biology that deals with **inheritance**—the transmission of characteristics from parents to offspring. We begin this unit by examining the structure of the genetic material, namely DNA, at the molecular and cellular levels. We will explore the structure and replication of DNA and how the DNA is packaged into chromosomes (Chapter 11). We then consider how segments of DNA are organized into units called genes and explore how genes are used to make products such as RNA and proteins (Chapters 12 and 13). The expression of genes is largely responsible for the characteristics of living organisms. We will also examine how mutations can alter the properties of genes and even lead to diseases such as cancer (Chapter 14).

In Chapter 15, we turn our attention to the mechanisms of how genes are transmitted from parent to offspring. This topic begins with a discussion of how chromosomes are sorted and transmitted during cell division. Chapters 16 and 17 explore the relationships between the transmission of genes and the outcome of an offspring's traits. We will look at genetic patterns called Mendelian inheritance, named after the 19th-century biologist who discovered them, as well as more complex patterns that could not have been predicted from Mendel's work.

Chapters 11 through 17 focus on the fundamental properties of the genetic material and heredity. The remaining chapters explore additional topics that are of interest to biologists. In Chapter 18, we will examine some of the unique genetic properties of bacteria and viruses. Chapter 19 considers how genes play a central role in the development of animals and plants from a fertilized egg to an adult. We end this unit by exploring genetic technologies that are used by researchers, clinicians, and biotechnologists to unlock the mysteries of genes and provide tools and applications that benefit humans (Chapters 20 and 21).

The following biology principles will be emphasized in this unit:

- **The genetic material provides a blueprint for reproduction:** *Throughout this unit, we will see how the genetic material carries the information to sustain life.*

- **Structure determines function:** *In Chapters 11 through 15, we will examine how the structures of DNA, RNA, genes, and chromosomes underlie their functions.*

- **Living organisms interact with their environment:** *In Chapters 16 and 17, we will explore the interactions between an organism's genes and its environment.*

- **Living organisms grow and develop:** *In Chapter 19, we will consider how a genetic program is involved in the developmental stages of animals and plants.*

- **Biology affects our society:** *In Chapters 20 and 21, we will examine genetic technologies that have many applications in our society.*

- **Biology is an experimental science:** *Every chapter in this unit has a Feature Investigation that describes a pivotal experiment that provided insights into our understanding of genetics.*

Nucleic Acid Structure, DNA Replication, and Chromosome Structure

11

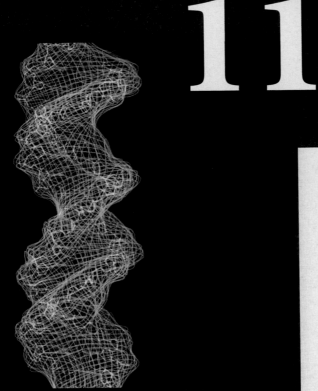

A molecular model for the structure of a DNA double helix.

ultimately the characteristics of unicellular and multicellular organisms. The past several decades have seen exciting advances in techniques and approaches to investigating and even to altering the genetic material. Not only have these advances greatly expanded our understanding of molecular genetics, such technologies are also widely used in related disciplines such as biochemistry, cell biology, and microbiology. Likewise, genetic techniques have many important applications in biotechnology and are used in criminal justice, including forensics, to provide evidence of guilt or innocence.

To a large extent, our understanding of genetics comes from our knowledge of the molecular structure of DNA. In this chapter, we begin by considering some classic experiments that provided evidence that DNA is the genetic material. We will then survey the molecular features of DNA, which allows us to appreciate how DNA can store information and be accurately copied. Though this chapter is largely concerned with DNA, we will also consider the components of ribonucleic acid (RNA), which show striking similarities to DNA. Lastly, we will examine the molecular composition of chromosomes where the DNA is found.

O n October 17, 2001, Mario K. was set free after serving 16 years in prison. He had been convicted of a sexual assault and murder that occurred in 1985. The charges were dropped because investigators discovered that another person, Edwin M., had actually committed the crime. How was Edwin M. identified as the real murderer? In 2001, he committed another crime, and his DNA was entered into a computer database. Edwin's DNA matched the DNA that had been collected from the victim in 1985, and other evidence was then gathered indicating that Edwin M. was the true murderer. Like Mario K., over 200 other inmates have been exonerated when DNA tests have shown that a different person was responsible for the crime.

Deoxyribonucleic acid, or **DNA**, is the genetic material that provides the blueprint to produce an individual's traits. Each person's DNA is distinct and unique. Even identical twins show minor differences in their DNA sequences. We begin our survey of genetics by examining DNA at the molecular level. Once we understand how DNA works at this level, it becomes easier to see how the function of DNA controls the properties of cells and

11.1 Biochemical Identification of the Genetic Material

Learning Outcomes:

1. List the four key criteria that the genetic material must fulfill.
2. Analyze the results of the experiments that identified DNA as the genetic material.

DNA carries the genetic instructions for the characteristics of living organisms. In the case of multicellular organisms such as plants and animals, the information stored in the genetic material enables a fertilized egg to develop into an embryo and eventually into an adult organism. In addition, the genetic material allows organisms to survive in their native environments. For example, an individual's DNA provides the blueprint to produce enzymes that are needed to metabolize nutrients in food. To fulfill its role, the genetic material must meet the following key criteria:

1. **Information:** The genetic material must contain the information necessary to construct an entire organism.
2. **Replication:** The genetic material must be accurately copied.

3. **Transmission:** After it is replicated, the genetic material can be passed from parent to offspring. It also must be passed from cell to cell during the process of cell division.

4. **Variation:** Differences in the genetic material must account for the known variation within each species and among different species.

How was the genetic material discovered? The quest to identify the genetic material began in the late 1800s, when a few scientists postulated that living organisms possess a blueprint that has a biochemical basis. In 1883, German biologist August Weismann and his Swiss colleague Karl Nägeli championed the idea that a chemical substance exists within living cells that is responsible for the transmission of traits from parents to offspring. During the next 30 years, experimentation along these lines centered on the behavior of **chromosomes**, the cellular structures that we now know contain the genetic material. Taken literally, chromosome is from the Greek words *chromo* and *soma*, meaning colored body, which refers to the observation of early microscopists that chromosomes are easily stained by colored dyes. By studying the transmission patterns of chromosomes from cell to cell and from parent to offspring, researchers were convinced that chromosomes carry the determinants that control the outcome of traits.

Ironically, the study of chromosomes initially misled researchers regarding the biochemical identity of the genetic material. Chromosomes contain two classes of macromolecules: proteins and DNA. Scientists of this era viewed proteins as being more biochemically complex because they are made from 20 different amino acids. Furthermore, biochemists already knew that proteins perform an amazingly wide range of functions, and complexity seemed an important prerequisite for the blueprint of an organism. By comparison, DNA seemed less complex, because it contains only four types of repeating units, called nucleotides, which will be described later in this chapter. In addition, the functional role of DNA in the nucleus had not been extensively investigated prior to the 1920s. Therefore, from the 1920s to the 1940s, most scientists were expecting research studies to reveal that proteins are the genetic material. Contrary to this expectation, however, the experiments described in this section were pivotal in showing that DNA carries out this critical role.

Griffith's Bacterial Transformation Experiments Indicated the Existence of a Genetic Material

Studies in microbiology were important in developing an experimental strategy for identifying the genetic material. In the late 1920s, an English microbiologist, Frederick Griffith, studied a type of bacterium known then as pneumococci and now classified as *Streptococcus pneumoniae*. Some strains of *S. pneumoniae* secrete a polysaccharide capsule, but other strains do not. When streaked on petri plates containing solid growth media, capsule-secreting strains have a smooth colony morphology. Those strains unable to secrete a capsule have a colony morphology that looks rough. In mammals, smooth strains of *S. pneumoniae* may cause pneumonia and other symptoms. In mice, such infections are usually fatal.

As shown in **Figure 11.1**, Griffith injected live and/or heat-killed bacteria into mice and then observed whether or not the bacteria caused them to die. He investigated the effects of two strains of *S. pneumoniae*:

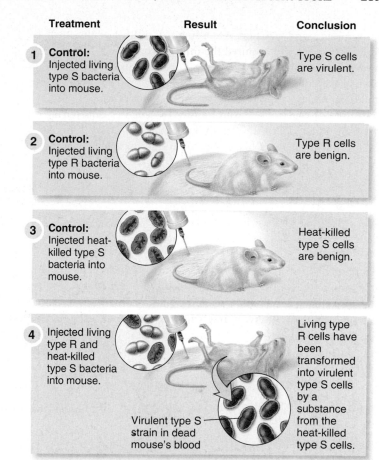

Treatment	Result	Conclusion
1 **Control:** Injected living type S bacteria into mouse.		Type S cells are virulent.
2 **Control:** Injected living type R bacteria into mouse.		Type R cells are benign.
3 **Control:** Injected heat-killed type S bacteria into mouse.		Heat-killed type S cells are benign.
4 Injected living type R and heat-killed type S bacteria into mouse.	Virulent type S strain in dead mouse's blood	Living type R cells have been transformed into virulent type S cells by a substance from the heat-killed type S cells.

Figure 11.1 Griffith's experiments that showed the transformation of bacteria by a "transformation principle." Note: To determine if a mouse's blood contained live bacteria, a sample of blood was applied to solid growth media to determine if smooth or rough bacterial colonies would form.

BioConnections: *Look ahead to Figure 18.18. How does bacterial transformation play a role in the transfer of genes, such as antibiotic resistance genes, from one bacterial species to another?*

type S for smooth and type R for rough. When injected into a live mouse, the type S strain killed the mouse (Figure 11.1, step 1). The capsule made by type S strains prevents the mouse's immune system from killing the bacterial cells. Following the death of the mouse, many type S bacteria were found in the mouse's blood. By comparison, when type R bacteria were injected into a mouse, the mouse survived, and after several days, living bacteria were not found in the live mouse's blood (Figure 11.1, step 2). In a follow-up to these results, Griffith also heat-killed the smooth bacteria and then injected them into a mouse. As expected, the mouse survived (Figure 11.1, step 3).

A surprising result occurred when Griffith mixed live type R bacteria with heat-killed type S bacteria and then injected them into a mouse—the mouse died (Figure 11.1, step 4). The blood from the dead mouse contained living type S bacteria! How did Griffith explain these results? He postulated that a substance from dead type S bacteria transformed the type R bacteria into type S bacteria. Griffith called this process **transformation**, and he termed the unidentified material responsible for this phenomenon the "transformation principle."

Let's consider what these observations mean with regard to the four criteria of the genetic material: information, replication, transmission, and variation. According to Griffith's results, the transformed bacteria had acquired the information (criterion 1) to make a capsule from the heat-killed cells. For the transformed bacteria to proliferate and thereby kill the mouse, the substance conferring the ability to make a capsule must be replicated (criterion 2) and then transmitted (criterion 3) from mother to daughter cells during cell division. Finally, Griffith already knew that variation (criterion 4) existed in the ability of his strains to produce a capsule (S strain) or not produce a capsule (R strain). Taken together, these observations are consistent with the idea that the formation of a capsule is governed by genetic material. The experiment of Figure 11.1, step 4, was consistent with the idea that some genetic material from the heat-killed type S bacteria had been transferred to the living type R bacteria and provided those bacteria with a new trait. At the time of his studies, however, Griffith could not determine the biochemical composition of the transforming substance.

FEATURE INVESTIGATION

Avery, MacLeod, and McCarty Used Purification Methods to Reveal That DNA Is the Genetic Material

Exciting discoveries sometimes occur when researchers recognize that another scientist's experimental approach may be modified and then used to dig deeper into a scientific question. In the 1940s, American physician Oswald Avery and American biologists Colin MacLeod and Maclyn McCarty were also interested in the process of bacterial transformation. During the course of their studies, they realized that Griffith's observations could be used as part of an experimental strategy to biochemically identify the genetic material. They asked the question, "What substance is being transferred from the dead type S bacteria to the live type R bacteria?"

To answer this question, Avery, MacLeod, and McCarty needed to purify the general categories of substances found in living cells. They used established biochemical procedures to purify classes of macromolecules, such as proteins, DNA, and RNA, from the type S streptococcal strain. Initially, they discovered that only the purified DNA could convert type R bacteria into type S. To further verify that DNA is the genetic material, they performed the investigation outlined in **Figure 11.2**. They purified DNA from the type S bacteria and mixed it with type R bacteria. After allowing time for DNA uptake,

Figure 11.2 The Avery, MacLeod, and McCarty experiments that identified DNA as Griffith's transformation principle—the genetic material.

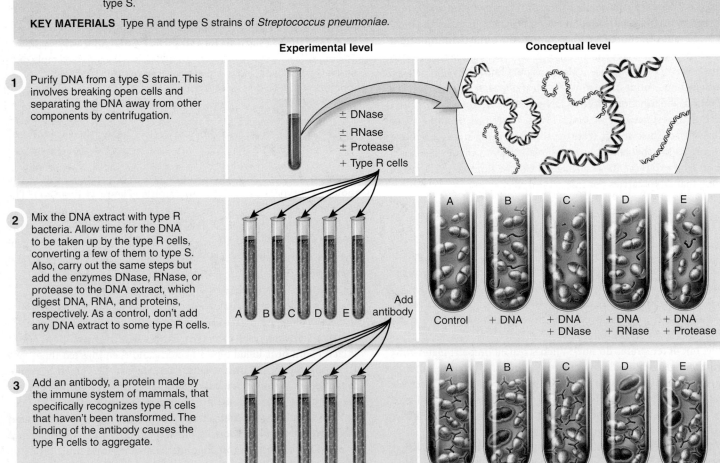

HYPOTHESIS A purified macromolecule from type S bacteria, which functions as the genetic material, will be able to convert type R bacteria into type S.

KEY MATERIALS Type R and type S strains of *Streptococcus pneumoniae*.

Experimental level   Conceptual level

1. Purify DNA from a type S strain. This involves breaking open cells and separating the DNA away from other components by centrifugation.

± DNase
± RNase
± Protease
+ Type R cells

2. Mix the DNA extract with type R bacteria. Allow time for the DNA to be taken up by the type R cells, converting a few of them to type S. Also, carry out the same steps but add the enzymes DNase, RNase, or protease to the DNA extract, which digest DNA, RNA, and proteins, respectively. As a control, don't add any DNA extract to some type R cells.

A B C D E   Add antibody

A   B   C   D   E
Control + DNA   + DNA   + DNA   + DNA
                  + DNase + RNase + Protease

3. Add an antibody, a protein made by the immune system of mammals, that specifically recognizes type R cells that haven't been transformed. The binding of the antibody causes the type R cells to aggregate.

A B C D E

A   B   C   D   E

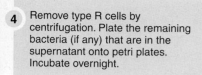

4 Remove type R cells by centrifugation. Plate the remaining bacteria (if any) that are in the supernatant onto petri plates. Incubate overnight.

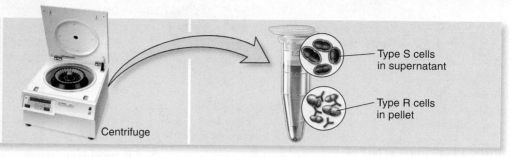

Centrifuge

Type S cells in supernatant

Type R cells in pellet

5 THE DATA

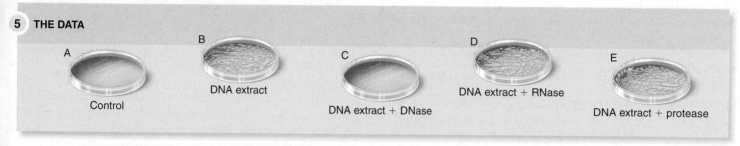

A Control

B DNA extract

C DNA extract + DNase

D DNA extract + RNase

E DNA extract + protease

6 CONCLUSION DNA is responsible for transforming type R cells into type S cells.

7 SOURCE Avery, O.T., MacLeod, C.M., and McCarty, M. 1944. Studies on the Chemical Nature of the Substance Inducing Transformation of Pneumococcal Types. *Journal of Experimental Medicine* 79:137–158.

they added an antibody that aggregated any nontransformed type R bacteria, which were then removed by centrifugation. The remaining bacteria were incubated overnight on petri plates.

As a control, if no DNA extract was added, no type S bacterial colonies were observed on the petri plates (see plate A in step 5). When they mixed their S strain DNA extract with type R bacteria, some of the bacteria were converted to type S bacteria (see plate B in step 5 of Figure 11.2). This result was consistent with the idea that DNA is the genetic material. Even so, a careful biochemist could argue that the DNA extract might not have been 100% pure. For this reason, the researchers realized that a small amount of contaminating material in the DNA extract could actually be the genetic material. The most likely contaminating substances in this case would be RNA or protein. To address this possibility, Avery, MacLeod, and McCarty treated the DNA extract with enzymes that digest DNA (called **DNase**), RNA (**RNase**), or protein (**protease**) (see step 2). When the DNA extracts were treated with RNase or protease, the type R bac-

teria were still converted into type S bacteria, suggesting that contaminating RNA or protein in the extract was not acting as the genetic material (see step 5, plates D and E). Moreover, when the extract was treated with DNase, it lost the ability to convert type R bacteria into type S bacteria (see plate C). Taken together, these results were consistent with the idea that DNA is the genetic material.

Experimental Questions

1. Avery, MacLeod, and McCarty worked with two strains of *Streptococcus pneumoniae* to determine the biochemical identity of the genetic material. Explain the characteristics of the *S. pneumoniae* strains that made them particularly well suited for such an experiment.

2. What is a DNA extract?

3. In the experiment of Avery, MacLeod, and McCarty, what was the purpose of using the protease, RNase, and DNase if only the DNA extract caused transformation?

Hershey and Chase Determined That DNA Is the Genetic Material of T2 Bacteriophage

In a second avenue of research conducted in 1952, the efforts of Alfred Hershey and Martha Chase centered on the study of a virus named T2. This virus infects bacterial cells, in this case *Escherichia coli*, and is therefore known as a **bacteriophage**, or simply a **phage**. A T2 phage has an outer covering called the phage coat that contains a head (capsid), sheath, tail fibers, and base plate (**Figure 11.3**). We now know the phage coat is composed entirely of protein. DNA is found inside the head of T2. From a biochemical perspective, T2 is very simple because it is composed of only proteins and DNA.

The genetic material of T2 provides a blueprint to make new phages. To replicate, all viruses must introduce their genetic material into the cytoplasm of a living host cell. In the case of T2, this involves attaching its tail fibers to the bacterial cell wall and injecting its genetic material into the cytoplasm (**Figure 11.3b**). However, at the time of Hershey and Chase's work, it was not known if the phage was injecting DNA or protein.

To determine whether DNA or protein is the genetic material of T2, Hershey and Chase devised a method for separating the phage coat, which is attached to the outside of the bacterium, from the genetic material, which is injected into the cytoplasm. They reasoned that the attachment of T2 on the surface of the bacterium could be

DNA

Protein

DNA

Phage head (capsid)

Sheath

Tail fiber

Base plate

E. coli cell

T2 genetic material being injected into *E. coli*

50 nm

Figure 11.3 The structure of T2 bacteriophage. The colorized electron micrograph in part **(b)** shows T2 phages attached to an *E. coli* cell and injecting their genetic material into the cell.

(a) Schematic drawing of T2 bacteriophage

(b) An electron micrograph of T2 bacteriophage infecting *E. coli*

disrupted if the cells were subjected to high shear forces such as those produced by a blender.

They also needed a way to distinguish T2 DNA from T2 proteins. Hershey and Chase used radioisotopes (described in Chapter 2) as a way to label these molecules. Sulfur atoms are found in phage proteins but not in DNA, whereas phosphorus atoms are found in DNA but not in phage proteins. They exposed T2-infected bacterial cells to

^{35}S (a radioisotope of sulfur) or to ^{32}P (a radioisotope of phosphorus). These infected cells produced phages that had incorporated either ^{35}S into their phage proteins or ^{32}P into their DNA. The ^{35}S- or ^{32}P-labeled phages were then used in the experiment shown in **Figure 11.4**.

Let's now consider the steps in this experiment. In separate tubes, they took samples of T2 phage, one in which the proteins were labeled with ^{35}S and the other in which the DNA was labeled with ^{32}P, and mixed

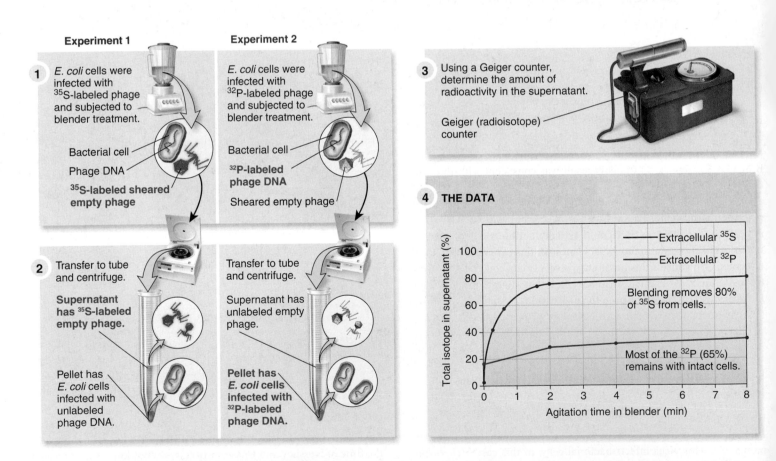

Experiment 1

1 *E. coli* cells were infected with ^{35}S-labeled phage and subjected to blender treatment.

Bacterial cell

Phage DNA

^{35}S-labeled sheared empty phage

2 Transfer to tube and centrifuge.

Supernatant has ^{35}S-labeled empty phage.

Pellet has *E. coli* cells infected with unlabeled phage DNA.

Experiment 2

E. coli cells were infected with ^{32}P-labeled phage and subjected to blender treatment.

Bacterial cell

^{32}P-labeled phage DNA

Sheared empty phage

Transfer to tube and centrifuge.

Supernatant has unlabeled empty phage.

Pellet has *E. coli* cells infected with ^{32}P-labeled phage DNA.

3 Using a Geiger counter, determine the amount of radioactivity in the supernatant.

Geiger (radioisotope) counter

4 **THE DATA**

Extracellular ^{35}S

Extracellular ^{32}P

Blending removes 80% of ^{35}S from cells.

Most of the ^{32}P (65%) remains with intact cells.

Total isotope in supernatant (%)

Agitation time in blender (min)

Figure 11.4 Hershey and Chase experiment showing that the genetic material of T2 phage is DNA. Green coloring indicates radiolabeling with either ^{35}S or ^{32}P. Note: The phages and bacteria are not drawn to scale; bacteria are much larger.

BIOLOGY PRINCIPLE Biology is an experimental science. This experiment, along with the previous one by Avery, MacLeod, and McCarty, was consistent with the idea that DNA is the genetic material.

Concept Check: *In these experiments, what was the purpose of using two different isotopes, ^{35}S and ^{32}P?*

them with *E. coli* cells for a short period of time. This allowed the phages enough time to inject their genetic material into the bacterial cells. The samples were then subjected to a shearing force, using a blender for up to 8 minutes. This treatment removed the phage coats from the surface of the bacterial cells without causing cell lysis. Each sample was then subjected to centrifugation at a speed that caused the heavier bacterial cells to form a pellet at the bottom of the tube, while the lighter phage coats remained in the supernatant, the liquid above the pellet. The amount of radioactivity in the supernatant (emitted from either ^{35}S or ^{32}P) was measured using an instrument called a Geiger counter.

As you can see in the data of Figure 11.4, most of the ^{35}S isotope (80%) was found in the supernatant. This represents the phage coats. In contrast, only about 35% of the ^{32}P was found in the supernatant following shearing. This indicates that most of the phage DNA (65%) was injected into the bacterial cells, which formed the pellet. This is the expected outcome if DNA is the genetic material of T2.

11.2   Nucleic Acid Structure

Learning Outcomes:

1. Outline the structural features of DNA at five levels of complexity.
2. Describe the structure of nucleotides, a DNA strand, and the DNA double helix.
3. Discuss and interpret the work of Franklin; Chargaff; and Watson and Crick.

A unifying principle in biology is that structure determines function. When biologists want to understand the function of a material at the molecular and cellular level, they focus some of their efforts on determining its biochemical structure. In this regard, an understanding of DNA's structure has proven to be particularly exciting because the structure makes it easier for us to understand how DNA can store information, how it is replicated and then transmitted from cell to cell, and how variation in its structure can occur.

DNA and its molecular cousin, RNA, are known as **nucleic acids**, polymers consisting of nucleotides, which are responsible for the storage, expression, and transmission of genetic information. This term is derived from the discovery of DNA by Swiss physician Friedrich Miescher in 1869. He identified a novel phosphorus-containing substance from the nuclei of white blood cells found in waste surgical bandages. He named this substance nuclein. As the structure of DNA and RNA became better understood, they were found to be acidic molecules, which means they release hydrogen ions (H^+) in solution and have a net negative charge at neutral pH. Thus, the name nucleic acid was coined.

DNA is a very large macromolecule composed of smaller building blocks. We can consider the structural features of DNA at different levels of complexity (**Figure 11.5**):

1. **Nucleotides** are the building blocks of DNA.
2. A **strand** of DNA is formed by the covalent linkage of nucleotides in a linear manner.
3. Two strands of DNA hydrogen-bond with each other to form a **double helix**. In a DNA double helix, two DNA strands are twisted together to form a structure that resembles a spiral staircase.
4. In living cells, DNA is associated with an array of different proteins to form chromosomes. The association of proteins with DNA organizes the long strands into a compact structure.

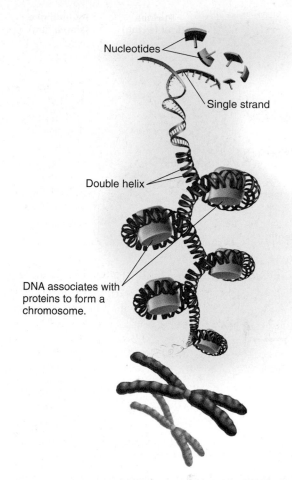

Figure 11.5 Levels of DNA structure to create a chromosome.

5. A **genome** is the complete complement of an organism's genetic material. For example, the genome of most bacteria is a single circular chromosome, whereas eukaryotic cells have DNA in their nucleus, mitochondria, and chloroplasts.

The first three levels of complexity will be the focus of this section. Level 4 will be discussed in Section 11.5, and level 5 is examined in Chapter 21.

Nucleotides Contain a Phosphate, a Sugar, and a Base

A nucleotide has three components: a phosphate group, a pentose (five-carbon) sugar, and a nitrogenous base. The nucleotides in DNA and RNA contain different sugars. Deoxyribose is found in DNA, and ribose is found in RNA. The base and phosphate group are attached to the sugar molecule at different sites (**Figure 11.6**).

Five different bases are found in nucleotides, although any given nucleotide contains only one base. The five bases are subdivided into two categories, the **purines** and the **pyrimidines**, due to differences in their structures (see Figure 11.6). The purine bases, **adenine (A)** and **guanine (G)**, have a double-ring structure, whereas the pyrimidine bases, **thymine (T)**, **cytosine (C)**, and **uracil (U)**, have a single-ring structure. Adenine, guanine, and cytosine are found in both DNA and RNA. Thymine is found only in DNA, whereas uracil is found only in RNA.

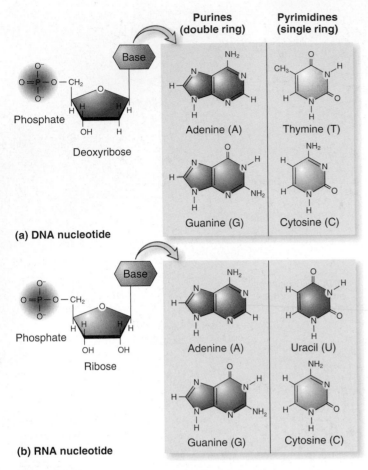

(a) DNA nucleotide

Purines (double ring) — Pyrimidines (single ring)

Adenine (A), Thymine (T), Guanine (G), Cytosine (C)

(b) RNA nucleotide

Adenine (A), Uracil (U), Guanine (G), Cytosine (C)

Figure 11.6 **Nucleotides and their components.** For simplicity, the carbon atoms in the ring structures are not shown.

Concept Check: *Which pyrimidine(s) is/are found in both DNA and RNA?*

A conventional numbering system describes the locations of carbon and nitrogen atoms in the sugars and bases (**Figure 11.7**). The prime symbol (′) is used to distinguish the numbering of carbons in the sugar. The atoms in the ring structures of the bases are not given the prime designation. The sugar carbons are designated 1′ (that is, "one prime"), 2′, 3′, 4′, and 5,′ with the carbon atoms numbered in a clockwise direction starting with the carbon atom to the right of the ring oxygen atom. The fifth carbon is outside the ring. A base is attached to the 1′ carbon atom, and a phosphate group is attached at the 5′ position. Compared with ribose (see Figure 11.6), deoxyribose lacks a single oxygen atom at the 2′ position; the prefix deoxy- (meaning without oxygen) refers to this missing atom.

A Strand Is a Linear Linkage of Nucleotides with Directionality

The next level of nucleotide structure is the formation of a strand of DNA or RNA in which nucleotides are covalently attached to each other in a linear fashion. **Figure 11.8** depicts a short strand of DNA with four nucleotides. The linkage is a phosphoester bond (a covalent bond between phosphorus and oxygen) involving a sugar molecule in one nucleotide and a phosphate group in the next nucleotide. Another

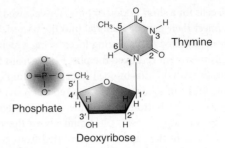

Figure 11.7 **Conventional numbering in a DNA nucleotide.** The carbons in the sugar are given a prime designation, whereas those in the base are not.

Concept Check: *What is the numbering designation of the carbon atom to which the phosphate is attached?*

way of viewing this linkage is to notice that a phosphate group connects two sugar molecules. From this perspective, the linkage in DNA and RNA strands is called a **phosphodiester linkage**, which has two phosphoester bonds. The phosphates and sugar molecules form the **backbone** of a DNA or RNA strand, and the bases project from the backbone. The backbone is negatively charged due to the negative charges of the phosphate groups.

An important structural feature of a nucleic acid strand is the orientation of the nucleotides. Each phosphate in a phosphodiester linkage is covalently bonded to the 5′ carbon in one nucleotide and to the 3′ carbon in the other. In a strand, all sugar molecules are oriented in the same direction. For example, in the strand shown in Figure 11.8, all of the 5′ carbons in every sugar molecule are above the 3′ carbons. A strand has a **directionality** based on the orientation of the sugar molecules within that strand. In Figure 11.8, the direction of the strand is said to be 5′ to 3′ when going from top to bottom. The 5′ end of a DNA strand has a phosphate group, whereas the 3′ end has an —OH group.

From the perspective of function, a key feature of DNA and RNA structure is that a strand contains a specific sequence of bases. In Figure 11.8, the sequence of bases is thymine—adenine—cytosine—guanine, or TACG. To indicate its directionality, the strand is abbreviated 5′–TACG–3′. Because the nucleotides within a strand are attached to each other by stable covalent bonds, the sequence of bases in a DNA strand remains the same over time, except in rare cases when mutations occur. The sequence of bases in DNA and RNA is the critical feature that allows them to store and transmit information.

A Few Key Experiments Paved the Way to Solving the Structure of DNA

What experimental approaches were used to analyze DNA structure? X-ray diffraction was a key experimental tool that led to the discovery of the DNA double helix. When a substance is exposed to X-rays, the atoms in the substance cause the X-rays to be scattered (**Figure 11.9**). If the substance has a repeating structure, the pattern of scattering, known as the diffraction pattern, is mathematically related to the structural arrangement of the atoms causing the scattering. The diffraction pattern is analyzed using mathematical theory to provide information regarding the three-dimensional structure

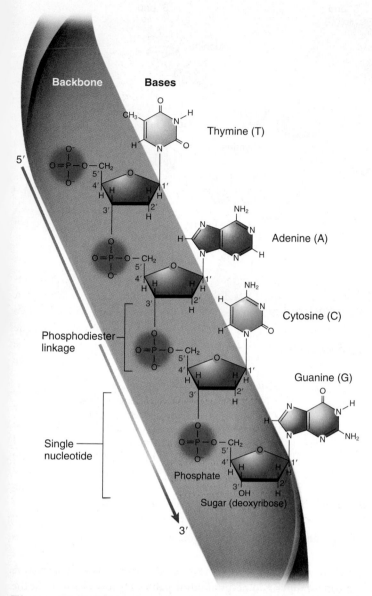

Figure 11.8 **The structure of a DNA strand.** Nucleotides are covalently bonded to each other in a linear manner. Notice the directionality of the strand and that it carries a particular sequence of bases. An RNA strand has a very similar structure, except the sugar is ribose rather than deoxyribose, and uracil is substituted for thymine.

BIOLOGY PRINCIPLE **The genetic material provides a blueprint for reproduction.** The covalent linkage of a sequence of bases allows DNA to store information.

Concept Check: *What is the difference between a phosphoester bond and a phosphodiester linkage?*

of the molecule. British biophysicist Rosalind Franklin, working in the 1950s in the same laboratory as Maurice Wilkins, was a gifted experimentalist who made marked advances in X-ray diffraction techniques involving DNA. The diffraction pattern of DNA fibers produced by Franklin suggested a helical structure with a diameter that is relatively uniform and too wide to be a single-stranded helix. In addition, the pattern provided information regarding the number of nucleotides per turn and was consistent with a 2-nm (nanometers)

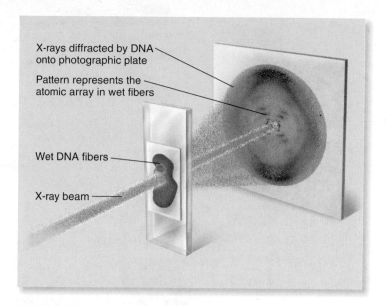

Figure 11.9 **Rosalind Franklin's X-ray diffraction of DNA fibers.** The exposure of DNA wet fibers to X-rays causes the X-rays to be scattered and the pattern of scattering is related to the position of the atoms in the DNA fibers.

spacing between the strands in which a purine (A or G) bonds with a pyrimidine (T or C).

Another piece of information that proved to be critical for the determination of the double helix structure came from the studies of Austrian-born American biochemist Erwin Chargaff. In 1950, Chargaff analyzed the base composition of DNA that was isolated from many different species. His experiments consistently showed that the amount of adenine in each sample was similar to the amount of thymine, and the amount of cytosine was similar to the amount of guanine (**Table 11.1**).

In the early 1950s, more information was known about the structure of proteins than that of nucleic acids. American biochemist Linus Pauling correctly proposed that some regions of proteins fold into a structure known as an α helix. To determine the structure of the α helix, Pauling built large models by linking together simple ball-and-stick

Table 11.1	Base Content in the DNA from a Variety of Organisms as Determined by Chargaff			
	Percentage of bases (%)			
Organism	**Adenine**	**Thymine**	**Guanine**	**Cytosine**
Escherichia coli (bacterium)	26.0	23.9	24.9	25.2
Streptococcus pneumoniae (bacterium)	29.8	31.6	20.5	18.0
Saccharomyces cerevisiae (yeast)	31.7	32.6	18.3	17.4
Turtle	28.7	27.9	22.0	21.3
Salmon	29.7	29.1	20.8	20.4
Chicken	28.0	28.4	22.0	21.6
Human	30.3	30.3	19.5	19.9

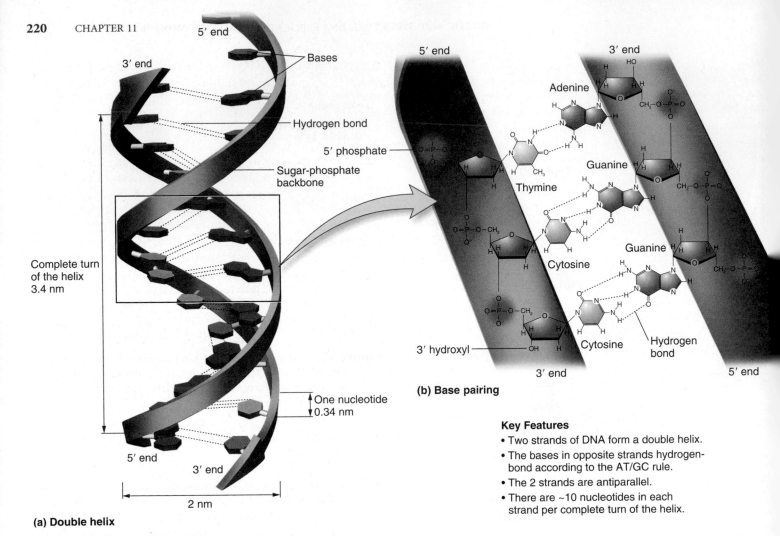

Figure 11.10 **Structure of the DNA double helix.** As seen in part (a), DNA is a helix composed of two antiparallel strands. Part (b) shows the AT/GC base pairing that holds the strands together via hydrogen bonds.

Concept Check: *If one DNA strand is 5'–GATTCGTTC–3', what is the complementary strand?*

units. In this way, he could see if atoms fit together properly in a complicated three-dimensional structure. This approach is still widely used today, except that now researchers construct three-dimensional models using computers. Use of the ball-and-stick approach was instrumental in solving the structure of the DNA double helix.

Watson and Crick Deduced the Double Helix Structure of DNA

Thus far, we have considered the experimental studies that led to the determination of the DNA double helix. American biologist James Watson and English biologist Francis Crick, working together at Cambridge University, assumed that nucleotides are linked together in a linear fashion and that the chemical linkage between two nucleotides is always the same. In collaboration with Wilkins, they then set out to build ball-and-stick models that incorporated all of the known experimental observations.

Modeling of chemical structures involves trial and error. Watson and Crick initially considered several incorrect models. One model was a double helix in which the bases were on the outside of the helix. In another model, each base formed hydrogen bonds with the identical base in the opposite strand (A to A, T to T, G to G, and C to

C). However, model-building revealed that purine-purine pairs were too wide and pyrimidine-pyrimidine pairs were too narrow to fit the uniform diameter of DNA revealed from Franklin's work. Eventually, they realized that the hydrogen bonding of adenine to thymine was structurally similar to that of guanine to cytosine. In both cases, a purine base (A or G) bonds with a pyrimidine base (T or C). With an interaction between A and T and between G and C, the ball-and-stick models showed that the two strands would form a double helix structure in which all atoms would fit together properly.

Watson and Crick proposed the structure of DNA, which was published in the journal *Nature* in 1953. In 1962, Watson, Crick, and Wilkins were awarded the Nobel Prize in Physiology or Medicine. Unfortunately, Rosalind Franklin had died before this time, and the Nobel Prize is awarded only to living recipients.

DNA Has a Repeating, Antiparallel Helical Structure Formed by the Complementary Base Pairing of Nucleotides

The structure that Watson and Crick proposed is a double-stranded, helical structure with the sugar-phosphate backbone on the outside and the bases on the inside (**Figure 11.10a**). This structure is stabilized by hydrogen bonding between the bases in opposite strands to form **base pairs**. A distinguishing feature of base pairing is its specificity. An adenine (A) base in one strand forms two hydrogen bonds with a thymine (T) base in the opposite strand, or a guanine (G) base forms three hydrogen bonds with a cytosine (C) (**Figure 11.10b**). This **AT/ GC rule** is consistent with Chargaff's observation that DNA contains equal amounts of A and T, and equal amounts of G and C. According to the AT/GC rule, purines (A and G) always bond with pyrimidines (T and C) (recall that purines have a double-ring structure, whereas pyrimidines have single rings). This keeps the width of the double helix relatively constant. One complete turn of the double helix is 3.4 nm in length and comprises 10 base pairs.

Due to the AT/GC rule, the base sequences of two DNA strands are **complementary** to each other. That is, you can predict the sequence in one DNA strand if you know the sequence in the opposite strand. For example, if one DNA strand has the sequence of 5′–GCGGATTT–3′, the opposite strand must be 3′–CGCCTAAA–5′. With regard to their 5′ and 3′ directionality, the two strands of a DNA double helix are **antiparallel**. If you look at Figure 11.10, one strand runs in the 5′ to 3′ direction from top to bottom, while the other strand is oriented 3′ to 5′ from top to bottom.

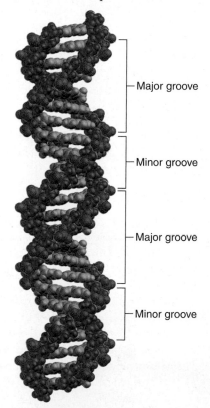

— Major groove

— Minor groove

— Major groove

— Minor groove

Figure 11.11 **A space-filling model of the DNA double helix.** In the sugar-phosphate backbone, sugar molecules are shown in blue, and phosphate groups are yellow. The backbone is on the outermost surface of the double helix. The atoms of the bases, shown in green, are more internally located within the double-stranded structure. Notice the major and minor grooves that are formed by this arrangement.

BIOLOGY PRINCIPLE Structure determines function. The major groove provides a binding site for proteins that control the expression of genes.

The DNA model in Figure 11.10a is called a ribbon model, which clearly shows the components of the DNA molecule. However, other models are also used to visualize DNA. The model for the DNA double helix shown in **Figure 11.11** is a space-filling model in which the atoms are depicted as spheres. Why is this model useful? This type of structural model emphasizes the surface of DNA. As you can see in this model, the sugar-phosphate backbone is on the outermost surface of the double helix; the backbone has the most direct contact with water. The atoms of the bases are more internally located within the double-stranded structure. The indentations where the atoms of the bases make contact with the surrounding water are termed grooves. Two grooves, called the **major groove** and the **minor groove**, spiral around the double helix. As discussed in later chapters, the major groove provides a location where a protein can bind to a particular sequence of bases and affect the expression of a gene (for example, look ahead to Figure 13.10).

11.3 An Overview of DNA Replication

Learning Outcomes:

1. Discuss and interpret the experiments of Meselson and Stahl.
2. Describe the double-stranded structure of DNA and explain how the AT/GC rule underlies the ability of DNA to be replicated semiconservatively.

The structure of DNA immediately suggested to Watson and Crick a mechanism by which DNA can be copied. They proposed that during this process, known as **DNA replication**, the original DNA strands are used as templates for the synthesis of new DNA strands. In this section, we will look at an early experiment that helped to determine the mechanism of DNA replication and then examine the structural characteristics that enable a double helix to be faithfully copied.

Meselson and Stahl Investigated Three Proposed Mechanisms of DNA Replication

Researchers in the late 1950s considered three different models for the mechanism of DNA replication (**Figure 11.12**). In all of these models, the two newly made strands are called the **daughter strands**, and the original strands are the **parental strands**. The first model is a **semiconservative mechanism** (Figure 11.12a). In this model, the double-stranded DNA is half conserved following the replication process so the new double-stranded DNA contains one parental strand and one daughter strand. This model is consistent with the proposal of Watson and Crick. However, other models were possible and had to be ruled out. According to a second model, called a **conservative mechanism**, both parental strands of DNA remain together following DNA replication (Figure 11.12b). The original arrangement of parental strands is completely conserved, and the two newly made daughter strands are also together following replication. Finally, a third possibility, called a **dispersive mechanism**, proposed that segments of parental DNA and newly made DNA are interspersed in both strands following the replication process (Figure 11.12c).

In 1958, American biologists Matthew Meselson and Franklin Stahl devised an experimental approach to distinguish among these

Original double helix   First round of replication   Second round of replication

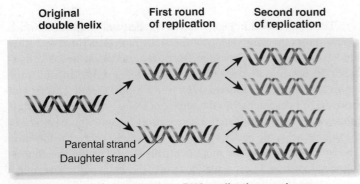

(a) Semiconservative mechanism. DNA replication produces DNA molecules with 1 parental strand and 1 newly made daughter strand.

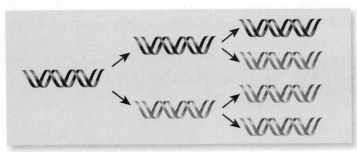

(b) Conservative mechanism. DNA replication produces 1 double helix with both parental strands and the other with 2 new daughter strands.

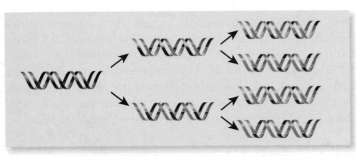

(c) Dispersive mechanism. DNA replication produces DNA strands in which segments of new DNA are interspersed with the parental DNA.

Figure 11.12 Three proposed mechanisms for DNA replication. The strands of the original (parental) double helix are shown in red. Two rounds of replication are illustrated with the daughter strands shown in blue.

three mechanisms. An important feature of their research was the use of isotope labeling. Nitrogen, which is found in DNA, occurs in a common light (^{14}N) form and a rare heavy (^{15}N) form. Meselson and Stahl studied DNA replication in the bacterium *Escherichia coli.* They grew *E. coli* cells for many generations in a medium that contained only the ^{15}N form of nitrogen (**Figure 11.13**). This produced a population of bacterial cells in which all of the DNA was heavy labeled. Then they switched the bacteria to a medium that contained only ^{14}N as its nitrogen source. The cells were allowed to divide, and samples were collected after one generation (that is, one round of DNA replication), two generations, and so on. Because the bacteria were doubling in a medium that contained only ^{14}N, all of the newly made DNA strands were labeled with light nitrogen, but the original strands would remain labeled with the heavy form.

1 Grow bacteria in ^{15}N media.

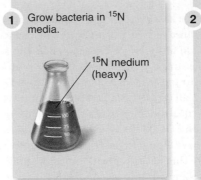

^{15}N medium (heavy)

2 Transfer to ^{14}N media and continue growth for <1, 1.0, 2.0, or 3 generations.

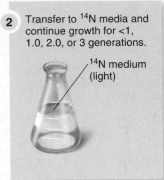

^{14}N medium (light)

3 Isolate DNA after each generation. Transfer DNA to CsCl gradient, and centrifuge.

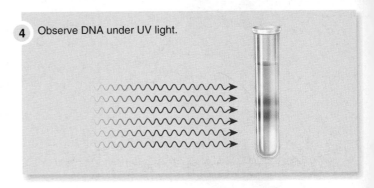

DNA

CsCl gradient

Centrifuge

4 Observe DNA under UV light.

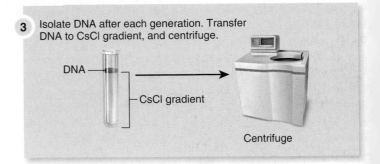

5 **THE DATA**

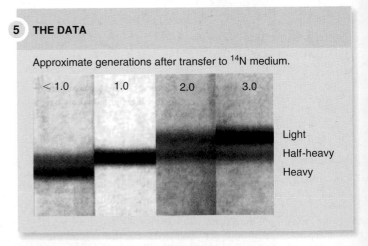

Approximate generations after transfer to ^{14}N medium.

< 1.0   1.0   2.0   3.0

Light
Half-heavy
Heavy

Figure 11.13 The Meselson and Stahl experiment showing that DNA replication is semiconservative.

Concept Check: If this experiment was conducted for four rounds of DNA replication (that is, four generations), what would be the expected fractions of light DNA and half-heavy DNA according to the semiconservative model?

How were the DNA molecules analyzed? Meselson and Stahl used centrifugation to separate DNA molecules based on differences in density. Samples were placed on the top of a solution that contained a salt gradient, in this case, cesium chloride (CsCl). A double helix containing all heavy nitrogen has a higher density and therefore travels closer to the bottom of the gradient. By comparison, if both DNA strands contained ^{14}N, the DNA would have a low density and remain closer to the top of the gradient. If one strand contained ^{14}N and the other strand contained ^{15}N, the DNA would be half-heavy and have an intermediate density, ending up near the middle of the gradient.

After one cell doubling (that is, one round of DNA replication), all of the DNA exhibited a density that was half-heavy or intermediate density (Figure 11.13, step 5). These results are consistent with both the semiconservative and dispersive models. In contrast, the conservative mechanism predicts two different DNA bands: one of high density and one of low density. Because the DNA was found in a single half-heavy band after one doubling, the conservative model was disproved.

After two cell doublings, both light DNA and half-heavy DNA bands were observed. This result was also predicted by the semiconservative mechanism of DNA replication, because half of the DNA molecules should contain all light DNA, while the other molecules should be half-heavy (see Figure 11.12a). However, in the dispersive mechanism, all of the DNA strands would have been 1/4 heavy after two generations. This mechanism predicts that the heavy nitrogen

would be evenly dispersed among four double helices, each strand containing 1/4 heavy nitrogen and 3/4 light nitrogen (see Figure 11.12c). This prediction did not agree with the data. Taken together, the results of the Meselson and Stahl experiment are consistent only with a semiconservative mechanism for DNA replication.

DNA Replication Proceeds According to the AT/GC Rule

As originally proposed by Watson and Crick, DNA replication relies on the complementarity of DNA strands according to the AT/GC rule. During the replication process, the two complementary strands of DNA separate and serve as **template strands**, also called parental strands, for the synthesis of daughter strands of DNA (**Figure 11.14a**). After the double helix has separated, individual nucleotides have access to the template strands in a region called the replication fork. First, individual nucleotides hydrogen-bond to the template strands according to the AT/GC rule: an adenine (A) base in one strand bonds with a thymine (T) base in the opposite strand, or a guanine (G) base bonds with a cytosine (C). Next, a covalent bond is formed between the phosphate of one nucleotide and the sugar of the previous nucleotide. The end result is that two double helices are made that have the same base sequence as the original DNA molecule (**Figure 11.14b**). This is a critical feature of DNA replication, because it enables the

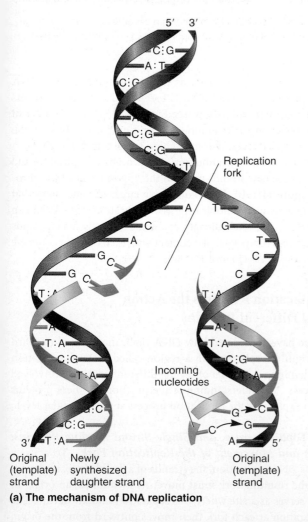

Original (template) strand   Newly synthesized daughter strand

Original (template) strand

(a) The mechanism of DNA replication

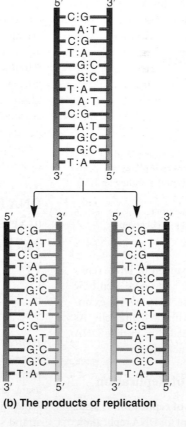

(b) The products of replication

Figure 11.14 **DNA replication according to the AT/GC rule.** **(a)** The mechanism of DNA replication as originally proposed by Watson and Crick. As we will see in Section 11.4, the synthesis of one newly made strand (the leading strand on the left side) occurs in the direction toward the replication fork, whereas the synthesis of the other newly made strand (the lagging strand on the right side) occurs in small segments away from the fork. **(b)** DNA replication produces two copies of DNA with the same sequence as the original DNA molecule.

BIOLOGY PRINCIPLE **Structure determines function.** A double-stranded structure that obeys the AT/GC rule underlies the function of DNA replication.

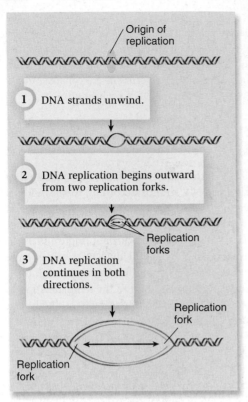

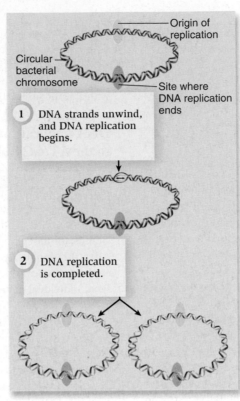

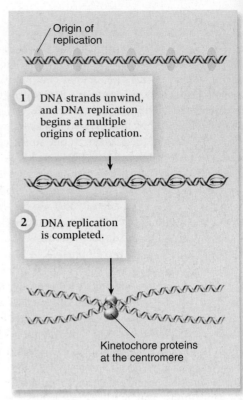

(a) Bidirectional replication   **(b) Single origin of replication in bacteria**   **(c) Multiple origins of replication in eukaryotes**

Figure 11.15 **The bidirectional replication of DNA. (a)** DNA replication proceeds in both directions from an origin of replication. **(b)** Bacterial chromosomes have a single origin of replication, whereas **(c)** eukaryotes have multiple origins. Following DNA replication in eukaryotes, the two copies remain attached to each other at the centromere via kinetochore proteins.

replicated DNA molecules to retain the same information (that is, the same base sequence) as the original molecule. In this way, DNA has the remarkable ability to direct its own duplication.

11.4 Molecular Mechanism of DNA Replication

Learning Outcomes:

1. Describe how the synthesis of new DNA strands begins at an origin of replication.
2. List the functions of helicase, topoisomerase, single-strand binding protein, primase, and DNA polymerase at the replication fork.
3. Outline the key differences between the synthesis of the leading and lagging strands.
4. List three reasons why DNA replication is very accurate.
5. Explain how DNA replication occurs at telomeres in eukaryotic chromosomes.

Thus far, we have examined the general mechanism of DNA replication, known as semiconservative replication, and we've seen how DNA synthesis obeys the AT/GC rule. In this section, we will examine the details of DNA replication as it occurs inside living cells. As you will learn, several different proteins are needed to initiate DNA replication and allow it to proceed quickly and accurately.

DNA Replication Begins at an Origin of Replication

Where does DNA replication begin? An **origin of replication** is a site within a chromosome that serves as a starting point for DNA replication.

At the origin, the two DNA strands unwind (Figure 11.15a). DNA replication proceeds outward from two **replication forks**, a process termed **bidirectional replication** (see Figure 11.15a). The number of origins of replication varies among different organisms. In bacteria, which have a small circular chromosome, a single origin of replication is found. Bidirectional replication starts at the origin of replication and proceeds until the new strands meet on the opposite side of the chromosome (Figure 11.15b). Eukaryotes have larger chromosomes that are linear. They require multiple origins of replication so the DNA can be replicated in a reasonable length of time. The newly made strands from each origin eventually make contact with each other to complete the replication process (Figure 11.15c).

DNA Replication Requires the Action of Several Different Proteins

Thus far, we have considered how DNA replication occurs outward from an origin of replication in a region called a DNA replication fork. In all living species, a set of several different proteins is involved in this process. An understanding of the functions of these proteins is critical to explaining the replication process at the molecular level.

Helicase, Topoisomerase, and Single-Strand Binding Proteins: Formation and Movement of the Replication Fork   To act as a template for DNA replication, the strands of a double helix must separate, and the resulting fork must move. As mentioned, an origin of replication serves as a site where this separation initially occurs. The strand separation at each fork then moves outward from the origin via the action of an enzyme called **DNA helicase**. At each fork, DNA helicase binds to one of the DNA strands and travels in the 5′ to 3′ direction toward the fork (**Figure 11.16**). It uses energy from ATP to separate the DNA strands and keeps the fork moving forward. The action of DNA helicase generates additional coiling just ahead of the replication fork that is alleviated by another enzyme called **DNA topoisomerase**, which helps to untwist the strands.

After the two template DNA strands have separated, they must remain that way until the complementary daughter strands have been made. The function of **single-strand binding proteins** is to coat both of the single strands of template DNA and prevent them from re-forming a double helix. In this way, the bases within the template strands are kept exposed so they can act as templates for the synthesis of complementary strands.

DNA Polymerase and Primase: Synthesis of DNA Strands

The enzyme **DNA polymerase** is responsible for covalently linking nucleotides together to form DNA strands. American biochemist Arthur Kornberg originally identified this enzyme in the 1950s. The structure of DNA polymerase resembles a human hand with the DNA threaded through it (**Figure 11.17a**). As DNA polymerase slides along the

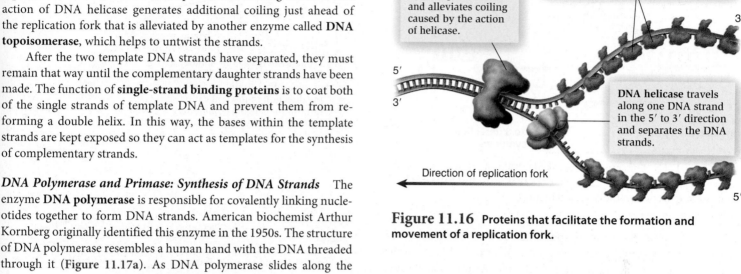

Figure 11.16 Proteins that facilitate the formation and movement of a replication fork.

Figure 11.17 Enzymatic synthesis of DNA. **(a)** Incoming deoxynucleoside triphosphates first hydrogen-bond to the template strand according to the AT/GC rule. DNA polymerase recognizes these deoxynucleoside triphosphates and attaches a deoxynucleoside monophosphate to the 3′ end of a growing strand. **(b)** DNA polymerase breaks the bond between the first and second phosphate in a deoxynucleoside triphosphate, causing the release of pyrophosphate. This provides the energy to form a covalent bond between the resulting deoxynucleoside monophosphate and the previous nucleotide In the growing strand. The pyrophosphate is broken down to two phosphates.

Concept Check: *Does the oxygen in a new phosphoester bond come from the sugar or from the phosphate?*

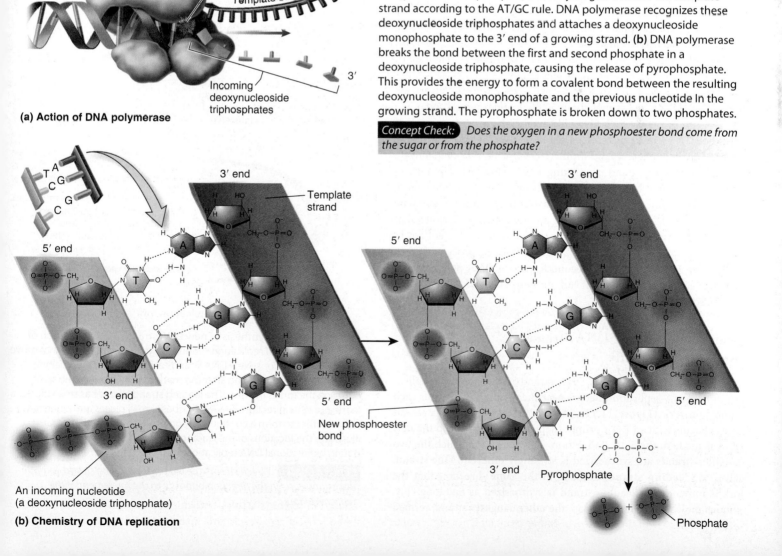

(a) Action of DNA polymerase

(b) Chemistry of DNA replication

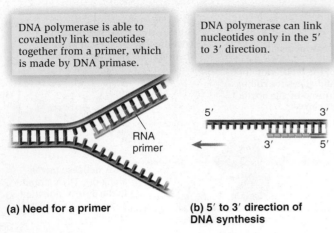

DNA polymerase is able to covalently link nucleotides together from a primer, which is made by DNA primase.

DNA polymerase can link nucleotides only in the 5′ to 3′ direction.

RNA primer

5′   3′
3′   5′

(a) Need for a primer

(b) 5′ to 3′ direction of DNA synthesis

Figure 11.18 Enzymatic features of DNA polymerase. (a) DNA polymerase needs a primer to begin DNA synthesis, and (b) it can synthesize DNA only in the 5′ to 3′ direction.

DNA, free nucleotides with three phosphate groups, called **deoxynucleoside triphosphates**, hydrogen-bond to the exposed bases in the template strand according to the AT/GC rule. At the catalytic site, DNA polymerase breaks a bond between the first and second phosphate and then attaches the resulting nucleotide with one phosphate group (a deoxynucleoside monophosphate) to the 3′ end of a growing strand via a phosphoester bond. The breakage of the covalent bond that releases pyrophosphate is an exergonic reaction that provides the energy to covalently connect adjacent nucleotides (Figure 11.17b). The pyrophosphate is broken down to two phosphates. The rate of synthesis is truly remarkable. In bacteria, DNA polymerase synthesizes DNA at a rate of 500 nucleotides per second, whereas eukaryotic species make DNA at a rate of about 50 nucleotides per second.

DNA polymerase has two additional enzymatic features that affect how DNA strands are made. First, if a DNA or RNA strand is already attached to a template strand, DNA polymerase can elongate such a pre-existing strand by making DNA. However, DNA polymerase is unable to begin DNA synthesis on a bare template strand. A different enzyme called **DNA primase** is required if the template strand is bare. DNA primase makes a complementary primer that is actually a short segment of RNA, typically 10 to 12 nucleotides in length. These short RNA strands start, or prime, the process of DNA replication (**Figure 11.18a**). A second feature of DNA polymerase is that once synthesis has begun, it can synthesize new DNA only in a 5′ to 3′ direction (**Figure 11.18b**).

Leading and Lagging DNA Strands Are Made Differently

Let's now consider how new DNA strands are made at a replication fork. DNA replication occurs near the opening that forms each replication fork (**Figure 11.19a**, step 1). The synthesis of a strand always begins with an RNA primer (depicted in yellow), and the new DNA is made in the 5′ to 3′ direction. The manner in which the two daughter strands are synthesized is strikingly different. One strand, called the **leading strand**, is made in the same direction that the fork is moving. The leading strand is synthesized as one long continuous molecule. By comparison, the other daughter strand, termed

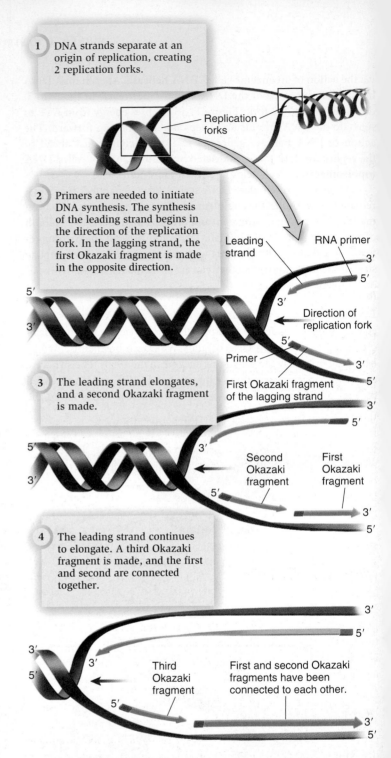

1 DNA strands separate at an origin of replication, creating 2 replication forks.

Replication forks

2 Primers are needed to initiate DNA synthesis. The synthesis of the leading strand begins in the direction of the replication fork. In the lagging strand, the first Okazaki fragment is made in the opposite direction.

Leading strand

RNA primer

3′
5′
5′
3′
3′

Direction of replication fork

5′

Primer

3′

5′

3 The leading strand elongates, and a second Okazaki fragment is made.

First Okazaki fragment of the lagging strand

3′
5′

Second Okazaki fragment

First Okazaki fragment

5′
3′
5′
3′

4 The leading strand continues to elongate. A third Okazaki fragment is made, and the first and second are connected together.

3′
5′

3′
5′

Third Okazaki fragment

First and second Okazaki fragments have been connected to each other.

5′

3′
5′

(a) DNA replication at one replication fork

Figure 11.19 Synthesis of new DNA strands. The separation of DNA at the origin of replication produces two replication forks that move in opposite directions. New DNA strands are made near the opening of each fork. (a) The leading strand is made continuously in the same direction the fork is moving. The lagging strand is made as small pieces in the opposite direction. Eventually, these small pieces are connected to each other to form a continuous lagging strand. (b) This diagram illustrates the locations of the leading and lagging strands that are made during bidirectional DNA replication from one origin of replication.

Concept Check: *Which strand, the leading or lagging strand, is made discontinuously in the direction opposite to the movement of the replication fork?*

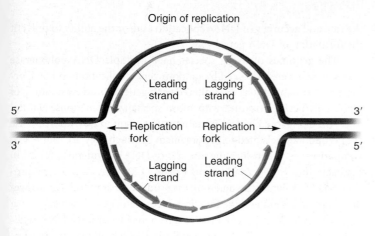

(b) Replication from an origin

the **lagging strand**, is made as a series of small fragments that are subsequently connected to each other to form a continuous strand. These DNA fragments are known as **Okazaki fragments**, after Japanese biologists Reiji and Tsuneko Okazaki, who initially discovered them in the late 1960s. The synthesis of Okazaki fragments occurs in the opposite direction of the replication fork. For example, the lower fragment seen in Figure 11.19a, steps 2 and 3, is synthesized from left to right. As shown in Figure 11.19a, step 4, the RNA primer is eventually removed, and adjacent Okazaki fragments are connected to each other to form a continuous strand of DNA. **Figure 11.19b** shows the leading and lagging strands that are made during bidirectional DNA replication from a single origin of replication.

Figure 11.19 was meant to emphasize the synthesis of new DNA strands. **Figure 11.20** shows the proteins involved with the synthesis of the leading and lagging strands in *E. coli*. In this bacterium, two different DNA polymerases, called DNA polymerase I and III, are primarily responsible for DNA replication. In the leading strand, DNA primase makes one RNA primer at the origin, and then DNA polymerase III attaches nucleotides in a 5′ to 3′ direction as it slides toward the opening of the replication fork. DNA polymerase III has a subunit called the clamp protein that allows the enzyme to slide along the template strand without falling off, a characteristic called **processivity**.

In the lagging strand, DNA is also synthesized in a 5′ to 3′ direction, but this synthesis occurs in the direction away from the replication fork. In the lagging strand, short segments of DNA are made discontinuously as a series of Okazaki fragments, each of which requires its own primer. DNA polymerase III synthesizes the remainder of the fragment (Figure 11.20, step 2). To complete the synthesis of Okazaki fragments within the lagging strand, three additional events occur: the removal of the RNA primers, the synthesis of DNA in the

Figure 11.20 Proteins involved with the synthesis of the leading and lagging strands in *E. coli*.

Concept Check: Briefly describe the movement of primase in the lagging strand in this figure. In which direction does it move when it is making a primer, from left to right or right to left? Describe how it must move after it is done making a primer and has to start making the next primer at a new location. Does it have to hop from left to right or from right to left?

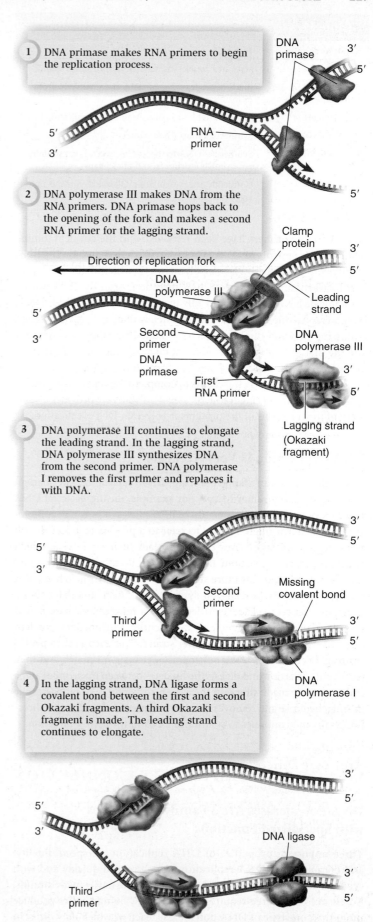

1 DNA primase makes RNA primers to begin the replication process.

2 DNA polymerase III makes DNA from the RNA primers. DNA primase hops back to the opening of the fork and makes a second RNA primer for the lagging strand.

3 DNA polymerase III continues to elongate the leading strand. In the lagging strand, DNA polymerase III synthesizes DNA from the second primer. DNA polymerase I removes the first primer and replaces it with DNA.

4 In the lagging strand, DNA ligase forms a covalent bond between the first and second Okazaki fragments. A third Okazaki fragment is made. The leading strand continues to elongate.

Table 11.2   Proteins Involved in DNA Replication

Common name	Function
DNA helicase	Separates double-stranded DNA into single strands
Single-strand binding protein	Binds to single-stranded DNA and prevents it from re-forming a double helix
Topoisomerase	Removes tightened coils ahead of the replication fork
DNA primase	Synthesizes short RNA primers
DNA polymerase	Synthesizes DNA in the leading and lagging strands, removes RNA primers, and fills in gaps
DNA ligase	Covalently attaches adjacent Okazaki fragments in the lagging strand

area where the primers have been removed, and the covalent joining of adjacent fragments of DNA (Figure 11.20, steps 3 and 4). The RNA primers are removed by DNA polymerase I, which digests the linkages between nucleotides in a 5′ to 3′ direction. After the RNA primer is removed, DNA polymerase I fills in the vacant region with DNA. However, once the DNA has been completely filled in, a covalent bond is missing between the last nucleotide added by DNA polymerase I and the first nucleotide in the adjacent Okazaki fragment. An enzyme known as **DNA ligase** catalyzes the formation of a covalent bond between these two DNA fragments to complete the replication process in the lagging strand (Figure 11.20, step 4). **Table 11.2** provides a summary of the functions of the proteins involved in DNA replication.

DNA Replication Is Very Accurate

Although errors can happen during DNA replication, permanent mistakes are extraordinarily rare. For example, during bacterial DNA replication, only 1 mistake per 100 million nucleotides is made. Biologists use the term "high fidelity" to refer to a process that occurs with relatively few mistakes. How can we explain such a remarkably high fidelity for DNA replication? First, hydrogen bonding between A and T or between G and C is more stable than between mismatched pairs. Second, the active site of DNA polymerase is unlikely to catalyze bond formation between adjacent nucleotides if a mismatched base pair is formed. Third, DNA polymerase can identify a mismatched nucleotide and remove it from the daughter strand. This event, called **proofreading**, occurs when DNA polymerase detects a mismatch and then reverses its direction and digests the linkages between nucleotides at the end of a newly made strand in the 3′ to 5′ direction. Once it passes the mismatched base and removes it, DNA polymerase then changes direction again and continues to synthesize DNA in the 5′ to 3′ direction.

GENOMES & PROTEOMES CONNECTION

DNA Polymerases Are a Family of Enzymes with Specialized Functions

Three important properties of DNA replication are speed, fidelity, and completeness. DNA replication must proceed quickly and with great accuracy, and gaps should not be left in the newly made strands. To ensure these three requirements are met, living species produce more than one type of DNA polymerase, each of which may differ in the rate and accuracy of DNA replication and/or the ability to prevent the formation of DNA gaps.

The genomes of living species have multiple DNA polymerase genes, which were produced by random gene duplication events. During evolution, mutations have altered each gene to produce a family of DNA polymerase enzymes with more specialized functions. Natural selection has favored certain mutations that result in DNA polymerase properties that are suited to the organism in which they are found. For comparison, let's consider the families of DNA polymerases found in the bacterium *E. coli* and humans (**Table 11.3**). Why does *E. coli* produce 5 DNA polymerases and humans produce 12 or more? The answer lies in specialization and the functional requirements of each species.

In *E. coli*, DNA polymerase III is responsible for most DNA replication. It synthesizes DNA very rapidly and with high fidelity. By comparison, the role of DNA polymerase I is to remove the RNA primers and fill in the short vacant regions with DNA. DNA polymerases II, IV, and V are involved in repairing DNA and in replicating DNA that has been damaged. DNA polymerases I and III become stalled when they encounter DNA damage and may be unable to make a complementary strand at such a site. By comparison, DNA polymerases II, IV, and V do not stall. Although their rate of synthesis is not as rapid as DNA polymerases I and III, they ensure that DNA replication is complete.

In human cells, DNA polymerase α (alpha) has its own "built-in" primase subunit. It synthesizes RNA primers followed by short DNA regions. Two other DNA polymerases, δ (delta) and ε (epsilon), then extend the DNA at a faster rate. DNA polymerase γ (gamma) functions in the mitochondria to replicate mitochondrial DNA.

When DNA replication occurs, the general DNA polymerases (α, δ, or γ) may be unable to replicate over an abnormality in DNA structure (a lesion). If this happens, lesion-replicating polymerases are attracted to the damaged DNA. These polymerases have special properties that enable them to synthesize a complementary strand

Table 11.3   DNA Polymerases in *E. coli* and Humans

Polymerase types*	Functions
E. coli	
III	Replicates most of the DNA during cell division
I	Removes RNA primers and fills in the gaps
II, IV, and V	Repairs damaged DNA and replicates over DNA damage
Humans	
α (alpha)	Makes RNA primers and synthesizes short DNA strands
δ (delta), ε (epsilon)	Displaces DNA polymerase α and then replicates DNA at a rapid rate
γ (gamma)	Replicates the mitochondrial DNA
η (eta), κ (kappa), ι (iota), ζ (zeta)	Replicates over damaged DNA
α, β (beta), δ, ε, σ (sigma), λ (lambda), μ (mu), φ (phi), θ (theta)	Repairs DNA or has other functions

*Certain DNA polymerases have more than one function.

over the lesion. Each type of lesion-replicating polymerase may be able to replicate over different kinds of DNA damage, thereby ensuring that DNA replication is complete.

Other human DNA polymerases play an important role in DNA repair. The need for multiple repair enzymes is rooted in the various ways that DNA can be damaged, as described in Chapter 14. Multicellular organisms must be particularly vigilant about repairing DNA, because unrepaired DNA can lead to cancer.

Telomerase Attaches DNA Sequences at the Ends of Eukaryotic Chromosomes

We will end our discussion of DNA replication by considering a specialized form of DNA replication that happens at the ends of eukaryotic chromosomes. This region, called the **telomere**, has a short nucleotide sequence that is repeated a few dozen to several hundred times in a row (**Figure 11.21**). The repeat sequence shown here, 5′–GGGTTA–3′, is the sequence found in human telomeres. Other organisms have different repeat sequences. For example, the sequence found in the telomeres of maize is 5′–GGGTTTA–3′. A telomere has a region at the 3′ end that is termed a 3′ overhang, because it does not have a complementary strand.

As discussed previously, DNA polymerase synthesizes DNA only in a 5′ to 3′ direction and requires a primer. For these reasons, DNA polymerase cannot copy the tip of a DNA strand with a 3′ end. Therefore, if this replication problem was not overcome, a linear chromosome would become progressively shorter with each round of DNA replication. In 1984, American molecular biologist Carol Greider and Australian-born American molecular biologist Elizabeth Blackburn discovered an enzyme called **telomerase** that prevents chromosome shortening by attaching many copies of a DNA repeat sequence to the ends of chromosomes (**Figure 11.22**). Telomerase contains both protein and RNA. The RNA part of telomerase has a sequence that is complementary to the DNA repeat sequence. This allows telomerase to bind to the 3′ overhang region of the telomere. Following binding, the RNA sequence beyond the binding site functions as a template, allowing telomerase to synthesize a 6-nucleotide sequence at the end of the DNA strand. The enzyme then moves to the new end of this DNA strand and attaches another 6 nucleotides to the end. This occurs many times, thereby greatly lengthening the 3′ end of the DNA

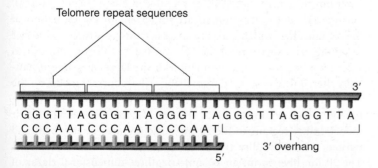

Figure 11.21 Telomere sequences at the end of a human chromosome. The telomere sequence shown here is found in humans and other mammals. The length of the telomere and the 3′ overhang varies among different species and cell types.

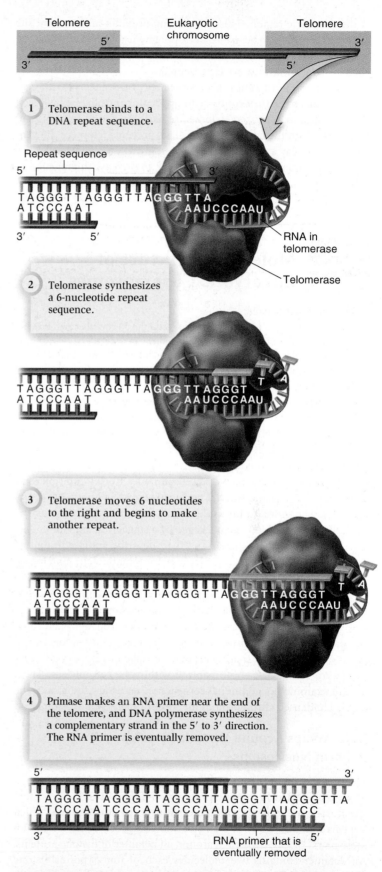

Figure 11.22 Mechanism of DNA replication by telomerase.

Concept Check: What does telomerase use as a template to make DNA?

in the telomeric region. This lengthening provides an upstream site for an RNA primer to be made. DNA polymerase then synthesizes the complementary DNA strand. In this way, the progressive shortening of eukaryotic chromosomes is prevented.

Telomerase function is also associated with cancer. When cells become cancerous, they continue to divide uncontrollably. In 90% of all types of human cancers, telomerase has been found to be present at high levels in the cancerous cells. This prevents telomere shortening and may play a role in the continued growth of cancer cells. The mechanism whereby cancer cells are able to increase the function of telomerase is not well understood and is a topic of active research.

Greider and Blackburn shared the 2009 Nobel Prize in Physiology or Medicine with Jack Szostak for their work on telomeres.

11.5 Molecular Structure of Eukaryotic Chromosomes

Learning Outcomes:

1. Describe the structure of nucleosomes and the 30-nm fiber, and how the 30-nm fiber forms radial loop domains.
2. Outline the various levels of compaction that lead to a metaphase chromosome.

We now turn our attention to the structure of eukaryotic chromosomes. A typical eukaryotic chromosome contains a single, linear, double-stranded DNA molecule that may be hundreds of millions of base pairs in length. If the DNA from a single set of human chromosomes were stretched end to end, the length would be over 1 meter! By comparison, most eukaryotic cells are only 10–100 μm (micrometers) in diameter, and the cell nucleus is typically about 2–4 μm in diameter. Therefore, to fit inside the nucleus, the DNA in a eukaryotic cell must be folded and packaged by a staggering amount.

The term chromosome is used to describe a discrete unit of genetic material. For example, a human somatic cell contains 46 chromosomes. By comparison, the term chromatin has a biochemical meaning. **Chromatin** is used to describe the complex of DNA and protein that makes up eukaryotic chromosomes. Chromosomes are very dynamic structures that alternate between tight and loose compaction states. In this section, we will focus our attention on two issues of chromosome structure. First, we will consider how chromosomes are compacted and organized within the cell nucleus. Then, we will examine the additional compaction necessary to produce the highly condensed chromosomes that occur during cell division.

DNA Wraps Around Histone Proteins to Form Nucleosomes

The first way DNA is compacted is by wrapping itself around a group of proteins called **histones**. As shown in **Figure 11.23**, a repeating structural unit of eukaryotic chromatin is the **nucleosome**, which is 11 nanometers (nm) in diameter and composed of 146 or 147 bp (base pairs) of DNA wrapped around an octamer of histone proteins. An octamer contains two molecules each of four types of histone proteins: H2A, H2B, H3, and H4. Histone proteins are very basic proteins because they contain a large number of positively charged

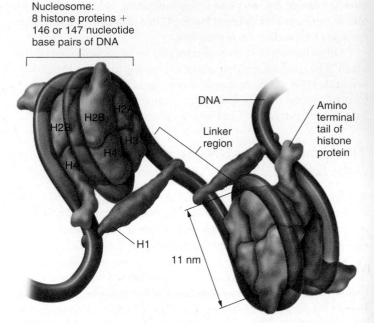

Figure 11.23 **Structure of a nucleosome.** A nucleosome is composed of double-stranded DNA wrapped around an octamer of histone proteins. A linker region connects two adjacent nucleosomes. Histone H1 is bound to the linker region, as are other proteins not shown in this figure.

lysine and arginine amino acids. The negative charges found in the phosphates of DNA are attracted to the positive charges on histone proteins. The amino terminal tail of each histone protein protrudes from the histone octamer. As discussed in Chapter 13, these tails can be covalently modified and play a key role in gene regulation.

The nucleosomes are connected by linker regions of DNA that vary in length from 20 to 100 bp, depending on the species and cell type. A particular histone named histone H1 is bound to the linker region, as are other types of proteins. The overall structure of connected nucleosomes resembles beads on a string. This structure shortens the length of the DNA molecule about sevenfold.

Nucleosomes Form a 30-nm Fiber

Nucleosome units are organized into a more compact structure that is 30 nm in diameter, known as the **30-nm fiber** (**Figure 11.24a**). Histone H1 and other proteins are important in the formation of the 30-nm fiber, which shortens the nucleosome structure another sevenfold. The structure of the 30-nm fiber has proven difficult to determine because the conformation of the DNA may be substantially altered when extracted from living cells. A current model for the 30-nm fiber was proposed by Rachel Horowitz-Scherer and Christopher Woodcock in the 1990s (**Figure 11.24b**). According to their model, linker regions in the 30-nm structure are variably bent and twisted, with little direct contact observed between nucleosomes. The 30-nm fiber forms an asymmetric, three-dimensional zigzag of nucleosomes. At this level of compaction, the overall picture of chromatin that emerges is an irregular, fluctuating structure with stable nucleosome units connected by bendable linker regions.

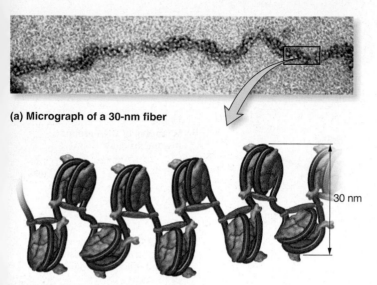

(a) Micrograph of a 30-nm fiber

30 nm

(b) Three-dimensional zigzag model

Figure 11.24 **The 30-nm fiber. (a)** A photomicrograph of the 30-nm fiber. **(b)** In this three-dimensional zigzag model, the linker DNA forms a bendable structure with little contact between adjacent nucleosomes.

Chromatin Loops Are Anchored to the Nuclear Matrix

Thus far, we have examined two mechanisms that compact eukaryotic DNA: the formation of nucleosomes and their arrangement into a 30-nm fiber. Taken together, these two events shorten the folded DNA about 49-fold. A third level of compaction involves interactions between the 30-nm fibers and a filamentous network of proteins in the nucleus called the **nuclear matrix**. This matrix consists of the **nuclear lamina**, which is composed of protein fibers that line the inner nuclear membrane (see Chapter 4, Figure 4.15), and an internal nuclear matrix that is connected to the lamina and fills the interior of the nucleus. The internal nuclear matrix is an intricate network of irregular protein fibers plus many other proteins that bind to these fibers. The nuclear matrix is involved in the compaction of the 30-nm fiber by participating in the formation of **radial loop domains**. These loops, often 25,000–200,000 bp in size, are anchored to the nuclear matrix (**Figure 11.25**).

How are chromosomes organized within the cell nucleus? In nondividing cells, each chromosome occupies its own discrete region in the cell nucleus that usually does not overlap with the territory of adjacent chromosomes (see Chapter 4, Figure 4.16). In other words, different chromosomes are not substantially intertwined with each other even when they are in a noncompacted condition.

The compaction level of chromosomes in the cell nucleus is not completely uniform. This variability can be seen with a light microscope and was first observed by German cytologist Emil Heitz in 1928. He used the term **heterochromatin** to describe the highly compacted regions of chromosomes. By comparison, the less condensed regions are known as **euchromatin**. Euchromatin is the form of chromatin in which the 30-nm fiber forms radial loop domains. In heterochromatin, these radial loop domains are compacted even further. In

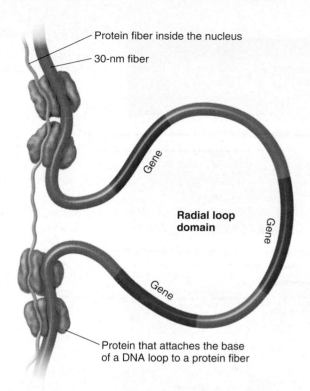

Protein fiber inside the nucleus

30-nm fiber

Gene

Radial loop domain

Gene

Gene

Protein that attaches the base of a DNA loop to a protein fiber

Figure 11.25 Attachment of the 30-nm fiber to a protein fiber to form a radial loop domain.

Concept Check: *What holds the bottoms of the loops in place?*

nondividing cells, most chromosomal regions are euchromatic, and some localized regions are heterochromatic.

During Cell Division, Chromosomes Undergo Maximum Compaction

When cells prepare to divide, the chromosomes become even more compacted or condensed. This aids in their proper alignment during metaphase, which is a stage of eukaryotic cell division described in Chapter 15. **Figure 11.26** illustrates the levels of compaction that contribute to the formation of a metaphase chromosome. DNA in the nucleus is always compacted by forming nucleosomes and condensing into a 30-nm fiber (Figure 11.26a,b,c). In euchromatin, the 30-nm fibers are arranged in radial loop domains that are relatively loose, meaning that a fair amount of space is between the 30-nm fibers (Figure 11.26d). The average width of such loops is about 300 nm.

By comparison, heterochromatin involves a much tighter packing of the loops, so little space is between the 30-nm fibers (Figure 11.26e). Heterochromatic regions tend to be wider, about 700 nm. When cells prepare to divide, all of the euchromatin becomes highly compacted. The compaction of euchromatin greatly shortens the chromosomes. In a metaphase chromosome, which contains two copies of the DNA (Figure 11.26f), the width averages about 1,400 nm, but the length of a metaphase chromosome is much shorter than the same chromosome in the nucleus of a nondividing cell.

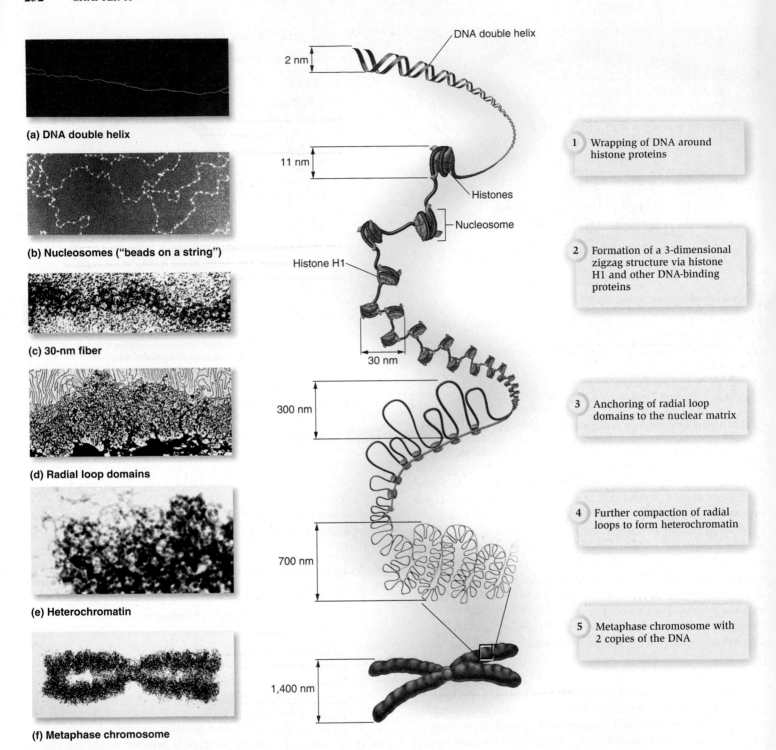

(a) DNA double helix

(b) Nucleosomes ("beads on a string")

(c) 30-nm fiber

(d) Radial loop domains

(e) Heterochromatin

(f) Metaphase chromosome

DNA double helix

2 nm

11 nm

Histones

Nucleosome

Histone H1

30 nm

300 nm

700 nm

1,400 nm

1 Wrapping of DNA around histone proteins

2 Formation of a 3-dimensional zigzag structure via histone H1 and other DNA-binding proteins

3 Anchoring of radial loop domains to the nuclear matrix

4 Further compaction of radial loops to form heterochromatin

5 Metaphase chromosome with 2 copies of the DNA

Figure 11.26 The steps in eukaryotic chromosomal compaction leading to the metaphase chromosome.

Concept Check: *After they have replicated and become compacted in preparation for cell division, chromosomes are often shaped like an X, as in part (f) of this figure. Which proteins are primarily responsible for this X shape?*

BioConnections: *Look ahead to Figure 15.8. Why do you think it is necessary for the chromosomes to become compact in preparation for cell division?*

Summary of Key Concepts

11.1 Biochemical Identification of the Genetic Material

- The genetic material carries information to produce the traits of organisms. It is accurately replicated and transmitted from cell to cell and parent to offspring. The genetic material carries differences that explain the variation among different organisms.

- Griffith's work with type S and type R bacteria indicated the existence of a genetic material, which he called the transformation principle (Figure 11.1).

- Avery, MacLeod, and McCarty used biochemical methods to show that DNA is the genetic material (Figure 11.2).

- Hershey and Chase labeled T2 phage with ^{35}S and ^{32}P and determined that DNA is the genetic material of this phage (Figures 11.3, 11.4).

11.2 Nucleic Acid Structure

- DNA is composed of nucleotides, which are covalently linked to form DNA strands. Two DNA strands are held together by hydrogen bonds between the bases to form a double helix. DNA associates with various proteins to form a chromosome (Figure 11.5).

- Nucleotides are composed of a phosphate, sugar, and nitrogenous base. The sugar can be deoxyribose (DNA) or ribose (RNA). The purine bases are adenine and guanine, and the pyrimidine bases are thymine (DNA only), cytosine, and uracil (RNA only). The atoms in a nucleotide are numbered in a conventional way (Figures 11.6, 11.7).

- In a strand of DNA (or RNA), the sugars are connected by covalent bonds in a 5′ to 3′ direction (Figure 11.8).

- The X-ray diffraction data of Franklin, the biochemical data of Chargaff (that is, the amount of A = T and the amount of G = C), and the ball-and-stick model approach of Pauling helped reveal the structure of DNA (Figure 11.9, Table 11.1).

- Watson and Crick determined that DNA is a double helix in which the DNA strands are antiparallel and obey the AT/GC rule (Figures 11.10, 11.11).

11.3 An Overview of DNA Replication

- Meselson and Stahl used ^{15}N- and ^{14}N-isotope labeling methods to show that DNA is replicated by a semiconservative mechanism in which the product of DNA replication is one original strand and one new strand (Figures 11.12, 11.13).

- During DNA replication, the parental double-stranded DNA separates and each strand serves as a template for the synthesis of daughter strands. Nucleotides hydrogen-bond to the template strands according to the AT/GC rule: an adenine (A) base in one strand bonds with a thymine (T) base in the opposite strand, or a guanine (G) base bonds with a cytosine. The result of DNA replication is two double helices with the same base sequence as the parental DNA (Figure 11.14).

11.4 Molecular Mechanism of DNA Replication

- DNA synthesis occurs bidirectionally from an origin of replication. The synthesis of new DNA strands happens near each replication fork (Figure 11.15).

- DNA helicase separates DNA strands, single-strand binding proteins keep them separated, and DNA topoisomerase alleviates coiling ahead of the fork (Figure 11.16).

- Deoxynucleoside triphosphates bind to the template strands according to the AT/GC rule. DNA polymerase recognizes these deoxynucleoside triphosphates and attaches a deoxynucleoside monophosphate to the 3′ end of a growing strand (Figure 11.17).

- DNA polymerase requires a primer and synthesizes new DNA strands only in the 5′ to 3′ direction (Figure 11.18).

- The leading strand is made continuously, in the same direction the fork is moving. The lagging strand is made in the opposite direction of the replication fork as short Okazaki fragments that are synthesized and connected together (Figure 11.19).

- DNA primase makes one RNA primer in the leading strand and multiple RNA primers in the lagging strand. In *E. coli*, DNA polymerase III extends these primers with DNA, and DNA polymerase I removes the primers when they are no longer needed and fills in with DNA. DNA ligase connects adjacent Okazaki fragments in the lagging strand (Figure 11.20, Table 11.2).

- DNA replication is very accurate because (1) hydrogen bonding according to the AT/CG rule is more stable; (2) DNA polymerase is unlikely to catalyze bond formation if a mismatched base pair is formed; and (3) DNA polymerase carries out proofreading.

- Living organisms have several different types of DNA polymerases with specialized functions (Table 11.3).

- The ends of linear, eukaryotic chromosomes have telomeres composed of repeat sequences. Telomerase binds to the telomere repeat sequence and synthesizes a 6-nucleotide repeat. This happens many times in a row to lengthen one DNA strand of the telomere. DNA primase, DNA polymerase, and DNA ligase are needed to synthesize the complementary DNA strand (Figures 11.21, 11.22).

11.5 Molecular Structure of Eukaryotic Chromosomes

- Chromosomes are structures in living cells that carry the genetic material. Chromatin is the name given to the complex of DNA and protein that makes up chromosomes.

- In eukaryotic chromosomes, the DNA is wrapped around histone proteins to form nucleosomes. Nucleosomes are further compacted into 30-nm fibers. The linker regions are variably twisted and bent into a zigzag pattern (Figures 11.23, 11.24).

- A third level of compaction of eukaryotic chromosomes involves the formation of radial loop domains in which the bases of 30-nm fibers are anchored to a network of proteins called the nuclear matrix. This level of compaction is called euchromatin. In heterochromatin, the loops are even more closely packed together (Figure 11.25).

- During cell division, chromosomes become even more condensed (Figure 11.26).

Assess and Discuss

Test Yourself

1. Why did researchers initially believe the genetic material was protein?
   a. Proteins are more biochemically complex than DNA.
   b. Proteins are found only in the nucleus, but DNA is found in many areas of the cell.
   c. Proteins are much larger molecules and can store more information than DNA.
   d. all of the above
   e. both a and c

2. Considering the components of a nucleotide, what component is always different when comparing nucleotides in a DNA strand or an RNA strand?
   a. phosphate group
   b. pentose sugar
   c. nitrogenous base
   d. both b and c
   e. a, b, and c

3. Which of the following equations is appropriate when considering DNA base composition?
   a. %A + %T = %G + %C
   b. %A = %G
   c. %A = %G = %T = %C
   d. %A + %G = %T + %C

4. If the sequence of a segment of DNA is 5′–CGCAACTAC–3′, what is the appropriate sequence for the opposite strand?
   a. 5′–GCGTTGATG–3′
   b. 3′–ATACCAGCA–5′
   c. 5′–ATACCAGCA–3′
   d. 3′–GCGTTGATG–5′

5. Of the following statements, which is correct when considering the process of DNA replication?
   a. New DNA molecules are composed of two completely new strands.
   b. New DNA molecules are composed of one strand from the old molecule and one new strand.
   c. New DNA molecules are composed of strands that are a mixture of sections from the old molecule and sections that are new.
   d. none of the above

6. Meselson and Stahl were able to demonstrate semiconservative replication in *E. coli* by
   a. using radioactive isotopes of phosphorus to label the old strand and visually determining the relationship of old and new DNA strands.
   b. using different enzymes to eliminate old strands from DNA.
   c. using isotopes of nitrogen to label the DNA and determining the relationship of old and new DNA strands by density differences of the new molecules.
   d. labeling viral DNA before it was incorporated into a bacterial cell and visually determining the location of the DNA after centrifugation.

7. During replication of a DNA molecule, the daughter strands are not produced in exactly the same manner. One strand, the leading strand, is made toward the replication fork, while the lagging strand is made in fragments in the opposite direction. This difference in the synthesis of the two strands is the result of which of the following?
   a. DNA polymerase is not efficient enough to make two "good" strands of DNA.
   b. The two template strands are antiparallel, and DNA polymerase makes DNA only in the 5′ to 3′ direction.
   c. The lagging strand is the result of DNA breakage due to UV light.
   d. The cell does not contain enough nucleotides to make two complete strands.

8. In eukaryotic cells, chromosomes consist of
   a. DNA and RNA.
   b. DNA only.
   c. RNA and proteins.
   d. DNA and proteins.
   e. RNA only.

9. A nucleosome is
   a. a dark-staining body composed of RNA and proteins found in the nucleus.
   b. a protein that helps organize the structure of chromosomes.
   c. another word for a chromosome.
   d. a structure composed of DNA wrapped around eight histones.
   e. the short arm of a chromosome.

10. The conversion of euchromatin into heterochromatin involves
   a. the formation of more nucleosomes.
   b. the formation of less nucleosomes.
   c. a greater compaction of loop domains.
   d. a lesser compaction of loop domains.
   e. both a and c.

Conceptual Questions

1. What are the four key characteristics of the genetic material? What was Frederick Griffith's contribution to the study of DNA, and why was it so important?

2. The Hershey and Chase experiment used radioactive isotopes to track the DNA and protein of phages as they infected bacterial cells. Explain how this procedure allowed them to determine that DNA is the genetic material of this particular virus.

3. A principle of biology is that *structure determines function*. Discuss how the structure of DNA underlies different aspects of its function.

Collaborative Questions

1. A trait that some bacterial strains exhibit is resistance to killing by antibiotics. For example, certain strains of bacteria are resistant to the drug tetracycline, whereas other strains are sensitive to this antibiotic. Describe an experiment you would carry out to demonstrate that tetracycline resistance is an inherited trait carried in the DNA of the resistant strain.

2. How might you provide evidence that DNA is the genetic material in mice?

Online Resource

www.brookerbiology.com

Stay a step ahead in your studies with animations that bring concepts to life and practice tests to assess your understanding. Your instructor may also recommend the interactive eBook, individualized learning tools, and more.

Gene Expression at the Molecular Level

12

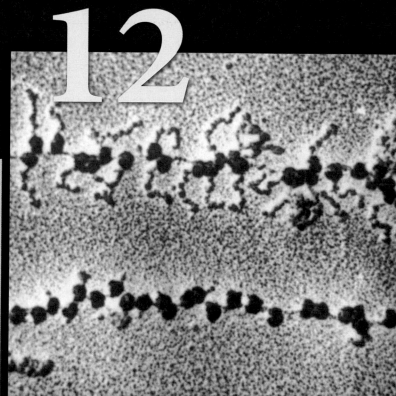

M ina, age 21, works part-time in an ice-cream shop and particularly enjoys the double-dark chocolate and chocolate fudge brownie flavors on her breaks. She exercises little and spends most of her time studying or watching television. Mina is effortlessly thin. She never worries about what or how much she eats. By comparison, her close friend, Rezzy, has struggled with her weight as long as she can remember. Compared with Mina, she feels like she must constantly deprive herself of food just to maintain her current weight—a weight she would describe as 30 pounds too much.

How do we explain the differences between Mina and Rezzy? Two fundamental factors are involved. Our weight is strongly influenced by the environment, especially our diet, as well as by social and behavioral factors. The amount and types of food we eat are correlated with weight gain. However, there is little doubt that our weight is also influenced by variation in our genes. Obesity, the condition of having too much body fat, runs in families. The degree of obesity is often similar between genetically identical twins who have been raised apart. Why has genetic variation resulted in some genes that cause certain people to gain weight? A popular hypothesis is that some people have inherited "thrifty genes" as hand-me-downs from their ancestors, who periodically faced famines and food scarcity. Such thrifty genes would be advantageous in allowing people to store body fat more easily and to use food resources more efficiently when times are lean. The negative side is that when food is abundant, unwanted weight gain—and associated diseases such as diabetes and heart disease—can constitute a serious health problem.

Why do we care about our genes? Let's consider this question with regard to obesity. Researchers have identified several key genes that influence a person's predisposition to becoming obese. Dozens more are likely to play a minor role. By identifying those genes and studying the proteins specified by those genes, researchers may gain a better understanding of how genetic variation causes certain people to gain weight more easily than others. In addition, this knowledge has led to the development of drugs that are used to combat obesity.

We can broadly define a gene as a unit of heredity. Geneticists view gene function at different biological levels. In Chapter 16, we will examine how genes affect the traits or characteristics of individuals. For example,

An electron micrograph of many ribosomes in the act of translating two mRNA molecules into many polypeptides. The complex of one mRNA and many ribosomes is called a polysome. Short polypeptides are seen emerging from the ribosomes.

we will consider how the transmission of genes from parents to offspring affects the color of the offspring's eyes and their likelihood of becoming color blind. In this chapter, we will explore how genes work at the molecular level. You will learn how DNA sequences are organized to form genes and how those genes are used as a template to make RNA copies, ultimately leading to the synthesis of a functional protein. The term **gene expression** can refer to gene function either at the level of traits or at the molecular level. In reality, the two phenomena are intricately woven together. The expression of genes at the molecular level affects the structure and function of cells, which, in turn, determine the traits that an organism expresses.

We begin this chapter by considering how researchers came to realize that most genes store the information to make proteins. We then explore the steps of gene expression as they occur at the molecular level. These steps include the use of a gene as a template to make an RNA molecule, the processing of the RNA into a functional molecule (in eukaryotes), and the use of RNA to direct the formation of a protein.

12.1 Overview of Gene Expression

Learning Outcomes:

1. Analyze the results of the experiments of Garrod and of Beadle and Tatum.
2. Outline the general steps of gene expression at the molecular level, which together constitute the central dogma.
3. Explain how proteins are largely responsible for determining an organism's characteristics.

Even before DNA was known to be the genetic material, scientists had asked the question, "How does the functioning of genes produce the traits of living organisms?" At the molecular level, a similar question can be asked. "How do genes affect the composition and/or function of molecules found within living cells?" An approach that was successful in answering these questions involved the study of **mutations**, which are changes in the genetic material that can be inherited. Mutations may affect the genetic blueprint by altering gene function. For this reason, research that focused on the effects of mutations proved instrumental in determining the molecular function of genes.

In this section, we will consider two early experiments in which researchers studied the effects of mutations in humans and in a bread mold. Both studies led to the conclusion that the role of some genes is to carry the information to produce enzymes, which are a type of protein. Then we will examine the general features of gene expression at the molecular level.

The Study of Inborn Errors of Metabolism Suggested That Some Genes Carry the Information to Make Enzymes

In 1908, Archibald Garrod, a British physician, proposed a relationship between genes and the production of enzymes. Prior to his work, biochemists had studied many metabolic pathways that consist of a series of conversions of one molecule to another, each step catalyzed by an enzyme. **Figure 12.1** illustrates part of the metabolic pathway for the breakdown of phenylalanine, an amino acid commonly found in human diets. The enzyme phenylalanine hydroxylase catalyzes the conversion of phenylalanine to tyrosine, another amino acid. A different enzyme, tyrosine aminotransferase, converts tyrosine into the next molecule, called p-hydroxyphenylpyruvic acid. In each case, a specific enzyme catalyzes a single chemical reaction.

Much of Garrod's early work centered on the inherited disease alkaptonuria, in which the patient's body accumulates abnormal levels of homogentisic acid (also called alkapton). This compound, which is bluish black, results in discoloration of the skin and cartilage and causes the urine to appear black. Garrod hypothesized that the accumulation of homogentisic acid in these patients is due to a defect in an enzyme, namely, homogentisic acid oxidase (see Figure 12.1). Furthermore, he already knew that alkaptonuria is an inherited condition that follows a recessive pattern of inheritance. As discussed in Chapter 16, if a disorder is recessive, an individual with the disease has inherited the mutant (defective) gene that causes the disorder from both parents.

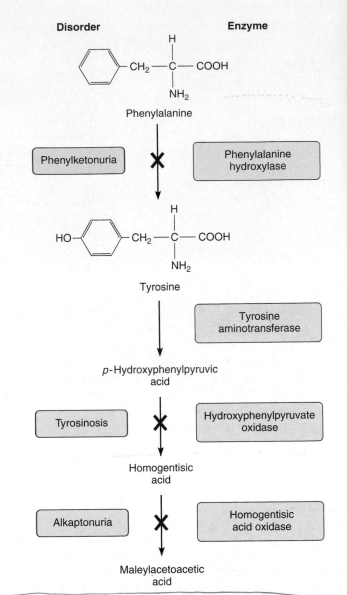

Figure 12.1 The metabolic pathway that breaks down phenylalanine and its relationship to certain genetic diseases. Each step in the pathway is catalyzed by a different enzyme, shown in the boxes on the right. If one of the enzymes is not functioning, the previous compound builds up, causing the disorders named in the boxes on the left.

Concept Check: What disease would occur if a person had inherited two defective copies of the gene that encodes phenylalanine hydroxylase?

How did Garrod explain these observations? In 1908, he proposed a relationship between the inheritance of a mutant gene and a defect in metabolism. In the case of alkaptonuria, if an individual inherited the mutant gene from both parents, she or he would not produce any normal enzyme and would be unable to metabolize homogentisic acid. Garrod described alkaptonuria as an **inborn error of metabolism**. An inborn error refers to a mutation in a gene that is inherited from one or both parents. At the turn of the last century, this was a particularly insightful idea because the structure and function of the genetic material were completely unknown.

Beadle and Tatum Proposed the One Gene–One Enzyme Hypothesis

In early 1940s, American geneticists George Beadle and Edward Tatum became aware of Garrod's work and were interested in the relationship between genes and enzymes. They focused their studies on *Neurospora crassa*, a common bread mold. *Neurospora* is easily grown in the laboratory and has only a few nutritional requirements: a carbon source (namely, sugar), inorganic salts, and one vitamin known as biotin. Otherwise, *Neurospora* has many different enzymes that synthesize the molecules, such as amino acids and vitamins, which are essential for growth.

Like Garrod, Beadle and Tatum hypothesized that genes carry the information to make specific enzymes. They reasoned that a mutation, or change in a gene, might cause a defect in an enzyme required for the synthesis of an essential molecule, such as a vitamin. A mutant *Neurospora* strain (one that carries such a mutation) would be unable to grow unless the vitamin was supplemented in the growth medium. Strains without a mutation are called wild-type. In their original study of 1941, Beadle and Tatum exposed *Neurospora* cells to X-rays, which caused mutations to occur, and studied the resulting cells. By plating the cells on growth media with or without vitamins, they were able to identify mutant strains that required vitamins for growth. In each case, a single mutation resulted in the requirement for a single type of vitamin in the growth media.

This early study by Beadle and Tatum led them to additional research and further investigation by others to study enzymes involved in the synthesis of other substances, including the amino acid arginine. At that time, the pathway leading to arginine synthesis was known to involve certain precursor molecules, including ornithine and citrulline. A simplified pathway for arginine synthesis is shown in **Figure 12.2a**. Each step is catalyzed by a different enzyme.

Researchers first isolated several different mutants that required arginine for growth. They hypothesized that each mutant strain might be blocked at only a single step in the consecutive series of reactions that lead to arginine synthesis. To test this hypothesis, the mutant strains were examined for their ability to grow in the presence of ornithine, citrulline, or arginine (**Figure 12.2b**). The wild-type strain could grow on minimal growth media that did not contain ornithine, citrulline, or arginine. Based on their growth properties, the mutant strains that had been originally identified as requiring arginine for growth could be placed into three groups, designated 1, 2, and 3. Group 1 mutants were missing enzyme 1, needed for the conversion of a precursor molecule into ornithine. They could grow only if ornithine, citrulline, or arginine was added to the growth medium. Group 2 mutants were missing the second enzyme in this pathway that is needed for the conversion of ornithine into citrulline. The group 2 mutants would not grow if only ornithine was added, but could grow if citrulline or arginine was added. Finally, the group 3 mutants were missing the enzyme needed for the conversion of citrulline into arginine. These mutants could grow only if arginine was added. How were these results interpreted? The researchers were able to order the

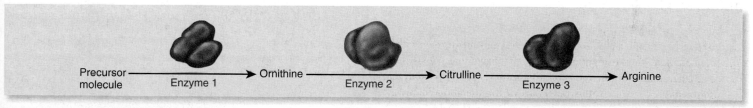

Precursor molecule → Enzyme 1 → Ornithine → Enzyme 2 → Citrulline → Enzyme 3 → Arginine

(a) Simplified pathway for arginine synthesis

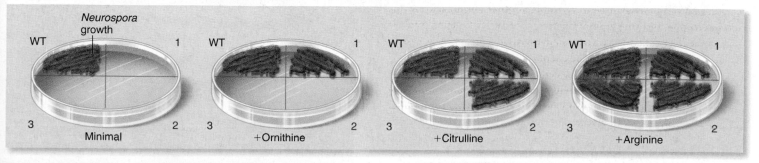

(b) Growth of strains on minimal and supplemented growth media

Figure 12.2 **An experiment that supported Beadle and Tatum's one-gene/one-enzyme hypothesis.** (a) This simplified metabolic pathway shows three enzymes that are required for arginine synthesis. (b) Growth of wild-type (WT) and mutant *Neurospora* strains (groups 1, 2, and 3) on minimal plates or in the presence of ornithine, citrulline, or arginine.

Concept Check: *What type of enzyme function is missing in group 2 mutants?*

functions of the genes involved in arginine synthesis in the following way:

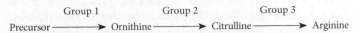

Group 1   Group 2   Group 3

Precursor ⟶ Ornithine ⟶ Citrulline ⟶ Arginine

From these results and earlier studies, Beadle and Tatum concluded that a single gene controlled the synthesis of a single enzyme. This was referred to as the **one-gene/one-enzyme hypothesis**. Beadle and Tatum received the 1958 Nobel Prize in Physiology or Medicine for their work on the role of genes in metabolism.

In later decades, this idea was modified in three ways. First, the information to make all proteins is contained within genes, and many proteins do not function as enzymes. Second, some proteins are composed of two or more different polypeptides. The term **polypeptide** refers to a linear sequence of amino acids; it denotes structure. Most genes carry the information to make a particular polypeptide. By comparison, the term **protein** denotes function. Some proteins are composed of one polypeptide. In such cases, a single gene does contain the information to make a single protein. In other cases, however, a functional protein is composed of two or more different polypeptides. An example is hemoglobin—the protein that carries oxygen in red blood cells—which is composed of two α-globin and two β-globin polypeptides. In this case, the expression of two genes (that is, the α-globin and β-globin genes) is needed to produce a functional protein. A third modification to the one-gene/one-enzyme hypothesis is that some genes encode RNAs that are not used to make polypeptides. For example, as discussed later in this chapter, some genes encode RNA molecules that form part of the structure of ribosomes. Because of these additional complexities, the one-gene/one-enzyme

hypothesis was modified as the definition of a gene became broader. As discussed later, a gene can be defined as a segment of DNA that is copied into RNA and produces a functional product.

Molecular Gene Expression Involves the Processes of Transcription and Translation

Thus far, we have considered two classic studies that led researchers to conclude that some genes carry the information to make enzymes. Let's now examine the general steps of gene expression at the molecular level. The first step, known as **transcription**, produces an RNA copy of a gene, also called an RNA transcript (**Figure 12.3**). The term transcription literally means the act of making a copy. Most genes, which are termed **structural genes**,[1] produce an RNA molecule that contains the information to specify a polypeptide with a particular amino acid sequence. This type of RNA is called **messenger RNA** (abbreviated **mRNA**), because its function is to carry information from the DNA to cellular components called ribosomes. As discussed later, ribosomes play a key role in the synthesis of polypeptides. The process of synthesizing a specific polypeptide on a ribosome is called **translation**. The term translation is used because a nucleotide sequence in mRNA is "translated" into an amino acid sequence of a polypeptide.

Together, the transcription of DNA into mRNA and the translation of mRNA into a polypeptide constitute the **central dogma** of gene expression at the molecular level, which was first proposed by Francis Crick in 1958 (see Figure 12.3). The central dogma applies equally to bacteria, archaea, and eukaryotes. However, in eukaryotes, an additional step occurs between transcription and translation.

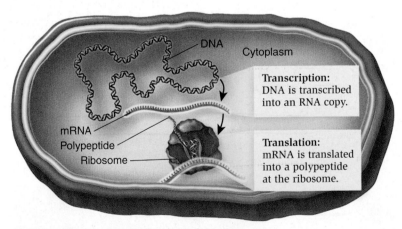

(a) Molecular gene expression in prokaryotes

Figure 12.3 The central dogma of gene expression at the molecular level. (a) In bacteria, transcription and translation occur in the cytoplasm. (b) In eukaryotes, transcription and RNA processing occur in the nucleus, whereas translation takes place in the cytosol.

Concept Check: What is the direction of flow of genetic information?

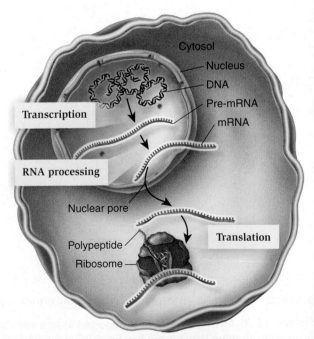

(b) Molecular gene expression in eukaryotes

[1] Geneticists commonly use the term structural gene to describe all genes that encode polypeptides, which is how it is used in this textbook. Some geneticists, however, distinguish structural genes from regulatory genes—genes that encode proteins regulating the expression of structural genes.

During **RNA processing**, which is described later in this chapter, the RNA transcript, termed **pre-mRNA**, is modified in ways that make it a functionally active mRNA (**Figure 12.3b**).

Another difference between bacteria and eukaryotes is the cellular location of transcription and translation. In bacteria, both events occur in the same location, namely, the cytoplasm. In eukaryotes, transcription occurs in the nucleus. The mRNA then exits the nucleus through a nuclear pore, and translation occurs in the cytosol.

Though the direction of information flow, that is, from DNA to RNA to protein, is the most common pathway, exceptions do occur. For example, certain viruses use RNA as a template to synthesize DNA. Such viruses are described in Chapter 18.

The Protein Products of Genes Determine an Organism's Characteristics

The genes that constitute the genetic material provide a blueprint for the characteristics of every organism. They contain the information necessary to produce an organism and allow it to favorably interact with its environment. Each structural gene stores the information for the production of a polypeptide, which then becomes a unit within a functional protein. The activities of proteins determine the structure and function of cells. Furthermore, the characteristics of an organism are rooted in the activities of cellular proteins.

The main purpose of the genetic material is to encode the production of proteins in the correct cell, at the proper time, and in suitable amounts. This is an intricate task, because living cells make thousands of different kinds of proteins. Genetic analyses have shown that a typical bacterium can make a few thousand different proteins, and estimates for eukaryotes range from several thousand in simpler eukaryotes to tens of thousands in more complex eukaryotes like humans.

12.2   Transcription

Learning Outcomes:

1. Describe how a gene is an organization of DNA sequences that can be transcribed into RNA.
2. Outline the three stages of transcription and the role of RNA polymerase in this process.
3. Explain how genes within the same chromosome vary in their direction of transcription.
4. Compare and contrast transcription in bacteria and eukaryotes.

DNA is an information storage unit. For genes to be expressed, the information in them must be accessed at the molecular level. Rather than accessing the information directly, however, a working copy of the DNA, composed of RNA, is made. This occurs by the process of transcription, in which a DNA sequence is copied into an RNA sequence. Importantly, transcription does not permanently alter the structure of DNA. Therefore, the same DNA can continue to store information even after an RNA copy has been made. In this section, we will examine the steps necessary for genes to act as transcriptional units. We will also consider some differences in these steps between bacteria and eukaryotes.

At the Molecular Level, a Gene Is Transcribed and Produces a Functional Product

nonstructural genes transfer + ribosomal RNA

What is a gene? At the molecular level, a **gene** is defined in the following way:

A gene is an organized unit of DNA sequences that enables a segment of DNA to be transcribed into RNA and ultimately results in the formation of a functional product.

When a structural gene is transcribed, an mRNA is made that specifies the amino acid sequence of a polypeptide. After it is made, the polypeptide becomes a functional product. The mRNA is an intermediary in polypeptide synthesis. Among all species, most genes are structural genes. However, for some genes, the functional product is the RNA itself. The RNA from a nonstructural gene is never translated. Two important products of nonstructural genes are transfer RNA and ribosomal RNA. **Transfer RNA (tRNA)** translates the language of mRNA into that of amino acids. **Ribosomal RNA (rRNA)** forms part of ribosomes, which provide the site where translation occurs. We'll learn more about these two types of RNA later in this chapter.

A gene is composed of specific base sequences organized in a way that allows the DNA to be transcribed into RNA. **Figure 12.4** shows the general organization of sequences in a structural gene. Transcription begins next to a site in the DNA called the **promoter**, whereas the **terminator** specifies the end of transcription. Therefore, transcription occurs between these two boundaries. As shown in Figure 12.4, the DNA is transcribed into mRNA from the end of the

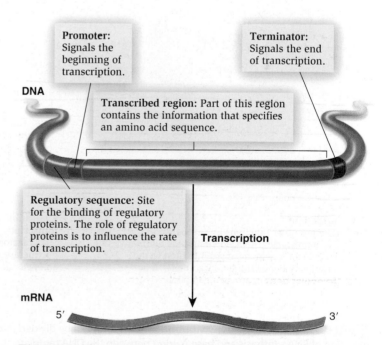

Promoter: Signals the beginning of transcription.

Terminator: Signals the end of transcription.

DNA

Transcribed region: Part of this region contains the information that specifies an amino acid sequence.

Regulatory sequence: Site for the binding of regulatory proteins. The role of regulatory proteins is to influence the rate of transcription.

Transcription

mRNA

5′   3′

Figure 12.4 A structural gene as a transcriptional unit.

BIOLOGY PRINCIPLE The genetic material provides a blueprint for reproduction. Transcription is the first step in accessing the information that is stored in DNA.

Concept Check: *How would removing a terminator from a gene affect transcription? Where would transcription end?*

DNA is transcribed to produce mRNA which is translated

promoter through the coding sequence to the terminator. Within this transcribed region is the information that will specify the amino acid sequence of a polypeptide when the mRNA is translated.

Other DNA sequences are involved in the regulation of transcription. These **regulatory sequences** function as sites for the binding of regulatory proteins, which are discussed in Chapter 13. When a regulatory protein binds to a regulatory sequence, the rate of transcription is affected. Some regulatory proteins enhance the rate of transcription, whereas others inhibit it.

During Transcription, RNA Polymerase Uses a DNA Template to Make RNA

Transcription occurs in three stages, called initiation, elongation, and termination, during which various proteins interact with DNA sequences (**Figure 12.5**). **Initiation** is a recognition step. In bacteria such as *E. coli*, a protein called **sigma factor** binds to **RNA polymerase**, the enzyme that synthesizes strands of RNA. Sigma factor also recognizes the base sequence of a promoter and binds there. An example of a promoter sequence is described in the legend

to Figure 12.5. The role of sigma factor is to cause RNA polymerase to bind to the promoter. The initiation stage is completed when the DNA strands are separated near the promoter to form an **open complex** that is approximately 10–15 bp long.

During **elongation**, RNA polymerase synthesizes the RNA transcript. For this to occur, sigma factor is released and RNA polymerase slides along the DNA in a way that maintains an open complex as it goes. The DNA strand that is used as a template for RNA synthesis is called the **template strand**. The opposite DNA strand is called the **coding strand**. The coding strand has the same sequence of bases as the resulting mRNA, except that thymine in the DNA is substituted for uracil in the RNA. The coding strand is so named because, like mRNA, it carries the information that codes for a polypeptide.

During the elongation stage of transcription, nucleotides bind to the template strand and are covalently connected in the 5′ to 3′ direction (see inset of step 2, Figure 12.5). The complementarity rule used in this process is similar to the AT/GC rule of DNA replication, except that uracil (U) in RNA substitutes for thymine (T) in DNA. For example, a DNA template with a sequence of 3′–TACAAT-GTAGCC–5′ will be transcribed into an RNA sequence reading

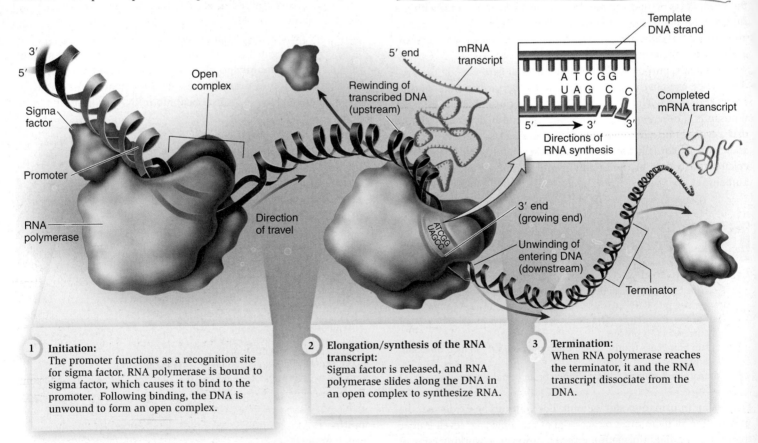

1 Initiation:
The promoter functions as a recognition site for sigma factor. RNA polymerase is bound to sigma factor, which causes it to bind to the promoter. Following binding, the DNA is unwound to form an open complex.

2 Elongation/synthesis of the RNA transcript:
Sigma factor is released, and RNA polymerase slides along the DNA in an open complex to synthesize RNA.

3 Termination:
When RNA polymerase reaches the terminator, it and the RNA transcript dissociate from the DNA.

Figure 12.5   Stages of transcription. Transcription can be divided into initiation, elongation, and termination. The inset emphasizes the direction of RNA synthesis and base pairing between the DNA template strand and RNA. An example of a promoter sequence in *E. coli* is:

5′-**TTGACA**TGATAGAAGCACTCTAC**TATATT**-3′
3′-**AACTGT**ACTATCTTCGTGAGATG**ATATAA**-5′

This region is 29 bp long. The bases that are specifically recognized by sigma factor are shown in red. The sequences of promoters for different genes are fairly diverse, particularly in eukaryotic species.

BioConnections: *Look back at DNA polymerase described in Figure 11.17. What are similarities and differences between the function of DNA polymerase and that of RNA polymerase?*

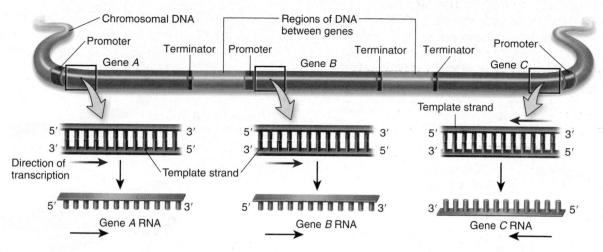

Figure 12.6 **The transcription of three different genes found in the same chromosome.** RNA polymerase synthesizes each RNA transcript in a 5′ to 3′ direction, sliding along a DNA template strand in a 3′ to 5′ direction. However, the use of the template strand can vary from gene to gene. For example, genes A and B use the bottom strand, while gene C uses the top strand.

5′–AUGUUACAUCGG–3′. In bacteria, the rate of RNA synthesis is about 40 nucleotides per second! Behind the open complex, the DNA rewinds back into a double helix. Eventually, RNA polymerase reaches a terminator, which causes it and the newly made RNA transcript to dissociate from the DNA. This event constitutes the **termination** of transcription.

When considering the transcription of multiple genes within a chromosome, the DNA strand that is used as the template strand varies among different genes. **Figure 12.6** shows three genes adjacent to each other within a chromosome. Genes A and B are transcribed from left to right, using the bottom DNA strand as the template strand. By comparison, gene C is transcribed from right to left, using the top DNA strand as a template strand. In all three cases, however, the synthesis of the RNA transcript begins at a promoter and always occurs in a 5′ to 3′ direction. The template strand is read in the 3′ to 5′ direction.

Transcription in Eukaryotes Involves More Proteins

The basic features of transcription are similar among all organisms. The genes of all species have promoters, and the transcription process occurs in the stages of initiation, elongation, and termination. However, compared with bacteria, the transcription of eukaryotic genes tends to involve a greater complexity of protein components. For example, three forms of RNA polymerase, designated I, II, and III, are found in eukaryotes. The catalytic portion of RNA polymerase responsible for the synthesis of RNA has a similar protein structure in all species. RNA polymerase II is responsible for transcribing the mRNA from eukaryotic structural genes, whereas RNA polymerases I and III transcribe nonstructural genes such as the genes that encode tRNAs and rRNAs. By comparison, bacteria have a single type of RNA polymerase that transcribes all genes, though many bacterial species have more than one type of sigma factor that can recognize different promoters.

The initiation stage of transcription in eukaryotes is also more complex. Recall that in bacteria such as *E. coli*, sigma factor recognizes the promoter of genes. By comparison, RNA polymerase II of eukaryotes always requires five general transcription factors to initiate transcription. **Transcription factors** are proteins that influence the ability of RNA polymerase to transcribe genes. In addition, the regulation of gene transcription in eukaryotes typically involves the function of several different proteins. The roles of eukaryotic transcription factors are considered in Chapter 13.

12.3   RNA Processing in Eukaryotes

Learning Outcomes:
1. Explain the process of splicing that produces mature eukaryotic mRNA.
2. Describe the addition of the 5′ cap and 3′ poly A tail to eukaryotic mRNA.

As noted previously, eukaryotic mRNA transcripts undergo modification, or RNA processing, to produce a functional mRNA. Transcription initially produces a longer RNA, called **pre-mRNA**, which undergoes certain processing events before it exits the nucleus. The final product is called a **mature mRNA**, or simply mRNA (**Figure 12.7**).

In the late 1970s, when the experimental tools became available to study eukaryotic genes at the molecular level, the scientific community was astonished by the discovery that the coding sequences within many eukaryotic structural genes are separated by DNA sequences that are transcribed but not translated into protein. These intervening sequences that are not translated are called **introns**, whereas sequences contained in the mature mRNA are termed **exons**. Exons are <u>ex</u>pressed regi<u>ons</u>, whereas introns are <u>inter</u>vening regi<u>ons</u> that are not expressed because they are removed from the mRNA.

To become a functional mRNA, the pre-mRNA undergoes a process known as **RNA splicing**, or simply splicing, in which introns are removed and the remaining exons are connected to each other (see Figure 12.7). In addition to splicing, eukaryotic pre-mRNA transcripts are modified in other ways, including the addition of caps and tails to the ends of the mRNA. After these modifications have been completed, the mRNA leaves the nucleus and enters the cytosol, where translation occurs. In this section, we will examine the molecular mechanisms that account for RNA processing events and consider why they are functionally important.

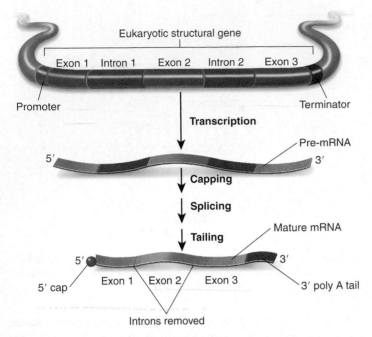

Figure 12.7 Modifications to eukaryotic pre-mRNA that are needed to produce a mature mRNA molecule.

Splicing Involves the Removal of Introns and the Linkage of Exons

Introns are found in many but not all eukaryotic genes. Splicing is less frequent among unicellular eukaryotic species, such as yeast, but is a widespread phenomenon among more complex eukaryotes. In animals and flowering plants, most structural genes have one or more introns. For example, an average human gene has about nine introns. The sizes of introns vary from a few dozen nucleotides to over 100,000! A few bacterial genes have been found to have introns, but they are rare among bacterial and archaeal species.

Introns are precisely removed from eukaryotic pre-mRNA by a large complex called a **spliceosome** that is composed of several different subunits known as snRNPs (pronounced "snurps"). Each snRNP contains small nuclear RNA and a set of proteins. This small nuclear RNA is the product of a nonstructural gene. Intron RNA is defined by a particular sequence within the intron termed the branch site and by two intron-exon boundaries, called the 5′ splice site and the 3′ splice site (**Figure 12.8**). Spliceosome subunits bind to specific sequences at these three locations. This binding causes the intron to loop outward, which brings the two exons close together. The 5′ splice site is then cut, and the 5′ end of the intron becomes covalently attached to the branch site. In the final step, the 3′ splice site is cut, and the two exons are covalently attached to each other. The intron is released and eventually degraded.

In some cases, the function of the spliceosome is regulated so the splicing of exons for a given mRNA can occur in two or more ways. This phenomenon, called **alternative splicing**, allows a single gene to encode two or more polypeptides with differences in their amino acid sequences. As described in Chapter 13, alternative splicing allows complex eukaryotic species to use the same gene to make different proteins at different stages of development or in different cell types. This increases the size of the proteome while minimizing the size of the genome.

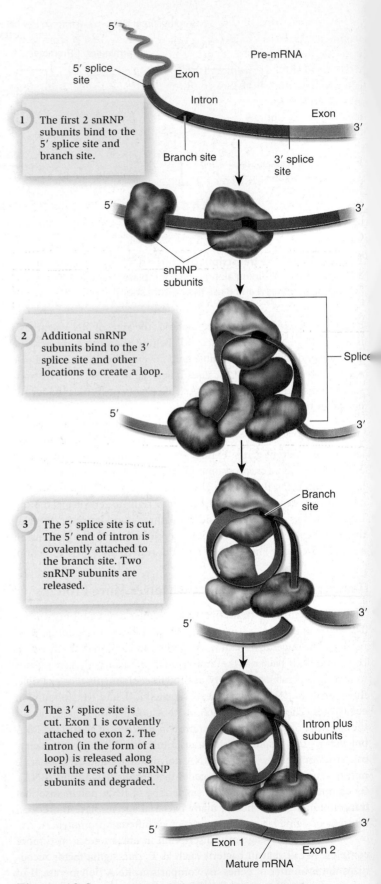

Figure 12.8 The splicing of a eukaryotic pre-mRNA by a spliceosome.

Although primarily found in mRNAs, introns occasionally occur in rRNA and tRNA molecules of certain species. These introns, however, are not removed by the action of a spliceosome. Instead, such rRNAs and tRNAs are **self-splicing**, which means the RNA itself can catalyze the removal of its own intron. Portions of the RNA act like an enzyme to cleave the covalent bonds at the intron-exon boundaries and connect the exons together. An RNA molecule that catalyzes a chemical reaction is termed a **ribozyme**.

RNA Processing Also Involves the Addition of a 5′ Cap and a 3′ Poly A Tail to Eukaryotic mRNAs

Mature mRNAs of eukaryotes have a modified form of guanine covalently attached at the 5′ end, an event known as **capping** (Figure 12.9a). Capping occurs while a pre-mRNA is being made by RNA polymerase, usually when the transcript is only 20 to 25 nucleotides in length. What are the functions of the cap? The 7-methylguanosine structure, called a **5′ cap**, is recognized by cap-binding proteins, which are needed for the proper exit of mRNAs from the nucleus. After an mRNA is in the cytosol, the cap structure helps to prevent mRNA degradation and is recognized by other cap-binding proteins that enable the mRNA to bind to a ribosome for translation.

At the 3′ end, most mature eukaryotic mRNAs have a string of adenine nucleotides, typically 100 to 200 nucleotides in length, referred to as a **poly A tail** (Figure 12.9b). The poly A tail is not encoded in the gene sequence. Instead, the tail is added enzymatically after a pre-mRNA has been completely transcribed. A long poly A tail aids in the export of mRNAs from the nucleus. It also causes a eukaryotic mRNA to be more stable and thereby exist for a longer period of time in the cytosol. Interestingly, new research has shown that some bacterial mRNAs also have poly A tails attached to them. However, the poly A tail has an opposite effect in bacteria, where it causes the mRNA to be rapidly degraded. The importance of a poly A tail in bacterial mRNAs is not well understood.

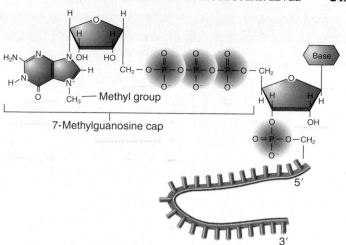

(a) Cap structure at the 5′ end of eukaryotic mRNA

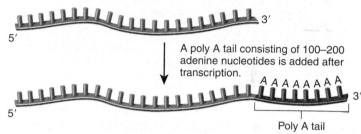

A poly A tail consisting of 100–200 adenine nucleotides is added after transcription.

Poly A tail

(b) Addition of a poly A tail at the 3′ end of eukaryotic mRNA

Figure 12.9 Modifications that occur at the ends of mRNA in eukaryotic cells. (a) A guanosine cap is attached to the 5′ end. This guanine base is modified by the attachment of a methyl group. The linkage between the cap and the mRNA is a 5′ to 5′ linkage. (b) A poly A tail is added to the 3′ end.

Concept Check: Do the ends of structural genes have a poly T region that provides a template for the synthesis of a poly A tail in mRNA? Explain.

12.4 Translation and the Genetic Code

Learning Outcomes:

1. Explain how the genetic code specifies the relationship between the sequence of codons in mRNA and the amino acid sequence of a polypeptide.
2. Analyze the experiments of Nirenberg and Leder that led to the deciphering of the genetic code.

In the two previous sections, we considered the first stages of the central dogma—how an RNA transcript is made from DNA and how eukaryotes process that transcript. Recall that this type of RNA is called messenger RNA (mRNA), because its function is to transmit information from DNA to cellular components called ribosomes, where polypeptide synthesis occurs. In this section, we will consider the next stage, translation, which is the synthesis of polypeptides using information from the mRNA. To understand the process of translation, we will first examine the **genetic code**, which specifies the relationship between the sequence of nucleotides in the mRNA and the sequence of amino acids in a polypeptide.

The Genetic Code Specifies the Amino Acids within a Polypeptide

The ability of mRNA to be translated into an amino acid sequence of a polypeptide relies on the genetic code. The code is read in groups of three nucleotide bases known as **codons**. The genetic code consists of 64 different codons (**Table 12.1**). The sequence of three bases in most codons specifies a particular amino acid. For example, the codon CCC specifies the amino acid proline, whereas the codon GGC encodes the amino acid glycine. From the analysis of many different species, including bacteria, archaea, protists, fungi, plants, and animals, researchers have found that the genetic code is nearly universal. Only a few rare exceptions to the genetic code have been discovered.

Why are there 64 codons, as shown in Table 12.1? Because there are 20 types of amino acids, at least 20 different codons are needed so each amino acid can be specified by a codon. With four types of bases in mRNA (U, C, A, and G), a genetic code containing two bases in a codon would not be sufficient, because only 4^2, or 16, different codons would be possible. A three-base system can specify 4^3, or 64, different codons, which is far more than the number of amino acids. The genetic code is said to be **degenerate** because more than one

Table 12.1   The Genetic Code*

		U	C	A	G	

Second position

First Position		U	C	A	G		Third Position
U		UUU } Phe	UCU }	UAU } Tyr	UGU } Cys	U	
		UUC }	UCC } Ser	UAC }	UGC }	C	
		UUA } Leu	UCA }	UAA Stop	UGA Stop	A	
		UUG }	UCG }	UAG Stop	UGG Trp	G	
C		CUU }	CCU }	CAU } His	CGU }	U	
		CUC } Leu	CCC } Pro	CAC }	CGC } Arg	C	
		CUA }	CCA }	CAA } Gln	CGA }	A	
		CUG }	CCG }	CAG }	CGG }	G	
A		AUU } Ile	ACU }	AAU } Asn	AGU } Ser	U	
		AUC }	ACC } Thr	AAC }	AGC }	C	
		AUA }	ACA }	AAA } Lys	AGA } Arg	A	
		AUG Met/start	ACG }	AAG }	AGG }	G	
G		GUU }	GCU }	GAU } Asp	GGU }	U	
		GUC } Val	GCC } Ala	GAC }	GGC } Gly	C	
		GUA }	GCA }	GAA } Glu	GGA }	A	
		GUG }	GCG }	GAG }	GGG }	G	

*Exceptions to the genetic code are sporadically found among various species. For example, AUA encodes methionine in yeast and mammalian mitochondria.

codon can specify the same amino acid (see Table 12.1). For example, the codons GGU, GGC, GGA, and GGG all code for the amino acid glycine. In most instances, the third base in the codon is the degenerate or variable base.

During Translation, mRNA Is Used to Make a Polypeptide with a Specific Amino Acid Sequence

Let's look at the organization of a bacterial mRNA to see how translation occurs (**Figure 12.10**). A ribosomal-binding site is located near the 5′ end of the mRNA. The **start codon**, which specifies the amino acid methionine, is only a few nucleotides from the ribosomal-binding site. Beyond this, a large portion of an mRNA functions as a **coding sequence**—a region that specifies the linear amino acid sequence of a polypeptide. A typical polypeptide is a few hundred amino acids in length. The coding sequence consists of a series of codons. Finally, one of three **stop codons** signals the end of translation. These codons, also known as **termination codons**, are UAA, UAG, and UGA.

The start codon also defines the **reading frame** of an mRNA, which refers to the order in which codons are read during translation. Beginning at the start codon, each adjacent codon is read as a group of three bases, also called a **triplet**, in the 5′ to 3′ direction. For example, look at the following two mRNA sequences and their corresponding amino acid sequences.

	Ribosomal-binding site	Start codon

mRNA 5′–<u>AUAAGGAGG</u>UUACG(<u>AUG</u>)(CAG)(CAG)(GGC)(UUU)(ACC)–3′

Polypeptide   Met - Gln - Gln - Gly - Phe - Thr

	Ribosomal-binding site	Start codon

mRNA 5′–<u>AUAAGGAGG</u>UUACG(<u>AUG</u>)(**U**CA)(GCA)(GGG)(CUU)(UAC)C–3′

Polypeptide   Met - Ser - Ala - Gly - Leu - Tyr

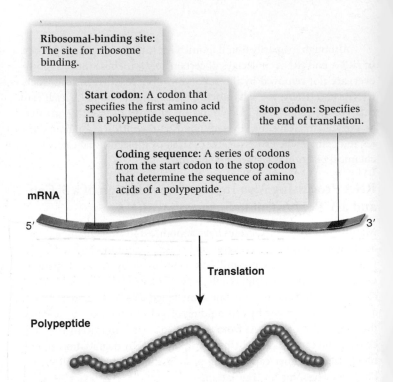

Figure 12.10 **The organization of a bacterial mRNA as a translational unit.** The string of blue balls represents a sequence of amino acids in a polypeptide. During and following translation, a sequence of amino acids folds into a more compact structure as described in Chapter 3 (see Figure 3.16).

Concept Check: *If a mutation eliminated the start codon from a gene, how would the mutation affect transcription, and how would it affect translation?*

The first sequence shows how the mRNA codons would be correctly translated into amino acids. In the second sequence, an additional U has been added to the same sequence after the start codon. This shifts the reading frame, thereby changing the codons as they occur in the 5′ to 3′ direction. The polypeptide produced from this series of codons has a very different sequence of amino acids. From this comparison, we can also see that the reading frame is not overlapping, which means that each base functions within a single codon.

DNA Stores Information, Whereas mRNA and tRNA Access That Information to Make a Polypeptide

The relationships among the DNA sequence of a gene, the mRNA transcribed from the gene, and the polypeptide sequence are shown schematically in **Figure 12.11**. Recall that the template strand is used to make mRNA. The resulting mRNA strand corresponds to the coding strand of DNA, except that U in the mRNA substitutes for T in the DNA. The 5′ end of the mRNA contains an untranslated region (5′ UTR) as does the 3′ end (3′ UTR). The middle portion contains a series of codons that specify the amino acid sequence of a polypeptide.

To translate a nucleotide sequence of mRNA into an amino acid sequence, recognition occurs between mRNA and transfer RNA (tRNA) molecules. Transfer RNA, which is described in Section 12.5, functions as the "translator" or intermediary between an mRNA

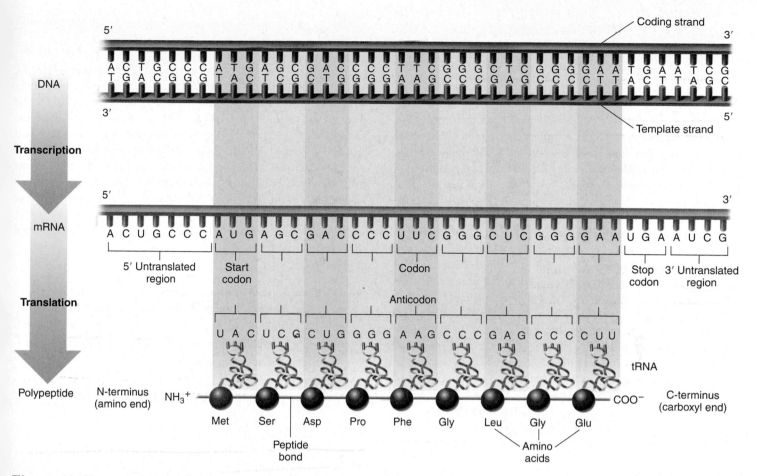

Figure 12.11 Relationships among the coding sequence of a gene, the codon sequence of an mRNA, the anticodons of tRNA, and the amino acid sequence of a polypeptide.

Concept Check: If an anticodon in a tRNA molecule has the sequence 3'–ACC–5', which amino acid does it carry?

codon and an amino acid. The **anticodon** is a three-base sequence in a tRNA molecule that is complementary to a codon in mRNA. Due to this complementarity, the anticodon in the tRNA and a codon in an mRNA bind to each other. Furthermore, the anticodon in a tRNA corresponds to the amino acid that it carries. For example, if the anticodon in a tRNA is 3'–AAG–5', it is complementary to a 5'–UUC–3' codon. According to the genetic code, a UUC codon specifies phenylalanine (Phe). Therefore, a tRNA with a 3'–AAG–5' anticodon must carry phenylalanine. As another example, a tRNA with a 3'–GGG–5' anticodon is complementary to a 5'–CCC–3' codon, which specifies proline. This tRNA must carry proline (Pro).

As seen at the bottom of Figure 12.11, the direction of polypeptide synthesis parallels the 5' to 3' orientation of mRNA. The first amino acid is said to be at the amino end, or **N-terminus**, of the polypeptide. The term N-terminus refers to the presence of a nitrogen atom (N) at this end, whereas amino end indicates the presence of an amino group (NH_2). **Peptide bonds** connect the amino acids together. These covalent bonds form between the carboxyl group (COOH) of the previous amino acid and the amino group of the next amino acid. The last amino acid in a completed polypeptide does not have another amino acid attached to its carboxyl group. This last amino acid is said to be located at the carboxyl end, or **C-terminus**. A carboxyl group is always found at this end of the polypeptide. Note that at neutral pH,

the amino group is positively charged (NH_3^+), whereas the carboxyl group is negatively charged (COO^-).

Synthetic RNA Helped to Decipher the Genetic Code

Now let's look at some early experiments that allowed scientists to decipher the genetic code. During the early 1960s, the genetic code was determined by the collective efforts of several researchers, including American biochemist Marshall Nirenberg, Spanish-American biochemist Severo Ochoa, and American geneticist Philip Leder. Prior to their studies, other scientists had discovered that bacterial cells can be broken open and components from the cytoplasm can synthesize polypeptides. This is termed an in vitro or cell-free translation system. Nirenberg and Ochoa made synthetic RNA molecules using an enzyme that covalently connects nucleotides together. Using this synthetic mRNA, they then determined which amino acids were incorporated into polypeptides. For example, if an RNA molecule had only adenine-containing nucleotides (for example, 5'–AAAAAAAAAAAAAAAAAAAA–3'), a polypeptide was produced that contained only lysine. This result indicated that the AAA codon specifies lysine.

Another method used to decipher the genetic code involved the chemical synthesis of short RNA molecules, as described next in the Feature Investigation.

FEATURE INVESTIGATION

Nirenberg and Leder Found That RNA Triplets Can Promote the Binding of tRNA to Ribosomes

In 1964, Nirenberg and Leder discovered that RNA molecules containing three nucleotides (that is, a triplet) can cause a tRNA molecule to bind to a ribosome. In other words, an RNA triplet acts like a codon within an mRNA molecule. To establish the relationship between triplet sequences and specific amino acids, Nirenberg and Leder made triplets with specific base sequences (**Figure 12.12**). For example, in one experiment they studied 5′–CCC–3′ triplets. This particular triplet was added to 20 different tubes. To each tube, they next added an in vitro translation system, which contained ribosomes and tRNAs that already had amino acids attached to them. However, each translation system had only one type of radiolabeled amino acid. One translation system had only proline that was radiolabeled, a second translation system had only serine that was radiolabeled, and so on.

As shown in step 2, the triplets became bound to the ribosomes just like the binding of mRNA to a ribosome. The tRNA with an anticodon that was complementary to the added triplet would bind to the triplet, which was already bound to the ribosome. For example, when the triplet was 5′–CCC–3′, a tRNA with a 3′–GGG–5′ anticodon would bind to the triplet/ribosome complex. This tRNA carries proline.

To determine which tRNA had bound, the contents from each tube were poured through a filter that trapped the large ribosomes but did not trap tRNAs that were not bound to ribosomes (see step 3). If the tRNA carrying the radiolabeled amino acid was bound to the triplet/ribosome complex, radioactivity would be trapped on the filter. Using a scintillation counter, the researchers determined the amount of radioactivity on each filter. Because only one amino acid was radiolabeled in each in vitro translation system, they could determine which triplet corresponded to which amino acid. In the example shown here, CCC corresponds to proline. Therefore, the in vitro translation system containing radiolabeled proline showed a large amount of radioactivity on the filter. As seen in the data, by studying triplets with different sequences, Nirenberg and Leder identified many codons of the genetic code.

Experimental Questions

1. Briefly explain how a triplet mimics the role of an mRNA molecule. How was this observation useful in the study done by Nirenberg and Leder?

2. What was the benefit of using radiolabeled amino acids in the Nirenberg and Leder experiment?

3. Predict the results that Nirenberg and Leder would have found for the following triplets: AUG, UAA, UAG, or UGA.

Figure 12.12 Nirenberg and Leder's use of triplet binding method to decipher the genetic code.

HYPOTHESIS An RNA triplet can bind to a ribosome and promote the binding of the tRNA that carries the amino acid that the RNA triplet specifies.

KEY MATERIALS The researchers made 20 in vitro translation systems, which included ribosomes, tRNAs, and 20 amino acids. The 20 translation systems differed with regard to which amino acid was radiolabeled. For example, in 1 translation system, radiolabeled glycine was added, and the other 19 amino acids were unlabeled. In another system, radiolabeled proline was added, and the other 19 amino acids were unlabeled. The in vitro translation systems also contained the enzymes that attach amino acids to tRNAs.

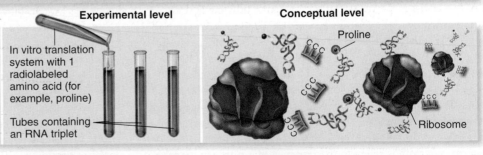

1 Mix together RNA triplets of a specific sequence and 20 in vitro translation systems. In the example shown here, the triplet is 5′–CCC–3′. Each translation system contained a different radiolabeled amino acid. (Note: Only 3 tubes are shown here.)

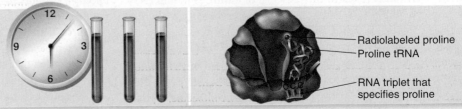

2 Allow time for the RNA triplet to bind to the ribosome and for the appropriate tRNA to bind to the RNA triplet.

3 Pour each mixture through a filter that allows the passage of unbound tRNA but does not allow the passage of ribosomes.

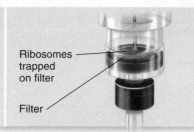

Ribosomes trapped on filter

Filter

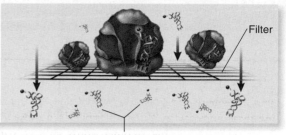

Filter

tRNAs not bound to a ribosome

4 Count radioactivity on the filter.

Scintillation counter

5 **THE DATA**

Triplet	Radiolabeled amino acid trapped on the filter	Triplet	Radiolabeled amino acid trapped on the filter
5′ – AAA – 3′	Lysine	5′ – GAC – 3′	Aspartic acid
5′ – ACA – 3′	Threonine	5′ – GCC – 3′	Alanine
5′ – ACC – 3′	Threonine	5′ – GGU – 3′	Glycine
5′ – AGA – 3′	Arginine	5′ – GGC – 3′	Glycine
5′ – AUA – 3′	Isoleucine	5′ – GUU – 3′	Valine
5′ – AUU – 3′	Isoleucine	5′ – UAU – 3′	Tyrosine
5′ – CCC – 3′	Proline	5′ – UGU – 3′	Cysteine
5′ – CGC – 3′	Arginine	5′ – UUG – 3′	Leucine
5′ – GAA – 3′	Glutamic acid		

6 **CONCLUSION** This method enabled the researchers to identify many of the codons of the genetic code.

7 **SOURCE** Leder, Philip, and Nirenberg, Marshall W. 1964. RNA Codewords and Protein Synthesis, III. On the nucleotide sequence of a cysteine and a leucine RNA codeword. *Proceedings of the National Academy of Sciences* 52:1521–1529.

12.5 The Machinery of Translation

Learning Outcomes:

1. Describe the structure and function of tRNA.
2. Explain how aminoacyl-tRNA synthases attach amino acids to tRNAs.
3. Outline the structural features of bacterial and eukaryotic ribosomes.
4. Analyze how ribosomal RNA (rRNA) is used to evaluate evolutionary relationships among different species.

Let's now turn our attention to the components found in living cells that are needed to use the genetic code and translate mRNA into polypeptides. Earlier in this chapter, we considered transcription, the first step in gene expression. To transcribe an RNA molecule, a preexisting DNA template strand is used to make a complementary RNA strand. A single enzyme, RNA polymerase, catalyzes this reaction.

By comparison, translation requires more components because the sequence of codons in an mRNA molecule must be translated into a sequence of amino acids according to the genetic code. A single protein cannot accomplish such a task. Instead, many different proteins and RNA molecules interact in an intricate series of steps to achieve the synthesis of a polypeptide. A cell must make many different components, including mRNAs, tRNAs, ribosomes, and translation factors, so polypeptides can be made (**Table 12.2**).

Though the estimates vary from cell to cell and from species to species, most cells use a substantial amount of their energy to translate mRNA into polypeptides. In *E. coli*, for example, approximately 90% of the cellular energy is used for this process. This value underscores the complexity and importance of translation in living organisms. In this section, we will focus on the components of the translation machinery. The last section of the chapter will describe the stages of translation as they occur in living cells.

Table 12.2	Components of the Translation Machinery
Component	**Function**
mRNA	Contains the information for a polypeptide sequence according to the genetic code.
tRNA	A molecule with two functional sites: one site, termed the anticodon, binds to a codon in mRNA, and a second site is where an appropriate amino acid is attached.
Ribosome	Composed of many proteins and rRNA molecules, the ribosome provides a location where mRNA and tRNA molecules can properly interact with each other. The ribosome also catalyzes the formation of covalent bonds between adjacent amino acids so that a polypeptide can be made.
Translation factors	Proteins needed for the three stages of translation. Initiation factors are required for the assembly of mRNA, the first tRNA, and ribosomal subunits. Elongation factors are needed to synthesize the polypeptide. Release factors are needed to recognize the stop codon and disassemble the translation machinery. Several translation factors use GTP as an energy source to carry out their functions.

Transfer RNAs Share Common Structural Features

To understand how tRNAs act as carriers of the correct amino acids during translation, researchers have examined their structural characteristics. The tRNAs of bacteria, archaea, and eukaryotes share common features. As originally proposed in 1965 by American biochemist Robert Holley, the two-dimensional structure of a tRNA exhibits a cloverleaf pattern. The structure has three stem-loops and a fourth stem with a 3' single-stranded region (**Figure 12.13a**). The stem in a stem-loop is a region where the RNA is double-stranded due to complementary base pairing via hydrogen binding, whereas the loop is a region without base pairing. The anticodon is located in the loop of the second stem-loop region. The 3' single-stranded region is the amino acid attachment site. The three-dimensional structure of tRNA molecules involves additional folding of the secondary structure (**Figure 12.13b**).

The cells of every organism make many different tRNA molecules, each encoded by a different gene. A tRNA is named according to the amino acid it carries. For example, tRNA^Ser carries a serine. Because the genetic code contains six different serine codons, as shown in Table 12.1, a cell produces more than one type of tRNA^Ser.

Aminoacyl-tRNA Synthetases Charge tRNAs by Attaching an Appropriate Amino Acid

To perform its role during translation, a tRNA must have the appropriate amino acid attached to its 3' end. The enzymes that catalyze the attachment of amino acids to tRNA molecules are known as **aminoacyl-tRNA synthetases**. Cells make 20 distinct types of aminoacyl-tRNA synthetase enzymes, with each type recognizing just one of the 20 different amino acids. Each aminoacyl-tRNA synthetase is named for the specific amino acid it attaches to tRNA. For example, alanyl-tRNA synthetase recognizes alanine and attaches this amino acid to all tRNAs with alanine anticodons.

Aminoacyl-tRNA synthetases catalyze chemical reactions involving an amino acid, a tRNA molecule, and ATP (**Figure 12.14**). First,

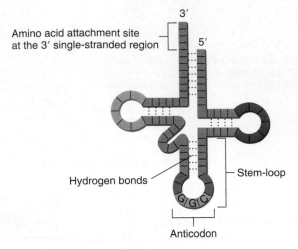

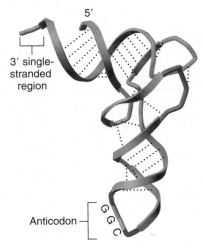

(a) **Two-dimensional structure of tRNA**

(b) **Three-dimensional structure of tRNA**

Figure 12.13 Structure of tRNA. (a) The two-dimensional or secondary structure of tRNA is that of a cloverleaf, with the anticodon within the middle stem-loop structure. The 3' single-stranded region (acceptor stem) is where an amino acid can attach. **(b)** The actual three-dimensional structure folds in on itself.

BIOLOGY PRINCIPLE   Structure determines function. The structure of tRNA has two functional sites: a 3' single-stranded region where an amino acid is attached and an anticodon that binds to a codon on mRNA.

Concept Check: *What is the function of the anticodon?*

a specific amino acid and ATP bind to the enzyme. Next, the amino acid is activated by the covalent attachment of an AMP molecule, and pyrophosphate is released. In a third step, the activated amino acid is covalently attached to the 3' end of a tRNA molecule, and AMP is released. Finally, the tRNA with its attached amino acid, called a **charged tRNA** or an **aminoacyl tRNA**, is released from the enzyme.

The ability of each aminoacyl-tRNA synthetase to recognize an appropriate tRNA has been called the second genetic code. A precise recognition process is necessary to maintain the fidelity of genetic information. If the wrong amino acid was attached to a tRNA, the amino acid sequence of the translated polypeptide would be incorrect. However, aminoacyl-tRNA synthetases are amazingly accurate enzymes. The wrong amino acid is attached to a tRNA less than once in 100,000 times! The anticodon region of the tRNA is usually

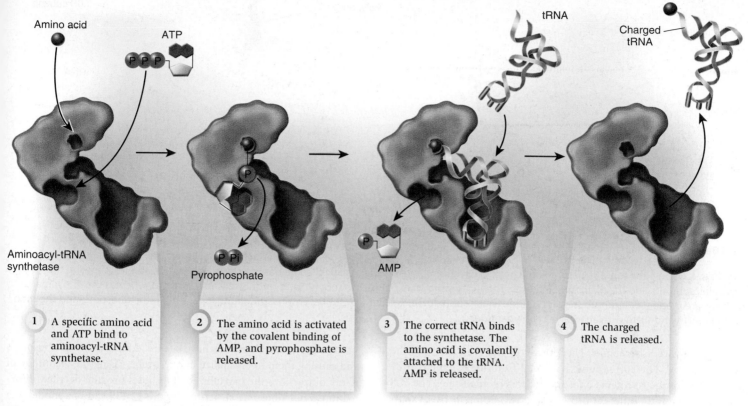

Figure 12.14 **Aminoacyl-tRNA synthetase charging a tRNA.**

BioConnections: Look back at Figure 6.3, which describes the hydrolysis of ATP. Why is ATP needed to charge a tRNA?

important for recognition by the correct aminoacyl-tRNA synthetase. In addition, the base sequences in other regions may facilitate binding to an aminoacyl-tRNA synthetase.

Ribosomes Are Assembled from rRNA and Proteins

Let's now turn our attention to the **ribosome**, the site where translation takes place. The ribosome is often described as a molecular machine. Bacterial cells have one type of ribosome, which translates all mRNAs in the cytoplasm. Because eukaryotic cells are compartmentalized into cellular organelles bounded by membranes, biochemically distinct ribosomes are found in different cellular compartments. The most abundant type of eukaryotic ribosome functions in the cytosol. In addition, mitochondria have ribosomes, and plant and algal cells have ribosomes in their chloroplasts. As you might expect from the endosymbiosis theory described in Chapter 4 (see Figure 4.27), the compositions of mitochondrial and chloroplast ribosomes are more similar to bacterial ribosomes than they are to eukaryotic cytosolic ribosomes. Unless otherwise noted, the term eukaryotic ribosome refers to ribosomes in the cytosol, not to those found in organelles.

A ribosome is a large complex composed of structures called the large and small subunits. The term subunit is perhaps misleading, because each ribosomal subunit is itself assembled from many different proteins and one or more RNA molecules. In the bacterium *E. coli*, the small ribosomal subunit is called 30S, and the large subunit is 50S (**Table 12.3**). The designations 30S and 50S refer to the rate at which these subunits sediment when subjected to a centrifugal force. This rate is described as a sedimentation coefficient in Svedberg units (S)

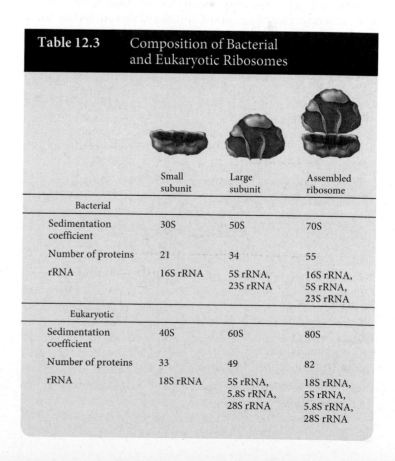

Table 12.3 Composition of Bacterial and Eukaryotic Ribosomes

	Small subunit	Large subunit	Assembled ribosome
Bacterial			
Sedimentation coefficient	30S	50S	70S
Number of proteins	21	34	55
rRNA	16S rRNA	5S rRNA, 23S rRNA	16S rRNA, 5S rRNA, 23S rRNA
Eukaryotic			
Sedimentation coefficient	40S	60S	80S
Number of proteins	33	49	82
rRNA	18S rRNA	5S rRNA, 5.8S rRNA, 28S rRNA	18S rRNA, 5S rRNA, 5.8S rRNA, 28S rRNA

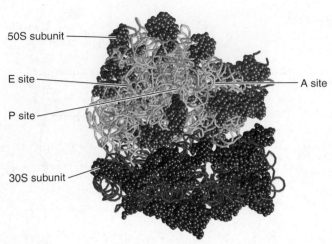

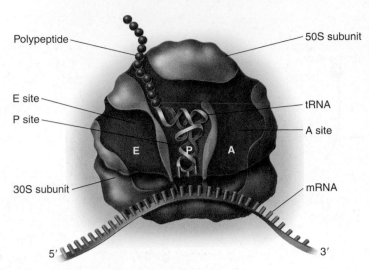

(a) Bacterial ribosome model based on X-ray diffraction studies   **(b) Schematic model for ribosome structure**

Figure 12.15 Ribosome structure. (a) A model for the structure of a bacterial ribosome based on X-ray diffraction studies, showing the large and small subunits and the major binding sites. The rRNA is shown in gray (large subunit) and turquoise (small subunit), whereas the ribosomal proteins are magenta (large subunit) and purple (small subunit). (b) A schematic model emphasizing functional sites in the ribosome, and showing bound mRNA and tRNA with an attached polypeptide.

in honor of Swedish chemist Theodor Svedberg, who invented the ultracentrifuge. The 30S subunit is formed from the assembly of 21 different ribosomal proteins and one 16S rRNA molecule. The 50S subunit contains 34 different proteins and two different rRNA molecules, called 5S and 23S. Together, the 30S and 50S subunits form a 70S ribosome. (Svedberg units don't add up linearly, because the sedimentation coefficient is a function of both size and shape.) In bacteria, ribosomal proteins and rRNA molecules are synthesized in the cytoplasm, and the ribosomal subunits are assembled there as well.

Eukaryotic ribosomes consist of subunits that are slightly larger than their bacterial counterparts (Table 12.3). In eukaryotes, 40S and 60S subunits combine to form an 80S ribosome. The 40S subunit is composed of 33 proteins and an 18S rRNA, and the 60S subunit has 49 proteins and 5S, 5.8S, and 28S rRNAs. The synthesis of eukaryotic rRNA occurs in the nucleolus, a region of the nucleus that is specialized for that purpose. The ribosomal proteins are made in the cytosol and imported into the nucleus. The rRNAs and ribosomal proteins are then assembled within the nucleolus to make the 40S and 60S subunits. The 40S and 60S subunits are exported into the cytosol, where they associate to form an 80S ribosome during translation.

Due to structural differences between bacterial and eukaryotic ribosomes, certain chemicals may bind to bacterial ribosomes but not to eukaryotic ribosomes, and vice versa. Some **antibiotics**, which are chemicals that inhibit the growth of certain microorganisms, bind only to bacterial ribosomes and inhibit translation. Examples include erythromycin and chloramphenicol. Because these chemicals do not inhibit eukaryotic ribosomes, they have been effective drugs for the treatment of bacterial infections in humans and domesticated animals.

Components of Ribosomal Subunits Form Functional Sites for Translation

To understand the structure and function of the ribosome at the molecular level, researchers have determined the locations and functional roles of individual ribosomal proteins and rRNAs. In recent

years, a few research groups have succeeded in purifying ribosomes and causing them to crystallize in a test tube. Using the technique of X-ray diffraction, the crystallized ribosomes provide detailed information about ribosome structure. **Figure 12.15a** shows a model of a bacterial ribosome.

During bacterial translation, the mRNA lies on the surface of the 30S subunit, within a space between the 30S and 50S subunits (**Figure 12.15b**). As a polypeptide is synthesized, it exits through a hole within the 50S subunit. Ribosomes contain discrete sites where tRNAs bind and the polypeptide is synthesized. In 1964, James Watson proposed a two-site model for tRNA binding to the ribosome. These sites are known as the **peptidyl site (P site)** and **aminoacyl site (A site)**. In 1981, German geneticists Knud Nierhaus and Hans-Jörg Rheinberger expanded this to a three-site model (Figure 12.15b). The third site is known as the exit site (E site). In Section 12.6, we will examine the roles of these sites in the synthesis of a polypeptide.

GENOMES & PROTEOMES CONNECTION

Comparisons of Small Subunit rRNAs Among Different Species Provide a Basis for Establishing Evolutionary Relationships

Translation is a fundamental process that is vital for the existence of all living species. Research indicates that the components needed for translation arose very early in the evolution of life on our planet in ancestors that gave rise to all known living species. For this reason, all organisms have translational components that are evolutionarily related to each other. For example, the rRNA found in the small subunit of ribosomes is similar in all forms of life, though it is slightly larger in eukaryotic species (18S) than in bacterial species (16S). In other words, the gene for the small subunit rRNA (SSU rRNA) is found in the genomes of all organisms.

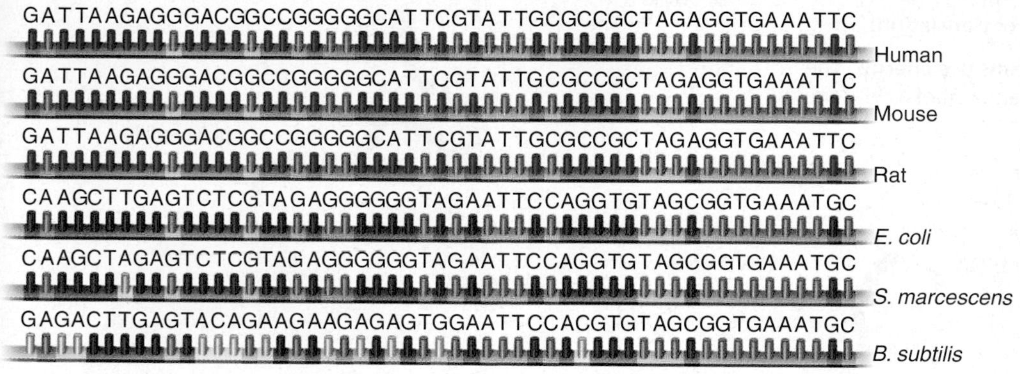

GATTAAGAGGGACGGCCGGGGGCATTCGTATTGCGCCGCTAGAGGTGAAATTC
Human

GATTAAGAGGGACGGCCGGGGGCATTCGTATTGCGCCGCTAGAGGTGAAATTC
Mouse

GATTAAGAGGGACGGCCGGGGGCATTCGTATTGCGCCGCTAGAGGTGAAATTC
Rat

CAAGCTTGAGTCTCGTAGAGGGGGGTAGAATTCCAGGTGTAGCGGTGAAATGC
E. coli

CAAGCTAGAGTCTCGTAGAGGGGGGTAGAATTCCAGGTGTAGCGGTGAAATGC
S. marcescens

GAGACTTGAGTACAGAAGAAGAGAGTGGAATTCCACGTGTAGCGGTGAAATGC
B. subtilis

Figure 12.16 Comparison of small subunit rRNA gene sequences from three mammalian and three bacterial species. Note the many similarities (yellow) and differences (green and red) among the sequences. The gray color indicates differences among the three bacterial species.

Concept Check: Based on the gene sequences shown here, pick two species that are closely related evolutionarily and two that are distantly related.

How is this observation useful? One way that geneticists explore evolutionary relationships is to compare the sequences of evolutionarily related genes. At the molecular level, gene evolution involves changes in DNA sequences. After two different species have diverged from each other during evolution, the genes of each species have an opportunity to accumulate changes, or mutations, that alter the sequences of those genes. After many generations, evolutionarily related species contain genes that are similar but not identical to each other, because each species accumulates different mutations. In general, if a very long time has elapsed since two species diverged evolutionarily, their genes tend to be quite different. In contrast, if two species diverged relatively recently on an evolutionary time scale, their genes tend to be more similar.

Figure 12.16 compares a portion of the sequence of the SSU rRNA gene from three mammalian and three bacterial species. The colors highlight different types of comparisons. The bases shaded in yellow are identical in five or six species. Sequences of bases that are identical or very similar in different species are said to be **evolutionarily conserved**. Presumably, these sequences were found in the primordial gene that gave rise to modern species. Perhaps because these sequences may have some critical function, they have not changed over evolutionary time. Those sequences shaded in green are identical in all three mammals, but differ compared with one or more bacterial species. Actually, if you scan the mammalian species, you may notice that all three sequences are identical in this region. The sequences shaded in red are identical or very similar in the bacterial species, but differ compared with the mammalian SSU rRNA genes. The sequences from *Escherichia coli* and *Serratia marcescens* are more similar to each other than the sequence from *Bacillus subtilis* is to either of them. This observation suggests that *E. coli* and *S. marcescens* are more closely related evolutionarily than either of them is to *B. subtilis*.

12.6 The Stages of Translation

Learning Outcomes:
1. Describe the three stages of translation.
2. Summarize the similarities and differences between translation in bacteria and eukaryotes.

As in transcription, the process of translation occurs in three stages called initiation, elongation, and termination. **Figure 12.17** provides an overview of the process. During initiation, an mRNA, the first

tRNA, and the ribosomal subunits assemble into a complex. Next, in the elongation stage, the ribosome moves in the 5′ to 3′ direction from the start codon in the mRNA toward the stop codon, synthesizing a polypeptide according to the sequence of codons in the mRNA. Finally, the process is terminated when the ribosome reaches a stop codon and the complex disassembles, releasing the completed polypeptide. In this section, we will examine the steps in this process as they occur in living cells.

Translation Is Initiated with the Assembly of mRNA, tRNA, and the Ribosomal Subunits

During **initiation**, a complex is formed between an mRNA molecule, the first tRNA, and the ribosomal subunits. In all species, the assembly of this complex requires the help of proteins called **initiation factors** that facilitate the interactions between these components (see Table 12.2). The assembly also requires an input of energy. Guanosine triphosphate (GTP) is hydrolyzed by certain initiation factors to provide the necessary energy.

In the absence of translation, the small and large ribosomal subunits exist separately. To begin assembly in bacteria, mRNA binds to the small ribosomal subunit (**Figure 12.18**). The binding of mRNA to this subunit is facilitated by a short ribosomal-binding site near the 5′ end of the mRNA. The ribosomal binding site is a sequence of bases that is complementary to a portion of the 16S rRNA within the small ribosomal subunit. The mRNA becomes bound to the ribosome because the ribosomal-binding site and rRNA hydrogen-bond to each other by base-pairing. The start codon is usually just a few nucleotides downstream (that is, toward the 3′ end) from the ribosomal-binding site. A specific tRNA, which functions as the initiator tRNA, recognizes the start codon in mRNA (AUG) and binds to it. In eukaryotes, this tRNA carries a methionine, whereas in bacteria it carries a methionine that has been modified by the attachment of a formyl group. To complete the initiation stage, the large ribosomal subunit associates with the small subunit. At the end of this stage, the initiator tRNA is located in the P site of the ribosome.

In eukaryotic species, the initiation phase of translation differs in two ways from the process in bacteria. First, instead of a RNA sequence that functions as a ribosomal-binding site, eukaryotic mRNAs have a guanosine cap (5′ cap) at their 5′ end. This 5′ cap is recognized by cap-binding proteins that promote the binding of the mRNA to the small ribosomal subunit. Also, unlike bacteria, in which the start codon is very close to a ribosomal-binding site, the location

Figure 12.17 An overview of the stages of translation.

BIOLOGY PRINCIPLE **Living organisms use energy.** The process of translation uses a sizeable amount of a cell's energy.

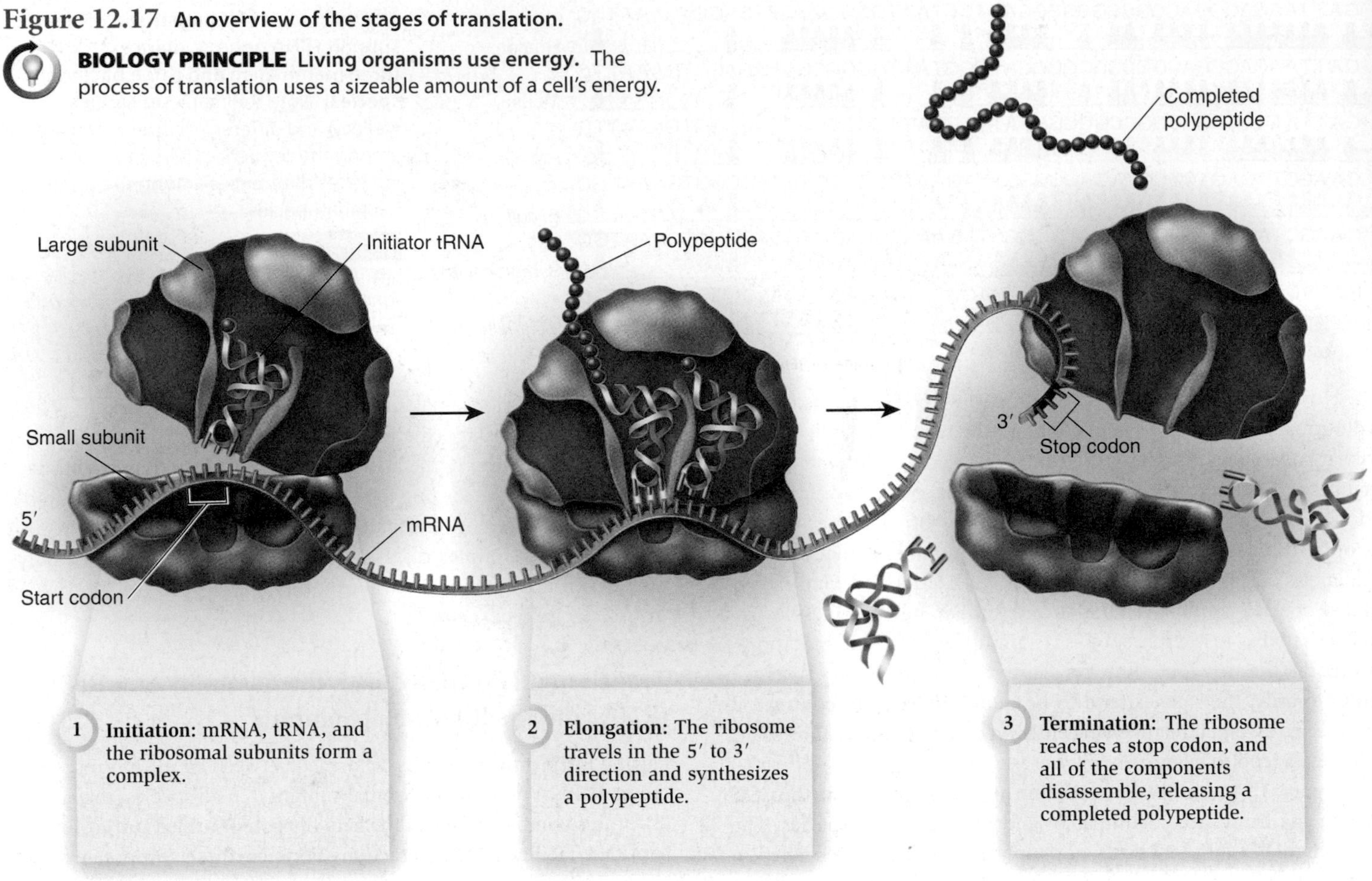

①	**Initiation:** mRNA, tRNA, and the ribosomal subunits form a complex.
②	**Elongation:** The ribosome travels in the 5′ to 3′ direction and synthesizes a polypeptide.
③	**Termination:** The ribosome reaches a stop codon, and all of the components disassemble, releasing a completed polypeptide.

of start codons in eukaryotes is more variable. In 1978, American biochemist Marilyn Kozak proposed that the small ribosomal subunit identifies a start codon by beginning at the 5′ end and then scanning along the mRNA in the 3′ direction in search of an AUG sequence. In many, but not all, cases the first AUG codon is used as a start codon. By analyzing the sequences of many eukaryotic mRNAs, Kozak and her colleagues discovered that the sequence around an AUG codon is important for it to be used as a start codon. The sequence for optimal start codon recognition is shown here:

Upstream of start codon	Start codon	Downstream coding region

. . . G C C (A or G) C C (**A U G**) G . . . .

Aside from an AUG codon itself, a guanine just past the start codon and the sequence of six bases directly upstream from the start codon are important for start codon selection. If the first AUG codon is within a site that deviates markedly from this optimal sequence, the small subunit may skip this codon and instead use another AUG codon farther downstream. Once the small subunit selects a start codon, an initiator tRNA binds to the start codon, and then the large ribosomal subunit associates with the small subunit to complete the assembly process.

Polypeptide Synthesis Occurs During the Elongation Stage

As its name suggests, the stage of translation called **elongation** involves the covalent bonding of amino acids to each other, one at a time, to produce a polypeptide. Even though this process involves several different components, translation occurs at a remarkable rate. Under normal cellular conditions, the translation machinery can elongate a polypeptide at a rate of 15 to 18 amino acids per second in bacteria and 6 amino acids per second in eukaryotes!

To elongate a polypeptide by one amino acid, a tRNA brings a new amino acid to the ribosome, where it is attached to the end of a growing polypeptide. In step 1 of **Figure 12.19**, translation has already proceeded to a point where a short polypeptide is attached to the tRNA located in the P site of the ribosome. This is called peptidyl tRNA. In the first step of elongation, a charged tRNA carrying a single amino acid binds to the A site. This binding occurs because the anticodon in the tRNA is complementary to the codon in the mRNA. The hydrolysis of GTP by proteins that function as **elongation factors** provides the energy for the binding of the tRNA to the A site (see Table 12.2). At this stage of translation, a peptidyl tRNA is in the P site and a charged tRNA (an aminoacyl tRNA) is in the A site. This is how the P and A sites came to be named.

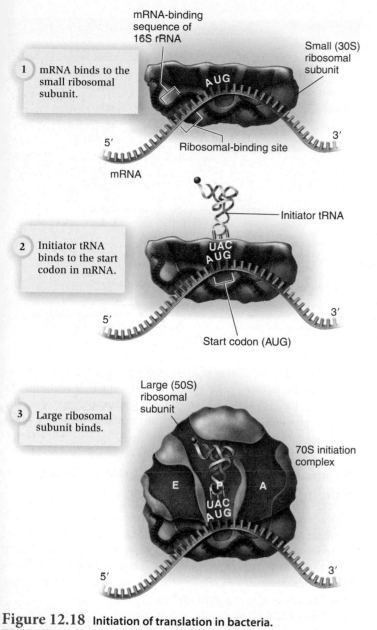

1 mRNA binds to the small ribosomal subunit.

mRNA-binding sequence of 16S rRNA

Small (30S) ribosomal subunit

Ribosomal-binding site

5′   3′

mRNA

2 Initiator tRNA binds to the start codon in mRNA.

Initiator tRNA

5′   3′

Start codon (AUG)

3 Large ribosomal subunit binds.

Large (50S) ribosomal subunit

70S initiation complex

E   P   A

5′   3′

Figure 12.18 Initiation of translation in bacteria.

Concept Check: What promotes the binding between the mRNA and the small ribosomal subunit?

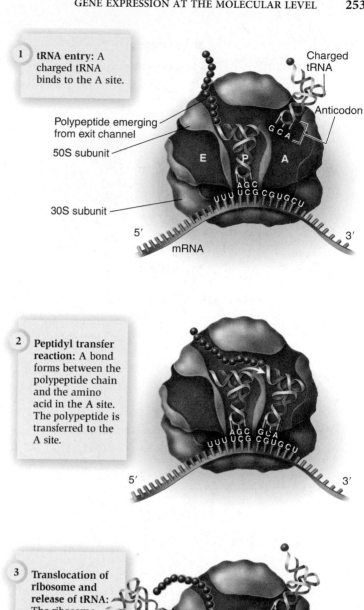

1 tRNA entry: A charged tRNA binds to the A site.

Charged tRNA

Polypeptide emerging from exit channel

50S subunit

Anticodon

E   P   A

30S subunit

5′   3′

mRNA

2 Peptidyl transfer reaction: A bond forms between the polypeptide chain and the amino acid in the A site. The polypeptide is transferred to the A site.

5′   3′

3 Translocation of ribosome and release of tRNA: The ribosome translocates 1 codon to the right. The uncharged tRNA is released from the E site. This process is repeated again and again until a stop codon is reached.

5′   3′

Figure 12.19 Elongation stage of translation in bacteria. In this drawing, the amino acids that were already contained within a polypeptide are shown in blue. The amino acids attached to incoming tRNAs in this figure are shown in yellow to distinguish them from the amino acids that were already in the polypeptide.

In the second step, a peptide bond is formed between the amino acid at the A site and the growing polypeptide, thereby lengthening the polypeptide by one amino acid. As this occurs, the polypeptide is removed from the tRNA in the P site and transferred to the amino acid at the A site, an event termed a **peptidyl transfer reaction**. This reaction is catalyzed by a region of the 50S subunit known as the peptidyltransferase center, which is composed of several proteins and rRNA. In 2000, American biochemist Thomas Steitz, American biophysicist Peter Moore, and their colleagues proposed that the rRNA is responsible for catalyzing the peptide bond formation between adjacent amino acids. It is now accepted that the ribosome is a ribozyme!

After the peptidyl transfer reaction is complete, the third step involves the movement or translocation of the ribosome toward the 3′ end of the mRNA by exactly one codon. This shifts the tRNAs in the

P and A sites to the E and P sites, respectively. The uncharged tRNA exits the E site. Notice that the next codon in the mRNA (GCU in Figure 12.19) is now exposed at the unoccupied A site. At this point, a charged tRNA can enter the A site, and the same series of steps will add the next amino acid to the polypeptide.

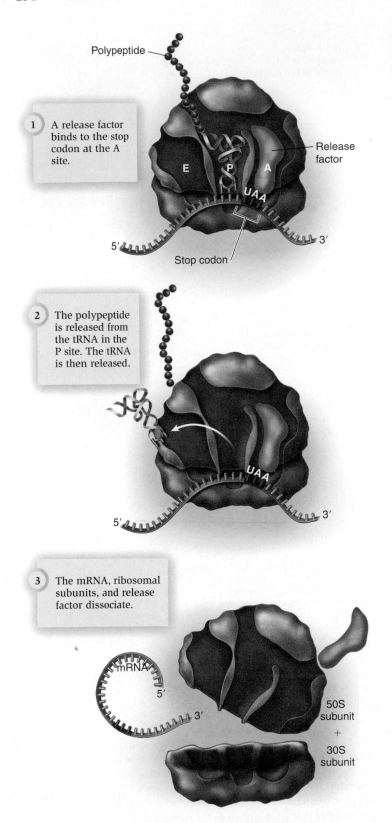

1 A release factor binds to the stop codon at the A site.

Release factor

E P A

UAA

5′ ⎓⎓⎓⎓⎓⎓⎓⎓⎓⎓⎓⎓⎓⎓ 3′

Stop codon

Polypeptide

2 The polypeptide is released from the tRNA in the P site. The tRNA is then released.

UAA

5′ ⎓⎓⎓⎓⎓⎓⎓⎓⎓⎓⎓⎓⎓⎓ 3′

3 The mRNA, ribosomal subunits, and release factor dissociate.

mRNA

5′

3′

50S subunit

+

30S subunit

Figure 12.20 Termination of translation in bacteria.

Table 12.4	Comparison of Bacterial and Eukaryotic Translation	
	Bacterial	**Eukaryotic**
Cellular location	Cytoplasm	Cytosol*
Ribosome composition	70S ribosomes:	80S ribosomes:
	30S subunit: 21 proteins + 1 rRNA	40S subunit: 33 proteins + 1 rRNA
	50S subunit: 34 proteins + 2 rRNAs	60S subunit: 49 proteins + 3 rRNAs
Initiator tRNA	tRNA$^{\text{Formyl-methionine}}$	tRNA^{Methionine}
Initial binding of mRNA	Requires a ribosomal-binding site	Requires a 7-methylguanosine cap
Selection of a start codon	Just downstream from the ribosomal-binding site	According to Kozak's sequences
Termination factors	Two factors: RF1 and RF2	One factor: eRF

*The components for eukaryotic translation described in this table refer to those that are used in the cytosol. Different types of ribosomes are used for translation inside mitochondria and chloroplasts.

Figure 12.19 considers a single ribosome in the act of translating an mRNA. In living cells, it is common for multiple ribosomes to be gliding along the same mRNA and synthesizing polypeptides. The complex of a single mRNA and multiple ribosomes is called a **polysome** (see Chapter opening micrograph).

Termination Occurs When a Stop Codon Is Reached in the mRNA

Elongation continues until a stop codon moves into the A site of a ribosome. The three stop codons, UAA, UAG, and UGA, are not recognized by a tRNA with a complementary sequence. Instead, they are recognized by a protein known as a **release factor**. The three-dimensional structure of a release factor protein mimics the structure of tRNAs, which allows it to fit into the A site.

Figure 12.20 illustrates the termination of translation. In step 1 of this figure, a release factor binds to the stop codon at the A site. The completed polypeptide is attached to a tRNA in the P site. In the second step, the bond between the polypeptide and the tRNA is hydrolyzed, causing the polypeptide and tRNA to be released from the ribosome. In the third step, the mRNA, ribosomal subunits, and release factor dissociate. The termination stage of translation is similar in bacteria and eukaryotes except that bacteria have two different termination factors that recognize stop codons (RF1 and RF2), whereas eukaryotes have only one (eRF). **Table 12.4** compares some of the key differences between bacterial and eukaryotic translation.

Summary of Key Concepts

12.1 Overview of Gene Expression

- Based on his studies of inborn errors of metabolism, Garrod hypothesized that certain genetic diseases are caused by a defect in a gene encoding an enzyme (Figure 12.1).

- By studying the nutritional requirements of bread mold, Beadle and Tatum proposed the one-gene/one-enzyme hypothesis in which a single gene controls the synthesis of a single enzyme (Figure 12.2).

- A polypeptide is a unit of structure. A protein, composed of one or more polypeptides, is a unit of function.

- At the molecular level, the central dogma states that most genes are transcribed into mRNA, and then the mRNA is translated into polypeptides. Eukaryotes modify their RNA transcripts to make them functional (Figure 12.3).

- The molecular expression of genes is an underlying factor that determines an organism's characteristics.

12.2 Transcription

- A site in a gene called a promoter specifies where transcription begins. A terminator specifies where transcription will end (Figure 12.4).

- In bacteria, the initiation of transcription begins when sigma factor binds to RNA polymerase and to a promoter. During elongation, an RNA transcript is synthesized due to base pairing of nucleotides to the template strand of DNA as RNA polymerase slides along the DNA. RNA polymerase and the RNA transcript dissociate from the DNA at the terminator (Figure 12.5).

- The genes along a chromosome are transcribed in different directions using either DNA strand as a template. RNA is always synthesized in a 5′ to 3′ direction (Figure 12.6).

12.3 RNA Processing in Eukaryotes

- In eukaryotes, transcription produces a pre-mRNA that is capped, spliced, and given a poly A tail (Figure 12.7).

- During RNA splicing, intervening sequences called introns are removed from eukaryotic pre-mRNA by a spliceosome (Figure 12.8).

- The 5′ cap is a methylated guanine base at the 5′ end of the mRNA. The poly A tail is a string of adenine nucleotides that is added to the 3′ end (Figure 12.9).

12.4 Translation and the Genetic Code

- Based on the genetic code, each of the 64 codons specifies a start codon (methionine), other amino acids, or a stop codon (Table 12.1, Figure 12.10).

- The template strand of DNA is used to make mRNA with a series of codons. Recognition between mRNA and many tRNA molecules determines the amino acid sequence of a polypeptide. A polypeptide has a directionality in which the first amino acid is at the N-terminus, or amino terminus, whereas the last amino acid is at the C-terminus, or carboxyl terminus (Figure 12.11).

- Nirenberg and Leder used the ability of RNA triplets to promote the binding of tRNA to ribosomes as a way to determine many of the codons of the genetic code (Figure 12.12).

12.5 The Machinery of Translation

- Translation requires mRNA, charged tRNAs, ribosomes, and many translation factors (Table 12.2).

- tRNA molecules have a cloverleaf structure. Two important sites are the amino acid attachment site at the 3′ end and the anticodon, which forms base-pairs with a codon in mRNA (Figure 12.13).

- The enzyme aminoacyl-tRNA synthetase attaches the correct amino acid to a tRNA molecule, producing a charged tRNA (Figure 12.14).

- Ribosomes are composed of a small and large subunit, each consisting of rRNA molecules and many proteins. Bacterial and eukaryotic ribosomes differ in their molecular composition (Table 12.3).

- Ribosomes have three sites, termed the A, P, and E sites, which are locations for the binding and release of tRNA molecules (Figure 12.15).

- The gene that encodes the small subunit rRNA (SSU rRNA) has been used to determine evolutionary relationships among different species (Figure 12.16).

12.6 The Stages of Translation

- Translation occurs in three stages called initiation, elongation, and termination (Figure 12.17).

- During initiation of translation, the mRNA assembles with the ribosomal subunits and the initiator tRNA molecule, which carries methionine, the initial amino acid (Figure 12.18).

- During elongation, amino acids are added one at a time to a growing polypeptide (Figure 12.19).

- Termination of translation occurs when the binding of a release factor to a stop codon causes the release of the completed polypeptide from the tRNA and the disassembly of the mRNA, ribosomal subunits, and release factor (Figure 12.20).

- Though translation in bacteria and eukaryotes is strikingly similar, some key differences have been observed (Table 12.4).

Assess and Discuss

Test Yourself

1. Which of the following best represents the central dogma of gene expression?
    a. During transcription, DNA codes for polypeptides.
    b. During transcription, DNA codes for mRNA, which codes for polypeptides during translation.
    c. During translation, DNA codes for mRNA, which codes for polypeptides during transcription.
    d. none of the above

2. Transcription of a gene begins at a site on DNA called ___ and ends at a site on DNA known as ___.
    a. the start codon, the stop codon
    b. a promoter, the stop codon
    c. the start codon, the terminator
    d. a promoter, the terminator
    e. none of the above

3. The functional product of a structural gene is
   a. tRNA.
   b. mRNA.
   c. rRNA.
   d. a polypeptide.
   e. a, b, and c.

4. During eukaryotic RNA processing, the nontranslated sequences that are removed are called
   a. exons.
   b. introns.
   c. promoters.
   d. codons.
   e. ribozymes.

5. The ___ is the site where the translation process takes place.
   a. mitochondria
   b. nucleus
   c. ribosome
   d. lysosome
   e. ribozyme

6. The small subunit of a ribosome is composed of
   a. a protein.
   b. an rRNA molecule.
   c. many proteins.
   d. many rRNA molecules.
   e. many proteins and one rRNA molecule.

7. The region of the tRNA that is complementary to a codon in mRNA is
   a. the acceptor stem.
   b. the codon.
   c. the peptidyl site.
   d. the anticodon.
   e. the adaptor loop.

8. During the initiation of translation, the first codon, ____, enters the _____ and associates with the initiator tRNA.
   a. UAG, A site
   b. AUG, A site
   c. UAG, P site
   d. AUG, P site
   e. AUG, E site

9. The movement of the polypeptide from the tRNA in the P site to the tRNA in the A site is referred to as
   a. peptide bonding.
   b. aminoacyl binding.
   c. translation.
   d. the peptidyl transfer reaction.
   e. elongation.

10. The synthesis of a polypeptide occurs during which stage of translation?
    a. initiation
    b. elongation
    c. termination
    d. splicing

Conceptual Questions

1. Describe the one-gene/one-enzyme hypothesis and the more modern modifications of this hypothesis. Briefly explain how studying the pathway that leads to arginine synthesis allowed Beadle and Tatum to conclude that one gene sometimes encodes one enzyme.

2. What is the function of an aminoacyl-tRNA synthetase?

3. A principle of biology is that *the genetic material provides a blueprint for reproduction.* Explain how the information within the blueprint is accessed at the molecular level.

Collaborative Questions

1. Why do you think some complexes, such as spliceosomes and ribosomes, have both protein and RNA components?

2. Discuss and make a list of the similarities and differences in the events that occur during the initiation, elongation, and termination stages of transcription and translation.

Online Resource

www.brookerbiology3e.com

Stay a step ahead in your studies with animations that bring concepts to life and practice tests to assess your understanding. Your instructor may also recommend the interactive eBook, individualized learning tools, and more.

Gene Regulation

13

E milio took a weight-lifting class in college and was surprised by the results. Within a few weeks, he was able to lift substantially more weight. He was inspired by this progress and continued lifting weights after the semester-long course ended. A year later, he was not only much stronger, but he could see physical changes in his body. Certain muscles, such as the biceps and triceps in his upper arms, were noticeably larger. How can we explain the increase in mass of Emilio's muscles? Unknowingly, when he was lifting weights, Emilio was affecting the regulation of his genes. Certain genes in his muscle cells were being "turned on" during his workouts, which then led to the synthesis of proteins that increased the mass of Emilio's muscles.

At the molecular level, **gene expression** is the process by which the information within a gene is made into a functional product, such as an RNA molecule or a protein. Most genes in all species are regulated so the proteins they specify are produced at appropriate times and in specific amounts. The term **gene regulation** refers to the ability of cells to control the expression of their genes. By comparison, some genes have relatively constant levels of expression in all conditions over time. These are called **constitutive genes**. Frequently, constitutive genes encode proteins that are always required for the survival of an organism, such as certain metabolic enzymes.

The importance of gene regulation is underscored by the number of genes devoted to this process in an organism. For example, in *Arabidopsis thaliana*, a plant that is studied by many plant geneticists, over 5% of its genome is involved with regulating gene transcription. This species has more than 1,500 different genes that encode proteins that regulate the transcription of other genes.

In this chapter, we will begin with an overview that emphasizes the benefits of gene regulation and the general mechanisms that achieve such regulation in bacteria and in eukaryotes. Later sections will describe how bacteria regulate gene expression in the face of environmental change and the more complex nature of gene regulation in eukaryotes.

A model for a protein that binds to DNA and regulates genes. The catabolite activator protein (CAP), shown in dark and light blue, is binding to the DNA double helix, shown in orange and white. The CAP, shown again in Figure 13.10, activates gene transcription.

13.1 Overview of Gene Regulation

Learning Outcomes:

1. Discuss the various ways that organisms benefit from gene regulation.
2. Identify where gene regulation can occur in the pathway of gene expression for bacteria and eukaryotes.

How do living organisms benefit from gene regulation? One reason is that it conserves energy. Proteins that are encoded by genes will be produced only when they are needed. In multicellular organisms, gene regulation also ensures that genes are expressed in the appropriate cell types and at the correct stage of development. In this section, we will examine a few examples that illustrate the important consequences of gene regulation. We will also survey the major points in the gene expression process at which genes are regulated in bacterial and eukaryotic cells.

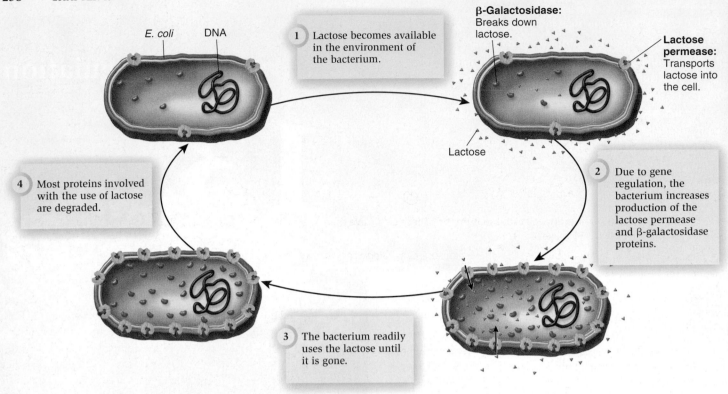

Figure 13.1 Gene regulation of lactose utilization in *E. coli*.

 BIOLOGY PRINCIPLE Living organisms use energy. Gene regulation provides a way for organisms to avoid wasting energy. They make proteins only when they are needed.

Bacteria Regulate Genes to Respond to Changes in Their Environment

The bacterium *Escherichia coli* can use many types of sugars as food sources, thereby increasing its chances of survival. With regard to gene regulation, we will focus on how it uses lactose, which is the sugar found in milk. *E. coli* carries genes that code for proteins that enable it to take up lactose from the environment and metabolize it.

Figure 13.1 illustrates the effects of lactose on the regulation of those genes. In order to utilize lactose, an *E. coli* cell requires a transporter, called lactose permease, that facilitates the uptake of lactose into the cell, and an enzyme, called β-galactosidase, that catalyzes the breakdown of lactose. When lactose is not present in the environment, an *E. coli* cell makes very little of these proteins. However, when lactose becomes available, the bacterium produces many more copies of these proteins, enabling it to readily use lactose from its environment. Eventually, all of the lactose in the environment is used up. At this point, the genes encoding these proteins will be shut off, and most of the proteins will be degraded. Overall, gene regulation conserves energy because it ensures that the proteins needed for lactose utilization are made only when lactose is present in the environment.

Eukaryotic Gene Regulation Produces Different Cell Types in a Single Organism

One of the most amazing examples of gene regulation is the phenomenon of **cell differentiation**, the process by which cells become specialized into particular types. In humans, for example, cells may differentiate into muscle cells, neurons, skin cells, or other types. **Figure 13.2** shows micrographs of three types of cells found in humans. As seen here, their morphologies are strikingly different. Likewise, their functions within the body are also quite different. Muscle cells are important in body movements, neurons function in cell signaling, and skin cells form a protective outer surface to the body.

Gene regulation is responsible for producing different types of cells within a multicellular organism. The three cell types shown in Figure 13.2 contain the same **genome**, meaning they carry the same set of genes. However, their **proteomes**—the collection of proteins they make—are quite different. Certain proteins are found in particular cell types but not in others. Alternatively, a protein may be present in all three cell types, but the relative amounts of the protein may be different. The amount of a given protein depends on many factors, including how strongly the corresponding gene is turned on and how much protein is synthesized from mRNA. Gene regulation plays a major role in determining the proteome of each cell type.

Eukaryotic Gene Regulation Enables Multicellular Organisms to Proceed Through Developmental Stages

In multicellular organisms that progress through developmental stages, certain genes are expressed at particular stages of development but not others. Let's consider an example of such gene regulation in mammals. Early stages of development occur in the uterus of female mammals. Following fertilization, an embryo develops inside the uterus. In humans, the embryonic stage lasts from fertilization to 8 weeks. During this stage, major developmental changes produce

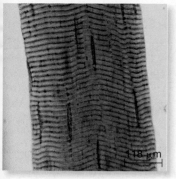

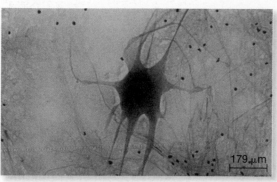

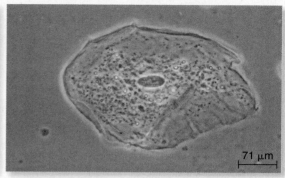

(a) Skeletal muscle cell   (b) Neuron   (c) Skin cell

Figure 13.2 **Examples of different cell types in humans.** These cells have the same genetic composition. Their unique morphologies are due to differences in the proteins they make.

Concept Check: *How does gene regulation underlie the different morphologies of these cells?*

the various body parts. The fetal stage occurs from 8 weeks to birth (41 weeks). This stage is characterized by continued refinement of body parts and a large increase in size.

The oxygen demands of a rapidly growing embryo and fetus are quite different from the needs of the mother. Gene regulation plays a vital role in ensuring that an embryo and fetus get the proper amount of oxygen. Hemoglobin is a protein that delivers oxygen to the cells of a mammal's body. A hemoglobin protein is composed of four globin polypeptides, two encoded by one globin gene and two encoded by another globin gene (**Figure 13.3**). The genomes of mammals carry several genes (designated with Greek letters) that encode slightly different globin polypeptides. During the embryonic stage of development, the epsilon (ε)- and zeta (ζ)-globin genes are turned on. At the fetal stage, these genes are turned off, and the alpha (α)- and gamma

(γ)-globin genes are turned on. Finally, at birth, the γ-globin gene is turned off, and the beta (β)-globin gene is turned on.

How do the embryo and fetus acquire oxygen from their mother's bloodstream? The hemoglobin produced during the embryonic and fetal stages has a higher binding affinity for oxygen than does the hemoglobin produced after birth. Therefore, the embryo and fetus can remove oxygen from the mother's bloodstream and use that oxygen for their own needs. This occurs across the placenta, where the mother's bloodstream is adjacent to the bloodstream of the embryo or fetus. In this way, gene regulation enables mammals to develop internally, even though the embryo and fetus are not breathing on their own. Gene regulation ensures that the correct hemoglobin protein is produced at the right time in development. We'll discuss how gene expression controls the process of development in greater detail in Chapter 19.

Gene Regulation Occurs at Different Points in the Process from DNA to Protein

Thus far, we have learned that gene regulation has a dramatic influence on the ability of organisms to respond to environmental changes, produce different types of cells, and progress through developmental stages. For genes that encode proteins, the regulation of gene expression can occur at any of the steps that are needed to produce a functional protein.

In bacteria, gene regulation most commonly occurs at the level of transcription, which means that bacteria regulate how much mRNA is made from genes (**Figure 13.4a**). When geneticists say a gene is "turned off," they mean that very little or no mRNA is made from that gene, whereas a gene that is "turned on" is transcribed into mRNA. Because transcription is the first step in gene expression, transcriptional regulation is a particularly efficient way to regulate genes because cells avoid wasting energy when the product of the gene is not needed. A second way for bacteria to regulate gene expression is to control the ability of an mRNA to be translated into protein. This form of gene regulation is less common in bacteria. Last, gene expression can be regulated at the protein or post-translational level.

In eukaryotes, gene regulation occurs at many levels, including transcription, RNA processing, translation, and after translation is completed (**Figure 13.4b**). As in their bacterial counterparts,

	Embryo	Fetus	Adult
Hemoglobin protein	2 ζ-globins 2 ε-globins	2 α-globins 2 γ-globins	2 α-globins 2 β-globins
Oxygen affinity	Highest	High	Moderate
Gene expression			
α-globin gene	Off	On	On
β-globin gene	Off	Off	On
γ-globin gene	Off	On	Off
ζ-globin gene	On	Off	Off
ε-globin gene	On	Off	Off

Figure 13.3 **Regulation of human globin genes at different stages of development.**

BIOLOGY PRINCIPLE **Living organisms grow and develop.** Gene regulation is an important process that allows organisms to proceed through developmental stages.

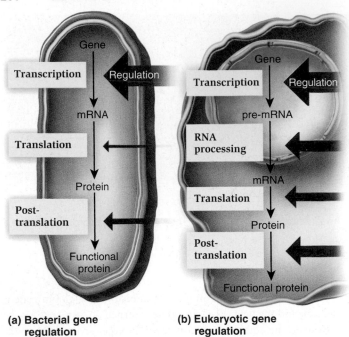

Figure 13.4 **Overview of gene regulation in (a) bacteria and (b) eukaryotes.** The relative width of the red arrows indicates the prominence with which gene regulation is used to control the production of functional proteins.

transcriptional regulation is a prominent form of gene regulation for eukaryotes. As discussed later in this chapter, eukaryotic genes are transcriptionally regulated in several different ways, some of which are not found in bacteria. As discussed in Chapter 12, eukaryotes process their mRNA transcripts in ways that do not commonly occur in bacteria (refer back to Figure 12.3). For example, RNA splicing is a widespread phenomenon in eukaryotes. Later in this chapter, we will examine how this process is regulated to produce two or more different types of mRNA from a single gene. Eukaryotes can also regulate an mRNA after its modification. The translation of mRNA may be regulated by small, inhibitory RNA molecules or by RNA-binding proteins that prevent translation from occurring.

As in bacteria, eukaryotic proteins can be regulated in a variety of ways other than gene regulation, including cellular regulation and biochemical regulation (such as feedback inhibition). These various types of regulation are best understood within the context of cell biology, so they were primarily discussed in Unit II (see Chapter 6 and Figure 6.13). Post-translational modifications are also summarized in Chapter 21 (look ahead to Figure 21.10b).

13.2 Regulation of Transcription in Bacteria

Learning Outcomes:

1. Explain how regulatory transcription factors and small effector molecules are involved in the regulation of transcription.
2. Describe the organization of the *lac* operon and how it is under negative and positive control.
3. Analyze the results of the experiments of Jacob, Monod, and Pardee.
4. Describe how the *trp* operon is under negative control.

As we have seen, when a bacterium is exposed to a particular nutrient in its environment, such as a sugar, the genes are expressed that encode proteins needed for the uptake and metabolism of that sugar. In addition, bacteria have genes that encode enzymes that synthesize molecules such as particular amino acids. In such cases, the control of gene expression often occurs at the level of transcription. In this section, we will examine the underlying molecular mechanisms that bring about transcriptional regulation in bacteria.

Transcriptional Regulation Involves Regulatory Transcription Factors and Small Effector Molecules

In most cases, regulation of transcription involves the actions of **regulatory transcription factors**—proteins that bind to **regulatory sequences** in the DNA in the vicinity of a promoter and affect the rate of transcription of one or more nearby genes. These transcription factors either decrease or increase the rate of transcription of a gene. **Repressors** are regulatory transcription factors that bind to the DNA and decrease the rate of transcription. This is a form of regulation called **negative control**. **Activators** bind to the DNA and increase the rate of transcription, a form of regulation termed **positive control** (**Figure 13.5a**).

In conjunction with regulatory transcription factors, molecules called **small effector molecules** often play a critical role in transcriptional regulation. A small effector molecule exerts its effects by binding to a regulatory transcription factor and causing a conformational change in the protein. In many cases, the effect of the conformational change determines whether or not the protein can bind to the DNA. **Figure 13.5b** illustrates an example involving a repressor. When the small effector molecule is not present in the cytoplasm, the repressor binds to the DNA and inhibits transcription. However, when the small effector molecule is subsequently found in the cytoplasm, it will bind to the repressor and cause a conformational change that inhibits the ability of the protein to bind to the DNA. Transcription can occur because the repressor is not able to bind to the DNA. Repressors and activators that respond to small effector molecules have two functional regions called domains. One domain is a site where the protein binds to the DNA, whereas the other is the binding site for the small effector molecule.

The *lac* Operon Contains Genes That Encode Proteins Involved in Lactose Metabolism

In bacteria, structural genes are sometimes clustered together and under the transcriptional control of a single promoter. This arrangement is known as an **operon**. The transcription of the genes occurs as a single unit and results in the production of a **polycistronic mRNA**, an mRNA that encodes more than one protein. What advantage is this arrangement? An operon organization allows a bacterium to coordinately regulate a group of genes that encode proteins whose functions are used in a common pathway.

The genome of *E. coli* carries an operon, called the *lac* **operon**, that contains the genes for the proteins that allow it to metabolize lactose (see Figure 13.1). **Figure 13.6a** shows the organization of this operon as it is found in the *E. coli* chromosome, as well as the polycistronic mRNA that is transcribed from it. The *lac* operon

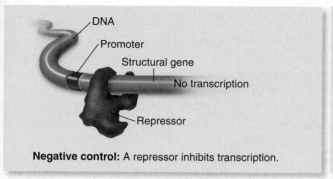

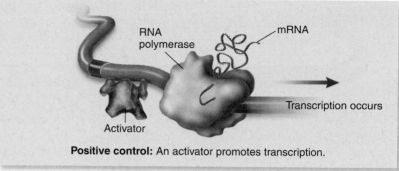

Negative control: A repressor inhibits transcription.

Positive control: An activator promotes transcription.

(a) Actions of regulatory transcription factors

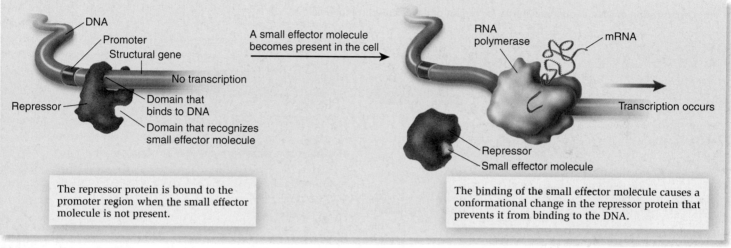

A small effector molecule becomes present in the cell

The repressor protein is bound to the promoter region when the small effector molecule is not present.

The binding of the small effector molecule causes a conformational change in the repressor protein that prevents it from binding to the DNA.

(b) Action of a small effector molecule on a repressor

Figure 13.5 **Actions of regulatory transcription factors and small effector molecules.** **(a)** Regulatory transcription factors are proteins that exert negative or positive control. **(b)** One way that a small effector molecule may exert its effects is by preventing a repressor protein from binding to the DNA.

contains a promoter, *lacP*, that is used to transcribe three structural genes: *lacZ*, *lacY*, and *lacA*. *LacZ* encodes β-galactosidase, which is an enzyme that breaks down lactose (**Figure 13.6b**). As a side reaction, β-galactosidase also converts a small percentage of lactose into allolactose, a structurally similar sugar or lactose analogue. As described later, allolactose is important in the regulation of the *lac* operon. The *lacY* gene encodes lactose permease, which is a membrane protein required for the transport of lactose into the cytoplasm of the bacterium. The *lacA* gene encodes galactoside transacetylase, which covalently modifies lactose and lactose analogues by attaching an acetyl group (—COCH₃). Although the functional necessity of this enzyme remains unclear, the attachment of acetyl groups to nonmetabolizable lactose analogues may prevent their toxic buildup in the cytoplasm.

Near the *lac* promoter are two regulatory sequences designated the operator and the CAP site (see Figure 13.6a). The **operator**, or *lacO* site, is a regulatory sequence in the DNA. The sequence of bases at the *lacO* site provides a binding site for a repressor protein. The **CAP site** is a regulatory sequence recognized by an activator protein.

Adjacent to the *lac* operon is the *lacI* gene, which encodes the **lac repressor**. This repressor protein is important for the regulation of the *lac* operon. The *lacI* gene, which is constitutively expressed at fairly low levels, has its own promoter called the *i* promoter. The *lacI*

gene is not considered a part of the *lac* operon. Let's now take a look at how the *lac* operon is regulated by the lac repressor.

The *lac* Operon Is Under Negative Control by a Repressor Protein

In the late 1950s, the first researchers to investigate gene regulation were French biologists François Jacob and Jacques Monod at the Pasteur Institute in Paris, France. Their focus on gene regulation stemmed from an interest in the phenomenon known as enzyme adaptation, which had been identified early in the 20th century. Enzyme adaptation occurs when a particular enzyme appears within a living cell only after the cell has been exposed to the substrate for that enzyme. Jacob and Monod studied lactose metabolism in *E. coli* to investigate this phenomenon. When they exposed bacteria to lactose, the levels of lactose-using enzymes in the cells increased by 1,000- to 10,000-fold. After lactose was removed, the synthesis of the enzymes abruptly stopped.

The first mechanism of regulation that Jacob and Monod discovered involved the lac repressor, which binds to the sequence of nucleotides found at the *lac* operator site. Once bound, the lac repressor prevents RNA polymerase from transcribing the *lacZ*, *lacY*, and

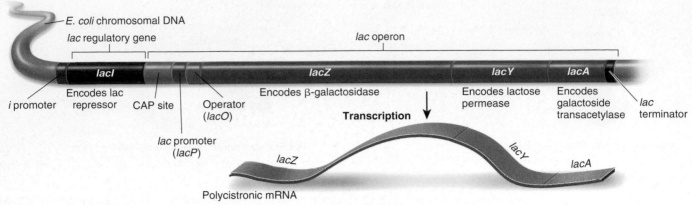

(a) Organization of DNA sequences in the *lac* region of the *E. coli* chromosome

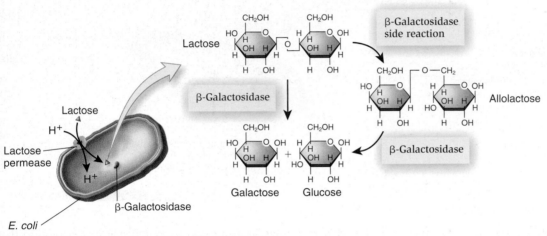

(b) Functions of lactose permease and β-galactosidase

Figure 13.6   The *lac* operon.   (a) This diagram depicts a region of the *E. coli* chromosome that contains the *lacI* gene and the adjacent *lac* operon, as well as the polycistronic mRNA transcribed from the operon. The mRNA is translated into three proteins: lactose permease, β-galactosidase, and galactoside transacetylase. **(b)** Lactose permease cotransports H⁺ with lactose. Bacteria maintain an H⁺ gradient across their cytoplasmic membrane that drives the active transport of lactose into the cytoplasm. β-Galactosidase cleaves lactose into galactose and glucose. As a side reaction, it can also convert lactose into allolactose.

Concept Check: *Which genes are under the control of the lac promoter?*

lacA genes (**Figure 13.7a**). RNA polymerase can bind to the promoter when the lac repressor is bound to the operator site, but cannot move past the operator to transcribe the *lacZ*, *lacY*, and *lacA* genes.

Whether or not the lac repressor binds to the operator site depends on allolactose, which is the previously mentioned side product of the β-galactosidase enzyme (see Figure 13.6b). How does allolactose control the lac repressor? Allolactose is an example of a small effector molecule. The lac repressor protein contains four identical subunits, each one recognizing a single allolactose molecule. When four allolactose molecules bind to the lac repressor, a conformational change occurs that prevents the repressor from binding to the operator. Under these conditions, RNA polymerase is free to transcribe the operon (**Figure 13.7b**).

The regulation of the *lac* operon enables *E. coli* to conserve energy because lactose-utilizing proteins are made only when lactose is present in the environment. Allolactose is **an inducer**, a small

effector molecule that increases the rate of transcription, and the *lac* operon is said to be an **inducible operon**. When the bacterium is not exposed to lactose, no allolactose is available to bind to the lac repressor. Therefore, the lac repressor binds to the operator site and inhibits transcription. In reality, the repressor does not completely inhibit transcription, so very small amounts of β-galactosidase, lactose permease, and galactoside transacetylase are made. Even so, the levels are far too low for the bacterium to readily use lactose. When the bacterium is exposed to lactose, a small amount can be transported into the cytoplasm via lactose permease, and β-galactosidase converts some of it to allolactose (see Figure 13.6b). The cytoplasmic level of allolactose gradually rises until allolactose binds to the lac repressor, which induces the *lac* operon and promotes a high rate of transcription of the *lacZ*, *lacY*, and *lacA* genes. Translation of the encoded polypeptides produces the proteins needed for lactose uptake and metabolism as described previously in Figure 13.1.

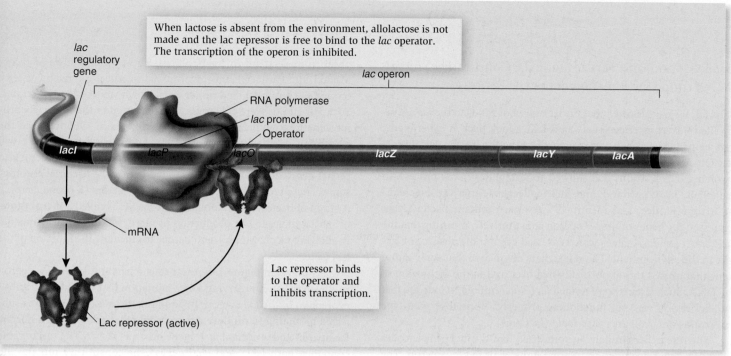

When lactose is absent from the environment, allolactose is not made and the lac repressor is free to bind to the *lac* operator. The transcription of the operon is inhibited.

lac regulatory gene

lac operon

RNA polymerase

lac promoter

Operator

lacI   lacP   lacO   lacZ   lacY   lacA

mRNA

Lac repressor binds to the operator and inhibits transcription.

Lac repressor (active)

(a) Lactose absent from the environment

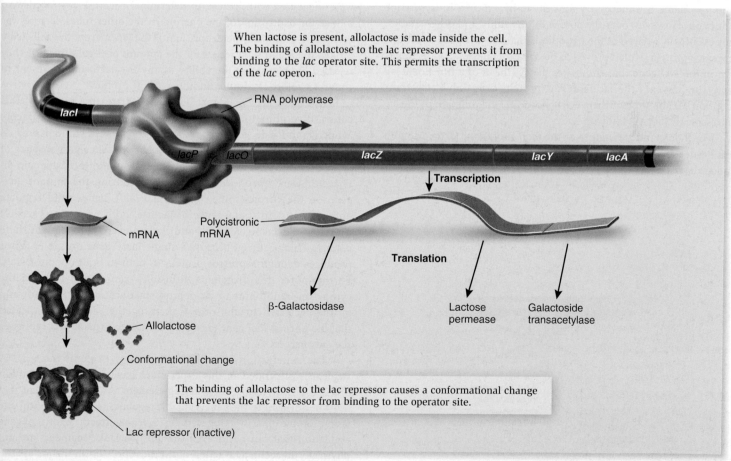

When lactose is present, allolactose is made inside the cell. The binding of allolactose to the lac repressor prevents it from binding to the *lac* operator site. This permits the transcription of the *lac* operon.

RNA polymerase

lacI   lacP   lacO   lacZ   lacY   lacA

Transcription

mRNA

Polycistronic mRNA

Translation

β-Galactosidase   Lactose permease   Galactoside transacetylase

Allolactose

Conformational change

The binding of allolactose to the lac repressor causes a conformational change that prevents the lac repressor from binding to the operator site.

Lac repressor (inactive)

(b) Lactose present

Figure 13.7 Negative control of an inducible set of genes: function of the lac repressor in regulating the *lac* operon.

Concept Check: *With regard to regulatory proteins and small effector molecules, explain the meaning of the terms "negative control" and "inducible."*

FEATURE INVESTIGATION

Jacob, Monod, and Pardee Studied a Constitutive Mutant to Determine the Function of the Lac Repressor

Thus far, we have learned that the lac repressor binds to the *lac* operator site to exert its effects. Let's now take a look back at experiments that helped researchers determine the function of the lac repressor. Our understanding of *lac* operon regulation came from studies involving *E. coli* strains that showed abnormalities in the process. In the 1950s, Jacob, Monod, and their colleague, American biochemist Arthur Pardee, had identified a few rare mutant bacteria that expressed the genes of the *lac* operon constitutively, meaning that the *lacZ*, *lacY*, and *lacA* genes were expressed even in the absence of lactose in the environment. The researchers discovered that some mutations that caused this abnormality had occurred in the *lacI* region of the DNA. Such strains were termed *lacI⁻* (*lacI* minus) to indicate that the *lacI* region was not functioning properly. Normal or wild-type *lacI* strains of *E. coli* are called *lacI⁺* (*lacI* plus).

The researchers initially hypothesized that the *lacI* gene encodes an enzyme that degrades an internal inducer of the *lac* operon. The *lacI⁻* mutation was thought to inhibit this enzyme, thereby allowing the internal inducer to always be synthesized. In this way, the *lacI⁻* mutation made it unnecessary for cells to be exposed to lactose for induction. However, over the course of this study and other studies, they eventually arrived at the hypothesis that the *lacI* gene encodes a repressor protein, which proved to be correct (**Figure 13.8**). A mutation in the *lacI* gene that eliminates the synthesis of a functional lac repressor prevents the lac repressor protein from inhibiting transcription. At the time of their work, however, the function of the lac repressor was not yet known.

To understand the nature of the *lacI⁻* mutation, Jacob, Monod, and Pardee applied a genetic approach. Although bacterial conjugation is described in Chapter 18, let's briefly examine this process in

order to understand this experiment. The earliest studies of Jacob, Monod, and Pardee in 1959 involved matings between recipient cells, termed F⁻ (F minus), and donor cells, which were called Hfr strains. Such Hfr strains were able to transfer a portion of the bacterial chromosome to a recipient cell. Later experiments in 1961 involved the transfer of circular segments of DNA known as F factors. We will consider this later type of experiment here. Sometimes an F factor also carries genes that were originally found within the bacterial chromosome. These types of F factors are called F′ factors (F prime factors). A strain of bacteria containing F′ factor genes is called a **merozygote**, or partial diploid. The production of merozygotes was instrumental in allowing Jacob, Monod, and Pardee to elucidate the function of the *lacI* gene.

As shown in **Figure 13.9**, these researchers studied the *lac* operon in a bacterial strain carrying a *lacI⁻* mutation that caused constitutive expression of the *lac* operon. In addition, the mutant strain was subjected to mating to produce a merozygote that also carried a normal *lac* operon and a normal *lacI⁺* gene on an F′ factor. The merozygote contained both *lacI⁺* and *lacI⁻* genes. The constitutive mutant and corresponding merozygote were grown separately in liquid media and then divided into two tubes each. In half of the tubes, the cells were incubated with lactose to determine if lactose was needed to induce the expression of the operon. In the other tubes, lactose was omitted. To monitor the expression of the *lac* operon, the cells were broken open and then tested for the amount of β-galactosidase they released by measuring the ability of any β-galactosidase present to convert a colorless compound into a yellow product.

The data table of Figure 13.9 summarizes the effects of this constitutive mutation and its analysis in a merozygote. As Jacob, Monod, and Pardee already knew, the *lacI⁻* mutant strain expressed the *lac* operon constitutively, in both the presence and absence of lactose. However, when a normal *lac* operon and *lacI⁺* gene on an F′ factor were introduced into a cell harboring the mutant *lacI⁻* gene on the chromosome, the normal *lacI⁺* gene could regulate both operons. In the absence of lactose, both operons were shut off. How did Jacob, Monod, and Pardee eventually explain these results? This occurred because a single *lacI⁺* gene on the F′ factor produces enough repressor protein to bind to both operator sites. Furthermore, this protein is diffusible—can spread through the cytoplasm—and binds to *lac* operons that are on the F′ factor and on the bacterial chromosome. Taken together, the data indicated that the normal *lacI* gene encodes a diffusible protein that represses the *lac* operon.

The interactions between regulatory proteins and DNA sequences illustrated in this experiment have led to the definition of three genetic terms. A **cis-acting element** is a DNA segment that must be adjacent to the gene(s) that it regulates. The *lac* operator site is an example of a *cis*-acting element. A **trans-effect** is a form of gene regulation that can occur even though two DNA segments are not physically adjacent. The action of the lac repressor on the *lac* operon is a *trans*-effect. A **cis-effect** is mediated by a *cis*-acting element that binds regulatory proteins, whereas a *trans*-effect is mediated by genes that encode diffusible regulatory proteins.

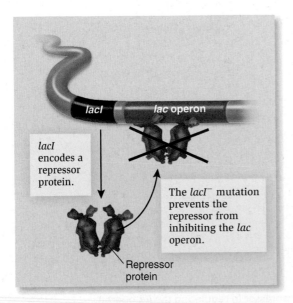

Figure 13.8 A hypothesis for the function of the *lacI* gene.

lacI encodes a repressor protein.

The *lacI⁻* mutation prevents the repressor from inhibiting the *lac* operon.

Repressor protein

Experimental Questions

1. What were the key observations made by Jacob, Monod, and Pardee that led to the development of their hypothesis regarding the *lacI* gene and the regulation of the *lac* operon?

2. What was the eventual hypothesis proposed by the researchers to explain the function of the *lacI* gene and the regulation of the *lac* operon?

3. How did Jacob, Monod, and Pardee test the hypothesis? What were the results of the experiment? How do these results support the idea that the *lacI* gene produces a repressor protein?

Figure 13.9 The experiment performed by Jacob, Monod, and Pardee to study a constitutive *lacI⁻* mutant.

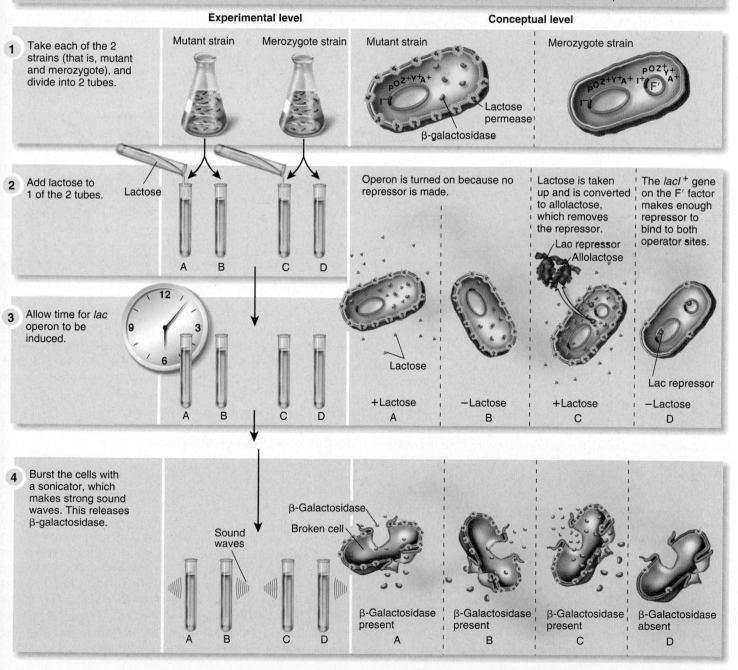

HYPOTHESIS The *lacI⁻* mutation inhibits the lac repressor and thereby allows the constitutive expression of the *lac* operon. Note: This correct hypothesis actually arose from the results of this study and other studies.

KEY MATERIALS A constitutive *lacI⁻* mutant strain was already characterized. An F′ factor carrying a normal *lacI⁺* gene and *lac* operon was introduced into this strain to produce a merozygote strain. Note: POZ⁺Y⁺A⁺ refers to a normal *lac* operon.

Experimental level / Conceptual level

1 Take each of the 2 strains (that is, mutant and merozygote), and divide into 2 tubes.

Mutant strain | Merozygote strain

Mutant strain | Merozygote strain

Lactose permease
β-galactosidase

2 Add lactose to 1 of the 2 tubes.

Lactose

A B   C D

Operon is turned on because no repressor is made.

Lactose is taken up and is converted to allolactose, which removes the repressor.

The *lacI⁺* gene on the F′ factor makes enough repressor to bind to both operator sites.

Lac repressor
Allolactose

3 Allow time for *lac* operon to be induced.

A B   C D

Lactose

+Lactose   −Lactose   +Lactose   −Lactose
   A   B   C   D

Lac repressor

4 Burst the cells with a sonicator, which makes strong sound waves. This releases β-galactosidase.

Sound waves

β-Galactosidase
Broken cell

A B   C D

β-Galactosidase present   β-Galactosidase present   β-Galactosidase present   β-Galactosidase absent
        A   B   C   D

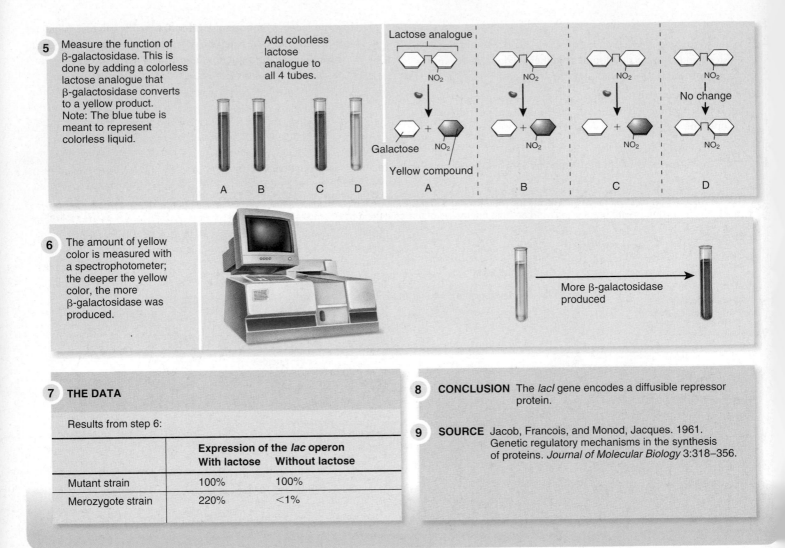

5. Measure the function of β-galactosidase. This is done by adding a colorless lactose analogue that β-galactosidase converts to a yellow product. Note: The blue tube is meant to represent colorless liquid.

Add colorless lactose analogue to all 4 tubes.

A   B   C   D

Lactose analogue

NO_2

Galactose NO_2

Yellow compound

A   B   C   D

No change

NO_2

6. The amount of yellow color is measured with a spectrophotometer; the deeper the yellow color, the more β-galactosidase was produced.

More β-galactosidase produced

7. **THE DATA**

Results from step 6:

	Expression of the *lac* operon With lactose	Without lactose
Mutant strain	100%	100%
Merozygote strain	220%	<1%

8. **CONCLUSION** The *lacI* gene encodes a diffusible repressor protein.

9. **SOURCE** Jacob, Francois, and Monod, Jacques. 1961. Genetic regulatory mechanisms in the synthesis of proteins. *Journal of Molecular Biology* 3:318–356.

The *lac* Operon Is Also Under Positive Control by an Activator Protein

In addition to negative control by a repressor protein, the *lac* operon is also positively regulated by an activator called the **catabolite activator protein (CAP)**. CAP is controlled by a small effector molecule, **cyclic AMP (cAMP)**, which is produced from ATP via an enzyme known as adenylyl cyclase. Gene regulation involving CAP and cAMP is an example of positive control (**Figure 13.10**). When cAMP binds to CAP, the cAMP-CAP complex binds to the CAP site near the *lac* promoter. This causes a bend in the DNA that enhances the ability of RNA polymerase to bind to the promoter. In this way, the rate of transcription is increased.

The key functional role of CAP is to allow *E. coli* to choose between different sources of sugar. In a process known as **catabolite repression**, the presence of a preferred energy source inhibits the use of other energy sources. In this case, transcription of the *lac* operon is inhibited by the presence of glucose, which is a catabolite (it is broken down—catabolized—inside the cell). This gene regulation allows *E. coli* to preferentially use glucose instead of other sugars, such as lactose. How does this occur? Glucose inhibits the production

of cAMP, thereby preventing the binding of CAP to the DNA. In this way, glucose blocks the activation of the *lac* operon, thereby inhibiting transcription. Though it may seem puzzling, the term catabolite repression was coined before the action of the cAMP-CAP complex was understood at the molecular level. Historically, the primary observation of researchers was that glucose (a catabolite) inhibited (repressed) lactose metabolism. Further experimentation revealed that CAP is actually an activator protein.

Figure 13.11 considers the four possible environmental conditions that an *E. coli* bacterium might experience with regard to these two sugars. When both lactose and glucose levels are high (Figure 13.11a), the rate of transcription of the *lac* operon is low, because CAP does not activate transcription. Under these conditions, the bacterium primarily uses glucose rather than lactose. Why is this a benefit to the bacterium? The bacterium conserves energy by using one type of sugar at a time. If lactose levels are high and glucose is low (Figure 13.11b), the transcription rate of the *lac* operon is very high because CAP is bound to the CAP site and the lac repressor is not bound to the operator site. Under these conditions, the bacterium metabolizes lactose. When lactose levels are low, the lac repressor prevents transcription of the *lac* operon, whether glucose levels are high or low (Figure 13.11c,d).

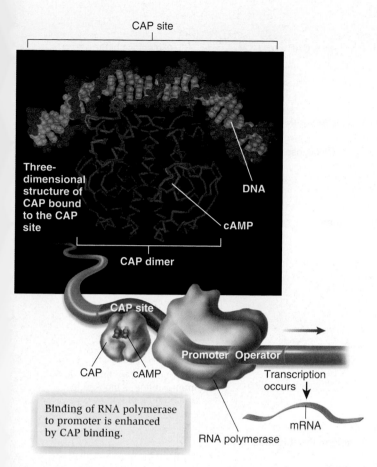

CAP site

Three-dimensional structure of CAP bound to the CAP site

DNA

cAMP

CAP dimer

CAP site

CAP   cAMP

Promoter Operator

Transcription occurs ↓

Binding of RNA polymerase to promoter is enhanced by CAP binding.

mRNA

RNA polymerase

Figure 13.10 **Positive control of the *lac* operon by the catabolite activator protein (CAP).** When cAMP is bound to CAP, CAP binds to the DNA and causes it to bend. This bend facilitates the binding of RNA polymerase.

BioConnections: *Look back at Figure 9.12. What is the function of cAMP in eukaryotic cells?*

The *trp* Operon Is Under Negative Control by a Repressor Protein

So far in this section, we have examined the regulation of the *lac* operon. Let's now consider an example of an operon that encodes enzymes involved in biosynthesis rather than breakdown. Our example is the **trp operon** of *E. coli*, which encodes enzymes that are required to make the amino acid tryptophan, a building block of cellular proteins. More specifically, the *trpE, trpD, trpC, trpB,* and *trpA* genes encode enzymes that are involved in a pathway that leads to tryptophan synthesis.

The *trp* operon is regulated by a repressor protein that is encoded by the *trpR* gene. The binding of the repressor to the *trp* operator site inhibits transcription. The ability of the trp repressor to bind to the *trp* operator is controlled by tryptophan, which is the product of the enzymes that are encoded by the operon. When tryptophan levels within the cell are very low, the trp repressor cannot bind to the operator site. Under these conditions, RNA polymerase readily transcribes the operon (**Figure 13.12a**). In this way, the cell expresses the

genes that encode enzymes that result in the synthesis of tryptophan, which is in short supply. Alternatively, when the tryptophan levels within the cell are high, tryptophan turns off the *trp* operon. Tryptophan acts as a small effector molecule, or **corepressor**, by binding to the trp repressor protein. This causes a conformational change in the repressor that allows it to bind to the *trp* operator site, inhibiting the ability of RNA polymerase to transcribe the operon (**Figure 13.12b**). Therefore, the bacterium does not waste energy making tryptophan when it is abundant.

When comparing the *lac* and *trp* operons, the actions of their small effector molecules are quite different. The lac repressor binds to its operator in the absence of its small effector molecule, whereas the trp repressor binds to its operator only in the presence of its small effector molecule. The *lac* operon is categorized as an inducible operon because allolactose, its small effector molecule, induces transcription. By comparison, the *trp* operon is considered to be a **repressible operon** because its small effector molecule, namely tryptophan, represses transcription.

13.3 Regulation of Transcription in Eukaryotes: Roles of Transcription Factors and Mediator

Learning Outcomes:
1. Explain the concept of combinatorial control.
2. Describe how RNA polymerase and general transcription factors initiate transcription at the core promoter.
3. Compare and contrast how activators, coactivators, repressors, TFIID, and mediator play a role in gene regulation.

Regulation of transcription in eukaryotes follows some of the same principles as those found in bacteria. For example, activator and repressor proteins are involved in regulating genes by influencing the ability of RNA polymerase to initiate transcription. In addition, many eukaryotic genes are regulated by small effector molecules. However, some important differences also occur. In eukaryotic species, genes are almost always organized individually, not in operons. In addition, eukaryotic gene regulation tends to be more intricate, because eukaryotes are faced with complexities that differ from their bacterial counterparts. For example, eukaryotes have more complicated cell structures that contain many more proteins and a variety of cell organelles. Many eukaryotes, such as animals and plants, are multicellular and contain different cell types. As discussed earlier in this chapter, animal cells may differentiate into neurons, muscle cells, and skin cells, and so on. Furthermore, animals and plants progress through developmental stages that require changes in gene expression.

By studying transcriptional regulation, researchers have discovered that most eukaryotic genes, particularly those found in multicellular species, are regulated by many factors. This phenomenon is called **combinatorial control** because the combination of many factors determines the expression of any given gene. At the level of

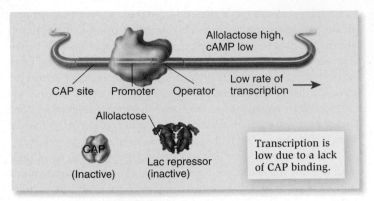

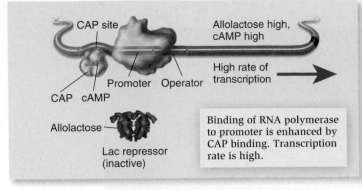

(a) Lactose high, glucose high

(b) Lactose high, glucose low

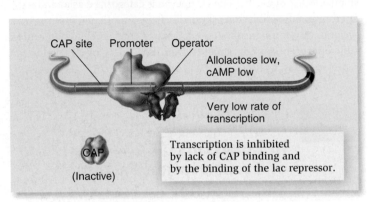

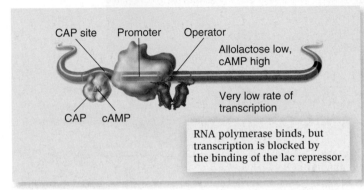

(c) Lactose low, glucose high

(d) Lactose low, glucose low

Figure 13.11 Effects of lactose and glucose on the expression of the *lac* operon.

Concept Check: What are the advantages of having both an activator and a repressor protein?

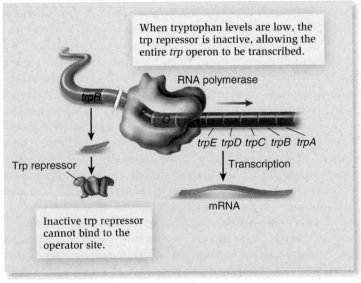

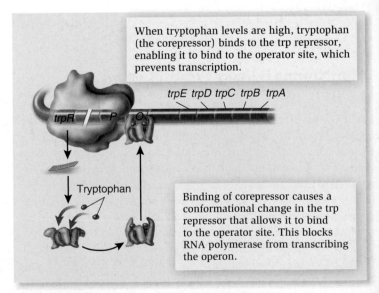

(a) Low tryptophan

(b) High tryptophan

Figure 13.12 Negative control of a repressible set of genes: function of the trp repressor and corepressor (tryptophan) in regulating the *trp* operon.

Concept Check: How are the functions of the lac repressor and trp repressor similar to each other, and how are they different?

transcription, common factors that contribute to combinatorial control include the following:

1. One or more activators may stimulate the ability of RNA polymerase to initiate transcription.
2. One or more repressors may inhibit the ability of RNA polymerase to initiate transcription.
3. The function of activators and repressors may be modulated in several ways, which include the binding of small effector molecules, protein-protein interactions, and covalent modifications.
4. Activators are necessary to alter chromatin structure in the region where a gene is located, thereby making it easier for the gene to be recognized and transcribed by RNA polymerase.
5. DNA methylation usually inhibits transcription, either by preventing the binding of an activator or by recruiting proteins that inhibit transcription.

All five of these factors may contribute to the regulation of a single gene, or possibly only three or four will play a role. In most cases, transcriptional regulation is aimed at controlling the initiation of transcription at the promoter. In this section and the following section, we will survey these basic types of gene regulation in eukaryotic species.

Eukaryotic Structural Genes Have a Core Promoter and Regulatory Elements

To understand gene regulation in eukaryotes, we first need to consider the DNA sequences that are needed to initiate transcription. For eukaryotic structural genes that encode proteins, three features are common among most promoters: **regulatory elements**, a **TATA box**, and a **transcriptional start site** (Figure 13.13).

The TATA box and transcriptional start site form the **core promoter**. The transcriptional start site is the place in the DNA where transcription actually begins. The TATA box, which is a

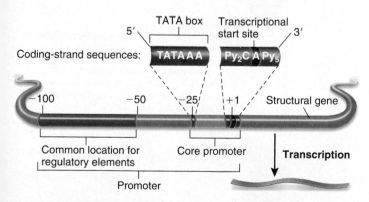

Figure 13.13   A common organization of sequences for the promoter of a eukaryotic structural gene. The core promoter has a TATA box and a transcriptional start site. The TATA box sequence is 5'–TATAAA–3'. However, not all structural genes in eukaryotes have a TATA box. The A highlighted in dark blue is the transcriptional start site. This A marks the site of the first A in the RNA transcript. The sequence that flanks the A of the transcriptional start site is two pyrimidines, then C, then five pyrimidines. Py refers to pyrimidine—cytosine or thymine. Regulatory elements, such as enhancers and silencers, are usually found upstream from the core promoter.

5'–TATAAA–3' sequence, is usually about 25 bp upstream from a transcriptional start site. The TATA box is important in determining the precise starting point for transcription. If it is missing from the core promoter, transcription may start at a variety of different locations. The core promoter, by itself, results in a low level of transcription that is termed **basal transcription**.

Regulatory elements (or regulatory sequences) are DNA segments that regulate eukaryotic genes. As described later, regulatory elements are recognized by regulatory transcription factors that control the ability of RNA polymerase to initiate transcription at the core promoter. Some regulatory elements, known as **enhancers**, play a role in the ability of RNA polymerase to begin transcription, thereby enhancing the rate of transcription. When enhancers are not functioning, most eukaryotic genes have very low levels of transcription. Other regulatory elements, known as **silencers**, prevent transcription of a given gene when its expression is not needed. When these sequences function, the rate of transcription is decreased.

A common location for regulatory elements is the region that is 50–100 bp upstream from the transcriptional start site (see Figure 13.13). However, the locations of regulatory elements vary greatly among different eukaryotic genes. Regulatory elements can be quite distant from the promoter, even 100,000 bp away, yet exert strong effects on the ability of RNA polymerase to initiate transcription at the core promoter! Regulatory elements were first discovered by Japanese molecular biologist Susumu Tonegawa and coworkers in the 1980s. While studying genes that play a role in immunity, they identified a region that was far away from the core promoter but was needed for high levels of transcription to take place.

RNA Polymerase II, General Transcription Factors, and Mediator Are Needed to Transcribe Eukaryotic Structural Genes

As discussed in Chapter 12, three forms of RNA polymerases, designated I, II, and III, are found in eukaryotes. RNA polymerase II transcribes structural genes that encode proteins. By studying transcription in a variety of eukaryotic species, researchers have identified three types of proteins that play a role in initiating transcription at the core promoter of structural genes. These are RNA polymerase II, five different proteins called **general transcription factors (GTFs)**, and a large protein complex called mediator.

RNA polymerase II and GTFs must come together at the TATA box of the core promoter so transcription can be initiated. A series of interactions occurs between these proteins so RNA polymerase II can bind to the DNA. The completed assembly of RNA polymerase II and GTFs at the TATA box is known as the **preinitiation complex** (Figure 13.14).

Another component needed for transcription in eukaryotes is the mediator protein complex. **Mediator** is composed of many proteins that bind to each other to form an elliptically shaped complex that partially wraps around RNA polymerase II and the GTFs. Mediator derives its name from the observation that it mediates interactions between the preinitiation complex and regulatory transcription factors such as activators or repressors that bind to enhancers or silencers. The function of mediator is to control the rate at which RNA polymerase can begin to transcribe RNA at the transcriptional start site.

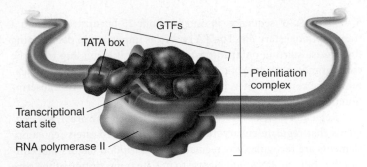

Figure 13.14   The preinitiation complex. General transcription factors (GTFs) and RNA polymerase II assemble into the preinitiation complex at the core promoter in eukaryotic structural genes.

Activators and Repressors May Influence the Function of GTFs or Mediator

In eukaryotes, regulatory transcription factors called activators and repressors bind to enhancers or silencers, respectively, and regulate the rate of transcription of genes. Activators and repressors commonly regulate the function of RNA polymerase II by binding to GTFs or mediator. As shown in **Figure 13.15**, some activators bind to an enhancer and then influence the function of GTFs. For example,

an activator may improve the ability of a GTF called transcription factor II D (TFIID) to initiate transcription. The function of TFIID is to recognize the TATA box and begin the assembly process. An activator may recruit TFIID to the TATA box, thereby promoting the assembly of GTFs and RNA polymerase II into the preinitiation complex. In contrast, repressors may bind to a silencer and inhibit the function of TFIID. Certain repressors exert their effects by preventing the binding of TFIID to the TATA box or by inhibiting the ability of TFIID to assemble other GTFs and RNA polymerase II at the core promoter.

In addition to affecting general transcription factors, a second way that regulatory transcription factors control RNA polymerase II is via mediator (**Figure 13.16**). In this example, an activator also interacts with a **coactivator**—a protein that increases the rate of transcription but does not directly bind to the DNA itself. The activator-coactivator complex stimulates the function of mediator, thereby causing RNA polymerase II to proceed to the elongation phase of transcription more quickly. Alternatively, repressors have the opposite effect to those seen in Figure 13.16. When a repressor inhibits mediator, RNA polymerase II cannot progress to the elongation stage.

A third way that regulatory transcription factors influence transcription is by recruiting proteins that affect chromatin structure in the promoter region, as described next.

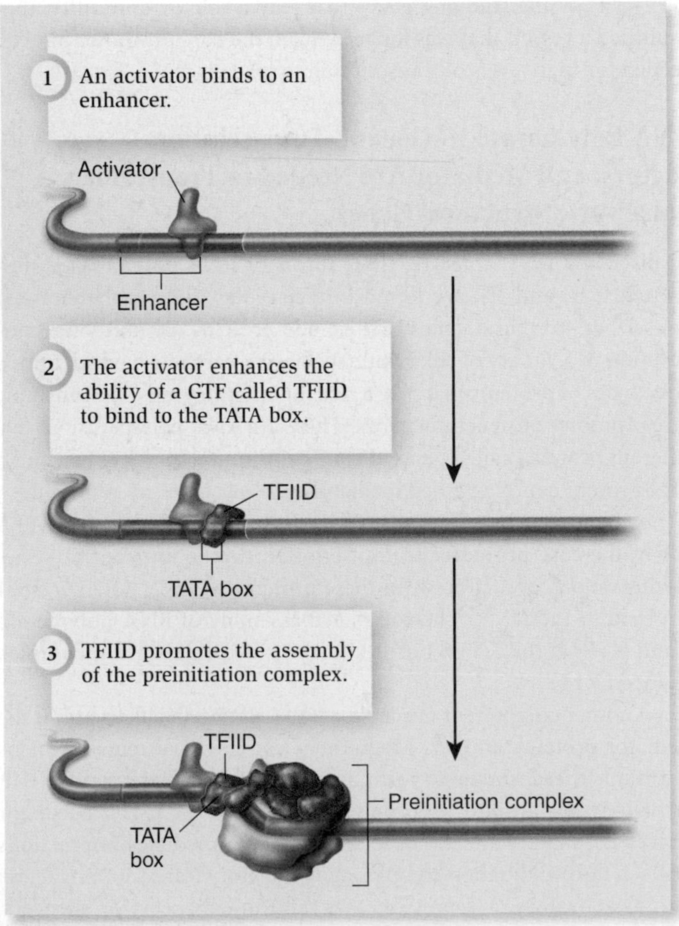

---

1 An activator binds to an enhancer.

2 The activator enhances the ability of a GTF called TFIID to bind to the TATA box.

3 TFIID promotes the assembly of the preinitiation complex.

Figure 13.15   Effect of an activator via TFIID, a general transcription factor.

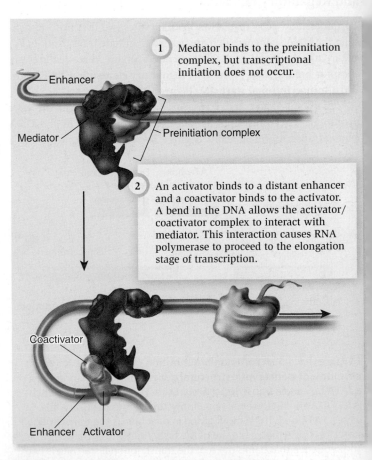

1 Mediator binds to the preinitiation complex, but transcriptional initiation does not occur.

2 An activator binds to a distant enhancer and a coactivator binds to the activator. A bend in the DNA allows the activator/coactivator complex to interact with mediator. This interaction causes RNA polymerase to proceed to the elongation stage of transcription.

Figure 13.16   Effect of an activator via mediator.

Concept Check: When an activator interacts with mediator, how does this affect the function of RNA polymerase?

13.4   Regulation of Transcription in Eukaryotes: Changes in Chromatin Structure and DNA Methylation

Learning Outcomes:

1. Describe how eukaryotic genes are flanked by nucleosome-free regions and how nucleosomes are altered during gene transcription.
2. Explain how DNA methylation affects transcription.

In eukaryotes, DNA is associated with proteins to form a structure called **chromatin**—the complex of DNA and proteins that makes up eukaryotic chromosomes (see Chapter 11, Figures 11.23 and 11.26). How does the structure of chromatin affect gene transcription? Recall from Chapter 11 that nucleosomes are composed of DNA wrapped around an octamer of histone proteins. Depending on the locations and arrangements of nucleosomes, a region containing a gene may be in a **closed conformation**, and transcription may be difficult or impossible. Transcription requires changes in chromatin structure that allow transcription factors to gain access to and bind to the DNA in the promoter region. Such chromatin, said to be in an **open conformation**, is accessible to GTFs and RNA polymerase II so transcription can take place. In this section, we will examine how chromatin is converted from a closed to an open conformation. We will also explore how **DNA methylation**—the attachment of methyl groups to the base cytosine—affects chromatin conformation and gene expression.

Transcription Is Controlled by Changes in Chromatin Structure

In recent years, geneticists have been trying to identify the steps that promote the interconversion between the closed and open conformations of chromatin. One way to change chromatin structure is through **ATP-dependent chromatin-remodeling complexes**, which are a group of proteins that alter chromatin structure. Such complexes use energy from ATP hydrolysis to drive a change in the locations and/or compositions of nucleosomes, thereby making the DNA more or less amenable to transcription. Therefore, chromatin remodeling is important for both the activation and repression of transcription.

How do ATP-dependent chromatin-remodeling complexes change chromatin structure? Three effects are possible. One result is that these complexes may bind to chromatin and change the locations of nucleosomes (**Figure 13.17a**). This may involve a shift of the relative positions of a few nucleosomes or a change in the relative spacing of nucleosomes over a long stretch of DNA. A second effect is that remodeling complexes may evict histone octamers from the DNA, thereby creating gaps where nucleosomes are not found (**Figure 13.17b**). A third possibility is that chromatin-remodeling complexes may change the composition of nucleosomes by removing standard histone proteins from an octamer and replacing them with histone variants (**Figure 13.17c**). A **histone variant** is a histone protein that has a slightly different amino acid sequence from the standard histone proteins described in Chapter 11. Some histone variants promote gene transcription, whereas others inhibit it.

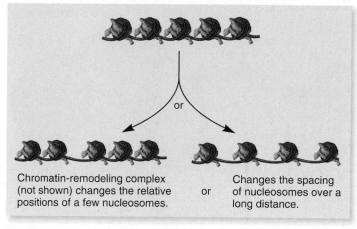

Chromatin-remodeling complex (not shown) changes the relative positions of a few nucleosomes. **or** Changes the spacing of nucleosomes over a long distance.

(a) Change in nucleosome position

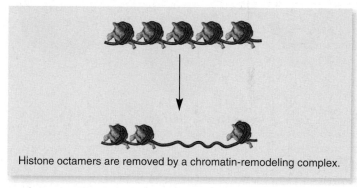

Histone octamers are removed by a chromatin-remodeling complex.

(b) Histone eviction

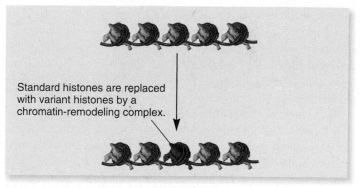

Standard histones are replaced with variant histones by a chromatin-remodeling complex.

(c) Replacement with variant histones

Figure 13.17 ATP-dependent chromatin remodeling. Chromatin-remodeling complexes may **(a)** change the locations of nucleosomes, **(b)** remove histones from the DNA, or **(c)** replace standard histones with variant histones. The chromatin-remodeling complex, which is composed of a group of proteins, is not shown in this figure.

Histone Modifications Affect Gene Transcription

In recent years, researchers have learned that the amino terminal tails of histone proteins are subject to several types of covalent modifications. For example, an enzyme called **histone acetyltransferase** attaches acetyl groups ($-COCH_3$) to the amino terminal tails of histone proteins. When acetylated, histone proteins do not bind as tightly to the DNA, which aids in transcription. Over 50 different

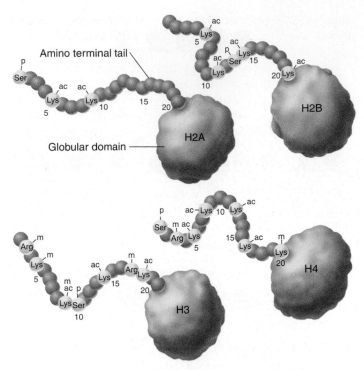

Figure 13.18 **Examples of covalent modifications that occur to the amino terminal tails of histone proteins.** The amino acids are numbered from the N-terminus, or amino end. The modifications shown here are m for methylation, p for phosphorylation, and ac for acetylation. Many more modifications can occur to the amino terminal tails. These modifications are reversible.

Concept Check: *What are the two opposing effects that histone modifications may have with regard to chromatin structure?*

enzymes have been identified in mammals that selectively modify amino terminal tails. **Figure 13.18** shows an example in the amino terminal tails of histone proteins H2A, H2B, H3, and H4 that can be modified by acetyl, methyl, and phosphate groups.

What are the effects of covalent modifications of histones? First, modifications may directly influence interactions between DNA and histone proteins, and between adjacent nucleosomes. As mentioned, the acetylation of histones loosens their binding to DNA and aids in transcription. Second, histone modifications provide binding sites that are recognized by other proteins. According to the **histone code**

hypothesis, proposed by American biologists Brian Strahl and David Allis in 2000, the pattern of histone modification is recognized by proteins much like a language or code. One pattern of histone modification may attract proteins that inhibit transcription. Alternatively, a different combination of histone modifications may attract proteins, such as ATP-dependent chromatin-remodeling complexes, that promote gene transcription. In this way, the histone code plays a key role in accessing the information within the genomes of eukaryotic species.

Eukaryotic Genes Are Flanked by Nucleosome-Free Regions

Studies over the last 10 years or so have revealed that many eukaryotic genes show a common pattern of nucleosome organization (**Figure 13.19**). For active genes or those genes that can be activated, the core promoter is found at a **nucleosome-free region (NFR)**, which is a site that is missing nucleosomes. The NFR is typically 150 bp in length. Although the NFR may be required for transcription, it is not, by itself, sufficient for gene activation. At any given time in the life of a eukaryotic cell, many genes that contain an NFR are not being actively transcribed. The NFR is flanked by two nucleosomes that are termed the –1 and +1 nucleosomes. These nucleosomes often contain histone variants that promote transcription. The nucleosomes downstream from the +1 nucleosome tend to be evenly spaced near the beginning of a eukaryotic gene, but their spacing becomes less regular farther downstream. The end of many eukaryotic genes is followed by another NFR. This arrangement at the end of genes may be important for transcriptional termination.

Transcriptional Activation Involves Changes in Nucleosome Locations, Composition, and Histone Modifications

A key role of certain activators is to recruit ATP-dependent chromatin-remodeling complexes and histone-modifying enzymes to the promoter region of eukaryotic genes. Though the order of recruitment may differ among specific activators, this appears to be critical for transcriptional initiation and elongation. In the scenario shown in **Figure 13.20**, an activator binds to an enhancer in the NFR. The activator then recruits chromatin-remodeling complexes and

A nucleosome-free region (NFR) is found at the beginning and end of many genes. Nucleosomes tend to be precisely positioned near the beginning and end of a gene, but are less regularly distributed elsewhere.

Figure 13.19 **Nucleosome arrangements in the vicinity of a eukaryotic structural gene.**

BioConnections: *Look back at Figure 11.23. What is the composition of a nucleosome?*

Many genes are flanked by nucleosome-free regions (NFR) and well-positioned nucleosomes.

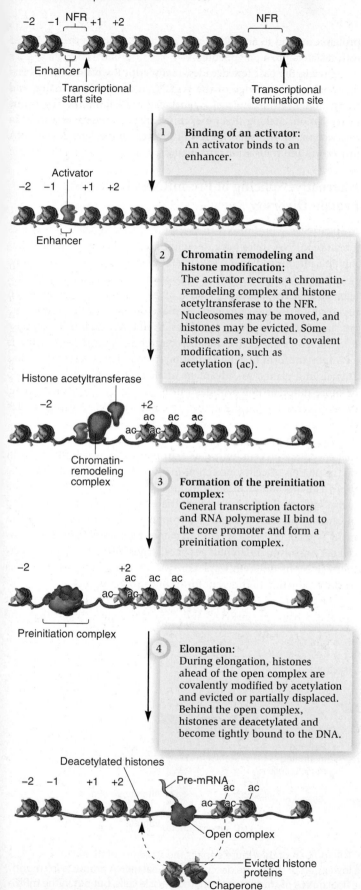

1 Binding of an activator:
An activator binds to an enhancer.

2 Chromatin remodeling and histone modification:
The activator recruits a chromatin-remodeling complex and histone acetyltransferase to the NFR. Nucleosomes may be moved, and histones may be evicted. Some histones are subjected to covalent modification, such as acetylation (ac).

3 Formation of the preinitiation complex:
General transcription factors and RNA polymerase II bind to the core promoter and form a preinitiation complex.

4 Elongation:
During elongation, histones ahead of the open complex are covalently modified by acetylation and evicted or partially displaced. Behind the open complex, histones are deacetylated and become tightly bound to the DNA.

Figure 13.20 A simplified model for the transcriptional activation of a eukaryotic structural gene.

histone-modifying enzymes to this region. The chromatin-remodeling complex may shift nucleosomes or temporarily evict nucleosomes from the promoter region. Nucleosomes containing certain histone variants are thought to be more easily removed from the DNA than those containing the standard histones. Histone-modifying enzymes, such as histone acetyltransferase, covalently modify histone proteins and may affect nucleosome contact with the DNA. The actions of chromatin-remodeling complexes and histone-modifying enzymes facilitate the binding of general transcription factors and RNA polymerase II to the core promoter, thereby allowing the formation of a preinitiation complex (see Figure 13.20, step 2).

Further changes in chromatin structure are necessary for elongation to occur. RNA polymerase II cannot transcribe DNA that is tightly wrapped in nucleosomes. For transcription to occur, histones are evicted, partially displaced, or destabilized so RNA polymerase II can pass. Evicted histones are then reassembled by chaperone proteins and placed back on the DNA behind the moving RNA polymerase II (see Figure 13.20). These histones may be deacetylated—had their acetyl groups removed—so they bind more tightly to the DNA.

DNA Methylation Inhibits Gene Transcription

Let's now turn our attention to a mechanism that usually silences gene expression. DNA structure can be modified by the covalent attachment of methyl groups ($-CH_3$) by an enzyme called **DNA methylase**. This modification, termed DNA methylation, is common in some eukaryotic species but not all. For example, yeast and *Drosophila* have little or no detectable methylation of their DNA, whereas DNA methylation in vertebrates and plants is relatively abundant. In mammals, approximately 5% of the DNA is methylated. Eukaryotic DNA methylation occurs on the cytosine base. The sequence that is methylated is shown here:

$$
\begin{array}{c}
CH_3 \\
| \\
5'-CG-3' \\
3'-GC-5' \\
| \\
CH_3
\end{array}
$$

DNA methylation usually inhibits the transcription of eukaryotic genes, particularly when it occurs in the vicinity of the promoter. In vertebrates and flowering plants, many genes contain sequences called **CpG islands** near their promoters. CpG refers to the nucleotides of C and G in DNA that are connected by a phosphodiester linkage. A CpG island is a cluster of CpG sites. Unmethylated CpG islands are usually correlated with active genes, whereas repressed genes contain methylated CpG islands. In this way, DNA methylation may play an important role in the silencing of particular genes.

How does DNA methylation inhibit transcription? This can occur in two general ways. First, methylation of CpG islands may prevent an activator from binding to an enhancer element, thus inhibiting the initiation of transcription. A second way that methylation inhibits transcription is by altering chromatin structure. Proteins known as **methyl-CpG-binding proteins** bind methylated sequences. Once bound to the DNA, the methyl-CpG-binding protein recruits other proteins to the region that inhibit transcription. As discussed in Chapter 17, DNA methylation is also associated with an inheritance pattern called **epigenetic inheritance** in which gene expression is altered in a way that is fixed during an individual's lifetime. Such epigenetic changes may affect the phenotype of the individual, but they are not permanent over the course of two or more generations.

13.5   Regulation of RNA Processing and Translation in Eukaryotes

Learning Outcomes:

1. Outline the process of alternative splicing and how it increases protein diversity.
2. Describe how RNA interference is used to regulate the expression of genes.
3. Explain how RNA-binding proteins can regulate the translation of specific mRNAs, using the regulation of iron absorption in mammals as an example.

In the preceding sections of this chapter, we focused on gene regulation at the level of transcription in bacteria and eukaryotes. Eukaryotic gene expression is also commonly regulated at the levels of RNA processing and translation. These added levels of regulation provide important benefits to eukaryotic species. First, by regulating RNA processing, eukaryotes can produce more than one mRNA transcript from a single gene. This allows a gene to encode two or more polypeptides, thereby increasing the complexity of eukaryotic proteomes. A second issue is timing. Regulation of transcription in eukaryotes takes a fair amount of time before its effects are observed at the cellular level. During transcription (1) the chromatin must be converted to an open conformation, (2) the gene must be transcribed, (3) the RNA must be processed and exported from the nucleus, and (4) the protein must be made via translation. All four steps take time, on the order of several minutes. One way to achieve faster regulation is to control steps that occur after an RNA transcript is made. In eukaryotes, regulation of translation provides a faster way to regulate the levels of gene products, namely, proteins. A small RNA molecule or RNA-binding

protein can bind to an mRNA and affect the ability of the mRNA to be translated into a polypeptide.

During the past few decades, many critical advances have been made in our knowledge of the regulation of RNA processing and translation. Even so, molecular geneticists are still finding new forms of regulation, making this an exciting area of modern research. In this section, we will survey a few of the known mechanisms of RNA processing and translational regulation.

Alternative Splicing of Pre-mRNAs Increases Protein Diversity

In eukaryotes, a pre-mRNA transcript is processed before it becomes a mature mRNA (refer back to Figure 12.9). When a pre-mRNA has multiple introns and exons, splicing may occur in more than one way, resulting in the production of two or more different polypeptides. Such **alternative splicing** is a form of gene regulation that allows an organism to use the same gene to make different proteins at different stages of development, in different cell types, and/or in response to a change in the environmental conditions. Alternative splicing is an important form of gene regulation in complex eukaryotes such as animals and plants. An advantage of alternative splicing is that two or more different polypeptides can be derived from a single gene, thereby increasing the size of the proteome while minimizing the size of the genome.

Let's consider an example of alternative splicing for a pre-mRNA that encodes a protein known as α-tropomyosin, which functions in the regulation of cell contraction in animals. It is located along the thin filaments found in smooth muscle cells, such as those in the uterus and small intestine, and in striated muscle cells that are found in cardiac and skeletal muscle. α-tropomyosin is also synthesized in many types of nonmuscle cells but in lower amounts. Within a multicellular organism, different types of cells must regulate their contractibility in subtly different ways. One way this may be accomplished is by the production of different forms of α-tropomyosin.

Figure 13.21 shows the intron-exon structure of the rat α-tropomyosin pre-mRNA and two alternative ways that the

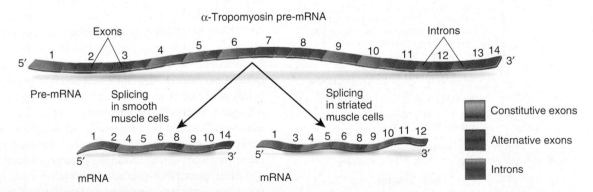

Figure 13.21 Alternative splicing of the rat α-tropomyosin pre-mRNA. The top part of this figure depicts the structure of the rat α-tropomyosin pre-mRNA. Exons are red or green, and introns are yellow. The lower part of the figure describes the final mRNA products in smooth and striated muscle cells after alternative splicing. Note: Exon 8 is found in the final mRNA of smooth and striated muscle cells, but not in the mRNA of certain other cell types. The junction between exons 13 and 14 contains a 3′ splice site that enables exon 13 to be separated from exon 14.

Concept Check: *What is the biological advantage of alternative splicing?*

pre-mRNA can be spliced. The pre-mRNA contains 14 exons, 6 of which are constitutive exons (shown in red), which are always found in the mature mRNA from all cell types. Presumably, constitutive exons encode polypeptide segments of the α-tropomyosin protein that are necessary for its general structure and function. By comparison, alternative exons (shown in green) are not always found in the mRNA after splicing has occurred. The polypeptide sequences encoded by alternative exons may subtly change the function of α-tropomyosin to meet the needs of the cell type in which it is found. For example, Figure 13.21 shows the predominant splicing products found in smooth muscle cells and striated muscle cells. Exon 2 encodes a segment of the α-tropomyosin protein that alters its function to make it suitable for smooth muscle cells. By comparison, the α-tropomyosin mRNA found in striated muscle cells does not include exon 2. Instead, this mRNA contains exon 3, which is more suitable for that cell type.

Table 13.1	Genome Size and Biological Complexity			
Species	Level of complexity	Genome size (million bp)	Approximate number of genes	Percentage of genes alternatively spliced
Escherichia coli	A unicellular bacterium	4.2	4,000	0
Saccharomyces cerevisiae	A unicellular eukaryote	12	6,000	<1
Caenorhabditis elegans	A tiny worm (about 1,000 cells)	97	19,000	2
Drosophila melanogaster	An insect	137	14,000	7
Arabidopsis thaliana	A flowering plant	142	26,000	11
Homo sapiens	A complex mammal	3,000	25,000	70

GENOMES & PROTEOMES CONNECTION

Alternative Splicing Tends to Be More Prevalent in Complex Eukaryotic Species

In the past few decades, many technical advances have improved our ability to analyze the genomes and proteomes of many different species. Researchers have been able to determine the amount of DNA from several species and estimate the total number of genes. In addition, scientists can also estimate the number of polypeptides if information is available about the degree of alternative splicing in a given species.

Table 13.1 compares six species: a bacterium (Escherichia coli), a eukaryotic single-celled organism (yeast—Saccharomyces cerevisiae), a small nematode worm (Caenorhabditis elegans), a fruit fly (Drosophila melanogaster), a small flowering plant (Arabidopsis thaliana), and a human (Homo sapiens). One general trend is that less complex organisms tend to have fewer genes. For example, unicellular organisms have only a few thousand genes, whereas multicellular species have tens of thousands. However, the trend is by no means a linear one. If we compare C. elegans and D. melanogaster, the fruit fly actually has fewer genes, even though it is morphologically more complex.

A second trend you can see in Table 13.1 concerns alternative splicing. This phenomenon does not occur in bacteria and is rare in S. cerevisiae. The frequency of alternative splicing increases from worms to flies to humans. For example, the level of alternative splicing is 10-fold higher in humans than in Drosophila. This trend can partially explain the increase in complexity among these species. Even though humans have only about 25,000 different genes, they can make well over 100,000 different proteins because most genes are alternatively spliced in multiple ways.

RNA Interference Blocks the Expression of mRNA

Let's now turn our attention to regulatory mechanisms that affect translation. **MicroRNAs (miRNAs)** and **short-interfering RNAs (siRNAs)** are RNA molecules that are processed to a small size, typically 22 nucleotides in length, and silence the expression of pre-existing mRNAs. The precursors of miRNAs are encoded by genes and usually form a hairpin structure. In most cases, miRNAs are partially complementary to certain cellular mRNAs and inhibit their translation. By comparison, short-interfering RNAs are derived from two RNA molecules that come together to form a double-stranded region. For example, a cellular RNA may bind to an RNA that is transcribed from viral genome. siRNAs are usually a perfect match to specific mRNAs and cause the mRNAs to be degraded.

Insight into the mechanism of miRNA inhibition came from the research of American biologists Andrew Fire and Craig Mello, who discovered the mechanism of action of miRNA (**Figure 13.22**). A pre-miRNA is first synthesized as a single-stranded molecule that folds back on itself to form a hairpin structure. (A pre-siRNA, which is not shown in this figure, would be composed of two RNA molecules that come together to form a double-stranded region.) The double-stranded region is trimmed to a 22-bp sequence by an enzyme called dicer. The 22-bp sequence becomes part of a complex called the **RNA-induced silencing complex (RISC)**, which also includes several proteins. One of the RNA strands is then degraded. The miRNA or siRNA in the complex binds to a target mRNA with a complementary sequence.

Upon binding, two different things may happen. When the miRNA and mRNA are not a perfect match or are only partially complementary, translation is inhibited. Alternatively, when an siRNA and mRNA are a perfect match or highly complementary, the mRNA is cut into two pieces and then degraded. Both miRNA and siRNA have the same effect—the expression of the mRNA is silenced. Fire and Mello called this **RNA interference (RNAi)**, because the miRNA interferes with the proper expression of an mRNA.

Since this study, researchers have discovered that genes encoding miRNAs are widely found in animals and plants. In humans, for example, approximately 200 different genes encode miRNAs. RNAi represents an important mechanism of gene regulation that results in mRNA silencing. In 2006, Fire and Mello were awarded the Nobel Prize in Physiology or Medicine for their studies of RNAi.

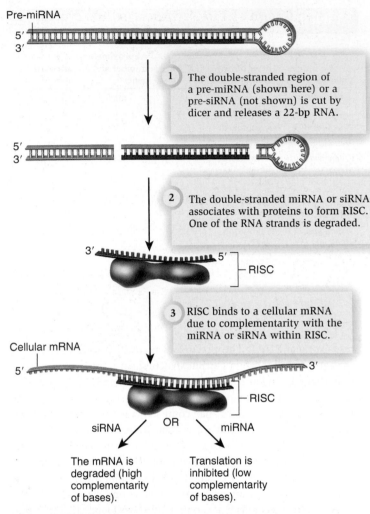

Pre-miRNA

① The double-stranded region of a pre-miRNA (shown here) or a pre-siRNA (not shown) is cut by dicer and releases a 22-bp RNA.

② The double-stranded miRNA or siRNA associates with proteins to form RISC. One of the RNA strands is degraded.

RISC

③ RISC binds to a cellular mRNA due to complementarity with the miRNA or siRNA within RISC.

Cellular mRNA

RISC

siRNA   OR   miRNA

The mRNA is degraded (high complementarity of bases).

Translation is inhibited (low complementarity of bases).

Figure 13.22 **Mechanism of action of microRNA (miRNA).** Note: Pre-siRNAs are also acted upon by dicer, but siRNAs are derived from two RNA molecules that form a double-stranded region rather than one RNA molecule that forms a hairpin.

🔄 **BIOLOGY PRINCIPLE** **Structure determines function.**
Because the structure of an miRNA or siRNA is complementary to an mRNA, it is able to inhibit the function of the mRNA.

The Prevention of Iron Toxicity in Mammals Involves the Regulation of Translation

Another way to regulate translation involves RNA-binding proteins that directly affect the initiation of translation. The regulation of iron absorption provides a well-studied example. Although iron is a vital cofactor for many cellular enzymes, it is toxic at high levels. To prevent toxicity, mammalian cells synthesize a protein called ferritin, which forms a hollow, spherical complex that stores excess iron.

The mRNA that encodes ferritin is controlled by an RNA-binding protein known as the **iron regulatory protein (IRP)**. When iron levels in the cytosol are low and more ferritin is not needed, IRP

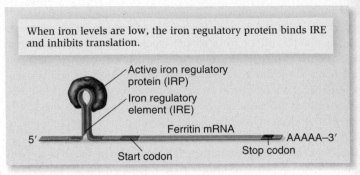

When iron levels are low, the iron regulatory protein binds IRE and inhibits translation.

Active iron regulatory protein (IRP)
Iron regulatory element (IRE)
Ferritin mRNA
5′   AAAAA–3′
Start codon   Stop codon

(a) Low iron levels

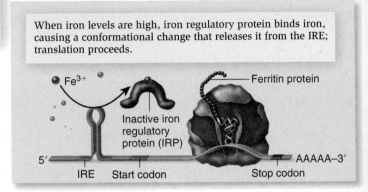

When iron levels are high, iron regulatory protein binds iron, causing a conformational change that releases it from the IRE; translation proceeds.

Fe^{3+}
Ferritin protein
Inactive iron regulatory protein (IRP)
5′   AAAAA–3′
IRE   Start codon   Stop codon

(b) High iron levels

Figure 13.23 **Translational regulation of ferritin mRNA by the iron regulatory protein (IRP).**

Concept Check: *Poisoning may occur when a young child finds a bottle of vitamins, such as those that taste like candy, and eats a large number of them. One of the toxic effects involves the ingestion of too much iron. How does the IRP protect people from the toxic effects of too much iron?*

binds to a regulatory element within the ferritin mRNA known as the **iron regulatory element (IRE)**. The IRE is located between the 5′ cap, where the ribosome binds, and the start codon where translation begins. Due to base pairing, it forms a stem-loop structure. The binding of IRP to the IRE inhibits translation of the ferritin mRNA (**Figure 13.23a**). However, when iron is abundant in the cytosol, the iron binds directly to IRP, which changes its conformation and prevents it from binding to the IRE. Under these conditions, the ferritin mRNA is translated to make more ferritin protein (**Figure 13.23b**).

Why is translational regulation of ferritin mRNA an advantage over transcriptional regulation of the ferritin gene? This mechanism of translational control allows cells to rapidly respond to changes in their environment. When cells are confronted with high levels of iron, they can quickly make more ferritin protein to prevent the toxic buildup of iron. This mechanism is faster than transcriptional regulation, which would require the activation of the ferritin gene and the transcription of ferritin mRNA prior to the synthesis of more ferritin protein.

Summary of Key Concepts

13.1 Overview of Gene Regulation

- Most genes are regulated so the level of gene expression can vary under different conditions. By comparison, constitutive genes are expressed at constant levels.

- Gene regulation ensures that gene products are made only when they are needed. An example is the synthesis of the gene products needed for lactose utilization in bacteria (Figure 13.1).

- In eukaryotes, gene regulation leads to the production of different cell types, such as neurons, muscle cells, and skin cells, within an organism (Figure 13.2).

- Eukaryote gene regulation enables gene products to be produced at different developmental stages (Figure 13.3).

- All organisms regulate gene expression at a variety of levels, including transcription, translation, and post-translation. Eukaryotes also regulate RNA processing (Figure 13.4).

13.2 Regulation of Transcription in Bacteria

- Repressors and activators are regulatory transcription factors that bind to the DNA and affect the transcription of genes. Small effector molecules control the ability of regulatory transcription factors to bind to DNA (Figure 13.5).

- An operon is an arrangement of several structural genes controlled by a promoter and operator. The *lac* operon is an example of an inducible operon. The lac repressor exerts negative control by binding to the operator site and preventing RNA polymerase from transcribing the operon. When allolactose binds to the repressor, a conformational change occurs that prevents the repressor from binding to the operator site so transcription can proceed (Figures 13.6, 13.7).

- By constructing a merozygote, Jacob, Monod, and Pardee determined that the *lacI* gene encodes a diffusible protein that represses the *lac* operon (Figures 13.8, 13.9).

- Positive control of the *lac* operon occurs when the catabolite activator protein (CAP) binds to the CAP site in the presence of cAMP. This causes a bend in the DNA, which promotes the binding of RNA polymerase to the promoter (Figure 13.10).

- Glucose inhibits cAMP production, which, in turn, inhibits the expression of the *lac* operon, because CAP cannot bind to the CAP site. This form of regulation provides bacteria with a more efficient utilization of their resources because the bacteria use one sugar at a time (Figure 13.11).

- The *trp* operon is an example of a repressible operon. The presence of tryptophan causes the trp repressor to bind to the *trp* operator and stop transcription. This prevents the excessive buildup of tryptophan in the cell, which would be a waste of energy (Figure 13.12).

13.3 Regulation of Transcription in Eukaryotes: Roles of Transcription Factors and Mediator

- Eukaryotic genes exhibit combinatorial control, meaning that many factors control the expression of a single gene. (See list on p. 269.)

- Eukaryotic promoters consist of a core promoter (containing a TATA box and transcriptional start site) and regulatory elements, such as enhancers or silencers, that regulate the rate of transcription (Figure 13.13).

- General transcription factors (GTFs) are needed for RNA polymerase II to bind to the core promoter, forming a preinitiation complex (Figure 13.14).

- Activators and repressors may regulate RNA polymerase II by interacting with TFIID (a GTF), or via mediator, a protein complex that wraps around RNA polymerase II (Figures 13.15, 13.16).

13.4 Regulation of Transcription in Eukaryotes: Changes in Chromatin Structure and DNA Methylation

- ATP-dependent chromatin-remodeling complexes change the positions and compositions of nucleosomes (Figure 13.17).

- The pattern of covalent modification of the amino terminal tails of histone proteins, also called the histone code, can inhibit or promote transcription (Figure 13.18).

- Eukaryotic genes are usually flanked by nucleosome-free regions (Figure 13.19).

- For eukaryotic genes, a pre-initiation complex forms at a nucleosome-free region. During elongation, nucleosomes are displaced ahead of RNA polymerase and re-form after RNA polymerase has passed (Figure 13.20).

- DNA methylation, which occurs at CpG islands near promoters, usually inhibits transcription by (1) preventing the binding of activator proteins or (2) promoting the binding of proteins that inhibit transcription.

13.5 Regulation of RNA Processing and Translation in Eukaryotes

- In alternative splicing, a single type of pre-mRNA can be spliced in more than one way, producing polypeptides with somewhat different sequences. This is a common way for complex eukaryotes to increase the size of their proteomes (Figure 13.21, Table 13.1).

- MicroRNAs (miRNAs) and short-interfering RNAs (siRNAs) inhibit mRNAs by inhibiting translation or by promoting the degradation of mRNAs, respectively (Figure 13.22).

- RNA-binding proteins can regulate the translation of specific mRNAs. An example is the regulation of iron absorption, in which the iron regulatory protein (IRP) regulates the translation of ferritin mRNA (Figure 13.23).

Assess and Discuss

Test Yourself

1. Genes that are expressed at all times at relatively constant levels are known as _____ genes.
   a. inducible
   b. repressible
   c. positive
   d. constitutive
   e. structural

2. Which of the following is *not* a form of gene regulation in bacteria?
   a. transcriptional
   b. RNA processing
   c. translational
   d. post-translational
   e. All of the above are levels at which bacteria are able to regulate gene expression.

3. Transcription factors that bind to DNA and stimulate transcription are
   a. repressors.
   b. small effector molecules.
   c. activators.
   d. promoters.
   e. operators.

4. In bacteria, the unit of DNA that contains multiple genes under the control of a single promoter is called ___. The mRNA produced from this unit is referred to as ___ mRNA.
   a. an operator, a polycistronic
   b. a template, a structural
   c. an operon, a polycistronic
   d. an operon, a monocistronic
   e. a template, a monocistronic

5. For the *lac* operon, what would be the expected effects of a mutation in the operator site that prevented the binding of the repressor protein?
   a. The operon would always be turned on.
   b. The operon would always be turned off.
   c. The operon would always be turned on, except when glucose is present.
   d. The operon would be turned on only in the presence of lactose.
   e. The operon would be turned on only in the presence of lactose and the absence of glucose.

6. The presence of _____ in the medium prevents CAP from binding to the DNA, resulting in _____ in transcription of the *lac* operon.
   a. lactose, an increase
   b. glucose, an increase
   c. cAMP, a decrease
   d. glucose, a decrease
   e. lactose, a decrease

7. The *trp* operon is considered _____ operon because the structural genes necessary for tryptophan synthesis are not expressed when the levels of tryptophan in the cell are high.
   a. an inducible
   b. a positive
   c. a repressible
   d. a negative
   e. Both c and d are correct.

8. Regulatory elements that function to increase transcription levels in eukaryotes are called
   a. promoters.
   b. silencers.
   c. enhancers.
   d. transcriptional start sites.
   e. activators.

9. DNA methylation in many eukaryotic organisms usually causes
   a. increased translation levels.
   b. decreased translation levels.
   c. increased transcription levels.
   d. decreased transcription levels.
   e. introns to be removed.

10. _____ refers to the phenomenon where a single type of pre-mRNA may give rise to multiple types of mRNAs due to different patterns of intron and exon removal.
    a. Spliceosomes
    b. Variable expression
    c. Alternative splicing
    d. Polycistronic mRNA
    e. Induced silencing

Conceptual Questions

1. What is the difference between inducible and repressible operons? Give an example of each.

2. Transcriptional regulation often involves a regulatory protein that binds to a segment of DNA and a small effector molecule that binds to the regulatory protein. Do the following terms apply to a regulatory protein, a segment of DNA, or a small effector molecule? a. repressor; b. inducer; c. operator site; d. corepressor; e. activator

3. A principle of biology is *the genetic material provides a blueprint for reproduction.* Explain how gene regulation is an important mechanism for reproduction and sustaining life.

Collaborative Questions

1. Discuss the advantages and disadvantages of genetic regulation at the different levels described in Figure 13.4.

2. Discuss the advantages and disadvantages of combinatorial control of eukaryotic genes.

Online Resource

www.brookerbiology.com

Stay a step ahead in your studies with animations that bring concepts to life and practice tests to assess your understanding. Your instructor may also recommend the interactive eBook, individualized learning tools, and more.

Mutation, DNA Repair, and Cancer

14

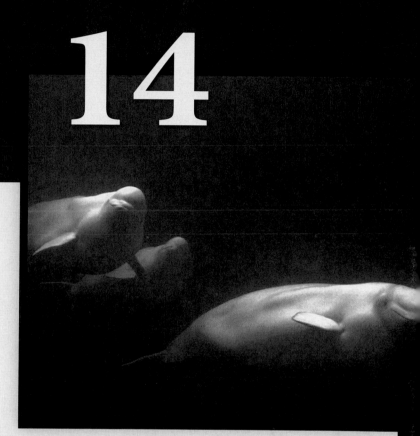

A
t a summer camp, the children enjoy ice cream, horseback riding, hay rides, swimming, and learning about the habits of owls. Not such an unusual camp, you might be thinking. However, what makes Camp Sundown unique is that the outdoor fun begins at dusk and runs all night. The children at this camp have inherited a disorder called xeroderma pigmentosum (XP), which makes them highly sensitive to sunlight. Their skin will blister or freckle on minimum Sun exposure. Of greater concern, however, is skin cancer. Persons with XP may have a 1,000-fold greater risk of developing skin cancer, though such a risk is greatly decreased if Sun exposure is minimized.

What explains the symptoms of XP? Individuals with this condition are highly susceptible to **mutation**, which is defined as a heritable change in the genetic material. When a mutation occurs, the order of nucleotide bases in a DNA molecule, its base sequence, is changed permanently, an alteration that can be passed from mother to daughter cells during cell division. Mutations that lead to cancer cause particular genes to be expressed in an abnormal way. For example, a mutation could affect the transcription of a gene, or it could alter the functional properties of the polypeptide that is specified by a gene.

Should we be afraid of mutations? Yes and no. On the positive side, mutations are essential to the long-term continuity of life. Mutations provide the foundation for evolutionary change. They supply the variation that enables species to evolve and become better adapted to their environments. On the negative side, however, new mutations are more likely to be harmful than beneficial to the individual. The genes within modern species are the products of billions of years of evolution and have evolved to work properly. Random mutations are more likely to disrupt genes rather than enhance their function. As we will see in this chapter, mutations can cause cancer. In addition, many forms of inherited diseases, such as XP and cystic fibrosis, are caused by gene mutations. For these and many other reasons, understanding the molecular nature of mutations is a compelling area of research.

Because mutations can be harmful, all species have evolved several ways to repair damaged DNA. Such DNA repair systems reverse DNA damage before a permanent mutation can occur. DNA repair systems are vital to the survival of all organisms. If these systems did not exist, mutations would be so prevalent that few species, if any, would survive. Persons with

During the past two decades, over 25% of the beluga whales in Canada's St. Lawrence Seaway have died of cancer. Biologists speculate that these deaths are caused by cancer-causing pollutants, such as polycyclic aromatic hydrocarbons (PAHs).

XP have an impaired DNA repair system, which is the underlying cause of their disorder. DNA damage from sunlight is normally corrected by DNA repair systems. In people with XP, damaged DNA often remains unrepaired, which can lead to cancer. In this chapter, we will examine how such DNA repair systems operate. But first, let's explore the molecular basis of mutation.

14.1 Mutation

Learning Outcomes:

1. List the different ways that mutations can alter the amino acid sequence of a polypeptide.
2. Analyze the replica plating experiments of the Lederbergs.
3. Distinguish between mutations in somatic cells and in germ-line cells.
4. Discuss the difference between spontaneous and induced mutations.
5. Analyze the results of an Ames test for determining if a substance is a mutagen.

How do mutations affect traits? To answer this question at the molecular level, we must understand how changes in the DNA sequence of a gene ultimately affect gene function. Most of our understanding of mutation has come from the study of experimental organisms, such as bacteria and *Drosophila*. Researchers can expose these organisms to agents that cause mutations and then study the consequences of the mutations that arise. In addition, because these organisms have a short generation time, researchers can investigate the effects of mutations when they are passed from parent to offspring over many generations.

The structure and amount of genetic material can be altered in a variety of ways. For example, the structure and number of chromosomes can change. We will examine these types of genetic changes in Chapter 15. In this section, we will focus our attention on gene mutations, which are relatively small changes in the sequence of bases in a particular gene. We will also consider how the timing of new mutations during an organism's development has important consequences. Finally, we will explore how environmental agents may bring about mutations and examine a testing method that is used to determine if an agent causes mutations.

Gene Mutations Alter the DNA Sequence of a Gene

Mutations cause two basic types of changes to a gene: (1) the base sequence within a gene can be changed; and (2) one or more base pairs can be added to or removed from a gene. A **point mutation** affects only a single base pair within the DNA. For example, the DNA sequence shown here has been altered by a **base substitution** in which a T (in the top strand) has been replaced by a G and the corresponding A in the bottom strand is replaced with a C:

```
5'-CCCGCTAGATA-3'              5'-CCCGCGAGATA-3'
                    ⟶
3'-GGGCGATCTAT-5'              3'-GGGCGCTCTAT-5'
```

A point mutation could also involve the addition or deletion of a single base pair to a DNA sequence. For example, in the following sequence, a single base pair (A-T) has been added to the DNA:

```
5'-GGCGCTAGATC-3'              5'-GGCAGCTAGATC-3'
                    ⟶
3'-CCGCGATCTAG-5'              3'-CCGTCGATCTAG-5'
```

Though point mutations may seem like small changes to a DNA sequence, they can have important consequences when genes are expressed, as we will see next.

Gene Mutations May Affect the Amino Acid Sequence of a Polypeptide

If a mutation occurs within the region of a structural gene that specifies the amino acid sequence, the mutation may alter that sequence in a variety of ways. **Table 14.1** considers the potential effects of point mutations. **Silent mutations** do not alter the amino acid sequence of the polypeptide, even though the nucleotide sequence has changed. As discussed in Chapter 12, the genetic code is degenerate, that is, more than one codon can specify the same amino acid. Silent mutations occur in the third base of many codons without changing the type of amino acid it encodes.

Table 14.1 Consequences of Point Mutations Within the Coding Sequence of a Structural Gene

Mutation in the DNA	Effect on polypeptide	Example*
None	None	ATGGCCGGCCCGAAAGAGACC — Met-Ala-Gly-Pro-Lys-Glu-Thr
Base substitution	**Silent**—causes no change	ATGGCCGGCCCCAAAGAGACC — Met-Ala-Gly-Pro-Lys-Glu-Thr
Base substitution	**Missense**—changes one amino acid	ATGCCCGGCCCGAAAGAGACC — Met-Pro-Gly-Pro-Lys-Glu-Thr
Base substitution	**Nonsense**—changes to a stop codon	ATGGCCGGCCCGTAAGAGACC — Met-Ala-Gly-Pro-STOP
Addition (or deletion) of single base	**Frameshift**—produces a different amino acid sequence	ATGGCCGGCACCGAAAGAGACC — Met-Ala-Gly-Thr-Glu-Arg-Asp

*DNA sequence in the coding strand. This sequence is the same as the mRNA sequence except that RNA contains uracil (U) instead of thymine (T).

A **missense mutation** is a base substitution that changes a single amino acid in a polypeptide sequence. A missense mutation may not alter protein function because it changes only a single amino acid within a polypeptide that is typically hundreds of amino acids in length. A missense mutation that substitutes an amino acid with a chemistry similar to the original amino acid is less likely to alter protein function. For example, a missense mutation that substitutes a glutamic acid for an aspartic acid may not alter protein function because both amino acids are negatively charged and have similar side chain structures (refer back to Figure 3.14).

Alternatively, some missense mutations have a dramatic effect on protein function. A striking example occurs in the human disease known as **sickle cell disease**. This disease involves a missense mutation in the β-globin gene, which encodes one of the polypeptide subunits that make up hemoglobin, the oxygen-carrying protein in red blood cells. In the most common form of this disease, a missense mutation alters the polypeptide sequence such that the sixth amino acid is changed from a glutamic acid to a valine (**Figure 14.1**). Because glutamic acid is hydrophilic but valine is hydrophobic, this single amino acid substitution alters the structure and function of the hemoglobin protein. The mutant hemoglobin subunits tend to stick to one another when the oxygen concentration is low. The aggregated proteins form fiber-like structures within red blood cells, which causes the cells to lose their normal disc-shaped morphology and become sickle-shaped. It seems amazing that a single amino acid substitution could have such a profound effect on the structure of cells.

Two other types of point mutations cause more dramatic changes to a polypeptide sequence. A **nonsense mutation** involves a change from a normal codon to a stop, or termination, codon. This causes translation to be terminated earlier than expected, producing

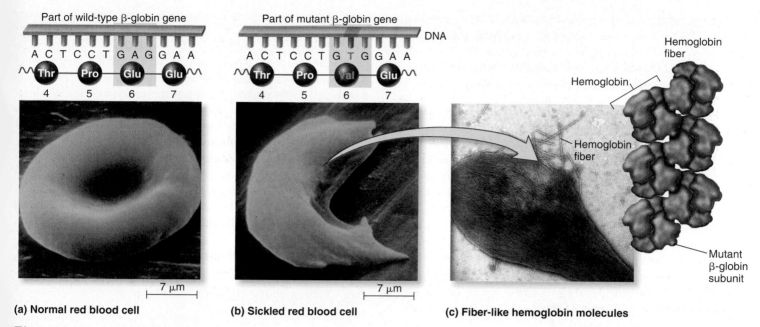

Part of wild-type β-globin gene

Part of mutant β-globin gene

DNA

A C T C C T G A G G A A
Thr Pro Glu Glu
4   5   6   7

A C T C C T G T G G A A
Thr Pro Val Glu
4   5   6   7

Hemoglobin fiber

Hemoglobin

Hemoglobin fiber

7 μm

7 μm

Mutant β-globin subunit

(a) Normal red blood cell   **(b) Sickled red blood cell**   **(c) Fiber-like hemoglobin molecules**

Figure 14.1   **A missense mutation that causes red blood cells to sickle in sickle cell disease.** Scanning electron micrographs of **(a)** normal red blood cell and **(b)** sickled red blood cell. As shown above the micrographs, a missense mutation in the β-globin gene (which codes for a subunit of hemoglobin) changes the sixth amino acid in the β-globin polypeptide from a glutamic acid (Glu) to a valine (Val). **(c)** This micrograph shows how this alteration to the structure of β-globin causes the formation of abnormal fiber-like structures. In normal cells, hemoglobin proteins do not form fibers.

Concept Check: *Based on the fiber-like structures seen in part (c), what aspect of hemoglobin structure does a glutamic acid at the sixth position in normal β-globin prevent? Speculate on how the charge of this amino acid may play a role.*

a truncated polypeptide (see Table 14.1). Compared with a normal polypeptide, a shorter polypeptide is much less likely to function properly. Finally, a **frameshift mutation** involves the addition or deletion of nucleotides that are not in multiples of three nucleotides. For example, a frameshift mutation could involve the addition or deletion of one, two, four, or five nucleotides. Because the codons are read in multiples of three, these types of insertions or deletions shift the reading frame so a completely different amino acid sequence occurs downstream from the mutation (see Table 14.1). Such a large change in polypeptide structure is likely to inhibit protein function.

Changes in protein function may affect the ability of an organism to survive and to reproduce. Except for silent mutations, new mutations are more likely to produce polypeptides that have reduced rather than enhanced function. However, mutations can occasionally produce a polypeptide that has an enhanced function. Such mutations may change in frequency in a population over the course of many generations due to natural selection. This topic is discussed in Chapter 24.

Gene Mutations That Occur Outside of Coding Sequences Can Influence Gene Expression

Thus far, we have focused our attention on mutations in the coding regions of structural genes. In Chapters 12 and 13, we explored the role of DNA sequences in gene expression. A mutation can occur within a noncoding DNA sequence and affect gene expression (**Table 14.2**). For example, a mutation may alter the sequence within

the promoter of a gene, thereby affecting the rate of transcription. A mutation that improves the ability of RNA polymerase to bind to the promoter may enhance transcription, whereas other mutations may inhibit transcription.

Mutations in regulatory elements or operator sites can alter the regulation of gene transcription. For example, in Chapter 13, we considered the roles of regulatory elements such as the *lac* operator site in *E. coli*, which is recognized by the lac repressor protein (refer back to Figure 13.7). Mutations in the *lac* operator site can disrupt the proper regulation of the *lac* operon. An operator mutation may change the DNA sequence so the lac repressor protein does not bind to it. This mutation would cause the operon to be constitutively expressed.

Table 14.2	Effects of Mutations Outside of the Coding Sequence of a Gene
Sequence	**Effect of mutation**
Promoter	May increase or decrease the rate of transcription
Transcriptional regulatory element/operator site	May alter the regulation of transcription
Splice sites	May alter the ability of pre-mRNA to be properly spliced
Translational regulatory element	May alter the ability of mRNA to be translationally regulated
Intergenic region	Not as likely to have an effect on gene expression

FEATURE INVESTIGATION

The Lederbergs Used Replica Plating to Show That Mutations Are Random Events

As we have seen, mutations affect the expression of genes in a variety of ways. Scientists considered the following question: Do mutations that affect the traits of an individual occur as a result of pre-existing circumstances, or are they random events that may happen in any gene of any individual? In the 19th century, French naturalist Jean Baptiste Lamarck proposed that physiological events (such as use or disuse) determine whether traits are passed along to offspring. For example, his hypothesis suggested that an individual who practiced

and became adept at a physical activity, such as the long jump, would pass that quality on to his or her offspring. Alternatively, geneticists in the early 1900s suggested that genetic variation occurs as a matter of chance. According to this view, those individuals whose genes happen to contain beneficial mutations are more likely to survive and pass those genes to their offspring.

These opposing views were tested in bacterial studies in the 1940s and 1950s. One such study, by American microbiologists Joshua and Esther Lederberg, focused on the occurrence of mutations in bacteria (**Figure 14.2**). First, they placed a large number of *E. coli* bacteria onto growth media and incubated them overnight, so each

Figure 14.2 **The experiment performed by the Lederbergs showing that mutations are random events.**

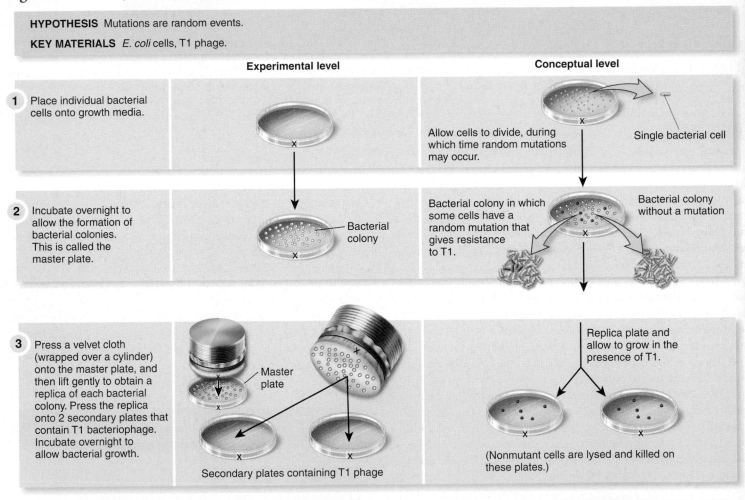

HYPOTHESIS Mutations are random events.

KEY MATERIALS *E. coli* cells, T1 phage.

Experimental level — **Conceptual level**

1 Place individual bacterial cells onto growth media.

Allow cells to divide, during which time random mutations may occur.

Single bacterial cell

2 Incubate overnight to allow the formation of bacterial colonies. This is called the master plate.

Bacterial colony

Bacterial colony in which some cells have a random mutation that gives resistance to T1.

Bacterial colony without a mutation

3 Press a velvet cloth (wrapped over a cylinder) onto the master plate, and then lift gently to obtain a replica of each bacterial colony. Press the replica onto 2 secondary plates that contain T1 bacteriophage. Incubate overnight to allow bacterial growth.

Master plate

Secondary plates containing T1 phage

Replica plate and allow to grow in the presence of T1.

(Nonmutant cells are lysed and killed on these plates.)

4 **THE DATA**

Colonies on each plate are in the same locations.

5 **CONCLUSION** Mutations are random events. In this case, the mutations occurred on the master plate prior to exposure to T1 bacteriophage.

6 **SOURCE** Lederberg, Joshua, and Lederberg, Esther M. 1952. Replica plating and indirect selection of bacterial mutants. *Journal of Bacteriology* 63:399–406.

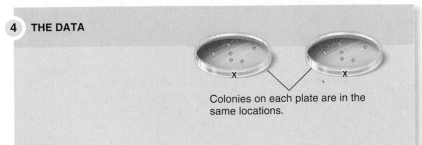

bacterial cell divided many times to form a bacterial colony composed of millions of cells. This is called the master plate. Using a technique known as **replica plating**, a sterile piece of velvet cloth was lightly touched to the master plate to pick up bacterial cells from each colony on the master plate. They then transferred this replica to two secondary plates containing an agent that selected for the growth of bacterial cells with a particular mutation.

In the example shown in Figure 14.2, the secondary plates contained T1 bacteriophages, which are viruses that infect bacteria and cause them to lyse. On these plates, only those rare cells that had acquired a mutation conferring resistance to T1, termed *ton^r*, could grow. All other cells were lysed by the proliferation of bacteriophages in the bacteria. Therefore, only a few colonies were observed on the secondary plates. Strikingly, these colonies occupied the same locations on each plate. How did the Lederbergs interpret these results?

The data indicated that the *ton^r* mutations occurred randomly while the bacterial cells were forming colonies on the nonselective master plate. The presence of T1 bacteriophages in the secondary plates did not cause the mutations to develop. Rather, the T1 bacteriophages simply selected for the growth of *ton^r* mutants that were already in the population. These results supported the idea that mutations are random events.

Experimental Questions

1. Explain the opposing views of mutation prior to the Lederbergs' study.

2. What hypothesis was being tested by the Lederbergs? What were the results of the experiment?

3. How did the results of the Lederbergs support or falsify the hypothesis?

Mutations Can Occur in Germ-Line or Somatic Cells

Let's now consider how the timing of a mutation may have an important influence on its potential effects. Multicellular organisms typically begin their lives as a single fertilized egg cell that divides many times to produce all the cells of an adult organism. A mutation can occur in any cell of the body, either very early in life, such as in a gamete (eggs or sperm) or a fertilized egg, or later in life, such as in the embryonic or adult stages. The number and location of cells with a mutation are critical both to the severity of the genetic effect and to whether the mutation can be passed on to offspring.

Geneticists classify the cells of animals into two types: germ-line and somatic cells. The term **germ line** refers to cells that give rise to gametes, such as egg and sperm cells. A germ-line mutation can occur directly in an egg or sperm cell, or it can occur in a precursor cell that produces the gametes. If a mutant human gamete participates in fertilization, all the cells of the resulting offspring will contain the mutation, as indicated by the red color in **Figure 14.3a**. Likewise, when such an individual produces gametes, the mutation may be transmitted to future generations of offspring. Because humans carry two copies of most genes, a new mutation in a single gene has a 50% chance of being transmitted from parent to offspring.

The **somatic cells** constitute all cells of the body except for the germ line. Examples include skin cells and muscle cells. Mutations can also occur within somatic cells at early or late stages of development. What are the consequences of a mutation that happens during the embryonic stage? As shown in **Figure 14.3b**, a mutation occurred within a single embryonic cell. This single somatic cell was the precursor for many cells of the adult. Therefore, in the adult, a patch of tissue contains cells that carry the mutation. The size of any patch depends on the timing of a new mutation. In general, the earlier a mutation occurs during development, the larger the patch. An individual with somatic regions that are genetically different from each other is called a **mosaic**.

Figure 14.4 illustrates a child who had a somatic mutation during an early stage of development. In this case, the child has a streak of white hair while the rest of his hair is black. Presumably, he initially had a single mutation happen in an embryonic cell that ultimately gave rise to the patch that produced the white hair.

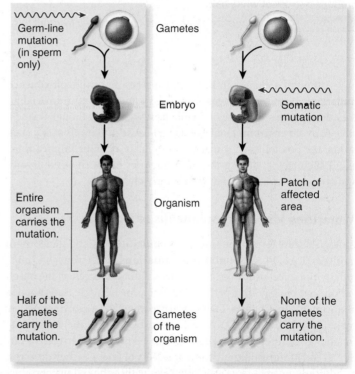

(a) Germ-line mutation   **(b) Somatic cell mutation**

Figure 14.3 **The effects of germ-line versus somatic cell mutations.** The red color indicates which cells carry the mutation. (a) If a mutation is passed via gametes, such germ-line mutations occur in every cell of the body. Because humans have two copies of most genes, a germ-line mutation in one of those two copies is transmitted to only half of the gametes. (b) Somatic mutations affect a limited area of the body and are not transmitted to offspring.

BIOLOGY PRINCIPLE **Living organisms grow and develop.** As a multicellular organism grows and develops, a germ-line mutation is transmitted to all cells of the body, whereas a somatic mutation is found only in a particular region.

Concept Check: *Why are somatic mutations unable to be transmitted to offspring?*

Figure 14.4 **Example of a somatic mutation.** This child has a streak of white hair. This is due to a somatic mutation in a single cell during embryonic development. This cell continued to divide to produce a streak of white hair.

Concept Check: *Can this child with a streak of white hair transmit this trait to his future offspring?*

Although a change in hair color is not a harmful consequence, mutations during early stages of life can be quite harmful, especially if they disrupt essential developmental processes. Even though it is sensible to avoid environmental agents that cause mutations at any stage of life, the possibility of somatic mutations is a compelling reason to avoid such agents during the early stages of life such as embryonic and fetal development, infancy, and early childhood.

Mutations May Be Spontaneous or Induced

Biologists categorize the causes of mutation as spontaneous or induced (**Table 14.3**). **Spontaneous mutations** result from abnormalities in biological processes. Spontaneous mutations reflect the observation that biology isn't perfect. Enzymes, for example, can function abnormally. In Chapter 11, we learned that DNA polymerase can make mistakes during DNA replication by putting the wrong base in a newly synthesized daughter strand. Though such errors are rare due to the proofreading function of DNA polymerase, they do occur. In addition, normal metabolic processes within the cell may produce toxic chemicals such as free radicals that can react directly with the DNA and alter its structure. Finally, the structure of nucleotides is not absolutely stable. On occasion, the structure of a base may spontaneously change, and such a change may cause a mutation if it occurs immediately prior to DNA replication.

The rates of spontaneous mutations vary from species to species and from gene to gene. Larger genes are usually more likely to incur a mutation than are smaller ones. A common rate of spontaneous mutation among various species is approximately 1 mutation for every 1 million genes per cell division, which equals 1 in 10^6, or simply 10^{-6}. This is the expected rate of spontaneous mutation, which creates the variation that is the raw material of evolution.

Induced mutations are caused by environmental agents that enter the cell and alter the structure of DNA. They cause the mutation

Table 14.3 Some Common Causes of Gene Mutations

Common causes of mutations	Description
Spontaneous:	
Errors in DNA replication	A mistake by DNA polymerase may cause a point mutation.
Toxic metabolic products	The products of normal metabolic processes may be reactive chemicals such as free radicals that can alter the structure of DNA.
Changes in nucleotide structure	On rare occasions, the linkage between purines and deoxyribose can spontaneously break. Changes in base structure (isomerization) may cause mispairing during DNA replication.
Transposons	As discussed in Chapter 21, transposons are small segments of DNA that can insert at various sites in the genome. If they insert into a gene, they may inactivate the gene.
Induced:	
Chemical agents	Chemical substances, such as benzo(a)pyrene, a chemical found in cigarette smoke, may cause changes in the structure of DNA.
Physical agents	Physical agents such as UV (ultraviolet) light and X-rays can damage the DNA.

rate to be higher than the spontaneous mutation rate. Agents that cause mutation are called **mutagens**. Mutagenic agents can be categorized as **chemical** or **physical mutagens** (**Table 14.4**). We will consider their effects next.

Mutagens Alter DNA Structure in Different Ways

Researchers have discovered that an enormous array of agents act as mutagens. We often hear in the news media that we should avoid these agents in our foods and living environments. We even use products such as sunscreens that help us avoid the mutagenic effects of ultraviolet (UV) light from the Sun. The public is often concerned about mutagens for two important reasons. First, mutagenic agents are usually involved in the development of human cancers. Second, because new mutations may be deleterious, people want to avoid mutagens to prevent mutations that may have harmful effects in their future offspring.

How do mutagens affect DNA structure? Some chemical mutagens act by covalently modifying the structure of nucleotides. For example, nitrous acid (HNO_2) deaminates bases by replacing amino groups with keto groups ($-NH_2$ to $=O$). This can change cytosine to uracil. When this altered DNA replicates, the modified base does not pair with the appropriate base in the newly made strand. In this case, uracil pairs with adenine (**Figure 14.5**).

Similarly, 5-bromouracil and 2-aminopurine, which are called base analogues, have structures that are similar to particular bases in DNA and can substitute for them. When incorporated into DNA, they also cause errors in DNA replication. Other chemical mutagens disrupt the appropriate pairing between nucleotides by alkylating bases within the DNA. During alkylation, methyl or ethyl groups are covalently attached to the bases. Examples of alkylating agents include nitrogen mustards (used as a chemical weapon during World War I) and ethyl methanesulfonate (EMS), which is used as a mutagen in laboratory experiments.

Table 14.4   Examples of Mutagens

Mutagen	Effect(s) on DNA structure
Chemical	
Nitrous acid	Deaminates bases
5-Bromouracil	Acts as a base analogue
2-Aminopurine	Acts as a base analogue
Nitrogen mustard	Alkylates bases
Ethyl methanesulfonate (EMS)	Alkylates bases
Benzo(a)pyrene	Inserts next to bases in the DNA double helix and causes additions or deletions
Physical	
X-rays	Causes base deletions, single nicks in DNA strands, crosslinking, and chromosomal breaks
UV light	Promotes pyrimidine dimer formation, which involves covalent bonds between adjacent pyrimidines (C or T)

Some chemical mutagens exert their effects by interfering with DNA replication. For example, benzo(a)pyrene, which is found in automobile exhaust, cigarette smoke, and charbroiled food, is metabolized to a compound (benzopyrene diol epoxide) that inserts in between the bases of the double helix, thereby distorting the helical structure. When DNA containing such a mutagen is replicated, single-nucleotide additions and deletions may be incorporated into the newly made strands.

DNA molecules are also sensitive to physical agents such as radiation. In particular, radiation of short wavelength and high energy, known as ionizing radiation, is known to alter DNA structure. Ionizing radiation includes X-rays and gamma rays. This type of radiation can penetrate deeply into biological materials, where it creates free radicals. These molecules can alter the structure of DNA in a variety of ways. Exposure to high doses of ionizing radiation causes base deletions, breaks in one DNA strand, and even a break in both DNA strands.

Nonionizing radiation, such as UV light, contains less energy, and so it penetrates only the surface of biological materials, such as the skin. Nevertheless, UV light is known to cause mutations. For example, UV light can cause the formation of a **thymine dimer**, which is a site where two adjacent thymine bases become covalently crosslinked to each other (**Figure 14.6**).

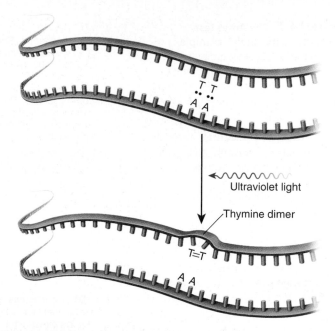

Figure 14.6 **Formation and structure of a thymine dimer.**

Concept Check: *Why is a thymine dimer harmful?*

Thymine dimers are typically repaired before or during DNA replication. However, if such repair fails to occur, a thymine dimer may cause a mutation when that DNA strand is replicated. When DNA polymerase attempts to replicate over a thymine dimer, proper base pairing does not occur between the template strand and the incoming nucleotides. This mispairing can cause gaps in the newly made strand or the incorporation of incorrect bases. Plants, in particular, must have effective ways to prevent UV damage because they are exposed to sunlight throughout the day.

Testing Methods Determine If an Agent Is a Mutagen

Because mutagens are harmful, researchers have developed testing methods to evaluate the ability of a substance to cause mutation. One commonly used test is the **Ames test**, which was developed by American biochemist Bruce Ames in the 1970s. This test uses a strain of a bacterium, *Salmonella typhimurium*, that cannot synthesize the amino acid histidine. This strain contains a point mutation within a gene that encodes an enzyme required for histidine biosynthesis. The mutation renders the enzyme inactive. The bacteria cannot grow unless histidine has been added to the growth medium. However, a second mutation may correct the first mutation, thereby restoring the ability to synthesize histidine. The Ames test monitors the rate at which this second mutation occurs and thereby indicates whether an agent increases the mutation rate above the spontaneous rate.

Figure 14.7 outlines the steps in the Ames test. The suspected mutagen is mixed with a rat liver extract and the bacterial strain of *S. typhimurium* that cannot synthesize histidine. Because some potential mutagens may require activation by cellular enzymes, the rat liver extract provides a mixture of enzymes that may cause such activation. This step improves the ability to identify agents that cause mutations in mammals. As a control, bacteria that have not been exposed to the mutagen are also tested. After an incubation period in which

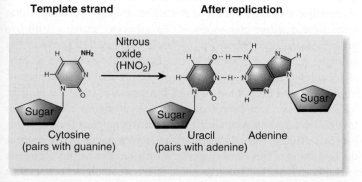

Template strand   **After replication**

Cytosine (pairs with guanine) → Uracil (pairs with adenine)   Adenine

Nitrous oxide (HNO₂)

Figure 14.5 **Deamination and mispairing of modified bases by a chemical mutagen.** Nitrous acid changes cytosine to uracil by replacing NH₂ with an oxygen. During DNA replication, uracil pairs with adenine, thereby creating a mutation in the newly replicated strand.

Figure 14.7 The Ames test for mutagenicity. In this example, 2 million bacterial cells were placed on plates lacking histidine. Two colonies arose from the control sample, whereas 44 arose from the sample exposed to a suspected mutagen.

 BIOLOGY PRINCIPLE Biology affects our society. Biologists have developed many methods, including the Ames test, for determining if a chemical is a mutagen. The results of these tests have prevented the use of many different chemicals in the production of food and also resulted in warning labels on products such as cigarettes.

> **Concept Check:** Based on the results seen in this figure, what is the rate of mutation that is caused by the suspected mutagen?

1 Mix together the *Salmonella typhimurium* strain, rat liver extract, and suspected mutagen and incubate. The suspected mutagen is omitted from the control sample. The rat liver extract is added because liver enzymes sometimes convert chemicals into mutagens.

Control

Rat liver extract

Rat liver extract

Suspected mutagen

S. typhimurium strain (requires histidine)

S. typhimurium strain (requires histidine)

2 Plate the mixtures onto petri plates that lack histidine. Incubate overnight to allow bacterial growth.

A large number of colonies suggests that the suspected mutagen causes mutation.

mutations may occur, a large number of bacteria are plated on a growth medium that does not contain histidine. The *S. typhimurium* strain is not expected to grow on these plates. However, if a mutation has occurred that allows a cell to synthesize histidine, the bacterium harboring this second mutation will proliferate during an overnight incubation period to form a visible bacterial colony.

To estimate the mutation rate, the colonies that grow in the absence of histidine are counted and compared with the total number of bacterial cells that were originally placed on the plate for both the suspected-mutagen sample and the control. The control condition is a measure of the spontaneous mutation rate, whereas the other sample measures the rate of mutation in the presence of the suspected mutagen. As an example, let's suppose that 2 million bacteria were plated from both the control and the suspected-mutagen tubes. In the control experiment, 2 bacterial colonies were observed. The spontaneous mutation rate is calculated by dividing 2 (the number of mutants) by 2 million (the number of original cells). This equals 1 in 1 million, or 1×10^{-6}. By comparison, 44 colonies arose from the suspected-mutagen sample (see Figure 14.7). In this case, the mutation rate would be 44 divided by 2 million, which equals 2.2×10^{-5}. The mutation rate in the presence of the mutagen is over 20 times higher than the spontaneous mutation rate.

How do we judge if an agent is a mutagen? Researchers compare the mutation rate in the presence and absence of the suspected mutagen. The experimental approach shown in Figure 14.7 is conducted several times. If statistics reveal that the mutation rate in the suspected-mutagen sample is significantly higher than in the control sample, they may tentatively conclude that the agent is a mutagen. Interestingly,

many studies have used the Ames test to compare the urine from cigarette smokers with that from nonsmokers. This research has shown that urine from smokers contains much higher levels of mutagens.

14.2 DNA Repair

Learning Outcomes:
1. List the general features of DNA repair systems.
2. Describe the steps of nucleotide excision repair.
3. Explain the connection between defects in DNA repair systems and the inherited human disease xeroderma pigmentosum.

In the previous section, we considered the causes and consequences of mutation. As we have seen, mutations are random events that often have negative consequences. To minimize mutation, all living organisms have the ability to repair changes that occur in the structure of DNA. For example, in Chapter 11 we considered how DNA polymerase has a proofreading function that helps to prevent mutations from happening during DNA replication. In this section, we will examine DNA repair systems that can detect abnormalities in DNA structure and repair them. The importance of these systems becomes evident when they are missing. For example, as discussed at the beginning of this chapter, persons with xeroderma pigmentosum are highly susceptible to the harmful effects of sunlight because they are missing a single DNA repair system.

How do organisms minimize the occurrence of mutations? Cells contain several DNA repair systems that can fix different types of DNA alterations (**Table 14.5**). Each repair system is composed of one or more

Table 14.5	Common Types of DNA Repair Systems
System	**Description**
Direct repair	A repair enzyme recognizes an incorrect structure in the DNA and directly converts it back to a correct structure.
Base excision and nucleotide excision repair	An abnormal base or nucleotide is recognized, and a portion of the strand containing the abnormality is removed. The complementary DNA strand is then used as a template to synthesize a normal DNA strand.
Methyl-directed mismatch repair	Similar to excision repair except that the DNA defect is a base pair mismatch in the DNA, not an abnormal nucleotide. The mismatch is recognized, and a strand of DNA in this region is removed. The complementary strand is used to synthesize a normal strand of DNA.

*Other types of repair systems exist; these are common examples.

proteins that play specific roles in the repair mechanism. DNA repair requires two coordinated events. In the first step, one or more proteins in the repair system detect an irregularity in DNA structure. In the second step, the abnormality is repaired. In some cases, the change in DNA structure can be directly repaired. For example, DNA may be modified by the attachment of an alkyl group, such as—CH_2CH_3, to a base. In **direct repair**, an enzyme removes this alkyl group, thereby restoring the structure of the original base. More commonly, however, the altered DNA is removed, and a new segment of DNA is synthesized. In this section, we will examine nucleotide excision repair as an example of how such systems operate. This system, which is found in all species, is an important mechanism of DNA repair.

Nucleotide Excision Repair Removes Segments of Damaged DNA

In **nucleotide excision repair (NER)**, a region encompassing several nucleotides in the damaged strand is removed from the DNA, and the intact undamaged strand is used as a template for the resynthesis of a normal complementary strand. NER can fix many different types of DNA damage, including UV-induced damage, chemically modified bases, missing bases, and various types of crosslinks (such as thymine dimers). The system is found in all species, although its molecular mechanism is better understood in bacteria.

In *E. coli*, the NER system is composed of four key proteins: UvrA, UvrB, UvrC, and UvrD. They are named Uvr because they are involved in ultraviolet light repair of thymine dimers, although these proteins are also important in repairing chemically damaged DNA. In addition, DNA polymerase and DNA ligase are required to complete the repair process.

How does the NER system work? Two UvrA proteins and one UvrB protein form a complex that tracks along the DNA (**Figure 14.8**). Damaged DNA will have a distorted double helix, which is sensed by the UvrA-UvrB complex. When the complex identifies a damaged site, the two UvrA proteins are released, and UvrC binds to UvrB at the site. The UvrC protein makes incisions in one DNA strand on both sides of the damaged site. After this incision process, UvrC is released. UvrD binds to UvrB. UvrD then begins to separate the DNA strands, and UvrB is released. The action of UvrD unravels the DNA,

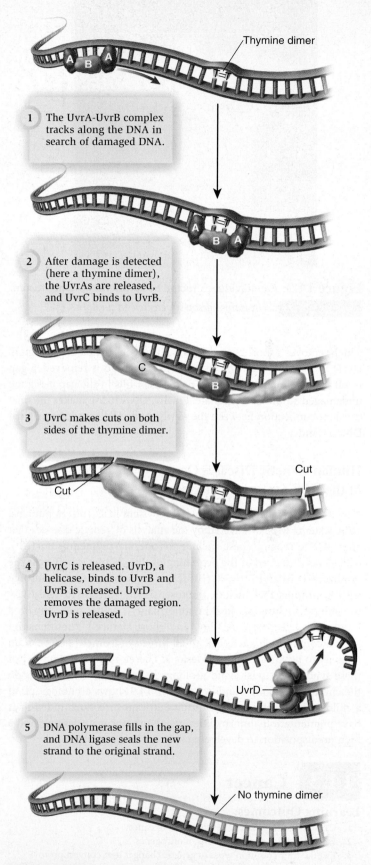

1 The UvrA-UvrB complex tracks along the DNA in search of damaged DNA.

2 After damage is detected (here a thymine dimer), the UvrAs are released, and UvrC binds to UvrB.

3 UvrC makes cuts on both sides of the thymine dimer.

4 UvrC is released. UvrD, a helicase, binds to UvrB and UvrB is released. UvrD removes the damaged region. UvrD is released.

5 DNA polymerase fills in the gap, and DNA ligase seals the new strand to the original strand.

Figure 14.8 Nucleotide excision repair in *E. coli*.

Concept Check: *Which components of NER are responsible for removing the damaged DNA?*

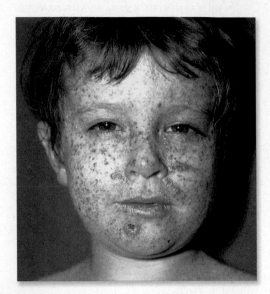

Figure 14.9 An individual affected by xeroderma pigmentosum.

Concept Check: Why is this person so sensitive to sunlight?

which removes a short DNA strand that contains the damaged region. UvrD is released. After the damaged DNA strand is removed, a gap is left in the double helix. DNA polymerase fills in the gap using the undamaged strand as a template. Finally, DNA ligase makes the final covalent connection between the newly made DNA and the original DNA strand.

Human Genetic Diseases Occur When a Component of the NER System Is Missing

Thus far, we have considered the NER system in *E. coli*. In humans, NER systems were discovered by the analysis of genetic diseases that affect DNA repair. These include xeroderma pigmentosum (XP), which was discussed at the beginning of this chapter, and Cockayne syndrome (CS) and PIBIDS. (PIBIDS is an acronym for a syndrome with symptoms that include photosensitivity [increased sensitivity to sunlight], ichthyosis [a skin abnormality], brittle hair, impaired intelligence, decreased fertility, and short stature.) Photosensitivity is a common characteristic in all three syndromes because of an inability to repair UV-induced lesions. Therefore, people with any of these syndromes must avoid prolonged exposure to sunlight, as do the children at Camp Sundown. **Figure 14.9** shows a photograph of a child with XP who had significant Sun exposure. Such individuals have pigmentation abnormalities, many precancerous lesions, and a high predisposition to developing skin cancer.

14.3 Cancer

Learning Outcomes:

1. Outline the steps in the development of cancer.
2. Describe the general functions of oncogenes.
3. List the four common types of genetic changes that convert proto-oncogenes into oncogenes.
4. Identify the two general functions of the proteins encoded by tumor-suppressor genes.
5. Describe three common ways that tumor-suppressor genes are silenced.

Cancer is a disease of multicellular organisms characterized by uncontrolled cell division. Worldwide, cancer is the second leading cause of death in humans, exceeded only by heart disease. In the United States, approximately 1.5 million people are diagnosed with cancer each year; over 0.5 million will die from the disease. Overall, about one in four Americans will die from cancer.

In about 10% of cancers, a higher predisposition to develop the disease is an inherited trait. Most cancers, though, perhaps 90%, do not involve genetic changes that are passed from parent to offspring. Rather, cancer is usually an acquired condition that typically occurs later in life. At least 80% of all human cancers are related to exposure to **carcinogens**, agents that increase the likelihood of developing cancer. Most carcinogens, such as UV light and certain chemicals in cigarette smoke, are mutagens that promote genetic changes in somatic cells. These genetic changes can alter gene expression in a way that ultimately affects cell division, leading to cancer. In this section, we will explore such genetic abnormalities.

How does cancer occur? In most cases, the development of cancer is a multistep process (**Figure 14.10**). Cancers originate from a single cell. This single cell and its lineage of daughter cells undergo a series of mutations that cause the cells to grow abnormally. At an early stage, the cells form a **tumor**, which is an overgrowth of cells. For most types of cancer, a tumor begins as a precancerous or **benign** growth. Such tumors do not invade adjacent tissues and do not spread throughout the body. This may be followed by additional mutations that cause some cells in the tumor to lose their normal growth regulation and become **malignant**. At this stage, the individual has cancer. Cancerous tumors invade healthy tissues and may spread through the bloodstream or surrounding body fluids, a process called **metastasis**. If left untreated, malignant cells will cause the death of the organism.

Over the past few decades, researchers have identified many genes that promote cancer when they are mutant. By comparing the function of each mutant gene with the corresponding nonmutant gene found in healthy cells, these genes have been placed into two categories. In some cases, a mutation causes a gene to be overactive—have an abnormally high level of expression. This overactivity contributes to the uncontrolled cell growth that is observed in cancer cells. This type of mutant gene is called an **oncogene**. Alternatively, when a **tumor-suppressor gene** is normal (that is, not mutant), it encodes a protein that helps to prevent cancer. However, when a mutation eliminates its function, cancer may occur. Thus, the two categories of cancer-causing genes are based on the effects of mutations. Oncogenes are the result of mutations that cause overactivity, whereas cancer-causing mutations in tumor-suppressor genes are due to a loss of activity. In this section, we will begin with a discussion of oncogenes and then consider tumor-suppressor genes.

Oncogenes May Result from Mutations That Cause the Overactivity of Proteins Involved with Cell Division

Over the past four decades, researchers have identified many oncogenes. A large number of oncogenes encode proteins that function in cell growth-signaling pathways. Cell division is regulated, in part, by growth factors, which are molecules that regulate cell division. A growth factor binds to a receptor, which results in receptor activation (**Figure 14.11**). This stimulates an intracellular signal transduction pathway that activates transcription factors. In this way, the

| 1 | Benign growth | | 2 | Malignant growth |

Initial tumor cell

Tumor

Cross section of bronchus

Lungs

3 | Metastasis occurs when cells enter the bloodstream or surrounding body fluids.

Lung tumor

Blood vessel

(a) Progression of cancer **(b) Normal lung (left) and cancerous lung (right)**

Figure 14.10 **Cancer: Its progression and effects.** **(a)** In a healthy individual, an initial mutation converts a normal cell into a tumor cell. This cell divides to produce a benign tumor. Additional genetic changes in the tumor cells may occur, leading to a malignant tumor. At a later stage in malignancy, the tumor cells invade surrounding tissues, and some malignant cells may metastasize by traveling through the bloodstream to other parts of the body. **(b)** On the left of the photo is a human lung that was obtained from a healthy nonsmoker. The lung shown on the right has been ravaged by lung cancer. This lung was taken from a person who was a heavy smoker.

BioConnections: *Look back at Figure 10.17. Explain how a disruption in the arrangement of epithelial cells could promote metastasis.*

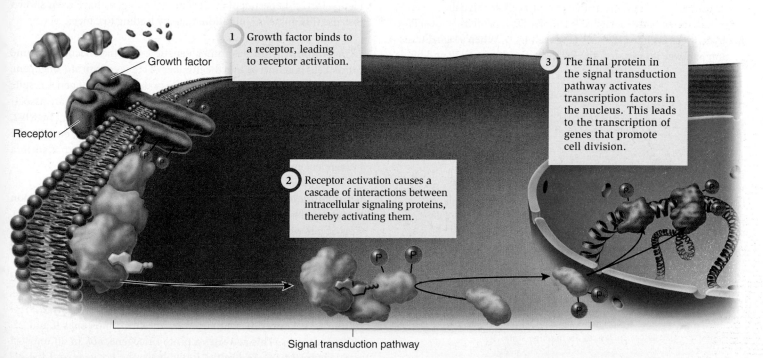

Growth factor

Receptor

1 | Growth factor binds to a receptor, leading to receptor activation.

3 | The final protein in the signal transduction pathway activates transcription factors in the nucleus. This leads to the transcription of genes that promote cell division.

2 | Receptor activation causes a cascade of interactions between intracellular signaling proteins, thereby activating them.

Signal transduction pathway

Figure 14.11 **General features of a growth factor-signaling pathway that promotes cell division.** A detailed description of this pathway is found in Chapter 9 (Figure 9.10).

Concept Check: *How does the presence of a growth factor ultimately affect the function of the cell?*

BioConnections: *Look back at Figure 9.10. Could drugs that inhibit protein kinases be used to combat cancer? Explain.*

Table 14.6	Examples of Genes Encoding Proteins of Growth Factor Signaling Pathways That Can Become Oncogenes
Gene*	**Cellular function**
erbB	Growth factor receptor for EGF (epidermal growth factor)
ras	Intracellular signaling protein
raf	Intracellular signaling protein
src	Intracellular signaling protein
fos	Transcription factor
jun	Transcription factor

*The genes described in this table are found in humans as well as other vertebrate species. Most of the genes have been given three-letter names that are abbreviations for the type of cancer the oncogene causes or the type of virus in which the gene was first identified.

transcription of specific genes is activated in response to a growth factor. After they are made, the gene products promote cell division.

Eukaryotic species produce many different growth factors that play a role in cell division. Likewise, cells have several different types of signal transduction pathways, which are composed of proteins that respond to growth factors and promote cell division. Mutations in the genes that encode these signal transduction proteins can change them into oncogenes (**Table 14.6**).

How does an oncogene promote cancer? In some cases, an oncogene may keep a cell division-signaling pathway in a permanent "on" position. One way oncogenes keep cell division turned on is by producing a functionally overactive protein. As a specific example, let's consider how a mutation alters an intracellular signaling protein called Ras (refer back to Figure 9.10). The Ras protein is a GTPase that hydrolyzes GTP to GDP + P_i (**Figure 14.12**). When a signal transduction pathway is activated, the Ras protein releases GDP and binds

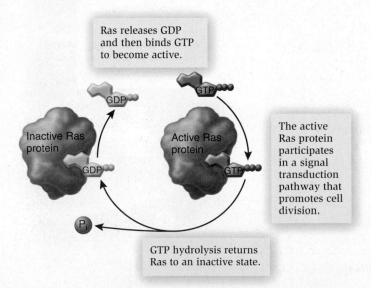

Ras releases GDP and then binds GTP to become active.

Inactive Ras protein

Active Ras protein

The active Ras protein participates in a signal transduction pathway that promotes cell division.

GTP hydrolysis returns Ras to an inactive state.

Figure 14.12   The function of Ras, a protein that is part of signal transduction pathways. When GTP is bound, the activated Ras protein promotes cell division. When GTP is hydrolyzed to GDP and P_i, Ras is inactivated, and cell division is inhibited.

GTP. When GTP is bound, the activated Ras protein promotes cell division. The Ras protein returns to its inactive state by hydrolyzing its bound GTP, and cell division is inhibited. Mutations that convert the normal *ras* gene into an oncogenic *ras* either decrease the ability of Ras protein to hydrolyze GTP or increase the rate of exchange of bound GDP for GTP. Both of these functional changes result in a greater amount of the active GTP-bound form of the Ras protein. In this way, these mutations keep the signaling pathway turned on when it should not be, resulting in uncontrolled cell division.

Mutations in Proto-Oncogenes Convert Them to Oncogenes

Thus far, we have examined the functions of proteins that cause cancer when they become overactive, resulting in uncontrolled cell division. Let's now consider the common types of genetic changes that create such oncogenes. A **proto-oncogene** is a normal gene that, if mutated, can become an oncogene. Several types of genetic changes may convert a proto-oncogene into an oncogene. **Figure 14.13** describes four common types: missense mutations, gene amplifications, chromosomal translocations, and retroviral insertions.

Missense Mutation   A missense mutation (Figure 14.13a), which changes a single amino acid in a protein, alters the function of the encoded protein in a way that promotes cancer. This type of mutation is responsible for the conversion of the *ras* gene into an oncogene. An example is a mutation in the *ras* gene that changes a specific glycine to a valine in the Ras protein. This mutation decreases the ability of the Ras protein to hydrolyze GTP, which promotes cell division (see Figure 14.12). Experimentally, chemical mutagens have been shown to cause this missense mutation, thereby leading to cancer.

Gene Amplification   Another genetic event that occurs in some cancer cells is an increase in the number of copies of a proto-oncogene (Figure 14.13b). An abnormal increase in the number of genes results in too much of the encoded protein. Many human cancers are associated with the amplification of particular proto-oncogenes. In 1982, American molecular biologist Mark Groudine discovered that the *myc* gene, which encodes a transcription factor, was amplified in a human leukemia.

Chromosomal Translocation   A third type of genetic alteration that can lead to cancer is a chromosomal translocation (Figure 14.13c). This occurs when one segment of a chromosome becomes attached to a different chromosome. In 1960, American pathologist Peter Nowell discovered that a form of leukemia called chronic myelogenous leukemia (CML)—a type of cancer involving blood cells—was correlated with the presence of a shortened version of a human chromosome. This shortened chromosome is the result of a chromosome translocation in which two different chromosomes, chromosomes 9 and 22, exchange pieces. This activates a proto-oncogene, *abl*, in an unusual way (**Figure 14.14**). In healthy individuals, the *bcr* gene and the *abl* gene are located on different chromosomes. In CML, these chromosomes break and rejoin in a way that causes the promoter and the first part of *bcr* to fuse with part of *abl*. This abnormal fusion event produces a **chimeric gene** composed of two gene fragments. This

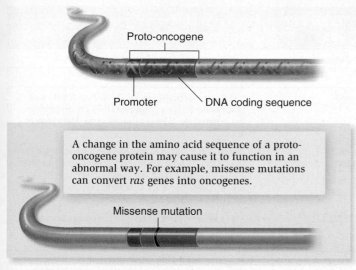

Proto-oncogene

Promoter — DNA coding sequence

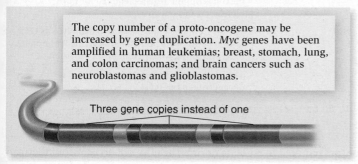

A change in the amino acid sequence of a proto-oncogene protein may cause it to function in an abnormal way. For example, missense mutations can convert *ras* genes into oncogenes.

Missense mutation

(a) Missense mutation

The copy number of a proto-oncogene may be increased by gene duplication. *Myc* genes have been amplified in human leukemias; breast, stomach, lung, and colon carcinomas; and brain cancers such as neuroblastomas and glioblastomas.

Three gene copies instead of one

(b) Gene amplification

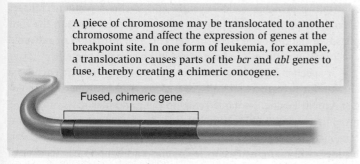

A piece of chromosome may be translocated to another chromosome and affect the expression of genes at the breakpoint site. In one form of leukemia, for example, a translocation causes parts of the *bcr* and *abl* genes to fuse, thereby creating a chimeric oncogene.

Fused, chimeric gene

(c) Chromosomal translocation

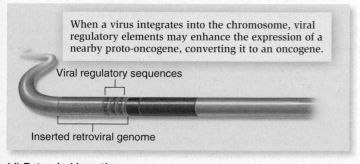

When a virus integrates into the chromosome, viral regulatory elements may enhance the expression of a nearby proto-oncogene, converting it to an oncogene.

Viral regulatory sequences

Inserted retroviral genome

(d) Retroviral Insertion

Figure 14.13 Genetic changes that convert proto-oncogenes to oncogenes. In addition to these, other types of genetic changes may also convert proto-oncogenes into oncogenes.

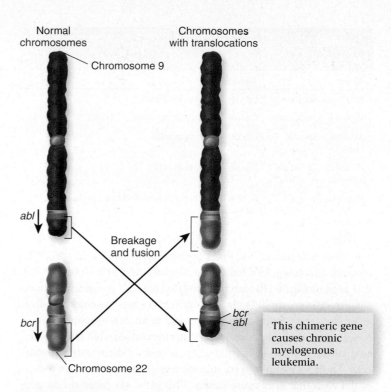

Normal chromosomes

Chromosomes with translocations

Chromosome 9

abl

Breakage and fusion

bcr

bcr
abl

This chimeric gene causes chronic myelogenous leukemia.

Chromosome 22

Figure 14.14 The formation of a chimeric gene found in people with certain forms of leukemia. The fusion of the *bcr* and *abl* genes creates a chimeric gene that encodes an abnormal fusion protein, leading to leukemia. The blue regions are the promoters for the *bcr* and *abl* genes.

Concept Check: *The bcr gene is normally expressed in blood cells. Explain how this observation is related to the type of cancer that the translocation causes.*

chimeric gene acts as an oncogene that encodes an abnormal fusion protein whose functional overactivity leads to leukemia.

Retroviral Insertion Certain types of viruses convert proto-oncogenes into oncogenes during the viral replication cycle (see Figure 14.13d). Retroviruses insert their DNA into the chromosomal DNA of the host cell. The viral genome contains promoter and regulatory elements that cause a high level of expression of viral genes. On occasion, the viral DNA may insert into a host chromosome in such a way that a viral promoter and regulatory elements are next to a proto-oncogene. This may result in the overexpression of the proto-oncogene, thereby promoting cancer. This is one way for a virus to cause cancer. Alternatively, a virus may cause cancer because it carries an oncogene in the viral genome. This phenomenon is described next.

Some Types of Cancer Are Caused by Viruses

The great majority of cancers are caused by mutagens that alter the structure and expression of genes that are found in somatic cells. A few viruses, however, are known to cause cancer in plants and animals, including humans (**Table 14.7**).

In 1911, the first cancer-causing virus to be discovered was isolated from chicken sarcomas by American pathologist Peyton Rous. A **sarcoma** is a tumor of connective tissue such as bone or cartilage.

Table 14.7   Examples of Viruses That Cause Cancer

Virus	Description
Rous sarcoma virus	Causes sarcomas in chickens
Simian sarcoma virus	Causes sarcomas in monkeys
Abelson leukemia virus	Causes leukemia in mice
Hardy-Zuckerman 4 feline sarcoma virus	Causes sarcomas in cats
Hepatitis B	Causes liver cancer in several species, including humans

The virus was named the Rous sarcoma virus (RSV). In the 1970s, research involving RSV led to the identification of a viral gene that acts as an oncogene. Researchers investigated RSV by using it to infect chicken cells grown in the laboratory. This causes the chicken cells to grow like cancer cells, continuously and in an uncontrolled manner. Researchers identified mutant RSV strains that infected and proliferated within chicken cells without transforming them into malignant cells. These RSV strains were missing a gene that is found in the form of the virus that does cause cancer. This gene was called the *src* gene because it causes sarcoma.

Americans, biologist Harold Varmus and microbiologist Michael Bishop, in collaboration with molecular biologist Peter Vogt, later discovered that normal (nonviral-infected) chicken cells also contain a copy of the *src* gene in their chromosomes. It is a proto-oncogene. When the *src* gene is incorporated into a viral genome, it is overexpressed because it is transcribed from a very active viral promoter. This ultimately produces too much of the Src protein in infected cells and promotes uncontrolled cell division.

Tumor-Suppressor Genes Prevent Mutation or Cell Proliferation

Thus far, we have examined one category of genes that promote cancer, namely oncogenes. We now turn our attention to the second category of genes, those called tumor-suppressor genes. The functioning of a normal (nonmutant) tumor-suppressor gene prevents cancerous growth. The proteins encoded by tumor-suppressor genes usually have one of two functions: maintenance of genome integrity or negative regulation of cell division (**Table 14.8**).

Maintenance of Genome Integrity   Some tumor-suppressor genes encode proteins that maintain the integrity of the genome by monitoring and/or repairing alterations in the genome. The proteins encoded by these genes are vital for the prevention of abnormalities such as gene mutations, DNA breaks, and improperly segregated chromosomes. Therefore, when these proteins are functioning properly, they minimize the chance that a cancer-causing mutation will occur. In some cases, the proteins encoded by tumor-suppressor genes prevent a cell from progressing through the cell cycle if an abnormality is detected. These are termed **checkpoint proteins** because their role is to check the integrity of the genome and prevent a cell from progressing past a certain point in the cell cycle. Checkpoint proteins are not

Table 14.8   Functions of Selected Tumor-Suppressor Genes

Gene	
Maintenance of genome integrity	
p53	p53 is a transcription factor that acts as a sensor of DNA damage. It can promote DNA repair, prevent the progression through the cell cycle, and promote apoptosis.
BRCA-1 *BRCA-2*	BRCA-1 and BRCA-2 proteins are both involved in the cellular defense against DNA damage. They play a role in sensing DNA damage and facilitate DNA repair. These genes are mutant in persons with certain inherited forms of breast cancer.
XPD	This represents one of several different genes whose products function in DNA repair. These genes are defective in patients with xeroderma pigmentosum.
Negative regulation of cell division	
Rb	The Rb protein is a negative regulator that represses the transcription of genes required for DNA replication and cell division.
NF1	The NF1 protein stimulates Ras to hydrolyze its GTP to GDP. Loss of NF1 function causes the Ras protein to be overactive, which promotes cell division.
p16	The p16 protein is a negative regulator of cyclin-dependent kinases (cdks).

always required to regulate normal, healthy cell division, but they can stop cell division if an abnormality is detected.

How do checkpoint proteins stop the cell cycle? One way is by controlling proteins called cyclins and cyclin-dependent kinases (cdks), which are responsible for advancing a cell through the four phases of the cell cycle (see Chapter 15). The formation of activated cyclin/cdk complexes can be stopped by checkpoint proteins.

A specific example of a tumor-suppressor gene that encodes a checkpoint protein is *p53*, discovered in 1979 by American biologist Arnold Levine. Its name refers to the molecular mass of the p53 protein, which is 53 kDa (kilodaltons). About 50% of all human cancers, including malignant tumors of the lung, breast, esophagus, liver, bladder, and brain, as well as leukemias and lymphomas (cancer of the lymphatic system), are associated with mutations in this gene.

As shown in **Figure 14.15**, p53 is a protein that controls the ability of cells to progress from the G_1 stage of the cell cycle to the S phase. The expression of the *p53* gene is induced when DNA is damaged. The p53 protein functions as a regulatory transcription factor that activates several different genes, leading to the synthesis of proteins that stop the cell cycle and other proteins that repair the DNA. If the DNA is eventually repaired, a cell may later proceed through the cell cycle.

Alternatively, if the DNA damage is too severe, the p53 protein will also activate other genes that promote programmed cell death. This process, called **apoptosis**, involves cell shrinkage and DNA degradation. As described in Chapter 9, enzymes known as caspases are activated during apoptosis (refer back to Figure 9.20). They function as proteases that are sometimes called the "executioners" of the cell. Caspases digest selected cellular proteins such as microfilaments,

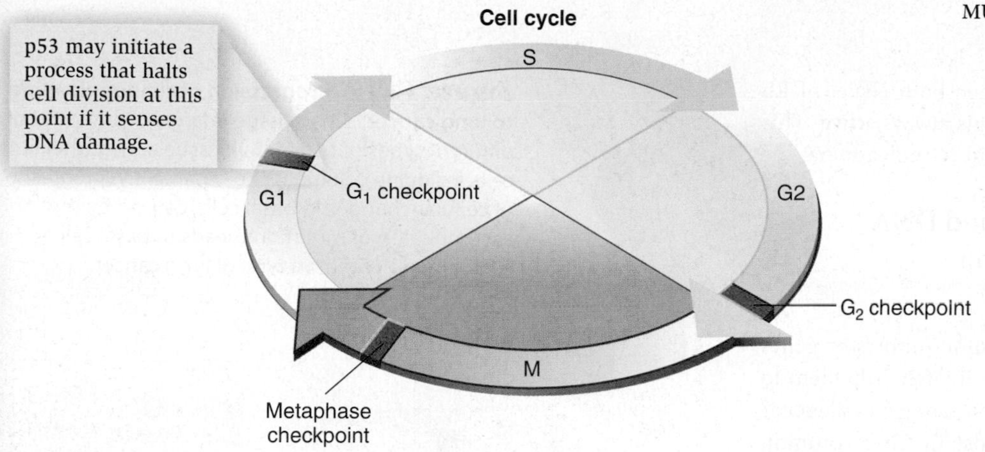

Cell cycle

p53 may initiate a process that halts cell division at this point if it senses DNA damage.

G_1 checkpoint

G1

S

G2

G_2 checkpoint

M

Metaphase checkpoint

Figure 14.15 The cell cycle and checkpoints. As discussed in Chapter 15, eukaryotic cells progress through a cell cycle composed of G_1, S, G_2, and M phases (look ahead to Figure 15.2). The yellow bars indicate common checkpoints that stop the cell cycle if genetic abnormalities are detected. The p53 protein stops a cell at the G_1 checkpoint if it senses DNA damage.

Concept Check: *Why is it an advantage for an organism to have checkpoints that can stop the cell cycle?*

which are components of the cytoskeleton. This causes the cell to break into small vesicles that are eventually phagocytized by cells of the immune system. It is beneficial for a multicellular organism to kill an occasional cell with cancer-causing potential.

When checkpoint genes such as *p53* are rendered inactive by mutation, the division of normal healthy cells may not be adversely affected. For example, mice that are missing the *p53* gene are born healthy. This indicates that checkpoint proteins such as p53 are not necessary for normal cell growth and division. However, these mice are very sensitive to mutagens such as UV light and easily develop cancer. The loss of p53 function makes it more likely that undesirable genetic changes will occur that could cause cancerous growth.

Negative Regulation of Cell Division   A second category of tumor-suppressor genes encodes proteins that are negative regulators or inhibitors of cell division. Their function is necessary to properly halt cell division. If their function is lost, cell division is abnormally accelerated.

An example of such a tumor-suppressor gene is the *Rb* gene. It was the first tumor-suppressor gene to be identified in humans by studying patients with a disease called retinoblastoma, a cancerous tumor that occurs in the retina of the eye. Some people have an inherited predisposition to develop this disease within the first few years of life. By comparison, the noninherited form of retinoblastoma, which is caused by environmental agents, is more likely to occur later in life.

Based on these differences, in 1971, American geneticist Alfred Knudson proposed a two-hit hypothesis for the occurrence of retinoblastoma. According to this hypothesis, retinoblastoma requires two mutations to occur. People have two copies of the *Rb* gene, one from each parent. Individuals with the inherited form of the disease already have received one mutant gene from one of their parents. They need only one additional mutation to develop the disease. Because the retina has more than 1 million cells, it is relatively likely that a mutation may occur in one of these cells at an early age, leading to the disease. However, people with the noninherited form of the disease must have two *Rb* mutations in the same retinal cell to cause the disease. Because two mutations are less likely than a single mutation, the noninherited form of this disease is expected to occur much later in life, and only rarely. Since Knudson's original work, molecular studies have confirmed the two-hit hypothesis for retinoblastoma.

The Rb protein negatively controls a regulatory transcription factor called E2F that activates genes required for cell cycle progression from G_1 to S phase. The binding of the Rb protein to E2F inhibits

its activity and prevents cell division (**Figure 14.16**). When a normal cell is supposed to divide, cyclins bind to cyclin-dependent kinases (cdks). This binding activates the kinases, which catalyze the transfer of a phosphate to the Rb protein. The phosphorylated form of the Rb protein is released from E2F, thereby allowing E2F to activate genes

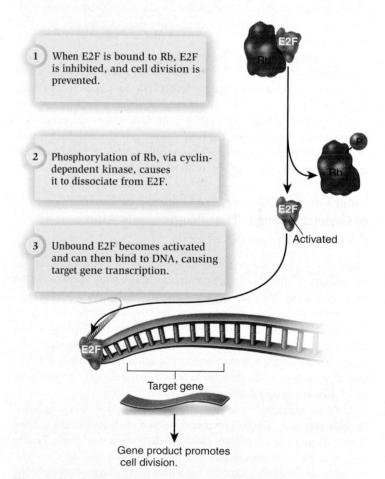

1   When E2F is bound to Rb, E2F is inhibited, and cell division is prevented.

2   Phosphorylation of Rb, via cyclin-dependent kinase, causes it to dissociate from E2F.

3   Unbound E2F becomes activated and can then bind to DNA, causing target gene transcription.

E2F

Rb

P

Rb

E2F

Activated

E2F

Target gene

Gene product promotes cell division.

Figure 14.16 Function of the Rb protein. The Rb protein inhibits the function of E2F, which turns on genes that cause a cell to divide. When cells are supposed to divide, Rb is phosphorylated by cyclin-dependent protein kinase, which allows E2F to function. If Rb protein is inactivated due to a mutation, E2F will always be active, and the cell will be stimulated to divide uncontrollably.

Concept Check: *Would cancer occur if both copies of the Rb gene and both copies of the E2F gene were rendered inactive due to mutations?*

needed to progress through the cell cycle. When both copies of Rb are defective due to mutations, the E2F protein is always active. This explains why uncontrolled cell division occurs in retinoblastoma.

Gene Mutations, Chromosome Loss, and DNA Methylation Can Inhibit the Expression of Tumor-Suppressor Genes

Cancer biologists want to understand how tumor-suppressor genes are inactivated, because this knowledge may ultimately help them to prevent or combat cancer. How are tumor-suppressor genes silenced? The function of tumor-suppressor genes is lost in three common ways. First, a mutation can occur within a tumor-suppressor gene to inactivate its function. For example, a mutation could abolish the function of the promoter for a tumor-suppressor gene or introduce an early stop codon in its coding sequence. Either of these would prevent the expression of a functional protein.

Chromosome loss is a second way that the function of a tumor-suppressor gene is lost. Chromosome loss may contribute to the progression of cancer if the missing chromosome carries one or more tumor-suppressor genes.

Recently, researchers have discovered a third way that these genes may be inactivated. Tumor-suppressor genes found in cancer cells are sometimes abnormally methylated. As discussed in Chapter 13, transcription is inhibited when CpG islands near a promoter region are methylated. Such DNA methylation near the promoters of tumor-suppressor genes has been found in many types of tumors, suggesting that this form of gene inactivation plays an important role in the formation and/or progression of malignancy.

Most Forms of Cancer Are Caused by a Series of Genetic Changes That Progressively Alter the Growth Properties of Cells

The discovery of oncogenes and tumor-suppressor genes has allowed researchers to study the progression of certain forms of cancer at the molecular level. Multiple genetic changes to the same cell lineage, perhaps in the range of 10 or more, are usually needed for cancer to occur. Many cancers begin with a benign genetic alteration that, over time and with additional mutations, leads to malignancy. Furthermore, a malignancy can continue to accumulate genetic changes that make it even more difficult to treat because the cells divide faster or invade surrounding tissues more readily.

As an example, let consider lung cancer, which is diagnosed in approximately 170,000 men and women each year in the United States. More than 1.2 million cases are diagnosed worldwide. Nearly 90% of these cases are caused by tobacco smoking and are thus preventable. Unlike other cancers for which early diagnosis is possible, lung cancer is usually detected only after it has become advanced and is difficult if not impossible to cure. The 5-year survival rate for lung cancer patients is approximately 15%.

What is the cellular basis for lung cancer? Most cancers of the lung are **carcinomas**—cancers of epithelial cells (**Figure 14.17**). (Epithelial cells, which form the lining of all internal and external body surfaces, are described in Chapter 10.) The top images in this figure show the normal epithelium found in a healthy lung. The rest of the figure shows the progression of a carcinoma that is due to mutations

Figure 14.17 **Progression of changes leading to lung cancer.** Lung tissue is largely composed of different types of connective tissue and epithelial cells, including columnar and basal cells. A progression of cellular changes in basal cells, caused by the accumulation of mutations, leads to basal cell carcinoma, a common type of lung cancer.

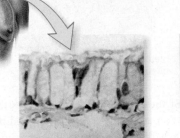

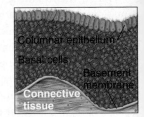

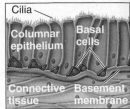
Normal lung epithelium

Hyperplasia

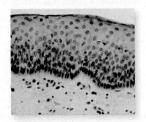
Loss of ciliated cells

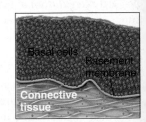
Dysplasia (initially precancerous, then cancerous)

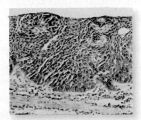
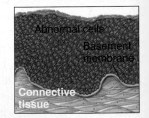

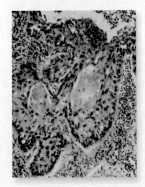
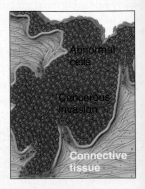
Invasive cancerous cells that can metastasize

in basal cells, a type of epithelial cell. Keep in mind that cancer occurs due to the accumulation of mutations in a cell lineage, beginning with an initial mutant cell that then divides multiple times to produce a population of many daughter cells (refer back to Figure 14.10). As mutations accumulate in a lineage of basal cells, their numbers increase dramatically. This causes a thickening of the epithelium, a condition called hyperplasia. The proliferation of such basal cells causes the loss of the ciliated, columnar epithelial cells that normally line the airways and help remove mucus and its trapped particles from the lungs. As additional mutations accumulate in this cell lineage, the basal cells develop more abnormal morphologies, a condition known as dysplasia. In the early stages of dysplasia, the abnormal basal cells are precancerous. If the source of chronic irritation (usually cigarette smoke) is eliminated, the abnormal cells are likely to disappear. Alternatively, if smoking continues, these abnormal cells may accumulate additional genetic changes and lose the ability to stop dividing. Such cells have become cancerous—the person has basal cell carcinoma.

The basement membrane is a sheetlike layer of extracellular matrix that provides a barrier between the lung cells and the bloodstream. If the cancer cells have not yet penetrated the basement membrane, they will not have metastasized, that is, spread into the blood and to other parts of the body. If the entire tumor is removed at this stage, the patient should be cured. The lower images in Figure 14.17 show a tumor that has broken through the basement membrane. The metastasis of these cells to other parts of the body will likely kill the patient, usually within a year of diagnosis.

The cellular changes that lead to lung cancer are correlated with genetic changes. These include the occurrence of mutations that create oncogenes and inhibit tumor-suppressor genes. The order of mutations is not absolute. It takes time for multiple changes to accumulate, so cancer is usually a disease of older people. Reducing your exposure to mutagens such as cigarette smoke throughout your lifetime helps minimize the risk of mutations to your genes that could promote cancer.

GENOMES & PROTEOMES CONNECTION

Mutations in Approximately 300 Human Genes May Promote Cancer

Researchers have identified a large number of genes that are mutated in cancer cells. Though not all of these mutant genes have been directly shown to affect the growth rate of cells, such mutations are likely to be found in tumors because they provide some type of growth advantage for the cell population from which the cancer developed. For example, certain mutations may affect the functions of proteins that enable cells to metastasize to neighboring locations. These mutations may not affect growth rate, but they provide the growth advantage that cancer cells are not limited to growing in a particular location. They can migrate to new locations.

How many genes can contribute to cancer when they become mutant? Researchers have estimated that about 300 different genes may play a role in the development of human cancer. With an approximate genome size of 20,000 to 25,000 genes, this observation indicates that over 1% of our genes have the potential to promote cancer if their function is altered by a mutation.

Summary of Key Concepts

14.1 Mutation

- A mutation is a heritable change in the genetic material; gene mutations are relatively small changes in the base sequence of a gene.

- Point mutations affect a single base pair and can alter the coding sequence of genes in several ways, including silent, missense, nonsense, and frameshift mutations (Table 14.1).

- Sickle cell disease is caused by a missense mutation that results in a single amino acid substitution in β-globin (Figure 14.1).

- Gene mutations also alter gene function by changing DNA sequences that are not within the coding region (Table 14.2).

- The Lederbergs used replica plating to show that mutations are random events (Figure 14.2).

- Germ-line mutations affect gametes, whereas mutations in somatic cells affect only a part of the body and cannot be passed to offspring (Figures 14.3, 14.4).

- Spontaneous mutations are the result of errors in natural biological processes. Induced mutations are caused by agents in the environment that alter DNA structure (Table 14.3).

- Mutagens are chemical or physical agents that lead to mutations in DNA (Table 14.4, Figures 14.5, 14.6).

- The Ames test is a method of testing whether an agent is a mutagen (Figure 14.7).

14.2 DNA Repair

- DNA repair systems involve proteins that sense DNA damage and repair it before a mutation occurs (Table 14.5).

- In nucleotide excision repair (NER) certain proteins recognize various types of DNA damage, such as thymine dimers. A region in the damaged strand is excised, and a new strand is synthesized, using the intact strand as a template (Figure 14.8).

- Certain inherited diseases in humans, such as xeroderma pigmentosum, are due to defects in the NER system (Figure 14.9).

14.3 Cancer

- Cancer is due to the accumulation of mutations in a lineage of cells that leads to uncontrolled cell growth (Figure 14.10).

- Mutations in proto-oncogenes that result in overactivity produce cancer-causing genes called oncogenes.

- Oncogenes often encode proteins involved in cell-signaling pathways that promote cell division (Figures 14.11, 14.12, Table 14.6).

- Four common types of genetic changes, namely, missense mutations, gene amplifications, chromosomal translocations, and retroviral insertions, can change proto-oncogenes into oncogenes (Figures 14.13, 14.14).

- Some types of cancer are caused by viruses (Table 14.7).

- The normal function of tumor-suppressor genes is to prevent cancer. Loss-of-function mutations in such genes promote cancer.

Tumor-suppressor genes often encode proteins that maintain the integrity of the genome or function as negative regulators of cell division (Table 14.8).

- Checkpoint proteins such as p53 monitor the integrity of the genome and prevent the cell from progressing through the cell cycle if abnormalities are detected (Figure 14.15).

- The Rb protein is an inhibitor of the cell cycle, because it negatively controls E2F, a transcription factor that promotes cell division (Figure 14.16).

- Tumor-suppressor genes can be inactivated by gene mutations, chromosome loss, and DNA methylation.

- Most forms of cancer, such as lung cancer, involve multiple genetic changes that lead to malignancy (Figure 14.17).

- Over 300 human genes, or over 1% of our genes, are known to be associated with cancer when they become mutant.

Assess and Discuss

Test Yourself

1. Point mutations that do not alter the amino acid sequence of the resulting gene product are called ___ mutations.
   a. frameshift
   b. natural
   c. silent
   d. nonsense
   e. missense

2. Some point mutations lead to an mRNA that produces a shorter polypeptide. This type of mutation is known as a ___ mutation.
   a. neutral
   b. silent
   c. missense
   d. nonsense
   e. chromosomal

3. A mutation in which of the following regions is least likely to affect gene function?
   a. promoter
   b. coding region
   c. splice junction
   d. intergenic region
   e. regulatory site

4. Mutagens can cause mutations by
   a. chemically altering DNA nucleotides.
   b. disrupting DNA replication.
   c. altering the genetic code of an organism.
   d. all of the above.
   e. a and b only.

5. The mutagenic effect of UV light is
   a. the alteration of cytosine bases to adenine bases.
   b. the formation of adenine dimers that interfere with genetic expression.
   c. the breaking of the sugar-phosphate backbone of the DNA molecule.
   d. the formation of thymine dimers that disrupt DNA replication.
   e. the deletion of thymine bases along the DNA molecule.

6. The Ames test
   a. provides a way to determine if any type of cell has experienced a mutation.
   b. provides a way to determine if an agent is a mutagen.
   c. allows researchers to experimentally disrupt gene activity by causing a mutation in a specific gene.
   d. provides a way to repair mutations in bacterial cells.
   e. does all of the above.

7. Xeroderma pigmentosum
   a. is a genetic disorder that results in uncontrolled cell growth.
   b. is a genetic disorder in which the NER system is not fully functional.
   c. is a genetic disorder that results in the loss of pigment in certain patches of skin.
   d. results from the lack of DNA polymerase proofreading.
   e. is both b and d.

8. If a mutation eliminated the function of UvrC, which aspect of nucleotide excision repair would not work?
   a. sensing a damaged DNA site
   b. endonuclease cleavage of the damaged strand
   c. removal of the damaged strand
   d. synthesis of a new strand, using the undamaged strand as a template
   e. none of the above

9. Cancer cells are said to be metastatic when they
   a. begin to divide uncontrollably.
   b. invade healthy tissue.
   c. migrate to other parts of the body.
   d. cause mutations in other healthy cells.
   e. do all of the above.

10. Oncogenes can be produced by
    a. missense mutations.
    b. gene amplification.
    c. chromosomal translocation.
    d. retroviral insertion.
    e. all of the above.

Conceptual Questions

1. Is a random mutation more likely to be beneficial or harmful? Explain your answer.

2. Distinguish between spontaneous and induced mutations. Which are more harmful? Which are avoidable?

3. A principle of biology is that the *genetic material provides a blueprint for reproduction*. Explain how mutations may cause alterations to the genetic material that are detrimental for reproduction and sustaining life.

Collaborative Questions

1. Discuss the pros and cons of mutation.

2. A large amount of research is aimed at studying mutation. However, there is not an infinite amount of research dollars. Where would you put your money for mutation research?
   a. testing of potential mutagens
   b. investigating molecular effects of mutagens
   c. investigating DNA repair mechanisms
   d. some other area

Online Resource

www.brookerbiology.com

Stay a step ahead in your studies with animations that bring concepts to life and practice tests to assess your understanding. Your instructor may also recommend the interactive eBook, individualized learning tools, and more.

The Eukaryotic Cell Cycle, Mitosis, and Meiosis

15

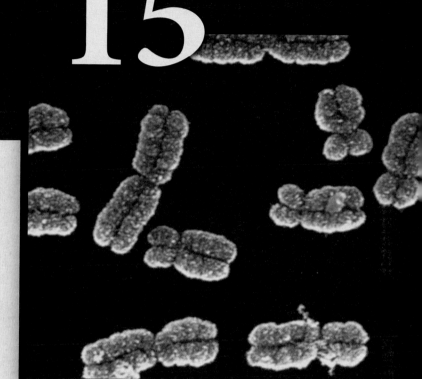

O ver 10,000,000,000,000! Researchers estimate the adult human body contains somewhere between 10 trillion to 50 trillion cells. It is almost an incomprehensible number. Even more amazing is the accuracy of the process that produces these cells. After a human sperm and egg unite, the fertilized egg goes through a long series of cell divisions to produce an adult with over 10 trillion cells. Let's suppose you randomly removed a cell from your arm and compared it with a cell from your foot. If you examined the chromosomes found in both cells under the microscope, they would look identical. Likewise, the DNA sequences along those chromosomes would also be the same, barring rare mutations. Similar comparisons could be made among the trillions of cells in your body. When you consider how many cell divisions are needed to produce an adult human, the precision of cell division is truly remarkable.

What accounts for this high level of accuracy? As we will examine in this chapter, **cell division**, the reproduction of cells, is a highly regulated process that distributes and monitors the integrity of the genetic material. The eukaryotic cell cycle is a series of phases needed for cell division. The cells of eukaryotic species follow one of two different sorting processes so that new daughter cells receive the correct number and types of chromosomes. The first sorting process we will explore, called mitosis, is needed so two daughter cells receive the same amount of genetic material as the mother cell that produced them. We will then examine another sorting process, called meiosis, which is needed for sexual reproduction. In meiosis, cells that have two sets of chromosomes produce daughter cells with a single set of chromosomes. Lastly, we will explore variation in the structure and number of chromosomes. As you will see, a variety of mechanisms that alter chromosome structure and number have important consequences for the organisms that carry them.

A scanning electron micrograph of human chromosomes. These chromosomes are highly compacted and found in a dividing cell.

Life is a continuum in which new living cells are formed by the division of pre-existing cells. The Latin axiom *omnis cellula e cellula*, meaning "Every cell originates from another cell," was first proposed in 1858 by Rudolf Virchow, a German biologist. From an evolutionary perspective, cell division has a very ancient origin. All living organisms, from unicellular bacteria to multicellular plants and animals, have been produced by a series of repeated rounds of cell growth and division extending back to the beginnings of life nearly 4 billion years ago.

A **cell cycle** is a series of events that leads to cell division. In all species, it is a highly regulated process so cell division occurs at the appropriate time. As discussed in Chapter 18, bacterial cells produce more cells via binary fission. The cell cycle in eukaryotes is more complex, in part, because eukaryotic cells have sets of chromosomes that need to be sorted properly. In this section, we will examine the phases of the eukaryotic cell cycle and see how the cell cycle is controlled by proteins that carefully monitor the division process to ensure its accuracy. But first, we need to consider some general features of chromosomes in eukaryotic species.

15.1 The Eukaryotic Cell Cycle

Learning Outcomes:

1. Describe the features of chromosomes and how sets of chromosomes are examined microscopically.
2. Outline the phases of the eukaryotic cell cycle.
3. Explain how cyclins and cdks work together to advance a cell through the eukaryotic cell cycle.

Chromosomes Are Inherited in Sets and Occur in Homologous Pairs

To understand the chromosomal composition of cells and the behavior of chromosomes during cell division, scientists observe cells and chromosomes with the use of microscopes. **Cytogenetics** is the field of genetics that involves the microscopic examination of chromosomes. When a cell prepares to divide, the chromosomes become more tightly compacted, a process that decreases their apparent length and increases their diameter. A consequence of this compaction is that distinctive shapes and numbers of chromosomes become visible under a light microscope.

Microscopic Examination of Chromosomes   Figure 15.1 shows the general procedure for preparing and viewing chromosomes from a eukaryotic cell. In this example, the cells were obtained from a sample of human blood. Specifically, the chromosomes within leukocytes (white blood cells) were examined. A sample of the blood cells was treated with drugs that stimulated them to divide. The actively dividing cells were centrifuged to concentrate them into a pellet, which was then mixed with a hypotonic solution that caused the cells to swell. The expansion of the cells causes the chromosomes to spread out from each other, making it easier to see each individual chromosome.

Next, the cells were concentrated by a second centrifugation and treated with a fixative, which chemically fixes them in place so the chromosomes can no longer move around. The cells were then exposed to a chemical dye, such as Giemsa, that binds to the chromosomes and stains them. This gives chromosomes a distinctive banding pattern that greatly enhances their contrast and ability to be uniquely identified; in this case, the bands are called G bands. The cells were then placed on a slide and viewed with a light microscope. In a cytogenetics laboratory, the microscopes are equipped with an electronic camera to photograph the chromosomes. On a computer screen, the chromosomes can be organized in a standard way, usually from largest to smallest. A photographic representation of the chromosomes, as in the photo in step 5 of Figure 15.1, is called a **karyotype**. A

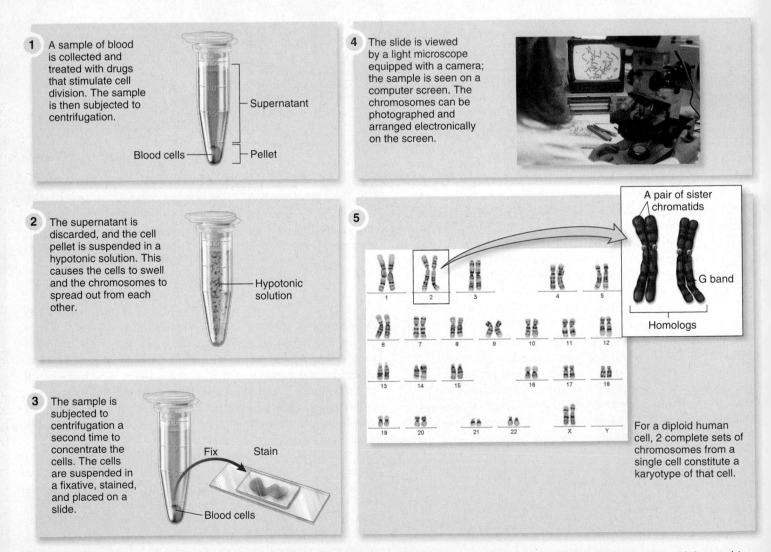

1   A sample of blood is collected and treated with drugs that stimulate cell division. The sample is then subjected to centrifugation.

Supernatant

Blood cells — Pellet

2   The supernatant is discarded, and the cell pellet is suspended in a hypotonic solution. This causes the cells to swell and the chromosomes to spread out from each other.

Hypotonic solution

3   The sample is subjected to centrifugation a second time to concentrate the cells. The cells are suspended in a fixative, stained, and placed on a slide.

Fix   Stain

Blood cells

4   The slide is viewed by a light microscope equipped with a camera; the sample is seen on a computer screen. The chromosomes can be photographed and arranged electronically on the screen.

5

A pair of sister chromatids

G band

Homologs

For a diploid human cell, 2 complete sets of chromosomes from a single cell constitute a karyotype of that cell.

Figure 15.1   The procedure for making a karyotype. In this example, the chromosomes were treated with the Giemsa stain, and the resulting bands are called G bands.

Concept Check: *Researchers usually treat cells with drugs that stimulate them to divide prior to the procedure for making a karyotype. Why is this useful?*

karyotype reveals the number, size, and form of chromosomes found within an actively dividing cell. It should also be noted that the chromosomes viewed in actively dividing cells have already replicated. The two copies are still joined to each other and referred to as a pair of **sister chromatids** (see inset to Figure 15.1).

Sets of Chromosomes   What type of information is learned from a karyotype? By studying the karyotypes of many species, scientists have discovered that eukaryotic chromosomes occur in sets. Each set is composed of several different types of chromosomes. For example, one set of human chromosomes contains 23 different types of chromosomes (see Figure 15.1). By convention, the chromosomes are numbered according to size, with the largest chromosomes having the smallest numbers. For example, human chromosomes 1, 2, and 3 are relatively large, whereas 21 and 22 are the two smallest. This numbering system does not apply to the **sex chromosomes**, which determine the sex of the individual. Sex chromosomes in humans are designated with the letters X and Y; females are XX and males are XY. The chromosomes that are not sex chromosomes are called **autosomes**. Humans have 22 different types of autosomes.

A second feature of many eukaryotic species is that most cells contain two sets of chromosomes. The karyotype shown in Figure 15.1 contains two sets of chromosomes, with 23 different chromosomes in each set. Therefore, this human cell contains a total of 46 chromosomes. Each cell has two sets because the individual inherited one set from the father and one set from the mother. When the cells of an organism carry two sets of chromosomes, that organism is said to be **diploid**. Geneticists use the letter n to represent a set of chromosomes. Diploid organisms are referred to as $2n$, because they have two sets of chromosomes. For example, humans are $2n$, where $n = 23$. Most human cells are diploid. An exception involves **gametes**, the sperm and egg cells. Gametes are **haploid**, or $1n$, which means they contain one set of chromosomes.

Homologous Pairs of Chromosomes   When an organism is diploid, the members of a pair of chromosomes are called **homologs** (see inset to Figure 15.1). The term **homology** refers to any similarity that is due to common ancestry. Pairs of homologous chromosomes are evolutionarily derived from the same chromosome. However, homologous chromosomes are not usually identical because over many generations they have accumulated some genetic changes that make them distinct.

How similar are homologous chromosomes to each other? Each of the two chromosomes in a homologous pair is nearly identical in size and contains a very similar composition of genetic material. A particular gene found on one copy of a chromosome is also found on the homolog. Because one homolog is received from each parent, the two homologs may vary in the way that a gene affects an organism's traits. As an example, let's consider a gene in humans called *OCA2*, which plays a major role in determining eye color. The *OCA2* gene is found on chromosome 15. One copy of chromosome 15 might carry the form of this eye color gene that confers brown eyes, whereas the gene on the homolog could confer blue eyes. The topic of how genes affect an organism's traits will be considered in Chapter 16.

The DNA sequences on homologous chromosomes are very similar. In most cases, the sequence of bases on one homolog differs by less than 1% from the sequence on the other homolog. For example, the DNA sequence of chromosome 1 that you inherited from your mother is likely to be more than 99% identical to the DNA sequence of chromosome 1 that you inherited from your father. Nevertheless, keep in mind that the sequences are not identical. The slight differences in DNA sequence provide important variation in gene function. Again, if we use the eye color gene *OCA2* as an example, a minor difference in DNA sequence distinguishes two forms of the gene, brown versus blue.

The striking similarity between homologous chromosomes does not apply to the sex chromosomes (for example, X and Y). These chromosomes differ in size and genetic composition. Certain genes found on the X chromosome are not found on the Y chromosome, and vice versa. The X and Y chromosomes are not considered homologous chromosomes, although they do have short regions of homology.

The Cell Cycle Is a Series of Phases That Lead to Cell Division

Eukaryotic cells that are destined to divide progress through the cell cycle, a series of changes that involves growth, replication, and division, and ultimately produces new cells. **Figure 15.2** provides an overview of the cell cycle. In this diagram, the mother cell has three pairs of chromosomes, for a total of six individual chromosomes. Such a cell is diploid ($2n$) and contains three chromosomes per set ($n = 3$). The paternal set is shown in blue, and the homologous maternal set is shown in red.

The phases of the cell cycle are G_1 (first gap), **S** (synthesis of DNA, the genetic material), G_2 (second gap), and **M phase** (mitosis and cytokinesis). The G_1 and G_2 phases were originally described as gap phases to indicate the periods between DNA synthesis and mitosis. In actively dividing cells, the G_1, S, and G_2 phases are collectively known as **interphase**. During interphase, the cell grows and copies its chromosomes in preparation for cell division. Alternatively, cells may exit the cell cycle and remain for long periods of time in a phase called G_0 (G zero). The G_0 phase is an alternative to proceeding through G_1. A cell in the G_0 phase has postponed making a decision to divide or, in the case of terminally differentiated cells (such as muscle cells in an adult animal), will never divide again. G_0 is a nondividing phase.

G_1 Phase   The G_1 phase is a period in a cell's life when it may become committed to divide. Depending on the environmental conditions and the presence of signaling molecules, a cell in the G_1 phase may accumulate molecular changes that cause it to progress through the rest of the cell cycle. Cell growth typically occurs during the G_1 phase.

S Phase   During the S phase, each chromosome is replicated to form a pair of sister chromatids (see Figure 15.1). When S phase is completed, a cell has twice as many chromatids as the number of chromosomes in the G_1 phase. For example, a human cell in the G_1 phase has 46 distinct chromosomes, whereas the same cell in G_2 would have 46 pairs of sister chromatids, for a total of 92 chromatids.

G_2 Phase   During the G_2 phase, a cell synthesizes the proteins necessary for chromosome sorting and cell division. Some cell growth may occur.

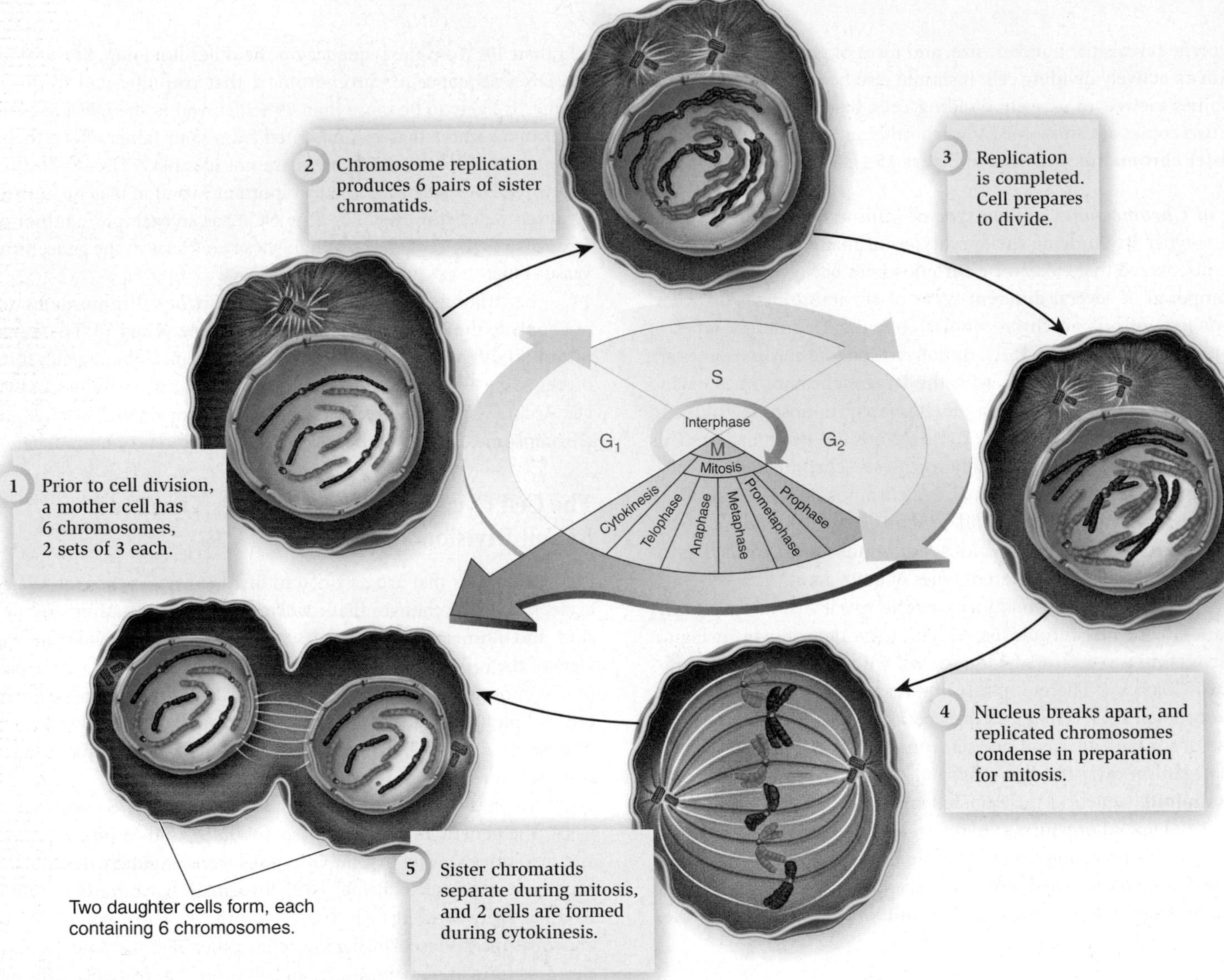

2 Chromosome replication produces 6 pairs of sister chromatids.

3 Replication is completed. Cell prepares to divide.

1 Prior to cell division, a mother cell has 6 chromosomes, 2 sets of 3 each.

4 Nucleus breaks apart, and replicated chromosomes condense in preparation for mitosis.

5 Sister chromatids separate during mitosis, and 2 cells are formed during cytokinesis.

Two daughter cells form, each containing 6 chromosomes.

S

Interphase

G_1

G_2

M

Mitosis

Cytokinesis

Telophase

Anaphase

Metaphase

Prometaphase

Prophase

Figure 15.2 The eukaryotic cell cycle. Dividing cells progress through a series of phases denoted G_1, S, G_2, and M. This diagram shows the progression of a cell through the cell cycle to produce two daughter cells. The original diploid cell had three pairs of chromosomes, for a total of six individual chromosomes. During S phase, these have replicated to yield 12 chromatids. After mitosis is complete, two daughter cells each contain six individual chromosomes. The width of the phases shown in this figure is not meant to reflect their actual length. G_1 is typically the longest phase of the cell cycle, whereas M phase is relatively short.

BIOLOGY PRINCIPLE Cells are the simplest units of life. The cells of eukaryotic species are made via cell division during the eukaryotic cell cycle.

Concept Check: *Which phases make up interphase?*

M Phase The first part of M phase is **mitosis**. The purpose of mitosis is to divide one cell nucleus into two nuclei, distributing the duplicated chromosomes so each daughter cell receives the same complement of chromosomes. As noted previously, a human cell in the G_2 phase has 92 chromatids, which are found in 46 pairs. During mitosis, these pairs of chromatids are separated and sorted so each daughter cell receives 46 chromosomes. In most cases, mitosis is followed by **cytokinesis**, which is the division of the cytoplasm to produce two distinct daughter cells.

The length of the cell cycle varies considerably among different cell types, ranging from several minutes in quickly growing embryos

to several months in slow-growing adult cells. For fast-dividing mammalian cells in adults, such as skin cells, the length of the cycle is often in the range of 10 to 24 hours. The various phases within the cell cycle also vary in length. G_1 is often the longest and also the most variable phase, and M phase is the shortest. For a cell that divides in 24 hours, the following lengths of time for each phase are typical:

- G_1 phase: 11 hours
- S phase: 8 hours
- G_2 phase: 4 hours
- M phase: 1 hour

What factors determine whether or not a cell will divide? First, cell division is controlled by external factors, such as environmental conditions and signaling molecules. The effects of growth factors on cell division are discussed in Chapter 9 (refer back to Figure 9.10). Second, internal factors affect cell division. These include cell cycle control molecules and checkpoints, as we will discuss next.

The Cell Cycle Is Controlled by Checkpoint Proteins

The progression through the cell cycle is a process that is highly regulated to ensure that the nuclear genome is intact and that the conditions are appropriate for a cell to divide. As discussed in Chapter 14, this is necessary to minimize the occurrence of mutations, which could have harmful effects and potentially lead to cancer. Proteins called **cyclins** and **cyclin-dependent kinases (cdks)** are responsible for advancing a cell through the phases of the cell cycle. Cyclins are so named because their amount varies throughout the cell cycle. To be active, the kinases controlling the cell cycle must bind to (are dependent on) a cyclin. The number of different types of cyclins and cdks varies from species to species.

Figure 15.3 gives a simplified description of how cyclins and cdks work together to advance a cell through G_1 and mitosis. During G_1, the amount of a particular cyclin termed G_1 cyclin increases in response to sufficient nutrients and growth factors. The G_1 cyclin binds to a cdk to form an activated G_1 cyclin/cdk complex. Once activated, cdk functions as a protein kinase that phosphorylates other proteins needed to advance the cell to the next phase in the cell cycle. For example, certain proteins involved with DNA synthesis are phosphorylated and activated, thereby allowing the cell to replicate its DNA in S phase. After the cell passes into the S phase, G_1 cyclin is degraded. Similar events advance the cell through other phases of the cell cycle. A different cyclin, called mitotic cyclin, accumulates late in

G_2. It binds to a cdk to form an activated mitotic cyclin/cdk complex. This complex phosphorylates proteins that are needed to advance the cell into M phase.

Three critical regulatory points called **checkpoints** are found in the cell cycle of eukaryotic cells (see Figure 15.3). At these checkpoints, a variety of proteins, referred to as checkpoint proteins, act as sensors to determine if a cell is in the proper condition to divide. The G_1 checkpoint, also called the **restriction point**, determines if conditions are favorable for cell division. In addition, G_1-checkpoint proteins can sense if the DNA has incurred damage. What happens if DNA damage is detected? The checkpoint proteins prevent the formation of active cyclin/cdk complexes, thereby stopping the progression of the cell cycle.

A second checkpoint exists in G_2. This checkpoint also checks the DNA for damage and ensures that all of the DNA has been replicated. In addition, the G_2 checkpoint monitors the levels of proteins that are needed to progress through M phase. A third checkpoint, called the metaphase checkpoint, senses the integrity of the spindle apparatus. As we will see later, the spindle apparatus is involved in chromosome sorting. Metaphase is a step in mitosis during which all of the chromosomes should be attached to the spindle apparatus. If a chromosome is not correctly attached, the metaphase checkpoint will stop the cell cycle. This checkpoint prevents cells from incorrectly sorting their chromosomes during division.

Checkpoint proteins delay the cell cycle until problems are fixed or prevent cell division when problems cannot be fixed. A primary aim of checkpoint proteins is to prevent the division of a cell that may have incurred DNA damage or harbors abnormalities in chromosome number. As discussed in Chapter 14, when the functions of checkpoint genes are lost due to mutation, the likelihood increases that undesirable genetic changes will occur that can cause additional mutations and cancerous growth.

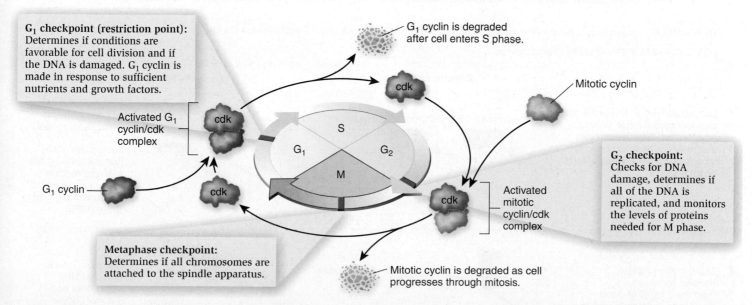

G_1 checkpoint (restriction point): Determines if conditions are favorable for cell division and if the DNA is damaged. G_1 cyclin is made in response to sufficient nutrients and growth factors.

G_1 cyclin is degraded after cell enters S phase.

Mitotic cyclin

Activated G_1 cyclin/cdk complex

cdk

G_1 cyclin

G_2 checkpoint: Checks for DNA damage, determines if all of the DNA is replicated, and monitors the levels of proteins needed for M phase.

Activated mitotic cyclin/cdk complex

Metaphase checkpoint: Determines if all chromosomes are attached to the spindle apparatus.

Mitotic cyclin is degraded as cell progresses through mitosis.

Figure 15.3 **Checkpoints in the cell cycle.** This is a general diagram of the eukaryotic cell cycle. Progression through the cell cycle requires the formation of activated cyclin/cdk complexes. Cells make different types of cyclin proteins, which are typically degraded after the cell has progressed to the next phase. The formation of activated cyclin/cdk complexes is regulated by checkpoint proteins.

BioConnections: *Look back at Figure 14.15. How do checkpoint proteins prevent cancer?*

FEATURE INVESTIGATION

Masui and Markert's Study of Oocyte Maturation Led to the Identification of Cyclins and Cyclin-Dependent Kinases

During the 1960s, researchers were intensely searching for the factors that promote cell division. In 1971, Japanese zoologist Yoshio Masui and American biologist Clement Markert developed a way to test whether a substance causes a cell to progress from one phase of the cell cycle to the next. They chose to study frog oocytes—cells that mature into egg cells. At the time of their work, researchers had already determined that frog oocytes naturally become dormant in the G_2 phase of the cell cycle for up to eight months (Figure 15.4). During mating season, female frogs produce a hormone called progesterone. After progesterone enters an oocyte and binds to intracellular receptors, the oocyte progresses from G_2 to the beginning of M phase, where the chromosomes condense and become visible under the microscope. This phenomenon is called maturation. When a sperm fertilizes the egg, M phase is completed, and the zygote continues to undergo cellular divisions.

Because progesterone is a signaling molecule, Masui and Markert speculated that this hormone affects the functions and/or amounts of proteins that trigger the oocyte to progress through the cell cycle. To test this hypothesis, they developed the procedure described in Figure 15.5, using the oocytes of the leopard frog (*Rana pipiens*). They began by exposing oocytes to progesterone in vitro and then incubated these oocytes for 2 hours or 12 hours. As a control, they

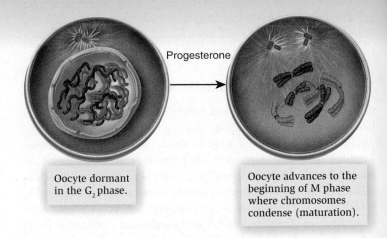

Oocyte dormant in the G_2 phase.

Progesterone

Oocyte advances to the beginning of M phase where chromosomes condense (maturation).

Figure 15.4 Oocyte maturation in certain species of frogs.

also used oocytes that had not been exposed to progesterone. These three types of cells were called the donor oocytes.

Next, they used a micropipette to transfer a small amount of cytosol from the three types of donor oocytes to recipient oocytes that had not been exposed to progesterone. As seen in the data, the recipient oocytes that had been injected with cytosol from the control donor oocytes or from oocytes that had been incubated with progesterone for only 2 hours did not progress to M phase. However, cytosol from donor oocytes that had been incubated with progesterone for

Figure 15.5 The experimental approach of Masui and Markert to identify cyclin and cyclin-dependent kinase (cdk).

HYPOTHESIS Progesterone induces the synthesis of a factor(s) that advances frog oocytes through the cell cycle from G_2 to M phase.

KEY MATERIALS Oocytes from *Rana pipiens*.

Experimental level	Conceptual level

1 Expose oocytes to progesterone, then incubate for 2 or 12 hours. As a control, also use oocytes that have not been exposed to progesterone. All 3 types are donor oocytes.

Progesterone   Progesterone   No progesterone (control)

02:00   12:00

Donor oocytes

Progesterone

Donor oocyte

Progesterone enters cell and activates intracellular receptor.

Factors are made that advance oocyte to M phase. One such factor is called maturation promoting factor (MPF).

2 Using a micropipette, transfer some cytosol from the 3 types of donor oocytes to recipient oocytes that have not been exposed to progesterone.

Micropipette tip

Donor cytosol

Donor oocytes   Recipient oocyte

Recipient oocyte   Cytosol   MPF

Recipient oocyte received MPF from donor oocyte if donor oocyte was incubated for 12 hours with progesterone.

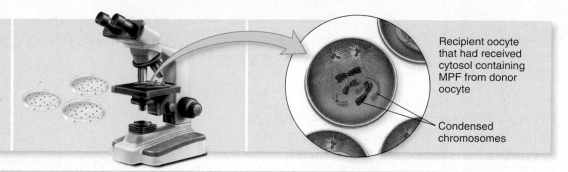

3 Incubate for several hours, and observe the recipient oocytes under the microscope to determine if the recipient oocytes advance to M phase. Advancement to M phase can be determined by the condensation of the chromosomes.

Recipient oocyte that had received cytosol containing MPF from donor oocyte

Condensed chromosomes

4 **THE DATA**

Donor oocytes	Recipient oocytes proceeded to M phase?
Control, no progesterone exposure	No
Progesterone exposure, incubation for 2 hours	No
Progesterone exposure, incubation for 12 hours	Yes

5 **CONCLUSION** Exposure of oocytes to progesterone for 12 hours results in the synthesis of a factor(s) that advances frog oocytes through the cell cycle from G_2 to M phase.

6 **SOURCE** Masui, Y., and Markert, C.L. 1971. Cytoplasmic control of nuclear behavior during meiotic maturation of frog oocytes. *Journal of Experimental Zoology* 177:129–145.

12 hours caused the recipient oocytes to advance to M phase. Masui and Markert concluded that a cytosolic factor, which required more than 2 hours to be synthesized after progesterone treatment, had been transferred to the recipient oocytes and induced maturation. The factor that caused the oocytes to progress (or mature) from G_2 to M phase was originally called the maturation-promoting factor (MPF).

After MPF was discovered in frogs, it was found in all eukaryotic species that researchers studied. MPF is important in the division of all types of cells, not just oocytes. It took another 17 years before Manfred Lohka, Marianne Hayes, and James Maller were able to purify the components that make up MPF. This was a difficult undertaking because these components are found in very small amounts in the cytosol and are easily degraded during purification procedures.

We now know that MPF is a complex made of a mitotic cyclin and a cyclin-dependent kinase (cdk), as described in Figure 15.3.

Experimental Questions

1. At the time of Masui and Markert's study shown in Figure 15.5, what was known about the effects of progesterone on oocytes?

2. What hypothesis did Masui and Markert propose to explain the function of progesterone? Explain the procedure used to test the hypothesis.

3. How did the researchers explain the difference between the results using 2-hour-exposed donor oocytes versus 12-hour-exposed donor oocytes?

15.2 Mitotic Cell Division

Learning Outcomes:

1. Describe how the replication of eukaryotic chromosomes produces sister chromatids.
2. Explain the structure and function of the mitotic spindle.
3. Outline the key events that occur during the phases of mitosis.

We now turn our attention to a mechanism of cell division and its relationship to chromosome replication and sorting. During the process of **mitotic cell division**, a cell divides to produce two new cells (the daughter cells) that are genetically identical to the original cell (the mother cell). Mitotic cell division involves mitosis—the division of one nucleus into two nuclei—and then cytokinesis in which the mother cell divides into two daughter cells.

Why is mitotic cell division important? One purpose is **asexual reproduction**, a process in which genetically identical offspring are produced from a single parent. Certain unicellular eukaryotic organisms, such as baker's yeast (*Saccharomyces cerevisiae*) and the amoeba, increase their numbers in this manner. A second important reason for mitotic cell division is the production and maintenance of multicellularity. Organisms such as plants, animals, and most fungi are derived from a single cell that subsequently undergoes repeated cellular divisions to become a multicellular organism.

In this section, we will explore how the process of mitotic cell division requires the replication, organization, and sorting of chromosomes. We will also examine how a single cell is separated into two daughter cells by cytokinesis.

In Preparation for Cell Division, Eukaryotic Chromosomes Are Replicated and Compacted to Produce Pairs Called Sister Chromatids

We now turn our attention to how chromosomes are replicated and sorted during cell division. In Chapter 11, we examined the molecular process of DNA replication. **Figure 15.6** describes the process at the chromosomal level. Prior to DNA replication, the DNA of each eukaryotic chromosome consists of a linear DNA double helix that is found in the nucleus and is not highly compacted. When the DNA is replicated, two identical copies of the original double helix are produced. As discussed earlier, these copies, along with associated proteins, lie side-by-side and are termed sister chromatids. When a cell prepares to divide, the sister chromatids become highly compacted and readily visible under the microscope. As shown in Figure 15.6b, the two sister chromatids are tightly associated at a region called the **centromere**. A protein called cohesin is necessary to hold the sister chromatids together. In addition, the centromere serves as an attachment site for a group of proteins that form the **kinetochore**, a structure necessary for sorting each chromosome.

The Mitotic Spindle Organizes and Sorts Chromosomes During Cell Division

What structure is responsible for organizing and sorting the chromosomes during cell division? The answer is the **mitotic spindle** (**Figure 15.7**). It is composed of microtubules—protein fibers that are components of the cytoskeleton (refer back to Table 4.1). In animal cells, microtubule growth and organization starts at two **centrosomes**, regions that are also referred to as microtubule organizing centers (MTOCs). A single centrosome duplicates during interphase. After they separate from each other during mitosis, each centrosome defines a **pole** of the spindle apparatus, one within each of the future daughter cells. The centrosome in animal cells has a pair of **centrioles**. Each one is composed of nine sets of triplet microtubules. However, centrioles are not found in many other eukaryotic species, such as plants, and are not required for spindle formation.

Each centrosome organizes the construction of the microtubules by rapidly polymerizing tubulin proteins. The three types of spindle microtubules are termed astral, polar, and kinetochore microtubules (see Figure 15.7). The astral microtubules, which extend away from the chromosomes, are important for positioning the spindle apparatus within the cell. The polar microtubules project into the region between the two poles. Polar microtubules that overlap with each other play a role in the separation of the two poles. Finally, the kinetochore microtubules are attached to kinetochores, which are bound to the centromere of each chromosome.

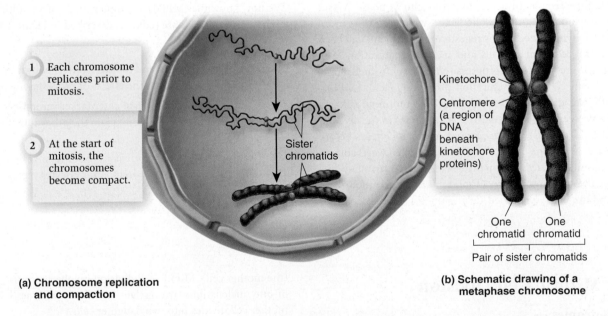

(a) **Chromosome replication and compaction**

(b) **Schematic drawing of a metaphase chromosome**

Figure 15.6 **Replication and compaction of chromosomes into pairs of sister chromatids.** (a) Chromosomal replication produces a pair of sister chromatids. While the chromosomes are elongated, they are replicated to produce two copies that are connected and lie parallel to each other. This is a pair of sister chromatids. Later, when the cell is preparing to divide, the sister chromatids condense into more compact structures that are easily seen with a light microscope. (b) A schematic drawing of a metaphase chromosome. This structure has two chromatids that lie side-by-side. The two chromatids are held together by cohesin proteins (not shown in this drawing). The kinetochore is a group of proteins that are attached to the centromere and play a role during chromosome sorting.

 BIOLOGY PRINCIPLE The genetic material provides a blueprint for reproduction. The process of mitosis ensures that each daughter cell receives a complete copy of the genetic material.

Concept Check: *Look back at the karyotype in Figure 15.1. In this micrograph, is each of the 46 objects a pair of sister chromatids?*

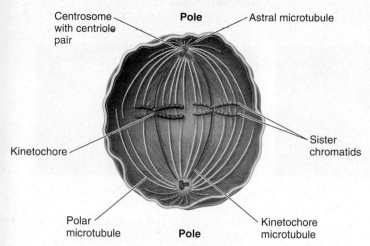

Centrosome with centriole pair

Pole

Astral microtubule

Kinetochore

Sister chromatids

Polar microtubule

Pole

Kinetochore microtubule

Figure 15.7 **The structure of the mitotic spindle.** The mitotic spindle in animal cells is formed by the centrosomes, which produce three types of microtubules. The astral microtubules emanate away from the region between the poles. The polar microtubules project into the region between the two poles. The kinetochore microtubules are attached to the kinetochores of sister chromatids. Note: For simplicity, this diagram shows only one pair of homologous chromosomes. Eukaryotic species typically have multiple chromosomes per set.

Concept Check: *What are the functions of the three types of microtubules?*

The Transmission of Chromosomes Requires a Sorting Process Known as Mitosis

Mitosis is the sorting process for dividing one cell nucleus into two nuclei. The duplicated chromosomes are distributed so each daughter cell receives the same complement of chromosomes. Mitosis was first observed microscopically in the 1870s by a German biologist, Walther Flemming, who coined the term (from the Greek *mitos*, meaning thread). He studied the large, transparent skin cells of salamander larvae as they were dividing and noticed that chromosomes are constructed of "threads" that are doubled in appearance along their length. These double threads divided and moved apart, one going to each of the two daughter nuclei. By this mechanism, Flemming pointed out, the two daughter cells receive an identical group of threads, the same as the number of threads in the mother cell.

Figure 15.8 depicts the process of mitosis in an animal cell, though the process is quite similar in a plant cell. Mitosis occurs as a continuum of phases known as prophase, prometaphase, metaphase, anaphase, and telophase. In the simplified diagrams shown along the bottom of Figure 15.8, the original cell contains six chromosomes. One set of chromosomes is depicted in red, whereas the homologous set is blue. These different colors represent maternal and paternal chromosomes.

Interphase Prior to mitosis, the cells are in interphase, which consists of the G_1, S, and G_2 phases of the cell cycle. The chromosomes have replicated in S phase and are decondensed and found in the nucleus (Figure 15.8a). The nucleolus, which is the site where the components of ribosomes assemble into ribosomal subunits, is visible during interphase.

Prophase At the start of mitosis, in **prophase**, the chromosomes have already replicated to produce 12 chromatids, joined as six pairs of sister chromatids that have condensed into highly compacted structures readily visible by light microscopy (Figure 15.8b). As prophase proceeds, the nuclear envelope begins to dissociate into small vesicles. The nucleolus is no longer visible.

Prometaphase During **prometaphase**, the nuclear envelope completely fragments into small vesicles, and the mitotic spindle is fully formed (Figure 15.8c). As prometaphase progresses, the centrosomes move apart and demarcate the two poles. Once the nuclear envelope has dissociated, the spindle fibers can interact with the sister chromatids. How do the sister chromatids become attached to the spindle apparatus? Initially, microtubules are rapidly formed and can be seen under a microscope growing out from the two poles. As it grows, if a microtubule happens to make contact with a kinetochore, it is said to be "captured" and remains firmly attached to the kinetochore. Alternatively, if a microtubule does not collide with a kinetochore, the microtubule eventually depolymerizes and retracts to the centrosome. This random process is how sister chromatids become attached to kinetochore microtubules. As the end of prometaphase nears, the two kinetochores on each pair of sister chromatids are attached to kinetochore microtubules from opposite poles. As these events are occurring, the sister chromatids are seen under the microscope to undergo jerky movements as they are tugged, back and forth, between the two poles by the kinetochore microtubules.

Metaphase Eventually, the pairs of sister chromatids are aligned in a single row along the **metaphase plate**, a plane halfway between the poles. When this alignment is complete, the cell is in **metaphase** of mitosis (Figure 15.8d). The chromatids can then be equally distributed into two daughter cells.

Anaphase During **anaphase**, the connections between the pairs of sister chromatids are broken (Figure 15.8e). Each chromatid, now an individual chromosome, is linked to only one of the two poles by one or more kinetochore microtubules. As anaphase proceeds, the kinetochore microtubules shorten, pulling the chromosomes toward the pole to which they are attached. In addition, the two poles move farther away from each other. This occurs because the overlapping polar microtubules lengthen and push against each other, thereby pushing the poles farther apart.

Telophase During **telophase**, the chromosomes have reached their respective poles and decondense. The nuclear envelope now re-forms to produce two separate nuclei. In Figure 15.8f, two nuclei are being produced that contain six chromosomes each.

Cytokinesis In most cases, mitosis is quickly followed by cytokinesis, in which the two nuclei are segregated into separate daughter cells. Whereas the phases of mitosis are similar between plant and animal cells, the process of cytokinesis is quite different. In animal cells, cytokinesis involves the formation of a **cleavage furrow**, which constricts like a drawstring to separate the cells (Figure 15.9a). In plants, vesicles from the Golgi apparatus move along microtubules to the center of the cell and coalesce to form a **cell plate** (Figure 15.9b), which then forms a cell wall between the two daughter cells.

(a) Interphase

(b) Prophase

(c) Prometaphase

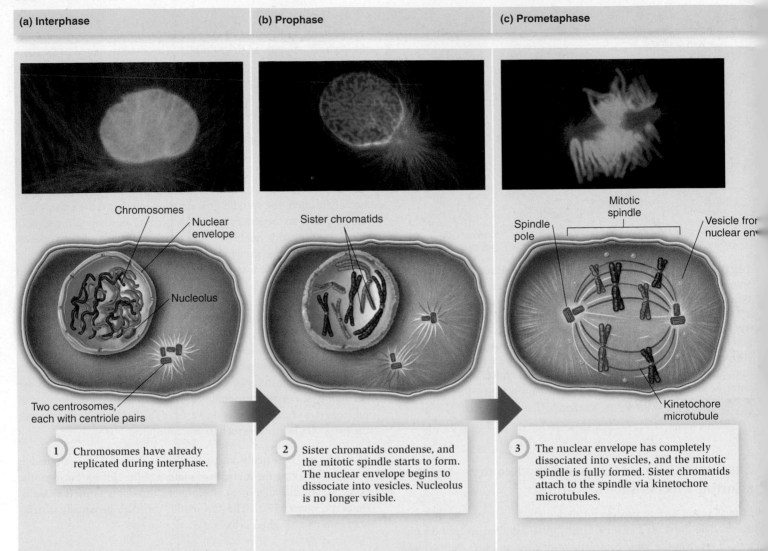

Chromosomes

Nuclear envelope

Nucleolus

Two centrosomes, each with centriole pairs

Sister chromatids

Spindle pole

Mitotic spindle

Vesicle from nuclear en[velope]

Kinetochore microtubule

1 Chromosomes have already replicated during interphase.

2 Sister chromatids condense, and the mitotic spindle starts to form. The nuclear envelope begins to dissociate into vesicles. Nucleolus is no longer visible.

3 The nuclear envelope has completely dissociated into vesicles, and the mitotic spindle is fully formed. Sister chromatids attach to the spindle via kinetochore microtubules.

Figure 15.8 **The process of mitosis in an animal cell.** The top panels illustrate the cells of a newt progressing through mitosis. The bottom panels are schematic drawings that emphasize the sorting and separation of the chromosomes in which the diploid mother cell had six chromosomes (three in each set). At the start of mitosis, these have already replicated into 12 chromatids. The final result is two daughter cells, each containing six chromosomes.

Concept Check: *With regard to chromosome composition, how does the mother cell compare with the two daughter cells?*

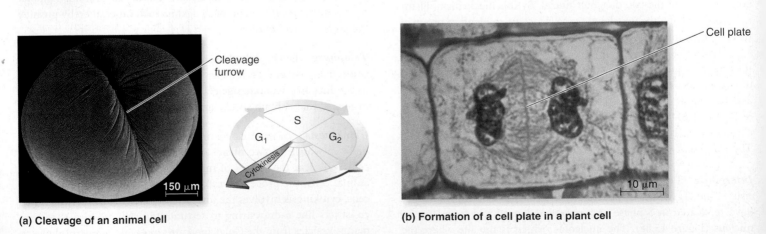

Cleavage furrow

S

G_1

G_2

Cytokinesis

150 µm

Cell plate

10 µm

(a) Cleavage of an animal cell

(b) Formation of a cell plate in a plant cell

Figure 15.9 Micrographs showing cytokinesis in animal and plant cells.

[Conc]ept Check: *What are the similarities and differences between cytokinesis in animal and plant cells?*

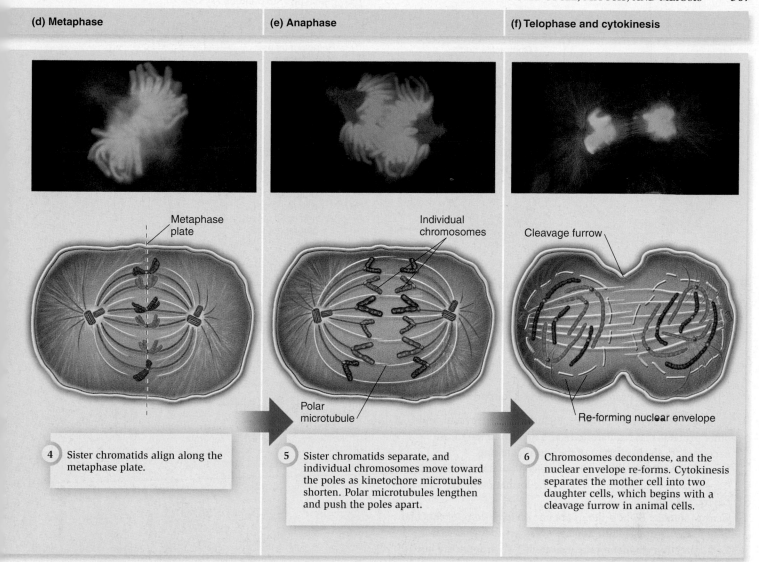

(d) Metaphase

Metaphase plate

4 Sister chromatids align along the metaphase plate.

(e) Anaphase

Individual chromosomes

Polar microtubule

5 Sister chromatids separate, and individual chromosomes move toward the poles as kinetochore microtubules shorten. Polar microtubules lengthen and push the poles apart.

(f) Telophase and cytokinesis

Cleavage furrow

Re-forming nuclear envelope

6 Chromosomes decondense, and the nuclear envelope re-forms. Cytokinesis separates the mother cell into two daughter cells, which begins with a cleavage furrow in animal cells.

What are the results of mitosis and cytokinesis? These processes ultimately produce two daughter cells with the same number of chromosomes as the mother cell. Barring rare mutations, the two daughter cells are genetically identical to each other and to the mother cell from which they were derived. The critical consequence of this sorting process is to ensure genetic consistency from one cell to the next. The development of multicellularity relies on the repeated process of mitosis and cytokinesis.

GENOMES & PROTEOMES CONNECTION

The Genomes of Diverse Animal Species Encode Approximately 20 Proteins Involved in Cytokinesis

To understand how a process works at the molecular and cellular level, researchers often try to identify the genes within a given species that encode proteins necessary for the process. Cytokinesis has been analyzed in this way. By comparing the results from vertebrates,

insects, and worms, researchers have identified approximately 20 proteins that are involved with cytokinesis in nearly all animal cells. In any given species, cytokinesis may also involve additional proteins beyond these 20, but these other proteins are not needed among all animal species. Evolutionary biologists would say the 20 proteins that are common to all animals are highly conserved, meaning their structure and function has been retained during the evolution of animals. The 20 conserved proteins are likely to play the most fundamental roles in the process of cytokinesis.

What are the functions of these 20 proteins? To appreciate their functions, we need to take a closer look at cytokinesis in animal cells (**Figure 15.10**). Animal cells produce a contractile ring that is attached to the plasma membrane to create the cleavage furrow. The contractile ring, which encircles a region of the mitotic spindle called the central spindle, is a network of actin (a cytoskeletal protein) and myosin (a motor protein). The motor activity of myosin moves actin filaments in a way that causes the contractile ring to constrict. Once the contractile ring becomes very small, membrane vesicles are inserted into the constricted site to achieve division of the plasma membranes in the two resulting cells.

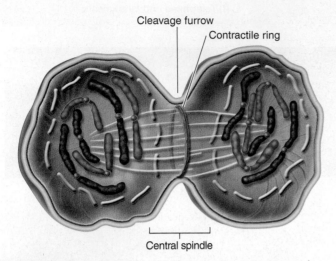

Figure 15.10 A closer look at cytokinesis in animal cells.

BioConnections: *Look back at Table 4.1 and Figure 4.11, which describe the structure and function of actin and myosin. How do you think the contractile ring contracts?*

The 20 conserved proteins perform one of four possible functions.

1. Contractile ring: Seven proteins, including actin, myosin, and other proteins that regulate actin and myosin function, are necessary for the formation of the contractile ring.
2. Signal transduction: Five proteins are components of a signal transduction pathway that initiates the formation of the contractile ring.
3. Central spindle: Eight proteins are known to be components that bind to the central spindle and are necessary for cytokinesis.
4. Cell separation via membrane insertion: Two proteins are needed for the final separation of the two daughter cells.

The 20 conserved proteins should be considered a minimum estimate. As we gain a deeper understanding of cytokinesis at the molecular level, it is likely that additional proteins may be discovered.

15.3 Meiosis and Sexual Reproduction

Learning Outcomes:

1. Describe the processes of synapsis and crossing over.
2. Outline the key events that occur during the phases of meiosis.
3. Compare and contrast mitosis and meiosis, focusing on key steps that account for the different outcomes of these two processes
4. Distinguish between the life cycles of diploid-dominant species, haploid-dominant species, and species that exhibit an alternation of generations.

We now turn our attention to **sexual reproduction**, a process in which two haploid gametes unite to form a diploid cell called a **zygote**. For multicellular species such as animals and plants, the zygote then grows and divides by mitotic cell divisions into a multicellular organ-
ith many diploid cells.

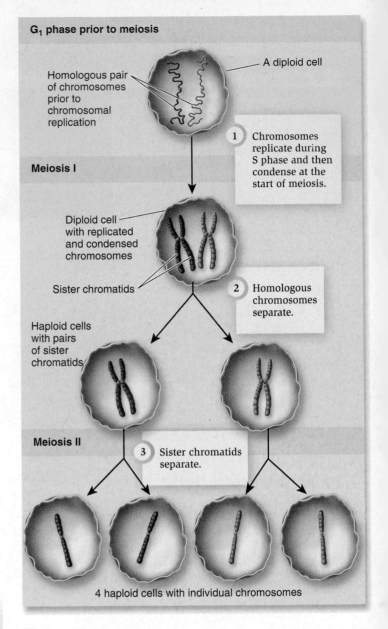

Figure 15.11 How the process of meiosis reduces chromosome number. This simplified diagram emphasizes the reduction in chromosome number as a diploid cell divides by meiosis to produce four haploid cells.

As discussed earlier, a diploid cell contains two homologous sets of chromosomes, whereas a haploid cell contains a single set. For example, a diploid human cell contains 46 chromosomes, but a human gamete—sperm or egg cell—is a haploid cell that contains only 23 chromosomes. **Meiosis** is the process by which haploid cells are produced from a cell that was originally diploid. The term meiosis, which means "to make smaller," refers to the fewer chromosomes found in cells following this process. For this to occur, the chromosomes must be correctly sorted and distributed in a way that reduces the chromosome number to half its original diploid value. In the case of human gametes, for example, each gamete must receive one chromosome from each of the 23 pairs. For this to happen, two rounds of divisions are necessary, termed meiosis I and meiosis II (**Figure 15.11**). When a cell begins meiosis, it contains chromosomes that are found in homologous pairs. When meiosis is completed, a single diploid cell with homologous pairs of chromosomes has produced four haploid cells.

In this section, we will examine the cellular events of meiosis that reduce the chromosome number from diploid to haploid. In addition, we will briefly consider how this process plays a role in the life cycles of animals, plants, fungi, and protists.

Bivalent Formation and Crossing Over Occur at the Beginning of Meiosis

Like mitosis, meiosis begins after a cell has progressed through the G_1, S, and G_2 phases of the cell cycle. However, two key events occur at the beginning of meiosis that do not occur in mitosis. First, homologous pairs of sister chromatids associate with each other, lying side by side to form a **bivalent**, also called a tetrad (**Figure 15.12**). The process of forming a bivalent is termed **synapsis**. In most eukaryotic species, a protein structure called the synaptonemal complex connects homologous chromosomes during a portion of meiosis. However, the synaptonemal complex is not required for the pairing of homologous chromosomes because some species of fungi completely lack such a complex, yet their chromosomes associate with each other correctly. At present, the precise role of the synaptonemal complex is not clearly understood.

The second event that occurs at the beginning of meiosis, but not usually during mitosis, is **crossing over**, which involves a physical exchange between chromosome segments of the bivalent (Figure 15.12). As discussed in Chapter 17, crossing over increases the genetic variation of sexually reproducing species. After crossing over occurs, the arms of the chromosomes tend to separate but remain adhered at a crossover site. This connection is called a chiasma (plural, chiasmata), because it physically resembles the Greek letter chi, χ. The

number of crossovers is carefully controlled by cells and depends on the size of the chromosome and the species. The range of crossovers for eukaryotic chromosomes is typically one or two to a couple dozen. During the formation of sperm in humans, for example, an average chromosome undergoes slightly more than two crossovers, whereas chromosomes in certain plant species may undergo 20 or more.

Meiosis I Separates Homologous Chromosomes

Now that we have an understanding of bivalent formation and crossing over, we are ready to consider the phases of meiosis (**Figure 15.13**). These simplified diagrams depict a diploid cell (*2n*) that contains a total of six chromosomes (as in our look at mitosis in Figure 15.8). Prior to meiosis, the chromosomes are replicated in S phase to produce pairs of sister chromatids. This single replication event is then followed by sequential divisions called meiosis I and II. Like mitosis, each of these is a continuous series of stages called prophase, prometaphase, metaphase, anaphase, and telophase. The sorting that occurs during **meiosis I** separates homologous chromosomes from each other (Figure 15.13a–e).

Prophase I During prophase I, the replicated chromosomes condense, the homologous chromosomes form bivalents, and crossing over occurs. The nuclear envelope then starts to fragment into small vesicles.

Prometaphase I In prometaphase I, the nuclear envelope is completely broken down into vesicles, and the spindle apparatus is entirely formed. The sister chromatids become attached to kinetochore microtubules. However, a key difference occurs between mitosis and meiosis I. In mitosis, a pair of sister chromatids is attached to both poles

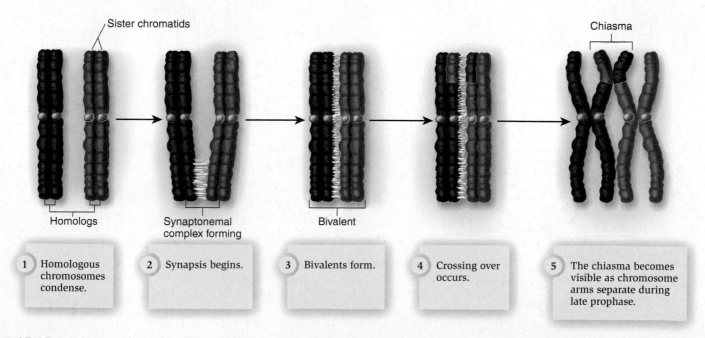

Sister chromatids

Chiasma

Homologs

Synaptonemal complex forming

Bivalent

1 Homologous chromosomes condense.

2 Synapsis begins.

3 Bivalents form.

4 Crossing over occurs.

5 The chiasma becomes visible as chromosome arms separate during late prophase.

Figure 15.12 Formation of a bivalent and crossing over during meiosis I. At the beginning of meiosis, homologous chromosomes pair with each other to form a bivalent, usually with a synaptonemal complex between them. Crossing over then occurs between homologous chromatids within the bivalent. During this process, homologs exchange segments of chromosomes.

Meiosis I

(a) Prophase I

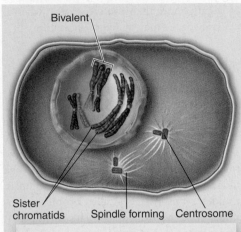

Bivalent

Sister chromatids   Spindle forming   Centrosome

1 Homologous chromosomes synapse to form bivalents, and crossing over occurs. Chromosomes condense, and the nuclear envelope begins to dissociate into vesicles.

(b) Prometaphase I

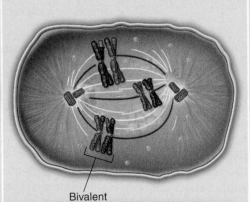

Bivalent

2 The nuclear envelope completely dissociates into vesicles, and bivalents become attached to kinetochore microtubules.

(c) Metaphase I

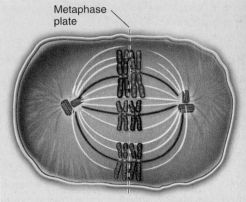

Metaphase plate

3 Bivalents randomly align along the metaphase plate. Each pair of sister chromatids is attached to one pole.

Meiosis II

(f) Prophase II

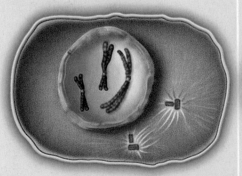

6 Sister chromatids condense, and the spindle starts to form. The nuclear envelope begins to dissociate into vesicles.

(g) Prometaphase II

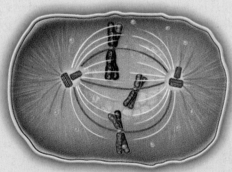

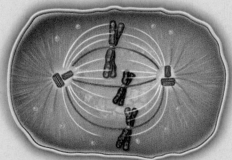

7 The nuclear envelope completely dissociates into vesicles. Sister chromatids attach to the spindle via kinetochore microtubules.

(h) Metaphase II

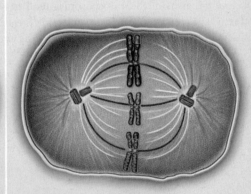

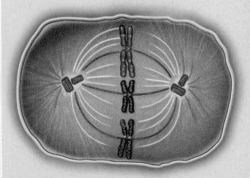

8 Sister chromatids align along the metaphase plate. Each pair of sister chromatids is attached to both poles.

(d) Anaphase I

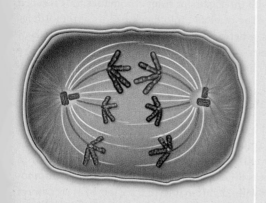

4 Homologous chromosomes separate and move toward opposite poles.

(e) Telophase I and cytokinesis

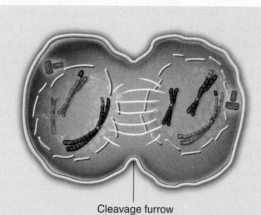

Cleavage furrow

5 The chromosomes decondense, and the nuclear envelope re-forms. The 2 daughter cells are separated by a cleavage furrow.

(I) Anaphase II

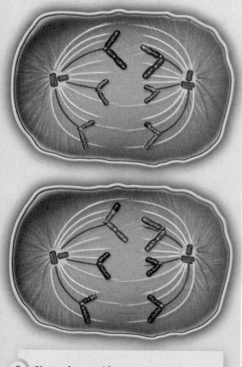

9 Sister chromatids separate, and individual chromosomes move toward the poles as kinetochore microtubules shorten. Polar microtubules lengthen and push the poles apart.

(j) Telophase II and cytokinesis

Four haploid cells

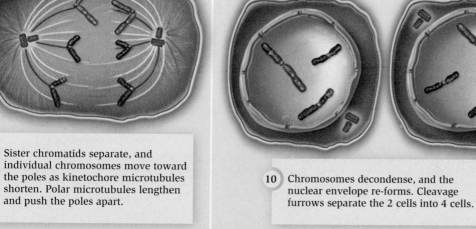

10 Chromosomes decondense, and the nuclear envelope re-forms. Cleavage furrows separate the 2 cells into 4 cells.

Figure 15.13 The phases of meiosis in an animal cell.

Concept Check: Relative to the original cell, what is the end result of meiosis?

(see Figure 15.8c). In meiosis I, a pair of sister chromatids is attached to just one pole via kinetochore microtubules (Figure 15.13b).

Metaphase I   At metaphase I, the bivalents are organized along the metaphase plate. Notice how this pattern of alignment is strikingly different from that observed during mitosis (see Figure 15.8d). In particular, the sister chromatids are aligned in a double row rather than a single row (as in mitosis). Furthermore, the arrangement of sister chromatids within this double row is random with regard to the (red and blue) homologs. (Remember that these different colors represent maternal and paternal chromosomes.) In Figure 15.13c, one of the red homologs is to the left of the metaphase plate, and the other two are to the right, whereas two of the blue homologs are to the left of the metaphase plate and the other one is to the right. In other cells, homologs could be arranged differently along the metaphase plate (for example, three blues to the left and none to the right, or none to the left and three to the right).

Because eukaryotic species typically have many chromosomes per set, maternal and paternal homologs can be randomly aligned along the metaphase plate in a variety of ways. For example, consider that humans have 23 chromosomes per set. The possible number of different, random alignments equals 2^n, where n equals the number of chromosomes per set. The reason why the random alignments equals 2^n is because each chromosome is found in a homologous pair and each member of the pair can align on either side of the metaphase plate. It is a matter of chance which daughter cell of meiosis I will get the maternal chromosome of a homologous pair, and which will get the paternal chromosome. In humans, 2^n equals 2^{23}, or over 8 million possibilities. Because the homologs are genetically similar but not identical, we see from this calculation that the random alignment of homologous chromosomes provides a mechanism to promote a vast amount of genetic diversity among the resulting haploid cells. When meiosis is complete, it is very unlikely that any two human gametes will have the same combination of homologous chromosomes.

Anaphase I   The segregation of homologs occurs during anaphase I (Figure 15.13d). The connections between bivalents break, but not the connections that hold sister chromatids together. Each joined pair of chromatids migrates to one pole, and the homologous pair of chromatids moves to the opposite pole, both pulled by kinetochore microtubules.

Telophase I   At telophase I, the sister chromatids have reached their respective poles and then decondense. The nuclear envelope now re-forms to produce two separate nuclei.

If we consider the end result of meiosis I, we see that two nuclei are produced, each with three pairs of sister chromatids; this is called a reduction division. The original diploid cell had its chromosomes in homologous pairs, whereas the two cells produced as a result of meiosis I and cytokinesis are considered haploid—they do not have pairs of homologous chromosomes.

Meiosis II Separates Sister Chromatids

Meiosis I is followed by cytokinesis and then **meiosis II** (see Figure 15.13f–j). DNA replication does not occur between meiosis I and meiosis II. The sorting events of meiosis II are similar to those of mitosis, but the starting point is different. For a diploid cell with six chromosomes, mitosis begins with 12 chromatids that are joined as six pairs of sister chromatids (see Figure 15.8). By comparison, the two cells that begin meiosis II each have six chromatids that are joined as three pairs of sister chromatids. Otherwise, the steps that occur during prophase, prometaphase, metaphase, anaphase, and telophase of meiosis II are analogous to a mitotic division. Sister chromatids are separated during anaphase II, unlike anaphase I in which bivalents are separated.

Mitosis and Meiosis Differ in a Few Key Steps

How are the outcomes of mitosis and meiosis different from each other? Mitosis produces two diploid daughter cells that are genetically identical. In our example shown in Figure 15.8, the starting cell had six chromosomes (three homologous pairs of chromosomes), and both daughter cells had copies of the same six chromosomes. By comparison, meiosis reduces the number of sets of chromosomes. In the example shown in Figure 15.13, the starting cell also had six chromosomes, whereas the resulting four daughter cells had only three chromosomes. However, the daughter cells did not contain a random mix of three chromosomes. Each haploid daughter cell contained one complete set of chromosomes, whereas the original diploid mother cell had two complete sets.

How do we explain the different outcomes of mitosis and meiosis? Table 15.1 emphasizes the differences between certain key steps in mitosis and meiosis that account for the different outcomes of these

Table 15.1   A Comparison of Mitosis, Meiosis I, and Meiosis II

Event	Mitosis	Meiosis I	Meiosis II
DNA replication:	Occurs prior to mitosis	Occurs prior to meiosis I	Does not occur between meiosis I and II
Synapsis during prophase:	No	Yes, bivalents are formed.	No
Crossing over during prophase:	Rarely	Commonly	Rarely
Attachment to poles at prometaphase:	A pair of sister chromatids is attached to kinetochore microtubules from both poles.	A pair of sister chromatids is attached to kinetochore microtubules from just one pole.	A pair of sister chromatids is attached to kinetochore microtubules from both poles.
Alignment along the metaphase plate:	Sister chromatids align.	Bivalents align.	Sister chromatids align.
Type of separation at anaphase:	Sister chromatids separate. A single chromatid, now called a chromosome, moves to each pole.	Homologous chromosomes separate. A pair of sister chromatids moves to each pole.	Sister chromatids separate. A single chromatid, now called a chromosome, moves to each pole.
result when the mother cell is oid:	Two daughter cells that are diploid	—	Four daughter cells that are haploid

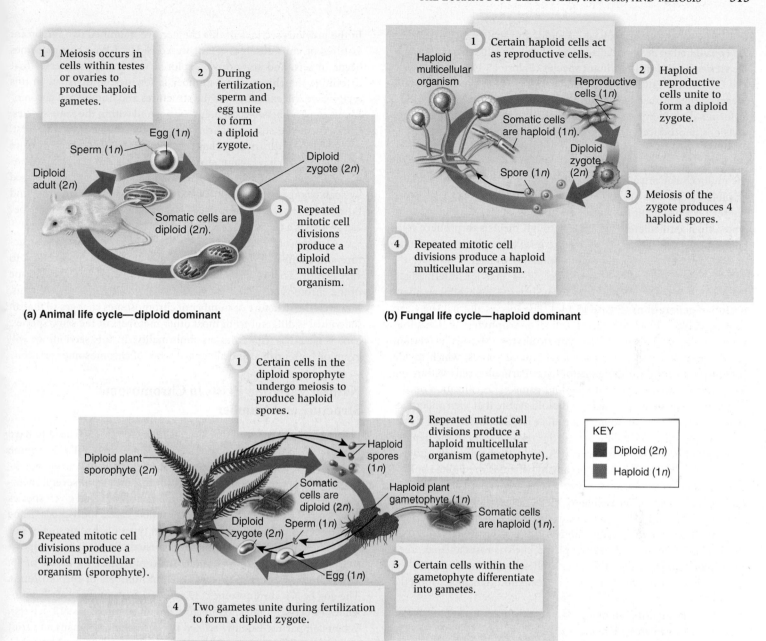

(a) Animal life cycle—diploid dominant

1. Meiosis occurs in cells within testes or ovaries to produce haploid gametes.
2. During fertilization, sperm and egg unite to form a diploid zygote.
3. Repeated mitotic cell divisions produce a diploid multicellular organism.

Sperm (1n)
Egg (1n)
Diploid adult (2n)
Somatic cells are diploid (2n).
Diploid zygote (2n)

(b) Fungal life cycle—haploid dominant

1. Certain haploid cells act as reproductive cells.
2. Haploid reproductive cells unite to form a diploid zygote.
3. Meiosis of the zygote produces 4 haploid spores.
4. Repeated mitotic cell divisions produce a haploid multicellular organism.

Haploid multicellular organism
Reproductive cells (1n)
Somatic cells are haploid (1n).
Diploid zygote (2n)
Spore (1n)

(c) Plant life cycle—alternation of generations

1. Certain cells in the diploid sporophyte undergo meiosis to produce haploid spores.
2. Repeated mitotic cell divisions produce a haploid multicellular organism (gametophyte).
3. Certain cells within the gametophyte differentiate into gametes.
4. Two gametes unite during fertilization to form a diploid zygote.
5. Repeated mitotic cell divisions produce a diploid multicellular organism (sporophyte).

Diploid plant sporophyte (2n)
Somatic cells are diploid (2n).
Haploid spores (1n)
Haploid plant gametophyte (1n)
Somatic cells are haploid (1n).
Diploid zygote (2n)
Sperm (1n)
Egg (1n)

KEY
■ Diploid (2n)
■ Haploid (1n)

Figure 15.14 A comparison of three types of sexual life cycles.

Concept Check: *What is the main reason for meiosis in animals? What is the main reason for mitosis in animals?*

two processes. DNA replication occurs prior to mitosis and meiosis I, but not between meiosis I and II. During prophase of meiosis I, the homologs synapse to form bivalents. This explains why crossing over occurs commonly during meiosis, but rarely during mitosis. During prometaphase of mitosis and meiosis II, pairs of sister chromatids are attached to both poles. In contrast, during meiosis I, each pair of sister chromatids (within a bivalent) is attached to a single pole. Bivalents align along the metaphase plate during metaphase of meiosis I, whereas sister chromatids align along the metaphase plate during metaphase of mitosis and meiosis II. At anaphase of meiosis I, the homologous chromosomes separate, but the sister chromatids remain together. In contrast, sister chromatid separation occurs during anaphase of mitosis and meiosis II. Taken together, the steps of mitosis produce two diploid cells that are genetically identical, whereas the steps of meiosis involve two sequential cell divisions that produce four haploid cells that may not be genetically identical.

Sexually Reproducing Species Produce Haploid and Diploid Cells at Different Times in Their Life Cycles

Let's now turn our attention to the relationship between mitosis, meiosis, and sexual reproduction in animals, plants, fungi, and protists. For any given species, the sequence of events that produces another generation of organisms is known as a **life cycle**. For sexually reproducing organisms, this usually involves an alternation between haploid cells or organisms and diploid cells or organisms (**Figure 15.14**).

Most species of animals are diploid, and their haploid gametes are considered to be a specialized type of cell. For this reason, animals are viewed as **diploid-dominant species** (Figure 15.14a). Certain diploid cells in the testes or ovaries undergo meiosis to produce haploid sperm or eggs, respectively. During fertilization, sperm and egg unite to form a diploid zygote, which then undergoes repeated mitotic cell divisions to produce a diploid multicellular organism.

By comparison, most fungi and some protists are just the opposite; they are **haploid-dominant species** (Figure 15.14b). In fungi, the multicellular organism is haploid ($1n$); only the zygote is diploid. Haploid fungal cells are most commonly produced by mitosis. During sexual reproduction, haploid cells unite to form a diploid zygote, which then immediately proceeds through meiosis to produce four haploid cells called spores. Each spore goes through mitotic cellular divisions to produce a haploid multicellular organism.

Plants and some algae have life cycles that are intermediate between diploid or haploid dominance. Such species exhibit an **alternation of generations** (Figure 15.14c). The species alternate between diploid multicellular organisms called **sporophytes**, and haploid multicellular organisms called **gametophytes**. Meiosis in certain cells within the sporophyte produces haploid spores, which divide by mitosis to produce the gametophyte. Particular cells within the gametophyte differentiate into haploid gametes. Fertilization occurs between two gametes, producing a diploid zygote that then undergoes repeated mitotic cell divisions to produce a sporophyte.

Among different plant species, the relative sizes of the haploid and diploid organisms vary greatly. In mosses, the haploid gametophyte is a visible multicellular organism, whereas the diploid sporophyte is smaller and remains attached to the haploid organism. In other plants, such as ferns (Figure 15.14c), both the diploid sporophyte and haploid gametophyte can grow independently. The sporophyte is considerably larger and is the organism we commonly think of as a fern. In seed-bearing plants, such as roses and oak trees, the diploid sporophyte is the large multicellular plant, whereas the gametophyte is composed of only a few cells and is formed within the sporophyte.

When comparing animals, plants, and fungi, it's interesting to consider how gametes are made. Animals produce gametes by meiosis. In contrast, plants and fungi produce reproductive cells by mitosis. The gametophyte of plants is a haploid multicellular organism that is created by mitotic cellular divisions of a haploid spore. Within the multicellular gametophyte, certain cells become specialized as gametes.

15.4 Variation in Chromosome Structure and Number

Learning Outcomes:

1. Describe how chromosomes can vary in size, centromere location, and number.
2. Identify the four ways that the structure of a chromosome can be changed via mutation.
3. Compare and contrast changes in the number of sets of chromosomes and changes in the number of individual chromosomes.
4. Give examples of how changes in chromosome number affect the characteristics of animals and plants.

In the previous sections of this chapter, we examined two important features of chromosomes. First, we considered how chromosomes occur in sets, and second, we explored two sorting processes that determine the chromosome number following cell division. In this section, we will examine how the structures and numbers of chromosomes can vary between different species and within the same species.

Why is the study of chromosomal variation important? First, geneticists have discovered that variations in chromosome structure and number can have major effects on the characteristics of an organism. We now know that several human genetic diseases are caused by such changes. In addition, changes in chromosome structure and number have been an important factor in the evolution of new species, which is a topic we will consider in Chapter 25.

Chromosome variation can be viewed in two ways. The structure and number of chromosomes among different species tend to vary greatly. There is also considerable variety in the size and shape of the chromosomes of a given species. On relatively rare occasions, however, the structure or number of chromosomes changes so that an individual is different from most other members of the same species. This is generally viewed as an abnormality. In this section, we will examine both normal and abnormal types of chromosome variation.

Natural Variation Exists in Chromosome Structure and Number

Before we begin to examine chromosome variation, we need to have a reference point for a normal set of chromosomes. To determine what the normal chromosomes of a species look like, a cytogeneticist microscopically examines the chromosomes from several members of the species. Chromosome composition within a given species tends to remain relatively constant. In most cases, individuals of the same species have the same number and types of chromosomes. For example, as mentioned previously, the usual chromosome composition of human cells is two sets of 23 chromosomes, for a total of 46. Other diploid species may have different numbers of chromosomes. The dog has 78 chromosomes (39 per set), the fruit fly has 8 chromosomes (4 per set), and the tomato has 24 chromosomes (12 per set). When comparing distantly related species, such as humans and fruit flies, major differences in chromosomal composition are observed.

The chromosomes of a given species also vary considerably in size and shape. Cytogeneticists have various ways to classify and identify chromosomes in their metaphase form. The three most commonly used features are size, location of the centromere, and banding patterns, which are revealed when the chromosomes are treated with stains. Based on centromere location, each chromosome is classified as **metacentric** (near the middle), **submetacentric** (off center), **acrocentric** (near one end), or **telocentric** (at the end) (**Figure 15.15**). Because the centromere is not exactly in the center of a chromosome, each chromosome has a short arm and a long arm. The short arm is designated with the letter "p" (for the French *petite*), and the long arm is designated with the letter "q." In the case of telocentric chromosomes, the short arm may be nearly nonexistent. When preparing a karyotype (see Figure 15.1), the chromosomes are aligned with the short arms on top and the long arms on the bottom.

Because different chromosomes often have similar sizes and centromeric locations, cytogeneticists must use additional methods to

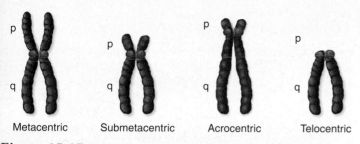

Metacentric   Submetacentric   Acrocentric   Telocentric

Figure 15.15 A comparison of centromeric locations among metaphase chromosomes.

accurately identify each type of chromosome within a karyotype. For detailed identification, chromosomes are treated with stains to produce characteristic banding patterns. Cytogeneticists use several different staining procedures to identify specific chromosomes. An example is Giemsa stain, which produces G bands (see Figure 15.1). The alternating pattern of G bands is unique for each type of chromosome.

The banding pattern of eukaryotic chromosomes is useful in two ways. First, individual chromosomes can be distinguished from each other, even if they have similar sizes and centromeric locations. Also, banding patterns are used to detect changes in chromosome structure that occur as a result of mutation.

Mutations Can Alter Chromosome Structure

Let's now consider how the structures of chromosomes can be modified by a mutation, a heritable change in the genetic material. Chromosomal mutations, which involve the breaking and rejoining of chromosomes, are categorized as deletions, duplications, inversions, and translocations (**Figure 15.16**).

Deletions and duplications are changes in the total amount of genetic material in a single chromosome. When a **deletion** occurs, a segment of chromosomal material is removed. The affected chromosome becomes deficient in a significant amount of genetic material. In a **duplication**, a section of a chromosome occurs two or more times in a row.

What are the consequences of a deletion or duplication? The possible effects depend on their size and whether they include genes or portions of genes that are vital to the development of the organism. When deletions or duplications have an effect, they are usually detrimental. Larger changes in the amount of genetic material tend to be more harmful because more genes are missing or duplicated.

Inversions and translocations are chromosomal rearrangements. An **inversion** is a change in the direction of the genetic material along a single chromosome. When a segment of one chromosome has been inverted, the order of G bands is opposite to that of a normal chromosome (Figure 15.16c). A **translocation** occurs when one segment of a chromosome becomes attached to a different chromosome. In a **simple translocation**, a single piece of chromosome is attached to another chromosome (Figure 15.16d). In a **reciprocal translocation**, two different types of chromosomes exchange pieces, thereby producing two abnormal chromosomes carrying translocations (Figure 15.16e).

Variation Occurs in the Number of Chromosome Sets and the Number of Individual Chromosomes

Variations in chromosome number can be categorized in two ways: variation in the number of sets of chromosomes and variation in the number of particular chromosomes within a set. The suffix -ploid or

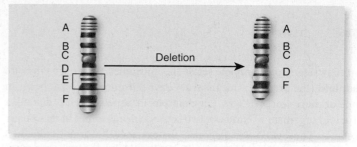

(a) Deletion: Removes a segment of chromosome.

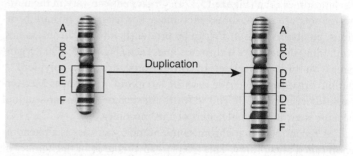

(b) Duplication: Doubles a particular region.

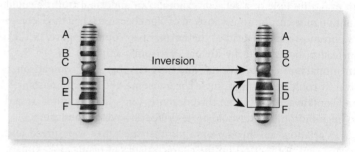

(c) Inversion: Flips a region to the opposite orientation.

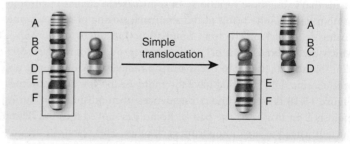

(d) Simple translocation: Moves a segment of 1 chromosome to another chromosome.

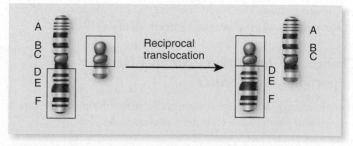

(e) Reciprocal translocation: Exchanges pieces between 2 different chromosomes.

Figure 15.16 Types of changes in chromosome structure. The letters alongside the chromosomes are placed there as frames of reference.

Concept Check: Which types of changes shown here do not affect the total amount of genetic material?

-ploidy refers to a complete set of chromosomes. Organisms that are **euploid** (the prefix eu- means true) have chromosomes that occur in one or more complete sets. For example, in a species that is diploid, a euploid organism would have two sets of chromosomes in its somatic cells. In *Drosophila melanogaster*, for example, a normal individual has eight chromosomes. The species is diploid, having two sets of four chromosomes each (**Figure 15.17a**). Organisms can vary in the number of sets of chromosomes they have. For example, on rare occasions, an abnormal fruit fly can be produced with 12 chromosomes, containing three sets of 4 chromosomes each (**Figure 15.17b**). Organisms with three or more sets of chromosomes are called **polyploid**. A diploid organism is referred to as $2n$, a **triploid** organism as $3n$, a **tetraploid** organism as $4n$, and so forth. All such organisms are euploid because they have complete sets of chromosomes.

A second way that chromosome number can vary is a phenomenon called **aneuploidy**. This refers to an alteration in the number of particular chromosomes, so the total number of chromosomes is not an exact multiple of a set. For example, an abnormal fruit fly could contain nine chromosomes instead of eight because it had three copies of chromosome 2 instead of the normal two copies (**Figure 15.17c**). Instead of being perfectly diploid, a trisomic animal is $2n + 1$. Such an animal is said to be trisomic and have **trisomy** 2. By comparison, a fruit fly could be lacking a single chromosome, such as chromosome 3, and contain a total of seven chromosomes ($2n - 1$). This animal is said to be monosomic and would be described as having **monosomy** 3.

Variations in chromosome number are fairly widespread and have a significant effect on the characteristics of plants and animals. For these reasons, researchers have wanted to understand the mechanisms that cause these variations. In some cases, a change in chromosome number is the result of the abnormal sorting of chromosomes during cell division. The term **nondisjunction** refers to an event in which the chromosomes do not separate properly during cell division. Nondisjunction can occur during meiosis I or meiosis II and produces haploid cells that have too many or too few chromosomes. **Figure 15.18** illustrates the consequences of nondisjunction during meiosis I. In this case, one pair of homologs moved into the cell on the left instead of separating from each other. This results in the production of aneuploid cells, with either too many or too few chromosomes. If such a cell becomes a gamete that fuses with another gamete during fertilization, the zygote and the resulting organism will have an abnormal number of chromosomes in all of its cells.

Changes in Chromosome Number Have Important Consequences

How do changes in chromosome number affect the characteristics of animals and plants? Let's consider a few examples.

Changes in Chromosome Number in Animals   In many cases, animals do not tolerate deviations from diploidy well. For example, polyploidy in mammals is generally a lethal condition. However, a few cases of naturally occurring variations from diploidy do occur in animals. Male bees, which are produced from unfertilized eggs, contain a single set of chromosomes and are therefore haploid organisms. By comparison, fertilized eggs become female bees, which are diploid. examples of vertebrate polyploid animals have been discovered.

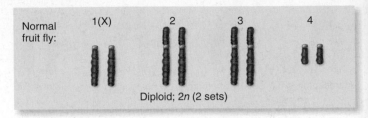

(a) Normal fruit fly chromosome composition

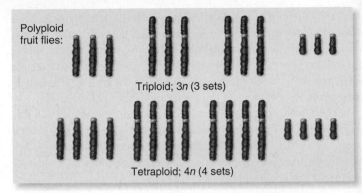

(b) Polyploidy

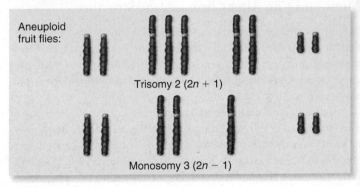

(c) Aneuploidy

Figure 15.17   Types of variation in chromosome number.
(a) The normal diploid number of chromosomes in *Drosophila*. The X chromosome is also called chromosome 1. Examples of chromosomes of **(b)** polyploid flies and **(c)** aneuploid flies.

Interestingly, on rare occasions, animals that are morphologically very similar to each other can be found as a diploid species as well as a separate polyploid species. This situation occurs among certain amphibians and reptiles. **Figure 15.19** shows photographs of a diploid and a tetraploid frog. As you can see, they look very similar.

One important reason that geneticists are so interested in aneuploidy is its relationship to certain inherited disorders in humans. Even though most people are born with 46 chromosomes, alterations in chromosome number occur at a surprising frequency during gamete formation. About 5% to 10% of all fertilized human eggs result in an embryo with an abnormality in chromosome number. In most cases, these abnormal embryos do not develop properly and result in a spontaneous abortion very early in pregnancy. Approximately 50% of all spontaneous abortions are due to alterations in chromosome number.

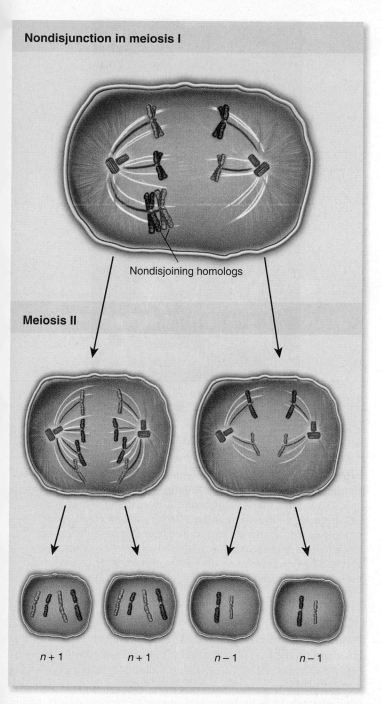

Figure 15.18 Nondisjunction during meiosis I. For simplicity, this cell shows only three pairs of homologous chromosomes. One of the three pairs does not disjoin properly, and both homologs have moved into the cell on the left. The resulting haploid cells shown at the bottom are all aneuploid, resulting in gametes with four chromosomes and two chromosomes, instead of three.

In some cases, an abnormality in chromosome number produces an offspring that can survive. Several human disorders are the result of abnormalities in chromosome number. The most common are trisomies of chromosomes 21, 18, or 13, or abnormalities in the number of the sex chromosomes (**Table 15.2**). These syndromes are most likely due to nondisjunction. For example, Turner syndrome (XO) may occur when a gamete that is lacking a sex chromosome due to nondisjunction has fused with a gamete carrying an X chromosome. By comparison, triple X syndrome (XXX) occurs when a gamete carrying two X chromosomes fuses with a gamete carrying a single X chromosome.

Most of the known trisomies involve chromosomes that are relatively small, so they carry fewer genes. Trisomies of the other human chromosomes and most monosomies are presumed to be lethal and have been found in spontaneously aborted embryos and fetuses.

Human abnormalities in chromosome number are influenced by the age of the parents. Older parents are more likely to produce children with abnormalities in chromosome number, possibly because meiotic nondisjunction is more likely to occur in older cells. **Down syndrome**, which was first described by the English physician John Langdon Down in 1866, provides an example. This disorder is caused by the inheritance of three copies of chromosome 21 (see Table 15.2). The incidence of Down syndrome rises with the age of either parent. In males, however, the rise occurs relatively late in life, usually past the age when most men have children. By comparison, the likelihood of having a child with Down syndrome rises dramatically during the later reproductive ages of women.

(a) *Hyla chrysoscelis* (diploid)

(b) *Hyla versicolor* (tetraploid)

Figure 15.19 Differences in chromosome number in two closely related frog species. The frog in **(a)** is diploid, whereas the frog in **(b)** is tetraploid. These frogs are in the act of performing their mating calls, which is why the skin under their mouths is protruding as a large bubble.

Table 15.2	Aneuploid Conditions in Humans		
Condition	Frequency (# of live births)	Syndrome	Characteristics
Autosomal			
Trisomy 21	1/800	Down	Mental impairment, abnormal pattern of palm creases, slanted eyes, flattened face, short stature
Trisomy 18	1/6,000	Edward	Mental and physical impairment, facial abnormalities, extreme muscle tone, early death
Trisomy 13	1/15,000	Patau	Mental and physical impairment, wide variety of defects in organs, large triangular nose, early death
Sex chromosomal			
XXY	1/1,000 (males)	Klinefelter	Sexual immaturity (no sperm), breast swelling (males)
XYY	1/1,000 (males)	Jacobs	Tall
XXX	1/1,500 (females)	Triple X	Tall and thin, menstrual irregularity
XO	1/5,000 (females)	Turner	Short stature, webbed neck, sexually undeveloped

(a) Wheat, *Triticum aestivum* (hexaploid)

(b) Diploid daylily (left) and tetraploid daylily (right)

Figure 15.20 Examples of polyploid plants. (a) Cultivated wheat, *Triticum aestivum*, is a hexaploid. It was derived from three different diploid species of grasses that originally were found in the Middle East and were cultivated by ancient farmers in that region. Modern varieties of wheat have been produced from this hexaploid species. **(b)** Differences in euploidy exist in these two closely related daylily species. The flower stems on the left are diploid, whereas those with the larger flowers on the right are tetraploid.

Changes in Chromosome Number in Plants In contrast to animals, plants commonly exhibit polyploidy. Polyploidy is also important in agriculture. In many instances, polyploid strains of plants display characteristics that are helpful to humans. They are often larger in size and more robust. These traits are clearly advantageous in the production of food. For example, the species of wheat that we use to make bread, *Triticum aestivum*, is a hexaploid (containing six sets of chromosomes) that arose from the union of diploid genomes from three closely related species (**Figure 15.20a**). During the course of its cultivation, two diploid species must have interbred to produce a tetraploid, and then a third species interbred with the tetraploid to produce a hexaploid. Plant polyploids tend to exhibit a greater adaptability, which allows them to withstand harsher environmental conditions. Polyploid ornamental plants commonly produce larger flowers than their diploid counterparts (**Figure 15.20b**).

Although polyploidy is often beneficial in plants, aneuploidy in all eukaryotic species usually has detrimental consequences on the characteristics of an organism. Why is aneuploidy usually detrimental? To answer this question, we need to consider the relationship between gene expression and chromosome number. For many, but not all genes, the level of gene expression is correlated with the number of genes per cell. Compared with a diploid cell, if a gene is carried on a chromosome that is present in three copies instead of two, approximately 150% of the normal amount of gene product is usually made. Alternatively, if only one copy of that gene is present due to a missing chromosome, only 50% of the gene product is typically made. For some genes, producing too much or too little of the gene product may not have adverse effects. However, for other genes, the over- or underexpression may interfere with the proper functioning of cells.

Summary of Key Concepts

15.1 The Eukaryotic Cell Cycle

- Cytogeneticists examine cells microscopically to determine their chromosome composition. A micrograph that shows the alignment of chromosomes from a given cell is called a karyotype. Eukaryotic chromosomes are inherited in sets. A diploid cell has two sets of chromosomes. The members of each pair are called homologs (Figure 15.1).

- The eukaryotic cell cycle consists of four phases called G_1 (first gap), S (synthesis of DNA), G_2 (second gap), and M phase (mitosis and cytokinesis). The G_1, S, and G_2 phases are collectively known as interphase (Figure 15.2).

- An interaction between cyclin and cyclin-dependent kinase is necessary for cells to progress through the cell cycle. Checkpoint proteins sense the environmental conditions and the integrity of the genome and control whether or not the cell progresses through the cell cycle (Figure 15.3).

- Masui and Markert studied the maturation of frog oocytes to identify a substance necessary for oocytes to progress through the cell cycle. This substance was initially called maturation promoting factor (MPF) and was later identified as a complex of mitotic cyclin and cyclin-dependent kinase (cdk) (Figures 15.4, 15.5).

15.2 Mitotic Cell Division

- In the process of mitotic cell division, a cell divides to produce two new cells (the daughter cells) that are genetically identical to the original cell.

- During S phase, eukaryotic chromosomes are replicated to produce a pair of identical sister chromatids that remain attached to each other (Figure 15.6).

- The mitotic spindle is a network of microtubules that plays a central role in chromosome sorting during cell division (Figure 15.7).

- Mitosis occurs in five phases called prophase, prometaphase, metaphase, anaphase, and telophase. During prophase, the chromosomes condense, and the nuclear envelope begins to dissociate. The spindle apparatus is completely formed by the end of prometaphase. At metaphase, the chromosomes are aligned in a single row along the metaphase plate of the spindle. During anaphase, the sister chromatids separate from each other and move to opposite poles; the poles themselves also move farther apart. During telophase, the chromosomes decondense, and the nuclear envelope re-forms (Figure 15.8).

- Cytokinesis, which occurs after mitosis, is the division of the cytoplasm to produce two distinct daughter cells. In animal cells, cytokinesis involves the formation of a cleavage furrow. In plant cells, two separate cells are produced by the formation of a cell plate. Among all animals, 20 different proteins are required for cytokinesis to occur (Figures 15.9, 15.10).

15.3 Meiosis and Sexual Reproduction

- The process of meiosis begins with a diploid cell and produces four haploid cells with one set of chromosomes each (Figure 15.11).

- During prophase of meiosis, homologous pairs of sister chromosomes synapse, and crossing over occurs. After crossing over, chiasmata—the site where crossing over occurs—become visible (Figure 15.12).

- Meiosis consists of two divisions—meiosis I and II—each composed of prophase, prometaphase, metaphase, anaphase, and telophase. During meiosis I, the homologs are separated into two different cells, and during meiosis II, the sister chromatids are separated into four different cells (Figure 15.13, Table 15.1).

- Animals are diploid-dominant species, whereas most fungi and some protists are haploid-dominant. Plants alternate between diploid and haploid forms (Figure 15.14).

15.4 Variation in Chromosome Structure and Number

- Chromosomes are classified as metacentric, submetacentric, acrocentric, and telocentric, based on their centromere location. Each type of chromosome can be uniquely identified by its banding pattern after staining (Figure 15.15).

- Deletions, duplications, inversions, and translocations are different ways in which mutations alter chromosome structure (Figure 15.16).

- A euploid organism has chromosomes that occur in complete sets. A polyploid organism has three or more sets of chromosomes. An organism that has one too many (trisomy) or one too few (monosomy) chromosomes is termed aneuploid. Aneuploidy can be caused by nondisjunction, an event in which the chromosomes do not separate properly during cell division (Figures 15.17, 15.18).

- Polyploid animals are relatively rare, but polyploid plants are common and tend to be larger and more robust than their diploid counterparts (Figures 15.19, 15.20).

- Aneuploidy in humans is responsible for several types of human genetic diseases, including Down syndrome (Table 15.2).

Assess and Discuss

Test Yourself

1. In which phase of the cell cycle are chromosomes replicated?
   a. G_1 phase
   b. S phase
   c. M phase
   d. G_2 phase
   e. none of the above

2. If two chromosomes are homologous, they
   a. look similar under the microscope.
   b. have very similar DNA sequences.
   c. carry the same types of genes.
   d. may carry different versions of the same gene.
   e. are all of the above.

3. Checkpoints during the cell cycle are important because they
   a. allow the organelle activity to catch up to cellular demands.
   b. ensure the integrity of the cell's DNA.
   c. allow the cell to generate sufficient ATP for cellular division.
   d. are the only time DNA replication can occur.
   e. do all of the above.

4. Which of the following is a reason for mitotic cell division?
   a. asexual reproduction
   b. gamete formation in animals
   c. multicellularity
   d. all of the above
   e. both a and c

5. A replicated chromosome is composed of
   a. two homologous chromosomes held together at the centromere.
   b. four sister chromatids held together at the centromere.
   c. two sister chromatids held together at the centromere.
   d. four homologous chromosomes held together at the centromere.
   e. one chromosome with a centromere.

6. Which of the following is *not* an event of anaphase of mitosis?
   a. The nuclear envelope breaks down.
   b. Sister chromatids separate.
   c. Kinetochore microtubules shorten, pulling the chromosomes to the pole.
   d. Polar microtubules push against each other, moving the poles farther apart.
   e. All of the above occur during anaphase.

7. A student is looking at cells under the microscope. The cells are from an organism that has a diploid number of 14. In one particular case, the cell has seven replicated chromosomes (sister chromatids) aligned at the metaphase plate of the cell. Which of the following statements accurately describes this particular cell?
   a. The cell is in metaphase of mitosis.
   b. The cell is in metaphase of meiosis I.
   c. The cell is in metaphase of meiosis II.
   d. All of the above are correct.
   e. Both b and c are correct.

8. Which of the following statements accurately describes a difference between mitosis and meiosis?
   a. Mitosis may produce diploid cells, whereas meiosis produces haploid cells.
   b. Homologous chromosomes synapse during meiosis but do not synapse during mitosis.
   c. Crossing over commonly occurs during meiosis, but it does not commonly occur during mitosis.
   d. All of the above are correct.
   e. Both a and c are correct.

9. During crossing over in meiosis I,
   a. homologous chromosomes are not altered.
   b. homologous chromosomes exchange genetic material.
   c. chromosomal damage occurs.
   d. genetic information is lost.
   e. cytokinesis occurs.

10. Aneuploidy may be the result of
    a. duplication of a region of a chromosome.
    b. inversion of a region of a chromosome.
    c. nondisjunction during meiosis.
    d. interspecies breeding.
    e. all of the above.

Conceptual Questions

1. Distinguish between homologous chromosomes and sister chromatids.

2. The *Oca2* gene, which influences eye color in humans, is found on chromosome 15. How many copies of this gene are found in the karyotype of Figure 15.1? Is it one, two, or four?

3. A principle of biology is that *cells are the simplest unit of life.* Explain how mitosis is a key process in the formation of new cells.

Collaborative Questions

1. Why is it necessary for chromosomes to condense during mitosis and meiosis? What do you think might happen if chromosomes did not condense?

2. A diploid eukaryotic cell has 10 chromosomes (five per set). As a group, take turns having one student draw the cell as it would look during a phase of mitosis, meiosis I, or meiosis II; then have the other students guess which phase it is.

Online Resource

www.brookerbiology.com

Stay a step ahead in your studies with animations that bring concepts to life and practice tests to assess your understanding. Your instructor may also recommend the interactive eBook, individualized learning tools, and more.

Simple Patterns of Inheritance

16

N tombi knew she looked different as long as she can remember. Born in Nigeria in 1991, she has accepted her appearance, though she still finds the occasional stare from strangers to be disturbing. Ntombi has albinism, a condition characterized by a total or a partial lack of pigmentation of the skin, hair, and eyes. As a result, she has very fair skin, blond hair, and blue eyes.* In contrast, her parents and three brothers have dark skin, black hair, and brown eyes, as do most of her relatives and most of the people in the city where she lives. Ntombi is very close to her aunt, who also has albinism.

Cases like Ntombi's have intrigued people for many centuries. How do we explain the traits that are found in people, plants, and other organisms? Can we predict what types of offspring two parents will produce? To answer such questions, researchers have studied the characteristics among related individuals and tried to make some sense of the data. Their goal is to understand **inheritance**—the acquisition of traits by their transmission from parent to offspring.

The first systematic attempt to understand inheritance was carried out by German plant breeder Joseph Kolreuter between 1761 and 1766. In crosses between two strains of tobacco plants, Kolreuter found that the offspring were usually intermediate in appearance between the two parents. He concluded that parents make equal genetic contributions to their offspring and that their genetic material blends together as it is passed to the next generation. This interpretation was consistent with the concept known as **blending inheritance**, which was widely accepted at that time. In the late 1700s, Jean Baptiste Lamarck, a French naturalist, hypothesized that physiological events (such as use or disuse) could modify traits and such modified traits would be inherited by offspring. For example, an individual who became adept at archery would pass that skill to his or her offspring. Overall, the prevailing view prior to the 1800s was that hereditary traits were rather malleable and could change and blend over the course of one or two generations.

In contrast, microscopic observations of chromosome transmission during mitosis and meiosis in the second half of the 19th century provided compelling evidence for **particulate inheritance**—the idea that the determinants of hereditary traits are transmitted in discrete units or particles from one generation to the next. Remarkably, this idea was first

An African girl with albinism. This condition results in very light skin and hair color.

put forward in the 1860s by a researcher who knew nothing about chromosomes. Gregor Mendel, remembered today as the "father of genetics," used statistical analysis of carefully designed plant breeding experiments to arrive at the concept of a gene, which is broadly defined as a unit of heredity. Forty years later, through the convergence of Mendel's work and that of cell biologists, this concept became the foundation of the modern science of genetics.

In this chapter, we will consider inheritance patterns and how the transmission of genes is related to the transmission of chromosomes. We will first consider the fundamental genetic patterns known as Mendelian inheritance and the relationship of these patterns to the behavior of chromosomes during meiosis. We will then examine the distinctive inheritance patterns of genes located on the X chromosome, paying special attention to the work of Thomas Hunt Morgan, whose investigation of these patterns confirmed that genes are on chromosomes. Finally, we will discuss the molecular basis of Mendelian inheritance and its variations and consider how probability calculations can be used to predict the outcome of crosses.

---

*In contrast to popular belief, most people with albinism have blue eyes, not pink eyes. This is particularly the case among Africans with albinism.

16.1 Mendel's Laws of Inheritance

Learning Outcomes:
1. List the advantages of using the garden pea to study inheritance.
2. Describe the difference between dominant and recessive traits.
3. Distinguish between genotype and phenotype.
4. Predict the outcome of genetic crosses using a Punnett square.
5. Define Mendel's law of segregation and law of independent assortment.

Gregor Johann Mendel (**Figure 16.1**) grew up on a small farm in northern Moravia, then a part of the Austrian Empire and now in the Czech Republic. At the age of 21, he entered the Augustinian monastery of St. Thomas in Brno, and was ordained a priest in 1847. Mendel then worked for a short time as a substitute teacher, but to continue teaching he needed a license. Surprisingly, he failed the licensing exam due to poor answers in physics and natural history, so he enrolled at the University of Vienna to expand his knowledge in these two areas. Mendel's training in physics and mathematics taught him to perceive the world as an orderly place, governed by natural laws that could be stated as simple mathematical relationships.

In 1856, Mendel began his historic studies on pea plants. For 8 years, he analyzed thousands of pea plants that he grew on a small plot in his monastery garden. In 1866, he published the results of his work in a paper entitled "Experiments on Plant Hybrids." This paper was largely ignored by scientists at that time, partly because of its title and because it was published in a somewhat obscure journal (*The Proceedings of the Brünn Society of Natural History*). Also, Mendel was clearly ahead of his time. During this period, biology had not yet become a quantitative, experimental science. In addition, the behavior of chromosomes during mitosis and meiosis, which provides a framework for understanding inheritance patterns, had yet to be studied. Prior to his death in 1884, Mendel reflected, "My scientific work has brought me a great deal of satisfaction and I am convinced it will be appreciated before long by the whole world." Sixteen years later, in 1900, Mendel's work was independently rediscovered by three biologists with an interest in plant genetics: Hugo de Vries of Holland, Carl Correns of Germany, and Erich von Tschermak of Austria. Within a few years, the influence of Mendel's landmark studies was felt around the world.

In this section, we will examine Mendel's experiments and how they led to the formulation of the basic genetic principles known as Mendel's laws. We will see that these principles apply not only to the pea plants Mendel studied, but also to a wide variety of sexually reproducing organisms, including humans.

Mendel Chose the Garden Pea to Study Inheritance

When two individuals of the same species with different characteristics are bred or crossed to each other, this is called **hybridization**, and the offspring are referred to as hybrids. For example, a hybridization experiment could involve breeding a purple-flowered plant to a white-flowered plant. Mendel was particularly intrigued by the consistency with which offspring of such crosses showed characteristics of one or the other parent in successive generations. His intellectual foundation in physics and the natural sciences led him to consider that this regularity might be rooted in natural laws that could be expressed mathematically. [To disco]ver these laws, he carried out quantitative experiments in which [he care]fully analyzed the numbers of offspring carrying specific traits.

Figure 16.1 Gregor Johann Mendel, the father of genetics.

Mendel chose the garden pea, *Pisum sativum*, to investigate the natural laws that govern inheritance. Why did he choose this species? Several properties of the garden pea were particularly advantageous for studying inheritance. First, it was available in many varieties that differed in characteristics, such as the appearance of seeds, pods, flowers, and stems. Such general features of an organism are called **characters**. **Figure 16.2** illustrates the seven characters that Mendel eventually chose to follow in his breeding experiments. Each of these characters was found in two discrete variants. For example, one character he followed was height, which had the variants known as tall and dwarf. Another was seed color, which had the variants yellow and green. A **trait** is an identifiable characteristic of an organism. The term trait usually refers to a variant for a character.* For example, seed color is a character, and green and yellow seed colors are traits.

A second important feature of garden peas is they are normally self-fertilizing. In **self-fertilization**, a female gamete is fertilized by a male gamete from the same plant. Like many flowering plants, peas have male and female sex organs in the same flower (**Figure 16.3**). Male gametes (sperm cells) are produced within pollen grains, which are formed in structures called stamens. Female gametes (egg cells) are produced in structures called ovules, which form within an organ called an ovary. For fertilization to occur, a pollen grain must land on the receptacle called a stigma, enabling a sperm to migrate to an ovule and fuse with an egg cell. In peas, the stamens and the ovaries are enclosed by a modified petal, an arrangement that greatly favors self-fertilization. Self-fertilization makes it easy to produce plants that breed true for a given trait, meaning the trait does not vary from generation to generation. For example, if a pea plant with yellow seeds breeds true for seed color, all the plants that grow from these seeds will also produce yellow seeds. A variety that continues to exhibit the same trait after several generations of self-fertilization is called a **true-breeding line**. Prior to conducting the studies described in this chapter, Mendel had already established that the seven characters he chose to study were true-breeding in the strains of pea plants he had obtained.

A third reason for using garden peas in hybridization experiments is the ease of making crosses: The flowers are quite large and easy to manipulate. In some cases, Mendel wanted his pea plants to self-fertilize, but in others, he wanted to cross plants that differed with respect to some character, a process called hybridization, or **cross-fertilization**. In garden peas, cross-fertilization requires

*Geneticists may also use the term trait to refer to a character.

Character	Variants (Traits)	
Flower color	Purple	White
Flower position	Axial	Terminal
Seed color	Yellow	Green
Seed shape	Round	Wrinkled
Pod color	Green	Yellow
Pod shape	Smooth	Constricted
Height	Tall	Dwarf

Figure 16.2 **The seven characters that Mendel studied.**

BIOLOGY PRINCIPLE **The genetic material provides a blueprint for reproduction.** The traits that Mendel studied in pea plants are governed by the genetic material of this species.

Concept Check: *Is having blue eyes a character, a variant, or both?*

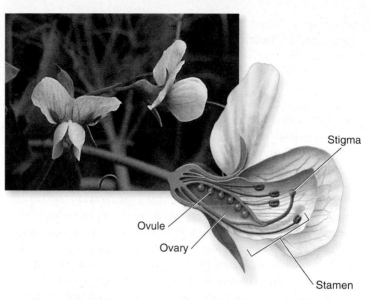

Figure 16.3 **Flower structure in pea plants.** The pea flower produces both male and female gametes. Sperm form in the pollen produced within the stamens; egg cells form in ovules within the ovary. A modified petal encloses the stamens and stigma, encouraging self-fertilization.

placing pollen from one plant onto the stigma of a flower on a different plant (**Figure 16.4**). Mendel would pry open an immature flower and remove the stamens before they produced pollen, so the flower could not self-fertilize. He then used a paintbrush to transfer pollen from another plant to the stigma of the flower that had its stamens removed. In this way, Mendel was able to cross-fertilize any two of his true-breeding pea plants and obtain any type of hybrid he wanted.

By Following the Inheritance Pattern of Single Traits, Mendel's Work Revealed the Law of Segregation

Mendel began his investigations by studying the inheritance patterns of pea plants that differed in a single character. A cross in which an experimenter follows the variants of only one character is called a **monohybrid cross**. As an example, we will consider a monohybrid

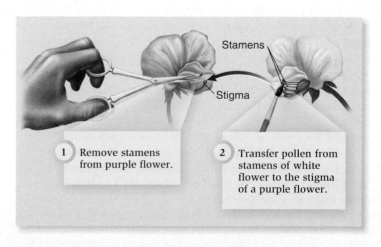

1 Remove stamens from purple flower.

2 Transfer pollen from stamens of white flower to the stigma of a purple flower.

Figure 16.4 **A procedure for cross-fertilizing pea plants.**

Concept Check: *Why are the stamens removed from the purple flower?*

cross in which Mendel followed the tall and dwarf variants for height (**Figure 16.5**). The left side of Figure 16.5a shows his experimental approach. The true-breeding parents are termed the **P generation** (parental generation), and their offspring constitute the F_1 **generation** (first filial generation, from the Latin *filius*, meaning son). When the true-breeding parents differ in a single character, their F_1 offspring are called single-trait hybrids, or **monohybrids**. When Mendel crossed true-breeding tall and dwarf plants, he observed that all plants of the F_1 generation were tall.

Next, Mendel followed the transmission of this character for a second generation. To do so, he allowed the F_1 monohybrids to self-fertilize, producing a generation called the F_2 **generation** (second filial generation). The dwarf trait reappeared in the F_2 offspring: Three-fourths of the plants were tall and one-fourth were dwarf. Mendel obtained similar results for each of the seven characters he studied, as shown in the data of Figure 16.5b. A quantitative analysis of his data allowed Mendel to postulate three important ideas about the properties and transmission of these traits from parents to offspring: (1) traits may exist in two forms: dominant and recessive; (2) an individual carries two genes for a given character, and genes have variant forms, which are now called **alleles**; and (3) the two alleles of a gene separate during gamete formation so that each sperm and egg receives only one allele.

Dominant and Recessive Traits   Perhaps the most surprising outcome of Mendel's work was that the data argued strongly against the prevailing notion of blending inheritance. In each of the seven cases, the F_1 generation displayed a trait distinctly like one of the two parents rather than an intermediate trait. Using genetic terms that Mendel originated, we describe the alternative traits as dominant and recessive. The term **dominant** describes the displayed trait, whereas the term **recessive** describes a trait that is masked by the presence of a dominant trait. Tall stems and purple flowers are examples of dominant traits; dwarf stems and white flowers are examples of recessive traits. In this case, we say that tall is dominant over dwarf, and purple is dominant over white.

Genes and Alleles   Mendel's results were consistent with particulate inheritance, in which the determinants of traits are inherited as unchanging, discrete units. In all seven cases, the recessive trait reappeared in the F_2 generation: Most F_2 plants displayed the dominant trait, whereas a smaller proportion showed the recessive trait. This observation led Mendel to conclude that the genetic determinants of traits are "unit factors" that are passed intact from generation to generation. These unit factors are what we now call **genes** (from the Greek *genos*, meaning birth), a term coined by the Danish botanist Wilhelm Johannsen in 1909. Mendel postulated that every individual carries two genes for a given character and that the gene for each character in his pea plant exists in two variant forms, which we now call alleles. For example, the gene controlling height in Mendel's pea plants occurs in two variants, called the tall allele and the dwarf allele. The right side of Figure 16.5a shows Mendel's conclusions, using genetic symbols (italic letters) that were adopted later. The letters *T* and *t* represent the alleles of the gene for plant height. By convention, the uppercase letter represents the dominant allele (in this case, tall), and the same letter in lowercase represents the recessive allele (dwarf).

gation of Alleles   When Mendel compared the numbers of ffspring exhibiting dominant and recessive traits, he noticed a

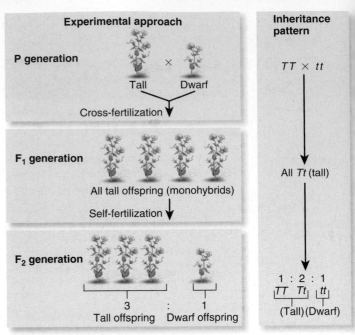

(a) Mendel's protocol for making monohybrid crosses

THE DATA

P cross	F_1 generation	F_2 generation	Ratio
Purple × white flowers	All purple	705 purple, 224 white	3.15:1
Axial × terminal flowers	All axial	651 axial, 207 terminal	3.14:1
Yellow × green seeds	All yellow	6,022 yellow, 2,001 green	3.01:1
Round × wrinkled seeds	All round	5,474 round, 1,850 wrinkled	2.96:1
Green × yellow pods	All green	428 green, 152 yellow	2.82:1
Smooth × constricted pods	All smooth	882 smooth, 299 constricted	2.95:1
Tall × dwarf stem	All tall	787 tall, 277 dwarf	2.84:1
Total	**All dominant**	**14,949 dominant, 5,010 recessive**	**2.98:1**

(b) Mendel's observed data for all 7 traits

Figure 16.5 Mendel's analyses of monohybrid crosses.

Concept Check: *Why do offspring of the F_1 generation exhibit only one variant of each character?*

recurring pattern. Although some experimental variation occurred, he always observed a 3:1 ratio between the dominant and the recessive trait (Figure 16.5b). How did Mendel interpret this ratio? He concluded that each parent carries two versions (alleles) of a gene and that the two alleles carried by an F_1 plant separate, or segregate, from each other during gamete formation, so each sperm or egg carries only one allele. The diagram in **Figure 16.6** shows that the segregation of the F_1 alleles should result in equal numbers of gametes carrying the dominant allele (*T*) and the recessive allele (*t*). If these gametes combine with one another randomly at fertilization, as shown in the figure, this would account for the 3:1 ratio of the F_2 generation. Note

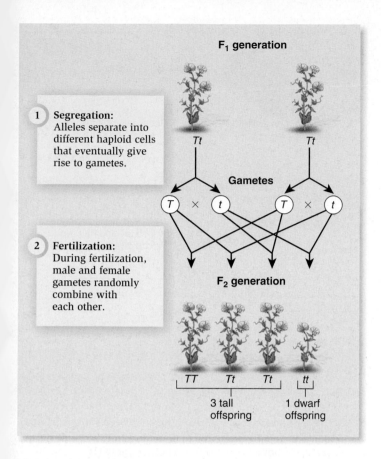

F₁ generation

1 **Segregation:** Alleles separate into different haploid cells that eventually give rise to gametes.

Gametes

$T \times t$ $T \times t$

2 **Fertilization:** During fertilization, male and female gametes randomly combine with each other.

F₂ generation

TT   Tt   Tt   tt

3 tall offspring   1 dwarf offspring

Figure 16.6 How the law of segregation explains Mendel's observed ratios. The segregation of alleles in the F₁ generation gives rise to gametes that carry just one of the two alleles. These gametes combine randomly during fertilization, producing the allele combinations TT, Tt, and tt in the F₂ offspring. The combination Tt occurs twice as often as either of the other two combinations because it can be produced in two different ways. The TT and Tt offspring are tall, whereas the tt offspring are dwarf.

Concept Check: *What is ratio of the T allele to the t allele in the F₂ generation? Does this ratio differ from the 3:1 phenotype ratio? If so, explain why.*

that a *Tt* individual can be produced by two different combinations of alleles—the *T* allele can come from the male gamete and the *t* allele from the female gamete, or vice versa. This accounts for the observation that *Tt* offspring are produced twice as often as either *TT* or *tt*. The idea that *the two alleles of a gene separate (segregate) during the formation of gametes so that every gamete receives only one allele* is known today as Mendel's **law of segregation**.

Genotype Describes an Organism's Genetic Makeup, Whereas Phenotype Describes Its Characteristics

To continue our discussion of Mendel's results, we need to introduce a few more genetic terms. The term **genotype** refers to the genetic composition of an individual. In the example shown in Figure 16.5a, *TT* and *tt* are the genotypes of the P generation, and *Tt* is the genotype of the F₁ generation. In the P generation, both parents are true-breeding plants, which means that each has identical copies of the allele of the gene for height. An individual with two identical alleles of a gene is said to be **homozygous** with respect to that gene. In the specific cross we are considering, the tall plant (*TT*) is homozygous for

T, and the dwarf plant (*tt*) is homozygous for *t*. In contrast, a **heterozygous** individual carries two different alleles of a gene. Plants of the F₁ generation are heterozygous, with the genotype *Tt*, because every individual carries one copy of the tall allele (*T*) and one copy of the dwarf allele (*t*). The F₂ generation includes both homozygous individuals (homozygotes) and heterozygous individuals (heterozygotes).

The term **phenotype** refers to the characteristics of an organism that are the result of the expression of its genes. In the example in Figure 16.5a, one of the parent plants is phenotypically tall, and the other is phenotypically dwarf. Although the F₁ offspring are heterozygous (*Tt*), they are phenotypically tall because each of them has a copy of the dominant tall allele. In contrast, the F₂ plants display both phenotypes in a ratio of 3:1. Later in the chapter, we will examine the underlying molecular mechanisms that produce phenotypes, but in our discussion of Mendel's results, the term simply refers to a visible characteristic such as flower color or height.

A Punnett Square Is Used to Predict the Outcome of Crosses

A common way to predict the outcome of simple genetic crosses is to make a **Punnett square**, a method originally proposed by the British geneticist Reginald Punnett. To construct a Punnett square, you must know the genotypes of the parents. What follows is a step-by-step description of the Punnett-square approach, using a cross of heterozygous tall plants.

Step 1. *Write down the genotypes of both parents.* In this example, a heterozygous tall plant is crossed to another heterozygous tall plant. The plant providing the pollen is considered the male parent and the plant providing the eggs, the female parent. (In self-pollination, a single individual produces both types of gametes.)

Male parent: *Tt*
Female parent: *Tt*

Step 2. *Write down the possible gametes that each parent can make.* Remember the law of segregation tells us that a gamete contains only one copy of each allele.

Male gametes: *T* or *t*
Female gametes: *T* or *t*

Step 3. *Create an empty Punnett square.* The number of columns equals the number of male gametes, and the number of rows equals the number of female gametes. Our example has two rows and two columns. Place the male gametes across the top of the Punnett square and the female gametes along the side.

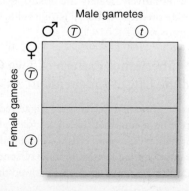

Male gametes

♂ *T*   *t*

♀ *T*

Female gametes

t

Step 4. *Fill in the possible genotypes of the offspring by combining the alleles of the gametes in the empty boxes.*

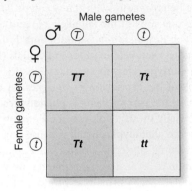

Step 5. *Determine the relative proportions of genotypes and phenotypes of the offspring.* The genotypes are obtained directly from the Punnett square. In this example, the genotypic ratios are $1TT : 2Tt : 1tt$. To determine the phenotypes, you must know which allele is dominant. For plant height, T (tall) is dominant to t (dwarf). The genotypes TT and Tt are tall, whereas the genotype tt is dwarf. Therefore, our Punnett square shows us that the phenotypic ratio is expected to be 3 tall: 1 dwarf. Keep in mind, however, these are predicted ratios for large numbers of offspring. If only a few offspring are produced, the observed ratios could deviate significantly from the predicted ratios. We will examine the topics of sample size and genetic prediction later in this chapter.

A Testcross Is Used to Determine an Individual's Genotype

When a character has two variants, one of which is dominant over the other, we know that an individual with a recessive phenotype is homozygous for the recessive allele. A dwarf pea plant, for example, must have the genotype tt. But an individual with a dominant phenotype may be either homozygous or heterozygous—a tall pea plant may have the genotype TT or Tt. How can we distinguish between these two possibilities? Mendel devised a method called a **testcross** to address this question. In a testcross, the researcher crosses the individual of interest to a homozygous recessive individual and observes the phenotypes of the offspring.

Figure 16.7 shows how this procedure can be used to determine the genotype of a tall pea plant. If the testcross produces some dwarf offspring, as shown in the Punnett square on the right side, these offspring must have two copies of the recessive allele, one inherited from each parent. Therefore, the tall parent must be a heterozygote, with the genotype Tt. Alternatively, if all of the offspring are tall, as shown in the Punnett square on the left, the tall parent is likely to be a homozygote, with the genotype TT.

Analyzing the Inheritance Pattern of Two Characters Demonstrated the Law of Independent Assortment

Mendel's analysis of monohybrid crosses suggested that traits are inherited as discrete units and that the alleles for a given gene segregate during the formation of haploid cells. To obtain additional insights into how genes are transmitted from parents to offspring, Mendel conducted crosses in which he simultaneously followed the inheritance of

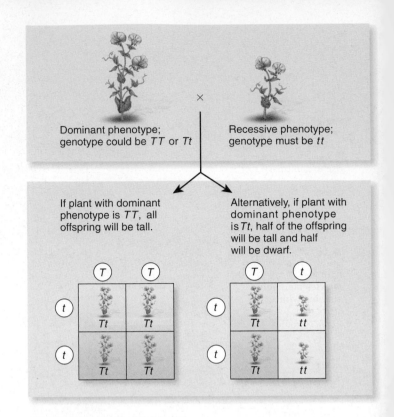

Figure 16.7 A testcross. The purpose of this experiment is to determine if the organism with the dominant phenotype, in this case a tall pea plant, is a homozygote (TT) or a heterozygote (Tt).

Concept Check: *Let's suppose you had a plant with purple flowers and unknown genotype and conducted a testcross to determine its genotype. You obtained 41 plants: 20 with white flowers and 21 with purple flowers. What was the genotype of the original purple-flowered plant?*

two different characters. A cross of this type is called a **dihybrid cross**. We will examine a dihybrid cross in which Mendel simultaneously followed the inheritance of seed color and seed shape (**Figure 16.8**). He began by crossing strains of pea plants that bred true for both characters. The plants of one strain had yellow, round seeds, and plants of the other strain had green, wrinkled seeds. He then allowed the F_1 offspring to self-fertilize and observed the phenotypes of the F_2 generation.

What are the possible patterns of inheritance for two characters? One possibility is that the two genes are linked in some way, so variants that occur together in the parents are always inherited as a unit. In our example, the allele for yellow seeds (Y) would always be inherited with the allele for round seeds (R), and the alleles for green seeds (y) would always be inherited with the allele for wrinkled seeds (r), as shown in Figure 16.8a. A second possibility is that the two genes are independent of one another, so their alleles are randomly distributed into gametes (Figure 16.8b). By following the transmission pattern of two characters simultaneously, Mendel could determine whether the genes that determine seed shape and seed color assort (are distributed) together as a unit or independently of each other.

What experimental results could Mendel predict for each of these two models? The two homozygous plants of the P generation can produce only two kinds of gametes, YR and yr, so in either case the F_1 offspring would be heterozygous for both genes; that is, they would have the genotypes $YyRr$. Because Mendel knew from his earlier experiments that yellow was dominant over green and round over wrinkled, he could predict that all the F_1 plants would have yellow, round seeds. In contrast, as shown in Figure 16.8, the ratios he

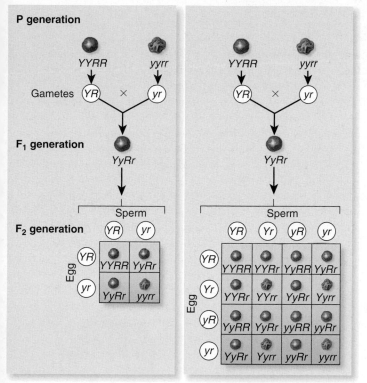

P generation

**(a) Hypothesis:
linked assortment**

**(b) Hypothesis:
independent assortment**

P cross	F₁ generation	F₂ generation
Yellow, round seeds × Green, wrinkled seeds	Yellow, round seeds	315 yellow, round seeds 101 yellow, wrinkled seeds 108 green, round seeds 32 green, wrinkled seeds

(c) The data observed by Mendel

Figure 16.8 **Two hypotheses for the assortment of two different genes.** In a cross between two true-breeding pea plants, one with yellow, round seeds and one with green, wrinkled seeds, all of the F₁ offspring have yellow, round seeds. When the F₁ offspring self-fertilize, the two hypotheses predict different phenotypes in the F₂ generation: **(a)** linked assortment, in which parental alleles stay associated with each other, or **(b)** independent assortment, in which each allele assorts independently. **(c)** Mendel's observations supported the independent assortment hypothesis.

Concept Check: *What ratio of offspring phenotypes would have occurred if the linked hypothesis had been correct?*

obtained in the F₂ generation would depend on whether the alleles of both genes assort together or independently.

If the parental genes are linked, as in Figure 16.8a, the F₁ plants could produce gametes that are only *YR* or *yr*. These gametes would combine to produce offspring with the genotypes *YYRR* (yellow, round), *YyRr* (yellow, round), or *yyrr* (green, wrinkled). The ratio of phenotypes would be 3 yellow, round to 1 green, wrinkled. Every F₂ plant would be phenotypically like one P-generation parent or the other. None would display a new combination of the parental traits. However, if the alleles assort independently, the F₂ generation would show a wider range of genotypes and phenotypes, as shown by the large Punnett square in Figure 16.8b. In this case, each F₁ parent

produces four kinds of gametes—*YR, Yr, yR,* and *yr*—instead of two, so the square is constructed with four rows on each side and shows 16 possible genotypes. The F₂ generation includes plants with yellow, round seeds; yellow, wrinkled seeds; green, round seeds; and green, wrinkled seeds, in a ratio of 9:3:3:1.

The actual results of this dihybrid cross are shown in Figure 16.8c. Crossing the true-breeding parents produced **dihybrid** offspring—offspring that are hybrids with respect to both traits. These F₁ dihybrids all had yellow, round seeds, confirming that yellow and round are dominant traits. This result was consistent with either hypothesis. However, the data for the F₂ generation were consistent only with the independent assortment hypothesis. Mendel observed four phenotypically different types of F₂ offspring, in a ratio that was reasonably close to 9:3:3:1.

In his original studies, Mendel reported that he had obtained similar results for every pair of characters he analyzed. His work supported the idea, now called the **law of independent assortment**, that *the alleles of different genes assort independently of each other during gamete formation.* Independent assortment means that a specific allele for one gene may be found in a gamete regardless of which allele for a different gene is found in the same gamete. In our example, the yellow and green alleles assort independently of the round and wrinkled alleles. The union of gametes from F₁ plants carrying these alleles produces the F₂ genotype and phenotype ratios shown in Figure 16.8b.

As we will see in Chapter 17, not all dihybrid crosses exhibit independent assortment. In some cases, the alleles of two genes that are physically located near each other on the same chromosome do not assort independently.

16.2 The Chromosome Theory of Inheritance

Learning Outcomes:

1. Outline the principles of the chromosome theory of inheritance.
2. Relate the behavior of chromosomes during meiosis to Mendel's laws of inheritance.

Mendel's studies with pea plants eventually led to the concept of a gene, which is the foundation for our understanding of inheritance. However, at the time of Mendel's work, the physical nature and location of genes were a complete mystery. The idea that inheritance has a physical basis was not even addressed until 1883, when German biologist August Weismann and Swiss botanist Karl Nägeli championed the idea that a substance in living cells is responsible for the transmission of hereditary traits. This idea challenged other researchers to identify the genetic material. Several scientists, including the German biologists Eduard Strasburger and Walther Flemming, observed dividing cells under the microscope and suggested that the chromosomes are the carriers of the genetic material. As we now know, the genetic material is the DNA within chromosomes.

In the early 1900s, the idea that chromosomes carry the genetic material dramatically unfolded as researchers continued to study the processes of mitosis, meiosis, and fertilization. It became increasingly clear that the characteristics of organisms are rooted in the continuity of cells during the life of an organism and from one generation to the next. Several scientists noted striking parallels between the segregation and assortment of traits noted by Mendel and the behavior of chromosomes during meiosis. Among these scientists were the German biologist Theodor Boveri and the American biologist Walter Sutton, who independently proposed the chromosome theory of inheritance. According to this theory, the inheritance patterns of traits can be explained by the transmission of chromosomes during meiosis and fertilization.

A modern view of the **chromosome theory of inheritance** consists of a few fundamental principles:

1. Chromosomes contain DNA, which is the genetic material. Genes are found within the chromosomes.
2. Chromosomes are replicated and passed from parent to offspring. They are also passed from cell to cell during the development of a multicellular organism.
3. The nucleus of a diploid cell contains two sets of chromosomes, which are found in homologous pairs. The maternal and paternal sets of homologous chromosomes are functionally equivalent; each set carries a full complement of genes.
4. At meiosis, one member of each chromosome pair segregates into one daughter nucleus, and its homolog segregates into the other daughter nucleus. During the formation of haploid cells, the members of different chromosome pairs segregate independently of each other.
5. Gametes are haploid cells that combine to form a diploid cell during fertilization, with each gamete transmitting one set of chromosomes to the offspring.

In this section, we will relate the chromosome theory of inheritance to Mendel's laws of inheritance.

Mendel's Law of Segregation Is Explained by the Segregation of Homologous Chromosomes During Meiosis

Now that you have an understanding of the basic tenets of the chromosome theory of inheritance, let's relate these ideas to Mendel's laws of inheritance. To do so, it will be helpful to introduce another genetic term. The physical location of a gene on a chromosome is called the gene's **locus** (plural, loci). As shown in **Figure 16.9**, each member of

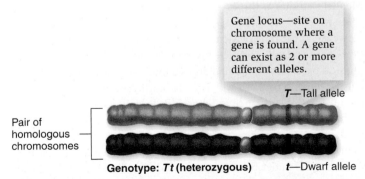

Gene locus—site on chromosome where a gene is found. A gene can exist as 2 or more different alleles.

T—Tall allele

Pair of homologous chromosomes

Genotype: *Tt* (heterozygous) *t*—Dwarf allele

Figure 16.9 **A gene locus.** The locus (location) of a gene is the same for each member of a homologous pair, whether the individual is homozygous or heterozygous for that gene. This individual is heterozygous (*Tt*) for a gene for plant height.

BioConnections: *Look back at Section 15.3 in Chapter 15. Explain the relationship between sexual reproduction and homologous chromosomes.*

a homologous chromosome pair carries an allele of the same gene at the same locus. The individual in this example is heterozygous (*Tt*), so each homolog has a different allele.

How can we relate the chromosome theory of inheritance to Mendel's law of segregation? **Figure 16.10** follows a pair of homologous chromosomes through the events of meiosis. This example involves a pea plant, heterozygous for height, *Tt*. The top of Figure 16.10 shows the two homologous chromosomes prior to DNA replication. When a cell prepares to divide, the homologs replicate to produce pairs of sister chromatids. Each chromatid carries a copy of the allele found on the original homolog, either *T* or *t*. During meiosis I, the homologs, each consisting of two sister chromatids, pair up and then segregate into two daughter cells. One of these cells has two copies of the *T* allele, and the other has two copies of the *t* allele. The

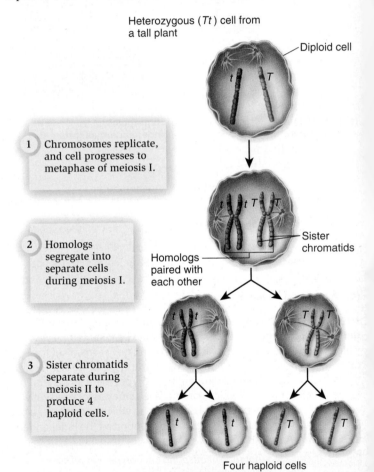

Heterozygous (*Tt*) cell from a tall plant

Diploid cell

1 Chromosomes replicate, and cell progresses to metaphase of meiosis I.

Sister chromatids

2 Homologs segregate into separate cells during meiosis I.

Homologs paired with each other

3 Sister chromatids separate during meiosis II to produce 4 haploid cells.

Four haploid cells

Figure 16.10 **The chromosomal basis of allele segregation.** This example shows a pair of homologous chromosomes in a cell of a pea plant. The blue chromosome was inherited from the male parent, and the red chromosome was inherited from the female parent. This individual is heterozygous (*Tt*) for a height gene. The two homologs segregate from each other during meiosis, leading to segregation of the tall allele (*T*) and the dwarf allele (*t*) into different haploid cells. Note: For simplicity, this diagram shows a single pair of homologous chromosomes, though eukaryotic cells typically have several different pairs of homologous chromosomes.

BioConnections: *When we say that alleles segregate, what does the word segregate mean? How is this related to meiosis, shown in Figure 15.11?*

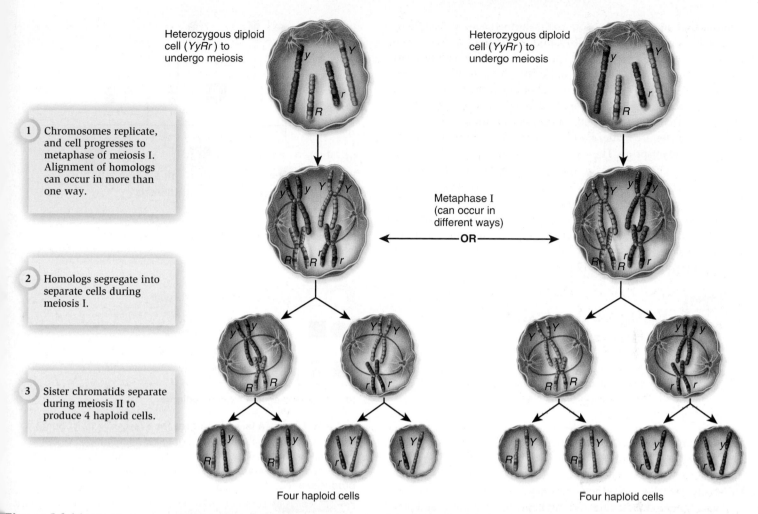

1. Chromosomes replicate, and cell progresses to metaphase of meiosis I. Alignment of homologs can occur in more than one way.

2. Homologs segregate into separate cells during meiosis I.

3. Sister chromatids separate during meiosis II to produce 4 haploid cells.

Heterozygous diploid cell (*YyRr*) to undergo meiosis

Metaphase I (can occur in different ways)

OR

Heterozygous diploid cell (*YyRr*) to undergo meiosis

Four haploid cells

Four haploid cells

Figure 16.11 **The chromosomal basis of independent assortment.** The alleles for seed color (*Y* or *y*) and seed shape (*R* or *r*) in peas are on different chromosomes. During metaphase of meiosis I, different arrangements of the two chromosome pairs lead to different combinations of the alleles in the resulting haploid cells. On the left, the chromosome carrying the dominant *R* allele has segregated with the chromosome carrying the recessive *y* allele. On the right, the two chromosomes carrying the dominant alleles (*R* and *Y*) have segregated together. Note: For simplicity, this diagram shows only two pairs of homologous chromosomes, though eukaryotic cells typically have several different pairs of homologous chromosomes.

Concept Check: Let's suppose that a cell is heterozygous for three different genes (Aa Bb Cc) and that each gene is on a different chromosome. How many different ways can these three pairs of homologous chromosomes align themselves during metaphase I, and how many different types of gametes can be produced?

sister chromatids separate during meiosis II, which produces four haploid cells. The end result of meiosis is that each haploid cell has a copy of just one of the two original homologs. Two of the cells have a chromosome carrying the *T* allele, and the other two have a chromosome carrying the *t* allele at the same locus. If the haploid cells shown at the bottom of Figure 16.10 give rise to gametes that combine randomly during fertilization, they produce diploid offspring with the genotypic and phenotypic ratios shown earlier in Figure 16.6.

Mendel's Law of Independent Assortment Is Explained by the Independent Alignment of Different Chromosomes During Meiosis

How can we relate the chromosome theory of inheritance to Mendel's law of independent assortment? **Figure 16.11** shows the alignment and segregation of two pairs of chromosomes in a pea plant. One

pair carries the gene for seed color: The yellow allele (*Y*) is on one chromosome, and the green allele (*y*) is on its homolog. The other pair of chromosomes carries the gene for seed shape: One member of the pair has the round allele (*R*), whereas its homolog carries the wrinkled allele (*r*). Therefore, this individual is heterozygous for both genes, with the genotype *YyRr*.

When meiosis begins, the DNA in each chromosome has already replicated, producing two sister chromatids. At metaphase I of meiosis, the two pairs of chromosomes randomly align themselves along the metaphase plate. This alignment can occur in two equally probable ways, shown on the two sides of the figure. On the left, the chromosome carrying the *y* allele is aligned on the same side of the metaphase plate as the chromosome carrying the *R* allele; *Y* is aligned with *r*. On the right, the opposite has occurred: *Y* is aligned with *R*, and *y* is with *r*. In each case, the chromosomes that aligned on the same side of the metaphase plate segregate into the same daughter cell. In this way, the random alignment of chromosome pairs during meiosis I leads to the independent assortment of alleles found on different chromosomes. For two genes found on different chromosomes, each with two variant alleles, meiosis produces four allele combinations in equal numbers (*Ry*, *rY*, *RY*, and *ry*), as seen at the bottom of the figure.

If a *YyRr* (dihybrid) plant undergoes self-fertilization, any two gametes can combine randomly during fertilization. Because four kinds of gametes are made, 4^2 or 16 possible allele combinations are possible in the offspring. These genotypes, in turn, produce four phenotypes in a 9:3:3:1 ratio, as seen earlier in Figure 16.8. This ratio is the expected outcome when a heterozygote for two genes on different chromosomes undergoes self-fertilization.

But what if two different genes are located on the same chromosome? In this case, the transmission pattern may not conform to the law of independent assortment. We will discuss this phenomenon, known as linkage, in Chapter 17.

16.3 Pedigree Analysis of Human Traits

Learning Outcomes:
1. Apply pedigree analysis to deduce inheritance patterns in humans.
2. Distinguish between recessively inherited disorders and dominantly inherited disorders.

As we have seen, Mendel conducted experiments by making selective crosses of pea plants and analyzing large numbers of offspring. Later geneticists also relied on crosses of experimental organisms, especially fruit flies (*Drosophila melanogaster*). However, geneticists studying human traits cannot use this approach, for ethical and practical reasons. Instead, human geneticists must rely on information from family trees, or pedigrees. In this approach, called **pedigree analysis**, an inherited trait is analyzed over the course of a few generations in one family. The results of this method may be less definitive than the results of breeding experiments because the small size of human families may lead to large sampling errors. Nevertheless, a pedigree analysis often provides important clues concerning human inheritance.

Pedigree analysis has been used to understand the inheritance of human genetic diseases that follow simple Mendelian patterns. Many genes that play a role in disease exist in two forms: the normal allele and an abnormal allele that has arisen by mutation. The disease symptoms are associated with the mutant allele. Pedigree analysis allows us to determine whether the mutant allele is dominant or recessive and to predict the likelihood of an individual being affected.

Let's consider a recessive condition to illustrate pedigree analysis. The pedigree in **Figure 16.12** concerns a human genetic disease known as cystic fibrosis (CF), which involves a mutation in a gene that encodes the cystic fibrosis transmembrane regulator (the *CFTR* gene, also see Figure 1.16). Approximately 3% of Americans of European descent are heterozygous carriers of the recessive *CFTR* allele. Carriers are usually phenotypically normal. Individuals who are homozygous for the *CFTR* allele exhibit the disease symptoms, which include abnormalities of the lungs, pancreas, intestine, and sweat glands. A human pedigree, like the one in Figure 16.12, shows the

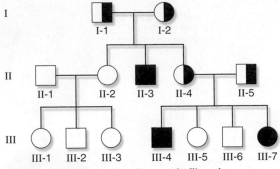

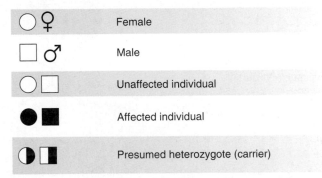

(a) Human pedigree showing cystic fibrosis

○ ♀	Female	
□ ♂	Male	
○ □	Unaffected individual	
● ■	Affected individual	
◐ ◨	Presumed heterozygote (carrier)	

(b) Symbols used in a human pedigree

Figure 16.12   A family pedigree for a recessive trait. Some members of the family in this pedigree are affected with cystic fibrosis. Phenotypically normal individuals I-1, I-2, II-4, and II-5 are presumed to be heterozygotes (carriers) because they have produced affected offspring.

Concept Check: Let's suppose a genetic disease is caused by a mutant allele. If two affected parents produce an unaffected offspring, can the mutant allele be recessive?

oldest generation (designated by the Roman numeral I) at the top, with later generations (II and III) below it. A male (represented by a square) and a female (represented by a circle) who produce offspring are connected by a horizontal line; a vertical line connects parents with their offspring. Siblings (brothers and sisters) are denoted by downward projections from a single horizontal line, from left to right in the order of their birth. For example, individuals I-1 and I-2 are the parents of individuals II-2, II-3, and II-4, who are all siblings. Individuals affected by the disease, such as individual II-3, are depicted by filled symbols.

Why does this pedigree indicate a recessive pattern of inheritance for CF? The answer is that two unaffected individuals can produce an affected offspring. Such individuals are presumed to be heterozygotes (designated by a half-filled symbol). However, the same unaffected parents can also produce unaffected offspring (depicted by an unfilled symbol), because an individual must inherit two copies of the mutant allele to exhibit the disease. A recessive mode of inheritance is also characterized by the observation that all of the offspring of two affected individuals are affected themselves. However, for genetic diseases like CF that limit survival or fertility, there are rarely if ever cases where two affected individuals produce offspring.

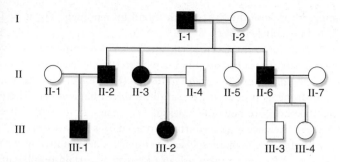

Figure 16.13 A family pedigree for a dominant trait. Huntington disease is caused by a dominant allele.

Concept Check: *What observation in a pedigree suggests a dominant pattern of inheritance?*

Although many of the alleles causing human genetic diseases are recessive, some are known to be dominant. Let's consider Huntington disease, a condition that causes the degeneration of brain cells involved in emotions, intellect, and movement. The symptoms of Huntington disease, which usually begin to appear when people are 30 to 50 years old, include uncontrollable jerking movements of the limbs, trunk, and face; progressive loss of mental abilities; and the development of psychiatric problems. If you examine the pedigree shown in **Figure 16.13**, you will see that every affected individual has one affected parent. This pattern is characteristic of most dominant disorders. However, affected parents do not always produce affected offspring. For example, II-6 is a heterozygote that has passed the normal allele to his offspring, thereby producing unaffected offspring (III-3 and III-4).

Most human genes are found on the paired chromosomes known as **autosomes**, which are the same in both sexes. Mendelian inheritance patterns involving these autosomal genes are described as autosomal inheritance patterns. Huntington disease is an example of a trait with an autosomal dominant inheritance pattern, whereas cystic fibrosis displays an autosomal recessive pattern. However, some human genes are located on sex chromosomes, which are different in males and females. These genes have their own characteristic inheritance patterns, which we will consider next.

16.4 Sex Chromosomes and X-Linked Inheritance Patterns

Learning Outcomes:
1. Describe different systems of sex determination in animals and plants.
2. Predict the outcome of crosses when genes are located on sex chromosomes.
3. Explain why X-linked recessive traits are more likely to occur in males.

In the first part of this chapter, we discussed Mendel's experiments that established the basis for understanding how traits are transmitted from parents to offspring. We also examined the chromosome theory of inheritance, which provided a framework for explaining Mendel's observations. Mendelian patterns of gene transmission are observed for most genes located on autosomes in a wide variety of eukaryotic species.

We will now turn our attention to genes located on **sex chromosomes**. As you learned in Chapter 15, this term refers to a distinctive pair of chromosomes that are different in males and females and that determine the sex of the individuals. Sex chromosomes are found in many but not all species with two sexes. The study of sex chromosomes proved pivotal in confirming the chromosome theory of inheritance. The distinctive transmission patterns of genes on sex chromosomes helped early geneticists show that particular genes are located on particular chromosomes. Later, other researchers became interested in these genes because some of them were found to cause inherited diseases in humans.

In this section, we will consider several mechanisms by which sex chromosomes in various species determine an individual's sex. We will then explore the inheritance patterns of genes on sex chromosomes and see that recessive alleles are expressed more frequently in males than in females. Last, we will examine some of the early research involving sex chromosomes that provided convincing evidence for the chromosome theory of inheritance.

In Many Species, Sex Differences Are Due to the Presence of Sex Chromosomes

Some early evidence supporting the chromosome theory of inheritance involved a consideration of sex determination. In 1901, American biologist C. E. McClung suggested that the inheritance of particular chromosomes is responsible for determining sex in fruit flies. Following McClung's initial observations, several mechanisms of sex determination were found in different species of animals. Some examples are described in **Figure 16.14**. All of these mechanisms involve chromosomal differences between the sexes, and most involve a difference in a single pair of sex chromosomes.

In the X-Y system of sex determination, which operates in mammals, the somatic cells of males have one X and one Y chromosome, whereas female somatic cells contain two X chromosomes (Figure 16.14a). For example, the 46 chromosomes carried by human cells consist of 22 pairs of autosomes and one pair of sex chromosomes (either XY or XX). Which chromosome, the X or Y, determines sex? In mammals, the presence of the Y chromosome causes maleness. This is known from the analysis of rare individuals who carry chromosomal abnormalities. For example, mistakes that occasionally occur during meiosis may produce an individual who carries two X chromosomes and one Y chromosome. Such an individual develops into a male. A gene called the *SRY* gene located on the Y chromosome of mammals plays a key role in the developmental pathway that leads to maleness.

The X-O system operates in many insects (Figure 16.14b). Unlike the X-Y system in mammals, the presence of the Y chromosome in the X-O system does not determine maleness. Females in this system have a pair of sex chromosomes and are designated XX. In some insect species that follow the X-O system, the male has only one sex chromosome, the X. In other X-O insect species, such as *Drosophila melanogaster*, the male has both an X chromosome and a Y chromosome. In all cases, an insect's sex is determined by the ratio between its X chromosomes and its sets of autosomes. If a fly has one X chromosome and is diploid for the autosomes (2*n*), this ratio is 1/2, or 0.5. This fly will become a male whether

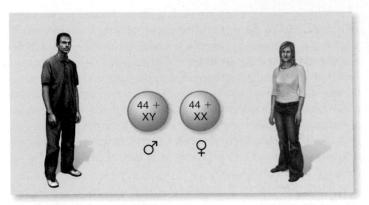

(a) The X-Y system in mammals

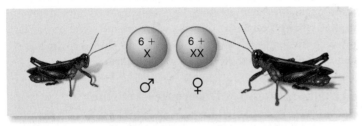

(b) The X-O system in certain insects

(c) The Z-W system in birds

(d) The haplodiploid system in bees

Figure 16.14 **Different mechanisms of sex determination in animals.** The numbers shown in the circles indicate the numbers of autosomes.

Concept Check: *If a person is born with only one X chromosome and no Y chromosome, would you expect that person to be a male or a female? Explain your answer.*

or not it receives a Y chromosome. On the other hand, if a diploid fly receives two X chromosomes, the ratio is 2/2, or 1.0, and the fly becomes a female.

Thus far, we have considered examples where females have two similar copies of a sex chromosome, the X. However, in some animal species, such as birds and some fish, the male carries two similar chromosomes (Figure 16.14c). This is called the Z-W system to

distinguish it from the X-Y system found in mammals. The male is ZZ, and the female is ZW.

Not all chromosomal mechanisms of sex determination involve a special pair of sex chromosomes. An interesting mechanism known as the haplodiploid system is found in bees (Figure 16.14d). The male bee, or drone, is produced from an unfertilized haploid egg. Therefore, male bees are haploid individuals. Females, both worker bees and queen bees, are produced from fertilized eggs and are diploid.

Although sex in many species of animals is determined by chromosomes, other mechanisms are also known. In certain reptiles and fish, sex is controlled by environmental factors such as temperature. For example, in the American alligator (*Alligator mississippiensis*), temperature controls sex development. When eggs of this alligator are incubated at 33°C, nearly all of them produce male individuals. When the eggs are incubated at a temperature significantly below 33°C, they produce nearly all females, whereas increasing percentages of females are produced above 34°C.

Most species of flowering plants, including pea plants, have a single type of diploid plant, or sporophyte, that makes both male and female gametophytes. However, the sporophytes of some species have two sexually distinct types of individuals, one with flowers that produce male gametophytes, and the other with flowers that produce female gametophytes. Examples include hollies, willows, poplars, and date palms. Sex chromosomes, designated X and Y, are responsible for sex determination in many such species. The male plant is XY, whereas the female plant is XX. However, in some plant species with separate sexes, microscopic examination of the chromosomes does not reveal distinct types of sex chromosomes.

In Humans, Recessive X-Linked Traits Are More Likely to Occur in Males

In humans, the X chromosome is rather large and carries over 1,000 genes, whereas the Y chromosome is quite small and has less than 100 genes. Therefore, many genes are found on the X chromosome but not on the Y; these are known as **X-linked genes**. By comparison, fewer genes are known to be Y linked, meaning they are found on the Y chromosome but not on the X. **Sex-linked genes** are found on one sex chromosome but not on the other. Because fewer genes are found on the Y chromosome, the term usually refers to X-linked genes. In mammals, a male cannot be described as being homozygous or heterozygous for an X-linked gene, because these terms apply to genes that are present in two copies. Instead, the term **hemizygous** is used to describe an individual with only one copy of a particular gene. A male mammal is said to be hemizygous for an X-linked gene.

Many recessive X-linked alleles cause diseases in humans, and these diseases occur more frequently in males than in females. As an example, let's consider the X-linked recessive disorder called classical hemophilia (hemophilia A). In individuals with hemophilia, blood does not clot normally, and a minor cut may bleed for a long time. Common accidental injuries that are minor in most people pose a threat of severe internal or external bleeding for hemophiliacs. Hemophilia A is caused by a recessive X-linked allele that encodes a defective form of a clotting protein. If a mother is a heterozygous carrier of hemophilia A, each of her children has a 50% chance of inheriting the recessive allele. The following Punnett quare shows a cross between an unaffected father and a heterozy-gous mother. X^H designates an X chromosome carrying the normal allele, and X^{h-A} is the X chromosome that carries the recessive allele or hemophilia A.

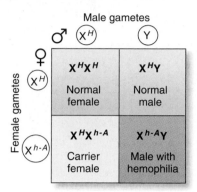

Male gametes

	X^H	Y
X^H	$X^H X^H$ Normal female	$X^H Y$ Normal male
X^{h-A}	$X^H X^{h-A}$ Carrier female	$X^{h-A} Y$ Male with hemophilia

Female gametes

Although each child has a 50% chance of inheriting the hemophilia allele from their mother, only 1/2 of the sons will exhibit the disorder. Because a son inherits only one X chromosome, a son who inherits the abnormal allele from his mother will have hemophilia. However, a daughter inherits an X chromosome from both her mother and her father. In this example, a daughter who inherits the hemophilia allele from her mother also inherits a normal allele from her father. This daughter will have a normal phenotype, but if she passes the abnormal allele to her sons, they will have hemophilia.

FEATURE INVESTIGATION

Morgan's Experiments Showed a Correlation Between a Genetic Trait and the Inheritance of a Sex Chromosome in *Drosophila*

The distinctive inheritance pattern of X-linked alleles provides a way of demonstrating that a specific gene is on an X chromosome. An X-linked gene was the first gene to be located on a specific chromosome. In 1910, the American geneticist Thomas Hunt Morgan began work on a project in which he reared large populations of fruit flies, *Drosophila melanogaster*, in the dark to determine if their eyes would atrophy from disuse and disappear in future generations. Even after many consecutive generations, the flies showed no noticeable changes. After 2 years of looking at many flies, Morgan happened to discover a male fly with white eyes rather than the normal red. The white-eye trait must have arisen from a new mutation that converted a red-eye allele into a white-eye allele.

To study the inheritance of the white-eye trait, Morgan followed an approach similar to Mendel's in which he made crosses and quantitatively analyzed their outcome. In the experiment described in Figure 16.15, Morgan crossed his white-eyed male to a red-eyed female. All of the F_1 offspring had red eyes, indicating that red is dominant to white. The F_1 offspring were then mated to each other to obtain an F_2 generation. As seen in the data table, this cross produced 1,011 red-eyed males, 782 white-eyed males, and 2,459

Figure 16.15 Morgan's crosses of red-eyed and white-eyed *Drosophila*.

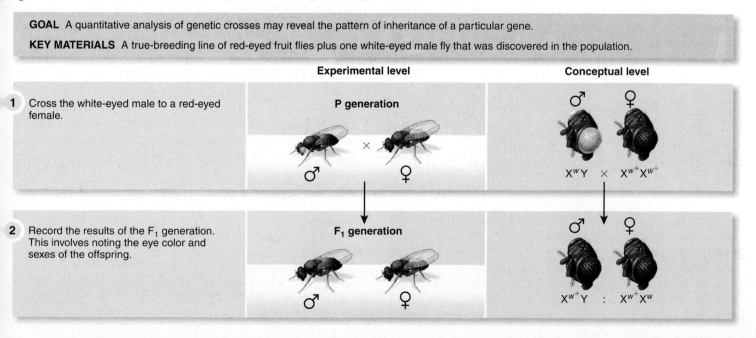

GOAL A quantitative analysis of genetic crosses may reveal the pattern of inheritance of a particular gene.

KEY MATERIALS A true-breeding line of red-eyed fruit flies plus one white-eyed male fly that was discovered in the population.

Experimental level   Conceptual level

1 Cross the white-eyed male to a red-eyed female.

P generation

♂   ♀

$X^w Y$ × $X^{w+} X^{w+}$

2 Record the results of the F_1 generation. This involves noting the eye color and sexes of the offspring.

F_1 generation

♂   ♀

$X^{w+} Y$: $X^{w+} X^w$

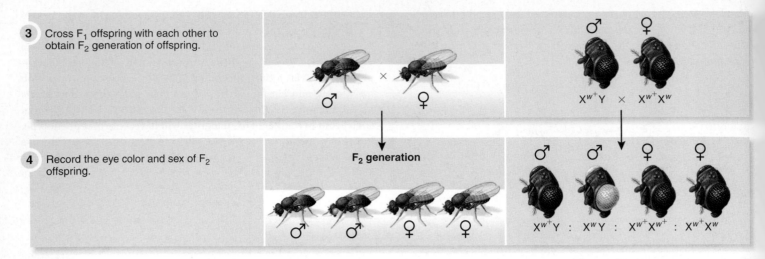

3 Cross F$_1$ offspring with each other to obtain F$_2$ generation of offspring.

$X^{w+}Y \times X^{w+}X^w$

4 Record the eye color and sex of F$_2$ offspring.

F$_2$ generation

$X^{w+}Y : X^wY : X^{w+}X^{w+} : X^{w+}X^w$

5 THE DATA

Cross	Results
Original white-eyed male to a red-eyed female	F$_1$ generation All red-eyed flies
F$_1$ males to F$_1$ females	F$_2$ generation 1,011 red-eyed males 782 white-eyed males 2,459 red-eyed females 0 white-eyed females

6 CONCLUSION The data are consistent with an inheritance pattern in which an eye-color gene is located on the X chromosome.

7 SOURCE Morgan, Thomas H. 1910. Sex limited inheritance in *Drosophila. Science* 32:120–122.

red-eyed females. Surprisingly, no white-eyed females were observed in the F$_2$ generation.

How did Morgan interpret these results? The results suggested a connection between the alleles for eye color and the sex of the offspring. As shown in the conceptual column of Figure 16.15 and in the following Punnett square, his data were consistent with the idea that the eye-color alleles in *Drosophila* are located on the X chromosome. X^{w+} is the chromosome carrying the normal allele for red eyes, and X^w is the chromosome with the mutant allele for white eyes.

F$_1$ male is $X^{w+}Y$
F$_1$ female is $X^{w+}X^w$

Male gametes

	♂ X^{w+}	Y
♀ X^{w+}	$X^{w+}X^{w+}$ Red, female	$X^{w+}Y$ Red, male
X^w	$X^{w+}X^w$ Red, female	X^wY White, male

Female gametes

The Punnett square predicts that the F$_2$ generation will not have any white-eyed females. This prediction was confirmed by Morgan's experimental data. However, it should also be pointed out that the experimental ratio of red eyes to white eyes in the F$_2$ generation is (2,459 + 1,011):782, which equals 4.4:1. This ratio deviates significantly from the ratio of 3:1 predicted in the Punnett square. The lower than expected number of white-eyed flies is explained by a decreased survival of white-eyed flies.

Following this initial discovery, Morgan carried out many experimental crosses that located specific genes on the *Drosophila* X chromosome. This research provided some of the most persuasive evidence for Mendel's laws and the chromosome theory of inheritance, which are the foundations of modern genetics. In 1933, Morgan became the first geneticist to receive a Nobel Prize (Physiology or Medicine).

Experimental Questions

1. Prior to the Feature Investigation, what was the original purpose of Morgan's experiments with *Drosophila*?

2. What results led Morgan to conclude that eye color was associated with the sex of the individual?

3. What crosses between fruit flies could yield female offspring with white eyes?

16.5   Variations in Inheritance Patterns and Their Molecular Basis

Learning Outcomes:

1. Relate dominant and recessive traits to protein function.
2. Describe pleiotropy and explain why it occurs.
3. Predict the outcome of crosses that exhibit incomplete dominance and codominance.
4. Discuss how the environment plays a critical role in determining the outcome of traits.

The term **Mendelian inheritance** describes the inheritance patterns of genes that segregate and assort independently. In the first section of this chapter, we considered the inheritance pattern of traits affected by a single gene that is found in two variants, one of which is dominant over the other. This pattern is called **simple Mendelian inheritance**, because the phenotypic ratios in the offspring clearly demonstrate Mendel's laws. In this section, we will discuss the molecular basis of dominant and recessive traits and see how the molecular expression of a gene can have widespread effects on an organism's phenotype. In addition, we will examine the inheritance patterns of genes that segregate and assort independently but do not display a simple dominant/recessive relationship. The transmission of these genes from parents to offspring does not usually produce the ratios of phenotypes we would expect on the basis of Mendel's observations. This does not mean that Mendel was wrong. Rather, the inheritance patterns of many traits are different from the simple patterns he chose to study. As described in **Table 16.1**, our understanding of gene function at the molecular level explains both simple Mendelian inheritance and other, more complex inheritance patterns that conform to Mendel's laws. This modern knowledge also sheds light on the role of the environment in producing an organism's phenotype, which we will discuss at the end of the section.

Protein Function Explains the Phenomenon of Dominance

As we discussed at the beginning of this chapter, Mendel studied seven characters that were found in two variants each (see Figure 16.2). The dominant variants are caused by the common alleles for these traits in pea plants. For any given gene, geneticists refer to a prevalent allele in a population as a **wild-type allele**. In most cases, a wild-type allele encodes a protein that is made in the proper amount and functions normally. By comparison, alleles that have been altered by mutation are called **mutant alleles**; these tend to be rare in natural populations. In the case of Mendel's seven characters in pea plants, the recessive alleles are due to rare mutations.

How do we explain why one allele is dominant and another allele is recessive? By studying genes and their gene products at the molecular level, researchers have discovered that a recessive allele is often defective in its ability to express a functional protein. In other words, mutations that produce recessive alleles are likely to decrease or eliminate the synthesis or functional activity of a protein. These are called loss-of-function alleles. To understand why many loss-of-function alleles are recessive, we need to take a quantitative look at protein function.

In a simple dominant/recessive relationship, the recessive allele does not affect the phenotype of the heterozygote. In this type of relationship, a single copy of the dominant (wild-type) allele is sufficient to mask the effects of the recessive allele. How do we explain the dominant phenotype of the heterozygote? **Figure 16.16** considers the example of flower color in a pea plant. The gene encodes an enzyme (protein P) that is needed to convert a colorless molecule into a purple pigment. The *P* allele is dominant because one *P* allele encodes enough of the functional protein—50% of the amount found in a normal homozygote—to provide a normal phenotype. Therefore, the *PP* homozygote and the *Pp* heterozygote both make enough of the purple pigment to yield purple flowers. The *pp* homozygote cannot make any of the functional protein required for pigment synthesis, so its flowers are white.

Table 16.1	Different Types of Mendelian Inheritance Patterns and Their Molecular Basis
Type	**Description**
Simple Mendelian inheritance	**Inheritance pattern:** Pattern of traits determined by a pair of alleles that display a dominant/recessive relationship and are located on an autosome. The presence of the dominant allele masks the presence of the recessive allele.
	Molecular basis: In many cases, the recessive allele is nonfunctional. Though a heterozygote may produce 50% of the functional protein compared with a dominant homozygote, this is sufficient to produce the dominant trait.
X-linked inheritance	**Inheritance pattern:** Pattern of traits determined by genes that display a dominant/recessive relationship and are located on the X chromosome. In mammals and fruit flies, males are hemizygous for X-linked genes. In these species, X-linked recessive traits occur more frequently in males than in females.
	Molecular basis: In a female with one recessive X-linked allele (a heterozygote), the protein encoded by the dominant allele is sufficient to produce the dominant trait. A male with a recessive X-linked allele (a hemizygote) does not have a dominant allele and does not make any of the functional protein.
Incomplete dominance	**Inheritance pattern:** Pattern that occurs when the heterozygote has a phenotype intermediate to the phenotypes of the homozygotes, as when a cross between red-flowered and white-flowered plants produces pink-flowered offspring.
	Molecular basis: Fifty percent of the protein encoded by the functional (wild-type) allele is not sufficient to produce the normal trait.
Codominance	**Inheritance pattern:** Pattern that occurs when the heterozygote expresses both alleles simultaneously. For example, a human carrying the A and B alleles for the ABO antigens of red blood cells produces both the A and the B antigens (has an AB blood type).
	Molecular basis: The codominant alleles encode proteins that function slightly differently from each other. In a heterozygote, the function of each protein affects the phenotype uniquely.

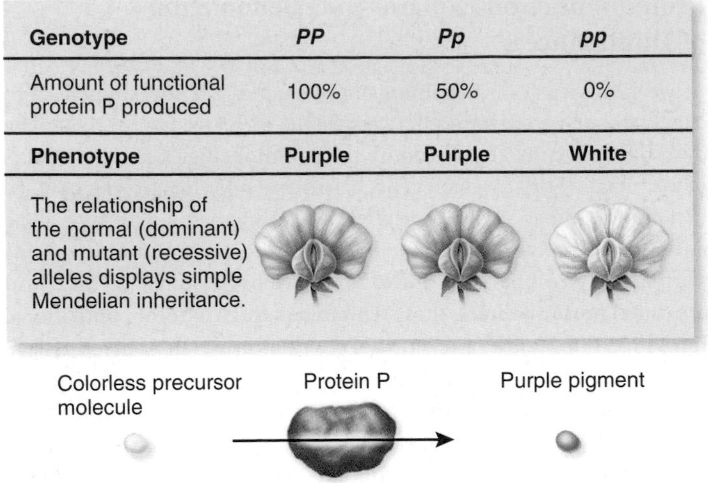

Genotype	PP	Pp	pp
Amount of functional protein P produced	100%	50%	0%
Phenotype	Purple	Purple	White

The relationship of the normal (dominant) and mutant (recessive) alleles displays simple Mendelian inheritance.

Colorless precursor molecule   Protein P   Purple pigment

Figure 16.16 **How genes give rise to traits during simple Mendelian inheritance.** In many cases, the amount of protein encoded by a single dominant allele is sufficient to produce the normal phenotype. In this example, the gene encodes an enzyme that is needed to produce a purple pigment. A plant with one or two copies of the normal allele produces enough pigment to produce purple flowers. In a *pp* homozygote, the complete lack of the normal protein (enzyme) results in white flowers.

This explanation—that 50% of the normal protein is enough—is true for many dominant alleles. In such cases, the normal homozygote is making much more of the protein than necessary, so if the amount is reduced to 50%, as it is in the heterozygote, the individual still has plenty of this protein to accomplish whatever cellular function it performs. In other cases, however, an allele may be dominant because the heterozygote actually produces more than 50% of the normal amount of functional protein. This increased production is due to the phenomenon of gene regulation. The normal gene is "up-regulated" in the heterozygote to compensate for the lack of function of the defective allele.

GENOMES & PROTEOMES CONNECTION

Recessive Alleles That Cause Diseases May Have Multiple Effects on Phenotype

The idea that recessive alleles usually cause a substantial decrease in the expression of a functional protein is supported by analyses of many human genetic diseases. Keep in mind that many genetic diseases are caused by rare mutant alleles. **Table 16.2** lists several examples of human genetic diseases in which a recessive allele fails to produce a specific cellular protein in its active form. Over 7,000 human disorders are caused by mutations in single genes; most of these are recessive alleles. With a human genome size of 20,000 to 25,000 genes, this means that roughly one-third of our genes are known to cause some kind of abnormality when mutations alter the expression or functionality of their gene product.

Single-gene disorders often illustrate the phenomenon of **pleiotropy**, which means that a mutation in a single gene can have multiple

Table 16.2	Examples of Recessive Human Genetic Diseases	
Disease	**Protein produced by the normal gene***	**Description**
Phenylketonuria	Phenylalanine hydroxylase	Inability to metabolize phenylalanine. Can lead to severe mental impairment and physical degeneration. The disease can be prevented by following a phenylalanine-free diet beginning early in life.
Cystic fibrosis	A chloride-ion transporter	Inability to regulate ion balance in epithelial cells. Leads to a variety of abnormalities, including production of thick lung mucus and chronic lung infections.
Tay-Sachs disease	Hexosaminidase A	Inability to metabolize certain lipids. Leads to paralysis, blindness, and early death.
α_1-Antitrypsin deficiency	α_1-Antitrypsin	Inability to prevent the activity of protease enzymes. Leads to a buildup of certain proteins that cause liver damage and emphysema.
Hemophilia A	Coagulation factor VIII	A defect in blood clotting due to a missing clotting factor. An accident may cause excessive bleeding or internal hemorrhaging.

*Individuals who exhibit the disease are homozygous (or hemizygous) for a recessive allele that results in a defect in the amount or function of the normal protein.

effects on an individual's phenotype. Pleiotropy occurs for several reasons, including the following:

1. The expression of a single gene can affect cell function in more than one way. For example, a defect in a microtubule protein may affect cell division and cell movement.
2. A gene may be expressed in different cell types in a multicellular organism.
3. A gene may be expressed at different stages of development.

In this genetics unit, we tend to discuss genes as they affect a single trait. This educational approach allows us to appreciate how genes function and how they are transmitted from parents to offspring. However, this focus may also obscure how amazing genes really are. In all or nearly all cases, the expression of a gene is pleiotropic with regard to the characteristics of an organism. The expression of any given gene influences the expression of many other genes in the genome, and vice versa. Pleiotropy is revealed when researchers study the effects of gene mutations.

As an example of a pleiotropic effect, let's consider cystic fibrosis (CF), which we discussed earlier as an example of a recessive human disorder (see Figure 16.12). In the late 1980s, the gene for CF was identified. The normal allele encodes a protein called the cystic fibrosis transmembrane conductance regulator (CFTR), which regulates ionic balance by allowing the transport of chloride ions (Cl⁻) across epithelial cell membranes. The mutation that causes CF diminishes the function of this Cl⁻ transporter, affecting several parts of the body in different ways. Because the movement of Cl⁻ affects water transport across membranes, the most severe symptom of CF is the production of thick mucus in the lungs, which occurs because of a water imbalance. In sweat glands, the normal Cl⁻ transporter has the function of recycling salt out of the glands and back into the skin before it can be lost to the outside world. Persons with CF have excessively salty sweat due to their inability to recycle salt back into their skin cells. A common test for CF is the measurement of salt on the skin. Another effect is seen in the reproductive systems of males who are homozygous for the mutant allele. Some males with CF are infertile because the vas deferens, the tubules that transport sperm from the testes, are absent or undeveloped. Presumably, a normally functioning Cl⁻ transporter is needed for the proper development of the vas deferens in the embryo. Taken together, we can see that a defect in CFTR has multiple effects throughout the body.

Incomplete Dominance Results in an Intermediate Phenotype

We will now turn our attention to examples in which the alleles for a given gene do not show a simple dominant/recessive relationship. In some cases, a heterozygote that carries two different alleles exhibits a phenotype that is intermediate between the corresponding homozygous individuals. This phenomenon is known as **incomplete dominance**.

In 1905, Carl Correns discovered this pattern of inheritance for alleles affecting flower color in the four-o'clock plant (*Mirabilis jalapa*). **Figure 16.17** shows a cross between two four-o'clock plants: a red-flowered homozygote and a white-flowered homozygote. The allele for red flower color is designated C^R, and the white allele is C^W. These alleles are designated with superscripts rather than upper- and lowercase letters because neither allele is dominant. The offspring of this cross have pink flowers—they are C^RC^W heterozygotes with an intermediate phenotype. If these F_1 offspring are allowed to self-fertilize, the F_2 generation has 1/4 red-flowered plants, 1/2 pink-flowered plants, and 1/4 white-flowered plants. This is a 1:2:1 phenotypic ratio rather than the 3:1 ratio observed for simple Mendelian inheritance. What is the molecular explanation for this ratio? In this case, the red allele encodes a functional protein needed to produce a red pigment, whereas the white allele is a mutant allele that is nonfunctional. In the C^RC^W heterozygote, 50% of the protein encoded by the C^R allele is not sufficient to produce the red-flower phenotype, but it does provide enough pigment to give pink flowers.

The degree to which we judge an allele to exhibit incomplete dominance may depend on how closely we examine an individual's phenotype. An example is an inherited human disease called phenylketonuria (PKU). This disorder is caused by a rare mutation in a gene that encodes an enzyme called phenylalanine hydroxylase. This enzyme is needed to metabolize the amino acid phenylalanine, which is found in milk, eggs, and other protein-rich foods in our diet. If left untreated, phenylalanine builds up, affecting various systems in the body. Homozygotes carrying the mutant allele suffer severe symptoms, including mental impairment, seizures, microcephaly (small head), poor development of tooth enamel, and decreased body growth. By comparison, heterozygotes appear phenotypically normal. For this reason, geneticists consider PKU to be a recessive disorder. However, biochemical analysis of the blood of heterozygotes shows they typically have a phenylalanine blood level twice as high as that

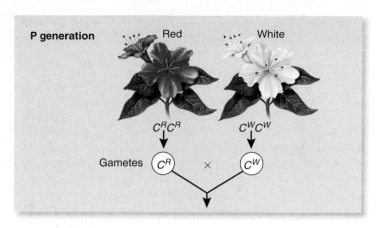

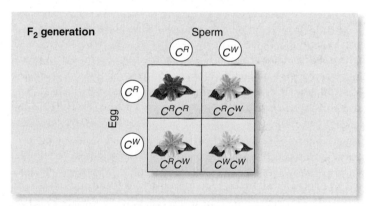

Figure 16.17 **Incomplete dominance in the four-o'clock plant.** When red-flowered and white-flowered homozygotes (C^RC^R and C^WC^W) are crossed, the resulting heterozygote (C^RC^W) has an intermediate phenotype of pink flowers.

of an individual carrying two normal copies of the gene. Individuals with PKU (homozygous recessive) typically have phenylalanine blood levels 30 times higher than normal. Therefore, at this closer level of examination, heterozygotes exhibit an intermediate phenotype relative to the homozygous dominant and recessive individuals. At this closer level of inspection, the relationship between the normal and mutant alleles is defined as incomplete dominance.

ABO Blood Type Is an Example of Multiple Alleles and Codominance

Although diploid individuals have only two copies of most genes, the majority of genes have three or more variants in natural populations. We describe such genes as occurring in **multiple alleles**. Particular

Table 16.3   The ABO Blood Group

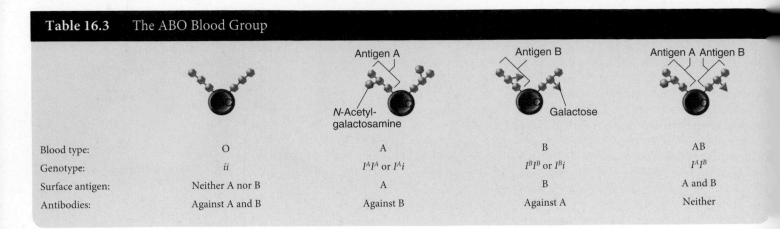

Blood type:	O	A	B	AB
Genotype:	ii	$I^A I^A$ or $I^A i$	$I^B I^B$ or $I^B i$	$I^A I^B$
Surface antigen:	Neither A nor B	A	B	A and B
Antibodies:	Against A and B	Against B	Against A	Neither

phenotypes depend on which two alleles each individual inherits. ABO blood types in humans are an example of phenotypes produced by multiple alleles.

As shown in **Table 16.3**, human red blood cells have structures on their plasma membrane known as surface antigens, which are constructed from several sugar molecules that are connected to form a carbohydrate tree. The carbohydrate tree is attached to lipids or membrane proteins to form glycolipids or glycoproteins, respectively. As noted in Chapter 5, glycolipids and glycoproteins often play a role in cell surface recognition.

Antigens are substances (in this case, carbohydrates) that may be recognized as foreign material when introduced into the body of an animal. Let's consider two types of surface antigens, known as A and B, which may be found on red blood cells. The synthesis of these antigens is determined by enzymes that are encoded by a gene that exists in three alleles, designated I^A, I^B, and i, respectively. The i allele is recessive to both I^A and I^B. A person who is ii homozygous does not produce surface antigen A or B and has blood type O. The red blood cells of an $I^A I^A$ homozygous or $I^A i$ heterozygous individual have surface antigen A (blood type A). Similarly, a homozygous $I^B I^B$ or heterozygous $I^B i$ individual produces surface antigen B (blood type B). A person who is $I^A I^B$ heterozygous makes both antigens, A and B, on every red blood cell (blood type AB). The phenomenon in which a single individual expresses two alleles is called **codominance**.

What is the molecular explanation for codominance? Biochemists have analyzed the carbohydrate tree produced in people of differing blood types. The differences are shown schematically in Table 16.3. In type O, the carbohydrate tree is smaller than in type A or type B because a sugar has not been attached to a specific site on the tree. People with blood type O have a loss-of-function mutation in the gene that encodes the enzyme that attaches a sugar at this site. This enzyme, called a glycosyl transferase, is inactive in type O individuals. In contrast, the type A and type B antigens have sugars attached to this site, but each of them has a different sugar. This difference occurs because the enzymes encoded by the I^A allele and the I^B allele have slightly different active sites. As a result, the enzyme encoded by the I^A allele attaches a sugar called N-acetylgalactosamine to the carbohydrate tree, whereas the enzyme encoded by the I^B allele attaches galactose. N-Acetylgalactosamine is represented by an orange hexagon in Table 16.3, and galactose by a green triangle. The importance

of surface antigens and blood type for safe blood transfusions is discussed in Chapter 53.

The Environment Plays a Vital Role in the Making of a Phenotype

In this chapter, we have been mainly concerned with the effects of genes on phenotypes. In addition, phenotypes are shaped by an organism's environment. An organism cannot exist without its genes or without an environment in which to live. Both are indispensable for life. An organism's genotype provides the plan to create a phenotype, and the environment provides nutrients and energy so that plan can be executed.

The **norm of reaction** is the phenotypic range that individuals with a particular genotype exhibit under differing environmental conditions. To evaluate the norm of reaction, researchers study members of true-breeding strains that have the same genotypes and subject them to different environmental conditions. For example, **Figure 16.18** shows the norm of reaction for genetically identical plants raised at different temperatures. As shown in the figure, these plants attain a maximal height when raised at 75°F. At 50°F and 85°F, the plants are substantially shorter. Growth cannot occur below 40°F or above 95°F.

The norm of reaction can be quite dramatic when we consider environmental influences on certain inherited diseases. A striking example is the human genetic disease PKU. As we discussed earlier in the chapter, this disorder is caused by a rare mutation in the gene that encodes the enzyme phenylalanine hydroxylase, which is needed to metabolize the amino acid phenylalanine. People with one or two functional copies of the gene can eat foods containing the amino acid phenylalanine and metabolize it correctly. However, individuals with two copies of the mutant gene cannot metabolize phenylalanine. When these individuals eat a standard diet containing phenylalanine, this amino acid accumulates within their bodies and becomes highly toxic. Under these conditions, PKU homozygotes manifest a variety of detrimental symptoms, including mental impairment, underdeveloped teeth, and foul-smelling urine. In contrast, when these individuals are identified at birth and given a restricted diet that is free of phenylalanine, they develop normally (**Figure 16.19**). This is a dramatic example of how genes and the environment interact to

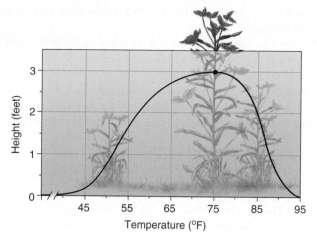

Figure 16.18 **The norm of reaction.** The norm of reaction is the range of phenotypes that a population of organisms with a particular genotype exhibit under different environmental conditions. In this example, genetically identical plants were grown at different temperatures in a greenhouse and then measured for height.

BIOLOGY PRINCIPLE **Living organisms interact with their environment.** As seen in this figure, the environment plays a key role in the outcome of traits.

Concept Check: *Could you study the norm of reaction in a wild population of squirrels?*

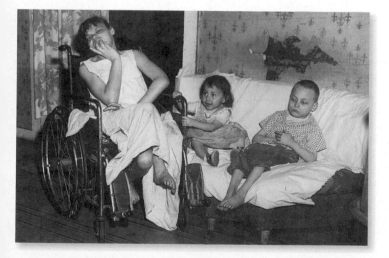

Figure 16.19 **Environmental influences on the expression of PKU within a single family.** All three children in this photo have inherited the alleles that cause PKU. The child in the middle was raised on a phenylalanine-free diet and developed normally. The other two children, born before the benefits of such a diet were known, were raised on diets containing phenylalanine. These two children have symptoms of PKU, including mental impairment.

BIOLOGY PRINCIPLE **Biology affects our society.** The study of genetic diseases has sometimes led to treatment options that prevent the harmful consequences of certain mutations, such as the one associated with PKU.

determine an individual's phenotype. In the United States, most newborns are tested for PKU, which occurs in about 1 in 10,000 babies. A newborn who is found to have this disorder can be raised on a phenylalanine-free diet and develop normally.

16.6 Genetics and Probability

Learning Outcomes:
1. Explain the concept of probability.
2. Apply the product rule and sum rule to problems involving genetic crosses.

As we have seen throughout this chapter, Mendel's laws of inheritance can be used to predict the outcome of genetic crosses. How is this useful? In agriculture, plant and animal breeders use predictions about the types and relative numbers of offspring their crosses will produce in order to develop commercially important crops and livestock. Also, people are often interested in the potential characteristics of their future children. This has particular importance to individuals who may carry alleles that cause inherited diseases. Of course, no one can see into the future and definitively predict what will happen. Nevertheless, genetic counselors can help couples predict the likelihood of having an affected child. This probability is one factor that may influence a couple's decision about whether to have children.

Earlier in this chapter, we considered how a Punnett square can be used to predict the outcome of simple genetic crosses. In addition to Punnett squares, we can apply the tools of mathematics and probability to solve more complex genetic problems. In this section, we will examine a couple of ways to calculate the outcomes of genetic crosses using these tools.

Genetic Predictions Are Based on the Rules of Probability

The chance that an event will have a particular outcome is called the **probability** of that outcome. The probability of a given outcome depends on the number of possible outcomes. For example, if you draw a card at random from a 52-card deck, the probability that you will get the jack of diamonds is 1 in 52, because there are 52 possible outcomes for the draw. In contrast, only two outcomes are possible when you flip a coin, so the probability is one in two (1/2, or 0.5, or 50%) that the heads side will be showing when the coin lands. The general formula for the probability (P) that a random event will have a specific outcome is

$$P = \frac{\text{Number of times an event occurs}}{\text{Total number of possible outcomes}}$$

Thus, for a single coin toss, the chance of getting heads is

$$P_{\text{heads}} = \frac{1 \text{ heads}}{(1 \text{ heads} + 1 \text{ tails})} = \frac{1}{2}$$

Earlier in this chapter, we used Punnett squares to predict the fractions of offspring with a given genotype or phenotype. In a cross between two pea plants that were heterozygous for the height gene (Tt), our Punnett square predicted that one-fourth of the offspring would be dwarf. We can make the same prediction by using a probability calculation.

$$P_{\text{dwarf}} = \frac{1\ tt}{(1\ TT + 2\ Tt + 1\ tt)} = \frac{1}{4} = 25\%$$

A probability calculation allows us to predict the likelihood that a future event will have a specific outcome. However, the accuracy of this prediction depends to a great extent on the number of events we observe—in other words, on the size of our sample. For example, if we toss a coin six times, the calculation we just presented for P_{heads} suggests we should get heads three times and tails three times. However, each coin toss is an independent event, meaning that every time we toss the coin there is a random chance that it will come up heads or tails, regardless of the outcome of the previous toss. With only six tosses, we would not be too surprised if we got four heads and two tails instead of the expected three heads and three tails. The deviation between the observed and expected outcomes is called the **random sampling error**. With a small sample, the random sampling error may cause the observed data to be quite different from the expected outcome. By comparison, if we flipped a coin 1,000 times, the percentage of heads would be fairly close to the predicted 50%. With a larger sample, we expect the sampling error to be smaller.

The Product Rule Is Used to Predict the Outcome of Independent Events

Punnett squares allow us to predict the likelihood that a genetic cross will produce an offspring with a particular genotype or phenotype. To predict the likelihood of producing multiple offspring with particular genotypes or phenotypes, we can use the **product rule**, which states that *the probability that two or more independent events will occur is equal to the product of their individual probabilities.* As we have already discussed, events are independent if the outcome of one event does not affect the outcome of another. In our previous coin-toss example, each toss is an independent event—if one toss comes up heads, another toss still has an equal chance of coming up either heads or tails. If we toss a coin twice, what is the probability that we will get heads both times? The product rule says that it is equal to the probability of getting heads on the first toss (1/2) times the probability of getting heads on the second toss (1/2), or one in four (1/2 × 1/2 = 1/4).

To see how the product rule can be applied to a genetics problem, let's consider a rare recessive human trait known as congenital analgesia. (Congenital refers to a condition present at birth; analgesia means insensitivity to pain.) People with this trait can distinguish between sensations such as sharp and dull, or hot and cold, but they do not perceive extremes of sensation as painful. The first known case of congenital analgesia, described in 1932, was a man who made his living entertaining the public as a "human pincushion." For a phenotypically normal couple, each heterozygous for the recessive allele causing congenital analgesia, we can ask, "What is the probability that their first three offspring will have the disorder?" To answer this question, we must first determine the probability of a single offspring having the abnormal phenotype. By using a Punnett square, we would find that the probability of an individual offspring being homozygous

recessive is 1/4. Thus, each of this couple's children has a one in four chance of having the disorder.

We can now use the product rule to calculate the probability of this couple having three affected offspring in a row. The phenotypes of the first, second, and third offspring are independent events; that is, the phenotype of the first offspring does not affect the phenotype of the second or third offspring. The product rule tells us that the probability of all three children having the abnormal phenotype is

$$\frac{1}{4} \times \frac{1}{4} \times \frac{1}{4} = \frac{1}{64} = 0.016$$

The probability of the first three offspring having the disorder is 0.016, or 1.6%. In other words, we can say that this couple's chance of having three children in a row with congenital analgesia is very small—only 1.6 out of 100.

The product rule can also be used to predict the outcome of a cross involving two or more genes. Let's suppose a pea plant with the genotype $TtYy$ was crossed to a plant with the genotype $Ttyy$. We could ask the question, "What is the probability that an offspring will have the genotype $ttYy$?" If the two genes independently assort, the probability of inheriting alleles for one gene is independent of the probability for other gene. Therefore, we can separately calculate the probability of the desired outcome for each gene. By constructing two small Punnett squares, we can determine the probability of genotypes for each gene individually, as shown here.

Cross: $TtYy \times Ttyy$

Probability that an offspring will be tt is 1/4, or 0.25.

Probability that an offspring will be Yy is 1/2, or 0.5.

We can now use the product rule to determine the probability that an offspring will be $ttYy$;

$$P = (0.25)(0.5) = 0.125, \text{ or } 12.5\%$$

The Sum Rule Is Used to Predict the Outcome of Mutually Exclusive Events

Let's now consider a second way to predict the outcome of particular crosses. In a cross between two heterozygous (Tt) pea plants, we may want to know the probability of a particular offspring being a homozygote. In this case we are asking, "What is the chance that this individual will be either homozygous TT or homozygous tt?" To answer an "either/or" question, we use the sum rule, which applies to events with mutually exclusive outcomes. When we say that outcomes are mutually exclusive, we mean they cannot occur at the same time. A pea plant can be tall or dwarf, but not both at the same time. The tall and dwarf phenotypes are mutually exclusive. Similarly, a plant with the genotype *TT* cannot be *Tt* or *tt*. Each of these genotypes is mutually exclusive of the other two. According to the **sum rule**, *the probability that one of two or more mutually exclusive outcomes will occur is the sum of the probabilities of the individual outcomes.*

To find the probability that an offspring will be either homozygous *TT* or homozygous *tt*, we add together the probability that it will be *TT* and the probability that it will be *tt*. If we constructed a Punnett square, we would find that the probability for each of these genotypes is one in four. We can now use the sum rule to determine the probability of an individual having one of these genotypes.

$$\frac{1}{4} \quad + \quad \frac{1}{4} \quad = \quad \frac{1}{2}$$

(probability of *TT*)   (probability of *tt*)   (probability of either *TT* or *tt*)

This calculation predicts that in crosses of two *Tt* parents, half of the offspring will be homozygotes—either *TT* or *tt*.

Summary of Key Concepts

16.1 Mendel's Laws of Inheritance

- Mendel studied seven characters found in garden peas that existed in two variants each (Figures 16.1, 16.2).
- Mendel allowed his peas to self-fertilize, or he carried out cross-fertilization, also known as hybridization (Figures 16.3, 16.4).
- By following the inheritance pattern of a single character (a monohybrid cross) for two generations, Mendel determined the law of segregation, which states that two alleles of a gene segregate during the formation of eggs and sperm so that every gamete receives only one allele (Figures 16.5, 16.6).
- The genotype is the genetic makeup of an organism. Alleles are alternative versions of the same gene. Phenotype is a description of the traits that an organism displays.
- A Punnett square is constructed to predict the outcome of crosses.
- A testcross is conducted to determine if an individual displaying a dominant trait is a homozygote or a heterozygote (Figure 16.7).
- By conducting a dihybrid cross, Mendel determined the law of independent assortment, which states that the alleles of different genes assort independently of each other during gamete formation. In a dihybrid cross, this yields a 9:3:3:1 ratio in the F_2 generation (Figure 16.8).

16.2 The Chromosome Theory of Inheritance

- The chromosome theory of inheritance explains how the behavior of chromosomes during meiosis accounts for Mendel's laws of inheritance. Each gene is located at a particular site, or locus, on a chromosome (Figures 16.9, 16.10, 16.11).

16.3 Pedigree Analysis of Human Traits

- The inheritance patterns in humans are determined from a pedigree analysis (Figures 16.12, 16.13).

16.4 Sex Chromosomes and X-Linked Inheritance Patterns

- Many species of animals and some species of plants have separate male and female sexes. In many cases, sex is determined by differences in sex chromosomes (Figure 16.14).
- X-linked genes are found on the X chromosome but not the Y chromosome. Recessive X-linked alleles in humans can cause diseases, such as hemophilia, which are more likely to occur in males.
- Morgan's experiments showed that an eye-color gene in *Drosophila* is located on the X chromosome (Figure 16.15).

16.5 Variations in Inheritance Patterns and Their Molecular Basis

- Several inheritance patterns have been discovered that obey Mendel's laws but yield differing ratios of offspring compared with Mendel's crosses (Table 16.1).
- Recessive inheritance is often due to a loss-of-function mutation. In many simple dominant/recessive relationships, the heterozygote has a dominant phenotype because 50% of the normal protein is sufficient to produce that phenotype (Figure 16.16).
- Mutant genes are responsible for many inherited diseases in humans. In many cases, the effects of a mutant gene are pleiotropic, meaning the gene affects several different aspects of bodily structure and function (Table 16.2).
- Incomplete dominance occurs when a heterozygote has a phenotype that is intermediate between either homozygote. This occurs because 50% of the functional protein is not enough to produce the same phenotype as a homozygote (Figure 16.17).
- ABO blood type is produced by the expression of a gene that exists in multiple alleles in a population. The I^A and I^B alleles show codominance, a phenomenon in which both alleles are expressed in the heterozygous individual (Table 16.3).
- Genes and the environment interact to determine an individual's phenotype. The norm of reaction is a description of how a phenotype may change under different environmental conditions (Figures 16.18, 16.19).

16.6 Genetics and Probability

- Probability is the likelihood that an event will occur in the future. Random sampling error is the deviation between observed and expected values.
- The product rule states that the probability of two or more independent events occurring is equal to the product of their individual probabilities. The sum rule states that the probability of two or more mutually exclusive events occurring is equal to the sum of their individual probabilities.

Assess and Discuss

Test Yourself

1. Based on Mendel's experimental crosses, what is the expected F_2 phenotypic ratio of a monohybrid cross?
   a. 1:2:1
   c. 3:1
   e. 4:1
   b. 2:1
   d. 9:3:3:1

2. During which phase of cellular division does Mendel's law of segregation physically occur?
   a. mitosis
   c. meiosis II
   e. b and c only
   b. meiosis I
   d. all of the above

3. An individual that has two different alleles of a particular gene is said to be
   a. dihybrid.
   d. heterozygous.
   b. recessive.
   e. hemizygous.
   c. homozygous.

4. Which of Mendel's laws cannot be observed in a monohybrid cross?
   a. segregation
   b. dominance/recessiveness
   c. independent assortment
   d. codominance
   e. All of the above can be observed in a monohybrid cross.

5. During a _____ cross, an individual with the dominant phenotype and unknown genotype is crossed with a _____ individual to determine the unknown genotype.
   a. monohybrid, homozygous recessive
   b. dihybrid, heterozygous
   c. test, homozygous dominant
   d. monohybrid, homozygous dominant
   e. test, homozygous recessive

6. A woman is heterozygous for an X-linked trait, hemophilia A. If she has a child with a man without hemophilia A, what is the probability that the child will be a male with hemophilia A? (Note: The child could be a male or female.)
   a. 100%
   c. 50%
   e. 0%
   b. 75%
   d. 25%

7. A gene that affects more than one phenotypic trait is said to be
   a. dominant.
   d. pleiotropic.
   b. wild type.
   e. heterozygous.
   c. dihybrid.

8. A hypothetical flowering plant species produces blue, light blue, and white flowers. To determine the inheritance pattern, the following crosses were conducted with the results indicated:

   blue × blue → all blue

   white × white → all white

   blue × white → all light blue

   What type of inheritance pattern does this represent?
   a. simple Mendelian
   d. incomplete dominance
   b. X-linked
   e. pleiotropy
   c. codominance

9. Genes located on a sex chromosome are said to be
   a. X-linked.
   c. hemizygous.
   e. autosomal.
   b. dominant.
   d. sex linked.

10. A man and woman are both heterozygous for the recessive allele that causes cystic fibrosis. What is the probability that their first 2 offspring will have the disorder?
    a. 1
    c. 1/16
    e. 0
    b. 1/4
    d. 1/32

Conceptual Questions

1. Describe one observation in a human pedigree that rules out a recessive pattern of inheritance. Describe an observation that rules out a dominant pattern.

2. A cross is made between individuals of the following genotypes: *AaBbCCDd* and *AabbCcdd*. What is the probability that an offspring will be *AABbCCDd*? Hint: Don't waste your time making a really large Punnett square. Make four small Punnett squares instead and use the product rule.

3. A principle of biology is that *living organisms interact with their environment*. Discuss how the environment plays a key role in determining the outcome of an individual's traits.

Collaborative Questions

1. Discuss the principles of the chromosome theory of inheritance. Which principles do you think were deduced via light microscopy, and which were deduced from crosses? What modern techniques could be used to support the chromosome theory of inheritance?

2. When examining a human pedigree, what observations do you look for to distinguish between X-linked recessive inheritance versus autosomal recessive inheritance? How would you distinguish X-linked dominant inheritance from autosomal dominant inheritance from an analysis of a human pedigree?

Online Resource

www.brookerbiology.com

Stay a step ahead in your studies with animations that bring concepts to life and practice tests to assess your understanding. Your instructor may also recommend the interactive eBook, individualized learning tools, and more.

Complex Patterns of Inheritance

17

A calico cat. **The inheritance of variegated coat colors in the calico cat can't be predicted by Mendel's laws.**

A s shown in the chapter opening photo, calico cats have patches of orange and black fur with a white underside. Calico refers to the pattern of orange and black patches, not to a particular breed of cat. Many different cat breeds, including Persian, British shorthair, Manx, and Japanese bobtail, are found in calico varieties. An interesting feature of this trait is that it is found only in female cats. It is caused by changes in the X chromosome that occur in female mammals. The calico pattern is an example of a complex pattern of inheritance, one that could not have been predicted from Mendel's laws.

In this chapter, we will explore inheritance patterns that would be difficult if not impossible to predict based solely on Mendel's laws of inheritance, which we discussed in Chapter 16. Some of them even violate the law of segregation or the law of independent assortment. Studies of complex inheritance patterns have helped us appreciate more fully how genes influence phenotypes. Such research has revealed an astounding variety of ways that inheritance occurs. The picture that emerges is of a wonderful web of diverse mechanisms by which genes give rise to phenotypes. **Table 17.1** provides a summary of Mendelian inheritance and the types of inheritance patterns we will consider in this chapter.

Table 17.1	Different Types of Inheritance Patterns
Type	**Description**
Mendelian	Inheritance patterns in which a single gene affects a single trait and the alleles obey the law of segregation. These patterns include simple Mendelian inheritance, X-linked inheritance, incomplete dominance, and codominance (refer back to Table 16.1).
Epistasis	A type of gene interaction in which the alleles of one gene mask the effects of a dominant allele of another gene.
Continuous variation	Inheritance pattern in which the offspring display a continuous range of phenotypes. This pattern is produced by the additive interactions of several genes, along with environmental influences.
Linkage	Inheritance pattern involving two or more genes that are close together on the same chromosome. Linked genes do not assort independently.
Extranuclear inheritance	Inheritance pattern of genes found in the genomes of mitochondria or chloroplasts. Usually these genes are inherited from the mother.
X inactivation	Phenomenon of female mammals in which one X chromosome is inactivated in every somatic cell, producing a mosaic phenotype.
Genomic imprinting	Inheritance pattern in which an allele from one parent is silenced in the somatic cells of the offspring, but the allele from the other parent is expressed.

17.1 Gene Interaction

Learning Outcomes:

1. Describe how the alleles of one gene can mask or be epistatic to the alleles of a different gene.
2. Explain why polygenic traits usually show a continuum of phenotype variation.

The study of single genes was pivotal in establishing the science of genetics. This focus allowed Mendel to formulate the basic laws of inheritance for traits with a simple dominant/recessive inheritance pattern. Likewise, this approach helped later researchers understand inheritance patterns involving incomplete dominance and codominance, as well as traits that are influenced by an individual's sex. However, all or nearly all traits are influenced by many genes. For example, in both plants and animals, height is affected by genes that encode proteins involved in the production of growth hormones, cell division, the uptake of nutrients, metabolism, and many other functions. Variation in any of the genes involved in these processes is likely to influence an individual's height.

If height is controlled by many genes, how was Mendel able to study the effects of a single gene that produced tall or dwarf pea plants? The answer lies in the genotypes of his strains. Although many genes affect the height of pea plants, Mendel chose true-breeding strains that differed with regard to only one of those genes. As a hypothetical example, let's suppose that pea plants have 10 genes affecting height, which we will call *K, L, M, N, O, P, Q, R, S,* and *T*. The genotypes of two hypothetical strains of pea plants may be:

Tall strain: *KK LL MM NN OO PP QQ RR SS TT*

Dwarf strain: *KK LL MM NN OO PP QQ RR SS tt*

In this example, the tall and dwarf strains differ at only a single gene. One strain is *TT* and the other is *tt*, and this accounts for the difference in their height. If we make crosses of tall and dwarf plants, the genotypes of the F₂ offspring will differ with regard to only one gene; the other nine genes will be identical in all of them. This approach allows a researcher to study the effects of a single gene even though many genes may affect a single character.

In this section, we will examine situations in which a single character is controlled by two or more different genes, each of which has two or more alleles. This phenomenon is called **gene interaction**. As you will see, allelic variation at two or more genes may affect the outcome of traits in different ways. First we will look at a gene interaction in which an allele of one gene prevents the phenotypic expression of an allele of a different gene. Then we will discuss an interaction in which multiple genes have additive effects on a single character. These additive effects, together with environmental influences, account for the continuous phenotypic variation that we see in most traits.

In an Epistatic Gene Interaction, the Alleles of One Gene Masks the Phenotypic Effects of a Different Gene

In some gene interactions, the alleles of one gene mask the expression of the alleles of another gene. This phenomenon is called **epistasis** (from the Greek *ephistanai*, meaning stopping). An example is

the unexpected gene interaction discovered by English geneticists William Bateson and Reginald Punnett in the early 1900s, when they were studying crosses involving the sweet pea, *Lathyrus odoratus*. A cross between a true-breeding purple-flowered plant and a true-breeding white-flowered plant produced an F₁ generation with all purple-flowered plants and an F₂ generation with a 3:1 ratio of purple- to white-flowered plants. Mendel's laws predicted this result. The surprise came when the researchers crossed two different true-breeding varieties of white-flowered sweet peas (**Figure 17.1**). All of the F₁ generation plants had purple flowers! When these plants were

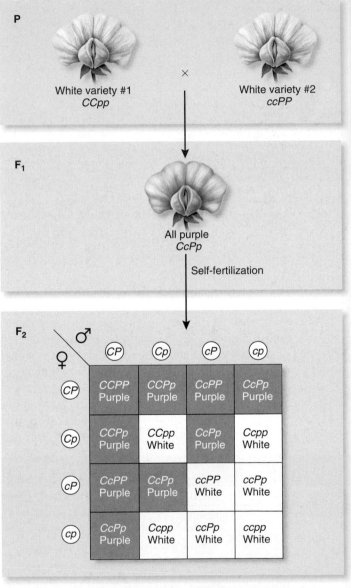

Figure 17.1 Epistasis in the sweet pea. The color of the sweet pea flower is controlled by two genes, each with a dominant and a recessive allele. Each of the dominant alleles (*C* and *P*) encodes an enzyme required for the synthesis of purple pigment. A plant that is homozygous recessive for either gene (*cc* or *pp*) cannot synthesize the pigment and will have white flowers.

Concept Check: In a *Ccpp* individual, which functional enzyme is missing? Is it the enzyme encoded by the *C* or *P* gene?

allowed to self-fertilize, the F$_2$ generation had purple-flowered and white-flowered plants in a 9:7 ratio. From these results, Bateson and Punnett deduced that two different genes were involved. To have purple flowers, a plant must have one or two dominant alleles for each of these genes. The relationships among the alleles are as follows:

C (one allele for purple) is dominant to *c* (white)

P (an allele of a different gene for purple) is dominant to *p* (white)

cc masks *P*, or *pp* masks *C*, in either case producing white flowers

A plant that was homozygous for either *c* or *p* would have white flowers even if it had a dominant purple-producing allele for the other gene.

How do we explain these results at the molecular and cellular level? Epistatic interactions often arise because two or more different proteins are involved in a single cellular function. For example, two or more proteins may be part of a metabolic pathway leading to the formation of a single product. This is the case for the formation of a purple pigment in the sweet pea strains we have been discussing:

Colorless precursor $\xrightarrow{\text{Enzyme C}}$ Colorless intermediate $\xrightarrow{\text{Enzyme P}}$ Purple pigment

In this example, a colorless precursor molecule must be acted on by two different enzymes to produce the purple pigment. Gene *C* encodes a functional protein called enzyme C, which converts the colorless precursor into a colorless intermediate. The recessive *c* allele results in a lack of production of enzyme C in the homozygote. Gene *P* encodes the functional enzyme P, which converts the colorless intermediate into the purple pigment. Like the *c* allele, the *p* allele results in an inability to produce a functional enzyme. A plant homozygous for either of the recessive alleles does not make any functional enzyme C or enzyme P. When either of these enzymes is missing, the plant cannot make the purple pigment and has white flowers. Note that the results observed in Figure 17.1 do not conflict with Mendel's laws of segregation or independent assortment. Mendel investigated the effects of only a single gene on a given character. The 9:7 ratio is due to a gene interaction in which two genes affect a single character.

Polygenic Inheritance and Environmental Influences Produce Continuous Phenotypic Variation

Until now, we have discussed the inheritance of characters with clearly defined phenotypic variants, such as red or white eyes in fruit flies or round or wrinkled seed shape in garden peas. These are known as **discrete traits**, because the phenotypes do not overlap. For most traits, however, the phenotypes cannot be sorted into discrete categories. Traits that show continuous variation over a range of phenotypes are called **quantitative traits**. In humans, quantitative traits include height, weight, skin color, metabolic rate, and heart size. In the case of domestic animals and plant crops, many of the traits that people consider desirable are quantitative in nature, such as the number of eggs a chicken lays, the amount of milk a cow produces, and the number of apples on an apple tree. Consequently, much of our modern understanding of quantitative traits comes from agricultural research.

Quantitative traits are usually **polygenic**, which means that multiple genes contribute to the outcome of the trait. For many polygenic traits, genes contribute to the phenotype in an additive way. As a hypothetical example, let's suppose that three different genes (*W1*, *W2*, and *W3*) affect weight in turkeys; each gene can occur in heavy (*W*) and light (*w*) alleles. A heavy allele contributes an extra pound to an individual's weight compared with the effect of a light allele. A turkey homozygous for all the heavy alleles (*W1W1 W2W2 W3W3*) would weigh 6 pounds more than an individual homozygous for all the light alleles (*w1w1 w2w2 w3w3*). A turkey heterozygous for all three genes (*W1w1 W2w2 W3w3*) would have an intermediate weight that would be 3 pounds lighter than the homozygous turkey carrying all of the heavy alleles, because the heterozygote carries three light alleles.

An individual's environment is another important factor affecting the expression of quantitative traits. As we learned in Chapter 16, the environment plays a vital role in the phenotypic expression of genes. Environmental factors often have a major effect on quantitative traits. For example, an animal's diet affects its weight, and the amount of rain and sunlight that fall on an apple tree affect how many apples it produces.

Because quantitative traits are polygenic and greatly influenced by environmental conditions, the phenotypes among different individuals may vary substantially in any given population. As an example, let's consider skin pigmentation in humans. This character is influenced by several genes that tend to interact in an additive way. As a simplified example, let's consider a population in which skin pigmentation in people is controlled by three genes, which we will designate *A*, *B*, and *C*. Each gene may exist as a dark allele, designated A^D, B^D, or C^D, or a light allele, designated A^L, B^L, or C^L, respectively. All of the alleles encode enzymes that cause the synthesis of skin pigment, but the enzymes encoded by dark alleles cause more pigment synthesis than the enzymes encoded by light alleles.

Figure 17.2 considers a hypothetical case in which people who were heterozygous for all three genes produced a large population of offspring. The bar graph shows the genotypes of the offspring, grouped according to the total number of light and dark alleles. As shown by the shading of the figure, skin pigmentation increases as the number of dark alleles increases. Offspring who have all light alleles or who have all dark alleles—that is, those who are homozygous for all three genes—are fewer in number than those with some combination of light and dark alleles. As seen in the bell-shaped curve above the bar graph, the phenotypes of the offspring fall along a continuum. This continuous phenotypic variation, which is typical of quantitative traits, is produced by genotypic differences together with environmental effects. A second bell-shaped curve (the dashed line) depicts the expected phenotypic range if the same population of offspring had been raised in a sunnier environment, which increases pigment production. This curve illustrates how the environment can also have a significant influence on the range of phenotypes.

In our discussion of genetics, we tend to focus on discrete traits because this makes it easier to relate a specific genotype with a phenotype. This is usually not possible for continuous traits. For example, as depicted in the middle bar of Figure 17.2, seven different genotypes can produce individuals with a medium amount of pigmentation. It is important to emphasize that the majority of traits in all organisms are continuous, not discrete. Most traits are influenced by multiple genes, and the environment has an important influence on the phenotypic outcome.

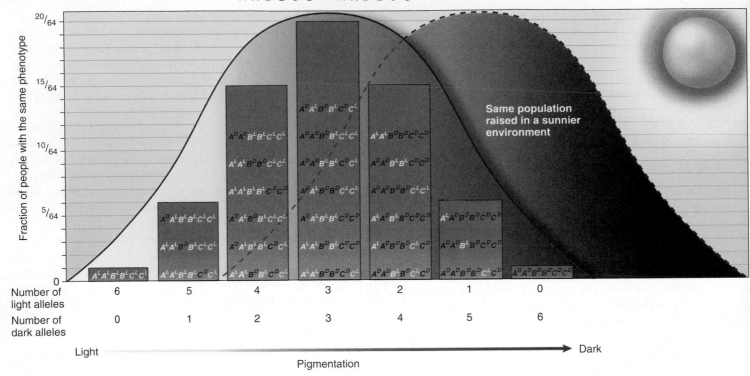

Figure 17.2 **Continuous variation in a polygenic trait.** Skin color is a polygenic character that displays a continuum of phenotypes. The bell curve on the left (solid line) shows the range of skin pigmentation in a hypothetical human population. The bar graphs below the curve show the additive effects of three genes that affect pigment production in this population; each bar shows the fraction of people with a particular number of dark alleles (A^D, B^D, and C^D) and light alleles (A^L, B^L, and C^L). The bell curve on the right (dashed line) represents the expected range of phenotypes if the same population was raised in a sunnier environment.

 BIOLOGY PRINCIPLE The genetic material provides the blueprint for reproduction. The genetic blueprint usually involves the expression of several different genes that affect the same trait. In many cases, this results in continuous variation.

17.2 Genes on the Same Chromosome: Linkage, Recombination, and Mapping

Learning Outcomes:

1. Describe how linkage violates the law of independent assortment.
2. Explain how experimental crosses can demonstrate linkage.
3. Calculate the distance between genes that are linked on the same chromosome.

In Chapter 16, we learned that the independent assortment of alleles is due to the random alignment of homologous chromosomes during meiosis (refer back to Figure 16.11). But what happens when the alleles of different genes are on the same chromosome and do not independently assort? A typical chromosome contains many hundreds or even a few thousand different genes. When two genes are close together on the same chromosome, they tend to be transmitted as a unit, a phenomenon known as **linkage**. A group of genes that usually stay together during meiosis is called a **linkage group**, and the genes in the group are said to be linked. In a dihybrid cross, linked genes that are close together on the same chromosome do not follow the law of independent assortment.

In this section, we begin by examining the first experimental cross that demonstrated linkage. This pattern was subsequently explained by Thomas Hunt Morgan, who proposed that different genes located close to each other on the same chromosome tend to be inherited together. We will also see how crossing over between such genes provided the first method of mapping genes along chromosomes.

FEATURE INVESTIGATION

Bateson and Punnett's Crosses of Sweet Peas Showed That Genes Do Not Always Assort Independently

The first study showing linkage between two different genes was a cross of sweet peas carried out by William Bateson and Reginald Punnett in 1911. A surprising result occurred when they conducted a two-factor cross involving flower color and pollen shape (**Figure 17.3**). One of the parent plants had purple flowers (*PP*) and long pollen (*LL*); the other had red flowers (*pp*) and round pollen (*ll*). As Bateson and Punnett expected, the F$_1$ plants all had purple flowers and long pollen (*PpLl*). The unexpected result came in the F$_2$ generation.

Figure 17.3 A cross of sweet peas showing that independent assortment does not always occur.

HYPOTHESIS The alleles of different genes assort independently of each other.

KEY MATERIALS True-breeding sweet pea strains that differ with regard to flower color and pollen shape.

	Experimental level	Conceptual level
1 Cross a plant with purple flowers and long pollen to a plant with red flowers and round pollen.	Purple flowers, long pollen × Red flowers, round pollen	$PPLL \times ppll$
2 Observe the phenotypes of the F₁ offspring.	Purple flowers, long pollen	$PpLl$
3 Allow the F₁ offspring to self-fertilize.	Purple flowers, long pollen × Purple flowers, long pollen	Meiosis PL and pl gametes — more frequent Pl and pL gametes — less frequent
4 Observe the phenotypes of the F₂ offspring.	Purple flowers, long pollen / Purple flowers, round pollen / Red flowers, long pollen / Red flowers, round pollen 15.6 : 1.0 : 1.4 : 4.5	Fertilization F₂ offspring having phenotypes of purple flowers with long pollen or red flowers with round pollen occurred more frequently than expected from Mendel's law of independent assortment.

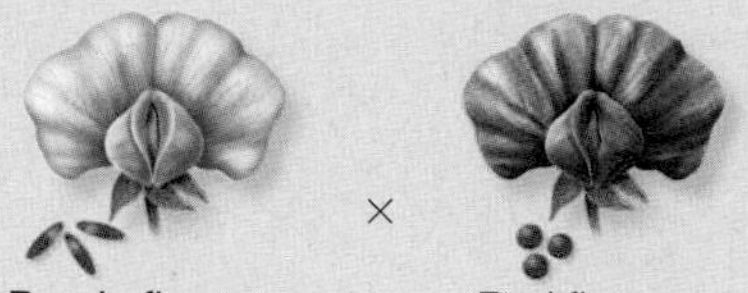

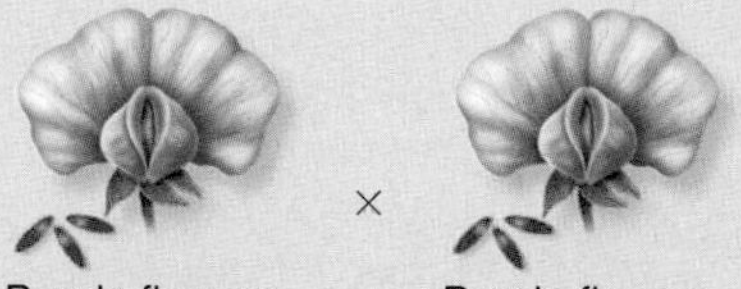

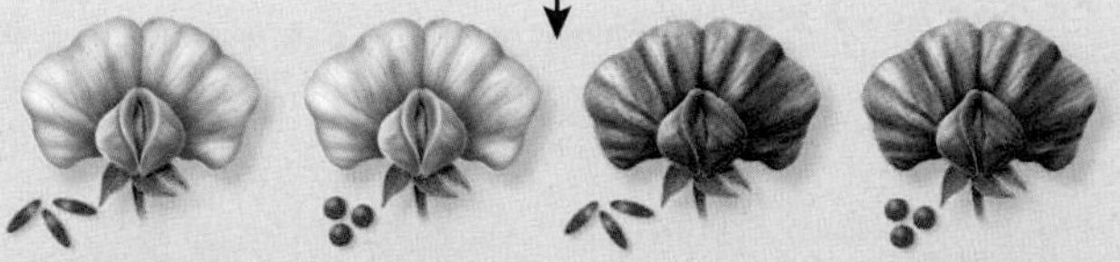

5 THE DATA

Phenotypes of F₂ offspring	Observed number	Observed ratio	Expected number	Expected ratio
Purple flowers, long pollen	296	15.6	240	9
Purple flowers, round pollen	19	1.0	80	3
Red flowers, long pollen	27	1.4	80	3
Red flowers, round pollen	85	4.5	27	1

6 CONCLUSION The data are not consistent with the law of independent assortment.

7 SOURCE Bateson, William, and Punnett, Reginald C. 1911. On the inter-relations of genetic factors. *Proceedings of the Royal Society of London, Series B*, 84:3–8.

Although the F$_2$ offspring displayed the four phenotypes predicted by Mendel's laws, the observed numbers of offspring did not conform to the predicted 9:3:3:1 ratio (refer back to Figure 16.8). Rather, as seen in the data in Figure 17.3, the F$_2$ generation had a much higher proportion of the two phenotypes found in the parental generation: purple flowers with long pollen, and red flowers with round pollen. How did Bateson and Punnett explain these results? They suggested that the transmission of flower color and pollen shape was somehow coupled, so these traits did not always assort indepen-

dently. Although the law of independent assortment applies to many other genes, in this example, the hypothesis of independent assortment was rejected.

Experimental Questions

1. What hypothesis was Bateson and Punnett testing when conducting the crosses in the sweet pea?
2. What were the expected results of Bateson and Punnett's cross?
3. How did the observed results differ from the expected results?

Linkage and Crossing Over Produce Parental and Recombinant Types

Bateson and Punnett realized their results did not conform to Mendel's law of independent assortment. However, they did not know why the genes were not assorting independently. A few years later, Thomas Hunt Morgan obtained similar ratios in crosses of fruit flies while studying the transmission pattern of genes in *Drosophila*. Like Bateson and Punnett, Morgan observed many more F$_2$ offspring with the combination of traits found in the parental generation than predicted on the basis of independent assortment. To explain his data, Morgan proposed three ideas:

1. When different genes are located on the same chromosome, the traits determined by those genes are more likely to be inherited together. This violates the law of independent assortment.
2. Due to crossing over during meiosis, homologous chromosomes can exchange pieces of chromosomes and create new combinations of alleles.
3. The likelihood of a crossover occurring in the region between two genes depends on the distance between the two genes. Crossovers between homologous chromosomes are much more likely to occur between two genes farther apart along a chromosome compared to two genes that are closer together.

To illustrate the first two ideas, **Figure 17.4** considers a series of crosses involving two genes linked on the same chromosome in *Drosophila*. The two genes are located on an autosome, not on a sex chromosome. The P generation cross is between flies that are homozygous for alleles that affect body color and wing shape. The female is homozygous for the dominant wild-type alleles that produce gray body color (b^+b^+) and straight (normal) wings (c^+c^+); the male is homozygous for recessive mutant alleles that produce black body color (bb) and curved wings (cc). The symbols for the genes are based on the name of the mutant allele; the dominant wild-type allele is indicated by a superscript plus sign ($^+$). The chromosomes next to the flies in Figure 17.4 show the arrangement of these alleles. If the two genes are on the same chromosome, we know the arrangement of alleles in the P generation flies because these flies are homozygous for both genes ($b^+b^+c^+c^+$ for one parent and $bbcc$ for the other parent). In the P generation female on the left, b^+ and c^+ are linked, whereas b and c are linked in the male on the right.

Let's now look at the outcome of the crosses in Figure 17.4. As expected, the F$_1$ offspring (b^+bc^+c) all had gray bodies and straight wings, confirming that these are the dominant traits. In the next cross, F$_1$ females were mated to males that were homozygous for both

recessive alleles ($bbcc$). Recall from Chapter 16 that a testcross was conducted to determine if an individual with a dominant phenotype is a homozygote or a heterozygote. However, in the crosses we are discussing here, the purpose of the testcross is to determine if the genes for body color and wing shape are linked. If the genes are on different chromosomes and assort independently, this testcross will produce F$_2$ offspring with the four possible phenotypes in a 1:1:1:1 ratio. The observed numbers clearly conflict with this prediction. The two most abundant phenotypes are those with the combinations of characteristics in the P generation: gray bodies and straight wings or black bodies and curved wings. These offspring are termed **nonrecombinants**, because this combination of traits has not changed from the parental generation. The smaller number of offspring that have a combination of traits not found in the parental generation—gray bodies and curved wings or black bodies and straight wings—are called **recombinants**.

How do we explain the occurrence of recombinants when genes are linked on the same chromosome? As shown beside the flies of the F$_2$ generation in Figure 17.4, each recombinant individual has a chromosome that is the product of a crossover. The crossover occurred while the F$_1$ female fly was making egg cells.

As shown below, four different egg cells are possible:

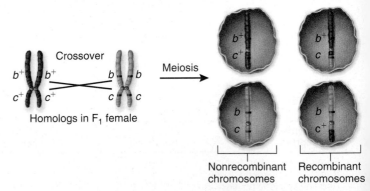

Due to crossing over, two of the four egg cells produced by meiosis have recombinant chromosomes. What happens when eggs containing such chromosomes are fertilized in the testcross? Each of the male fly's sperm cells carries a chromosome with the two recessive alleles. If the egg contains the recombinant chromosome carrying the b^+ and c alleles, the testcross will produce an F$_2$ offspring with a gray body and curved wings. If the egg contains the recombinant chromosome carrying the b and c^+ alleles, F$_2$ offspring will have a black body and straight wings. Therefore, crossing over in the F$_1$ female can explain the occurrence of both types of F$_2$ recombinant offspring.

Morgan's third idea regarding linkage was that the frequency of crossing over between linked genes depends on the distance between

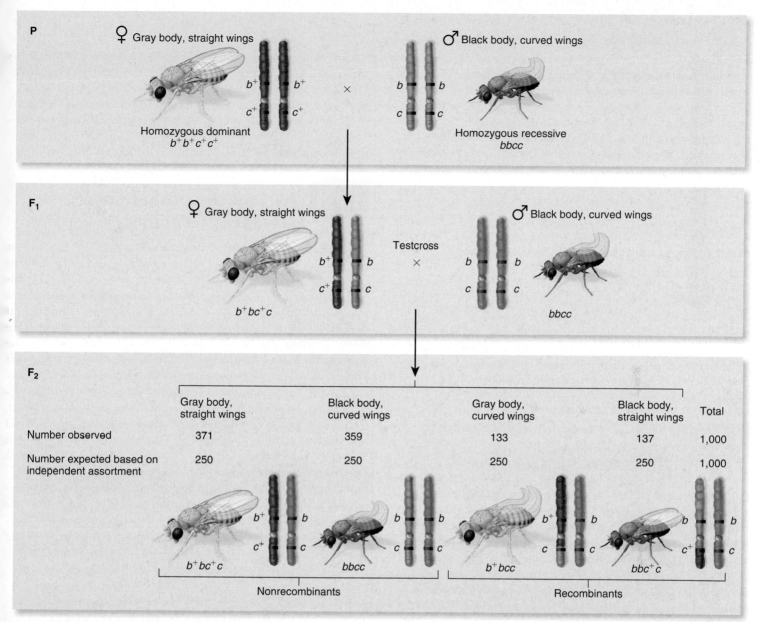

Figure 17.4 **Linkage and recombination of alleles.** An experimenter crossed $b^+b^+c^+c^+$ and $bbcc$ flies to produce F_1 heterozygotes. F_1 females were then testcrossed to $bbcc$ males. The large number of nonrecombinant phenotypes in the F_2 generation suggests that the two genes are linked on the same chromosome. F_2 recombinant phenotypes occur because the alleles can be rearranged by crossing over. Note: The b^+ and c^+ alleles are dominant, and the b and c alleles are recessive.

Concept Check: *In which fly or flies did crossing over occur to produce the recombinant offspring of the F_2 generation?*

BioConnections: *Look back at Figure 15.13. When does crossing over occur?*

them. This suggested a method for determining the relative positions of genes on a chromosome, as we will discuss next.

Recombination Frequencies Provide a Method for Mapping Genes Along Chromosomes

The study of the arrangement of genes in a species' genome is called **genetic mapping**. As depicted in **Figure 17.5**, the linear order of genes along a chromosome is shown in a chart known as a **genetic map**. Each gene has its own physical location, or locus, on a chromosome. For example, the gene for black body color (*b*) discussed earlier is located near the middle of the chromosome, whereas the gene for curved wings (*c*) is closer to one end. The first genetic map, showing

five genes on the *Drosophila* X chromosome, was constructed in 1911 by American geneticist Alfred Sturtevant, an undergraduate student who studied in Morgan's laboratory.

Genetic mapping allows us to estimate the relative distances between linked genes based on the likelihood that a crossover will occur between them. This likelihood is proportional to the distance between the genes, as Morgan first proposed. If the genes are very close together, a crossover is unlikely to occur in the region between them. However, if the genes are very far apart, a crossover is more likely to be initiated in the region between the genes and thereby recombine the alleles. Therefore, in a testcross involving two genes on the same chromosome, the percentage of recombinant offspring is correlated with the distance between the genes. If a two-factor testcross produces many recombinants, the

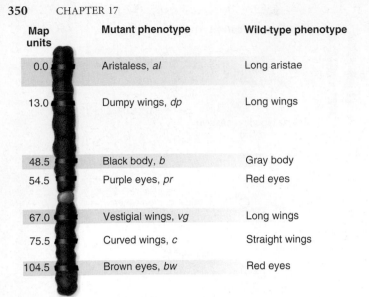

Map units	Mutant phenotype	Wild-type phenotype
0.0	Aristaless, *al*	Long aristae
13.0	Dumpy wings, *dp*	Long wings
48.5	Black body, *b*	Gray body
54.5	Purple eyes, *pr*	Red eyes
67.0	Vestigial wings, *vg*	Long wings
75.5	Curved wings, *c*	Straight wings
104.5	Brown eyes, *bw*	Red eyes

Figure 17.5   A simplified genetic map. This map shows the relative locations of a few genes along chromosome number 2 in *Drosophila melanogaster*. The name of each gene is based on the mutant phenotype. The numbers on the left are map units (mu). The distance between two genes, in mu's, corresponds to their recombination frequency in testcrosses.

Concept Check: *How would you set up a testcross to determine the distance between the al and dp genes? What would be the genotypes of the P, F_1, and F_2 generations?*

experimenter concludes that the two genes are far apart. If very few recombinants are observed, the two genes must be close together.

To find the distance between two genes, the experimenter must determine the frequency of crossing over between them, called their **recombination frequency**. This is accomplished by conducting a testcross. As an example, let's refer back to the *Drosophila* testcross described in Figure 17.4. As we discussed, the genes for body color and wing shape are on the same chromosome. The recombinants are the result of crossing over during egg formation in the F_1 female. We can use the data from the testcross shown in Figure 17.4 to estimate the distance between these two genes. The **map distance** between two genes is defined as the number of recombinants divided by the total number of offspring times 100.

$$\text{Map distance} = \frac{\text{Number of recombinants}}{\text{Total number of offspring}} \times 100$$

$$= \frac{133+137}{371+359+133+137} \times 100$$

$$= 27.0 \text{ map units}$$

The units of distance are called **map units (mu)**, or sometimes **centiMorgans (cM)** in honor of Thomas Hunt Morgan. One map unit is equivalent to a 1% recombination frequency. In this example, 270 out of 1,000 offspring are recombinants, so the recombination frequency is 27%, and the two genes are 27.0 mu apart.

Genetic mapping has been useful for analyzing the genes of organisms that are easily crossed and produce many offspring in a short time. It has been used to map the genes of several plant species and of certain species of animals, such as *Drosophila*. However, for

most organisms, including humans, genetic mapping via crosses is impractical due to long generation times or the inability to carry out experimental crosses. Fortunately, many alternative methods of gene mapping have been developed in the past few decades that are faster and do not depend on crosses. These newer cytological and molecular approaches, which we will discuss in Chapter 20, are also used to map genes in a wide variety of organisms.

17.3   Extranuclear Inheritance: Organelle Genomes

Learning Outcomes:

1. Describe the general features of mitochondrial and chloroplast genomes.
2. Predict the outcome of crosses that exhibit maternal inheritance.
3. List human diseases associated with mutations in mitochondrial genes.

In the previous section, we examined the inheritance patterns of linked genes that violate the law of independent assortment. In this section, we will explore inheritance patterns that violate the law of segregation. The segregation of genes is explained by the pairing and segregation of homologous chromosomes during meiosis. However, some genes are not found on the chromosomes in the cell nucleus, and these genes do not segregate in the same way. The transmission of genes located outside the cell nucleus is called **extranuclear inheritance**. Two important types of extranuclear inheritance patterns involve genes found in chloroplasts and mitochondria. Extranuclear inheritance is also called cytoplasmic inheritance because these organelles are in the cytoplasm of the cell. In this section, we will examine the transmission patterns observed for genes found in the chloroplast and mitochondrial genomes and consider how mutations in these genes may affect an individual's traits.

GENOMES & PROTEOMES CONNECTION

Chloroplast and Mitochondrial Genomes Are Relatively Small, but Contain Genes That Encode Important Proteins

As we discussed in Chapter 4, mitochondria and chloroplasts are found in eukaryotic cells because of an ancient endosymbiotic relationship. They contain their own genetic material, called the mitochondrial genome and chloroplast genome, respectively (**Figure 17.6**). Mitochondrial and chloroplast genomes are composed of a single, circular DNA molecule. The mitochondrial genome of many mammalian species has been analyzed and usually contains a total of 37 genes. Twenty-four genes encode tRNAs and rRNAs, which are needed for translation inside the mitochondrion, and 13 genes encode proteins that are involved in oxidative phosphorylation. As discussed in Chapter 7, the primary function of the mitochondrion is the synthesis of ATP via oxidative phosphorylation. Among different species of plants, chloroplast genomes typically contain about 110 to 120 genes. Many of these genes encode proteins that are vital to the process of photosynthesis, which we discussed in Chapter 8.

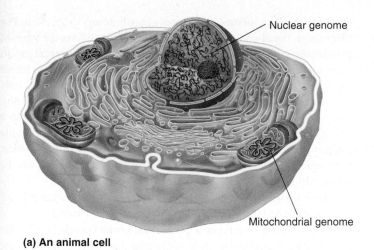

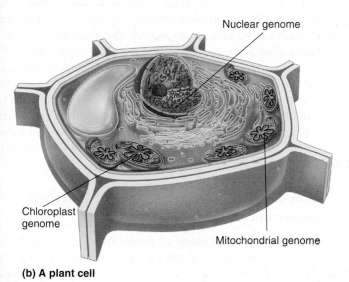

Figure 17.6 The locations of genetic material in animal and plant cells.
The chromosomes in the cell nucleus are collectively known as the nuclear genome. Mitochondria and chloroplasts have small circular chromosomes called the mitochondrial and chloroplast genomes, respectively.

BioConnections: *Look back at Figure 4.27. What is the evolutionary origin of mitochondria and chloroplasts in eukaryotic cells?*

Chloroplast Genomes Are Often Maternally Inherited

One of the first experiments showing an extranuclear inheritance pattern was carried out by German botanist Carl Correns in 1909. Correns discovered that leaf pigmentation in the four-o'clock plant (*Mirabilis jalapa*) follows a pattern of inheritance that does not obey Mendel's law of segregation. Four-o'clock leaves may be green, white, or variegated. Correns observed that the pigmentation of the offspring depended solely on the pigmentation of the female parent, a phenomenon called **maternal inheritance** (**Figure 17.7**). If the female parent had white leaves, all of the offspring had white leaves. Similarly, if the female was green, so were all of the offspring. The offspring of a variegated female parent could be green, white, or variegated.

What accounts for maternal inheritance? At the time, Correns did not understand that chloroplasts contain genetic material. Subsequent

Figure 17.7 Maternal inheritance in the four-o'clock plant.
In four-o'clocks, the egg contains all of the proplastids, which develop into chloroplasts, that are inherited by the offspring. The phenotype of the offspring is determined by the maternal parent. The green phenotype is due to the presence of normal chloroplasts. The white phenotype is due to chloroplasts with a mutant allele that greatly reduces green pigment production. The variegated phenotype is due to a mixture of normal and mutant chloroplasts.

Concept Check: *In this example, where is the gene located that causes the green color of four-o'clock leaves? How is this gene transmitted from parent to offspring?*

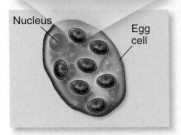

Normal proplastid will produce chloroplasts with a normal amount of green pigment.

Mutant proplastid will produce chloroplasts with very little pigment.

Nucleus

Egg cell

(a) Egg cell from a maternal parent with green leaves

(b) Egg cell from a maternal parent with white leaves

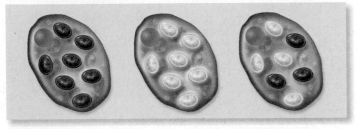

(c) Possible egg cells from a maternal parent with variegated leaves

Figure 17.8 Plastid compositions of egg cells from green, white, and variegated four-o'clock plants. In this drawing of four-o'clock egg cells, normal proplastids are represented as green and mutant proplastids as white. (Note: This drawing is schematic. Proplastids do not differentiate into chloroplasts in egg cells, and they are not actually green.) **(a)** A green plant produces eggs carrying normal proplastids. **(b)** A white plant produces eggs carrying mutant proplastids. **(c)** A variegated plant produces eggs that may contain either or both types of proplastids.

research identified DNA present in chloroplasts as responsible for the unusual inheritance pattern observed. We now know that the pigmentation of four-o'clock leaves can be explained by the occurrence of genetically different types of chloroplasts in the leaf cells. As discussed in Chapter 8, chloroplasts are the site of photosynthesis, and their green color is due to the presence of the pigment called chlorophyll. Certain genes required for chlorophyll synthesis are found within the chloroplast DNA. The green phenotype is due to the presence of chloroplasts that have normal genes and synthesize the usual quantity of chlorophyll. The white phenotype is caused by a mutation in a gene within the chloroplast DNA that prevents the synthesis of most of the chlorophyll. (Enough chlorophyll is made for the plant to survive.) The variegated phenotype occurs in leaves that have a mixture of the two types of chloroplasts.

Leaf pigmentation follows a maternal inheritance pattern because the chloroplasts in four-o'clocks are transmitted only through the cytoplasm of the egg (**Figure 17.8**). In most species of plants, the egg cell provides most of the zygote's cytoplasm, whereas the much smaller male gamete often provides little more than a nucleus. Therefore, chloroplasts are most often inherited via the egg. Recall from Chapter 4 that chloroplasts are derived from proplastids. In four-o'clocks, the egg cell contains several proplastids that are inherited by

the offspring. The sperm cell does not contribute any proplastids. For this reason, the phenotype of a four-o'clock plant reflects the types of proplastids it inherits from the maternal parent. If the maternal parent transmits only normal proplastids, all offspring will have green leaves (Figure 17.8a). Alternatively, if the maternal parent transmits only mutant proplastids, all offspring will have white leaves (Figure 17.8b). Because an egg cell contains several proplastids, an offspring from a variegated maternal parent may inherit only normal proplastids, only mutant proplastids, or a mixture of normal and mutant proplastids. Consequently, the offspring of a variegated maternal parent can be green, white, or variegated individuals (Figure 17.8c).

How do we explain the variegated phenotype at the cellular level? This phenotype is due to events that occur after fertilization. As a zygote containing both types of proplastids grows via cellular division to produce a multicellular plant, some cells may receive mostly those that develop into normal chloroplasts. Further division of these cells gives rise to a patch of green tissue. Alternatively, as a matter of chance, other cells may receive all or mostly mutant chloroplasts that are defective in chlorophyll synthesis. The result is a patch of white tissue.

In seed-bearing plants, maternal inheritance of chloroplasts is the most common transmission pattern. However, certain species exhibit a pattern called **biparental inheritance**, in which both the pollen and the egg contribute chloroplasts to the offspring. Others exhibit **paternal inheritance**, in which only the pollen contributes these organelles. For example, most types of pine trees show paternal inheritance of chloroplasts.

Mitochondrial Genomes Are Maternally Inherited in Humans and Most Other Species

Mitochondria are found in nearly all eukaryotic species. As with the transmission of chloroplasts in plants, maternal inheritance is the most common pattern of mitochondrial transmission in eukaryotes, although some species do exhibit biparental or paternal inheritance.

In humans, mitochondria are maternally inherited. Researchers have discovered that mutations in human mitochondrial genes cause a variety of rare diseases (**Table 17.2**). These are usually chronic

Table 17.2	Examples of Human Mitochondrial Disease
Disease	**Causes and symptoms**
Leber's hereditary optic neuropathy (LHON)	A mutation in one of several mitochondrial genes that encode electron transport proteins. The main symptom is loss of vision.
Neurogenic muscle weakness	A mutation in a mitochondrial gene that encodes a subunit of mitochondrial ATP synthase, which is required for ATP synthesis. Symptoms involve abnormalities in the nervous system that affect the muscles and eyes.
Maternal myopathy and cardiomyopathy	A mutation in a mitochondrial gene that encodes a tRNA for leucine. The primary symptoms involve muscle abnormalities, most notably in the heart.
Myoclonic epilepsy and ragged-red muscle fibers	A mutation in a mitochondrial gene that encodes a tRNA for lysine. Symptoms include epilepsy, dementia, blindness, deafness, and heart and kidney malfunctions.

degenerative disorders that affect organs and cells, such as the brain, eyes, heart, muscle, kidney, and endocrine glands, that require high levels of ATP. For example, Leber's hereditary optic neuropathy (LHON) affects the optic nerve and leads to the progressive loss of vision in one or both eyes. LHON is caused by point mutations in several different mitochondrial genes.

17.4 Epigenetic Inheritance

Learning Outcomes:

1. Describe the process of X inactivation and how it affects the phenotype of heterozygous females.
2. Explain the molecular basis of genomic imprinting and predict how it affects inheritance patterns.

We will end our discussion of complex inheritance patterns by considering examples in which the timing and control of gene expression result in inheritance patterns that are determined by the sex of the individual or by the sex of the parents. We will consider two patterns, called X inactivation and genomic imprinting, which are types of **epigenetic inheritance**. In epigenetic inheritance, modification of a gene or chromosome occurs during egg formation, sperm formation, or early stages of embryo growth. This modification does not alter the DNA sequence, but it affects gene expression in a way that is fixed during an individual's lifetime. Such epigenetic changes affect the phenotype of the individual, but they are not permanent over the course of two or more generations. For example, a gene may undergo an epigenetic change that inactivates the gene for an individual's entire life, so it is never expressed in that individual. However, when the same individual produces gametes, the gene may become activated and remain active during the lifetime of an offspring that inherits the gene.

In Female Mammals, One X Chromosome Is Inactivated in Each Somatic Cell

In 1961, the British geneticist Mary Lyon proposed the epigenetic phenomenon of **X inactivation**, in which one of the two copies of the X chromosome in the somatic cells of female mammals is inactivated, meaning that its genes are not expressed. X inactivation is based on two lines of evidence. The first came from microscopic studies of mammalian cells. In 1949, Canadian physicians Murray Barr and Ewart Bertram identified a highly condensed structure in the cells of female cats that was not found in the cells of male cats. This structure was named a **Barr body** after one of its discoverers (**Figure 17.9**). In 1960, Asian American geneticist Susumu Ohno correctly proposed that a Barr body is a highly condensed X chromosome. Lyon's second line of evidence was the inheritance pattern of variegated coat colors in certain female mammals. A classic case is the calico cat, which has randomly distributed patches of black and orange fur (see chapter opening photo).

How do we explain this patchwork phenotype? According to Lyon's hypothesis, the calico pattern is due to the permanent inactivation of one X chromosome in each cell that forms a patch of the

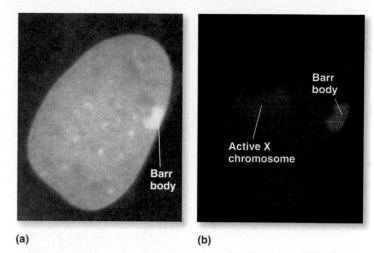

(a)   **(b)**

Figure 17.9   X-chromosome inactivation in female mammals.
(a) A Barr body is seen on the periphery of a human nucleus (during interphase) after staining with a DNA-specific dye. Because it is compact, the Barr body is the most brightly stained. **(b)** The same nucleus was labeled using a yellow fluorescent probe that recognizes the X chromosome. The Barr body is more compact than the active X chromosome, which is to the left of the Barr body.

Concept Check: *How is the Barr body different from the other X chromosome in this cell?*

cat's skin, as shown in **Figure 17.10**. The gene involved is an X-linked gene that occurs as an orange allele, X^O, and a black allele, X^B. A female cat heterozygous for this gene will be calico. (The cat's white underside is due to a dominant allele of a different autosomal gene.) At an early stage of embryonic development, one of the two X chromosomes is randomly inactivated in each of the cat's somatic cells, including those that will give rise to the hair-producing skin cells. As the embryo grows and matures, the pattern of X inactivation is maintained during subsequent cell divisions. Skin cells derived from a single embryonic cell in which the X^B-carrying chromosome has been inactivated produce a patch of orange fur, because they express only the X^O allele that is carried on the active chromosome. Alternatively, a group of skin cells in which the chromosome carrying X^O has been inactivated express only the X^B allele, producing a patch of black fur. If female mammals are heterozygous for X-linked genes, approximately half of their somatic cells express one allele, whereas the rest of their somatic cells express the other allele. The result is an animal with randomly distributed patches of black and orange fur. These heterozygotes are called **mosaics** because they are composed of two types of cells.

For many X-linked traits in humans, females who are heterozygous for recessive X-linked alleles usually show the dominant trait because the expression of the dominant allele in 50% of their cells is sufficient to produce the dominant phenotype. For example, let's consider the recessive X-linked form of hemophilia that we discussed in Chapter 16 (hemophilia A). This type of hemophilia is caused by a defect in a gene that encodes a blood-clotting protein, called factor VIII, which is made by cells in the liver and secreted into the bloodstream. In a heterozygous female, approximately half of her liver cells make and secrete this clotting factor, which is sufficient to prevent

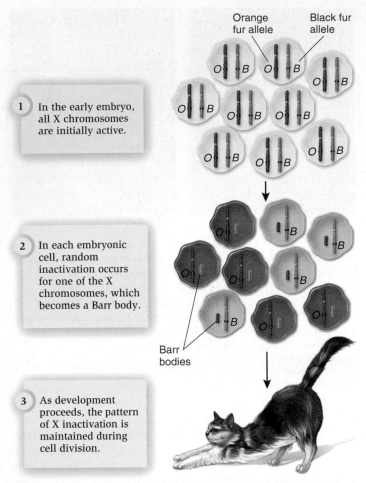

1 In the early embryo, all X chromosomes are initially active.

Orange fur allele   Black fur allele

2 In each embryonic cell, random inactivation occurs for one of the X chromosomes, which becomes a Barr body.

Barr bodies

3 As development proceeds, the pattern of X inactivation is maintained during cell division.

Figure 17.10 X-chromosome inactivation in a calico cat. The calico pattern is due to random X-chromosome inactivation in a female that is heterozygous for an X-linked gene with black and orange alleles. The cells at the top of this figure represent a small mass of cells making up the very early embryo. In these cells, both X chromosomes are active. At an early stage of embryonic development, one X chromosome is randomly inactivated in each cell. The initial inactivation pattern is maintained in the descendents of each cell as the embryo matures into an adult. The pattern of orange and black fur in the adult cat reflects the pattern of X inactivation in the embryo.

BIOLOGY PRINCIPLE The genetic material provides a blueprint for reproduction. In this example, the process of X inactivation produces a variegated pattern of fur color.

hemophilia. Therefore, she exhibits the dominant trait of normal blood clotting.

On rare occasions, a female who is heterozygous may show mild or even severe disease symptoms. How is this possible? X inactivation in humans occurs when an embryo is 10 days old. At this stage, the liver contains only about a dozen cells. In most females who are heterozygous for the normal and hemophilia alleles, roughly half of their liver cells express the normal allele. However, on rare occasions, all or most of the dozen embryonic liver cells may inactivate the X chromosome carrying the dominant normal allele. Following growth and development, such a female will have a very low level of factor VIII and as a result shows symptoms of hemophilia.

Why does X inactivation occur? Researchers have proposed that X inactivation achieves **dosage compensation**, a process that equalizes the expression of X-linked genes in male and female mammals. The inactivation of one X chromosome in the female reduces the number of expressed copies (doses) of X-linked genes from two to one. As a result, the expression of X-linked genes in females and males is roughly equal.

The X Chromosome Has an X Inactivation Center That Controls Compaction into a Barr Body

After Lyon's hypothesis was confirmed, researchers became interested in the genetic control of X inactivation. The cells of humans and other mammals have the ability to count their X chromosomes and allow only one of them to remain active. Additional X chromosomes are converted to Barr bodies. In normal females, two X chromosomes are counted and one is inactivated. In normal males, one X chromosome is counted and none inactivated.

On rare occasions, people are born with abnormalities in the number of their sex chromosomes (refer back to Table 15.2). In the disorders known as Turner syndrome, triple X syndrome, and Klinefelter syndrome, the cells inactivate the number of X chromosomes necessary to leave a single active chromosome (**Table 17.3**). For example, in triple X syndrome, in which an extra X chromosome is found in each cell, two X chromosomes are converted to Barr bodies. In spite of X inactivation, people with these three syndromes do exhibit some phenotypic abnormalities. The symptoms associated with these disorders may be due to effects that occur prior to X inactivation or because not all of the genes on the Barr body are completely silenced.

Although the genetic control of inactivation is not entirely understood at the molecular level, a short region on the X chromosome called the **X inactivation center (Xic)** is known to play a critical role. Finnish-born American geneticist Eeva Therman and German-born American geneticist Klaus Patau determined that X inactivation is accomplished by counting the number of Xics and inactivating all X chromosomes except for one. In cells with two X chromosomes, if one of them is missing its Xic due to a chromosome mutation, neither X chromosome will be inactivated, because only one Xic is counted. Having two active X chromosomes is a lethal condition for a human female embryo.

Table 17.3	Relationship Between X Inactivation and the Number of X Chromosomes		
Phenotype	Chromosome composition	Number of Barr bodies	Number of active X chromosomes
Normal female	XX	1	1
Normal male	XY	0	1
Turner syndrome (female)	XO	0	1
Triple X syndrome (female)	XXX	2	1
Klinefelter syndrome (male)	XXY	1	1

The expression of a specific gene within the Xic is required for compaction of the X chromosome into a Barr body. This gene, discovered in 1991, is named *Xist* (for X inactive specific transcript). The *Xist* gene product is a long RNA molecule that does not encode a protein. Instead, the role of *Xist* RNA is to coat one of the two X chromosomes during the process of X inactivation. After coating, proteins associate with the *Xist* RNA and promote compaction of the chromosome into a Barr body. The *Xist* gene on the Barr body continues to be expressed after other genes on this chromosome have been silenced. The expression of the *Xist* gene also maintains a chromosome as a Barr body during cell division. Whenever a somatic cell divides in a female mammal, the Barr body is replicated to produce two Barr bodies.

For Imprinted Genes, the Gene from Only One Parent Is Expressed

As we have seen, X inactivation is a type of epigenetic inheritance in which a chromosome is modified in the early embryo, permanently altering gene expression in that individual. Other types of epigenetic inheritance occur when genes or chromosomes are modified in the gametes of a parent, permanently altering gene expression in the offspring. **Genomic imprinting**, which was discovered in the early 1980s, refers to an inheritance pattern in which a segment of DNA is imprinted or marked so that gene expression occurs only from the genetic material inherited from one parent. It occurs in numerous species, including insects, plants, and mammals.

Genomic imprinting may involve a single gene, a part of a chromosome, an entire chromosome, or even all of the chromosomes inherited from one parent. It is permanent in the somatic cells of a given individual, but the marking of the DNA is altered from generation to generation. Imprinted genes do not follow a Mendelian pattern of inheritance because imprinting causes the offspring to distinguish between maternally and paternally inherited alleles. Depending on how a particular gene is marked by each parent, the offspring expresses either the maternal or the paternal allele, but not both.

One of the first imprinted genes to be identified is a gene called *Igf2* that is found in mice and other mammals. This gene encodes a growth hormone called insulin-like growth factor 2 (Igf2) that is needed for proper growth. If a normal copy of this gene is not expressed, a mouse will be dwarf. The *Igf2* gene is known to be located on an autosome, not on a sex chromosome. Because mice are diploid, they have two copies of this gene, one from each parent.

Researchers have discovered mutations in the *Igf2* gene that block the function of the Igf2 hormone. When mice carrying normal or mutant alleles are crossed to each other, a bizarre result is obtained (**Figure 17.11**). If the male parent is homozygous for the normal allele and the female is homozygous for the mutant allele (left), all the offspring grow to a normal size. In contrast, if the male is homozygous for the mutant allele and the female is homozygous for the normal allele (right), all the offspring are dwarf. The reason this result is so surprising is that the normal and dwarf offspring have the same genotype (*Igf2 Igf2⁻*) but different phenotypes! In mice, the *Igf2* gene is imprinted in such a way that only the paternal allele is expressed,

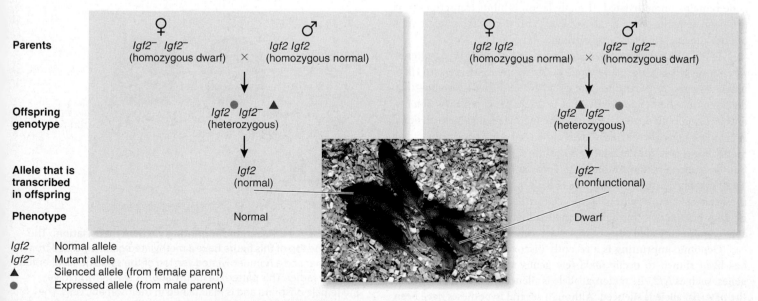

Figure 17.11 An example of genomic imprinting in the mouse. In the cross on the left, a homozygous male with the normal *Igf2* allele was crossed to a homozygous female carrying a defective allele, *Igf2⁻*. Offspring are phenotypically normal because the paternal allele is expressed. In the cross on the right, a homozygous male carrying the defective allele was crossed to a homozygous normal female. In this case, offspring are dwarf because the paternal allele is defective and the maternal allele is not expressed. The photograph shows normal-size (left) and dwarf littermates (right) derived from a cross between a wild-type female (*Igf2 Igf2*) and a heterozygous male carrying a loss-of-function allele (*Igf2 Igf2⁻*) (courtesy of A. Efstratiadis). The loss-of-function allele was made using methods described in Chapter 20.

Concept Check: If you cross an *Igf2 Igf2⁻* male mouse to an *Igf2 Igf2* female mouse, what would be the expected results?

which means it is transcribed into mRNA. The maternal allele is not transcribed. The baby mice shown on the left side of the photograph of Figure 17.11 are normal because they express a functional paternal allele. In contrast, the baby mice on the right are dwarf because the paternal gene is a mutant allele that results in a nonfunctional hormone.

The Transcription of an Imprinted Gene Depends on Methylation

Why is the maternal gene encoding Igf2 not transcribed into mRNA? To answer this question we need to consider the regulation of gene transcription in eukaryotes. As discussed in Chapter 13, DNA methylation, which is the attachment of methyl ($-CH_3$) groups to bases of DNA, can alter gene transcription. Researchers have discovered that DNA methylation is the marking process that occurs during the imprinting of certain genes, including the *Igf2* gene. For most genes, DNA methylation silences gene expression by inhibiting the initiation of transcription or by causing the chromatin in a region to become more compact. In contrast, for a few imprinted genes, DNA methylation may enhance gene expression by attracting activator proteins to the promoter or by preventing the binding of repressor proteins.

Figure 17.12 shows the imprinting process in which a maternal gene is methylated. The left side of the figure follows the marking process during the life of a female individual; the right side follows the same process in a male. Both individuals received a methylated gene from their mother and a nonmethylated copy of the same gene from their father. Via cell division, the zygote develops into a multicellular organism. Each time a somatic cell divides, enzymes in the cell maintain the methylation of the maternal gene, but the paternal gene remains unmethylated. If methylation inhibits transcription of this gene, only the paternal copy will be expressed in the somatic cells of both the male and female offspring.

The methylation state of an imprinted gene may be altered when individuals make gametes. First, the methylation is erased (Figure 17.12, step 2). Next, the gene may be methylated again, but that depends on whether the individual is a female or male. In females making eggs, both copies of the gene are methylated; in males making sperm, neither copy is methylated. When we consider the effects of methylation over the course of two or more generations, we can see how this phenomenon results in an epigenetic transmission pattern. The male in Figure 17.12 has inherited a methylated gene from his mother that is transcriptionally silenced in his somatic cells. Although he does not express this gene during his lifetime, he can pass on an active, nonmethylated copy of this exact same gene to his offspring.

Genomic imprinting is a recently discovered phenomenon that has been shown to occur for a few genes in mammals. For some genes, such as Igf2, the maternal allele is silenced, but for other genes, the paternal allele is silenced. Although several hypotheses have been advanced, biologists are still trying to understand the reason for this curious marking process.

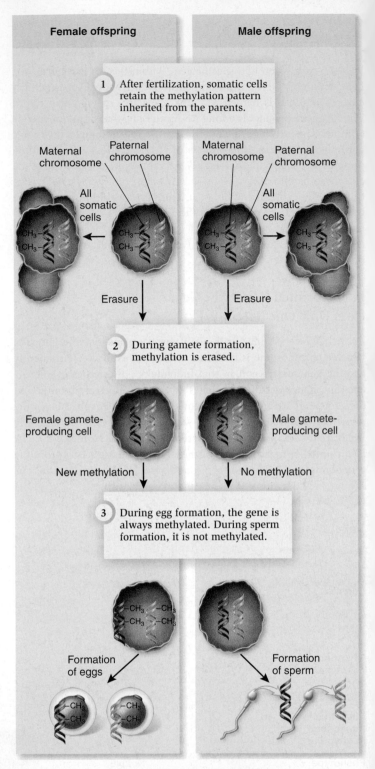

Figure 17.12 Genomic imprinting via DNA methylation. The cells at the top of this figure have a methylated gene inherited from the mother and a nonmethylated version of the same gene inherited from the father. This pattern of methylation is the same in male and female offspring and is maintained in their somatic cells. The methylation is erased during gamete formation, but in females, the gene is methylated again at a later stage in the formation of eggs. Therefore, females always transmit a methylated, transcriptionally silent copy of this gene, whereas males transmit a nonmethylated, transcriptionally active copy.

Summary of Key Concepts

- A variety of inheritance patterns are now known and some of these do not obey one or both of Mendel's laws of inheritance (Table 17.1).

17.1 Gene Interaction

- Epistasis is a gene interaction that occurs when the alleles of one gene mask the effects of the alleles of a different gene (Figure 17.1).

- Quantitative traits such as height and weight are polygenic, which means that multiple genes govern the trait. Often, the alleles of such genes contribute in an additive way to the phenotype and are greatly affected by the environment. This produces continuous variation in the trait, which is graphed as a bell-shaped curve (Figure 17.2).

17.2 Genes on the Same Chromosome: Linkage, Recombination, and Mapping

- When two different genes are on the same chromosome, they are said to be linked. Linked genes tend to be inherited as a unit, unless crossing over separates them (Figures 17.3, 17.4).

- Genetic mapping allows us to determine the order of genes along a chromosome and the relative distances between them, based on the frequency of crossing over observed in testcrosses (Figure 17.5).

17.3 Extranuclear Inheritance: Organelle Genomes

- Mitochondria and chloroplasts carry a small number of genes. The inheritance of such genes is called extranuclear inheritance (Figure 17.6).

- Chloroplasts in the four-o'clock plant are transmitted via the egg, a pattern called maternal inheritance (Figures 17.7, 17.8).

- Several human diseases are known to be caused by mutations in mitochondrial genes, which follow a maternal inheritance pattern (Table 17.2).

17.4 Epigenetic Inheritance

- Epigenetic inheritance refers to a modification of a gene or chromosome that affects the expression of one or more genes but does not alter the DNA sequence. Such changes may remain through the life of an organism, but are not permanent over the course of two or more generations.

- X inactivation in female mammals occurs when one X chromosome in every somatic cell is randomly inactivated. If the female is heterozygous for an X-linked gene, this can lead to a mosaic phenotype, with some of the somatic cells expressing one allele and some expressing the other (Figures 17.9, 17.10, Table 17.3).

- In genomic imprinting, offspring express either a maternal or paternal allele, depending on how a particular gene is marked, or imprinted. During gamete formation, DNA methylation of an allele from one parent is a mechanism to achieve imprinting (Figures 17.11, 17.12).

Assess and Discuss

Test Yourself

1. When two genes are located on the same chromosome they are said to be
   a. homologous.
   b. allelic.
   c. epistatic.
   d. linked.
   e. polygenic.

2. Based on the ideas proposed by Morgan, which of the following statements concerning linkage is *not* true?
   a. Traits determined by genes located on the same chromosome are likely to be inherited together.
   b. Crossing over between homologous chromosomes can create new allele combinations.
   c. A crossover is more likely to occur in a region between two genes that are close together than in a region between two genes that are farther apart.
   d. The probability of crossing over depends on the distance between the genes.
   e. Genes that tend to be transmitted together are physically located on the same chromosome.

3. In linkage mapping, 1 map unit is equivalent to
   a. 100 base pairs.
   b. 1 base pair.
   c. 10% recombination frequency.
   d. 1% recombination frequency.
   e. 1% the length of the chromosome.

4. Extranuclear inheritance occurs because
   a. certain genes are found on the X chromosome.
   b. chromosomes in the nucleus may be transferred to the cytoplasm.
   c. some organelles contain DNA.
   d. the nuclear membrane breaks down during cell division.
   e. both a and c.

5. In many organisms, organelles such as the mitochondria are transmitted only by the egg. This phenomenon is known as
   a. biparental inheritance.
   b. paternal inheritance.
   c. X-linked inheritance.
   d. maternal inheritance.
   e. both c and d.

6. Modification of a gene during gamete formation or early development that alters the way the gene is expressed during the individual's lifetime but is not permanent over two or more generations is called
   a. maternal inheritance.
   b. epigenetic inheritance.
   c. epistasis.
   d. multiple allelism.
   e. alternative splicing.

7. A male mouse that is homozygous for the normal allele of the *Igf2* gene is mated to a female that is heterozygous, carrying one normal copy and one defective copy of the gene. What would be the expected outcome of this cross?
   a. all normal offspring
   b. 1/2 normal and 1/2 dwarf
   c. all dwarf
   d. 3/4 normal and 1/4 dwarf
   e. none of the above

8. When a gene is inactivated during gamete formation and that gene is maintained in an inactivated state in the somatic cells of offspring, such an inheritance pattern is called
   a. linkage.
   b. X inactivation.
   c. epistasis.
   d. genomic imprinting.
   e. polygenic inheritance.

9. Calico coat pattern in cats is the result of
   a. X inactivation.
   b. epistasis.
   c. organelle heredity.
   d. genomic imprinting.
   e. maternal inheritance.

10. Genomic imprinting can be explained by
    a. DNA methylation of genes during gamete formation.
    b. epistasis.
    c. the spreading of X inactivation from the Xic locus.
    d. the inheritance of alleles that contribute additively to a trait.
    e. none of the above.

Conceptual Questions

1. Two genes (called gene *A* and gene *B*) are located on the same chromosome and are 12 mu apart. An *AABB* individual was crossed to an *aabb* individual. The F_1 (*AaBb*) offspring were crossed to *aabb* individuals. What percentage of the F_2 offspring would you expect to be *Aabb*?

2. Certain forms of human color blindness are inherited as X-linked recessive traits. Heterozygous females are not usually color blind, but on rare occasions, a female may exhibit partial color blindness or may be color blind in just one eye. Explain how this could happen.

3.  A principle of biology is that *Biology is as an experimental science*. Describe how the phenomenon of linkage enables biologists to conduct experiments that are aimed at the mapping of genes along a chromosome.

Collaborative Questions

1. As discussed in Chapter 16, Mendel studied seven traits in pea plants, and the garden pea happens to have seven different chromosomes. It has been pointed out that Mendel was very lucky not to have conducted crosses involving two traits that are closely linked on the same chromosome because the results would have confounded his theory of independent assortment. It has even been suggested that Mendel may not have published data involving traits that were linked. An article by Blixt ("Why Didn't Gregor Mendel Find Linkage?" *Nature* 256:206[1975]) considers this issue. Look up this article and discuss why Mendel did not find linkage.

2. Discuss the similarities and differences between X inactivation and genomic imprinting.

Online Resource

www.brookerbiology.com

Stay a step ahead in your studies with animations that bring concepts to life and practice tests to assess your understanding. Your instructor may also recommend the interactive eBook, individualized learning tools, and more.

Genomes, Proteomes, and Bioinformatics

21

Genomes and computer technology. The amount of data derived from the analyses of genomes is so staggering in size and complexity that researchers have turned to computers to unravel the amazing information that genomes contain.

I magine a book that is incredibly long and has taken billions of years to write. Such an analogy applies to the human genome, which is written in only four letters—A, T, G, and C—and is over 3 billion base pairs long. If the entire human genome were typed in a textbook like this, with about 3,000 letters per page, it would be over 1 million pages long! Our genome contains many unsolved mysteries that researchers are trying to unravel, such as: "What are the functions of every gene in the genome? How do gene mutations cause disease? How are humans evolutionarily related to other species?" As you will learn, genomes are full of surprises. For example, did you know that most of your DNA has no known function?

The unifying theme of biology is evolution. The genome of every living species is the product of approximately 4 billion years of evolution. We can understand the unity of modern organisms by realizing that all species evolved from an interrelated group of ancestors. Throughout this textbook, a recurring theme is a series of "Genomes & Proteomes Connections"—topics that highlight the evolutionary connections among all forms of life and underscore how the genetic material produces the form and function of living organisms. By now, you may feel familiar with the concept of a

genome, the complete genetic composition of a cell, organism, or species. The genome of each species is critical to its existence in several ways:

- The genome stores information in the form of genes, which provide a genetic blueprint to produce the characteristics of organisms.

- The genome is copied and transmitted from generation to generation.

- The accumulation of genetic changes (mutations) over the course of many generations produces the evolutionary changes that alter species and produce new species.

An extension of genome analysis is the study of proteomes. The term **proteome** refers to the entire complement of proteins that a cell or organism makes. The function of most genes is to encode proteins, which are the key determinants of cell structure and function. Analyzing the proteomes of organisms allows researchers to understand many aspects of biology, including the structure and function of cells, the complexity of multicellular organisms, and the interactions between organisms and their environment.

In the first two sections of this chapter, we will consider genome characteristics of bacteria, archaea, and eukaryotes. We then turn our attention to proteomes and examine the roles of the proteins that a species can make. From a molecular perspective, genomes and proteomes contain extensive and complex information, which is studied using computer technology. In the last section of this chapter, we will consider how the field of bioinformatics, which employs computers and statistical techniques to analyze biological information, is critical to the study of genomes and proteomes.

21.1 Bacterial and Archaeal Genomes

Learning Outcomes:
1. List the key characteristics of bacterial and archaeal genomes.
2. Describe the method of shotgun DNA sequencing.

The past decade has seen remarkable advances in our overall understanding of the entire genome of many species. As genetic technology has progressed, researchers have gained an increasing ability to analyze the composition of genomes as a whole unit. For many species, we now know their complete DNA sequence, which provides the most detailed description available of an organism's genome at the molecular level. In this section, we will survey the sizes and composition of genomes in selected species of bacteria and archaea.

The Genomes of Bacteria and Archaea Typically Consist of a Circular Chromosome with a Few Thousand Genes

Geneticists have made great progress in the study of bacterial and archaeal genomes. Some of the key features of bacterial chromosomes are described in Chapter 18 (refer back to Figure 18.10). Why are researchers interested in the genomes of bacteria and archaea? First, bacteria cause many different diseases that affect humans as well as other animals and plants. Studying the genomes of bacteria reveals important clues about the process of infection, which may also help us find ways to combat bacterial infection. A second reason for studying bacterial and archaeal genomes is that the information we learn about these microscopic organisms often applies to larger and more complex organisms. For example, basic genetic mechanisms, such as DNA replication and gene regulation, were first understood in the bacterium *Escherichia coli*. That knowledge provided a critical foundation to understand how these processes work in humans and other eukaryotic species. A third reason is evolution. The origin of the first eukaryotic cell probably involved a union between an archaeal and a bacterial cell, as we will explore in Chapter 22. The study of bacterial and archaeal genomes helps us understand how all living species evolved. Finally, another reason to study the genomes of bacteria is because we use them as tools in research and biotechnology, which was discussed in Chapter 20.

As of 2011, the genomes of over 700 bacterial and archaeal species have been completely sequenced and analyzed. The chromosomes of bacteria and archaea are usually a few million base pairs in length. Genomic researchers refer to 1 million base pairs as 1 megabase pair, abbreviated Mb. Most bacteria and archaea contain a single type of chromosome, though multiple copies may be present in a single cell. However, some bacteria are known to have different chromosomes. For example, *Vibrio cholerae*, the bacterium that causes the diarrheal disease known as cholera, has two different chromosomes in each cell, one 2.9 Mb and the other 1.1 Mb.

Bacterial and archaeal chromosomes are usually circular. For example, the two chromosomes in *V. cholerae* are circular, as is the single type of chromosome found in *E. coli*. However, linear chromosomes are found in some species, such as *Borrelia burgdorferi*, the bacterium that causes Lyme disease, the most common tick-borne disease in the U.S. Certain bacterial species may even contain both linear and circular chromosomes. *Agrobacterium tumefaciens*, which infects plants and causes a disease called crown gall, has one linear chromosome (2.1 Mb) and one circular chromosome (3.0 Mb).

Table 21.1 compares the sequenced genomes from several bacterial and archaeal species. They range in size from 1.7 to 5.2 Mb.

Table 21.1 Examples of Bacterial and Archaeal Genomes That Have Been Sequenced*

Species	Genome size (Mb)[†]	Number of genes[‡]	Description
Methanobacterium thermoautotrophicum	1.7	1,869	An archaeon that produces methane
Haemophilus influenzae	1.8	1,743	One of several different bacterial species that causes respiratory illness and meningitis
Sulfolobus solfataricus	3.0	3,032	An archaeon that metabolizes sulfur-containing compounds
Lactobacillus plantarum	3.3	3,052	A type of lactic acid bacterium used in the production of cheese and yogurt
Mycobacterium tuberculosis	4.4	4,294	The bacterium that causes the respiratory disease tuberculosis
Escherichia coli	4.6	4,289	A naturally occurring intestinal bacterium; certain strains can cause human illness
Bacillus anthracis	5.2	5,439	The bacterium that causes the disease anthrax

*Bacterial and archaeal species often exist in different strains that may differ slightly in their genome size and number of genes. The data are from common strains of the indicated species. The species shown in this table have only one type of chromosome.
[†]Mb equals 1 million base pairs, or a megabase pair.
[‡]The number of genes is an estimate based on the analysis of genome sequences.

The total number of genes is correlated with the total genome size. Roughly 1,000 genes are found for every megabase pair of DNA. Compared with eukaryotic genomes, bacterial and archaeal genomes are less complex. Their chromosomes lack centromeres and telomeres and have a single origin of replication. Also, chromosomes of bacteria and archaea have relatively little repetitive DNA, whereas repetitive sequences are usually abundant in eukaryotic genomes.

In addition to one or more chromosomes, bacteria often have plasmids, circular pieces of DNA that exist independently of the bacterial chromosome. Plasmids are typically small, in the range of a few thousand to tens of thousands of base pairs in length, though some can be quite large, even hundreds of thousands of base pairs. The various functions of plasmids are described in Chapter 18, and their use as vectors in gene cloning is discussed in Chapter 20.

FEATURE INVESTIGATION

Venter, Smith, and Colleagues Sequenced the First Genome in 1995

The first genome to be entirely sequenced was that of the bacterium *Haemophilus influenzae*. This bacterium causes a variety of diseases in humans, including respiratory illnesses and bacterial meningitis. *H. influenzae* has a relatively small genome consisting of approximately 1.8 Mb of DNA in a single circular chromosome.

A common strategy for sequencing an entire genome is called **shotgun DNA sequencing**. In this approach, researchers use a DNA sequencing method, such as the dideoxy chain-termination method (see Figure 20.9), to randomly sequence many DNA fragments from the genome. As a matter of chance, some of the fragments are overlapping—the end of one fragment contains the same DNA region as the beginning of another fragment. Computers are used to align the overlapping regions and assemble the DNA fragments into a contiguous sequence identical to that found in the intact chromosome. The advantage of shotgun DNA sequencing is that it does not require extensive mapping, a process that can be time-consuming. A disadvantage is that researchers may waste time sequencing the same region of DNA more times than necessary in order to assemble the sequence correctly.

To obtain a complete sequence of a genome with the shotgun approach, how do researchers decide how many fragments to sequence? We can calculate the probability that a base will not be sequenced (*P*) using this equation:

$$P = e^{-m}$$

where *e* is the base of the natural logarithm (*e* = 2.72), and *m* is the number of sequenced bases divided by the total genome size. For example, in the case of *H. influenzae*, with a genome size of 1.8 Mb, if researchers sequenced 9.0 Mb, *m* = 5 (that is, 9.0 Mb divided by 1.8 Mb):

$$P = e^{-m} = e^{-5} = 0.0067, \text{ or } 0.67\%.$$

This means that if we randomly sequence 9.0 Mb, which is five times the length of a single genome, we are likely to miss only 0.67% of the genome. With a genome size of 1.8 Mb, we would miss about 12,000 nucleotides out of approximately 1.8 million. Such missed sequences are typically on small DNA fragments that, as a matter of random chance, did not happen to be sequenced. The missing links in the genome are identified using mapping methods, which are described in Chapter 20.

In their discovery based investigation, American biologists Craig Venter and Hamilton Smith and their colleagues used a shotgun DNA sequencing approach (**Figure 21.1**). The researchers isolated chromosomal DNA from *H. influenzae* and used sound waves to break the DNA into small fragments of approximately 2,000 bp in length. These fragments were randomly inserted into vectors, allowing the DNA to be propagated in *E. coli*. Each *E. coli* clone carried a vector with a different piece of DNA from *H. influenzae*. The complete set of vectors, each containing a different fragment of DNA, is called a **DNA library** (refer back to Figure 20.4). The researchers then subjected many of these clones to the procedure of DNA sequencing. They sequenced a total of approximately 10.8 Mb of DNA.

The outcome of this genome-sequencing project was a very long DNA sequence. In 1995, Venter, Smith, and colleagues published the entire DNA sequence of *H. influenzae*. The researchers then analyzed the genome sequence using a computer to obtain information about the properties of the genome. Questions they asked included, "How many genes does the genome contain, and what are the likely functions of those genes?" Later in this chapter, we will learn how scientists can answer such questions with the use of computers. The data in Figure 21.1 summarize these researchers' results. The *H. influenzae* genome is composed of 1,830,137 bp of DNA. The computer analysis predicted 1,743 genes. Based on their similarities to sequences of genes identified in other species, the researchers also predicted the functions of proteins encoded by nearly two-thirds of those genes.

Figure 21.1 Determination of the complete genome sequence of *Haemophilus influenzae* by Venter, Smith, and colleagues.

GOAL The goal is to obtain the entire genome sequence of *Haemophilus influenzae*. This information will reveal its genome size and also which genes the organism has.

KEY MATERIALS A strain of *H. influenzae*.

Experimental level   **Conceptual level**

1 Purify DNA from a strain of *H. influenzae*. This involves breaking the cells open by adding phenol and chloroform. Most protein and lipid components go into the phenol-chloroform phase. DNA remains in the aqueous (water) phase.

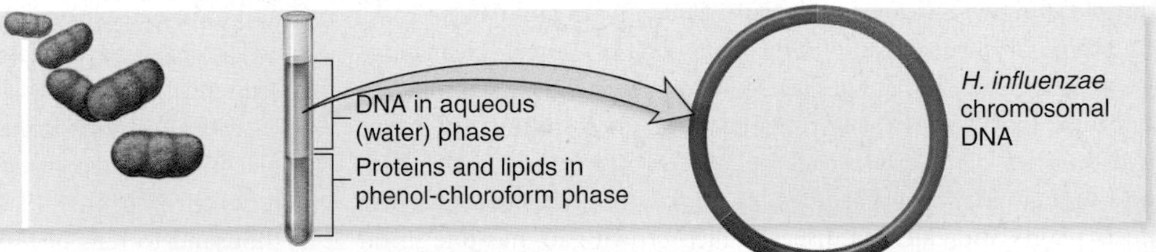

DNA in aqueous (water) phase
Proteins and lipids in phenol-chloroform phase
H. influenzae chromosomal DNA

2 Sonicate the DNA to break it into small fragments of about 2,000 bp in length.

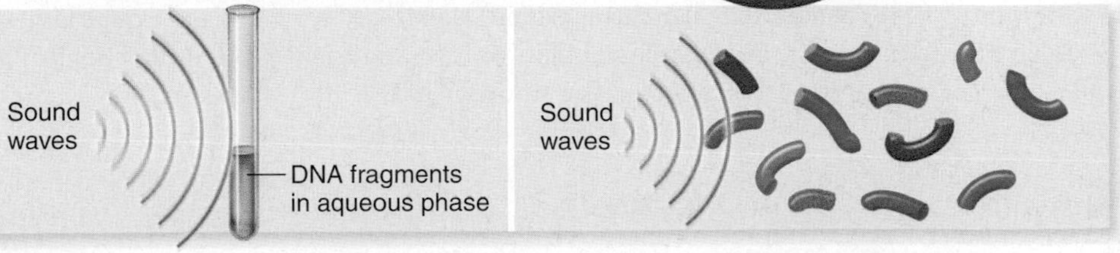

Sound waves
DNA fragments in aqueous phase
Sound waves

3 Clone the DNA fragments into vectors. The procedures for cloning are described in Chapter 20. This produces a DNA library.

Refer back to Figures 20.2 and 20.3.

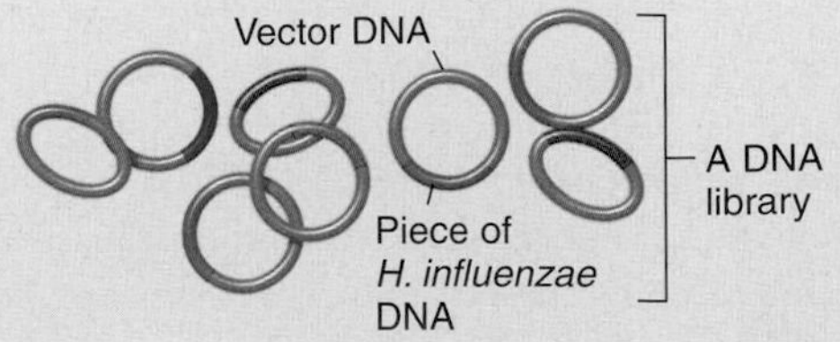

Vector DNA
Piece of *H. influenzae* DNA
A DNA library

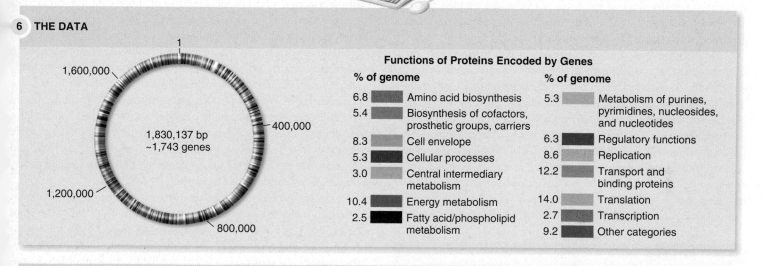

4 Subject many clones to the procedure of dideoxy sequencing, also described in Chapter 20. A total of 10.8 Mb was sequenced.

Refer back to Figure 20.9.

Produces a large number of sequences with overlapping regions.

5 Use tools of bioinformatics, described in the last section of this chapter, to identify various types of genes in the genome.

CCATGCCATGGCCCC...

Explores the genome sequence and identifies and characterizes genes.

6 THE DATA

1,830,137 bp
~1,743 genes

Functions of Proteins Encoded by Genes

% of genome		% of genome	
6.8	Amino acid biosynthesis	5.3	Metabolism of purines, pyrimidines, nucleosides, and nucleotides
5.4	Biosynthesis of cofactors, prosthetic groups, carriers		
8.3	Cell envelope	6.3	Regulatory functions
5.3	Cellular processes	8.6	Replication
3.0	Central intermediary metabolism	12.2	Transport and binding proteins
10.4	Energy metabolism	14.0	Translation
2.5	Fatty acid/phospholipid metabolism	2.7	Transcription
		9.2	Other categories

7 CONCLUSION *H. influenzae* has a genome size of 1.83 Mb with approximately 1,743 genes. The functions of many of those genes could be inferred by comparing them to genes in other species.

8 SOURCE Fleischmann et al. 1995. Whole-genome random sequencing and assembly of *Haemophilus influenzae* Rd. *Science* 269:496–512.

The diagram shown in the data of Figure 21.1 places proteins in various categories based on their predicted function. These results gave the first comprehensive "genome picture" of a living organism!

Experimental Questions

1. What was the goal of the experiment conducted by Venter, Smith, and their colleagues?

2. How does shotgun DNA sequencing differ from procedures that involve mapping? Name an advantage and a disadvantage of the shotgun DNA sequencing approach.

3. What were the results of the study described in Figure 21.1?

21.2 Eukaryotic Genomes

Learning Outcomes:

1. Describe the key features of eukaryotic genomes.
2. Name the two major types of transposable elements and describe how they differ.
3. Explain how gene duplications can occur and lead to the formation of gene families.
4. Outline the goals and results of the Human Genome Project.

Thus far, we have examined bacterial and archaeal genomes. In this section, we turn to eukaryotes, which include protists, fungi, animals, and plants. As you will learn, their genomes are larger and more complex than their bacterial and archaeal counterparts. In addition to genes, eukaryotic genomes often have abundant amounts of

noncoding sequences, whose function is largely unknown. For example, eukaryotic genomes typically have a substantial amount of short repeated sequences called repetitive DNA. We will explore how certain types of repetitive DNA sequences are formed by a process called transposition. We will also examine how the duplication of genes can lead to families of related genes.

The Nuclear Genomes of Eukaryotes Are Sets of Linear Chromosomes That Vary Greatly in Size and Composition Among Different Species

As discussed in Chapter 15, the genome located in the nucleus of eukaryotic species is usually found in sets of linear chromosomes. In humans, for example, one set contains 23 linear chromosomes—22 autosomes and one sex chromosome, X or Y. In addition, certain organelles in eukaryotic cells contain a small amount of DNA. These include the mitochondrion, which plays a role in ATP synthesis, and the chloroplast (found in plants and algae), which carries out photosynthesis. The genetic material in these organelles is referred to as the mitochondrial or the chloroplast genome to distinguish it from the nuclear genome, which is located in the cell nucleus. In this chapter, we will focus on the nuclear genome of eukaryotes.

Sizes of Nuclear Genomes   In the past decade or so, the DNA sequence of entire nuclear genomes has been determined for over 100 eukaryotic species, including more than two dozen mammalian genomes. Examples are shown in **Table 21.2**.

Motivation to sequence these genomes comes from four main sources. First, the availability of genome sequences makes it easier for researchers to identify and characterize the genes of model organisms. This was the impetus for genome projects involving baker's yeast (*Saccharomyces cerevisiae*), the fruit fly (*Drosophila melanogaster*), a nematode worm (*Caenorhabditis elegans*), the plant called thale cress (*Arabidopsis thaliana*), and the mouse (*Mus musculus*). A second reason for genome sequencing is to gather more information to identify and treat human diseases, which is an important aim for sequencing the human genome. Knowing the DNA sequence of the human genome will help to identify genes in which mutation plays a role in disease. Third, by sequencing the genomes of agriculturally important species, new strains of livestock and plant species with improved traits can be developed. Fourth, biologists are increasingly relying on genome sequences as a way to establish evolutionary relationships.

Relationship Between Genome Sizes and Repetitive Sequences
Eukaryotic genomes are generally larger than bacterial and archaeal genomes, both in terms of the number of genes and genome size. The genomes of simpler eukaryotes, such as yeast, carry several thousand different genes, whereas the genomes of more complex eukaryotes contain tens of thousands of genes (see Table 21.2). Note that the number of genes is not the same as genome size. When we speak of genome size, this means the total amount of DNA, often measured in megabase pairs. The relative sizes of nuclear genomes vary dramatically among different eukaryotic species (**Figure 21.2a**). In general, increases in the amount of DNA are correlated with increases in cell size, cell complexity, and body complexity. For example, yeast have smaller genomes than animals. However, major variations in genome sizes are observed among organisms that are similar in form and function. For example, the total amount of DNA found within different species of amphibians varies over 100-fold.

The amount of DNA in closely related species can also vary. As an example, let's consider two closely related species of the plant called the globe thistle, *Echinops bannaticus* and *Echinops nanus* (**Figure 21.2b,c**). These species have similar numbers of chromosomes, but *E. bannaticus* has nearly double the amount of DNA compared to *E. nanus*. What is the explanation for the larger genome of

Table 21.2	Examples of Eukaryotic Nuclear Genomes That Have Been Sequenced		
Species	**Nuclear genome size (Mb)**	**Number of genes**	**Description**
Saccharomyces cerevisiae (baker's yeast)	12.1	6,294	One of the simplest eukaryotic species; it has been extensively studied by researchers to understand eukaryotic molecular biology.
Caenorhabditis elegans (nematode worm)	100	~19,000	A model organism used to study animal development.
Drosophila melanogaster (fruit fly)	180	~14,000	A model organism used to study many genetic phenomena, including development.
Arabidopsis thaliana (thale cress)	120	~26,000	A model organism studied by plant biologists.
Oryza sativa (rice)	440	~40,000	A cereal grain with a relatively small genome; it is very important worldwide as a food crop.
Mus musculus (mouse)	2,500	~20,000–25,000	A model mammalian organism used to study genetics, cell biology, and development.
Homo sapiens (humans)	3,200	~20,000–25,000	Our own genome, the sequencing of which will help to elucidate our understanding of inherited traits and to aid in the identification and treatment of diseases.

Note: The genome size refers to the number of megabase (Mb) pairs in one set of chromosomes. For species with sex chromosomes, it would include both sex chromosomes.

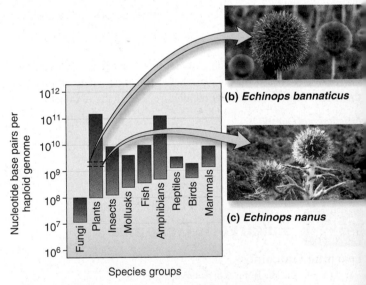

(b) *Echinops bannaticus*

(c) *Echinops nanus*

(a) Genome size

Figure 21.2   **Genome sizes among selected groups of eukaryotes. (a)** Genome sizes among various groups of eukaryotes are shown on a log scale. As an example for comparison, two closely related species of globe thistle are pictured. These species have similar characteristics, but *Echinops bannaticus* **(b)** has nearly double the amount of DNA as does *E. nanus* **(c)** due to the accumulation of repetitive DNA sequences.

Concept Check: *What are two reasons why the groups of species shown in (a) vary in their total amount of DNA?*

E. bannaticus? The genome of *E. bannaticus* is not likely to contain twice as many genes. Rather, its genome composition includes many **repetitive sequences**, which are short DNA sequences that are present in many copies throughout the genome. Repetitive sequences are often abundant in eukaryotic species.

Types of Repetitive Sequences Repetitive sequences fall into two broad categories, moderately and highly repetitive. Sequences that are repeated a few hundred to several thousand times are called **moderately repetitive sequences**. In some cases, these sequences are multiple copies of the same gene. For example, the genes that encode ribosomal RNA (rRNA) are found in many copies. The cell needs a large amount of rRNA for its cellular ribosomes. This is accomplished by having and expressing multiple copies of the genes that encode rRNA. In addition, other types of functionally important sequences can be moderately repetitive. For example, multiple copies of origins of replication are found in eukaryotic chromosomes. Other moderately repetitive sequences may play a role in the regulation of gene transcription and translation.

Highly repetitive sequences are those that are repeated tens of thousands to millions of times throughout the genome. Each copy of a highly repetitive sequence is relatively short, ranging from a few nucleotides to several hundred nucleotides in length. Most of these sequences have no known function, and whether or not they benefit the organism is a matter of debate. A widely studied example is the *Alu* family of sequences found in humans and other primates. The *Alu* sequence is approximately 300 bp long. This sequence derives its name from the observation that it contains a site for cleavage by a restriction enzyme known as *Alu*I. It represents about 10% of the total human DNA and occurs (on average) approximately every 5,000–6,000 bases. Evolutionary studies suggest that the *Alu* sequence arose 65 million years ago (mya) from a section of a single ancestral gene known as the 7SL RNA gene. Remarkably, over the course of 65 million years, the *Alu* sequence has been copied and inserted into the human genome so often that it now occurs more than 1 million times! The mechanism for the proliferation of *Alu* sequences will be described later.

Some highly repetitive sequences, like the *Alu* family, are interspersed throughout the genome. However, other highly repetitive sequences are clustered together in a tandem array, in which a very short nucleotide sequence is repeated many times in a row. In *Drosophila*, for example, 19% of the chromosomal DNA is highly repetitive DNA found in tandem arrays. An example is shown here:

```
AATATAATATATAATATAATATAATATAT
TTATATTATATATTATATTATATTATATA
```

In this particular tandem array, two related sequences, AATAT and AATATAT (in the top strand), are repeated multiple times. Highly repetitive sequences, which contain tandem arrays of short sequences, can be quite long, sometimes more than 1 million bp in length!

Figure 21.3 shows the composition of the relative classes of DNA sequences found in the nuclear genome of humans. Surprisingly, exons, the coding regions of structural genes, and the genes that give rise to rRNA and tRNA make up only about 2% of our genome! The other 98% is composed of noncoding sequences. Though we often

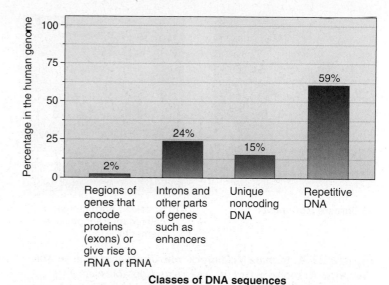

Figure 21.3 **The composition of DNA sequences that are found in the nuclear genome of humans.** Only about 2% of our genome codes for proteins. Most of our genome is made up of repetitive sequences.

BIOLOGY PRINCIPLE **The genetic material provides the blueprint for reproduction.** Only a small percentage of the human genome is involved with encoding the proteins that are largely responsible for human traits.

think of genomes as being the repository of sequences that code for proteins, most eukaryotic genomes are largely composed of other types of sequences. Intron DNA comprises about 24% of the human genome, and unique noncoding DNA, whose function is largely unknown, constitutes 15%. Repetitive DNA makes up 59% of the DNA in the genome. Much of the repetitive DNA is derived from transposable elements, stretches of DNA that can move from one location to another, which are described next.

Transposable Elements Move from One Chromosomal Location to Another

During a process called **transposition**, a short segment of DNA moves from its original site to a new site in the genome. Such segments are known as **transposable elements (TEs)**. They range from a few hundred to several thousand base pairs in length. TEs have sometimes been referred to as "jumping genes," because they are inherently mobile. American cytogeneticist Barbara McClintock first identified transposable elements in the late 1940s from her studies with corn plants (Figure 21.4). She identified a segment of DNA that could move into and out of a gene that affected the color of corn kernels, producing a speckled appearance. Since that time, biologists have discovered many different types of TEs in nearly all species examined.

Though McClintock identified TEs in corn in the late 1940s, her work was met with great skepticism because many researchers had trouble believing that DNA segments could be mobile. The advent of molecular technology in the 1960s and 1970s allowed scientists to understand more about the characteristics of TEs that enable their movement. Most notably, research involving bacterial TEs eventually

(a) Barbara McClintock

(b) Speckled corn kernels caused by transposable elements

Figure 21.4 Barbara McClintock, who discovered transposable elements. As shown in part **(b)**, when a transposable element is found within a pigment gene in corn, its frequent movement disrupts the gene, causing the kernel color to be speckled.

progressed to a molecular understanding of the transposition process. In 1983, more than 30 years after her initial discovery, McClintock was awarded the Nobel Prize in Physiology or Medicine.

Researchers have studied TEs from many species, including bacteria, archaea, and eukaryotes. They have discovered that TEs fall into two groups, based on different mechanisms of movement.

DNA Transposons Transposable elements that move via a DNA molecule are called **DNA transposons**. Both ends of DNA transposons usually have inverted repeats (IRs)—DNA sequences that are identical (or very similar) but run in opposite directions (**Figure 21.5a**), such as the following:

5′-CTGACTCTT-3′ and 5′-AAGAGTCAG-3′
3′-GACTGAGAA-5′   3′-TTCTCAGTC-5′

Depending on the particular TE, inverted repeats range from 9 to 40 bp in length. In addition, DNA transposons may contain a central region that encodes **transposase**, an enzyme that facilitates transposition.

As shown in **Figure 21.5b**, transposition of DNA transposons occurs by a cut-and-paste mechanism. Transposase first recognizes the inverted repeats (IR) in the transposon and then removes the DNA transposon from its original site. Next, the transposase/transposon complex moves to a new location, where transposase cleaves the target DNA and inserts the transposon into the site. Transposition may occur when a cell is in the process of DNA replication. If a TE is removed from a site that has already replicated and is inserted into a chromosomal site that has not yet replicated, the transposon will increase in number after DNA replication is complete. This is one way for transposons to become more prevalent in a genome.

Retroelements Another category of TE moves via an RNA intermediate. This form of transposition is very common but is found only in eukaryotic species. These types of elements are known as **retroelements** or **retrotransposons**. The *Alu* sequence in the human genome is an example of a retroelement. Some retroelements contain

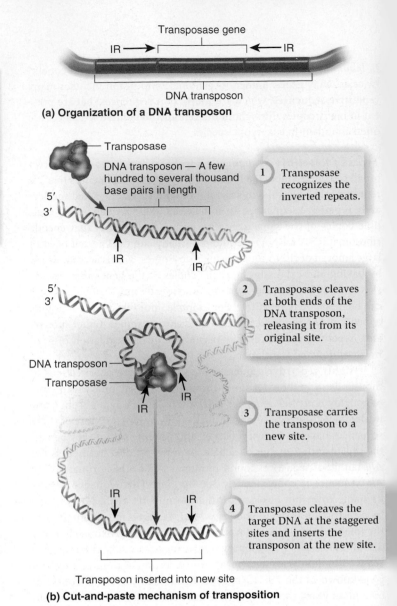

(a) Organization of a DNA transposon

1 Transposase recognizes the inverted repeats.

2 Transposase cleaves at both ends of the DNA transposon, releasing it from its original site.

3 Transposase carries the transposon to a new site.

4 Transposase cleaves the target DNA at the staggered sites and inserts the transposon at the new site.

Transposon inserted into new site

(b) Cut-and-paste mechanism of transposition

Figure 21.5 DNA transposons and their mechanism of transposition. **(a)** DNA transposons contain inverted repeat (IR) sequences at each end and may contain a gene that encodes transposase in the middle. **(b)** Transposition occurs by a cut-and-paste mechanism.

Concept Check: What is the role of the inverted repeats in the mechanism of transposition?

genes that encode the enzymes reverse transcriptase and integrase, which are needed in the transposition process (**Figure 21.6a**). Recall from Chapter 18 that reverse transcriptase uses RNA as a template to synthesize a complementary copy of DNA. Retroelements may also contain repeated sequences called terminal repeats at each end that facilitate their recognition.

The mechanism of retroelement movement is shown in **Figure 21.6b**. First, the enzyme RNA polymerase transcribes the retroelement into RNA. Reverse transcriptase uses this RNA as a template to synthesize a double-stranded DNA molecule. The ends of the double-stranded DNA are then recognized by integrase, which catalyzes the insertion of the DNA into the host chromosomal DNA. The integration of retroelements can occur at many locations within the

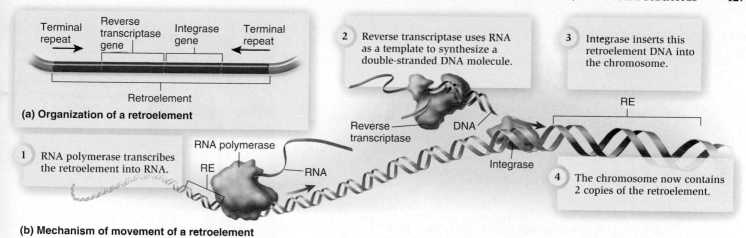

Figure 21.6 **Retroelements and their mechanism of transposition.** Retroelements are found only in eukaryotic species. **(a)** Some retroelements contain terminal repeats and genes that encode the enzymes reverse transcriptase and integrase, which are needed in the transposition process. **(b)** The process that adds a copy of a retroelement into a host chromosome. Note: In addition to using RNA as a template, some forms of reverse transcriptase can also use a DNA template to make a complementary DNA strand. As depicted here, these forms can make double-stranded DNA using a strand of RNA as a starting material. However, some forms of reverse transcriptase can make DNA only using an RNA template. In those cases, reverse transcriptase makes a complementary DNA strand from the RNA template and then the opposite DNA strand is made via a host-cell DNA polymerase.

Concept Check: *Based on their mechanism of movement, which type of TEs do you think would proliferate more rapidly in a genome, DNA transposons (see Figure 21.5b) or retroelements?*

genome. Furthermore, because a single retroelement can be copied into many RNA transcripts, retroelements may accumulate rapidly within a genome. This explains how the *Alu* element in the human genome was able to proliferate and constitute 10% of our genome.

Role of Transposable Elements What is the biological significance of TEs? The question is not resolved. According to the **selfish DNA hypothesis**, TEs exist solely because they have characteristics that allow them to insert themselves into the host cell DNA. In other words, they resemble parasites in that they inhabit the host without offering any advantage. They can proliferate within the host as long as they do not harm the host to the extent that they significantly disrupt its survival. However, TEs can do harm. For example, if they jump into the middle of an important gene and thereby disrupt its function, this may have a negative effect on the phenotype of an organism.

Other biologists have argued that TEs may provide benefits to a given species. For example, bacterial TEs often carry an antibiotic-resistance gene that provides the organism with a survival advantage. In addition, TEs may cause greater genetic diversity by promoting chromosomal rearrangements. As discussed next, such rearrangements can cause a misaligned crossover during meiosis and promote the formation of a gene family.

Gene Duplications Provide Additional Material for Genome Evolution, Sometimes Leading to the Formation of Gene Families

Let's now turn our attention to a way that the number of genes in a genome can increase. These gene duplications are important because they provide raw material for the addition of more genes into a species' genome. Such duplications can produce **homologous genes**, two or more genes that are derived from the same ancestral gene

(**Figure 21.7a**). Over the course of many generations, each version of the gene accumulates different mutations, resulting in genes with similar but not identical DNA sequences.

How do gene duplications occur? One mechanism that produces gene duplications is a misaligned crossover (**Figure 21.7b**). In this example, two homologous chromosomes have paired with each other during meiosis, but the homologs are misaligned. If a crossover occurs, this produces one chromosome with a gene duplication, one with a gene deletion, and two normal chromosomes. Each of these chromosomes are segregated into different haploid cells. If a haploid cell carrying the chromosome with the gene duplication participates in fertilization with another gamete, an offspring with a gene duplication is produced. In this way, gene duplications can form and be transmitted to future generations. The presence of multiple copies of the same transposable element in a genome can foster this process because the chromosomes may misalign while attempting to align TEs that are at different locations in the same chromosome.

During evolution, gene duplications can occur several times. Two or more homologous genes within a single species are also called paralogous genes, or **paralogs**. Multiple gene duplications followed by the accumulation of mutations in each paralog can result in a **gene family**—a group of paralogs that carry out related functions. A well-studied example is the globin gene family found in animals. The globin genes encode polypeptides that are subunits of proteins that function in oxygen binding. Hemoglobin, which is made in red blood cells, carries oxygen throughout the body. In humans, the globin gene family is composed of 14 paralogs that were originally derived from a single ancestral globin gene (**Figure 21.8**). According to an evolutionary analysis, the ancestral globin gene duplicated between 500 and 600 mya. Since that time, additional duplication events and chromosomal rearrangements have occurred to produce the current number of 14 genes on three different human chromosomes. Four of these

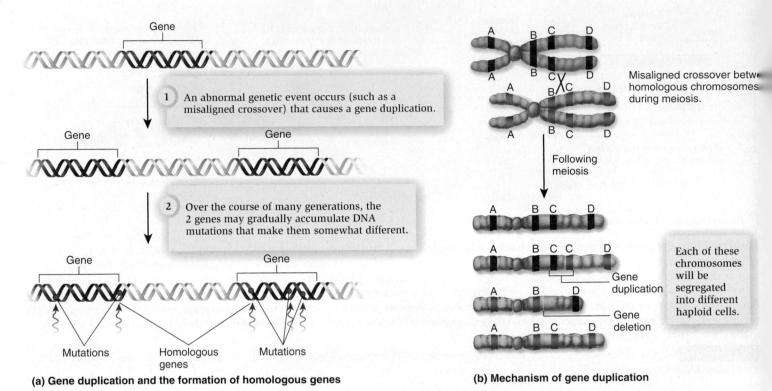

(a) Gene duplication and the formation of homologous genes

(b) Mechanism of gene duplication

Figure 21.7 **Gene duplication and the evolution of homologous genes.** **(a)** A gene duplication produces two copies of the same gene. Over time, these copies accumulate different random mutations, which results in homologous genes with similar but not identical DNA sequences. **(b)** Mechanism of gene duplication. If two homologous chromosomes misalign during meiosis, a crossover will produce a chromosome with a gene duplication.

BIOLOGY PRINCIPLE **Populations of organisms evolve from one generation to the next.** In this example, evolution involves two different types of genetic changes. First, a gene duplication occurs and, second, each copy of the gene accumulates different mutations.

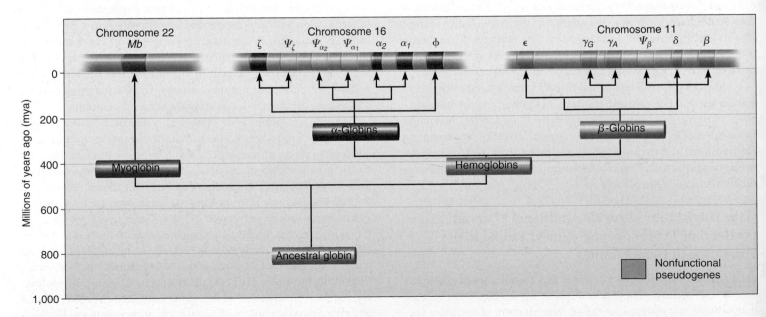

Figure 21.8 **The evolution of the globin gene family in humans.** The globin gene family evolved from a single ancestral globin gene.

BioConnections: Look back to Figure 13.3. How do different gene family members vary in their affinity for oxygen?

are pseudogenes—genes that have been produced by gene duplication but have accumulated mutations that make them nonfunctional, so they are not transcribed into RNA.

The accumulation of different mutations in the various family members has produced globins that are specialized in their function. For example, myoglobin binds and stores oxygen in muscle cells, whereas the hemoglobins bind and transport oxygen via red blood cells. Also, different globin genes are expressed during different stages of development. The zeta (ζ)-globin and epsilon (ε)-globin genes are expressed very early in embryonic life. During the second trimester of gestation, the alpha (α)-globin and gamma (γ)-globin genes are turned on. Following birth, the γ-globin genes are turned off, and the β-globin gene is turned on. These differences in the expression of the globin genes reflect the differences in the oxygen transport needs of humans during the embryonic, fetal, and postpartum stages of life (refer back to Figure 13.3).

The Human Genome Project Has Stimulated Genomic Research

Before ending our discussion of genomes, let's consider the **Human Genome Project**, a research effort to identify and map all human genes. Scientists had been discussing how to undertake this project since the mid-1980s. In 1988, the National Institutes of Health (NIH) in Bethesda, Maryland, established an Office of Human Genome Research with James Watson as its first director. The Human Genome Project officially began on October 1, 1990, and was largely finished by the end of 2003. It was an international consortium that included research institutions in the U.S., U.K., France, Germany, Japan, and China. From its outset, the Human Genome Project had the following goals:

1. *To identify all human genes.* This involved mapping the locations of genes throughout the entire genome. The data from the Human Genome Project suggest that humans have about 20,000 to 25,000 different genes.

2. *To obtain the DNA sequence of the entire human genome.* The first draft of a nearly completed DNA sequence was published in February 2001, and a second draft was published in 2003. The entire genome is approximately 3.2 billion base pairs in length.

3. *To develop technology for the generation and management of human genome information.* Some of the efforts of the Human Genome Project have involved improvements in molecular genetic technology, such as gene cloning, DNA sequencing, and so forth. The Human Genome Project has also developed computer tools to allow scientists to easily access up-to-date information from the project and analytical tools to interpret genomic information.

4. *To analyze the genomes of model organisms.* These include *E. coli, S. cerevisiae, D. melanogaster, C. elegans, A. thaliana,* and *M. musculus.*

5. *To develop programs focused on understanding and addressing the ethical, legal, and social implications of the results obtained from the Human Genome Project.* The Human Genome Project raised many ethical issues regarding genetic information and genetic engineering. Who should have access to genetic information? Should employers, insurance companies, law enforcement agencies, and schools have access to our genetic makeup? Another controversial topic is gene patenting. Should the blueprints of life be considered patentable, like any other invention, or should there be limits to the patenting of genes? In the U.S., genes can be patented for a variety of reasons. For example, the patenting of genes has been associated with the commercial development of diagnostic tests for genetic diseases. Some argue that patenting fosters greater investment in research and development; others say it can impede basic research and scientific innovation. The answers to such questions are complex and will require discussion among many groups.

Some current and potential applications of the Human Genome Project include the improved diagnosis and treatment of genetic diseases such as cystic fibrosis, Huntington disease, and Duchenne muscular dystrophy. The project may also enable researchers to identify the genetic basis of common disorders such as cancer, diabetes, and heart disease, which involve alterations in several genes.

21.3 Proteomes

Learning Outcomes:
1. Distinguish between a proteome and a genome.
2. List the major categories of proteins in a proteome.
3. Explain how the number of proteins in an organism's proteome can be greater than the number of genes in its genome.

Thus far in this chapter, we have considered the genome characteristics of many different species, including humans. Because most genes encode proteins, a logical next step is to examine the functional roles of the proteins that a species can make. As mentioned, the entire collection of proteins that a cell or organism produces is called a proteome. As we move through the 21st century, a key challenge facing molecular biologists is the study of proteomes. Much like the study of genomes, this will require the collective contributions of many scientists, as well as improvements in technologies to investigate the complexities of the proteome. In this section, we will begin by considering the functional categories of proteins and then examine their relative abundance in the proteome. We also will explore the molecular mechanisms that cause an organism's proteome to be much larger than its genome.

The Proteome Is a Diverse Array of Proteins with Many Kinds of Functions

As we have seen, the genomes of simple, unicellular organisms such as bacteria and yeast contain thousands of structural genes, whereas the genomes of complex, multicellular organisms contain tens of thousands. Such genome sizes can produce proteomes with tens of thousands to hundreds of thousands of different proteins. To bring some order to this large amount of complex information, researchers often organize proteins into different categories based on their functions. **Table 21.3** describes some general categories of protein function and provides examples of each type. Many approaches are used to categorize proteins. Table 21.3 shows just one of the more general ways to categorize protein function. Note that the data of Figure 21.1

Table 21.3   Categories of Proteins Found in the Proteome

Function	Examples
Metabolic enzymes—accelerate chemical reactions in the cell.	Hexokinase: Phosphorylates glucose during the first step in glycolysis. Glycogen synthetase: Uses glucose to synthesize a large carbohydrate known as glycogen.
Structural proteins—provide shape and protection to cells.	Tubulin: Forms cytoskeletal structures known as microtubules. Collagen: Forms large fibers in the extracellular matrix (ECM) of animals.
Motor proteins—facilitate intracellular movements and the movements of whole cells.	Myosin: Involved in muscle cell contraction. Kinesin: Involved in the movement of chromosomes during cell division.
Cell-signaling proteins—allow cells to respond to environmental signals and send signals to each other.	Insulin: Influences target cell metabolism and growth. Insulin receptor: Recognizes insulin and initiates a cellular response.
Transport proteins—involved in the transport of ions and molecules across membranes and throughout the body.	Lactose permease: Transports lactose across the bacterial cell membrane. Hemoglobin: Found in red blood cells and transports oxygen throughout the body.
Gene expression and regulatory proteins—involved in transcription, mRNA modification, translation, and gene regulation.	Transcription factors: Regulate the expression of genes. Ribosomal proteins: Components of ribosomes, which are needed for the synthesis of new proteins.
Defense and protective proteins—help cells and organisms to fight disease and survive environmental stress.	Antibodies: Fight viral and bacterial infections in vertebrate species. Chaperones such as heat shock proteins: Play a role in protein folding, thereby helping cells cope with stresses such as abrupt increases in temperature.

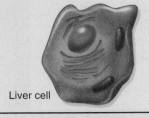

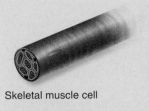

Liver cell

Abundance in genome	
Genes for metabolic enzymes	25%
Genes for structural proteins	5%
Genes for motor proteins	< 2%

Abundance in cell	
Metabolic enzymes	> 50%
Structural proteins	< 10%
Motor proteins	< 5%

Skeletal muscle cell

Abundance in genome	
Genes for metabolic enzymes	25%
Genes for structural proteins	5%
Genes for motor proteins	< 2%

Abundance in cell	
Metabolic enzymes	< 10%
Structural proteins	20–30%
Motor proteins	25–40%

Figure 21.9   A comparison of the proteomes in human liver and skeletal muscle cells. Because all cells of the human body carry the same genome, the percentages of proteins encoded in the genome are the same in each cell type. However, the relative amounts of proteins made in different cell types can be vastly different, as seen here.

Concept Check: *What genetic process explains the differences in protein abundance in liver cells versus muscle cells?*

displays the functions of proteins encoded by genes in a different, more detailed way.

The relative abundance of proteins can be viewed at two levels. First, we can consider abundance in the genome—the numbers of genes in the genome that encode a particular type or category of protein. For example, if an entire genome encodes 10,000 different types of proteins and 1,500 of these are different types of transporters, we would say that 15% of the genome is composed of transporters. However, such an analysis ignores the phenomenon that genes are expressed at different levels. In other words, various proteins are made in different amounts. Therefore, a second way to view protein abundance is to consider abundance in the cell—the amount of a given protein or protein category actually made by a living cell. For example, less than 1% of human genes encode proteins, such as collagen, that are found in the extracellular matrix (ECM). Even so, these genes are highly expressed in certain cells, so a large amount of this type of protein is made compared with other types.

Figure 21.9 is a general comparison of protein abundance in two cell types in humans: liver and muscle cells. Liver cells play a key role in metabolism, whereas muscle cells are involved in bodily movements. Both liver and muscle cells have the same genes. Therefore, at the level of the genome, the percentages of the different protein categories are identical. However, at the cellular level, the relative abundance of certain protein categories is quite different. Liver cells make a large number of different enzymes that play a role in the metabolism of fats, proteins, and carbohydrates. By comparison, their level of structural and motor proteins is relatively small. In contrast, muscle cells have fairly low levels of enzymes but make a high percentage of structural and motor proteins. These differences in protein composition between liver and muscle cells are largely due to differential gene regulation.

The Number of Different Proteins in a Species' Proteome Is Larger Than the Number of Genes in Its Genome

From the sequencing and analysis of genomes, researchers can identify all or nearly all of the genes of a given species. For example, the human genome is believed to contain between 20,000 and 25,000

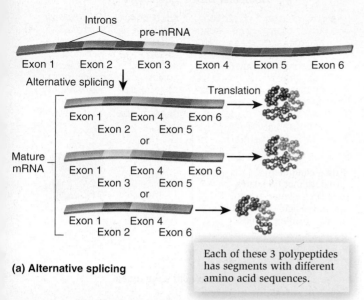

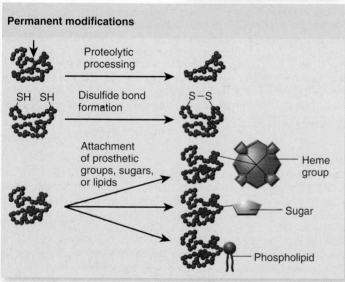

(a) Alternative splicing

Each of these 3 polypeptides has segments with different amino acid sequences.

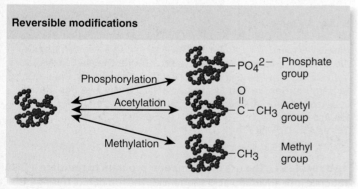

(b) Post-translational covalent modification

Figure 21.10 **Cellular mechanisms that increase protein diversity.** (a) Following alternative splicing, the pattern of exons in the resulting mature mRNA can be different, producing multiple types of polypeptides from the same gene. (b) In post-translational covalent modification, after a protein is made, it can be modified in a variety of ways, some of which are permanent and some reversible.

BioConnections: *Look back at Figure 9.13. How is reversible phosphorylation used in cell signaling?*

different genes that encode proteins. Even so, humans can make many more than 25,000 different types of proteins. How is this possible? The larger size of the proteome relative to the genome is primarily due to two types of cellular processes: alternative splicing and post-translational covalent modification, as described next.

Alternative Splicing   Due to **alternative splicing**, different mRNA molecules can be produced from the same pre-mRNA transcript (refer back to Figure 13.21). For many genes, a single pre-mRNA can be spliced in more than one way, resulting in the production of two or more polypeptides with different amino acid sequences (**Figure 21.10a**). The splicing is often cell specific or may be related to environmental conditions. Alternative splicing is widespread, particularly among more complex eukaryotes (refer back to Table 13.1). It can lead to the production of several or perhaps dozens of different polypeptide sequences from the same pre-mRNA. This greatly increases the number of proteins in a species' proteome, while minimizing the size of the genome.

Post-translational Covalent Modification   A second process that greatly diversifies the composition of a proteome is the phenomenon of **post-translational covalent modification**, the modification of the structure of a protein after its translation (**Figure 21.10b**). Such modifications can be permanent or reversible. Permanent modifications are often involved with the assembly and construction of functional proteins. These alterations include proteolytic processing (the cleavage of a polypeptide to a smaller unit), disulfide bond formation, and the attachment of prosthetic groups (such as heme, a component of hemoglobin), sugars, or lipids. In Chapter 6, we also considered the attachment of ubiquitin to a protein, which targets it for degradation. By comparison, reversible modifications, such as phosphorylation, acetylation, and methylation, often transiently affect the function of a protein (see Figure 21.10b). Molecules are covalently attached and later removed by cellular enzymes. Because a given type of protein may be subjected to several different types of modifications, this can greatly increase the forms of a particular protein that are found in a cell at any given time.

21.4   Bioinformatics

Learning Outcomes:
1. Describe how scientists use bioinformatics.
2. Define database.
3. Explain how the BLAST program works and why it is useful.

In the previous sections, we learned that the number of genes in a genome and the number of proteins made by a given cell type are extremely large. In the 1960s and 1970s, when the tools of molecular biology first became available, researchers tended to focus on the study of just one or a few genes and proteins at a time. Although this is a useful approach, scientists came to realize that certain properties of life emerge from complex interactions involving the expression of many genes and the functioning of many different proteins. The study of such complex interactions is called **systems biology**. This new perspective, coupled with the wealth of data produced by the genomics projects described previously in the chapter, challenged researchers to invent new tools to study many genes and proteins simultaneously.

As a very general definition, **bioinformatics** is the use of computers, mathematical tools, and statistical techniques to record, store, and analyze biological information. Why do we need bioinformatics? Simply put, the main issues are size and speed. Earlier in this chapter, we learned that the human genome has been sequenced and that it is approximately 3.2 billion base pairs long. A single person, or even a group of talented mathematicians, could not, in a reasonable length of time, analyze such an enormous amount of data. Instead, the data are put into computers, and scientists devise computational procedures to study and evaluate it.

In this section, we will consider the branch of bioinformatics that focuses on using molecular information to study biology. This area, also called **computational molecular biology**, uses computers to characterize the molecular components of living things. Molecular genetic data, which comes in the form of DNA, RNA, or protein sequences, are particularly amenable to computer analysis. In this section, we will first survey the fundamental concepts that underlie the analysis of genetic sequences. We will then consider how these methods are used to provide knowledge about how biology works at the molecular level.

Sequence Files Are Stored and Analyzed by Computers

The first steps in bioinformatics are to collect and store data in a computer. As an example, let's consider a gene sequence as a type of data. The gene sequence must first be determined experimentally using the technique of DNA sequencing. After the sequence is obtained, the next step is to put those data into a file on a computer. Typically, genetic sequence data are entered into a computer file by laboratory instruments that can read experimental data—such as data from a DNA-sequencing experiment—and enter the sequence directly into a computer.

Genetic sequence data in a computer data file can then be investigated in many different ways, corresponding to the many questions a researcher might ask about the sequence and its functional significance, including the following:

1. Does a sequence contain a gene?
2. Does a gene sequence contain a mutation that might cause a disease?
3. Where are functional sequences, such as promoters, regulatory sites, and splice sites, located within a particular gene?
4. From the sequence of a structural gene, what is the amino acid sequence of the polypeptide encoded by that gene?
5. Is there an evolutionary relationship between two or more genetic sequences?

To answer these and many other questions, computer programs have been written to analyze genetic sequences in particular ways. As an example, let's consider a computer program aimed at translating a DNA sequence into an amino acid sequence. **Figure 21.11** shows a short computer data file of a DNA sequence that is presumed to be part of the coding sequence of a structural gene. In this figure, only the coding strand of DNA is shown. A computer program can analyze this sequence and print out the possible amino acid sequences that this DNA sequence would encode. The program relies on the genetic code (refer back to Table 12.1). In the example shown in Figure 21.11, the computer program shows the results for all three possible reading frames, beginning at nucleotide 1, 2, or 3, respectively. In a newly

Computer DNA sequence file

```
5' GTGTCCACGC  GGTCCTGGAA  AACCCAGGCT  TGGGCAGGAA
   ACTCTCTGAC  TTTGGACAGG  AAACAAGCTA  TATTGAAGAC
   AACTGCAATC  AAAATGGTGC  CATATCACTG  ATCTTCTCAC
   TCAAAGAAGA  AGTTGGTGCA  TTGGCCAAAG  TATTGCGCTT
   ATTTGAGGAG  AATGATGTAA  ACCTGACCCA  CATTGAATCT
   AGACCTTCTC  GTTTAAAGAA  AGATGAGTAT  GAATTTTTCA
   CCCATTTGGA  TAAACGTAGC  CTGCCTGCTC  TGACAAACAT
   CATCAAGATC  TTGAGGCATG  ACATTGGTGC  CACTGTCCAT
   GAGCTTTCAC  GAGATAAGAA  GAAAGACACA  GTGCCCTGGT
   TTCCCAAG 3'
```

Run a computer program that translates this DNA sequence into an amino acid sequence in all 3 reading frames.

Possible amino acid sequences

5' ➞ 3' Frame 1
Val Ser Thr Arg Ser Trp Lys Thr Gln Ala Trp Ala Gly Asn Ser Leu Thr Leu Asp Arg Lys Gln Ala Ile Leu Lys Thr Thr Ala Ile Lys Met Val Pro Tyr His **STOP** Ser Ser His Ser Lys Lys Lys Leu Val His Trp Pro Lys Tyr Cys Ala Tyr Leu Arg Arg Met Met **STOP** Thr **STOP** Pro Thr Leu Asn Leu Asp Leu Leu Val **STOP** Arg Lys Met Ser Met Asn Phe Ser Pro Ile Trp Ile Asn Val Ala Cys Leu Leu **STOP** Gln Thr Ser Ser Arg Ser **STOP** Gly Met Thr Leu Val Pro Leu Ser Met Ser Phe His Glu Ile Arg Arg Lys Thr Gln Cys Pro Gly Ser Gln

5' ➞ 3' Frame 2
Cys Pro Arg Gly Pro Gly Lys Pro Arg Leu Gly Gln Glu Thr Leu **STOP** Leu Trp Thr Gly Asn Lys Leu Tyr **STOP** Arg Gln Leu Gln Ser Lys Trp Cys His Ile Thr Asp Leu Leu Thr Gln Arg Arg Ser Trp Cys Ile Gly Gln Ser Ile Ala Leu Ile **STOP** Gly Glu **STOP** Cys Lys Pro Asp Pro His **STOP** Ile **STOP** Thr Phe Ser Phe Lys Glu Arg **STOP** Val **STOP** Ile Phe His Pro Phe Gly **STOP** Thr **STOP** Pro Ala Cys Ser Asp Lys His His Gln Asp Leu Glu Ala **STOP** His Trp Cys His Cys Pro **STOP** Ala Phe Thr Arg **STOP** Glu Glu Arg His Ser Ala Leu Val Pro Lys

5' ➞ 3' Frame 3
Val His Ala Val Leu Glu Asn Pro Gly Leu Gly Arg Lys Leu Ser Asp Phe Gly Gln Glu Thr Ser Tyr Ile Glu Asp Asn Cys Asn Gln Asn Gly Ala Ile Ser Leu Ile Phe Ser Leu Lys Glu Glu Val Gly Ala Leu Ala Lys Val Leu Arg Leu Phe Glu Glu Asn Asp Val Asn Leu Thr His Ile Glu Ser Arg Pro Ser Arg Leu Lys Lys Asp Glu Tyr Glu Phe Phe Thr His Leu Asp Lys Arg Ser Leu Pro Ala Leu Thr Asn Ile Ile Lys Ile Leu Arg His Asp Ile Gly Ala Thr Val His Glu Leu Ser Arg Asp Lys Lys Lys Asp Thr Val Pro Trp Phe Pro

Figure 21.11   The use of a computer program to translate a DNA sequence into an amino acid sequence. The top part of this figure shows the sequence of a segment of the coding strand of a structural gene (divided into groups of 10 bases for ease of reading). A computer program translates the DNA sequence into an amino acid sequence based on the genetic code. The program produces three different amino acid sequences, as shown at the bottom of the figure. In this example, reading frame 3 is likely to be the correct one because it does not contain any stop codons.

Concept Check: *Why is it helpful to use a computer program to translate a genetic sequence rather than doing it by hand?*

Table 21.4 Examples of Major Genetic Databases

Nucleotide sequences	DNA sequence data are collected into three internationally collaborating databases: GenBank (a U.S. database), EMBL (European Molecular Biology Laboratory Nucleotide Sequence Database), and DDBJ (DNA Data Bank of Japan). These databases receive sequence and sequence annotation data from genome projects, sequencing centers, individual scientists, and patent offices. New and updated entries are exchanged daily.
Amino acid sequences	Protein sequence data are collected into a few international databases, including Swiss-Prot (Swiss protein database), PIR (Protein Information Resource), TrEMBL (translated sequences from the EMBL database), and Genpept (translated peptide sequences from the GenBank database).

obtained DNA sequence, a researcher would not know the proper reading frame—the series of codons read in groups of three, which begins with the start codon. Therefore, the computer program provides all three. If you look at the results, reading frames 1 and 2 include several stop codons, whereas reading frame 3 does not. From these results, reading frame 3 is likely to be the correct one. Also, for a new DNA sequence, a researcher may not know which DNA strand is the coding strand. Therefore, the sequence of the other DNA strand, which is not shown in this figure, would also be analyzed by this computer program.

The Scientific Community Has Collected Computer Data Files and Stored Them in Large Databases

Over the past several decades, the amount of genetic information generated by researchers and clinicians has become enormous. With these advances, scientists have realized that another critical use of computers is to store the staggering amount of data produced from genetic research.

A large amount of data that is collected, stored in a single location, and organized for rapid search and retrieval is called a **database**. The files within databases are often annotated, which means they contain a concise description of each gene sequence, the name of the organism from which the sequence was obtained, and the function of the encoded protein, if it is known. The file may also provide a published reference that contains the sequence.

The research community has collected genetic information from thousands of research laboratories and created several large databases. **Table 21.4** describes some of the major genetic databases in use worldwide, all of which can be accessed online. These databases enable researchers to access and compare genetic sequences that are obtained by many laboratories. Later in this chapter, we will learn how researchers use databases to analyze genetic sequences.

Many programs are freely available over the Internet to utilize the information within databases. For example, the National Center for Biotechnology Information (NCBI), which is a part of the U.S. National Institutes of Health, manages a website called "Tools for Data Mining," where anyone can run various types of programs that are used to analyze genetic sequences (www.ncbi.nlm.nih.gov/Tools). Like conventional mining, in which a precious mineral is extracted from a large area of land, **data mining** is the extraction of useful information and often previously unknown relationships from sequence files and large databases.

Computer Programs Can Identify Homologous Sequences

Let's now turn our attention to genes that are evolutionarily related. Organisms that are closely related evolutionarily tend to have genes with similar DNA sequences. As an example, let's consider the gene that encodes β-globin. As described earlier in Figure 21.8, β-globin is a polypeptide found in hemoglobin, which carries oxygen in red blood cells. The β-globin gene is found in humans and other vertebrates.

Figure 21.12a compares a short region of the β-globin gene from the laboratory mouse (*Mus musculus*) with that from a laboratory rat (*Rattus norvegicus*). As you can see, the gene sequences are similar

Mouse

GGGCAGGTTGGTATCCAGGTTACAAGG**C**AGCTC**AC**AAGTAGAAG**CTG**GGTGCTTGGAGAC
|||||||||||||||||||||||||||| ||||| |||||| |||||| ||||||||||||
GGGCAGGTTGGTATCCAGGTTACAAGG**T**AGCTC**CT**AAGTAGAAG**TTT**GGTGCTTGGAGAC

Rat

(a) A comparison of one DNA strand of the mouse and rat β-globin genes

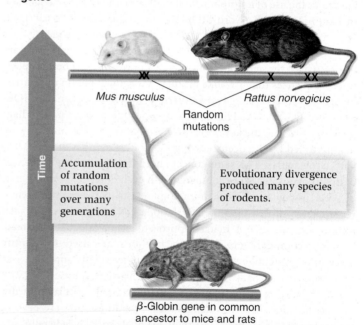

(b) The formation of homologous β-globin genes during evolution of mice and rats

Figure 21.12 Structure and formation of the homologous β-globin genes in mice and rats. (a) A comparison of a short region of the gene that encodes β-globin in laboratory mice (*Mus musculus*) and rats (*Rattus norvegicus*). Only one DNA strand is shown. Bases that are identical between the two sequences are connected by a vertical line. (b) Schematic view of the formation of these homologous β-globin genes during evolution. An ancestral β-globin gene was found in an ancestor common to both mice and rats. This ancestral species later diverged into different species, which gave rise to modern rodent species. During this process, the β-globin genes accumulated different random mutations, resulting in DNA sequences that are slightly different from each other.

Concept Check: *Is it possible for orthologs from two different species to have exactly the same DNA sequence? Explain.*

but not identical. In this 60-nucleotide sequence, five differences are observed. The reason for the sequence similarity is that the genes are derived from the same ancestral gene. This idea is shown schematically in **Figure 21.12b**. An ancestral gene was found in a rodent species that was a common ancestor to both mice and rats. During evolution, this ancestral species diverged into different species, which eventually gave rise to several modern rodent species, including mice and rats. Following divergence, the β-globin genes accumulated distinct mutations that produced somewhat different base sequences for this gene. Therefore, in mice and rats, the β-globin genes have homologous sequences—sequences that are similar because they are derived from the same ancestral gene, but not identical because each species has accumulated a few different random mutations. Homologous genes in different species are also called orthologous genes or **orthologs**. Analyzing orthologs helps biologists understand the evolutionary relationships among modern species, a topic that we will consider in more detail in Units IV and V.

How do researchers, with the aid of computers, determine if two genes are homologous to each other? To evaluate the similarity between two sequences, a matrix can be constructed. **Figure 21.13** illustrates the use of a simplified dot matrix to evaluate two sequences. In Figure 21.13a, the word BIOLOGY is compared with itself. Each point in the grid corresponds to one position of each sequence. The matrix allows all such pairs to be compared simultaneously. Dots are placed where the same letter occurs at the two corresponding positions. Sequences that are alike produce a diagonal line on the matrix. Figure 21.13b compares two similar but different sequences: BIOLOGY and ECOLOGY. This comparison produces only a partial diagonal line. Overall, the key observation is that regions of similarity are distinguished by the occurrence of many dots along a diagonal line within the matrix. This same concept holds true when base sequences of homologous genes are compared with each other.

To discover whether homology exists between two genes, researchers must compare relatively long DNA sequences. For such long sequences, a dot matrix approach is not adequate. Instead, dynamic computer programming methods are used to identify optimal alignments between genetic sequences. This approach was first proposed by Saul Needleman and Christian Wunsch in 1970. Dynamic programming methods are theoretically similar to a dot matrix, but they involve mathematical operations that are beyond the scope of this textbook. In their original work, Needleman and Wunsch demonstrated that whale myoglobin and human β-globin genes have similar sequences.

A Database Can Be Searched to Identify Similar Sequences and Thereby Infer Homology and Gene Function

Why is it useful to identify homology between different genes? Because they are derived from the same ancestral gene, homologous genes usually carry out similar or identical functions. In many cases, the first way to identify the function of a newly determined gene sequence is to find a homologous gene whose function is already known. An example is the gene that is altered in cystic fibrosis patients. After this gene was identified in humans, bioinformatic methods revealed that it is homologous to several genes found in other species. A few of the

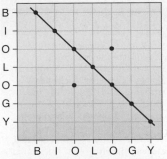
(a) Comparison of two identical words

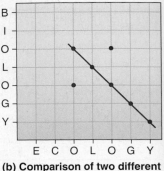
(b) Comparison of two different words

Figure 21.13 The use of a simple dot matrix. In these comparisons, a diagonal line indicates sequence similarity. **(a)** The word BIOLOGY is compared with itself. Dots are placed where the same letter occurs at the two corresponding positions. Notice the diagonal line that is formed. **(b)** Two similar but different sequences, BIOLOGY and ECOLOGY, are compared with each other. Notice that only a partial line is formed by this comparison.

homologous genes were already known to encode proteins that function in the transport of ions and small molecules across the plasma membrane. This observation provided an important clue that cystic fibrosis involves a defect in membrane transport.

The ability of computer programs to identify homology between genetic sequences provides a powerful tool for predicting the function of genetic sequences. In 1990, American mathematician Stephen Altschul, his colleague biologist David Lipman, and their coworkers developed a program called **BLAST** (for basic local alignment search tool). The BLAST program has been described by many biologists as the single most important tool in computational molecular biology. This computer program can start with a particular genetic sequence—either a nucleotide or an amino acid sequence—and then locate homologous sequences within a large database.

As an example of how the BLAST program works, let's consider the human enzyme phenylalanine hydroxylase, which functions in the metabolism of phenylalanine, an amino acid. Recessive mutations in the gene that encodes this enzyme are responsible for the disease called phenylketonuria (PKU). The computational experiment shown in **Table 21.5** started with the amino acid sequence of this protein and used the BLAST program to search the Swiss-Prot database, which contains hundreds of thousands of different protein sequences. The BLAST program can determine which sequences in the Swiss-Prot database are the closest matches to the amino acid sequence of human phenylalanine hydroxylase. Table 21.5 shows some of the results, which includes 10 of the matches to human phenylalanine hydroxylase that were identified by the program. Because this enzyme is found in nearly all eukaryotic species, the program identified phenylalanine hydroxylase from many different species. The column to the right of the match number shows the percentage of amino acids that are identical between the species indicated and the human sequence. Because the human phenylalanine hydroxylase sequence is already in the Swiss-Prot database, the closest match of human phenylalanine hydroxylase is to itself. The next nine sequences are in order of similarity. The next most similar sequence is from the orangutan, a primate that is a close relative of humans. This is followed by two other mammals, the mouse and rat, and then five vertebrates that are not mammals. The 10th best match is from *Drosophila*, an invertebrate.

Table 21.5 Results from a BLAST Program Comparing Human Phenylalanine Hydroxylase with Database Sequences

Match	Percentage of identical amino acids*	Species	Function of sequence†
1	100	Human (*Homo sapiens*)	Phenylalanine hydroxylase
2	99	Orangutan (*Pongo pygmaeus*)	Phenylalanine hydroxylase
3	95	Mouse (*Mus musculus*)	Phenylalanine hydroxylase
4	95	Rat (*Rattus norvegicus*)	Phenylalanine hydroxylase
5	89	Chicken (*Gallus gallus*)	Phenylalanine hydroxylase
6	82	Pipid frog (*Xenopus tropicalis*)	Phenylalanine hydroxylase
7	82	Green pufferfish (*Tetraodon nigroviridis*)	Phenylalanine hydroxylase
8	82	Zebrafish (*Danio rerio*)	Phenylalanine hydroxylase
9	80	Japanese pufferfish (*Takifugu rubripes*)	Phenylalanine hydroxylase
10	75	Fruit fly (*Drosophila melanogaster*)	Phenylalanine hydroxylase

*The number indicates the percentage of amino acids that are identical with the amino acid sequence of human phenylalanine hydroxylase. Note: These matches were randomly selected from a long list of matches.

†In some cases, the function of the sequence was determined by biochemical assay. In other cases, the function was inferred due to the high degree of sequence similarity with other species.

As you may have noticed, the order of the matches follows the evolutionary relatedness of the various species to humans. The similarity between any two sequences is related to the time that has passed since they diverged from a common ancestor. Among the species listed in this table, humans are most closely related to the orangutan, other mammals, other vertebrates, and finally invertebrates.

Overall, Table 21.5 is an example of the remarkable computational abilities of current computer technology. In less than a minute, the amino acid sequence of human phenylalanine hydroxylase can be compared with hundreds of thousands of different sequences to yield the data shown in this table! The main power of the BLAST program is its use with newly identified sequences, in which a researcher does not know the function of a gene or an encoded protein. When the BLAST program identifies a match to a sequence whose function is already known, it is likely that the newly identified sequence has an identical or similar function.

Summary of Key Concepts

21.1 Bacterial and Archaeal Genomes

- The genome is the complete genetic makeup of a cell, organism, or species.
- Bacterial and archaeal genomes are typically a single circular chromosome with a few million base pairs of DNA. Such genomes usually have a few thousand different genes. Bacteria often have plasmids (Table 21.1).

- Venter, Smith, and colleagues used a shotgun DNA sequencing strategy to sequence the first genome, that of the bacterium *Haemophilus influenzae* (Figure 21.1).

21.2 Eukaryotic Genomes

- The nuclear genomes of eukaryotic species are composed of sets of linear chromosomes with a total length of several million to billions of base pairs. They typically contain several thousand to tens of thousands of genes (Table 21.2).
- Genome sizes vary among eukaryotic species. In many cases, variation is due to the accumulation of noncoding regions of DNA, particularly repetitive DNA sequences (Figures 21.2, 21.3).
- Much of the repetitive DNA is derived from transposable elements, segments of DNA that can move from one site to another through a process called transposition (Figure 21.4).
- Transposable elements fall into two groups that move by different molecular mechanisms. DNA transposons move by a cut-and-paste mechanism facilitated by the enzyme transposase. Retroelements move to new sites in the genome via RNA intermediates (Figures 21.5, 21.6).
- Gene duplication may occur by a misaligned crossover during meiosis. This is one mechanism that can produce a gene family, two or more homologous genes in a species that have related functions (Figures 21.7, 21.8).
- The Human Genome Project, an international effort to map and sequence the entire human genome, was completed by an international consortium in 2003.

21.3 Proteomes

- A proteome is the collection of proteins that a given cell or species makes.
- Proteins are often placed into broad categories based on their functions. These include metabolic enzymes, structural proteins, motor proteins, cell-signaling proteins, transport proteins, proteins involved with gene expression and regulation, and those involved with protection and defense (Table 21.3).
- Protein abundance refers to the number of genes encoding a particular type of protein or the amount of a protein made by a cell (Figure 21.9).
- Protein diversity increases via mechanisms such as alternative splicing and post-translational covalent modifications (Figure 21.10).

21.4 Bioinformatics

- Bioinformatics involves the use of computers, mathematical tools, and statistical techniques to record, store, and analyze biological information, particularly genetic data such as DNA and protein sequences.
- Genetic information is stored in large genetics databases that are analyzed using computer programs (Figure 21.11, Table 21.4).
- Homologous genes are derived from the same ancestral gene and have accumulated random mutations that make their sequences slightly different (Figure 21.12).
- Scientists use computer programs to determine if gene sequences are homologous (Figure 21.13).
- Computer programs, such as BLAST, identify homologous genes that are found in a database (Table 21.5).

Assess and Discuss

Test Yourself

1. The entire collection of proteins produced by a cell or organism is
   - a. a genome.
   - b. bioinformatics.
   - c. a proteome.
   - d. a gene family.
   - e. a protein family.

2. Important reasons for studying the genomes of bacteria and archaea include all of the following except
   - a. it may provide information that helps us understand how bacteria infect other organisms.
   - b. it may provide a basic understanding of cellular processes that allow us to determine eukaryotic cellular function.
   - c. it may provide the means of understanding evolutionary processes.
   - d. it will reveal the approximate number of genes that an organism has in its genome.
   - e. all of the above are important reasons.

3. The enzyme that allows short segments of DNA to move within a cell from one location in the genome to another is
   - a. transposase.
   - b. DNA polymerase.
   - c. protease.
   - d. restriction endonuclease.
   - e. DNA ligase.

4. A gene family includes
   - a. one specific gene found in several different species.
   - b. all of the genes on the same chromosome.
   - c. two or more homologous genes found within a single species.
   - d. genes that code for structural proteins.
   - e. both a and c.

5. Which of the following was *not* a goal of the Human Genome Project?
   - a. identify all human genes
   - b. sequence the entire human genome
   - c. address the legal and ethical implications resulting from the project
   - d. develop programs to manage the information gathered from the project
   - e. be able to clone a human

6. Bioinformatics is
   - a. the analysis of DNA by molecular techniques.
   - b. the use of computers to analyze and store biological information.
   - c. a collection of gene sequences from a single individual.
   - d. cloning.
   - e. all of the above.

7. Using bioinformatics, evolutionary relationships among species can be characterized by identifying and analyzing
   - a. phenotypes of selected organisms.
   - b. homologous DNA sequences from different organisms.
   - c. fossils of ancestral species.
   - d. all of the above.
   - e. a and b only.

8. Repetitive sequences
   - a. are short DNA sequences that are found many times throughout the genome.
   - b. may be multiple copies of the same gene found in the genome.
   - c. are more common in eukaryotes.
   - d. all of the above
   - e. a and c only

9. The BLAST program is a tool for
   - a. inserting many DNA fragments into a cell at the same time.
   - b. translating a DNA sequence into an amino acid sequence.
   - c. identifying homology between a selected sequence and genetic sequences in databases.
   - d. all of the above.
   - e. both b and c.

10. Let's suppose you used the BLAST program beginning with a DNA sequence from a *Drosophila* hexokinase gene. (Hexokinase is an enzyme involved with glucose metabolism.) Which of the following choices would you expect to be the closest match?
    - a. a *Drosophila* globin gene
    - b. a human hexokinase gene
    - c. a house fly hexokinase gene
    - d. an *Arabidopsis* hexokinase gene
    - e. an amoeba hexokinase gene

Conceptual Questions

1. Briefly describe whether or not each of the following could be appropriately described as a genome.
   - a. the *E. coli* chromosome
   - b. human chromosome 11
   - c. a complete set of 10 chromosomes in corn
   - d. a copy of the single-stranded RNA packaged into human immunodeficiency virus (HIV)

2. Describe two main reasons why the proteomes of eukaryotes species are usually much larger than their genomes.

3. A principle of biology is that *the genetic material provides a blueprint for reproduction*. Explain the roles of the genome and proteome with regard to this principle.

Collaborative Questions

1. Compare and contrast the genomes of bacteria, archaea, and eukaryotes.

2. The following is a DNA sequence from one strand of a gene. (The bases are shown in groups of 10 each.) Go to the NCBI website (www.ncbi.nlm.nih.gov/Tools) and select the Basic Local Alignment Search Tool (BLAST) program to determine which gene it is and in which species it is found.

```
GTGAAGGCTC ATGGCAAGAA AGTGCTCGGT GCCTTTAGTG
ATGGCCTGGC TCACCTGGAC AACCTCAAGG GCACCTTTGC
CACACTGAGT GAGCTGCACT GTGACAAGCT GCACGTGGAT
CCTGAGAACT TCAGGGTGAG TCTATGGGAC GCTTGATGTT
TTCTTTCCCC TTCTTTTCTA TGGTTAAGTT CATGTCATAG
GAAGGGGATA AGTAACAGGG TACAGTTTAG AATGGGAAAC
AGACGAATGA TTGCATCAGT GTGGAAGTCT CAGGATCGTT
TTAGTTTCTT TTATTTGCTG TTCATAACAA TTGTTTTCTT
TTGTTTAATT CTTGCTTTCT TTTTTTTTCT TCTCCGCAAT
```

Online Resource

www.brookerbiology.com

Stay a step ahead in your studies with animations that bring concepts to life and practice tests to assess your understanding. Your instructor may also recommend the interactive eBook, individualized learning tools, and more.

UNIT IV
EVOLUTION

Evolution is a heritable change in one or more characteristics of a population from one generation to the next. This process not only alters the characteristics of populations, it also leads to the formation of new species.

We will begin Unit IV with a discussion of the hypotheses that have been proposed to explain the origin of life on Earth, and then examine a timeline for the evolution of species from 4 billion years ago to the present. In Chapter 23, you will be introduced to the fundamental concepts of evolution, with an emphasis on natural selection. We will examine observations of evolutionary change, which includes (1) the fossil record, (2) a comparison of the characteristics of modern species, and (3) an analysis of molecular data. Chapter 24 continues our discussion of evolution at the molecular level and focuses on how changes in allele and genotype frequencies from one generation to the next are driven by a variety of different factors. By comparison, Chapter 25 shifts the emphasis of evolution to the level of species. We will examine how species are identified and discuss the mechanisms by which new species arise via evolution. Finally, in Chapter 26, we will examine how biologists determine the evolutionary relationships among different species and produce "trees" that describe those relationships.

The following biology principles will be emphasized in this unit:

- **Populations of organisms evolve from one generation to the next.** *This concept will be emphasized throughout the entire unit.*

- **Living organisms interact with their environment.** *As discussed in Chapters 23 and 24, natural selection is a process in which certain individuals have greater reproductive success. This success is often due to their ability to survive in a given environment.*

- **Structure determines function.** *Chapters 23 and 24 will also consider how structural features change during the evolution of new species. Such changes are related to changes in function.*

- **All species (past and present) are related by an evolutionary history.** *Chapter 26 is devoted to examining how biologists determine evolutionary relationships among different species.*

- **Biology is an experimental science.** *Every chapter has a Feature Investigation that describes a pivotal experiment that provided insights into our understanding of evolution.*

The Origin and History of Life on Earth

22

A fossil fish. This 50-million-year-old fossil of a unicorn fish (*Naso rectifrons*) is an example of the many different kinds of organisms that have existed during the history of life on Earth.

The amazing origin of the universe is difficult to comprehend. Astronomers think the universe began with a cosmic explosion called the Big Bang about 13.7 billion years ago (bya), when the first clouds of the elements hydrogen and helium were formed. Over a long time period, gravitational forces collapsed these clouds to create stars that converted hydrogen and helium into heavier elements, including carbon, nitrogen, and oxygen, which are the atomic building blocks of life on Earth. These elements were returned to interstellar space by exploding stars called supernovas, which created clouds in which simple molecules such as water, carbon monoxide, and hydrocarbons formed. The clouds then collapsed to make a new generation of stars and solar systems.

Our solar system began about 4.6 bya after one or more local supernova explosions. According to one widely accepted scenario, hundreds of planetesimals consisting of bodies such as asteroids and comets, occupied the region where Venus, Earth, and Mars are now found. The Earth, which is estimated to be 4.55 billion years old, grew from the aggregation of such planetesimals over a period of 100 to 200 million years. For the

first half billion years or so after its formation, the Earth was too hot to allow liquid water to accumulate on its surface. By 4 bya, the Earth had cooled enough for the outer layers of the planet to solidify and for oceans to begin to form.

The period between 4.0 and 3.5 bya marked the emergence of life on our planet. The first forms of life that we know about produced well-preserved microscopic fossils, such as those found in western Australia. These fossils, estimated to be about 3.5 billion years old, resemble modern cyanobacteria, which are photosynthetic bacteria (**Figure 22.1**). Researchers cannot travel back through time and observe how the first life-forms came into being. However, plausible hypotheses regarding how life first arose have emerged from our understanding of modern life.

This chapter, the first in the Evolution unit, emphasizes when particular forms of life arose. The first section surveys a variety of hypotheses regarding (1) the origin of organic molecules on Earth, (2) the formation of complex molecules such as DNA, RNA, and proteins, (3) the formation of primitive cell-like structures, and (4) the process that gave rise to the first living cells. We will then consider fossils, the preserved remains of organisms that existed in the past. Starting 3.5 bya, the formation of fossils, such as the one shown in the chapter opening photo, has provided biologists with evidence of the history of life on Earth from its earliest beginnings to the present day. The last section provides a broad overview of the geologic time scale and the major events in the history of life on Earth.

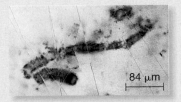

(a) Fossil prokaryote

(b) Modern cyanobacteria

Figure 22.1 Earliest fossils and living cyanobacteria. (a) A fossilized prokaryote about 3.5 billion years old that is thought to be an early cyanobacterium. (b) A modern cyanobacterium, which has a similar morphology. Cyanobacterial cells are connected to each other to form chains, as shown here.

22.1 Origin of Life on Earth

Learning Outcomes:

1. Outline the four overlapping stages that are hypothesized to have led to the origin of life.
2. List various hypotheses about how complex organic molecules formed.
3. Analyze the results of Bartel and Szostak that indicated that chemical evolution is possible.
4. Explain the concept of an RNA world and how it could have evolved into a DNA/RNA/protein world.

As we have seen, living cells are complex collections of molecules and macromolecules. DNA stores genetic information, RNA acts as an intermediary in the process of protein synthesis and plays other important roles, and proteins form the foundation for the structure and activities of living cells. Life as we know it requires this interplay between DNA, RNA, and proteins for its existence and perpetuation. On modern Earth, every living cell is made from a pre-existing cell.

But how did life get started? As described in Chapter 1, living organisms have several characteristics that distinguish them from nonliving materials. Because DNA, RNA, and proteins are the central players in the enterprise of life, scientists who are interested in the origin of life have focused much of their attention on the formation of these macromolecules and their building blocks, namely, nucleotides and amino acids. To understand the origin of life, we can view the process as occurring in four overlapping stages:

Stage 1: Nucleotides and amino acids were produced prior to the existence of cells.

Stage 2: Nucleotides became polymerized to form RNA and/or DNA, and amino acids become polymerized to form proteins.

Stage 3: Polymers became enclosed in membranes.

Stage 4: Polymers enclosed in membranes acquired cellular properties.

Researchers have followed a variety of experimental approaches to determine how life may have begun, including the synthesis of organic molecules in the laboratory without the presence of living cells or cellular material. This work has led researchers to propose a variety of hypotheses regarding the origin of life. In this section, we will examine the origin of life at each of these stages and consider a few scientific viewpoints that wrestle with the question, "How did life on Earth begin?"

Stage 1: Organic Molecules Formed Prior to the Existence of Cells

Let's begin our inquiry into the first stage of the origin of life by considering how nucleotides and amino acids may have been made prior to the existence of living cells. In the 1920s, the Russian biochemist Alexander Oparin and the Scottish biologist J.B.S. Haldane independently proposed that organic molecules, such as nucleotides and amino acids, arose spontaneously under the conditions that occurred on early Earth. According to this hypothesis, the spontaneous appearance of organic molecules produced what they called a "primordial soup," which eventually gave rise to living cells.

The conditions on early Earth, which were much different from today, may have been more conducive to the spontaneous formation of organic molecules. Current hypotheses suggest that organic molecules, and eventually macromolecules, formed spontaneously. This is termed prebiotic (before life) or abiotic (without life) synthesis. These slowly forming organic molecules accumulated because there was little free oxygen gas, so they were not spontaneously oxidized, and there were as yet no living organisms, so they were also not metabolized. The slow accumulation of these molecules in the early oceans over a long period of time formed what is now called the **prebiotic soup**. The formation of this medium was a key event that preceded the origin of life.

Though most scientists agree that life originated from the assemblage of nonliving matter on early Earth, the mechanism of how and where these molecules originated is widely debated. Many intriguing hypotheses have been proposed, which are not mutually exclusive. A few of the more widely debated ideas are the reducing atmosphere hypothesis, the extraterrestrial hypothesis, and the deep-sea vent hypothesis.

Reducing Atmosphere Hypothesis Based largely on geological data, many scientists in the 1950s proposed that the atmosphere on early Earth was rich in water vapor (H_2O), hydrogen gas (H_2), methane (CH_4), and ammonia (NH_3). These components, along with a lack of atmospheric oxygen (O_2), produce a reducing atmosphere because methane and ammonia readily give up electrons to other molecules, thereby reducing them. Such oxidation-reduction reactions, or redox reactions, are required for the formation of complex organic molecules from simple inorganic molecules.

In 1953, American chemist Stanley Miller, a student in the laboratory of the physical chemist Harold Urey, was the first scientist to use experimentation to test whether the prebiotic synthesis of organic molecules is possible. His experimental apparatus was intended to simulate the conditions on early Earth that were postulated in the 1950s (**Figure 22.2**). Water vapor from a flask of boiling water rose into another chamber containing hydrogen gas (H_2), methane (CH_4), and ammonia (NH_3). Miller inserted two electrodes that sent electrical discharges into the chamber to simulate lightning bolts. A condenser jacket cooled some of the gases from the chamber, causing droplets to form that fell into a trap. He then took samples from this trap for chemical analysis. In his first experiments, he observed the formation of hydrogen cyanide (HCN) and formaldehyde (CH_2O). Such molecules are precursors of more complex organic molecules. These precursors also combined to make larger molecules such as the amino acid glycine. At the end of 1 week of operation, 10–15% of the carbon had been incorporated into organic compounds. Later experiments by Miller and others demonstrated the formation of sugars, a few types of amino acids, lipids, and nitrogenous bases found in nucleic acids (for example, adenine).

In a study published in 2011, researchers analyzed samples that Miller had preserved from a 1958 experiment in which he used a mixture of CH_4, NH_3, hydrogen sulfide (H_2S), and carbon dioxide (CO_2). For unknown reasons, Miller had not analyzed what products were made in this experiment. When these preserved samples were analyzed using modern technology, they were found to contain 23 different amino acids and 4 amines (another type of organic molecule), more organic compounds than seen in Miller's classic experiments.

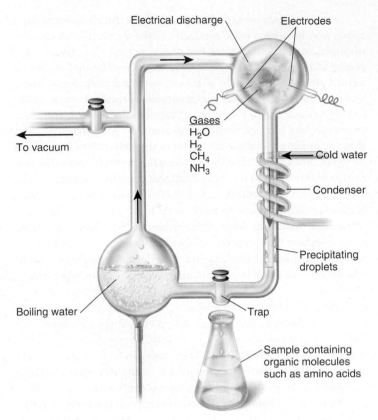

Gases
H_2O
H_2
CH_4
NH_3

Figure 22.2 Testing the reducing atmosphere hypothesis for the origin of life—the Miller and Urey experiment.

BIOLOGY PRINCIPLE Biology is an experimental science. By conducting experiments, researchers were able to demonstrate the feasibility of the synthesis of organic molecules prior to the emergence of living cells.

Concept Check: *With regard to the origin of life, why are biologists interested in the prebiotic synthesis of organic molecules?*

Why were these studies important? The work of Miller and Urey was the first attempt to apply scientific experimentation to our quest to understand the origin of life. Their pioneering strategy showed that the prebiotic synthesis of organic molecules is possible, although it could not prove that it really happened that way. In spite of the importance of these studies, critics of the so-called reducing atmosphere hypothesis have argued that Miller and Urey were wrong about the composition of early Earth's environment. More recently, many scientists have suggested that the atmosphere on early Earth was not reducing, but instead was a neutral environment composed mostly of carbon monoxide (CO), carbon dioxide (CO_2), nitrogen gas (N_2), and H_2O. These newer ideas are derived from studies of volcanic gas, which has much more CO_2 and N_2 than CH_4 and NH_3, and from the observation that ultraviolet (UV) radiation destroys CH_4 and NH_3, so these molecules would have been short-lived on early Earth, which had high levels of UV radiation. Nevertheless, since the experiments of Miller and Urey, many newer investigations have shown that organic molecules can be made under a variety of conditions. For example, organic molecules can be made prebiotically from a neutral environment composed primarily of CO, CO_2, N_2, and H_2O.

Extraterrestrial Hypothesis Many scientists have argued that sufficient organic molecules may have been present in the materials from asteroids and comets that reached the surface of early Earth in the form of meteorites. A significant proportion of meteorites belong to a class known as carbonaceous chondrites. Such meteorites may contain a substantial amount of organic carbon, including amino acids and nucleic acid bases. Based on this observation, some scientists have postulated that such meteorites could have transported a significant amount of organic molecules to early Earth.

Opponents of this hypothesis argue that most of this material would have been destroyed by the intense heating that accompanies the passage of large bodies through the atmosphere and their subsequent collision with the surface of the Earth. Though some organic molecules are known to reach the Earth via such meteorites, the degree to which heat would have destroyed many of the organic molecules remains a matter of controversy.

Deep-Sea Vent Hypothesis In 1988, the German lawyer and organic chemist Günter Wächtershäuser proposed that key organic molecules may have originated in deep-sea vents, which are cracks in the Earth's surface where superheated water rich in metal ions and hydrogen sulfide (H_2S) mixes abruptly with cold seawater. These vents release hot gaseous substances from the interior of the Earth at temperatures in excess of 300°C (572°F). Supporters of this hypothesis propose that biologically important molecules may have been formed in the temperature gradient between the extremely hot vent water and the cold water that surrounds the vent (**Figure 22.3a**).

Experimentally, the temperatures within this gradient are known to be suitable for the synthesis of molecules that form components of biological molecules. For example, the reaction between iron and H_2S yields pyrites and H_2 and has been shown to provide the energy necessary for the reduction of N_2 to NH_3. Nitrogen is an essential component of both nucleic acids and amino acids—the molecular building blocks of life. But N_2, which is found abundantly on Earth, is chemically inert, so it is unlikely to have given rise to life. The conversion of N_2 to NH_3 at deep-sea vents may have led to the production of amino acids and nucleic acids.

Interestingly, complex biological communities are found in the vicinity of modern deep-sea vents. Various types of fish, worms, clams, crabs, shrimp, and bacteria are found in significant abundance in those areas (**Figure 22.3b**). Unlike most other forms of life on our planet, these organisms receive their energy from chemicals in the vent and not from the Sun. In 2007, American scientist Timothy Kusky and colleagues discovered 1.43 billion-year-old fossils of deep-sea microbes near ancient deep-sea vents. This study provided more evidence that life may have originated on the bottom of the ocean. However, debate continues as to the primary way that organic molecules were made prior to the existence of life on Earth.

Stage 2: Organic Polymers May Have Formed on the Surface of Clay

The preceding three hypotheses provide reasonable mechanisms whereby small organic molecules could have accumulated on early Earth. Scientists hypothesize that the second stage in the origin of life was a period in which simple organic molecules polymerized to

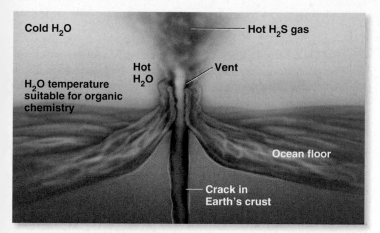

(a) Deep-sea vent hypothesis

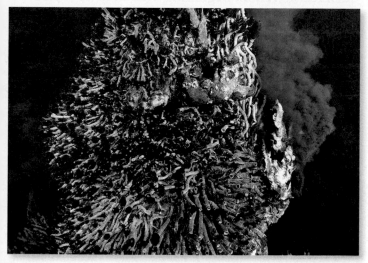

(b) A deep-sea vent community

Figure 22.3 The deep-sea vent hypothesis for the origin of life. (a) Deep-sea vents are cracks in the Earth's surface that release hot gases such as hydrogen sulfide (H_2S). This heats the water near the vent and results in a gradient between the very hot water adjacent to the vent and the cold water farther from the vent. The synthesis of organic molecules occurs in this gradient. (b) Photograph of a biological community near a deep-sea vent, which includes giant tube worms and crabs.

Concept Check: *What properties of deep-sea vents made them suitable for the prebiotic synthesis of molecules?*

form more complex organic polymers such as DNA, RNA, or proteins. Most ideas regarding the origin of life assume that polymers with lengths of at least 30–60 monomers are needed to store enough information to make a viable genetic system. Because hydrolysis competes with polymerization, many scientists have speculated that the synthesis of polymers did not occur in a watery prebiotic soup, but instead took place on a solid surface or in evaporating tidal pools.

In 1951, Irish X-ray crystallographer John Bernal first suggested that the prebiotic synthesis of polymers took place on clay. In his book *The Physical Basis of Life*, he wrote that "clays, muds and inorganic crystals are powerful means to concentrate and polymerize organic molecules." Many clay minerals are known to bind organic molecules such as nucleotides and amino acids. Experimentally, many research groups have demonstrated the formation of nucleic acid polymers

and polypeptides on the surface of clay, given the presence of monomer building blocks. During the prebiotic synthesis of RNA, the purine bases of the nucleotides interact with the silicate surfaces of the clay. Cations, such as Mg^{2+}, bind the nucleotides to the negative surfaces of the clay, thereby positioning the nucleotides in a way that promotes bond formation between the phosphate of one nucleotide and the ribose sugar of an adjacent nucleotide. In this way, polymers such as RNA may have been formed.

Though the formation of polymers on clay remains a reasonable hypothesis, studies by American chemist Luke Leman and his colleagues English chemist Leslie Orgel and Iranian-American chemist M. Reza Ghadiri indicate that polymers can also form in aqueous solutions, which is contrary to popular belief. Their work in 2004 showed that carbonyl sulfide, a simple gas present in volcanic gases and deep-sea vent emissions, can bring about the formation of peptides from amino acids under mild conditions in water. These results indicate that the synthesis of polymers could have taken place in the prebiotic soup.

Stage 3: Cell-Like Structures May Have Originated When Polymers Were Enclosed by a Boundary

The third stage in the origin of living cells is hypothesized to be the formation of a boundary that separated the internal polymers such as RNA from the environment. The term **protobiont** is used to describe an aggregate of prebiotically produced molecules and macromolecules that acquired a boundary, such as a lipid bilayer, that allowed it to maintain an internal chemical environment distinct from that of its surroundings. What characteristics make protobionts possible precursors of living cells? Scientists envision the existence of four key features:

1. A boundary, such as a membrane, separated the internal contents of the protobiont from the external environment.
2. Polymers inside the protobiont contained information.
3. Polymers inside the protobiont had catalytic functions.
4. The protobionts eventually developed the capability of self-replication.

Protobionts were not capable of precise self-reproduction like living cells, but could divide to increase in number. Such protobionts are thought to have exhibited basic metabolic pathways in which the structures of organic molecules were changed. In particular, the polymers inside protobionts must have gained the catalytic ability to link organic building blocks to produce new polymers. This would have been a critical step in the process that eventually provided protobionts with the ability to self-replicate. According to this scenario, metabolic pathways became more complex, and the ability of protobionts to self-replicate became more refined over time. Eventually, these structures exhibited the characteristics that we attribute to living cells. As described next, researchers have hypothesized that protobionts may have exhibited different types of structures, such as coacervates and liposomes.

In 1924 Alexander Oparin hypothesized that living cells evolved from **coacervates**, droplets that form spontaneously from the association of charged polymers such as proteins, carbohydrates, or nucleic acids surrounded by water. Their name derives from the Latin *coacervare*, meaning to assemble together or cluster. Coacervates measure

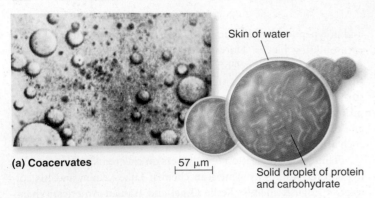

(a) Coacervates

Skin of water

57 μm

Solid droplet of protein and carbohydrate

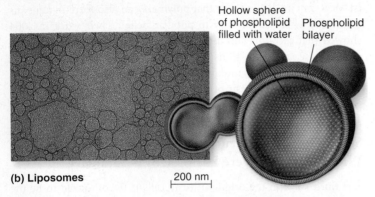

Hollow sphere of phospholipid filled with water

Phospholipid bilayer

(b) Liposomes   200 nm

Figure 22.4 **Protobionts and their lifelike functions.** Primitive cell-like structures such as coacervates and liposomes could have given rise to living cells. **(a)** A micrograph and illustration of coacervates, which are droplets of protein and carbohydrate surrounded by a skin of water molecules. **(b)** An electron micrograph and illustration of liposomes. Each liposome is made of a phospholipid bilayer surrounding an aqueous compartment.

Concept Check: *Which protobiont seems most similar to real cells? Explain.*

BioConnections: *Look back at Figure 3.12. What is the physical/chemical reason why phospholipids tend to form a bilayer?*

1–100 μm (micrometers) across, are surrounded by a tight skin of water molecules, and possess osmotic properties (**Figure 22.4a**). This boundary allows the selective absorption of simple molecules from the surrounding medium.

Enzymes trapped within coacervates can perform primitive metabolic functions. For example, researchers have made coacervates containing the enzyme glycogen phosphorylase. When glucose-1-phosphate was made available to the coacervates, it was taken up into them, and starch was produced. The starch merged with the wall of the coacervates, which increased in size and eventually divided into two. When the enzyme amylase was included, the starch was broken down to maltose, which was released from the coacervates.

As a second possibility, protobionts may have resembled **liposomes**—vesicles surrounded by a lipid bilayer (**Figure 22.4b**). When certain types of lipids are dissolved in water, they spontaneously form liposomes. As discussed in Chapter 5, lipid bilayers are selectively permeable (refer back to Figure 5.11), and some liposomes can even store energy in the form of an electrical gradient. Such liposomes can discharge this energy in a neuron-like fashion, showing rudimentary signs of excitability, which is characteristic of living cells.

In 2003, Danish chemist Martin Hanczyc, American chemist Shelly Fujikawa, and Canadian American biologist Jack Szostak showed that clay can catalyze the formation of liposomes that grow and divide, a primitive form of self-replication. Furthermore, if RNA was on the surface of the clay, the researchers discovered that liposomes that enclosed RNA were formed. These experiments are compelling because they showed that the formation of membrane vesicles containing RNA molecules is a plausible explanation for the emergence of cell-like structures based on simple physical and chemical properties.

Stage 4: Cellular Characteristics May Have Evolved via Chemical Selection, Beginning with an RNA World

The majority of scientists favor RNA as the first macromolecule that was found in protobionts. Unlike other polymers, RNA exhibits three key functions:

1. RNA has the ability to store information in its nucleotide base sequence.
2. Due to base pairing, its nucleotide sequence has the capacity for self-replication.
3. RNA can perform a variety of catalytic functions. The results of many experiments have shown that some RNA molecules can function as **ribozymes**—RNA molecules that catalyze chemical reactions.

By comparison, DNA and proteins are not as versatile as RNA. DNA has very limited catalytic activity, and proteins are not known to undergo self-replication. RNA can perform functions that are characteristic of proteins and, at the same time, can serve as genetic material with replicative and informational functions.

How did the RNA molecules that were first made prebiotically evolve into more complex molecules that produced cell-like characteristics? Researchers propose that a process called chemical selection was responsible. **Chemical selection** occurs when a chemical within a mixture has special properties or advantages that cause it to increase in number relative to other chemicals in the mixture. (As we will discuss in Chapter 23, natural selection is a similar process except that it describes the changing of a population of living organisms over time due to survival and reproductive advantages.) Chemical selection results in **chemical evolution**—a population of molecules changes over time to become a new population with a different chemical composition.

Scientists speculate that initially the special properties that enabled certain RNA molecules to undergo chemical selection were its ability to self-replicate and to perform other catalytic functions. As a way to understand the concept of chemical selection, let's consider a hypothetical scenario showing two steps of chemical selection. Step 1 of **Figure 22.5** shows a group of protobionts that contain RNA molecules that were made prebiotically. RNA molecules inside these protobionts can be used as templates for the prebiotic synthesis of complementary RNA molecules. Such a process of self-replication, however, would be very slow because it would not be catalyzed by enzymes in the protobiont. In a first step of chemical selection, the sequence of one of the RNA molecules has undergone a mutation that gives it the catalytic ability to attach nucleotides together, using RNA molecules as a template. This protobiont would have an advantage

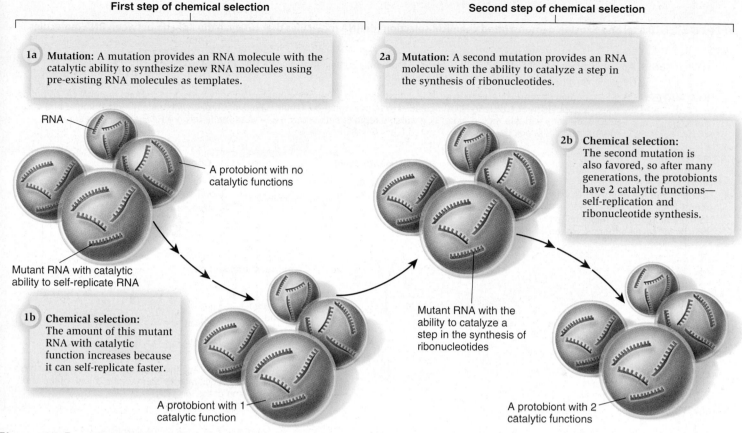

First step of chemical selection

1a **Mutation:** A mutation provides an RNA molecule with the catalytic ability to synthesize new RNA molecules using pre-existing RNA molecules as templates.

RNA

A protobiont with no catalytic functions

Mutant RNA with catalytic ability to self-replicate RNA

1b **Chemical selection:** The amount of this mutant RNA with catalytic function increases because it can self-replicate faster.

A protobiont with 1 catalytic function

Second step of chemical selection

2a **Mutation:** A second mutation provides an RNA molecule with the ability to catalyze a step in the synthesis of ribonucleotides.

2b **Chemical selection:** The second mutation is also favored, so after many generations, the protobionts have 2 catalytic functions— self-replication and ribonucleotide synthesis.

Mutant RNA with the ability to catalyze a step in the synthesis of ribonucleotides

A protobiont with 2 catalytic functions

Figure 22.5 **A hypothetical scenario illustrating the process of chemical selection.** This figure shows a two-step scenario. In the first step, RNAs that can self-replicate are selected, and in the second step, RNAs with the ability to catalyze a step in ribonucleotide synthesis are selected.

Concept Check: *What is meant by the term chemical selection?*

over the others because it would be capable of faster self-replication of its RNA molecules. Over time, due to its enhanced rate of replication, protobionts carrying such RNA molecules would increase in number compared with the others. Eventually, the group of protobionts shown in the figure contains only this type of catalytic RNA.

In the second step of chemical selection (Figure 22.5, right side), a second mutation in an RNA molecule could produce the catalytic function that would help to promote the synthesis of ribonucleotides, the building blocks of RNA. For example, a hypothetical ribozyme may catalyze the attachment of a base to a ribose, thereby catalyzing one of the steps necessary for making a ribonucleotide. This protobiont would not solely rely on the prebiotic synthesis of ribonucleotides, which also is a very slow process. Therefore, the protobiont having the ability to both self-replicate and synthesize ribonucleotides would have an advantage over a protobiont that could only self-replicate. Over time, the faster rate of self-replication and ribonucleotide

synthesis would cause an increase in the numbers of the protobionts with both functions.

The **RNA world** is a hypothetical period on early Earth when both the information needed for life and the catalytic activity of living cells were contained solely in RNA molecules. In this scenario, lipid membranes enclosing RNA exhibited the properties of life due to RNA genomes that were copied and maintained through the catalytic function of RNA molecules. Over time, scientists envision that mutations occurred in these RNA molecules, occasionally introducing new functional possibilities. Chemical selection would have eventually produced an increase in complexity in these cells, with RNA molecules accruing activities such as the ability to link amino acids together into proteins and other catalytic functions.

But is an RNA world a plausible scenario? As described next in the Feature Investigation, chemical selection of RNA molecules in the laboratory can result in chemical evolution.

FEATURE INVESTIGATION

Bartel and Szostak Demonstrated Chemical Evolution in the Laboratory

Remarkably, scientists have been able to perform experiments in the laboratory that can select for RNA molecules with a particular function. American biologist David Bartel and Jack Szostak conducted the

first study of this type in 1993 (**Figure 22.6**). Using molecular techniques, they synthesized a mixture of 10^{15} RNA molecules that we will call the long RNA molecules. Each long RNA in this mixture contained two regions. The first region at the 5′ end was a constant region that formed a stem-loop. Its sequence was identical among all 10^{15} molecules. The constant region was next to a second region that was

Figure 22.6 Bartel and Szostak demonstrated chemical selection for RNA molecules that catalyze the linkage between RNA molecules.

HYPOTHESIS Among a large pool of RNA molecules, some of them may contain the catalytic ability to make a covalent bond between nucleotides; these can be selected for in the laboratory.

KEY MATERIALS Many copies of short RNA were synthesized that had a tag sequence that binds tightly to column packing material called beads. Also, a population of 10^{15} long RNA molecules was made that contained a constant region with a stem-loop structure and a 220-nucleotide variable region. Note: The variable regions of the long RNAs were made using a PCR step that caused mutations in this region.

| | **Experimental level** | **Conceptual level** |

1 Mix together the short RNAs with the 10^{15} different long RNAs. Allow time for covalent connections to form if the long RNA happens to have the catalytic activity for covalent bond formation.

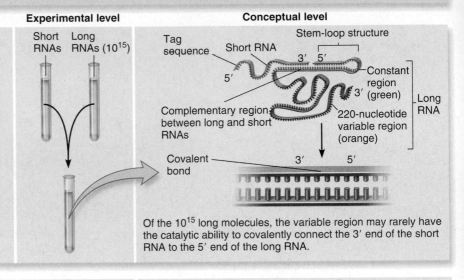

Of the 10^{15} long molecules, the variable region may rarely have the catalytic ability to covalently connect the 3′ end of the short RNA to the 5′ end of the long RNA.

2 Pass the mixture through a column of beads that binds the tag sequence found on the short RNA. Add additional liquid to flush out long RNAs that are not covalently attached to short RNAs.

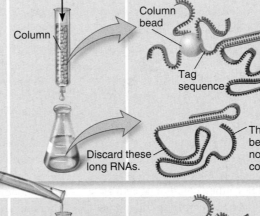

Tag sequences promote the binding of the short RNA to the column beads. Long RNAs covalently attached to a short RNA will also be bound.

This long RNA does not bind to the beads because the variable region does not possess the catalytic ability to covalently attach to the short RNA.

Discard these long RNAs.

3 Add a low pH solution to prevent the tag sequence from binding to the beads. This causes the tightly bound RNAs to be flushed out of the column.

Low pH wash

4 The flushed-out RNAs are termed pool #1. Use pool #1 to make a second batch of long RNA molecules. This involved a PCR step using reverse transcriptase to make cDNA. The PCR primers recognized the beginning and end of the long RNA sequence and copied only this region. The cDNA was then used as a template to make long RNA via RNA polymerase.

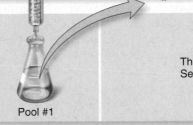

Pool #1

This involved using PCR. See Figure 20.6 for a description of PCR.

5 Repeat procedure to generate 10 consecutive pools of RNA molecules.

Pool #1   Pool #2   Pool #3   Pool #4   Pool #5   Pool #6   Pool #7   Pool #8   Pool #9   Pool #10

6 Test a sample of the original population and each of the 10 pools for the catalytic ability to make a covalent bond between adjacent nucleotides.

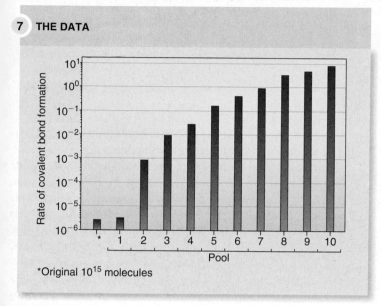

Gap

Covalent bond

7 THE DATA

*Original 10^{15} molecules

Rate of covalent bond formation (y-axis: 10^1, 10^0, 10^{-1}, 10^{-2}, 10^{-3}, 10^{-4}, 10^{-5}, 10^{-6})

Pool (x-axis: *, 1, 2, 3, 4, 5, 6, 7, 8, 9, 10)

8 CONCLUSION The increase in covalent bond formation from pool 1 to pool 10 indicates that chemical selection can occur.

9 SOURCE Bartel, David P., and Szostak, Jack W. 1993. Isolation of new ribozymes from a large pool of random sequences. *Science* 261:1411–1418.

220 nucleotides in length. A key feature of the second region is that its sequence varied among the long RNA molecules. The researchers hypothesized that this variation could occasionally result in a long RNA molecule with the ability to catalyze a covalent bond between two adjacent nucleotides.

They also made another type of RNA molecule, which we will call the short RNA, with two important properties. First, the short RNA had a region that was complementary to a site in the constant region of the long RNA molecules. Second, the short RNA had a tag sequence that caused it to bind tightly to column material referred to as beads. The short RNAs did not have a variable region; they were all the same.

To begin this experiment, the researchers incubated a large number of the long and short RNA molecules together. During this incubation period, long and short RNA molecules hydrogen-bonded to each other due to their complementary regions. Although hydrogen bonding is not permanent, this step allowed the long and short RNAs to recognize each other for a short time. The researchers reasoned that a long RNA with the catalytic ability to form a covalent bond between nucleotides would make this interaction more permanent by catalyzing a bond between the long and short RNA molecules. Following this incubation, the mixture of RNAs was passed through a column with beads that specifically bound the short RNA. The aim of this approach was to select for longer RNA molecules that had covalently bonded to the short RNA molecule (see the Conceptual level of step 2).

The vast majority of long RNAs would not have the catalytic ability to catalyze a permanent covalent bond between nucleotides. These would pass out of the column at step 2, because hydrogen bonding between the long and short RNAs is not sufficient to hold them together for very long. Such unbound long RNAs would be discarded. Long RNAs with the ability to catalyze a covalent bond to the short RNA would remain bound to the column beads at step 2. These catalytic RNAs were then flushed out at step 3 to generate a mixture of RNAs termed pool #1. The researchers expected this pool to contain several different long RNA molecules with varying abilities to catalyze a covalent bond between nucleotides.

To further the chemical selection process, the scientists used the first pool of long RNA molecules flushed out at step 3 to make more long RNA molecules. This was accomplished via polymerase chain reaction (PCR). This next batch also had the constant and variable regions but did not have the short RNA covalently attached. Because the variable regions of these new RNA molecules were derived from the variable regions of pool #1 RNA molecules, they were expected to have catalytic activity. The researchers reasoned that additional variation might occasionally produce an RNA molecule with improved catalytic activity. This second batch of long RNA molecules (pool #2) was subjected to the same steps as was the first batch of 10^{15} molecules. In this case, the group of long molecules flushed out at step 3 was termed pool #2. This protocol was followed eight more times to generate 10 consecutive pools of RNA molecules. During this work, the researchers analyzed the original random collection of 10^{15} RNA molecules and each of the 10 pools for the catalytic ability to covalently link RNA molecules. As seen in the data, each successive pool became enriched for molecules with higher catalytic activity. Pool #10 showed catalytic activity that was approximately 3 million times higher than the original random pool of molecules!

Like the work of Miller and Urey, Bartel and Szostak showed the feasibility of another phase of the prebiotic process that led to life. In this case, chemical selection resulted in chemical evolution. The results showed that chemical selection can change the functional characteristics of a group of RNA molecules over time by increasing the proportion of those molecules with enhanced function.

Experimental Questions

1. What is chemical selection? What hypothesis did Bartel and Szostak test?

2. In conducting the selection experiment among pools of long RNA molecules with various catalytic abilities, what was the purpose of using the short RNA molecules?

3. What were the results of the experiment conducted by Bartel and Szostak? How did this study influence our understanding of the evolution of life on Earth?

The RNA World Was Superseded by the Modern DNA/RNA/Protein World

Assuming that an RNA world was the origin of life, researchers have asked the question, "Why and how did the RNA world evolve into the DNA/RNA/protein world we see today?" The RNA world may have been superseded by a DNA/RNA world or an RNA/protein world before the emergence of the modern DNA/RNA/protein world. Let's now consider the advantages of a DNA/RNA/protein world as opposed to the simpler RNA world and explore how this modern biological world might have come into being.

Information Storage   RNA can store information in its base sequence. If so, why did DNA take over that function, as is the case in modern cells? During the RNA world, RNA had to perform two roles: the storage of information and the catalysis of chemical reactions. Scientists have speculated that the incorporation of DNA into cells would have relieved RNA of its informational role, thereby allowing RNA to perform a greater variety of other functions. For example, if DNA stored the information for the synthesis of RNA molecules, such RNA molecules could bind cofactors, have modified bases, or bind peptides that might enhance their catalytic function. Cells with both DNA and RNA would have had an advantage over those with just RNA, and so they would have been selected. Another advantage of DNA is its stability. Compared with RNA, DNA strands are less likely to spontaneously break.

A second issue is how DNA came into being. Scientists have proposed that an ancestral RNA molecule had the ability to make DNA using RNA as a template. This function, known as reverse transcription, is described in Chapter 18 in the discussion of retroviruses. Interestingly, modern eukaryotic cells can use RNA as a template to make DNA. For example, an RNA sequence in the enzyme telomerase copies the ends of chromosomes, thus preventing progressive shortening of the chromosomes (refer back to Figure 11.22).

Metabolism and Other Cellular Functions   Now let's consider the origin of proteins. The emergence of proteins as catalysts may have been a great benefit to early cells. Due to the different chemical properties of the 20 amino acids, proteins have vastly greater catalytic ability than do RNA molecules, again providing a major advantage to cells that had both RNA and proteins. In modern cells, proteins have taken over most, but not all, catalytic functions. In addition, proteins can perform other important tasks. For example, cytoskeletal proteins carry out structural roles, and certain membrane proteins are responsible for the uptake of substances into living cells.

How would proteins have come into being in an RNA world? Chemical selection experiments have shown that RNA molecules can catalyze the formation of peptide bonds and even attach amino acids to primitive tRNA molecules. Similarly, modern protein synthesis still involves a central role for RNA in the synthesis of polypeptides. First, mRNA provides the information for a polypeptide sequence. Second, tRNA molecules act as adaptors for the formation of a polypeptide chain. And finally, ribosomes containing rRNA provide a site for polypeptide synthesis. Furthermore, rRNA within the ribosome acts as a ribozyme to catalyze peptide bond formation. Taken together, the analysis of translation in modern cells is consistent with an evolutionary history in which RNA molecules were instrumental in the emergence and formation of proteins.

22.2   The Fossil Record

Learning Outcomes:

1. Describe how fossils are formed.
2. Explain how radiometric dating is used to estimate the age of a fossil.
3. List several factors that affect the completeness of the fossil record.

We will now turn our attention to a process that has given us a window into the history of life over the past 3.5 billion years. **Fossils** are the preserved remains of past life on Earth. They can take many forms, including bones, shells, and leaves, and the impression of cells or other evidence, such as footprints or burrows. Scientists who study fossils are called **paleontologists** (from the Greek *palaios*, meaning ancient). Because our understanding of the history of life is derived primarily from the fossil record, it is important to appreciate how fossils are formed and dated and to understand why the fossil record cannot be viewed as complete.

Fossils Are Formed Within Sedimentary Rock

How are fossils usually formed? Many of the rocks observed by paleontologists are sedimentary rocks that were formed from particles of older rocks broken apart by water or wind. These particles, such as gravel, sand, and mud, settle and bury living and dead organisms at the bottoms of rivers, lakes, and oceans. Over time, more particles pile up, and sediments at the bottom of the pile eventually become rock. Gravel particles form rock called conglomerate, sand becomes sandstone, and mud becomes shale. Most fossils are formed when organisms are buried quickly, and then during the process of sedimentary rock formation, their hard parts are gradually replaced over millions of years by minerals, producing a recognizable representation of the original organism (see, for example, the chapter opening photo).

The relative ages of fossils can sometimes be revealed by their locations in sedimentary rock formations. Because sedimentary rocks are formed particle by particle and bed by bed, the layers are piled one on top of the other. In a sequence of layered rocks, the lower rock layers are usually older than the upper layers. Paleontologists often study changes in life-forms over time by studying the fossils in layers from bottom to top (**Figure 22.7**). The more ancient life-forms are found in the lower layers, and newer species are found in the upper layers. However, such an assumption can occasionally be misleading when geological processes such as folding have flipped the layers.

The Analysis of Radioisotopes Is Used to Date Fossils

A common way to estimate the age of a fossil is by analyzing the decay of radioisotopes within the accompanying rock, a process called **radiometric dating**. As discussed in Chapter 2, elements may be found in multiple forms, called isotopes, that differ in the number of neutrons they contain. A radioisotope is an unstable isotope of an element that decays spontaneously, releasing radiation at a constant rate. The **half-life** is the length of time required for a radioisotope to decay to exactly one-half of its initial quantity. Each radioisotope has its own unique half-life (**Figure 22.8a**). Within a sample of rock, scientists can measure the amount of a given radioisotope as well as the

amount of the decay product—the isotope that is produced when the original isotope decays. For dating geological materials, several types of isotope decay patterns are particularly useful: carbon to nitrogen, potassium to argon, rubidium to strontium, and uranium to lead (**Figure 22.8b**).

To determine the age of a rock using radiometric dating, paleontologists need to have a way to set the clock—extrapolate back to a starting point in which a rock did not have any amount of the decay product. Except for fossils less than 50,000 years old, in which carbon-14 (^{14}C) dating can be employed, fossil dating is not usually conducted on the fossil itself or on the sedimentary rock in which the fossil is found. Most commonly, igneous rock—rock formed through the cooling and solidification of lava—in the vicinity of the sedimentary rock is dated. Why is igneous rock chosen? One reason is that igneous rock derived from an ancient lava flow initially contains uranium-235 (^{235}U) but no lead-207 (^{207}Pb). The decay product of ^{235}U is ^{207}Pb. By comparing the relative proportions of ^{235}U and ^{207}Pb in a sample, the age of igneous rock can be accurately determined.

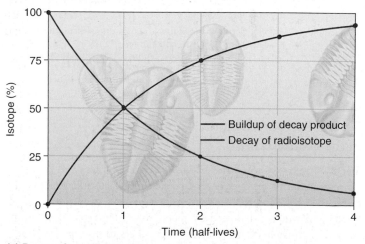

(a) Decay of a radioisotope

Radioisotope	Decay product	Half-life (years)	Useful dating range (years)
Carbon-14	Nitrogen-14	5,730	100–50,000
Potassium-40	Argon-40	1.3 billion	100,000–4.5 billion
Rubidium-87	Strontium-87	47 billion	10 million–4.5 billion
Uranium-235	Lead-207	710 million	10 million–4.5 billion
Uranium-238	Lead-206	4.5 billion	10 million–4.5 billion

(b) Radioisotopes that are useful for geological dating

Figure 22.8 **Radiometric dating of fossils.** **(a)** A rock can be dated by measuring the relative amounts of a radioisotope and its decay product within the rock. **(b)** These five isotopes are particularly useful for the dating of fossils.

Concept Check: If you suspected a fossil is 50 million years old, which pair of radioisotopes would you choose to analyze?

Figure 22.7 **An example of layers of sedimentary rock that contain fossils.**

Concept Check: Which rock layer in this photo is most likely to be the oldest?

Table 22.1	Factors That Affect the Fossil Record
Factor	**Description**
Anatomy	Organisms with hard body parts, such as animals with a skeleton or thick shell, are more likely to be preserved than are organisms composed of soft tissues.
Size	The fossil remains of larger organisms are more likely to be found than those of smaller organisms.
Number	Species that existed in greater numbers or over a larger area are more likely to be preserved within the fossil record than those that existed in smaller numbers or in a smaller area.
Environment	Inland species are less likely to become fossilized than are those that lived in a marine environment or near the edge of water because sedimentary rock is more likely to be formed in or near water.
Time	Organisms that lived relatively recently or existed for a long time are more likely to be found as fossils than organisms that lived very long ago or for a relatively short time.
Geological processes	Due to the chemistry of fossilization, certain organisms are more likely to be preserved than are other organisms.
Paleontology	Certain types of fossils may be more interesting to paleontologists. In addition, a significant bias exists with regard to the locations where paleontologists search for fossils. For example, they tend to search in regions where other fossils have already been found.

Several Factors Affect the Completeness of the Fossil Record

The fossil record should not be viewed as a complete and balanced representation of the species that existed in the past. Several factors affect the likelihood that extinct organisms have been preserved as fossils and will be identified by paleontologists (**Table 22.1**). First, certain organisms are more likely than others to become fossilized. Organisms with hard shells or bones tend to be over-represented. Factors such as anatomy, size, number, and the environment and time in which they lived also play important roles in determining the likelihood that organisms will be preserved in the fossil record. In addition, geological processes may favor the fossilization of certain types of organisms. Finally, unintentional biases arise that are related to the efforts of paleontologists. For example, scientific interests may favor searching for and analyzing certain species over others. For example, researchers have been greatly interested in finding the remains of dinosaurs.

Although the fossil record is incomplete, it has provided a wealth of information regarding the history of the types of life that existed on Earth. The rest of this chapter will survey the emergence of life-forms from 3.5 bya to the present.

22.3 History of Life on Earth

Learning Outcomes:
1. List the types of environmental changes that have affected the history of life on Earth.
2. Describe the cell structure and energy utilization of the first living organisms that arose during the Archaean eon.
3. Explain how the origin of eukaryotic cells involved a union between bacterial and archaeal cells.
4. Describe the key features of multicellular organisms, which arose during the Proterozoic eon.
5. Outline the major events and changes in species diversity during the Paleozoic, Mesozoic, and Cenozoic eras.

Thus far, we have considered hypotheses of how the first cells came into existence, and we have also examined the characteristics of fossils. The first known fossils of single-celled organisms were preserved approximately 3.5 bya. In this section, we will begin with a brief description of the geological changes on Earth that have affected the emergence of new forms of life and then examine some of the major changes in life that have occurred since it began.

Many Environmental Changes Have Occurred Since the Origin of the Earth

The **geological timescale** is a time line of the Earth's history and major events from its origin approximately 4.55 bya to the present (**Figure 22.9**). This time line is subdivided into four eons—the Hadean, Archaean, Proterozoic, and Phanerozoic—and then further subdivided into eras. The first three eons are collectively known as the Precambrian because they preceded the Cambrian era, a geological era that saw a rapid increase in the diversity of life. The names of several eons and eras end in -*zoic* (meaning animal life), because we often recognize these time intervals on the basis of animal life. We will examine these time periods later in this chapter.

The changes that occurred in living organisms over the past 4 billion years are the result of two interactive processes. First, as discussed in the next several chapters, genetic changes in organisms can affect their characteristics. Such changes can influence organisms' abilities to survive and reproduce in their native environment. Second, the environment on Earth has undergone dramatic changes that have profoundly influenced the types of organisms that have existed during different periods of time. In some cases, an environmental change has allowed new types of organisms to flourish. Alternatively, environmental changes have resulted in **extinction**—the complete loss of a species or group of species. Major types of environmental changes are described next.

Temperature   During the first 2.5 billion years of its existence, the surface of the Earth gradually cooled. However, during the last 2 billion years, the Earth has undergone major fluctuations in temperature, producing Ice Ages that alternate with warmer periods. Furthermore, the temperature on Earth is not uniform, which produces a range of environments where the temperatures are quite different, such as tropical rain forests and the arctic tundra.

Atmosphere   The chemical composition of the gases surrounding the Earth has changed substantially over the past 4 billion years. One notable change involves the amount of oxygen. Prior to 2.4 bya, relatively little oxygen gas was in the atmosphere, but at that time, levels of oxygen in the form of O_2 began to rise significantly. The emergence of organisms that are capable of photosynthesis added oxygen to the atmosphere. Our current atmosphere contains about 21% O_2.

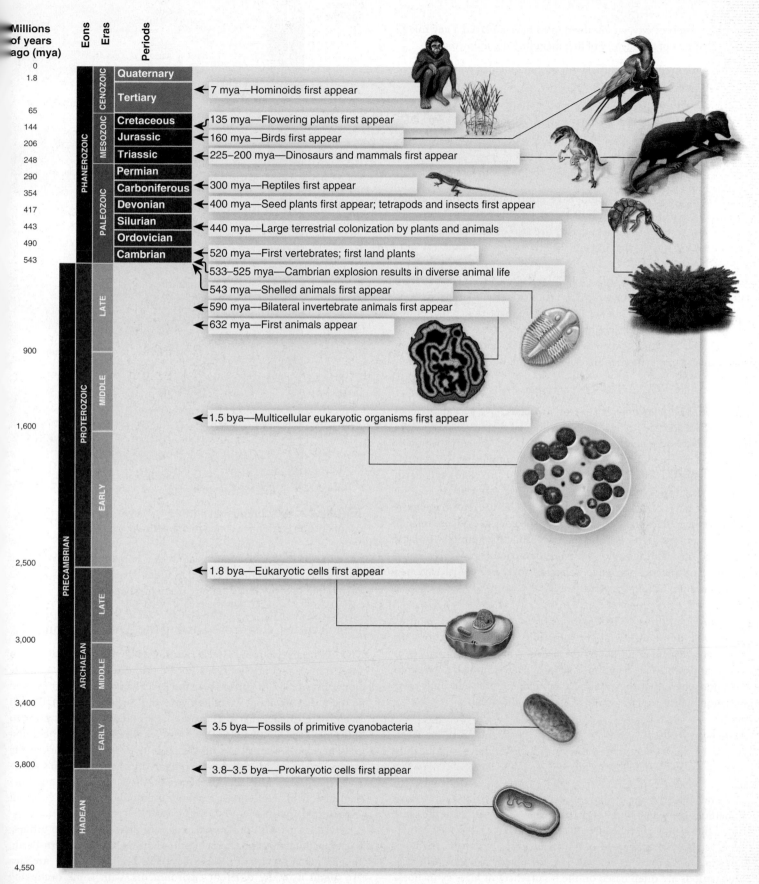

Millions of years ago (mya)	Eons	Eras	Periods	
0			Quaternary	
1.8		CENOZOIC	Tertiary	← 7 mya—Hominoids first appear
65			Cretaceous	135 mya—Flowering plants first appear
144		MESOZOIC	Jurassic	← 160 mya—Birds first appear
206	PHANEROZOIC		Triassic	← 225–200 mya—Dinosaurs and mammals first appear
248			Permian	
290			Carboniferous	← 300 mya—Reptiles first appear
354		PALEOZOIC	Devonian	← 400 mya—Seed plants first appear; tetrapods and insects first appear
417			Silurian	← 440 mya—Large terrestrial colonization by plants and animals
443			Ordovician	
490			Cambrian	← 520 mya—First vertebrates; first land plants
543				533–525 mya—Cambrian explosion results in diverse animal life
		LATE		543 mya—Shelled animals first appear
				← 590 mya—Bilateral invertebrate animals first appear
				← 632 mya—First animals appear
900	PROTEROZOIC	MIDDLE		
1,600				← 1.5 bya—Multicellular eukaryotic organisms first appear
		EARLY		
2,500	PRECAMBRIAN	LATE		← 1.8 bya—Eukaryotic cells first appear
3,000				
3,400	ARCHAEAN	MIDDLE		
3,800		EARLY		← 3.5 bya—Fossils of primitive cyanobacteria
				← 3.8–3.5 bya—Prokaryotic cells first appear
	HADEAN			
4,550				

Figure 22.9 The geological timescale and an overview of the history of life on Earth.

Increased levels of oxygen are thought to have a played a key role in various aspects of the history of life, including the following:

- The origin of many animal body plans coincided with a rise in atmospheric O_2.
- The conquest of land by arthropods (about 410 million years ago [mya]) and a second conquest by arthropods and vertebrates (about 350 mya) occurred during periods in which O_2 levels were high or increasing.
- Increases in animal body sizes are associated with higher O_2 levels.

Higher levels of O_2 could have contributed to these events because higher O_2 levels may enhance the ability of animals to carry out aerobic respiration. These events are also discussed later in this chapter and in more detail in Unit VI.

Landmasses   As the Earth cooled, landmasses formed that were surrounded by bodies of water. This produced two different environments: terrestrial and aquatic. Furthermore, over the course of billions of years, the major landmasses, known as the continents, have shifted their positions, changed their shapes, and separated from each other. This phenomenon, called **continental drift**, is shown in **Figure 22.10**.

Floods and Glaciations   Catastrophic floods have periodically had major effects on the organisms in the flooded regions. Glaciers have periodically moved across continents and altered the composition of species on those landmasses. As an extreme example, in 1992, American geobiologist Joseph Kirschvink proposed the "Snowball Earth hypothesis," which suggests that the Earth was entirely covered by ice during parts of the period from 790 to 630 mya. This hypothesis was developed to explain various types of geological evidence including sedimentary deposits of glacial origin that are found at tropical latitudes. Although the prior existence of a completely frozen Earth remains controversial, massive glaciations over our planet have had an important effect on the history of life.

Volcanic Eruptions   The eruptions of volcanoes harm organisms in the vicinity of the eruption, sometimes causing extinctions. In addition, volcanic eruptions in the oceans lead to the formation of new islands. Massive eruptions may also spew so much debris into the atmosphere that they affect global temperatures and limit solar radiation, which restricts photosynthetic production.

Meteorite Impacts   During its long history, the Earth has been struck by many meteorites. Large meteorites have significantly affected the Earth's environment.

The effects of one or more of the changes described above have sometimes caused large numbers of species to go extinct at the same time. Such events are called **mass extinctions**. Five large mass extinctions occurred near the end of the Ordovician, Devonian, Permian, Triassic, and Cretaceous periods. The boundaries between geological time periods are often based on the occurrences of mass extinctions. A recurring pattern seen in the history of life is the extinction of some species and the emergence of new ones. The rapid extinction of many

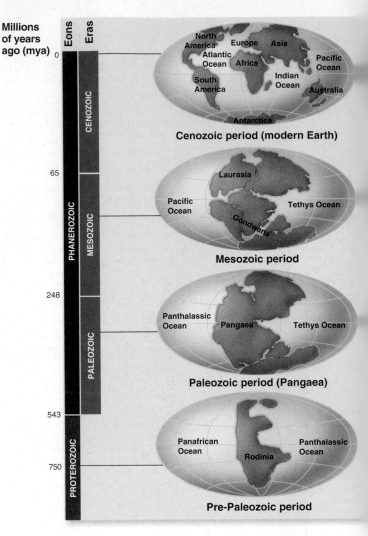

Figure 22.10   Continental drift. The relative locations of the continents on Earth have changed dramatically over time.

modern species due to human activities is sometimes referred to as the sixth mass extinction. We will examine mass extinctions and the current biodiversity crisis in more detail in Chapter 60.

Prokaryotic Cells Arose During the Archaean Eon

The Archaean (from the Greek, meaning ancient) was an eon when diverse microbial life flourished in the primordial oceans. As mentioned previously, the first known fossils of living cells were preserved in rocks that are about 3.5 billion years old (see Figure 22.1), though scientists postulate that cells arose many millions of years prior to this time. Based on the morphology of fossilized remains, these first cells were prokaryotic. During the more than 1 billion years of the Archaean eon, all life-forms were prokaryotic. Because Earth's atmosphere had very little free oxygen (O_2), the single-celled microorganisms of this eon almost certainly used only anaerobic (without oxygen) respiration.

Organisms with prokaryotic cells are divided into two groups: bacteria and archaea. Bacteria are more prevalent on modern Earth, though many species of archaea have also been identified. Archaea are found in many different environments, with some occupying extreme environments such as hot springs. Both bacteria and archaea share fundamental similarities, indicating that they are derived from a common ancestor. Even so, certain differences suggest that these two types of prokaryotes diverged from each other quite early in the history of life. In particular, bacteria and archaea show some interesting differences in metabolism, lipid composition, and genetic pathways (look ahead to Chapter 26, Table 26.1).

Biologists Are Undecided About Whether Heterotrophs or Autotrophs Came First

An important factor that greatly influenced the emergence of new species is the availability of energy. As we learned in Unit II, all organisms require energy to survive and reproduce. Organisms may follow two different strategies to obtain energy. Some are **heterotrophs**, which means their energy is derived from the chemical bonds within organic molecules they consume. Because the most common sources of organic molecules today are other organisms, heterotrophs typically consume other organisms or materials from other organisms. Alternatively, many organisms are **autotrophs**, which directly harness energy from either inorganic molecules or light. Among modern species, plants are an important example of autotrophs. Plants can directly absorb light energy and use it (via photosynthesis) to synthesize organic molecules such as glucose. On modern Earth, heterotrophs ultimately rely on autotrophs for the production of food.

Were the first forms of life heterotrophs or autotrophs? The answer is not resolved. Some biologists have speculated that autotrophs, such as those living near deep-sea vents, may have arisen first. These organisms would have used chemicals that were made near the vents as an energy source to make organic molecules. Alternatively, many scientists have hypothesized that the first living cells were heterotrophs. They reason that it would have been simpler for the first primitive cells to use the organic molecules in the prebiotic soup as a source of energy.

If heterotrophs came first, why were cyanobacteria preserved in the earliest fossils, rather than heterotrophs? One possible reason is related to their manner of growth. Certain cyanobacteria promote the formation of a layered structure called a **stromatolite** (Figure 22.11). The aquatic environment where these cyanobacteria survive is rich in minerals such as calcium. The cyanobacteria grow in large mats that form layers. As they grow, they deplete the carbon dioxide (CO_2) in the surrounding water. This causes calcium carbonate in the water to gradually precipitate over the bacterial cells, calcifying the older cells in the lower layers and also trapping grains of sediment. Newer cells produce a layer on top. Over time, many layers of calcified cells and sediment are formed, thereby producing a stromatolite. This process still occurs today in places such as Shark Bay in western Australia, which is renowned for the stromatolites along its beaches (Figure 22.11).

The emergence and proliferation of ancient cyanobacteria had two critical consequences. First, the autotrophic nature of these bacteria enabled them to produce organic molecules from CO_2. This prevented the depletion of organic foodstuffs that would have been exhausted if only heterotrophs existed. Second, cyanobacteria produce oxygen (O_2) as a waste product of photosynthesis. During the Archaean and Proterozoic eons, the activity of cyanobacteria led to the gradual rise in O_2 discussed earlier. The increase in O_2 spelled doom for many anaerobic species, which became restricted to a few anoxic (without oxygen) environments, such as deep within the soil. However, O_2 enabled the formation of new bacterial and archaeal

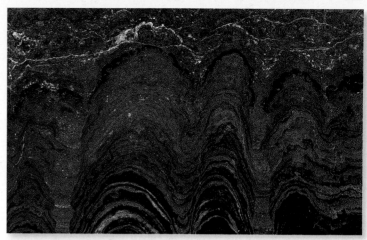

(a) Fossil stromatolite

(b) Modern stromatolites

Figure 22.11   **Fossil and modern stromatolites: Evidence of autotrophic cyanobacteria.** Each stromatolite is a rocklike structure, typically 1 meter in diameter. **(a)** Section of a fossilized stromatolite. These layers are mats of mineralized cyanobacteria, one layer on top of the other. The existence of fossil stromatolites provides evidence of early autotrophic organisms. **(b)** Modern stromatolites that have formed in western Australia.

species that used aerobic (with oxygen) respiration (see Chapter 7). In addition, aerobic respiration is likely to have played a key role in the emergence and eventual explosion of eukaryotic life-forms, which typically have high energy demands. These eukaryotic life-forms are described next.

GENOMES & PROTEOMES CONNECTION

The Origin of Eukaryotic Cells Involved a Union Between Bacterial and Archaeal Cells

Eukaryotic cells arose during the Proterozoic eon, which began 2.5 bya and ended 543 mya (see Figure 22.9). The manner in which the first eukaryotic cell originated is not entirely understood. In modern eukaryotic cells, genetic material is found in three distinct organelles. All eukaryotic cells contain DNA in the nucleus and mitochondria, and plant and algal cells also have DNA in their chloroplasts. To address the issue of the origin of eukaryotic species, scientists have examined the DNA sequences found in these three organelles. From such studies, the nuclear, mitochondrial, and chloroplast genomes appear to be derived from once-separate cells that came together.

Nuclear Genome   From a genome perspective, both bacteria and archaea have contributed substantially to the nuclear genome of eukaryotic cells. Eukaryotic nuclear genes encoding proteins involved in metabolic pathways and lipid biosynthesis appear to be derived from ancient bacteria, whereas genes involved with transcription and translation appear to be derived from an archaeal ancestor. To explain the origin of the nuclear genome, several hypotheses have been proposed. The most widely accepted involves an association between ancient bacteria and archaea, which is hypothesized to be endosymbiotic. In an **endosymbiotic** relationship, a smaller organism (the endosymbiont) lives inside a larger organism (the host).

Researchers have suggested that an archaeal species evolved the ability to invaginate its plasma membrane, which could have two results (**Figure 22.12**). First, it could eventually lead to the formation of an extensive internal membrane system and enclose the genetic material in a nuclear envelope. Second, the ability to invaginate the plasma membrane would provide a mechanism to take up materials from the environment via endocytosis, which is described in Chapter 5. In the scenario described in Figure 22.12, an ancient archaeon engulfed a bacterium via endocytosis, maintaining the bacterium in its cytoplasm as an endosymbiont. Over time, some genes from the bacterium were transferred to the archaeal host cell, and the resulting genetic material eventually became the nuclear genome.

Mitochondrial and Chloroplast Genomes   As discussed in Chapter 4, the analyses of genes from mitochondria, chloroplasts, and bacteria are consistent with the endosymbiosis theory, which proposes that mitochondria and chloroplasts originated from bacteria that took up residence within a primordial eukaryotic cell (refer back to Figure 4.28). Mitochondria found in eukaryotic cells are likely derived from a bacterial species that resembled modern α-proteobacteria, a diverse group of bacteria that carry out oxidative phosphorylation to make ATP. One possibility is that an endosymbiotic event involving an ancestor of this bacterial species produced the first eukaryotic cell and that the mitochondrion is a remnant of that event. Alternatively, endosymbiosis may have produced the first eukaryotic cell, and then a subsequent endosymbiosis resulted in mitochondria (see Figure 22.12). DNA-sequencing data indicate that chloroplasts were derived from a separate endosymbiotic relationship between a primitive eukaryotic cell and a cyanobacterium. As discussed in Chapter 28, plastids, such as chloroplasts, have arisen on several independent occasions via primary, secondary, and tertiary endosymbiosis (see Figure 28.13).

Interestingly, an endosymbiotic relationship involving two different proteobacteria was reported in 2001. In mealybugs, bacteria survive within the cytoplasm of large host cells of a specialized organ called a bacteriome. Recent analysis has shown that different species of bacteria inside the host cells share their own endosymbiotic relationship. In particular, γ-proteobacteria live endosymbiotically inside β-proteobacteria. Such an observation demonstrates that an endosymbiotic relationship can occur between two bacterial species.

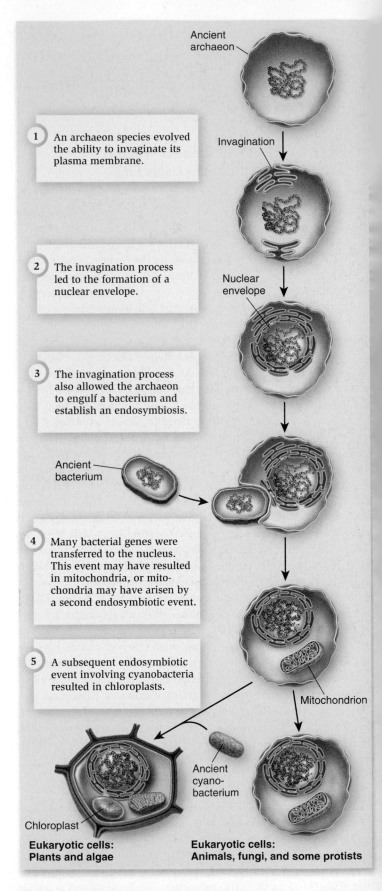

1   An archaeon species evolved the ability to invaginate its plasma membrane.

2   The invagination process led to the formation of a nuclear envelope.

3   The invagination process also allowed the archaeon to engulf a bacterium and establish an endosymbiosis.

4   Many bacterial genes were transferred to the nucleus. This event may have resulted in mitochondria, or mitochondria may have arisen by a second endosymbiotic event.

5   A subsequent endosymbiotic event involving cyanobacteria resulted in chloroplasts.

Ancient archaeon

Invagination

Nuclear envelope

Ancient bacterium

Mitochondrion

Ancient cyanobacterium

Chloroplast

Eukaryotic cells: Plants and algae

Eukaryotic cells: Animals, fungi, and some protists

Figure 22.12 Possible endosymbiotic relationships that gave rise to the first eukaryotic cells.

BioConnections: *Look back at Figure 5.24. Explain how endocytosis played a role in endosymbiosis.*

Flagella

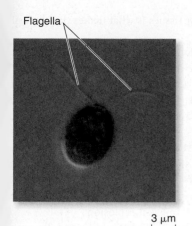

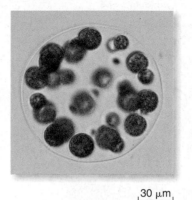

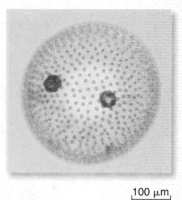

|3 μm| |10 μm| |30 μm| |100 μm|

(a) *Chlamydomonas reinhardtii,* a unicellular alga

(b) *Gonium pectorale,* composed of 16 identical cells

(c) *Pleodorina californica,* composed of 64 to 128 cells, has 2 cell types, somatic and reproductive

(d) *Volvox aureus,* composed of about 1,000 to 2,000 cells, has 2 cell types, somatic and reproductive

Figure 22.13 Variation in the level of multicellularity among volvocine algae.

 BIOLOGY PRINCIPLE New properties of life emerge from complex interactions. The formation of different cell types is an emergent property of multicellularity.

Multicellular Eukaryotes and the Earliest Animals Arose During the Proterozoic Eon

The first multicellular eukaryotes are thought to have emerged about 1.5 bya, in the middle of the Proterozoic eon. The oldest fossil evidence for multicellular eukaryotes was an organism that resembled modern red algae; this fossil was dated at approximately 1.2 billion years old.

Simple multicellular organisms are believed to have originated in one of two different ways. One possibility is that several individual cells found each other and aggregated to form a colony. Cellular slime molds, discussed in Chapter 28, are examples of modern organisms in which groups of single-celled organisms can come together to form a small multicellular organism. According to the fossil record, such organisms have remained very simple for hundreds of millions of years.

Alternatively, another way that multicellularity can occur is when a single cell divides and the resulting cells stick together. This pattern occurs in many simple multicellular organisms, such as algae and fungi, as well as in species with more complex body plans, such as plants and animals. Biologists cannot be certain whether the first multicellular organisms arose by an aggregation process or by cell division and adhesion. However, the development of complex, multicellular organisms now occurs by cell division and adhesion.

An interesting example showing changes in the level of complexity from unicellular organisms to more complex multicellular organisms is found among evolutionarily related species of volvocine green algae. These algae exist as unicellular species, as small clumps of cells of the same cell type, or as larger groups of cells with two distinct cell types. **Figure 22.13** compares four species of volvocine algae. *Chlamydomonas reinhardtii* is a unicellular alga (Figure 22.13a). It is called a biflagellate because each cell has two flagella. *Gonium pectorale* is a multicellular organism composed of 16 cells (Figure 22.13b). This simple multicellular organism is formed from a single cell by cell division and adhesion. All of the cells in this species are biflagellate.

Other volvocine algae have evolved into larger and more complex organisms. *Pleodorina californica* has 64–128 cells (Figure 22.13c), and *Volvox aureus* has about 1,000–2,000 cells (Figure 22.13d). A feature of these more complex organisms is they have two cell types: somatic and reproductive cells. The somatic cells are biflagellate cells, but the reproductive cells are not. When comparing *P. californica* and *V. aureus, V. aureus* has a higher percentage of somatic cells than *P. californica*.

Overall, an analysis of these four species of algae illustrates three important principles found among complex multicellular species:

1. Multicellular organisms arise from a single cell that divides to produce daughter cells that adhere to one another.
2. The daughter cells can follow different fates, thereby producing multicellular organisms with different cell types.
3. As organisms get larger, a greater percentage of the cells tend to be somatic cells. The somatic cells carry out the activities required for the survival of the multicellular organism, whereas the reproductive cells are specialized for the sole purpose of producing offspring.

Toward the end of the Proterozoic eon, multicellular animals emerged. The first animals were invertebrates—animals without a backbone. Most animals, except for organisms such as sponges and jellyfish, exhibit bilateral symmetry—a two-sided body plan with a right and left side that are mirror images. Because each side of the body has appendages such as legs, one advantage of bilateral symmetry is that it facilitates locomotion. Bilateral animals also have anterior and posterior ends, with the mouth at the anterior end, as described in Chapter 19. In southern China in 2004, Chinese paleontologist Jun-Yuan Chen, American paleobiologist David Bottjer, and their colleagues discovered a fossil of the earliest known ancestor of animals with bilateral symmetry. This minute creature, with a shape like a flattened helmet, is barely visible to the naked eye (**Figure 22.14**). The fossil is approximately 580–600 million years old.

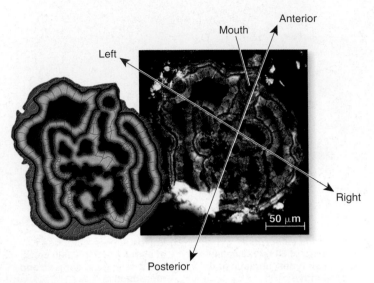

Figure 22.14 **Fossil of an early invertebrate animal showing bilateral symmetry.** This fossil of an early animal, *Vernanimalcula guizhouena*, dates from 580 to 600 mya.

Concept Check: *Name three other species that exhibit bilateral symmetry.*

Phanerozoic Eon: The Paleozoic Era Saw the Diversification of Invertebrates and the Colonization of Land by Plants and Animals

The proliferation of multicellular eukaryotic life has been extensive during the Phanerozoic eon, which started 543 mya and extends to the present day. Phanerozoic means "well-displayed life," referring to the abundance of fossils of plants and animals that have been identified from this eon. As described in Figure 22.9, the Phanerozoic eon is subdivided into three eras: the Paleozoic, Mesozoic, and Cenozoic. Because they are relatively recent and we have many fossils from these eras, each of them is further subdivided into periods. We will consider each era with its associated conditions and prevalent forms of life separately.

The term Paleozoic means ancient animal life. The Paleozoic era covers approximately 300 million years, from 543 to 248 mya, and is subdivided into six periods: the Cambrian, Ordovician, Silurian, Devonian, Carboniferous, and Permian. Periods are usually named after regions where rocks and fossils of that age were first discovered.

Cambrian Period (543–490 mya) The climate in the Cambrian period was generally warm and wet, with no evidence of ice at the poles. During this time, the diversity of animal species increased rapidly, an event called the **Cambrian explosion**. However, recent evidence suggests that many types of animal groups present during the Cambrian period actually arose prior to this period.

Many fossils from the Cambrian period were found in the Canadian Rockies in a rock bed called the Burgess Shale, which was discovered by American paleontologist Charles Walcott in 1909. At this site, both soft- and hard-bodied (shelled) invertebrates were buried in an underwater mudslide and preserved in water that was so deep and oxygen-free that decomposition was minimal (**Figure 22.15a**). The

excellent preservation of the softer tissues is what makes this deposit unique (**Figure 22.15b**).

By the middle of the Cambrian period, all of the existing major types of marine invertebrates were present, plus many others that no longer exist. These include over 100 major animal groups with significantly different body plans. Examples that still exist include echinoderms (sea urchins and starfish), arthropods (insects, spiders, and crustaceans), mollusks (clams and snails), chordates (organisms with a dorsal nerve chord), and vertebrates (animals with backbones). Interestingly, although many new species of animals have arisen since this time, these later species have not shown a major reorganization of body plan, but instead exhibit variations on themes that were established during or prior to the Cambrian explosion.

The cause of the Cambrian explosion is not understood. Because it occurred shortly after marine animals evolved shells, some scientists have speculated that the changes observed in animal species may have allowed them to exploit new environments. Alternatively, others have suggested that the increase in diversity may be related to atmospheric oxygen levels. During this period, oxygen levels were increasing, and perhaps more complex body plans became possible only after the atmospheric oxygen surpassed a certain threshold. In addition, as atmospheric oxygen reached its present levels, an ozone (O_3) layer was produced that screens out harmful ultraviolet radiation, thereby allowing complex life to live in shallow water and eventually on land. Another possible contributor to the Cambrian explosion was an "evolutionary arms race" between interacting species. The ability of predators to capture prey and the ability of prey to avoid predators may have been a major factor that resulted in a diversification of animals into many different species.

Ordovician Period (490–443 mya) As in the Cambrian period, the climate of the early and middle parts of the Ordovician period was warm, and the atmosphere was moist. During this period, a diverse group of hard-shelled marine invertebrates, including trilobites and brachiopods, appeared in the fossil record (**Figure 22.16**). Marine communities consisted of invertebrates, algae, early jawless fishes (a type of early vertebrate), mollusks, and corals. Fossil evidence also suggests that early land plants and arthropods may have first invaded the land during this period.

Toward the end of the Ordovician period, the climate changed rather dramatically. Large glaciers formed, which drained the relatively shallow oceans, causing the water levels to drop. This resulted in a mass extinction in which as much as 60% of the existing marine invertebrates became extinct.

Silurian Period (443–417 mya) In contrast to the dramatic climate changes observed during the Ordovician period, the climate during the Silurian was relatively stable. The glaciers largely melted, which caused the ocean levels to rise. No new major types of invertebrate animals appeared during this period, but significant changes were observed among existing vertebrate and plant species. Many new types of fishes appeared in the fossil record. In addition, coral reefs made their first appearance during this period.

The Silurian marked a major colonization of land by terrestrial plants and animals. For this to occur, certain species evolved adaptations that prevented them from drying out, such as an external cuticle. Ancestral relatives of spiders and centipedes became prevalent.

(a) The Burgess Shale

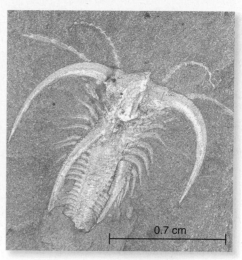

0.7 cm

(b) A fossilized arthropod, *Marrella*

Figure 22.15 **The Cambrian explosion and the Burgess Shale.** (a) This photograph shows the original site in the Canadian Rockies discovered by Charles Walcott. Since its discovery, this site has been made into a quarry for the collection of fossils. (b) A fossil of an extinct arthropod, Marrella, which was found at this site.

2 cm

(a) Trilobite

3 cm

(b) Brachiopod

Figure 22.16 **Shelled, invertebrate fossils of the Ordovician period.** Trilobites existed for millions of years before becoming extinct about 250 mya. Many species of brachiopods exist today.

The earliest fossils of vascular plants, which have tissues that are specialized for the transport of water, sugar, and salts throughout the plant body, were observed in this period.

Devonian Period (417–354 mya)   In the Devonian period, generally dry conditions occurred across much of the northern landmasses. However, the southern landmasses were mostly covered by cool, temperate oceans.

The Devonian saw a major increase in the number of terrestrial species. At first, the vegetation consisted primarily of small plants, only a meter tall or less. Later, ferns, horsetails, and seed plants, such as gymnosperms, also emerged. By the end of the Devonian, the first trees and forests were formed. A major expansion of terrestrial animals also occurred. Insects first appeared in the fossil record, and other invertebrates became plentiful. In addition, the first tetrapods— vertebrates with four legs—are believed to have arisen in the Devonian. Early tetrapods included amphibians, which lived on land but required water in which to lay their eggs.

In the oceans, many types of invertebrates flourished, including brachiopods, echinoderms, and corals. This period is sometimes called the Age of Fishes, as many new types of fishes emerged. During a period of approximately 20 million years near the end of the Devonian period, a prolonged series of extinctions eliminated many marine species. The cause of this mass extinction is not well understood.

Carboniferous Period (354–290 mya)   The term Carboniferous refers to the rich deposits of coal, a sedimentary rock primarily composed of carbon, that were formed during this period. The Carboniferous had the ideal conditions for the subsequent formation of coal. It was a cooler period, and much of the land was covered by forest swamps. Coal was formed over many millions of years from compressed layers of rotting vegetation.

Plants and animals further diversified during the Carboniferous period. Very large plants and trees became prevalent. For example, tree ferns such as *Psaronius* grew to a height of 15 meters or more (**Figure 22.17**). The first flying insects emerged. Giant dragonflies with

Psaronius

Figure 22.17 **A giant tree fern, *Psaronius*, from the Carboniferous period.** This genus became extinct during the Permian. The illustration is a re-creation based on fossil evidence. The inset shows a fossilized section of the trunk, also known as petrified wood.

a wingspan of over 2 feet inhabited the forest swamps. Terrestrial vertebrates also became more diverse. Amphibians were very prevalent. One innovation that seemed particularly beneficial was the amniotic egg. In reptiles, the amniotic egg was covered with a leathery or hard shell, which prevented the desiccation of the embryo inside. This innovation was critical for the emergence of reptiles during this period.

Permian Period (290–248 mya) At the beginning of the Permian, continental drift had brought much of the total land together into a supercontinent known as Pangaea (see Figure 22.10). The interior regions of Pangaea were dry, with great seasonal fluctuations. The forests of fernlike plants were replaced with gymnosperms. Species resembling modern conifers first appeared in the fossil record. Amphibians were prevalent, but reptiles became the dominant vertebrate species.

At the end of the Permian period, the largest known mass extinction in the history of life on Earth occurred; 90–95% of marine species and a large proportion of terrestrial species were eliminated. The cause of the Permian extinction is the subject of much research and controversy. One possibility is that glaciation destroyed the habitats of terrestrial species and lowered ocean levels, which would have caused greater competition among marine species. Another hypothesis is that enormous volcanic eruptions in Siberia produced large ash clouds that abruptly changed the climate on Earth.

Phanerozoic Eon: The Mesozoic Era Saw the Rise and Fall of the Dinosaurs

The Permian extinction marks the division between the Paleozoic and Mesozoic eras. Mesozoic means "middle animals." It was a time period that saw great changes in animal and plant species. This era is sometimes called the Age of Dinosaurs, which flourished during this time. The climate during the Mesozoic era was consistently hot, and terrestrial environments were relatively dry. Little if any ice was found at either pole. The Mesozoic is divided into three periods: the Triassic, Jurassic, and Cretaceous.

Figure 22.18 *Megazostrodon,* **the first known mammal of the Triassic period.** The illustration is a re-creation based on fossilized skeletons. The *Megazostrodon* was 10 to 12 cm long.

BioConnections: *Look ahead to Table 34.1. What are the common characteristics of mammals?*

Triassic Period (248–206 mya) Reptiles were plentiful in this period, including new groups such as crocodiles and turtles. The first dinosaurs emerged during the middle of the Triassic, as did the first mammals, such as the small *Megazostrodon* (**Figure 22.18**). Gymnosperms were the dominant land plant. Volcanic eruptions near the end of the Triassic are thought to have caused global warming, resulting in mass extinctions that eliminated many marine and terrestrial species.

Jurassic Period (206–144 mya) Gymnosperms, such as conifers, continued to be the dominant vegetation. Mammals were not prevalent. Reptiles continued to be the dominant land vertebrate. These included dinosaurs, which were predominantly terrestrial reptiles that shared certain anatomical features, such as an erect posture. Some dinosaurs attained enormous sizes, including the massive *Brachiosaurus*, which reached a length of 25 m (80 ft) and weighed up to 100 tons! Modern birds are descendents of a dinosaur lineage called theropod (meaning "beast-footed") dinosaurs. *Tyrannosaurus rex* is one of the best known theropod dinosaurs. An early birdlike animal, *Archaeopteryx* (**Figure 22.19**), emerged in the Jurassic period. However, paleontologists are debating whether or not *Archaeopteryx* is a true ancestor of modern birds.

Cretaceous Period (144–65 mya) On land, dinosaurs continued to be the dominant animals. The earliest flowering plants, called angiosperms, which form seeds within a protective chamber, emerged and began to diversify.

The end of the Cretaceous witnessed another mass extinction, which brought an end to many previously successful groups of organisms. Except for the lineage that gave rise to birds, dinosaurs abruptly died out, as did many other species. As with the Permian extinction, the cause or causes of this mass extinction are still debated. One plausible hypothesis suggests that a large meteorite hit the region that is now the Yucatan Peninsula of Mexico, lifting massive amounts of debris into the air and thereby blocking the sunlight from reaching the Earth's surface. Such a dense haze could have cooled the Earth's

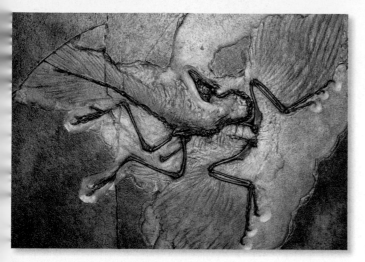

Figure 22.19 A fossil of an early birdlike animal, *Archaeopteryx*, which emerged in the Jurassic period.

surface by 11–15°C (20–30°F). Evidence also points to strong volcanic eruptions as a contributing factor for this mass extinction.

Phanerozoic Eon: Mammals and Flowering Plants Diversified During the Cenozoic Era

The Cenozoic era spans the most recent 65 million years. It is divided into two periods: the Tertiary and Quaternary. In many parts of the world, tropical conditions were replaced by a colder, drier climate. During this time, mammals became the largest terrestrial animals, which is why the Cenozoic is sometimes called the Age of Mammals. However, the Cenozoic era also saw an amazing diversification of many types of organisms, including birds, fishes, insects, and flowering plants.

Tertiary Period (65–1.8 mya) On land, the mammals that survived from the Cretaceous began to diversify rapidly during the early part of the Tertiary period. Angiosperms became the dominant land plant, and insects became important for their pollination. Fishes also diversified, and sharks became abundant.

Toward the end of the Tertiary period, about 7 mya, hominoids came into existence. **Hominoids** include humans, chimpanzees, gorillas, orangutans, and gibbons, plus all of their recent ancestors. The subset of hominoids called hominins includes modern humans, extinct human species (for example, of the *Homo* genus), and our immediate ancestors. In 2002, a fossil of the earliest known hominin, *Sahelanthropus tchadensis*, was discovered in Central Africa. This fossil was dated at between 6 and 7 million years old. Another early hominin genus, called *Australopithecus*, first emerged in Africa about 4 mya. Australopithecines walked upright and had a protruding jaw, prominent eyebrow ridges, and a small braincase.

Quaternary Period (1.8 mya–present) Periodic Ice Ages have been prevalent during the last 1.8 million years, covering much of Europe and North America. This period has witnessed the widespread extinction of many species of mammals, particularly larger ones. Certain species of hominins became increasingly more like living humans. Near the beginning of the Quaternary period, fossils were discovered of *Homo habilis*, or handy man, so called because stone tools were found with the fossil remains. Fossils that are classified as *Homo sapiens*—modern humans—first appeared about 170,000 years ago. The evolution of hominins is discussed in more detail in Chapter 34.

▮ Summary of Key Concepts

- Life began on Earth from nonliving material between 3.5 and 4.0 bya (Figure 22.1).

22.1 Origin of Life on Earth

- Life on Earth is hypothesized to have occurred in four overlapping stages. The first stage involved the synthesis of organic molecules to form a prebiotic soup. Possible scenarios of how this occurred are the reducing atmosphere, extraterrestrial, and deep-sea vent hypotheses (Figures 22.2, 22.3).
- The second stage was the formation of polymers from simple organic molecules. This may have occurred on the surface of clay.
- The third stage occurred when polymers became enclosed in structures called protobionts that separated them from the external environment (Figure 22.4).
- In the fourth stage, polymers enclosed in membranes acquired properties of cells, such as self-replication and other catalytic functions (Figure 22.5).
- In the hypothesized period called the RNA world, the first living cells used RNA for both information storage and catalytic functions.
- Bartel and Szostak demonstrated that chemical selection for RNA molecules, which can catalyze covalent bond formation, is possible experimentally (Figure 22.6).
- The RNA world was eventually superseded by the modern DNA/RNA/protein world.

22.2 The Fossil Record

- Fossils, which are preserved remnants of past life-forms, are formed in sedimentary rock (Figure 22.7).
- Radiometric dating is one way of estimating the age of a fossil. Fossils provide an extensive record of the history of life, though the record is incomplete (Figure 22.8, Table 22.1).

22.3 History of Life on Earth

- The geological time scale, which is divided into four eons and many eras and periods, charts the major events that occurred during the history of life on Earth (Figure 22.9).
- The formation of species, as well as mass extinctions, are correlated with changes in temperature, amount of O_2 in the atmosphere, landmass locations, floods and glaciation, volcanic eruptions, and meteorite impacts (Figure 22.10).
- During the Archaean eon, bacteria and archaea arose. The proliferation of cyanobacteria led to a gradual rise in O_2 levels (Figure 22.11).
- Eukaryotic cells arose during the Proterozoic eon. This origin involved a union between bacterial and archaeal cells that is hypothesized to have been endosymbiotic. The origin of mitochondria and chloroplasts was an endosymbiotic relationship (Figure 22.12).
- Multicellular eukaryotes arose about 1.5 bya during the Proterozoic eon. Multicellularity now occurs via cell division and the adherence of the resulting cells to each other. A multicellular organism can produce multiple cell types (Figure 22.13).

- The first bilateral animal emerged toward the end of the Proterozoic eon (Figure 22.14).
- The Phanerozoic eon is subdivided into the Paleozoic, Mesozoic, and Cenozoic eras. During the Paleozoic era, invertebrates greatly diversified, particularly during the Cambrian explosion, and the land became colonized by plants and animals. Terrestrial vertebrates, including tetrapods, became more diverse (Figures 22.15, 22.16, 22.17).
- Dinosaurs were prevalent during the Mesozoic era, particularly during the Jurassic period. Mammals and birds also emerged (Figures 22.18, 22.19).
- During the Cenozoic era, mammals diversified, and flowering plants became the dominant plant species. The first hominoids emerged approximately 7 mya. Fossils classified as *Homo sapiens*, our species, appeared about 170,000 years ago.

Assess and Discuss

Test Yourself

1. The prebiotic soup was
   a. the assemblage of unicellular prokaryotes that existed in the oceans of early Earth.
   b. the accumulation of organic molecules in the oceans of early Earth.
   c. the mixture of organic molecules found in the cytoplasm of the earliest cells on Earth.
   d. a pool of nucleic acids that contained the genetic information for the earliest organisms.
   e. none of the above.

2. Which of the following is *not* a characteristic of protobionts necessary for the evolution of living cells?
   a. a membrane-like boundary separating the external environment from an internal environment
   b. polymers capable of functioning in information storage
   c. polymers capable of catalytic activity
   d. self-replication
   e. compartmentalization of metabolic activity

3. RNA is believed to be the first functional macromolecule in protobionts because it
   a. is easier to synthesize compared with other macromolecules.
   b. has the ability to store information, self-replicate, and perform catalytic activity.
   c. is the simplest of the macromolecules commonly found in living cells.
   d. All of the above are correct.
   e. Only a and c are correct.

4. The movement of landmasses that have changed their positions, shapes, and association with other landmasses is called
   a. glaciation.   d. biogeography.
   b. Pangaea.   e. geological scale.
   c. continental drift.

5. Paleontologists estimate the dates of fossils by
   a. the layer of rock in which the fossils are found.
   b. analysis of radioisotopes found in nearby igneous rock.
   c. the complexity of the body plan of the organism.
   d. all of the above.
   e. a and b only.

6. The fossil record does not give us a complete picture of the history of life because
   a. not all past organisms have become fossilized.
   b. only organisms with hard skeletons can become fossilized.
   c. fossils of very small organisms have not been found.
   d. fossils of early organisms are located too deep in the crust of the Earth to be found.
   e. all of the above.

7. The endosymbiosis hypothesis explaining the evolution of eukaryotic cells is supported by
   a. DNA-sequencing analysis comparing bacterial genomes, mitochondrial genomes, and eukaryotic nuclear genomes.
   b. naturally occurring examples of endosymbiotic relationships between bacterial cells and eukaryotic cells.
   c. the presence of DNA in mitochondria and chloroplasts.
   d. all of the above.
   e. a and b only.

8. Which of the following explanations of multicellularity in eukaryotes is seen in the development of complex, multicellular organisms today?
   a. endosymbiosis
   b. aggregation of cells to form a colony
   c. division of cells with the resulting cells adhering together
   d. multiple cell types aggregating to form a complex organism
   e. none of the above

9. The earliest fossils of vascular plants were formed during the _____ period.
   a. Ordovician   c. Devonian   e. Jurassic
   b. Silurian   d. Triassic

10. The appearance of the first hominoids dates to the _____ period.
    a. Triassic   c. Cretaceous   e. Quaternary
    b. Jurassic   d. Tertiary

Conceptual Questions

1. What are the four stages that led to the origin of living cells?

2. How are the ages of fossils determined? In your answer, you should discuss which types of rocks are analyzed and explain the concepts of radiometric dating and half-life.

3. Two principles of biology are (1) *living organisms interact with their environment* and (2) *populations of organisms evolve from one generation to the next.* Describe two examples in which changes in the global climate affected the evolution of species.

Collaborative Questions

1. Discuss possible hypotheses of how organic molecules were first formed.

2. Discuss the key features of a protobiont. What distinguishes a protobiont from a living cell?

Online Resource

www.brookerbiology.com

Stay a step ahead in your studies with animations that bring concepts to life and practice tests to assess your understanding. Your instructor may also recommend the interactive eBook, individualized learning tools, and more.

An Introduction to Evolution

23

O rganic life beneath the shoreless waves
Was born and nurs'd in Ocean's pearly caves
First forms minute, unseen by spheric glass,
Move on the mud, or pierce the watery mass;
These, as successive generations bloom,
New powers acquire, and larger limbs assume;
Whence countless groups of vegetation spring,
And breathing realms of fin, and feet, and wing.

From *The Temple of Nature* by Erasmus Darwin,
grandfather of Charles Darwin. Published posthumously in 1803.

The term **evolution** is used to describe a heritable change in one or more characteristics of a population from one generation to the next. Evolution can be viewed on a small scale (**microevolution**) as it relates to changes in a single gene or allele frequencies in a population over time, or it can be viewed on a larger scale (**macroevolution**) as it relates to the formation of new species or groups of related species.

It is helpful to begin our discussion of evolution with a working definition of a species. Biologists often define a **species** as a group of related organisms that share a distinctive form. Among species that reproduce sexually, such as plants and animals, members of the same species are capable of interbreeding in nature to produce viable and fertile offspring. The term **population** refers to all members of a species that live in the same area at the same time and have the opportunity to interbreed. As we will see in Chapter 25, some of the emphasis in the study of evolution is on understanding how populations change over the course of many generations to produce new species.

In the first part of this chapter, we will examine the development of evolutionary thought and some of the basic tenets of evolution, particularly those proposed by the British naturalist Charles Darwin in the mid-1800s. The theory of evolution has been refined over the past 150 years or so, but the fundamental principle of evolution remains unchanged and has provided a cornerstone for our understanding of biology. Ukrainian-born American geneticist Theodosius Dobzhansky, an influential evolutionary scientist of the 1900s, once said, "Nothing in biology makes sense except in the light of evolution." The extraordinarily diverse and often seemingly bizarre array of species on our planet can be explained within the context of evolution. As is the case with all scientific theories, evolution is called a theory because it is supported by a substantial body of evidence and because it explains a wide range of observations. The theory of evolution provides answers to many questions related to the diversity of life. In biology, theories such as this are viewed as scientific knowledge.

Selective breeding. The horses in this race have been bred for a particular trait, in this case, speed. Such a practice, called selective breeding, can dramatically change the traits of organisms over several generations.

In the second part of this chapter, we will survey the extensive data that illustrate the processes by which evolution occurs. These data not only support the theory of evolution but also allow us to understand the interrelatedness of different species, whose similarities are often due to descent from a common ancestor. Much of the early evidence supporting evolution came from direct observations and comparisons of living and extinct species. More recently, advances in molecular genetics, particularly those related to DNA sequencing and genomics, have revolutionized the study of evolution. Scientists now have information that allows us to understand how evolution involves changes in the DNA sequences of a given species. These changes affect both a species' genes and the proteins they encode. **Molecular evolution** refers to the process of evolution at the level of genes and proteins. Comparisons of gene or protein sequences in different organisms can reveal evolutionary relationships that cannot be seen in morphology. A major focus of this textbook, namely genomes and proteomes, is rooted in an understanding of these changes. In the last section of this chapter, we consider some of the exciting new ways of exploring evolutionary change at the molecular level. In the following chapters of this unit, we will examine how such changes are acted upon by evolutionary factors in ways that alter the traits of a given species and may eventually lead to the formation of new species.

23.1 The Theory of Evolution

Learning Outcomes:

1. Define the theory of evolution.
2. Describe the factors that led Darwin to the theory of evolution.
3. Explain the process of natural selection.

Undoubtedly, the question, "Where did we come from?" has been asked and debated by people for thousands of years. Many of the early ideas regarding the existence of living organisms were strongly influenced by religion and philosophy. Some of these ideas suggested that all forms of life have remained the same since their creation. In the 1600s, however, scholars in Europe began a revolution that created the basis of empirical and scientific thought. **Empirical thought** relies on observation to form an idea or hypothesis rather than trying to understand life from a nonphysical or spiritual point of view. As described in this section, the shift toward empirical thought encouraged scholars to look for the basic rationale behind a given process or phenomenon. This perspective played a key role in developing the theory of evolution.

The Work of Several Scientists Set the Stage for Darwin's Ideas

In the mid- to late-1600s, the first scientist to carry out a thorough study of the living world was an English naturalist named John Ray, who developed an early classification system for plants and animals based on anatomy and physiology. He established the modern concept of a species, noting that organisms of one species do not interbreed with members of another and used it as the basic unit of his classification system. Ray's ideas on classification were later expanded by the Swedish naturalist Carolus Linnaeus. How did their work contribute to the development of evolutionary theory? Neither Ray nor Linnaeus proposed that evolutionary change promotes the formation of new species. However, their systematic classification of plants and animals helped scholars of this period perceive the similarities and differences among living organisms.

Late in the 1700s, a small number of European scientists began to quietly suggest that life-forms are not fixed and unchanging. A French zoologist, George Buffon, actually proposed that living things change through time. However, Buffon was careful to hide his views in a 44-volume series of books on natural history. Around the same time, a French naturalist named Jean-Baptiste Lamarck suggested an intimate relationship between variation and evolution. By examining fossils, he realized that some species had remained the same over the millennia and others had changed. Lamarck hypothesized that species change over the course of many generations by adapting to new environments. He believed that living things evolved in a continuously upward direction, from dead matter, through simple to more complex forms, toward "human perfection." According to Lamarck, organisms altered their behavior in response to environmental change. He thought that behavioral changes could modify traits and hypothesized that these modified traits were inherited by offspring. He called this idea the **inheritance of acquired characteristics**. For example, according to Lamarck's hypothesis, giraffes developed their elongated necks and front legs by feeding on the leaves at the top of trees. The exercise of stretching up to the leaves altered the neck and legs, and Lamarck presumed that these acquired characteristics were transmitted to offspring. However, further research has rejected Lamarck's idea that acquired traits can be inherited. Even so, Lamarck's work was important in promoting the idea of evolutionary change.

Interestingly, Erasmus Darwin, the grandfather of Charles Darwin, was a contemporary of Buffon and Lamarck and an early advocate of evolutionary change. He was a physician, a plant biologist, and also a poet (see poem at the beginning of the chapter). He was aware that modern species were different from similar types of fossilized organisms and also saw how plant and animal breeders used breeding practices to change the traits of domesticated species (see chapter opening photo). He knew that offspring inherited features from their parents and went so far as to say that life on Earth could have descended from a common ancestor.

Darwin Suggested That Existing Species Are Derived from Pre-existing Species

Charles Darwin played a central role in developing the theory that existing species have evolved from pre-existing ones. Darwin's unique perspective and his ability to formulate evolutionary theory were shaped by several different fields of study, including ideas of his time about geological and biological processes.

Two main hypotheses about geological processes predominated in the early 19th century. Catastrophism was first proposed by French zoologist and paleontologist Georges Cuvier to explain the age of the Earth. Cuvier suggested that the Earth was just 6,000 years old and that only catastrophic events had changed its geological structure. This idea fit well with certain religious teachings. Alternatively, uniformitarianism, proposed by Scottish geologist James Hutton and popularized by fellow Scotsman geologist Charles Lyell, suggested that changes in the Earth are directly caused by recurring events. For example, they suggested that geological processes such as erosion existed in the past and happened at the same gradual rate as they do now. For such slow geological processes to eventually lead to substantial changes in the Earth's characteristics, a great deal of time was required. Hutton and Lyell were the first to propose that the age of the Earth is well beyond 6,000 years. The ideas of Hutton and Lyell helped to shape Darwin's view of the world.

Darwin's thinking was also influenced by a paper published in 1798 called *Essay on the Principle of Population* by Thomas Malthus, an English economist. Malthus asserted that the population size of humans can, at best, increase linearly due to increased land usage and improvements in agriculture, whereas our reproductive potential is exponential (for example, doubling with each generation). He argued that famine, war, and disease, especially among the poor, keep population growth within existing resources. The relevant message from Malthus's work was that not all members of any population will survive and reproduce.

Darwin's ideas, however, were most influenced by his own experiences and observations. His work as a young man aboard the HMS *Beagle*, a survey ship, lasted from 1831 to 1836 and involved a careful examination of many different species (**Figure 23.1**). The main mission

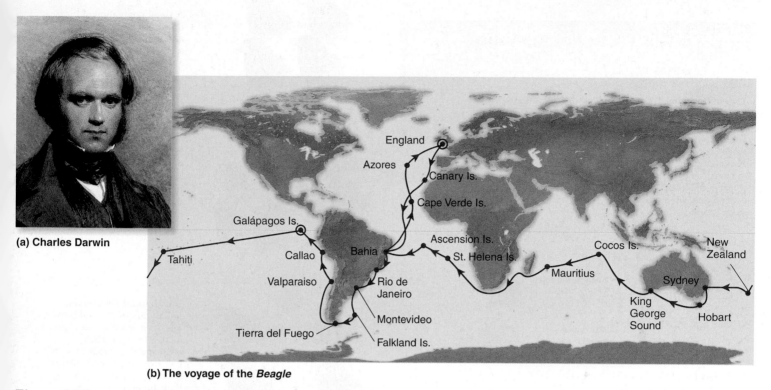

(a) Charles Darwin

(b) The voyage of the *Beagle*

Figure 23.1 **Charles Darwin and the voyage of the *Beagle*, 1831–1836.** **(a)** A portrait of Charles Darwin (1809–1882) at age 31. **(b)** Darwin's voyage on the *Beagle*, which took almost 5 years to circumnavigate the world.

of the *Beagle* was to map the coastline of southern South America and take oceanographic measurements. As the ship's naturalist, Darwin's job was to record information about the weather, geological features, plants, animals, fossils, rocks, minerals, and indigenous people.

Though Darwin made many interesting observations on his journey, he was particularly struck by the distinctive traits of island species. For example, Darwin observed several species of finches found on the Galápagos Islands, a group of volcanic islands 600 miles from the coast of Ecuador. Though it is often assumed that Darwin's personal observations of these finches directly inspired his theory of evolution, this is not the case. Initially, Darwin thought the birds were various species of blackbirds, grosbeaks, and finches. Later, however, the bird specimens from the islands were given to the British ornithologist John Gould, who identified them as several new finch species. Gould's observations helped Darwin in the later formulation of his theory.

As seen in **Table 23.1**, the finches differed widely in the size and shape of their beaks and in their feeding habits. For example, the ground and vegetarian finches have sturdy, crushing beaks they use to crush various sizes of seeds or buds. The tree finches have grasping beaks they use to pick up insects from trees. The mangrove, woodpecker, warbler, and cactus finches have pointed, probing beaks. They use their beaks to search for insects in crevices. The cactus finches use their probing beaks to open cactus fruits and eat the seeds. One species, the woodpecker finch, even uses twigs or cactus spines to extract insect larvae from holes in dead tree branches. Darwin clearly saw the similarities among these species, yet he noted the differences that provided them with specialized feeding strategies. It is now known these finches all evolved from a single species similar to the dull-colored

grassquit finch (*Tiaris obscura*), commonly found along the Pacific Coast of South America. Once they arrived on the Galápagos Islands, the finches' ability to survive and reproduce in their new habitat depended, in part, on changes in the size and shape of their beaks over many generations. These specializations enabled succeeding generations to better obtain particular types of food.

With an understanding of geology and population growth, and his observations from his voyage on the *Beagle*, Darwin had formulated his theory of evolution by the mid-1840s. He had also catalogued and described all of the species he had collected on his *Beagle* voyage except for one type of barnacle. Some have speculated that Darwin may have felt that he should establish himself as an expert on one species before making generalizations about all of them. Therefore, he spent several additional years studying barnacles. During this time, the geologist Charles Lyell, who had greatly influenced Darwin's thinking, strongly encouraged Darwin to publish his theory of evolution. In 1856, Darwin began to write a long book to explain his ideas. In 1858, however, Alfred Wallace, a British naturalist working in the East Indies, sent Darwin an unpublished manuscript to read prior to its publication. In it, Wallace proposed the same ideas concerning evolution. In response to this, Darwin decided to use some of his own writings on this subject, and two papers, one by Darwin and one by Wallace, were published in the *Proceedings of the Linnaean Society of London*. These papers were not widely recognized. A year later, however, Darwin finished his book *On the Origin of Species* (1859), which described his ideas in greater detail and included observational support. This book, which received high praise from many scientists and scorn from others, started a great debate concerning evolution.

Table 23.1   A Comparison of Beak Type and Diet Among the Galápagos Finches That Darwin Studied

Type of finch/diet	Species	Type of beak
Ground finches		
Ground finches have beaks shaped to crush various sizes of seeds; large beaks can crush large seeds, whereas smaller beaks are better for crushing small seeds.	Large ground finch (*Geospiza magnirostris*)	Crushing
	Medium ground finch (*G. fortis*)	
	Small ground finch (*G. fuliginosa*)	
	Sharp-billed ground finch (*G. difficilis*)	
Vegetarian finch		
Vegetarian finches have crushing beaks to pull buds from branches.	Vegetarian finch (*Platyspiza crassirostris*)	Crushing
Tree finches		
Tree finches have grasping beaks to pick insects from trees. Those with heavier beaks can also break apart wood in search of insects.	Large tree finch (*Camarhynchus psittacula*)	Grasping
	Medium tree finch (*Camarhynchus pauper*)	
	Small tree finch (*Camarhynchus parvulus*)	
Tree and warbler finches		
These finches have probing beaks to search for insects in crevices and then to pick them up. The woodpecker finch can also use a cactus spine for probing.	Mangrove finch (*Cactospiza heliobates*)	Probing
	Woodpecker finch (*Camarhynchus pallidus*)	
	Warbler finch (*Certhidea olivacea*)	
Cactus finches		
Cactus finches have probing beaks to open cactus fruits and take out seeds.	Large cactus finch (*G. conirostris*)	Probing
	Cactus finch (*G. scandens*)	

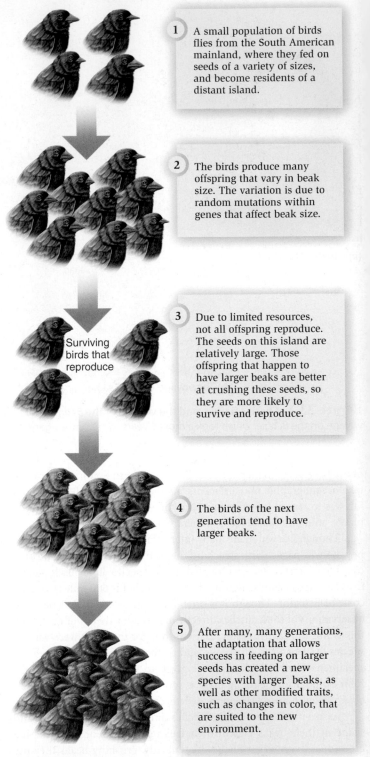

1. A small population of birds flies from the South American mainland, where they fed on seeds of a variety of sizes, and become residents of a distant island.

2. The birds produce many offspring that vary in beak size. The variation is due to random mutations within genes that affect beak size.

Surviving birds that reproduce

3. Due to limited resources, not all offspring reproduce. The seeds on this island are relatively large. Those offspring that happen to have larger beaks are better at crushing these seeds, so they are more likely to survive and reproduce.

4. The birds of the next generation tend to have larger beaks.

5. After many, many generations, the adaptation that allows success in feeding on larger seeds has created a new species with larger beaks, as well as other modified traits, such as changes in color, that are suited to the new environment.

Figure 23.2 Evolutionary adaptation to a new environment via natural selection. The example shown here involves a species of finch adapting to a new environment on a distant island. According to Darwin's theory of evolution, the process of adaptation can lead to the formation of a new species with traits that are better suited to the new environment.

Concept Check: The phrase "an organism evolves" is incorrect. Explain why.

BioConnections: Look back at Figure 22.5. How is natural selection similar to chemical selection? How are they different?

Although some of his ideas were incomplete because the genetic basis of traits was not understood at that time, Darwin's work remains a foundation of our understanding of biology.

Natural Selection Changes Populations from Generation to Generation

Darwin hypothesized that existing life-forms on our planet result from the modification of pre-existing life-forms. He expressed this concept of evolution as "the theory of descent with modification through variation and natural selection." The term evolution refers to change. What factors bring about evolutionary change? According to Darwin's ideas, evolution occurs from generation to generation due to two interacting factors, genetic variation and natural selection:

1. Variation in traits may occur among individuals of a given species. The heritable traits are then passed from parents to offspring. The genetic basis for variation within a species was not understood at the time Darwin proposed his theory of evolution. We now know that such variation is due to different types of genetic changes such as random mutations in genes. Even though Darwin did not fully appreciate the genetic basis of variation, he and many other people before him observed that offspring resemble their parents more than they do unrelated individuals. Therefore, he assumed that some traits are passed from parent to offspring.

2. In each generation, many more offspring are usually produced than will survive and reproduce. Often times, resources in the environment are limiting for an organism's survival. During the process of **natural selection**, individuals with heritable traits that make them better suited to their native environment tend to flourish and reproduce, whereas other individuals are less likely to survive and reproduce. As a result of natural selection, certain traits that favor reproductive success become more prevalent in a population over time.

As an example, we can consider a population of finches that migrates from the South American mainland to a distant island (**Figure 23.2**). Variation exists in the beak sizes among the migrating birds. Let's suppose the seeds produced on the distant island are larger than those produced on the mainland. Those birds with larger beaks would be better able to feed on these larger seeds and therefore would be more likely to survive and pass that trait to their offspring. What are the consequences of this selection process? In succeeding generations, the population tends to have a greater proportion of finches with larger beaks. Alternatively, if a trait happens to be detrimental to an individual's ability to survive and reproduce, natural selection is likely to eliminate this type of variation. For example, if a finch in the same environment had a small beak, this bird would be less likely to acquire food, which would decrease its ability to survive and pass this trait to its offspring. Natural selection may ultimately result in a new species with a combination of multiple traits that are quite different from those of the original species, such as finches with larger beaks and changes in coloration. In other words, the newer species has evolved from a pre-existing one. Let's look at a scientific study involving one such change in a population over time.

FEATURE INVESTIGATION

The Grants Observed Natural Selection in Galápagos Finches

Since 1973, British evolutionary biologists Peter Grant, Rosemary Grant, and their colleagues have studied natural selection in finches found on the Galápagos Islands. For over 30 years, the Grants have focused much of their work on one of the Galápagos Islands known as Daphne Major (**Figure 23.3a**). This small island (0.34 km²) has a moderate degree of isolation (it is 8 km from the nearest island), an undisturbed habitat, and a resident population of *Geospiza fortis*, the medium ground finch (**Figure 23.3b**).

To study natural selection, the Grants observed various traits in finches over the course of many years. One trait they observed is beak size. The medium ground finch has a relatively small crushing beak, allowing it to more easily feed on small, tender seeds (see Table 23.1). The Grants quantified beak size among the medium ground finches of Daphne Major by carefully measuring beak depth—a measurement of the beak from top to bottom (**Figure 23.4**). The small size of the island made it possible for them to measure a large percentage of birds and their offspring. During the course of their studies, they compared the beak depths of parents and offspring by examining many broods over several years and found that the depth of the beak was transmitted from parents to offspring, regardless of environmental conditions, indicating that differences in beak depths are due to genetic differences in the population. In other words, they found that beak depth was a heritable trait.

(a) Daphne Major   **(b) Medium ground finch**

Figure 23.3 The Grants' investigation of natural selection in finches. **(a)** Daphne Major, one of the Galápagos Islands. **(b)** One of the medium ground finches (*Geospiza fortis*) that populate this island.

 **BIOLOGY PRINCIPLE** Populations of organisms evolve from one generation to the next. This study was aimed at analyzing how beak size may change from one generation to the next.

By measuring many birds every year, the Grants were able to assemble a detailed portrait of natural selection in action. In the study shown in Figure 23.4, they measured beak depth from 1976 to 1978. In the wet year of 1976, the plants of Daphne Major produced an abundance of the small, tender seeds that these finches could easily eat. However, a severe drought occurred in 1977. During this year,

Figure 23.4 The Grants and natural selection of beak size among the medium ground finch.

HYPOTHESIS Dry conditions produce larger seeds and may result in larger beaks in succeeding generations of *Geospiza fortis* due to natural selection.

KEY MATERIALS A population of *G. fortis* on the Galápagos Island called Daphne Major.

		Experimental level	Conceptual level
1	In 1976, measure beak depth in parents and offspring of the species *G. fortis*.	Capture birds and measure beak depth. 	This is a way to measure a trait that may be subject to natural selection.
2	Repeat the procedure on offspring that were born in 1978 and had reached mature size. A drought had occurred in 1977 that caused plants on the island to produce mostly large dry seeds and relatively few small seeds.	Capture birds and measure beak depth. 	This is a way to measure a trait that may be subject to natural selection.

3 THE DATA

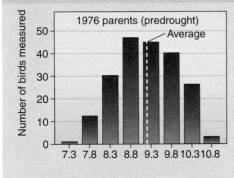
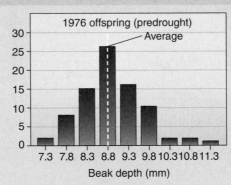
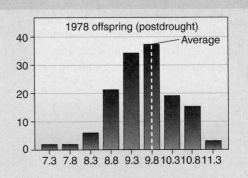

Number of birds measured — Beak depth (mm)

4 CONCLUSION Because a drought produced larger seeds, birds with larger beaks were more likely to survive and reproduce. The process of natural selection produced postdrought offspring that had larger beaks compared to predrought offspring.

5 SOURCE Grant, B. Rosemary, and Grant, Peter R. 2003. What Darwin's Finches Can Teach Us about the Evolutionary Origin and Regulation of Biodiversity. *Bioscience* 53:965–975.

the plants on Daphne Major tended to produce few of the smaller seeds, which the finches rapidly consumed. Therefore, the finches resorted to eating larger, drier seeds, which are harder to crush. As a result, birds with larger beaks were more likely to survive and reproduce because they were better at breaking open the large seeds. As shown in the data, the average beak depth of birds in the population increased substantially, from 8.8 mm in predrought offspring to 9.8 mm in postdrought offspring. How do we explain these results? According to evolutionary theory, birds with larger beaks were more likely to survive and pass this trait to their offspring. Overall, these results illustrate the power of natural selection to alter the features of a trait—in this case, beak depth—in a given population over time.

Experimental Questions

1. What features of Daphne Major made it a suitable field site for studying the effects of natural selection?

2. Why is beak depth in finches a good trait for a study of natural selection? What environmental conditions were important to allowing the Grants to collect information concerning natural selection?

3. What were the results of the Grants' study following the drought in 1977? What effect did these results have on the theory of evolution?

23.2 Evidence of Evolutionary Change

Learning Outcomes:

1. Summarize the different types of evidence for evolutionary change, including the fossil record, biogeography, convergent traits, selective breeding, and homologies.
2. Provide examples of three types of homologies.

Evidence that supports the theory of evolution has been gleaned from many sources (**Table 23.2**). As we have already seen, the Grants were able to observe changes in a finch population as a result of a drought. Historically, the first evidence of biological evolution came from studies of the fossil record, the distribution of related species on our planet, selective breeding experiments, and the comparison of similar anatomical features in different species. More recently, additional evidence that illustrates the process of evolution has been found at the molecular level. By comparing DNA sequences from many different species, evolutionary biologists have gained great insight into the relationship between the evolution of species and the associated

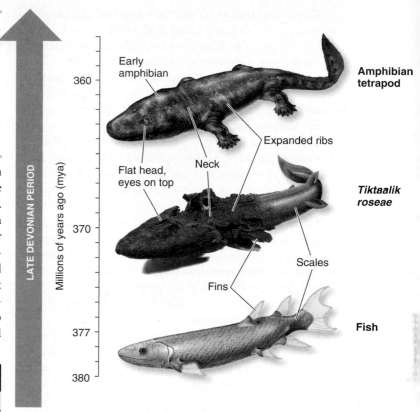

Figure 23.5 A transitional form in the tetrapod lineage. This figure shows two early tetrapod ancestors, a Devonian fish and the transitional form *Tiktaalik roseae*, as well as one of their descendants, an early amphibian. An analysis of the fossils shows that *T. roseae*, also known as a fishapod, had both fish and amphibian characteristics, so it was likely able to survive brief periods out of the water.

changes in the genetic material. In this section, we will survey the various types of evidence that show the process of evolutionary change.

Fossils Show Successive Evolutionary Change

As discussed in Chapter 22, the fossil record has provided biologists with evidence of the history of life on Earth. Today, scientists have access to a far more extensive fossil record than was available to Darwin and other scientists of his time. Even though the fossil record is still incomplete, the many fossils that have been discovered provide detailed information regarding evolutionary change in a series of related organisms. When fossils are compared according to their age, from oldest to youngest, successive evolutionary change becomes apparent.

Let's consider a couple of examples in which paleontologists have observed evolutionary change. In 2005, fossils of *Tiktaalik roseae*, nicknamed fishapod, were discovered by paleontologists Ted Daeschler, Neil Shubin, and Farish Jenkins. The discovery of fishapod illuminates one of several steps that led to the evolution of tetrapods, which are animals with four legs. *T. roseae* is called a **transitional form** because it displays an intermediate state between an ancestral form and the form of its descendants (**Figure 23.5**). In this case, the fishapod is a transitional form between fishes, which have

Table 23.2	Evidence of Biological Evolution
Type of evidence	**Description**
Studies of natural selection	By following the characteristics of populations over time, researchers have observed how natural selection alters such populations in response to environmental changes (see Figure 23.4).
Fossil record	When fossils are compared according to their age, from oldest to youngest, successive evolutionary change becomes apparent.
Biogeography	Unique species found on islands and other remote areas have arisen because the species in these locations have evolved in isolation from the rest of the world.
Convergent evolution	Two different species from different lineages sometimes become anatomically similar because they occupy similar environments. This indicates that natural selection results in adaptation to a given environment.
Selective breeding	The traits in domesticated species have been profoundly modified by selective breeding (also called artificial selection) in which breeders choose the parents that have desirable traits.
Homologies	
Anatomical	Homologous structures are structures that are anatomically similar to each other because they evolved from a structure in a common ancestor. In some cases, such structures have lost their original function and become vestigial.
Developmental	An analysis of embryonic development often reveals similar features that point to past evolutionary relationships.
Molecular	At the molecular level, certain characteristics are found in all living cells, suggesting that all living species are derived from an interrelated group of common ancestors. In addition, species that are closely related evolutionarily have DNA sequences that are more similar to each other than they are to distantly related organisms.

fins for locomotion, and tetrapods, which are four-limbed animals. Unlike a true fish, *T. roseae* had a broad skull, a flexible neck, and eyes mounted on the top of its head like a crocodile. Its interlocking rib cage suggests it had primitive lungs. Perhaps the most surprising discovery was that its pectoral fins (those on the side of the body) revealed the beginnings of a primitive wrist and five finger-like bones. These appendages would have allowed *T. roseae* to support its body on shallow river bottoms and lift its head above the water to search for prey and perhaps even move out of the water for short periods. During the Devonian period (417–354 mya), this could have been an important advantage in the marshy floodplains of large rivers.

One of the best-studied observations of evolutionary change through the fossil record is that of the horse family, modern members of which include horses, zebras, and donkeys. These species, which are large, long-legged animals adapted to living in open grasslands, are the remaining descendants of a long lineage that produced many species that have subsequently become extinct since its origin approximately 55 mya. Examination of the horse lineage through fossils provides a particularly interesting case of how evolution involves adaptation to changing environments.

The earliest known fossils of the horse family revealed that the animals were small with short legs and broad feet (**Figure 23.6**). Early horses, such as *Hyracotherium*, lived in wooded habitats and are thought to have browsed on leaves. The fossil record has revealed changes in size, foot anatomy, and tooth morphology among this group of related species over time. Early horses were the size of dogs, whereas modern horses typically weigh more than a half ton. *Hyracotherium*, an early horse, had four toes on its front feet and three on its hind feet. The toes were encased in fleshy pads. By comparison, the feet of modern horses have a single toe, enclosed in a tough, bony hoof. The fossil record shows an increase in the length of the central toe, the development of a bony hoof, and the loss of the other toes. Finally, the teeth of *Hyracotherium* were relatively small compared with those of modern horses. Over the course of millions of years, horse molars have increased in size and developed a complex pattern of ridges.

How do evolutionary biologists explain these changes in horse characteristics? The changes can be attributed to natural selection, which acted on existing variation and resulted in adaptations to changes in global climates. Over North America, where much of horse evolution occurred, changes in climate caused large areas of dense forests to be replaced with grasslands. The increase in size and changes in foot structure enabled horses to escape predators more easily and travel greater distances in search of food. The changes seen in horses' teeth are consistent with a shift from eating the tender leaves of bushes and trees to eating grasses and other vegetation that are abrasive and require more chewing.

Biogeography Indicates That Species in a Given Area Have Evolved from Pre-existing Species

Biogeography is the study of the geographic distribution of extinct and living species. Patterns of past evolution are often found in the natural geographic distribution of related species. From such studies, scientists have discovered that isolated continents and island groups have evolved their own distinct plant and animal communities. As

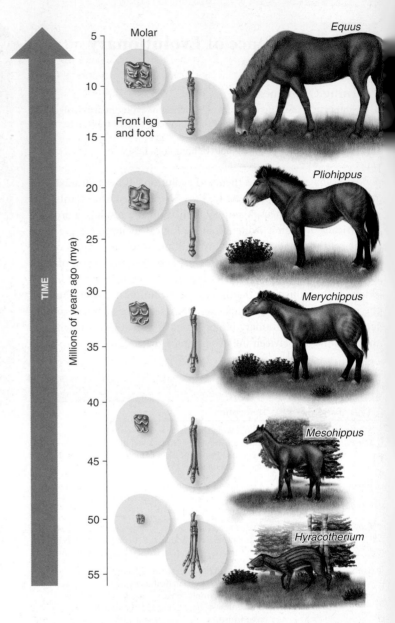

Figure 23.6 Evolutionary changes in horse morphology. Some major changes observed in the fossil record relate to body size, foot anatomy, and tooth morphology. These anatomical changes are hypothesized to be due to adaptations to a changing environment over the last 55 million years. Note: This figure is meant to emphasize general anatomical changes in horse morphology. The evolutionary pathway that produced modern horses involves several branches and is described in Chapter 26.

BIOLOGY PRINCIPLE All species (past and present) are related by an evolutionary history. This diagram shows the morphological changes that occurred in the evolution of the horse.

mentioned earlier, Darwin observed several species of finches found on the Galápagos Islands that had unique characteristics, such as beak shapes, when compared with similar finches found on the mainland. Scientists now hypothesize these island species evolved from mainland birds that had migrated to the islands and then became adapted to a variety of new feeding habits (see Figure 23.2).

Islands, which are isolated from other large landmasses, provide numerous examples in which geography has played a key role in the evolution of new species. Islands often have many species of plants and animals that are **endemic**, which means they are naturally found only in a particular location. Most endemic island species have closely related relatives on nearby islands or the mainland. For example, consider the island fox (*Urocyon littoralis*), which lives on the Channel Islands located off the coast of Santa Barbara in southern California (**Figure 23.7**). This type of fox is found nowhere else in the world. It weighs about 3–6 pounds and feeds largely on insects, mice, and fruits. The island fox evolved from the mainland gray fox (*Urocyon cinereoargenteus*), which is much larger, usually 7–11 pounds. During the last Ice Age, about 16,000–18,000 years ago, the Santa Barbara channel was frozen and narrow enough for ancestors of the mainland gray fox to cross over to the Channel Islands. When the Ice Age ended, the ice melted and sea levels rose, causing the foxes to be cut off from the mainland. Over the last 16,000–18,000 years, the population of foxes on the Channel Islands evolved into the smaller island fox, which is now considered a different species from the larger gray fox. The gray fox is still found on the mainland. The smaller size of the island fox is an example of island dwarfing, a phenomenon in which the size of large animals on an isolated island shrinks dramatically over many generations. It is the result of natural selection in which a smaller size provides a survival and reproductive advantage, probably because of limited food and other resources.

The evolution of major animal groups is also correlated with known changes in the distribution of landmasses on the Earth. The first mammals arose approximately 200 mya, when the area that is now Australia was still connected to the other continents. However, the first placental mammals, which have a long internal gestation and give birth to well-developed offspring, evolved much later, after continental drift had separated Australia from the other continents (refer back to Figure 22.10). Except for a few species of bats and rodents that have migrated to Australia more recently, Australia lacks any of the larger, terrestrial placental mammals. How do biologists explain this observation? It is consistent with the idea that placental mammals first arose somewhere other than Australia, and that the barrier of a large ocean prevented most terrestrial placental mammals from migrating there. On the other hand, Australia has more than 100 species of kangaroos, koalas, and other marsupials, most of which are not found on any other continent. Marsupials are a group of mammal species in which young are born in a very immature condition and then develop further in the mother's abdominal pouch, which covers the mammary glands. Evolutionary theory is consistent with the idea that the existence of these unique Australian species is due to their having evolved in isolation from the rest of the world for millions of years.

Convergent Evolution Suggests Adaptation to the Environment

The process of natural selection is also evident in the study of plants and animals that have similar characteristics, even though they are not closely related evolutionarily. This similarity is the result of **convergent evolution**, in which two species from different lineages have independently evolved similar characteristics because they occupy similar environments. For example, both the giant anteater

(a) Island fox
(*Urocyon littoralis*)

California

Santa Barbara

Channel Islands

Santa Barbara channel

San Miguel

Santa Rosa

Santa Cruz

Anacapa

(b) Gray fox (*Urocyon cinereoargenteus*)

Figure 23.7 **The evolution of an endemic island species from a mainland species.** (a) The smaller island fox found on the Channel Islands evolved from (b) the gray fox found on the California mainland.

Concept Check: *Explain how geography played a key role in the evolution of the island fox.*

(*Myrmecophaga tridactyla*), found in South America, and the echidna (*Tachyglossus aculeatus*), found in Australia, have a long snout and tongue. Both species independently evolved these adaptations that enable them to feed on ants (**Figure 23.8a**). The giant anteater is a placental mammal, whereas the echidna is an egg-laying mammal known as a monotreme, so they are not closely related evolutionarily.

Another example of convergent evolution involves aerial rootlets found in vines such as English ivy (*Hedera helix*) and wintercreeper (*Euonymus fortunei*) (**Figure 23.8b**). Based on differences in their structures, these aerial rootlets appear to have developed independently as an effective means of clinging to the support on which a vine attaches itself.

A third example of convergent evolution is revealed by the molecular analysis of fishes that live in very cold water. Antifreeze

(a) The long snouts and tongues of the giant anteater (left) and the echidna (right) allow them to feed on ants.

(b) The aerial rootlets of English ivy (left) and wintercreeper (right) enable them to climb up supports.

Figure 23.8 **Examples of convergent evolution.** All three pairs of species shown in this figure are not closely related evolutionarily but occupy similar environments, suggesting that natural selection results in similar adaptations to a particular environment.

Concept Check: *Can you think of another example in which two species that are not closely related have a similar adaptation?*

(c) The sea raven (left) and the longhorn sculpin (right) have antifreeze proteins that enable them to survive in frigid waters.

proteins enable certain species of fishes to survive the subfreezing temperatures of Arctic and Antarctic waters by inhibiting the formation of ice crystals in body fluids. Researchers have determined that these fishes are an interesting case of convergent evolution (**Figure 23.8c**). Among different species of fishes, one of five different genes has independently evolved to produce antifreeze proteins. For example, in the sea raven (*Hemitripterus americanus*), the antifreeze protein is rich in the amino acid cysteine, and the secondary structure

of the protein is in a β sheet conformation. In contrast, the antifreeze protein in the longhorn sculpin (*Trematomus nicolai*) is encoded by an entirely different gene. The antifreeze protein in this species is rich in the amino acid glutamine, and the secondary structure of the protein is largely composed of α helices.

The similar characteristics in the examples shown in Figure 23.8— for example, the snouts of the anteater and the echidna—are called **analogous structures** or convergent traits. They represent cases in

(a) Bulldog

(b) Greyhound

(c) Dachshund

Figure 23.9 **Common breeds of dogs that have been obtained by selective breeding.** By selecting individuals carrying the alleles that influence traits desirable to humans, dog breeders have produced breeds with distinctive features. All the dogs in this figure carry the same kinds of genes (for example, genes that affect their size, shape, and fur color). However, the alleles for many of these genes are different among these dogs, thereby allowing dog breeders to select for or against them and produce breeds with strikingly different phenotypes.

which characteristics have arisen independently, two or more times, because different species have occupied similar types of environments on the Earth.

Selective Breeding Is a Human-Driven Form of Selection

The term **selective breeding** refers to programs and procedures designed to modify traits in domesticated species. This practice, also called **artificial selection**, is related to natural selection. In forming his theory of evolution, Charles Darwin was influenced by his observations of selective breeding by pigeon breeders. The primary difference between natural and artificial selection is how the parents are chosen. Natural selection occurs because of genetic variation in reproductive success. Organisms that are able to survive and reproduce are more likely to pass their genes to future generations. Environmental factors often determine which individuals will be successful parents. In artificial selection, the breeder chooses as parents those individuals with traits that are desirable from a human perspective.

The underlying phenomenon that makes selective breeding possible is genetic variation. Within a population, variation may exist in a trait of interest. For selective breeding to be successful, the underlying cause of the phenotypic variation is usually related to differences in **alleles**, variant forms of a particular gene, that determine the trait. The breeder chooses parents with desirable phenotypic characteristics. For centuries, humans have employed selective breeding to obtain domesticated species with interesting or agriculturally useful characteristics. For example, many common breeds of dog are the result of selective breeding strategies (**Figure 23.9**). All dogs are members of the same species, *Canis lupus*, subspecies *familiaris*, so they can interbreed to produce offspring. Selective breeding can dramatically modify the traits in a species. When you compare certain breeds of dogs (for example, a greyhound and a dachshund), they hardly look

like members of the same species! Recent work in 2007 by American geneticist Nathan Sutter and colleagues indicates that the size of dogs may be determined by alleles in the *Igf1* gene that encodes a growth hormone called insulin-like growth factor 1. A particular allele of this gene was found to be common to all small breeds of dogs and nearly absent from very large breeds, suggesting that this allele is a major contributor to body size in small breeds of dogs.

Likewise, most of the food we eat—including products such as grains, fruits, vegetables, meat, milk, and juices—is obtained from species that have been profoundly modified by selective breeding strategies. For example, certain characteristics in the wild mustard plant (*Brassica oleracea*) have been modified by selective breeding to produce several varieties of domesticated crops, including broccoli, Brussels sprouts, cabbage, and cauliflower (**Figure 23.10**). The wild mustard plant is native to Europe and Asia, and plant breeders began to modify its traits approximately 4,000 years ago. As seen here, certain traits in the domestic strains differ dramatically from those of the original wild species. These varieties are all members of the same species. They can interbreed to produce viable offspring. For example, in the grocery store you may have seen broccoflower, a vegetable produced from a cross between broccoli and cauliflower.

As another example, **Figure 23.11** shows the results of a selective breeding experiment on corn begun at the University of Illinois Agricultural Experiment Station in 1896, several years before the rediscovery of Mendel's laws. This study began with 163 ears of corn with an oil content ranging from 4 to 6%. In each of 80 succeeding generations, corn plants were divided into two separate groups. In one group, members with the highest oil content in the kernels were chosen as parents of the next generation. In the other group, members with the lowest oil content were chosen. After many generations, the oil content in the first group rose to over 18%. In the other group, it dropped to less than 1%. These results show that selective breeding can modify a trait in a very directed manner.

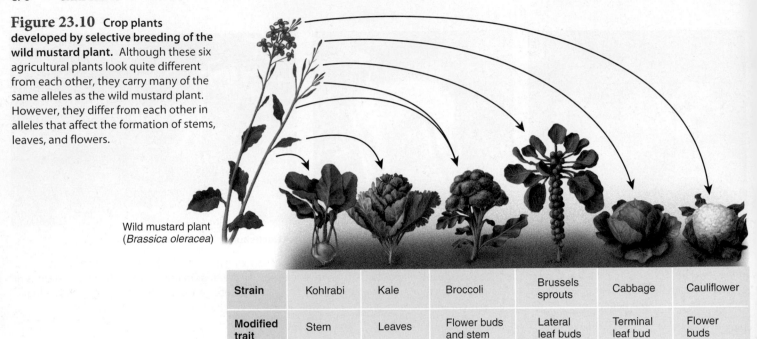

Figure 23.10 Crop plants developed by selective breeding of the wild mustard plant. Although these six agricultural plants look quite different from each other, they carry many of the same alleles as the wild mustard plant. However, they differ from each other in alleles that affect the formation of stems, leaves, and flowers.

Wild mustard plant (*Brassica oleracea*)

Strain	Kohlrabi	Kale	Broccoli	Brussels sprouts	Cabbage	Cauliflower
Modified trait	Stem	Leaves	Flower buds and stem	Lateral leaf buds	Terminal leaf bud	Flower buds

A Comparison of Homologies Shows Evolution of Related Species from a Common Ancestor

Let's now consider other widespread observations of the process of evolution among living organisms. In biology, the term **homology** refers to a similarity that occurs due to descent from a common ancestor. Two species may have a similar trait because the trait was originally found in a common ancestor. As described next, such homologies may involve anatomical, developmental, or molecular features.

Anatomical Homologies As noted by Theodosius Dobzhansky, many observations regarding the features of living organisms simply cannot be understood in any meaningful scientific way except as a result of evolution. A comparison of vertebrate anatomy is a case in point. An examination of the limbs of modern vertebrate species reveals similarities that indicate the same set of bones has undergone evolutionary changes, becoming modified to perform different functions in different species. As seen in **Figure 23.12**, the forelimbs of vertebrates have a strikingly similar pattern of bone arrangements. These are termed **homologous structures**—structures that are similar to each other because they are derived from a common ancestor. The forearm has developed different functions among various vertebrates, including grasping, walking, flying, swimming, and climbing. The theory of evolution explains how these animals have descended from a common ancestor and how natural selection has resulted in modifications to the structure of the original set of bones in ways that ultimately allowed them to be used for several different functions.

Another result of evolution is the phenomenon of **vestigial structures**, anatomical features that have no current function but resemble structures of their presumed ancestors (**Table 23.3**). An interesting case is found in humans. People have a complete set of muscles for moving their ears, even though most people are unable to do so. By comparison, many modern mammals can move their ears, and presumably this was an important trait in a distant human ancestor. Why would organisms have structures that are no longer useful? Within the context of evolutionary theory, vestigial structures are evolutionary relics. Organisms having vestigial structures share a common ancestry with organisms in which the structure is functional. Natural selection maintains functional structures in a population of individuals. However, if a species changes its lifestyle so the structure loses its purpose, the selection that would normally keep the structure in a functional condition is no longer present. When this occurs, the structure may degenerate over the course of many generations due to the accumulation of mutations that limit its size and shape. Natural selection may eventually eliminate such traits due to the inefficiency and cost of producing unused structures.

Developmental Homologies Another example of homology is the way that animals undergo embryonic development. Species that differ substantially at the adult stage often bear striking similarities during early stages of embryonic development. These temporary similarities are called developmental homologies. In addition, evolutionary history is revealed during development in certain organisms, such as vertebrates. For example, if we consider human development, several features are seen in the embryo that are not present at birth. Human embryos have rudimentary gill ridges like a fish embryo, even though human embryos receive oxygen via the umbilical cord. The presence of gill ridges indicates that humans evolved from an aquatic species that had gill slits. A second observation is that every human embryo has a bony tail. It is difficult to see the advantage of such a structure in utero, but easier to understand its presence assuming that an ancestor of the human lineage possessed a tail. These observations, and many others, illustrate that closely related species share similar developmental pathways.

Molecular Homologies Our last examples of homology due to evolution involve molecular studies. Similarities between organisms at the molecular level due to descent from a common ancestor are

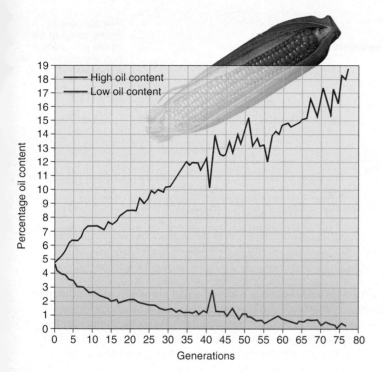

Figure 23.11 **Results of selective breeding for oil content in corn plants.** In this example, corn plants were selected for breeding based on high or low oil content of the kernels. Over the course of many generations, this had a major influence on the amount of corn oil (an agriculturally important product) made by the two groups of plants.

BIOLOGY PRINCIPLE **Populations of organisms evolve from one generation to the next.** This study illustrates how a trait in corn, namely oil content, may change over time due to human intervention.

Concept Check: *When comparing Figures 23.9, 23.10, and 23.11, what general effects of artificial selection do you observe?*

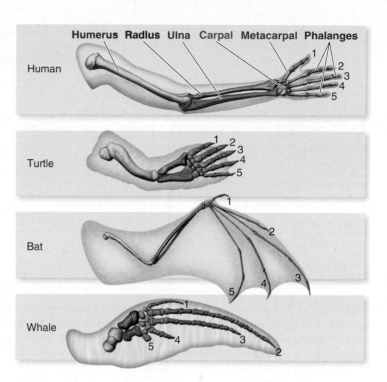

Figure 23.12 **An example of anatomical homology: Homologous structures found in vertebrates.** The same set of bones is found in the human arm, turtle arm, bat wing, and whale flipper, although their relative sizes and shapes differ significantly. This homology suggests that all of these animals evolved from a common ancestor.

BIOLOGY PRINCIPLE **Structure determines function.** These homologous sets of bones have evolved into somewhat different structures due to differences in their functions in humans, turtles, bats, and whales.

Table 23.3	Examples of Vestigial Structures in Animals
Organism	**Vestigial structure(s)**
Humans	Tail bone and muscles to wiggle ears in adult
Boa constrictors	Skeletal remnants of hip and hind leg bones
Whales	Skeletal remnants of a pelvis
Manatees	Fingernails on the flippers
Hornbills and cuckoos	Fibrous cords that were derived from the common carotid arteries. In certain families of birds, both of the common carotid arteries are nonfunctional, fibrous cords. Their vascular function has been assumed by other vessels.

called **molecular homologies**. For example, all living species use DNA to store information and rely on the genetic code to translate mRNA into proteins. Furthermore, certain biochemical pathways are found in all or nearly all species, although minor changes in the structure and function of proteins involved in these pathways have occurred. For example, all species that use oxygen, which constitutes the great majority of species on our planet, have similar proteins that together make up an electron transport chain and an ATP synthase (refer back to Figure 7.8). In addition, nearly all living organisms can break down glucose via a metabolic pathway that is described in Chapter 7. How do we explain these types of observations? Taken together, they indicate that such molecular phenomena arose very early in the origin of life and have been passed to all or nearly all modern forms.

A very compelling observation at the molecular level indicating that modern life-forms are derived from an interrelated group of common ancestors is revealed by analyzing genetic sequences. The same type of gene is often found in diverse organisms. Furthermore, the degree of similarity between genetic sequences from different species reflects the evolutionary relatedness of those species.

As an example, let's consider the *p53* gene, which encodes the p53 protein—a checkpoint protein of the cell cycle (see Chapter 14, Figure 14.15). **Figure 23.13** shows a short amino acid sequence that makes up part of the p53 protein from a variety of species, including five mammals, one bird, and three fish. The top sequence is the human p53 sequence, and the right column describes the percentages of amino acids within the entire sequence that are identical

	Short amino acid sequence within the p53 protein	Percentages of amino acids in the whole p53 protein that are identical to human p53
Human (*Homo sapiens*)	Val Pro Ser Gln Lys Thr Tyr Gln Gly Ser Tyr Gly Phe Arg Leu Gly Phe Leu His Ser Gly Thr	100
Rhesus monkey (*Macaca mulatta*)	Val Pro Ser Gln Lys Thr Tyr His Gly Ser Tyr Gly Phe Arg Leu Gly Phe Leu His Ser Gly Thr	95
Green monkey (*Cercopithecus aethiops*)	Val Pro Ser Gln Lys Thr Tyr His Gly Ser Tyr Gly Phe Arg Leu Gly Phe Leu His Ser Gly Thr	95
Rabbit (*Oryctolagus cuniculus*)	Val Pro Ser Gln Lys Thr Tyr His Gly Asn Tyr Gly Phe Arg Leu Gly Phe Leu His Ser Gly Thr	86
Dog (*Canis lupus familiaris*)	Val Pro Ser Pro Lys Thr Tyr Pro Gly Thr Tyr Gly Phe Arg Leu Gly Phe Leu His Ser Gly Thr	80
Chicken (*Gallus gallus*)	Val Pro Ser Thr Glu Asp Tyr Gly Gly Asp Phe Asp Phe Arg Val Gly Phe Val Glu Ala Gly Thr	53
Channel catfish (*Ictalurus punctatus*)	Val Pro Val Thr Ser Asp Tyr Pro Gly Leu Leu Asn Phe Thr Leu His Phe Gln Glu Ser Ser Gly	48
European flounder (*Platichthys flesus*)	Val Pro Val Val Thr Asp Tyr Pro Gly Glu Tyr Gly Phe Gln Leu Arg Phe Gln Lys Ser Gly Thr	46
Congo puffer fish (*Tetraodon miurus*)	Val Pro Val Thr Thr Asp Tyr Pro Gly Glu Tyr Gly Phe Lys Leu Arg Phe Gln Lys Ser Gly Thr	41

Figure 23.13 **An example of genetic homology: A comparison of a short amino acid sequence within the p53 protein from nine different animals.** This figure compares a short region of the p53 protein, a tumor suppressor that plays a role in preventing cancer. Amino acids are represented by three-letter abbreviations. The orange-colored amino acids in the sequences are identical to those in the human sequence. The numbers in the right column indicate the percentage of amino acids within the whole p53 protein that is identical with the human p53 protein, which is 393 amino acids in length. For example, 95% of the amino acids, or 373 of 393, are identical between the p53 sequence found in humans and in Rhesus monkeys.

Concept Check: In the sequence shown in this figure, how many amino acid differences occur between the following pairs: Rhesus and green monkeys, Congo puffer fish and European flounder, and Rhesus monkey and Congo puffer fish? What do these differences tell you about the evolutionary relationships among these four species?

BioConnections: Look back at Table 21.5. How are genetic sequences that are retrieved from a database using the BLAST program correlated with the evolutionary relatedness of the species?

to those in the entire human sequence. Amino acids in the other species that are identical to those in humans are highlighted in orange. The sequences from the two monkeys are the most similar to those in humans, followed by the other two mammalian species (rabbit and dog). The three fish sequences are the least similar to the human sequence, but the fish sequences tend to be similar to each other.

Taken together, the data shown in Figure 23.13 illustrate two critical points about gene evolution. First, specific genes are found in a diverse array of species such as mammals, birds, and fishes. Second, the sequences of closely related species tend to be more similar to each other than they are to distantly related species. The mechanisms for this second observation are discussed in the next section.

23.3 The Molecular Processes That Underlie Evolution

Learning Outcomes:

1. Explain how paralogs and orthologs are produced.
2. Describe how new types of genes arise via exon shuffling.
3. Distinguish between vertical evolution and horizontal gene transfer.

Historically, the study of evolution was based on a comparison of the anatomies of extinct and modern species to identify similarities between related species. However, the advent of molecular approaches for analyzing DNA sequences has revolutionized the field of evolutionary biology. Now we can analyze how changes in the genetic material are associated with changes in phenotype. In this section, we will examine some of the molecular changes in the genetic material that reveal evolutionary change.

Homologous Genes Are Derived from a Common Ancestral Gene

Two or more genes derived from the same ancestral gene are called **homologous genes**. The analysis of homologous genes reveals evidence of evolutionary change at the molecular level. How do homologous genes arise? As an example, let's consider a gene in two different species of bacteria that encodes a transport protein involved in the uptake of metal ions into bacterial cells. Homologous genes that are in different species are termed **orthologs**. Millions of years ago, these two species had a common ancestor (**Figure 23.14**). Over time, the common ancestor diverged into additional species, eventually evolving into *Escherichia coli*, *Clostridium acetylbutylicum*, and many other species. Since this divergence, the metal transporter gene has accumulated mutations that altered its sequence, though

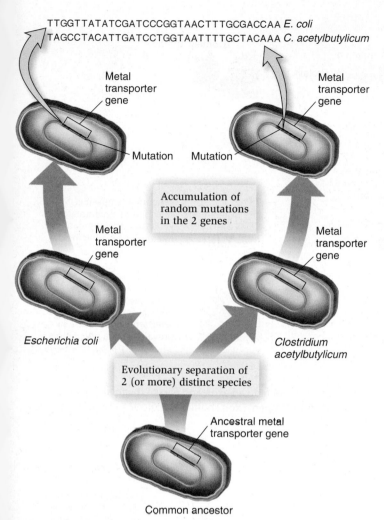

```
TTGGTTATATCGATCCCGGTAACTTTGCGACCAA E. coli
TAGCCTACATTGATCCTGGTAATTTTGCTACAAA C. acetylbutylicum
```

Figure 23.14 **The evolution of orthologs, homologous genes from different species.** After the two species diverged from each other, the genes accumulated random mutations that resulted in similar, but not identical, gene sequences called orthologs. These orthologs in *E. coli* and *C. acetylbutylicum* encode metal transporters. Only one of the two DNA strands is shown from each of the genes. Bases that are identical between the two genes are shown in orange.

Concept Check: *Why do these orthologs have similar gene sequences? Why aren't they identical?*

the similarity between the *E. coli* and the *C. acetylbutylicum* genes remains striking. In this case, the two sequences are similar because they were derived from the same ancestral gene, but they are not identical due to the independent accumulation of different random mutations.

Gene Duplications Produce Gene Families

Evidence of evolutionary change is also found within a single species. Two or more homologous genes within a single species are termed **paralogs** of each other. Rare gene duplication events produce multiple copies of a gene and ultimately lead to the formation of a **gene family**—a set of paralogs within the genome of a single species. A well-studied example of a gene family is the globin gene family in humans, which is composed of 14 genes that are hypothesized to be derived from a

single ancestral globin gene (refer back to Figure 21.8). According to an evolutionary analysis, the ancestral globin gene first duplicated between 500 and 600 mya. Since that time, additional duplication events and chromosomal rearrangements have produced the current number of 14 genes on three different human chromosomes.

What is the advantage of a gene family? Even though all of the globin polypeptides are subunits of proteins that play a role in oxygen binding, the accumulation of changes in the various family members has produced globins that differ in the timing of their expression and in their functional properties. The various globin genes are expressed at different stages of development in humans. The functional differences of the globin proteins correlate with the oxygen transport needs of humans during the embryonic, fetal, and postpartum stages of life (refer back to Figure 13.3).

What is the evolutionary significance of the globin gene family regarding adaptation? On land, egg cells and small embryos are very susceptible to drying out if they are not protected in some way. Species such as birds and reptiles lay eggs with a protective shell around them. Most mammals, however, have become adapted to a terrestrial environment by evolving internal gestation. The ability to develop young internally has been an important factor in the survival and proliferation of humans and other mammals. The embryonic and fetal forms of hemoglobin allow the embryo and fetus to capture oxygen from the bloodstream of the mother.

GENOMES & PROTEOMES CONNECTION

New Genes in Eukaryotes Have Evolved via Exon Shuffling

Thus far, we have considered how evolutionary change results in the formation of homologous genes, either orthologs or paralogs. Evolutionary mechanisms are also revealed when exons, the parts of genes that encode protein domains, are compared within a single species. Many proteins, particularly those found in eukaryotic species, have a modular structure composed of two or more domains with different functions. By comparing the modular structure of eukaryotic proteins with the genes that encode them, geneticists have discovered that each domain tends to be encoded by one exon or by a series of two or more adjacent exons.

During the evolution of eukaryotic species, many new genes have been produced by a type of mutation known as **exon shuffling**. During this process, an exon and parts of the flanking introns from one gene are inserted into another gene, thereby producing a new gene that encodes a protein with an additional domain (**Figure 23.15**). This process may also involve the duplication and rearrangement of exons. Exon shuffling can result in novel genes that express proteins with new combinations of functional domains. Such proteins may alter traits in the organism and therefore be subjected to natural selection.

Exon shuffling may occur by more than one mechanism. One possibility is that a double crossover could promote the insertion of an exon into another gene (as seen in Figure 23.15). Alternatively, transposable elements, described in Chapter 21, may promote the movement of exons into other genes.

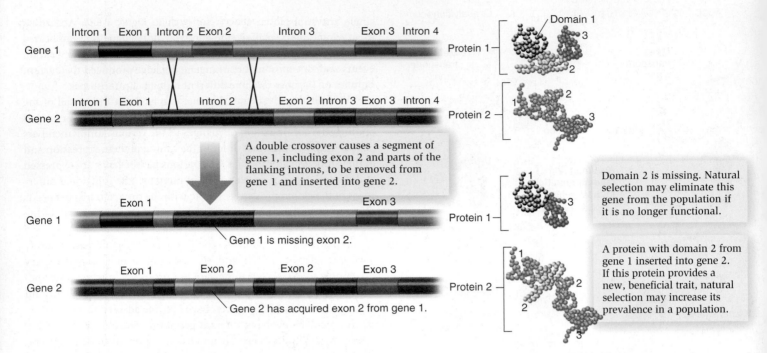

Figure 23.15 **The process of exon shuffling.** In this example, a segment of one gene containing an exon and part of the flanking introns has been inserted into another gene. A rare, abnormal double crossover event may cause this to happen. Exon shuffling results in proteins that have new combinations of domains and new combinations of functions.

Concept Check: *What is the evolutionary advantage of exon shuffling?*

Horizontal Gene Transfer Contributes to the Evolution of Species

At the molecular level, the type of evolutionary change depicted in Figures 23.13 through 23.15 is called **vertical evolution**. In these cases, new species arise from pre-existing species by the accumulation of genetic changes, such as gene mutations, gene duplications, and exon shuffling. Vertical evolution involves genetic changes in a series of ancestors that form a lineage. In addition to vertical evolution, species accumulate genetic changes by **horizontal gene transfer**—a process in which an organism incorporates genetic material from another organism without being the offspring of that organism. Horizontal gene transfer can involve the exchange of genetic material between members of the same species or different species.

How does horizontal gene transfer occur? **Figure 23.16** illustrates one possible mechanism for horizontal gene transfer. In this example, a paramecium, which is a eukaryotic organism, has engulfed a bacterial cell. During the degradation of the bacterium in a phagocytic vesicle, a bacterial gene escapes to the nucleus of the cell, where it is inserted into one of the chromosomes. In this way, a gene has been transferred from a bacterial species to a eukaryotic species. By analyzing gene sequences among many different species, researchers have discovered that horizontal gene transfer is a common phenomenon. This process can occur from bacteria and archaea to eukaryotes, from eukaryotes to bacteria and archaea, between different species of bacteria and archaea, and between different species of eukaryotes. Therefore, when we view evolution, it is not simply a matter of one species evolving into one or more new species via the accumulation of random mutations. It also involves the horizontal transfer of genes

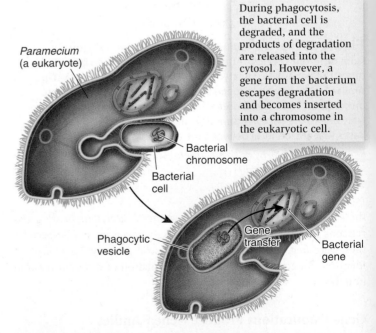

During phagocytosis, the bacterial cell is degraded, and the products of degradation are released into the cytosol. However, a gene from the bacterium escapes degradation and becomes inserted into a chromosome in the eukaryotic cell.

Figure 23.16 **Horizontal gene transfer from a bacterium to a eukaryote.** In this example, a bacterium is engulfed by a paramecium (a ciliated protist), and a bacterial gene is transferred to one of the paramecium's chromosomes.

BioConnections: *Look back at Table 18.3. What are three mechanisms of gene transfer that could result in horizontal gene transfer between two different bacterial species?*

among different species, enabling those species to acquire new traits that foster the evolutionary process.

Horizontal gene transfer among bacterial species is relatively widespread. As discussed in Chapter 18, bacterial species may carry out three natural mechanisms of gene transfer known as conjugation, transformation, and transduction. By analyzing the genomes of bacterial species, scientists have determined that many genes within a given bacterial genome are derived from horizontal gene transfer. Genome studies have suggested that as much as 20–30% of the variation in the genetic composition of modern bacterial species can be attributed to this process. The roles of the genes acquired by horizontal gene transfer are quite varied, though they commonly involve functions that are beneficial for survival and reproduction. These include genes that confer antibiotic resistance, the ability to degrade toxic compounds, and pathogenicity (the ability to cause disease).

Evolution at the Genomic Level Involves Changes in Chromosome Structure and Number

Thus far, we have considered several ways a species might acquire new genetic variation. These include mutations within pre-existing genes, gene duplications that produce gene families, exon shuffling, and horizontal gene transfer. Evolution also involves changes in chromosome structure and number. When comparing the chromosomes of closely related species, changes in chromosome structure and/or number are common.

As an example, **Figure 23.17** compares the banding patterns of the three largest chromosomes in humans and the corresponding chromosomes in chimpanzees, gorillas, and orangutans. (Refer back to Chapter 15, Figure 15.1 for an example of chromosome banding.) The banding patterns in the chromosomes are strikingly similar because these species are closely related evolutionarily. Chromosome 1 looks very similar in all species. Even so, you can see some interesting differences. Humans have one large chromosome 2, but this chromosome is divided into two separate chromosomes in the other three species. This explains why human cells have 23 pairs of chromosomes, whereas cells of chimpanzees, gorillas, and orangutans have 24. The fusion of the two smaller chromosomes during the development of the human lineage may have caused this difference in chromosome number. Another interesting change in chromosome structure is seen in chromosome 3. The banding patterns

among humans, chimpanzees, and gorillas are very similar, but the orangutan has a large inversion that flips the order of the bands in the centromeric region. As discussed in Chapter 25, changes in chromosome structure and number may affect the ability of two organisms to breed with one another. In this way, such changes have been important in the establishment of new species.

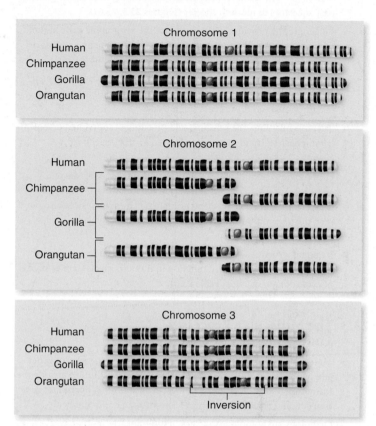

Figure 23.17 Evolutionary changes in chromosome structure and number found in primates. This figure is a comparison of the three largest human chromosomes and the corresponding chromosomes in the chimpanzee, gorilla, and orangutan. It is a schematic drawing of Giemsa-stained chromosomes. The differences between these chromosomes illustrate the changes that have occurred during the evolution of these related primate species.

Concept Check: *Describe two changes in chromosome structure that have occurred among these chromosomes.*

Summary of Key Concepts

23.1 The Theory of Evolution

- Evolution is a heritable change in one or more characteristics of a population from one generation to the next.

- Charles Darwin proposed the theory of evolution based on his understanding of geology and population growth and his observations of species in their natural settings. His voyage on the *Beagle*, during which he studied many species, including finches on the Galápagos Islands, was particularly influential in the development of his ideas (Figure 23.1, Table 23.1).

- Darwin expressed his theory of evolution as descent with modification through variation and natural selection. As a result of natural selection, genetic variation changes from generation to generation to produce populations of organisms with traits (adaptations) that favor greater reproductive success (Figure 23.2).

- The Grants' research on finches showed how differences in beak size (a heritable trait) were driven by natural selection (Figures 23.3, 23.4).

23.2 Evidence of Evolutionary Change

- Evidence of evolutionary change is found in studies of natural selection, the fossil record, biogeography, convergent evolution, selective breeding, and homologies (Table 23.2).

- Fossils provide evidence of evolutionary change in a series of related organisms. The fossil record often reveals transitional forms that link past ancestors to modern species (Figures 23.5, 23.6).

- Biogeography provides information on the geographic distribution of related species. When populations become isolated on islands or continents, they often evolve into new species (Figure 23.7).

- In convergent evolution, independent adaptations result in similar characteristics, or analogous structures, because different species occupy similar environments (Figure 23.8).

- Selective breeding, the selecting and breeding of individual organisms having desired traits, is a human-driven form of selection (Figures 23.9, 23.10, 23.11).

- Homologies are similarities that occur due to descent from a common ancestor. The set of bones in the forearms of vertebrates is an example of an anatomical homology. Homologies can also be seen during embryonic development and at the molecular level (Figures 23.12, 23.13).

- Vestigial structures, structures that were functional in an ancestor but no longer have a useful function in modern species, are evidence of evolutionary change (Table 23.3).

23.3 The Molecular Processes That Underlie Evolution

- Molecular evolution is the process of evolution at the level of genes and proteins. Molecular processes that underlie evolution include the formation of orthologs and paralogs, exon shuffling, horizontal gene transfer, and changes in chromosome structure and number.

- Orthologs are homologous genes in different species that have accumulated random mutations over time (Figure 23.14).

- Paralogs are homologous genes in the same species that are produced by gene duplication events. Gene duplication can result in the formation of a gene family such as the globin gene family, which supported the evolutionary adaptation of internal gestation.

- Exon shuffling is a process in which exons from one gene are inserted into another gene, producing proteins that have additional functions (Figure 23.15).

- Another mechanism that produces genetic variation is horizontal gene transfer, in which genetic material is transferred from one organism to another organism that is not its offspring. Such genetic changes are subject to natural selection (Figure 23.16).

- Molecular evolution can also involve changes in chromosome structure and number (Figure 23.17).

 Assess and Discuss

Test Yourself

1. A change in one or more characteristics of a population that is heritable and occurs from one generation to the next is called
   a. natural selection.
   b. sexual selection.
   c. population genetics.
   d. evolution.
   e. inheritance of acquired characteristics.

2. Lamarck's vision of evolution differed from Darwin's in that Lamarck believed
   a. living things evolve in an upward direction.
   b. behavioral changes modify heritable traits.
   c. genetic differences among individuals in the population allow for evolution.
   d. a and b only.
   e. none of the above.

3. Which of the following scientists influenced Darwin's views on the nature of population growth?
   a. Cuvier   c. Lyell   e. Wallace
   b. Malthus   d. Hutton

4. An evolutionary change in which a population of organisms changes its characteristics over many generations in ways that make it better suited to its environment is
   a. natural selection.   d. evolution.
   b. an adaptation.   e. both a and c.
   c. an acquired characteristic.

5. Vestigial structures are anatomical structures
   a. that have more than one function.
   b. that were functional in an ancestor but no longer have a useful function.
   c. that look similar in different species but have different functions.
   d. that have the same function in different species but have very different appearances.
   e. of the body wall.

6. Which of the following is an example of a developmental homology seen in human embryonic development and other vertebrate species that are not mammals?
   a. gill ridges   c. tail   e. all of the above
   b. umbilical cord   d. both a and c

7. Two or more homologous genes found within a particular species are called
   a. homozygous.   c. paralogs.   e. duplicates.
   b. orthologs.   d. alleles.

8. The phenomenon of exon shuffling
   a. produces new gene products by changing the pattern of intron removal in pre-mRNA.
   b. produces new genes by inserting exons and flanking introns into a different gene sequence, thereby introducing a new domain in a protein.
   c. deletes one or more bases in a single gene.
   d. rearranges the introns in a particular gene, producing new proteins.
   e. both a and d.

9. Horizontal gene transfer
   a. is a process in which an organism incorporates genetic material from another organism without being the offspring of that organism.
   b. can involve the exchange of genetic material among individuals of the same species.
   c. can involve the exchange of genetic material among individuals of different species.
   d. can be all of the above.
   e. can be a and b only.

10. Genetic variation can occur as a result of
    a. random mutations in genes.
    b. exon shuffling.
    c. gene duplication.
    d. horizontal gene transfer.
    e. all of the above.

Conceptual Questions

1. Evolution that results in adaptation is rooted in two phenomena: genetic variation and natural selection. In a very concise way (three sentences or less), describe how genetic variation and natural selection can bring about evolution.

2. What is convergent evolution? How does it support the theory of evolution?

3. A principle of biology is that *populations of organisms evolve from one generation to the next.* Explain how the homologous forelimbs of vertebrates indicate that populations evolve from one generation to the next.

Collaborative Questions

1. The term natural selection is sometimes confused with the term evolution. Discuss the meanings of these two terms. Explain how the terms are different and how they are related to each other.

2. Make a list of the observations made by biologists that support the theory of evolution. Which of the observations on your list do you find the most convincing and the least convincing?

Online Resource

www.brookerbiology.com

Stay a step ahead in your studies with animations that bring concepts to life and practice tests to assess your understanding. Your instructor may also recommend the interactive eBook, individualized learning tools, and more.

Population Genetics

Colorful African cichlids. Color is a factor that influences the choice of mates in populations of cichlids.

K imbareta, age 19, lives in the Democratic Republic of Congo (formerly Zaire) with his parents, one brother, and two sisters. Kimbareta has sickle cell disease, which causes his red blood cells to occasionally form a crescent or sickled shape. The sickled cells may block the flow of blood through his vessels. This results in tissue and organ damage along with painful episodes (also called crises) involving his arms, legs, chest, and abdomen. In some people with this disease, stroke may even occur. Sickle cell disease follows a recessive pattern of inheritance. It is caused by a mutation in a gene that encodes β-globin, a subunit of hemoglobin that carries oxygen in the red blood cells.

Many different recessive diseases have been identified by geneticists. Most of them are very rare. However, in the village where Kimbareta lives, sickle cell disease is surprisingly common. Nearly 2% of the inhabitants have the disease—an incidence that is similar to other places in the country. How can we explain such a high occurrence of a serious inherited disease? If natural selection tends to eliminate detrimental genetic variation, as we saw in Chapter 23, why does the sickle cell allele persist in this population? As we will see later, biologists have discovered that the effect of the allele in heterozygotes is the underlying factor. Heterozygotes, who

carry one copy of the sickle cell allele and one copy of the more common (non-disease-causing) allele, have an increased resistance to malaria.

Population genetics is the study of genes and genotypes in a population. A **population** is a group of individuals of the same species that occupy the same environment at the same time. For sexually reproducing species, members of a given population can interbreed with one another. The central issue in population genetics is genetic variation—its extent within populations, why it exists, how it is maintained, and how it changes over the course of many generations. Population genetics helps us understand how underlying genetic variation is related to phenotypic variation.

Population genetics emerged as a branch of genetics in the 1920s and 1930s. Its mathematical foundations were developed by theoreticians who extended the principles of Darwin and Mendel by deriving equations to explain the occurrence of genotypes within populations. These foundations can be largely attributed to British evolutionary biologists J. B. S. Haldane and Ronald Fisher, and American geneticist Sewall Wright. As we will see, several researchers who analyzed the genetic composition of natural and experimental populations provided support for their mathematical theories. More recently, population geneticists have used techniques to probe genetic variation at the molecular level. In addition, the staggering improvements in computer technology have aided population geneticists in the analysis of data and the testing of genetic hypotheses.

We will begin this chapter by exploring the extent of genetic variation that occurs in populations and how such variation is subject to change. In many cases, genetic changes are associated with evolutionary adaptations, which are characteristics of a species that have evolved over a long period of time by the process of natural selection. In the second half of the chapter, we will examine the various evolutionary mechanisms that promote genetic change in a population, including natural selection, genetic drift, migration, and nonrandom mating.

24.1 Genes in Populations

Learning Outcomes:

1. Define a gene pool.
2. Distinguish between allele and genotype frequency.
3. Use the Hardy-Weinberg equation to calculate allele and genotype frequencies of a given population.
4. List the conditions that must be met for a population to be in Hardy-Weinberg equilibrium.
5. Describe the factors that cause microevolution to happen.

Population genetics is an extension of our understanding of Darwin's theory of natural selection, Mendel's laws of inheritance, and newer studies in molecular genetics. All of the alleles for every gene in a given population make up the **gene pool**. Each member of the population receives its genes from its parents, which, in turn, are members of the gene pool. Individuals that reproduce contribute to the gene pool of the next generation. Population geneticists study the genetic variation within the gene pool and how such variation changes from one generation to the next. The emphasis is often on understanding the variation in alleles among members of a population. In this section, we will examine some of the general features of populations and gene pools.

Populations Are Dynamic Units

Recall that a population is a group of individuals of the same species that occupy the same environment at the same time and can interbreed with one another. Certain species occupy a wide geographic range and are divided into discrete populations due to geographic isolation. For example, distinct populations of a given species may be located on different sides of a physical barrier, such as a mountain.

Populations change from one generation to the next. How might populations become different? Populations may change in size and geographic location. As the size and locations of a population change, their genetic composition generally changes as well. Some of the genetic changes involve adaptation, in which a population becomes better suited to its environment, making it more likely to survive and reproduce. For example, a population of mammals may move from a warmer to a colder geographic location. Over the course of many generations, natural selection may change the population such that the fur of most animals is thicker and provides better insulation against the colder temperatures.

GENOMES & PROTEOMES CONNECTION

Genes Are Usually Polymorphic

The term **polymorphism** (from the Greek, meaning many forms) refers to the presence of two or more variants or traits for a given character within a population. **Figure 24.1** illustrates a striking example of polymorphism in the elder-flowered orchid (*Dactylorhiza sambucina*). Throughout the range of this species in Europe, both yellow- and red-flowered individuals are prevalent.

Polymorphism in a character is usually due to two or more alleles of a gene that influences the character. Geneticists also use the term polymorphism to describe the variation in the DNA sequence of genes. A gene that commonly exists as two or more alleles in a population is a **polymorphic gene**. To be considered polymorphic, a gene must exist in at least two alleles, and each allele must occur at a frequency that is greater than 1%. By comparison, a **monomorphic gene** exists predominantly as a single allele in a population. When 99% or more of the alleles of a given gene are identical in a population, the gene is considered to be monomorphic.

What types of molecular changes cause genes to be polymorphic? A polymorphism may involve various types of changes, such as a deletion of a significant region of the gene, a duplication of a

Figure 24.1 An example of polymorphism: The two color variations found in the orchid *Dactylorhiza sambucina*.

region, or a change in a single nucleotide. This last type of variation is called a **single-nucleotide polymorphism (SNP)**. SNPs ("snips") are the smallest type of genetic variation that can occur within a given gene and also the most common. For example, the sickle cell allele discussed at the beginning of the chapter involves a single-nucleotide change in the β-globin gene, which encodes a subunit of the oxygen-carrying protein called hemoglobin. The non-disease-causing allele and sickle cell allele represent a SNP of the β-globin gene:

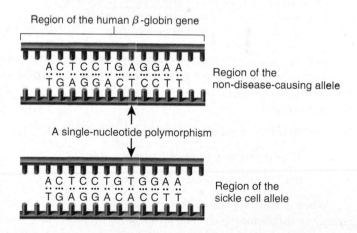

Relative to the non-disease-causing allele, this is a single-nucleotide substitution of an A (in the top strand) to a T in the sickle cell allele.

SNPs represent 90% of all variation in human DNA sequences that occurs among different people. In human populations, a gene that is 2,000–3,000 bp in length, on average, contains 10 different SNPs. Likewise, SNPs with a frequency of 1% or more are found very frequently among genes of nearly all species. Polymorphism is the norm for relatively large, healthy populations of nearly all species, as evidenced by the occurrence of SNPs within most genes.

Why do we care about SNPs? One reason is their importance in human health. By analyzing SNPs in human genes, researchers have determined that these small variations in DNA sequences can affect the function of the proteins encoded by the genes. These effects on the proteome, in turn, may influence how humans develop diseases, such as heart disease, diabetes, and sickle cell disease. Variations in SNPs in the human population are also associated with how people respond to viruses, drugs, and vaccines. The analysis of SNPs may be instrumental in the current and future development of **personalized medicine**— a medical practice in which information about a patient's genotype is used to tailor her or his medical care. For example, an analysis of a person's SNPs may be used to select between different types of medication or customize the dosage. In addition, SNP analysis may reveal that a person has a high predisposition to develop a particular disease, such as heart disease. Such information may be used to initiate preventative measures to minimize the chances of developing the disease.

Population Genetics Is Concerned with Allele and Genotype Frequencies

One approach to analyzing genetic variation in populations is to consider the frequency of specific alleles and genotypes in a quantitative way. Two fundamental calculations are central to population genetics: **allele frequency** and **genotype frequency**. Allele and genotype frequency are defined as follows:

$$\text{Allele frequency} = \frac{\text{Number of copies of a specific allele in a population}}{\text{Total number of all alleles for that gene in a population}}$$

$$\text{Genotype frequency} = \frac{\text{Number of individuals with a particular genotype in a population}}{\text{Total number of individuals in a population}}$$

Although allele and genotype frequencies are related, make sure you clearly distinguish between them. As an example, let's consider a population of 100 four-o'clock plants (*Mirabilis jalapa*) with the following genotypes:

49 red-flowered plants with the genotype $C^R C^R$

42 pink-flowered plants with the genotype $C^R C^W$

9 white-flowered plants with the genotype $C^W C^W$

When calculating an allele frequency for a diploid species, remember that homozygous individuals have two copies of a given allele, whereas heterozygotes have only one. For example, in tallying the C^W allele, each of the 42 heterozygotes has one copy of the C^W allele, and each white-flowered plant has two copies. Therefore, the allele frequency for C^W (the white color allele) equals

$$\text{Frequency of } C^W = \frac{(C^R C^W) + 2(C^W C^W)}{2(C^R C^R) + 2(C^R C^W) + 2(C^W C^W)}$$

$$\text{Frequency of } C^W = \frac{42 + (2)(9)}{(2)(49) + (2)(42) + (2)(9)}$$

$$= \frac{60}{200} = 0.3, \text{ or } 30\%$$

This result tells us that the allele frequency of C^W is 0.3. In other words, 30% of the alleles for this gene in the population are the white color (C^W) allele.

Let's now calculate the genotype frequency of $C^W C^W$ homozygotes (white-flowered plants).

$$\text{Frequency of } C^W C^W = \frac{9}{49 + 42 + 9}$$

$$= \frac{9}{100} = 0.09, \text{ or } 9\%$$

We see that 9% of the individuals in this population have the white-flower genotype.

The Hardy-Weinberg Equation Relates Allele and Genotype Frequencies in a Population

In 1908, Godfrey Harold Hardy, an English mathematician, and Wilhelm Weinberg, a German physician, independently derived a simple mathematical expression, now called the Hardy-Weinberg equation, that describes the relationship between allele and genotype frequencies when a population is not evolving. Let's examine the Hardy-Weinberg equation using the population of four-o'clock plants that we just considered. If the allele frequency of C^R is denoted by the symbol p and the allele frequency of C^W by q, then

$$p + q = 1$$

For example, if $p = 0.7$, then q must be 0.3. In other words, if the allele frequency of C^R equals 70%, the remaining 30% of alleles must be C^W, because together they equal 100%.

For a gene that exists in two alleles, the **Hardy-Weinberg equation** states that

$$p^2 + 2pq + q^2 = 1$$

If we apply this equation to our flower color gene, then

p^2 = the genotype frequency of $C^R C^R$ homozygotes

$2pq$ = the genotype frequency of $C^R C^W$ heterozygotes

q^2 = the genotype frequency of $C^W C^W$ homozygotes

If $p = 0.7$ and $q = 0.3$, then

$$\text{Frequency of } C^R C^R = p^2 = (0.7)^2 = 0.49$$

$$\text{Frequency of } C^R C^W = 2pq = 2(0.7)(0.3) = 0.42$$

$$\text{Frequency of } C^W C^W = q^2 = (0.3)^2 = 0.09$$

In other words, if the allele frequency of C^R is 70% and the allele frequency of C^W is 30%, the expected genotype frequency of $C^R C^R$ is 49%, $C^R C^W$ is 42%, and $C^W C^W$ is 9%.

Figure 24.2 uses a Punnett square to illustrate the relationship between allele frequencies and the way that gametes combine to produce genotypes. To be valid, the Hardy-Weinberg equation carries the assumption that two gametes combine randomly with each

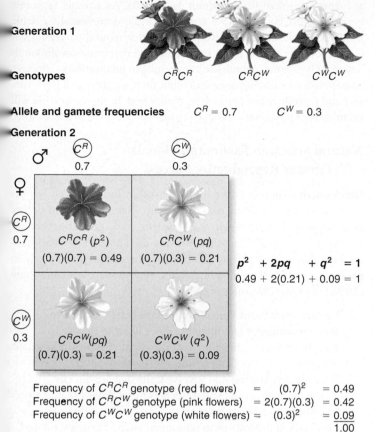

Generation 1

Genotypes $C^R C^R$ $C^R C^W$ $C^W C^W$

Allele and gamete frequencies $C^R = 0.7$ $C^W = 0.3$

Generation 2

♂ C^R C^W
     0.7   0.3

♀

	C^R 0.7	C^W 0.3
C^R 0.7	$C^R C^R$ (p^2) (0.7)(0.7) = 0.49	$C^R C^W$ (pq) (0.7)(0.3) = 0.21
C^W 0.3	$C^R C^W$ (pq) (0.7)(0.3) = 0.21	$C^W C^W$ (q^2) (0.3)(0.3) = 0.09

$$p^2 + 2pq + q^2 = 1$$
$$0.49 + 2(0.21) + 0.09 = 1$$

Frequency of $C^R C^R$ genotype (red flowers) = $(0.7)^2$ = 0.49
Frequency of $C^R C^W$ genotype (pink flowers) = 2(0.7)(0.3) = 0.42
Frequency of $C^W C^W$ genotype (white flowers) = $(0.3)^2$ = 0.09
                                         1.00

Figure 24.2 **Calculating allele and genotype frequencies with the Hardy-Weinberg equation.** A population of four-o'clock plants has allele and gamete frequencies of 0.7 for the C^R allele and 0.3 for the C^W allele. Knowing the allele frequencies allows us to calculate the genotype frequencies in the population.

Concept Check: *What would be the frequency of pink flowers in a population in which the allele frequency of C^R is 0.4 and the population is in Hardy-Weinberg equilibrium? Assume that C^R and C^W are the only two alleles.*

other to produce offspring. In a population, the frequency of a gamete carrying a particular allele is equal to the allele frequency in that population. For example, if the allele frequency of C^R equals 0.7, the frequency of a gamete carrying the C^R allele also equals 0.7. The probability of producing a $C^R C^R$ homozygote with red flowers is 0.7 × 0.7 = 0.49, or 49%. The probability of inheriting both C^W alleles, which produces white flowers, is 0.3 × 0.3 = 0.09, or 9%. Two different gamete combinations produce heterozygotes with pink flowers. An offspring could inherit the C^R allele from the pollen and C^W from the egg, or C^R from the egg and C^W from the pollen. Therefore, the frequency of heterozygotes is $pq + pq$, which equals $2pq$. In our example, this is 2(0.7)(0.3) = 0.42, or 42%. Note that the frequencies for all three genotypes total 100%.

The Hardy-Weinberg equation predicts that allele and genotype frequencies will remain the same, generation after generation, provided that a population is in equilibrium. To be in equilibrium, evolutionary mechanisms that can change allele and genotype frequencies

are not acting on a population. For this to occur, the following conditions must be met:

- No new mutations occur to alter allele frequencies.
- No natural selection occurs; that is, no survival or reproductive advantage exists for any of the genotypes.
- The population is so large that allele frequencies do not change due to random chance.
- No migration occurs between different populations, altering the allele frequencies.
- Random mating occurs; that is, the members of the population mate with each other without regard to their genotypes.

Why is the Hardy-Weinberg equilibrium a useful concept? An equilibrium is a null hypothesis, which suggests that evolutionary change is not occurring. In reality, however, populations rarely achieve an equilibrium, though in large natural populations with little migration and negligible natural selection, the Hardy-Weinberg equilibrium may be nearly approximated for certain genes. Sometimes, when researchers experimentally examine allele and genotype frequencies for one or more genes in a given species, they discover that the frequencies are not in Hardy-Weinberg equilibrium. In such cases, they assume that one or more of the conditions are being violated—in other words, mechanisms of evolutionary change are affecting the population. Conservation biologists and wildlife managers may wish to determine why such disequilibrium has occurred because it may affect the future survival of the species. Next, we will take a look at the mechanisms that cause evolutionary change.

Microevolution Involves Changes in Allele Frequencies from One Generation to the Next

The term **microevolution** is used to describe changes in a population's gene pool, such as changes in allele frequencies, from generation to generation. What causes microevolution to happen? Such change is rooted in two related phenomena (**Table 24.1**). First, the introduction of new genetic variation into a population is one essential aspect of microevolution. New alleles of preexisting genes arise by random mutation and, as discussed in Chapter 23, new genes can be introduced into a population by gene duplication, exon shuffling, and horizontal gene transfer. Such mutations, albeit rare, provide a continuous source of new variation to populations. In 1926, the Russian geneticist Sergei Chetverikov was the first to suggest that random mutations are the raw material for evolution. However, due to their low rate of occurrence, mutations by themselves do not play a major role in changing allele frequencies in a population over time. They do not significantly disrupt a Hardy-Weinberg equilibrium.

The second phenomenon that is required for evolution to occur is one or more mechanisms that alter the prevalence of a given allele or genotype in a population. These mechanisms are natural selection, genetic drift, migration, and nonrandom mating (see Table 24.1). Over the course of many generations, these mechanisms may promote widespread genetic changes in a population. In the remainder of this chapter, we will examine how natural selection, genetic drift, migration, and nonrandom mating affect the type of genetic variation that occurs when a gene exists as two alleles in a population.

Table 24.1   Factors That Govern Microevolution

Sources of new genetic variation*

New mutations within genes that produce new alleles	Random mutations within pre-existing genes introduce new alleles into populations, but at a very low rate. New mutations may be neutral, deleterious, or beneficial. Because mutations are rare, the change from one generation to the next is generally very small. For alleles to rise to a significant percentage in a population, evolutionary mechanisms, such as natural selection, genetic drift, and migration, must operate on them.
Gene duplication[†]	Abnormal crossover events and transposable elements may increase the number of copies of a gene. Over time, the additional copies accumulate random mutations and constitute a gene family.
Exon shuffling[‡]	Abnormal crossover events and transposable elements may promote gene rearrangements in which one or more exons from one gene are inserted into another gene. The protein encoded by such a gene may display a novel function that is acted on by evolutionary mechanisms.
Horizontal gene[‡] transfer	Genes from one species may be introduced into another species. The transferred gene may be acted on by evolutionary mechanisms.

Evolutionary mechanisms that alter the frequencies of existing genetic variation

Natural selection	The process in which individuals that possess certain traits are more likely to survive and reproduce than individuals without those traits. Over the course of many generations, beneficial traits that are heritable become more common and detrimental traits become less common.
Genetic drift	A change in genetic variation from generation to generation due to random chance. Allele frequencies may change as a matter of chance from one generation to the next. Genetic drift has a greater influence in a small population.
Migration	Migration can occur between two populations that have different allele frequencies. The introduction of migrants into a recipient population may change the allele frequencies of that population.
Nonrandom mating	The phenomenon in which individuals select mates based on their phenotypes or genetic lineage. This alters the relative proportion of homozygotes and heterozygotes that is predicted by the Hardy-Weinberg equation, but it does not change allele frequencies.

* These are examples that affect single genes. Other events, such as crossing over, independent assortment, and changes in chromosome structure and number, may alter the genetic variation among many genes.

[†] Described in Chapter 21. See Figures 21.7 and 21.8.

[‡] Described in Chapter 23. See Figures 23.15 and 23.16.

24.2   Natural Selection

Learning Outcomes:

1. Explain how natural selection can result in a population that is better adapted to its environment and more successful at reproduction.
2. Calculate the fitness values of given genotypes.
3. List and distinguish between four different types of natural selection.

Recall from Chapter 23 that **natural selection** is the process in which individuals with certain heritable traits tend to survive and reproduce

at higher rates than those without those traits. As a result, favorable heritable traits become more common, while detrimental heritable traits become less common. Keep in mind that natural selection itself is not evolution. Rather it is a key mechanism that causes evolution to happen. Over time, natural selection results in **adaptations**—changes in populations of living organisms that increase their ability to survive and reproduce in a particular environment. In this section, we will examine various ways that natural selection produces such adaptations.

Natural Selection Favors Individuals with Greater Reproductive Success

Reproductive success is the likelihood of an individual contributing fertile offspring to the next generation. Natural selection occurs because some individuals in a population have greater reproductive success compared to other individuals. Those individuals having heritable traits that favor reproductive success are more likely to pass those traits to their offspring. Reproductive success is commonly attributed to two categories of traits:

1. Certain characteristics make organisms better adapted to their environment and therefore more likely to survive to reproductive age. Therefore, natural selection favors individuals with characteristics that provide a survival advantage.
2. Reproductive success may involve traits that are directly associated with reproduction, such as the abilities to find a mate and produce viable gametes and offspring. Traits that enhance the ability of individuals to reproduce, such as brightly colored plumage in male birds, are often subject to natural selection.

As discussed in Chapter 23, Charles Darwin and Alfred Wallace independently proposed the theory of evolution by natural selection. A modern description of the principles of natural selection can relate our knowledge of molecular genetics to the process of evolution:

1. Within a population, allelic variation arises from random mutations that cause differences in DNA sequences. A mutation that creates a new allele may alter the amino acid sequence of the encoded protein. This, in turn, may alter the function of the protein.
2. Some alleles encode proteins that enhance an individual's survival or reproductive capability over that of other members of the population. For example, an allele may produce a protein that is more efficient at a higher temperature, conferring on the individual a greater probability of survival in a hot climate.
3. Individuals with beneficial alleles are more likely to survive and contribute their alleles to the gene pool of the next generation.
4. Over the course of many generations, allele frequencies of many different genes may change through natural selection, thereby significantly altering the characteristics of a population. The net result of natural selection is a population that is better adapted to its environment and more successful at reproduction.

Fitness Is a Quantitative Measure of Reproductive Success

As mentioned earlier, Haldane, Fisher, and Wright developed mathematical relationships to explain the phenomenon of natural selection. To begin our quantitative discussion of natural selection, we need to consider the concept of **fitness**, which is the relative likelihood that one genotype will contribute to the gene pool of the next generation compared with other genotypes. Although this property often correlates with physical fitness, the two ideas should not be confused. Fitness is a measure of reproductive success. An extremely fertile individual may have a higher fitness than a less fertile individual that appears more physically fit.

To examine fitness, let's consider an example of a hypothetical gene existing in *A* and *a* alleles. We can assign fitness values to each of the three possible genotypes according to their relative reproductive success. For example, let's suppose the average reproductive successes of the three genotypes are

> *AA* produces 5 offspring
> *Aa* produces 4 offspring
> *aa* produces 1 offspring

By convention, the genotype with the highest reproductive success is given a fitness value of 1.0. Fitness values are denoted by the variable *w*. The fitness values of the other genotypes are assigned values relative to this 1.0 value.

> Fitness of *AA*: $w^{AA} = 1.0$
>
> Fitness of *Aa*: $w^{Aa} = 4/5 = 0.8$
>
> Fitness of *aa*: $w^{aa} = 1/5 = 0.2$

Variation in fitness occurs because certain genotypes result in individuals that have a greater reproductive success than other genotypes.

Likewise, the effects of natural selection can be viewed at the level of a population. The average reproductive success of members of a population is called the **mean fitness of the population**. Over many generations, as individuals with higher fitness values become more prevalent, natural selection also increases the mean fitness of the population. In this way, the process of natural selection results in a population of organisms that is well adapted to its native environment and more likely to be successful at reproduction.

Natural Selection Follows Different Patterns

By studying species in their native environments, population geneticists have discovered that natural selection can occur in several ways. In most of the examples described next, natural selection leads to adaptations in which certain members of a species are more likely to survive to reproductive age.

Directional Selection   During **directional selection**, individuals at one extreme of a phenotypic range have greater reproductive success in a particular environment. Different phenomena may initiate the process of directional selection. A common reason for directional selection is that a population may be exposed to a prolonged change in its living environment. Under the new environmental conditions, the relative fitness values may change to favor one genotype, which will promote the elimination of other genotypes. As an example, let's suppose a population of finches on a mainland already has genetic variation that affects beak size (refer back to Figure 23.2). A small number of birds migrate to an island where the seeds are generally larger than on the mainland. In this new environment, birds with

larger beaks have a higher fitness because they are better able to crack open the larger seeds and thereby survive to reproduce. Over the course of many generations, directional selection would produce a population of birds carrying alleles that promote larger beak size.

Another way that directional selection may arise is that a new allele may be introduced into a population by mutation, and the new allele may confer a higher fitness in individuals that carry it (**Figure 24.3**). What are the long-term effects of such directional selection? If the homozygote carrying the favored allele has the highest fitness value, directional selection may cause this favored allele to eventually predominate in the population, perhaps even leading to a monomorphic gene.

Stabilizing Selection   A type of natural selection called **stabilizing selection** favors the survival of individuals with intermediate phenotypes and selects against those with extreme phenotypes. Stabilizing selection tends to decrease genetic diversity. An example of stabilizing selection involves clutch size (number of eggs laid) in birds, which was first studied by British biologist David Lack in 1947. Under stabilizing selection, birds that lay too many or too few eggs per nest have lower fitness values than do those that lay an intermediate number. When a bird lays too many eggs, many offspring die due to inadequate parental care and food. In addition, the strain on the parents themselves may decrease their likelihood of survival and consequently their ability to produce more offspring. Having too few offspring, however, does not contribute many individuals to the next generation. Therefore, the most successful parents are those that produce an intermediate clutch size. In the 1980s, Swedish evolutionary biologist Lars Gustafsson and his colleagues examined the phenomenon of stabilizing selection in the collared flycatcher (*Ficedula albicollis*) on the Swedish island of Gotland. They discovered that Lack's hypothesis concerning an optimal clutch size appears to be true for this species (**Figure 24.4**).

Diversifying Selection   **Diversifying selection** (also known as disruptive selection) favors the survival of two or more different genotypes that produce different phenotypes. In diversifying selection, the fitness values of a particular genotype are higher in one environment and lower in a different one, whereas the fitness values of the second genotype vary in an opposite manner. Diversifying selection is likely to occur in populations that occupy heterogeneous environments, so some members of the species are more likely to survive in each type of environmental condition.

An example of diversifying selection involves colonial bentgrass (*Agrostis capillaris*) (**Figure 24.5**). In certain locations where this grass is found, such as South Wales, isolated places occur where the soil is contaminated with high levels of heavy metals due to mining. The relatively recent metal contamination has selected for the proliferation of mutant strains of *A. capillaris* that are tolerant of the heavy metals (Figure 24.5a). Such genetic changes enable these mutant strains to grow on contaminated soil but tend to inhibit their growth on normal, noncontaminated soil. These metal-resistant plants often grow on contaminated sites that are close to plants that grow on uncontaminated land and do not show metal tolerance.

Balancing Selection   Contrary to a popular misconception, natural selection does not always cause the elimination of "weaker" or less-fit

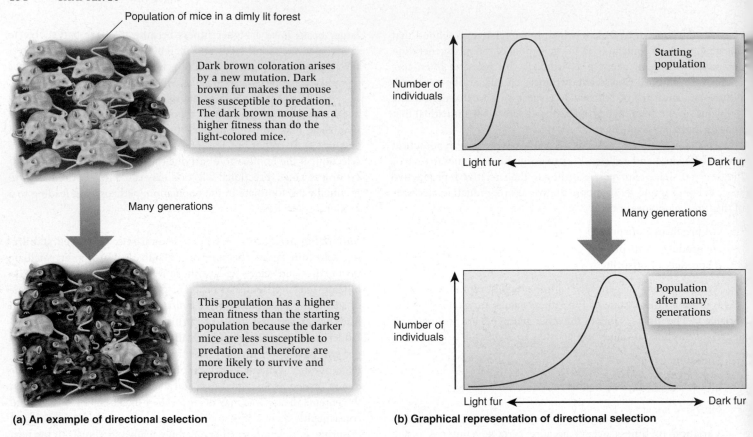

Population of mice in a dimly lit forest

Dark brown coloration arises by a new mutation. Dark brown fur makes the mouse less susceptible to predation. The dark brown mouse has a higher fitness than do the light-colored mice.

Many generations

This population has a higher mean fitness than the starting population because the darker mice are less susceptible to predation and therefore are more likely to survive and reproduce.

(a) An example of directional selection

Number of individuals

Light fur ← → Dark fur

Starting population

Many generations

Number of individuals

Light fur ← → Dark fur

Population after many generations

(b) Graphical representation of directional selection

Figure 24.3 Directional selection. This pattern of natural selection selects for one extreme of a phenotype that confers the highest fitness in the population's environment. **(a)** In this example, a mutation causing darker fur arises in a population of mice. This new genotype confers higher fitness, because mice with darker fur can evade predators and are more likely to survive and reproduce. Over many generations, directional selection favors the prevalence of individuals with darker fur. **(b)** These graphs show the change in fur color phenotypes before and after directional selection.

Concept Check: *Let's suppose the climate on an island abruptly changed such that the average temperature was 10°C higher. The climate change is permanent. How would directional selection affect the genetic diversity in a population of mice on the island (1) over the short run and (2) over the long run?*

alleles. **Balancing selection** is a type of natural selection that maintains genetic diversity in a population. Over many generations, balancing selection results in a **balanced polymorphism**, in which two or more alleles are kept in balance and therefore are maintained in a population over many generations.

How does balancing selection maintain a polymorphism? Population geneticists have identified two common ways that balancing selection occurs. First, for genetic variation involving a single gene, balancing selection can favor the heterozygote over either corresponding homozygote. This situation is called **heterozygote advantage**. Heterozygote advantage sometimes explains the persistence of alleles that are deleterious in a homozygous condition.

Figure 24.4 Stabilizing selection. In this pattern of natural selection, the extremes of a phenotypic distribution are selected against. Those individuals with intermediate traits have the highest fitness. These graphs show the results of stabilizing selection on clutch size in a population of collared flycatchers (*Ficedula albicollis*). This process results in a population with less diversity and more uniform traits.

Concept Check: *Why does stabilizing selection decrease genetic diversity?*

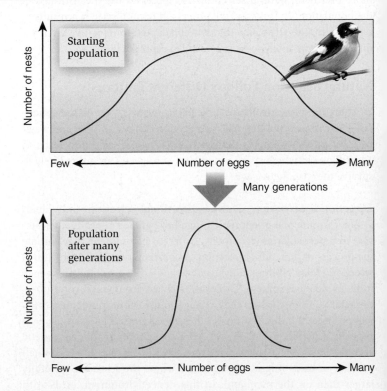

Number of nests

Starting population

Few ← Number of eggs → Many

Many generations

Number of nests

Population after many generations

Few ← Number of eggs → Many

(a) Growth of *Agrostis capillaris* on contaminated soil

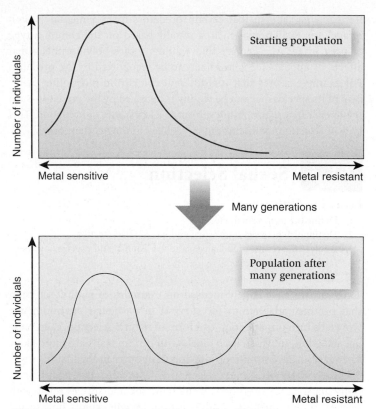

(b) Graphical representation of disruptive selection

Figure 24.5 **Diversifying selection.** This pattern of natural selection selects for two different phenotypes, each of which is most fit in a particular environment. **(a)** In this example, random mutations have resulted in metal-resistant alleles in colonial bentgrass (*Agrostis capillaris*) that allow it to grow on contaminated soil. In uncontaminated soils, the grass does not show metal tolerance. The existence of both metal-resistant and metal-sensitive alleles in the population is an example of diversifying selection due to heterogeneous environments. **(b)** Graphs showing the change in phenotypes in this bentgrass population before and after diversifying selection.

BIOLOGY PRINCIPLE **Populations of organisms evolve from one generation to the next.** In this example, the frequencies of metal-resistant alleles become more prevalent when populations of *A. capillaris* are exposed to toxic metals in the soil.

A classic example of heterozygote advantage involves the H^S allele of the human β-globin gene. A homozygous $H^S H^S$ individual, such as Kimbareta, discussed at the beginning of the chapter, has sickle cell disease. This disease causes the red blood cells to form a sickle shape. Sickle-shaped cells deliver less oxygen to the body's tissues and can block the flow of blood through the vessels. The $H^S H^S$ homozygote has a lower fitness than a homozygote with two copies of the more common β-globin allele, $H^A H^A$. Heterozygotes, $H^A H^S$, do not typically show symptoms of the disease, but they have an increased resistance to malaria. Compared with $H^A H^A$ homozygotes, heterozygotes have the highest fitness because they have a 10–15% better chance of surviving if infected by the malarial parasite *Plasmodium falciparum*. Therefore, the H^S allele is maintained in populations where malaria is prevalent, such as the Democratic Republic of Congo, even though the allele is detrimental in the homozygous state (**Figure 24.6**). This balanced polymorphism results in a higher mean fitness of the population. In areas where malaria is endemic, a population composed of all $H^A H^A$ individuals would have a lower mean fitness.

Negative frequency-dependent selection is a second way that natural selection produces a balanced polymorphism. In this pattern of natural selection, the fitness of a genotype decreases when its frequency becomes higher. In other words, common individuals have a lower fitness, and rare individuals have a higher fitness. Therefore, common individuals are less likely to reproduce, whereas rare individuals are more likely to reproduce, thereby producing a balanced polymorphism in which no genotype becomes too rare or too common.

Negative frequency-dependent selection is thought to maintain polymorphisms among species that are preyed upon by predators.

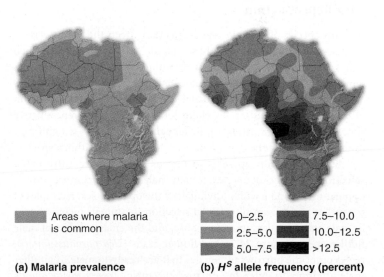

Areas where malaria is common		0–2.5	7.5–10.0
		2.5–5.0	10.0–12.5
		5.0–7.5	>12.5

(a) Malaria prevalence   **(b) H^S allele frequency (percent)**

Figure 24.6 **Balancing selection and heterozygote advantage.** **(a)** The geographic prevalence of malaria in Africa. **(b)** The frequency of the H^S allele of the β-globin gene in the same area. In the homozygous condition, the H^S allele causes sickle cell disease. This allele is maintained in human populations in areas where malaria is prevalent, because the heterozygote ($H^A H^S$) has a higher fitness than either of the corresponding homozygotes ($H^A H^A$ or $H^S H^S$).

Concept Check: *If malaria was eradicated, what would you expect to happen to the frequencies of the H^A and H^S alleles over the long run?*

Research has shown that certain predators form a mental "search image" for their prey, which is usually based on the common type of prey in an area. A prey that exhibits a rare polymorphism that affects its appearance is less likely to be recognized by the predator. For example, a prey that is a different color from most other members of its species may not be readily recognized by the predator. Such relatively rare organisms are subject to a lower rate of predation. This type of selection maintains polymorphism among certain prey.

24.3   Sexual Selection

Learning Outcomes:

1. Define the term sexual selection.
2. Distinguish between intrasexual and intersexual selection.
3. Analyze the results of Seehausen and van Alphen and explain how they relate to sexual selection.

Thus far, we have largely focused on examples of natural selection that produce adaptations for survival in particular environments. Now let's turn our attention to a form of natural selection, called **sexual selection**, in which individuals with certain traits are more likely to engage in successful reproduction than other individuals. Darwin originally described sexual selection as "the advantage that certain individuals have over others of the same sex and species solely with respect to reproduction." In this section, we will explore how sexual selection alters traits that play a key role in reproduction.

Sexual Selection Is a Type of Natural Selection Pertaining to Traits That Are Directly Involved with Reproduction

In many species of animals, sexual selection affects the characteristics of males more intensely than those of females. Unlike females, which tend to be fairly uniform in their reproductive success, male success tends to be more variable, with some males mating with many females and others not mating at all. Sexual selection results in the evolution of traits, called secondary sex characteristics, that favor reproductive success. The process can result in **sexual dimorphism**—a significant difference between the appearances of the two sexes within a species.

Sexual selection operates in one of two ways. In **intrasexual selection**, members of one sex, usually males, directly compete for the opportunity to mate with individuals of the opposite sex. Examples of traits that result from intrasexual selection in animals include horns in male sheep, antlers in male moose, and the enlarged claw of male fiddler crabs (**Figure 24.7a**). In fiddler crabs (*Uca paradussumieri*), males enter the burrows of females that are ready to mate. If another male attempts to enter the burrow, the male already inside stands in the burrow shaft and blocks the entrance with his enlarged claw. Males with the largest claws are more likely to be successful at driving off their rivals and being able to mate and therefore more likely to pass on their genes to future generations.

In **intersexual selection**, also called mate choice, members of one sex, usually females, choose their mates from individuals of the other sex on the basis of certain desirable characteristics. This type of sexual selection often results in showy characteristics in males. **Figure 24.7b** shows a classic example that involves the Indian peafowl

(*Pavo cristatus*), the national bird of India. Male peacocks have long and brightly colored tail feathers, which they fan out as a mating behavior. Female peahens select among males based on feather color and pattern as well as the physical prowess of the display.

A less obvious type of intersexual selection is cryptic female choice, in which the female reproductive system influences the relative success of sperm. As an example of cryptic female choice, the female genital tract of certain animals selects for sperm that tend to be genetically unrelated to the female. Sperm from males closely related to the female, such as brothers or cousins, are less successful than are sperm from genetically unrelated males. The selection for sperm may occur over the journey through the reproductive tract. The egg itself may even have mechanisms to prevent fertilization by genetically related sperm. Cryptic female choice occurs in species in which females may mate with more than one male, such as many species of reptiles and ducks. A similar mechanism is found in many plant species in which pollen from genetically related plants, perhaps from the same flower, is unsuccessful at fertilization, whereas pollen from unrelated plants is successful. One possible advantage of cryptic female choice is that it inhibits inbreeding (described later in this chapter). At the population level, cryptic female choice may promote genetic diversity by favoring interbreeding among genetically unrelated individuals.

Sexual selection is sometimes a combination of both intrasexual and intersexual selection. During breeding season, male elk (*Cervus elaphus*) become aggressive and bugle loudly to challenge other male elk. Males spar with their antlers, which usually turns into a pushing match to determine which elk is stronger. Female elk then choose the strongest bulls as their mates.

Sexual selection can explain the existence of traits that could decrease an individual's chances of survival but increase their chances of reproducing. For example, the male guppy (*Poecilia reticulata*) is brightly colored compared with the female (**Figure 24.7c**). In nature, females prefer brightly colored males. However, brightly colored males are more likely to be seen and eaten by predators. In places with few predators, the males tend to be brightly colored. In contrast, where predators are abundant, brightly colored males are less plentiful because they are subject to predation. In this case, the relative abundance of brightly and dully colored males depends on the balance between sexual selection, which favors bright coloring, and escape from predation, which favors dull coloring.

Many animals have secondary sexual characteristics, and evolutionary biologists generally agree that sexual selection is responsible for such traits. But why should males compete, and why should females be choosy? Researchers have proposed various hypotheses to explain the underlying mechanisms. One possible reason is related to the different roles that males and females play in the nurturing of offspring. In some animal species, the female is the primary caregiver, whereas the male plays a minor role. In such species, mating behavior may influence the fitness of both males and females. Males increase their fitness by mating with multiple females. This increases their likelihood of passing their genes on to the next generation. By comparison, females may produce relatively fewer offspring, and their reproductive success may not be limited by the number of available males. In these circumstances, females will have higher fitness if they choose males that are good defenders of their territory and

(a) Intrasexual selection

(b) Intersexual selection

(c) Sexual selection balanced by predation

Figure 24.7 Examples of the results of sexual selection, a type of natural selection. (a) An example of intrasexual selection. The enlarged claw of the male fiddler crab is used in direct male-to-male competition. In this photograph, a male inside a burrow is extending its claw out of the burrow to prevent another male from entering and mating with the female. (b) An example of intersexual selection. Female peahens choose male peacocks based on the males' colorful and long tail feathers and the robustness of their display. (c) Male guppies (on the right) are brightly colored to attract a female (on the left), but brightly colored males are less common where predation is high. Note: These photos also illustrate the concept of sexual dimorphism.

Concept Check: *Male birds of many species have loud and elaborate courtship songs. Is this likely to be the result of intersexual or intrasexual selection? Explain.*

have alleles that confer a survival advantage to their offspring. One measure of alleles that confer higher fitness is age. Males that live to an older age are more likely to carry beneficial alleles. Many research studies involving female choice have shown that females tend to select traits that are more likely to be well developed in older males than in immature ones. For example, in certain species of birds, females tend to choose males with a larger repertoire of songs, which is more likely to occur in older males. Sexual selection is governed by the same processes involved in the evolution of traits that are not directly related to sex. Sexual selection can occur by directional, stabilizing, diversifying, or balancing selection. For example, the evolution of the large and brightly colored tail of the male peacock reflects directional selection.

FEATURE INVESTIGATION

Seehausen and van Alphen Found That Male Coloration in African Cichlids Is Subject to Female Choice

In 1998, population geneticists Ole Seehausen and Jacques van Alphen investigated the possible role of sexual selection as it pertains to male coloration of two species of cichlid—a tropical freshwater fish popular among aquarium enthusiasts. The Cichlidae family is composed of more than 3,000 species that vary in body shape, coloration, behavior, and feeding habits, making it one of the largest and most diverse vertebrate families. By far, the greatest diversity of these fish is found in Lake Victoria, Lake Malawi, and Lake Tanganyika in East Africa, where more than 1,800 species are found.

Cichlids have complex mating behavior, and females play an important role in choosing males with particular characteristics, such as color (see chapter opening photo). In some locations, *Pundamilia pundamilia* and *P. nyererei* do not readily interbreed and behave like two distinct biological species, whereas in other places, they behave like a single interbreeding species with two color morphs. Males of both species have blackish underparts and blackish vertical bars on their sides (**Figure 24.8a**). *P. pundamilia* males are grayish white on top and on the sides, and they have a metallic blue and red dorsal

P. pundamilia

P. nyererei

(a) Males of two species in normal light

P. pundamilia

P. nyererei

(b) Males of two species in artificial light

Figure 24.8 Male coloration in African cichlids. (a) Two males (*Pundamilia pundamilia*, top, and *Pundamilia nyererei*, bottom) under normal illumination. (b) The same species under orange monochromatic light, which obscures their color differences.

Figure 24.9 A study by Seehausen and van Alphen evaluating the effects of male coloration on female choice in African cichlids.

HYPOTHESIS Female African cichlids choose mates based on the males' coloration.

KEY MATERIALS Two species of cichlid, *Pundamilia pundamilia* and *P. nyererei*, were chosen. The males differ with regard to their coloration. A total of 8 males and 8 females (4 males and 4 females from each species) were tested.

Experimental level   Conceptual level

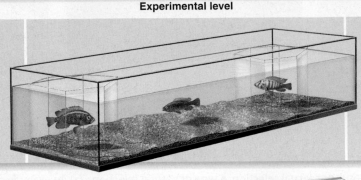

1 Place 1 female and 2 males in an aquarium. Each male is within a separate glass enclosure. The enclosures contain 1 male from each species.

This is a method to evaluate sexual selection via female choice in 2 species of cichlid.

2 Observe potential courtship behavior for 1 hour. If a male exhibited lateral display (a courtship invitation) and then the female approached the enclosure that contained the male, this was scored as a positive encounter. This protocol was performed under normal light and under orange monochromatic light.

3 THE DATA

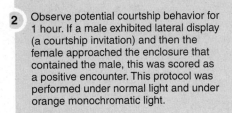

Female	Male	Light condition	Percentage of positive encounters*
P. pundamilia	*P. pundamilia*	Normal	16
P. pundamilia	*P. nyererei*	Normal	2
P. nyererei	*P. nyererei*	Normal	16
P. nyererei	*P. pundamilia*	Normal	5
P. pundamilia	*P. pundamilia*	Monochromatic	20
P. pundamilia	*P. nyererei*	Monochromatic	18
P. nyererei	*P. nyererei*	Monochromatic	13
P. nyererei	*P. pundamilia*	Monochromatic	18

*A positive encounter occurred when a male's lateral display was followed by the female approaching the male.

4 CONCLUSION Under normal light, where colors can be distinguished, *P. pundamilia* females prefer *P. pundamilia* males, and *P. nyererei* females prefer *P. nyererei* males.

5 SOURCE Seehausen, O., and van Alphen, J.J.M. 1998. The effect of male coloration on female mate choice in closely related Lake Victoria cichlids (*Haplochromis nyererei* complex). *Behav. Ecol. Sociobiol.* 42:1–8.

fin—the uppermost fin. *P. nyererei* males are red-orange on top and yellow on their sides.

Seehausen and van Alphen hypothesized that females choose males for mates based, in part, on the males' coloration. The researchers took advantage of the observation that colors are obscured under orange monochromatic light. As seen in **Figure 24.8b**, males of both species look similar under these conditions. In their study, a female

of one species was placed in an aquarium that contained one male of each species within an enclosure (**Figure 24.9**). The males were within glass enclosures to avoid direct competition with each other, which would have likely affected female choice. The goal of the experiment was to determine which of the two males a female would prefer. Courtship between a male and female begins when a male swims toward a female and exhibits a lateral display (that is, shows the side of his body to the female). If the female is interested, she will approach the male, and then the male will display a quivering motion. Such courtship behavior was examined under normal light and under orange monochromatic light.

As seen in the data, Seehausen and van Alphen found that the females' preference for males was dramatically different depending on the illumination conditions. Under normal light, *P. pundamilia* females preferred *P. pundamilia* males, and *P. nyererei* females preferred *P. nyererei* males. However, such mating preference was lost when colors were masked by artificial light. If the light conditions in their native habitats are similar to the normal light used in this experiment, female choice would be expected to separate cichlids into two populations, with *P. pundamilia* females mating with *P. pundamilia* males and *P. nyererei* females mating with *P. nyererei* males. In this case, sexual selection appears to have followed a diversifying mecha-

nism in which certain females prefer males with one color pattern, whereas other females prefer males with a different color pattern. A possible outcome of such sexual selection is that it can separate one large population into smaller populations that selectively breed with each other and eventually become distinct species. We will discuss the topic of species formation in more depth in Chapter 25.

Experimental Questions

1. What hypothesis is tested in the Seehausen and van Alphen experiment?

2. Describe the experimental design for this study, illustrated in Figure 24.9. What was the purpose of conducting the experiment under the two different light conditions?

3. What were the results of the experiment in Figure 24.9?

24.4   Genetic Drift

Learning Outcomes:

1. Define genetic drift and explain its effects on allele frequencies over time.
2. Compare and contrast the bottleneck and founder effects.
3. Explain how neutral mutations can spread through a population.

Thus far, we have focused on natural selection as a mechanism that can promote widespread genetic changes in a population. Let's now turn our attention to a second important way the gene pool of a population can change. In the 1930s, Sewall Wright played a large role in developing the concept of **genetic drift** (also called random genetic drift), which refers to changes in allele frequencies due to random chance. The term genetic drift is derived from the observation that allele frequencies may "drift" randomly from generation to generation as a matter of chance.

Changes in allele frequencies due to genetic drift happen regardless of the fitness of individuals that carry those alleles. For example, an individual with a high fitness value may, by chance, not encounter a member of the opposite sex. Likewise, random chance can influence which alleles happen to be found in the gametes that fuse with each other in a successful fertilization. In this section, we will examine how genetic drift alters allele frequencies in populations.

Genetic Drift Has a Greater Effect in Small Populations

What are the effects of genetic drift? Over the long run, genetic drift favors either the elimination or the fixation of an allele, that is, when its frequency reaches 0% or 100% in a population, respectively. However, the number of generations it takes for an allele to be lost or fixed greatly depends on the population size. **Figure 24.10** illustrates the potential consequences of genetic drift in one large (*N* = 1,000) and two small (*N* = 10) populations. This simulation

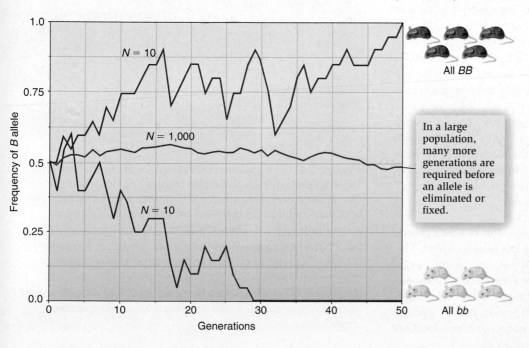

In a large population, many more generations are required before an allele is eliminated or fixed.

Figure 24.10   Genetic drift and population size. This graph shows three hypothetical simulations of genetic drift and their effects on small and large populations of black (*B* allele) and white (*b* allele) mice. In all cases, the starting allele frequencies are *B* = 0.5 and *b* = 0.5. The red lines illustrate two populations of mice in which *N* = 10; the blue line shows a population in which *N* = 1,000.

involves the frequency of hypothetical *B* and *b* alleles of a gene for fur color in a population of mice—*B* is the black allele, and *b* is the white allele.

At the beginning of this hypothetical simulation, which runs for 50 generations, all three populations had identical allele frequencies: $B = 0.5$ and $b = 0.5$. In the small populations, the allele frequencies fluctuated substantially from generation to generation. Eventually, in one population, the *b* allele was eliminated; in another, it was fixed at 100%. These small populations would then consist of only black mice or white mice, respectively. At this point, the gene has become monomorphic and cannot change any further. By comparison, the frequencies of *B* and *b* in the large population fluctuated much less. As discussed in Chapter 16, the relative effect of random chance, also termed random sampling error, is much smaller when the sample size is large. Nevertheless, genetic drift can eventually lead to allele loss or fixation even in large populations, but this will take many more generations to occur than it does in small populations.

In nature, genetic drift may rapidly alter allele frequencies when the size of a population dramatically decreases. Two examples of this phenomenon are the bottleneck effect and the founder effect, which are described next.

Bottleneck Effect   A population can be dramatically reduced in size by events such as earthquakes, floods, drought, and human destruction of habitat. These occurrences may eliminate most members of the population without regard to their genetic composition. The population is said to have passed through a bottleneck. The change in allele frequencies of the resulting population due to genetic drift is called the **bottleneck effect**. Some alleles may be overrepresented whereas others may even be eliminated. Such changes may happen for two reasons. First, the surviving population often has allele frequencies that differ from those of the original population that was much larger. Second, as we saw in Figure 24.10, genetic drift acts more quickly to reduce genetic variation when the population size is small. Eventually, a population that has gone through a bottleneck may regain its original size. However, the new population is likely to have less genetic variation than the original one.

A hypothetical example of the bottleneck effect is shown with a population of frogs in **Figure 24.11**. In this example, a starting population of frogs is found in three phenotypes: yellow, dark green, and striped. Due to a bottleneck caused by a drought, the dark green variety is lost from the population.

As a real-life example, the Northern elephant seal (*Mirounga angustirostris*) has lost much of its genetic variation. This was caused by a bottleneck effect in which the population decreased to approximately 20 to 30 surviving members in the 1890s due to hunting. The species has rebounded in numbers to over 100,000, but the bottleneck reduced its genetic variation to very low levels.

Founder Effect   Another common phenomenon in which genetic drift may rapidly alter allele frequencies is the **founder effect**. This occurs when a small group of individuals separates from a larger population and establishes a colony in a new location. For example, a few individuals may migrate from a large population on a continent and become the founders of an island population. The founder effect differs from a bottleneck in that it occurs in a new location,

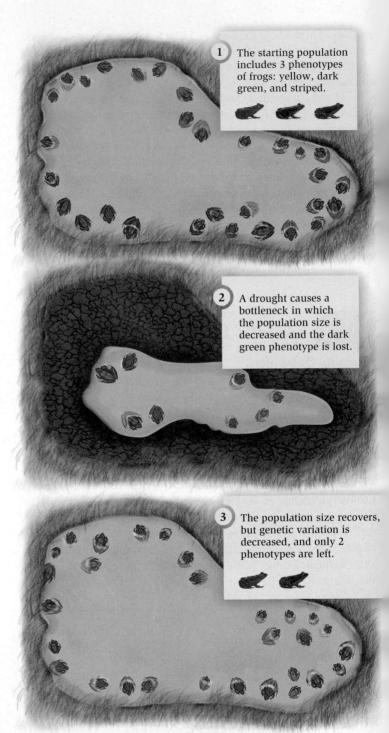

1. The starting population includes 3 phenotypes of frogs: yellow, dark green, and striped.

2. A drought causes a bottleneck in which the population size is decreased and the dark green phenotype is lost.

3. The population size recovers, but genetic variation is decreased, and only 2 phenotypes are left.

Figure 24.11 A hypothetical example of the bottleneck effect. This example involves a population of frogs in which a drought dramatically reduced population size, resulting in a bottleneck. The bottleneck reduced the genetic diversity in the population.

BIOLOGY PRINCIPLE Populations of organisms evolve from one generation to the next. Genetic drift randomly changes allele frequencies and (in the long run) leads to a loss or fixation of an allele.

Concept Check: *How does the bottleneck effect undermine the efforts of conservation biologists who are trying to save species nearing extinction?*

although both effects are related to a reduction in population size. The founder effect has two important consequences. First, the founding population, which is relatively small, is expected to have less genetic variation than the larger original population from which it was derived. Second, as a matter of chance, the allele frequencies in the founding population may differ markedly from those of the original population.

Population geneticists have studied many examples in which isolated populations were founded via colonization by members of another population. For example, in the 1960s, American geneticist Victor McKusick studied allele frequencies in the Amish of Lancaster County, Pennsylvania. At that time, this group included about 8,000 people, descended from just three couples that immigrated to the U.S. in 1770. Among this population of 8,000, a genetic disease known as Ellis–van Creveld syndrome (a recessive form of dwarfism) was found at a frequency of 0.07, or 7%. By comparison, this disorder is extremely rare in other human populations, even the population from which the founding members had originated. Evidence suggests that the high frequency in the Lancaster County population can be traced to one couple, one of whom carried the mutated gene that causes the syndrome.

Genetic Drift Plays an Important Role in Promoting Genetic Change

In 1968, Japanese evolutionary biologist Motoo Kimura proposed that much of the DNA sequence variation seen in genes in natural populations is the result of genetic drift rather than natural selection. Genetic drift is a random process that does not preferentially select for any particular allele—it can alter the frequencies of both beneficial and deleterious alleles. Much of the time, genetic drift promotes **neutral variation**—changes in genes and proteins that do not have an effect on reproductive success.

According to Kimura, most variation in DNA sequences is due to the accumulation of neutral mutations that have attained high frequencies in a population via genetic drift. For example, a new mutation within a gene that changes a glycine codon from GGG to GGC would not affect the amino acid sequence of the encoded protein. Both genotypes are equal in fitness. However, such new mutations can spread throughout a population due to genetic drift (**Figure 24.12**). This phenomenon has been called **non-Darwinian evolution** and also "survival of the luckiest." Kimura agreed with Darwin that natural selection is responsible for adaptive changes in a species during evolution. The long neck of the giraffe is the result of natural selection. His main idea is that much of the variation in DNA sequences is explained by neutral variation rather than adaptive variation.

The sequencing of genomes from many species is consistent with Kimura's proposal. When we examine changes of the coding sequence within structural genes, we find that nucleotide substitutions are more prevalent in the third base of a codon than in the first or second base. Mutations in the third base are often neutral; that is, they do not change the amino acid sequence of the protein (refer back to Table 12.1). In contrast, random mutations at the first or second base are more likely to be harmful than beneficial and tend to be eliminated from a population.

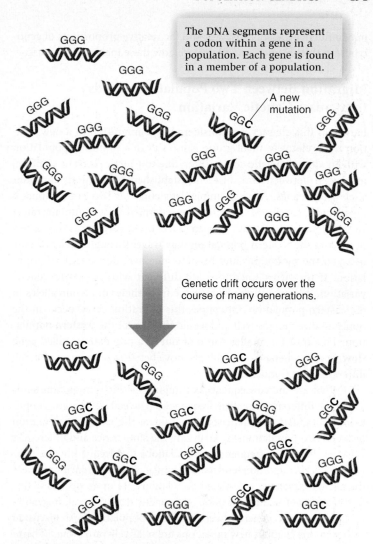

The DNA segments represent a codon within a gene in a population. Each gene is found in a member of a population.

A new mutation

Genetic drift occurs over the course of many generations.

Figure 24.12 Neutral evolution in a population. In this example, a mutation within a gene changes a glycine codon from GGG to GGC, which does not affect the amino acid sequence of the encoded protein. Each gene shown represents a copy of the gene in a member of a population. Over the course of many generations, genetic drift may cause this neutral allele to become prevalent in the population, perhaps even monomorphic.

BioConnections: *Look back at the genetic code described in Table 12.1. Describe three different genetic changes that you would expect to be neutral.*

24.5 Migration and Nonrandom Mating

Learning Outcomes:
1. Describe how gene flow affects genetic variation in neighboring populations.
2. Define inbreeding and explain how it may have detrimental consequences.

Thus far, we have considered how natural selection and genetic drift are key mechanisms that cause evolution to happen. In addition, migration between neighboring populations and nonrandom mating may influence genetic variation and the relative proportions of genotypes. In this section, we will explore how these mechanisms work.

Migration Between Two Populations Tends to Increase Genetic Variation

Earlier in this chapter, we considered how migration to a new location by a relatively small group can result in a founding population with an altered genetic composition due to genetic drift. In addition, migration between two different established populations can alter allele frequencies. As an example, let's consider two populations of a particular species of deer that are separated by a mountain range running north and south (**Figure 24.13**). On rare occasions, a few deer from the western population may travel through a narrow pass between the mountains and become members of the eastern population. If the two populations are different with regard to genetic variation, this migration will alter the frequencies of certain alleles in the eastern population. Of course, this migration could occur in the opposite direction as well and would then affect the western population. This transfer of alleles into or out of a population, called **gene flow**, occurs whenever individuals move between populations having different allele frequencies.

What are the consequences of migration? First, migration tends to reduce differences in allele frequencies between neighboring populations. Population geneticists can evaluate the extent of migration between two populations by analyzing the similarities and differences between their allele frequencies. Populations that frequently mix their gene pools via migration tend to have similar allele frequencies, whereas the allele frequencies of isolated populations are more disparate, due to the effects of natural selection and genetic drift. Second, migration tends to increase genetic diversity within populations. As discussed earlier in this chapter, new mutations are relatively rare events. Therefore, a new mutation may arise in only one population, and migration may then introduce this new allele into a neighboring population.

Nonrandom Mating Affects the Relative Proportion of Homozygotes and Heterozygotes in a Population

As mentioned earlier, one of the conditions required to establish Hardy-Weinberg equilibrium is random mating, which means that members of a population choose their mates irrespective of their genotypes or phenotypes. In many species, including human populations, this condition is violated. Such **nonrandom mating** takes different forms. Assortative mating occurs when individuals with similar phenotypes are more likely to mate. If the similar phenotypes are due to similar genotypes, assortative mating tends to increase the proportion of homozygotes and decrease the proportion of heterozygotes in the population. The opposite situation, where dissimilar phenotypes mate preferentially, causes heterozygosity to increase.

Another form of nonrandom mating involves the choice of mates based on their genetic history rather than their phenotypes. Individuals may choose a mate that is part of the same genetic lineage. The mating of two genetically related individuals, such as cousins, is called **inbreeding**. This sometimes occurs in human societies and is more likely to take place in nature when population size becomes very small.

In the absence of other evolutionary factors, nonrandom mating does not affect allele frequencies in a population. However, it will

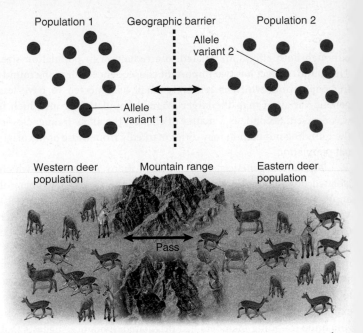

Figure 24.13 Migration and gene flow. In this example, two populations of a deer species are separated by a mountain range. On rare occasions, a few deer from one population travel through a narrow pass and become members of the other population. If the two populations differ in regard to genetic variation, this migration will alter the frequencies of alleles in the populations.

Concept Check: *How does migration affect the genetic compositions of populations?*

alter the balance of genotypes predicted by the Hardy-Weinberg equilibrium. As an example, let's consider a human pedigree involving a mating between cousins (**Figure 24.14**). Individuals III-2 and III-3 are cousins and have produced the daughter labeled IV-1. She is said to be inbred, because her parents are genetically related. The parents of an inbred individual have one or more common ancestors. In the pedigree of Figure 24.14, I-2 is the grandfather of both III-2 and III-3.

Inbreeding increases the relative proportions of homozygotes and decreases the likelihood of heterozygotes in a population. Why does this happen? An inbred individual has a higher chance of being homozygous for any given gene because the same allele for that gene could be inherited twice from a common ancestor. For example, individual I-2 is a heterozygote, *Cc*. The *c* allele could pass from I-2 to II-2 to III-2 and finally to IV-1 (see red lines in Figure 24.14). Likewise, the *c* allele could pass from I-2 to II-3 to III-3 and then to IV-1. Therefore, IV-1 has a chance of being homozygous because she inherited both copies of the *c* allele from a common ancestor to both of her parents. Inbreeding does not favor any particular allele—it does not favor *c* over *C*—but it does increase the likelihood that an individual will be homozygous for any given gene.

Although inbreeding by itself does not affect allele frequencies, it may have negative consequences with regard to recessive alleles. Rare recessive alleles that are harmful in the homozygous condition are found in all populations. Such alleles do not usually pose a problem because heterozygotes carrying a rare recessive allele are also rare, making it very unlikely that two such heterozygotes will mate with each other. However, related individuals share some of their genes, including recessive alleles. Therefore, if inbreeding occurs, homozygous offspring are more likely to be produced. For example, rare recessive diseases in humans are more frequent when inbreeding occurs.

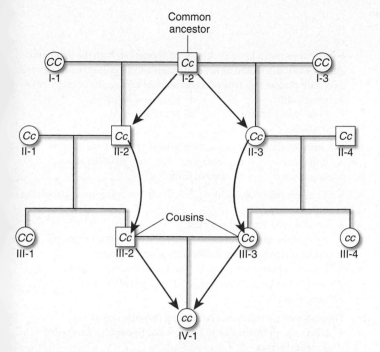

Figure 24.14 **A human pedigree containing inbreeding.** The parents of individual IV-1 are genetically related (cousins), and, therefore, individual IV-1 is inbred. Inbreeding increases the likelihood that an individual will be homozygous for any given gene. The red arrows show how IV-1 could become homozygous by inheriting the same allele (*c*) from the common ancestor (I-2) to both of her parents.

BioConnections: *Many inherited human diseases show a recessive pattern of inheritance (see Table 16.2). Explain whether inbreeding would increase or decrease the likelihood of such diseases.*

In natural populations, inbreeding lowers the mean fitness of the population if homozygous offspring have lower fitness values. This can be a serious problem as natural populations become smaller due to human destruction of habitat. As the population shrinks, inbreeding becomes more likely because individuals have fewer potential mates from which to choose. The inbreeding, in turn, produces homozygotes that are less fit, thereby decreasing the reproductive success of the population. This phenomenon is called **inbreeding depression**. Conservation biologists sometimes try to circumvent this problem by introducing individuals from one population into another. For example, the endangered Florida panther (*Puma concolor coryi*) suffers from inbreeding-related defects, which include poor sperm quality and quantity, and morphological abnormalities. To alleviate these effects, panthers from Texas have been introduced into the Florida population of panthers.

Summary of Key Concepts

24.1 Genes in Populations

- Population genetics is the study of genes and genotypes in a population. A population is a group of individuals of the same species that occupy the same environment and can interbreed. All of the alleles for every gene in a population constitute a gene pool.

- Polymorphism, which is very common in nearly all populations, refers to two or more variants of a character in a population. A monomorphic gene exists as a single allele (>99%) in a population (Figure 24.1).

- Allele frequency is the number of copies of a specific allele divided by the total number of all alleles in a population. Genotype frequency is the number of individuals with a given genotype divided by the total number of individuals in a population.

- The Hardy-Weinberg equation ($p^2 + 2pq + q^2 = 1$) predicts that allele and genotype frequencies will remain in equilibrium if no new mutations are formed, no natural selection occurs, the population size is very large, migration does not occur, and mating is random (Figure 24.2).

- Sources of new genetic variation include random gene mutations, gene duplications, exon shuffling, and horizontal gene transfer. Natural selection, genetic drift, migration, and nonrandom mating may alter allele and genotype frequencies and cause a population to evolve (Table 24.1).

24.2 Natural Selection

- Natural selection is the process in which individuals with certain heritable traits that favor survival and reproduction tend to become more prevalent in a population. Fitness, the relative likelihood that a genotype will contribute to the gene pool of the next generation, is a measure of reproductive success.

- Directional selection is the process in which one extreme of a phenotypic distribution is favored (Figure 24.3).

- Stabilizing selection is the process in which an intermediate phenotype is favored (Figure 24.4).

- Diversifying selection is the process in which two or more phenotypes are favored. An example is a population that occupies a diverse environment (Figure 24.5).

- Balancing selection maintains genetic polymorphism in a population. Examples include heterozygote advantage and negative frequency-dependent selection (Figure 24.6).

24.3 Sexual Selection

- Sexual selection is a form of natural selection in which individuals with certain traits are more likely than others to engage in successful mating. In intrasexual selection, members of one sex compete for the opportunity to mate with individuals of the opposite sex. In intersexual selection, members of one sex choose their mates on the basis of certain desirable characteristics (Figure 24.7).

- Seehausen and van Alphen discovered that female cichlids' choice of mates is influenced by male coloration. This is an example of sexual selection (Figures 24.8, 24.9).

24.4 Genetic Drift

- Genetic drift involves changes in allele frequencies over time due to chance events. It occurs more rapidly in small populations and leads to either the elimination or the fixation of alleles (Figure 24.10).

- In the bottleneck effect, an environmental event dramatically reduces a population size and the allele frequencies of the resulting population change due to genetic drift (Figure 24.11).

- The founder effect occurs when a small population moves to a new geographic location and genetic drift alters the genetic composition of that population.

- Kimura proposed that genetic drift promotes the accumulation of neutral genetic changes that do not affect reproductive success. Much of the genetic variation in DNA sequences in populations appears to be the result of genetic drift rather than natural selection (Figure 24.12).

24.5 Migration and Nonrandom Mating

- Gene flow occurs when individuals migrate between populations with different allele frequencies. It reduces differences in allele frequencies between populations and enhances genetic diversity (Figure 24.13).

- Inbreeding, a form of nonrandom mating in which genetically related individuals have offspring with each other, tends to increase the proportion of homozygotes relative to heterozygotes. When the resulting homozygotes have lower fitness, this phenomenon is called inbreeding depression (Figure 24.14).

Assess and Discuss

Test Yourself

1. Population geneticists are interested in the genetic variation in populations. The most common type of genetic change that causes polymorphism in a population is
   a. a deletion of a gene sequence.
   b. a duplication of a region of a gene.
   c. a rearrangement of a gene sequence.
   d. a single-nucleotide substitution.
   e. an inversion of a segment of a chromosome.

2. The Hardy-Weinberg equation characterizes the allele and genotype frequencies
   a. of a population that is experiencing selection for mating success.
   b. of a population that is extremely small.
   c. of a population that is very large and not evolving.
   d. of a community of species that is not evolving.
   e. of a community of species that is experiencing selection.

3. In the Hardy-Weinberg equation, what portion of the equation would be used to calculate the frequency of individuals that do not exhibit a recessive disease but are carriers of a recessive allele?
   a. q c. $2pq$ e. both b and d
   b. p^2 d. q^2

4. By itself, which of the following is not likely to have a major influence on allele frequencies?
   a. natural selection   d. inbreeding
   b. genetic drift   e. both c and d
   c. mutation

5. Which of the following statements is correct regarding mutations?
   a. Mutations are not important in evolution.
   b. Mutations provide the source for genetic variation, but other evolutionary factors are more important in determining allele frequencies in a population.
   c. Mutations occur at such a high rate that they promote major changes in the gene pool from one generation to the next.
   d. Mutations are of greater importance in smaller populations than in larger ones.
   e. Mutations are of greater importance in larger populations than in smaller ones.

6. In a population of fish, body coloration varies from a light shade, almost white, to a very dark shade of green. If changes in the environment resulted in decreased predation of individuals with the lightest coloration, this would be an example of _____ selection.
   a. diversifying   c. directional   e. artificial
   b. stabilizing   d. sexual

7. Considering the same population of fish described in question 6, if the stream environment included several areas of sandy, light-colored

bottom areas and a lot of dark-colored vegetation, both the light- and dark-colored fish would have selective advantage and increased survival in certain places. This type of scenario could explain the occurrence of
   a. genetic drift.   d. stabilizing selection.
   b. diversifying selection.   e. sexual selection.
   c. mutation.

8. The microevolutionary factor most sensitive to population size is
   a. mutation.   c. selection.   e. all of the above.
   b. migration.   d. genetic drift.

9. Kimura's proposal regarding neutral mutations differs from Darwinian evolution in that
   a. natural selection does not exist.
   b. most of the genetic variation in a population is due to neutral mutations, which do not affect reproductive success.
   c. neutral variation alters survival and reproductive success.
   d. neutral mutations are not affected by population size.
   e. both b and c.

10. Populations that experience inbreeding may also experience
   a. a decrease in fitness due to an increased frequency of recessive genetic diseases.
   b. an increase in fitness due to increases in heterozygosity.
   c. very little genetic drift.
   d. no apparent change.
   e. increased mutation rates.

Conceptual Questions

1. The percentage of individuals exhibiting a recessive disease in a population is 0.04, which is 4%. Based on a Hardy-Weinberg equilibrium, what percentage of individuals would be expected to be heterozygous carriers?

2. Compare and contrast the four patterns of natural selection that lead to environmental adaptation. You should also discuss sexual selection.

3. A principle of biology is that *populations of organisms evolve from one generation to the next.* Explain how genetic drift results in evolution.

Collaborative Questions

1. Antibiotics are commonly used to combat bacterial and fungal infections. During the past several decades, however, antibiotic-resistant strains of microorganisms have become alarmingly prevalent. This has undermined the ability of physicians to treat many types of infectious disease. Discuss how the following processes that alter allele frequencies may have contributed to the emergence of antibiotic-resistant strains:
   a. random mutation
   b. genetic drift
   c. natural selection

2. Discuss the similarities and differences among directional, disruptive, balancing, and stabilizing selection.

Online Resource

www.brookerbiology.com

Stay a step ahead in your studies with animations that bring concepts to life and practice tests to assess your understanding. Your instructor may also recommend the interactive eBook, individualized learning tools, and more.

Origin of Species and Macroevolution

25

Two different species of zebras. Grevy's zebra (*Equus grevyi*) is shown on the left, and Grant's zebra (*Equus quagga boehmi*), which has fewer and thicker stripes, is shown on the right.

T he origin of living organisms has been described by philosophers as the great "mystery of mysteries." Perhaps that is why so many different views have been put forth to explain the existence of living species. At the time of Aristotle (4th century B.C.E.), most people believed that some living organisms came into being by spontaneous generation—the idea that nonliving materials can give rise to living organisms. For example, it was commonly believed that worms and frogs could arise from mud, and mice could come from grain. By comparison, many religious teachings contend that species were divinely made and have remained the same since their creation. In contrast to these ideas, the work of Charles Darwin provided the scientific theory of evolution by descent with modification. Darwin's work, and that of subsequent biologists, helps us to understand the diversity of life, and in particular, it presents a logical explanation for how new species can evolve from pre-existing species.

This chapter provides an exciting way to build on the information that we have considered in previous chapters. In Chapter 22, we examined how the first primitive cells in an RNA world could have evolved into prokaryotic cells and eventually eukaryotes. Chapter 23 surveyed the tenets on which the theory of evolution is built, and in Chapter 24, we viewed microevolution—evolution on a small scale as it relates to allele frequencies in a population. In this chapter, we will consider evolution on a larger scale. **Macroevolution** refers to evolutionary changes that produce new species and groups of species.

To biologists, the concept of a **species** has come to mean a group of related organisms that share a distinctive set of attributes in nature. Members of the same species share an evolutionary history, which makes them more genetically similar to each other than they are to members of a different species. You may already have an intuitive sense of this concept. It is obvious that zebras and mice are different species. However, as we will learn in the first section of this chapter, the distinction between different, closely related species is often blurred in natural environments. Two closely related species may look very similar, as the chapter opening photo illustrates. Species identification has several practical uses. For example, it allows biologists to plan for the preservation and conservation of endangered species. In addition, it is often important for a physician to correctly identify the bacterial species that is causing a disease in a patient so the proper medication can be prescribed.

In this chapter, we will also focus on the mechanisms that promote the formation of new species, a phenomenon called **speciation**. Such macroevolution typically occurs by the accumulation of microevolutionary

changes, those that occur in single genes (see Chapter 24). We will also consider how macroevolution can happen at a fast or slow pace and explore how variations in the genes that control development play a role in the evolution of new species.

25.1 Identification of Species

Learning Outcomes:

1. Outline the characteristics that biologists use to distinguish different species.
2. Describe different species concepts.
3. Compare and contrast prezygotic and postzygotic isolating mechanisms.

How many different species are on Earth? The number is astounding. A study done by American biologist E. O. Wilson and colleagues in 1990 estimated the known number of species at approximately 1.4 million. Currently, about 1.3 million species have been identified and catalogued. However, a vast number of species have yet to be classified. This is particularly true among bacteria and archaea, which are difficult to categorize into distinct species. Also, new invertebrate and even vertebrate species are still being found in the far reaches of pristine habitats. Common estimates of the total number of species range from 5 to 50 million!

When studying natural populations, evolutionary biologists are often confronted with situations in which some differences between two populations are apparent, but it is difficult to decide whether the two populations truly represent separate species. When two or more geographically restricted groups of the same species display one or more traits that are somewhat different but not enough to warrant their placement into different species, biologists sometimes classify such groups as **subspecies**. Similarly, many bacterial species are subdivided into **ecotypes**. Each ecotype is a genetically distinct population adapted to its local environment. In this section, we will consider the characteristics that biologists examine when deciding if two groups of organisms constitute different species.

Each Species Is Established Using Characteristics and Histories That Distinguish It from Other Species

As mentioned, a species is a group of organisms that share a distinctive set of attributes in nature. In the case of sexually reproducing species, members of one species usually cannot successfully interbreed with members of other species. Members of the same species share an evolutionary history that is distinct from other species. Although this may seem like a reasonable way to characterize a given species, biologists would agree that distinguishing between species is a more difficult undertaking. What criteria do we use to distinguish species? How many differences must exist between two populations to classify them as different species? Such questions are often difficult to answer.

The characteristics that a biologist uses to identify a species depend, in large part, on the species in question. For example, the traits used to distinguish insect species are quite different from those used to identify different bacterial species. The relatively high level of horizontal gene transfer among bacteria presents special challenges in the grouping of bacterial species. Among bacteria, it is sometimes very difficult and perhaps arbitrary to divide closely related organisms into separate species.

The most commonly used characteristics for identifying species are morphological traits, the ability to interbreed, molecular features, ecological factors, and evolutionary relationships. A comparison of these concepts will help you appreciate the various approaches that biologists use to identify the bewildering array of species on our planet.

Morphological Traits
One way to establish that a population constitutes a unique species is based on their physical characteristics. Organisms are classified as the same species if their anatomical traits appear to be very similar. Likewise, microorganisms can be classified according to morphological traits at the cellular level. By comparing many different morphological traits, biologists may be able to decide that certain populations constitute a unique species.

Although an analysis of morphological traits is a common way for biologists to establish that a particular group constitutes a species, this approach has drawbacks. First, researchers may have difficulty deciding how many traits to consider. In addition, quantitative traits, such as size and weight, that vary in a continuous way among members of the same species are not easy to analyze. Another drawback is that the degree of dissimilarity that distinguishes different species may not show a simple relationship. The members of the same

(a) Frogs of the same species

(b) Frogs of different species

Figure 25.1 **Difficulties of using morphological traits to identify species.** In some cases, members of the same species appear quite different. In other cases, members of different species look very similar. **(a)** Two frogs of the same species, the dyeing poison frog (*Dendrobates tinctorius*). **(b)** Two different species of frog, the Northern leopard frog (*Rana pipiens*, left) and the Southern leopard frog (*Rana utricularia*, right).

Concept Check: *Can you think of another example of two different species that look very similar?*

species sometimes look very different, and conversely, members of different species sometimes look remarkably similar to each other. For example, **Figure 25.1a** shows two different frogs of the species *Dendrobates tinctorius*, commonly called the dyeing poison frog. This species exists in many different-colored morphs, which are individuals of the same species that have noticeably dissimilar appearances. In contrast, **Figure 25.1b** shows two different species of frogs, the Northern leopard frog (*Rana pipiens*) and the Southern leopard frog (*Rana utricularia*), which look fairly similar.

Reproductive Isolation
Why would biologists describe two species, such as the Northern leopard frog and Southern leopard frog, as being different if they are morphologically similar? One reason is that biologists have discovered that they are unable to breed with each other in nature. Therefore, a second way of identifying a species is by its ability to interbreed. In the late 1920s, geneticist Theodosius Dobzhansky proposed that each species is reproductively isolated from other species. Such **reproductive isolation** prevents one species from successfully interbreeding with other species. In 1942, German evolutionary biologist Ernst Mayr expanded on the ideas of Dobzhansky to provide a reproductive definition of a species. According to Mayr, a key feature of sexually reproducing species is that, in nature, the members of one species have the potential to interbreed with one another to produce viable, fertile offspring but cannot successfully interbreed with members of other species. As discussed later in this section, reproductive isolation among species of plants and animals occurs by an amazing variety of different mechanisms.

Reproductive isolation has been used to distinguish many plant and animal species, especially those that look alike but do not interbreed. Even so, this criterion suffers from four main problems. First, in nature, it may be difficult to determine if two populations are reproductively isolated, particularly if the populations have nonoverlapping geographic ranges. Second, biologists have noted many cases in which two different species can interbreed in nature yet consistently maintain themselves as separate species. For example, different species of yucca plants, such as *Yucca pallida* and *Yucca constricta*, do interbreed in nature yet typically maintain populations with distinct characteristics. For this reason, they are viewed as distinct species. A third drawback of reproductive isolation is that it does not apply to asexual species such as bacteria. Likewise, some species of plants and fungi reproduce only asexually. Finally, a fourth drawback is that it cannot be applied to extinct species. For these reasons, reproductive isolation has been primarily used to distinguish closely related species of modern animals and plants that reproduce sexually.

Molecular Features   Molecular features are now commonly used to determine if two different populations are different species. Evolutionary biologists often compare DNA sequences within genes, gene order along chromosomes, chromosome structure, and chromosome number in order to identify similarities and differences among different populations. For example, researchers may compare the DNA sequence of the *16S rRNA* gene between different bacterial populations as a way of determining if the two populations represent different species. When the sequences are very similar, such populations would probably be judged as the same species. However, it may be difficult to draw the line when separating groups into different species. How much difference must be present for species to be considered separate? Is a 2% difference in their genome sequences sufficient to warrant placement into two different species, or do we need a 5% difference?

Ecological Factors   A variety of factors related to an organism's habitat are used to distinguish one species from another. For example, certain species of warblers are distinguished by the habitat in which they forage for food. Some species search the ground for food, others forage in bushes or small trees, and some species primarily forage in tall trees. Such habitat differences are used to distinguish different species that look morphologically similar.

Many bacterial species have been categorized as distinct based on ecological factors. Bacterial cells of the same species are likely to use the same types of resources (such as sugars and vitamins) and grow under the same types of conditions (such as temperature and pH). However, a drawback of this approach is that different groups of bacteria sometimes display very similar growth characteristics, and even the same species may show great variation in the growth conditions it will tolerate.

Evolutionary Relationships   In Chapter 26, we will examine the methods that are used to produce evolutionary trees that describe the relationships between ancestral species and modern species. In some cases, such relationships are based on an analysis of the fossil record. For example, in Chapter 26, we will consider how the fossil record was used to construct a tree that shows the ancestors that led to modern horse species. Alternatively, another way of establishing evolutionary relationships is by the analysis of DNA sequences. Researchers obtain samples of cells from different individuals and compare the genes within those cells to see how similar or different they are.

Biologists Have Proposed Different Species Concepts

A **species concept** is a way of defining the concept of a species and/or of providing an approach to distinguish one species from another. However, even Darwin realized the difficulty in defining a species. In 1859, he said, "No one definition [of species] has as yet satisfied all naturalists; yet every naturalist knows vaguely what he means when he speaks of a species." Since 1942, over 20 different species concepts have been proposed by a variety of evolutionary biologists. Ernst Mayr proposed one of the first species concepts, called the **biological species concept**. According to Mayr's concept, a species is a group of individuals whose members have the potential to interbreed with one another in nature to produce viable, fertile offspring but cannot successfully interbreed with members of other species. The biological species concept emphasizes reproductive isolation as the most important criterion for delimiting species.

Another example is the **evolutionary lineage concept** proposed by American paleontologist George Gaylord Simpson in 1961. A **lineage** is a series of species that forms a line of descent, with each new species the direct result of speciation from an immediate ancestral species. According to Gaylord, species should be defined based on the separate evolution of lineages. A third example is the **ecological species concept**, described by American evolutionary biologist Leigh Van Valen in 1976. According to this viewpoint, each species occupies an ecological niche, which is the unique set of habitat resources that a species requires, as well as its influence on the environment and other species.

Most evolutionary biologists would agree that different methods are needed to distinguish the vast array of species on Earth. Even so, some evolutionary biologists have questioned whether it is valid to have many different species concepts. In 1998, American zoologist Kevin de Queiroz suggested that there is only a single general species concept, which concurs with Simpson's evolutionary lineage concept and includes all previous concepts. According to de Queiroz's **general lineage concept**, each species is a population of an independently evolving lineage. Each species has evolved from a specific series of ancestors and, as a consequence, forms a group of organisms with a particular set of characteristics. Multiple criteria are used to determine if a population is part of an independent evolutionary lineage, and thus a species, which is distinct from others. Typically, researchers use analyses of morphology, reproductive isolation, DNA sequences, and ecology to determine if a population or group of populations is distinct from others. Because of its generality, the general lineage concept has received significant support.

Reproductive Isolating Mechanisms Help to Maintain the Distinctiveness of Each Species

Thus far we have considered various ways of differentiating species. In our discussion, you may have realized that the identification of a species is not always a simple matter. The phenomenon of reproductive isolation has played a major role in the way biologists study plant and animal species, partly because it identifies a possible mechanism for the process of forming new species. For this reason, much research has been done to try to understand **reproductive isolating mechanisms**, the mechanisms that prevent interbreeding between different species. Why do reproductive isolating mechanisms occur? Populations do not intentionally erect these reproductive barriers. Rather, reproductive isolation is a consequence of genetic changes that occur usually because a species becomes adapted to its own particular environment. The view of evolutionary biologists is that reproductive isolation typically evolves as a by-product of genetic divergence. Over time, as a species evolves its own unique characteristics, some of those traits are likely to prevent breeding with other species.

Reproductive isolating mechanisms fall into two categories: **prezygotic isolating mechanisms**, which prevent the formation of a zygote, and **postzygotic isolating mechanisms**, which block the development of a viable and fertile individual after fertilization has taken place. **Figure 25.2** summarizes some of the more common ways that reproductive isolating mechanisms prevent reproduction between different species. When two species do produce offspring, such an offspring is called an **interspecies hybrid**.

Prezygotic Isolating Mechanisms We will consider five types of prezygotic isolating mechanisms.

Habitat Isolation: One obvious way to prevent interbreeding is for members of different species to never come in contact with each other. This phenomenon, called habitat isolation, may involve a geographic barrier to interbreeding. For example, a large body of water may separate two different plant species that live on nearby islands.

Temporal Isolation: In temporal isolation, species happen to reproduce at different times of the day or year. In the northeastern U.S., for example, the two most abundant field crickets, *Gryllus veletis* and *Gryllus pennsylvanicus* (spring and fall field crickets, respectively), do not differ in song or habitat and are morphologically very similar (**Figure 25.3**). How do the two species maintain reproductive isolation? *G. veletis* matures in the spring, whereas *G. pennsylvanicus* matures in the fall. This minimizes interbreeding between the two species.

Behavioral Isolation: In the case of animals, mating behavior and anatomy often play key roles in promoting reproductive isolation. An example of the third type of prezygotic isolation, behavioral isolation, is found between the western meadowlark (*Sturnella neglecta*) and eastern meadowlark (*Sturnella magna*). Both species are nearly identical in shape, coloration, and habitat, and their ranges overlap in the central U.S. (**Figure 25.4**). For many years, they were thought to be the same species. When biologists discovered that the western meadowlark is a separate species, it was given the species name *S. neglecta* to reflect the long delay in its recognition. In the zone of overlap, very little interspecies mating takes place between western and eastern meadowlarks, largely due to differences in their songs. The song of the western meadowlark is a long series of flutelike gurgling notes that go down the scale. By comparison, the eastern meadowlark's song is a simple series of whistles, typically about four or five notes. These differences in songs enable meadowlarks to recognize potential mates as members of their own species.

Mechanical Isolation: A fourth type of prezygotic isolation, called mechanical isolation, occurs when morphological features such as size or incompatible genitalia prevent two species from interbreed-

Species 1	Species 2

Prezygotic isolating mechanisms

Habitat isolation: Species occupy different habitats, so they never come in contact with each other.

Temporal isolation: Species have different mating or flowering seasons or times of day or become sexually mature at different times of the year.

Behavioral isolation: Sexual attraction between males and females of different animal species is limited due to differences in behavior or physiology.

Attempted mating

Mechanical isolation: Morphological features such as size and incompatible genitalia prevent 2 members of different species from interbreeding.

Gametic isolation: Gametic transfer takes place, but the gametes fail to unite with each other. This can occur because the male and female gametes fail to attract, because they are unable to fuse, or because the male gametes are inviable in the female reproductive tract of another species. In plants, the pollen of one species usually cannot generate a pollen tube to fertilize the egg cells of another species.

Fertilization

Postzygotic isolating mechanisms

Hybrid inviability: The egg of one species is fertilized by the sperm from another species, but the fertilized egg fails to develop past the early embryonic stages.

Hybrid sterility: An interspecies hybrid survives, but it is sterile. For example, the mule, which is sterile, is produced from a cross between a male donkey (*Equus asinus*) and a female horse (*Equus caballus*).

Hybrid breakdown: The F_1 interspecies hybrid is viable and fertile, but succeeding generations (F_2, and so on) become increasingly inviable. This is usually due to the formation of less-fit genotypes by genetic recombination.

Interspecies hybrid

Figure 25.2 Reproductive isolating mechanisms. These mechanisms prevent successful breeding between different species. They can occur prior to fertilization (prezygotic) or after fertilization (postzygotic).

BioConnections: *Look back at Figure 24.9. Is female choice an example of a prezygotic or postzygotic isolating mechanism?*

(a) Spring field cricket (*Gryllus veletis*)

(b) Fall field cricket (*Gryllus pennsylvanicus*)

Figure 25.3 **Temporal isolation.** Interbreeding between these two species of crickets does not usually occur because *Gryllus veletis* matures in the spring, whereas *Gryllus pennsylvanicus* matures in the fall.

Concept Check: *Is this an example of a prezygotic or a postzygotic isolating mechanism?*

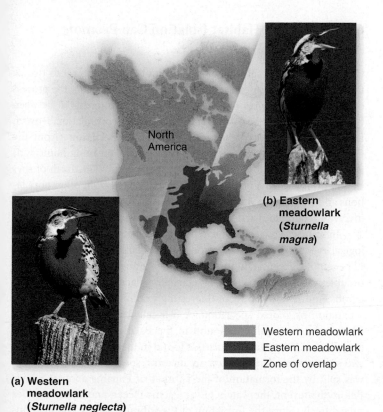

North America

Western meadowlark
Eastern meadowlark
Zone of overlap

(b) Eastern meadowlark (*Sturnella magna*)

(a) Western meadowlark (*Sturnella neglecta*)

Figure 25.4 **Behavioral isolation.** **(a)** The western meadowlark (*Sturnella neglecta*) and **(b)** eastern meadowlark (*Sturnella magna*) are very similar in appearance. The red region in this map shows where the two species' ranges overlap. However, very little interspecies mating takes place due to differences in their songs.

BIOLOGY PRINCIPLE **Populations of organisms evolve from one generation to the next.** For these two species of meadowlarks, one evolutionary change that took place is that their mating songs became different.

ing. For example, male dragonflies use a pair of special appendages to grasp females during copulation. When a male tries to mate with a female of a different species, his grasping appendages do not fit her body shape.

Gametic Isolation: A fifth type of prezygotic isolating mechanism occurs when two species attempt to interbreed, but the gametes fail to unite in a successful fertilization event. This phenomenon, called gametic isolation, is widespread among plant and animal species. In aquatic animals that release sperm and egg cells into the water, gametic isolation is important in preventing interspecies hybrids. For example, closely related species of sea urchins may release sperm and eggs into the water at the same time. Researchers have discovered that sea urchin sperm have a protein on their surface called bindin, which mediates sperm-egg attachment and membrane fusion. The structure of bindin is significantly different among different sea urchin species, thereby ensuring that fertilization occurs only between sperm and egg cells of the same species.

In flowering plants, gametic isolation is commonly associated with pollination. As discussed in Chapter 39, plant fertilization is initiated when a pollen grain lands on the stigma of a flower and sprouts a pollen tube that ultimately reaches an egg cell (look ahead to Figure 39.4). When pollen is released from a plant, it could be transferred to the stigma of many different plant species. In most cases, when a pollen grain lands on the stigma of a different species, it either fails to generate a pollen tube or the tube does not grow properly and reach the egg cell.

Postzygotic Isolating Mechanisms Let's now turn to postzygotic mechanisms of reproductive isolation, of which there are three common types.

Hybrid Inviability: The mechanism of hybrid inviability occurs when an egg of one species is fertilized by a sperm from another species, but the fertilized egg cannot develop past the early embryonic stages.

Hybrid Sterility: A second postzygotic isolating mechanism is hybrid sterility, in which an interspecies hybrid may be viable but sterile. A classic example of hybrid sterility is the mule, which is produced by a mating between a male donkey (*Equus asinus*) and a female horse (*Equus ferus caballus*) (**Figure 25.5**). All male mules and most female mules are sterile. Why are mules usually sterile? Two reasons explain the sterility. Because the horse has 32 chromosomes per set and a donkey has 31, a mule inherits 63 chromosomes (32 + 31). Due to the uneven number, all of the chromosomes cannot pair evenly. Also, the chromosomes of the horse and donkey have structural differences, which either prevent them from pairing correctly or lead to chromosomal abnormalities if crossing over occurs during meiosis. For these reasons, mules usually produce inviable gametes. Note that the mule has no species name because it is not considered a species due to this sterility.

Hybrid Breakdown: Finally, interspecies hybrids may be viable and fertile, but the subsequent generation(s) may harbor genetic abnormalities that are detrimental. This third mechanism, called hybrid breakdown, can be caused by changes in chromosome structure. The chromosomes of closely related species may have structural differences from each other, such as inversions. In hybrids, a crossover

 ×

Male donkey (*Equus asinus*)   **Female horse (*Equus ferus caballus*)**

Mule

Figure 25.5 Hybrid sterility. When a male donkey (*Equus asinus*) mates with a female horse (*Equus ferus caballus*), their offspring is a mule, which is usually sterile.

Concept Check: Is this an example of a prezygotic or a postzygotic isolating mechanism?

may occur in the region that is inverted in one species but not the other. This will produce gametes with too little or too much genetic material. Such hybrids often have offspring with developmental abnormalities.

Postzygotic isolating mechanisms tend to be uncommon in nature compared with prezygotic mechanisms. Why are postzygotic mechanisms rare? One explanation is that they are more costly in terms of energy and resources used. For example, a female mammal would use a large amount of energy to produce an offspring that is sterile. Evolutionary biologists hypothesize that natural selection has favored prezygotic isolating mechanisms because they do not waste a lot of energy.

25.2 Mechanisms of Speciation

Learning Outcomes:

1. Describe how allopatric speciation can occur and how it can lead to adaptive radiation.
2. Outline three different mechanisms of sympatric speciation.

Speciation, the formation of a new species, is caused by genetic changes in a particular group that make it different from the species from which it was derived. As discussed in Chapter 24, mutations in genes can be acted on by natural selection and other evolutionary mechanisms to alter the genetic composition of a population. New species commonly evolve in this manner. In addition, interspecies matings, changes in chromosome number, and horizontal gene

transfer may also cause new species to arise. In all of these cases, the underlying cause of speciation is the accumulation of genetic changes that ultimately promote enough differences so we judge a population to constitute a unique species.

Even though genetic changes account for the phenotypic differences observed among living organisms, such changes do not fully explain the existence of many distinct species on our planet. Why does life often diversify into the more or less discrete populations that we recognize as species? Two main explanations have been proposed:

1. In some cases, speciation may occur due to abrupt events, such as changes in chromosome number, that cause reproductive isolation.
2. More commonly, species arise as a consequence of adaptation to different ecological niches. For sexually reproducing organisms, reproductive isolation is typically a by-product of that adaptation.

Depending on the species involved, one or both factors may play a dominant role in the formation of new species. In this section, we will consider how reproductive isolating mechanisms and adaptation to particular environments are critical aspects of the speciation process.

Geographic and Habitat Isolation Can Promote Allopatric Speciation

Cladogenesis is the splitting or diverging of a population into two or more species. In the case of sexually reproducing organisms, the process of cladogenesis requires that gene flow becomes interrupted between two or more populations, limiting or eliminating reproduction between members of different populations. **Allopatric speciation** (from the Greek *allos*, meaning other, and the Latin *patria*, meaning homeland) is the most prevalent way for cladogenesis to occur. This form of speciation occurs when a population becomes isolated from other populations and evolves into one or more species. Typically, this isolation may involve a geographic barrier such as a large area of land or body of water.

In some cases, geographic separation may be caused by slow geological events that eventually produce quite large geographic barriers. For example, a mountain range may emerge and split one species that occupies the lowland regions, or a creeping glacier may divide a population. **Figure 25.6** shows an interesting example in which geological separation promoted speciation. A fish called the Panamic porkfish (*Anisotremus taeniatus*) is found in the Pacific Ocean, whereas the porkfish (*Anisotremus virginicus*) is found in the Caribbean Sea. These two species were derived from an ancestral species whose population was split by the formation of the Isthmus of Panama about 3.5 mya. Before that event, the waters of the Pacific Ocean and Caribbean Sea mixed freely. Since the formation of the isthmus, the two populations have been geographically isolated and have evolved into distinct species.

Allopatric speciation can also occur when a small population moves to a new location that is geographically isolated from the main population. For example, a storm may force a small group of birds from a mainland to a distant island. In this case, migration between the island and the mainland population is an infrequent event. In a relatively short period of time, the small founding population on the island may evolve into a new species. How does speciation occur rapidly? Because the environment on the island may differ significantly from the mainland environment, natural selection may rapidly alter

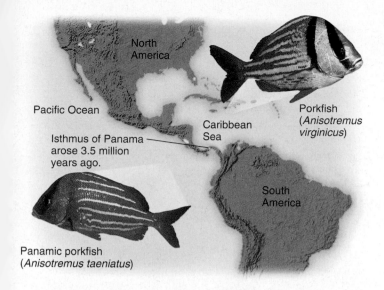

North America

Pacific Ocean

Caribbean Sea

Porkfish (*Anisotremus virginicus*)

Isthmus of Panama arose 3.5 million years ago.

South America

Panamic porkfish (*Anisotremus taeniatus*)

Figure 25.6 **Allopatric speciation.** An ancestral fish population was split into two by the formation of the Isthmus of Panama about 3.5 mya. Since that time, different genetic changes occurred in the two populations. These changes eventually led to the formation of different species: the Panamic porkfish (*Anisotremus taeniatus*) is found in the Pacific Ocean, and the porkfish (*Anisotremus virginicus*) is found in the Caribbean Sea.

🔘 **BIOLOGY PRINCIPLE** **All species (past and present) are related by an evolutionary history.** These two species of fish look similar because they share a common ancestor that existed in the fairly recent past.

investigated several examples of **adaptive radiation**, in which a single ancestral species has evolved into a wide array of descendant species that differ in their habitat, form, or behavior. For example, approximately 1,000 species of *Drosophila* are found dispersed throughout the Hawaiian Islands. Evolutionary studies suggest that these evolved from a single colonization by one species of fruit fly! Natural selection resulted in changes in body form and function that produced the amazing diversity of *Drosophila* species that are now found on the islands.

As shown in **Figure 25.7**, an example of adaptive radiation is seen with a family of birds called honeycreepers (*Drepanidinae*). Researchers estimate that the honeycreepers' ancestor arrived in

the genetic composition of the population, leading to adaptation to the new environment. In addition, as discussed in Chapter 24, a form of genetic drift known as the founder effect can have a larger influence in small founding populations.

The Hawaiian Islands are a showcase of allopatric speciation. The islands' extreme isolation coupled with their phenomenal array of ecological niches has enabled a small number of founding species to evolve into a vast assortment of different species. Biologists have

Asia

Eurasian rosefinch

Hawaiian Islands

(a) Migration of ancestor to the Hawaiian Islands

Figure 25.7 **Adaptive radiation.** **(a)** The honeycreepers' ancestor is believed to be related to a Eurasian rosefinch that arrived on the Hawaiian Islands approximately 3–7 mya. Since that time, at least 54 different species of honeycreepers (*Drepanidinae*) have evolved on the islands. **(b)** Adaptations to feeding have produced honeycreeper species with notable differences in beak morphology.

BioConnections: *Look back at Figure 24.5b. Discuss how diversifying selection played a role in the diversity of honeycreepers on the Hawaiian Islands.*

Hawaiian honeycreepers

Palila

Nihoa finch

Seed eaters

Maui Alauahio

Akikiki

Insect eaters

I'iwi

Akohekohe

Nectar feeders

(b) Examples of Hawaiian honeycreepers

Hawaii 3–7 mya. This ancestor was a single species of finch, possibly a Eurasian rosefinch (genus *Carpodacus*) or, less likely, the North American house finch (*Carpodacus mexicanus*). At least 54 different species of honeycreepers, many of which are now extinct, evolved from this founding event to fill available niches in the islands' habitats. Natural selection resulted in the formation of many species with different feeding strategies. Seed eaters have stouter, stronger bills capable of cracking tough husks. Insect-eating honeycreepers have thin, warbler-like bills adapted for picking insects from foliage or strong, hooked bills to root out wood-boring insects. The curved bills of nectar-feeding honeycreepers enable them to extract nectar from the flowers of Hawaii's endemic plants.

Before ending our discussion of allopatric speciation, let's consider a common situation in which geographic separation is not complete. The zones where two populations can interbreed are known as **hybrid zones**. **Figure 25.8** shows a hybrid zone along a mountain pass that connects two deer populations. For speciation to occur, the amount of gene flow within hybrid zones must become very limited. How does this happen? As the two populations accumulate different genetic changes, the ability of individuals from different populations to mate with each other in the hybrid zone may decrease. For example, natural selection in the western deer population may favor an increase in body size that is not favored in the eastern population. Over time, as this size difference between members of the two populations becomes greater, breeding in the hybrid zone may decrease. Larger individuals may not interbreed easily with smaller ones due to

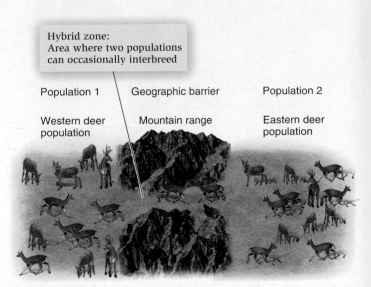

Figure 25.8 Hybrid zones. Two populations of deer are separated by a mountain range. A hybrid zone exists in a mountain pass, where occasional interbreeding may occur.

mechanical isolation. In addition, larger individuals may prefer larger individuals as mates, and smaller individuals may also prefer each other. Once gene flow through the hybrid zone is greatly diminished, the two populations are reproductively isolated. Over the course of many generations, such populations may evolve into distinct species.

FEATURE INVESTIGATION

Podos Found That an Adaptation to Feeding May Have Promoted Reproductive Isolation in Finches

In 2001, American evolutionary biologist Jeffrey Podos analyzed the songs of Darwin's finches on the Galápagos Islands to determine how environmental adaptation may contribute to reproductive isolation. As in honeycreepers, the differences in beak sizes and shapes among the various species of finches are adaptations to different feeding strategies. Podos hypothesized that changes in beak morphology could also affect the songs that the birds produce, thereby having the potential to affect mate choice. The components of the vocal tract of birds, including the trachea, larynx, and beak, work collectively to produce a bird's song. Birds actively modify the shape of their vocal tracts during singing, and beak movements are normally very rapid and precise.

Podos focused on two aspects of a bird's song. The first feature is the frequency range, which is a measure of the minimum and maximum frequencies in a bird's song, measured in kilohertz (kHz). The second feature is the trill rate. A trill is a series of notes or group of notes repeated in succession. **Figure 25.9** shows a graphical depiction of the songs of Darwin's finches. As you can see, the song patterns of these finches are quite different from each other.

To quantitatively study the relationship between beak size and song, Podos first captured male finches on Santa Cruz, one of the Galápagos Islands, and measured their beak sizes (**Figure 25.10**). The birds were banded and then released into the wild. The banding pro-

vided a way of identifying the birds whose beaks had already been measured. After release, the songs of the banded birds were recorded on a tape recorder, and their range of frequencies and trill rate were analyzed. Podos then compared the data for the Galápagos finches to a large body of data that had been collected on many other bird species. This comparison was used to evaluate whether beak size, in this case, beak depth—the measurement of the beak from top to bottom, at its base—constrained either the frequency range and/or the trill rate of the finches.

The results of this comparison are shown in the data of Figure 25.10. As seen here, the relative constraint on vocal performance became higher as the beak depth became larger. This means that birds with larger beaks had a narrower frequency range and/or a slower trill rate. Podos proposed that as jaws and beaks became adapted for strength to crack open larger, harder seeds, they became less able to perform the rapid movements associated with certain types of songs. In contrast, the finches with smaller beaks adapted to probe for insects or eat smaller seeds had less constraint on their vocal performance. From the perspective of evolution, the changes observed in song patterns for the Galápagos finches could have played an important role in promoting reproductive isolation, because song pattern is an important factor in mate selection in birds. Therefore, a by-product of beak adaptation for feeding is that it also appears to have affected song pattern, possibly promoting reproductive isolation and eventually the formation of distinct species.

Figure 25.9 **Differences in the songs of Galápagos finches.** These spectrograms depict the frequency of each bird's song over time, measured in kilohertz (kHz). The songs are produced in a series of trills that have a particular pattern and occur at regular intervals. Notice the differences in frequency and trill rate between different species of birds.

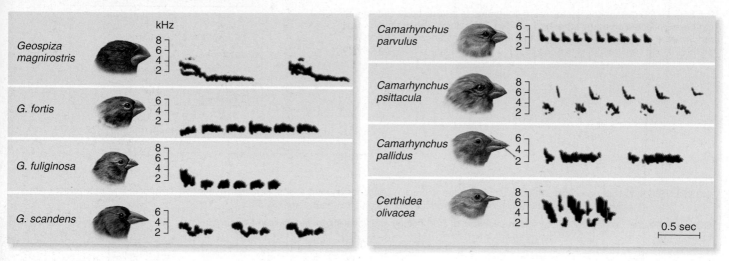

Figure 25.10 **Study by Podos investigating the effects of beak depth on song among different species of Galápagos finches.**

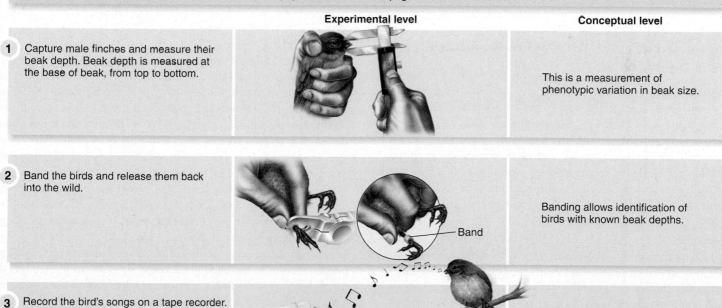

HYPOTHESIS Changes in beak morphology that are an adaptation to feeding may also affect the songs of Galápagos finches and thereby lead to reproductive isolation between species.

KEY MATERIALS This study was conducted on finch populations of the Galápagos Island of Santa Cruz.

	Experimental level	Conceptual level
1 Capture male finches and measure their beak depth. Beak depth is measured at the base of beak, from top to bottom.		This is a measurement of phenotypic variation in beak size.
2 Band the birds and release them back into the wild.	Band	Banding allows identification of birds with known beak depths.
3 Record the bird's songs on a tape recorder.		This is a measurement of phenotypic variation in song.
4 Analyze the songs with regard to frequency range and trill rate.		The frequency range is the value between high and low frequencies. The trill rate is the number of repeats per unit time.

5 THE DATA

The data for the Galápagos finches were compared to a large body of data that had been collected on many other bird species. The relative constraint on vocal performance is higher if a bird has a narrower frequency range and/or a slower trill rate. These constraints were analyzed with regard to each bird's beak depth.

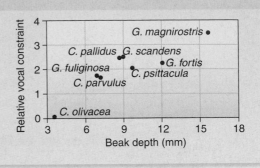

6 CONCLUSION Larger beak size, which is an adaptation to cracking open large, hard seeds, constrains vocal performance. This may affect mating song patterns and thereby promote reproductive isolation and, in turn, speciation.

7 SOURCE Podos, Jeffrey. 2001. Correlated evolution of morphology and vocal signal structure in Darwin's finches. *Nature* 409:185–188.

Experimental Questions

1. What did Podos hypothesize regarding the effects of beak size on a bird's song? How could changes in beak size and shape lead to reproductive isolation among the finches?

2. How did Podos test the hypothesis that beak morphology caused changes in the birds' songs?

3. Did the results of Podos's study support his original hypothesis? Explain. What is meant by the phrase "by-product of adaptation," and how does it apply to this particular study?

Sympatric Speciation Occurs When Populations Are in Direct Contact

Sympatric speciation (from the Greek *sym*, meaning together) occurs when members of a species that are within the same range diverge into two or more different species even though there are no physical barriers to interbreeding. Although sympatric speciation is believed to be less common than allopatric speciation, particularly in animals, evolutionary biologists have discovered several ways in which it can occur. These include polyploidy, adaptation to local environments, and sexual selection.

Polyploidy   A type of genetic change that can cause immediate reproductive isolation is **polyploidy**, in which an organism has more than two sets of chromosomes. Plants tend to be more tolerant of changes in chromosome number than animals. For example, many crops and decorative species of plants are polyploid. How does polyploidy occur? One mechanism is complete nondisjunction of chromosomes, which increases the number of chromosome sets in a given species (autopolyploidy). Such changes can result in an abrupt sympatric speciation. For example, nondisjunction could produce a tetraploid plant with four sets of chromosomes from a species that was diploid with two sets. A cross between a tetraploid and a diploid produces a triploid offspring with three sets of chromosomes. Triploid offspring are usually sterile because an odd number of chromosomes cannot be evenly segregated during meiosis. This hybrid sterility causes reproductive isolation between the tetraploid and diploid species.

Another mechanism that leads to polyploidy is interspecies breeding. An **alloploid** organism contains at least one set of chromosomes from two or more different species. This term refers to the occurrence of chromosome sets (ploidy) from the genomes of different (allo-) species. Interbreeding between two different species may produce an allodiploid, an organism that has only one set of chromosomes from each species. Species that are close evolutionary relatives are most likely to breed and produce allodiploid offspring. For example, closely related species of grasses may interbreed to produce allodiploids. An organism containing two or more complete sets of chromosomes from two or more different species is called an allopolyploid. An allopolyploid can be the result of interspecies breeding between species that are already polyploid, or it can occur as a result of nondisjunction in an allodiploid organism. For example, complete nondisjunction in an allodiploid could produce an allotetraploid, which is an allopolyploid with two complete sets of chromosomes from two species for a total of four sets.

The formation of an allopolyploid can also abruptly lead to reproductive isolation, thereby promoting speciation. As an example, let's consider the origin of a natural species of a plant called the common hemp nettle, *Galeopsis tetrahit*. This species is thought to be an allotetraploid derived from two diploid species, *Galeopsis pubescens* and *Galeopsis speciosa* (**Figure 25.11a**). These two diploid species contain 16 chromosomes each ($2n = 16$), whereas *G. tetrahit* contains 32 chromosomes. Though the origin of *G. tetrahit* is not completely certain, research suggests it may have originated from an interspecies cross between *G. pubescens* and *G. speciosa*, which initially produced

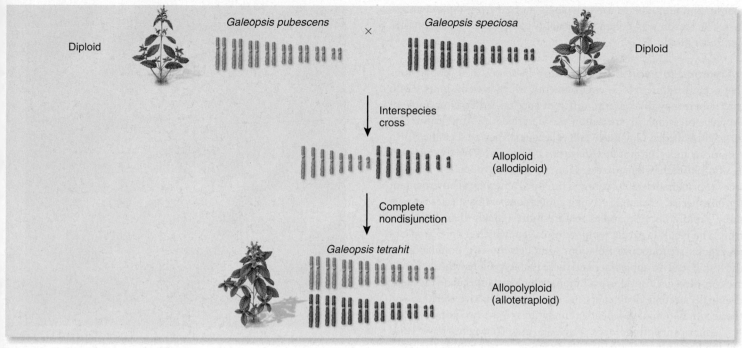

(a) Possible formation of *G. tetrahit*

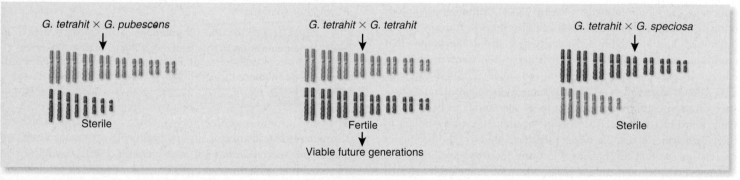

(b) Outcome of breeding among *G. tetrahit*, *G. pubescens*, and *G. speciosa*

Figure 25.11 Polyploidy and sympatric speciation. (a) *Galeopsis tetrahit* may have arisen by an interspecies cross between *Galeopsis pubescens* and *Galeopsis speciosa*, which was followed by a subsequent nondisjunction event. (b) Polyploidy may have caused reproductive isolation between these three natural species of hemp nettle. If *G. tetrahit* is mated with either of the other two species, the resulting offspring would be monoploid for one chromosome set and diploid for the other set, making them sterile. Therefore, *G. tetrahit* is reproductively isolated from the diploid species, making it a new species.

Concept Check: *Suppose that G. tetrahit was crossed to G. pubescens to produce an interspecies hybrid as shown at the left side of part (b). If this interspecies hybrid was crossed to G. tetrahit, how many chromosomes do you think an offspring would have? The answer you give should be a range, not a single number.*

an allodiploid with 16 chromosomes (one set from each species). The allodiploid then underwent complete nondisjunction to become an allotetraploid carrying four sets of chromosomes—two from each species.

How do these genetic changes cause reproductive isolation? The allotetraploid, *G. tetrahit*, is fertile, because all of its chromosomes occur in homologous pairs that can segregate evenly during meiosis. However, a cross between *G. tetrahit* and a diploid, *G. pubescens* or *G. speciosa*, produces an offspring that is monoploid for one chromosome set and diploid for the other set (**Figure 25.11b**). The

chromosomes of the monoploid set cannot be evenly segregated during meiosis. These offspring are expected to be sterile, because they will produce gametes that have incomplete sets of chromosomes. This hybrid sterility causes the allotetraploid to be reproductively isolated from both diploid species. Therefore, this process could have led to the formation of a new species, *G. tetrahit*, by sympatric speciation.

Polyploidy is so frequent in plants that it is a major mechanism of their speciation. In ferns and flowering plants, about 40–70% of the species are polyploid. By comparison, polyploidy can occur in animals, but it is much less common. For example, less than 1% of reptiles and amphibians are polyploids derived from diploid ancestors. The reason why polyploidy is not usually tolerated in animals is not understood.

Adaptation to Local Environments   In some cases, populations that occupy different local environments, which are continuous with each other, may diverge into different species. An early example of this type of sympatric speciation was described by American biologists Jeffrey Feder, Guy Bush, and colleagues. They studied the North American apple maggot fly (*Rhagoletis pomenella*). This fly originally fed on native hawthorn trees. However, the introduction of apple trees approximately 200 years ago provided a new local environment for this species. The apple-feeding populations of this species develop more rapidly because apples mature more quickly than hawthorn fruit. The result is partial temporal isolation, which is an example of prezygotic reproductive isolation. Although the two populations—those that feed on apple trees and those that feed on hawthorn trees—are considered subspecies, evolutionary biologists speculate they may eventually become distinct species due to reproductive isolation and the accumulation of independent mutations in the two populations.

American entomologist Sara Via and colleagues have studied the beginnings of sympatric speciation in pea aphids (*Acyrthosiphon pisum*), a small, plant-eating insect. Pea aphids in the same geographic area can be found on both alfalfa (*Medicago sativa*) and red clover (*Trifolium pratenae*) (**Figure 25.12**). Although pea aphids on these two host plants look identical, they show significant genetic differences and are highly ecologically specialized. Pea aphids that are found on alfalfa exhibit a lower fitness when transferred to red clover, whereas pea aphids found on red clover exhibit a lower fitness when transferred to alfalfa. The same traits involved in this host specialization cause these two groups of pea aphids to be substantially reproductively isolated. Taken together, the observations of the North American apple maggot fly, pea aphids, and other insect species suggest that diversifying selection (described in Chapter 24) occurs because some members within the same range evolve to feed on a different host. This may be an important mechanism of sympatric speciation among insects.

Sexual Selection   Another mechanism that may promote sympatric speciation is sexual selection. As discussed in Chapter 24, one type of sexual selection is mate choice (refer back to Figures 24.8 and 24.9). Ole Seehausen and Jacques van Alphen found that male coloration in African cichlids is subject to female choice. In this case, sexual selection appears to have followed a diversifying mechanism in which certain females prefer males with one color pattern, and other females prefer males with a different color pattern. A possible outcome of such sexual selection is that it can separate one large sympatric population into smaller populations that eventually become distinct species because they selectively breed among themselves.

25.3   The Pace of Speciation

Learning Outcome:

1. Compare and contrast the concepts of gradualism and punctuated equilibria.

Figure 25.12 Pea aphids, a possible example of sympatric speciation in progress. Some pea aphids prefer alfalfa, whereas others prefer red clover. These two populations may be in the process of sympatric speciation.

BIOLOGY PRINCIPLE Populations of organisms evolve from one generation to the next. Populations of pea aphids are evolving based on preference for different food sources—alfalfa or red clover. The populations may eventually evolve into separate species.

Concept Check: *How may host preference eventually lead to speciation?*

Throughout the history of life on Earth, the rate of evolutionary change and speciation has not been constant. Even Darwin himself suggested that evolution can be fast or slow. **Figure 25.13** illustrates two contrasting views concerning the rate of evolutionary change. These ideas are not mutually exclusive but represent two different ways to consider the tempo of evolution. The concept of **gradualism** suggests that each new species evolves continuously over long spans of time (Figure 25.13a). The principal idea is that large phenotypic differences that produce new species are due to the gradual accumulation of many small genetic changes. By comparison, the concept of **punctuated equilibrium**, advocated in the 1970s by American paleontologist and evolutionary biologist Niles Eldredge and Stephen Jay Gould, suggests that the tempo of evolution is more sporadic (Figure 25.13b). According to this hypothesis, species exist relatively unchanged for many generations. During this equilibrium period, genetic changes are likely to accumulate, particularly neutral changes. However, genetic changes that significantly alter phenotype do not substantially change the overall composition of a population. These long periods of equilibria are punctuated by relatively short periods (that is, on a geological timescale) during which the frequencies of certain phenotypes in a population change substantially at a far more rapid rate.

A rapid rate of evolution could commonly occur via allopatric speciation in which a small group migrates away from a larger

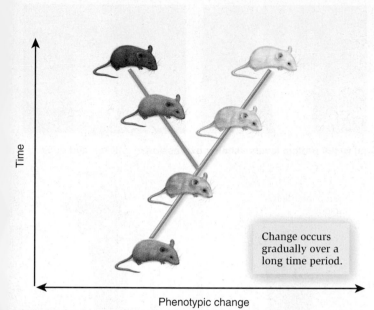

Time

Change occurs gradually over a long time period.

Phenotypic change

(a) Gradualism

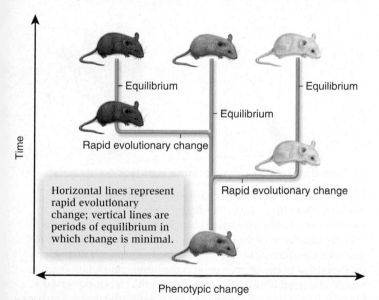

Time

Equilibrium

Equilibrium

Equilibrium

Rapid evolutionary change

Rapid evolutionary change

Horizontal lines represent rapid evolutionary change; vertical lines are periods of equilibrium in which change is minimal.

Phenotypic change

(b) Punctuated equilibrium

Figure 25.13 **A comparison of gradualism and punctuated equilibrium.** **(a)** During gradualism, the phenotypic characteristics of a species gradually change due to the accumulation of small genetic changes. **(b)** During punctuated equilibrium, long periods of equilibrium in which species exist essentially unchanged are punctuated by relatively short periods of evolutionary change during which phenotypic characteristics may change rapidly.

BIOLOGY PRINCIPLE **Populations of organisms evolve from one generation to the next.** Gradualism and punctuated equilibrium are two different views regarding the pace of evolution.

population to a new environment in which different alleles provide better adaptation to the surroundings. By natural selection, the small population may rapidly evolve into a new species. In addition, events such as polyploidy may abruptly produce individuals with new phenotypic traits. On an evolutionary timescale, these types of events can

be rather rapid, because a few genetic changes can have a major influence on phenotype.

In conjunction with genetic changes, species may also be subjected to sudden environmental shifts that quickly drive the gene pool in a particular direction via natural selection. For example, the climate may change or a new predator may infiltrate the geographic range of the species. Natural selection may lead to a rapid evolution of the gene pool by favoring those alleles that allow members of the population to survive the climatic change or to have phenotypic characteristics that allow them to avoid the predator.

Which viewpoint is correct, punctuated equilibrium or gradualism? Both have merit. The occurrence of punctuated equilibrium is often supported by the fossil record. New species seem to arise rather suddenly in a layer of rocks, persist relatively unchanged for a very long period of time, and then become extinct. In such cases, scientists hypothesize that the period during which a previous species evolved into a new species was so short that few, if any, of the transitional forms of the species were preserved as fossils. Even so, these rapid periods of change were probably followed by long periods that likely involved the additional accumulation of many small genetic changes, consistent with gradualism.

Finally, another issue associated with the speed of speciation is generation time. Species of large animals with long generation times tend to evolve much more slowly than do microbial species with short generations. Many new species of bacteria will come into existence during our lifetime, whereas new species of large animals tend to arise on a much longer timescale. This is an important consideration because bacteria have great environmental effects. They are decomposers of organic materials and pollutants in the environment, and they play a role in many diseases of plants and animals, including humans.

25.4 Evo-Devo: Evolutionary Developmental Biology

Learning Outcomes:

1. Describe how the spatial expression of genes, such as *BMP4* and *Gremlin*, affects pattern formation.
2. Explain the relationship between the number of *Hox* genes and the body plan of an animal species.
3. Outline how differences in the growth rates of body parts can change the characteristics of species.
4. Describe how the study of the *Pax6* gene suggests that the eyes of different animal species evolved from a common ancestor.

As we have learned, the origin of new species involves genetic changes that lead to adaptations to environmental niches and/or to reproductive isolating mechanisms that prevent closely related species from interbreeding. These genetic changes result in morphological and physiological differences that distinguish one species from another. In recent years, many evolutionary biologists have begun to investigate how genetic variation produces species and groups of species with novel shapes and forms. The underlying reasons for such changes are often rooted in the developmental pathways that control an organism's morphology.

Evolutionary developmental biology (referred to as **evo-devo**) is an exciting and relatively new field of biology that compares the development of different organisms in an attempt to understand ancestral relationships between organisms and the mechanisms that bring about evolutionary change. During the past few decades, developmental geneticists have gained a better understanding of biological development at the molecular level. Much of this work has involved the discovery of genes that control development in model organisms. As the genomes of more organisms have been analyzed, researchers have become interested in the similarities and differences that occur between closely related and distantly related species. The field of evolutionary developmental biology has arisen in response to this trend.

How do new morphological forms come into being? For example, how does a nonwebbed foot evolve into a webbed foot? How does a new organ, such as an eye, come into existence? As we will learn, such novelty arises through genetic changes, also called genetic innovations. Certain types of genetic innovations have been so advantageous they have resulted in groups of new species. For example, the innovation of wings resulted in the evolution of many different species of birds. In this section, we will see that proteins that control developmental changes, such as cell-signaling proteins and transcription factors, often play a key role in promoting the morphological changes that occur during evolution.

The Spatial Expression of Genes That Affect Development Has a Dramatic Effect on Phenotype

In Chapter 19, we considered the role of genetics in the development of plants and animals. As we learned, genes that play a role in development influence cell division, cell migration, cell differentiation, and cell death. The interplay among these four processes produces an organism with a specific body pattern, a process called **pattern formation**. As you might imagine, developmental genes are very important to the phenotypes of individuals. They affect traits such as the shape of a bird's beak, the length of a giraffe's neck, and the size of a plant's flower. In recent years, the study of development has indicated that developmental genes are key players in the evolution of many types of traits. Changes in such genes affect traits that can be acted on by natural selection. Furthermore, variation in the expression of these genes may be commonly involved in the acquisition of new traits that promote speciation.

As an example, let's compare the formation of a chicken's foot with that of a duck. Developmental biologists have discovered that the morphological differences between a nonwebbed and a webbed foot are due to the differential expression of two different cell-signaling proteins called bone morphogenetic protein 4 (BMP4) and gremlin. The *BMP4* gene is expressed throughout the developing limb of both the chicken and duck; this is shown in **Figure 25.14a**, in which the BMP4 protein is stained purple. The BMP4 protein causes cells to undergo apoptosis and die. The gremlin protein, which is stained brown in **Figure 25.14b**, inhibits the function of BMP4, thereby allowing cells to survive. In the developing chicken limb, the *Gremlin* gene is expressed throughout the limb, except in the regions between each digit. Therefore, in these regions, the cells die, and a chicken develops a nonwebbed foot (**Figure 25.14c**). By comparison, in the duck, *Gremlin* is expressed throughout the entire limb, including the interdigit regions, and the duck develops a webbed foot. Interestingly, researchers have been able to introduce gremlin protein into

Chicken   Duck

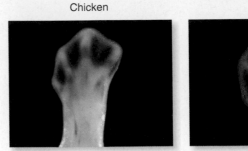
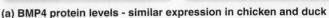

(a) BMP4 protein levels - similar expression in chicken and duck

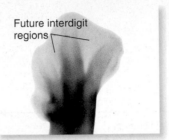

Future interdigit regions

(b) Gremlin protein levels - not expressed in interdigit region in chicken

(c) Comparison of a chicken foot and a duck foot

Figure 25.14 **The role of cell-signaling proteins in the morphology of birds' feet.** This figure shows how changes in developmental gene expression can affect webbing between the toes. **(a)** Expression of the *BMP4* gene in the developing limbs. BMP4 protein is stained purple here and is expressed throughout the limb. **(b)** Expression of the *Gremlin* gene in the developing limbs. Gremlin protein is stained brown here. Note that *Gremlin* is not expressed in the interdigit regions of the chicken but is expressed in these regions of the duck. Gremlin inhibits BMP4, which causes programmed cell death. **(c)** Because BMP4 is not inhibited in the interdigit regions in the chicken, the cells in this region die, and the foot is not webbed. By comparison, inhibition of BMP4 in the interdigit regions in the duck results in a webbed foot.

Concept Check: *What would you expect to happen to the morphology of the feet of ducks if the Gremlin gene was under expressed?*

the interdigit regions of developing chicken limbs. This produces a chicken with webbed feet!

How are these observations related to evolution? During the evolution of birds, genetic variation arose such that some individuals expressed the *Gremlin* gene in the regions between each digit, but others did not. This variation determined whether or not a bird's feet were webbed. In terrestrial settings, having nonwebbed feet is an advantage because it enables the individual to hold onto perches, run along the ground, and snatch prey. Therefore, natural selection would favor nonwebbed feet in terrestrial environments. This process explains the occurrence of nonwebbed feet in chickens, hawks, crows, and many other terrestrial birds. In aquatic environments, however, webbed feet are an advantage because they act as paddles for swimming, so genetic variation that produced webbed feet in aquatic birds would have been acted on by natural selection. Over time, this gave rise to the webbed feet now found in a wide variety of aquatic birds, including ducks, geese, and penguins.

The *Hox* Genes Have Been Important in the Evolution of a Variety of Body Plans

The study of developmental genes has revealed interesting trends among large groups of species. *Hox* genes, which are discussed in Chapter 19, are found in nearly all animals, indicating they have originated very early in animal evolution. *Hox* genes are homeotic genes, which specify the fate of a particular segment or region of the body.

Developmental biologists have hypothesized that variation in the *Hox* genes has spawned the formation of many new body plans. As shown in **Figure 25.15**, the number and arrangement of *Hox* genes varies considerably among different types of animals. Sponges, the simplest of animals, have at least one gene that is homologous to *Hox* genes. Insects typically have nine or more *Hox* genes. In most cases, multiple *Hox* genes occur in a cluster in which the genes are close to each other along a chromosome. In mammals, *Hox* gene clusters have been duplicated twice during the course of evolution to form four clusters, all slightly different, containing a total of 38 genes.

Researchers propose that increases in the number of *Hox* genes have been instrumental in the evolution of many animal species with greater complexity in body structure. To understand how, let's first consider *Hox* gene function. All *Hox* genes encode transcription factors that act as master control proteins for directing the formation of particular regions of the body. Each *Hox* gene controls a hierarchy of many regulatory genes that regulate the expression of genes encoding

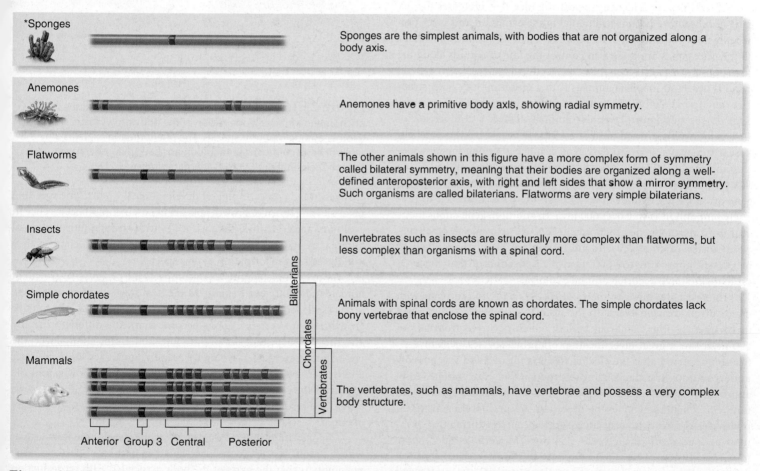

Figure 25.15 *Hox* **gene number and body complexity in different types of animals.** Researchers speculate that the duplication of *Hox* genes and *Hox* gene clusters played a key role in the evolution of more complex body plans in animals. A correlation is observed between increasing numbers of *Hox* genes and increasing complexity of body structure. The *Hox* genes are divided into four groups, called anterior, group 3, central, and posterior, based on their relative similarities. Each group is represented by a different color in this figure. *Note: Sponges, which are the simplest animals with no true tissues, do not have true *Hox* genes, though they have an evolutionarily related gene called an *NK-like* gene. Some species of sponges have more than one copy of this gene.

Concept Check: *What is the relationship between the total number of Hox genes in an animal species and its morphological complexity?*

BioConnections: *Look back at Figures 19.16 and 19.17. How is the expression of Hox genes related to segmentation and the anteroposterior axis?*

proteins that ultimately affect the morphology of the organism. The evolution of complex body plans is associated with an increase not only in the number of regulatory genes—as evidenced by the increase in *Hox* gene complexity during evolution—but also in genes that encode proteins that directly affect an organism's form and function.

How would an increase in *Hox* genes enable more complex body forms to evolve? Part of the answer lies in the spatial expression of the *Hox* genes. Different *Hox* genes are expressed in different regions of the body along the anteroposterior axis (refer back to Figure 19.16). Therefore, an increase in the number of *Hox* genes allows each of these master control genes to become more specialized in the region that it controls. In fruit flies, one segment in the middle of the body can be controlled by a particular *Hox* gene and form wings and legs, whereas a segment in the head region can be controlled by a different *Hox* gene and develops antennae. Therefore, research suggests that one way for new, more complex body forms to evolve is by increasing the number of *Hox* genes, thereby making it possible to form many specialized parts of the body that are organized along a body axis.

Three lines of evidence support the idea that increases in *Hox* gene number have been instrumental in the evolution and speciation of animals with different body patterns. First, as discussed in Chapter 19, *Hox* genes are known to control the fate of regions along the anteroposterior axis. Second, as described in Figure 25.15, a general trend is observed in which animals with a more complex body structure tend to have more *Hox* genes and *Hox* clusters in their genomes than do the genomes of simpler animals. Third, a comparison of *Hox* gene evolution and animal evolution bears striking parallels. Researchers have analyzed *Hox* gene sequences among modern species and made estimates regarding the timing of past events. Using this type of approach, geneticists have estimated when the first *Hox* gene arose by gene innovation. Though the date is difficult to precisely pinpoint, it is well over 600 mya. In addition, gene duplications of this primordial gene produced clusters of *Hox* genes in other species. Clusters such as those found in modern insects were likely to be present approximately 600 mya. A duplication of that cluster is estimated to have occurred around 520 mya.

Interestingly, these estimates of *Hox* gene origins correlate with major diversification events in the history of animals. As described in Chapter 22, the Cambrian period, which occurred from 543 to 490 mya, saw a great diversification of animal species. This diversification occurred after the *Hox* cluster was formed and was possibly undergoing its first duplication to produce two *Hox* clusters. Also, approximately 420 mya, a second duplication produced species with four *Hox* clusters. This event preceded the proliferation of tetrapods—vertebrates with four limbs—that occurred during the Devonian period, approximately 417–354 mya. Modern tetrapods have four *Hox* clusters. This second duplication may have been a critical event that led to the evolution of complex terrestrial vertebrates with four limbs, such as amphibians, reptiles, and mammals.

Variation in Growth Rates Can Have a Dramatic Effect on Phenotype

Another way that genetic variation can influence morphology is by controlling the relative growth rates of different parts of the body during development. The term **heterochrony** refers to evolutionary

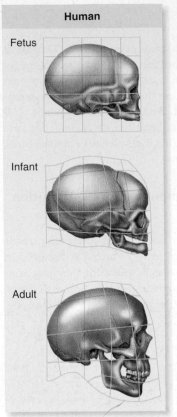
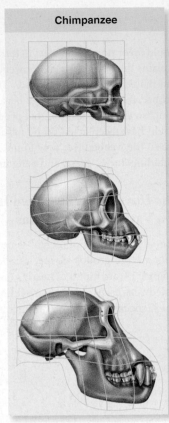

Figure 25.16 **Heterochrony.** Heterochrony refers to the phenomenon in which one region of the body grows faster than another among different species. The phenomenon explains why the skulls of adult chimpanzees and humans have different shapes even though their fetal skull shapes are quite similar.

changes in the rate or timing of developmental events. The speeding up or slowing down of growth appears to be a common occurrence in evolution and leads to different species with striking morphological differences. With regard to the pace of evolution, such changes may rapidly lead to the formation of new species.

As an example, **Figure 25.16** compares the progressive growth of human and chimpanzee skulls. At the fetal stage, the size and shape of the skulls look fairly similar. However, after this stage, the relative growth rates of certain regions become markedly different, thereby affecting the shape and size of the adult skull. In the chimpanzee, the jaw region grows faster, giving the adult chimpanzee a much larger and longer jaw. In the human, the jaw grows more slowly, and the region of the skull that surrounds the brain—the cranium—grows faster. The result is that adult humans have smaller jaws but a larger cranium.

Changes in growth rates also affect the developmental stage at which certain species reproduce. This can occur in two ways. One possibility is that the parts of the body associated with reproduction develop faster than the rest of the body. Alternatively, reproduction may occur at the same absolute age, but the development of nonreproductive body parts is slowed down. In either case, the morphological result is the same—reproduction is observed at an earlier stage in one species than it is in another. In such cases, the sexually mature organism may retain traits typical of the juvenile stage of the organism's ancestor, a condition called **paedomorphosis** (from the Greek *paedo*, meaning young or juvenile, and *morph*, meaning the form of an

Figure 25.17 Paedomorphosis. Paedomorphosis occurs when an adult species retains characteristics that are juvenile traits in another related species. Cope's giant salamander reproduces at the tadpole stage.

organism). It is particularly common among salamanders. Typically when salamanders mature, they lose their gills and tail fins, features associated with aquatic life. Paedomorphic species retain certain juvenile features as adults, but have the ability to reproduce successfully. For example, Cope's giant salamander (*Dicamptodon copei*) becomes mature and reproduces in the aquatic form, without changing into a terrestrial adult as do other salamander species (**Figure 25.17**). The adult form of Cope's giant salamander has gills and a large paddle-shaped tail, features that resemble those of the larval (tadpole) stage of other salamander species. Such a change in morphology was likely a contributing factor to the formation of this species or an ancestral species to Cope's giant salamander.

GENOMES & PROTEOMES CONNECTION

The Study of the *Pax6* Gene Indicates That Different Types of Eyes Evolved from a Simpler Form

Thus far in this section, we have focused on the roles of particular genes as they influence the development of species with novel shapes and forms. Explaining how a complex organ comes into existence is another major challenge for evolutionary biologists. Although it is relatively easy to comprehend how a limb could undergo evolutionary modifications to become a wing, flipper, or arm, it is more difficult to understand how a body structure, such as a limb, comes into being in the first place. In his book *The Origin of Species*, Charles Darwin addressed this question and admitted that the evolution and development of a complex organ such as the eye was difficult to understand. As noted by Darwin, the eyes of vertebrate species are exceedingly complex, being able to adjust focus, let in different amounts of light, and detect a spectrum of colors. Darwin speculated that such complex eyes must have evolved from a simpler structure through the process of descent with modification. With amazing insight, he suggested that a very simple eye would be composed of two cell types, a photoreceptor cell and an adjacent pigment cell. The photoreceptor cell, which is a type of nerve cell, is able to absorb light and respond to it. The function of the pigment cell is to stop the light from reaching one side of the photoreceptor cell. This primitive, two-cell arrangement would

allow an organism to sense both light and the direction from which the light comes.

A primitive eye would provide an additional way for an organism to sense its environment, possibly allowing it to avoid predators or locate food. Vision is nearly universal among animals, which indicates a strong selective advantage for eyesight. Over time, eyes could become more complex by enhancing the ability to absorb different amounts and wavelengths of light and also by refinements in structures such as the addition of lenses that focus the incoming light.

Since the time of Darwin, many evolutionary biologists have wrestled with the question of eye evolution. From an anatomical point of view, researchers have discovered many different types of eyes. For example, the eyes of fruit flies, squid, and humans are quite different from each other. This observation led evolutionary biologists such as Austrian zoologist Luitfried von Salvini-Plawen and German evolutionary biologist Ernst Mayr to propose that eyes may have independently arisen multiple times during evolution. Based solely on morphology, such a hypothesis seemed reasonable and for many years was accepted by the scientific community.

The situation took a dramatic turn when geneticists began to study eye development. Researchers identified a master control gene, *Pax6*[1]. The protein encoded by the *Pax6* gene is a transcription factor that controls the expression of many other genes, including those involved in the development of the eye in both rodents and humans. In mice and rats, a mutation in the *Pax6* gene results in small eyes. A mutation in the human *Pax6* gene causes an eye disorder called aniridia, in which the iris and other structures of the eye do not develop properly. Similarly, *Drosophila* has a gene named *eyeless* that also causes a defect in eye development when mutant. *Eyeless* and *Pax6* are homologous genes; they are derived from the same ancestral gene.

In 1995, Swiss geneticist Walter Gehring and his colleagues were able to show experimentally that the expression of the *eyeless* gene in parts of *Drosophila* where it is normally inactive could promote the formation of additional eyes. For example, using genetic engineering techniques, they were able to express the *eyeless* gene in the region where antennae should form. As seen in **Figure 25.18a**, this resulted in the formation of an eye where antennae are normally found! Remarkably, the expression of the mouse *Pax6* gene in *Drosophila* can also cause the formation of eyes in unusual places. For example, **Figure 25.18b** shows the formation of an eye on the leg of *Drosophila*.

Note that when the mouse *Pax6* master control gene switches on eye formation in *Drosophila*, the eye produced is a *Drosophila* eye, not a mouse eye. Why does this occur? It happens because the *Pax6* master control gene activates genes from the *Drosophila* genome. In *Drosophila*, the *Pax6* homolog called *eyeless* switches on a cascade involving several hundred genes required for eye morphogenesis. In organisms with simpler eyes, the *Pax6* gene would be expected to control a cascade of fewer genes.

Since the discovery of the *Pax6* and *eyeless* genes, homologs of this gene have been discovered in many different species. In all cases where it has been tested, this gene is involved with eye development. Gehring and colleagues have hypothesized that the eyes of many different species have evolved from a common ancestral form consisting

---

[1]Pax is an abbreviation for <u>pa</u>ired bo<u>x</u>. The protein encoded by this gene contains a domain called a paired box.

(a) **Abnormal expression of the *Drosophila eyeless* gene in the antenna region**

Normal eye

Eye where an antenna is normally found

(b) **Abnormal expression of the mouse *Pax6* gene in a fruit fly leg**

Eye on the side of a leg

Figure 25.18 Formation of additional eyes in *Drosophila* due to the abnormal expression of a master control gene for eye morphogenesis. (a) When the *Drosophila eyeless* gene is expressed in the antenna region, eyes are formed where antennae should be located. (b) When the mouse *Pax6* gene is expressed in the leg region of *Drosophila*, a small eye is formed there.

Concept Check: *What do you think would happen if the Drosophila eyeless gene was expressed at the tip of a mouse's tail?*

of, as proposed by Darwin, one photoreceptor cell and one pigment cell (**Figure 25.19**). As mentioned, such a very simple eye can accomplish a rudimentary form of vision by detecting light and its direction. Eyes such as these are still found in modern species, such as the larvae of certain types of mollusks. Over time, simple eyes evolved into more complex types of eyes by modifications that resulted in the addition of more types of cells, such as lens cells and nerve cells. Alternatively, other researchers propose that *Pax6* may control only certain features of eye development and that different types of eyes may have evolved independently. Future research will be needed to resolve this controversy.

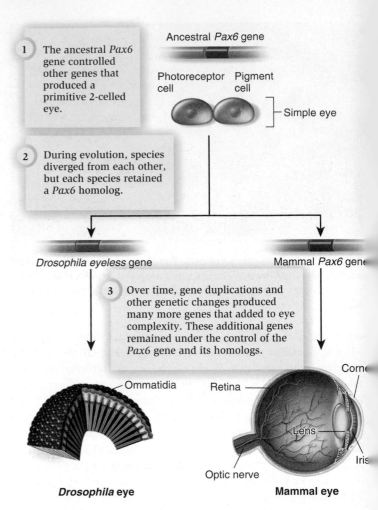

1 The ancestral *Pax6* gene controlled other genes that produced a primitive 2-celled eye.

Ancestral *Pax6* gene

Photoreceptor cell   Pigment cell

Simple eye

2 During evolution, species diverged from each other, but each species retained a *Pax6* homolog.

Drosophila eyeless gene   Mammal *Pax6* gene

3 Over time, gene duplications and other genetic changes produced many more genes that added to eye complexity. These additional genes remained under the control of the *Pax6* gene and its homologs.

Ommatidia   Retina   Cornea

Lens

Iris

Optic nerve

***Drosophila* eye**   **Mammal eye**

Figure 25.19 Genetic control of eye evolution. In this diagram, genetic changes, under the control of the ancestral *Pax6* gene, led to the evolution of different types of eyes.

Summary of Key Concepts

25.1 Identification of Species

- A species is a group of related organisms that shares a distinctive set of attributes in nature. Speciation is the process by which new species are formed. Macroevolution refers to evolutionary changes that produce new species and groups of species.

- Different characteristics, including morphological traits, reproductive isolation, molecular features, ecological factors, and evolutionary relationships, are used to identify species (Figure 25.1).

- Reproductive isolating mechanisms prevent two different species from breeding with each other (Figure 25.2).

- Prezygotic isolating mechanisms include habitat isolation, temporal isolation, behavioral isolation, mechanical isolation, and gametic isolation (Figures 25.3, 25.4).

- Postzygotic isolating mechanisms include hybrid inviability, hybrid sterility, and hybrid breakdown (Figure 25.5).

25.2 Mechanisms of Speciation

- Allopatric speciation occurs when a population becomes isolated from other populations and evolves into one or more new species. When speciation from a single ancestral species occurs multiple

times, the process is called adaptive radiation. If two populations are incompletely separated, interbreeding may occur in hybrid zones (Figures 25.6, 25.7, 27.8).

- Podos hypothesized that changes in beak depth, associated with adaptation to feeding, promoted reproductive isolation by altering the song pattern of finches (Figures 25.9, 25.10).

- Sympatric speciation involves the formation of different species in populations that are not geographically isolated from one another. Polyploidy, adaptation to local environments, and sexual selection are mechanisms that promote sympatric speciation (Figures 25.11, 25.12).

25.3 The Pace of Speciation

- The pace of evolution may seem relatively constant or it may vary. Gradualism involves steady evolution due to many small genetic changes, whereas punctuated equilibrium is a pattern of evolution in which new species arise more rapidly and then remain unchanged for long periods of time (Figure 25.13).

25.4 Evo-Devo: Evolutionary Developmental Biology

- Evolutionary developmental biology compares the development of different species in order to understand ancestral relationships and the mechanisms that bring about evolutionary change. These changes often involve variation in the expression of cell-signaling proteins and transcription factors.

- The spatial expression of genes that affect development can affect phenotypes dramatically, as shown by the expression of the *BMP4* and *Gremlin* genes in birds with nonwebbed or webbed feet (Figure 25.14).

- An increase in the number of *Hox* genes played an important role in the evolution of more complex body forms in animals (Figure 25.15).

- A difference in the relative growth rates of body parts among different species is called heterochrony. Paedomorphosis occurs when an adult organism retains characteristics that are typical of the juvenile stage in another related species (Figures 25.16, 25.17).

- The *Pax6* gene and its homolog in other species are master control genes that control eye development in animals (Figures 25.18, 25.19).

Assess and Discuss

Test Yourself

1. Macroevolution refers to evolutionary changes that
   a. occur in multicellular organisms.
   b. produce new species and groups of species.
   c. occur over long periods of time.
   d. cause changes in allele frequencies.
   e. occur in large mammals.

2. The biological species concept classifies a species based on
   a. morphological characteristics.
   b. reproductive isolation.
   c. the niche the organism occupies in the environment.
   d. genetic relationships between an organism and its ancestors.
   e. both a and b.

3. Which of the following is considered an example of a postzygotic isolating mechanism?
   a. incompatible genitalia
   b. different mating seasons
   c. incompatible gametes
   d. mountain range separating two populations
   e. fertilized egg fails to develop normally

4. Hybrid breakdown occurs when species hybrids
   a. do not develop past the early embryonic stages.
   b. have a reduced life span.
   c. are infertile.
   d. are fertile but produce offspring with reduced viability and fertility.
   e. produce offspring that express the traits of only one of the original species.

5. The evolution of one species into two or more species is called
   a. gradualism.
   b. punctuated equilibrium.
   c. cladogenesis.
   d. horizontal gene transfer.
   e. microevolution.

6. A large number of honeycreeper species on the Hawaiian Islands is an example of
   a. adaptive radiation.
   b. genetic drift.
   c. stabilizing selection.
   d. horizontal gene transfer.
   e. microevolution.

7. A major mechanism of speciation in plants but not in animals is
   a. adaptation to new environments.
   b. polyploidy.
   c. hybrid breakdown.

   d. genetic changes that alter the organism's niche.
   e. both a and d.

8. The concept of punctuated equilibrium suggests that
   a. the rate of evolution is constant, with short time periods of no evolutionary change.
   b. evolution occurs gradually over time.
   c. small genetic changes accumulate over time to allow for phenotypic change and speciation.
   d. long periods of little evolutionary change are interrupted by short periods of major evolutionary change.
   e. both b and c.

9. Researchers suggest that an increase in the number of *Hox* genes
   a. leads to reproductive isolation in all cases.
   b. could explain the evolution of color vision.
   c. allows for the evolution of more complex body forms in animals.
   d. results in the decrease in the number of body segments in insects.
   e. does all of the above.

10. The observation that the mammalian *Pax6* gene and the *Drosophila eyeless* gene are homologous genes that promote the formation of different types of eyes suggests that
    a. *Drosophila* eyes are more complex.
    b. mammalian eyes are more complex.
    c. eyes arose once during evolution.
    d. eyes arose at least twice during evolution.
    e. eye development is a simple process.

Conceptual Questions

1. What is the key difference between prezygotic and postzygotic isolating mechanisms? Give an example of each type. Which type is more costly from the perspective of energy?

2. What are the key differences between gradualism and punctuated equilibrium? How are genetic changes related to these two models?

3. A principle of biology is that *populations of organisms evolve from one generation to the next.* Describe one example in which genes that control development played an important role in the evolution of different species.

Collaborative Questions

1. What is a species? Discuss how geographic isolation can lead to speciation, and explain how reproductive isolation plays a role.

2. Discuss the type of speciation (allopatric or sympatric) that is most likely to occur under each of the following conditions:
   a. A pregnant female rat is transported by an ocean liner to a new continent.
   b. A meadow containing several species of grasses is exposed to a pesticide that promotes nondisjunction.
   c. In a very large lake containing several species of fishes, the water level gradually falls over the course of several years. Eventually, the large lake becomes subdivided into smaller lakes, some of which are connected by narrow streams.

Online Resource

www.brookerbiology.com

Stay a step ahead in your studies with animations that bring concepts to life and practice tests to assess your understanding. Your instructor may also recommend the interactive eBook, individualized learning tools, and more.

Appendix A

Periodic Table of the Elements

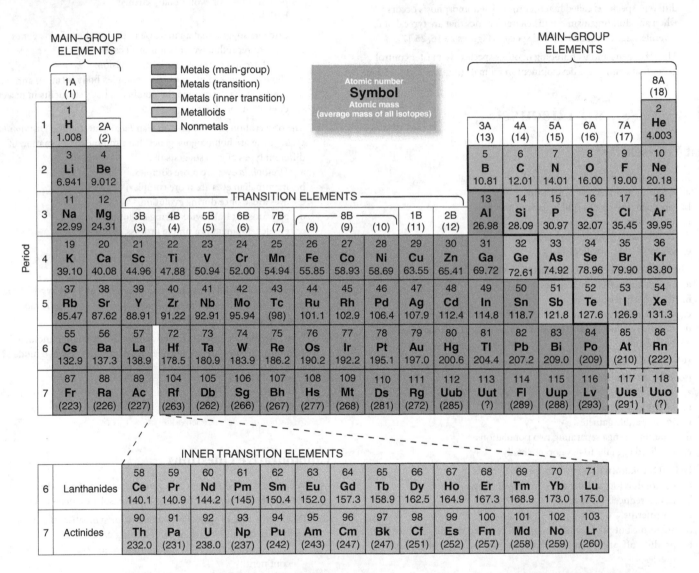

The complete Periodic Table of the Elements. Group numbers are different in some cases from those presented in Figure 2.5, because of the inclusion of transition elements. In some cases, the average atomic mass has been rounded to one or two decimal places, and in others only an estimate is given in parentheses due to the short-lived nature or rarity of those elements. The symbols and names of some of the elements between 112–118 are temporary until the chemical characteristics of these elements become better defined. Element 117 is currently not confirmed as a true element, and little is known about element 118. The International Union of Pure and Applied Chemistry (IUPAC) has recently proposed adopting the name copernicium (Cp) for element 112 in honor of scientist and astronomer Nicolaus Copernicus.

Appendix B

Answer Key

Answers to Collaborative Questions can be found on the website.

Chapter 1

Concept Checks

Figure 1.5 It would be at the population level.

Figure 1.6 In monkeys, the tail has been modified to grasp onto things, such as tree branches. In skunks, the tail is modified with a bright stripe; the tail can stick up and act as a warning signal to potential predators. In cattle, the tail has long hairs and is used to swat insects. Many more examples are possible.

Figure 1.7 Natural selection is a process that causes evolution to happen.

Figure 1.9 A tree of life suggests that all living organisms evolved from a single ancestor by vertical evolution with mutation. A web of life assumes that both vertical evolution with mutation and horizontal gene transfer were important mechanisms in the evolution of new species.

Figure 1.11 Taxonomy helps us appreciate the unity and diversity of life. Organisms that are closely related evolutionarily are placed in smaller groups.

Figure 1.12 The genome stores the information to make an organism's proteins. In and of itself, the genome is merely DNA. The traits of cells and organisms are largely determined by the structures and functions of the hundreds or thousands of different proteins they make.

Figure 1.13 Male and female clownfish have the same genomes. Hormones affect the expression of their genes, thereby altering their proteomes. Differences in proteomes determine the morphological differences between males and females.

Figure 1.15 A researcher can compare the results in the experimental group and control group to determine if a single variable is causing a particular outcome in the experimental group.

Figure 1.16 After the *CF* gene was identified by discovery-based science, researchers realized that the *CF* gene was similar to other genes that encoded proteins that were already known to be transport proteins. This provided an important clue that the *CF* gene also encodes a transport protein.

BioConnections

Figure 1.4 This figure is emphasizing that living organisms grow and develop.

Figure 1.10 Fungi are more closely related to animals.

Feature Investigation Questions

1. In discovery-based science, a researcher does not need to have a preconceived hypothesis. Experimentation is conducted in the hope that it may have practical applications or may provide new information that will lead to a hypothesis. By comparison, hypothesis testing occurs when a researcher forms a hypothesis that makes certain predictions. Experiments are conducted to see if those predictions are correct. In this way, the hypothesis may be accepted or rejected.

2. This strategy may be described as a five-stage process:

   1. Observations are made regarding natural phenomena.
   2. These observations lead to a hypothesis that tries to explain the phenomena. A useful hypothesis is one that is testable because it makes specific predictions.
   3. Experimentation is conducted to determine if the predictions are correct.
   4. The data from the experiment are analyzed.
   5. The hypothesis is accepted or rejected.

3. In an ideal experiment, the control and experimental groups differ by only one factor. Biologists apply statistical analyses to their data to determine if the control and experimental groups are likely to be different from each other because

of the single variable that is different between the two groups. This provides an objective way to accept or reject a hypothesis.

Test Yourself

1. d 2. a 3. c 4. c 5. d 6. b 7. d 8. d 9. a 10. b

Conceptual Questions

1. Principles (a) through (f) apply to individuals whereas (g) and (h) apply to populations.

2. The unity among different species occurs because modern species have evolved from a group of related ancestors. Some of the traits in those ancestors are also found in modern species, which thereby unites them. The diversity is due to the variety of environments on the Earth. Each species has evolved to occupy its own unique environment. For every species, many traits are evolutionary adaptations to survival in a specific environment. For this reason, evolution also promotes diversity.

3. The principles are outlined in Figure 1.4. Students can rephrase these principles in their own words.

Chapter 2

Concept Checks

Figure 2.4 An energy shell is a region outside the nucleus of an atom occupied by electrons of a given energy level. More than one orbital can be found within an electron shell. An orbital may be spherical or dumbbell-shaped and contains up to two electrons.

Figure 2.9 The octet rule states that atoms are stable when they have eight electrons in their outermost shell. Oxygen has six electrons in its outer shell. When two oxygen atoms share two pairs of electrons, each atom has eight electrons in its outer shell, at least part of the time.

Figure 2.11 Strand separation requires energy, because the DNA strands are held together by a large number of hydrogen bonds. Although each hydrogen bond is weak, collectively the vast number of such bonds in a molecule of DNA adds up to a considerable strength.

Figure 2.17 The oil would be in the center of the soap micelles.

Figure 2.20 It is 10^{-6} M. Since $[H^+][OH^-]$ always equals 10^{-14} M, if $[H^+] = 10^{-8}$ M (that is, pH 8.0), then $[OH^-]$ must be 10^{-6} M.

BioConnections

Figure 2.20 At a pH of 5.0, the H^+ concentration would be 10^{-5}M, as can be seen from the figure but which can also be calculated by the equation $pH = -\log_{10}[H^+]$. (From this information, you can also determine that the OH^- concentration must be 10^{-9} M, because the product of the H^+ and OH^- concentrations must be equal to 10^{-14} M).

Feature Investigation Questions

1. Scientists were aware that atoms contained charged particles. Many believed that the positive charges and mass were evenly distributed throughout the atom.

2. Rutherford was testing the hypothesis that atoms are composed of positive charges evenly distributed throughout the atom. Based on this model of the structure of the atom, alpha particles, which are positively charged nuclei of helium atoms, should be deflected as they pass through the foil, due to the presence of positive charges spread throughout the gold foil.

3. Instead of detecting slight deflection of most alpha particles as they passed through the gold foil, the majority, 98%, of the alpha particles passed directly through the gold foil without deflection. A much smaller percentage either

deflected or bounced back from the gold foil. Rutherford suggested that since most of the alpha particles passed unimpeded through the gold foil, most of the volume of atoms is empty space. Rutherford also proposed that the bouncing back of some of the alpha particles indicated that most of the positively charged particles were concentrated in a compact area. These results ran counter to the hypothesized model.

Test Yourself

1. b   2. b   3. b   4. d   5. e   6. e   7. e   8. c   9. e   10. b

Conceptual Questions

1. Covalent bonds are bonds in which atoms share electrons. A hydrogen bond is a weak polar covalent bond that forms when a hydrogen atom from one polar molecule becomes electrically attracted to an electronegative atom. A nonpolar covalent bond is one between two atoms of similar electronegativities, such as two carbon atoms. The van der Waal forces are temporary, weak bonds, resulting from random electrical forces generated by the changing distributions of electrons in the outer shells of nearby atoms. The strong attraction between two oppositely charged atoms forms an ionic bond.

2. Within limits, bonds within molecules can rotate and thereby change the shape of a molecule. This is important because it is the shape of a molecule that determines, in part, the ability of that molecule to interact with other molecules. Also, when two molecules do interact through such forces as hydrogen bonds, the shape of one or both molecules may change as a consequence. The change in shape is often part of the mechanism by which signals are sent within and between cells.

3. A good example of emergent properties at the molecular level is that of the formation of sodium chloride (NaCl), a solid white crystalline compound that is very important for most living organisms. In their elemental states, sodium is a soft, highly reactive metal and chlorine is a toxic gas. When they combine through ionic bonds, the two elements produce a completely new and harmless substance found in all the world's oceans and soils. Another example described in this chapter is water, a liquid that is vital for all life but which is formed from two gases, hydrogen and oxygen, with very different properties.

Chapter 3
Concept Checks

Figure 3.1 Due to the fact that he had earlier purified urea from urine and then formed urea crystals, he already knew what urea crystals looked like. As seen in this figure, they are quite distinctive looking. Therefore, when he reacted ammonia and cyanic acid and got a compound that formed crystals, the distinctive look of the crystals made him realize that he had synthesized urea.

Figure 3.6 One reason is that the binding of a molecule to an enzyme depends on the spatial arrangements of the atoms in that molecule. Enantiomers have different spatial relationships that are mirror images of each other. Therefore, one may bind very tightly to an enzyme and the other may not be recognized at all.

Figure 3.7 Recall from Figure 3.5 that the reverse of a dehydration reaction is called a hydrolysis reaction, in which a molecule of water is added to the molecule being broken down, resulting in the formation of monomers.

Figure 3.11 Hydrogenation is the addition of hydrogens to double-bonded carbon atoms, changing them from unsaturated to saturated. This causes them to be solid at room temperature.

Figure 3.12 The phospholipids would be oriented such that their polar regions dissolved in the water layer and the nonpolar regions dissolved in the oil. Thus, the phospholipids would form a layer at the interface between the water and oil.

Figure 3.15 71; one less than the number of amino acids in the polypeptide.

Figure 3.19 If the primary structure of protein 1 were altered in some way, this would, in turn, most likely alter the secondary and tertiary structures of protein 1. Therefore, it is possible that the precise fit between proteins 1 and 2 would be lost and that the two proteins would lose the ability to interact.

Figure 3.24 Yes. The opposite strand must be the mirror image of the first strand, because pairs can form only between A and T, and G and C. For instance, if a portion of the first strand is AATGCA, the opposite strand along that region would be TTACGT.

BioConnections

Figure 3.8 Cellulose is believed to be the most abundant organic molecule on earth. In addition to being part of plant cells, it is also found in many other organisms, including many protists.

Figure 3.21 Many intracellular signaling molecules, such as those described in Chapter 9, are not proteins and therefore do not have domain structure. Some are very small molecules with a relatively simple structure; some are actually ions like Ca^{2+}.

Feature Investigation Questions

1. Many scientists assumed that protein folding was directed by some cellular factor, meaning some other molecule in the cytoplasm, and therefore, protein folding could not occur spontaneously. Others assumed that protein folding was determined somehow by the ribosome, because this organelle is primarily responsible for synthesizing proteins.

2. Anfinsen was testing the hypothesis that the information necessary for determining the three-dimensional shape of a protein is contained within the protein itself. In other words, the chemical characteristics of the amino acids that make up a protein determines the three-dimensional shape.

3. The urea disrupts hydrogen bonds and ionic interactions that are necessary for protein folding. The mercaptoethanol disrupted the $S-S$ bonds that also form between certain amino acids of the same polypeptide chains. Both substances essentially allow the polypeptide chain to unfold, disrupting the three-dimensional shape. Anfinsen removed the urea and mercaptoethanol from the protein solution by size-exclusion chromatography. After removing the urea and mercaptoethanol, Anfinsen discovered that the protein refolded into its proper three-dimensional shape and became functional again. This was important because the solution contained only the protein and lacked any other cellular material that could possibly assist in protein folding. This demonstrated that the protein could refold into the functional conformation.

Test Yourself

1. b   2. b   3. e   4. b   5. c   6. b   7. b   8. d   9. b   10. b

Conceptual Questions

1. Isomers are two structures with an identical molecular formula but with different structures and arrangements of atoms within the molecule. There are two major types of isomers: structural and stereoisomers. Because many chemical reactions in biology depend on the actions of enzymes, which are often highly specific for the spatial arrangement of atoms in a molecule, one isomer of a pair may have biological functions, and the other may not.

2. Saturated fatty acids are saturated with hydrogen and have only single (C—C) bonds, whereas unsaturated fatty acids have one or more double (C=C) bonds. The double bonds in unsaturated fatty acids alters their shape, resulting in a kink in the structure. Saturated fatty acids are unkinked and are better able to stack tightly together. Fats containing saturated fatty acids have a higher melting point than those containing mostly unsaturated fatty acids; consequently, saturated fats tend to be solids at room temperatures, and unsaturated fatty acids are usually liquids at room temperature.

3. The structures of macromolecules in all cases determines their function. For example, the structure of a protein determines its three-dimensional shape. This, in turn, allows a protein to interact specifically with certain other molecules. Certain intracellular signaling molecules, for example, have shapes that are determined by the structural arrangement of various protein domains; by themselves, these domains may have no function, but when combined in a precise way they create a functional protein. Likewise, the structure of different lipids determines such functional characteristics as male/female differences, cellular membrane formation, and energy storage. The different structures of polysaccharides determine their usefulness as energy stores, or as components of plant cell walls.

Chapter 4
Concept Checks

Figure 4.1 You would use transmission electron microscopy. The other methods do not have good enough resolution.

Figure 4.3 The primary advantage is that it gives an image of the 3-D surface of a material.

Figure 4.6 They have different proteomes.

Figure 4.7 Centrioles: Not found in plant cells; their role is not entirely clear, but they are found in the centrosome, which is where microtubules are anchored.

Chloroplasts: Not found in animal cells; function in photosynthesis.

Cell wall: Not found in animal cells; important in cell shape.

Figure 4.12 Both dynein and microtubules are anchored in place. Using ATP as a source of energy, dynein tugs on microtubules. Because the microtubules are anchored, they bend in response to the force exerted by dynein.

Figure 4.15 The nuclear lamina organizes the nuclear envelope and also helps to organize/anchor the chromosomes. The nuclear matrix is inside the nucleus and helps to organize the chromosomes into chromosome territories.

Figure 4.18 The protein begins its synthesis in the cytosol and then is further synthesized into the ER. It travels via vesicles to the *cis-*, *medial-*, and *trans*-Golgi and then is secreted.

Figure 4.22 Of these three choices, membrane transport is probably the most important because it regulates which molecules can enter the cell and participate in metabolism and which products of metabolism are exported from the cell. Cell signaling may affect metabolism, but its overall effect is probably less important than membrane transport.

Figure 4.24 It increases the surface area where ATP synthesis takes place, thereby making it possible to increase the amount of ATP synthesis.

Figure 4.27 Bacteria and mitochondria are similar in size; they both have circular chromosomes; they both divide by binary fission; and they both make ATP. Bacterial chromosomes are larger, and they make all of their own cellular proteins. Mitochondria chromosomes are smaller, and they import most of their proteins from the cytosol.

Figure 4.29 The signal sequence of an ER protein is recognized by SRP, which halts translation. The emerging protein and its ribosome are then transferred to the ER membrane, where translation resumes.

Figure 4.31 If chaperone proteins were not found in the cytosol, the mitochondrial matrix protein would start to fold, which might prevent it from being able to pass through the channel in the outer and inner mitochondrial membrane. Normally, a protein is threaded through this channel in an unfolded state.

BioConnections

Figure 4.6 Alternative splicing produces proteins with slightly different structures, because they have certain regions that have different amino acid sequences. The functions of such proteins are often similar, but specialized for the cell type in which they are expressed.

Figure 4.8 The surfaces of cells involved with gas exchange are highly convoluted. This provides a much greater surface area, thereby facilitating the movement of gasses across the membrane.

Figure 4.11 The type of movement shown in part (b) occurs during muscle contraction.

Figure 4.13 Cilia carry out a variety of functions, including motility, moving food particles into a feeding groove, and dispersing across moist surfaces.

Figure 4.16 During cell division, the chromosomes condense and form more compact structures.

Figure 4.26 These processes are very similar in that DNA replication occurs and then mitochondria or bacterial cells split in two. They are different in that bacteria have cell walls and septa must form between the two daughter cells, which does not occur when mitochondria divide.

Feature Investigation Questions

1. In a pulse-chase experiment, radioactive material is provided to cells. This is referred to as the pulse, or single administration of the radioactive material to the cells. After a few minutes, a large amount of nonradioactive material is provided to the cells to remove or "chase away" any of the remaining radioactive material.

    The researchers were attempting to determine the movement of proteins through the different compartments of a cell. Radioactive amino acids were used to label the proteins and enable the researchers to visualize where the proteins were at different times.

2. Pancreatic cells produce large numbers of proteins that are secreted from the cell. The number and final location of the proteins would allow the researchers an ideal system for studying protein movement through the cell.

3. Using electron microscopy, the researchers found that the proteins, indicated by radioactivity, were first found in the ER of the cells. Later the radioactivity moved to the Golgi and then into vesicles near the plasma membrane.

    The researchers concluded that secreted proteins move through several cellular compartments before they are secreted from the cell. Also, the movement of proteins through these compartments is not random but follows a particular pathway: ER, Golgi, secretory vesicles, plasma membrane, and, finally, secreted.

Test Yourself

1. d 2. d 3. b 4. c 5. e 6. a 7. e 8. e 9. a It would go there first, because targeting to the ER occurs cotranslationally. 10. c It is true they carry out metabolism, but so do eukaryotic cells.

Conceptual Questions

1. There are a lot of possibilities. The interactions between a motor protein (dynein) and cytoskeletal filaments (microtubules) cause a flagellum to bend. The interaction between V-snares and T-snares causes a vesicle to fuse with the correct target membrane.

2. If the motor is bound to a cargo and the motor can walk along a filament that is fixed in place, this will cause the movement of the cargo when the motor is activated. If the motor is fixed in place and the filament is free to move, this will cause the filament to move when the motor is activated. If both the motor and filament are fixed in place, the activation of the motor will cause the filament to bend.

3. ATP synthesis occurs along the inner mitochondrial membrane. The invaginations of this membrane greatly increase its surface area, thereby allowing for a greater amount of ATP synthesis.

Chapter 5
Concept Checks

Figure 5.3 Probably not. The hydrophobic tails of both leaflets touch each other, so the heavy metal would probably show a single, thick dark line. Osmium tetroxide shows two parallel lines because it labels the polar head groups, which are separated by the hydrophobic interior of the membrane.

Figure 5.4 More double bonds and shorter fatty acyl tails make the membrane more fluid. Changing the cholesterol concentration can also affect fluidity, but that depends on the starting level of cholesterol. If cholesterol was at a level that maximized stability, increasing the cholesterol concentration would probably increase fluidity.

Figure 5.5 The low temperature prevents lateral diffusion of membrane proteins. Therefore, after fusion, all of the mouse proteins would stay on one side of the fused cell, and all of the human proteins would remain on the other.

Figure 5.7 Lipids are transferred to the other leaflet of the ER via enzymes called flippases.

Figure 5.8 The most common way for a transmembrane segment to form is that it contains a stretch (about 20) of amino acids that mostly have hydrophobic (nonpolar) side chains.

Figure 5.12 Although both of these molecules penetrate the bilayer fairly quickly, methanol has a polar −OH group and therefore crosses a bilayer more slowly than methane.

Figure 5.15 Water will move from outside to inside, from the hypotonic medium into the hypertonic medium.

Figure 5.17 The purpose of gating is to regulate the function of channels.

Figure 5.22 The Na^+/K^+-ATPase could reach the point where the protein was covalently phosphorylated and Na^+ was released on the outside. At that stage, the reaction would stop, because it needs K^+ to proceed through the rest of the cycle.

Figure 5.23 The protein coat is needed for the membrane to bud from its site and form a vesicle.

BioConnections

Figure 5.6 Transmembrane proteins called cell adhesion molecules bind to each other to promote cell-to-cell adhesion. In addition, they can bind to molecules in the extracellular matrix, such as collagen fibers, thereby causing a cell to adhere to the extracellular matrix.

Figure 5.11 Leucine would cross an artificial membrane more easily because it is more hydrophobic than lysine.

Figure 5.13 Gradients of sodium and potassium ions are important for the conduction of action potentials.

Feature Investigation Questions

1. Most cells allow movement of water across the cell membrane by passive diffusion. However, it was noted that certain cell types had a much higher rate of water movement, indicating that something different was occurring in these cells.

2. The researchers identified water channels by characterizing proteins that are present in red blood cells and kidney cells but not other types of cells. Red blood cells and kidney cells have a faster rate of water movement across the membrane than other cell types. These cells are more likely to have water channels. By identifying proteins that are found in both of these types of cells but not in other cells, the researchers were identifying possible candidate proteins that function as water channels. In addition, CHIP28 had a structure that resembled other known channel proteins.

Agre and his associates experimentally created multiple copies of the gene that produces the CHIP28 protein and then artificially transcribed the genes to produce many mRNAs. The mRNAs were injected into frog oocytes where they could be translated to make the CHIP28 proteins. After altering the frog oocytes by introducing the CHIP28 mRNAs, they compared the rate of water transport in the altered oocytes versus normal frog oocytes. This procedure allowed them to introduce the candidate protein to a cell type that normally does not have the protein present.

3. After artificially introducing the candidate protein into the frog oocytes, the researchers found that the experimental oocytes took up water at a much faster rate in a hypotonic solution as compared to the control oocytes. The results indicated that the presence of the CHIP28 protein did increase water transport into cells.

Test Yourself

1. c   2. c   3. b   4. d   5. b   6. e   7. d   8. e   9. e   10. c

Conceptual Questions

1. See Figure 5.1 for the type of drawing you should have made. The membrane is considered a mosaic of lipid, protein, and carbohydrate molecules. The membrane exhibits properties that resemble a fluid because lipids and proteins can move relative to each other within the membrane.

2. Integral membrane proteins can contain transmembrane segments that cross the membrane, or they may contain lipid anchors. Peripheral membrane proteins are noncovalently bound to integral membrane proteins or to the polar heads of phospholipids.

3. Lipid bilayers, channels, and transporters cause the plasma membrane to be selectively permeable. This allows a cell to take up needed nutrients from its extracellular environment and to export waste products into the environment.

Chapter 6

Concept Checks

Figure 6.2 The solution of dissolved Na^+ and Cl^- has more entropy. A salt crystal is very ordered, whereas the ions in solution are much more disordered.

Figure 6.4 If a large amount of ADP was broken down, it would be more difficult for the cell to make ATP, which is made by the attachment of a phosphate group to ADP. The ATP cycle would be inhibited.

Figure 6.5 It speeds up the rate. When the activation energy is lower, it takes less time for reactants to reach a transition state where a chemical reaction can occur. It does not affect the direction of a reaction.

Figure 6.6 The activation energy is lowered during the second step when the substrates undergo induced fit.

Figure 6.7 At a substrate concentration of 0.5 mM, enzyme A would have a higher velocity. Enzyme A would be very near its V_{max}, whereas enzyme B would be well below its V_{max}.

Figure 6.12 The oxidized form is NAD^+.

Figure 6.15 Protein degradation eliminates proteins that are worn out, misfolded, or no longer needed by the cell. Such proteins could interfere with normal cell function. In addition, the recycling of amino acids saves the cell energy.

BioConnections

Figure 6.8 Thermophilic bacteria have enzymes that function at a very high temperature, perhaps with a temperature optimum of 50 to 70°C.

Figure 6.9 Without RNase P, the tRNAs could not be converted to their mature forms. The pre-tRNAs would be too large to fit into the ribosome. Therefore, translation would be inhibited.

Figure 6.13 Feedback inhibition prevents the excessive breakdown of carbohydrates and thereby prevents the excessive synthesis of ATP. Cells don't waste energy making ATP if they don't need it.

Feature Investigation Questions

1. RNase P has both a protein and RNA subunit. To determine which subunit has catalytic function, it was necessary to purify them individually and then see which one is able to cleave ptRNA.

2. The experimental strategy was to incubate RNase P or subunits of RNase P with ptRNA and then run a gel to determine if ptRNA had been cleaved to a mature tRNA and a 5′ fragment. The control without protein was to determine if the RNA alone could catalyze the cleavage. The control without RNA was to determine if some other factor in the experiment (for instance, Mg^{2+} or protein) was able to cleave the ptRNA.

3. The critical results occurred when the researchers incubated the purified RNA subunit at high Mg^{2+} concentrations with the ptRNA. Under these conditions, the ptRNA was cleaved. These results indicate that the RNA subunit has catalytic activity. A high Mg^{2+} concentration is needed to keep it catalytically active in the absence of a protein subunit.

Test Yourself

1. d   2. e   3. b   4. d   5. a   6. c   7. b   8. c   9. e   10. a

Conceptual Questions

1. Exergonic reactions are spontaneous. They proceed in a particular direction. An exergonic reaction could be slow or fast. By comparison, an endergonic reaction is not spontaneous. It will not proceed in a particular direction unless free energy is supplied. An endergonic reaction can be fast or slow.

2. During feedback inhibition, the product of a metabolic pathway binds to an allosteric site on an enzyme that acts earlier in the pathway. The product inhibits this enzyme, thereby preventing the overaccumulation of the product.

3. Recycling of amino acids and nucleotides is important because it conserves a great deal of energy. Cells don't have to remake these building blocks, which would require a large amount of energy. Eukaryotes primarily use the proteasome to recycle proteins.

Chapter 7

Concept Checks

Figure 7.2 The first phase is named the energy investment phase because some ATP is used up. The second phase is called the cleavage phase because a 6-carbon molecule is broken down into two 3-carbon molecules. The energy liberation phase is so named because NADH and ATP are made.

Figure 7.3 The molecules that donate phosphates are 1,3-bisphosphoglycerate and phosphoenolpyruvate.

Figure 7.6 For each acetyl group that is oxidized, the main products are 2 CO_2, 3 NADH, 1 $FADH_2$, and 1 GTP.

Figure 7.8 It is called cytochrome oxidase because it removes electrons from (oxidizes) cytochrome *c*. Another possible name would be oxygen reductase because it reduces oxygen.

Figure 7.10 No. The role of the electron transport chain is to make an H^+ electrochemical gradient. It is the H^+ electrochemical gradient that drives ATP synthase. If the H^+ electrochemical is made another way, such as by bacteriorhodopsin, the ATP synthase still makes ATP.

Figure 7.11 The γ subunit turns clockwise, when viewed from the intermembrane space. The β subunit in the back right is in conformation 3, and the one on the left is in conformation 1.

Figure 7.14 The advantage is that the cell can use the same enzymes to metabolize different kinds of organic molecules. This saves the cell energy because it is costly to make a lot of different enzymes, which are composed of proteins.

BioConnections

Figure 7.2 Glycolytic muscle fibers rely on glycolysis for their ATP needs. Because glycolysis does not require oxygen, such muscle fibers can function without oxygen.

Figure 7.4 FDG is radiolabeled so it can be specifically detected by a PET scan.

Feature Investigation Questions

1. The researchers attached an actin filament to the γ subunit of ATP synthase. The actin filament was fluorescently labeled so the researchers could determine if the actin filament moved when viewed under the fluorescence microscope.

2. When functioning in the hydrolysis of ATP, the actin filament was seen to rotate. The actin filament was attached to the γ subunit of ATP synthase. The rotational movement of the filament was the result of the rotational movement of the enzyme. In the control experiment, no ATP was added to stimulate enzyme activity. In the absence of ATP, no movement was observed.

3. No, the observation of counterclockwise rotation is the opposite of what would be expected inside the mitochondria. During the experiment, the enzyme was not functioning in ATP synthesis but instead was running backwards and hydrolyzing ATP.

Test Yourself

1. a 2. d 3. b 4. b 5. a 6. d 7. b 8. d 9. d 10. b

Conceptual Questions

1. The purpose of the electron transport chain is to pump H$^+$ across the inner mitochondrial membrane to establish a H$^+$ electrochemical gradient. When the H$^+$ flows back across the membrane through ATP synthase, ATP is synthesized.

2. The movement of H$^+$ through the *c* subunits causes the γ subunit to rotate. As it rotates, it sequentially alters the conformation of the subunits, where ATP is made. This causes (1) ADP and P$_i$ to bind with moderate affinity, (2) ADP and P$_i$ to bind very tightly such that ATP is made, and (3) ATP to be released.

3. As discussed in this chapter, the phases of glucose metabolism are regulated in a variety of ways. For example, key enzymes in glycolysis and the citric acid cycle are regulated by the availability of substrates and by feedback inhibition. The electron transport chain is regulated by the ATP/ADP ratio. Such regulation ensures that a cell does not waste energy making ATP when it is in sufficient supply. Also, the production of too much NADH is potentially harmful because at high levels it has the potential to haphazardly donate its electrons to other molecules and promote the formation of free radicals, highly reactive chemicals that damage DNA and cellular proteins.

Chapter 8
Concept Checks

Figure 8.1 Both heterotrophs and autotrophs carry out cellular respiration.

Figure 8.3 The Calvin cycle can occur in the dark as long as there is sufficient CO$_2$, ATP, and NADPH.

Figure 8.4 Gamma rays have higher energy than radio waves.

Figure 8.5 To drop down to a lower orbital at a lower energy level, an electron could release energy in the form of heat, release energy in the form of light, or transfer energy to another electron by resonance energy transfer.

Figure 8.7 By having different pigment molecules, plants can absorb a wider range of wavelengths of light.

Figure 8.8 ATP and NADPH are made in the stroma. O$_2$ is made in the thylakoid lumen.

Figure 8.9 Noncyclic electron flow produces equal amounts of ATP and NADPH. However, plants usually need more ATP than NADPH. Cyclic photophosphorylation allows plants to make just ATP, thereby increasing the relative amount of ATP.

Figure 8.10 Because these two proteins are homologous, this means that the genes that encode them were derived from the same ancestral gene. Therefore, the amino acid sequences of these two proteins are expected to be very similar, though not identical. Because the amino acid sequence of a protein determines its structure, two proteins with similar amino acid sequences would be expected to have similar structures.

Figure 8.13 No. The enhancement effect occurs because the flashes activate both photosystem II and photosystem I. Light at 700 nm is needed to activate P700 in photosystem I.

Figure 8.14 An electron has its highest amount of energy just after it has been boosted by light in PSI.

Figure 8.15 NADPH reduces organic molecules and makes them more able to form C−C and C−H bonds.

Figure 8.18 The arrangement of cells in C$_4$ plants makes the level of CO$_2$ high and the level of O$_2$ low in the bundle sheath cells.

Figure 8.19 When there is plenty of moisture and it is not too hot, C$_3$ plants are more efficient. However, under hot and dry conditions, C$_4$ and CAM plants have the advantage because they lose less water and avoid photorespiration.

BioConnections

Figure 8.2 Two guard cells make up one stoma.

Figure 8.18 Water is taken up by the roots of plants and moves via the vascular system to the leaves.

Feature Investigation Questions

1. The researchers were attempting to determine the biochemical pathway of the process of carbohydrate synthesis in plants. The researchers wanted to identify different molecules produced in plants over time to determine the steps of the biochemical pathway.

2. The purpose for using ^{14}C was to label the different carbon molecules produced during the biochemical pathway. The researchers could "follow" the carbon molecules from CO$_2$ that were incorporated into the organic molecules during photosynthesis. The radioactive isotope provided the researchers with a method of labeling the different molecules.

   The purpose of the experiment was to determine the steps in the biochemical pathway of photosynthesis. By examining samples from different times after the introduction of the labeled carbon source, the researchers would be able to determine which molecules were produced first and, thus, products of the earlier steps of the pathway versus products of later steps of the pathway.

   The researchers used two-dimensional paper chromatography to separate the different molecules from each other. Afterward, the different molecules were identified by different chemical methods. The text describes the method of comparing two-dimensional paper chromatography results of unknown molecules to known molecules and identifying the unknown with the known molecule it matched.

3. The researchers were able to determine the biochemical process that plants use to incorporate CO$_2$ into organic molecules. The researchers were able to identify the biochemical steps and the molecules produced at these steps in what is now called the Calvin cycle.

Test Yourself

1. c 2. c 3. c 4. a 5. b 6. b 7. c 8. b 9. e 10. c

Conceptual Questions

1. The two stages of photosynthesis are the light reactions and the Calvin cycle. The key products of the light reactions are ATP, NADPH, and O$_2$. The key product of the Calvin cycle is carbohydrate. The initial product is G3P, which is used to make sugars and other organic molecules.

2. NADPH is used during the reduction phase of the Calvin cycle. It donates its electrons to 1,3-BPG.

3. At the level of the biosphere, the role of photosynthesis is to incorporate carbon dioxide into organic molecules. These organic molecules can then be broken down, by autotrophs and by heterotrophs, to make ATP. The organic molecules made during photosynthesis are also used as starting materials to synthesize a wide variety of organic molecules and macromolecules that are made by cells.

Chapter 9
Concept Checks

Figure 9.1 It is glucose.

Figure 9.3 Endocrine signals are more likely to exist for a longer period of time. This is necessary because endocrine signals called hormones travel relatively long distances to reach their target cells. Therefore, the hormone must exist long enough to reach its target cells.

Figure 9.4 The effect of a signaling molecule is to cause a cellular response. Most signaling molecules do not enter the cell. Therefore, to exert an effect, they must alter the conformation of a receptor protein, which, in turn, stimulates an intracellular signal transduction pathway that leads to a cellular response.

Figure 9.6 Phosphorylation of a protein via a kinase involves ATP hydrolysis, which is an exergonic reaction. The energy from this reaction usually alters the conformation of the phosphorylated protein, thereby influencing its function. Phosphorylation is used to regulate protein function.

Figure 9.7 The α subunit has to hydrolyze its GTP to GDP. This changes the conformation of the α subunit so that it can reassociate with the β and γ subunits.

Figure 9.12 The signal transduction pathway begins with the G protein and ends with protein kinase A being activated. The cellular response involves the phosphorylation of target proteins. The phosphorylation of target proteins will change their function in some way, which is how the cell is responding.

Figure 9.13 Depending on the protein involved, phosphorylation can activate or inhibit protein function. Phosphorylation of phosphorylase kinase and glycogen phosphorylase activates their function, whereas it inhibits glycogen synthase.

Figure 9.14 Signal amplification allows a single signaling molecule to affect many proteins within a cell, thereby amplifying a cellular response.

Figure 9.20 The initiator caspase is part of the death-inducing signaling complex. It is directly activated when a cell receives a death signal. The initiator caspase then activates the executioner caspases, which degrade various cellular proteins and thereby cause the destruction of the cell.

BioConnections

Figure 9.2 Auxin causes cells to elongate. The cells on the nonilluminated side accumulate more auxin, which causes this side to grow faster and bend toward the light.

Figure 9.5 Most receptors and enzymes bind their ligands noncovalently and with high specificity. Enzymes, however, convert their ligands (which are reactants) into products, whereas receptors undergo a conformation change after a ligand binds.

Figure 9.10 The GTP-bound form of Ras is active and promotes cell division. To turn the pathway off, Ras hydrolyzes GTP to GDP. If this cannot occur due to a mutation, the pathway will be continuously on, and uncontrolled cell division will result.

Feature Investigation Questions

1. Compared with control rats, those injected with prednisolone alone would be expected to have a decrease in the number of cells because it suppresses ACTH synthesis. Therefore, apoptosis would be higher. By comparison, prednisolone + ACTH would have a normal number of cells because the addition of ACTH would compensate for effects of prednisolone. ACTH alone would be expected to have a greater number of cells; apoptosis would be inhibited.

2. Yes, when injected with ACTH, prednisolone probably inhibited the ability of the rats to make their own ACTH. Even so, they were given ACTH by injection, so they didn't need to make their own ACTH to prevent apoptosis.

3. The lowest level of apoptosis would occur in the ACTH alone group, because they could make their own ACTH plus they were given ACTH. With such high levels of ACTH, they probably had the lowest level of apoptosis; it was already known that ACTH promotes cell division.

Test Yourself

1. d   2. c   3. d   4. e   5. a   6. d   7. e   8. e   9. e   10. b

Conceptual Questions

1. Cells need to respond to a changing environment, and cells need to communicate with each other.

2. In the first stage, a signaling molecule binds to a receptor, causing receptor activation. In the second stage, one type of signal is transduced or converted to a different signal inside the cell. In the third stage, the cell responds in some way to the signal, possibly by altering the activity of enzymes, structural proteins, or transcription factors. When the estrogen receptor is activated, the second stage, signal transduction, is not needed because the estrogen receptor is an intracellular receptor that directly activates the transcription of genes to elicit a cellular response.

3. Cell signaling allows cells to respond to environmental changes. For example, if a yeast cell is exposed to glucose, cell signaling will allow it to adapt to that change and utilize glucose more readily. Likewise, cell signaling allows plants to grow toward light. In addition, cells in a multicellular organism respond to changes in signaling molecules, such as hormones, and thereby coordinate their activities.

Chapter 10

Concept Checks

Figure 10.1 The four functions of the ECM in animals are strength, structural support, organization, and cell signaling.

Figure 10.2 The extension sequences of procollagen prevent fibers from forming intracellularly.

Figure 10.3 The proteins would become more linear, and the fiber would come apart.

Figure 10.4 GAGs are highly negatively charged molecules that tend to attract positively charged ions and water. Their high water content gives GAGs a gel-like character, which makes them difficult to compress.

Figure 10.5 Because the secondary cell wall is usually rigid, it prevents cell growth. If it were made too soon, it might prevent a cell from attaining its proper size.

Figure 10.7 Adherens junctions and desmosomes are cell-to-cell junctions, whereas hemidesomosomes and focal adhesions are cell-to-ECM junctions.

Figure 10.9 Tight junctions in your skin prevent harmful things like toxins and viruses from entering your body. They also prevent materials like nutrients from leaking out of your body.

Figure 10.10 As opposed to the results shown in Figure 10.10, the dye would be on the side of the cell layer facing the intestinal tract. You would see dye up to the tight junction on this side of the cells, but not on the side of the tight junction facing the blood.

Figure 10.13 Middle lamellae are similar to anchoring junctions and desmosomes in that they all function in cell-to-cell adhesion. However, their structures are quite different. Middle lamellae are composed primarily of carbohydrates that involve linkages between negatively charged carbohydrates and divalent cations. By comparison, anchoring junctions and desmosomes hold cells together via proteins such as cadherins and integrins.

Figure 10.15 Connective tissue would have the most extensive ECM.

Figure 10.16 Dermal tissue would be found on the surfaces of leaves, stems, and roots.

Figure 10.19 Simple epithelium and epidermis are one cell layer thick, whereas stratified epithelium and periderm are several cell layers thick. All of these types of tissues form coverings on the surfaces of animals and plants and (in animals) on the surfaces that line internal organs.

Figure 10.21 Both ground tissue in plants and connective tissue in animals are important in supporting the organism. These tissues have a large amount of ECM that provides structural support.

BioConnections

Figure 10.9 If tight junctions did not exist, substances in the lumen of your intestine might directly enter your blood. This could be potentially harmful if you consumed something with a toxic molecule in it. Likewise, materials from blood could be lost by diffusing into the lumen of your small intestine.

Figure 10.14 Plasmodesmata facilitate the movement of nutrients in a cell-to-cell manner. This is called symplastic transport.

Feature Investigation Questions

1. The purpose of this study was to determine the sizes of molecules that can move through gap junctions from one cell to another.

2. The researchers used fluorescent dyes to visibly monitor the movement of material from one cell to an adjacent cell through the gap junctions. First, single layers of rat liver cells were cultured. Next, fluorescent dyes with molecules of various masses were injected into particular cells. The researchers then used fluorescence microscopy to determine whether or not the dyes were transferred from one cell to the next.

3. The researchers found that molecules of masses less than 1,000 daltons (Da) could pass through the gap junction channels. Molecules of masses larger than 1,000 Da could not pass through the gap junctions. Further experimentation revealed variation in gap junction channel size of different cell types. However, the upper limit of the gap junction channel size was determined to usually be around 1,000 Da.

Test Yourself

1. e   2. c   3. b   4. e   5. e   6. d   7. e   8. d   9. e   10. a

Conceptual Questions

1. The primary cell wall is synthesized first between the two newly made daughter cells. It is relatively thin and allows cells to expand and grow. The secondary cell wall is made in layers by the deposition of cellulose fibrils and other components. In many cell types, it is relatively thick.

2. Cadherins and integrins are both membrane proteins that function as cell adhesion molecules. They also can function in cell signaling. Cadherins bind one cell to another cell, whereas integrins bind a cell to the extracellular matrix. Cadherins require calcium ions to function, but integrins do not.

3. Cell junctions are important in the proper arrangement of cells in a multicellular organism. In animals, for example, cells junctions allow cells to recognize and bind to each other. This is very important during embryonic development. In addition, cell junctions adhere cells to the extracellular matrix. Likewise, in plants, the cell wall and middle lamella are important in forming connections between plant cells that gives plants their correct morphology and function.

Chapter 11

Concept Checks

Figure 11.4 ^{35}S was used to label phage proteins, whereas ^{32}P was used to label phage DNA.

Figure 11.6 Cytosine is found in both DNA and RNA.

Figure 11.7 The phosphate is attached to the number 5′ carbon in a single nucleotide. In a DNA strand, it is attached to both the 5′ carbon and 3′ carbon.

Figure 11.8 A phosphoester bond is a single covalent bond between a phosphorus atom and an oxygen atom. A phosphodiester linkage involves two phosphoester bonds. This linkage occurs along the backbone of DNA and RNA strands.

Figure 11.10 Because it is antiparallel and obeys the AT/GC rule, it would be 3′–CTAAGCAAG–5′.

Figure 11.13 It would be 1/8 half-heavy and 7/8 light.

Figure 11.17 The oxygen in a new phosphoester bond comes from the sugar.

Figure 11.19 The lagging strand is made discontinuously in the direction opposite to the movement of the replication fork.

Figure 11.20 When primase is synthesizing a primer in the lagging strand, it moves from left to right in this figure. After it is done making a primer, it needs to hop to the opening of the replication fork to make a new primer. This movement is from right to left in this figure.

Figure 11.22 Telomerase uses a short strand of RNA as template to make the DNA repeat sequence.

Figure 11.25 Proteins hold the bottoms of the loops in place.

Figure 11.26 Proteins that compact the radial loop domains are primarily responsible for the X shape.

BioConnections

Figure 11.1 When a bacterium dies, it may release some of its DNA into the environment. Such DNA can be taken up via transformation by living bacteria, even bacteria of other species. If the DNA that is taken up encodes an antibiotic resistance gene, such a gene may be incorporated into the genome of the living bacterium and make it resistant to an antibiotic.

Figure 11.26 If chromosomes did not become compact, they might get tangled up with others during cell division, which would prevent the even segregation of chromosomes into the two daughter cells.

Feature Investigation Questions

1. Previous studies had indicated that mixing different strains could lead to transformation or the changing of a strain into a different one. Griffith had shown that mixing heat-killed type S with living type R would result in the transformation of the type R to type S. Though mutations could cause the changing of the identity of certain strains, the type R to type S transformation was not due to mutation but was more likely due to the transmission of a biochemical substance between the two strains. Griffith recognized this and referred to the biochemical substance as the "transformation principle." If Avery, MacCleod, and McCarty could determine the biochemical identity of this "transformation principle," they could identify the genetic material for this organism.

2. A DNA extract contains DNA that has been purified from a sample of cells.

3. The researchers could not verify that the DNA extract was completely pure and did not have small amounts of contaminating molecules, such as proteins and RNA. The researchers were able to treat the extract with enzymes to remove proteins (using protease), RNA (using RNase), or DNA (using DNase). Removing the proteins or RNA did not alter the transformation of the type R to type S strains. Only the enzymatic removal of DNA disrupted the transformation, indicating that DNA is the genetic material.

Test Yourself

1. a 2. b 3. d 4. d 5. b 6. c 7. b 8. d 9. d 10. c

Conceptual Questions

1. The genetic material must contain the information necessary to construct an entire organism. The genetic material must be accurately copied and transmitted from parent to offspring and from cell to cell during cell division in multicellular organisms. The genetic material must contain variation that can account for the known variation within each species and among different species.

Griffith discovered something called the transformation principle, and his experiments showed the existence of biochemical genetic information. In addition, he showed that this genetic information can move from one individual to another of the same species. In his experiments, Griffith took heat-killed type S bacteria and mixed them with living type R bacteria and injected them into a live mouse, which died after the injection. By themselves, these two strains would not kill the mouse, but when they were put together, the genetic information from the heat-killed type S bacteria was transferred into the living type R bacteria, thus transforming the type R bacteria into type S.

2. In the case of the Hershey and Chase experiment, a radioactive isotope of sulfur was used to label the protein in the viral protein coat. The DNA was labeled

using a radioactive isotope of phosphorus. This was an ideal way of labeling the different components, because sulfur is found in proteins but not DNA, and phosphorus is found in DNA but not proteins. By labeling the two candidate molecules with the radioactive isotopes, Hershey and Chase could determine the genetic material by seeing which isotope entered the bacterial cells.

3. In a DNA double helix, the two strands hydrogen-bond with each other according to the AT/GC rule. This provides the basis for DNA replication. In addition, as described in later chapters, hydrogen bonding between complementary bases is the basis for the transcription of RNA, which is needed for gene expression.

Chapter 12

Concept Checks

Figure 12.1 A person with two defective copies of phenylalanine hydroxylase would have phenylketonuria.

Figure 12.2 The ability to convert ornithine into citrulline is missing.

Figure 12.3 The usual direction of flow of genetic information is from DNA to RNA to protein, though exceptions occur.

Figure 12.4 If a terminator was removed, transcription would occur beyond the normal stopping point. Eventually, RNA polymerase would encounter a terminator from an adjacent gene, and transcription would end.

Figure 12.9 The ends of structural genes do not have a poly T region that acts as a template for the synthesis of a poly A tail. Instead, the poly A tail is added after the pre-mRNA is made by an enzyme that attaches many adenine nucleotides in a row.

Figure 12.10 A structural gene would still be transcribed into RNA if the start codon was missing. However, it would not be translated properly into a polypeptide.

Figure 12.11 It would bind to a 5′–UGG–3′ codon, and it would carry tryptophan.

Figure 12.13 The function of the anticodon in tRNA is to recognize a codon in an mRNA.

Figure 12.16 Each mammal is closely related to the other mammals, and *E. coli* and *Serratia marcescens* are also closely related. The mammals are relatively distantly related to the bacterial species.

Figure 12.18 A region near the 5′ end of the mRNA is complementary to a region of rRNA in the small subunit. These complementary regions hydrogen-bond with each other to promote the binding of the mRNA to the small ribosomal subunit.

BioConnections

Figure 12.5 Both DNA and RNA polymerase use DNA strands as a template and connect nucleotides to each other in a 5′ to 3′ direction based on the complementarity of base pairing. One difference is that DNA polymerase needs a pre-existing strand, such as a RNA primer, to begin DNA replication, whereas RNA polymerase can begin the synthesis of RNA on a bare template strand. Another key difference is that DNA polymerase connects deoxyribonucleotides, whereas RNA polymerase connects ribonucleotides.

Figure 12.14 The attachment of an amino acid to a tRNA is an endergonic reaction. ATP provides the energy to catalyze this reaction.

Feature Investigation Questions

1. A triplet mimics mRNA because it can cause a specific tRNA to bind to the ribosome. This was useful to Nirenberg and Leder because it allowed them to correlate the binding of a tRNA carrying a specific amino acid with a triplet sequence.

2. The researchers were attempting to match codons with appropriate amino acids. By labeling one amino acid in each of the 20 tubes for each codon, the researchers were able to identify the correct relationship by detecting which tube resulted in radioactivity on the filter.

3. The AUG triplet would have shown radioactivity in the methionine test tube. Even though AUG acts as the start codon, it also codes for the amino acid methionine. The other three codons act as stop codons and do not code for an amino acid. In these cases, the researchers would not have found radioactivity trapped on filters.

Test Yourself

1. b 2. d 3. d 4. b 5. c 6. e 7. d 8. d 9. d 10. b

Conceptual Questions

1. Beadle and Tatum had the insight from their studies that a single gene controlled the synthesis of a single enzyme. In later years, it became apparent that genes code for all proteins and that some proteins consist of more than

one polypeptide chain. So the modern statement is one gene codes for each polypeptide.

Confirmation of their hypothesis came from studies involving arginine biosynthesis. Biochemists had already established that particular enzymes are involved in a pathway to produce arginine. Intermediates in this pathway are ornithine and citrulline. Mutants in single genes disrupted the ability of cells to catalyze just one reaction in this pathway, thereby suggesting that a single gene encodes a single enzyme.

2. Each of these 20 enzymes catalyzes the attachment of a specific amino acid to a specific tRNA molecule.

3. During transcription, a DNA strand is used as a template for the synthesis of RNA. Most genes encode mRNAs, which contain the information to make polypeptides. During translation, an mRNA binds to a ribosome and a polypeptide is made, which becomes a unit within a functional protein.

Chapter 13

Concept Checks

Figure 13.2 Gene regulation causes each cell type to express its own unique set of proteins, which, in turn, are largely responsible for the morphologies and functions of cells.

Figure 13.6 The *lacZ*, *lacY*, and *lacA* genes are under the control of the *lac* promoter.

Figure 13.7 Negative control refers to the action of a repressor protein, which inhibits transcription when it binds to the DNA. Inducible refers to the action of a small effector molecule. When it is present, it promotes transcription.

Figure 13.11 In this case, the repressor keeps the *lac* operon turned off unless lactose is present in the environment. The activator allows the bacterium to choose between glucose and lactose.

Figure 13.12 Both proteins are similar in that they repress transcription. They prevent RNA polymerase from transcribing the operons. They are different with regard to the effects of their small effector molecules. For the lac repressor, the binding of allolactose causes a conformational change that prevents the repressor from binding to its operator site. In contrast, the binding of tryptophan to the trp repressor allows it to bind to its operator site. Another difference is that the lac repressor binds to the DNA sequence found in the *lac* operator site, whereas the trp repressor recognizes a different DNA sequence that is found in the *trp* operator site.

Figure 13.16 When an activator interacts with mediator, it causes RNA polymerase to proceed to the elongation phase of transcription.

Figure 13.18 Some histone modifications may promote a loosening of chromatin structure, whereas others cause the chromatin to become more compact.

Figure 13.21 The advantage of alternative splicing is that it allows a single gene to encode two or more polypeptides. This enables organisms to have smaller genomes, which is more efficient and easier to package into a cell.

Figure 13.23 When iron levels rise in the cell, the iron binds to IRP and removes it from the mRNA that encodes ferritin. This results in the rapid translation of ferritin protein, which can store excess iron. Unfortunately, ferritin storage does have limits, so iron poisoning can occur if too much is ingested.

BioConnections

Figure 13.10 In eukaryotic cells, cAMP acts as a second messenger in signal transduction pathways.

Figure 13.19 A nucleosome is composed of DNA wrapped around an octamer of histone proteins.

Feature Investigation Questions

1. The first observation was the identification of rare bacterial strains that had constitutive expression of the *lac* operon. Normally, the genes are expressed only when lactose is present. These mutant strains expressed the genes all the time. The researchers also observed that some of these strains had mutations in the *lacI* gene. These two observations were key to the development of hypotheses explaining the relationship between the *lacI* gene and the regulation of the *lac* operon.

2. The correct hypothesis is that the *lacI* gene encodes a repressor protein that inhibits the operon.

3. The researchers used an F′ factor to introduce the wild-type *lacI* gene into the cell. In this case, the cells that contained the F′ factor had both a mutant copy of the gene and a normal copy of the gene. By creating a merozygote with an F′ factor with a normal copy of the *lacI* gene, regulation of the *lac* operon was restored. The researchers concluded that the normal *lacI* gene produced

adequate amounts of a diffusible protein that could interact with the operator on the chromosomal DNA as well as the F′ factor DNA and regulate transcription.

Test Yourself

1. d 2. b 3. c 4. c 5. c 6. d 7. c 8. c 9. d 10. c

Conceptual Questions

1. In an inducible operon, the presence of a small effector molecule causes transcription to occur. In repressible operons, a small effector molecule inhibits transcription. The effects of these small molecules are mediated through regulatory proteins that bind to the DNA. Repressible operons usually encode anabolic enzymes, and inducible operons encode catabolic enzymes.

2. a. regulatory protein; b. small effector molecule; c. segment of DNA; d. small effector molecule; and e. regulatory protein.

3. Gene regulation offers key advantages such as (1) proteins are made only when they are needed; (2) proteins are made in the correct cell type; and (3) proteins are made at the correct stage of development. These advantages are important for reproduction and sustaining life.

Chapter 14

Concept Checks

Figure 14.1 At neutral pH, glutamic acid is negatively charged. Perhaps the negative charges repel each other and prevent hemoglobin proteins from aggregating into fiber-like structures.

Figure 14.3 Only germ-line cells give rise to gametes (sperm or egg cells). A somatic cell cannot give rise to a gamete and therefore cannot be passed to offspring.

Figure 14.4 This is a mutation that occurred in a somatic cell, so it cannot be transmitted to an offspring.

Figure 14.6 A thymine dimer is harmful because it can cause errors in DNA replication.

Figure 14.7 If we divide 44 by 2 million, the rate is 2.2×10^{-5}.

Figure 14.8 UvrC and UvrD are responsible for removing the damaged DNA. UvrC makes cuts on both sides of the damage, and then UvrD removes the damaged region.

Figure 14.9 The Sun has UV rays and other harmful radiation that could damage the DNA. This person has a defect in the nucleotide excision repair pathway. Therefore, his DNA is more likely to suffer mutations, which cause growths on the skin.

Figure 14.11 Growth factors turn on a signaling pathway that ultimately leads to cell division.

Figure 14.14 The type of cancer associated with this fusion is leukemia, which is a cancer of blood cells. The gene fusion produces a chimeric gene that is expressed in blood cells because it has the *bcr* promoter. The abnormal fusion protein promotes cancer in these cells.

Figure 14.15 Checkpoints prevent cell division if a genetic abnormality is detected. This helps to properly maintain the genome, thereby minimizing the possibility that a cell harboring a mutation will divide to produce two daughter cells.

Figure 14.16 Cancer would not occur if both copies of the *Rb* gene and both copies of the *E2F* gene were rendered inactive due to mutations. An active copy of the *E2F* gene is needed to promote cell division.

BioConnections

Figure 14.10 Epithelial cells form sheets that separate certain tissues from each other. When the integrity of the sheet is compromised, metastasis may occur.

Figure 14.11 Drugs that inhibit protein kinases may be used to combat cancer if they target the protein kinases that are overactive in certain forms of cancer.

Feature Investigation Questions

1. Some biologists believed that heritable traits may be altered by physiological events. This suggests that mutations may be stimulated by certain needs of the organism. Others believed that mutations are random. If a mutation had a beneficial effect that improved survival and/or reproductive success, these mutations would be maintained in the population through natural selection.

2. The Lederbergs were testing the hypothesis that mutations are random events. By subjecting the bacteria to some type of environmental stress, the bacteriophage, the researchers would be able to see if the stress induced mutations or if mutations occurred randomly.

3. When looking at the number and location of colonies that were resistant to viral infection, the pattern was consistent among the secondary plates. This indicates that the mutation that allowed the colonies to be resistant to viral infection occurred on the master plate. The secondary plates introduced the selective agent that allowed the resistant bacteria colonies to survive and reproduce while the other colonies were destroyed. Thus, mutations occurred randomly in the absence of any selective agent.

Test Yourself

1. c   2. d   3. d   4. e   5. d   6. b   7. b   8. b   9. c   10. e

Conceptual Questions

1. Random mutations are more likely to be harmful than beneficial. The genes within each species have evolved to work properly. They have functional promoters, coding sequences, terminators, and so on, that allow the genes to be expressed. Mutations are more likely to disrupt these sequences. For example, mutations within the coding sequence may produce early stop codons, frame-shift mutations, and missense mutations that result in a nonfunctional polypeptide. On rare occasions, however, mutations are beneficial; they may produce a gene that is expressed better than the original gene or produce a polypeptide that functions better.

2. A spontaneous mutation originates within a living cell. It may be due to spontaneous changes in nucleotide structure, errors in DNA replication, or products of normal metabolism that may alter the structure of DNA. The causes of induced mutations originate from outside the cell. They may be physical agents, such as UV light or X-rays, or chemicals that act as mutagens. Both spontaneous and induced mutations may cause a harmful phenotype such as a cancer. In many cases, induced mutations are avoidable if the individual can prevent exposure to the environmental agent that acts as a mutagen.

3. Mutations may alter the expression of a gene and/or alter the function of a protein encoded by a gene. In many cases, such changes are harmful because a gene may not be expressed at the correct level, or the protein may not function as well as the normal (nonmutant) protein.

Chapter 15
Concept Checks

Figure 15.1 Chromosomes are readily seen when they are compacted in a dividing cell. By adding such a drug, you increase the percentage of cells that are actively dividing.

Figure 15.2 Interphase consists of the G_1, S, and G_2 phases of the cell cycle.

Figure 15.6 As shown in the inset, each object is a pair of sister chromatids.

Figure 15.7 The astral microtubules, which extend away from the chromosomes, are important for positioning the spindle apparatus within the cell. The polar microtubules project into the region between the two poles. Polar microtubules that overlap with each other play a role in the separation of the two poles. Kinetochore microtubules are attached to kinetochores at the centromeres and are needed to sort the chromosomes.

Figure 15.8 The mother cell (in G_1 phase) and the daughter cells have the same chromosome composition. They are genetically identical.

Figure 15.9 Cytokinesis in both animal and plant cells separates a mother cell into two daughter cells. In animal cells, cytokinesis involves the formation of a cleavage furrow, which constricts like a drawstring to separate the cells. In plants, the two daughter cells are separated by the formation of a cell plate, which forms a cell wall between the two daughter cells.

Figure 15.13 The mother cell is diploid with two sets of chromosomes, whereas the four resulting cells are haploid with one set of chromosomes.

Figure 15.14 The reason for meiosis in animals is to produce gametes. These gametes combine during fertilization to produce a diploid organism. Following fertilization, the purpose of mitosis is to produce a multicellular organism.

Figure 15.16 Inversions and the translocations shown here do not affect the total amount of genetic material.

BioConnections

Figure 15.3 Checkpoints prevent cancer by checking the integrity of the genome. If abnormalities in DNA structure are detected or if a chromosome is not properly attached to the spindle, the checkpoint will delay cell division until the problem is fixed. If it cannot be fixed, the checkpoint will initiate the process of apoptosis, thereby killing a cell that may harbor mutations. This prevents the proliferation of cells that have the potential to be cancerous.

Figure 15.10 Though the process is not entirely understood, myosin motor proteins tug on the actin filaments. Actin monomers are gradually released during this process, which makes the contractile ring get smaller and smaller.

Feature Investigation Questions

1. Researchers had demonstrated that the binding of progesterone to receptors in oocytes caused the cells to progress from the G_2 phase of the cell cycle to mitosis. It appeared that progesterone acted as a signaling molecule for the progression through the cell cycle.

2. The researchers proposed that progesterone acted as a signaling molecule that led to the synthesis of molecules that cause the cell to progress through the cell cycle. These changes led to the maturation of the oocyte.
   To test their hypothesis, donor eggs were exposed to progesterone for either 2 or 12 hours. Control donor oocytes were not exposed to progesterone. Cytosol from each treatment was then transferred to recipient oocytes. The researchers recorded whether or not the recipient oocytes underwent maturation.

3. The oocytes that were exposed to the progesterone for only 2 hours did not induce maturation in the recipient oocytes, whereas the oocytes that were exposed to progesterone for 12 hours did induce maturation in the recipient oocytes. The researchers suggested that a time span greater than 2 hours is needed to accumulate the proteins that are necessary to promote maturation.

Test Yourself

1. b   2. e   3. b   4. e   5. c   6. a   7. c   8. d   9. b   10. c

Conceptual Questions

1. In diploid species, chromosomes are present in pairs, one from each parent, and contain similar gene arrangements. Such chromosomes are homologous. When DNA is replicated, two identical copies are created, and these are sister chromatids.

2. There are four copies. A karyotype shows homologous chromosomes that come in pairs. Each member of the pair has replicated to form a pair of sister chromatids. Therefore, four copies of each gene are present. See the inset to Figure 15.1.

3. Mitosis is a process that produces two daughter cells with the same genetic material as the original daughter cell. In the case of plants and animals, this allows a fertilized egg to develop into a multicellular organism composed of many, genetically identical cells.

Chapter 16
Concept Checks

Figure 16.2 Having blue eyes is a variant (also called a trait). A character is a more general term, which in this case would refer to eye color.

Figure 16.4 In this procedure, stamens are removed from the purple flower to prevent self-fertilization.

Figure 16.5 The reason why offspring of the F_1 generation exhibit only one variant of each character is because one trait is dominant over the other.

Figure 16.6 The ratio of alleles (T to t) is 1:1. The reason why the phenotypic ratio is 3:1 is because T is dominant to t.

Figure 16.7 It was Pp. To produce white offspring, which are pp, the original plant had to have at least one copy of the p allele. Because it had purple flowers, it also had to have one copy of the P allele. So, its genotype must be Pp.

Figure 16.8 If the linked hypothesis had been correct, the ratio would have been 3 round, yellow to 1 wrinkled, green.

Figure 16.10 The word segregate means that alleles are separated into different places. In this case, the alleles are segregated into different cells during the process of meiosis. Alleles are located on chromosomes. A diploid cell has two copies of each allele. During meiosis, a diploid cell divides twice to produce four haploid cells that each have only one copy of an allele.

Figure 16.11 There would be four possible ways of aligning the chromosomes, and eight different types of gametes (ABC, abc, ABc, abC, Abc, aBC, AbC, aBc) could be produced.

Figure 16.12 No. If two parents are affected with the disease, they must be homozygous for the mutant allele if it's recessive. Two homozygous parents would have to produce all affected offspring. If they don't, then the inheritance pattern is not recessive.

Figure 16.13 All affected offspring having at least one affected parent suggests a dominant pattern of inheritance.

Figure 16.14 The person would be a female. In mammals, the presence of the Y chromosome causes maleness. Therefore, without a Y chromosome, a person with a single X chromosome would develop into a female.

Figure 16.18 No. You need a genetically homogenous population to study the norm of reaction. A wild population of squirrels is not genetically homogenous, so it could not be used.

BioConnections

Figure 16.9 Sexual reproduction is the process in which two haploid gametes (for example, sperm and egg) combine with each other to begin the life of a new individual. Each gamete contributes one set of chromosomes. The resulting zygote has chromosomes that occur in pairs (one from each parent). The members of each pair are called homologs of each other; they carry the same types of genes.

Figure 16.10 Alleles segregate from each other during the process of meiosis. Meiosis begins with a diploid mother cell that has pairs of genes, which may be found in different alleles. During meiosis, these pairs of genes separate and end up in different haploid cells. Therefore, each haploid cell has only one copy of each gene. In other words, each haploid cell has only one allele of a given gene.

Feature Investigation Questions

1. Morgan was testing the hypothesis of use and disuse. This hypothesis suggests that if a structure is not used, over time, it will diminish and/or disappear. In Morgan's experiments, originally he was testing to see if flies reared in the dark would lose some level of eye development.

2. When the F_1 individuals were crossed, only male F_2 offspring expressed the white eye color. At this time, Morgan was aware of sex chromosome differences between male and female flies. He realized that since males only possess one copy of X-linked genes, this would explain why only F_2 males exhibited the recessive trait.

3. In a cross between a white-eyed male and a female that is heterozygous for the white and red alleles, 1/2 of the female offspring would have white eyes. Also, a cross between a white-eyed male and a white-eyed female would yield all offspring with white eyes.

Test Yourself

1. c   2. b   Mendel's law of segregation refers to the separation of the two alleles into separate cells. Meiosis is the cellular division process that produces haploid cells. During the first meiotic division, a diploid cell divides to produce haploid cells. This is the phase in which the two alleles segregate, or separate, from each other.   3. d   4. c   5. e   6. d   7. d   8. d   9. d   10. c

Conceptual Questions

1. Two affected parents having an unaffected offspring would rule out recessive inheritance. If two unaffected parents had an affected offspring, dominant inheritance is ruled out. However, it should be noted that this answer assumes that no new mutations are happening. In rare cases, a new mutation could cause or alter these results. For recessive inheritance, two affected parents could have an unaffected offspring if the offspring had a new mutation that converted the recessive allele to the dominant allele. Similarly for dominant inheritance, two unaffected parents could have an affected offspring if the offspring inherited a new mutation that was dominant. Note: New mutations are expected to be relatively rare.

2. The individual probabilities are as follows: $AA = 0.25$; $bb = 0.5$; $CC = 0.5$; and $Dd = 0.5$. These are determined by making small Punnett squares. We use the product rule to calculate the probability of $AAbbCCDd = (0.25)(0.5)(0.5)(0.5) = 0.03125$, or 3.125%.

3. The environment is needed so that genes can be expressed. For example, organic molecules and energy are needed for transcription and translation. In addition, environmental factors influence the outcome of traits. For example, sunlight can cause a tanning response, thereby affecting the darkness of the skin.

Chapter 17

Concept Checks

Figure 17.1 The recessive allele is the result of a loss-of-function mutation. In a $Ccpp$ individual, the enzyme encoded by the P gene is defective.

Figure 17.4 Crossing over occurred during oogenesis in the heterozygous female of the F_1 generation to produce the recombinant offspring of the F_2 generation.

Figure 17.5 One strategy would be to begin with two true-breeding parental strains: $alal\ dpdp$ and $al^+al^+\ dp^+dp^+$ and cross them together to get F_1 heterozygotes al^+al

dp^+dp. Then testcross female F_1 heterozygotes to male $alal\ dpdp$ homozygotes. In the F_2 generation, the recombinant offspring would be $al^+al\ dpdp$ and $alal\ dp^+dp$, and the nonrecombinants would be $al^+al\ dp^+dp$, and $alal\ dpdp$.

Figure 17.7 The gene is located in the chloroplast DNA. In this species, chloroplasts are transmitted from parent to offspring via eggs but not via sperm.

Figure 17.9 The Barr body is much more compact than the other X chromosome in the cell. This compaction prevents most of the genes on the Barr body from being expressed.

Figure 17.11 Only the male genes are transcriptionally active in the offspring. In this case, half the offspring would be normal, and half would be dwarf. The dwarf offspring would have inherited the $Igf-2$ allele from their father.

BioConnections

Figure 17.4 Crossing over occurs during prophase of meiosis I.

Figure 17.6 The evolutionary origin of these organelles is an ancient endosymbiotic relationship. Mitochondria are derived from purple bacteria, and chloroplasts are derived from cyanobacteria.

Feature Investigation Questions

1. Bateson and Punnett were testing the hypothesis that the gene pairs that influence flower color and pollen shape would assort independently of each other. The two traits were expected to show a pattern consistent with Mendel's law of independent assortment.

2. The expected results were a phenotypic ratio of 9:3:3:1. The researchers expected 9/16 of the offspring would have purple flowers and long pollen, 3/16 of the offspring would have purple flowers and round pollen, 3/16 of the offspring would have red flowers and long pollen, and 1/16 of the offspring would have red flowers and round pollen.

3. Though all four of the expected phenotype groups were seen, they were not in the predicted ratio of 9:3:3:1. The number of individuals with the phenotypes found in the parental generation (purple flowers and long pollen or red flowers and round pollen) was much higher than expected. Bateson and Punnett suggested that the gene controlling flower color was somehow coupled with the gene that controls pollen shape. This would explain why these traits did not always assort independently.

Test Yourself

1. d   2. c   3. d   4. c   5. d   6. b   7. a   8. d   9. a   10. a

Conceptual Questions

1. The correct answer is 6%. Individuals that are $Aabb$ are recombinants that occurred as a result of crossing over. Because the genes are 12 map units apart, we expect that 12% will be recombinants. However, there are two types of recombinants: $Aabb$ and $aaBb$, which would occur in equal amounts. Therefore, we expect 6% to be $Aabb$.

2. This may happen due to X inactivation. As a matter of bad luck, a female embryo may preferentially inactivate the X chromosome carrying the normal allele in the embryonic cells that will give rise to the eyes. If the X chromosome carrying the allele for color blindness is preferentially expressed, one or both eyes may show color blindness to some degree.

3. When genes are linked along the same chromosome, researchers can set up testcrosses and determine the percentage of recombinant offspring that results from those testcrosses. This percentage can be used as a map distance between genes.

Chapter 18

Concept Checks

Figure 18.3 Viruses vary with regard to their structure and their genomes. Genome variation is described in Table 18.1.

Figure 18.5 The advantage of the lytic cycle is that the virus can make many copies of itself and proliferate. However, sometimes the growth conditions may not be favorable to make new viruses. The advantage of the lysogenic cycle is that the virus can remain latent until conditions become favorable to make new viruses.

Figure 18.9 There appears to be three nucleoids in the bacterial cell to the far right.

Figure 18.11 The loop domains are held in place by proteins that bind to the DNA at the bases of the loops. The proteins also bind to each other.

Figure 18.12 Bacterial chromosomes and plasmids are similar in that they typically contain circular DNA molecules. However, bacterial chromosomes are usually much longer than plasmids and carry many more genes. Also, bacterial chromosomes tend to be more compacted due to the formation of loop domains and supercoiling.

Figure 18.13 16 hours is the same as 32 doublings. So, 2^{32} = 4,294,967,296. (The actual number would be much less because the cells would deplete the growth media and grow more slowly than the maximal rate.)

Figure 18.16 Yes. The two strains would have mixed together, allowing them to conjugate. Therefore, there would have been colonies on the plates.

Figure 18.17 During conjugation, only one strand of the DNA from an F factor is transferred from the donor to the recipient cell. The single-stranded DNA in both cells is then used as a template to create double-stranded F factor DNA in both cells.

Figure 18.19 Transduction is not a normal part of the phage life cycle. It is a mistake in which a piece of the bacterial chromosome is packaged into a phage coat and is then transferred to another bacterial cell.

BioConnections

Figure 18.4 Viral release occurs as a budding process in which a membrane vesicle is formed that surrounds the capsid. Similarly, exocytosis involves the formation of a membrane vesicle that encloses some type of cargo.

Figure 18.9 A nucleoid is not a membrane-bound organelle. It is simply a region where a bacterial chromosome is found. A cell nucleus in a eukaryotic cell has an envelope with a double membrane.

Figure 18.18 Griffiths was able to show that genetic material was transferred to type R bacteria, which converted them to type S. This occurred via transformation. Later, Avery, MacLeod, and McCarty determined that DNA was the material that was being transferred.

Feature Investigation Questions

1. Lederberg and Tatum were testing the hypothesis that genetic material could be transferred from one bacterial strain to another.

2. The experimental growth medium lacked particular amino acids and biotin. The mutant strains were unable to synthesize these particular amino acids or biotin. Therefore, they were unable to grow due to the lack of the necessary nutrients. The two strains used in the experiment each lacked the ability to make two essential nutrients necessary for growth. The appearance of colonies growing on the experimental growth medium indicated that some bacterial cells had acquired the normal genes for the two mutations they carried. By acquiring these normal genes, the ability to synthesize the essential nutrients was restored.

3. Bernard Davis placed samples of the two bacterial strains in different arms of a U-tube. A filter allowed the free movement of the liquid in which the bacterial cells were suspended, but prevented the actual contact between the bacterial cells. After incubating the strains in this environment, Davis found that genetic transfer did not take place. He concluded that physical contact between cells of the two strains was required for genetic transfer.

Test Yourself

1. c   2. e   3. c   4. b   5. e   6. a   7. d   8. d   9. b   10. c

Conceptual Questions

1. Viruses are similar to living cells in that they contain a genetic material that provides a blueprint to make new viruses. However, viruses are not composed of cells, and by themselves, they do not carry out metabolism, use energy, maintain homeostasis, or even reproduce. A virus or its genetic material must be taken up by a living cell to replicate.

2. Conjugation—The process involves a direct physical contact between two bacterial cells in which a donor cell transfers a strand of DNA to a recipient cell.
Transformation—This occurs when a living bacteria takes up genetic information that has been released from a dead bacteria.
Transduction—When a virus infects a donor cell, it incorporates a fragment of bacterial chromosomal DNA into a newly made virus particle. The virus then transfers this fragment of DNA to a recipient cell.

3. Horizontal gene transfer is the transfer of genes from another organism without being the offspring of that organism. These acquired genes sometimes increase survival and therefore may have an evolutionary advantage. Such genes may even promote the formation of new species. From a medical perspective, an important example of horizontal gene transfer is when one bacterium acquires antibiotic resistance from another bacterium and then itself becomes resistant to that antibiotic. This phenomenon is making it increasingly difficult to treat a wide variety of bacterial diseases.

Chapter 19

Concept Checks

Figure 19.3 Cell division and cell migration are common in the earliest stages of development, whereas cell differentiation and apoptosis are more common as tissues and organs start to form.

Figure 19.4 If apoptosis did not occur, the fingers would be webbed.

Figure 19.5 During development, positional information may a cause a cell to respond in one of four ways: cell division, cell migration, cell differentiation, and cell death.

Figure 19.6 Cell division and migration would be the most prevalent in the early phases of development, such as phase 1 and 2.

Figure 19.8 The larva would have anterior structures at both ends and would lack posterior structures such as a spiracle.

Figure 19.9 The Bicoid protein functions as a transcription factor. Its function is highest in the anterior end of the embryo.

Figure 19.11 This embryo has 15 pink stripes, each of which corresponds to a portion of the 15 segments in the embryo.

Figure 19.14 The last abdominal segment would have legs!

Figure 19.18 Stem cells can divide, and they can differentiate into specific cell types.

Figure 19.20 Hematopoietic stem cells are multipotent.

Figure 19.23 Most stem cells in plants are found in meristems, which are located at the tips of roots and shoots.

Figure 19.24 The pattern would be sepal, petal, stamen, stamen.

BioConnections

Figure 19.3 First, the nucleus and cell shrink. Next, multiple extensions (blebs) are formed from the plasma membrane. Finally, this blebbing continues to occur until the cell is broken up into small fragments.

Figure 19.5 Some receptors recognize signals that convey positional information. After the signal binds to this type of receptor, a signal transduction pathway is activated that may cause a cell to divide, migrate, differentiate, or undergo apoptosis.

Figure 19.17 As the number of *Hox* genes increases, the body plans of animals become more complex.

Feature Investigation Questions

1. The researchers were interested in the factors that cause cells to differentiate. For this particular study, the researchers were attempting to identify genes involved in the differentiation of muscle cells.

2. Using genetic technology, the researcher compared the gene expression in cells that could differentiate into muscle cells with the gene expression in cells that could not differentiate into muscle cells. Though many genes were expressed in both, the researchers were able to isolate three genes that were expressed in muscle cell lines that were not expressed in the nonmuscle cell lines.

3. Again, using genetic technology, each of the candidate genes was introduced into a cell that normally did not give rise to skeletal muscle. This procedure was used to test whether or not these genes played a key role in muscle cell differentiation. If the genetically engineered cell gave rise to muscle cells, the researchers would have evidence that a particular candidate gene was involved in muscle cell differentiation. Of the three candidate genes, only one was shown to be involved in muscle cell differentiation. When the *MyoD* gene was expressed in fibroblasts, these cells differentiated into skeletal muscle cells.

Test Yourself

1. c   2. d   3. e   4. b   5. c   6. e   7. a   8. a   9. b   10. d

Conceptual Questions

1. a. This would be consistent with a defect in a segmentation gene, such as a gap gene.

b. This would be consistent with a mutation in a homeotic gene because the characteristics of a particular segment have been changed.

2. Both types of genes encode transcription factors that bind to the DNA and regulate the expression of other genes. The effects of *Hox* genes are to determine the characteristics of certain regions of the body, whereas the *myoD* gene is cell specific—it causes a cell to become a skeletal muscle cell.

3. Maternal effect genes control the formation of body axes, such as the anteroposterior and dorsoventral axes. Next, the segmentation genes divide the embryo into segments, though visible segments are lost in many animal species at later stages of development. Finally, the homeotic genes determine the characteristics of each segment.

Chapter 20

Concept Checks

Figure 20.2 No. A recombinant vector has been made, but it has not been cloned. In other words, many copies of the recombinant vector have not been made yet.

Figure 20.3 The insertion of chromosomal DNA into the vector disrupts the *lacZ* gene, thereby preventing the expression of β-galactosidase. The functionality of *lacZ* can be determined by providing the growth medium with a colorless compound, X-Gal, which is cleaved by β-galactosidase into a blue dye. Bacterial colonies containing recircularized vectors form blue colonies, whereas colonies containing recombinant vectors carrying a segment of chromosomal DNA will be white.

Figure 20.5 The 600-bp piece would be closer to the bottom. Smaller pieces travel faster through the gel.

Figure 20.6 The primers are complementary to sequences at each end of the DNA region to be amplified.

Figure 20.7 It means that part of their inserts are exactly the same, but other regions are not.

Figure 20.9 If a dideoxynucleotide ddNTP is added to a growing DNA strand, the strand can no longer grow because the 3′−OH group, the site of attachment for the next nucleotide, is missing.

Figure 20.10 A fluorescent spot identifies a cDNA that is complementary to a particular DNA sequence. Because the cDNA was generated from mRNA, this technique identifies a gene that has been transcribed in a particular cell type under a given set of conditions.

Figure 20.11 The reason why the A and B chains are made as fusion proteins is because the A and B chains are rapidly degraded when expressed in bacterial cells by themselves. The fusion proteins, however, are not.

Figure 20.13 Only the T DNA within the Ti plasmid is transferred to a plant cell.

Figure 20.15 Not all of Dolly's DNA came from a mammary cell. Her mitochondrial DNA came from the oocyte donor.

Figure 20.16 The bands match suspect 2.

BioConnections

Figure 20.2 Plasmids are small, circular molecules of DNA that exist independently of the bacterial chromosome. They have their own origin of replication. Many plasmids carry genes that convey some type of selective advantage to the host cell, such as antibiotic resistance.

Figure 20.6 Primers are needed in a PCR experiment because DNA polymerase cannot begin DNA replication on a bare template strand.

Feature Investigation Questions

1. Gene therapy is the introduction of cloned genes into living cells to correct genetic mutations. The hope is that the cloned genes will correct or restore the normal gene function, thereby eliminating the clinical effects of the disease.
   ADA deficiency is a recessive genetic disorder in which an enzyme, adenosine deaminase, is not functional. The absence of this enzyme causes a buildup of deoxyadenosine, which is toxic to lymphocytes. When lymphocytes are destroyed, a person's immune system begins to fail, leading to a severe combined immunodeficiency disease (SCID).

2. The researchers introduced normal copies of the ADA gene into lymphocytes, restoring normal cell metabolism. The researchers isolated lymphocytes from the patient and used a viral vector to introduce the gene into the lymphocytes. These lymphocytes were then reintroduced back into the patient.

3. Following several rounds of treatment with gene therapy, researchers were able to document continued production of the correct enzyme by the lymphocytes over the course of 4 years. However, because the patients were also receiving other forms of treatment, it was not possible to determine if the gene therapy reduced the negative effects of the genetic disease.

Test Yourself

1. e   2. d   3. b   4. b   5. b   6. c   7. d   8. c   9. e   10. e

Conceptual Questions

1. The restriction enzyme cuts the plasmid at a specific site, leaving sticky ends. The gene of interest, cut with the same enzyme, has complementary sticky ends that allow hydrogen bonding between the gene of interest and the plasmid. The connections are then made permanent, using DNA ligase that connects the DNA backbones.

2. A ddNTP is missing an oxygen at the 3′ position. This prevents the further growth of a DNA strand, thereby causing chain termination.

3. One example is Bt corn in which corn plants carry genes that make it herbicide- and pest-resistant. These types of strains have become very popular among farmers. A similar approach was used to create Bt cotton. You may find other examples by searching the web.

Chapter 21

Concept Checks

Figure 21.2 One reason is that more complex species tend to have more genes. A second reason is that species vary with regard to the amount of repetitive DNA present in their genome.

Figure 21.5 For DNA transposons, inverted repeats are recognized by transposase, which cleaves the DNA and inserts the transposon into a new location.

Figure 21.6 Retroelements. A single retroelement can be transcribed into multiple copies of RNA, which can be converted to DNA by reverse transcriptase, and inserted into multiple sites in the genome.

Figure 21.9 Differential gene regulation. Genes that encode metabolic enzymes are highly expressed in liver cells, whereas those same genes are expressed in lower amounts in muscle cells. Conversely, genes that encode cytoskeletal and motor proteins are highly expressed in muscle cells, but less so in liver cells.

Figure 21.11 The two main advantages of having a computer program translate a genetic sequence are that it's faster and probably more accurate.

Figure 21.12 It is possible for orthologs to have exactly the same DNA sequence if neither of them has accumulated any new mutations that would cause their sequences to become different. This is likely only for closely related species that have diverged relatively recently from each other.

BioConnections

Figure 21.8 The family members that are expressed at early stages of development (embryonic and fetal stages) have a higher affinity for oxygen than the adult form. This allows the embryo and fetus to obtain oxygen from its mother's bloodstream.

Figure 21.10 Reversible post-translation covalent modifications provide a way to modulate protein function. Certain types can turn off protein function, whereas others can turn on protein function. These modifications provide a rapid way for a cell to control protein function.

Feature Investigation Questions

1. The goal of the experiment was to sequence the entire genome of *Haemophilus influenzae*. By conducting this experiment, the researchers would have information about genome size and the types of genes the bacterium has.

2. One strategy requires mapping the genome prior to sequencing. After mapping is completed, each region of the genome is then sequenced. The shotgun approach does not require mapping of the genome prior to sequencing. Instead, many fragments are randomly sequenced.
   The advantage of the shotgun approach is the speed at which the sequencing can be conducted because the researchers do not have to spend time mapping the genome first. The disadvantage is that because the researchers are sequencing random fragments, some fragments may be sequenced more than necessary.

3. The researchers were successful in sequencing the entire genome of the bacterium. The genome size was determined to be 1,830,137 base pairs, with a predicted 1,743 structural genes. The researchers were also able to predict the function of many of these genes. More importantly, the results were the first complete genomic sequence of a living organism.

Test Yourself

1. c   2. e   3. a   4. c   5. e   6. b   7. b   8. d   9. c   10. c

Conceptual Questions

1. a. yes

   b. No, it's only one chromosome in the nuclear genome.

c. yes

d. yes

2. The two main reasons why the proteomes of eukaryote species are usually much larger than their genomes are alternative splicing and post-translational covalent modifications. During alternative splicing, a pre-mRNA is spliced in two or more different ways to yield two or more different polypeptides. Post-translational covalent modifications can affect protein structure in a variety of ways, including proteolytic processing; disulfide bond formation; the attachment of prosthetic group, sugars, or lipids; phosphorylation; acetylation; and methylation.

3. The genome contains the information for the production of cellular proteins; it is a blueprint. The production of proteins is largely responsible for determining cellular characteristics, which, in turn, determine an organism's traits.

Chapter 22
Concept Checks

Figure 22.2 Organic molecules form the chemical foundation for the structure and function of living organisms. Modern organisms can synthesize organic molecules. However, to explain how life got started, biologists need to explain how organic molecules were made prior to the existence of living cells.

Figure 22.3 These vents release hot gaseous substances from the interior of the Earth. Organic molecules can form in the temperature gradient between the extremely hot vent water and the cold water that surrounds the vent.

Figure 22.4 A liposome is more similar to real cells, which are surrounded by a membrane that is composed of a phospholipid bilayer.

Figure 22.5 Certain chemicals, such as RNA molecules, have properties that provide advantages and therefore cause them to increase in number relative to other molecules.

Figure 22.7 In a sedimentary rock formation, the layer at the bottom is usually the oldest.

Figure 22.8 For this time frame, you would analyze the relative amounts of the rubidium-87 and strontium-87 isotopes.

Figure 22.14 Most animal species, including fruit flies, fishes, and humans, exhibit bilateral symmetry.

BioConnections

Figure 22.4 Phospholipids are amphipathic molecules; they have a polar end (the head groups) and a nonpolar end (the two fatty acyl tails). Phospholipids form a bilayer such that the heads interact with water, whereas the tails are shielded from the water. This is an energetically favorable structure.

Figure 22.12 First, the process of membrane invagination created the nuclear envelope. Second, endocytosis may have enabled an ancient archaeon to take up a bacterial cell. Over time, bacterial genes were transferred to the nucleus, which gave rise to the eukaryotic nuclear genome. An engulfed bacterial cell eventually became a mitochondrion, and an engulfed cyanobacterial cell became a chloroplast in algae and plants.

Figure 22.18 Two key features are mammary glands and hair. They also have specialized teeth, external ears, and enlarged skulls that harbor highly developed brains. Mammals are typically endothermic.

Feature Investigation Questions

1. Chemical selection occurs when a particular chemical in a mixture has advantageous properties that allow it to increase in number compared to the other chemicals in the mixture. Bartel and Szostak hypothesized that variation in the catalytic abilities of RNA molecules would allow for chemical selection in the laboratory. Bartel and Szostak proposed to select for RNA molecules with higher catalytic abilities.

2. The short RNA molecules allowed the researchers to physically separate the mixture of longer RNA molecules based on catalytic properties. Long RNA molecules with catalytic abilities would covalently bond with the short RNA molecules. The short RNA molecules had a specific region that caused them to be attracted to column beads in the experimental apparatus. The long RNA molecules that did not have catalytic abilities passed through the column and therefore could be separated from the ones that had catalytic activity and became bound to the column beads.

3. The researchers found that with each round of selection, the enzymatic activity of the selected pool of RNA molecules increased. These results provided evidence that chemical selection could improve the functional characteristics of a group of molecules. Much of the explanation of the evolution of life on Earth is

theoretical, meaning it is based on scientific principles but has not been experimentally verified. Researchers are attempting to develop laboratory experiments that test the explanations of the evolution of life. The experiment conducted by Bartel and Szostak provided experimental data to support the hypothesis of chemical selection as a possible mechanism for the early evolutionary process that led to living cells.

Test Yourself

1. b 2. e 3. b 4. c 5. e 6. a 7. d 8. c 9. b 10. d

Conceptual Questions

1. Nucleotides and amino acids were produced prior to the existence of cells.

Nucleotides and amino acids became polymerized to form DNA, RNA, and proteins.

Polymers became enclosed in membranes.

Polymers enclosed in membranes evolved cellular properties.

2. The relative ages of fossils can be determined by the locations in sedimentary rock formation. Older fossils are found in lower layers. A common way to determine the ages of fossils is via radioisotope dating, which is often conducted using a piece of igneous rock from the vicinity of the fossil. A radioisotope is an unstable isotope of an element that decays spontaneously, releasing radiation at a constant rate. The half-life is the length of time required for a radioisotope to decay to exactly one-half of its initial value. To determine the age of a rock (and that of a nearby fossil), scientists can measure the amount of a given radioisotope as well as the amount of the decay product.

3. Several examples are described in this chapter. In some cases, catastrophic events like volcanic eruptions and glaciers caused mass extinctions, which allowed new species to evolve and flourish. In other cases, changing environmental conditions (for example, changes in temperature and moisture) played key roles. One interesting example is adaptation to terrestrial environments. Plant species evolved seeds that are dessication resistant, whereas animal species evolved eggs. Mammalian species evolved internal gestation.

Chapter 23
Concept Checks

Figure 23.2 A single organism does not evolve. Populations may evolve from one generation to the next.

Figure 23.7 Due to a changing global climate, the island fox became isolated from the mainland species. Over time, natural selection resulted in adaptations for the population on the island and eventually resulted in a new species with characteristics that are somewhat different from the mainland species.

Figure 23.8 Many answers are possible. One example is the wing of a bird and the wing of a bat.

Figure 23.11 The relative sizes of traits are changing. For example, in dogs, the lengths of legs, body size, and so on, are quite different. Artificial selection is often aimed at changing the relative sizes of body parts.

Figure 23.13 Rhesus and green monkeys = 0, Congo puffer fish and European flounder = 2, and Rhesus monkey and Congo puffer fish = 10. Pairs that are closely related evolutionarily have fewer differences than do pairs that are more distantly related.

Figure 23.14 Orthologs have similar gene sequences because they are derived from the same ancestral gene. The sequences are not identical because after the species diverged, each one accumulated different random mutations that changed their sequences.

Figure 23.15 It creates multifunctional proteins that may have new properties that can be acted upon by natural selection.

Figure 23.17 Humans have one large chromosome 2, but this chromosome is divided into two separate chromosomes in the other three species. In chromosome 3, the banding patterns among humans, chimpanzees, and gorillas are very similar, but the orangutan has a large inversion that flips the arrangement of bands in the centromeric region.

BioConnections

Figure 23.2 Both natural selection and chemical selection involve processes in which the relative proportions of something in a population increases compared to something else. In natural selection, it is the relative proportions of individuals with certain traits that increases. In chemical selection, molecules with certain characteristics increase their relative numbers compared with other molecules.

Figure 23.13 When comparing homologous genes or proteins, species that are closely related evolutionarily have more similar sequences than do more distantly related species.

Figure 23.16 The three mechanisms of horizontal gene transfer between bacterial species are conjugation, transformation and transduction.

Feature Investigation Questions

1. The island has a moderate level of isolation but is located near enough to the mainland to have some migrants. The island is an undisturbed habitat, so the researchers would not have to consider the effects of human activity on the study. Finally, the island had an existing population of ground finches that would serve as the study organism over many generations.

2. First, the researchers were able to show that beak depth is a genetic trait that has variation in the population. Second, the depth of the beak is an indicator of the types of seeds the birds can eat. The birds with larger beaks can eat larger and drier seeds; therefore, changes in the types of seeds available could act as a selective force on the bird population.

    During the study period, annual changes in rainfall occurred, which affected the seed sizes produced by the plants on the island. In the drier year, fewer small seeds were produced, so the birds would have to eat larger, drier seeds.

3. The researchers found that following the drought in 1978, the average beak depth in the finch population increased. This indicated that birds with larger beaks were better able to adapt to the environmental changes due to the drought and produce more offspring. This is direct evidence of the phenomenon of natural selection.

Test Yourself

1. d   2. d   3. b   4. b   5. b   6. d   7. c   8. b   9. d   10. e

Conceptual Questions

1. Some random mutations result in a phenotype with greater reproductive success. If so, natural selection results in a greater proportion of such individuals in succeeding generations. These individuals are more likely to survive and reproduce, which means they have evolved to be better adapted to their environment.

2. The process of convergent evolution produces two different species from different lineages that show similar characteristics because they occupy similar environments. An example is the long snout and tongue of both the giant anteater, found in South America, and the echidna, found in Australia. This enables these animals to feed on ants, but the two structures evolved independently. These observations support the idea that evolution results in adaptations to particular environments.

3. Homologous structures are two or more structures that are similar because they are derived from a common ancestor. An example is the same set of bones that is found in the human arm, turtle arm, bat wing, and whale flipper. The forearms in these species have been modified to perform different functions. This supports the idea that all of these animals evolved from a common ancestor by descent with modification.

Chapter 24

Concept Checks

Figure 24.2 If C^R is 0.4, then C^W must be 0.6, because the allele frequencies add up to 1.0. The heterozygote ($2pq$) equals 2(0.4)(0.6), which equals 0.48, or 48%.

Figure 24.3 Over the short run, alleles that confer better fitness would be favored and increase in frequency, perhaps enhancing diversity. Over the long run, however, an allele that confers high fitness in the homozygous state may become monomorphic, thereby reducing genetic diversity.

Figure 24.4 Stabilizing selection eliminates alleles that give phenotypes that deviate significantly from the average phenotype. For this reason, it tends to decrease genetic diversity.

Figure 24.6 If malaria was eradicated, there would be no selective advantage for the heterozygote. The H^S allele would eventually be eliminated because the $H^S H^S$ homozygote has a lower fitness. Directional selection would occur.

Figure 24.7 This is likely to be a form of intersexual selection. Such traits are likely to be involved in mate choice.

Figure 24.11 The bottleneck effect decreases genetic diversity. This may eliminate adaptations that promote survival and reproductive success. Therefore, the bottleneck effect makes it more difficult for a population to survive.

Figure 24.13 Gene flow tends to make the allele frequencies in neighboring populations more similar to each other. It also promotes genetic diversity by introducing new alleles into populations.

BioConnections

Figure 24.12 There are lots of possibilities. The idea is that you are changing one codon to another codon that specifies the same amino acid. For example, changing a codon from GGA to GGG is likely to be neutral because both codons specify glycine.

Figure 24.14 Inbreeding favors homozygotes. Initially, inbreeding would result in more homozygotes in a population. Over the long run, however, if a homozygote has a lower fitness, inbreeding would accelerate the elimination of the allele from the population.

Feature Investigation Questions

1. The two species of cichlids used in the experiment are distinguishable by coloration, and the researchers were testing the hypothesis that the females make mate choices based on this variable.

2. Individual females were placed in tanks that contained one male from each species. The males were held in small glass tanks to limit their movement but allowed the female to see each of the males. The researchers recorded the courtship behavior between the female and males and the number of positive encounters between the female and each of the different males. This procedure was conducted under normal lighting and under monochromatic lighting that obscured the coloration differences between the two species. Comparing the behavior of the females under normal light conditions and monochromatic light conditions allowed the researchers to determine the importance of coloration in mate choice.

3. The researchers found that the female was more likely to select a mate from her own species in normal light conditions. However, under monochromatic light conditions, the species-specific mate choice was not observed. Females were as likely to choose males of the other species as they were males of their own species. This indicated that coloration is an important factor in mate choice in these species of fish.

Test Yourself

1. d   2. c   3. c   4. e   5. b   6. c   7. b   8. d   9. b   10. a

Conceptual Questions

1. The frequency of the disease is a genotype frequency because it represents individuals with the disease. If we let q^2 represent the genotype frequency, then q equals the square root of 0.04, which is 0.2. If $q = 0.2$, then $p = 1 - q$, which is 0.8. The frequency of heterozygous carriers is $2pq$, which is 2(0.8)(0.2) = 0.32, or 32%.

2. Directional selection—This is when natural selection favors an extreme phenotype that makes the organism better suited to survive and reproduce in its environment. As a result, the extreme phenotype will become predominant in the population. This can occur either through new mutation or through a prolonged environmental change. In addition to selecting for a certain phenotype, the opposite end of the extreme is removed from the gene pool.

    - Stabilizing selection—In this type of selection, natural selection favors individuals with intermediate phenotypes, whereas organisms with extreme phenotypes are less likely to reproduce. This selection tends to prevent major changes in the phenotypes of populations.
    - Disruptive selection—This type of selection favors both extremes and removes the intermediate phenotype. It is also known as diversifying selection.
    - Balancing selection—This type of selection results in a balanced polymorphism in which two or more alleles are stably maintained in a population. Examples include heterozygote advantage, as in the sickle cell allele, and negative frequency-dependent selection, as in certain prey.
    - Sexual selection—This is a type of natural selection that is directly aimed at reproductive success. It can occur by any of the previous four mechanisms. Male coloration in African cichlids is an example.

3. Genetic drift involves random changes in the genetic composition of a population from one generation to the next. Neutral changes in DNA sequences may happen randomly, and these are most likely to accumulate in a population due to genetic drift. This is evolution at the level of DNA, but it does not affect phenotype.

Chapter 25

Concept Checks

Figure 25.1 There are a lot of possibilities. Certain grass species look quite similar. Elephant species look very similar. And so on.

Figure 25.3 Temporal isolation is an example of a prezygotic isolating mechanism. Because the species breed at different times of the year, hybrid zygotes are not formed between the two species.

Figure 25.5 Hybrid sterility is a type of postzygotic isolating mechanism. A hybrid forms between the two species, but it is sterile.

Figure 25.11 The offspring would inherit 16 chromosomes from *Galeopsis tetrahit*, and from the hybrid, it would inherit anywhere from 8 to 16. So the answer is 24 to 32. The hybrid parent would always pass the 8 chromosomes that are found in pairs. With regard to the 8 chromosomes not found in pairs, it could pass 0 to 8 of them.

Figure 25.12 The insects on different host plants would tend to breed with each other, and natural selection would favor the development of traits that are an advantage for feeding on that host. Over time, the accumulation of genetic changes may lead to reproductive isolation between the populations of insects.

Figure 25.14 If the *Gremlin* gene was underexpressed, less Gremlin protein would be produced. Because Gremlin protein inhibits apoptosis, more cell death would occur, and the result would probably be smaller feet, and maybe they would not be webbed.

Figure 25.15 By comparing the number of *Hox* genes in many different animal species, a general trend is observed that animals with more complex body structures have a greater number of *Hox* genes.

Figure 25.18 The tip of the mouse's tail might have a mouse eye!

BioConnections

Figure 25.2 Female choice is a prezygotic isolating mechanism.

Figure 25.7 The Hawaiian Islands have many different ecological niches that can be occupied by birds. The first founding bird inhabitants evolved to occupy those niches, thereby evolving into many different species.

Figure 25.15 The *Hox* genes expressed along the anteroposterior axis during early embryonic development are homeotic genes. In insects that contain discrete body segments, each *Hox* gene determines the structures that will ultimately form in those segments. Although more complex animals such as mammals do not display discrete segments, the expression of the *Hox* genes controls what structures will form along the anteroposterior axis.

Feature Investigation Questions

1. Podos hypothesized that the morphological changes in the beak would also affect the birds' songs. A bird's song is an important component for mate choice. If changes in the beak alter the song of the bird, reproductive ability would be affected. Podos suggested that changes in the beak morphology could thus lead to reproductive isolation among the birds.

2. Podos first caught male birds in the field and collected data on beak size. The birds were banded for identification and released. Later, the banded birds' songs were recorded and analyzed for range of frequencies and trill rates. The results were then compared with similar data from other species of birds to determine if beak size constrained the frequency range and trill rate of the song.

3. The results of the study did indicate that natural selection on beak size due to changes in diet could lead to changes in song. Considering the importance of bird song to mate choice, the changes in the song could also lead to reproductive isolation.

   The phrase "by-product of adaptation" refers to changes in the phenotype that are not directly acted on by natural selection. In the case of the Galápagos finches, the changes in beak size were directly related to diet; however, as a consequence of that selection, the song pattern was also altered. The change in song pattern was a by-product.

Test Yourself

1. b   2. b   3. e   4. d   5. c   6. a   7. b   8. d   9. c   10. c

Conceptual Questions

1. Prezygotic isolating mechanisms prevent the formation of the zygote. An example is mechanical isolation, the incompatibility of genitalia. Postzygotic isolating mechanisms act after the formation of the zygote. An example is inviability of the hybrid that is formed. (Other examples shown in Figure 25.2 would also be correct.) Postzygotic mechanisms are more costly because some energy is spent in the formation of a zygote and its subsequent growth.

2. The concept of gradualism suggests that each new species evolves continuously over long spans of time (Figure 25.13a). The principal idea is that large phenotypic differences that produce new species are due to the accumulation of many small genetic changes. According to the punctuated equilibrium model, species

exist relatively unchanged for many generations. During this period, the species is in equilibrium with its environment. These long periods of equilibrium are punctuated by relatively short periods during which evolution occurs at a far more rapid rate. This rapid evolution is caused by relatively few genetic changes.

3. One example involves the *Hox* genes, which control morphological features along the anteroposterior axis in animals. An increase in the number of *Hox* genes during evolution is associated with an increase in body complexity and may have spawned many different animal species.

Chapter 26

Concept Checks

Figure 26.2 A phylum is broader than a family.

Figure 26.3 Yes. They can have many common ancestors, depending on how far back you go in the tree. For example, dogs and cats have a common ancestor that gave rise to mammals, and an older common ancestor that gave rise to vertebrates. The most recent common ancestor is the point at which two species diverged from each other.

Figure 26.4 An order is a smaller taxon that would have a more recent common ancestor.

Figure 26.9 A hinged jaw is the character common to the salmon, lizard, and rabbit, but not to the lamprey.

Figure 26.10 Changing the second G to an A is common to species A, B, and C, but not to species G.

Figure 26.13 The kiwis are found in New Zealand. Even so, the kiwis are more closely related to Australian and African flightless birds than they are to the moas, which were found in New Zealand.

Figure 26.15 Gorillas and humans would be expected to have fewer genetic differences because their common ancestor (named C) is more recent than that of orangutans and gorillas, which is ancestor B.

Figure 26.16 Monophyletic groups are based on the concept that a particular group of species descended from a common ancestor. When horizontal gene transfer occurs, not all of the genes in a species were inherited from the common ancestor, so this muddles the concept of monophyletic groups.

BioConnections

Figure 26.1 The domains Bacteria and Archaea have organisms with prokaryotic cells.

Figure 26.14 There are lots of possibilities. The idea is that you are changing one codon to another codon that specifies the same amino acid. For example, changing a codon from GGA to GGG is likely to be neutral because both codons specify glycine.

Feature Investigation Questions

1. Molecular paleontology is the sequencing and analysis of DNA obtained from extinct species. Tissue samples from specimens of extinct species may contain DNA molecules that can be extracted, amplified, and sequenced. The DNA sequences can then be compared with living species to study evolutionary relationships between modern and extinct species.

   The researchers extracted DNA from tissue samples of moas, extinct flightless birds that lived in New Zealand. The DNA sequences from the moas were compared with the DNA sequences of modern species of flightless birds to determine the evolutionary relationships of this particular group of organisms.

2. The researchers compared the DNA sequences of the extinct moas and modern kiwis of New Zealand to the emu and cassowary of Australia and New Guinea, the ostrich of Africa, and rheas of South America. All of the birds are flightless. With the birds selected, the researchers could look for similarities between birds over a large geographic area.

3. The sequences were very similar among the different species of flightless birds. Interestingly, the sequences of the kiwis of New Zealand were more similar to those of the modern species of flightless birds found on other land masses than they were to those of the moas found in New Zealand.

   The researchers constructed a new evolutionary tree that suggests that kiwis are more closely related to the emu, cassowary, and ostrich. Also, based on the results of this study, the researchers suggested that New Zealand was colonized twice by ancestors of flightless birds. The first ancestor gave rise to the now-extinct moas. The second ancestor gave rise to the kiwis.

Test Yourself

1. c   2. d   3. e   4. d   5. b   6. d   7. b   8. b   9. c   10. e

Conceptual Questions

1. The scientific name of every species has two parts, which are the genus name and the species epithet. The genus name is always capitalized, but the species name is not. Both names are italicized. An example is *Canis lupus*.

2. If neutral mutations occur at a relatively constant rate, they act as a molecular clock on which to measure evolutionary time. Genetic diversity between species that is due to neutral mutation gives an estimate of the time elapsed since the last common ancestor. A molecular clock can provide a timescale to a phylogenetic tree.

3. Morphological analysis focuses on morphological features of extinct and modern species. Many traits are analyzed to obtain a comprehensive picture of two species' relatedness. Convergent evolution leads to similar traits that arise independently in different species as they adapt to similar environments. Convergent evolution can, therefore, cause errors if a researcher assumes that a particular trait arose only once and that all species having the trait have the same common ancestor.

Chapter 27

Concept Checks

Figure 27.5 The cell will tend to float because it is full of intact gas vesicles.

Figure 27.11 The motion of the stiff filament of a prokaryotic flagellum is more like that of a propeller shaft than the flexible arms of a human swimmer.

Figure 27.13 Cells having pili tend to move with a twitching or gliding motion.

Figure 27.14 When DNA sequencing studies show that samples contain many uncultured bacterial species, the fluorescence method is preferred, though it requires the use of a fluorescence microscope. Under such conditions, the culture method will underestimate the bacterial numbers. But when the goal is to estimate numbers of bacteria whose culture preferences are known, the culture method may provide good estimates.

Figure 27.15 Endospores allow bacterial cells to survive treatments and environmental conditions that would kill ordinary cells.

Figure 27.18 Structural similarities to bacterial flagella and pili indicate that these types of attack systems evolved from these structures.

BioConnections

Figure 27.6 Like the bacterium *Magnetospirillum magnetotacticum*, birds such as homing pigeons and migratory fishes such as rainbow trout have the capacity to sense and respond to magnetic fields.

Figure 27.2 The microscopic protist *Giardia intestinalis* likewise uses flagella to move within the human small intestine.

Figure 27.14 Two.

Feature Investigation Questions

1. Many bacteria are known to produce organic compounds that function as antibiotics, and are potential food sources for chemoheterotrophic bacteria.

2. Researchers isolated and cultivated bacteria from different types of soils, then grew the cultured bacteria on media that contained one of several common types of antibiotics as the only source of organic food.

3. It was important to know if soil bacteria are a source of antibiotic resistance that can be medically significant.

Test Yourself

1. c   2. b   3. c   4. d   5. a   6. a   7. b   8. e   9. d   10. d

Conceptual Questions

1. Small cell size and simple division processes allow many bacteria to divide much more rapidly than eukaryotes. This helps to explain why food can spoil so quickly and why infections can spread very rapidly within the body. Other factors also influence these rates.

2. Pathogen populations naturally display genetic variation in their susceptibility to antibiotics. When such populations are exposed to antibiotics, even if initially only a few cells are resistant, the numbers of resistant cells will eventually increase and could come to dominate natural populations.

3. Humans. When humans pollute natural waters with high levels of fertilizers originating from sewage effluent or crop field runoff, cyanobacterial populations are able to grow large enough to produce harmful blooms.

Chapter 28

Concept Checks

Figure 28.7 After particles are ingested via feeding grooves, particles are enclosed by membrane vesicles and then digested by enzymes.

Figure 28.8 The intestinal parasite *Giardia intestinalis* is transmitted from one person to another via fecal wastes, whereas the urogenital parasite *Trichomonas vaginalis* can be transmitted by sexual activity.

Figure 28.17 Flagellar hairs function like oars, helping to pull cells through the water.

Figure 28.18 Kelps are harvested for the production of industrially useful materials. In addition, they nurture fishes and other wildlife of economic importance.

Figure 28.21 Genes that encode cell adhesion and extracellular matrix proteins are likely essential to modern choanoflagellates' ability to attach to surfaces, where they feed. Similar proteins are involved in the formation of multicellular tissues in animals. Evolutionary biologists would say that ancient choanoflagellates were preadapted for the later evolution of multicellular tissues in early animals.

Figure 28.24 Cysts allow protists to survive conditions that are not suitable for growth. One such condition would be the dry or cold environment outside a parasitic protist's warm, moist host tissues.

Figure 28.29 Gametes of *Plasmodium falciparum* undergo fusion to produce zygotes while in the mosquito host.

BioConnections

Figure 28.5 The amoebocytes of sponges, which carry food to other cells, move similarly to amoeboid protists.

Figure 28.25 Because the only cell in the *Chlamydomonas* life cycle that is diploid is the zygote, other phases of the life cycle are haploid, and therefore homologous copies do not affect gene expression.

Figure 28.27 The life cycle of diatoms is similar to that of animals.

Feature Investigation Questions

1. One strain had earlier been reported to be toxic to fishes, whereas the other had been reported to be nontoxic, a difference that could be attributed to differing experimental conditions. The investigators wanted to determine the degree of toxicity of the two strains when grown under the same conditions.

2. Producing toxins requires considerable ATP and other resources, so many organisms produce such compounds only when needed. In the case of *Pfiesteria shumwayae*, this might be when a major food source, fish, was present, but not when they fed primarily upon algal cells. The investigators needed to know if this dinoflagellate produces toxin even when feeding on algae alone (which would not require toxin production) or only when exposed to fishes.

3. The team knew that fishermen and scientists had suffered amnesia and other neurological impairments when they were near water containing large populations of the genus *Pfiesteria*. These observations suggested that the toxin was volatile or suspended in water droplets that people could inhale. As a precaution, they used the biohazard containment system to avoid personal harm. The use of biohazard containment systems is generally recommended for scientists who work with hazardous or potentially hazardous biological materials.

Test Yourself

1. c   2. a   3. b   4. b   5. e   6. b   7. e   8. d   9. b   10. c

Conceptual Questions

1. Protists are amazingly diverse, reflecting the occurrence of extensive adaptive radiation after the origin of eukaryotic cells, widespread occurrence of endosymbiosis, and adaptation to many types of moist habitats, including the tissues of animals and plants. As a result of this extensive diversity, protists cannot be classified into a single kingdom or phylum.

2. Several protists, including the apicomplexans *Cryptosporidium parvum* and *Plasmodium falciparum* and the kinetoplastids *Leishmania major* and *Trypanosoma brucei*, cause many cases of illness around the world, but few treatments are available, and organisms often evolve drug resistance. Genomic data allow researchers to identify metabolic features of these parasites that are not present in humans and are therefore good targets for development of new drugs. An

example is provided by metabolic pathways of the apicoplast, a reduced plastid that is present in cells of the genus *Plasmodium*. Because the apicoplast plays essential metabolic roles in the protist but is absent from humans, drugs that disable apicoplast metabolism would kill the parasite without harming the human host.

3. Most protist cells cannot survive outside moist environments, but cysts have tough walls and dormant cytoplasm that allow them to persist in habitats that are unfavorable for growth. While cysts play important roles in the asexual reproduction and survival of many protists, they also allow protist parasites such as *Entamoeba histolytica* (the cause of amoebic dysentery) to spread to human hosts who consume food or water that have been contaminated with cysts. Widespread contamination can sicken thousands of people at a time.

Chapter 29

Concept Checks

Figure 29.3 Liverworts grow very close to surfaces such as soil or tree trunks. Raising their sporophytes off the surface helps to disperse spores into air currents.

Figure 29.4 Wind speed varies, so if the moss released all the spores at the same time into a weak air current, the spores would not travel very far and might have to compete with the parent plant for scarce resources. By releasing spores gradually, some spores may enter strong gusts of wind that carry them long distances, reducing competition with the parent.

Figure 29.8 Larger sporophytes are able to capture more resources for use in producing larger numbers of progeny and therefore have greater fitness than do smaller sporophytes.

Figure 29.13 The capacity to produce both wood and seeds are key features of lignophytes.

Figure 29.15 The polyester cutin found in cuticle, sporopollenin on spore walls, and lignin on water-conducting tracheids of vascular tissues are resistant to decay and thus help plants fossilize.

Figure 29.16 During the Carboniferous period (Coal Age), atmospheric oxygen levels reached historic high levels that were able to supply the large needs of giant insects, which obtain oxygen by diffusion.

Figure 29.21 Because the veins of fern leaves reflect the vascular systems of branched-stem systems, you might infer that leaves evolved from more highly branched-stem systems would be more densely veined, that is, have more veins per unit area than fern leaves. This is actually the case for leaves of seed plants.

Figure 29.22 Although some angiosperm seeds, such as those of corn and coconut, contain abundant endosperm, many angiosperm embryos consume most or all of the nutritive endosperm during their development.

Figure 29.24 Because the lacy integument of *Runcaria* does not completely enclose the megasporangium, it probably did not function to protect the megasporangium before fertilization nor as an effective seed coat after fertilization, as do the integuments of modern seed plants. However, the lacy integument of *Runcaria* might have retained the megasporangium on the parent sporophyte during the period of time when nutrients flowed from parent to developing ovule and seed. That function would prevent megasporangia from dropping off the parent plant before fertilization occurred, allow the parent plant to provide nutrients needed during embryo development, and allow seeds time to absorb and store more nutrients from the parent. Such a function would illustrate how one mutation having a positive reproductive benefit can lay the foundation for subsequent mutations that confer additional fitness. *Runcaria* illustrates a first step in the multistage evolutionary process that gave rise to modern seeds.

BioConnections

Figure 29.19 Microvilli characteristic of the animal placenta and small intestine, like the transfer cell-wall protrusions that occur in the plant placenta, vastly increase cell membrane area, thereby providing space for many transport proteins, resulting in relatively high flux of materials across the cell membrane.

Figure 29.23 The amniotic egg characteristic of many animals, like the seeds of plants, provides protection and nutrients to the developing embryo.

Feature Investigation Questions

1. The experimental goals were to determine the rate at which organic molecules produced by gametophyte photosynthesis were able to move into sporophytes and to investigate the effect of sporophyte size on the amount of organic molecules transferred from the gametophyte.

2. The investigators shaded sporophytes with black glass covers to ensure that all of the radioactive organic molecules detected in sporophytes at the end of the experiment came originally from the gametophyte.

3. The investigators measured the amount of radioactivity in gametophytes and sporophytes, and in sporophytes of different sizes. These measurements indicated the relative amounts of labeled organic compounds that were present in different plant tissues.

Test Yourself

1. c   2. d   3. d   4. e   5. b   6. a   7. c   8. e   9. c   10. b

Conceptual Questions

1. Charophycean algae, particularly the complex genera *Chara* and *Coleochaete*, share many features of structure, reproduction, and biochemistry with land plants. Examples include cell division similarities and plasmodesmata and sexual reproduction by means of flagellate sperm and eggs.

2. Bryophytes are well adapted for sexual reproduction when water is available for fertilization. Their green gametophytes efficiently transfer nutrients to developing embryos, enhancing their growth into sporophytes. Their sporophytes are able to produce many genetically diverse spores as the result of meiosis and effectively disperse these spores by means of wind.

3. Vascular tissues allow tracheophytes to effectively conduct water from roots to stems and to leaves. Waxy cuticle helps prevent loss of water by evaporation through plant surfaces. Stomata allow plants to achieve gas exchange under moist conditions and help them avoid losing excess water under arid conditions.

Chapter 30

Concept Checks

Figure 30.4 The nitrogen-fixing cyanobacteria that often occur within the coralloid roots of cycads are photosynthetic organisms that require light. If coralloid roots occurred underground, symbiotic cyanobacteria would not receive enough light to survive.

Figure 30.10 Ways in which conifer leaves are adapted to resist water loss include low surface area/volume, needle- or scale-shape, thick surface coating of waxy cuticle, and stomata that are sunken into the leaf and are therefore less exposed to drying winds.

Figure 30.12 Wide vessels are commonly present in the water transport tissues of angiosperms and much less commonly in other plants. The vessels occasionally found in nonangiosperms are thought to have evolved independently from those of angiosperms.

Figure 30.20 A large, showy perianth would not be useful to grass plants because they are wind pollinated; such a perianth would interfere with pollination in grasses. By not producing a showy perianth, grasses increase the chances of successful pollination and save resources that would otherwise be consumed during perianth development.

Figure 30.24 The flower characteristics of *Brighamia insignis* shown in this figure (white color and deep, narrow nectar tubes) are consistent with pollination by a moth (see Table 30.1).

Figure 30.26 Importantly, ears of modern *Zea mays* do not readily shatter when the fruits are mature, as do those of teosinte. This feature enables human harvesting of the fruits.

BioConnections

Figure 30.2 Modern forests are dominated by seed plants, gymnosperms and angiosperms, whereas nonseed plants dominated *Archaeopteris* forests.

Figure 30.8 The wind-dispersed seeds of the gymnosperm pine resemble the wind-dispersed seeds of the flowering plant maple in bearing winglike structures that enhance transport in air.

Feature Investigation Questions

1. The investigators obtained many samples from around the world because they wanted to increase their chances of finding as many species as possible.

2. The researchers grew plants in a greenhouse under consistent environmental conditions because they wanted to reduce the possible effect of environmental variation on the ratio of cannabinoids produced.

3. Although cannabinoids are produced in glandular hairs that cover the plant surface, these compounds are most abundant on leaves near the flowers. Collecting such leaves reduces the chances that compounds might be missed by the analysis.

Test Yourself

1. d   2. a   3. e   4. e   5. b   6. d   7. e   8. c   9. d   10. e

Conceptual Questions

1. Consult Figure 30.15 to see how plant biologists think stamens and pistils might have evolved from leaves that bore sporangia. Then consider how green leaves surrounding stamens and pistils might have been transformed into petals, sepals, or tepals.

2. Apple, strawberry, and cherry plants coevolved with animals that use the fleshy, sweet portion of the fruits as food and excrete the seeds, thereby dispersing them. Humans have sensory systems similar to those of the target animals and likewise are attracted by the same colors, odors, and tastes.

3. A sunflower is not a single flower, but rather is an inflorescence, a group of flowers.

Chapter 31

Concept Checks

Figure 31.4 Fungal hyphae growing into a substrate having a much higher solute concentration will tend to lose cell water to the substrate, a process that could inhibit fungal growth. This process explains how salting or drying foods helps to protect them from fungal degradation and thus are common preservation techniques.

Figure 31.6 You might filter the air entering the patient's room and limit the entry of visitors and materials that could introduce fungal spores from the outside environment.

Figure 31.27 Modern AM (arbuscular mycorrhizal fungi), also known as Glomeromycota, do not occur separately from plant hosts, as far as is known.

Figure 31.28 Ectomycorrhizal fungi provide their plant partners with water and minerals absorbed from a much larger area of soil than plant roots can exploit on their own.

BioConnections

Figure 31.7 The *Saccharomyces cerevisiae* genome is only 12 million base pairs in size, relatively small for a eukaryote.

Figure 31.10 The amanitin toxin, by interfering with the function of RNA polymerase II, inhibits transcription in eukaryotic cells.

Feature Investigation Questions

1. Plants growing on soils up to 65°C would be expected to have fungal endophytes that aid in heat stress tolerance.

2. The investigators cured some of their *Curvularia protuberata* cultures of an associated virus; then they compared the survival of plants infected with fungal endophytes that had virus versus endophytes lacking virus under conditions of heat stress. Only plants having fungal endophytes that possessed the virus were able to survive growth on soils of high temperature.

3. The fungus *C. protuberata* might be used to confer heat stress tolerance to crop plants, as the investigators demonstrated in tomato.

Test Yourself

1. c   2. b   3. e   4. b   5. a   6. d   7. e   8. b   9. e   10. a

Conceptual Questions

1. Fungi are like animals in being heterotrophic, having absorptive nutrition, and storing surplus organic compounds in their cells as glycogen. Fungi are like plants in having rigid cell walls and reproducing by means of walled spores that are dispersed by wind, water, or animals.

2. Toxic or hallucinogenic compounds likely help to protect the fungi from organisms that would consume them.

3. Some fungi partner with algae or cyanobacteria to form lichens. Some fungi associate with plant roots to form mycorrhizae. Some fungi grow as endophytes within the bodies of plants. In all cases, the heterotrophic fungi receive photosynthetic products from the autotrophic partner.

Chapter 32

Concept Checks

Figure 32.4 Simple choanoflagellates are single-celled organisms. Only later, when such organisms became colonial and groups of cells acquired specialized functions, as in sponges, can we consider them early animals.

Figure 32.8 The coelom functions as a hydrostatic skeleton, which aids in movement. This feature permitted increased burrowing activity and contributed to the development of a profusion of wormlike body shapes.

Figure 32.12 The main members of the Ecdysozoa are the arthropods (insects, spiders, and crustaceans) and the nematodes.

BioConnections

Figure 32.6 A shared derived character.

Figure 32.11 Yellow

Feature Investigation Questions

1. The researchers sequenced the complete gene that encodes small subunit rRNA from a variety of representative taxa of animals to determine their phylogenetic relationships, particularly the relationships of arthropods to other animal taxa.

2. The results indicated a monophyletic clade containing arthropods and nematodes, plus several other smaller phyla. This clade was called the Ecdysozoa. The results of this study indicated that nematodes were more closely related to the arthropods than previously believed.

3. The fruit fly, *Drosophila melanogaster*, and the nematode, *Caenorhabditis elegans*, have been widely studied to understand early development. Under the traditional phylogeny, these two species were not considered to be closely related, so similarities in development were assumed to have arisen early in animal evolution. With the closer relationship indicated by this study, these similarities may have evolved after the divergence of the Ecdysozoan clade. This puts into question the applicability of studies of these organisms to the understanding of human biology.

Test Yourself

1. b   2. c   3. e   4. c   5. c   6. d   7. d   8. d   9. b   10. e

Conceptual Questions

1. (1) Absence or existence of different tissue types. (2) Type of body symmetry. (3) Patterns of embryonic development.

2. The evolution of a coelom cushioned the internal organs in fluid, preventing injury from external forces. In addition, the coelom enabled the internal organs to grow and move independently of the outer body wall. Finally, in some invertebrates, the coelom acts as a hydrostatic skeleton that supports the body and permits movement.

3. Polyphyletic.

Chapter 33

Concept Checks

Figure 33.2 Sponges aren't eaten by other organisms because they produce toxic chemicals and contain needle-like silica spicules that are hard to digest.

Figure 33.4 The dominant life stages are jellyfish: medusa; sea anemone: polyp; Portuguese man-of-war: polyp (in a large floating colony).

Figure 33.5 Cnidocytes are not reused. New ones form to replace the old used ones.

Figure 33.7 Having no specialized respiratory or circulatory system, flatworms obtain oxygen by diffusion. A flattened shape ensures no cells are too far from the body surface.

Figure 33.11 (1) A ciliary feeding device, and (2) a respiratory device are the two main functions of the lophophore.

Figure 33.12 Technically, most mollusks pump hemolymph into vessels and then into tissues. The hemolymph collects in open, fluid-filled cavities called sinuses, which flow into the gills and then back to the heart. This is known as an open circulatory system. Only closed circulatory systems pump blood, as occurs in the cephalopods.

Figure 33.17 Some advantages of segmentation are organ duplication, minimization of body distortion during movement, and specialization of some segments.

Figure 33.19 An annelid is segmented and possesses a true coelom, whereas a nematode is unsegmented and has a pseudocoelom. In addition, nematodes molt, but annelids do not.

Figure 33.20 Other parasitic nematodes in humans are roundworms, *Ascaris lumbricoides*; hookworms, *Necator americanus*; and pinworms, *Enterobius vermicularis*.

Figure 33.25 All arachnids have a body consisting of two tagmata: a cephalothorax and an abdomen. Insects have three tagmata: a head, thorax, and abdomen.

Figure 33.27 Two key insect adaptations are the development of wings and an exoskeleton that reduced water loss and aided in the colonization of land.

Figure 33.33 In embryonic development, deuterostomes have radial cleavage, indeterminate cleavage, and the blastopore becomes the anus. (In protostomes, cleavage is spiral and determinate, and the blastopore becomes the mouth.)

Figure 33.34 Two unique features of an echinoderm are an internal skeleton of calcified plates and a water vascular system.

BioConnections

Figure 33.14 Mollusks arose in the Cambrian period, 543–490 mya. Three hundred million years later ammonites flourished, yet none are alive today.

Figure 33.21 Because most species can excrete urine that is isoosmotic or hyperosmotic to the body fluids.

Figure 33.27 Some insects, such as flies, have chemoreceptors on their feet, whereas others, such as moths, smell through their antennae.

Figure 33.30 These organs, called statocysts, are located at the base of the antennules.

Feature Investigation Questions

1. The researchers tested the hypothesis that an octopus can learn by observing the behavior of another octopus.

2. The results indicated that the observer learned by watching the training of the other octopus. The observer was much more likely to choose the same color ball that the demonstrator was trained to attack. These results seem to support the hypothesis that octopuses can learn by observing the behavior of others.

3. The untrained octopuses had no prior exposure to the demonstrators. The results indicated that these octopuses were as likely to attack the white ball as the red ball. No preference for either color was indicated. The untrained octopuses acted as a control. This is an important factor to ensure the results from the trials using observers indicate response to learning and not an existing preference for a certain color.

Test Yourself

1. b   2. d   3. d   4. d   5. b   6. c   7. b   8. a   9. c   10. a

Conceptual Questions

1. The five main feeding methods used by animals are (1) suspension feeding, (2) decomposition, (3) herbivory, (4) predation, and (5) parasitism. Suspension feeding is usually used to filter out food particles from the water column. A great many phyla, including sponges, rotifers, lophophorates, some mollusks and echinoderms and tunicates, are filter feeders. Decomposers usually feed on dead material such as animal carcasses or dead leaves. For example, many fly and beetle larvae feed on dead animals, and earthworms consume dead leaves from the surface of the Earth. Earthworms and crabs also sift through soil or mud, eating the substrate and digesting the soil-dwelling bacteria, protists, and dead organic material. Herbivores eat plants or algae and are especially common in the arthropoda. Adult moths and butterflies also consume nectar. Snails are also common plant feeders. Predators feed on other animals, killing their prey, and may be active hunters or sit-and-wait predators. Many scorpions and spiders actively pursue their prey, whereas web-spinning spiders ambush their prey using webs. Parasites also feed on other animals but do not normally kill their hosts. Endoparasites, which includes flukes, tapeworms, and nematodes, live inside their hosts. Ectoparasites (ticks and lice) live on the outside of their hosts.

2. Gametes dry out on land, and internal fertilization prevents this from happening. Also, water facilitates movement of gametes, reducing the need for internal fertilization.

3. Complete metamorphosis has four stages: egg, larva, pupa, and adult. The larval stage is often spent in an entirely different habitat from that of the adult, and larval and adult forms utilize different food sources. Incomplete metamorphosis has only three stages: egg, nymph, and adult. Young insects, called nymphs, look like miniature adults when they hatch from their eggs.

Chapter 34
Concept Checks

Figure 34.1 Vertebrates (but not invertebrates) usually possess a (1) notochord; (2) dorsal hollow nerve chord; (3) pharyngeal slits; (4) postanal tail, exhibited by all chordates; (5) vertebral column; (6) cranium; (7) endoskeleton of cartilage or bone; (8) neural crest; and (9) a diversity of internal organs.

Figure 34.7 Ray-finned fishes (but not sharks) have a (1) bony skeleton; (2) mucus-covered skin; (3) swim bladder; and (4) operculum covering the gills.

Figure 34.9 Both lungfishes and coelocanths are Sarcopterygians, having lobe fins.

Figure 34.11 The advantages to animals that moved onto land included an oxygen-rich environment and a bonanza of food in the form of terrestrial plants and the insects that fed on them.

Figure 34.14 No. Caecilians and some salamanders give birth to live young.

Figure 34.15 Besides the amniotic egg, other critical innovations in amniotes are thoracic breathing; internal fertilization; a thicker, less permeable skin; and more efficient kidneys.

Figure 34.17 Snakes evolved from tetrapod ancestors but subsequently lost their limbs. Some species have tiny vestigial limbs.

Figure 34.21 Adaptations in birds to reduce body weight for flight include a lightweight skull; reduction of organ size; and a reduction of organs outside of breeding season. Also female birds have one ovary and relatively few eggs, and no urinary bladder.

Figure 34.29 Defining features of primates are grasping hands; eyes situated on the front of the head to facilitate binocular vision; a large brain; and digits with flat nails instead of claws.

BioConnections

Figure 34.5 Collagen-secreting cells. Cartilage is not mineralized and is softer and more flexible than bone.

Figure 34.13 Yes, the blood vessels to the lungs close and those to skin open wider. The opposite occurs when on land and frogs breath air.

Figure 34.18 Both classes have four-chambered hearts and care for their young.

Figure 34.21 Air is constantly being moved across the lungs, both in inhalation and exhalation. Also, birds employ a cross-current blood supply to the lungs.

Figure 34.27 None. The bloodstreams of fetus and mother are brought into close contact in the placenta, but they do not mix.

Feature Investigation Questions

1. The researchers were interested in determining the method in which *Hox* genes controlled limb development.

2. The researchers bred mice that were homozygous for certain mutations in specific *Hox* genes. This allowed the researchers to determine the function of individual genes.

3. The researchers found that homozygous mutants would develop limbs of shorter lengths compared to the wild-type mice. The reduced length was due to the lack of development of particular bones in the limb, specifically, the radius, ulna, and some carpels. These results indicated that simple mutations in a few genes could lead to dramatic changes in limb development.

Test Yourself

1. c   2. d   3. a   4. d   5. d   6. c   7. c   8. a   9. c   10. d

Conceptual Questions

1. Both taxa have external limbs that move when the attached muscles contract or relax. The difference is that arthropods have external skeletons with the muscles attached internally, whereas vertebrates have internal skeletons with the muscles attached externally.

2. Endothermy (warm-bloodedness) probably evolved independently in both birds and mammals. If the common ancestor of reptiles and birds were endothermic, the chances are that all reptiles would be endothermic.

3. Possibly. Both birds and reptiles lay amniotic eggs and possess scales, though these only cover the legs in birds. Birds and crocodilians also share a four-chambered heart. Finally, birds share many skeletal similarities with certain dinosaurs.

Chapter 35

Concept Checks

Figure 35.6 As in the case of shoots, the capacity to divide the root into two equal pieces by means of a line drawn from the circular edges through the center would indicate that a root has superficial radial symmetry. In order to determine that an organ has radial symmetry at the cellular level, you would have to compare the microscopic views of randomly chosen, wedge-shaped pieces of cross slices. If the structure of the wedges is similar, the organ has radial symmetry at the microscopic level.

Figure 35.8 Locating stomata on the darker and cooler lower leaf surface helps reduce water loss from the leaf.

Figure 35.12 A twig having five sets of bud scale scars is likely to be approximately 6 years old.

Figure 35.17 Cactus stems are green and photosynthetic, playing the role served by the leaves of most plants.

Figure 35.21 A woody stem builds up a thicker layer of wood than inner bark in part because older tracheids and vessel element walls are not lost during shedding of bark, which is the case for secondary phloem. In addition, plants typically produce a greater volume of xylem than phloem tissue per year, in part because vessel elements are relatively wide. A large volume of water-conducting tissue helps plants maintain a large amount of internal water.

Figure 35.25 Lateral roots are produced from internal meristematic tissue because roots do not produce axillary buds like those from which shoot branches develop. Internal production of branch roots helps to prevent them from shearing off as the root tip grows through abrasive soil.

BioConnections

Figure 35.5 Apical-basal polarity of the plant body resembles anterior-posterior polarity in the animal body.

Figure 35.9 Plant cells often possess a large vacuole, whereas animal cell vacuoles are relatively small.

Figure 35.11 There is no difference in microtubule structure among eukaryotes.

Feature Investigation Questions

1. The advantages of using natural plants include the opportunity to avoid influencing plants with unnatural environmental factors, such as artificial light, and the exposure of all experimental plants to similar growth conditions. In addition, the investigators studied the leaves of some large trees, which would be hard to accommodate in a greenhouse.

2. Pinnately veined leaves were splinted to prevent their breaking, since they were cut at the single main vein, which has both support and conducting functions.

3. Sack and associates measured leaf water conduction at two or more places on each leaf because the effect of cutting a vein might have affected some portions of leaves more than others.

Test Yourself

1. d   2. c   3. b   4. a   5. c   6. a   7. d   8. e   9. b   10. d

Conceptual Questions

1. If overall plant architecture were bilaterally symmetrical, plants would be shaped like higher animals, with a distinct front (ventral surface) and back (dorsal surface). By comparison with radially symmetrical organisms, bilaterally symmetrical plants would have reduced ability to deploy branches and leaves in a way that would fill available lighted space and would thus be unable to take optimal photosynthetic advantage of their habitats.

2. If leaves were generally radially symmetrical (shaped like spheres or cylinders), leaves would not have maximal ability to absorb sunlight, and they would not be able to optimally disperse excess heat from their surfaces.

3. Although tall herbaceous plants exist (palms and bamboo are examples), the additional support and water-conducting capacity that are provided by secondary xylem allow woody plants to grow tall.

Chapter 36

Concept Checks

Figure 36.4 Auxin efflux carriers could be located on the upper sides of root cells, thereby allowing auxin to move upward in roots.

Figure 36.6 Once a callus has been established from a single plant having desirable characteristics using plant tissue culture, the callus can be divided into many small calluses. A grower could transfer these to separate containers having the appropriate hormone mixtures to induce root and shoot growth, then transplant the young plant clones to soil. This would allow the grower to produce many identical plants.

Figure 36.9 The triple response of dicot seedlings to internally produced ethylene allows them to protect the delicate apical meristem from damage as the seedling emerges through the soil.

Figure 36.10 The active conformation of phytochrome absorbs far-red light. Such absorption causes the active conformation of phytochrome to change to the inactive conformation and to move out of the nucleus and into the cytosol.

Figure 36.11 The inactive conformation of phytochrome would absorb the red portion of sunlight, thereby converting phytochrome into the active conformation.

Figure 36.12 Exposing plants to brief periods of darkness during the daytime will have no effect on flowering because flowering is determined by night length.

Figure 36.14 Yes, just as shoots exhibit negative gravitropism in upward growth, roots are capable of using negative phototropism to grow downward, because light decreases with depth in the soil.

Figure 36.16 In some plants, aerenchyma development is genetically determined and occurs even in the absence of flooding. In other cases, aerenchyma develops only under flooding conditions as a result of controlled cell death.

Figure 36.17 Predators are more likely to be able to find their prey if the latter are concentrated and exposed while feeding on plants. Plants benefit when predation removes herbivores, a process that lessens damage to plants.

Figure 36.19 Similar suites of protective plant hormones, such as jasmonic acid, are used in both types of defenses.

BioConnections

Figure 36.3 The defense hormone/plasma membrane receptor is the plant signaling system most similar to the general diagram shown in Figure 9.4.

Figure 36.18 The lipopolysaccharide envelope characteristic of Gram-negative bacteria is a feature by which plants recognize pathogens.

Feature Investigation Questions

1. The experimental procedure that Briggs would use to test the hypothesis that light destroys auxin would follow a similar protocol as his other experiment. The figure on the next page shows this experimental protocol.

2. Hypothetically, auxin enhances the rate at which cell membrane proton pumps acidify the plant cell wall, thereby allowing cells to extend. Although the evidence for acid effects on cell-wall extension is strong, the molecular basis of possible auxin effects on proton pumps is not as yet clear.

3. A small number of seedling tips could display atypical responses for a variety of reasons. The investigators actually performed the experiment with many replicate seedling tips (coleoptiles), in order to gain confidence that the responses are general.

Test Yourself

1. c   2. c   3. a   4. e   5. d   6. d   7. c   8. d   9. d   10. d

Conceptual Questions

1. Behavior is defined as the responses of living things to a stimulus. Therefore, because plants display many kinds of responses to diverse stimuli, they display behavior.

2. Many kinds of disease-causing bacteria and fungi occur in nature, and these organisms evolve very quickly, producing diverse elicitors. Thus, plants must maintain a stock of resistance genes, each having many alleles.

3. Talking implies a conversation with "listeners" who detect a message and respond to it. Thus, plants that exude volatile compounds that attract enemies of herbivores could be interpreted as "talking" to those enemies. The message is "Hey, you guys, there's food for you over here." In addition, research has revealed that some plants near those under attack respond to volatile compounds by building up defenses. "Talking" to other plants does not enhance the "talker's" fitness. But the ability to "listen" enhances the "listener's" fitness, because it can take preemptive actions to prevent attack.

(b) Briggs experiment 1

HYPOTHESIS Light destroys auxin on lit side of shoot tips, causing unequal auxin distribution. Unlit side should grow more than lit side.

STARTING MATERIALS Corn seedlings.

Experimental level   Conceptual level

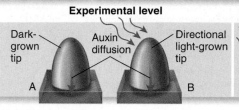

1   Collect auxin into agar blocks from:
    A   dark-grown tips
    B   tips grown with directional light

Dark-grown tip   Auxin diffusion   Directional light-grown tip

A   B

If light destroys auxin on one side, less auxin will enter the block.

2   Place agar blocks on right side of decapitated shoots.

Agar block   Dark-grown   Shoot   Light-grown

A   B

If the block on the right side has less auxin, it will cause less bending.

3   **THE DATA**

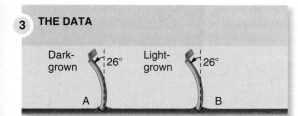

Dark-grown   26°   Light-grown   26°

A   B

4   **CONCLUSION**

Similar bending demonstrates that light did not destroy auxin in the directionally lit shoot tip. If it had, less auxin would have been present in the agar block in B, and the degree of bending would have been less. The hypothesis described under conceptual level (above) is incorrect.

Chapter 37

Concept Checks

Figure 37.5 Plastids that occur in a cluster near the nucleus would have more rubisco than plastids at the periphery.

Figure 37.6 Chlorosis is not always a sign of iron deficiency; it can be a deficiency symptom for several mineral nutrients, including zinc in corn.

Figure 37.10 Mineral leaching occurs more readily from sandy soils than from clay soils.

Figure 37.12 Soil crusts containing nitrogen-fixing cyanobacteria increase soil fertility, fostering the growth of larger plants that stabilize soils against erosion and provide forage for animals.

Figure 37.13 Oxygen, which makes up 21% of Earth's present atmosphere, can bind to the active site of nitrogenase, thereby inactivating it.

BioConnections

Figure 37.7 Land whose topsoil has been damaged will likely not function normally to support a wild community or agriculture; rehabilitation might be accomplished by restoring topsoil and planting vegetation that holds the soils in place and increases its fertility.

Figure 37.20 Both the tapeworm and the dodder obtain organic food from a host, an animal or plant, respectively.

Feature Investigation Questions

1. During this period of time, the amount of phosphorus in plant tissues had significantly decreased, but plant growth had not yet been affected. Thus, a monitoring system based on gene expression changes that occur during this time would allow farmers time to apply fertilizer in order to prevent crop losses resulting from nutrient deficiency.

2. *SDQ1* expression is induced by phosphorus deficiency. This gene fosters replacement of plastid phospholipids with sulfur-containing lipids, thereby reducing the plant's phosphorus requirement.

3. They used genetic engineering techniques to place a reporter gene under the control of the *SQD1* promoter, so that when *SQD1* was expressed, the reporter gene was expressed also. After growing plants in nutrient solutions containing various levels of phosphorus, they removed sample leaves and treated them with a compound that turns blue when the reporter gene is expressed. When

they saw blue leaves, the investigators could infer (1) that the plants from which those leaves had been taken were beginning to experience phosphorus deficiency, and (2) that application of fertilizer at this point could prevent damage to the plants.

Test Yourself

1. e   2. a   3. c   4. b   5. e   6. c   7. d   8. d   9. a   10. b

Conceptual Questions

1. Agricultural experts are concerned that adding excess fertilizer to crop fields increases the costs of crop production. Ecologists are concerned that excess fertilizers will wash from crop fields into natural waters and cause harmful overgrowths of cyanobacteria, algae, and aquatic plants. Methods for closely monitoring crop nutrient needs so that only the appropriate amount of fertilizer is applied would help to allay both groups' concerns.

2. Use Figure 37.10 as a reference. A first arrow could be drawn from a root to rhizobia in the soil, and the arrow labeled "flavonoids." A second arrow could be drawn from rhizobia to roots and labeled "Nod factors." A third arrow from rhizobia to roots could be labeled "infection proteins." A fourth arrow from roots to rhizobia could be labeled "nodulins" and the resulting nodule environmental conditions, which influence the formation of bacteroids. A fifth arrow could represent the flow of fixed nitrogen from bacteroids to plant. A sixth arrow could represent the flow of organic compounds from plant to bacteroids.

Chapter 38

Concept Checks

Figure 38.5 When placed in pure water, a turgid cell having a water potential of 1.0 will lose water, because 1 is greater than 0. When placed in pure water, a plasmolyzed cell having a water potential of –1.0 MPa will gain water. When placed in pure water, a flaccid cell having a water potential of –0.5 MPa will gain water. This is because water moves from a region of higher water potential to a region of lower water potential, and 0 is greater than –0.5.

Figure 38.11 You would likely see stained rings or helical ribbons extending up the insides of the long walls of extensible tracheids. You would not see staining at the ends of tracheids, where they connect to form cell files.

Figure 38.12 The large perforations in vessel element end walls allow an air bubble to extend from one element to another, thereby clogging vessels and preventing water flow through them. In contrast, the much smaller pores in the end walls of tracheids do not allow water to flow as efficiently as it does through vessels, but these smaller pores also retard the movement of air bubbles. As a result, air bubbles are confined to a single tracheid where they do little harm.

Figure 38.13 Root pressure can help to reverse embolism, thereby aiding water flow through xylem.

Figure 38.16 The evaporation of water has a powerful cooling effect because it disperses heat so effectively. Water has the highest heat of vaporization of any known liquid.

Figure 38.17 You could model a stomatal guard cell with an elongate balloon by partially inflating it, then attaching thick tape along one side to represent thickened inner walls and circles of string or thin tape to represent radial cellulose, then adding more air to the balloon. The balloon should curve as it expands, just as a guard cell does when the stomatal pore opens. Two such balloons could be used to model both guard cells and the stomatal pore.

Figure 38.19 In its desert habitat, times of drought and contrasting availability of water sufficient to support the development and photosynthetic function of leaves do not occur at predictable times, as is the case for temperate forests. For this reason, ocotillo leaf abscission is not amenable to the evolution of genetic mechanisms that allow leaf drop to be precisely timed in anticipation of the onset of drought.

Figure 38.25 You could note the relatively few genes that are plotted along the middle left side of the triangle, then try to localize the encoded proteins within the tissues of very young stem tissue, using microscopy.

BioConnections

Figure 38.8 Tight junctions of intestinal epithelium and Casparian strips of endodermal cells of plant roots both incorporate materials that form a tight seal, preventing movement of materials from one location to another.

Figure 38.21 Stomatal guard cell and phloem companion cell development both begin with an unequal cell division.

Feature Investigation Questions

1. This design allowed investigators to compensate for variation among plants, which might have influenced the results had they used separate plants for experiments and controls.

2. Transpiration! Water evaporating from the surfaces of leaves exerted a tension on the water column of the xylem, pulling sap and water through it.

3. The effects of ions on sap flow rates did not directly depend on a biological process, so xylem sap of the same ionic concentration moved through dead plants at the same rate as in living plants.

Test Yourself

1. c   2. b   3. e   4. d   5. a   6. e   7. d   8. e   9. a   10. c

Conceptual Questions

1. In the case of plant fertilizers, more is not better, because the ion concentration of overfertilized soil may become so high as to draw water from plant cells. In this case, the cells would be bathed in a hypertonic solution and would likely lose water to the solution. If plant cells lose too much water, they will die.

2. When the natural vegetation is removed, transpiration stops, so water is not transported from the ground to the atmosphere, where it may be an important contributor to local rainfall. Extensive removal of plants actually changes local climates in ways that reduce agricultural productivity and human survival.

3. You cannot assume that an ocotillo plant lacking leaves is dead, because this plant responds to drought by shedding its leaves, and living plants can produce new leaves when the drought stress is relieved. However, if the ocotillo plants do not produce new leaves after normal rainstorms, you might suspect that they have died.

Chapter 39

Concept Checks

Figure 39.2 Because gametophytes are haploid, they lack the potential for allele variation at each gene locus that is present in diploid sporophytes. Hence, gametophytes are more vulnerable to environmental stresses. By living within the diploid tissues of flowers, flowering plant gametophytes are protected to some extent, and the plant does not lose its gamete-producing life cycle stage.

Figure 39.3 Some flowers lack some of the major flower parts.

Figure 39.4 By clustering its stamens around the pistil, the hibiscus flower increases the chance that a pollinator will both pick up pollen and deliver pollen from another hibiscus flower on the same trip.

Figure 39.7 The absence of showy petals often correlates with wind pollination, because large petals would interfere with the shedding of pollen in the wind.

Figure 39.10 The rim flowers of *Gerbera* inflorescences have bilateral symmetry, conferred by expression of a *CYCLOIDEA*-like gene. Rim flowers also possess showy petals that attract pollinators, but lack pollen-producing stamens. By contrast, central flowers display radial symmetry, lack showy petals, and possess pollen-producing stamens.

Figure 39.12 The maximum number of cells in a mature male gametophyte of a flowering plant is three: a tube cell and two sperm cells.

Figure 39.13 Female gametophytes are not photosynthetic and cannot produce their own food. Enclosed within ovules, female gametophytes lack direct access to the outside environment. Carpels contain veins of vascular tissue that bring nutrients from sporophytic tissue to ovules.

Figure 39.16 An embryo in which the TOPLESS genes were nonfunctional would have two roots and no shoots.

Figure 39.17 During their maturation, the cotyledons of eudicot seeds absorb the nutrients originally present in endosperm.

BioConnections

Figure 39. 15 The plant pollen tube is analogous in function to a human penis in that both structures accomplish internal fertilization. The plant pollen tube grows long enough to deposit sperm at the micropyle within the body of the female gametophyte, much as an animal penis deposits sperm within the female's body. In both cases, sperm are more likely to survive and accomplish fertilization than if they were deposited outside the female body.

Figure 39.21 The plant is similar to the animal *Obelia* because both can reproduce asexually by means of multicellular structures that when released can grow into an adult.

Feature Investigation Questions

1. The large flowers of this lily enabled investigators to more easily mark petals and record the positions of marks over time.

2. Time-lapse video reduced the amount of time investigators would have to spend recording changes in the positions of petal marks.

3. Results obtained by using mathematical models can be compared with actual measurements to assess the accuracy of the models. An accurate mathematical model indicates a relatively full understanding of the physical processes involved. If models are sufficiently accurate, they can be utilized in other situations.

Test Yourself

1. a   2. b   3. d   4. b   5. d   6. e   7. b   8. c   9. d   10. c

Conceptual Questions

1. Pollen grains are vulnerable to mechanical damage and microbial attack during the journey through the air from the anthers of a flower to a stigma. Sporopollenin is an extremely tough polymer that helps to protect pollen cells from these dangers. The function of the beautiful sculptured patterns of sporopollenin on pollen surfaces is unclear.

2. The embryos within seeds are vulnerable to mechanical damage and microbial attack after they are dispersed. Seed coats protect embryos from these dangers and also help to prevent seeds from germinating until conditions are favorable for seedling survival and growth.

3. Flower diversity is an evolutionary response to diverse pollination circumstances. For example, plants such as oak and corn that are wind-pollinated produce flowers having a poorly developed perianth. If such wind-pollinated flowers had large, showy perianths, they would get in the way of pollen dispersal or acquisition. On the other hand, flowers that are pollinated by animals often have diverse shapes and attractive petals of differing colors or fragrances that have coevolved with different types of animal pollinators.

Chapter 40

Concept Checks

Figure 40.2 Locomotion is the movement of an animal's body from one place to another. This is achieved by the actions of skeletal muscle. However, smooth muscle contraction promotes movement of internal structures, like those of the digestive system, and contraction of cardiac muscle causes movement (beating) of the heart.

Figure 40.6 No. The brain, for example, does not contain muscle tissue (although the blood vessels supplying the brain do contain smooth muscle).

Figure 40.7 Blood, including plasma and blood cells, would leak out of the blood vessel into the interstitial space. The fluid level of the bloodstream would decrease, and that of the interstitial space near the site of the injury would increase. Eventually the blood that entered the interstitial space would be degraded by enzymes, resulting in the characteristic skin appearance of a bruise. If the injury were very severe, the fluid level in the blood could decrease to a point where the various tissues and organs of the body would not receive sufficient nutrients and oxygen to function normally.

Figure 40.8 A decrease in intracellular fluid volume, like that shown in the cell in this figure, would result in an increase in intracellular solute concentration (likewise, an increase in intracellular fluid volume would decrease intracellular solute concentrations). This may have drastic consequences on cell function. For example, some solutes, like Ca^{2+} and certain other ions, are toxic to cells at high concentrations.

Figure 40.10 Surface area is important to any living organism that needs to exchange materials with the environment. A good example of a high surface area/volume ratio is that of most tree leaves. This makes leaves ideally suited for such processes as light absorption (required for photosynthesis; see Chapter 8) and the exchange of gases and water with the environment.

Figure 40.12 No, not necessarily. Body temperature, for example, is maintained at different set points in birds and mammals. Other vertebrates and most invertebrates do not have temperature set points; their body temperature simply conforms close to that of the environment. As another example, a giraffe has a set point for blood pressure that is higher than that of a human being, because a giraffe's circulatory system must generate enough pressure to pump blood up its long neck to its brain.

Figure 40.15 In nature, an animal such as a horse would have the same type of responses shown here if threatened by a predator. Upon sensing the presence of the predator, the horse's respiratory and circulatory systems would begin increasing their activities in preparation for the possibility that the horse might have to flee or defend itself. This would occur even before the horse began to flee.

BioConnections

Figure 40.6 Note that both the stomach and the intestine depicted in Figures 40.6 and 45.9 contain layers of muscle wrapped around the lumen. Although you will learn later that the stomach and intestine have many different functions, this similarity in anatomy suggests that both of these organs may perform the similar activity of mechanically breaking apart chunks of food, and propelling the contents from one region to another.

Feature Investigation Questions

1. Pavlov studied feedforward regulation of saliva production that occurs in hungry dogs even before they receive food. He hypothesized that the feedforward response could be conditioned to other, nonrelevant stimuli such as sounds, as long as the sounds were presented simultaneously with food.

2. Pavlov remained outside the room where the dog was housed when the conditioning stimulus—a metronome—was started. In addition, the room was carefully sealed to prevent any other stimuli, including smells, sights, and sounds, from interfering with the conditioning response.

3. He measured the amount of saliva secreted by salivary glands in the dog's mouth by collecting the saliva through a tube and funnel, and then recording the number of drops. He discovered that once a dog had become conditioned to hearing the sound of the metronome whenever presented with food, the sound itself was sufficient to stimulate the feedforward response of salivation. This experiment revealed that feedforward processes could be modulated by experience and learning.

Test Yourself

1. d   2. c   3. d   4. b   5. c   6. c   7. d   8. b   9. d   10. e

Conceptual Questions

1. Structure and function are related in that the function of a given organ, for example, depends in part on the organ's size, shape, and cellular and tissue arrangement. Clues about a physical structure's function can often be obtained by examining the structure's form. For example, the extensive surface area of a moth's antennae suggests that the antennae are important in detecting the presence of airborne chemicals. Likewise, any structure that contains a large surface area for its volume is likely involved in some aspect of signal detection,

cell-cell communication, or transport of materials within the animal or between the animal and the environment. Surface area increases by a power of 2, and volume increases by a power of 3 as an object enlarges; this means that in order to greatly increase surface area of a structure such as an antenna, without occupying enormous volumes, specializations must be present (such as folds) to package the structure in a small space.

2. Homeostasis is the ability of animals to maintain a stable internal environment by adjusting physiological processes, despite changes in the external environment. Examples include maintenance of salt and water balance, pH of body fluids, and body temperature. Some animals conform to their external environment to achieve homeostasis, but others regulate their internal environment themselves.

3. Maintaining homeostasis requires continual supplies of energy. Animals consume food, and the energy from that food helps sustain activities that maintain variables such as body temperature and pH, and synthesis of complex molecules. Without this energy, it would be difficult or impossible for animals to maintain many important biological processes within a narrow range despite changes in the environment.

Chapter 41
Concept Checks

Figure 41.4 Many reflexes, such as the knee-jerk reflex, cannot be prevented once started. Others, however, can be controlled to an extent. Open your eyes widely and gently touch your eyelashes. A reflex that protects your eye will tend to make you close your eyelid. However, you can overcome this reflex with a bit of difficulty if you need to, for example, when you are putting in contact lenses.

Figure 41.5 The squid axon is not coated in myelin sheaths. This is another feature of the squid giant axon that makes it a convenient model for conducting in vitro experiments such as the one depicted in this figure.

Figure 41.7 Yes, the flow of K^+ down its chemical gradient does create an electrical gradient because K^+ is electrically charged. The net flow of K^+ will stop when the chemical gradient balances the electrical gradient. This occurs at the equilibrium potential.

Figure 41.10 When the K^+ channels open (at 1 msec), the Na^+ channels would still be opened, so the part of the curve that slopes downward would not occur as rapidly, and perhaps the cell would not be able to restore its resting potential.

Figure 41.12 The action potential can move faster down an axon. This is especially important for long axons, such as those that carry signals from the spinal cord to distant muscles.

Figure 41.14 In the absence of such enzymes, neurotransmitters would remain in the synapse for too long, and the postsynaptic cell could become overstimulated. In addition, the ability of the postsynaptic cell to respond to multiple, discrete inputs from the presynaptic cell would be compromised.

BioConnections

Figure 41.1 This is an example of a feedforward response, most famously demonstrated by the conditioning experiments of Ivan Pavlov. In this case, the peripheral and central nervous systems interact to prepare the hyena for feeding.

Figure 41.8 Water molecules move through membrane channels called aquaporins.

Feature Investigation Questions

1. Loewi was aware that electrical stimulation of the vagus nerve associated with heart muscle would slow down the rate of heart contractions in a frog. Also, he knew that electrical stimulation of other nerves associated with the frog heart produced opposite results. If the effects of the different nerves on heart muscle were mediated directly by electrical activity only, the heart muscle cells would have no way to distinguish between stimulatory and inhibitory signals. Loewi hypothesized that nerves released chemicals onto heart muscle cells and that it was these different chemicals that produced the varied effects on the heart.

2. Loewi placed two hearts in separate chambers, one heart with its vagus nerve intact and the other with its vagus nerve removed. He electrically stimulated the vagus nerve of the first heart, then removed some of the saline solution surrounding the heart and transferred it to the second heart. He then observed whether or not the second heart responded as if its vagus nerve had been intact and had been stimulated.

3. When fluid from the saline solution around the stimulated heart was added to the saline solution of the second, unstimulated heart, the rate of contraction in the second heart was decreased just as if its own vagus nerve had been intact

and was stimulated. This suggested that chemicals were released into the saline solution of the first heart following the electrical stimulation of its vagus nerve, and that it was these chemicals that caused the cardiac muscle to slow its rate of contraction. The results did support Loewi's hypothesis.

Test Yourself

1. c   2. d   3. e   4. e   5. b   6. d   7. b   8. e   9. a   10. e

Conceptual Questions

1. In a graded potential, a weak stimulus causes a small change in the membrane potential, whereas a strong stimulus produces a greater change. Graded potentials occur along the dendrites and cell body. If a graded potential reaches the threshold potential at the axon hillock, an action potential results. This is a change in the membrane potential that is of a constant value and is propagated from the axon hillock to the axon terminal.

2. An increase in extracellular Na^+ concentration would slightly depolarize neurons, thereby changing the resting membrane potential. This effect would be minimal, however, because the resting membrane is not very permeable to Na^+. However, the shape of the action potentials in such neurons would be a little steeper, and the peak a little higher, because the electrochemical gradient favoring Na^+ entry into the cell through voltage-gated channels would be greater.

3. Neurons are among the most highly complex cells in an animal's body, with numerous extensions of the cell body. These extensions provide considerable surface area that allows for an extraordinary number of cell-to-cell contacts with other neurons, making them ideally suited for intercellular communication. In addition, myelin sheaths provide a structure that speeds up electric signaling along the axon, facilitating communication even more.

Chapter 42

Concept Checks

Figure 42.4 Not necessarily. Brain mass is not the sole determinant of intelligence or the ability to perform complex tasks. The degree of folding of the cerebral cortex is also important.

Figure 42.6 A spinal nerve is composed of both afferent and efferent neurons.

Figure 42.7 The major symptom experienced by patients undergoing a lumbar puncture is headache, in part because the brain is no longer cushioned adequately by CSF. Within 24–48 hours, however, the CSF is replenished to normal levels.

Figure 42.9 Damage to the cerebellum would result in loss of balance and a lack of fine motor control, such as picking up small objects or making graceful, smooth movements.

Figure 42.11 It was in her right hand.

Figure 42.16 Thinking requires energy! Even daydreaming requires energy; imagine how much energy the brain uses when you concentrate for 60 minutes on a difficult exam. In fact, you just expended energy thinking about this question!

BioConnections

Figure 42.1 As defined in Chapter 32, animals are multicellular heterotrophs (cannot make their own food) whose cells lack a cell wall. Most animals have a nervous system, muscles, the ability to move about during at least some phase of their life cycle, and to reproduce sexually.

Feature Investigation Questions

1. Gaser and Schlaug hypothesized that repeated exposure to musical training would increase the size of certain areas of the brain associated with motor, auditory, and visual skills. All three skills are commonly used in reading and performing musical pieces.

2. The researchers used MRI to examine the areas of the brain associated with motor, auditory, and visual skills in three groups of individuals: professional musicians, amateur musicians, and nonmusicians. The researchers found that certain areas of the brain were larger in the professional musicians compared to the other groups, and larger in the amateur musicians compared to the nonmusicians.

3. Schmithorst and Holland found that, when exposed to music, certain regions of the brains of musicians were activated differently compared with the brains of nonmusicians. This study supports the hypothesis that there is a difference in the brains of musicians versus nonmusicians.

The experiment conducted by Gaser and Schlaug compared the size of certain regions of the brain among professional musicians, amateur musicians, and nonmusicians. Schmithorst and Holland, however, were also able to detect functional differences between musicians and nonmusicians.

Test Yourself

1. b   2. a   3. e   4. c   5. c   6. b   7. e   8. b   9. a   10. d

Conceptual Questions

1. All animals with nervous systems have reflexes, which allow rapid behavioral responses to changes in the environment. When a cnidarian senses a tactile stimulus, its nerve net responds immediately and the animal reflexively contracts nearly all of its muscles, making the animal a smaller target. This behavior protects the animal from predators. When you hear a loud, unexpected, and frightening sound (such as a firecracker), you hunch your shoulders and slightly lower your head; this reflex protects you from danger by minimizing exposure of your neck and head to danger. Dilation of the pupils of the eyes in darkness, and constriction of the pupils in bright light, are reflexes that help us see in the dark and protect our retinas in bright light. Reflexes are particularly adaptive because they occur rapidly, typically with very few synapses involved, and without the need for conscious thought.

2. White matter consists of the myelinated axons that are bundled together in large tracts in the central nervous system and which connect different CNS regions. The lipid-rich myelin gives the tracts a whitish appearance. It is distinguished from gray matter, which are the cell bodies, dendrites, and some unmyelinated axons of neurons in the CNS.

3. The activities of animal nervous systems are replete with examples of new properties emerging from complex interactions. For example, you learned about reflexes in this chapter, which are behaviors that emerge from interactions between individual neurons that form communication circuits between the peripheral and central nervous systems. You also learned about such "higher" properties such as conscious thought, which also emerges from the interactions between many individual cells, each of which is in communication with up to hundreds of thousands of other cells. Individually, the cells cannot "think," but networked together in elaborate ways, a person like yourself can think, remember, plan ahead, and interpret your environment.

Chapter 43

Concept Checks

Figure 43.3 To think about what types of touch you are aware of, let's take the example of sitting in a chair reading this textbook while holding it on your lap. You are aware of the constant weight of the book, the brush of the pages on your fingertips as you turn a page, a gentle breeze that may be circulating in your environment, the deep pressure from regularly adjusting your posture in your chair, an itch you may have on your skin, and the heat or cold of the room. Even a simple exercise such as this one is filled with stimuli of numerous types and durations.

Figure 43.10 This orientation permits animals to detect circular or angular movement of the head in three different planes. The fluid in a canal that is oriented in the same plane as the plane of movement will respond maximally to the movement. For example, the canal that is oriented horizontally would respond greatest to horizontal movements, while the other two canals would not. Overall, by comparing the signals from the three canals, the brain can interpret the motion in three dimensions.

Figure 43.19 Because red-green color blindness is a sex-linked recessive gene, males require only a single defective allele on an X chromosome, whereas females require two defective alleles, one on each X chromosome.

Figure 43.27 Salt is a vital nutrient needed to maintain plasma membrane potentials and fluid balance in animals' bodies. Sugar provides glucose and other monosaccharides, important energy-yielding compounds. Sour (acidic) foods, like citrus fruits, provide nutrients and important antioxidants (vitamin C, for example) that protect against disease. Bitter substances are often toxic, and their bad taste discourages animals from eating them.

BioConnections

Figure 43.1 The term sensory receptor refers to a type of cell that can respond to a particular type of stimulus. The term membrane receptor refers to a protein within a cell membrane that binds a ligand, thereby generating signals that initiate a cellular response.

Figure 43.4 Cilia are cell extensions that contain in their internal structure microtubules and motor proteins that cause the cilia to beat, or move, in a coordinated fashion. Stereocilia are membrane projections that are not motile, but instead are deformed by the movements of surrounding fluids.

Figure 43.9 Statoliths are also found in the roots and shoots of plants. They serve as a gravity-detection mechanism that results in roots growing downward, and shoots upward.

Feature Investigation Questions

1. One possibility is that many different types of odor molecules might bind to one or just a few types of receptor proteins, with the brain responding differently depending on the number or distribution of the activated receptors. The second hypothesis is that organisms can make a large number of receptor proteins, each type binding a particular odor molecule or group of odor molecules. According to this hypothesis, it is the *type* of receptor protein, and not the number or distribution of receptors, that is important for olfactory sensing.

   The researchers extracted RNA molecules from the olfactory receptor cells of the nasal epithelium. They then used this RNA to identify genes that encoded G-protein-coupled receptor proteins.

2. In their study, they identified 18 different genes that encoded different G-protein-coupled receptor proteins.

3. The results of the experiment conducted by Buck and Axel support the hypothesis that animals discriminate between different odors based on having a variety of receptor proteins that recognize different odor molecules. Current research suggests that each olfactory receptor cell has a single type of receptor protein that is specific to particular odor molecules. Because most odors are due to multiple chemicals that activate many different types of odor receptor proteins, the brain detects odors based on the combination of the activated receptor proteins. Odor seems to be discriminated by many olfactory receptor proteins, which are in the membrane of separate olfactory receptor cells.

Test Yourself

1. d 2. d 3. a 4. c 5. e 6. d 7. b 8. b 9. d 10. b

Conceptual Questions

1. Sensory transduction—The process by which incoming stimuli are converted into neural signals. An example would be the signals generated in the retina when a photon of light strikes a photoreceptor.

   Perception—An awareness of the sensations that are experienced. An example would be an awareness of what a particular visual image is.

2. The organ of Corti contains the hair cells and sensory neurons that initiate signaling. The hair cells sit on top of the basilar membrane, and their stereocilia are embedded in the tectorial membrane at the top of the organ of Corti. Pressure waves of different frequencies cause the basilar membrane to vibrate at particular sites. This bends the stereocilia of hair cells back and forth, sending oscillating signals to the sensory neurons. Consequently, the sensory neurons send intermittent action potentials to the CNS via the auditory nerve. Hair cells at the end of the basilar membrane closest to the oval window respond to high-pitched sounds, and lower-pitched sounds trigger hair cell movement further along the basilar membrane.

3. Of the various senses, the sense of olfaction (smell) is least important for the survival of humans. As diurnal animals, we rely largely on our visual sense. Sounds are a critical way to learn about impending danger, such as a car horn, but also is our major means of communication. Other senses, such as the ability to sense pain, have acutely important functions from time to time. Olfaction, though often a pleasurable sense and at times a protective one (think of the smell of spoiled food), nonetheless provides little survival advantage to us. In fact, many people spend much of their lives with greatly diminished olfactory abilities, whether from chronic allergies or other problems, and are not hindered in any significant way. The story is very different for animals such as nocturnal mammals, which rely very heavily on olfaction to find food, locate mates, and avoid predators.

Chapter 44

Concept Checks

Figure 44.1 Yes. In addition to not having a requirement to shed their skeletons periodically, animals with endoskeletons can use their skin as an efficient means of heat transfer (and, to an extent in amphibians, water transfer). In addition, the body surface of such animals is often a highly sensitive sensory organ.

Figure 44.3 If a tendon is torn, its ability to link a muscle to bone is reduced or lost. Therefore, when a muscle such as the one shown in this illustration contracts, it will not be able to move the bone from which the tendon has become dislodged.

Figure 44.8 The ATP concentration in cells becomes depleted after death, because oxygen and nutrients are not being provided to cells. Consequently, the cross-bridge cycle becomes locked before step 3. Without ATP, the cross-bridges cannot dissociate until many hours later, when the muscle tissue sufficiently decomposes.

Figure 44.11 Na^+ enters the muscle cell because all cells have an electrochemical gradient for Na^+ that favors diffusion of Na^+ from extracellular to intracellular fluid (see Chapter 41). This is because cells have a negative membrane potential and because Na^+ concentrations are higher in the extracellular fluid. The acetylcholine receptor on skeletal muscle cells is also a ligand-gated ion channel; when acetylcholine binds the receptor, it induces a shape change that opens the channel. This allows the entry of Na^+ into the cell.

Figure 44.14 No. The data are expressed "per kg"; this means that when normalized to a standard body mass (1 kg), the amount of energy expended for any type of locomotion by a small animal tends to be greater than that of a larger animal. However, these are *relative* values. For example, the *absolute* amount of energy expended by a tiny minnow is much less than that of a large tuna over any given distance.

BioConnections

Figure 44.10 Voltage-gated Ca^{2+} channels exist in the terminals of all axons that communicate by chemical signaling (neurotransmitter release). In those cases, depolarization of the axon terminal opens Ca^{2+} channels, allowing Ca^{2+} to enter the terminal and trigger exocytosis of stored vesicles containing neurotransmitter molecules.

Figure 44.11 As described in Figures 41.2 and 41.12, myelin is a lipid-rich membrane sheath that speeds up conduction of action potentials along an axon. Action potentials are regenerated at discrete lengths along the axon wherever the myelin sheath is interrupted by a node of Ranvier. This is known as saltatory conduction.

Feature Investigation Questions

1. PPAR-δ is a nuclear receptor that regulates the expression of genes that enable cells to more efficiently burn fat instead of glucose for energy.

2. Evans suggested that if PPAR-δ were highly activated in mice, the mice would lose weight because of the high level of fat metabolism.

3. They developed transgenic mice with highly activated PPAR-δ. Then they fed the transgenic mice and a strain of normal mice high-fat diets. They then compared the weights of the two strains of mice to determine if the change in PPAR-δ activity affected weight. The weights of the transgenic mice were considerably lower than those of the normal mice. These results supported the hypothesis that highly activated PPAR-δ would lead to lower weight gain due to fat metabolism. Interestingly, the researchers also discovered that the transgenic mice could perform prolonged exercise for a much longer time than the normal mice. The muscle tissue of the transgenic mice was more specialized for long-term exercise.

Test Yourself

1. c 2. e 3. d 4. c 5. e 6. c 7. a 8. e 9. c 10. e

Conceptual Questions

1. Exoskeletons are on the outside of an animal's body, and endoskeletons are inside the body. Both function in support and protection, but only exoskeletons protect an animal's outer surface. Exoskeletons must be shed when an animal grows, whereas endoskeletons grow with an animal.

2. a. The cycle begins with the binding of an energized myosin cross-bridge to an actin molecule on a thin filament.

   b. The cross-bridge moves, and the thin filaments slide past the thick filaments.

   c. The ATP binds to myosin, causing the cross-bridge to detach.

   d. The ATP bound to myosin is hydrolyzed by ATPase, re-forming the energized state of myosin.

3. The use of energy released by the hydrolysis of ATP is fundamental to muscle function and locomotion. Recall that ATP must be hydrolyzed during the cross-bridge cycle for skeletal muscle cells to shorten. Energy is also used to maintain calcium ion balance in the sarcoplasmic reticulum and is used in all forms of locomotion. The amount of energy expended by an animal during locomotion reflects how well they are adapted to the environment in which they must move.

Chapter 45

Concept Checks

Figure 45.4 After a large blood meal, the body mass of a flying blood-sucking animal increases sufficiently as to make it nearly impossible to fly. The problem is solved, however, by a unique adaptation that allows such animals to concentrate the nutrients from blood and excrete most of the water portion of blood as soon as they begin eating. By the time the meal is finished, much of the water they consumed has already been excreted.

Figure 45.7 Sauropod dinosaurs were herbivores that probably contained a gizzard-type stomach in which stones helped to grind coarse vegetation. Such stones would have become smooth after months or even years of rumbling around in the gizzard. Some of these sauropods are known to have lacked the sort of grinding teeth characteristic of modern mammalian herbivores, and thus a gizzard would have aided in their digestion much as it does in modern birds.

Figure 45.10 By having bile stored in a gallbladder, bile can be released precisely when needed in response to a meal, which is particularly useful for animals that consume large or infrequent meals. In the absence of a gallbladder, bile flows into the intestine continuously and cannot be increased to match the amount or timing of food intake.

Figure 45.11 Secondary active transport requires energy provided by ATP. Thus, absorption of nutrients by this mechanism is an energy-requiring event, and some portion of an animal's regular nutrient consumption is used to provide the energy required to absorb the nutrients.

BioConnections

Figure 45.11 Transmembrane transport processes are not unique to animals, and one or more types are found in virtually all cells.

Figure 45.13 CCK inhibits stomach activity. This is an example of negative feedback. The arrival of chyme in the small intestine stimulates CCK, which promotes digestion as shown in the figure. At the same time, CCK inhibits contraction of the smooth muscles of the stomach so that the entry of chyme into the small intestine is slowed down. This allows time for controlled digestion and absorption of nutrients in the intestine, without the intestine becoming overfilled with chyme. Simultaneously, CCK inhibits acid production by the stomach so that the pH of the intestine does not become dangerously low before bicarbonate ions are able to neutralize it.

Feature Investigation Questions

1. The researchers severed the nerves that connected to the small intestine in a dog. Following the removal of the nerves, the researchers introduced an acidic solution directly into the intestine of the dog. The introduction of the acid into the intestine caused pancreatic secretion. This suggested that non-neural factors must have mediated communication between the digestive tract and the secretory cells of the pancreas.

2. Other researchers were not convinced that all the nerves were dissected from the intestine, because of the technical difficulty in performing such a procedure. To provide more conclusive evidence of other regulatory factors that were produced by the intestine, the researchers conducted a second experiment. First, they dissected a portion of a small intestine from a dog, treated it with acid, ground it up to produce a mash, and then filtered the mash to obtain an extract. The extract—which was expected to contain any secretions of the intestine that occurred following acid exposure—was then injected into the circulatory system of a second dog. The results indicated that the second dog had pancreatic secretion following the injection.

3. The results suggested that factors were secreted by the small intestine following exposure of the intestine to acid, as would occur when chyme enters the intestine from the stomach. These factors probably reached the pancreas through the bloodstream. The researchers called these factors hormones. Thus, the digestive system was regulated not only by the nervous system, but also by chemical secretions, and different parts of the digestive system were able to communicate with each other via hormones.

Test Yourself

1. d 2. e 3. e 4. b 5. c 6. b 7. d 8. c 9. a 10. e

Conceptual Questions

1. Digestion is the breakdown of large molecules into smaller ones by the action of enzymes and acid. Absorption is the transport of digested molecules and small molecules that do not require digestion, across the epithelial cells of the alimentary canal and from there into the extracellular fluid of an animal.

2. The crop is a dilation of the esophagus, which stores and softens food. The gizzard contains swallowed pebbles that help pulverize food. Both of these functions are adaptations that assist digestion in birds, which do not have teeth and therefore do not chew food. Humans, like many animals, can chew food before swallowing.

3. Carnivores eat live animal flesh and/or fluids or may scavenge dead animals. Carnivores' teeth are adapted for seizing, grasping, piercing, biting, slicing, tearing, or holding prey; they generally do not chew their food extensively, but may chew to facilitate swallowing. Herbivores have powerful jaw muscles and large, broad molars for grinding tough, fibrous plant material; they may also have incisors adapted for nipping grass or other vegetation. Simply examining the type of teeth an animal has is often sufficient to determine whether that animal eats vegetation, animals, or both.

Chapter 46

Concept Checks

Figure 46.3 The time required for the vesicles to move to the plasma membrane and fuse with it is much shorter than the time required for new GLUTs to be synthesized by activation of GLUT genes. Thus, the action of insulin on cells is very quick, because the GLUTs are already synthesized.

Figure 46.4 The glycerol and fatty acids used to make glucose are the breakdown products of triglycerides that were stored in adipose tissue during the absorptive period. The amino acids used to make glucose are derived from the breakdown of protein in muscle and other tissue.

Figure 46.6 Even though the goose was resting, sampling the air from the mask would be only a rough estimate of BMR. That is because the artificial setting and the placement of the mask would be enough of a stimulus to affect the activity and behavior of the goose, thereby increasing its metabolism.

Figure 46.7 As shown in Figure 46.7, for humans exercise is a voluntary activity. In nature, however, "exercise" is often a component of the fight-or-flight reaction, such as when an animal attempts to escape danger. During such times, digestion and absorption of food are less important than providing as much blood flow, oxygen, and nutrients as possible to skeletal muscle. The gut, therefore, temporarily reduces its activity and requires less blood flow.

Figure 46.8 Nearly all animals today show a similar relationship between body mass and metabolic rate, and there is no reason why it should not always have been true. Thus, the tiny 1-foot-tall ancestral horse *Eohippus* most likely had a higher BMR than do today's larger horses.

Figure 46.11 Humans are homeothermic endotherms. We maintain our body temperature within a very narrow range, and we supply our own body heat.

BioConnections

Figure 46.3 Exocytosis, a feature characteristic of animal cells, involves the fusion of intracellular vesicles with the plasma membrane, resulting in the release of the vesicle contents into the extracellular fluid. See Figure 5.26 for a general description, and Figure 41.14 for a specific example unique to animal cells.

Feature Investigation Questions

1. Scientists were interested in knowing why animals seemed to regulate their body mass around a particular level, even though many animals experience changes in food supply throughout the year. This seemed to indicate that a mechanism existed within the body that monitored when fuel stores were higher or lower than normal, and that initiated changes in behavior and metabolism to compensate.

2. Coleman hypothesized that communication regarding energy status must take place between the brain and the rest of the body. He suggested that chemical signals were transported through the blood from outside the brain to feeding or satiety centers within the brain, where they regulated appetite and thus body weight. He tested this by linking the blood circulations of normal mice and genetically obese mice and then monitoring the mice for changes in body weight.

3. In most cases, the obese mice lost weight and ate less during the experimental procedure. This confirmed that something in the bloodstream of the wild-type mice was regulating body weight but was missing in the obese mice. When the unknown factor crossed into the bloodstream of the obese mice, it caused them to lose weight. In another group of parabiosed mice, however, the wild-type

mice lost weight, but the obese mice did not. Coleman concluded that these obese mice were not able to respond to the chemical signal that regulates body weight, even though they made the signal themselves and it was active in their parabiosed wild-type partners.

Test Yourself

1. c   2. a   3. d   4. c   5. a   6. e   7. e   8. c   9. c   10. e

Conceptual Questions

1. Insulin acts on adipose and skeletal muscle cells to facilitate the diffusion of glucose from extracellular fluid into the cell cytosol. This is accomplished by increasing the translocation of glucose-transporter (GLUT) proteins from the cytosol to sites within the plasma membrane of insulin-sensitive cells. Insulin also inhibits glycogenolysis and gluconeogenesis in the liver, which decreases the amount of glucose secreted into the blood by the liver. Insulin is required for glucose transport because like many other polar molecules, glucose cannot move across the lipid bilayer of a plasma membrane by simple diffusion. The inhibitory effects of insulin on liver function help to ensure that liver glycogen stores will be spared for the postabsorptive period.

2. Appetite is controlled by a satiety center in the brain that receives signals from the stretched stomach and intestines after a meal. When digestion and absorption are complete, the stomach and intestines return to their original size, and the brain no longer senses that an animal feels "full." In addition, appetite is controlled by leptin, a hormone secreted by adipose cells in direct proportion to the amount of fat stored in an animal's body. When leptin levels in the blood are high, appetite is suppressed. When leptin levels are low, as occurs when an animal is losing weight, appetite is increased. The presence of a hormone that is released into the blood in proportion to fat mass in the body allows the brain to monitor the amount of energy stored in the body. A decrease in the concentration of leptin in the blood, for example, is the mechanism that communicates to the brain that fat stores are lower than normal. This initiates the sensation of hunger, which encourages an animal to seek food.

3. Countercurrent heat exchange is a mechanism for retaining body heat. The physical arrangement (structure) of arteries and veins in an animal's body can contribute to the very important function of thermoregulation. As warm blood travels through arteries down a bird's leg, for example, heat moves by conduction from the artery to adjacent veins carrying cooler blood in the other direction, toward the heart. By the time the arterial blood reaches the tip of the leg, its temperature has dropped considerably, reducing the amount of heat loss to the environment, while the heat is returned to the body's core via the warmed veins.

Chapter 47

Concept Checks

Figure 47.2 Open circulatory systems evolved prior to closed systems. However, this does not mean that open systems are in some way inferior to closed circulatory systems. It is better to think of open systems as being ideally suited to the needs of those animals that have them. Arthropods are an incredibly successful order of animals, with the greatest number of species, and inhabiting virtually every ecological niche on the planet. Clearly, their type of circulatory system has not prevented arthropods from achieving their great success.

Figure 47.3 Keeping oxygenated and deoxygenated blood fully separate allows the arterial blood of birds and mammals to provide the maximum amount of oxygen to tissues. This means that those tissues can achieve higher metabolisms and be more active at all times.

Figure 47.6 Each hemoglobin molecule contains four subunits, each of which has an iron atom at its core. Each iron binds one oxygen molecule (O_2); therefore, a total of eight oxygen atoms can bind to one hemoglobin molecule.

Figure 47.11 Body fluids, both extracellular and intracellular, contain large amounts of charged ions, which are capable of conducting electricity. The slight electric currents generated by the beating heart muscle cells are conducted through the surrounding body fluids by the movements of ions in those fluids. This is recorded by the surface electrodes and amplified by the recording machine.

Figure 47.13 When the animal is active, the arterioles of its leg muscle would dilate, bringing more blood and, consequently, nutrients and oxygen to the active muscle tissue.

Figure 47.16 The valves open toward the heart. When the head is upright, the valves are open, and blood drains from the head to the right atrium by gravity. When the

giraffe lowers its head to drink, however, gravity would prevent the venous blood from reaching the heart; instead, blood would pool in the head and could raise pressure in the head and brain. The valves in the neck veins work the same way as those in the legs of other animals, helping to propel blood against gravity to the heart.

BioConnections

Figure 47.1 Water circulation mixes food with enzymes and brings digested food into close contact with all interior cells.

Figure 47.5 Immune defenses are found in most living organisms. Many bacteria produce antibacterial secretions that kill other bacteria. Plants, as shown in Figure 36.19, have a wide array of pathogen-fighting mechanisms.

Figure 47.19 Baroreceptors are mechanoreceptors. Like all mechanoreceptors (for example, those in distensible or deformable structures such as the urinary bladder and stomach), their ion channels are opened by physical deformation or stretching of the plasma membrane. They are, therefore, mechanically gated ion channels.

Feature Investigation Questions

1. Furchgott noted that acetylcholine had different effects on the rabbit aorta depending on the manner in which the aorta was isolated and prepared. When applied to flattened strips of the aorta, acetylcholine caused contraction of the aorta smooth muscle; however, when applied to circular rings of the aorta, acetylcholine caused relaxation. Furchgott suggested that the difference was due to the absence of the endothelial layer of tissue in the flattened strips of aorta.

2. Furchgott hypothesized that acetylcholine stimulated the endothelial cells to secrete a substance that functioned as a vasodilator, causing the muscle layer to relax. Furchgott performed several experiments to test his hypothesis. He compared the effects of acetylcholine on circular rings of aorta that either had the endothelial layer intact or experimentally removed. The results of this experiment demonstrated that when the endothelial layer was present, relaxation occurred in the presence of acetylcholine. Removal of the endothelial layer, however, resulted in contraction of muscle in the presence of acetylcholine. In a second experiment, a strip of the aorta with the endothelial layer removed was put in contact with a strip of aorta with an intact endothelial layer. When this "sandwiched" treatment was exposed to acetylcholine, both muscle layers relaxed.

3. Furchgott concluded that the endothelial layer produced a vasodilator in the presence of acetylcholine. The vasodilator diffused from the intact strip of muscle to the denuded strip and caused the muscle layer to relax.

Test Yourself

1. b   2. a   3. c   4. b   5. a   6. d   7. c   8. d   9. c   10. d

Conceptual Questions

1. The three main components of a circulatory system are (1) blood or hemolymph, an internal body fluid containing dissolved solutes; (2) blood vessels, a system of hollow tubes within the body through which blood travels; and (3) one or more hearts, muscular structures that pump blood through the blood vessels.

2. **Closed circulatory system**—In a closed circulatory system, the blood and interstitial fluid are contained within tubes called blood vessels and are transported by a pump called the heart. All of the nutrients and oxygen that tissues require are delivered directly to them by the blood vessels. Advantages of closed circulatory systems are that different parts of an animal's body can receive blood flow in proportion to that body part's metabolic requirements at any given time. Due to its efficiency, a closed circulatory system allows organisms to become larger.

   Open circulatory system—In an open circulatory system, the organs are bathed in hemolymph that ebbs and flows into and out of the heart(s) and body cavity, rather than blood being directed to all cells. Like a closed circulatory system, there are a pump and blood vessels, but these two structures are less developed and less complex compared to a closed circulatory system. Partly as a result, organisms such as mollusks and arthropods are generally limited to being relatively small, although exceptions do exist.

3. A circulatory system permits delivery of the nutrients and oxygen required by cells to maintain energy-demanding processes, such as pumping ions across cellular membranes, contracting muscle cells including those of the heart, cell division, protein synthesis, and many others. In addition, the circulatory system removes soluble waste products, which, if allowed to accumulate, would be toxic to cells. Many circulatory systems are capable of adapting to changing metabolic requirements, thus ensuring that homeostasis is maintained whether an animal is resting or active.

Chapter 48

Concept Checks

Figure 48.2 Regardless of whether the atmosphere is measured on Mt. Everest or at sea level, the percentage of gas molecules that are oxygen remains close to 21%. However, the pressure exerted by those gas molecules decreases as one ascends in elevation.

Figure 48.3 If a lungless salamander were to dry out, its capacity for gas exchange would be greatly reduced. Gases diffuse into and out of the body of the salamander by dissolving in the moist fluid layer on the skin.

Figure 48.5 Imagine holding several thin sheets of a wet substance, such as paper. If you wave them in the air, what happens? The sheets stick to one another because of surface tension and other properties of moist surfaces. This is what happens to the lamellae in gills when they are in air. When the lamellae stick to each other, the surface area available for gas exchange is reduced and the fish suffocates.

Figure 48.7 Several factors probably limit insect body size, but the respiratory system most likely is one such factor. If an insect grew to the size of a human, for example, the trachea and tracheoles would be so large and extensive that there would be little room for any other internal organs in the body! Also, the mass of the animal's body and the forces generated during locomotion would probably collapse the tracheoles. Finally, diffusion of oxygen from the surface of the body to the deepest regions of a human-sized insect would take far too long to support the metabolic demands of internal structures.

Figure 48.12 Because fishes have the most efficient means of extracting oxygen from their environment, one might conclude that this is an adaptation to cope with low environmental oxygen. Based on that logic, you would conclude that the oxygen content of water was less than that of air, which is indeed correct.

Figure 48.14 The waters off the coast of Antarctica are extremely cold, rarely warmer than 0.30°C. As we saw earlier in this chapter, more oxygen dissolves in cold water than in warm water, and therefore icefish have the potential to obtain more oxygen across their gills. Cold temperatures also decrease the metabolic rate of the animals, because all chemical reactions slow down at low temperature. Thus, the oxygen demands of icefish are lower than those of warm-water fish. Several other adaptations have evolved to enable these animals to live without hemoglobin. Large gills with exceptionally high surface area facilitate diffusion of oxygen into the animal's blood. In addition, cardiovascular adaptations evolved to help increase the total amount of oxygen in the blood and its ability to be pumped to all body tissues. For example, icefish have larger blood volumes and a larger heart than warm-water fish of a similar size. Also, the absence of red blood cells makes the blood less viscous (makes it "thinner") and therefore easier to pump through the body.

Figure 48.15 An increase in the blood concentration of HCO_3^- would favor the reaction $HCO_3^- + H^+ \rightarrow H_2CO_3 \rightarrow CO_2 + H_2O$. This would reduce the H^+ concentration of the blood, thereby raising the pH; the CO_2 formed as a result would be exhaled. These changes would shift the hemoglobin curve to the left of the usual position.

BioConnections

Figure 48.16 The brainstem includes the midbrain, pons and medulla oblongata. See Figure 42.9 for an illustration of the major parts of the human brain.

Feature Investigation Questions

1. The study conducted by Schmidt-Neilsen intended to determine the route of air through the avian respiratory system. This would provide a better understanding of the functions of the air sacs and the process of gas exchange in birds.

2. The first experiment by Schmidt-Neilsen compared the composition of air between the posterior and anterior air sacs. Oxygen content was high in the posterior sacs but low in the anterior sacs. Carbon dioxide levels, however, were low in the posterior sacs but high in the anterior sacs. The researchers concluded that when inhaled, the air moves first to the posterior sacs; then to the lungs where oxygen diffuses into the blood and carbon dioxide diffuses into the lungs; and, finally, to the anterior sacs before being exhaled.

3. The second experiment by Schmidt-Neilsen was conducted to verify the pathway of air through the respiratory system of the bird. In this experiment, the researcher monitored oxygen levels by surgically implanting oxygen probes in the anterior and posterior air sacs. The bird was fitted with a face mask and allowed to take one breath of pure oxygen. The researcher was then able to track the movement of this oxygen through the respiratory tract. Schmidt-Neilsen concluded that it takes two complete breaths for air to move from the environment through the lungs and back out again to the environment. The two breaths are required to move the air from the posterior air sacs through the lungs and, finally, to the anterior air sacs before exiting the body.

Test Yourself

Conceptual Questions

1. Countercurrent exchange maximizes the amount of oxygen that can be obtained from the water in fishes. Oxygenated water flows across the lamellae of a fish gill in the opposite direction in which deoxygenated blood flows through the capillaries of the lamellae. In this way, a diffusion gradient for oxygen is maintained along the entire length of the lamellae, facilitating diffusion of oxygen even when much of it has already entered the blood.

2. Animals that live at high altitudes face the special challenge of obtaining oxygen where the atmospheric pressure is low. When atmospheric pressure is low, the partial pressure of oxygen in the air is also low. This means that there is less of a driving force for the diffusion of oxygen from the air into the body of the animal. Several adaptations have arisen that help animals cope with such habitats. For example, many high-altitude animals have more red blood cells and have hemoglobin with a higher affinity for oxygen than that of sea-level animals. This means their hemoglobin can bind oxygen even at the low partial pressures of high altitudes, thereby saturating their blood with oxygen. In addition, such animals generally have larger hearts and lungs for their body size than animals that live at lower altitudes. Animals that move to high altitude show increases in the number of red blood cells in their circulation and in respiratory rates. The number of capillaries in skeletal muscle increases to facilitate oxygen diffusion into the muscle cells. Myoglobin content of muscle cells also increases, expanding the reservoir of oxygen in the cytosol.

3. Hemoglobin is a protein with quaternary structure (see Chapter 3) in which the different subunits cooperate to bind up to a total of four oxygen molecules. It is the structure of the subunits and their relationship to each other that contributes to their ability to bind O_2 and to the nonlinear relationship of the oxygen-hemoglobin dissociation curve. In addition, however, interactions of hemoglobin with other molecules, such as CO_2, change the structure of hemoglobin in such a way that its properties change. Under such conditions, hemoglobin is less able to bind O_2 and consequently it releases the gas. Any molecule that binds to hemoglobin will alter its structure and change its properties; these revert to the original state once the bound molecules are released. A particularly dramatic example of the structure and function of hemoglobin being related is that which occurs in sickle cell disease, due to a mutation.

Chapter 49

Concept Checks

Figure 49.1 No, obligatory exchanges must always occur, but animals can minimize obligatory losses through modifications in behavior. For example, terrestrial animals that seek shade on a hot, sunny day reduce evaporative water loss. As another example, reducing activity minimizes water loss due to respiration.

Figure 49.4 Humans cannot survive by drinking seawater because we do not possess specialized salt glands to rid ourselves of the excess sodium and other ions ingested with seawater. The human kidneys cannot eliminate that much salt. The high blood levels of sodium and other ions would cause changes in cellular membrane potentials, disrupting vital functions of electrically excitable tissue such as cardiac muscle and nerve tissue.

Figure 49.6 Secretion of substances into excretory organ tubules is advantageous because it increases the amount of a substance that gets removed from the body by the excretory organs. This is important, because many substances that get secreted are potentially toxic. Filtration, though efficient, is limited by the volume of fluid that can leave the capillaries and enter the excretory tubule.

BioConnections

Figure 49.12 A brush border composed of microvilli is also present along the epithelial cell layer of the vertebrate small intestine (see Chapter 45). In the intestine, the brush border serves to increase the absorption of nutrients. In both the intestine and the proximal tubule of nephrons, therefore, a brush border provides extensive surface area for the transport of substances between a lumen and the epithelial cells (and from there to extracellular fluid).

Figure 49.14 Epithelial cells like those in the kidney tubules can distribute proteins between the luminal and basolateral sides of the plasma membrane. In this way, the Na^+/K^+-ATPase pumps that are stimulated by aldosterone are present and active only on one side of the cell, the basolateral surfaces. If the pumps were activated on the luminal surface of the cell, aldosterone would not be able to promote reabsorption of

Na$^+$ and water, because Na$^+$ would also be transported from the cell into the tubule lumen.

Feature Investigation Questions

1. Symptoms of prolonged, heavy exercise include fatigue, muscle cramps, and even occasionally seizures. Fatigue results from the reduction in blood flow to muscles and other organs. Muscle cramps and seizures are the results of imbalances in plasma electrolyte levels. Cade and his colleagues hypothesized that maintaining proper water and electrolyte levels would prevent these problems, and that if water and electrolyte levels were maintained, athletic performance should not decrease as rapidly with prolonged exercise.

2. To test their hypothesis, the researchers created a drink that would restore the correct proportions of lost water and electrolytes within the athletes. If the athletes consumed the drink during exercise, they should not experience as much fatigue or muscle cramping, and thus their performance should be enhanced compared with a control group of athletes that drank only water.

3. The performance of a group of exercising athletes given the electrolyte-containing drink was better than that of the control group that drank only water during exercise. This could be attributed to the replacement of normal electrolyte levels by the drink.

Test Yourself

1. e   2. e   3. d   4. c   5. a   6. c   7. e   8. d   9. a   10. b

Conceptual Questions

1. Nitrogenous wastes are the breakdown products of the metabolism of proteins and nucleic acids. They consist of ammonia, ammonium ions, urea, and uric acid. The predominant type of waste excreted depends in part on an animal's environment. For example, aquatic animals typically excrete ammonia and ammonium ions, whereas many terrestrial animals excrete primarily urea and uric acid. Urea and uric acid are less toxic than the other types but require energy to be synthesized. Urea and uric acid also result in less water excreted, an adaptation that is especially useful for organisms that must conserve water, such as many terrestrial species.

2. During filtration, an organ acts like a sieve or filter, removing some of the water and its small solutes from the blood, interstitial fluid, or hemolymph, while retaining blood cells and large solutes such as proteins. Reabsorption is the process whereby epithelial cells of an excretory organ recapture useful solutes that were filtered. Secretion is the process whereby epithelial cells of an excretory organ transport unneeded or harmful solutes from the blood to the excretory tubules for elimination. Some substances such as glucose and amino acids are reabsorbed but not secreted, while some other substances such as toxic compounds are not reabsorbed and are secreted. Still other substances, namely proteins, are not filtered at all.

3. Salt glands contain a network of secretory tubules that actively transport NaCl from the extracellular fluid into the tubule lumen. This solution then moves through a central duct and to the outside environment through pores in the nose, around the eyes, and in other locations. The ability to remove salt from body fluids is an adaptation for many marine reptiles and birds, which do not have ready access to fresh water and would otherwise run the risk of having very high levels of salts in their blood and other body fluids.

Chapter 50

Concept Checks

Figure 50.10 Not all mammals use the energy of sunlight to synthesize vitamin D. Many animals, such as those that inhabit caves or that are strictly nocturnal, rarely are exposed to sunlight. Some of these animals get their vitamin D from dietary sources. How others maintain calcium balance without dietary or sunlight-derived active vitamin D remains uncertain.

Figure 50.12 Sodium and potassium ion balance is of vital importance for most animals because of the critical role these ions play in nervous system and muscle function. It is more the rule than the exception that such important physiological variables are under multiple layers of control. This grants a high degree of fine-tuning capability such that these ions—and other similarly important molecules—rarely exceed or fall below the normal range of concentrations for a given animal.

Figure 50.13 The great height of the twin on the left in Figure 50.13 clearly indicates that his condition arose prior to puberty. The enlarged bones further suggest that the disease continued for a time after puberty, when further linear bone growth was no longer possible.

Figure 50.15 Because 20-hydroxyecdysone is a steroid hormone, you would predict that its receptor would be intracellular. All steroid hormones interact with receptors located either in the cytosol or, more commonly, in the nucleus. The hormone-receptor complex then acts to promote or inhibit transcription of one or more genes. The receptor for 20-hydroxyecdysone is indeed found in cell nuclei.

BioConnections

Figure 50.4 When dopamine is secreted from an axon terminal into a synapse where it diffuses to a postsynaptic cell, it is considered a neurotransmitter. When it is secreted from an axon terminal into the extracellular fluid, from where it diffuses into the blood, it is considered a hormone.

Figure 50.7 In addition to the pancreas, certain other organs in an animal's body may contain both exocrine and endocrine tissue or cells. For example, you learned in Chapters 45 and 46 that the vertebrate alimentary canal is composed of several types of secretory cells. Some of these cells release hormones into the blood that regulate the activities of the pancreas and other structures, such as the gallbladder. Other cells of the alimentary canal secrete exocrine products such as acids or mucus into the gut lumen that directly aid in digestion or act as a protective coating, respectively.

Feature Investigation Questions

1. Banting and Best based their procedure on a medical condition that results when pancreatic ducts are blocked. The exocrine cells will deteriorate in a pancreas that has obstructed ducts; however, the islet cells are not affected. The researchers proposed to experimentally replicate the condition to isolate the cells suspected of secreting the glucose-lowering factor. From these cells, they assumed they would be able to extract the substance of interest without contamination or degradation due to exocrine products.

2. The extracts obtained by Banting and Best did contain insulin, the glucose-lowering factor, but were of low strength and purity. Collip developed a procedure to obtain a more purified extract with higher concentrations of insulin.

3. The researchers chose to use bovine pancreases as their starting material for preparing the extracts. Because of the large size of these animals and their availability at local slaughterhouses, the researchers were able to obtain great yields of insulin. Second, Collip developed a highly sensitive assay for monitoring changes in blood glucose levels after injection of insulin. This allowed the researchers to better estimate how much insulin was in a preparation and how much was necessary to give to a patient.

Test Yourself

1. b   2. e   3. b   4. e   5. b   6. e   7. c   8. d   9. b   10. d

Conceptual Questions

1. Leptin acts in the hypothalamus to reduce appetite and increase metabolic rate. Because adipose tissue is typically the most important and abundant source of stored energy in an animal's body, the ability to relay information to the appetite and metabolism centers of the brain about the amount of available adipose tissue is a major benefit. In this way, the brain's centers can indirectly monitor the minute-to-minute energy status in the body. A decrease in leptin, for example, would indicate that a decrease in adipose tissue existed—as might occur during a fast. Removal of the leptin signal would cause appetite to increase and metabolism to decrease, thereby conserving energy. The presence of an appetite and the subjective sensations associated with hunger is a motivation that drives an animal to seek food at the expense of other activities, such as seeking shelter, finding a mate, and so on.

2. Type 1 DM is characterized by insufficient production of insulin due to the immune system destroying the insulin-producing cells of the pancreas. In type 2 DM, insulin is still produced by the pancreas, but adipose and muscle cells do not respond normally to insulin.

3. Insulin acts to lower blood glucose concentrations, for example, after a meal, whereas glucagon elevates blood glucose, for example, during fasting. Insulin acts by stimulating the insertion of glucose transporter proteins into the cell membrane of muscle and fat cells. Glucagon acts by stimulating glycogenolysis in the liver. If a high dose of glucagon were injected into an animal, including humans, the blood concentration of glucagon would increase rapidly. This would stimulate increased glycogenolysis, resulting in blood glucose concentrations that were above normal.

Chapter 51

Concept Checks

Figure 51.4 Aquatic environments in which the water is stagnant or only gently moving, as shown in this figure, are generally best for external fertilization. Fast-moving bodies of water reduce the likelihood of a sperm contacting an egg and increase the chances that gametes will be washed away in the current. Many river-dwelling fishes lay eggs in gently moving streams, and many marine fishes do so in relatively shallow waters.

Figure 51.7 The elevated testosterone levels would inhibit LH and FSH production through negative feedback. This would result in reduced spermatogenesis and possibly even infertility (an inability to produce sufficient sperm to cause a pregnancy).

Figure 51.10 FSH and LH concentrations do not surge in males, but instead remain fairly steady, because the testes do not show cyclical activity. Sperm production in males is constant throughout life after puberty.

Figure 51.14 Pregnancy and subsequent lactation require considerable energy and, therefore, nutrient ingestion. Consuming the placenta provides the female with a rich source of protein and other important nutrients.

BioConnections

Figure 51.11 In addition to its other functions, the placenta must serve the function of the lungs for the fetus, because the fetus' lungs are not breathing air during this time. Arteries always carry blood away from the heart; veins carry blood to the heart. Consequently, blood leaving the heart of the fetus and traveling through arteries to the placenta is deoxygenated. As blood leaves the placenta and returns to the heart, the blood has become oxygenated as oxygen diffuses from the maternal blood into fetal blood. That oxygenated blood then gets pumped from the fetal heart through other arteries to the rest of the fetus' body.

Feature Investigation Questions

1. Using *Daphnia*, Paland and Lynch compared the accumulation of mitochondrial mutations between sexually reproducing populations and asexually reproducing populations.

2. The results—that sexually reproducing populations had a lower rate of deleterious mutations compared with asexually reproducing populations—indicate that sexual reproduction does decrease the accumulation of deleterious mutations, at least in this species.

3. Sexual reproduction allows for mixing of the different alleles of genes with each generation, thereby increasing genetic variation within the population. This could prevent the accumulation of deleterious alleles in the population.

Test Yourself

1. d   2. c   3. e   4. a   5. b   6. c   7. b   8. c   9. b   10. c

Conceptual Questions

1. In viviparity, most of embryonic development occurs within the mother, and the animal is born alive, as occurs in most mammals. If all or most of embryonic development occurs outside the mother and the embryo depends exclusively on yolk from an egg for nourishment, the process is called oviparity; this occurs in most vertebrates and in insects. In ovoviviparity, which occurs in some reptiles, sharks, and some invertebrates, fertilized eggs covered with a very thin shell hatch inside the mother's body, but the offspring receive no nourishment from the mother. Humans are viviparous. An advantage of viviparity is that the embryo and fetus develop in a protected environment.

2. Cells of the hypothalamus produce two important hormones that regulate reproduction. GnRH stimulates the anterior pituitary gland to release two gonadotropic hormones, LH and FSH. These two hormones regulate the production of gonadal hormones and development of gametes in both sexes. In addition, increased secretion of GnRH contributes to the initiation of puberty. The hypothalamus also produces oxytocin, a hormone that is stored in the posterior pituitary gland and that acts to stimulate milk release during lactation. Finally, changes in neuroendocrine activity in the hypothalamus are linked to seasonal changes in day length and therefore contribute to seasonal breeding in certain mammals.

3. Sexual reproduction requires that males and females of a species produce different gametes and that these gametes come into contact with each other. This requires males and females to expend energy to locate mates. It also may require specialized organs for copulation and in some cases requires the production of very large numbers of gametes to increase the likelihood that the eggs are fertilized. These costs are outweighed by the genetic diversity afforded by sexual reproduction.

Chapter 52

Concept Checks

Figure 52.14 Different concentrations of a signaling protein can exert different effects on cells when, for example, different cells express different isoforms of a plasma membrane receptor for the protein. If one cell expresses a high-affinity receptor and another cell a low-affinity receptor, the two cells would respond to the signaling protein at different concentrations. Likewise, the different receptors may be linked with different second-messenger molecules generated within the cell. These messengers, such as cAMP and Ca^{2+}, may have different effects on cell function.

BioConnections

Figure 52.1 The process by which a tadpole develops into an adult frog is called metamorphosis. This process is widespread in animals and occurs in many arthropods, certain fishes, numerous marine invertebrates such as gastropods, and amphibia.

Figure 52.5 No, all vertebrates do not use internal fertilization. External fertilization is common in fishes and amphibia; these animals lay unfertilized eggs, over which males deposit sperm (see Chapter 51).

Feature Investigation Questions

1. Knowing the genes expressed in this region of a developing embryo would provide important information about the control of the patterning of embryonic tissues and structures.

2. Harland and colleagues tested the hypothesis that cells within the Spemann organizer expressed certain genes important in the development of dorsal structures, such as the notochord.

3. The scientists used a procedure called expression cloning. In this process, they isolated the various mRNAs that were present in the tissue of the dorsal lip of the embryo. After purifying these mRNAs, they produced a cDNA library. This library contained all the genes expressed in the particular tissue at that particular time of development. The scientists then transcribed the different genes in the cDNA library into mRNAs and injected these into UV-damaged eggs, which were subsequently fertilized. UV-damaged fertilized eggs fail to develop dorsal structures. The scientists were interested in any mRNA that "rescued" the developing embryo and restored some level of normal development. One protein, noggin, was found to rescue the embryos and acted as a morphogen.

Test Yourself

1. a   2. c   3. c   4. d   5. b   6. c   7. b   8. e   9. e   10. e

Conceptual Questions

1. Autonomous specification results from the asymmetrical distribution of intracellular proteins and mRNAs during the cleavage events of embryonic development. The resulting daughter cells will contain different amounts of these cytoplasmic determinants, and this will direct these cells into different developmental fates. Conditional specification results from the interactions of proteins on the extracellular surface of the cell membranes of different cells or from proteins secreted from one cell and acting on another cell. This type of specification determines where a cell ends up within the embryo and what type of cell develops.

2. The timing of the final development of an embryo's organs is typically linked with the requirement for that organ's function. In mammals, for example, the heart is required early in development to pump blood through the embryonic and fetal circulation, thereby delivering nutrients and removing wastes. Fully functional lungs, however, are not required until the animal is born and begins breathing air for the first time.

3. Embryonic development is the process by which a fertilized egg is transformed into an organism with distinct physiological systems and body parts. Cell differentiation is the process by which different cells within a developing organism acquire specialized forms and functions, due to the expression of cell-specific genes. Growth is the enlargement of an embryo, as cells divide and/or enlarge.

Chapter 53

Concept Checks

Figure 53.2 Although swelling is one of the most obvious manifestations of inflammation, it has no significant adaptive value of its own. It is a consequence of fluid leaking out of blood vessels into the interstitial space. It can, however, contribute to pain sensations, because the buildup of fluid may cause distortion of connective tissue structures such as tendons and ligaments. Pain, while obviously unpleasant, is an important signal that alerts many animals to the injury and serves as a reminder to protect the injured site.

Figure 53.4 Recall from Chapter 47 that as blood circulates, a portion of the plasma—the fluid part of blood—exits venules and capillaries and enters the interstitial fluid. Most of the plasma is reabsorbed back into the capillaries, but a portion gets left behind. That excess fluid is drained away by lymph vessels and becomes lymph. Without lymph vessels, fluid would accumulate outside of the blood, in the interstitial fluid.

Figure 53.14 Because an animal may encounter the same type of pathogen many times during its life, having a secondary immune response means that future infections will be fought off much more efficiently.

BioConnections

Figure 53.2 When histamine receptors are blocked by antihistamines, histamine cannot promote wakefulness and thus drowsiness ensues. Some antihistamines are designed such that they cannot get into the extracellular fluid of the brain; these drugs are still effective in inhibiting allergic reactions but do not cause drowsiness.

Feature Investigation Questions

1. The amino acid sequence of Toll protein shared similarities with a portion of a protein known to be involved in immune responses in vertebrates. In addition, activation of Toll protein and the vertebrate immune protein (a cytokine receptor) resulted in the generation of some of the same intracellular signals. This suggested that in addition to its characterized role in embryonic development, Toll may also be important in immune functions in flies.

2. No, Toll protein is not a receptor that recognizes pathogen-associated molecular patterns (PAMPs) expressed on microbial surfaces, and thus it is distinguishable from Toll-like receptors in vertebrates. Toll is, however, a transmembrane protein that binds to extracellular signals; these signals arise, however, not from the microbes themselves but rather from proteins that are endogenous to flies and that are generated during infections.

3. Yes, the results of the survival study clearly implicated Toll as a protein required for the induction of antimicrobial proteins and the ability to withstand fungal infection. Thus, the investigators' hypothesis was supported.

Test Yourself
1. e 2. b 3. c 4. c 5. a 6. d 7. b 8. a 9. d 10. b

Conceptual Questions

1. Innate immunity is present at birth and is found in all animals. These defenses recognize general, conserved features common to a wide array of pathogens and include external barriers, such as the skin, and internal defenses involving phagocytes and other cells. Acquired immunity develops *after* an animal has been exposed to a *particular* antigen. The responses include humoral and cell-mediated defenses. Acquired immunity appears to be largely restricted to vertebrates. Unlike innate immunity, in acquired immunity, the response to an antigen is greatly increased if an animal is exposed to that antigen again at some future time.

2. Cytotoxic T cells are "attack" cells that are responsible for cell-mediated immunity. Once activated, they migrate to the location of their targets, bind to the targets by combining with an antigen on them, and directly kill the targets via secreted chemicals.

3. Pathogens are disease-causing microorganisms and include bacteria, viruses, and eukaryotic parasites such as certain protists, fungi and small worms. Bacteria are single-celled prokaryotes that lack a true nucleus but are capable of reproducing on their own, whereas viruses are nucleic acids packaged in a protein coat that require a host cell to reproduce.

Chapter 54

Concept Checks

Figure 54.4 Higher predation would occur where locust numbers are highest. This means that predators would be responding to an increase in prey density by eating more individuals.

Figure 54.6 Cold water suppresses the ability of the coral-building organisms to secrete their calcium carbonate shell.

Figure 54.9 In some areas when fire is prevented, fuel, in the form of old leaves and branches, can accumulate. When a fire eventually occurs, it can be so large and hot that it destroys everything in its path, even reaching high into the tree canopy.

Figure 54.11 Temperature and rainfall.

Figure 54.16 Acid soils are low in essential plant and animal nutrients such as calcium and nitrogen and are lethal to some soil microorganisms that are important in decomposition and nutrient cycling.

Figure 54.18 This occurs because increasing cloudiness and rain at the tropics maintain fairly constant temperatures across a wide latitudinal range.

Figure 54.22 Soil conditions can also influence biome type. Nutrient-poor soils, for example, may support vegetation different from that of the surrounding area.

Figure 54.23 Taiga.

BioConnections

Chapter Opener The main causes of extinctions are introduced species, direct exploitation, habitat destruction, and climate change. All are human-induced.

Figure 54.15 Plants cannot readily absorb salty water because of its highly negative water potential.

Feature Investigation Questions

1. Most believe that invasive species succeed in new environments due to the lack of natural enemies and that diseases and predators present in the original environment controlled the growth of the population. When these organisms are introduced into a novel environment, the natural enemies are usually absent. This allows for an unchecked increase in the population of the invasive species.

2. Callaway and Aschehoug were able to demonstrate through a controlled experiment that the presence of *Centaurea*, an invasive species, reduced the biomass of three other native species of grasses by releasing allelochemicals. Similar experiments using species of grasses that are found in the native region of *Centaurea* indicate that these species have evolved defenses against the allelochemicals.

3. The activated charcoal helps to remove the allelochemical from the soil. The researchers conducted this experiment to provide further evidence that the chemical released by the *Centaurea* was reducing the biomass of the native Montana grasses. With the removal of the chemicals by the addition of the charcoal, the researchers showed an increase in biomass of the native Montana grasses compared with the experiments lacking the charcoal.

Test Yourself
1. b 2. e 3. a 4. b 5. a 6. a 7. d 8. d 9. a 10. a

Conceptual Questions

1. Mountains are cooler than valleys because of adiabatic cooling. Air at higher altitudes expands because of decreased pressure. As it expands, air cools, at a rate of 10°C for every 1,000 m in elevation. As a result, mountain tops can be much cooler than the plains or valleys that surround them.

2. For several reasons. First, lightning strikes from electrical storms are usually more frequent in prairies than in deserts. Second, the vegetation in a prairie is more continuous and the biomass more extensive than in a desert, so fires burn more frequently and for longer.

3. Florida is a peninsula that is surrounded by the Atlantic Ocean and the Gulf of Mexico. Differential heating between the land and the sea creates onshore sea breezes on both the east and west coasts. These breezes often drift across the whole peninsula, bringing heavy rain.

Chapter 55

Concept Checks

Figure 55.3 In classical conditioning, an involuntary response comes to be associated with a stimulus that did not originally elicit the response, as with Pavlov's dogs salivating at the sound of a metronome.

Figure 55.5 The ability to sing the same distinctive song must be considered innate behavior because the cuckoo has had no opportunity to learn its song from its parents.

Figure 55.7 Tinbergen manipulated pinecones, but not all digger wasp nests are surrounded by pinecones. You could manipulate branches, twigs, stones, and leaves to determine the necessary size and dimensions of objects that digger wasps use as landmarks.

Figure 55.8 This is an unusual example because the return trip involves several different generations to complete: One generation overwinters in Mexico, but these individuals lay eggs and die on the return journey, and their offspring continue the return trip.

Figure 55.14 The individuals in the center of the group are less likely to be attacked than those on the edge of the group. This is referred to as the geometry of the selfish herd.

Figure 55.16 Because of the genetic benefit, the answer is nine cousins. Consider Hamilton's rule, expressed in the formula $rB > C$. Using cousins, $B = 9$, $r = 0.125$, and $C = 1$, and $1.125 > 1$. Using sisters, $B = 2$, $r = 0.5$, and $C = 1$. Because rB would not be greater than C, there would be no net genetic benefit in self-sacrifice.

Figure 55.17 All the larvae in the group are likely to be the progeny of one egg mass from one adult female moth. The death of the one caterpillar teaches a predator to avoid the pattern and benefits the caterpillar's close kin.

Figure 55.24 Because sperm are cheaper to produce than eggs, males try to maximize their fitness through attracting multiple females, whereas female fitness is maximized by choosing a mate with good genetic quality and parenting skills. Colorful plumage and elaborate adornments may be signals of the male's overall health.

Figure 55.25 The males aren't careful because it is likely the pups were fathered in the previous year by a different male. Being a harem master is demanding, and males may often only perform this role for a year or two.

BioConnections

Figure 55.3 Toxic or bad-tasting prey species converge on the same color patterns to reinforce the basic distasteful design.

Figure 55.4 According to studies of humans and other animals, learning a task increases the size of the brain regions that are associated with learning and memory.

Figure 55.25 One claw is enlarged and used in fights over females and to block burrows containing females so that other males cannot enter.

Feature Investigation Questions

1. Tinbergen observed the activity of digger wasps as they prepared to leave the nest. Each time, the wasp hovered and flew around the nest for a period of time before leaving. Tinbergen suggested that during this time, the wasp was making a mental map of the nest site. He hypothesized that the wasp was using characteristics of the nest site, particularly landmarks, to help relocate it.

2. Tinbergen placed pinecones around the nest of the wasps. When the wasps left the nest, he removed the pinecones from the nest site and set them up in the same pattern a distance away, constructing a sham nest. For each trial, the wasps would go directly to the sham nest, which had the pinecones around it. This indicated to Tinbergen that the wasps identified the nest based on the pinecone landmarks.

3. No. Tinbergen also conducted an experiment to determine if the wasps were responding to the visual cue of the pinecones or the chemical cue of the pinecone scent. The results of this experiment indicated that the wasps responded to the visual cue of the pinecones and not their scent.

Test Yourself

1. d 2. d 3. d 4. c 5. c 6. d 7. b 8. c 9. a 10. c

Conceptual Questions

1. The donation of the male's body to the female is the ultimate nuptial gift. It is possible that this meal enables the females to produce more eggs. In this way, the male's genes will be passed on to future generations.

2. Certainty of paternity influences degree of parental care. With internal fertilization, certainty of paternity is relatively low. With external fertilization, eggs and sperm are deposited together, and paternity is more certain. This explains why males of some species, such as mouth-breeding cichlid fish, are more likely to engage in parental care.

3. As male bears are killed by hunters, new males move into a territory and kill existing cubs. Thus, not only are bears killed directly by hunters, but population growth is also slowed as cubs are killed and population recovery is prolonged.

Chapter 56

Concept Checks

Figure 56.2 The total population size, N, would be estimated to be $110 \times 100/20$, or 550.

Figure 56.3 In a half-empty classroom, the distribution is often clumped because friends sit together.

Figure 56.7 (a) type III, (b) type II

Figure 56.11 $dN/dt = 0.1 \times 500 (1000 - 500)/1000 = 25$.

Figure 56.13 Only density-dependent factors operate in this way.

Figure 56.19 There were very few juveniles in the population and many mature adults. The population would be in decline.

Figure 56.22 Many different ecological footprint calculators are available on the Internet. Does altering inputs such as type of transportation, amount of meat eaten, or amount of waste generated make a difference?

BioConnections

Figure 56.3 Uniform. Territorial marking is likely to keep cheetahs well separated from each other.

Figure 56.14 It has lost the ability to produce viable seeds but it makes thousands of fully formed plantlets, borne on its leaves.

Feature Investigation Questions

1. It became apparent that the sheep population was declining. Some individuals felt that the decline in the population was due to increased wolf predation having a negative effect on population growth. This led to the suggestion of culling the wolf population to reduce the level of predation on the sheep population.

2. The survivorship curve is very similar to a typical type I survivorship curve. This suggests that survival is high among young and reproductively active members of the population and that mortality rates are higher for older members of the population. One difference between the actual survivorship curve and a typical type I curve is that the mortality rate of very young sheep was higher in the actual curve, and then it leveled off after the second year. This suggests that very young and older sheep are more at risk for predation.

3. It was concluded that wolf predation was not the primary reason for the drop in the sheep population. It appeared that wolves prey on the vulnerable members of the population and not on the healthy, reproductively active members. The Park Service determined that several cold winters may have had a more important effect on the sheep population than wolf predation did. Based on these conclusions, the Park Service ended a wolf population control program.

Test Yourself

1. b 2. e 3. b 4. c 5. c 6. b 7. c 8. d 9. c 10. c

Conceptual Questions

1. Increase. Instead of recapturing 5 tagged fish, we only recapture 4. Population size is now estimated as $50 \times 40/4 = 2000/4 = 500$. Our population estimate has increased to 500 when in fact it is more likely that 400 fish occur in the lake.

2. At medium values of N, $(K - N)/K$ is closer to a value of 1, and population growth is relatively large. If $K = 1,000$, $N = 500$, and $r = 0.1$, then

$$\frac{dN}{dt} = (0.1)(500) \times \frac{(1,000 - 100)}{1,000}$$

$$\frac{dN}{dt} = 25$$

However, if population sizes are low ($N = 100$), $(K - N)/K$ is so small that growth is low.

$$\frac{dN}{dt} = (0.1)(100) \times \frac{(1,000 - 100)}{1,000}$$

$$\frac{dN}{dt} = 9$$

By comparing these two examples with that shown in Section 56.3, we see that growth is small at high and low values of N and is greatest at immediate values of N. Growth is greatest when $N = K/2$. However, when expressed as a percentage, growth is greatest at low population sizes. Where $N = 100$, percentage growth = $9/100 = 9\%$. Where $N = 500$, percentage growth = $25/500 = 5\%$, and where $N = 900$, percentage growth = $9/100 = 1\%$.

3. In the ponds that dry out, species would tend to be semelparous, producing all their offspring in a single reproductive rate while water is present. In the permanently wet ponds, species would be iteroparous, reproducing repeatedly over the course of the year.

Chapter 57

Concept Checks

Figure 57.2 Individual vultures often fight one another over small carcasses. These interactions would constitute intraspecific interference competition.

Figure 57.3 There would be 10 possible pairings (AB, AC, AD, AE, BC, BD, BC, CD, CE, DE), of which only neighboring species (AB, BC, CD, DE) competed. Therefore, competition would be expected in 4/10 pairings, or 40% of the cases.

Figure 57.7 A 1974 review by Tom Schoener examined segregation in a more wide-ranging literature review of over 80 species, including slime molds, mollusks, and insects, as well as birds. He found segregation by habitat occurred in the majority of the examples, 55%. The other most common form of segregation was by food type, 40%.

Figure 57.8 Omnivores, such as bears, can feed on both plant material, such as berries, and animals, such as salmon. As such, omnivores may act as both predators and herbivores depending on what they are feeding on.

Figure 57.9 Batesian mimicry has a positive effect for the mimic, and the model is unaffected, so it is a +/0 relationship, like commensalism. Müllerian mimicry has a positive effect on both species, so it is a +/+ relationship, like mutualism.

Figure 57.11 Because there is no evolutionary history between invasive predators and native prey, the native prey often have no defenses against these predators and are very easily caught and eaten.

Figure 57.13 Invertebrate herbivores can eat around mechanical defenses; therefore, chemical defenses are probably most effective against invertebrate herbivores.

Figure 57.20 It's an example of facultative mutualism, because in this case, both species can live without the other.

Figure 57.23 Fertilizer increases plant quality and hence herbivore density, which, in turn, increases the density of spiders. This is a bottom-up effect.

BioConnections

Figure 57.10 Most mollusks are heavily armored. However, sea slugs have lost their shells. These species are aposematically colored, advertising a poisonous body. In addition, some octopuses are poisonous, and most can eject an inky chemical smoke screen.

Figure 57.13 Red hot chili peppers.

Figure 57.20 Mycorrhizae.

Figure 57.21 Red.

Feature Investigation Questions

1. The two species of barnacles can be found in the same intertidal zone, but there is a distinct difference in niche of each species. *Chthamalus stellatus* is found only in the upper intertidal zone. *Semibalanus balanoides* is found only in the lower tidal zone.

2. Connell moved rocks with young *Chthamalus* from the upper intertidal zone into the lower intertidal zone to allow *Semibalanus* to colonize the rocks. After the rocks were colonized by *Semibalanus*, he removed *Semibalanus* from one side of each rock and returned the rocks to the lower intertidal zone. This allowed Connell to observe the growth of *Chthamalus* in the presence and the absence of *Semibalanus*.

3. Connell observed that *Chthamalus* was more resistant to desiccation than *Semibalanus*. Though *Semibalanus* was the better competitor in the lower intertidal zone, the species was at a disadvantage in the upper intertidal zone when water levels were low. This allowed *Chthamalus* to flourish and outcompete *Semibalanus* in a different region of the intertidal zone.

Test Yourself

1. d   2. c   3. b   4. d   5. c   6. b   7. d   8. b   9. b   10. c

Conceptual Questions

1. Interspecific and interference competition.

2. Yes, it is possible that by removing parasites from a neighbor, an individual may be reducing the likelihood of the parasite spreading. You scratch my back, I'll scratch yours, and together we will both be better off.

3. There are at least three reasons why we don't see more herbivory in nature. First, plants possess an array of defensive chemicals, including alkaloids, phenolics, and terpenes. Second, many herbivore populations are reduced by the action of natural enemies. We see evidence for this in the world of biological control. Third, the low nutritive value of plants ensures herbivore populations remain low and unlikely to affect plant populations.

Chapter 58

Concept Checks

Figure 58.5 Species richness of trees doesn't increase because rainfall in the western United States is low compared with that in the east.

Figure 58.6 Hurricanes, tropical storms, heavy rainfall, and mudslides are disturbances that maintain a mosaic of disturbed and undisturbed habitats, favoring high species richness in the tropics.

Figure 58.10 As we walk forward from the edge of the glacier to the mouth of the inlet, we are walking backward in ecological time to communities that originated hundreds of years ago.

Figure 58.11 No, competition is also important. For example, the shade from later-arriving species, such as spruce trees, causes competitive exclusion of some of the original understory species.

Figure 58.13 Competition features more prominently. Although early colonists tend to make the habitat more favorable for later colonists, it is the later colonists who outcompete the earlier ones, and this fuels species change.

Figure 58.14 If a small island was extremely close to the mainland, it could continually receive migrating species from the source pool. Even though these species could not complete their life cycle on such a small island, extinctions would rarely be recorded because of this continual immigration.

Figure 58.15 At first glance, the change looks small, but the data are plotted on a log scale. On this scale, an increase in bird richness from 1.2 to 1.6 equals an increase from 16 to 40 species, a change of over 100%.

BioConnections

Figure 58.1 A hypothesis is a proposed idea, whereas a theory is a broad explanation backed by extensive evidence.

Figure 58.11 *Frankia*.

Figure 58.14 The model helps conservationists design the best shaped and optimally placed nature reserves.

Feature Investigation Questions

1. Simberloff and Wilson were testing the three predictions of the theory of island biogeography. One prediction suggested that the number of species should increase with increasing island size. Another prediction suggested that the number of species should decrease with increasing distance of the island from the source pool. Finally, the researchers were testing the prediction that the turnover of species on islands should be considerable.

2. Simberloff and Wilson used the information gathered from the species survey to determine whether the same types of species recolonized the islands or if colonizing species were random.

3. The data suggested that species richness did increase with island size. Also, the researchers found that in all but one of the islands, the number of species was similar to the number of species before fumigation.

Test Yourself

1. c   2. c   3. d   4. b   5. c   6. d   7. a   8. d   9. b   10. c

Conceptual Questions

1. Much of what we learned about secondary metabolites in Chapter 57 related to how these chemicals reduced herbivory. This graph shows that a tree's range influences species richness of herbivores. As such it suggests a reduced role for secondary metabolites in influencing herbivore species richness, although abundance of individual herbivore species may still be influenced by the presence of secondary metabolites.

Disturbance	Frequency	Severity of Effects
Forest fire	Low to high, depending on lightning frequency	High to low, depending on frequency
Hurricane	Low	Severe
Tornado	Very low	Severe
Floods	Medium to high in riparian areas	Fairly low; many communities can recover quickly
Disease epidemics	Low	High; may cause catastrophic losses of species
Droughts	Low	Potentially severe
High winds	High	May kill large trees and create light gaps
Hard freezes	Low	May cause deaths to tropical species, such as mangroves

2. Facilitation. *Calluna* litter enriches the soil with nitrogen, facilitating the growth of the grasses. Adding fertilizer also increases soil nitrogen.

Chapter 59

Concept Checks

Figure 59.3 It depends on the trophic level of their food, whether dead vegetation or dead animals. Many decomposers feed at multiple trophic levels.

Figure 59.6 The production efficiency is $(16/823) \times 100$, or 1.9%.

Figure 59.13 On a population level, plant secondary metabolites can deter herbivores from feeding. However, on an ecosystem level, these effects are not as important because higher primary production tends to result in higher secondary production.

Figure 59.18 The greatest stores are in rocks and fossil fuels.

Figure 59.19 It fluctuates because less CO_2 is emitted from vegetation in the summer and more is emitted in the winter. This pattern is driven by the large land masses of the Northern Hemisphere relative to the smaller land masses of the Southern Hemisphere.

BioConnections

Figure 59.2 Cyanobacteria.

Figure 59.3 Basidiomycetes and Zygomycetes.

Figure 59.9 In organic fertilizers, most minerals are bound to organic molecules and are released relatively slowly. In inorganic fertilizers, the minerals are not bound up in this way and are immediately available to plants. However, they are also more easily leached out by heavy rainfall.

Figure 59.18 Oxygen, hydrogen, and nitrogen.

Figure 59.19 About 450 mya, in the Ordovician period.

Feature Investigation Questions

1. The researchers were testing the effects of increased carbon dioxide levels on the forest ecosystem. The researchers were testing the effects of increased CO_2 levels on primary production as well as other trophic levels in the ecosystem.

2. By increasing the CO_2 levels in only half of the chambers, the researchers were maintaining the control treatments necessary for all scientific studies. By maintaining equal numbers of control and experimental treatments, the researchers could compare data to determine what effects the experimental treatment had on the ecosystem.

3. The increased CO_2 levels led to an increase in primary productivity, as expected. Since photosynthetic rate is limited by CO_2 levels, increases in the available CO_2 should increase photosynthetic rates. Interestingly, though, the increase in primary productivity did not lead to an increase in herbivory. The results indicated that herbivory actually decreased with increased CO_2 levels.

Test Yourself

1. d   2. d   3. d   4. a   5. a   6. d   7. a   8. b   9. c   10. d

Conceptual Questions

1. Carrion beetles are decomposers. They feed on dead animals such as mice, at trophic level 3 or 4. Mice generally feed on vegetative material (trophic level 1)

or crawling arthropods (trophic level 2), so mice themselves feed at trophic level 2 or 3.

2. Chain lengths are short in food webs because there is low production efficiency and only a 10% rate of energy transfer from one level to another, so only a few links can be supported.

3. A unit of energy passes through a food web only once and energy is lost at each transfer between trophic levels. In contrast, chemicals cycle repeatedly through food webs and may become more concentrated at higher trophic levels.

Chapter 60

Concept Checks

Figure 60.3 It is possible that the results are driven by what is known as a sampling effect. As the numbers of species in the community increase, so does the likelihood of including a "superspecies," a species with exceptionally large individuals that would use up resources. In communities with higher diversity, care has to be taken that increased diversity is driving the results, not the increased likelihood of including a superspecies.

Figure 60.6 The extinction rate could increase because an increasing human population requires more space to live, work, and grow food, resulting in less available habitat and resources for other species.

Figure 60.8 No, some species, such as self-fertilizing flowers, appear to be less affected by inbreeding.

Figure 60.9 The effective population size (N_e) would be = $(4 \times 125 \times 500) / (125 + 500)$, or 400.

Figure 60.12 Corridors might also promote the movement of invasive species or the spread of fire between areas.

Figure 60.13 They act as habitat corridors because they permit movement of species between forest fragments.

BioConnections

Figure 60.2 A protist. Mosquitoes are the vectors.

Figure 60.19 Genetic cloning could be used to save threatened species or even to resurrect recently extinct species. Cloning may theoretically be able to increase genetic variability of populations if it were possible to use cells from deceased animals. However, cloning is not a panacea because habitat loss, poaching, or invasive species may still prevent reintroductions of species back into the wild.

Feature Investigation Questions

1. The researchers hoped to replicate terrestrial communities that differed only in their level of biodiversity. This would allow the researchers to determine the relationship between biodiversity and ecological function.

2. The hypothesis was that ecological function was directly related to biodiversity. If biodiversity increased, the hypothesis suggested that ecological function should increase.

3. The researchers tested for ecosystem function by monitoring community respiration, decomposition, nutrient retention rates, and productivity. All of these indicate the efficiency of nutrient production and use in the ecosystem.

Test Yourself

1. d   2. e   3. a   4. c   5. c   6. e   7. e   8. a   9. c   10. b

Conceptual Questions

1. To reduce the risks associated with inbreeding in especially small populations.

2. The most vulnerable are those with small population sizes, low rates of population growth, *K*-selected (Chapter 56), with inbreeding and possible harem mating structure, tame and unafraid of humans, possibly limited to islands, flightless, possibly valuable to humans as timber, a source of meat or fur, or desirable by collectors (Chapter 60).

3. Increased species diversity increases ecosystem function. Ecosystem functions such as nutrient cycling, regulation of atmospheric gasses, pollination of crops, pest regulation, water purity, storm protection, and sewage purification are all likely to be increased by increased species diversity. In addition, increased plant species diversity increases likely availability of new medicines for humans.

Glossary

A

A band A wide, dark band in a myofibril produced by the orderly parallel arrangement of the thick filaments in the middle of each sarcomere.

abiotic The term used to describe interactions between organisms and their nonliving environment.

abortion A procedure or circumstance that causes the death of an embryo or fetus after implantation.

abscisic acid One of several plant hormones that help a plant cope with environmental stress.

abscission The process by which plants drop their leaves.

absolute refractory period The period during an action potential when the inactivation gate of the voltage-gated sodium channel is closed; during this time, it is impossible to generate another action potential.

absorption The process in which digested nutrients are transported from the digestive cavity into an animal's circulatory system.

absorption spectrum A diagram that depicts the wavelengths of electromagnetic radiation that are absorbed by a pigment.

absorptive nutrition The process whereby an organism uses enzymes to digest organic materials and absorbs the resulting small food molecules into its cells.

absorptive state One of two alternating phases in the utilization of nutrients; occurs when ingested nutrients enter the blood from the gastrointestinal tract. The other phase is the postabsorptive state.

acclimatization A long-term and persistent physiological adaptation to an extreme environment.

accommodation In the vertebrate eye, the process in which contraction and relaxation of the ciliary muscles adjust the lens according to the angle at which light enters the eye.

acetylcholinesterase An enzyme located on membranes of postsynaptic cells that respond to the neurotransmitter acetylcholine, such as in muscle fibers in a neuromuscular junction; breaks down excess acetylcholine released into the synaptic cleft.

acid A molecule that releases hydrogen ions (H^+) in solution.

acid hydrolase A hydrolytic enzyme found in lysosomes that functions at acidic pH and uses a molecule of water to break a covalent bond.

acid rain Precipitation with a pH of less than 5.6; results from the burning of fossil fuels.

acidic A solution that has a pH below 7.

acoelomate An animal that lacks a fluid-filled body cavity.

acquired antibiotic resistance The common phenomenon of a previously susceptible strain of bacteria becoming resistant to a specific antibiotic.

acquired immunity A specific immune defense that develops only after an animal is exposed to a foreign substance; believed to be unique to vertebrates.

acquired immunodeficiency syndrome (AIDS) A disease caused by the human immunodeficiency virus (HIV) that leads to a defect in the immune system of infected individuals.

acrocentric A chromosome in which the centromere is near one end.

acromegaly A condition in which a person's growth hormone level is abnormally elevated, causing many bones to thicken and enlarge.

acrosomal reaction An event in fertilization in which enzymes released from a sperm's acrosome break down the outer layers of an egg cell, allowing the entry of the sperm cell's nucleus into the egg cell.

acrosome A special structure at the tip of a sperm's head containing proteolytic enzymes that break down the protective outer layers of the egg cell at fertilization.

actin A cytoskeletal protein.

actin filament A thin type of protein filament composed of actin proteins that forms part of the cytoskeleton and supports the plasma membrane; plays a key role in cell strength, shape, and movement.

action potential An electrical signal along a cell's plasma membrane; occurs in animal neuron axons and muscle cells and in some plant cells.

action spectrum The rate of photosynthesis plotted as a function of different wavelengths of light.

activation energy An initial input of energy in a chemical reaction that allows the molecules to get close enough to cause a rearrangement of bonds.

activator A transcription factor that binds to DNA and increases the rate of transcription.

active immunity An animal's ability to fight off a pathogen to which it has been previously exposed. Active immunity can develop as a result of natural infection or artificial immunization.

active site The location in an enzyme where a chemical reaction takes place.

active transport The transport of a solute across a membrane against its gradient (from a region of low concentration to a region of higher concentration). Active transport requires an input of energy.

adaptations The processes and structures by which organisms adjust to changes in their environment.

adaptive radiation The process whereby a single ancestral species evolves into a wide array of descendant species that differ greatly in their habitat, form, or behavior.

adenine (A) A purine base found in DNA and RNA.

adenosine triphosphate (ATP) A molecule that is a common energy source for all cells.

adenylyl cyclase An enzyme in the plasma membrane that synthesizes cAMP from ATP.

adherens junction A mechanically strong cell junction between animal cells that typically occurs in bands. The cells are connected to each other via cadherins, and the cadherins are linked to actin filaments on the inside of the cells.

adhesion The ability of two different substances to bind to each other; the ability of water to be attracted to, and thereby adhere to, a surface that is not electrically neutral.

adiabatic cooling The process in which increasing elevation leads to a decrease in air temperature.

adventitious root A root that is produced on the surfaces of stems (and sometimes leaves) of vascular plants; also, roots that develop at the bases of stem cuttings.

aerenchyma Spongy plant tissue with large air spaces.

aerobe An organism that requires oxygen to survive.

aerobic respiration A type of cellular respiration in which O_2 is consumed and CO_2 is released.

aerotolerant anaerobe A microorganism that does not use oxygen but is not poisoned by it either.

afferent arterioles Blood vessels that provide a pathway for blood into the glomeruli of the vertebrate kidney.

affinity The degree of attraction between an enzyme and its substrate.

aflatoxins Fungal toxins that cause liver cancer and are a major health concern worldwide.

age-specific fertility rate The rate of offspring production for females of a certain age; used to calculate how a population grows.

age structure The relative numbers of individuals of each defined age group in a population.

AIDS *See* acquired immunodeficiency syndrome.

air sac A component of the avian respiratory system; air sacs—not lungs—expand when a bird inhales and shrink when it exhales. They do not participate in gas exchange, but help direct air through the lungs.

akinete A thick-walled, food-filled cell produced by certain bacteria or protists that enables them to survive unfavorable conditions in a dormant state.

aldosterone A steroid hormone made by the adrenal glands that regulates salt and water balance in vertebrates.

algae (singular, **alga**) A term that applies to about 10 phyla of protists, including both photosynthetic and nonphotosynthetic species; often also includes cyanobacteria.

alimentary canal In animals, the single elongated tube of a digestive system, with an opening at either end through which food and eventually wastes pass from one end to the other.

alkaline A solution with a pH above 7.

alkaloids A group of secondary metabolites that contain nitrogen and usually have a cyclic, ringlike structure. Examples include caffeine and nicotine.

allantois One of the four extraembryonic membranes in the amniotic egg. It serves as a disposal sac for metabolic wastes.

Allee effect The phenomenon that some individuals will fail to mate successfully purely by chance, for example, because of the failure to find a mate.

allele A variant form of a gene.

allele frequency The number of copies of a particular allele in a population divided by the total number of alleles in that population.

allelochemical A powerful plant chemical, often a root exudate, that kills other plant species.

allelopathy The suppressed growth of one species due to the release of toxic chemicals by another species.

allergy Hypersensitivity reaction to a harmless substance.

allopatric The term used to describe species occurring in different geographic areas.

allopatric speciation A form of speciation that occurs when a population becomes geographically isolated from other populations and evolves into one or more new species.

alloploid An organism having at least one set of chromosomes from two or more different species.

alloploidy *See* alloploid.

allosteric site A site on an enzyme where a molecule can bind noncovalently and affect the function of the active site.

alpha (α) helix A type of protein secondary structure in which a polypeptide forms a repeating helical structure stabilized by hydrogen bonds.

alternation of generations The phenomenon that occurs in plants and some protists in which the life cycle alternates between multicellular diploid organisms, called sporophytes, and multicellular haploid organisms, called gametophytes.

alternative splicing The splicing of pre-mRNA in more than one way to create two or more different polypeptides.

altruism Behavior that appears to benefit others at a cost to oneself.

alveolus (plural, **alveoli**) 1. Saclike structures in the lungs where gas exchange occurs. 2. Saclike cellular features of the protists known as alveolates.

Alzheimer disease (AD)   The leading worldwide cause of dementia; characterized by a loss of memory and intellectual and emotional function (formerly called Alzheimer's disease).

AM fungi   A phylum of fungi that forms mycorrhizal associations with plants.

amensalism   One-sided competition between species, in which the interaction is detrimental to one species but not to the other.

Ames test   A test that helps ascertain whether or not an agent is a mutagen by using a strain of a bacterium, *Salmonella typhimurium*.

amino acid   The building blocks of proteins. Amino acids have a common structure in which a carbon atom, called the α-carbon, is linked to an amino group (NH_2) and a carboxyl group (COOH). The α-carbon also is linked to a hydrogen atom and a particular side chain.

aminoacyl site (A site)   One of three sites for tRNA binding in the ribosome during translation; the other two are the peptidyl site (P site) and the exit site (E site). The A site is where incoming tRNA molecules bind to the mRNA (except for the initiator tRNA).

aminoacyl tRNA   *See* charged tRNA.

aminoacyl-tRNA synthetase   An enzyme that catalyzes the attachment of amino acids to tRNA molecules.

amino terminus   *See* N-terminus.

ammonia (NH_3)   A highly toxic nitrogenous waste typically produced by many aquatic animal species.

ammonification   The conversion of organic nitrogen to NH_3 and NH_4^+ during the nitrogen cycle.

amnion   The innermost of the four extraembryonic membranes in the amniotic egg. It protects the developing embryo in a fluid-filled sac called the amniotic cavity.

amniotes   A group of tetrapods with amniotic eggs that includes turtles, lizards, snakes, crocodiles, birds, and mammals.

amniotic egg   A type of egg produced by amniotic animals that contains the developing embryo and the four separate extraembryonic membranes that it produces: the amnion, the yolk sac, the allantois, and the chorion.

amoeba (plural, **amoebae**)   A protist that moves by pseudopodia, which involves extending cytoplasm into filaments or lobes.

amoebocyte   A mobile cell within a sponge's mesophyl that absorbs food from choanocytes, digests it, and carries the nutrients to other cells.

amphibian   An ectothermic, vertebrate animal that metamorphoses from a water-breathing to an air-breathing form but must return to the water to reproduce.

amphipathic   Molecules containing a hydrophobic (water-fearing) region and a hydrophilic (water-loving) region.

ampulla (plural, **ampullae**)   1. A muscular sac at the base of each tube foot of an echinoderm; used to store water. 2. A bulge in the walls of the semicircular canals of the mammalian inner ear; important for sensing circular motions of the head.

amygdala   An area of the vertebrate forebrain known to be critical for understanding and remembering emotional situations.

amylase   A digestive enzyme in saliva and the pancreas involved in the digestion of starch.

anabolic reaction   A metabolic pathway that involves the synthesis of larger molecules from smaller precursor molecules. Such reactions usually require an input of energy.

anabolism   A metabolic pathway that results in the synthesis of cellular molecules and macromolecules; requires an input of energy.

anaerobic   Refers to a process that occurs in the absence of oxygen; a form of metabolism that does not require oxygen.

anaerobic respiration   The breakdown of organic molecules in the absence of oxygen.

anagenesis   The pattern of speciation in which a single species is transformed into a different species over the course of many generations.

analogous structure   A structure that is the result of convergent evolution. Such structures have arisen independently, two or more times, because species have occupied similar types of environments on Earth.

anaphase   The phase of mitosis during which the sister chromatids separate from each other and move to opposite poles; the poles themselves also move farther apart.

anchoring junction   A type of junction between animal cells that attaches cells to each other and to the extracellular matrix (ECM).

androecium   The aggregate of stamens that forms the third whorl of a flower.

androgens   Steroid hormones produced by the male testes (and, to a lesser extent, the adrenal glands) that affect most aspects of male reproduction.

anemia   A condition characterized by lower than normal levels of hemoglobin, which reduces the amount of oxygen that can be stored in the blood.

aneuploidy   An alteration in the number of particular chromosomes so that the total number of chromosomes is not an exact multiple of a set.

angina pectoris   Chest pain during exertion due to the heart being deprived of oxygen.

angiosperm   A flowering plant. The term means enclosed seed, which reflects the presence of seeds within fruits.

animal cap assay   A type of experiment used to identify proteins secreted by embryonic cells that induce cells in the animal pole to differentiate into mesoderm.

animal pole   In triploblast organisms, the pole of the egg with less yolk and more cytoplasm.

Animalia   A eukaryotic kingdom of the domain Eukarya.

animals   Multicellular heterotrophs with cells that lack cell walls. Most animals have nerves, muscles, the capacity to move at some point in their life cycle, and the ability to reproduce sexually, with sperm fusing directly with eggs.

anion   An ion that has a net negative charge.

annual   A plant that dies after producing seed during its first year of life.

anorexia nervosa   An eating disorder characterized by aversion to food, starvation, and illness secondary to malnourishment.

antagonist   A muscle or group of muscles that produces oppositely directed movements at a joint.

antenna complex   *See* light-harvesting complex.

anterior   Refers to the end of an animal where the head is found.

anteroposterior axis   In bilateral animals, one of the three axes along which the adult body pattern is organized; the others are the dorsoventral axis and the right-left axis.

anther   The uppermost part of a flower stamen, consisting of a cluster of microsporangia that produce and release pollen.

antheridia   Round or elongate gametangia that produce sperm in plants.

anthropoidea   A member of a group of primates that includes the monkeys and the hominoidea; these species are larger-brained and diurnal.

antibiotic   A chemical, usually made by microorganisms, that inhibits the growth of certain other microorganisms.

antibody   A protein secreted by plasma cells that is part of the immune response; antibodies travel all over the body to reach antigens identical to those that stimulated their production, combine with these antigens, then guide an attack that eliminates the antigens or the cells bearing them.

anticodon   A three-nucleotide sequence in tRNA that is complementary to a codon in mRNA.

antidiuretic hormone (ADH)   A hormone secreted by the posterior pituitary gland that acts on kidney cells to decrease urine production.

antigen   Any foreign molecule that the host does not recognize as self and that triggers a specific immune response.

antigen-presenting cell (APC)   Cells bearing fragments of antigen, called antigenic determinants or epitopes, complexed with the cell's major histocompatibility complex (MHC) proteins.

antiparallel   The arrangement in DNA where one strand runs in the 5′ to 3′ direction while the other strand is oriented in the 3′ to 5′ direction.

antiporter   A type of transporter that binds two or more ions or molecules and transports them in opposite directions across a membrane.

anus   The final portion of the alimentary canal through which solid wastes are expelled.

aorta   In vertebrates, a large blood vessel that exits a ventricle of the heart and leads to the systemic circulation.

apical-basal-patterning genes   A category of genes that are important in early stages of plant development during which the apical and basal axes are formed.

apical-basal polarity   An architectural feature of plants in which they display an upper, apical pole and a lower, basal pole; shoot apical meristem occurs at the apical pole, and root apical meristem occurs at the basal pole.

apical constriction   A cellular process during gastrulation that occurs in bottle cells, where a reduction in the diameter of the actin rings connected to the adherens junctions causes the cells to elongate toward their basal end.

apical meristem   In plants, a group of actively dividing cells at a growing tip.

apical region   The region of a plant seedling that produces the leaves and flowers.

apomixis   A natural asexual reproductive process in which plant fruits and seeds are produced in the absence of fertilization.

apoplast   The continuum of water-soaked cell walls and intercellular spaces in a plant.

apoplastic transport   The movement of solutes through cell walls and the spaces between cells.

apoptosis   Programmed cell death.

aposematic coloration   Warning coloration that advertises an organism's unpalatable taste.

aquaporin   A transport protein in the form of a channel that allows the rapid diffusion of water across the cell membrane.

aqueous humor   A thin liquid in the anterior cavity behind the cornea of the vertebrate eye.

aqueous solution   A solution made with water.

aquifer   An underground water supply.

arbuscular mycorrhizae   Symbiotic associations between AM fungi and the roots of vascular plants.

Archaea   One of the three domains of life; the other two are Bacteria and Eukarya.

archaea   When not capitalized, refers to a cell or species within the domain Archaea.

archegonia   Flask-shaped plant gametangia that enclose an egg cell.

archenteron   A cavity formed in an animal embryo during gastrulation that will become the organism's digestive tract.

area hypothesis   The proposal that larger areas contain more species than smaller areas because they can support larger populations and a greater range of habitats.

arteriole   A single-celled layer of endothelium surrounded by one or two layers of smooth muscle and connective tissue that delivers blood to the capillaries and distributes blood to regions of the body in proportion to metabolic demands.

artery   A blood vessel that carries blood away from the heart.

artificial selection   *See* selective breeding.

asci (singular, **ascus**)   Fungal sporangia shaped like sacs that produce and release sexual ascospores.

ascocarp   The type of fruiting body produced by ascomycete fungi.

ascomycetes   A phylum of fungi that produce sexual spores in saclike asci located at the surfaces of fruiting bodies known as ascocarps.

ascospore   The type of sexual spore produced by the ascomycete fungi.

aseptate   The condition of not being partitioned into smaller cells; usually refers to fungal cells.

asexual reproduction   A reproductive strategy that occurs when offspring are produced from a single parent, without the fusion of gametes from two parents. The offspring are therefore clones of the parent.

A site   *See* aminoacyl site.

assimilation   During the nitrogen cycle, the process by which plants and animals incorporate the ammonia and NO_3^- formed through nitrogen fixation and nitrification.

assisted reproductive technologies (ART)   Any of a group of methods used to produce a pregnancy by artificial mechanisms.

associative learning   A change in behavior due to an association between a stimulus and a response.

asthma   A disease in which the smooth muscles around the bronchioles contract more than usual, decreasing airflow in the lungs.

AT/GC rule   Refers to the phenomenon that an A in one DNA strand always hydrogen-bonds with a T in the opposite strand, and a G in one strand always bonds with a C.

atherosclerosis   The condition in which large plaques may occlude (block) the lumen of an artery.

atmospheric (barometric) pressure   The pressure exerted by the gases in air on the body surfaces of animals.

atom   The smallest functional unit of matter that forms all chemical substances and cannot be further broken down into other substances by ordinary chemical or physical means.

atomic mass   An atom's mass relative to the mass of other atoms. By convention, the most common form of carbon, which has six protons and six neutrons, is assigned an atomic mass of exactly 12.

atomic nucleus   The center of an atom; contains protons and neutrons.

atomic number   The number of protons in an atom.

ATP   *See* adenosine triphosphate.

ATP-dependent chromatin remodeling enzyme   An enzyme that catalyzes a change in the positions of nucleosomes.

ATP synthase   An enzyme that utilizes the energy stored in a H^+ electrochemical gradient for the synthesis of ATP via chemiosmosis.

atrial natriuretic peptide (ANP)   A peptide secreted from the atria of the heart whenever blood levels of sodium increase; ANP causes a natriuresis by decreasing sodium reabsorption in the kidney tubules.

atrioventricular (AV) node   Specialized cardiac cells in most vertebrates that sit near the junction of the atria

and ventricles and conduct the electrical events from the atria to the ventricles.

atrioventricular (AV) valve   A one-way valve into the ventricles of the vertebrate heart through which blood moves from the atria.

atrium   In the heart, a chamber to collect blood from the tissues.

atrophy   A reduction in the size of a structure, such as a muscle.

audition   The ability to detect and interpret sound waves; present in vertebrates and arthropods.

autoimmune disease   In humans and many other vertebrates, a disorder in which the body's normal state of immune tolerance breaks down, with the result that attacks are directed against the body's own cells and tissues.

autonomic nervous system   The division of the peripheral nervous system that regulates homeostasis and organ function.

autonomous specification   The unequal acquisition of cytoplasmic factors during cell division in a developing vertebrate embryo.

autophagosome   A double-membrane structure enclosing cellular material destined to be degraded; produced by the process of autophagy.

autophagy   A process whereby cellular material, such as a worn-out organelle, becomes enclosed in a double membrane and is degraded.

autopolyploidy   The condition of having more than two copies of the entire nuclear genome, which may result when all homologous chromosome pairs do not separate during meiosis.

autosomes   All of the chromosomes found in the cell nucleus of eukaryotes except for the sex chromosomes.

autotomy   In echinoderms, the ability to detach a body part, such as a limb, that will later regenerate.

autotroph   An organism that has metabolic pathways that use energy from either inorganic molecules or light to make organic molecules.

auxin   One of several types of hormones considered to be "master" plant hormones because they influence plant structure, development, and behavior in many ways.

auxin efflux carrier   One of several types of PIN proteins, which transport auxin out of plant cells.

auxin influx carrier   A plasma membrane protein that transports auxin into plant cells.

auxin-response genes   Plant genes that are regulated by the hormone auxin.

avirulence gene (*Avr* gene)   A gene in a plant pathogen that encodes a virulence-enhancing elicitor, which causes plant disease.

Avogadro's number   As first described by Italian physicist Amedeo Avogadro, 1 mole of any element contains the same number of atoms—6.022×10^{23}.

axillary bud   A bud that occurs in the axil, the upper angle where a twig or leaf emerges from a stem.

axillary meristem   A meristem produced in the axil, the upper angle where a twig or leaf emerges from a stem. Axillary meristems generate axillary buds, which produce flowers or branches.

axon   An extension of the plasma membrane of a neuron that is involved in sending signals to neighboring cells.

axon hillock   The part of the axon closest to the cell body; typically where an action potential begins.

axon terminal   The end of the axon that sends electrical or chemical messages to other cells.

axoneme   The internal structure of eukaryotic flagella and cilia consisting of microtubules, the motor protein dynein, and linking proteins.

B

bacilli (singular, **bacillus**)   Rod-shaped prokaryotic cells.

backbone   The linear arrangement of phosphates and sugar molecules in a DNA or RNA strand.

Bacteria   One of the three domains of life; the other two are Archaea and Eukarya.

bacteria (singular, **bacterium**)   When not capitalized, refers to a cell or species within the domain Bacteria.

bacterial artificial chromosome (BAC)   A cloning vector derived from F factors that can contain large DNA inserts.

bacterial colony   A clone of genetically identical cells formed from a single cell.

bacteriophage   A virus that infects bacteria.

bacteroid   A modified bacterial cell of the type known as rhizobia present in mature root nodules of some plants.

balanced polymorphism   The phenomenon in which two or more alleles are kept in balance and maintained in a population over the course of many generations.

balancing selection   A type of natural selection that maintains genetic diversity in a population.

balloon angioplasty   A common treatment to restore blood flow through a blood vessel. A thin tube with a tiny, inflatable balloon at its tip is threaded through the artery to the diseased area; inflating the balloon compresses the plaque against the arterial wall, widening the lumen.

barometric pressure   *See* atmospheric pressure.

baroreceptor   A pressure-sensitive region within the walls of certain arteries that contains the endings of nerve cells; these regions sense and help to maintain blood pressure in the normal range for an animal.

Barr body   A highly condensed X chromosome present in female mammals.

basal body   A site at the base of flagella or cilia from which microtubules grow. Basal bodies are anchored on the cytosolic side of the plasma membrane.

basal metabolic rate (BMR)   The metabolic rate of an animal under resting conditions, in a postabsorptive state, and at a standard temperature.

basal nuclei   Clusters of neuronal cell bodies in the vertebrate forebrain that surround the thalamus and lie beneath the cerebral cortex; involved in planning and learning movements.

basal region   The region of a plant seedling that produces the roots.

basal transcription   A low level of transcription resulting from just the core promoter.

basal transcription apparatus   In a eukaryotic structural gene, refers to the complex of RNA polymerase II, general transcription factors (GTFs), and a DNA sequence containing a TATA box.

base   1. A molecule that when dissolved in water lowers the H^+ concentration. 2. A component of nucleotides that is a single or double ring of carbon and nitrogen atoms.

base pair   The structure in which two bases in opposite strands of DNA hydrogen-bond with each other.

base substitution   A mutation that involves the substitution of a single base in the DNA for another base.

basic local alignment search tool (BLAST)   *See* BLAST.

basidia   Club-shaped cells that produce sexual spores in basidiomycete fungi.

basidiocarp   The type of fruiting body produced by basidiomycete fungi.

basidiomycetes   A phylum of fungi whose sexual spores are produced on the surfaces of club-shaped structures (basidia).

basidiospore   A sexual spore of the basidiomycete fungi.

basilar membrane   A component of the mammalian ear that vibrates back and forth in response to sound and bends the stereocilia in one direction and then the other.

basophil A type of leukocyte that secretes the anticlotting factor heparin at the site of an infection, which helps flush out the infected site; basophils also secrete histamine, which attracts infection-fighting cells and proteins.

Batesian mimicry The mimicry of an unpalatable species (the model) by a palatable one (the mimic).

Bayesian method One method used to evaluate a phylogenetic tree based on an evolutionary model.

B cell A type of lymphocyte responsible for specific immunity.

behavior The observable response of organisms to external or internal stimuli.

behavioral ecology A subdiscipline of organismal ecology that focuses on how the behavior of an individual organism contributes to its survival and reproductive success, which, in turn, eventually affects the population density of the species.

benign tumor A precancerous mass of abnormal cells.

beta (β) pleated sheet A type of protein secondary structure in which regions of a polypeptide lie parallel to each other and are held together by hydrogen bonds to form a repeating zigzag shape.

bidirectional replication The process in which DNA replication proceeds outward from the origin in opposite directions.

biennial A plant that does not reproduce during the first year of life but may reproduce within the following year.

bilateral symmetry An architectural feature in which the body or organ of an organism can be divided along a vertical plane at the midline to create two halves.

Bilateria Bilaterally symmetric animals.

bile A substance produced by the liver that contains bicarbonate ions, cholesterol, phospholipids, a number of organic wastes, and a group of substances collectively termed bile salts. Bile emulsifies fats so they can be absorbed by the small intestine.

bile salts A group of substances produced in the liver that solubilize dietary fat and increase its accessibility to digestive enzymes.

binary fission The process of cell division in bacteria and archaea in which one cell divides into two cells.

binocular (or stereoscopic) vision A type of vision in animals having two eyes located at the front of the head; the overlapping images coming into both eyes are processed together in the brain to form one perception. Binocular vision enables depth perception.

binomial nomenclature The standard method for naming species. Each species has a genus name and species epithet.

biochemistry The study of the chemistry of living organisms.

biodiversity The diversity of life forms in a given location.

biodiversity crisis The idea that there is currently an elevated loss of species on Earth, far beyond the normal historical extinction rate of species.

biofilm An aggregation of microorganisms that secrete adhesive mucilage, thereby gluing themselves to surfaces.

biogeochemical cycle The continuous movement of nutrients such as nitrogen, carbon, sulfur, and phosphorus from the physical environment to organisms and back.

biogeographic region One of six geographic regions which divide up the world's biota: Nearctic, Palearctic, Neotropical, Ethopian, Oriental, and Australian.

biogeography The study of the geographic distribution of extinct and modern species.

bioinformatics A field of study that uses computers to study biological information.

biological control The use of an introduced species' natural enemies to control its proliferation.

biological diversity See biodiversity.

biological nitrogen fixation Nitrogen fixation that is performed in nature by certain prokaryotes.

biological species concept An approach used to distinguish species, which states that a species is a group of individuals whose members have the potential to interbreed with one another in nature to produce viable, fertile offspring but cannot successfully interbreed with members of other species.

biology The study of life.

bioluminescence A phenomenon in living organisms in which chemical reactions give off light rather than heat.

biomagnification The increase in the concentration of a substance in living organisms from lower to higher trophic levels in a food web.

biomass A quantitative estimate of the total mass of living matter in a given area, usually measured in grams or grams per square meter.

biome A major type of habitat characterized by distinctive plant and animal life.

bioremediation The use of living organisms, usually microbes or plants, to detoxify polluted habitats such as dump sites or oil spills.

biosphere The regions on the surface of the Earth and in the atmosphere where living organisms exist.

biosynthetic reaction Also called an anabolic reaction; a chemical reaction in which small molecules are used to synthesize larger molecules.

biotechnology The use of living organisms or the products of living organisms for human benefit.

biotic The term used to describe interactions among organisms.

biparental inheritance An inheritance pattern in which both the male and female gametes contribute organellar genes to the offspring.

bipedal Having the ability to walk on two feet.

bipolar cells Cells in the vertebrate eye that make synapses with photoreceptors and relay responses to the ganglion cells.

bivalent Homologous pairs of sister chromatids associated with each other, lying side by side.

blade The flattened portion of a leaf.

BLAST (basic local alignment search tool) A computer program that can identify homologous genes that are found in a database.

blastocoel A cavity formed in a cleavage-stage vertebrate embryo (blastula); provides a space into which cells of the future digestive tract will migrate.

blastocyst The mammalian counterpart of a blastula.

blastoderm A flattened disc of dividing cells in the embryo of animals that undergo incomplete cleavage; occurs in birds and some fishes.

blastomere The two half-size daughter cells produced by each cell division during cleavage.

blastopore A small opening created when a band of tissue invaginates during gastrulation. It forms the primary opening of the archenteron to the outside.

blastula An animal embryo at the stage when it forms an outer epithelial layer and an inner cavity.

blending inheritance An early hypothesis of inheritance that stated that the genetic material that dictates hereditary traits blends together from generation to generation, and the blended traits are then passed to the next generation.

blood A fluid connective tissue in animals consisting of cells and (in mammals) cell fragments suspended in a solution of water containing dissolved nutrients, proteins, gases, and other molecules.

blood-doping An example of hormone misuse in which the number of red blood cells in the circulation is boosted to increase the oxygen-carrying capacity of the blood.

blood pressure The force exerted by blood on the walls of blood vessels; blood pressure is responsible for moving blood through the vessels.

body mass index (BMI) A method of assessing body fat and health risk that involves calculating the ratio of weight compared with height; weight in kilograms is divided by the square of the height in meters.

body plan The organization of cells, tissues, and organs within a multicellular organism; also known as a body pattern.

bone A relatively hard component of the vertebrate skeleton; a living, dynamic tissue composed of organic molecules and minerals.

bottleneck effect A situation in which a population size is dramatically reduced and then rebounds. While the population is small, genetic drift may rapidly reduce the genetic diversity of the population.

Bowman's capsule A saclike structure that houses the glomerulus at the beginning of the tubular component of a nephron in the mammalian kidney.

brain Organ of the central nervous system of animals that functions to process and integrate information.

brainstem The part of the vertebrate brain composed of the medulla oblongata, the pons, and the midbrain.

brassinosteroid One of several plant hormones that help a plant to cope with environmental stress.

bronchi (singular, **bronchus**) Tubes branching from the trachea and leading into the lungs.

bronchiole A thin-walled, small tube branching from the bronchi and leading to the alveoli in mammalian lungs.

bronchodilator A compound that binds to the muscles of the bronchioles of the lung and causes them to relax, thereby widening the bronchioles and easing breathing.

brown adipose tissue A specialized tissue in small mammals such as hibernating bats, small rodents living in cold environments, and many newborn mammals, including humans, that can help to generate heat and maintain body temperature.

brush border The collective name for the microvilli in the vertebrate small intestine.

bryophytes Liverworts, mosses, and hornworts, the modern nonvascular land plants.

buccal pumping A form of breathing in which animals take in water or air into their mouths, then raise the floor of the mouth, creating a positive pressure that pumps water or air across the gills or into the lungs; found in fishes and amphibians.

bud A miniature plant shoot having a dormant shoot apical meristem.

budding A form of asexual reproduction in which a portion of the parent organism pinches off to form a complete new individual.

buffer A compound that acts to minimize pH fluctuations in the fluids of living organisms. Buffer systems can raise or lower pH as needed.

bulbourethral gland Paired accessory glands in the human male reproductive system that secrete an alkaline mucus that protects sperm by neutralizing the acidity in the urethra.

bulimia nervosa An eating disorder characterized by cycles of binge eating followed by purging and vomiting to reduce body weight.

bulk feeders Animals that eat food in large pieces.

bulk flow The mass movement of liquid in a plant caused by pressure, gravity, or both.

C

C_3 plant   A plant that incorporates CO_2 into organic molecules via RuBP to make 3PG, a three-carbon molecule.

C_4 plant   A plant that uses PEP carboxylase to initially fix CO_2 into a four-carbon molecule and later uses rubisco to fix CO_2 into simple sugars; an adaptation to hot, dry environments.

cadherin   A cell adhesion molecule found in animal cells that promotes cell-to-cell adhesion.

calcitonin   A hormone that plays a role in Ca^{2+} homeostasis in some vertebrates.

calcium wave   A brief increase in cytosolic Ca^{2+} concentrations in an egg that has been penetrated by a sperm cell; the change in Ca^{2+} moves through the cell and contributes to the slow block to polyspermy.

callose   A carbohydrate that plays crucial roles in plant development and plugging wounds in plant phloem.

calorie   The amount of heat required to raise the temperature of 1 gram of water 1°C. The Calorie (dietary unit) is equivalent to a kilocalorie, or 1,000 calories.

Calvin cycle   The second stage in the process of photosynthesis. During this cycle, ATP is used as a source of energy, and NADPH is used as a source of high-energy electrons so that CO_2 can be incorporated into carbohydrate.

calyx   The sepals that form the outermost whorl of a flower.

Cambrian explosion   An event during the Cambrian period (543–490 mya) in which there was an abrupt increase (on a geological scale) in the diversity of animal species.

cAMP   *See* cyclic adenosine monophosphate.

CAM (crassulacean acid metabolism) plants C_4 plants that open their stomata at night to take up CO_2.

cancer   A disease caused by gene mutations that lead to uncontrolled cell growth.

canopy   The uppermost layer of tree foliage.

capillary   A tiny thin-walled vessel that is the site of gas and nutrient exchange between the blood and interstitial fluid.

capping   The process in which a 7-methylguanosine is covalently attached at the 5′ end of mature mRNAs of eukaryotes.

capsid   A protein coat enclosing a virus's genome.

CAP site   One of two regulatory sites near the *lac* promoter; this site is a DNA sequence recognized by the catabolite activator protein (CAP).

capsule   A very thick, gelatinous glycocalyx produced by certain strains of bacteria that may help them avoid being destroyed by an animal's immune (defense) system.

carapace   The hard protective cuticle covering the cephalothorax of a crustacean.

carbohydrate   An organic molecule often with the general formula, $C(H_2O)$; a carbon-containing compound that includes starches, sugars, and cellulose.

carbon fixation   A process in which carbon from inorganic CO_2 is incorporated into an organic molecule such as a carbohydrate.

carboxyl terminus   *See* C-terminus.

carcinogen   An agent that increases the likelihood of developing cancer, usually a mutagen.

carcinoma   A cancer of epithelial cells.

cardiac cycle   The events that produce a single heartbeat, which can be divided into two phases, diastole and systole.

cardiac muscle   A type of muscle tissue found only in hearts in which physical and electrical connections between individual cells enable many of the cells to contract simultaneously.

cardiac output (CO)   The amount of blood the heart pumps per unit time, usually expressed in units of L/min.

cardiovascular disease   Diseases affecting the heart and blood vessels.

carnivore   An animal that consumes animal flesh or fluids.

carotenoid   A type of photosynthetic or protective pigment found in plastids that imparts a color that ranges from yellow to orange to red.

carpel   A flower shoot organ that produces ovules that contain female gametophytes.

carrier   *See* transporter.

carrying capacity (K)   The upper boundary for a population size.

Casparian strips   Suberin ribbons on the walls of endodermal cells of plant roots; prevent apoplastic transport of ions into vascular tissues.

caspase   An enzyme that is activated during apoptosis.

catabolic reaction   A metabolic pathway in which a molecule is broken down into smaller components, usually releasing energy.

catabolism   A metabolic pathway that results in the breakdown of larger molecules into smaller molecules. Such reactions are often exergonic.

catabolite activator protein (CAP)   An activator protein for the *lac* operon.

catabolite repression   In bacteria, a process whereby transcriptional regulation is influenced by the presence of glucose.

catalase   An enzyme within peroxisomes that breaks down hydrogen peroxide to water and oxygen gas.

catalyst   An agent that speeds up the rate of a chemical reaction without being consumed during the reaction.

cataract   An accumulation of protein in the lens of the eye; causes blurring and poor night vision.

cation   An ion that has a net positive charge.

cation exchange   With regard to soil, the process in which hydrogen ions are able to replace mineral cations on the surfaces of humus or clay particles.

cDNA   *See* complementary DNA.

cDNA library   A type of DNA library in which the inserts are derived from cDNA.

cecum   The first portion of a vertebrate's large intestine.

cell   The simplest unit of a living organism.

cell adhesion   A vital function of the cell membrane that allows cells to bind to each other. Cell adhesion is critical in the formation of multicellular organisms and provides a way to convey positional information between neighboring cells.

cell adhesion molecule (CAM)   A membrane protein found in animal cells that promotes cell adhesion.

cell biology   The study of individual cells and their interactions with each other.

cell body   A part of a neuron that contains the cell nucleus and other organelles.

cell coat   Also called the glycocalyx, the carbohydrate-rich zone on the surface of animal cells that shields the cell from mechanical and physical damage.

cell communication   The process through which cells can detect and respond to signals in their extracellular environment. In multicellular organisms, cell communication is also needed to coordinate cellular activities within the whole organism.

cell cycle   The series of phases a eukaryotic cell progresses through from its origin until it divides by mitosis.

cell differentiation   The phenomenon by which cells become specialized into particular cell types.

cell division   The process in which one cell divides into two cells.

cell doctrine   *See* cell theory.

cell junctions   Specialized structures that adhere cells to each other and to the ECM.

cell-mediated immunity   A type of specific immunity in which cytotoxic T cells directly attack and destroy infected body cells, cancer cells, or transplanted cells.

cell nucleus   The membrane-bound area of a eukaryotic cell in which the genetic material is found.

cell plate   In plant cells, a structure that forms a cell wall between the two daughter cells during cytokinesis.

cell signaling   A vital function of the plasma membrane that involves cells sensing changes in their environment and communicating with each other.

cell surface receptor   A receptor found in the plasma membrane that enables a cell to respond to different kinds of signaling molecules.

cell theory   A theory that states that all organisms are made of cells, cells are the smallest units of living organisms, and new cells come from pre-existing cells by cell division.

cell-to-cell communication   A form of cell communication that occurs between two different cells.

cellular differentiation   The process by which different cells within a developing organism acquire specialized forms and functions due to the expression of cell-specific genes.

cellular respiration   A process by which living cells obtain energy from organic molecules and release waste products.

cellular response   Adaptation at the cellular level that involves a cell responding to signals in its environment.

cellulose   The main macromolecule of the primary cell wall of plants and many algae; a polymer made of repeating molecules of glucose attached end to end.

cell wall   A relatively rigid, porous structure located outside the plasma membrane of prokaryotic, plant, fungal, and certain protist cells; provides support and protection.

centiMorgan (cM)   *See* map unit (mu).

central cell   In the female gametophyte of a flowering plant, a large cell that contains two nuclei; after double fertilization, it forms the first cell of the nutritive endosperm tissue.

central dogma   Refers to the steps of gene expression at the molecular level. DNA is transcribed into mRNA, and mRNA is translated into a polypeptide.

central nervous system (CNS)   In vertebrates, the brain and spinal cord.

central region   The region of a plant seedling that produces stem tissue.

central vacuole   An organelle that often occupies 80% or more of the cell volume of plant cells and stores a large amount of water, enzymes, and inorganic ions.

central zone   The area of a plant shoot meristem where undifferentiated stem cells are maintained.

centrioles   A pair of structures within the centrosome of animal cells. Most plant cells and many protists lack centrioles.

centromere   The region where the two sister chromatids are tightly associated; the centromere is an attachment site for kinetochore proteins.

centrosome   A single structure often near the cell nucleus of eukaryotic cells that forms a nucleating site for the growth of microtubules; also called the microtubule-organizing center.

cephalization   The localization of a brain and sensory structures at the anterior end of the body of animals.

cephalothorax   The fused head and thorax structure in species of the class Arachnida and Crustacea.

cerebellum   The part of the vertebrate hindbrain, along with the pons, responsible for monitoring and coordinating body movements.

cerebral cortex   The surface layer of gray matter that forms the outer part of the cerebrum of the vertebrate brain.

cerebral ganglia A paired structure in the head of invertebrates that receives input from sensory cells and controls motor output.

cerebrospinal fluid Fluid that exists in ventricles within the central nervous system and surrounds the exterior of the brain and spinal cord; it absorbs physical shocks to the brain resulting from sudden movements or blows to the head.

cerebrum A region of the vertebrate forebrain that is responsible for the higher functions of conscious thought, planning, and emotion, as well as control of motor function.

cervix A fibrous structure at the end of the female vagina that forms the opening to the uterus.

channel A transmembrane protein that forms an open passageway for the direct diffusion of ions or molecules across a membrane.

chaperone A protein that keeps other proteins in an unfolded state during the process of post-translational sorting.

character A characteristic of an organism, such as the appearance of seeds, pods, flowers, or stems.

character displacement The tendency for two species to diverge in morphology and thus resource use because of competition.

character state A particular variant of a given character.

charged tRNA A tRNA with its attached amino acid; also called aminoacyl tRNA.

charophyceans The lineages of freshwater green algae that are most closely related to the land plants.

checkpoint One of three critical regulatory points found in the cell cycle of eukaryotic cells. At these checkpoints, a variety of proteins act as sensors to determine if a cell is in the proper condition to divide.

checkpoint protein A protein that senses if a cell is in the proper condition to divide and prevents a cell from progressing through the cell cycle if it is not.

chemical energy The potential energy contained within covalent bonds in molecules.

chemical equilibrium A state in a chemical reaction in which the rate of formation of products equals the rate of formation of reactants.

chemical mutagen A chemical that causes mutations.

chemical reaction The formation and breaking of chemical bonds, resulting in a change in the composition of substances.

chemical selection Occurs when a chemical within a mixture has special properties or advantages that cause it to increase in amount. May have played a key role in the formation of an RNA world.

chemical synapse A synapse in which a chemical called a neurotransmitter is released from the axon terminal of a neuron and acts as a signal from the presynaptic to the postsynaptic cell.

chemiosmosis A process for making ATP in which energy stored in an ion electrochemical gradient is used to make ATP from ADP and P_i.

chemoautotroph An organism able to use energy obtained by chemical modifications of inorganic compounds to synthesize organic compounds.

chemoheterotroph An organism that must obtain organic molecules both for energy and as a carbon source.

chemoreceptor A sensory receptor in animals that responds to specific chemical compounds.

chiasma The connection at a crossover site of two chromosomes.

chimeric gene A gene formed from the fusion of two gene fragments to each other.

chitin A tough, nitrogen-containing polysaccharide that forms the external skeleton of many insects and the cell walls of fungi.

chlorophyll A photosynthetic green pigment found in the chloroplasts of plants, algae, and some bacteria.

chlorophyll *a* A type of chlorophyll pigment found in plants, algae, and cyanobacteria.

chlorophyll *b* A type of chlorophyll pigment found in plants, green algae, and some other photosynthetic organisms.

chloroplast A semiautonomous organelle found in plant and algal cells that carries out photosynthesis.

chloroplast genome The chromosome found in chloroplasts.

chlorosis The yellowing of plant leaves caused by various types of mineral deficiencies.

choanocyte A specialized cell of sponges that functions to trap and eat small particles.

chondrichthyans Members of the class Chondrichthyes, including sharks, skates, and rays.

chordate An organism that has or at some point in its life has had a notochord and a hollow dorsal nerve cord; includes all vertebrates and some invertebrates.

chorion One of the four extraembryonic membranes in the amniotic egg. It exchanges gases between the embryo and the surrounding air.

chorionic gonadotropin A luteinizing hormone (LH)-like hormone made by the blastocyst and placenta that maintains the corpus luteum.

chromatin Refers to the biochemical composition of chromosomes, which contain DNA and many types of proteins.

chromosome A discrete unit of genetic material composed of DNA and associated proteins. Eukaryotes have chromosomes in their cell nuclei and in plastids and mitochondria.

chromosome territory A distinct, nonoverlapping area where each chromosome is located within the cell nucleus of eukaryotic cells.

chromosome theory of inheritance An explanation of how the steps of meiosis account for the inheritance patterns observed by Mendel.

chylomicron Large fat droplet coated with amphipathic proteins that perform an emulsifying function similar to that of bile salts; chylomicrons are formed in intestinal epithelial cells from absorbed fats in the diet.

chyme A solution of water and partially digested food particles in the stomach and small intestine.

chymotrypsin A protease involved in the breakdown of proteins in the small intestine.

chytrids Simple, early-diverging phyla of fungi; commonly found in aquatic habitats and moist soil, where they produce flagellate reproductive cells.

cilia (singular, cilium) Cell appendages that have the same internal structure as flagella and function like flagella to facilitate cell movement; cilia are shorter and more numerous on cells than are flagella.

ciliate A protist that moves by means of cilia, which are tiny hairlike extensions that occur on the outside of cells and have the same internal structure as flagella.

circadian rhythm Internal biological clock system that can be found in plants, animals, and other organisms.

circulatory system A system that transports necessary materials to all cells of an animal's body and transports waste products away from cells. Three basic types are gastrovascular cavities, open systems, and closed systems.

***cis*-acting element** See *cis*-effect.

***cis*-effect** A DNA segment that must be adjacent to the gene(s) that it regulates. The *lac* operator site is an example of a *cis*-acting element.

cisternae Flattened, fluid-filled tubules of the endoplasmic reticulum.

***cis/trans* isomers** Organic molecules with the same chemical composition but existing in two different configurations determined by the positions of hydrogen atoms on the two carbons of a CC double bond. When the hydrogen atoms are on the same side of the double bond, it is called a *cis* isomer; when on the opposite sides of the double bond, it is a *trans* isomer.

citric acid cycle A cycle that results in the breakdown of carbohydrates to CO_2; also known as the Krebs cycle.

clade A group of species derived from a single common ancestor.

cladistic approach An approach used to construct a phylogenetic tree by comparing primitive and shared derived characters.

cladogenesis A pattern of speciation in which a species is divided into two or more species.

cladogram A phylogenetic tree constructed by using a cladistic approach.

clamp connection In basidiomycete fungi, a structure that helps distribute nuclei during cell division.

clasper An extension of the pelvic fin of a chondrichthyan, used by the male to transfer sperm to the female.

class In taxonomy, a subdivision of a phylum.

classical conditioning A type of associative learning in which an involuntary response comes to be associated positively or negatively with a stimulus that did not originally elicit the response.

cleavage A succession of rapid cell divisions with no significant growth that produces a hollow sphere of cells called a blastula.

cleavage furrow In animal cells, an area that constricts like a drawstring to separate the cells during cytokinesis.

climate The prevailing weather pattern of a given region.

climax community A distinct end point of succession.

clitoris Located at the anterior part of the female labia minora, erectile tissue that becomes engorged with blood during sexual arousal and is very sensitive to sexual stimulation.

clonal deletion One of two mechanisms that explain why normal individuals lack active lymphocytes that respond to self components; T cells with receptors capable of binding self proteins are destroyed by apoptosis.

clonal inactivation One of two mechanisms that explain why normal individuals lack active lymphocytes that respond to self components; the process occurs outside the thymus and causes potentially self-reacting T cells to become nonresponsive.

clonal selection The process by which an antigen-stimulated lymphocyte divides and forms a clone of cells, each of which recognizes that particular antigen.

cloning Making many copies of something such as a DNA molecule.

closed circulatory system A circulatory system in which blood flows throughout an animal entirely within a series of vessels and is kept separate from the interstitial fluid.

closed conformation Tightly packed chromatin that cannot be transcribed into RNA.

clumped The most common pattern of dispersion within a population, in which individuals are gathered in small groups.

cnidocil On the surface of a cnidocyte, a hairlike trigger that detects stimuli.

cnidocyte A characteristic feature of cnidarians; a stinging cell that functions in defense or the capture of prey.

coacervates Droplets that form spontaneously from the association of charged polymers such as proteins, carbohydrates, or nucleic acids surrounded by water.

coactivator A protein that increases the rate of transcription but does not directly bind to the DNA itself.

coat protein A protein that surrounds a membrane vesicle and facilitates vesicle formation.

cocci Sphere-shaped prokaryotic cells.

cochlea   A coiled structure in the inner ear of mammals that contains the auditory receptors (organ of Corti).

coding sequence   The region of a gene or a DNA molecule that encodes the information for the amino acid sequence of a polypeptide.

coding strand   The DNA strand opposite to the template (or noncoding strand).

codominance   The phenomenon in which a single individual expresses two alleles.

codon   A sequence of three nucleotide bases that specifies a particular amino acid or a stop codon; codons function during translation.

coefficient of relatedness (r)   The probability that any two individuals will share a copy of a particular gene.

coelom   A fluid-filled body cavity in an animal.

coelomate   An animal with a true coelom.

coenzyme   An organic molecule that participates in a chemical reaction with an enzyme but is left unchanged after the reaction is completed.

coevolution   The process by which two or more species of organisms influence each other's evolutionary pathway.

cofactor   Usually an inorganic ion that temporarily binds to the surface of an enzyme and promotes a chemical reaction.

cognitive learning   The ability to solve problems with conscious thought and without direct environmental feedback.

cohesion   The ability of like molecules to noncovalently bind to each other; the attraction of water molecules for each other.

cohesion-tension theory   The explanation for long-distance water transport as the combined effect of the cohesive forces of water and evaporative tension.

cohort   A group of organisms of the same age.

coleoptile   A protective sheath that encloses the first bud of the epicotyl in a mature monocot embryo.

coleorhiza   A protective envelope that encloses the young root of a monocot.

colinearity rule   The phenomenon whereby the order of homeotic genes along the chromosome correlates with their expression along the anteroposterior axis of the body.

collagen   A protein secreted from animal cells that forms large fibers in the extracellular matrix.

collecting duct   A tubule in the mammalian kidney that collects urine from nephrons.

collenchyma cells   Flexible cells that make up collenchyma tissue.

collenchyma tissue   A plant ground tissue that provides support to plant organs.

colligative property   A property of a solution that depends only on the concentration of solute molecules.

colloid   A gel-like substance in the follicles of the thyroid gland.

colon   A part of a vertebrate's large intestine consisting of three relatively straight segments—the ascending, transverse, and descending portions. The terminal portion of the descending colon is S-shaped, forming the sigmoid colon, which empties into the rectum.

colony hybridization   A method that uses a labeled probe to identify bacterial colonies that contain a desired gene.

combinatorial control   The phenomenon whereby a combination of many factors determines the expression of any given gene.

commensalism   An interaction that benefits one species and leaves the other unaffected.

communication   The use of specially designed visual, chemical, auditory, or tactile signals to modify the behavior of others.

community   An assemblage of populations of different species that live in the same place at the same time.

community ecology   The study of how populations of species interact and form functional communities.

compartmentalization   A characteristic of eukaryotic cells in which many organelles separate the cell into different regions. Cellular compartmentalization allows a cell to carry out specialized chemical reactions in different places.

competent   The term used to describe bacterial strains that have the ability to take up DNA from the environment.

competition   An interaction that affects two or more species negatively, as they compete over food or other resources.

competitive exclusion principle   The proposal that two species with the same resource requirements cannot occupy the same niche.

competitive inhibitor   A molecule that binds to the active site of an enzyme and inhibits the ability of the substrate to bind.

complement   The family of plasma proteins that provides a means for extracellular killing of microbes without prior phagocytosis.

complementary   Describes the specific base pairing that occurs between strands of nucleic acids; A pairs only with T (in DNA) or U (in RNA), and G pairs only with C.

complementary DNA (cDNA)   DNA molecules that are made from mRNA as a starting material.

complete flower   A flower that possesses all four types of flower organs.

complete metamorphosis   During development in the majority of insects, a dramatic change in body form from larva to a very different looking adult.

compound   A molecule composed of two or more different elements.

compound eye   A type of image-forming eye in arthropods and some annelids consisting of several hundred to several thousand light detectors called ommatidia.

computational molecular biology   An area of study that uses computers to characterize the molecular components of living things.

concentration   The amount of a solute dissolved in a unit volume of solution.

condensation reaction   A chemical reaction in which two or more molecules are combined into one larger molecule by covalent bonding, with the loss of a small molecule.

conditional specification   The acquisition by cells of specific properties through a variety of cell-to-cell signaling mechanisms in a developing vertebrate embryo.

conditioned response   The learned response that is elicited by a newly conditioned stimulus.

conditioned stimulus   A new stimulus that is delivered at the same time as an old stimulus, and that over time, is sufficient to elicit the same response.

condom   A sheathlike membrane worn over the penis; in addition to their contraceptive function, condoms significantly reduce the risk of contracting and transmitting sexually transmitted diseases.

conduction   The process in which the body surface loses or gains heat through direct contact with cooler or warmer substances.

cone pigment   Any of several types of visual pigments found in the cones of the vertebrate eye.

cones   1. Photoreceptors found in the vertebrate eye; they are less sensitive to low levels of light but can detect color. 2. The reproductive structures of coniferous plants.

congenital hypothyroidism   A condition characterized by poor differentiation of the central nervous system due to a failure of neurons to become myelinated in fetal development; results in profound mental defects.

congestive heart failure   The condition resulting from the failure of the heart to pump blood normally; results in fluid buildup in the lungs (congestion).

conidia   A type of asexual reproductive cell produced by many fungi.

conifers   A phylum of gymnosperm plants, Coniferophyta.

conjugation   A type of genetic transfer between bacteria that involves a direct physical interaction between two bacterial cells.

connective tissue   Clusters of cells that connect, anchor, and support the structures of an animal's body; includes blood, adipose (fat-storing) tissue, bone, cartilage, loose connective tissue, and dense connective tissue.

connexon   A channel that forms gap junctions consisting of six connexin proteins in one cell aligned with six connexin proteins in an adjacent cell.

conservation biology   The study that uses principles and knowledge from molecular biology, genetics, and ecology to protect the biological diversity of life.

conservative mechanism   In this incorrect model for DNA replication, both parental strands of DNA remain together (are conserved) following DNA replication. The two newly made daughter strands also occur together.

consortia   A community of many microbial species.

constant region   The portions of amino acid sequences in the heavy and light chains that are identical for all immunoglobulins of a given class.

constitutive gene   An unregulated gene that has constant levels of expression in all conditions over time.

contig   A series of clones that contain overlapping pieces of chromosomal DNA.

continental drift   The process by which, over the course of billions of years, the major landmasses, known as the continents, have shifted their positions, changed their shapes, and, in some cases, have become separated from each other.

contraception   The use of birth control procedures to prevent fertilization or implantation of a fertilized egg.

contractile vacuole   A small, membrane enclosed, water-filled compartment that eliminates excess liquid from the cells of certain protists.

contrast   In microscopy, relative differences in the lightness, darkness, or color between adjacent regions in a sample.

control group   The sample in an experiment that is treated just like an experimental group except that it is not subjected to one particular variable.

convection   The transfer of heat by the movement of air or water next to the body.

convergent evolution   The process whereby two different species from different lineages show similar characteristics because they occupy similar environments.

convergent extension   A cellular process during gastrulation that is crucial to development; two rows of cells merge to form a single elongated layer.

convergent trait   *See* analogous structure.

coprophagy   The practice of certain birds and mammals in which feces are consumed to maximize absorption of water and nutrients.

copulation   The process of sperm being deposited within the reproductive tract of the female.

corepressor   A small effector molecule that binds to a repressor protein to inhibit transcription.

core promoter   Refers to the TATA box and the transcriptional start site of a eukaryotic structural gene.

Coriolis effect   The effect of the Earth's rotation on the surface flow of wind.

cork cambium   A secondary meristem in a plant that produces cork tissue.

cornea A thin, clear layer on the front of the vertebrate eye.

corolla The petals of a flower, which occur in the whorl to the inside of the calyx and the outside of the stamens.

corona The ciliated crown of members of the phylum Rotifera.

coronary artery An artery that carries oxygen and nutrients to the heart muscle.

coronary artery bypass A common treatment to restore blood flow through a coronary artery. A small piece of healthy blood vessel is removed from one part of the body and surgically grafted onto the coronary circulation in order to bypass the diseased artery.

coronary artery disease A condition that occurs when plaques form in the coronary arteries.

corpus callosum The major tract that connects the two hemispheres of the cerebrum.

corpus luteum A structure that develops from a ruptured follicle following ovulation; it is responsible for secreting hormones that stimulate the development of the uterus during pregnancy.

correlation A meaningful relationship between two variables.

cortex The area of a plant stem or root beneath the epidermis that is largely composed of parenchyma tissue.

cortical reaction An event in fertilization in which IP_3 and calcium signaling produces barriers to more than one sperm cell binding to and uniting with an egg; called the slow block to polyspermy.

cortisol A steroid hormone made by the adrenal cortex.

cotranslational sorting The sorting process in which the synthesis of certain eukaryotic proteins begins in the cytosol and then halts temporarily until the ribosome has become bound to the ER membrane.

cotransporter See symporter.

cotyledon An embryonic seed leaf.

countercurrent exchange 1. An arrangement of water and blood flow in which water enters a fish's mouth and flows between the lamellae of the gills in the opposite direction to blood flowing through the lamellar capillaries. 2. An arrangement of blood vessels under the skin of vertebrates that contributes to heat retention.

countercurrent multiplication system The mechanism by which the vertebrate loop of Henle reabsorbs salts and water along it length.

covalent bond A chemical bond in which two atoms share a pair of electrons.

CpG island A cluster of CpG sites. CG refers to the nucleotides of C and G in DNA, and p refers to a phosphodiester linkage.

cranial nerve A nerve in the peripheral nervous system that is directly connected to the brain.

cranium A protective bony or cartilaginous housing that encases the brain of a craniate.

crenation The process of cell shrinkage that occurs if animal cells are placed in a hypertonic medium.

cristae Projections of the highly invaginated inner membrane of a mitochondrion.

critical innovations New features that foster the diversification of phyla.

critical period A limited period of time in which many animals develop species-specific patterns of behavior.

crop A storage organ that is a dilation of the lower esophagus; found in most birds and many invertebrates, including insects and some worms.

cross-bridge A region of myosin molecules that extend from the surface of the thick filaments toward the thin filaments in skeletal muscle.

cross-bridge cycle During muscle contraction, the sequence of events that occurs between the time when a cross-bridge binds to a thin filament and when it is set to repeat the process.

cross-fertilization Fertilization that involves the union of a female gamete and a male gamete from different individuals.

crossing over The exchange of genetic material between homologous chromosomes during meiosis; allows for increased variation in the genetic information that each parent may pass to the offspring.

cross-pollination The process in which a stigma receives pollen from a different plant of the same species.

cryptic coloration The blending of an organism with the background color of its habitat; also known as camouflage.

cryptochrome A type of blue-light receptor in plants and protists.

cryptomycota A newly discovered group of eukaryotes proposed to be an early-diverging lineage of fungi.

C-terminus The location of the last amino acid in a polypeptide; also known as the carboxyl terminus.

CT scan Computerized tomography, which is an X-ray technique used to examine the structure of bones and soft tissues, including the brain.

cupula A gelatinous structure within the lateral line organ of fishes that detects changes in water movement.

cuticle A coating of wax and cutin that helps to reduce water loss from plant surfaces. Also, a nonliving covering that serves to both support and protect an animal.

cycads A phylum of gymnosperm plants, Cycadophyta.

cyclic adenosine monophosphate (cAMP) A small effector molecule that acts as a second messenger and is produced from ATP.

cyclic AMP (cAMP) See cyclic adenosine monophosphate.

cyclic electron flow See cyclic photophosphorylation.

cyclic photophosphorylation During photosynthesis, a pattern of electron flow in the thylakoid membrane that is cyclic and generates ATP alone.

cyclin A protein responsible for advancing a cell through the phases of the cell cycle by binding to a cyclin-dependent kinase.

cyclin-dependent kinase (cdk) A protein responsible for advancing a cell through the phases of the cell cycle. Its function is dependent on the binding of a cyclin.

cyst A one-to-few celled structure that often has a thick, protective wall and can remain dormant through periods of unfavorable climate or low food availability.

cytogenetics The field of genetics that involves the microscopic examination of chromosomes.

cytokines A family of proteins that function in both nonspecific and specific immune defenses by providing a chemical communication network that synchronizes the components of the immune response.

cytokinesis The division of the cytoplasm to produce two distinct daughter cells.

cytokinin A type of plant hormone that promotes cell division.

cytoplasm The region of the cell that is contained within the plasma membrane.

cytoplasmic inheritance See extranuclear inheritance.

cytosine (C) A pyrimidine base found in DNA and RNA.

cytoskeleton In eukaryotes, a network of three different types of protein filaments in the cytosol called microtubules, intermediate filaments, and actin filaments.

cytosol The region of a eukaryotic cell that is inside the plasma membrane and outside the organelles.

cytotoxic T cell A type of lymphocyte that travels to the location of its target, binds to the target by combining with an antigen on it, and directly kills the target via secreted chemicals.

D

dalton (Da) A measure of atomic mass. One dalton equals one-twelfth the mass of a carbon atom.

data mining The extraction of useful information and often previously unknown relationships from sequence files and large databases.

database A large number of computer data files that are collected, stored in a single location, and organized for rapid search and retrieval.

daughter strand The newly made strand in DNA replication.

day-neutral plant A plant that flowers regardless of the night length, as long as day length meets the minimal requirements for plant growth.

deafness Hearing loss, usually caused by damage to the hair cells within the cochlea.

death-inducing signaling complex (DISC) A complex consisting of death receptors, adaptor proteins, and procaspase that initiates apoptosis via the extrinsic pathway.

death receptor A type of receptor found in the plasma membrane of eukaryotic cells that can promote apoptosis when it becomes activated.

decomposer A consumer that gets its energy from the remains and waste products of other organisms.

defecation The expulsion of feces that occurs through the anus of an animal's digestive canal.

defensive mutualism A mutually beneficial interaction often involving an animal defending a plant or herbivore in return for food or shelter.

deforestation The conversion of forested areas by humans to nonforested land.

degenerate In the genetic code, the observation that more than one codon can specify the same amino acid.

dehydration A reduction in the amount of water in the body.

dehydration reaction A type of condensation reaction in which a molecule of water is lost.

delayed implantation A reproductive cycle in which a fertilized egg reaches the uterus but does not implant until later, when environmental conditions are more favorable for the newly produced young.

delayed ovulation A reproductive cycle in which the ovarian cycle in females is halted before ovulation and sperm are stored and nourished in the female's uterus over the winter. Upon arousal from hibernation in the spring, the female ovulates one or more eggs, which are fertilized by the stored sperm.

deletion A type of mutation in which a segment of genetic material is missing.

demographic transition The shift in birth and death rates accompanying human societal development.

demography The study of birth rates, death rates, age distributions, and the sizes of populations.

dendrite A treelike extension of the plasma membrane of a neuron that receives electrical signals from other neurons.

dendritic cell A type of cell derived from bone marrow stem cells that plays an important role in nonspecific immunity; these cells are scattered throughout most tissues, where they perform various macrophage functions.

denitrification The reduction of nitrate (NO_3^-) to gaseous nitrogen (N_2).

density In the context of populations, the numbers of organisms in a given unit area.

density-dependent factor   A mortality factor whose influence increases with the density of the population.

density-independent factor   A mortality factor whose influence is not affected by changes in population density.

deoxynucleoside triphosphates   Individual nucleotides with three phosphate groups.

deoxyribonucleic acid (DNA)   One of two classes of nucleic acids; the other is ribonucleic acid (RNA). A DNA molecule consists of two strands of nucleotides coiled around each other to form a double helix, held together by hydrogen bonds according to the AT/GC rule.

deoxyribose   A five-carbon sugar found in DNA.

depolarization   The change in the membrane potential that occurs when a cell becomes less polarized, that is, less negative relative to the surrounding fluid.

dermal tissue   The covering on various parts of a plant.

descent with modification   Darwin's theory that existing life-forms on our planet are the product of the modification of pre-existing life-forms.

desertification   The overstocking of land with domestic animals that can greatly reduce grass coverage through overgrazing, turning the area more desert-like.

desmosome   A mechanically strong cell junction between animal cells that typically occurs in spotlike rivets.

determinate cleavage   In animals, a characteristic of protostome development in which the fate of each embryonic cell is determined very early.

determinate growth   A type of growth in plants that is of limited duration, such as the growth of flowers.

determined   The term used to describe a cell that is destined to differentiate into a particular cell type.

detritivore   *See* decomposer.

detritus   Unconsumed plants that die and decompose, along with the dead remains of animals and animal waste products.

deuterostome   An animal whose development exhibits radial, indeterminate cleavage and in which the blastopore becomes the anus; includes echinoderms and vertebrates.

development   In biology, a series of changes in the state of a cell, tissue, organ, or organism; the underlying process that gives rise to the structure and function of living organisms.

developmental genetics   A field of study aimed at understanding how gene expression controls the process of development.

diaphragm   A large muscle that subdivides the thoracic cavity from the abdomen in mammals; contraction of the diaphragm enlarges the thoracic cavity during inhalation.

diarrhea   A common intestinal disorder arising from ingested microbes or other causes; usually runs its course within one or two days but, in serious cases, can require hospitalization.

diastole   The phase of the cardiac cycle in which the ventricles fill with blood coming from the atria through the open AV valves.

diazotroph   A bacterium that fixes nitrogen.

dideoxy chain-termination method   The most common method of DNA sequencing; utilizes dideoxynucleotides as a reagent.

differential gene regulation   The phenomenon in which the expression of genes differs under various environmental conditions and in specialized cell types.

diffusion   In a solution, the process that occurs when a solute moves from a region of high concentration to a region of lower concentration.

digestion   The process of breaking down nutrients in food into smaller molecules that can be absorbed across the intestinal epithelia and directly used by cells.

digestive system   In animals, the long tube through which food is processed. In a vertebrate, this system consists of the alimentary canal plus several associated structures.

dihybrid   An offspring that is a hybrid with respect to two traits.

dihybrid cross   A cross in which the inheritance of two different traits is followed.

dikaryotic   The occurrence of two genetically distinct nuclei in the cells of fungal hyphae after mating has occurred.

dikaryotic mycelium   A fungal body that is made of cells that each possess two genetically distinct nuclei.

dimorphic fungi   Fungi that can exist in two different morphological forms.

dinosaur   A term, meaning "terrible lizard," used to describe some of the extinct fossil reptiles.

dioecious   The term to describe plants that produce staminate and carpellate flowers on separate plants.

diploblastic   Having two distinct germ layers—ectoderm and endoderm—but not mesoderm.

diploid   Refers to cells containing two sets of chromosomes; designated as $2n$.

diploid-dominant species   Species in which the diploid organism is the prevalent organism in the life cycle. Animals are an example.

direct calorimetry   A method of determining basal metabolic rate that involves quantifying the amount of heat generated by the animal.

direct repair   Refers to a DNA repair system in which an enzyme finds an incorrect structure in the DNA and directly converts it back to the correct structure.

directionality   In a DNA or RNA strand, refers to the orientation of the sugar molecules within that strand. Can be 5′ to 3′ or 3′ to 5′.

directional selection   A pattern of natural selection that favors individuals at one extreme of a phenotypic distribution.

disaccharide   A carbohydrate composed of two monosaccharides.

discovery-based science   The collection and analysis of data without the need for a preconceived hypothesis; also called discovery science.

discrete trait   A trait with clearly defined phenotypic variants.

dispersion   A pattern of spacing in which individuals in a population are clustered together or spread out to varying degrees.

dispersive mechanism   In this incorrect model for DNA replication, segments of parental DNA and newly made DNA are interspersed in both strands following the replication process.

dispersive mutualism   A mutually beneficial interaction often involving plants and pollinators that disperse their pollen, and plants and fruit eaters that disperse the plant's seeds.

dissociation constant   An equilibrium constant between a ligand and a protein, such as a receptor or an enzyme.

distal tubule   The segment of the tubule of the nephron through which fluid flows into one of the many collecting ducts in the kidney.

disulfide bridge   Covalent chemical bond formed between two cysteine residues in a protein; important in the tertiary structure of proteins.

diversifying selection   A pattern of natural selection that favors the survival of two or more different genotypes that produce different phenotypes.

diversity-stability hypothesis   The proposal that species-rich communities are more stable than those with fewer species.

DNA (deoxyribonucleic acid)   The genetic material that provides a blueprint for the organization, development, and function of living things.

DNA fingerprinting   A technology that identifies particular individuals using properties of their DNA.

DNA helicase   An enzyme that uses ATP to separate DNA strands during DNA replication.

DNA library   A collection of recombinant vectors, each containing a particular fragment of chromosomal DNA (cDNA).

DNA ligase   An enzyme that catalyzes the formation of a covalent bond between nucleotides in adjacent DNA fragments to complete the replication process.

DNA methylase   An enzyme that attaches methyl groups to bases in DNA.

DNA methylation   A process in which methyl groups are attached to bases in DNA.

DNA microarray   A technology used to monitor the expression of thousands of genes simultaneously.

DNA polymerase   An enzyme responsible for covalently linking nucleotides together during DNA replication.

DNA primase   An enzyme that synthesizes a primer for DNA replication.

DNA repair systems   One of several systems to reverse DNA damage before a permanent mutation can occur.

DNA replication   The process by which DNA is copied.

DNase   An enzyme that digests DNA.

DNA sequencing   A method to determine the base sequence of DNA.

DNA supercoiling   A method of compacting chromosomes through the formation of additional coils around the long, thin DNA molecule.

DNA topoisomerase   An enzyme that alleviates DNA supercoiling during DNA replication.

DNA transposon   A type of transposable element that moves as a DNA molecule.

domain   1. A defined region of a protein with a distinct structure and function. 2. One of the three major categories of life: Bacteria, Archaea, and Eukarya.

domestication   A process that involves artificial selection of plants or animals for traits desirable to humans.

dominant   A term that describes the displayed trait in a heterozygote.

dominant species   A species that has a large effect in a community because of its high abundance or high biomass.

dormancy   A phase of metabolic slowdown in a plant.

dorsal   Refers to the upper side of an animal.

dorsoventral axis   In bilateral animals, one of the three axes along which the adult body pattern is organized; the others are the anteroposterior axis and the right-left axis.

dosage compensation   The phenomenon that gene dosage is compensated between males and females. In mammals, the inactivation of one X chromosome in the female reduces the number of expressed copies (doses) of X-linked genes from two to one.

double bond   A bond that occurs when the atoms of a molecule share two pairs of electrons.

double fertilization   In angiosperms, the process in which two different fertilization events occur, producing both a zygote and the first cell of a nutritive endosperm tissue.

double helix   Two strands of DNA hydrogen-bonded with each other. In a DNA double helix, two DNA strands are twisted together to form a structure that resembles a spiral staircase.

Down syndrome   A human disorder caused by the inheritance of three copies of chromosome 21.

Duchenne muscular dystrophy   An inherited, X-linked disorder of humans causing muscle weakness and muscle degeneration.

duodenum   The first part of the vertebrate small intestine arising from the stomach.

duplication   A type of mutation in which a section of a chromosome occurs two or more times.

dynamic instability   The oscillation of a single microtubule between growing and shortening phases; important in many cellular activities, including the sorting of chromosomes during cell division.

E

Ecdysis   The process by which an animal molts, or breaks out of its old exoskeleton, and secretes a newer, larger one.

Ecdysozoa   A clade of molting animals that encompasses primarily the arthropods and nematodes.

echolocation   The phenomenon in which certain species listen for echoes of high-frequency sound waves in order to determine the distance and location of an object.

ECM   *See* extracellular matrix.

ecological footprint   The amount of productive land needed to support each person on Earth.

ecological species concept   An approach used to distinguish species; considers a species within its native environment and states that each species occupies its own ecological niche.

ecology   The study of interactions among organisms and between organisms and their environments.

ecosystem   The biotic community of organisms in an area as well as the abiotic environment affecting that community.

ecosystem engineer   A keystone species that creates, modifies, and maintains habitats.

ecosystems ecology   The study of the flow of energy and cycling of nutrients among organisms within a community and between organisms and the environment.

ecotypes   Genetically distinct populations adapted to their local environments.

ectoderm   In animals, the outermost layer of cells formed during gastrulation that covers the surface of the embryo and differentiates into the epidermis and nervous system.

ectomycorrhizae   Beneficial interactions between temperate forest trees and soil fungi that coat their roots.

ectoparasite   A parasite that lives on the outside of the host's body.

ectotherm   An animal that largely depends on the environment to warm its body.

ectothermic   Referring to an animal that is an ectotherm.

edge effect   A special physical condition that exists at the boundary or edge of an area.

effective population size   The number of individuals that contribute genes to future populations, often smaller than the actual population size.

effector   A molecule that directly influences cellular responses.

effector cell   A cloned lymphocyte that carries out the attack response during specific immunity.

efferent arteriole   A blood vessel that carries blood away from a glomerulus of the vertebrate kidney.

egestion   In animals, the process of undigested material passing out of the body.

egg   The mature female gamete; also called an ovum.

ejaculation   The movement of semen through the urethra by contraction of muscles at the base of the penis.

ejaculatory duct   The structure in the male reproductive system through which sperm leave the vas deferens and enter the urethra.

elastin   A protein that makes up elastic fibers in the extracellular matrix of animals.

electrical synapse   A synapse that directly passes electric current from the presynaptic to the postsynaptic cell via gap junctions.

electrocardiogram (ECG)   A record of the electrical impulses generated by the cells of the heart during the cardiac cycle.

electrochemical gradient   The combined effect of both an electrical and chemical gradient across a membrane; determines the direction that an ion will move.

electrogenic pump   A pump that generates an electrical gradient across a membrane.

electromagnetic receptor   A sensory receptor in animals that detects radiation within a wide range of the electromagnetic spectrum, including visible, ultraviolet, and infrared light, as well as electrical and magnetic fields in some animals.

electromagnetic spectrum   All possible wavelengths of electromagnetic radiation, from relatively short wavelengths (gamma rays) to much longer wavelengths (radio waves).

electron   A negatively charged particle found in orbitals around an atomic nucleus.

electron microscope   A microscope that uses an electron beam for illumination.

electron shell   The region around an atom's nucleus where electrons reside; larger atoms have more electron shells than smaller atoms.

electron transport chain (ETC)   A group of protein complexes and small organic molecules within the inner membranes of mitochondria and chloroplasts and the plasma membrane of prokaryotes. The components accept and donate electrons to each other in a linear manner and produce a H^+ electrochemical gradient.

electronegativity   A measure of an atom's ability to attract electrons to its outer shell from another atom.

element   A substance composed of specific types of atoms that cannot be further broken down by ordinary chemical or physical means.

elicitor   A compound produced by bacterial and fungal pathogens that promotes virulence.

elongation factor   A protein that is needed for the growth of a polypeptide during translation.

elongation stage   The second step in transcription or translation where RNA strands or polypeptides are made, respectively.

embryo   The early stages of development in a multicellular organism during which the organization of the organism is largely formed.

embryogenesis   The process by which embryos develop from single-celled zygotes by mitotic divisions.

embryonic development   The process by which a fertilized egg is transformed into an organism with distinct physiological systems and body parts.

embryonic germ cell (EG cell)   A cell in the early mammalian embryo that later gives rise to sperm or egg cells. These cells are pluripotent.

embryonic stem cell (ES cell)   A cell in the early mammalian embryo that can differentiate into almost every cell type of the body. These cells are pluripotent.

embryophyte   A synonym for the land plants.

emerging virus   A newly arising virus.

emphysema   A progressive disease characterized by a loss of elastic recoil ability of the lungs, usually resulting from chronic tobacco smoking.

empirical thought   Thought that relies on observation to form an idea or hypothesis, rather than trying to understand life from a nonphysical or spiritual point of view.

emulsification   A process during digestion that disrupts large lipid droplets into many tiny droplets, thereby increasing their total surface area and exposure to lipase action.

enantiomer   One of a pair of stereoisomers that exist as mirror images.

endangered species   Those species that are in danger of extinction throughout all or a significant portion of their range.

endemic   The term to describe organisms that are naturally found only in a particular location.

endergonic   Refers to chemical reactions that require an addition of free energy and do not proceed spontaneously.

endocrine disruptor   A chemical found in polluted water and soil that resembles a natural hormone; a common example are chemicals that resemble estrogen and can bind to estrogen receptors in animals.

endocrine glands   Structures that contain epithelial cells that secrete hormones into the bloodstream, where they circulate throughout the body.

endocrine system   All the endocrine glands and other organs containing hormone-secreting cells.

endocytosis   A process in which the plasma membrane invaginates, or folds inward, to form a vesicle that brings substances into the cell.

endoderm   In animals, the innermost layer of cells formed during gastrulation; lines the gut and gives rise to many internal organs.

endodermis   In vascular plants, a thin cylinder of root tissue that forms a barrier between the root cortex and the central core of vascular tissue.

endomembrane system   A network of membranes that includes the nuclear envelope, the endoplasmic reticulum, Golgi apparatus, lysosomes, vacuoles, and plasma membrane.

endomycorrhizae   Partnerships between plants and fungi in which the fungal hyphae grow into the spaces between root cell walls and plasma membranes.

endoparasite   A parasite that lives inside the host's body.

endophyte   A mutualistic fungus that lives compatibly within the tissues of various types of plants.

endoplasmic reticulum (ER)   A convoluted network of membranes in a cell's cytoplasm that forms flattened, fluid-filled tubules or cisternae.

endoskeleton   An internal hard skeleton covered by soft tissue; present in echinoderms and vertebrates.

endosperm   A nutritive tissue that increases the efficiency with which food is stored and used in the seeds of flowering plants.

endospore   A cell with a tough coat that is produced in certain bacteria and then released when the enclosing bacterial cell dies and breaks down.

endosporic gametophyte   A plant gametophyte that grows within the confines of microspore or megaspore walls.

endosymbiont   A smaller species that lives within a larger species in a symbiotic relationship.

endosymbiosis   A symbiotic relationship in which the smaller species—the symbiont—lives inside the larger species.

endosymbiosis theory   A theory that mitochondria and chloroplasts originated from bacteria that took up residence within a primordial eukaryotic cell.

endosymbiotic   Describes a relationship in which one organism lives inside the other.

endothelium   The single-celled inner layer of a blood vessel; forms a smooth lining in contact with the blood.

endotherm   An animal that generates most of its body heat by metabolic processes.

endothermic   Referring to an animal that is an endotherm.

energy   The ability to promote change or to do work.

energy flow   The movement of energy through an ecosystem.

energy intermediate   A molecule such as ATP or NADH that stores energy and is used to drive endergonic reactions in cells.

energy shell   In an atom, an energy level of electrons occupied by one or more orbitals; each energy level is a characteristic distance from the nucleus, with outer shells having more energy than inner shells.

enhancement effect   The phenomenon in which maximal activation of the pigments in photosystems I and II is achieved when organisms are exposed to two wavelengths of light.

enhancer   A response element in eukaryotes that increases the rate of transcription.

enthalpy (*H*)   The total energy of a system.

entomology   The study of insects.

entropy   The degree of disorder of a system.

environmental science   The application of ecology to real-world problems.

enzyme   A protein that acts as a catalyst to speed up a chemical reaction in a cell.

enzyme-linked receptor   A receptor found in all living species that typically has two important domains: an extracellular domain, which binds a signaling molecule, and an intracellular domain, which has a catalytic function.

enzyme-substrate complex   The binding between an enzyme and its substrate.

eosinophil   A type of phagocyte found in large numbers in mucosal surfaces lining the gastrointestinal, respiratory, and urinary tracts, where they fight off parasitic infections.

epicotyl   The portion of an embryonic plant stem with two tiny leaves in a first bud; located above the point of attachment of the cotyledons.

epidermis   A layer of dermal tissue that helps protect a plant from damage.

epididymis   A coiled, tubular structure located on the surface of the testis in which sperm complete their differentiation.

epigenetic inheritance   An inheritance pattern in which modification of a gene or chromosome during egg formation, sperm formation, or early stages of embryonic growth alters gene expression in a way that is fixed during an individual's lifetime.

epinephrine   A hormone secreted by the adrenal glands; also known as adrenaline.

episome   A plasmid that can integrate into a bacterial chromosome.

epistasis   A gene interaction in which the alleles of one gene mask the expression of the alleles of another gene.

epithalamus   A region of the vertebrate forebrain that includes the pineal gland.

epithelial tissue   In animals, a sheet of densely packed cells that covers the body, covers individual organs, and lines the walls of various cavities inside the body.

epitope   Antigenic determinant; the peptide fragments of an antigen that are complexed to MHC proteins and presented to a helper T cell.

equilibrium   1. In a chemical reaction, occurs when the rate of the forward reaction is balanced by the rate of the reverse reaction. 2. In a population, the situation in which the population size stays the same.

equilibrium model of island biogeography   A model to explain the process of succession on new islands; states that the number of species on an island tends toward an equilibrium number that is determined by the balance between immigration rates and extinction rates.

equilibrium potential   In membrane physiology, the membrane potential at which the flow of an ion is at equilibrium, with no net movement in either direction.

ER lumen   A single compartment enclosed by the ER membrane.

ER signal sequence   A sorting signal in a polypeptide usually located near the amino terminus that is recognized by SRP (signal recognition particle) and directs the polypeptide to the ER membrane.

erythrocyte   A cell that serves the critical function of transporting oxygen throughout an animal's body; also known as a red blood cell.

erythropoietin (EPO)   A hormone made by the liver and kidneys in response to any situation where additional red blood cells are required.

E site   *See* exit site.

esophagus   In animals, the tubular structure that forms a pathway from the pharynx to the stomach.

essential amino acid   An amino acid that is required in the diet of particular organisms.

essential fatty acid   A polyunsaturated fatty acid, such as linoleic acid, that cannot be synthesized by animal cells and must therefore be consumed in the diet.

essential element   In plants, a chemical element that is required for metabolism, sometimes by functioning as an enzyme cofactor.

essential nutrient   In animals, a compound that cannot be synthesized from any ingested or stored precursor molecule and so must be obtained in the diet in its complete form. In plants, those substances needed to complete reproduction while avoiding the symptoms of nutrient deficiency.

estradiol   The major estrogen in many vertebrates, including humans.

estrogens   Steroid hormones produced by the ovaries that affect most aspects of female reproduction.

ethology   Scientific studies of animal behavior.

ethylene   A plant hormone that is particularly important in coordinating plant developmental and stress responses.

euchromatin   The less condensed regions of a chromosome; areas that are capable of gene transcription.

eudicots   One of the two largest lineages of flowering plants in which the embryo possesses two seed leaves.

Eukarya   One of the three domains of life; the other two are Bacteria and Archaea.

eukaryote   One of the two categories into which all forms of life can be placed. The distinguishing feature of eukaryotes is cell compartmentalization, including a cell nucleus; includes protists, fungi, plants, and animals.

eukaryotic   Refers to organisms having cells with internal compartments that serve various functions; includes all members of the domain Eukarya.

Eumetazoa   A subgroup of animals having more than one type of tissue and, for the most part, different types of organs.

euphyll   A leaf with branched veins.

euphyllophytes   The clade that includes pteridophytes and seed plants.

euploid   An organism that has a chromosome number that is a multiple of a chromosome set (1*n*, 2*n*, 3*n*, etc.).

eusociality   An extreme form of altruism in social insects in which the vast majority of females, known as workers, do not reproduce. Instead, they help one reproductive female (the queen) raise offspring.

Eustachian tube   In mammals, a connection from the middle ear to the pharynx; maintains the pressure in the middle ear at atmospheric pressure.

eustele   In plants, a ring of vascular tissue arranged around a central pith of nonvascular tissue; typical of progymnosperms, gymnosperms, and angiosperms.

eutherian   A placental mammal and member of the subclass Eutheria.

eutrophic   Waters that contain relatively high levels of nutrients such as phosphate or nitrogen and typically exhibit high levels of primary productivity and low levels of biodiversity.

eutrophication   The process by which elevated nutrient levels in a body of water lead to an overgrowth of algae or aquatic plants and a subsequent depletion of water oxygen levels when these photosynthesizers decay.

evaporation   The transformation of water from the liquid to the gaseous state at normal temperatures. Animals use evaporation as a means of losing excess body heat.

evapotranspiration rate   The rate at which water moves into the atmosphere through the processes of evaporation from the soil and transpiration of plants.

evolution   The phenomenon that populations of organisms change from one generation to the next. As a result, some organisms become more successful at survival and reproduction.

evolutionarily conserved   The term used to describe homologous DNA sequences that are very similar or identical between different species.

evolutionary developmental biology (evo-devo)   A field of biology that compares the development of different organisms in an attempt to understand ancestral relationships between organisms and the developmental mechanisms that bring about evolutionary change.

evolutionary lineage concept   An approach used to distinguish species; states that a species is derived from a single distinct lineage and has its own evolutionary tendencies and historical fate.

excitable cell   The term used to describe neurons and muscle cells because they have the capacity to generate electrical signals.

excitation-contraction coupling   The sequence of events by which an action potential in the plasma membrane of a muscle fiber leads to cross-bridge activity.

excitatory postsynaptic potential (EPSP)   The response from an excitatory neurotransmitter that depolarizes the postsynaptic membrane; the depolarization brings the membrane potential closer to the threshold potential that would trigger an action potential.

excretion   In animals, the process of expelling waste or harmful materials from the body.

exercise   Any physical activity that increases an animal's metabolic rate.

exergonic   Refers to chemical reactions that release free energy and occur spontaneously.

exit site (E site)   One of three sites for tRNA binding in the ribosome during translation; the other two are the peptidyl site (P site) and the aminoacyl site (A site). The uncharged tRNA exits from the E site.

exocrine gland   A gland in which epithelial cells secrete chemicals into a duct, which carries those molecules directly to another structure or to the outside surface of the body.

exocytosis   A process in which material inside a cell is packaged into vesicles and excreted into the extracellular medium.

exon   A portion of RNA that is found in the mature mRNA molecule after splicing is finished.

exon shuffling   A form of mutation in which exons and their flanking introns are inserted into genes and thereby create proteins with additional functional domains.

exonuclease   An enzyme that cleaves off nucleotides, one at a time, from the end of a DNA or RNA molecule.

exoskeleton   An external skeleton made of chitin and protein that surrounds and protects most of the body surface of animals such as insects.

exosome   A multiprotein complex that degrades mRNA.

expansin   A protein that occurs in the plant cell wall and fosters cell enlargement.

experimental group   The sample in an experiment that is subjected to some type of variation that does not occur for the control group.

exploitation competition   Competition in which organisms compete indirectly through the consumption of a limited resource.

exponential growth   Rapid population growth that occurs when the per capita growth rate remains above zero.

extensor   A muscle that straightens a limb at a joint.

external fertilization   Fertilization that occurs in aquatic environments, when eggs and sperm are released into the water in close enough proximity for fertilization to occur.

external intercostal muscles   Muscles of the rib cage that contract during inhalation, thereby expanding the chest.

extinction   The end of the existence of a species or a group of species.

extinction vortex   A downward spiral toward extinction from which a species cannot naturally recover.

extracellular fluid   The fluid in an organism's body that is outside of the cells.

extracellular matrix (ECM)   A network of material that is secreted from animal cells and forms a complex meshwork outside of cells. The ECM provides strength, support, and organization.

extranuclear inheritance   In eukaryotes, the transmission of genes that are located outside the cell nucleus.

extremophile   An organism that occurs primarily in extreme habitats.

eye   The visual organ in animals that detects light and sends signals to the brain.

eyecup   An eye in planaria that detects light and its direction but which does not form an image.

F

facilitated diffusion   A method of passive transport of solutes down a concentration gradient that involves the aid of a transport protein.

facilitation   A mechanism for succession in which a species facilitates or makes the environment more suitable for subsequent species.

facultative anaerobe   A microorganism that can use oxygen in aerobic respiration, obtain energy via anaerobic fermentation, or use inorganic chemical reactions to obtain energy.

facultative mutualism   An interaction between mutualistic species that is beneficial but not essential to the survival and reproduction of either species.

family   In taxonomy, a subdivision of an order.

fast block to polyspermy   A depolarization of the egg that blocks other sperm from binding to the egg membrane proteins.

fast fiber   A skeletal muscle fiber containing myosin with a high rate of ATP hydrolysis.

fast-glycolytic fiber   A skeletal muscle fiber that has high myosin ATPase activity but cannot make as much ATP as oxidative fibers because its source of ATP is glycolysis; best suited for rapid, intense actions.

fast-oxidative fiber   A skeletal muscle fiber that has high myosin ATPase activity and can make large amounts of ATP; used for long-term activities.

fate   The ultimate morphological features that a cell or a group of cells will adopt.

fate mapping   A technique in which a small population of cells within an embryo is specifically labeled with a harmless dye, and the fate of these labeled cells is followed to a later stage of embryonic development.

feedback inhibition   A form of regulation in which the product of a metabolic pathway inhibits an enzyme

that acts early in the pathway, thus preventing the overaccumulation of the product.

feedforward regulation   The process by which an animal's body begins preparing for a change in some variable before it even occurs.

female-enforced monogamy hypothesis   The hypothesis that a male is monogamous due to various actions employed by his female mate.

female gametophyte   A haploid multicellular plant generation that produces one or more eggs but does not produce sperm cells.

fermentation   The breakdown of organic molecules to produce energy without any net oxidation of an organic molecule.

fertilization   The union of two gametes, such as an egg cell with a sperm cell, to form a zygote.

fertilizer   A soil addition that enhances plant growth by providing essential elements.

fetal alcohol syndrome   The physical and mental defects that may arise in a child born to a woman who consumes alcohol during pregnancy.

fetus   The maturing embryo after the eighth week of gestation in humans.

fever   An increase in an animal's temperature, typically due to infection.

F factor   A type of bacterial plasmid called a fertility factor that plays a role in bacterial conjugation.

F_1 generation   The first generation in a genetic cross.

F_2 generation   The second generation in a genetic cross.

fiber   A type of tough-walled plant cell that provides support.

fibrin   A protein that forms a meshwork of threadlike fibers that wrap around and between platelets and blood cells, enlarging and thickening a blood clot.

fibrous root system   The root system of monocots, which consists of multiple adventitious roots that grow from the stem base.

fight-or-flight   The response of vertebrates to real or perceived danger; associated with increased activity of the sympathetic branch of the autonomic nervous system.

filament   1. The elongate portion of a flower's stamen; contains vascular tissue that delivers nutrients from parental sporophytes to anthers. 2. In fishes, a part of the gills.

filtrate   In the process of filtration in an excretory system, the material that passes through the filter and enters the excretory organ for either further processing or excretion.

filtration   The passive removal of water and small solutes from the blood during the production of urine.

finite rate of increase   In ecology, the ratio of a population size from one year to the next.

first law of thermodynamics   States that energy cannot be created or destroyed; also called the law of conservation of energy.

fitness   The relative likelihood that a genotype will contribute to the gene pool of the next generation as compared with other genotypes.

5′ cap   The 7-methylguanosine cap structure at the 5′ end of most mature mRNAs in eukaryotes.

fixed action pattern (FAP)   An animal behavior that, once initiated, will continue until completed.

fixed nitrogen   Atmospheric nitrogen that has been combined with other elements into a form of nitrogen that can be used by plants. An example is ammonia, NH_3.

flaccid   A plant cell in which the concentration of solutes is the same as that in the external fluid environment. A flaccid cell has a water content higher than a plasmolyzed cell, but lower than a turgid cell.

flagella (singular, **flagellum**)   Relatively long cell appendages that facilitate cellular movement or the movement of extracellular fluids.

flagellate   A protist that uses one or more flagella to move in water or cause water motions useful in feeding.

flagship species   A single large or instantly recognizable species.

flame cell   A cell that exists primarily to maintain osmotic balance between an organism's body and surrounding fluids; present in flatworms.

flavonoid   A type of phenolic secondary metabolite that provides plants with protection from ultraviolet damage or imparts color to flowers.

flexor   A muscle that bends a limb at a joint.

florigen   The hypothesized flowering hormone, now identified as the FT (flowering time) protein that moves from leaves, where it is produced, into the shoot apex.

flower   A reproductive shoot; a short stem that produces reproductive organs instead of leaves.

flowering plants   The angiosperms, which produce ovules within the protective ovaries of flowers. The ovules develop into seeds, and the ovaries develop into fruits, which function in seed dispersal.

flow-through system   The method of ventilation in fishes in which water moves unidirectionally such that the gills are constantly in contact with fresh, oxygenated water. Buccal pumping and ram ventilation are examples.

fluid-feeder   An animal that licks or sucks fluid from plants or animals and does not need teeth except to puncture an animal's skin.

fluidity   A property of biomembranes in which individual molecules remain in close association yet have the ability to move rotationally or laterally within the plane of the membrane. Membranes are semifluid.

fluid-mosaic model   The accepted model of the plasma membrane; its basic framework is the semifluid phospholipid bilayer with a mosaic of proteins. Carbohydrates may be attached to the lipids or proteins.

fMRI   *See* functional magnetic resonance imaging.

focal adhesion   A mechanically strong cell junction that connects an animal cell to the extracellular matrix (ECM).

follicle   A structure within an animal ovary where each ovum undergoes growth and development before it is released.

follicle-stimulating hormone (FSH)   A gonadotropin that stimulates follicle development.

food chain   A linear depiction of energy flow between organisms, with each organism feeding on and deriving energy from the preceding organism.

food-induced thermogenesis   A rise in metabolic rate for a few hours after eating that produces heat.

food vacuole   *See* phagocytic vacuole.

food web   A complex model of interconnected food chains in which there are multiple links between species.

foot   In mollusks, a muscular structure usually used for movement.

forebrain   One of three major divisions of the vertebrate brain; the other two divisions are the midbrain and hindbrain.

fossil   Recognizable preserved remains of past life on Earth.

fossil fuel   A fuel formed in the Earth from protist, plant, or animal remains, such as coal, petroleum, and natural gas.

founder effect   Genetic drift that occurs when a small group of individuals separates from a larger population and establishes a colony in a new location.

fovea   A small area on the retina directly behind the lens, where an image is most sharply focused.

frameshift mutation A mutation that involves the addition or deletion of a number of nucleotides that are not in multiples of three.

free energy (G) In living organisms, the amount of available energy that can be used to do work.

free radical A molecule containing an atom with a single, unpaired electron in its outer shell. A free radical is unstable and interacts with other molecules by removing electrons from their atoms.

frequency In regard to sound, the number of complete wavelengths that occur in 1 second, measured in hertz (Hz).

frontal lobe One of four lobes of the cerebral cortex of the human brain; important in a variety of functions, including judgment and conscious thought.

fruit A structure that develops from flower organs, encloses seeds, and fosters seed dispersal in the environment.

fruiting bodies The visible fungal reproductive structures that are composed of densely packed hyphae that typically grow out of the substrate.

functional genomics Genomic methods aimed at studying the expression of a genome.

functional group A group of atoms with chemical features that are functionally important. Each functional group exhibits the same properties in all molecules in which it occurs.

functional magnetic resonance imaging (fMRI) A technique used to determine changes in brain activity while a person is performing specific tasks.

fundamental niche The optimal range in which a particular species best functions.

fungi A eukaryotic kingdom of the domain Eukarya.

fungus-like protists Heterotrophic protists that often resemble true fungi in having threadlike, filamentous bodies and absorbing nutrients from their environment.

G

G_0 A phase in which cells exit the cell cycle and postpone making the decision to divide.

G_1 The first gap phase of the cell cycle.

G_2 The second gap phase of the cell cycle.

gallbladder In many vertebrates, a small sac underneath the liver that is a storage site for bile; allows the release of large amounts of bile to be precisely timed to the consumption of fats.

gametangia Specialized structures produced by many land plants in which developing gametes are protected by a jacket of tissue.

gamete A haploid cell that is involved with sexual reproduction, such as a sperm or egg cell.

gametic life cycle A type of life cycle where all cells except the gametes are diploid, and gametes are produced by meiosis.

gametogenesis The formation of gametes.

gametophyte In plants and many multicellular protists, the haploid stage that produces gametes by mitosis.

ganglion A group of neuronal cell bodies in the peripheral nervous system that is involved in a similar function.

ganglion cells Cells in the vertebrate eye that send their axons into the optic nerve.

gap gene A type of segmentation gene; a mutation in this type of gene may cause several adjacent segments to be missing in the larva.

gap junction A type of junction between animal cells that provides a passageway for intercellular transport.

gas exchange The process of moving oxygen and carbon dioxide in opposite directions between the environment and blood and between blood and cells.

gas vesicle A cytoplasmic structure used to adjust buoyancy in cyanobacteria and certain other bacteria that live in aquatic habitats.

gastrin A hormone secreted by cells of the vertebrate stomach that stimulates acid production by stomach cells.

gastrovascular cavity In certain invertebrates such as cnidarians, a body cavity with a single opening to the outside; it functions as both a digestive system and circulatory system.

gastrula A stage of an animal embryo that is the result of gastrulation and has three cellular layers: the ectoderm, endoderm, and mesoderm.

gastrulation In animals, a process in which an area in the blastula invaginates and folds inward, creating different embryonic cell layers called germ layers.

gated A property of many channels that allows them to open and close to control the diffusion of solutes through a membrane.

gel electrophoresis A technique used to separate macromolecules by using an electric field that causes them to pass through a gel matrix.

gene A unit of heredity that contributes to the characteristics or traits of an organism. At the molecular level, a gene is composed of organized sequences of DNA.

gene addition The insertion of a cloned gene into the genome of an organism.

gene amplification An increase in the copy number of a gene.

gene cloning The process of making multiple copies of a gene of interest.

gene expression Gene function both at the level of traits and at the molecular level.

gene family A group of homologous genes within a single species.

gene flow Occurs when individuals migrate between different populations and results in changes in the genetic composition of the resulting populations.

gene interaction A situation in which a single trait is controlled by two or more genes.

gene knockout An organism in which both copies of a functional gene have been replaced with nonfunctional copies. Experimentally, this can occur via gene replacement.

gene mutation A relatively small change in DNA structure that alters a particular gene.

gene pool All of the genes in a population.

genera (singular, genus) In taxonomy, a subdivision of a family.

general lineage concept A widely accepted approach used to distinguish species; states that each species is a population of an independently evolving lineage.

general transcription factors (GTFs) Five different proteins that play a role in initiating transcription at the core promoter of structural genes in eukaryotes.

generative cell In a seed plant, one of the cells resulting from the division of a microspore; a generative cell divides to produce two sperm cells.

gene regulation The ability of cells to control their level of gene expression.

gene replacement The phenomenon in which a cloned gene recombines with the normal gene on a chromosome and replaces it.

gene therapy The introduction of cloned genes into living cells in an attempt to cure disease.

genetic code A code that specifies the relationship between the sequence of nucleotides in the codons found in mRNA and the sequence of amino acids in a polypeptide.

genetic drift The random change in a population's allele frequencies from one generation to the next that is attributable to chance. It occurs more quickly in small populations.

genetic engineering The direct manipulation of genes for practical purposes.

genetic map A chart that shows the linear arrangement of genes along a chromosome.

genetic mapping The use of genetic crosses to determine the linear order of genes that are linked to each other along the same chromosome.

genetically modified organisms (GMOs) See transgenic.

gene transfer The process by which genetic material is transferred from one bacterial cell to another.

genome The complete genetic composition of a cell or a species.

genomic imprinting A phenomenon in which a segment of DNA is imprinted, or marked, in a way that affects gene expression throughout the life of the individual who inherits that DNA.

genomic library A type of DNA library in which the inserts are derived from chromosomal DNA.

genomics Techniques that are used in the molecular analysis of the entire genome of a species.

genotype The genetic composition of an individual.

genotype frequency In a population, the number of individuals with a given genotype divided by the total number of individuals.

geological timescale A time line of the Earth's history from its origin about 4.55 bya to the present.

germination In plants, the process in which an embryo absorbs water, becomes metabolically active, and grows out of the seed coat, producing a seedling.

germ layer An embryonic cell layer such as ectoderm, mesoderm, or endoderm.

germ line Cells that give rise to gametes such as egg and sperm cells.

germ plasm Cytoplasmic determinants that help define and specify the primordial germ cells in the gastrula stage of animal development.

gestation See pregnancy.

giant axon A very large axon in certain species such as squids that facilitates high-speed neuronal conduction and rapid responses to stimuli.

gibberellic acid A type of gibberellin.

gibberellin A plant hormone that stimulates both cell division and cell elongation.

gills Specialized filamentous organs in aquatic animals that are used to obtain oxygen and eliminate carbon dioxide.

ginkgos A phylum of gymnosperms; Ginkgophyta.

gizzard The muscular portion of the stomach of birds and some reptiles that is capable of grinding food into smaller fragments.

glaucoma A condition in which drainage of aqueous humor in the eye becomes blocked and the pressure inside the eye increases. If untreated, this pressure damages cells in the retina and leads to irreversible loss of vision.

glia Cells that surround the neurons; a major class of cells in nervous systems that perform various functions.

global warming A gradual elevation of the Earth's surface temperature caused by an increasing greenhouse effect.

glomerular filtration rate (GFR) The rate at which a filtrate of plasma is formed in all the glomeruli of the vertebrate kidneys.

glomerulus A cluster of interconnected, fenestrated capillaries in the renal corpuscle of the kidney; the site of filtration in the kidney.

glucagon A hormone found in animals that stimulates the processes of glycogenolysis, gluconeogenesis, and the synthesis of ketones in the liver.

glucocorticoid A steroid hormone that regulates glucose balance and helps prepare the body for stress situations.

gluconeogenesis   A mechanism for maintaining blood glucose level; enzymes in the liver convert noncarbohydrate precursors into glucose, which is then secreted into the blood.

glucose sparing   A metabolic adjustment that reserves the glucose produced by the liver for use by the nervous system.

glycocalyx   1. An outer viscous covering surrounding a bacterium that traps water and helps protect bacteria from drying out. 2. A carbohydrate-rich zone on the surface of animal cells; also called a cell coat.

glycogen   A polysaccharide found in animal cells (especially liver and skeletal muscle) and sometimes called animal starch; also, the major carbohydrate storage of fungi.

glycogenolysis   A mechanism for maintaining blood glucose level; stored glycogen can be broken down into molecules of glucose which are then secreted into the blood.

glycolipid   A lipid that has carbohydrate attached to it.

glycolysis   A metabolic pathway that breaks down glucose to pyruvate.

glycolytic fiber   A skeletal muscle fiber that has few mitochondria but possesses both a high concentration of glycolytic enzymes and large stores of glycogen.

glycoprotein   A protein that has carbohydrate attached to it.

glycosaminoglycan   The most abundant type of polysaccharide in the extracellular matrix (ECM) of animals, consisting of repeating disaccharide units that give a gel-like character to the ECM of animals.

glycosidic bond   A bond formed between two sugar molecules.

glycosylation   The attachment of carbohydrate to a protein or lipid, producing a glycoprotein or glycolipid.

glyoxysome   A specialized organelle within plant seeds that contains enzymes needed to convert fats to sugars.

gnathostomes   All vertebrate species that possess jaws.

gnetophytes   A phylum of gymnosperms; Gnetophyta.

Golgi apparatus   A stack of flattened, membrane-bound compartments that performs three overlapping functions: secretion, processing, and protein sorting.

gonadotropins   Hormones secreted by the anterior pituitary gland that are the same in both sexes; gonadotropins influence the ability of the testes and ovaries to produce the sex steroids.

gonads   The testes in males and the ovaries in females, where the gametes are formed.

G protein   An intracellular protein that binds guanosine triphosphate (GTP) and guanosine diphosphate (GDP) and participates in intracellular signaling pathways.

G-protein-coupled receptors (GPCRs)   A common type of receptor found in the cells of eukaryotic species that interacts with G proteins to initiate a cellular response.

graded potential   A depolarization or hyperpolarization in a neuron that varies with the strength of a stimulus.

gradualism   A concept suggesting that species evolve continuously over long spans of time.

grain   The characteristic single-seeded fruit of cereal grasses such as rice, corn, barley, and wheat.

Gram stain   A staining process that can help to identify bacteria and predict their responses to antibiotics.

granum   A structure composed of stacked membrane-bound thylakoids within a chloroplast.

gravitropism   Plant growth in response to the force of gravity.

gray matter   Brain tissue that consists of neuronal cell bodies, dendrites, and some unmyelinated axons.

greenhouse effect   The process in which short-wave solar radiation passes through the atmosphere to warm the Earth but is radiated back to space as long-wave infrared radiation. Much of this radiation is reflected by atmospheric gases back to Earth's surface, causing its temperature to rise.

groove   In the DNA double helix, an indentation where the atoms of the bases make contact with the surrounding water.

gross primary production (GPP)   The measure of biomass production by photosynthetic organisms; equivalent to the carbon fixed during photosynthesis.

ground meristem   In plants, a type of primary plant tissue meristem that gives rise to ground tissue.

ground tissue   Most of the body of a plant, which has a variety of functions, including photosynthesis, storage of carbohydrates, and support. Ground tissue can be subdivided into three types: parenchyma, collenchyma, and sclerenchyma.

group selection   A premise that attempts to explain altruism. States that natural selection produces outcomes beneficial for the whole group or species rather than for individuals.

growth   An increase in weight or size.

growth factors   Proteins in animals that stimulate certain cells to grow and divide.

growth hormone (GH)   A hormone produced in vertebrates by the anterior pituitary gland; GH acts on the liver to produce insulin-like growth factor-1 (IGF-1).

guanine (G)   A purine base found in DNA and RNA.

guard cell   A specialized plant cell that allows epidermal pores (stomata) to close when conditions are too dry and to open under moist conditions, allowing the entry of CO_2 needed for photosynthesis.

gustation   The sense of taste.

gut   The gastrointestinal (GI) tract of an animal.

guttation   Droplets of water at the edges of leaves that are the result of root pressure.

gymnosperm   A plant that produces seeds that are exposed rather than seeds enclosed in fruits.

gynoecium   The aggregate of carpels that forms the innermost whorl of a flower.

H

habituation   The form of nonassociative learning in which an organism learns to ignore a repeated stimulus.

hair cell   A mechanoreceptor in animals that is a specialized epithelial cell with deformable stereocilia.

half-life   1. In the case of organic molecules in a cell, refers to the time it takes for 50% of the molecules to be broken down and recycled. 2. In the case of radioisotopes, the time it takes for 50% of the molecules to decay and emit radiation.

halophile   A bacterium or archaeon that can live in an extremely salty environment.

halophyte   A plant that can tolerate higher than normal salt concentrations and can occupy coastal salt marshes or saline deserts.

Hamilton's rule   The proposal that an altruistic gene will be favored by natural selection when $rB > C$, where r is the coefficient of relatedness of the donor (the altruist) to the recipient, B is the benefit received by the recipient, and C is the cost incurred by the donor.

haplodiploid system   A genetic system in which females develop from fertilized eggs and are diploid but males develop from unfertilized eggs and are haploid.

haploid   Containing one set of chromosomes; designated as $1n$.

haploid-dominant species   Species in which the haploid organism is the prevalent organism in the life cycle. Examples include fungi and some protists.

haplorrhini   Larger-brained diurnal species of primates; includes monkeys, gibbons, orangutans, gorillas, chimpanzees, and humans.

Hardy-Weinberg equation   An equation ($p^2 + 2pq + q^2 = 1$) that relates allele and genotype frequencies; the equation predicts an equilibrium if no new mutations are formed, no natural selection occurs, the population size is very large, the population does not migrate, and mating is random.

heart   A muscular structure that pumps blood through blood vessels.

heart attack   *See* myocardial infarction (MI).

heartburn   More properly called gastroesophageal reflux; the movement of acidic stomach contents upward into the esophagus, typically causing pain.

heat of fusion   The amount of heat energy that must be withdrawn or released from a substance to cause it to change from the liquid to the solid state.

heat of vaporization   The heat required to vaporize 1 mole of any substance at its boiling point under standard pressure.

heavy chain   A part of an immunoglobulin molecule.

H⁺ electrochemical gradient   A transmembrane gradient for H⁺ composed of both a membrane potential and a concentration difference for H⁺ across a membrane.

helper T cell   A type of lymphocyte that assists in the activation and function of B cells and cytotoxic T cells.

hematocrit   The volume of blood that is composed of red blood cells, usually between 40 and 65% in vertebrates.

hemidesmosome   A mechanically strong cell junction that connects an animal cell to the extracellular matrix (ECM).

hemiparasite   A parasitic organism that photosynthesizes, but lacks a root system to draw water and thus depends on its host for that function.

hemispheres   The two halves of the cerebrum.

hemizygous   The term used to describe the single copy of an X-linked gene in a male.

hemocyanin   A copper-containing pigment that binds oxygen and gives blood or hemolymph a bluish tint.

hemodialysis   A medical procedure used to artificially perform the kidneys' function.

hemoglobin   An iron-containing protein that binds oxygen and is found within the cytosol of red blood cells.

hemolymph   Blood and interstitial fluid combined in one fluid compartment; present in many invertebrates.

hemophilia   An inherited disorder characterized by the deficiency of a specific blood clotting factor.

hemorrhage   A loss of blood from a ruptured blood vessel.

herbaceous plant   A plant that produces little or no wood and is composed mostly of primary vascular tissues.

herbivore   An animal that eats only plants.

herbivory   Refers to herbivores feeding on plants.

hermaphrodite   In animals, an individual that can produce both sperm and eggs.

hermaphroditism   A form of sexual reproduction in which individuals have both male and female reproductive systems.

heterochromatin   The highly compacted regions of chromosomes that are usually transcriptionally inactive because of their tight conformation.

heterochrony   Evolutionary changes in the rate or timing of developmental events.

heterocyst   A specialized cell of some cyanobacteria in which nitrogen fixation occurs.

heterospory   In plants, the formation of two different types of spores: microspores and megaspores; microspores produce male gametophytes, and megaspores produce female gametophytes.

heterotherm   An animal that has a body temperature that is not constant; both ectotherms and endotherms may be heterotherms.

heterotroph   Organisms that cannot produce their own organic molecules and thus must obtain organic food from other organisms.

heterotrophic   Requiring organic food from the environment.

heterozygote advantage   A phenomenon in which a heterozygote has a higher Darwinian fitness than either corresponding homozygote.

heterozygous   An individual with two different alleles of the same gene.

hibernation   The state of torpor in an animal that can last for months.

highly repetitive sequence   A DNA sequence found tens of thousands or even millions of times throughout a genome.

hindbrain   One of three major divisions of the vertebrate brain; the other two divisions are the midbrain and forebrain.

hippocampus   The area of the vertebrate forebrain that functions in establishing memories for spatial locations, facts, and the sequence of events.

histone acetyltransferase   An enzyme that loosens the compaction of chromatin by attaching acetyl groups to histone proteins.

histone code hypothesis   Refers to the pattern of histone modification recognized by particular proteins. The pattern of covalent modifications of amino terminus tails provides binding sites for proteins that subsequently affect the degree of chromatin compaction.

histones   A group of proteins involved in the formation of nucleosomes that aid in the compaction of eukaryotic DNA.

HIV   *See* human immunodeficiency virus.

holoblastic cleavage   A complete type of cell cleavage in certain animals in which the entire zygote is bisected into two equal-sized blastomeres.

holoparasite   A parasitic organism that lacks chlorophyll and is totally dependent on a host plant for its water and nutrients.

homeobox   A 180-bp sequence within the coding sequence of homeotic genes.

homeodomain   A region of a homeotic protein that functions in binding to the DNA.

homeostasis   The process whereby living organisms regulate their cells and bodies to maintain relatively stable internal conditions.

homeostatic control system   A system designed to regulate particular variables in an animal's body, such as body temperature; consists of a set point, sensor, integrator, and effectors.

homeotherm   An animal that maintains its body temperature within a narrow range.

homeotic gene   A gene that controls the developmental fate of particular segments or regions of an animal's body.

hominin   Either an extinct or modern species of humans.

hominoidea (hominoid)   A member of a group of primates that includes gibbons, orangutans, gorillas, chimpanzees, and humans.

homologous genes   Genes derived from the same ancestral gene that have accumulated random mutations that make their sequences slightly different.

homologous structures   Structures that are similar to each other because they are derived from the same ancestral structure.

homolog   A member of a pair of chromosomes in a diploid organism.

homology   A fundamental similarity that occurs due to descent from a common ancestor.

homozygous   An individual with two identical copies of an allele.

horizontal gene transfer   A process in which an organism incorporates genetic material from another organism without being the offspring of that organism.

hormone   A chemical messenger that is produced in a gland or other structure and acts on distant target cells in one or more parts of an animal or plant.

hornworts   A phylum of bryophytes; Anthocerophyta.

host   The prey organism in a parasitic association.

host cell   1. A cell that is infected by a virus, fungus, or a bacterium. 2. A eukaryotic cell that contains photosynthetic or nonphotosynthetic endosymbionts.

host plant resistance   The ability of plants to prevent herbivory.

host range   The number of species and cell types that a virus or bacterium can infect.

hot spot   A human-impacted geographic area with a large number of endemic species. To qualify as a hot spot, a region must contain at least 1,500 species of endemic vascular plants and have lost at least 70% of its original habitat.

***Hox* genes**   In animals, a class of genes involved in pattern formation in early embryos.

Human Genome Project   A 13-year international effort coordinated by the U.S. Department of Energy and the National Institutes of Health that characterized and sequenced the entire human genome.

human immunodeficiency virus (HIV)   A retrovirus that is the causative agent of acquired immune deficiency syndrome (AIDS).

humoral immunity   A type of specific immunity in which plasma cells secrete antibodies that bind to antigens.

humus   A collective term for the organic constituents of soils.

hybridization   A situation in which two individuals with different characteristics are mated or crossed to each other; the offspring are referred to as hybrids.

hybrid zone   An area where two populations can interbreed.

hydrocarbon   Molecules with predominantly hydrogen–carbon bonds.

hydrogen bond   A weak chemical attraction between a partially positive hydrogen atom of a polar molecule and a partially negative atom of another polar molecule.

hydrolysis reaction   A chemical reaction that utilizes water to break apart molecules.

hydrophilic   Refers to ions and molecules that contain polar covalent bonds and will dissolve in water.

hydrophobic   Refers to molecules that do not have partial charges and therefore are not attracted to water molecules. Such molecules are composed predominantly of carbon and hydrogen and are relatively insoluble in water.

hydrostatic skeleton   A fluid-filled body cavity in certain soft-bodied invertebrates that is surrounded by muscles and provides support and shape.

hydroxide ion   An anion with the formula, OH^-.

hypermutation   A process that primarily involves numerous C to T point mutations that are crucial to enabling lymphocytes to produce a diverse array of immunoglobulins capable of recognizing many different antigens.

hyperpolarization   The change in the membrane potential that occurs when the cell becomes more polarized.

hypersensitive response (HR)   A plant's local defensive response to pathogen attack.

hypertension   High blood pressure.

hyperthermophile   An organism that thrives in extremely hot temperatures.

hyperthyroidism   A medical condition resulting from a hyperactive thyroid gland.

hypertonic   Any solution that causes a cell to shrink due to osmosis of water out of the cell.

hypha   A microscopic, branched filament of the body of a fungus.

hypocotyl   The portion of an embryonic plant stem located below the point of attachment of the cotyledons.

hypothalamus   A part of the vertebrate brain located below the thalamus; it controls functions of the gastrointestinal and reproductive systems, among others, and regulates many basic behaviors such as eating and drinking.

hypothesis   In biology, a proposed explanation for a natural phenomenon based on previous observations or experimental studies.

hypothesis testing   Also known as the scientific method, a strategy for testing the validity of a hypothesis.

hypothyroidism   A medical condition resulting from an underactive thyroid gland.

hypotonic   Any solution that causes a cell to swell when placed in that solution.

H zone   In a myofibril, a narrow, light region in the center of the A band that corresponds to the space between the two sets of thin filaments in each sarcomere.

I

I band   In a myofibril, a light band that lies between the A bands of two adjacent sarcomeres.

idiosyncratic hypothesis   The possibility that ecosystem function changes as the number of species increases or decreases but that the amount and direction of change is unpredictable.

immune system   The cells and organs within an animal's body that contribute to immune defenses.

immune tolerance   The process by which the body distinguishes between self and nonself components.

immunity   The ability of an animal to ward off internal threats, including harmful microorganisms, foreign molecules, and abnormal cells such as cancer cells.

immunoglobulin   A Y-shaped protein with two heavy chains and two light chains that provides immunity to foreign substances; antibodies are a type of immunoglobulin.

immunological memory   The immune system's ability to produce a secondary immune response.

imperfect flower   A flower that lacks either stamens or carpels.

implantation   The first event of pregnancy, when the blastocyst embeds within the uterine endometrium.

imprinting   1. The development of a species-specific pattern of behavior that occurs during a critical period; a form of learning, with a large innate component. 2. In genetics, the marking of DNA that occurs differently between males and females.

inactivation gate   A string of amino acids that juts out from a channel protein into the cytosol and blocks the movement of ions through the channel.

inborn error of metabolism   A genetic defect in the ability to metabolize certain compounds.

inbreeding   Mating among genetically related relatives.

inbreeding depression   The phenomenon whereby inbreeding produces homozygotes that are less fit, thereby decreasing the reproductive success of a population.

inclusive fitness   The term used to designate the total number of copies of genes passed on through one's relatives, as well as one's own reproductive output.

incomplete dominance   The phenomenon in which a heterozygote that carries two different alleles exhibits a phenotype that is intermediate between the corresponding homozygous individuals.

incomplete flower   A flower that lacks one or more of the four flower organ types.

incomplete metamorphosis   During development in some insects, a gradual change in body form from a nymph into an adult.

incurrent siphon A structure in a tunicate used to draw water through the mouth.

indeterminate cleavage In animals, a characteristic of deuterostome development in which each cell produced by early cleavage retains the ability to develop into a complete embryo.

indeterminate growth Growth in which plant shoot apical meristems continuously produce new stem tissues and leaves, as long as conditions remain favorable.

indicator species A species whose status provides information on the overall health of an ecosystem.

indirect calorimetry A method of determining basal metabolic rate in which the rate at which an animal uses oxygen is measured.

individualistic model A view of the nature of a community that considers it to be an assemblage of species coexisting primarily because of similarities in their physiological requirements and tolerances.

individual selection The proposal that adaptive traits generally are selected for because they benefit the survival and reproduction of the individual rather than the group.

induced fit Occurs when a substrate(s) binds to an enzyme and the enzyme undergoes a conformational change that causes the substrate(s) to bind more tightly to the enzyme.

induced mutation A mutation brought about by environmental agents that enter the cell and then alter the structure of DNA.

inducer In transcription, a small effector molecule that increases the rate of transcription.

inducible operon In this type of operon, the presence of a small effector molecule causes transcription to occur.

induction 1. In development, the process by which a cell or group of cells governs the developmental fate of neighboring cells. 2. In molecular genetics, refers to the process by which transcription has been turned on by the presence of a small effector molecule.

industrial nitrogen fixation The human activity of producing nitrogen fertilizers.

infertility The inability to produce viable offspring.

inflammation An innate local response to infection or injury characterized by local redness, swelling, heat, and pain.

inflorescence A cluster of flowers on a plant.

infundibular stalk The structure that physically connects the hypothalamus to the pituitary gland.

ingestion In animals, the act of taking food into the body.

ingroup In a cladogram, a group of interest.

inheritance The acquisition of traits by their transmission from parent to offspring.

inheritance of acquired characteristics Jean-Baptiste Lamarck's incorrect hypothesis that species change over the course of many generations by adapting to new environments.

inhibition A mechanism for succession in which early colonists exclude subsequent colonists.

inhibitory postsynaptic potential (IPSP) The response from an inhibitory neurotransmitter that hyperpolarizes the postsynaptic membrane; this hyperpolarization reduces the likelihood of an action potential.

initiation factor A protein that facilitates the interactions between mRNA, the first tRNA, and the ribosomal subunits during the initiation stage of translation.

initiation stage The first step in the process of transcription or translation.

initiator tRNA A specific tRNA that recognizes the start codon AUG in mRNA and binds to it, initiating translation.

innate The term used to describe behaviors that seem to be genetically programmed.

innate immunity The body's defenses that are present at birth and act against foreign materials in much the same way regardless of their specific identity; includes the skin and mucous membranes, plus various cellular and chemical defenses.

inner bark The thin layer of secondary phloem that carries out most of the sugar transport in a woody stem.

inner ear One of the three main compartments of the mammalian ear. The inner ear is composed of the bony cochlea and the vestibular system, which plays a role in balance.

inner segment The part of the vertebrate photoreceptors (rods and cones) that contains the cell nucleus and cytoplasmic organelles.

inorganic chemistry The study of the nature of atoms and molecules, with the exception of those that contain rings or chains of carbon.

insulin A hormone found in animals that regulates metabolism in several ways, primarily by regulating the blood glucose concentration.

insulin-like growth factor-1 (IGF-1) A hormone in mammals that stimulates the elongation of bones, especially during puberty.

integral membrane protein A protein that cannot be released from the membrane unless it is dissolved with an organic solvent or detergent. Includes transmembrane proteins and lipid-anchored proteins.

integrase An enzyme, sometimes encoded by viruses, that catalyzes the integration of the viral genome into a host-cell chromosome.

integrator The part of a homeostatic control system in which a variable is compared to a set point; typically a nucleus in the brain.

integrin A cell adhesion molecule found in animal cells that connects cells to the extracellular matrix.

integument In plants, a structure that encloses the megasporangium to form an ovule.

interference competition Competition in which organisms interact directly with one another by physical force or intimidation.

interferon A protein that generally inhibits viral replication inside host cells.

intermediate-disturbance hypothesis The proposal that moderately disturbed communities are more diverse than undisturbed or highly disturbed communities.

intermediate filament A type of protein filament of the cytoskeleton that helps maintain cell shape and rigidity.

internal fertilization Fertilization that occurs in terrestrial animals in which sperm are deposited within the reproductive tract of the female during copulation.

interneuron A type of neuron that forms interconnections between other neurons.

internode The region of a plant stem between adjacent nodes.

interphase The G_1, S, and G_2 phases of the cell cycle. It is the portion of the cell cycle during which the chromosomes are decondensed and found in the nucleus.

intersexual selection Sexual selection between members of the opposite sex.

interspecies hybrid The offspring resulting from the mating of two different species.

interspecific competition Competition between individuals of different species.

interstitial fluid The fluid that surrounds cells.

intertidal zone The area where the land meets the sea, which is alternately submerged and exposed by the daily cycle of tides.

intracellular fluid The fluid inside cells.

intranuclear spindle A spindle that forms within an intact nuclear envelope during nuclear division in fungi and some protists.

intrasexual selection Sexual selection between members of the same sex.

intraspecific competition Competition between individuals of the same species.

intrauterine device (IUD) A small object that is placed in the uterus and interferes with the endometrial preparation required for acceptance of the blastocyst; used as a form of contraception.

intrinsic rate of increase The situation in which conditions are optimal for a population and the per capita growth rate is at its maximum rate.

introduced species A species moved by humans from a native location to another location.

intron Intervening DNA sequences that are found in between the coding sequences of genes.

invaginate The act of pinching inward, as during early embryonic development in animals.

invasive cell A cancer cell that can invade healthy tissues.

invasive species Introduced species that spread on their own, often outcompeting native species for space and resources.

inverse density-dependent factor A mortality factor whose influence decreases as population size or density increases.

inversion A type of mutation that involves a change in the direction of the genetic material along a single chromosome.

invertebrate An animal that lacks vertebrae.

in vitro Meaning, "in glass" as in a test tube. An alternative to studying a process in a living organism that involves studying components outside of their natural locations. This can involve studying cells or components of cells in the laboratory.

in vivo Meaning, "in life." Studying a process in living organisms.

involution During embryogenesis, the folding back of sheets of surface cells into the interior of an embryo.

iodine-deficient goiter An overgrown thyroid gland that is incapable of making thyroid hormone due to a lack of dietary iodine.

ion An atom or molecule that gains or loses one or more electrons and acquires a net electric charge.

ion electrochemical gradient A dual gradient for an ion that is composed of both an electrical gradient and a chemical gradient for that ion.

ionic bond The bond that occurs when a cation binds to an anion.

ionotropic receptor One of two types of postsynaptic receptors, the other being a metabotropic receptor. Consists of a ligand-gated ion channel that opens in response to binding of a neurotransmitter.

iris The circle of pigmented smooth muscle and connective tissue that is responsible for eye color.

iron regulatory element (IRE) A response element within the ferritin mRNA to which the iron regulatory protein binds.

iron regulatory protein (IRP) An RNA-binding protein that regulates the translation of the mRNA that encodes ferritin.

islets of Langerhans Spherical clusters of endocrine cells that are scattered throughout the pancreas; the cells secrete insulin or glucagon, among other hormones.

isomers Two structures with an identical molecular formula but different structures and characteristics.

isotonic Condition in which the solute concentrations on both sides of a plasma membrane are equal, which does not cause a cell to shrink or swell.

isotope An element that exists in multiple forms that differ in the number of neutrons they contain.

iteroparity   The pattern of repeated reproduction at intervals throughout an organism's life cycle.

J

joint   The juncture where two or more bones of a vertebrate endoskeleton come together.

juvenile hormone   A hormone made in arthropods that inhibits maturation from a larva into a pupa.

K

karyogamy   The process of nuclear fusion.

karyotype   A photographic representation of the chromosomes in an actively dividing cell.

K_d The dissociation constant between a ligand and its receptor.

ketones   Small compounds generated from fatty acids. Ketones are made in the liver and released into the blood to provide an important energy source during prolonged fasting for many tissues, including the brain.

keystone hypothesis   The idea that ecosystem function plummets as soon as biodiversity declines from its natural levels.

keystone species   A species within a community that has a role out of proportion to its abundance.

kidney   The major excretory organ found in all vertebrates.

kcal (kilocalorie)   One thousand calories; the amount of heat energy required to raise the temperature of 1 kg of water by 1°C.

kinesis   A movement in response to a stimulus, but one that is not directed toward or away from the source of the stimulus.

kinetic energy   Energy associated with movement.

kinetic skull   A characteristic of lizards and snakes in which the joints between various parts of the skull are extremely mobile.

kinetochore   A group of proteins that bind to a centromere and are necessary for sorting each chromosome.

kingdom   A taxonomic group; the second largest division after domain.

kin selection   Selection for behavior that lowers an individual's own fitness but enhances the reproductive success of a relative.

K_M The substrate concentration at which an enzyme-catalyzed reaction is half of its maximal value.

knowledge   The awareness and understanding of information.

Koch's postulates   A series of steps used to determine whether a particular organism causes a specific disease.

K-selected species   A type of life history strategy where species have a low rate of per capita population growth but good competitive ability.

K/T event   An ancient cataclysm that involved at least one large meteorite or comet that crashed into the Earth near the present-day Yucatán Peninsula in Mexico about 65 mya.

L

labia majora   In the female mammalian genitalia, large outer folds that surround the external opening of the reproductive tract.

labia minora   In the female mammalian genitalia, smaller, inner folds near the external opening of the reproductive tract.

labor   The strong rhythmic contractions of the uterus that serve to deliver a fetus during childbirth.

lac operon   An operon in the genome of E. coli that contains the genes for the enzymes that allow it to metabolize lactose.

lac repressor   A repressor protein that regulates the lac operon.

lactation   In mammals, a period after birth in which the young are nurtured by milk produced by the mother.

lacteal   A lymphatic vessel in the center of each intestinal villus; lipids are absorbed by the lacteals, which eventually empty into the circulatory system.

lagging strand   During DNA replication, a DNA strand made as a series of small Okazaki fragments that are eventually connected to each other to form a continuous strand.

lamellae (singular, lamella)   Platelike structures in the internal gills of fishes that branch from structures called filaments; gas exchange occurs here.

larva   A free-living organism that is morphologically very different from the embryo and adult.

larynx   The segment of the respiratory tract that contains the vocal cords.

latent   The term used to describe a prophage or provirus that remains inactive for a long time.

lateral line system   Microscopic sensory organs in fishes and some toads that allows them to detect movement in surrounding water.

lateral meristem   See secondary meristem.

law of independent assortment   States that the alleles of different genes assort independently of each other during gamete formation.

law of segregation   States that two copies of a gene segregate from each other during gamete formation and during transmission from parent to offspring.

leaching   The dissolution and removal of inorganic ions as water percolates through materials such as soil.

leading strand   During DNA replication, a DNA strand made in the same direction that the replication fork is moving. The strand is synthesized as one long continuous molecule.

leaf abscission   The process by which a leaf drops after the formation of an abscission zone.

leaflet   1. Half of a phospholipid bilayer. 2. A portion of a compound leaf.

leaf primordia   Small outgrowths that occur at the sides of a shoot apical meristem and develop into young leaves.

leaf vein   In plants, a bundle of vascular tissue in a leaf.

learning   The ability of an animal to make modifications to a behavior based on previous experience; the process by which new information is acquired.

leaves   Flattened plant organs that emerge from stems and function in photosynthesis.

left-right axis   In bilaterally symmetric animals, the left and right sides of the body.

leghemoglobin   A protein found in legume plants that helps to regulate local oxygen concentrations around rhizobial bacteroids in root nodules.

legume   A member of the pea (bean) family; also their distinctive fruits.

lek   A designated communal courting area in certain species of birds.

lens   1. A structure of the eye that focuses light. 2. The glass components of a light microscope or the electromagnetic parts of an electron microscope that allow the production of magnified images of microscopic structures.

lentic   Refers to a freshwater habitat characterized by standing water.

lenticels   Passages in the outer bark of a woody plant stem that allow inner stem tissues to accomplish gas exchange.

leptin   A hormone produced by adipose cells in proportion to fat mass; controls appetite and metabolic rate.

leukocyte   A cell that develops from the marrow of certain bones of vertebrates; all leukocytes (also known as white blood cells) perform vital functions that defend the body against infection and disease.

lichens   The mutualistic association between particular fungi and certain photosynthetic green algae or cyanobacteria. This association results in a body form distinctive from that of either partner alone.

Liebig's law of the minimum   States that species' biomass or abundance is limited by the scarcest factor.

life cycle   The sequence of events that characterize the steps of development of the individuals of a given species.

life table   A table that provides data on the number of living individuals in a population in particular age classes.

ligand   An ion or molecule that binds to a protein, such as an enzyme or a receptor.

ligand-gated ion channel   A type of cell surface receptor that binds a ligand and functions as an ion channel. Ligand binding either opens or closes a channel.

ligand-receptor complex   The structure formed when a ligand and its receptor noncovalently bind.

light chain   1. A part of an immunoglobulin molecule. 2. Two of the polypeptides that make up each myosin molecule.

light-harvesting complex   A component of photosystem II and photosystem I composed of several dozen pigment molecules that are anchored to proteins in the thylakoid membranes of a chloroplast. The role of these complexes is to absorb photons of light.

light microscope   A microscope that utilizes light for illumination.

light reactions   The first of two stages in the process of photosynthesis. During the light reactions, photosystem II and photosystem I absorb light energy and produce ATP, NADPH, and O_2.

lignin   A tough polymer that adds strength and decay resistance to cell walls of tracheids, vessel elements, and other cells of plants.

lignophytes   Modern and fossil seed plants and seedless ancestors that produced wood.

limbic system   In the vertebrate forebrain, the areas involved in the formation and expression of emotions; also plays a role in learning, memory, and the perception of smells.

limiting factor   A factor whose amount or concentration limits the rate of a biological process or a chemical reaction.

lineage   A progression of changes in a series of ancestors.

line transect   A sampling technique used by plant ecologists in which the number of plants located along a length of string are counted.

linkage   The phenomenon that two genes close together on the same chromosome are transmitted as a unit.

linkage group   A group of genes that usually stay together during meiosis.

lipase   The major fat-digesting enzyme from the pancreas.

lipid   A molecule composed predominantly of hydrogen and carbon atoms. Lipids are nonpolar and therefore very insoluble in water. They include fats (triglycerides), phospholipids, waxes, and steroids.

lipid-anchored protein   A type of integral membrane protein that is attached to the membrane via a lipid molecule.

lipid-exchange protein   A protein that extracts a lipid from one membrane, diffuses through the cell, and inserts the lipid into another membrane.

lipid raft   In a membrane, a group of lipids and proteins that float together as a unit in a larger sea of lipids.

lipolysis   The enzymatic breakdown of triglycerides into fatty acids and either monoglycerides or glycerol.

lipopolysaccharides   Lipids with covalently bound carbohydrates; prevalent in the thin, outer envelope that encloses the cell walls of Gram-negative bacteria.

liposome   A vesicle surrounded by a lipid bilayer.

liver   An organ in vertebrates that performs diverse metabolic functions and is the site of bile production.

liverworts A phylum of bryophytes; formally called Hepatophyta.

loam A type of soil that contains a mixture of sand, silt, and clay and is ideal for plant cultivation.

lobe fins The Actinistia (coelacanths), Dipnoi (lungfishes), and tetrapods; also called Sarcopterygii.

lobe-finned fishes Fishes in which the fins are part of the body; the fins are supported by skeletal extensions of the pectoral and pelvic areas.

locomotion The movement of an animal from place to place.

locus The physical location of a gene on a chromosome.

logistic equation An equation that relates the growth of populations to their carrying capacity, K.

logistic growth The pattern in which the growth of a population typically slows down as it approaches the carrying capacity.

long-day plant A plant that flowers in spring or early summer, when the night period is shorter (and thus the day length is longer) than a defined period.

long-term potentiation (LTP) The long-lasting strengthening of the connection between neurons that is believed to be part of the mechanism of learning and memory.

loop domain In bacteria, a chromosomal segment that is folded into loops by the attachment to proteins; a method of compacting bacterial chromosomes.

loop of Henle A segment of the tubule of the nephron of the kidney containing a sharp hairpin-like loop that contributes to reabsorption of ions and water. It consists of a descending limb coming from the proximal tubule and an ascending limb leading to the distal tubule.

lophophore A horseshoe-shaped crown of tentacles used for feeding in several invertebrate species.

Lophotrochozoa A clade of animals that encompasses the mollusks, annelids, and several other phyla; they are distinguished by two morphological features: the lophophore, a crown of tentacles used for feeding, and the trochophore larva, a distinct larval stage.

lotic Refers to a freshwater habitat characterized by running water.

lumen The internal space or hollow cavity of an organelle or an organ, such as the stomach or a blood vessel.

lungfishes The Dipnoi; fish with primitive lungs that live in oxygen-poor freshwater swamps and ponds.

lung In terrestrial vertebrates, internal paired structures used to bring O_2 into the circulatory system and remove CO_2.

luteinizing hormone (LH) A gonadotropin that controls the production of sex steroids in both males and females.

lycophyll A relatively small leaf having a single unbranched vein; produced by lycophytes.

lycophytes Members of a phylum of vascular land plants whose leaves are lycophylls, Lycopodiophyta.

lymphatic system A system of vessels along with a group of organs and tissues where most leukocytes reside. The lymphatic vessels collect excess interstitial fluid and return it to the blood.

lymphocyte A type of leukocyte that is responsible for specific immunity; the two types are B cells and T cells.

lysogenic cycle The growth cycle of a bacteriophage consisting of integration, prophage replication, and excision.

lysosome A small organelle found in animal cells that contains acid hydrolases that degrade macromolecules.

lytic cycle The growth cycle of a bacteriophage in which the production and release of new viruses lyses the host cell.

M

macroalgae Photosynthetic protists that can be seen with the unaided eye; also known as seaweeds.

macroevolution Evolutionary changes that create new species and groups of species.

macromolecule Many molecules bonded together to form a polymer. Carbohydrates, proteins, and nucleic acids (for example, DNA and RNA) are important macromolecules found in living organisms.

macronutrient An element required by plants in amounts of at least 1 g/kg of plant dry matter.

macroparasite A parasite that lives in a host but releases infective juvenile stages outside the host's body.

macrophage A type of phagocyte capable of engulfing viruses and bacteria.

macular degeneration An eye condition in which photoreceptor cells in and around the fovea of the retina are lost; one of the leading causes of blindness in the U.S.

madreporite A sievelike plate on the surface of an echinoderm where water enters the water vascular system.

magnetic resonance imaging (MRI) An imaging method that relies on the use of magnetic fields and radio waves to visualize the internal structure of an organism's body.

magnification The ratio between the size of an image produced by a microscope and a sample's actual size.

major depressive disorder A neurological disorder characterized by feelings of despair and sadness, resulting from an imbalance in neurotransmitter levels in the brain.

major groove A groove that spirals around the DNA double helix; provides a location where a protein can bind to a particular sequence of bases and affect the expression of a gene.

major histocompatibility complex (MHC) A gene family that encodes the plasma membrane self proteins that must be complexed with an antigen for T-cell recognition to occur.

male-assistance hypothesis A hypothesis to explain the existence of monogamy that maintains that males remain with females to help them rear their offspring.

male gametophyte A haploid multicellular plant life cycle stage that produces sperm.

malignant tumor A growth of cells that has progressed to the cancerous stage.

Malpighian tubules Delicate projections from the digestive tract of insects and some other taxa that function as an excretory organ.

mammal A vertebrate that is a member of the class Mammalia that nourishes its young with milk secreted by the female's mammary glands. Another distinguishing feature is hair.

mammary gland A gland in female mammals that secretes milk.

manganese cluster A site where the oxidation of water occurs in photosystem II during photosynthesis.

mantle In mollusks, a fold of skin draped over the visceral mass that secretes a shell in those species that form shells.

mantle cavity The chamber in a mollusk mantle that houses delicate gills.

many-eyes hypothesis The idea that increased group size decreases predators' success because of increased detection of predators.

map distance The distance between genes along chromosomes, which is calculated as the number of recombinant offspring divided by the total number of offspring times 100.

mapping The process of determining the relative locations of genes or other DNA segments along a chromosome.

map unit (mu) A unit of distance on a chromosome equivalent to a 1% recombination frequency.

mark-recapture technique The capture and tagging of animals so they can be released and recaptured, allowing an estimate of population size.

marsupial A member of a group of seven mammalian orders and about 280 species found in the subclass Metatheria.

mass extinction When many species become extinct at the same time.

mass-specific BMR The amount of energy expended per gram of body mass.

mastax The circular muscular pharynx in the mouth of rotifers.

mast cell A type of cell derived from bone marrow stem cells that plays an important role in nonspecific immunity.

mate-guarding hypothesis The hypothesis that a male is monogamous to prevent his mate from being fertilized by other males.

maternal effect An inheritance pattern in which the genotype of the mother determines the phenotype of her offspring.

maternal effect gene A gene that follows a maternal effect inheritance pattern.

maternal inheritance A phenomenon in which offspring inherit particular genes only from the female parent (through the egg).

matrotrophy In plants, the phenomenon in which zygotes remain enclosed within gametophyte tissues, where they are sheltered and fed.

matter Anything that has mass and takes up space.

maturation-promoting factor (MPF) A factor, now known to be a complex of cyclin and cyclin-dependent kinase, important in the division of all types of eukaryotic cells.

mature mRNA In eukaryotes, transcription produces a long RNA, pre-mRNA, which undergoes certain processing events before it exits the nucleus; mature mRNA is the final functional product.

maximum likelihood One method used to evaluate a phylogenetic tree based on an evolutionary model.

mean fitness of the population The average reproductive success of members of a population.

mechanoreceptor A sensory receptor in animals that transduces mechanical energy such as pressure, touch, stretch, movement, and sound.

mediator A large protein complex that plays a role in initiating transcription at the core promoter of structural genes in eukaryotes.

medulla oblongata The part of the vertebrate hindbrain that coordinates many basic reflexes and bodily functions, such as breathing.

medusa A type of cnidarian body form that is motile and usually floats mouth down.

megadiversity country Those countries with the greatest numbers of species; used in targeting areas for conservation.

megaspore In seed plants and some seedless plants, a large spore that produces a female gametophyte within the spore wall.

meiosis The process by which haploid cells are produced from a cell that was originally diploid.

meiosis I The first division of meiosis in which the homologs are separated into different cells.

meiosis II The second division of meiosis in which sister chromatids are separated into different cells.

Meissner's corpuscle Structures that sense touch and light pressure and lie just beneath the skin surface of an animal.

melatonin A hormone produced by the pineal gland of vertebrates; plays a role in light-dependent behaviors such as seasonal reproduction and daily rhythms.

membrane attack complex (MAC)   A multiunit protein formed by the activation of complement proteins; the complex creates water channels in the microbial plasma membrane and causes the microbe to swell and burst.

membrane potential   The difference between the electric charges outside and inside a cell; also called a potential difference (or voltage).

membrane transport   The movement of ions or molecules across a cell membrane.

memory   The retention of information over time.

memory cell   A cloned lymphocyte that remains poised to recognize a returning antigen; a component of specific immunity.

Mendelian inheritance   The inheritance patterns of genes that segregate and assort independently.

meninges   Three layers of sheathlike membranes that cover and protect the brain and spinal cord.

meningitis   A potentially life-threatening infectious disease in which the meninges become inflamed.

menopause   The event during which a woman permanently stops having ovarian cycles.

menstrual cycle   The cyclical changes that occur in the uterus in parallel with the ovarian cycle in a female mammal. Also called the uterine cycle.

menstruation   A period of bleeding at the beginning of the menstrual cycle in a female mammal.

meristem   In plants, an organized tissue that includes actively dividing cells and a reservoir of stem cells.

meroblastic cleavage   An incomplete type of cell cleavage in which only the region of the egg containing cytoplasm at the animal pole undergoes cell division. Occurs in birds and some fishes.

merozygote   A strain of bacteria containing an F′ factor.

mesoderm   In animals, a layer of cells formed during gastrulation that develops between the ectoderm and endoderm; gives rise to the skeleton, muscles, and much of the circulatory system.

mesoglea   A gelatinous substance between the epidermis and the gastrodermis in the Radiata.

mesohyl   A gelatinous, protein-rich matrix in between the choanocytes and the epithelial cells of a sponge.

mesophyll   The internal tissue of a plant leaf; the site of photosynthesis.

messenger RNA (mRNA)   RNA that contains the information to specify a polypeptide with a particular amino acid sequence.

metabolic cycle   A biochemical cycle in which particular molecules enter while others leave; the process is cyclical because it involves a series of organic molecules that are regenerated with each turn of the cycle.

metabolic pathway   In living cells, a series of chemical reactions in which each step is catalyzed by a specific enzyme.

metabolic rate   The total energy expenditure of an organism per unit of time.

metabolism   The sum total of all chemical reactions that occur within an organism. Also, a specific set of chemical reactions occurring at the cellular level.

metabotropic receptor   A G-protein-coupled receptor that initiates a signaling pathway in response to a neurotransmitter. One of two types of postsynaptic receptors, the other being an ionotropic receptor.

metacentric   A chromosome in which the centromere is near the middle.

metagenomics   A field of study that seeks to identify and analyze the collective microbial genomes contained in a community of organisms, including those not easily cultured in the laboratory.

metamorphosis   The process in which a pupal or juvenile organism changes into a mature adult with very different characteristics.

metanephridia   Excretory filtration organs found in a variety of invertebrates.

metaphase   The phase of mitosis during which the chromosomes are aligned along the metaphase plate.

metaphase plate   A plane halfway between the poles of the spindle apparatus on which the sister chromatids align during the metaphase stage of mitosis.

metastasis   The process by which cancer cells spread from their original location to distant parts of the body.

Metazoa   The collective term for animals.

methanogens   Several groups of anaerobic archaea that convert CO_2, methyl groups, or acetate to methane, and release it from their cells.

methanotroph   An aerobic bacterium that consumes methane.

methyl-CpG-binding protein   A protein that binds methylated sequences and inhibits transcription.

micelle   The sphere formed by long amphipathic molecules when they are mixed with water. In animals, micelles aid in the absorption of poorly soluble products during digestion.

microbiome   All of the microorganisms in a particular environment.

microclimate   Local variations of the climate within a given area.

microevolution   Changes in a population's gene pool from generation to generation.

microfilament   *See* actin filament.

micrograph   An image taken with the aid of a microscope.

micronutrient   An element required by plants in amounts at, or less than, 0.1 g/kg of plant dry matter; also known as a trace element.

microparasite   A parasite that multiplies within its host, usually within the cells.

micropyle   A small opening in the integument of a seed plant ovule through which a pollen tube grows.

microRNAs (miRNAs)   Small RNA molecules, typically 22 nucleotides in length, that silence the expression of specific mRNAs by inhibiting translation.

microscope   A magnification tool that enables researchers to study very small structures such as cells.

microspore   In seed plants and some seedless plants, a relatively small spore that produces a male gametophyte within the spore wall.

microsporidia   Single-celled fungi that parasitize animal cells.

microtubule   A type of hollow protein filament composed of tubulin proteins that is part of the cytoskeleton and is important for cell shape, organization, and movement.

microtubule-organizing center   *See* centrosome.

microvillus (plural microvilli)   Small projections in the surface membranes of epithelial cells in the small intestine and many other absorptive cells.

midbrain   One of three major divisions of the vertebrate brain; the other two divisions are the hindbrain and the forebrain.

middle ear   One of the three main compartments of the mammalian ear; contains three small bones called ossicles that connect the eardrum with the oval window.

middle lamella   An extracellular layer in plants composed primarily of carbohydrate; cements adjacent plant cell walls together.

migration   Long-range seasonal movement among animals in order to feed or breed.

mimicry   The resemblance of an organism (the mimic) to another organism (the model).

mineral   An inorganic ion or inorganic molecule required by a living organism.

mineralization   The general process by which phosphorus, nitrogen, CO_2, and other minerals are released from organic compounds.

mineralocorticoid   A steroid hormone such as aldosterone that regulates the balance of sodium and potassium ions in the body.

minor groove   A smaller groove that spirals around the DNA double helix.

miRNA   *See* microRNAs.

missense mutation   A base substitution that changes a single amino acid in a polypeptide sequence.

mitochondrial genome   The chromosome found in mitochondria.

mitochondrial matrix   A compartment inside the inner membrane of a mitochondrion.

mitochondrion   A semiautonomous organelle found in eukaryotic cells that supplies most of a cell's ATP.

mitogen-activated protein kinase (MAP kinase)   A type of protein kinase that is involved with promoting cell division.

mitosis   In eukaryotes, the process in which nuclear division results in two nuclei, each of which receives the same complement of chromosomes.

mitotic cell division   A process whereby a eukaryotic cell divides to produce two new cells that are genetically identical to the original cell.

mitotic spindle   The structure responsible for organizing and sorting the chromosomes during mitosis; also called the mitotic spindle apparatus.

mixotroph   An organism that is able to use autotrophy as well as phagotrophy or osmotrophy to obtain organic nutrients.

M line   In a myofibril, a narrow, dark band in the center of the H zone where proteins link the central regions of adjacent thick filaments.

model organism   An organism studied by many different researchers so they can compare their results and determine scientific principles that apply more broadly to other species.

moderately repetitive sequence   A DNA sequence found a few hundred to several thousand times in a genome.

molar   A term used to describe a solution's molarity; a 1 molar solution contains 1 mole of a solute in 1 L of water.

molarity   The number of moles of a solute dissolved in 1 L of water.

mole   The amount of any substance that contains the same number of particles as there are atoms in exactly 12 g of carbon.

molecular biology   A field of study spawned largely by genetic technology that looks at the structure and function of the molecules of life.

molecular clock   A method for estimating evolutionary time; based on the observation that neutral mutations occur at a relatively constant rate.

molecular evolution   The molecular changes in genetic material that underlie the phenotypic changes associated with evolution.

molecular formula   A representation of a molecule that consists of the chemical symbols for all of the atoms present and subscripts that indicate how many of those atoms are present.

molecular homologies   Similarities at the molecular level that indicate that living species evolved from a common ancestor or interrelated group of common ancestors.

molecular mass   The sum of the atomic masses of all the atoms in a molecule.

molecular pharming   An avenue of research that involves the production of medically important proteins in agricultural crops or animals.

molecular systematics   A field of study that involves the analysis of genetic data, such as DNA sequences, to

GLOSSARY

identify and study genetic homology and construct phylogenetic trees.

molecule   Two or more atoms that are connected by chemical bonds.

monoclonal antibodies   Antibodies of a specific type that are derived from a single clone of cells.

monocots   One of the two largest lineages of flowering plants in which the embryo produces a single seed leaf.

monocular vision   A type of vision in animals that have eyes on the sides of the head; the animal sees a wide area at one time, though depth perception is reduced.

monocyte   A type of phagocyte that circulates in the blood for only a few days, after which it takes up permanent residence in various organs as a macrophage.

monoecious   The term to describe plants that produce carpellate and staminate flowers on the same plant.

monogamy   A mating system in which one male mates with one female, and most individuals have mates.

monohybrid   The F$_1$ offspring, also called single-trait hybrids, of true-breeding parents that differ with regard to a single trait.

monohybrid cross   A cross in which the inheritance of only one trait is followed.

monomer   An organic molecule that can be used to form larger molecules (polymers) consisting of many repeating units of the monomer.

monomorphic gene   A gene that exists predominantly as a single allele in a population.

monophagous   The term used to describe parasites that feed on one or a few closely related species.

monophyletic group   A group of species, a taxon, consisting of the most recent common ancestor and all of its descendants.

monosaccharide   A simple sugar.

monosomic   An aneuploid organism that has one too few chromosomes.

monotreme   A member of the mammalian order Monotremata, which consists of three species found in Australia and New Guinea: the duck-billed platypus and two species of echidna.

morphogen   A molecule that imparts positional information and promotes developmental changes at the cellular level.

morphogenetic field   A group of cells believed to differentiate into a single body structure.

morphology   The structure or form of a body part or an entire organism.

morula   An early stage in a mammalian embryo in which physical contact between cells is maximized by compaction.

mosaic   An individual with somatic cells that are genetically different from each other.

mosses   A phylum of bryophytes; Bryophyta.

motor end plate   The region of a skeletal muscle cell that lies beneath an axon terminal at the neuromuscular junction.

motor neuron   A neuron that sends signals away from the central nervous system and elicits some type of response from a gland, muscle or other structure.

motor protein   A category of cellular proteins that uses ATP as a source of energy to promote movement; consists of three domains called the head, hinge, and tail.

movement corridor   Thin strips of habitat that may permit the movement of individuals between larger habitat patches.

M phase   The sequential events of mitosis and cytokinesis.

mRNA   See messenger RNA.

Müllerian mimicry   A type of mimicry in which many noxious species converge to look the same, thus reinforcing the basic distasteful design.

multicellular   Describes an organism consisting of more than one cell, particularly when cell-to-cell adherence and signaling processes and cellular specialization can be demonstrated.

multimeric protein   A protein with more than one polypeptide chain; also said to have a quarternary structure.

multiple alleles   Refers to the occurrence of a gene that exists as three or more alleles in a population.

multiple sclerosis (MS)   A disease in which the patient's own body attacks and destroys myelin as if it were a foreign substance; impairs the function of myelinated neurons that control movement, speech, memory, and emotion.

multipotent   A term used to describe a stem cell that can differentiate into several cell types, but far fewer than pluripotent cells.

muscle   A grouping of muscle cells (fibers) bound together by a succession of connective tissue layers.

muscle fiber   Individual cell within a muscle.

muscle tissue   Bundles of muscle fibers that are specialized to contract when stimulated.

muscular dystrophy   A group of diseases associated with progressive degeneration of skeletal and cardiac muscle fibers.

mutagen   An agent known to cause mutation.

mutant allele   An allele that has been altered by mutation.

mutation   A heritable change in the genetic material of an organism.

mutualism   A symbiotic interaction in which both species benefit.

myasthenia gravis   A disease characterized by loss of acetylcholine receptors on skeletal muscle, due to the body's own immune system destroying the receptors.

mycelium   A fungal body composed of microscopic branched filaments known as hyphae.

mycorrhizae (singular, **mycorrhiza**)   Associations between the hyphae of certain fungi and the roots of plants.

myelin sheath   In the nervous system, an insulating layer made up of specialized glial cells wrapped around the axons.

myocardial infarction (MI)   The death of cardiac muscle cells, which can occur if a region of the heart is deprived of blood for an extended time.

myofibril   Rodlike collection of myofilaments within a muscle fiber (cell); contains thick and thin filaments.

myogenic heart   A heart in which the signaling mechanism that initiates contraction resides within the cardiac muscle itself.

myoglobin   An oxygen-binding protein that provides an intracellular reservoir of oxygen for muscle fibers.

myosin   A motor protein found abundantly in muscle cells and also in other cell types.

N

NAD⁺   Nicotinamide adenine dinucleotide; a dinucleotide that functions as an energy intermediate molecule. It combines with two electrons and H⁺ to form NADH.

NADPH   Nicotinamide adenine dinucleotide phosphate; an energy intermediate that provides the energy and electrons to drive the Calvin cycle during photosynthesis.

natural killer (NK) cell   A type of leukocyte that participates in both nonspecific and specific immunity; recognizes general features on the surface of cancer cells or any virus-infected cells.

natural selection   The process that eliminates those individuals that are less likely to survive and reproduce in a particular environment, while allowing other individuals with traits that confer greater reproductive success to increase in numbers.

nauplius   The first larval stage in a crustacean.

navigation   A mechanism of migration that involves the ability not only to follow a compass bearing but also to set or adjust it.

negative control   Transcriptional regulation by repressor proteins.

negative feedback loop   A homeostatic system in animals in which a change in the variable being regulated brings about responses that move the variable in the opposite direction.

negative frequency-dependent selection   A pattern of natural selection in which the fitness of a genotype decreases when its frequency becomes higher; the result is a balanced polymorphism.

negative pressure filling   The mechanism by which reptiles, birds, and mammals ventilate their lungs.

nekton   Free-swimming animals in the open ocean that can swim against currents to locate food.

nematocyst   In a cnidarian, a powerful capsule with an inverted coiled and barbed thread that functions to immobilize small prey.

neocortex   The layer of the brain that evolved most recently in mammals.

nephron   One of several million single-cell-thick tubules that are the functional units of the mammalian kidney.

Nernst equation   The formula that gives the equilibrium potential for an ion at any given concentration gradient: $E = 60$ mV $\log_{10}([X_{extracellular}]/[X_{intracellular}])$.

nerve   A structure found in the peripheral nervous system that is composed of multiple myelinated neurons bound by connective tissue; carries information to or from the central nervous system.

nerve cord   In many invertebrates, a ventral structure that extends from the anterior end of the animal to the tail; a dorsal nerve cord is found in chordates.

nerve net   Interconnected neurons with no central control organ.

nervous system   Groups of cells that sense internal and environmental changes and transmit signals that enable an animal to respond in an appropriate way.

nervous tissue   Clusters of cells that initiate and conduct electrical signals from one part of an animal's body to another part.

net primary production (NPP)   Gross primary production minus the energy lost in plant cellular respiration.

net reproductive rate   The population growth rate per generation.

neural crest   In vertebrates, a group of embryonic cells derived from ectoderm that disperse throughout the embryo and contribute to the development of the skeleton and other structures, including peripheral nerves.

neural tube   In chordates, a structure formed from ectoderm located dorsal to the notochord; all neurons and their supporting cells in the central nervous system originate from neural precursor cells derived from the neural tube.

neurogenesis   The production of new neurons by cell division.

neurogenic heart   A heart that will not beat unless it receives regular electrical impulses from the nervous system.

neurohormone   A hormone made in and secreted by neurons whose cell bodies are in the hypothalamus.

neuromodulator   Another term for a neuropeptide, which is a neurotransmitter that can alter or modulate the response of a postsynaptic neuron to other neurotransmitters.

neuromuscular junction   The junction between a motor neuron's axon and a skeletal or cardiac muscle fiber.

neuron   A highly specialized cell found in nervous systems of animals that communicates with other cells by electrical or chemical signals.

neuroscience The scientific study of nervous systems.

neurotransmitter A small signaling molecule that is released from an axon terminal and diffuses to a postsynaptic cell where it elicits a response.

neurulation The embryological process responsible for initiating central nervous system formation.

neutral theory of evolution States that most genetic variation is due to the accumulation of neutral mutations that have attained high frequencies in a population via genetic drift.

neutral variation Genetic variation in which natural selection does not favor any particular genotype.

neutron A neutral particle found in the center of an atom.

neutrophil A type of phagocyte and the most abundant type of leukocyte. Neutrophils engulf bacteria by endocytosis.

niche The unique set of habitat resources a species requires as well as its effect on the ecosystem.

nitrification The conversion by soil bacteria of ammonia (NH_3) or ammonium (NH_4^+) to nitrate (NO_3^-), a form of nitrogen commonly used by plants.

nitrogen fixation A specialized metabolic process in which certain prokaryotes use the enzyme nitrogenase to convert inert atmospheric nitrogen gas (N_2) into ammonia (NH_3); also, the industrial process by which humans produce NH_3 fertilizer from N_2.

nitrogenase An enzyme used in the biological process of fixing nitrogen.

nitrogen-limitation hypothesis The proposal that organisms select food based on its nitrogen content.

nitrogenous waste Degradation product of proteins and nucleic acids that are toxic at high concentrations and must be eliminated from the body.

nociceptor A sensory receptor in animals that responds to extreme heat, cold, and pressure, as well as to certain molecules such as acids; also known as a pain receptor.

node The region of a plant stem from which one or more leaves, branches, or buds emerge.

nodes of Ranvier Exposed areas in the axons of myelinated neurons that contain many voltage-gated Na^+ channels and are the sites of regeneration of action potentials.

Nod factor Nodulation factor; a substance produced by nitrogen-fixing bacteria in response to flavonoids secreted from the roots of potential host plants. Nod factors bind to receptors in plant root membranes, starting a process that allows the bacteria to invade roots.

nodule A small swelling on a plant root that contains nitrogen-fixing bacteria.

nodulin One of several plant proteins that foster root nodule development.

noncoding strand *See* template strand.

noncompetitive inhibitor A molecule that binds to an enzyme at a location that is outside the active site and inhibits the enzyme's function.

noncyclic electron flow The combined action of photosystem II and photosystem I in which electrons flow in a linear manner to produce NADPH.

non-Darwinian evolution The idea that much of the modern variation in gene sequences is explained by neutral variation rather than adaptive variation.

nondisjunction An event in which the chromosomes do not sort properly during cell division.

nonpolar covalent bond A strong bond formed between two atoms of similar electronegativities in which electrons are shared between the atoms.

nonpolar molecule A molecule composed predominantly of nonpolar bonds.

nonrandom mating The phenomenon that individuals choose their mates based on their genotypes or phenotypes.

nonrecombinant An offspring whose combination of traits has not changed from the parental generation.

nonsense codon *See* stop codon.

nonsense mutation A mutation that changes a normal codon into a stop codon; this causes translation to be terminated earlier than expected, producing a truncated polypeptide.

nonshivering thermogenesis An increase in an animal's metabolic rate that is not due to increased muscle activity; occurs primarily in brown adipose tissue.

nonspecific immunity *See* innate immunity.

nonvascular plant A plant that does not produce lignified vascular tissue; includes the bryophytes.

norepinephrine A type of neurotransmitter; also known as noradrenaline.

norm of reaction A description of how a trait may change depending on environmental conditions.

notochord A defining characteristic of all chordate embryos; consists of a flexible rod that lies between the digestive tract and the nerve cord.

N-terminus The location of the first amino acid in a polypeptide; also known as the amino terminus.

nuclear envelope A double-membrane structure that encloses the cell's nucleus.

nuclear genome The chromosomes found in the nucleus of a eukaryotic cell.

nuclear lamina A collection of filamentous proteins that line the inner nuclear membrane; part of the nuclear matrix.

nuclear matrix A filamentous network of proteins that is found inside the nucleus and lines the inner nuclear membrane. The nuclear matrix serves to organize the chromosomes.

nuclear pore A passageway for the movement of molecules and macromolecules into and out of the nucleus; formed where the inner and outer nuclear membranes make contact with each other.

nucleic acid An organic molecule composed of nucleotides. The two types of nucleic acids are deoxyribonucleic acid (DNA) and ribonucleic acid (RNA).

nucleoid region A site in a bacterial cell where the genetic material (DNA) is located.

nucleolus A prominent region in the nucleus of nondividing cells where ribosome assembly occurs.

nucleosome A structural unit of eukaryotic chromosomes composed of an octamer of histones (eight histone proteins) wrapped with DNA.

nucleotide An organic molecule having three components: one or more phosphate groups, a five-carbon sugar (either deoxyribose or ribose), and a single or double ring of carbon and nitrogen atoms known as a base.

nucleotide excision repair (NER) A common type of DNA repair system that removes (excises) and repairs a region of the DNA where damage has occurred.

nucleus (plural, nuclei) 1. In cell biology, an organelle found in eukaryotic cells that contains most of the cell's genetic material. 2. In chemistry, the region of an atom that contains protons and neutrons. 3. In neurobiology, a group of neuronal cell bodies in the brain that are devoted to a particular function.

nutrient Any substance taken up by a living organism that is needed for survival, growth, development, repair, or reproduction.

nutrition The means of providing nutrients for cell survival.

O

obese According to current National Institutes of Health guidelines, a person having a body mass index (BMI) of 30 kg/m² or more.

obligate aerobes Microorganisms that require oxygen.

obligate anaerobes Microorganisms that are poisoned by oxygen.

obligatory mutualism An interaction in which two mutualistic species cannot live without each other.

occipital lobe One of four lobes of the cerebral cortex of the human brain; controls aspects of vision and color recognition.

ocelli Photosensitive organs in some animal species.

octet rule The phenomenon that some atoms are most stable when their outer shell is full with eight electrons.

Okazaki fragments Short segments of DNA synthesized in the lagging strand during DNA replication.

olfaction The sense of smell.

olfactory bulbs Part of the limbic system of the forebrain of vertebrates; the olfactory bulbs carry information about odors to the brain.

oligodendrocytes Glial cells that produce the myelin sheath around neurons in the central nervous system.

oligotrophic The term used to describe aquatic systems that are low in nutrients such as phosphate and combined nitrogen and are consequently low in primary productivity and biomass, but typically high in species diversity.

ommatidium (plural, ommatidia) An independent visual unit in the eye of insects that functions as a separate photoreceptor capable of forming an independent image.

omnivore An animal that can survive on plants and animals for food and which typically consumes both.

oncogene A type of mutant gene derived from a proto-oncogene. An oncogene is overactive, thus contributing to uncontrolled cell growth and promoting cancer.

one-gene/one-enzyme hypothesis An early hypothesis by Beadle and Tatum that suggested that one gene encodes one enzyme. It was later modified to the one-gene/one-polypeptide theory.

one-gene/one-polypeptide theory The concept that one structural gene codes for one polypeptide.

oogenesis Gametogenesis in a female animal resulting in the production of an egg cell.

oogonium (plural, oogonia) In animals, diploid germ cells that give rise to the female gametes, the eggs.

open circulatory system In animals, a circulatory system in which hemolymph, which is not different than the interstitial fluid, flows throughout the body and is not confined to special vessels.

open complex Also called the transcription bubble; a small bubble-like structure between two DNA strands that occurs during transcription.

open conformation Loosely packed chromatin that can be transcribed into RNA.

operant conditioning A form of behavior modification; a type of associative learning in which an animal's behavior is reinforced by a consequence, either a reward or a punishment.

operator A DNA sequence in bacteria that is recognized by activator or repressor proteins that regulate the level of gene transcription.

operculum A protective flap that covers the gills of a bony fish.

operon An arrangement of two or more genes in bacteria that are under the transcriptional control of a single promoter.

opsin A protein that is a component of visual pigments in the vertebrate eye.

opsonization The process by which an antibody binds to a pathogen and provides a means to link the pathogen with a phagocyte.

optic disc In vertebrates, the point on the retina where the optic nerve leaves the eye.

optic nerve A structure of the vertebrate eye that carries electrical signals to the brain.

optimal foraging   The concept that in a given circumstance, an animal seeks to obtain the most energy possible with the least expenditure of energy.

optimality theory   The theory that predicts an animal should behave in a way that maximizes the benefits of a behavior minus its costs.

orbital   The region surrounding the nucleus of an atom where the probability is high of finding a particular electron.

order   In taxonomy, a subdivision of a class.

organ   Two or more types of tissue combined to perform a common function.

organelle   A subcellular structure or membrane-bound compartment with its own unique structure and function.

organic chemistry   The study of carbon-containing molecules.

organic farming   The production of crops without the use of commercial inorganic fertilizers, growth substances, and pesticides.

organic molecule   A carbon-containing molecule, so named because they are found in living organisms.

organism   A living thing that maintains an internal order that is separated from the environment.

organismal ecology   The investigation of how adaptations and choices by individuals affect their reproduction and survival.

organismic model   A view of the nature of a community that considers it to be equivalent to a superorganism; individuals, populations, and communities have a relationship to each other that resembles the associations found between cells, tissues, and organs.

organizing center   A group of cells in a plant shoot meristem that ensures the proper organization of the meristem and preserves the correct number of actively dividing stem cells.

organ of Corti   Coiled structure in the vertebrate ear responsible for detecting sound.

organogenesis   The developmental stage during which cells and tissues form organs in animal embryos.

organ system   Different organs that work together to perform an overall function in an organism.

orientation   A mechanism of migration in which animals have the ability to follow a compass bearing and travel in a straight line.

origin of replication   A site within a chromosome that serves as a starting point for DNA replication.

ortholog   A homologous gene in different species.

osmoconformer   An animal whose osmolarity conforms to that of its environment.

osmolarity   The solute concentration of a solution of water, expressed as milliosmoles/liter (mOsm/L).

osmoregulator   An animal that maintains stable internal salt concentrations and osmolarities, even when living in water with very different osmolarities than its body fluids.

osmosis   The movement of water across membranes to balance solute concentrations. Water diffuses from a solution that is hypotonic (lower solute concentration) into a solution that is hypertonic (higher solute concentration).

osmotic adjustment   The process by which a plant cell modifies the solute concentration of its cytosol.

osmotic lysis   Occurs when a cell in a hypotonic environment takes up so much water that it ruptures.

osmotic pressure   The hydrostatic pressure required to stop the net flow of water across a membrane due to osmosis.

osmotroph   An organism that relies on osmotrophy (uptake of small organic molecules) as a form of nutrition.

osteichythan   A clade that includes all vertebrates with a bony skeleton.

osteomalacia   Bone deformation in adults due to inadequate mineral intake or absorption from the intestines.

osteoporosis   A disease in which the mineral and organic components of bone are reduced.

otolith   Granules of calcium carbonate found in the gelatinous substance that embeds hair cells in the vertebrate ear.

outer bark   Protective layers of mostly dead cork cells that cover the outside of woody stems and roots.

outer ear   One of the three main compartments of the mammalian ear; consists of the external ear, or pinna, and the auditory canal.

outer segment   The highly convoluted plasma membranes found in the rods and cones of the eye.

outgroup   In a cladogram, a species or group of species that does not exhibit one or more shared derived characters found in the ingroup.

ovarian cycle   The events beginning with the development of an ovarian follicle, followed by release of a secondary oocyte, and concluding with formation and subsequent degeneration of a corpus luteum.

ovary   1. In animals, the female gonad where eggs are formed. 2. In plants, the lowermost portion of the pistil that encloses and protects the ovules.

oviduct   A thin tube with undulating fimbriae (finger-like structures) that is connected to the uterus and extends out to the ovary; also called the Fallopian tube.

oviparity   Development of an embryo outside the mother, usually in a protective shell or other structure from which the young hatch.

oviparous   An animal whose young hatch from eggs laid outside the mother's body.

ovoviparous   An animal that retains fertilized eggs covered by a protective sheath or other structure within the body, where the young hatch.

ovoviviparity   Development of an embryo involving aspects of both viviparity and oviparity; fertilized eggs covered with a protective sheath are produced and hatch inside the mother's body, but the offspring receive no nourishment from the mother.

ovulation   The process by which a mature oocyte is released from an ovary.

ovule   In a seed plant, a megaspore-producing megasporangium and enclosing tissues known as integuments.

ovum (plural, **ova**)   *See* egg.

oxidation   A process that involves the removal of electrons; occurs during the breakdown of small organic molecules.

oxidative fiber   A skeletal muscle fiber that contains numerous mitochondria and has a high capacity for oxidative phosphorylation.

oxidative phosphorylation   A process during which NADH and $FADH_2$ are oxidized to make more ATP via the phosphorylation of ADP.

oxygen-hemoglobin dissociation curve   A curve that represents the relationship between the partial pressure of oxygen and the binding of oxygen to hemoglobin proteins.

oxytocin   A hormone secreted by the posterior pituitary gland that stimulates contractions of the smooth muscles in the uterus of a pregnant mammal, facilitating the birth process; after birth, it is important in milk secretion.

P

pacemaker   *See* sinoatrial (SA) node.

Pacinian corpuscle   Structure located deep beneath the surface of an animal's skin that responds to deep pressure or vibration.

paedomorphosis   The retention of juvenile traits in an adult organism.

pair-rule gene   A type of segmentation gene; a mutation in this gene may cause alternating segments or parts of segments to be deleted.

paleontologist   A scientist who studies fossils.

palisade parenchyma   Photosynthetic ground tissue of the plant leaf mesophyll that consists of closely packed, elongate cells adapted to efficiently absorb sunlight.

palmate   A type of leaf vein pattern in which veins radiate outward, resembling an open hand.

pancreas   In vertebrates, an elongated gland located behind the stomach that secretes digestive enzymes and a fluid rich in bicarbonate ions.

parabronchi   In birds, a series of parallel air tubes that make up the lungs and are the regions of gas exchange.

paracrine   Refers to a type of cellular communication in which molecules are released into the interstitial fluid and act on nearby cells.

paralogs   Homologous genes within a single species.

paraphyletic group   A group of organisms that contains a common ancestor and some, but not all, of its descendants.

parapodia   Fleshy, footlike structures in the polychaetes that are pushed into the substrate to provide traction during movement.

parasite   A predatory organism that feeds off another organism but does not normally kill it.

parasitism   A symbiotic association in which one organism feeds off another but does not normally kill it.

parasympathetic division   The division of the autonomic nervous system that is involved in maintaining and restoring body functions.

parathyroid hormone (PTH)   A hormone that acts on bone to stimulate the activity of cells that dissolve the mineral part of bone.

Parazoa   A subgroup of animals lacking specialized tissue types or organs, although they may have several distinct types of cells; the one phylum in this group is the Porifera (sponges).

parenchyma cell   A type of plant cell that is thin-walled and alive at maturity.

parenchyma tissue   A plant ground tissue that is composed of parenchyma cells.

parental strand   The original strand in DNA replication.

parietal lobe   One of four lobes of the cerebral cortex of the human brain; receives and interprets sensory input from visual and somatic pathways.

parthenogenesis   An asexual process in which an offspring develops from an unfertilized egg.

partial pressure   The individual pressure of each gas in the air; the sum of these pressures is known as atmospheric pressure.

particulate inheritance   The idea that the determinants of hereditary traits are transmitted intact from one generation to the next.

parturition   The birth of an organism.

passive diffusion   Diffusion through a membrane without the aid of a transport protein.

passive immunity   A type of acquired immunity that confers protection against disease through the direct transfer of antibodies from one individual to another.

passive transport   The diffusion of a solute across a membrane in a process that is energetically favorable and does not require an input of energy.

paternal inheritance   A pattern in which only the male gamete contributes particular genes to the offspring.

pathogen   A microorganism that causes disease symptoms in its host.

pathogen associated molecular pattern (PAMP) Common molecules found in many pathogens that trigger an innate immune response.

pattern formation The process that gives rise to a plant or animal with a particular body structure.

pedal glands Glands in the foot of a rotifer that secrete a sticky substance that aids in attachment to the substrate.

pedicel 1. A flower stalk. 2. A narrow, waistlike point of attachment between the body parts of spiders and some insects.

pedigree analysis An examination of the inheritance of human traits in families.

pedipalps In spiders, a pair of appendages that have various sensory, predatory, or reproductive functions.

peer-review process A procedure in which experts in a particular area evaluate papers submitted to scientific journals.

pelagic zone The open ocean, where the water depth averages 4,000 m and nutrient concentrations are typically low.

penis A male external accessory sex organ found in many animals that is involved in copulation.

pentadactyl limb A limb ending in five digits.

PEP carboxylase An enzyme in C_4 plants that adds CO_2 to phosphoenolpyruvate (PEP) to produce the four-carbon compound oxaloacetate.

pepsin An active enzyme in the stomach that begins the digestion of protein.

peptide bond The covalent bond that links amino acids in a polypeptide.

peptidoglycan A polymer composed of carbohydrates crosslinked with peptides that is an important component of the cell walls of most bacteria.

peptidyl site (P site) One of three sites for tRNA binding in the ribosome during translation; the other two are the aminoacyl site (A site) and the exit site (E site). The P site holds the tRNA carrying the growing polypeptide chain.

peptidyl transfer reaction During translation, the transfer of the polypeptide from the tRNA in the P site to the amino acid at the A site.

per capita growth rate The per capita birth rate minus the per capita death rate; the rate that determines how populations grow over any time period.

perception An awareness of the sensations that are experienced.

perennial A plant that lives for more than 2 years, often producing seeds each year after it reaches reproductive maturity.

perfect flower A flower that has both stamens and carpels.

perianth The term that refers to flower petals and sepals collectively.

pericarp The wall of a plant's fruit.

pericycle A cylinder of plant tissue having cell division (meristematic) capacity that encloses the root vascular tissue.

periderm The outer layers of a woody stem, composed of cork cambium, layers of cork tissue produced by the cork cambium, and associated parenchyma cells, together forming outer bark.

peripheral membrane protein A protein that is noncovalently bound to regions of integral membrane proteins that project out from the membrane, or they are noncovalently bound to the polar head groups of phospholipids.

peripheral nervous system (PNS) In vertebrates, all nerves and ganglia outside the brain and spinal cord.

peripheral zone The area of a plant shoot meristem that contains dividing cells that will eventually differentiate into plant structures.

periphyton Communities of microorganisms that are attached by mucilage to underwater surfaces such as rocks, sand, and plants.

peristalsis In animals, the rhythmic, spontaneous waves of muscle contractions that propel food through the digestive system.

peritubular capillary A capillary near the junction of the cortex and medulla that surrounds the nephron of the mammalian kidney.

permafrost A layer of permanently frozen soil found in tundra.

peroxisome A relatively small organelle found in all eukaryotic cells that catalyzes detoxifying reactions.

personalized medicine A medical practice in which information about a patient's genotype is used to individualize their medical care.

petal A flower organ that usually serves to attract insects or other animals for pollen transport.

petiole A stalk that connects a leaf to the stem of a plant.

P generation The parental generation in a genetic cross.

pH The mathematical expression of a solution's hydrogen ion (H^+) concentration, defined as the negative logarithm to the base 10 of the H^+ concentration.

phage *See* bacteriophage.

phagocyte A cell capable of phagocytosis; phagocytes provide nonspecific defense against pathogens that enter the body.

phagocytic vacuole A vacuole that functions in the degradation of food particles or bacteria; also called a food vacuole.

phagocytosis A form of endocytosis that involves the formation of a membrane vesicle, called a phagocytic vacuole, which engulfs a particle such as a bacterium.

phagotroph An organism that specializes in phagotrophy (particle feeding) by means of phagocytosis as a form of nutrition.

pharyngeal slit A defining characteristic of all chordate embryos. In early-diverging chordates, pharyngeal slits develop into a filter-feeding device, and in some advanced chordates, they form gills.

pharynx A portion of the vertebrate alimentary canal; also known as the throat.

phenolics A group of secondary metabolites that contain a benzene ring covalently linked to a single hydroxyl group. Includes tannins, lignins, and flavonoids.

phenotype The characteristics of an organism that are the result of the expression of its genes.

pheromone A powerful chemical attractant used to manipulate the behavior of others.

phloem A specialized conducting tissue in a plant's stem.

phloem loading The process of conveying sugars to sieve-tube elements for long-distance transport.

phoresy A form of commensalism in which individuals of one species use individuals of a second species for transportation.

phosphodiesterase An enzyme that breaks down cAMP into AMP.

phosphodiester linkage Refers to a double linkage (two phosphoester bonds) that holds together adjacent nucleotides in DNA and RNA strands.

phospholipid A class of lipids that are similar in structure to triglycerides, but the third hydroxyl group of glycerol is linked to a phosphate group instead of a fatty acid; a key component of biological membranes.

phospholipid bilayer The basic framework of the cellular membrane, consisting of two layers of lipids.

phosphorylation The attachment of a phosphate to a molecule.

photic zone A fairly narrow zone close to the surface of an aquatic environment, where light is sufficient to allow photosynthesis to exceed respiration.

photoautotroph An organism that uses the energy from light to make organic molecules from inorganic sources.

photoheterotroph An organism that is able to use light energy to generate ATP but must take in organic compounds from the environment.

photon A discrete particle that makes up light. A photon is massless and travels in a wavelike pattern.

photoperiodism A plant's ability to measure and respond to amounts of light; used as a way of detecting seasonal change.

photopsin A protein in the cone cell of an animal's eye; detects color vision.

photoreceptor A specialized cell in an animal that responds to visible light energy; in plants, molecules that respond to light.

photorespiration The metabolic process occurring in C_3 plants that occurs when the enzyme rubisco combines with O_2 instead of CO_2 and produces only one molecule of 3PG instead of two, thereby reducing photosynthetic efficiency.

photosynthesis The process whereby light energy is captured by plant, algal, or bacterial cells and is used to synthesize organic molecules from CO_2 and H_2O (or H_2S).

photosystem I (PSI) A distinct complex of proteins and pigment molecules in chloroplasts that absorbs light during the light reactions of photosynthesis.

photosystem II (PSII) A distinct complex of proteins and pigment molecules in chloroplasts that generates oxygen from water during the light reactions of photosynthesis.

phototropin The main blue-light sensor involved in phototropism in plants.

phototropism The tendency of a plant to grow toward a light source.

phylogenetic tree A diagram that describes a phylogeny; such a tree is a hypothesis of the evolutionary relationships among various species, based on the information available to and gathered by systematists.

phylogeny The evolutionary history of a species or group of species.

phylum (plural, phyla) In taxonomy, a subdivision of a kingdom.

physical mutagen A physical agent, such as ultraviolet light, that causes mutations.

physiological ecology A subdiscipline of organismal ecology that investigates how organisms are physiologically adapted to their environment and how the environment impacts the distribution of species.

phytochrome A red and far-red-light receptor in plants.

phytoplankton Microscopic photosynthetic protists that float in the water column or actively move through water.

phytoremediation The process of removing harmful metals from soils by growing hyperaccumulator plants on metal-contaminated soils, then harvesting and burning the plants to ashes for disposal and/or metal recovery.

pigment A molecule that can absorb light energy.

pili (singular, pilus) Threadlike surface appendages that allow bacteria to attach to each other during conjugation or to move across surfaces.

piloting A mechanism of migration in which an animal moves from one familiar landmark to the next.

pinnate A type of leaf vein pattern in which veins appear feather-like.

pinocytosis A form of endocytosis that involves the formation of membrane vesicles from the plasma membrane as a way for cells to internalize the extracellular fluid.

pistil A flower structure that may consist of a single carpel or multiple, fused carpels and is differentiated into stigma, style, and ovary.

pit A thin-walled circular area in a plant cell wall where secondary wall materials such as lignin are absent and through which water moves.

pitch The tone of a sound wave that depends on its length and frequency.

pituitary giant A person who has a tumor of the GH-secreting cells of the anterior pituitary gland and thus produces excess GH during childhood and, if untreated, during adulthood; the person can grow very tall before growth ceases after puberty.

pituitary gland A multilobed endocrine gland sitting directly below the hypothalamus of the brain.

placenta A structure through which humans and other eutherian mammals retain and nourish their young within the uterus via the transfer of nutrients and gases.

placental transfer tissue In plants, a nutritive tissue that aids in the transfer of nutrients from maternal parent to embryo.

plant A multicellular eukaryotic organism that is photosynthetic, generally lives on land, and is adapted in many ways to cope with the environmental stresses of life on land.

Plantae A eukaryotic kingdom of the domain Eukarya.

plant tissue culture A laboratory process to produce thousands of identical plants having the same desirable characteristics.

plaques 1. Deposits of lipids, fibrous tissue, and smooth muscle cells that may develop inside arterial walls. 2. A bacterial biofilm that may form on the surfaces of teeth.

plasma The fluid part of blood that contains water and dissolved solutes.

plasma cell A cell that synthesizes and secretes antibodies.

plasma membrane The biomembrane that separates the internal contents of a cell from its external environment.

plasmid A small circular piece of DNA found naturally in many strains of bacteria and occasionally in eukaryotic cells; can be used as a vector in cloning experiments.

plasmodesma (plural, plasmodesmata) A membrane-lined, ER-containing channel that connects the cytoplasm of adjacent plant cells.

plasmogamy The fusion of the cytoplasm between two gametes.

plasmolysis The shrinkage of algal or plant cytoplasm that occurs when water leaves the cell by osmosis, with the result that the plasma membrane no longer presses on the cell wall.

plastid A general name given to organelles found in plant and algal cells that are bound by two membranes and contain DNA and large amounts of either chlorophyll (in chloroplasts), carotenoids (in chromoplasts), or starch (in amyloplasts).

platelets Cell fragments in the blood of mammals that play a crucial role in the formation of blood clots.

pleiotropy The phenomenon in which a mutation in a single gene can have multiple effects on an individual's phenotype.

pleural sac A double layer of moist sheathlike membranes that encases each lung.

pluripotent Refers to the ability of embryonic stem cells to differentiate into almost every cell type of the body.

point mutation A mutation that affects only a single base pair within DNA or that involves the addition or deletion of a single base pair to a DNA sequence.

polar cell The highest latitude cell in the three-cell model of atmospheric circulation.

polar covalent bond A covalent bond between two atoms that have different electronegativities; the shared electrons are closer to the atom of higher electronegativity than the atom of lower

electronegativity. This distribution of electrons around the atoms creates a polarity, or difference in electric charge, across the molecule.

polarized 1. In cell biology, refers to cells that have different sides, such as the apical and basal sides of epithelial cells. 2. In neuroscience, refers to the electrical gradient across a neuron's plasma membrane.

polar molecule A molecule containing significant numbers of polar bonds.

polar transport The process whereby auxin flows primarily downward in shoots.

pole A structure of the spindle apparatus defined by each centrosome.

pollen In seed plants, tiny male gametophytes enclosed by sporopollenin-containing microspore walls.

pollen coat A layer of material that covers the sporopollenin-rich pollen wall.

pollen grain The immature male gametophyte of a seed plant.

pollen tube In seed plants, a long, thin tube produced by a pollen grain that delivers sperm to the ovule.

pollen wall A tough, sporopollenin wall at the surface of a pollen grain.

pollination The process in which pollen grains are transported to an angiosperm flower or a gymnosperm cone primarily by means of wind or animal pollinators.

pollination syndromes The pattern of coevolved traits between particular types of flowers and their specific pollinators.

pollinator An animal that carries pollen between angiosperm flowers or cones of gymnosperms.

polyandry A mating system in which one female mates with several males, but males mate with only one female.

poly A tail A string of adenine nucleotides at the 3′ end of most mature mRNAs in eukaryotes.

polycistronic mRNA An mRNA that contains the coding sequences for two or more structural genes.

polycythemia A condition of increased hemoglobin due to increased hematocrit.

polygenic A trait in which several or many genes contribute to the outcome of the trait.

polygyny A mating system in which one male mates with several females in a single breeding season, but females mate with only one male.

polyketides A group of secondary metabolites produced by diverse organisms. Examples include streptomycin, erythromycin, and tetracycline.

polymer A large molecule formed by linking many smaller molecules called monomers.

polymerase chain reaction (PCR) A technique to make many copies of a gene in vitro; primers are used that flank the region of DNA to be amplified.

polymorphic gene A gene that commonly exists as two or more alleles in a population.

polymorphism The phenomenon that many traits or genes may display variation within a population.

polyp A type of cnidarian body form that is sessile and occurs mouth up.

polypeptide A linear sequence of amino acids; the term denotes structure.

polyphagous Parasites that feed on many host species.

polyphyletic group A group of organisms that consists of members of several evolutionary lines and does not include the most recent common ancestor of the included lineages.

polyploid An organism that has three or more sets of chromosomes.

polyploidy In an organism, the state of having three or more sets of chromosomes.

polysaccharide Many monosaccharides linked to form long polymers.

pons The part of the vertebrate hindbrain, along with the cerebellum, responsible for monitoring and coordinating body movements.

population A group of individuals of the same species that occupy the same environment and can interbreed with one another.

population ecology The study of how populations grow and what factors promote or limit growth.

population genetics The study of genes and genotypes in a population.

portal vein A vein that not only collects blood from capillaries—like all veins—but also forms another set of capillaries, as opposed to returning the blood directly to the heart.

positional information Molecules that are provided to a cell that allow it to determine its position relative to other cells.

positive control Transcriptional regulation by activator proteins.

positive feedback loop In animals, the acceleration of a process, leading to what is sometimes called an explosive system.

positive pressure filling The method by which amphibians ventilate their lungs. The animals gulp air and force it under pressure into the lungs, as if inflating a balloon.

postabsorptive state One of two alternating phases in the utilization of nutrients; occurs when the gastrointestinal tract is empty of nutrients and the body's own stores must supply energy. The other phase is the absorptive state.

postanal tail A defining characteristic of all chordate embryos; consists of a tail of variable length that extends posterior to the anal opening.

posterior Refers to the rear (tail-end) of an animal.

postsynaptic cell The cell that receives the electrical or chemical signal sent from a neuron.

post-translational covalent modification A process of changing the structure of a protein, usually by covalently attaching functional groups; this process greatly increases the diversity of the proteome.

post-translational sorting The uptake of proteins into the nucleus, mitochondria, chloroplasts, or peroxisomes that occurs after the protein is completely made in the cytosol (that is, completely translated).

postzygotic isolating mechanism A mechanism that prevents interbreeding by blocking the development of a viable and fertile individual after fertilization has taken place.

potential energy The stored energy that a substance possesses due to its structure or location.

power stroke In muscle, a conformation change in the myosin cross-bridge that results in binding between myosin and actin and the movement of the actin filament.

P protein Phloem protein; the proteinaceous material used by plant phloem as a response to wounding.

prebiotic soup The medium formed by the slow accumulation of organic molecules in the early oceans over a long period of time prior to the existence of life.

predation An interaction in which the action of a predator results in the death of its prey.

predator An animal that kills its prey.

prediction An expected outcome based on a hypothesis that can be shown to be correct or incorrect through observation or experimentation.

pregnancy The time during which a developing embryo and fetus grows within the uterus of the mother. The period of pregnancy is also known as gestation.

preinitiation complex The structure of the completed assembly of RNA polymerase II and GTFs at the TATA box prior to transcription of eukaryotic structural genes.

pre-mRNA In eukaryotes, the mRNA transcript prior to any processing.

pressure-flow hypothesis Explains sugar translocation in plants as a process driven by differences in turgor pressure between cells of a sugar source, where sugar is produced, and cells of a sugar sink, where sugar is consumed.

pressure potential (P) The component of water potential due to hydrostatic pressure.

presynaptic cell The neuron that sends an electrical or chemical signal to another cell.

prezygotic isolating mechanism A mechanism that stops interbreeding by preventing the formation of a zygote.

primary active transport A type of transport that involves pumps that directly use energy to transport a solute against a gradient.

primary cell wall In plants, a relatively thin and flexible cell wall that is synthesized first between two newly made daughter cells.

primary consumer An organism that obtains its food by eating primary producers; also called a herbivore.

primary electron acceptor The molecule to which a high-energy electron from an excited pigment molecule such as P680* is transferred during photosynthesis.

primary endosymbiosis The process by which a eukaryotic host cell acquires prokaryotic endosymbionts. Mitochondria and the plastids of green and red algae are examples of organelles that originated with primary endosymbiosis.

primary growth Plant growth that occurs from primary meristems and produces primary tissues and organs of diverse types.

primary immune response The response to an initial exposure to an antigen.

primary meristem A meristematic tissue that increases plant length and produces new organs.

primary metabolism The synthesis and breakdown of molecules and macromolecules that are found in all forms of life and are essential for cell structure and function.

primary oocyte In animals, a cell that undergoes meiosis to begin the process of egg production.

primary plastid A plastid that originated from a prokaryote as the result of primary endosymbiosis.

primary production Production by autotrophs, normally green plants.

primary spermatocyte In animals, a cell that undergoes meiosis to begin the process of sperm production.

primary structure The linear sequence of amino acids of a polypeptide; one of four levels of protein structure.

primary succession Succession on newly exposed sites that were not previously occupied by soil and vegetation.

primary vascular tissue Plant tissue composed of primary xylem and phloem, which is the conducting tissue of nonwoody plants.

primer A short segment of RNA, typically 10 to 12 nucleotides in length, that is needed to begin DNA replication.

primordial germ cells (PGCs) In animals, the embryonic cells that eventually give rise to gametes.

principle of parsimony The concept that the preferred hypothesis is the one that is the simplest.

principle of species individuality A view of the nature of a community in which each species is distributed according to its physiological needs and population dynamics; most communities intergrade continuously, and competition does not create distinct vegetational zones.

prion An infectious protein that causes disease by inducing the abnormal folding of other protein molecules.

probability The chance that an event will have a particular outcome.

proboscis The coiled tongue of a butterfly or moth, which can be uncoiled, enabling it to drink nectar from flowers.

procambium In plants, a type of primary tissue meristem that produces vascular tissue.

producer An organism that synthesizes the organic compounds used by other organisms for food.

product The end result of a chemical reaction.

production efficiency The percentage of energy assimilated by an organism that becomes incorporated into new biomass.

productivity hypothesis The proposal that greater production by plants results in greater overall species richness.

product rule The probability that two or more independent events will occur is equal to the product of their individual probabilities.

progesterone A hormone secreted by the female ovaries that plays a key role in pregnancy.

progymnosperms An extinct group of plants having wood but not seeds, which evolved before the gymnosperms.

prokaryote One of the two categories into which all forms of life can be placed. Prokaryotes lack a nucleus and include bacteria and archaea.

prokaryotic Refers to organisms having cells lacking a membrane-enclosed nucleus and cell compartmentalization; includes all members of the domains Bacteria and Archaea.

prometaphase The phase of mitosis during which the mitotic spindle is completely formed.

promiscuous In ecology, a term for animals that have different sexual mates every year or breeding season.

promoter The site in the DNA where transcription begins.

proofreading The ability of DNA polymerase to identify a mismatched nucleotide and remove it from the daughter strand.

prophage Refers to the DNA of a phage that has become integrated into a bacterial chromosome.

prophase The phase of mitosis during which the chromosomes condense and the nuclear membrane begins to vesiculate.

proplastid Unspecialized structures that form plastids.

prostate gland A structure in the male reproductive system that secretes a thin fluid that protects sperm once they are deposited within the female reproductive tract.

prosthetic group Small molecules that are permanently attached to the surface of an enzyme and aid in catalysis.

protandrous Describes an animal that is born male but that may become phenotypically female under certain conditions.

protease An enzyme that cuts proteins into smaller polypeptides.

proteasome A molecular machine that is the primary pathway for protein degradation in archaea and eukaryotic cells.

protein A functional unit composed of one or more polypeptides. Each polypeptide is composed of a linear sequence of amino acids.

protein kinase An enzyme that transfers phosphate groups from ATP to a protein.

protein kinase cascade The sequential activation of multiple protein kinases.

protein phosphatase An enzyme responsible for removing phosphate groups from proteins.

protein-protein interactions The specific interactions between proteins that occur during many critical cellular processes.

protein subunit An individual polypeptide within a functional protein; most functional proteins are composed of two or more polypeptides.

proteoglycan A glycosaminoglycan in the extracellular matrix linked to a core protein.

proteolysis A processing event within a cell in which enzymes called proteases cut proteins into smaller polypeptides.

proteome The complete complement of proteins that a cell or organism can make.

proteomics Techniques used to identify and study groups of proteins.

prothoracicotropic hormone (PTTH) A hormone produced in certain invertebrates that stimulates a pair of endocrine glands called the prothoracic glands.

protist A eukaryotic organism that is not a member of the animal, plant, or fungal kingdoms; lives in moist habitats and is typically microscopic in size.

Protista Formerly a eukaryotic kingdom. Protists are now placed into seven eukaryotic supergroups.

protobiont The term used to describe the first nonliving structures that evolved into living cells.

protoderm In plants, a type of primary tissue meristem that generates the outermost dermal tissue.

protogynous Describes an hermaphroditic animal born female but which is capable of assuming a male phenotype at some point in its life history.

proton A positively charged particle found in the nucleus of an atom. The number of protons in an atom is called the atomic number and defines each type of element.

protonephridia Simple excretory organs found in flatworms that are used to filter out wastes and excess water.

proton-motive force *See* H^+ electrochemical gradient.

proto-oncogene A normal gene that, if mutated, can become an oncogene.

protostome An animal whose development exhibits spiral determinate cleavage and in which the blastopore becomes the mouth; includes mollusks, annelid worms, and arthropods.

protozoa A term commonly used to describe diverse heterotrophic protists.

proventriculus The glandular portion of the stomach of a bird.

provirus Refers to viral DNA that has become incorporated into a eukaryotic chromosome.

proximal tubule The segment of the tubule of the nephron in the kidney that drains Bowman's capsule.

proximate cause A specific genetic and physiological mechanism of behavior.

pseudocoelomate An animal with a pseudocoelom.

P site *See* peptidyl site.

pteridophytes A phylum of vascular plants having euphylls, but not seeds; Pteridophyta.

pulmocutaneous circulation The routing of blood from the heart to the gas exchange organs (lungs and skin) of frogs and some other amphibians.

pulmonary circulation The pumping of blood from the right side of the heart to the lungs to pick up oxygen from the atmosphere and release carbon dioxide.

pulmonary hypertension A condition that usually results from a diseased or damaged left ventricle that fails to pump out the usual amount of blood with each beat of the heart. This causes blood to back up in the pulmonary vessels, raising their pressure.

pulmonary trunk A major artery leaving the heart of some air-breathing vertebrates including humans that splits into the left and right pulmonary arteries and brings blood to the lungs.

pulse-chase experiment A procedure in which researchers administer a pulse of radioactively labeled materials to cells so that they make radioactive products. This is followed by the addition of nonlabeled materials called a chase.

pump A transporter that directly couples its conformational changes to an energy source, such as ATP hydrolysis.

punctuated equilibrium   A concept that suggests that the tempo of evolution is more sporadic than gradual. Species rapidly evolve into new species followed by long periods of equilibrium with little evolutionary change.

Punnett square   A common method for predicting the outcome of simple genetic crosses.

pupa   A developmental stage in some insects that undergo metamorphosis; occurs between the larval and adult stages.

pupil   A small opening in the eye of a vertebrate that transmits different patterns of light emitted from images in the animal's field of view.

purine   The bases adenine (A) and guanine (G), with double rings of carbon and nitrogen atoms.

pyramid of biomass   A measure of trophic-level transfer efficiency in which the organisms at each trophic level are weighed.

pyramid of energy   A measure of trophic-level transfer efficiency in which rates of energy production are used rather than biomass.

pyramid of numbers   An expression of trophic-level transfer efficiency in which the number of individuals decreases at each trophic level, with a huge number of individuals at the base and fewer individuals at the top.

pyrimidine   The bases thymine (T), cytosine (C), and uracil (U) with a single ring of carbon and nitrogen atoms.

Q

quadrat   A sampling device used by plant ecologists consisting of a square frame that often encloses $0.25 \, m^2$.

quantitative trait   A trait that shows continuous variation over a range of phenotypes.

quaternary structure   The association of two or more polypeptides to form a protein; one of four levels of protein structure.

quorum sensing   A mechanism by which prokaryotic cells are able to communicate by chemical means when they reach a critical population size.

R

radial cleavage   A mechanism of animal development in which the cleavage planes are either parallel or perpendicular to the vertical axis of the embryo.

radial loop domain   A loop of chromatin, often 25,000 to 200,000 base pairs in size, that is anchored to the nuclear matrix.

radial pattern   A characteristic of the body pattern of plants.

radial symmetry   1. In plants, an architectural feature in which embryos display a cylindrical shape, which is retained in the stems and roots of seedlings and mature plants. In addition, new leaves or flower parts are produced in circular whorls, or spirals, around shoot tips. 2. In animals, an architectural feature in which the body can be divided into symmetrical halves by many different longitudinal planes along a central axis.

Radiata   Radially symmetric animals; includes cnidarians and ctenophores.

radiation   The emission of electromagnetic waves by the surfaces of objects; a method of heat exchange in animals.

radicle   An embryonic root, which extends from the plant hypocotyl.

radioisotope   An isotope found in nature that is inherently unstable and usually does not exist for long periods of time. Such isotopes decay and emit energy in the form of radiation.

radioisotope dating   A common way to estimate the age of a fossil by analyzing the elemental isotopes within the accompanying rock.

radula   A unique, protrusible, tonguelike organ in a mollusk that has many teeth and is used to eat plants, scrape food particles off of rocks, or bore into shells of other species.

rain shadow   An area on the side of a mountain that is sheltered from the wind and experiences less precipitation.

ram ventilation   A mechanism used by fishes to ventilate their gills; fishes swim or face upstream with their mouths open, allowing water to enter into their buccal cavity and across their gills.

random   The rarest pattern of dispersion within a population, in which the location of individuals lacks a pattern.

random sampling error   The deviation between the observed and the expected outcomes.

rate-limiting step   The slowest step in a pathway.

ray-finned fishes   The Actinopterygii, which includes all bony fishes except the coelacanths and lungfishes.

reabsorption   In the production of urine, the process in which useful solutes in the filtrate are recaptured and transported back into the body fluids of an animal.

reactant   A substance that participates in a chemical reaction and becomes changed by that reaction.

realized niche   The actual range of an organism in nature.

reading frame   Refers to the way in which codons are read during translation, in groups of three bases beginning with the start codon.

receptacle   The enlarged region at the tip of a flower peduncle to which flower parts are attached.

receptor   1. A cellular protein that recognizes a signaling molecule. 2. A structure capable of detecting changes in the environment of an animal, such as a touch receptor.

receptor-mediated endocytosis   A common form of endocytosis in which a receptor is specific for a given cargo.

receptor potential   The membrane potential in a sensory receptor cell of an animal.

receptor tyrosine kinase   A type of enzyme-linked receptor found in animal cells that can attach phosphate groups onto tyrosines that are found in the receptor itself or in other cellular proteins.

recessive   A term that describes a trait that is masked by the presence of a dominant trait in a heterozygote.

reciprocal translocation   A type of mutation in which two different types of chromosomes exchange pieces, thereby producing two abnormal chromosomes carrying translocations.

recombinant   An offspring that has a different combination of traits from the parental generation.

recombinant DNA technology   The use of laboratory techniques to isolate and manipulate fragments of DNA.

recombinant vector   A vector containing a piece of chromosomal DNA.

recombination frequency   The frequency of crossing over between two genes.

rectum   The last segment of the large intestine of animals that empties into the anus, the posterior opening of the alimentary canal to the external environment.

red blood cell   *See* erythrocyte.

redox reaction   A type of reaction in which an electron that is removed during the oxidation of an atom or molecule is transferred to another atom or molecule, which becomes reduced; short for a reduction-oxidation reaction.

reduction   A process that involves the addition of electrons to an atom or molecule.

reductionism   An approach that involves reducing complex systems to simpler components as a way to understand how the system works. In biology, reductionists study the parts of a cell or organism as individual units.

redundancy hypothesis   A biodiversity proposal that is an alternative to the rivet hypothesis. In this model, most species are said to be redundant because they could simply be eliminated or replaced by others with no effect.

reflex arc   A simple circuit that allows an organism to respond rapidly to inputs from sensory neurons and consists of only a few neurons.

regeneration   A form of asexual reproduction in which a complete organism forms from small fragments of its body.

regulatory element   In eukaryotes, a DNA sequence that is recognized by regulatory transcription factors and regulates the expression of genes.

regulatory gene   A gene whose function is to regulate the expression of other genes.

regulatory sequence   In the regulation of transcription, a DNA sequence that functions as a binding site for genetic regulatory proteins. Regulatory sequences control whether a gene is turned on or off.

regulatory transcription factor   A protein that binds to DNA in the vicinity of a promoter and affects the rate of transcription of one or more nearby genes.

relative abundance   The frequency of occurrence of species in a community.

relative refractory period   The period near the end of an action potential when voltage-gated potassium channels are still open; during this time a new action potential can be generated if a stimulus is sufficiently strong to raise the membrane potential to threshold.

relative water content (RWC)   The property often used to gauge the water content of a plant organ or entire plant; RWC integrates the water potential of all cells within an organ or plant and is thus a measure of relative turgidity.

release factor   A protein that recognizes a stop codon in the termination stage of translation and promotes the termination of translation.

renal corpuscle   A filtering component in the nephron of the kidney.

repetitive sequence   Short DNA sequences that are present in many copies in a genome.

replica plating   A technique in which a replica of bacterial colonies is transferred from one petri plate to a new petri plate.

replication   1. The copying of DNA strands. 2. The performing of experiments several or many times.

replication fork   The area where two DNA strands have separated and new strands are being synthesized.

repressible operon   In this type of operon, a small effector molecule inhibits transcription.

repressor   A transcription factor that binds to DNA and inhibits transcription.

reproduction   The generation of offspring by sexual or asexual means.

reproductive cloning   The cloning of a multicellular organism, such as a plant or animal.

reproductive isolating mechanisms   Mechanisms that prevent interbreeding between different species.

reproductive isolation   Refers to the concept that a species cannot successfully interbreed with other species.

reproductive success   The likelihood of contributing fertile offspring to the next generation.

resistance (R)   The tendency of blood vessels to slow down the flow of blood through their lumens.

resistance gene (*R* gene)   A plant gene that has evolved as part of a defense system in response to pathogen attack.

resolution   In microscopy, the ability to observe two adjacent objects as distinct from one another; a measure of the clarity of an image.

resonance energy transfer   The process by which energy (not an electron itself) can be transferred to adjacent pigment molecules during photosynthesis.

resource partitioning   The differentiation of niches, both in space and time, that enables similar species to coexist in a community.

respiration   Metabolic reactions that a cell uses to get energy from food molecules and release waste products.

respiratory centers   Several regions of the brainstem in vertebrates that initiate expansion of the lungs.

respiratory chain   *See* electron transport chain.

respiratory distress syndrome of the newborn   The situation in which a human baby is born prematurely, before sufficient surfactant is produced in the lungs, causing the collapse of many alveoli.

respiratory pigment   A large protein that contains one or more metal atoms that bind to oxygen.

respiratory system   All components of the body that contribute to the exchange of gas between the external environment and the blood; in mammals, includes the nose, mouth, airways, and lungs and the muscles and connective tissues that encase these structures within the thoracic (chest) cavity.

resting potential   The difference in charges across the plasma membrane in an unstimulated neuron.

restoration ecology   The full or partial repair or replacement of biological habitats and/or their populations that have been damaged.

rest-or-digest   The response of vertebrates to situations associated with nonstressful states, such as feeding; mediated by the parasympathetic branch of the autonomic nervous system.

restriction enzyme   An enzyme that recognizes particular DNA sequences and cleaves the DNA backbone at two sites.

restriction point   A point in the cell cycle in which a cell has become committed to divide.

restriction sites   The base sequences recognized by restriction enzymes.

reticular formation   An array of nuclei in the brainstem of vertebrates that plays a major role in controlling states such as sleep and arousal.

retina   A sheetlike layer of photoreceptors at the back of the vertebrate eye.

retinal   A derivative of vitamin A that is capable of absorbing light energy; a component of visual pigments in the vertebrate eye.

retroelement   A type of transposable element that moves via an RNA intermediate.

retrovirus   An RNA virus that utilizes reverse transcription to produce viral DNA that can be integrated into the host cell genome.

reverse transcriptase   A viral enzyme that catalyzes the synthesis of viral DNA starting with viral RNA as a template.

rhizobia   The collective term for proteobacteria involved in nitrogen-fixation symbioses with plants.

rhodopsin   The visual pigment in the rods of the vertebrate eye.

ribonucleic acid (RNA)   One of two classes of nucleic acids; the other is deoxyribonucleic acid (DNA). RNA consists of a single strand of nucleotides.

ribonucleoprotein   A complex between an RNA molecule and a protein.

ribose   A five-carbon sugar found in RNA.

ribosomal RNA (rRNA)   An RNA that forms part of ribosomes, which provide the site where translation occurs.

ribosome   A structure composed of proteins and rRNA that provides the site where polypeptide synthesis occurs.

ribozyme   A biological catalyst that is an RNA molecule.

rickets   A condition in children characterized by bone deformations due to inadequate mineral intake or malabsorption in the intestines.

right-left axis   In bilateral animals, one of the three axes along which the adult body pattern is organized; the others are the dorsoventral axis and the anteroposterior axis.

ring canal   A central disc in the water vascular system of echinoderms.

RNA   *See* ribonucleic acid.

RNA-induced silencing complex (RISC)   A complex consisting of miRNA or siRNA and proteins; mediates RNA interference.

RNA interference (RNAi)   Refers to a type of mRNA silencing; miRNA or siRNA interferes with the proper expression of an mRNA.

RNA polymerase   The enzyme that synthesizes strands of RNA during gene transcription.

RNA processing   A step in gene expression between transcription and translation in eukaryotes; the RNA transcript, termed pre-mRNA, is modified in ways that make it a functionally active mRNA.

RNase   An enzyme that digests RNA.

RNA world   A hypothetical period on primitive Earth when both the information needed for life and the enzymatic activity of living cells were contained solely in RNA molecules.

rod   Type of photoreceptor found in the vertebrate eye; they are very sensitive to low-intensity light but do not readily discriminate different colors. Rods are utilized mostly at night, and they send signals to the brain that generate a black-and-white visual image.

root   A plant organ that provides anchorage in the soil and also fosters efficient uptake of water and minerals.

root apical meristem (RAM)   The region of rapidly dividing cells at plant root tips.

root hair   A specialized, long, thin root epidermal cell that functions to absorb water and minerals, usually from soil.

root meristem   The collection of cells at the root tip that generate all of the tissues of a plant root.

root pressure   Osmotic pressure within roots that causes water to rise for some distance through a plant stem, under conditions of high soil moisture or low transpiration.

root-shoot axis   The general body pattern of plants in which the root grows downward and the shoot grows upward.

root system   The collection of roots and root branches produced by root apical meristems.

rough endoplasmic reticulum (rough ER)   The part of the ER that is studded with ribosomes; this region plays a key role in the initial synthesis and sorting of proteins that are destined for the ER, Golgi apparatus, lysosomes, vacuoles, plasma membrane, or outside of the cell.

rRNA   *See* ribosomal RNA.

r-selected species   A type of life history strategy, where species have a high rate of per capita population growth but poor competitive ability.

rubisco   The enzyme that catalyzes the first step in the Calvin cycle in which CO_2 is incorporated into an organic molecule.

Ruffini corpuscle   Tactile (touch) receptors in the skin of mammals that respond to deep pressure and vibration.

ruminants   Animals such as sheep, goats, llamas, and cows that have complex stomachs consisting of several chambers.

S

saltatory conduction   The conduction of an action potential along an axon in which the action potential is regenerated at each node of Ranvier instead of along the entire length of the axon.

sarcoma   A tumor of connective tissue such as bone or cartilage.

sarcomere   One complete unit of the repeating pattern of thick and thin filaments within a myofibril.

sarcoplasmic reticulum   A cellular organelle that provides a muscle fiber's source of the calcium involved in muscle contraction; a specialized form of the endoplasmic reticulum.

satiety   A feeling of fullness.

saturated fatty acid   A fatty acid in which all the carbons are linked by single covalent bonds.

scanning electron microscopy (SEM)   A type of microscopy that utilizes an electron beam to produce an image of the three-dimensional surface of biological samples.

scavenger   An animal that eats the remains of dead animals.

Schwann cells   The glial cells that form myelin on axons that travel outside the brain and spinal cord.

science   In biology, the observation, identification, experimental investigation, and theoretical explanation of natural phenomena.

scientific method   A series of steps to test the validity of a hypothesis. This approach often involves a comparison between control and experimental groups.

sclera   The white of the vertebrate eye; a strong outer sheath that in the front is continuous with a thin, clear layer known as the cornea.

sclereid   Star- or stone-shaped plant cells having tough, lignified cell walls.

sclerenchyma tissue   A rigid plant ground tissue composed of tough-walled fibers and sclereids.

secondary active transport   A type of membrane transport that involves the utilization of a pre-existing gradient to drive the active transport of another solute.

secondary cell wall   A thick rigid plant cell wall that is synthesized and deposited between the plasma membrane and the primary cell wall after a plant cell matures and has stopped increasing in size.

secondary consumer   An organism that eats primary consumers; also called a carnivore.

secondary endosymbiosis   A process that occurs when a eukaryotic host cell acquires a eukaryotic endosymbiont having a primary plastid.

secondary growth   Plant growth that occurs from secondary meristems and increases the girth of woody plant stems and roots.

secondary immune response   An immediate and heightened production of additional specific antibodies against the particular antigen that previously elicited a primary immune response.

secondary meristem   A meristem in woody plants forming a ring of actively dividing cells that encircle the stem.

secondary metabolism   The synthesis of chemicals that are not essential for cell structure and growth and are usually not required for cell survival but are advantageous to the organism.

secondary metabolite   Molecules that are produced by secondary metabolism.

secondary oocyte   In animals, the large haploid cell that is produced when a primary oocyte undergoes meiosis I during oogenesis.

secondary phloem   The inner bark of a woody plant.

secondary plastid   A plastid that has originated by the endosymbiotic incorporation of a eukaryotic cell containing a primary plastid into a eukaryotic host cell.

secondary production   The measure of production of heterotrophs and decomposers.

GLOSSARY

secondary spermatocytes In animals, the haploid cells produced when a primary spermatocyte undergoes meiosis I during spermatogenesis.

secondary structure The bending or twisting of proteins into α helices or β sheets; one of four levels of protein structure.

secondary succession Succession on a site that has previously supported life but has undergone a disturbance.

secondary xylem In plants, a type of secondary vascular tissue that is also known as wood.

second law of thermodynamics States that the transfer of energy or the transformation of energy from one form to another increases the entropy, or degree of disorder, of a system.

second messengers Small molecules or ions that relay signals inside the cell.

secretion 1. The export of a substance from a cell. 2. In the production of urine, the process in which some solutes are actively transported into the tubules of the excretory organ; this supplements the amount of a solute that would normally be removed by filtration alone.

secretory pathway A pathway for the movement of larger substances, such as carbohydrates and proteins, out of a cell.

secretory vesicle A membrane vesicle carrying different types of materials that fuses with the cell's plasma membrane to release the contents extracellularly.

seed A reproductive structure having specialized tissues that enclose plant embryos; produced by gymnosperms and flowering plants, usually as the result of sexual reproduction.

seed coat A hard and tough covering that develops from the ovule's integuments and protects a plant embryo.

seed plant The informal name for gymnosperms and angiosperms.

segmentation The division of an animal's body into clearly defined regions.

segmentation gene A gene that controls the segmentation pattern of an animal embryo.

segment-polarity gene A type of segmentation gene; a mutation in this gene causes portions of segments to be missing either an anterior or a posterior region and for adjacent regions to become mirror images of each other.

segregate To separate, as in chromosomes during mitosis.

selectable marker A gene whose presence can allow organisms (such as bacteria) to grow under a certain set of conditions. For example, an antibiotic-resistance gene is a selectable marker that allows bacteria to grow in the presence of the antibiotic.

selective breeding Programs and procedures designed to modify traits in domesticated species.

selectively permeable The property of membranes that allows the passage of certain ions or molecules but not others.

selective serotonin reuptake inhibitors Drugs used to treat major depressive disorder that act by increasing concentrations of serotonin in the brain.

self-compatible The reproductive state of plants that can serve as both mother and father to their progeny.

self-fertilization Fertilization that involves the union of a female gamete and male gamete from the same individual.

self-incompatibility (SI) Rejection of pollen that is genetically too similar to the pistil of a plant.

selfish DNA hypothesis The hypothesis that transposable elements exist because they have the characteristics that allow them to insert themselves into the host cell DNA but do not provide any advantage.

self-pollination The process in which pollen from the anthers of a flower is transferred to the stigma of the same flower or between flowers of the same plant.

self-splicing The phenomenon that RNA itself can catalyze the removal of its own intron(s); occurs in rRNA and tRNA.

SEM *See* scanning electron microscopy.

semelparity A reproductive pattern in which organisms produce all of their offspring in a single reproductive event.

semen A mixture containing fluid and sperm that is released during ejaculation.

semicircular canal Structures of the vertebrate ear that can detect a range of motions of the head.

semiconservative mechanism The correct model for DNA replication; double-stranded DNA is half conserved following replication, resulting in new double-stranded DNA containing one parental strand and one daughter strand.

semifluid A type of motion within biomembranes; considered two-dimensional because movement occurs only within the plane of the membrane.

semilunar valves One-way valves into the systemic and pulmonary arteries through which blood is pumped from the ventricles.

seminal vesicles Paired accessory glands in the male reproductive system that secrete fructose, the main nutrient for sperm, into the urethra.

seminiferous tubule A tightly packed tubule in the testis, where spermatogenesis takes place.

senescent Cells that have doubled many times and have reached a point where they have lost the capacity to divide any further.

sense A system in an animal that consists of sensory cells that respond to a specific type of chemical or physical stimulus and send signals to the central nervous system, where the signals are received and interpreted.

sensor A structure such as a sensory receptor or a nucleus in the brain that detects a signal in a homeostatic control system.

sensory neuron A neuron that detects or senses information from the outside world, such as light, sound, touch, and heat; sensory neurons also detect internal body conditions such as blood pressure and body temperature.

sensory receptor In animals, a specialized cell whose function is to receive sensory inputs.

sensory transduction The process by which incoming stimuli are converted into neural signals.

sepal A flower organ that occurs in a whorl located outside whorls of petals of eudicot plants.

septum (plural, septa) A cross wall; examples include the cross walls that divide the hyphae of most fungi into many small cells and the structure that separates the old and new chambers of a nautilus.

sere Each phase of succession in a community; also called a seral stage.

setae Chitinous bristles in the integument of many invertebrates.

set point The normal value for a controlled variable, such as blood pressure, in an animal.

sex chromosomes A distinctive pair of chromosomes that are different in males and females.

sex-influenced inheritance The phenomenon in which an allele is dominant in one sex but recessive in the other.

sex linked Refers to genes that are found on one sex chromosome but not on the other.

sex pili Hairlike structures made by bacterial F^+ cells that bind specifically to other F^- cells.

sexual dimorphism A pronounced difference in the morphologies of the two sexes within a species.

sexual reproduction A process that requires a fertilization event in which two gametes unite to produce a cell called a zygote.

sexual selection A type of natural selection that is directed at certain traits of sexually reproducing species that make it more likely for individuals to find or choose a mate and/or engage in successful mating.

Shannon diversity index (H_S) A means of measuring the diversity of a community; $H_S = -\Sigma p_i \ln p_i$.

shared derived character A trait that is shared by a group of organisms but not by a distant common ancestor.

shared primitive character A trait shared with a distant ancestor.

shattering The process by which ears of wild grain crops break apart and disperse seeds.

shell A tough, protective covering on an amniotic egg that is impermeable to water and prevents the embryo from drying out.

shivering thermogenesis Rapid muscle contractions in an animal, without any locomotion, in order to raise body temperature.

shoot The portion of a plant comprised of stems and leaves.

shoot apical meristem (SAM) The region of rapidly dividing plant cells at plant shoot apices.

shoot meristem The tissue that produces all aerial parts of the plant, which include the stems as well as lateral structures such as leaves and flowers.

shoot system The collection of plant organs produced by shoot apical meristems.

short-day plant A plant that flowers only when the night length is longer than a defined period.

short stature A condition characterized by stunted growth; formerly called pituitary dwarfism.

short tandem repeat sequences (STRs) Short sequences repeated many times in a row and found in multiple sites in the genome of humans and other species; often vary in length among different individuals.

shotgun DNA sequencing A strategy for sequencing an entire genome by randomly sequencing many different DNA fragments.

sickle cell disease A disease due to a genetic mutation in a hemoglobin gene in which sickle-shaped red blood cells are less able to move smoothly through capillaries and can block blood flow, resulting in severe pain and cell death of the surrounding tissue.

sieve plate The perforated end wall of a mature sieve-tube element.

sieve plate pore One of many perforations in a plant's sieve plate.

sieve-tube elements A component of the phloem tissues of flowering plants; thin-walled cells arranged end to end to form transport pipes.

sigma factor A protein that plays a key role in bacterial promoter recognition and recruits RNA polymerase to the promoter.

signal Regarding cell communication, an incoming or outgoing agent that influences the properties of cells.

signal recognition particle (SRP) A protein/RNA complex that recognizes the ER signal sequence of a polypeptide, pauses translation, and directs the ribosome to the ER to complete translation.

signal transduction pathway A group of proteins that convert an initial signal to a different signal inside a cell.

sign stimulus In animals, a trigger that initiates a fixed-action pattern of behavior.

silencer A regulatory element in eukaryotes that prevents transcription of a given gene.

silencing RNAs (siRNAs) Small RNA molecules, typically 22 nucleotides in length, that silence the expression of specific mRNAs by promoting their degradation.

silent mutation A gene mutation that does not alter the amino acid sequence of the polypeptide, even though the nucleotide sequence has changed.

simple Mendelian inheritance The inheritance pattern of traits affected by a single gene that is found in two variants, one of which is completely dominant over the other.

simple translocation A type of mutation in which a single piece of chromosome is attached to another chromosome.

single-factor cross *See* monohybrid cross.

single lens eye Type of eye found in vertebrates and some invertebrates with only one lens, as opposed compound eyes of insects with many lenses.

single nucleotide polymorphism (SNP) A type of genetic variation in a population in which a particular gene sequence varies at a single nucleotide.

single-strand binding protein A protein that binds to both of the single strands of parental DNA and prevents them from re-forming a double helix during DNA replication.

sinoatrial (SA) node A collection of modified cardiac cells in the right atrium of most vertebrates that spontaneously and rhythmically generates action potentials that spread across the entire atria; also known as the pacemaker of the heart.

siRNAS *See* silencing RNAs.

sister chromatids The two duplicated chromatids that are still joined to each other after DNA replication.

skeletal muscle A type of muscle tissue that is attached by tendons to bones in vertebrates and to the exoskeleton of invertebrates.

skeleton A structure or structures that serve one or more functions related to support, protection, and locomotion.

sliding filament mechanism The way in which a muscle fiber shortens during muscle contraction.

SLOSS debate In conservation biology, the debate over whether it is preferable to protect one single, large reserve or several smaller ones.

slow block to polyspermy Events initiated by the release of Ca^{2+} that produce barriers to more sperm penetrating an already fertilized egg.

slow fiber A skeletal muscle fiber containing myosin with a low rate of ATP hydrolysis.

slow-oxidative fiber A skeletal muscle fiber that has a low rate of myosin ATP hydrolysis but has the ability to make large amounts of ATP; used for prolonged, regular activity.

small effector molecule With regard to transcription, refers to a molecule that exerts its effects by binding to a regulatory transcription factor, causing a conformational change in the protein.

small intestine In vertebrates, a tube that leads from the stomach to the large intestine where nearly all digestion of food and absorption of food nutrients and water occur.

smooth endoplasmic reticulum (smooth ER) The part of the ER that is not studded with ribosomes. This region is continuous with the rough ER and functions in diverse metabolic processes such as detoxification, carbohydrate metabolism, accumulation of calcium ions (Ca^{2+}), and synthesis and modification of lipids.

smooth muscle A type of muscle tissue that surrounds hollow tubes and cavities inside the body's organs; it is not under conscious control.

soil horizon Layers of soil, ranging from topsoil to bedrock.

solute A substance dissolved in a liquid.

solute potential (S) The component of water potential due to the presence of solute molecules.

solution A liquid that contains one or more dissolved solutes.

solvent The liquid in which a solute is dissolved.

somatic cell The type of cell that constitutes all cells of an animal or plant body except those that give rise to gametes.

somatic embryogenesis The production of plant embryos from body (somatic) cells.

somatic nervous system The division of the peripheral nervous system that senses the external environmental conditions and controls skeletal muscles.

somites Blocklike structures resulting from the segmentation of mesoderm during neurulation.

soredia An asexual reproductive structure produced by lichens consisting of small clumps of hyphae surrounding a few algal cells that can disperse in wind currents.

sorting signal A short amino acid sequence in a protein that directs the protein to its correct location; also known as a traffic signal.

source pool The pool of species on the mainland that is available to colonize an island.

spatial summation Occurs when two or more postsynaptic potentials are generated at one time along different regions of the dendrites and their depolarizations and hyperpolarizations sum together.

speciation The formation of new species.

species A group of related organisms that share a distinctive form in nature and (for sexually reproducing species) are capable of interbreeding.

species-area effect The relationship between the amount of available area and the number of species present.

species concepts Different approaches for distinguishing species.

species diversity A measure of biological diversity that incorporates both the number of species in an area and the relative distribution of individuals among species.

species interactions A part of the study of population ecology that focuses on interactions such as predation, competition, parasitism, mutualism, and commensalism.

species richness The numbers of species in a community.

specific heat The amount of energy required to raise the temperature of 1 gram of a substance by 1°C.

specific immunity *See* acquired immunity.

specificity Refers to the concept that enzymes recognize specific substrates.

Spemann's organizer An extremely important morphogenetic field in the early gastrula; the organizer secretes morphogens responsible for inducing the formation of a new embryonic axis.

sperm Refers to a male gamete that is generally smaller than the female gamete (egg).

spermatid In animals, a haploid cell produced when the secondary spermatocytes undergo meiosis II; these cells eventually differentiate into sperm cells.

spermatogenesis Gametogenesis in a male animal resulting in the production of sperm.

spermatogonium In animals, a diploid germ cell that gives rise to the male gametes, the sperm.

spermatophytes All of the living and fossil seed plant phyla.

sperm storage A method of synchronizing the production of offspring with favorable environmental conditions in which female animals store and nourish sperm in their reproductive tract for long periods of time.

S phase The DNA synthesis phase of the cell cycle.

spicules Needle-like structures that are usually made of silica and form lattice-like skeletons in sponges, possibly helping to reduce predation.

spina bifida A developmental abnormality of the neural tube, which fails to close.

spinal cord In chordates, the structure that connects the brain to all areas of the body and together with the brain constitutes the central nervous system.

spinal nerve A nerve that connects the peripheral nervous system and the spinal cord.

spiracle One of several pairs of pores on the body surface of insects through which air enters and exits the body.

spiral cleavage A mechanism of animal development in which the planes of cell cleavage are oblique to the axis of the embryo.

spirilli Rigid, spiral-shaped prokaryotic cells.

spirochaetes Flexible, spiral-shaped prokaryotic cells.

spliceosome A complex of several subunits known as snRNPs that removes introns from eukaryotic pre-mRNA.

splicing The process whereby introns are removed from RNA and the remaining exons are connected to each other.

spongin A tough protein that lends skeletal support to a sponge.

spongocoel A central cavity in the body of a sponge.

spongy parenchyma Photosynthetic ground tissue of the plant leaf mesophyll that contains round cells separated by abundant air spaces.

spontaneous mutation A mutation resulting from abnormalities in biological processes.

sporangia Structures that produce and disperse the spores of plants, fungi, or protists.

sporangium Singular of sporangia.

spore A haploid, typically single-celled reproductive structure of fungi and plants that is dispersed into the environment and is able to grow into a new fungal mycelium or plant gametophyte in a suitable habitat.

sporic life cycle *See* alternation of generations.

sporophyte The diploid generation of plants or multicellular protists that have a sporic life cycle; this generation produces haploid spores by the process of meiosis.

sporopollenin The tough material that composes much of the walls of plant spores and helps to prevent cellular damage during transport in air.

stabilizing selection A pattern of natural selection that favors the survival of individuals with intermediate phenotypes.

stamen A flower organ that produces the male gametophyte, pollen.

standard metabolic rate (SMR) The metabolic rate of ectotherms measured at a standard temperature for each species—one that approximates the average temperature that a species normally encounters.

standing crop The total biomass in an ecosystem at any one point in time.

starch A polysaccharide composed of repeating glucose units that is produced by the cells of plants and some algal protists.

start codon A three-base sequence—usually AUG—that specifies the first amino acid in a polypeptide.

statocyst An organ of equilibrium found in many invertebrate species.

statolith 1. Tiny granules of sand or other dense objects located in a statocyst that aid equilibrium in many invertebrates. 2. In plants, a starch-heavy plastid that allows both roots and shoots to detect gravity.

stem A plant organ that produces buds, leaves, branches, and reproductive structures.

stem cell A cell that divides so that one daughter cell remains a stem cell and the other can differentiate into a specialized cell type. Stem cells construct the bodies of all animals and plants.

stereocilia Deformable projections from epithelial cells called hair cells that are bent by movements of fluid or other stimuli.

stereoisomers   Isomers with identical bonding relationships, but different spatial positioning of their atoms.

sternum   The breastbone of a vertebrate.

steroid   A lipid containing four interconnected rings of carbon atoms; functions as a hormone in animals and plants.

steroid receptor   A transcription factor that recognizes a steroid hormone and usually functions as a transcriptional activator.

sticky ends   Single-stranded ends of DNA fragments that will hydrogen-bond to each other due to their complementary sequences.

stigma   In a flower, the topmost portion of the pistil, which receives and recognizes pollen of the appropriate species or genotype.

stomach   A saclike organ in some animals that most likely evolved as a means of storing food; it partially digests some of the macromolecules in food and regulates the rate at which the contents empty into the small intestine.

stomata   Surface pores on plant surfaces that can be closed to retain water or open to allow the entry of CO_2 needed for photosynthesis and the exit of O_2 and water vapor.

stop codon   One of three three-base sequences—UAA, UAG, and UGA—that signals the end of translation; also called termination codon or nonsense codon.

strain   Within a given species, a lineage that has genetic differences compared to another lineage.

strand   A structure of DNA (or RNA) formed by the covalent linkage of nucleotides in a linear manner.

strepsirrhini   Smaller species of primates; includes bush babies, lemurs, and pottos.

streptophyte   Land pants (embryophytes) and close relatives among the green algae.

streptophyte algae   The green algae that are closely related to land plants (embryophytes).

stretch receptor   A type of mechanoreceptor found widely in an animal's organs and muscle tissues that can be distended.

striated muscle   Skeletal and cardiac muscle with a series of light and dark bands perpendicular to the muscle's long axis.

stroke   The condition that occurs when blood flow to part of the brain is disrupted.

stroke volume (SV)   The amount of blood ejected with each beat, or stroke, of the heart.

stroma   The fluid-filled region of the chloroplast between the thylakoid membrane and the inner membrane.

stromatolite   A layered calcium carbonate structure in an aquatic environment generally produced by cyanobacteria.

strong acid   An acid that completely ionizes in solution.

structural gene   Refers to most genes, which produce an mRNA molecule that contains the information to specify a polypeptide with a particular amino acid sequence.

structural isomers   Isomers that contain the same atoms but in different bonding relationships.

style   In a flower, the elongate portion of the pistil through which the pollen tube grows.

stylet   A sharp, piercing organ in the mouth of nematodes and some insects.

submetacentric   A chromosome in which the centromere is off center.

subsidence zones   Areas of high pressure that are the sites of the world's tropical deserts because the subsiding air is relatively dry, having released all of its moisture over the equator.

subspecies   A subdivision of a species; this designation is used when two or more geographically restricted groups of the same species differ, but not enough to warrant their placement into separate species.

substrate   1. The reactant molecules and/or ions that bind to an enzyme at the active site and participate in a chemical reaction. 2. The organic compounds such as soil or rotting wood that fungi use as food.

substrate-level phosphorylation   A method of synthesizing ATP that occurs when an enzyme directly transfers a phosphate from an organic molecule to ADP.

succession   The gradual and continuous change in species composition and community structure over time.

sugar sink   The plant tissues or organs in which more sugar is consumed than is produced by photosynthesis.

sugar source   The plant tissues or organs that produce more sugar than they consume in respiration.

sum rule   The probability that one of two or more mutually exclusive outcomes will occur is the sum of the probabilities of the possible outcomes.

supergroup   One of the seven subdivisions of the domain Eukarya.

surface area-to-volume (SA/V) ratio   The ratio between a structure's surface area and the volume in which the structure is contained.

surface tension   A measure of how difficult it is to break the interface between a liquid and air.

surfactant   A mixture of proteins and amphipathic lipids produced in certain alveolar cells that prevents the collapse of alveoli by reducing surface tension in the lungs.

survivorship curve   A graphical plot of the numbers of surviving individuals at each age in a population.

suspension feeder   An aquatic animal that sifts water, filtering out the organic matter and expelling the rest.

suspensor   A short chain of cells at the base of an early angiosperm embryo that provides anchorage and nutrients.

swim bladder   A gas-filled, balloon-like structure that helps a fish to remain buoyant in the water even when the fish is completely stationary.

symbiosis   An intimate association between two or more organisms of different species.

symbiotic   Describes a relationship in which two or more different species live in direct contact with each other.

sympathetic division   The division of the autonomic nervous system that is responsible for rapidly activating body systems to provide immediate energy in response to danger or stress.

sympatric   The term used to describe species occurring in the same geographic area.

sympatric speciation   A form of speciation that occurs when members of a species that initially occupy the same habitat within the same range diverge into two or more different species.

symplast   All of a plant's protoplasts (the cell contents without the cell walls) and plasmodesmata.

symplastic transport   The movement of a substance from the cytosol of one cell to the cytosol of an adjacent cell via membrane-lined channels called plasmodesmata.

symplesiomorphy   *See* shared primitive character.

symporter   A type of transporter that binds two or more ions or molecules and transports them in the same direction across a membrane; also called a cotransporter.

synapomorphy   *See* shared derived character.

synapse   A junction where a nerve terminal meets a target neuron, muscle cell, or gland and through which an electrical or chemical signal passes.

synapsis   The process of forming a bivalent.

synaptic cleft   The extracellular space between a neuron and its target cell.

synaptic plasticity   The formation of additional synaptic connections that occurs as a result of learning.

synaptic signaling   A specialized form of paracrine signaling that occurs in the nervous system of animals.

synergids   In the female gametophyte of a flowering plant, the two cells adjacent to the egg cell that help to import nutrients from maternal sporophyte tissues.

syntrophy   The phenomenon in which one species lives off the products of another species.

systematics   The study of biological diversity and evolutionary relationships among organisms, both extinct and modern.

systemic acquired resistance (SAR)   A whole-plant defensive response to pathogenic microorganisms.

systemic circulation   The pumping of blood from the left side of an animal's heart to the body to drop off O_2 and nutrients and pick up CO_2 and wastes. The blood then returns to the right side of the heart.

systemic hypertension   An arterial blood pressure above normal; in humans, normal blood pressure ranges from systolic/diastolic pressures of about 90/60 to 120/80 mmHg; often called hypertension or high blood pressure.

systems biology   A field of study in which researchers investigate living organisms in terms of their underlying networks—groups of structural and functional connections—rather than their individual molecular components.

systole   The second phase of the cardiac cycle, in which the ventricles contract and eject the blood through the open semilunar valves.

T

tagmata   The fusion of body segments into functional units.

taproot system   The root system of eudicots, consisting of one main root with many branch roots.

taste buds   Structures located in the mouth and tongue of vertebrates that contain the sensory cells, supporting cells, and associated neuronal endings that contribute to taste sensation.

TATA box   One of three features found in most eukaryotic promoters; the others are the transcriptional start site and regulatory elements.

taxis   A directed type of response to a stimulus that is either toward or away from the stimulus.

taxon   A group of species that are evolutionarily related to each other. In taxonomy, each species is placed into several taxons that form a hierarchy from large (domain) to small (genus).

taxonomy   The field of biology that is concerned with the theory, practice, and rules of classifying living and extinct organisms and viruses.

T cells   A type of lymphocyte that directly kills infected, mutated, or transplanted cells.

telocentric   A chromosome in which the centromere is at the end.

telomerase   An enzyme that catalyzes the replication of the telomere.

telomere   A region at the ends of eukaryotic chromosomes where a specialized form of DNA replication occurs.

telophase   The phase of mitosis during which the chromosomes decondense and the nuclear membrane re-forms.

TEM   *See* transmission electron microscopy.

temperate phage   A bacteriophage that may spend some of its time in the lysogenic cycle.

template strand   The DNA strand that is used as a template for RNA synthesis or DNA replication.

temporal lobe   One of four lobes of the cerebral cortex of human brain; necessary for language, hearing, and some types of memory.

temporal summation   Occurs when two or more postsynaptic potentials arrive at the same location in a dendrite in quick succession and their depolarizations and hyperpolarizations sum together.

tepal   A flower perianth part that cannot be distinguished by appearance as a petal or a sepal.

termination codon   *See* stop codon.

termination stage   The final stage of transcription or translation in which the process ends.

terminator   A sequence that specifies the end of transcription.

terpenoids   A group of secondary metabolites synthesized from five-carbon isoprene units. An example is β-carotene, which gives carrots their orange color.

territory   A fixed area in which an individual or group excludes other members of its own species, and sometimes other species, by aggressive behavior or territory marking.

tertiary consumer   An organism that feeds on secondary consumers.

tertiary endosymbiosis   The acquisition by eukaryotic protist host cells of plastids from cells that possess secondary plastids.

tertiary plastid   A plastid acquired by the incorporation into a host cell of an endosymbiont having a secondary plastid.

tertiary structure   The three-dimensional shape of a single polypeptide; one of four levels of protein structure.

testcross   A cross to determine if an individual with a dominant phenotype is a homozygote or a heterozygote. Also, a cross to determine if two different genes are linked.

testis (plural, **testes**)   In animals, the male gonad, where sperm are produced.

testosterone   The primary androgen in many vertebrates, including humans.

tetrad   *See* bivalent.

tetraploid   An organism or cell that has four sets of chromosomes.

tetrapod   A vertebrate animal having four legs or leglike appendages.

thalamus   A region of the vertebrate forebrain that plays a major role in relaying sensory information to appropriate parts of the cerebrum and, in turn, sending outputs from the cerebrum to other parts of the brain.

theory   In biology, a broad explanation of some aspect of the natural world that is substantiated by a large body of evidence. Biological theories incorporate observations, hypothesis testing, and the laws of other disciplines such as chemistry and physics. A theory makes valid predictions.

thermodynamics   The study of energy interconversions.

thermoreceptor   A sensory receptor in animals that responds to cold and heat.

theropods   A group of bipedal saurischian dinosaurs.

thick filament   A section of the repeating pattern in a myofibril composed almost entirely of the motor protein myosin.

thigmotropism   Touch responses in plants.

thin filament   A section of the repeating pattern in a myofibril that contains the cytoskeletal protein actin, as well as two other proteins—troponin and tropomyosin—that play important roles in regulating contraction.

30-nm fiber   Nucleosome units organized into a more compact structure that is 30 nm in diameter.

thoracic breathing   Breathing in which coordinated contractions of muscles expand the rib cage, creating a negative pressure to suck air in and then forcing it out later; found in amniotes.

threatened species   Those species that are likely to become endangered in the future.

threshold concentration   The concentration above which a morphogen will exert its effects but below which it is ineffective.

threshold potential   The membrane potential, typically around –50 to –55 mV, which is sufficient to trigger an action potential in an electrically excitable cell such as a neuron.

thrifty genes   Genes that boosted our ancestors' ability to store fat from each feast in order to sustain them through the next famine.

thrombocyte   Intact cell in the blood of vertebrates other than mammals that plays a crucial role in the formation of blood clots; in mammals, cell fragments called platelets serve this function.

thylakoid   A flattened, platelike membranous region found in cyanobacterial cells and the chloroplasts of photosynthetic protists and plants; the location of the light reactions of photosynthesis.

thylakoid lumen   The fluid-filled compartment within the thylakoid.

thylakoid membrane   A membrane within the chloroplast that forms many flattened, fluid-filled tubules that enclose a single, convoluted compartment. It contains chlorophyll and is the site where the light-dependent reactions of photosynthesis occurs.

thymine (T)   A pyrimidine base found in DNA.

thymine dimer   In DNA, a type of pyrimidine dimer that can cause a mutation; a site where two adjacent thymine bases become covalently crosslinked to each other.

thyroglobulin   A protein found in the colloid of the thyroid gland that is involved in the formation of thyroid hormones.

thyroxine (T_4)   A weakly active thyroid hormone that contains iodine and helps regulate metabolic rate; it is converted by cells into the more active triiodothyronine (T_3).

tidal ventilation   A type of breathing in mammals in which the lungs are inflated with air and then the chest muscles and diaphragm relax and recoil back to their original positions as an animal exhales. During exhalation, air leaves via the same route that it entered during inhalation, and no new oxygen is delivered to the airways at that time.

tidal volume   The volume of air that is normally breathed in and out at rest.

tight junction   A type of junction between animal cells that forms a tight seal between adjacent epithelial cells and thereby prevents molecules from leaking between cells; also called an occluding junction.

Ti plasmid   Tumor-inducing plasmid found in *Agrobacterium tumefaciens*; it is used as a cloning vector to transfer genes into plant cells.

tissue   The association of many cells of the same type, for example, muscle tissue.

tolerance   A mechanism for succession in which any species can start the succession, but the eventual climax community is reached in a somewhat orderly fashion; early species neither facilitate nor inhibit subsequent colonists.

Toll-like receptor   Receptor proteins that recognize nonspecific antigens in microbes; key part of the innate immune system.

tonoplast   The membrane of the central vacuole in a plant or algal cell.

topsoil   The uppermost layer of a soil.

torpor   The strategy in endotherms of lowering internal body temperature to just a few degrees above that of the environment in order to conserve energy.

torus   The nonporous, flexible central region of a conifer pit that functions like a valve.

total fertility rate   The average number of live births a female has during her lifetime.

total peripheral resistance (TPR)   The sum of all the resistance in all arterioles.

totipotent   The ability of a fertilized egg to produce all of the cell types in the adult organism; also the ability of unspecialized plant cells to regenerate an adult plant.

toxins   Compounds that have adverse effects in living organisms; often produced by various protist and plant species.

trace element   An element that is essential for normal function in living organisms but is required in extremely small quantities.

trachea   1. A sturdy tube arising from the spiracles of an insect's body; involved in respiration. 2. The name of the tube leading to the lungs of air-breathing vertebrates.

tracheal system   The respiratory system of insects consisting of a series of finely branched air tubes called tracheae; air enters and exits the tracheae through spiracles, which are pores on the body surface.

tracheary elements   Water-conducting cells in plants that, when mature, are always dead and empty of cytosol; include tracheids and vessel elements.

tracheid   A type of dead, lignified plant cell in xylem that conducts water, along with dissolved minerals; also provides structural support.

tracheophytes   A term used to describe vascular plants.

tract   A parallel bundle of myelinated axons in the central nervous system.

traffic signal   *See* sorting signal.

trait   An identifiable characteristic; usually refers to a variant.

transcription   The use of a gene sequence to make a copy of RNA.

transcriptional start site   The site in a eukaryotic promoter where transcription begins.

transcription factor   A protein that influences the ability of RNA polymerase to transcribe genes.

transduction   A type of genetic transfer between bacteria in which a virus infects a bacterial cell and then subsequently transfers some of that cell's DNA to another bacterium.

***trans*-effect**   In both prokaryotes and eukaryotes, a form of genetic regulation that can occur even though two DNA segments are not physically adjacent. The action of the lac repressor on the *lac* operon is a *trans*-effect.

transepithelial transport   The process of moving solutes across an epithelium, such as in the gut of animals.

transfer RNA (tRNA)   An RNA that carries amino acids and is used to translate mRNA into polypeptides.

transformation   A type of genetic transfer between bacteria in which a segment of DNA from the environment is taken up by a competent cell and incorporated into the bacterial chromosome.

transgenic   The term used to describe an organism that carries genes that were introduced using molecular techniques such as gene cloning.

transitional form   An organism that provides a link between earlier and later forms in evolution.

transition state   In a chemical reaction, a state in which the original bonds have stretched to their limit; once this state is reached, the reaction can proceed to the formation of products.

translation   The process of synthesizing a specific polypeptide on a ribosome.

translocation   1. A type of mutation in which one segment of a chromosome becomes attached to a different chromosome. 2. A process in plants in which phloem transports substances from a source to a sink.

transmembrane gradient   A situation in which the concentration of a solute is higher on one side of a membrane than on the other.

transmembrane protein   A protein that has one or more regions that are physically embedded in the hydrophobic region of a cell membrane's phospholipid bilayer.

transmembrane segment   A region of a membrane protein that is a stretch of nonpolar amino acids that spans or traverses the membrane from one leaflet to the other.

transmembrane transport   The export of material from one cell into the intercellular space and then into an adjacent cell.

transmission electron microscopy (TEM)   A type of microscopy in which a beam of electrons is transmitted through a biological sample to form an image on a photographic plate or screen.

transpiration   The evaporative loss of water from plant surfaces into sun-heated air.

transporter   A membrane protein that binds a solute and undergoes a conformational change to allow the movement of the solute across a membrane; also called a carrier.

transport protein   Proteins embedded within the phospholipid bilayer that allow plasma membranes to be selectively permeable by providing a passageway for the movement of some but not all substances across the membrane.

transposable element (TE)   A segment of DNA that can move from one site to another.

transposase   An enzyme that facilitates transposition.

transposition   The process in which a short segment of DNA moves within a cell from its original site to a new site in the genome.

transverse tubules (T-tubules)   Invaginations of the plasma membrane of skeletal muscle cells that open to the extracellular fluid and conduct action potentials from the outer surface to the myofibrils.

triacylglycerol   *See* triglyceride.

trichome   A projection, often hairlike, from the epidermal tissue of a plant that offers protection from excessive light, ultraviolet radiation, extreme air temperature, or attack by herbivores.

triglyceride   A molecule composed of three fatty acids linked by ester bonds to a molecule of glycerol; also known as a triacylglycerol.

triiodothyronine (T$_3$)   A thyroid hormone that contains iodine and helps regulate metabolic rate.

triplet   A group of three bases that function as a codon.

triploblastic   Having three distinct germ layers: endoderm, ectoderm, and mesoderm.

triploid   An organism or cell that has three sets of chromosomes.

trisomic   An aneuploid organism that has one too many chromosomes.

tRNA   *See* transfer RNA.

trochophore larva   A distinct larval stage of many invertebrate phyla.

trophectoderm   The outer layer of cells in a developing mammalian blastocyst; continuous with the ectoderm layer.

trophic level   Each feeding level in a food chain.

trophic-level transfer efficiency   The amount of energy at a trophic level that is acquired by the trophic level above and incorporated into biomass.

trophic mutualism   A mutually beneficial interaction between two species in which both species receive the benefit of resources.

tropism   In plants, a growth response that is dependent on a stimulus that occurs in a particular direction.

tropomyosin   A rod-shaped protein that plays an important role in regulating muscle contraction.

troponin   A small globular-shaped protein that plays an important role in regulating muscle contraction through its ability to bind Ca^{2+}.

trp operon   An operon of *E. coli* that encodes enzymes required to make the amino acid tryptophan, a building block of cellular proteins.

true-breeding line   A strain that continues to exhibit the same trait after several generations of self-fertilization or inbreeding.

trypsin   A protease involved in the breakdown of proteins in the small intestine.

T-snare   A protein in a target membrane that recognizes a V-snare in a membrane vesicle.

tubal ligation   A means of contraception that involves the cutting and sealing of the fallopian tubes in a woman, thereby preventing movement of a fertilized egg into the uterus.

tube cell   In a seed plant, one of the cells resulting from the division of a microspore; stores proteins and forms the pollen tube.

tube feet   Echinoderm structures that function in movement, gas exchange, feeding, and excretion.

tumor   An abnormal overgrowth of cells.

tumor-suppressor gene   A gene that when normal (that is, not mutant) encodes a protein that prevents cancer; however, when a mutation eliminates its function, cancer may occur.

tunic   A nonliving structure that encloses a tunicate, made of protein and a cellulose-like material called tunicin.

turgid   The term used to describe a plant cell whose cytosol is so full of water that the plasma membrane presses right up against the cell wall; as a result, turgid cells are firm or swollen.

turgor pressure   *See* osmotic pressure.

20-hydroxyecdysone   A hormone produced by the prothoracic glands of arthropods that stimulates molting.

two-factor cross   *See* dihybrid cross.

type 1 diabetes mellitus (T1DM)   A disease in which the pancreas does not produce sufficient insulin; as a result, extracellular glucose cannot cross plasma membranes, and glucose accumulates to very high concentrations in the blood.

type 2 diabetes mellitus (T2DM)   A disease in which the pancreas produces sufficient insulin, but the cells of the body lose much of their ability to respond to insulin.

U

ubiquitin   A small protein in eukaryotic cells that directs unwanted proteins to a proteasome by its covalent attachment.

ulcer   An erosion of the mucosal surface of the alimentary canal; typically occurs in the lower esophagus, stomach, or duodenum.

ultimate cause   The reason a particular behavior evolved, in terms of its effect on reproductive success.

umbrella species   A species whose habitat requirements are so large that protecting them would protect many other species existing in the same habitat.

unconditioned response   An action that is elicited by an unconditioned stimulus.

unconditioned stimulus   A trigger that elicits an original response.

uniform   A pattern of dispersion within a population in which individuals maintain a certain minimum distance between themselves to produce an evenly spaced distribution.

uniporter   A type of transporter that binds a single ion or molecule and transports it across a membrane.

unipotent   A term used to describe a stem cell found in the adult that can produce daughter cells that differentiate into only one cell type.

unsaturated   The quality of certain lipids containing one or more CwC double bonds.

unsaturated fatty acid   A fatty acid that contains one or more CwC double bonds.

upwelling   In the ocean, a process that carries mineral nutrients from the bottom waters to the surface.

uracil (U)   A pyrimidine base found in RNA.

urea   A nitrogenous waste commonly produced by many terrestrial species, including mammals.

uremia   A condition characterized by the presence of nitrogenous wastes, such as urea, in the blood; typically results from kidney disease.

ureter   A structure in the mammalian urinary system through which urine flows from the kidney into the urinary bladder.

urethra   The structure in the mammalian urinary system through which urine is eliminated from the body.

uric acid   A nitrogenous waste produced by birds, insects, and reptiles.

urinary bladder   The structure in the mammalian urinary system that collects urine before it is eliminated.

urinary system   The structures that collectively act to filter blood or hemolymph and excrete wastes, while recapturing useful compounds.

urine   The part of the filtrate formed in the kidney that remains after all reabsorption of solutes and water is complete.

uterine cycle   *See* menstrual cycle.

uterus   A small, pear-shaped organ capable of enlarging and specialized for carrying a developing fetus in female mammals.

V

vaccination   The injection into the body of small quantities of weakened or dead pathogens, resulting in the development of immunity to those pathogens without causing disease.

vacuole   Specialized compartments found in eukaryotic cells that function in storage, the regulation of cell volume, and degradation.

vagina   The birth canal of female mammals; also functions to receive sperm during copulation.

vaginal diaphragm   A barrier method of preventing fertilization in which a diaphragm is placed in the upper part of the vagina just prior to intercourse; blocks movement of sperm to the cervix.

valence electron   An electron in the outer shell of an atom that is available to combine with other atoms. Such electrons allow atoms to form chemical bonds with each other.

van der Waals forces   Attractive forces between molecules in close proximity to each other, caused by the variations in the distribution of electron density around individual atoms.

variable region   A unique domain within an immunoglobulin that serves as the antigen-binding site.

vasa recta capillaries   Capillaries in the medulla in the nephron of the kidney.

vascular bundle   Primary plant vascular tissues that occur in a cluster.

vascular cambium   A secondary meristematic tissue of plants that produces both wood and inner bark.

vascular plant   A plant that contains vascular tissue. Includes all modern plant species except liverworts, hornworts, and mosses.

vascular tissue   Plant tissue that provides both structural support and conduction of water, minerals, and organic compounds.

vas deferens   A muscular tube through which sperm leave the epididymis.

vasectomy A surgical procedure in men that severs the vas deferens, thereby preventing the release of sperm at ejaculation.

vasoconstriction A decrease in blood vessel radius; an important mechanism for directing blood flow away from specific regions of the body.

vasodilation An increase in blood vessel radius; an important mechanism for directing blood flow to specific regions of the body.

vasotocin A peptide hormone that is responsible for regulating salt and water balance in the blood of nonmammalian vertebrates.

vector A type of DNA that acts as a carrier of a DNA segment that is to be cloned.

vegetal pole In triploblast organisms, the pole of the egg where the yolk is most concentrated.

vegetative growth The production of new nonreproductive tissues by the shoot apical meristem and root apical meristem during seedling development and growth of mature plants.

vein 1. In animals, a blood vessel that returns blood to the heart. 2. In plants, a bundle of vascular tissue in a leaf.

veliger In mollusks, a free-swimming larva that has a rudimentary foot, shell, and mantle.

ventilation The process of bringing oxygenated water or air into contact with a respiratory surface such as gills or lungs.

ventral Refers to the lower side of an animal.

ventricle In the heart, a chamber that pumps blood out of the heart.

venule A small, thin-walled extension of a capillary that empties into larger vessels called veins that return blood to the heart for another trip around the circulation.

vertebrae A bony or cartilaginous column of interlocking structures that provides support and also protects the nerve cord, which lies within its tubelike structure.

vertebrate An organism with a backbone.

vertical evolution A process in which species evolve from pre-existing species by the accumulation of mutations.

vesicle A small membrane-enclosed sac within a cell.

vessel In a plant, a pipeline-like file of dead, water-conducting vessel elements.

vessel element A type of plant cell in xylem that conducts water, along with dissolved minerals and certain organic compounds.

vestibular system The organ of balance in vertebrates, located in the inner ear next to the cochlea.

vestigial structure An anatomical feature that has no apparent function but resembles a structure of a presumed ancestor.

vibrios Comma-shaped prokaryotic cells.

villus (plural, **villi**) Finger-like projections extending from the luminal surface into the lumen of the small intestine; these are specializations that aid in digestion and absorption.

viral envelope A structure enclosing a viral capsid that consists of a membrane derived from the plasma membrane of the host cell; is embedded with virally encoded spike glycoproteins.

viral genome The genetic material of a virus.

viral reproductive cycle The series of steps that result in the production of new viruses during a viral infection.

viral vector A type of vector used in cloning experiments that is derived from a virus.

viroid An RNA particle that infects plant cells.

virulence The ability of a microorganism to cause disease.

virulent phage A phage that follows only the lytic cycle.

virus A small infectious particle that consists of nucleic acid enclosed in a protein coat.

visceral mass In mollusks, a structure that rests atop the foot and contains the internal organs.

vitamin An organic nutrient that serves as a coenzyme for metabolic and biosynthetic reactions.

vitamin D A vitamin that is converted into a hormone in the body; regulates the calcium level in the blood through an effect on intestinal transport of calcium ions.

vitreous humor A thick liquid in the large posterior cavity of the vertebrate eye, which helps maintain the shape of the eye.

viviparity Development of an embryo within the mother, resulting in a live birth.

viviparous The term used to describe an animal whose embryos develop within the uterus, receiving nourishment from the mother via a placenta.

V_{max} The maximal velocity of an enzyme-catalyzed reaction.

volt A unit of measurement of potential difference in charge (electrical force) such as the difference between the interior and exterior of a cell.

voltage-gated ion channels Ion channels that open and close in response to changes in the amount of electric charge across a membrane.

V-snare A protein incorporated into a vesicle membrane during vesicle formation that is recognized by a T-snare in a target membrane.

W

water potential The potential energy of water.

water vascular system A network of canals powered by water pressure generated by the contraction of muscles; enables extension and contraction of the tube feet, allowing echinoderms to move slowly.

wavelength The distance from the peak of one sound wave or light wave to the next.

waxy cuticle A protective, waterproof layer of polyester and wax present on most surfaces of vascular plant sporophytes.

weak acid An acid that only partially ionizes in solution.

weathering The physical and chemical breakdown of rock.

white blood cell *See* leukocyte.

white matter Brain tissue that consists of myelinated axons that are bundled together in large numbers to form tracts.

whorls In a flower, concentric rings of sepals and petals (or tepals), stamens, and carpels.

wild-type allele One or more prevalent alleles in a population.

wood A secondary plant tissue composed of numerous pipelike arrays of dead, empty, water-conducting cells whose walls are strengthened by an exceptionally tough secondary metabolite known as lignin.

woody plant A type of plant that produces both primary and secondary vascular tissues.

X

X inactivation The phenomenon in which one X chromosome in the somatic cells of female mammals is inactivated, meaning that its genes are not expressed.

X inactivation center (Xic) A short region on the X chromosome known to play a critical role in X inactivation.

X-linked gene A gene found on the X chromosome but not on the Y.

X-linked inheritance The pattern displayed by pairs of dominant and recessive alleles located on X chromosomes.

X-ray crystallography A technique in which researchers purify molecules and cause them to form a crystal. When a crystal is exposed to X-rays, the resulting pattern can be analyzed mathematically to determine the three-dimensional structure of the crystal's components.

xylem A specialized conducting tissue in plants that transports water, minerals, and some organic compounds.

xylem loading The process by which root xylem parenchyma cells transport ions and water across their membranes into the long-distance conducting cells of the xylem, which include the vessel elements and tracheids.

Y

yeast A fungus that can occur as a single cell and that reproduces by budding.

yolk sac One of the four extraembryonic membranes in the amniotic egg. The yolk sac encloses a stockpile of nutrients, in the form of yolk, for the developing embryo.

Z

zero population growth The situation in which no changes in population size occur.

Z line A network of proteins in a myofibril that anchors thin filaments at the ends of each sarcomere.

zona pellucida The glycoprotein covering that surrounds a mature oocyte.

zone of elongation The area above the root apical meristem of a plant where cells extend by water uptake, thereby dramatically increasing root length.

zone of maturation The area above the zone of elongation in a plant root where root cell differentiation and tissue specialization occur.

zooplankton Aquatic organisms drifting in the open ocean or fresh water; includes minute animals consisting of some worms, copepods, tiny jellyfish, and the small larvae of invertebrates and fishes.

Z scheme A model depicting the series of energy changes of an electron during the light reactions of photosynthesis. The electron absorbs light energy twice, resulting in an energy curve with a zigzag shape.

zygomycete A phylum of fungi that produces distinctive, large zygospores as the result of sexual reproduction.

zygospore A dark-pigmented, thick-walled spore that matures within the zygosporangium of zygomycete fungi during sexual reproduction.

zygote A diploid cell formed by the fusion of two haploid gametes.

zygotic life cycle The type of life cycle of most unicellular protists in which haploid cells develop into gametes. Two gametes then fuse to produce a diploid zygote.

Photo Credits

Front Matter: Page v: © Ian J. Quitadamo, Ph.D.

Contents: I: © Dr. Parvinder Sethi; II: © PCN Photography; III: © Daniel Gage, University of Connecticut. Appeared in Schultz, S. C., Shields, G. C. and Steitz, T. A. (1991) "Crystal structure of a CAP-DNA complex: the DNA is bent by 90 degrees," *Science*, 253:1001; IV: © George Bernard/SPL/Photo Researchers, Inc.; V: © Morales/Getty Images; VI: © Gerald & Buff Corsi/Visuals Unlimited; VII: © John Rowley/Getty Images RF; VIII: © Mike Lockhart.

Chapter 1: Opener: © Georgette Douwma/Photo Researchers, Inc.; 1.1: © Photo W. Wüster, courtesy Instituto Butantan; 1.2: © blickwinkel/Alamy; 1.3: © SciMAT/Photo Researchers, Inc.; 1.4a: © David Scharf/Photo Researchers, Inc.; 1.4b: © Alexis Rosenfeld/Photo Researchers, Inc.; 1.4c: © Cathlyn Melloan/Stone/Getty Images; 1.4d: © Adam Jones/Visuals Unlimited; 1.4e: © Patti Murray/Animals Animals; 1.4f: © Paul Hanna/Reuters/Corbis; 1.4g: © Mehgan Murphy, National Zoo/AP Photo; 1.4h: © HPH Publishing/Getty Images; 1.4i: © Louise Pemberton; 1.4j: © Maria Teijeiro/Getty Images RF; 1.4k: © Corbis/SuperStock RF; 1.4l: © Bill Barksdale/agefotostock; 1.10a: © Dr. David M. Phillips/Visuals Unlimited; 1.10b: © B. Boonyaratanakornkit & D.S. Clark, G. Vrdoljak/EM Lab, U of C Berkeley/Visuals Unlimited; 1.10c (protists): © Dr. Dennis Kunkel Microscopy/Visuals Unlimited; 1.10c (plants): © Kent Foster/Photo Researchers, Inc.; 1.10c (fungi): © Carl Schmidt-Luchs/Photo Researchers, Inc.; 1.10c (animals): © Fritz Polking/Visuals Unlimited; 1.13: © Georgette Douwma/Photo Researchers, Inc.; 1.14a: © Fred Bavendam/Minden Pictures; 1.14b: © Eastcott/Momatiuk/Animals Animals; 1.14c: © Ton Koene/Visuals Unlimited; 1.14d: © Northwestern, Shu-Ling Zhou/AP Photo; 1.14e: © Andrew Brookes/Corbis; 1.14e (inset): © Alfred Pasieka/Photo Researchers, Inc.; 1.17: © Dita Alangkara/AP Photo.

Unit I: 2: © Dr. Parvinder Sethi; 3: © de Vos, A. M., Ultsch, M., Steitz, A.A., (1992), "Human growth hormone and extracellular domain of its receptor: crystal structure of the complex," *Science*, 255(306). Image by Daniel Gage, University of Connecticut.

Chapter 2: Opener: © Dr. Parvinder Sethi; 2.6: © The McGraw-Hill Companies, Inc./Al Telser, photographer; 2.12b: © Charles D. Winters/Photo Researchers, Inc.; 2.17 (top right): © Jeremy Burgess/Photo Researchers, Inc.; 2.19b: © Aaron Haupt/Photo Researchers, Inc.; 2.19d: © Chris McGrath/Getty Images; 2.19e: © Dana Tezarr/Getty Images; 2.19f: © Anthony Bannister/Gallo Images/Corbis; 2.19g: © Hermann Eisenbeiss/Photo Researchers, Inc.

Chapter 3: Opener: © de Vos, A. M., Ultsch, M., Steitz, A.A., (1992), "Human growth hormone and extracellular domain of its receptor: crystal structure of the complex," *Science*, 255(306). Image by Daniel Gage, University of Connecticut; 3.1: © The McGraw-Hill Companies, Inc./Al Telser, photographer; 3.11a: © Tom Pantages; 3.11b: © Felicia Martinez/PhotoEdit; 3.13: © Adam Jones/Photo Researchers, Inc.

Unit II: 4: © Biophoto Associates/Photo Researchers, Inc.; 5: © Tom Pantages; 6: © 3660 Group Inc./Custom Medical Stock Photo; 7: © PCN Photography; 8: © Travel Pix Ltd/Getty Images; 9: © David McCarthy/SPL/Photo Researchers, Inc.; 10: © altrendo panoramic/Getty Images.

Chapter 4: Opener: © Biophoto Associates/Photo Researchers, Inc.; 4.2a-b: © Images courtesy of Molecular Expressions; 4.3a: © Dr. Donald Fawcett & L. Zamboni/Visuals Unlimited; 4.3b, 4.4b: © Dr. Dennis Kunkel Microscopy/Visuals Unlimited; 4.6a: © Ed Reschke/Getty Images; 4.6b: © Eye of Science/Photo Researchers, Inc.; Table 4.1(1): © Thomas Deerinck/Visuals Unlimited; Table 4.1(2-3): © Dr. Gopal Murti/Visuals Unlimited; 4.12a: © Courtesy Charles Brokaw/California Institute of Technology, 1991. "Microtubule sliding in swimming sperm flagella, direct and indirect measurements on sea urchin and tunicate spermatozoa," *Journal of Cell Biology*, 114:1201–15, issue cover image; 4.12b: Courtesy of Dr. Barbara Surek, Culture Collection of Algae at the University of Cologne (CCAC); 4.12c: © SPL/Photo Researchers, Inc.; 4.13 (top left): © Aaron J. Bell/Photo Researchers, Inc.; 4.13 (middle): © Dr. William Dentler/University of Kansas; 4.15 (top right): © Dr. Donald Fawcett/Visuals Unlimited; 4.15 (middle right): © Dr. Richard Kessel & Dr. Gene Shih/Visuals Unlimited; 4.16: Courtesy of Felix A. Habermann; 4.17 (right): © Dennis Kunkel Microscopy, Inc./Phototake; 4.19: © Lucien G. Caro, Ph.D., and George E. Palade, M.D., 1964. "Protein synthesis, storage, and discharge in the pancreatic exocrine: an autoradiographic study," *Journal of Cell Biology*, 20:473–95, Fig. 3; 4.20a: © E.H. Newcomb & S.E. Frederick/Biological Photo Service; 4.20b: Courtesy Dr. Peter Luykx, Biology, University of Miami; 4.20c: © Dr. David Patterson/Photo Researchers, Inc.; 4.21 (inset) © The McGraw-Hill Companies, Inc./Al Telser, photographer; 4.24: © Dr. Donald Fawcett/Visuals Unlimited; 4.25: © Dr. Jeremy Burgess/Photo Researchers, Inc.; 4.26: © T. Kanaseki and Dr. Donald Fawcett/Visuals Unlimited.

Chapter 5: Opener: © Tom Pantages; 5.3a-b: © The McGraw-Hill Companies, Inc./Al Telser, photographer; 5.16(1–2): © Carolina Biological Supply/Visuals Unlimited; 5.18: Courtesy Dr. Peter Agre. From GM Preston, TP Carroll, WP Guggino, P Agre (1992), "Appearance of water channels in *Xenopus* oocytes expressing red cell CHIP28 protein," *Science*, 256(5055):385–7.

Chapter 6: Opener: © 3660 Group Inc./Custom Medical Stock Photo; 6.1a: © moodboard/Corbis RF; 6.1b: © amanaimages/Corbis RF; 6.10(4–5): From Altman, S., (1990). Nobel Lecture, "Enzymatic Cleavage of RNA by RNA," *Bioscience Reports*, 10:317–37, Fig. 7. © The Nobel Foundation; 6.14: © Liu, Q., Greimann, J.C., and Lima, C.D., (2006), "Reconstitution, activities, and structure of the eukaryotic exosome," *Cell*, 127:1223–37. Graphic generated using DeLano, W.L. (2002), The PyMOL Molecular Graphics System (San Carlos, CA, USA, DeLano Scientific). With permission from Elsevier.

Chapter 7: Opener: © PCN Photography; 7.4: © Custom Medical Stock Photo; 7.13: From Noji, H., Yoshida, M. (2001), "The rotary machine in the cell, ATP Synthase," *Journal of Biological Chemistry*, 276(3):1665–8. © 2001 The American Society for Biochemistry and Molecular Biology; 7.14: © Ernie Friedlander/Cole Group/Getty Images RF; 7.16a: © Homer W Sykes/Alamy; 7.16b: © Jeff Greenberg/The Image Works.

Chapter 8: Opener: © Travel Pix Ltd/Getty Images; 8.2(1): © Norman Owen Tomalin/Bruce Coleman Inc./Photoshot; 8.2(2): © J. Michael Eichelberger/Visuals Unlimited; 8.2(3): © Dr. George Chapman/Visuals Unlimited; 8.12b: © Reproduction of Fig. 1A from

Ferreira, K.N., Iverson, T.M., Maghlaoui, K., Barber, J. and Iwata, S., "Architecture of the photosynthetic oxygen evolving center," *Science*, 303(5665):1831–8 © 2004. With permission from AAAS; 8.16(6): Calvin, M., "The path of carbon in photosynthesis," *Nobel Lecture, December 11, 1961*, pp. 618–44, Fig. 4. © The Nobel Foundation; 8.17a: © David Noton Photography/Alamy; 8.17b: © David Sieren/Visuals Unlimited; 8.19(1): © Wesley Hitt/Getty Images; 8.19(2): © John Foxx/Getty Images RF.

Chapter 9: Opener: © David McCarthy/SPL/Photo Researchers, Inc.; 9.2 (inset): © Robert J. Erwin/Photo Researchers, Inc.; 9.15(1–2): Courtesy of Brian J. Bacskai, from Bacskai et al., *Science*, 260:222–6, 1993. With permission from AAAS; 9.18(1–4): © Prof. Guy Whitley/Reproductive and Cardiovascular Disease Research Group at St. George's University of London; 9.19(4): © Dr. Thomas Caceci, Virginia–Maryland Regional College of Veterinary Medicine.

Chapter 10: Opener: © altrendo panoramic/Getty Images; 10.1 (left): © Dr. Dennis Kunkel Microscopy/Visuals Unlimited/Corbis; 10.1 (right): Courtesy of Dr. Joseph Buckwalter/University of Iowa; 10.6: © Dr. Dennis Kunkel Microscopy/Visuals Unlimited; 10.10: © Dr. Daniel Friend; 10.11: Courtesy Dr. Dan Goodenough/Harvard Medical School; 10.13: © Purbasha Sarkar; 10.14: © E.H. Newcomb & W.P. Wergin/Biological Photo Service; 10.19a: © Ed Reschke/Getty Images; 10.19b: © Biodisc/Visuals Unlimited; 10.20: © Robert Brons/Biological Photo Service; 10.21: © J.N.A. Lott/Biological Photo Service.

Unit III: 11: © Jean Claude Revy/ISM/Phototake; 12: © Kiseleva and Dr. Donald Fawcett/Visuals Unlimited; 13: © Daniel Gage, University of Connecticut. Appeared in Schultz, S. C., Shields, G. C., and Steitz, T. A. (1991) "Crystal structure of a CAP-DNA complex: the DNA is bent by 90 degrees," *Science*, 253:1001; 14: © Yvette Cardozo/Workbook Stock/Getty Images; 15: © Biophoto Associates/Photo Researchers, Inc.; 16: © Radu Sigheti/Reuters; 17: © Dave King/Dorling Kindersley/Getty Images; 18: © CAMR/A. Barry Dowsett/Photo Researchers, Inc.; 19: © Medical-on-Line/Alamy; 20: © Corbis; 21: © Coston Stock/Alamy.

Chapter 11: Opener: © Jean Claude Revy/ISM/Phototake; 11.3b: © Eye of Science/Photo Researchers, Inc.; 11.13: © Meselson, M., Stahl, F., (1958) "The replication of DNA in *Escherichia coli*," *PNAS*, 44(7):671–82, Fig. 4a; 11.24a: Photo courtesy of Dr. Barbara Hamkalo; 11.26a: © Dr. Gopal Murti/Visuals Unlimited; 11.26b: © Ada L. Olins and Donald E. Olins/Biological Photo Service; 11.26c: Courtesy Dr. Jerome B. Rattner, Cell Biology and Anatomy, University of Calgary; 11.26d: Courtesy of Paulson, J.R. & Laemmli, U.K. James R. Paulson, U.K. Laemmli, "The structure of histone-depleted metaphase chromosomes," *Cell*, 12:817–28, Copyright Elsevier 1977; 11.26e-f: © Peter Engelhardt/Department of Virology, Haartman Institute.

Chapter 12: Opener: © Kiseleva and Dr. Donald Fawcett/Visuals Unlimited; 12.15a: Reprinted from Seth A. Darst, "Bacterial RNA polymerase," *Current Opinion in Structural Biology*, 11(2):155–62, © 2001, with permission from Elsevier.

Chapter 13: Opener: © Daniel Gage, University of Connecticut. Appeared in Schultz, S. C., Shields, G. C. and Steitz, T. A. (1991) "Crystal structure of a CAP-

DNA complex: the DNA is bent by 90 degrees," *Science*, 253:1001; 13.2a: © Ed Reschke/Getty Images; 13.2b: © Triarch/Visuals Unlimited; 13.2c: © SIU BioMed/ Custom Medical Stock Photo; 13.10: © Thomas Steitz, Howard Hughes Medical Institution, Yale University.

Chapter 14: Opener: © Yvette Cardozo/Workbook Stock/Getty Images; 14.1a-b: © Stan Flegler/Visuals Unlimited; 14.1c: Courtesy of Thomas Wellems and Robert Josephs. Electron Microscopy and Image Processing Laboratory, University of Chicago; 14.4: © Otero/gtphoto; 14.9: © Dr. Kenneth Greer/Visuals Unlimited; 14.10b: © St. Bartholomew's Hospital/Photo Researchers, Inc.; 14.17(1–5): © Dr. Oscar Auerbach, reproduced with permission.

Chapter 15: Opener: © Biophoto Associates/Photo Researchers, Inc.; 15.1(4): © Burger/Photo Researchers, Inc.; 15.1(5): Courtesy of the Genomic Centre for Cancer Research and Diagnosis, CancerCare Manitoba, University of Manitoba, Winnipeg, Manitoba, Canada; 15.8a-f: Photographs by Conly L. Rieder, East Greenbush, New York, 12061; 15.9a: © Dr. David M. Phillips/Visuals Unlimited; 15.9b: © Carolina Biological Supply Company/ Phototake; 15.19a-b: © A. B. Sheldon; 15.20a: © Sylvan Wittwer/Visuals Unlimited; 15.20b: © B. Runk/S. Schoenberger/Grant Heilman Photography.

Chapter 16: Opener: © Radu Sigheti/Reuters; 16.1: © SPL/Photo Researchers, Inc.; 16.3: © Nigel Cattlin/ Photo Researchers, Inc.; 16.19: © March of Dimes.

Chapter 17: Opener: © Dave King/Dorling Kindersley/ Getty Images; 17.9a-b: Courtesy of I. Solovei, University of Munich (LMU); 17.11: Courtesy of Dr. Argiris Efstratiadis.

Chapter 18: Opener: © CAMR/A. Barry Dowsett/ Photo Researchers, Inc.; 18.1: © Norm Thomas/Photo Researchers, Inc.; 18.3a: © Robley C. Williams/Biological Photo Service; 18.3b: Reprinted from R.C. Valentine and H.G. Pereira, "Antigens and structure of the adenovirus," *Journal of Molecular Biology*, 13(2):71–83, © 1965, with permission from Elsevier; 18.3c: © Chris Bjornberg/Photo Researchers, Inc.; 18.3d: © Omikron/ Photo Researchers, Inc.; 18.6: © Cynthia Goldsmith/ CDC; 18.7: © Photograph by J. W. Randles, at Albay Research Center, Philippines; 18.8: © Eye of Science/ Photo Researchers, Inc.; 18.9: Carl Robinow & Eduard Kellengerger, "The bacterial nucleoid revisited," *Microbiological Reviews*, 1994 June, 58(2):211–32. Fig. 4 © American Society for Microbiology; 18.12 (right): © Stanley Cohen/Photo Researchers, Inc.; 18.13 (bottom): © Dr. Jeremy Burgess/SPL/Photo Researchers, Inc.; 18.17: © Dr. L. Caro/SPL/Photo Researchers, Inc.

Chapter 19: Opener: © Medical-on-Line/Alamy; 19.1a: © Herman Eisenbeiss/Photo Researchers, Inc.; 19.1b: © Sinclair Stammers/Photo Researchers, Inc.; 19.1c: © J-M. Labat/Photo Researchers, Inc.; 19.1d: © Mark Smith/Photo Researchers, Inc.; 19.1e: © Nigel Cattlin/ Photo Researchers, Inc.; 19.4a–19.6(1): Courtesy of the National Museum of Health and Medicine, Washington, D.C.; 19.6(2): © Congenital Anomaly Research Center of Kyoto University; 19.6(3–4): Courtesy of the National Museum of Health and Medicine, Washington, D.C.; 19.9b–19.11(1): Christiane Nüsslein-Volhard, "Determination of the embryonic axes of *Drosophila*," *Development*, Supplement 1, 1991, pp. 1–10, Fig. 5, © The Company of Biologists Limited 1991; 19.11(2–4): © Jim Langeland, Steve Paddock and Sean Carroll/University of Wisconsin-Madison; 19.12a-b: Courtesy of the Archives, California Institute of Technology; 19.14a: © Juergen Berger/Photo Researchers, Inc.; 19.14b: © F. R. Turner,

Indiana University; 19.24a: © Darwin Dale/Photo Researchers, Inc.; 19.24b-c: © John Bowman.

Chapter 20: Opener: © Corbis; 20.10 (bottom): © Alfred Pasieka/Photo Researchers, Inc.; 20.14a: © Bill Barksdale/Agstockusa/agefotostock; 20.15(6): © Roslin Institute/Phototake; 20.16a: © Leonard Lessin.

Chapter 21: Opener: © Coston Stock/Alamy; 21.2b: © The Picture Store/SPL/Photo Researchers, Inc.; 21.2c: © Photo by Michael Beckmann, Institute of Geobotany and Botanical Garden, Halle, Germany; 21.4a: © Topham/ The Image Works; 21.4b: © Jerome Wexler/Visuals Unlimited.

Unit IV: 22: © George Bernard/SPL/Photo Researchers, Inc.; 23: © Mark Dadswell/Getty Images; 24: © Dynamic Graphics Group/IT StockFree/Alamy RF; 25: © Frederic B. Siskind; 26: © Peter Weimann/Animals Animals.

Chapter 22: Opener: © George Bernard/SPL/Photo Researchers, Inc.; 22.1a: © Stanley M. Awramik/Biological Photo Service; 22.1b: © Michael Abbey/Visuals Unlimited; 22.3b: © CSSF/NEPTUNE Canada; 22.4a: A.I. Oparin. From *The Origin of Life*, New York: Dover, 1952; 22.4b: © Mary Kraft; 22.7: © Simon Fraser/SPL/Photo Researchers, Inc.; 22.11a: © Dirk Wiersma/SPL/Photo Researchers, Inc.; 22.11b: © Roger Garwood & Trish Ainslie/Corbis; 22.13a: Courtesy of Dr. Barbara Surek, Culture Collection of Algae at the University of Cologne (CCAC); 22.13b: © Bill Bourland/micro*scope; 22.13c-d: © Dr. Cristian A. Solari, Department of Ecology and Evolutionary Biology, University of Arizona; 22.14: We thank Prof. Jun-yuan Chen for permission to use this image; 22.15a: © Newman & Flowers/Photo Researchers, Inc.; 22.15b: Courtesy of the Smithsonian Institution, Photograph by Chip Clark. *Marrella splendens*, most commonly occurring fossil from the Burgess Shale. Collected by Charles D. Walcott for the Smithsonian Research Collections; 22.16a: © Francois Gohier/Photo Researchers, Inc.; 22.16b: © DK Limited/ Corbis; 22.17: © Ken Lucas/Visuals Unlimited; 22.19: © Jason Edwards/Getty Images RF.

Chapter 23: Opener: © Mark Dadswell/Getty Images; 23.1a: © PoodlesRock/Corbis; 23.3a: © Worldwide Picture Library/Alamy; 23.3b: © Gerald & Buff Corsi/Visuals Unlimited; 23.5 (middle): © T. Daeschler/VIREO; 23.7a: © Wm. Grenfell/Visuals Unlimited; 23.7b: © Prisma Bildagentur AG/Alamy; 23.8a (left): © Tom Brakefield/ Corbis; 23.8a (right): © Tom McHugh/Photo Researchers, Inc.; 23.8b (left): © David Sieren/Visuals Unlimited; 23.8b (right): © 2003 Steve Baskauf/bioimages.vanderbilt.edu; 23.8c (left): © Jonathan Bird/Getty Images; 23.8c (right): © David Wrobel/SeaPics.com; 23.9a: © Mark Raycroft/ Minden Pictures; 23.9b: © Martin Rugner/agefotostock; 23.9c: © Juniors Bildarchiv/agefotostock.

Chapter 24: Opener: © Dynamic Graphics Group/ IT StockFree/Alamy RF; 24.1: © Paul Harcourt Davies/ SPL/Photo Researchers, Inc.; 24.5a: Courtesy Mark McNair, University of Exeter; 24.7a: © Gerald Cubitt; 24.7b: © Topham/The Image Works; 24.7c: © Photo by Darren P. Croft, University of Exeter UK; 24.8a-b: © Ole Seehausen.

Chapter 25: Opener: © Frederic B. Siskind; 25.1a (left): © Mark Smith/Photo Researchers, Inc.; 25.1a (right): © Pascal Goetgheluck/ardea.com; 25.1b (left): © Gary Meszaros/Visuals Unlimited; 25.1b (right): © robin chittenden/Alamy; 25.3a: © C. Allan Morgan/ Getty Images; 25.3b: © Bryan E. Reynolds; 25.4a: © Rod Planck/Photo Researchers, Inc.; 25.4b: © Ron Austing/ Photo Researchers, Inc.; 25.5 (top left): © Mark Boulton/ Photo Researchers, Inc.; 25.5 (top right): © Carolina

Biological Society/Visuals Unlimited; 25.5 (bottom): © Stephen L. Saks/Photo Researchers, Inc.; 25.6 (left): © Hal Beral/V&W/imagequestmarine.com; 25.6 (right): © Amar and Isabelle Guillen/Guillen Photography/Alamy; 25.7 (top right): © FLPA/Alamy; 25.7b(1–3, 6): © Jack Jeffrey Photography; 25.7b(4–5): © Jim Denny; 25.12: © Dr. Sara Via, Department of Biology and Department of Entomology, University of Maryland; 25.14a: Courtesy Ed Laufer; 25.14b-c: Courtesy of Dr. J.M. Hurle. Originally published in *Development*. 1999 Dec. 126(23):5515–22; 25.17: © Gary Nafis; 25.18a-b: © Prof. Walter J. Gehring, University of Basel.

Chapter 26: Opener: © Peter Weimann/Animals Animals.

Unit V: 27: © Dr. Jeremy Burgess/SPL/Photo Researchers, Inc.; 28: © Photograph by H. Cantor-Lund reproduced with permission of the copyright holder J. W. G. Lund; 29: © Craig Tuttle/Corbis; 30: © Gallo Images/Corbis; 31: © Brian Lightfoot/naturepl.com; 32: © Morales/Getty Images; 33: © Georgie Holland/ agefotostock; 34: © Ken Catania/Visuals Unlimited.

Chapter 27: Opener: © Dr. Jeremy Burgess/SPL/ Photo Researchers, Inc.; 27.2a: © Linda Graham: 27.2b: © Eye of Science/Photo Researchers, Inc.; Table 27.1(1): © Dr. David M. Phillips/Visuals Unlimited; Table 27.1(2): © Michael J. Daly, Uniformed Services University of the Health Sciences, Bethesda, MD, U.S.A.; Table 27.1(3): © Wim van Egmond/Visuals Unlimited; Table 27.1(4): © Prof. Dr. Hans Reichenbach/GBF; 27.3a: © Linda Graham; 27.3b: © Wim van Egmond/Visuals Unlimited; 27.3c: © Michael Abbey/Visuals Unlimited; 27.3d: © Lee W. Wilcox; 27.4: © Nigel Cattlin/Visuals Unlimited; 27.5: © H. Stuart Pankratz/Biological Photo Service; 27.6: © Dr. Richard P. Blakemore, University of New Hampshire; 27.7a: © SciMAT/Photo Researchers, Inc.; 27.7b-d: © Dennis Kunkel Microscopy; 27.8: © Science Photo Library/Alamy RF; 27.9a: © CNRI/ Photo Researchers, Inc.; 27.9b: © Lee W. Wilcox; 27.12a: © Dennis Kunkel Microscopy/Phototake; 27.12b: © Scientifica/Visuals Unlimited; 27.13: © Dr. Terry Beveridge/Visuals Unlimited; 27.14a: © Scientifica/RML/ Visuals Unlimited; 27.14b: © Michael Gabridge/Visuals Unlimited; 27.14c–27.15a: © Lee W. Wilcox; 27.15b: © Dr. Kari Lounatmaa/Photo Researchers, Inc.; 27.17: © Peter Durben.

Chapter 28: Opener & 28.1: © Photographs by H. Cantor-Lund reproduced with permission of the copyright holder J. W. G. Lund; 28.2: © Andrew Syred/ Photo Researchers, Inc.; 28.3a: © Brian P. Piasecki; 28.3b: © Roland Birke/Phototake; 28.3c-e: © Linda Graham; 28.4: © Dr. Dennis Kunkel Microscopy/Visuals Unlimited; 28.5: © Dr. Stanley Flegler/Visuals Unlimited; 28.8a: © Dr. David M. Phillips/Visuals Unlimited; 28.8b: © Jerome Paulin/Visuals Unlimited; 28.9a: © Wim van Egmond/Visuals Unlimited; 28.9b: © Ross Waller, University of Melbourne, Australia; 28.9c: © Eye of Science/Photo Researchers, Inc.; 28.11a: © Doug Sokell/ Visuals Unlimited; 28.11b: © Andrew J. Martinez/Photo Researchers, Inc.; 28.12: © Joe Scott, Department of Biology, College of William and Mary, Williamsburg, VA 23187; 28.14a: © Dennis Kunkel Microscopy; 28.14b: © Isao Inouye; 28.14c: © Stockbyte/Getty Images RF; 28.16a: © Lee W. Wilcox; 28.16b: Cover photograph of *Eukaryotic Cell*, March 2007, 6(3). Related article: Alvin C. M. Kwok, Carmen C. M. Mak, Francis T. W. Wong, Joseph T. Y. Wong, "Novel method for preparing spheroplasts from cells with an internal cellulosic cell wall," pp. 563–7. doi: 10.1128/EC.00301–06. Copyright © 2007 American Society for Microbiology. Reproduced with permission from American Society for Microbiology;

© The Company of Biologists Limited 1999; 35.17a: © Ed Reschke/Getty Images; 35.17b: © John Farmar; 35.17c: © Steve Terrill/Corbis; 35.17d: © John Gerlach/Animals Animals; 35.18–35.19: © Lee W. Wilcox; 35.21: © Bruce Iverson; 35.22a: © Stephen Ingram/Animals Animals; 35.22b: © Peter E. Smith, Natural Sciences Image Library; 35.25: © Lee W. Wilcox.

Chapter 36: Opener: © Gerald & Buff Corsi/Visuals Unlimited; 36.1a: © Digital Photography by Ash Kaushesh, University of Central Arkansas, Conway, Arkansas 72035 USA/Image courtesy Botanical Society of America, www.botany.org, St. Louis, MO 63110; 36.1b: © Lee W. Wilcox; 36.11(1–5): © Prof. and Mrs. M. B. Wilkins/University of Glasgow; 36.12 (top left): © Pat O'Hara/Corbis; 36.12 (top right): © Henry Schleichkorn/Custom Medical Stock Photo; 36.12 (middle left): © Robert Maier/Animals Animals; 36.12 (middle right): © Michael Gadomski/Animals Animals; 36.12 (bottom left): © Pat O'Hara/Corbis; 36.12 (bottom right): © Henry Schleichkorn/Custom Medical Stock Photo; 36.13: © Lee W. Wilcox; 36.16: Courtesy Dr. Malcolm Drew, Texas A&M University; 36.18 (inset): © G. R. "Dick" Roberts/Natural Sciences Image Library.

Chapter 37: Opener: © Dwight Kuhn; 37.2: © Robert Ziemba/agefotostock; 37.3a-b: © Raymon Donahue; 37.4: © Royal Botanical Gardens Kew/Wellcome Trust Medical Photographic Library; 37.5: Confocal fluorescence micrograph courtesy Simon D.X. Chuong; 37.6: © Geoff Kidd/SPL/Photo Researchers, Inc.; 37.7b: Courtesy of C.A. Stiles, University of Wisconsin; 37.7c: © Ruddy Gold/agefotostock; 37.8; USDA Photo; 37.12: Photo courtesy of Jayne Belnap, U.S. Geological Survey; 37.16: © J. Hyvönen; 37.16 (inset): Photo by Birgitta Bergman, Department of Botany, Stockholm University (Sweden); 37.17: © M. Kalab/Custom Medical Stock Photo; 37.19a: © Dani/Jeske/Animals Animals; 37.19b: © Breck P. Kent/agefotostock; 37.20: © Charles T. Bryson, USDA Agricultural Research Service, Bugwood.org.

Chapter 38: Opener: © Barry Mason/Alamy RF; 38.8 (right): © James S. Busse; 38.10: © Jerry Cooke, Inc./Animals Animals; 38.11b: © Astrid & Hanns/Frieder Michler/Photo Researchers, Inc.; 38.12b-c: © John N.A. Lott/Biological Photo Service; 38.13: © David Q. Cavagnaro/Getty Images; 38.16: © Adalberto Rios Szalay/Sexto Sol/Stockbyte/Getty Images RF; 38.17a: © Andrew Syred/Photo Researchers, Inc.; 38.19a: © Dan Suizo/Photo Researchers, Inc.; 38.19b: © Dr. William J. Weber/Visuals Unlimited; 38.20a–38.22: © Lee W. Wilcox.

Chapter 39: Opener: © E.R. Degginger/Animals Animals; 39.3b: © Lee W. Wilcox; 39.5a: © Natural Sciences Image Library; 39.5b: © Lee W. Wilcox; 39.7a: © Scott Sinklier/agefotostock; 39.7b: © Chris Russell, 11eggs.com; 39.8a: © Richard Shiell/Animals Animals; 39.8b: © Richard Jorgensen; 39.9a-b: Courtesy of John Innes Centre; 39.10: © Burke/Triolo Productions/Getty Images RF; 39.11(6): Haiyi Liang and L. Mahadevana, "Growth, geometry, and mechanics of a blooming lily," *PNAS*, April 5, 2011, 108(14): 5516–21, Fig. 2c; 39.12b: © RMF/Scientifica/Visuals Unlimited; 39.14 (top left): © Biodisc/Visuals Unlimited; 39.15: Courtesy J.M. Escobar-Restrepo and A.J. Johnston, University of Zurich, Institute of Plant Biology. From Bernasconi et al., "Evolutionary ecology of the prezygotic stage," *Science*, 303(5660):971–5, Fig. 2, © 2004. Reprinted with permission from AAAS; 39.18–39.21: © Lee W. Wilcox.

Unit VII: 40: © John Rowley/Getty Images RF; 41: © James Cavallini/Photo Researchers, Inc.; 42: Courtesy Ann-Shyn Chiang, Tsing Hua Chair Professor/Brain Research Center & Institute of Biotechnology/

National Tsing Hua University; 43: © Jane Burton/Bruce Coleman Inc./Photoshot; 44: © Stephen Dalton/Photo Researchers, Inc.; 45: © Richard Hutchings/PhotoEdit; 46: © The Rockefeller University/AP Photo; 47: © SPL/Photo Researchers, Inc.; 48: © brianlatino/Alamy RF; 49: © Guido Alberto Rossi/agefotostock; 50: © Sovereign/ISM/Phototake; 51: © David Liebman/Pink Guppy; 52: Matsui et al., "Effects of ethanol on photoreceptors and visual function in developing zebrafish," *Investigative Ophthalmology & Visual Science*, October 2006, 47(10):4589–97, Fig. 1. © Association for Research in Vision and Ophthalmology. Images Courtesy of Jonathan Matsui; 53: © SPL/Photo Researchers, Inc.

Chapter 40: Opener: © John Rowley/Getty Images RF; 40.2 (left): © Michael Abbey/Photo Researchers, Inc.; 40.2 (middle): © Sinclair Stammers/Photo Researchers, Inc.; 40.2 (right): © Dr. Richard Kessel/Visuals Unlimited; 40.5 (blood): © Dennis Kunkel Microscopy, Inc./Phototake; 40.5 (adipose tissue): © Ed Reschke/Getty Images; 40.5 (bone): © Innerspace Imaging/Photo Researchers, Inc.; 40.5 (cartilage): © Dr. John D. Cunningham/Visuals Unlimited; 40.5 (loose connective tissue, dense connective tissue): © The McGraw-Hill Companies, Inc./Al Telser, photographer; 40.8 (left, middle): © Dr. Stanley Flegler/Visuals Unlimited; 40.8 (right): © Dr. David M. Phillips/Visuals Unlimited; 40.10a: © Biophoto Associates/Photo Researchers, Inc.; 40.10b: © Pete Oxford/Minden Pictures; 40.10c: © Thomas Deerinck/Visuals Unlimited; 40.10d: © Anthony Bannister/Photo Researchers, Inc.; 40.15 (top left): © Mitch Wojnarowicz/The Image Works.

Chapter 41: Opener: © James Cavallini/Photo Researchers, Inc.; 41.2a: © James Cavallini/BSIP/Phototake; 41.5a: Courtesy of Dr. R. F. Rakowski, Ohio University, Athens, OH; 41.14b: © The McGraw-Hill Companies, Inc./Al Telser, photographer.

Chapter 42: Opener: Courtesy Ann-Shyn Chiang, Tsing Hua Chair Professor/Brain Research Center & Institute of Biotechnology/National Tsing Hua University; 42.6b: © Jan Leestma, M.D./Custom Medical Stock Photo; 42.14a: © Premaphotos/Alamy; 42.16a-b: © Dr. Scott T. Grafton/Visuals Unlimited; 42.18 (left): © The McGraw-Hill Companies, Inc./Al Telser, photographer.

Chapter 43: Opener: © Jane Burton/Bruce Coleman Inc./Photoshot; 43.8: © Gary Meszaros/Photo Researchers, Inc.; 43.12: © Daniel Heuclin/Photo Researchers, Inc.; 43.14a: © Eye of Science/Photo Researchers, Inc.; 43.16: © Omikron/Photo Researchers, Inc.; 43.17 (right): © Dr. Donald Fawcett/Visuals Unlimited; 43.19b: © Steve Allen/Getty Images RF; 43.23a: © Corbis/SuperStock RF; 43.23b: © Cal Vornberger/Getty Images; 43.24b: Courtesy of Russell Jurenka, Iowa State University; 43.24c (left): © Anthony Bannister/Photo Researchers, Inc.; 43.24c (right): Courtesy of Louisa Howard, Dartmouth College; 43.28a-c: © The Royal Society for the Blind of South Australia Inc.

Chapter 44: Opener: © Stephen Dalton/Photo Researchers, Inc.; 44.1a (right): © Dwight Kuhn; 44.1b: © Michele Hall/SeaPics.com; 44.1c (left): © Georgette Douwma/Photo Researchers, Inc.; 44.1c (right): © The Natural History Museum, London; 44.5b: © Dr. H.E. Huxley; 44.7: © Hansell H. Stedman, M.D.; 44.11a: © Dr. Donald Fawcett/Photo Researchers, Inc.; 44.12 (right): © Mark Richards/PhotoEdit; 44.15a: © Dr. LR/Photo Researchers, Inc.; 44.15b: © Tim Arnett, University College London.

Chapter 45: Opener: © Richard Hutchings/PhotoEdit; 45.2: © Daniel Hornbach and Tony Deneka, Courtesy of

Daniel Hornbach, Macalester College; 45.2b: © Armin May forest/Getty Images; 45.3a: © David A. Northcott/Corbis; 45.3b: © John Giustina/Getty Images RF; 45.3c: © Kim Karpeles/agefotostock; 45.3d: © Reinhard Dirscherl/Getty Images; 45.3e: © CFranke/F1Online RF/Photolibrary; 45.4a: © Royalty-Free/Corbis; 45.4b: © Sarah Klockars-Clauser/agefotostock; 45.15c: © Javier Domingo/Phototake.

Chapter 46: Opener: © The Rockefeller University/AP Photo; 46.9a: © Paul McCormick/Getty Images; 46.9b: © William S. Clark/Frank Lane Picture Agency/Corbis; 46.13: © Nutscode/T Service/Photo Researchers, Inc.; 46.15b: Courtesy of Uffe Midtgård, University of Copenhagen; 46.16: CDC.

Chapter 47: Opener: © SPL/Photo Researchers, Inc.; 47.5: © Dr. David M. Phillips/Visuals Unlimited; 47.7: © Dennis Kunkel Microscopy; 47.11: © The McGraw-Hill Companies, Inc./Rick Brady, photographer; 47.12b: © Carolina Biological Supply/Visuals Unlimited; 47.14: © Ed Reschke/Getty Images; 47.20: © Biophoto Associates/SPL/Photo Researchers, Inc.; 47.21: © Sovereign/TSM/Phototake.

Chapter 48: Opener: © brianlatino/Alamy RF; 48.3 (top): © Ken Lucas/Visuals Unlimited; 48.3 (bottom): © Todd Pierson; 48.4a: © Hal Beral/V&W/The Image Works; 48.4b: © Jane Burton/Bruce Coleman Inc./Photoshot; 48.5a: © Jane Burton/naturepl.com; 48.5c: © Electron Microscopy Unit, Royal Holloway, University of London; 48.7 (top left): © Microfield Scientific Ltd/Photo Researchers, Inc.; 48.7 (right): © Ed Reschke/Getty Images; 48.10b: © Pr. M. Brauner/Photo Researchers, Inc.; 48.17 (left): © Astrid & Hanns-Frieder Michler/SPL/Photo Researchers, Inc.; 48.17 (right): © Dr. John D. Cunningham/Visuals Unlimited.

Chapter 49: Opener: © Guido Alberto Rossi/agefotostock; 49.12: © Steve Gschmeissner/SPL/Photo Researchers, Inc.

Chapter 50: Opener: © Sovereign/ISM/Phototake; 50.6a (left, right insets): © S. Goodwin & Dr. Max Hincke, Division of Clinical and Functional Anatomy, University of Ottawa; 50.6b: © Bob Daemmrich/The Image Works; 50.7 (bottom left): © Carolina Biological Supply/Visuals Unlimited; 50.13: From Robert F. Gagel, M.D., and Ian E. McCutcheon, M.D., "Pituitary Gigantism," *New England Journal of Medicine*, 1999, 340:524, Fig. 1A. © 2007 Massachusetts Medical Society. All rights reserved; 50.14b: © blickwinkel/Alamy.

Chapter 51: Opener: © David Liebman/Pink Guppy; 51.1a: © Clouds Hill Imaging Ltd./Corbis; 51.1b: © WaterFrame/Alamy; 51.3b: © Dr. Stanley Flegler/Visuals Unlimited; 51.3d: © P.M. Motta & G. Familiari/Univ. La Sapienza/Photo Researchers, Inc.; 51.4: © FLPA/Alamy; 51.12a: © Claude Edelmann/Photo Reseachers, Inc.; 51.12b: © Nestle/Petit Format/Photo Researchers, Inc.; 51.12c: © Photo Lennart Nilsson/Scanpix; 51.15 (diaphragm, condoms, oral contraceptive): © The McGraw-Hill Companies, Inc./Jill Braaten, photographer.

Chapter 52: Opener: Matsui et al., "Effects of ethanol on photoreceptors and visual function in developing zebrafish," *Investigative Ophthalmology & Visual Science*, October 2006, 47(10):4589–97, Fig. 1. © Association for Research in Vision and Ophthalmology. Images Courtesy of Jonathan Matsui; 52.2: Courtesy Dr. M. Whitaker, University of Newcastle upon Tyne; 52.4 (top row, middle row): © Dr. Richard Kessel & Dr. Gene Shih/Visuals Unlimited; 52.4 (bottom row): © Tom Fleming; 52.6 (bottom): Courtesy Hiroki Nishida, Biological Sciences, Osaka University; 52.10a: Courtesy Dr. Laurence D. Etkin, University of

Page numbers followed by *f* denote figures; those followed by *t* denote tables.

G

G$_1$ phase, 299, 300, 301, 301f
G$_2$ phase, 299, 300, 301, 301f
Gage, Fred, 868–69
galactose, 47, 47f, 933, 934f
galactoside transacetylase, 261, 262f
Galápagos finches. *See* finches
Galápagos Islands, 461, 463–64
Galeopsis tetrahit, 504–5
gallbladder, 932f, 933
Galliformes, 702t
galls, 412, 413, 536, 537f
Gallus gallus, 381
Galvani, Luigi, 834
gametangia, 579, 584f, 626
gametes. *See also* sexual reproduction
    of bryophytes, 579
    defined, 1056
    differences among eukaryotes, 314
    DNA methylation, 356
    epigenetic inheritance and, 355, 356
    flowering plants, 717
    formation, 1059–61
    fungi, 623, 626, 627, 628f
    haploid nature, 299
    hormonal control of development, 1050
    linkage and crossing over effects, 348–50
    maternal inheritance and, 352
    mutations, 283, 283f
    of protists, 567, 568f
    recording in Punnett square, 325–26
    self-fertilization, 322
gametic isolation, 498f, 499
gametic life cycles of protists, 568, 570f
gametogenesis, 1059–61, 1066–67
gametophytes
    of bryophytes, 578, 578f, 579, 580
    defined, 313f, 314
    development in flower tissues, 719
    in flowering plant life cycle, 717, 794
    lycophyte and pteridophyte, 583, 584f
    production in flowers, 795
    structure and function in flowering plants, 802–4
gametophytic SI, 803, 803f
γ-aminobutyric acid, 845t, 846, 848–49
γ cytokine receptor, 416
γ^c-globin genes, 429, 1070
gamma globulin, 1104
gamma rays, 157, 285
ganglia, 858
ganglion cells of retina, 890
gannets (*Morus bassanus*), 1155, 1155f
gap genes, 387, 388f
gap junctions
    basic features, 198, 198t
    cardiac muscle, 176, 201, 971
    channel size, 202, 202f
    mechanisms of action, 201, 201f
Garces, Helena, 809
garden pea (*Pisum sativum*), 322–23, 807, 808f
Garrod, Archibald, 236–37
Garstang, Walter, 680
gaseous neurotransmitters, 846
Gaser, Christian, 870, 871
gases, 845t, 986–88
gas exchange, 986, 987f
gas gangrene, 544
gastric brooding frog (*Rheobatrachus* spp.), 1244
gastric ulcers, 940, 941f
gastrin, 937, 937f, 1031f
gastroenteritis, 361f
gastroesophageal reflux, 940
Gastropoda, 661, 662f

gastropod locomotion, 916
gastrovascular cavity
    as circulatory system, 965, 965f
    digestion via, 927, 927f
    in flatworms, 657
    in Radiata, 654
gastrula, 642, 1088
gastrulation, 642, 643f, 1081–83
gated channels, 109, 109f, 110f, 838–42
Gatorade, 1015
gaur (*Bos gaurus*), 1261
Gause, Georgyi, 1189
Gaut, Brandon, 615
GDP. *See* guanosine diphosphate (GDP)
geese
    egg-rolling response, 1147, 1147f
    imprinted behavior, 1150, 1150f
Gehring, Walter, 511
gel electrophoresis, 126, 127f, 404f, 405, 407
gemmae, 578f
Gemmata obscuriglobus, 539
GenBank database, 433t
gene addition, 411
gene amplification, 290, 291f
gene cloning
    DNA libraries, 404–5
    gel electrophoresis and PCR, 405–6
    steps, 400–404, 401f
gene duplication, 427–29, 428f, 481, 482t
gene expression. *See also* inheritance
    defined, 235, 257
    early studies, 236–38
    genetic code, 243–47, 244t, 245f
    genotype vs. phenotype, 325
    hormone effects, 13
    molecular-level steps, 238–39
    in organizers, 1089–91
    RNA processing in eukaryotes, 241–43, 242f
    transcription, 239–41, 240f, 241f
    translation basics, 244–45, 247–51
    translation stages, 251–54, 252f, 253f, 254f
    xylem, phloem, and nonvascular tissue, 789–90
gene expression and regulatory proteins, 430t
gene families, 427–29, 473, 1070
gene flow, 492
gene interactions, 344–46
gene knockout, 411
gene pools, 479
genera, 516
generalist herbivores, 1197
general lineage concept, 497
General Sherman tree, 193, 193f
general transcription factors, 269, 270, 270f
generation times, 507
generative cells, 802
gene regulation
    defined, 257
    microarray data, 410t
    occurrence in eukaryotes and bacteria, 259–60
    overview, 130
    purpose, 258–59
    RNA processing in eukaryotes, 274–75
    transcription in bacteria, 259, 260–67
    transcription in eukaryotes, 267–74
    translation in eukaryotes, 275–76
gene replacement, 411–12
gene repressors, 740
genes
    altruism, 1159–61
    Alzheimer disease related, 872
    avirulence, 752, 753f
    basic functions, 4, 69, 239
    control of flower structures, 798–802
    current theory, 15

defined, 4, 239
differential regulation, 188, 196
duplications, 427–29, 473
early association with enzymes, 236, 237–38
early discoveries, 327
evolution, 472–75
extranuclear, 350–53
homologous, 161, 162f, 471–72
interactions between, 344–46
linked, 346–50
loci, 328
Mendel's observations, 324
for muscle cell differentiation, 393–95
mutations, 280–86, 294, 295, 336–37, 380, 389, 482
percentage encoding transmembrane proteins, 99–100
polymorphic, 479
resistance, 752, 753f
role in behavior, 1147–48, 1149–50
structural vs. regulatory, 238
transfer between species, 7–8, 377–78, 474–75, 667
gene sequences. *See also* DNA sequences
    evolution evidence from, 471–72
    from extinct organisms, 524–25
    homologous, 520
    mechanisms producing, 472–75
    neutral variation, 491
    shared derived characters, 522, 523f
gene silencing, 269, 799
gene therapy, 416–17
genetically modified organisms, 411
genetic code, 243–47
genetic disorders
    adenosine deaminase (ADA) deficiency, 416–17
    aniridia, 380
    biotechnology efforts against, 411–12, 416–17
    cleft palate, 1091–92
    congenital analgesia, 340
    cystic fibrosis, 16–17, 330, 336–37, 411–12
    Down syndrome, 317, 1091, 1092
    Ehlers-Danlos syndrome, 196
    Huntington disease, 331
    Klinefelter syndrome, 318t, 354, 354t
    nucleotide excision repair systems, 288
    pedigree analysis, 330–31
    phenylketonuria, 336t, 337, 338–39, 339f
    recessive alleles causing, 330, 336–37, 336t
    sickle cell disease, 280, 281f, 478
    triple X syndrome, 317, 318t, 354, 354t
    Turner syndrome, 317, 318t, 354, 354t
    xeroderma pigmentosum, 279, 288, 288f
    X-linked, 332–33, 353–54
genetic diversity
    chromosome structure and, 314
    impact on small populations, 1252–54
    importance, 1245
    random chromosome alignment and, 312
genetic drift
    effect on populations, 489–91
    role in microevolution, 481, 482t
    small populations and, 1252–53
genetic engineering. *See also* biotechnology
    of animals, 411–12, 414–15
    defined, 400
    of plants, 412–13, 764–66, 1198, 1232
genetic mapping, 349–50, 350f
genetic material
    as characteristic of life, 3f, 4
    current theory, 15
    DNA discoveries, 212–17
    early discoveries, 327
    locations in eukaryotic cells, 351f, 423–24
    in mitochondria and chloroplasts, 88–89
    mutations, 280–86